ACCOUNTING PRINCIPLES

ACCOUNTING PRINCIPLES

Lanny M. Solomon
The University of Texas at Arlington

Richard J. Vargo
University of the Pacific

Richard G. Schroeder
Texas A & M University

1817

HARPER & ROW, PUBLISHERS, New York
Cambridge, Philadelphia, San Francisco,
London, Mexico City, São Paulo, Sydney

Sponsoring Editor: John Greenman
Development Editor: Johnna G. Barto
Project Editor: Cynthia L. Indriso
Designer: Gayle Jaeger
Production Manager: Willie Lane
Compositor: York Graphic Services, Inc.
Printer and Binder: The Murray Printing Company
Cover Photograph: Bill Longcore

ACCOUNTING PRINCIPLES

Library of Congress Cataloging in Publication Data
Solomon, Lanny M., 1946–
Accounting principles.
1. Accounting. I. Vargo, Richard J. II. Schroeder, Richard G. III. Title.
HF5635.S688 1983 657 82-15449
ISBN 0-06-046348-1

CONTENTS

[1] Titles marked by an asterisk (*) denote chapter articles.

PREFACE

During the past ten years accounting enrollments throughout the country have risen dramatically. Dedicated (and not so dedicated) students have crowded into classrooms to learn the whys and wherefores of accounting and financial reporting in order to improve their chances of future employment. Interestingly, during the same period, professorial complaints regarding students' reading and analytical abilities and their unwillingness to work diligently have increased. It is these very problems that prompted the development and publication of *Accounting Principles.*

The authors recognize that introductory accounting courses at many colleges and universities are failing to meet the needs of both faculty and students. Often these courses are of the service variety required of all business administration majors. Consequently, such classes usually contain a substantial number of students who quickly lose interest in the subject matter, which they regard as relatively difficult and which requires considerable study time. To complicate matters, instructors assigned to such courses sometimes have difficulty generating enthusiasm for elementary explorations of debit-credit rules, posting, payroll, bond interest computations, the preparation of master budgets, and a number of other topics basic to our discipline.

What does *Accounting Principles* do to overcome these problems? While we do not claim to perform miracles, we are confident that our text has a proven ability to arouse students' interest in accounting, thereby creating a more dynamic instructional environment. This ability grows out of the text's heavy emphasis on real-world experience. It uses real data from corporate financial reports, interesting excerpts from periodicals, and a truly managerial approach to management accounting. It also includes a number of controversial yet exciting accounting topics. Although we constantly strive to add pizzazz to the study of accounting, we do not lose sight of our main objective: to provide a readable, solid, well-balanced presentation of the principles, practices, and procedures that affect the measurement, reporting, and management of financial activity. Class testing of the text at various kinds of colleges and universities has shown that our objectives have been met. Both faculty and student users were enthusiastic about the book's clarity, accuracy, readability, and comprehensiveness.

MAJOR FEATURES

Throughout the twenty-eight chapters, we have implemented several planned features that distinguish this text.

Heavy Real-World Emphasis

Many accounting texts resort to using hypothetical firms in their illustrations and examples. We have found that students show an increased interest in the subject matter when exposed to the accounting practices of real firms. Consequently, we include annual report data from over 125 different companies, including McDonald's, Holiday Inn, Apple Computer, American Airlines, Coca-Cola, and the Atlanta Braves. We have carefully selected firms from industries with which students themselves have contact. Importantly, all examples are scaled down to an introductory level. Obviously, in a principles text, real firms cannot entirely replace hypothetical ones because of the level of simplicity required, but we have used real-world examples whenever possible.

Strong Problem Material

All problem material included in this text was carefully designed to accurately reflect current accounting principles and practices. Questions, exercises, problems, and cases range in scope from the simple to the complex; all were written and solved by the authors to assure close coordination with the text presentation. To further ensure accuracy and reliability, we not only reviewed all results of class testing, but obtained independently worked solutions from four additional experienced accounting instructors. Furthermore, the *Instructor's Solutions Manual* has been triple-checked by the authors and yet two other accounting instructors. While perfection is impossible in any undertaking of this magnitude, we are confident that the end-of-chapter materials are as trouble-free as repeated multiple checking can make them. They will provide a solid, well-rounded foundation for accounting students and a varied resource for instructors.

Our problem material generally requires the standard calculations. Often, however, we go one step further and ask the student to think beyond the numbers. For example, the student may be directed to comment on limitations of the calculation and/or method used or to pursue a managerial application of the data generated. The exercises and problems require consideration of both the how and the why. *All* requirements are answerable from either the text presentation or good common sense.

Occasionally, we have used problems from past CPA and CMA examinations. However, only elementary problems have been employed, and to reduce unnecessary complexity in such items, many have been modified extensively (indicated by the term "modified" as opposed to "adapted").

Finally, in addition to paying close attention to quality in our problem material, we have also been conscious of the need for quantity. You will find an abundant collection of exercises and problems for homework and in-class assignments. For the most part, these materials reflect the authors' preference for variety rather than duplication. For instructors desiring some duplicative material for classroom illustration, for use in multiple sections, and/or for the second or third year of text use, five alternate problems per chapter are provided. These problems are identical or very similar to others in the chapter, but use different information. For ease in problem assignments, each problem's topic coverage and purpose is labeled in boldface type.

Excerpts from Periodicals

We feel the integration of excerpts from journal and newspaper articles is an excellent way to further bridge the gap between academia and Main Street. The selected articles relate to the subject matter at hand and were adapted to avoid theoretical and conceptual material. The emphasis is on practical, interesting applications. Excerpts are from such popular periodicals as *The Wall Street Journal, Forbes, Fortune,* and a host of other sources. Typical examples include:

> "Does the IRS Play Favorites?"
> "The Nagging Feeling of Undetected Fraud"
> "Considering Accounting as a Career?"

A Truly Managerial Section

The final chapters of an accounting principles text are normally devoted to cost and managerial accounting topics. The usual approach is to have students calculate, calculate, and calculate, while paying very little attention to the use or impact of the data they are generating. Our approach is to focus on the how *and why* of planning, control, performance evaluation, and decision making and to show their practical applications whenever possible. This balanced (as opposed to highly procedural) presentation should appeal to a wide variety of instructors, including those who currently use separate texts for their financial and managerial coverage.

HIGHLIGHTS OF COVERAGE

The text offers a comprehensive presentation of topics usually covered in an accounting principles course. The following list highlights some of the text's strongest features:

1 Particular attention is paid to topics that tend to give students the most difficulty, including adjusting entries, deferrals and accruals, corporate equity, bonds, present value, and the statement of changes in financial position.

2 To aid the student, learning objectives for each chapter and numerous summary (demonstration) problems with solutions are included.

3 Selected accounting principles are introduced early, along with an innovative way of explaining the impact of transactions on the fundamental accounting equation. (Chapter 1)

4 Where appropriate, we present a systems emphasis, including the operation of a merchandising system, the function of an audit trail, and the use and design of adequate internal control. And, we stress the interaction of accounting and computers by discussing benefits and problems (including computer fraud), as opposed to a detailed presentation of how a computer works. (Chapters 4, 5)

5 A financial statement orientation occurs early in the text. The student is exposed to realistic reporting issues (e.g., earnings per share, contingencies, and segment reporting) on a *scaled-down level* to show that financial accounting is really more sophisticated and exciting than debits and credits, posting, and the completion of the accounting cycle. (Chapter 6)

6 The growing impact of inflation on inventories and investments in property, plant, and equipment is emphasized. Our major discussion of inflation accounting is contained in the same chapter as horizontal, vertical, and ratio analysis so as to provide a sound foundation for the evaluation of financial statements. (Chapters 9, 10, 19)

7 The Accelerated Cost Recovery System is introduced. (Chapter 10)

8 A clear and meaningful discussion of present value is achieved by close comparisons with compound interest. (Chapters 15, 16, 28)

9 A heavily class-tested, diagramatic approach for understanding the working capital and cash approaches to the statement of changes in financial position is employed. (Chapter 17)

10 In addition to presentation of the objectives of financial reporting and generally accepted accounting principles, there is a discussion of the impact of generally accepted accounting alternatives (practices) on financial statements. (Chapter 18)

11 The problems of service industries and nonprofit organizations in performance measurement, cost accumulation, and budgeting are covered. (Chapters 21, 22, 23)

12 The presentation integrates behavioral issues as they relate to budgeting, responsibility accounting, standard costs and variance analysis, and decision making. (Chapters 23, 25, 26, 27)

13 For instructors desiring such material, there is a brief introduction to the use of quantitative methods (namely, expected value) in decision making. This topic is treated in a separate section of the chapter and may be omitted without any loss of continuity. (Chapter 27)

SUPPLEMENTARY MATERIALS

A complete set of supplementary materials accompanies this text:

1 ***Instructor's Solutions Manual.*** A comprehensive manual is available in two volumes that contain the solutions to all questions, exercises, problems, and cases. A suggested completion time and difficulty index is provided for each problem and case.

2 ***Test Bank.*** A test bank, available in both printed and computerized form, is free to adopters. The test bank contains forty multiple-choice questions for each of the text's twenty-eight chapters. Each question has an assigned difficulty level. In addition, many of the numerical calculation questions are structured so that the answer choices may be omitted, thereby allowing for conversion to short exercises if desired by the instructor.

3 ***Study Guide.*** An innovative study guide has been prepared by Wanda A. Wallace and James J. Wallace of Southern Methodist University to reinforce the material presented in the text. The study guide contains chapter learning objectives; a chapter synopsis; a discussion of technical points in the text; multiple-choice, true-false, and matching questions, along with answers *and* explanations; short exercises; chapter demonstration problems; and crossword puzzles.

4 ***Achievement Tests.*** Nine sets of objective tests, each covering two to four chapters, are available in alternate forms. These require 50 to 60 minutes to complete; alternate forms permit varied use for different sections or semesters. In addition, we offer two comprehensive tests in alternate forms for Chapters 1–14 and Chapters 15–28; these require 100 to 120 minutes to administer.

5 ***Working Papers.*** Two volumes of working papers have been prepared. Volume I covers Chapters 1–14; Volume II pertains to Chapters 15–28. Many of the working papers are partially filled in, thereby allowing students to concentrate on accounting concepts as opposed to the pencil pushing associated with problem setup.

6 ***Practice Sets.*** The authors have written two practice sets that tie together a number of the issues discussed in the text. The first practice set, Winchester's Fine Jewelry, covers Chapters 1–6 and helps students to understand the accounting cycle, the functions of an accounting system, and the preparation of financial statements. The second practice set, Dutton Manufacturing Corporation, covers Chapters 21–27 and is managerial in orientation. While some transaction processing is included, students are asked to concentrate on such issues as budget preparation, variance analysis, and decision making. The solutions to the practice sets are contained in the *Instructor's Solutions Manual.*

7 ***Computer Simulation.*** For those schools desiring to integrate microcomputers into the management accounting section, a computer simulation game is available. Developed by Gaylord Smith of Albion College, the game asks teams of students to manage Briton Manufacturing Company and make accounting-related business decisions. The related software and *Instructor's Manual* will be furnished to adopters. A *Student Manual* is available to help guide team players.

8 ***Transparencies.*** A set of over 500 transparencies is free to adopters. The transparencies contain solutions to a wide variety of problems and cases.

ACKNOWLEDGMENTS

A project of this nature and magnitude is a team effort, entailing much cooperation, thoughtfulness, and patience. To our team members we owe a tremendous debt of gratitude. Those persons participating in focus groups, class testing our material, checking our problems, and reviewing chapters were especially helpful with their comments and suggestions. Therefore, many thanks to the following people:

Focus group participants

Barbara Adams, *Texas Southern University*
Frank Barton, *Memphis State University*
Dale Buckmaster, *University of Delaware*
Gary Bulmash, *American University*
Dan Etnier, *University of Wisconsin, Eau Claire*
Gail Farrelly, *George Washington University*
Lorraine Hicks, *State Technical Institute*
Dolan Hinson, *University of North Carolina, Charlotte*
Roderick Holmes, *Baylor University*
Gordon Hosch, *University of New Orleans*
Hans Johnson, *University of Texas, San Antonio*
Richard Jones, *Lamar University*
William Jones, *Seton Hall University*
Clinton Kind, *Mankato State University*
Paul W. Parkinson, *Ball State University*
H. Lee Schlorff, *Bentley College*
Bert Scott, *University of Montana*
Robert Shirley, *Oregon State University*
Claude Smith, *Eastern Kentucky University*
William Smith, *University of Southern California*
Barbara Vinson, *University of Akron*
Thomas Weirich, *Central Michigan University*

Class-testers

Lawrence Ozzello, *University of Wisconsin, Eau Claire*
Howard L. Royer, *Miami-Dade Community College*
Betty M. Strauss, *Towson State University*
Charlotte Wright, *Oklahoma State University*

Problem checkers

Thomas Gavin, *University of Tennessee, Chattanooga*
Robert Landry, *Massasoit Community College*
Raymond Larsen, *Appalachian State University*
Richard Rivers, *Southern Illinois University*
Bevie Sanders, *Arizona State University*

Reviewers

Barbara Adams, *Texas Southern University*
Roy E. Baker, *University of Missouri, Kansas City*
Alfred Brown, *Monmouth College*
Gary Bulmash, *American University*
Harold Cannon, *State University of New York, Albany*
Kenneth Elvik, *Iowa State University*
Wilbert Fischer, *Moorhead State University*
Dale Flesher, *University of Mississippi*
Thomas Gavin, *University of Tennessee, Chattanooga*
Raymond Green, *Texas Tech University*
Galen Hadley, *University of South Dakota*
Larzette Hale, *Utah State University*
Dolan Hinson, *University of North Carolina, Charlotte*
John Kostolansky, *Loyola University, Chicago*
Raymond Larsen, *Appalachian State University*
Scott Meisel, *Indiana State University*
Lawrence Peterson, *County College of Morris*
Richard Rivers, *Southern Illinois University*
Bevie Sanders, *Arizona State University*
H. Lee Schlorff, *Bentley College*
Michael Sheffey, *University of Wisconsin, Parkside*

Frank Singer, *University of Massachusetts*
Helen Tekell, *Virginia Polytechnic Institute*
Delbert Williamson, *California State University, Long Beach*

A special thank you for various chores related to the text's development goes to Judy Cassidy, Flora Chance, James Cook, Richard Mark, Lola Rhodes, Sue Strickland, Mel Sullivan, Peggy Thurmond, Larry Walther, and Terry Witt, all of the University of Texas at Arlington; Janet Ferguson, Terry Kalenda, Charles Kelliher, JoAnn Mikula, and Janice Taylor of Texas A & M University; Myrtle Clark of the University of Kentucky; Larry Konrath of the University of Toledo; and Katherine Moffeitt of North Texas State University.

Sherry Cash, Beverly Kale, Janet King, Brenda Lovelady, Jan Herdrich, Mary Kiszlowski, Jean Eliceche, and Paula Freeman did the majority of typing on the manuscript and put up with our unique handwriting, short tempers, and unreasonable deadlines.

The assistance from Harper & Row in developing this manuscript was extremely helpful. We appreciate the work of Bonnie Binkert, John Greenman, Cindy Indriso, and especially Johnna Barto, who reviewed the many drafts of each chapter, offered numerous valuable suggestions, and provided constant encouragement during the years that the text and ancillary materials were under development.

We are grateful to the American Institute of Certified Public Accountants and the Institute of Management Accounting for permission to use selected problems from past CPA and CMA examinations, respectively.

And finally, we are deeply appreciative of the support from our families that enabled us to pursue this project. To Nancy, Scott, and Deborah Solomon; Melinda, Blaine, Michael, and Matthew Vargo; and Betty, Carolyn, and John Schroeder—we love you.

Comments from users are welcomed and appreciated.

Lanny M. Solomon
Richard J. Vargo
Richard G. Schroeder

ABOUT THE AUTHORS

Lanny M. Solomon is currently an associate professor of accounting at the University of Texas at Arlington. He holds a Ph.D. in accounting and information systems from Case Western Reserve University and the Certificate in Management Accounting (CMA). Professor Solomon has published articles in *The Accounting Review, Journal of Accountancy, Cost and Management,* and various journals of state CPA societies. In addition, he has presented numerous papers at technical accounting meetings. Professor Solomon is an active member of the American Accounting Association, the National Association of Accountants, and the Institute of Management Accounting, and has been the recipient of several outstanding teaching awards.

Richard J. Vargo received his doctorate in accounting from the University of Washington. He is currently professor of accounting at the University of the Pacific. He has public accounting experience with Deloitte Haskins & Sells. Articles by Professor Vargo have appeared in the *Journal of Accountancy, CPA Journal,* and other professional journals. He is the author of several other accounting and business books, including one prepared for the American Institute of Certified Public Accountants. Professor Vargo is actively involved in the American Accounting Association, and has served as a member of the editorial board of *The Accounting Review* and the Professional Examinations Committee. He has acted as a consultant to a number of businesses on accounting and financial reporting matters.

Richard G. Schroeder is an associate professor at Texas A & M University. Professor Schroeder received his doctorate from Arizona State University. A certified public accountant, he is the author of numerous publications and has published articles in *Accounting, Organizations and Society, The Accounting Review, Management Accounting,* the *CPA Journal, The Internal Auditor,* and *Managerial Planning.* Additionally, he is the coauthor of *Intermediate Accounting* and *Accounting Theory: Text and Readings.* Professor Schroeder was also the corecipient of a Peat, Marwick, Mitchell Foundation Research in Auditing grant and has held a number of official positions in the American Accounting Association, the American Institute of Certified Public Accountants, and the National Association of Accountants.

1 AN INTRODUCTION TO ACCOUNTING

LEARNING OBJECTIVES

After reading this chapter you should:

1 Be familiar with the broad scope of accounting services and accounting-related careers.

2 Understand the entity assumption, the principle of historical cost, and the fundamental accounting equation.

3 Understand the meaning of assets, liabilities, and owners' equity.

4 Be aware of the four items that cause owners' equity to change: specifically, owner investments, owner withdrawals, net income, and net loss.

5 Understand the impact of various transactions on the accounting equation.

6 Understand the content and be able to prepare an income statement, statement of owners' equity, and balance sheet.

CHAPTER 1

Assets, dividends, expenses, net income, and *earnings per share* are terms that have a specific meaning to accountants and many others engaged in business operations. Perhaps you have encountered these terms in your working experience and readings. They are frequently used in daily conversations among managers and often appear in financial reports, newspapers, and periodicals. Consider, for example, the following information, which appeared in a report to the directors and owners of McDonald's Corporation, a firm engaged in the operation of fast-food restaurants:

> *McDonald's reached a number of milestones. Systemwide sales exceeded $6 billion, [and this was] the first year in which an individual McDonald's topped the $4 million annual sales mark. Total revenues surpassed $2 billion. Revenues include (a) sales by Company-owned restaurants, (b) revenues from franchised restaurants, and (c) other revenues, including gains on sales of Company-owned restaurant businesses and interest income.*
>
> *Revenues from franchised restaurants consist primarily of fees provided for by agreements that are part of the overall franchise arrangement with each franchisee. These fees are based upon a percentage of sales with a specified minimum payment and, under current agreements, generally amount to 11.5% of a restaurant's sales.*
>
> *By design, [the year-end] current ratio was 0.7. Because working capital generated from operations is more significant relative to funds required, and because the Company has $300 million of long-term bank credit under existing agreements, a lesser amount of cash, certificates of deposit, and short-term investments need be maintained to meet current obligations. Therefore, excess funds are used to reduce long-term debt.*

As is apparent from this illustration, it is necessary to possess some knowledge of accounting to converse intelligently with professionals regarding financial matters.

The purpose of this text is to acquaint you with the essentials of accounting. You will be exposed to principles, practices, and procedures. Rather than taking a strictly theoretical overview of the field, the text emphasizes the "real world." A presentation of some theory and conceptual material is mandatory, however, for understanding the basis for what accountants do. Consequently, this book integrates theory with practice by utilizing many examples similar to the report to the directors and owners of McDonald's. In addition, each chapter contains excerpts from periodicals and realistic case problems. Upon completion of the text you will have a fundamental understanding of the dynamic field of accounting, a discipline characterized by growth, excitement, and challenge. Furthermore, you will see that a familiarity with accounting is an indispensable tool for success, now and in the future.

WHAT IS ACCOUNTING?

Constructing a definition of accounting is not an easy task. The field is broad and the work an accountant performs is varied. An accountant may keep a set of records for a small retail establishment to determine the establishment's profit or loss, or perhaps design a computerized information system so managers will receive timely reports for decision making and control of daily operations. Or the accountant may be conducting research in the area of federal income tax paid to the government. A publication from an accounting firm notes the following:

> *Historically, [accounting] suffered from an image problem—the Bob Cratchit syndrome—which portrayed it as dull, routine work. If this view were ever true, it certainly isn't today.*[1]

Observing the accountants' work and the profession of which they are members, few would find fault with the following definition:

> **Accounting** *is a set of theories, concepts, and techniques by which financial data is processed into information for reporting, planning, controlling, and decision-making purposes.*

To expand, most disciplines are based on theories and assumptions. Accounting is no exception. The foundation for many of the accountant's actions, procedures, and methodologies is a set of underlying principles and practices that have been generally accepted by the accounting profession. Given these principles and practices, various techniques have been developed for their implementation. The accountant uses these techniques to process the financial transactions of firms as complex as Boeing Corporation or as simple in structure as the family-owned corner market. In a sense the accountant is creating meaningful information from a series of facts and figures (data). This information is ultimately delivered to a user, who might employ it in deciding whether to add a new product, lease a new machine, or expand a firm's service area. The information might be used to report the results of past operations to interested parties such as the firm's owners or trade associations, or perhaps referenced to aid in the budgeting of future cash inflows and outflows.

Accounting encompasses extensive subject matter. Financial reporting, taxation, systems, planning, and decision making are only a few of its numerous elements. This text makes no attempt to cover in-depth all of accounting's vital components. Instead we will concentrate on an introduction to the fundamentals of financial and managerial accounting.

Financial accounting is primarily concerned with external reporting; that is, reporting the results of financial activities to parties outside the firm. Stockholders and governmental agencies such as the Securities and Exchange Commission (SEC) are included in this group. The financial reporting activities concentrate on a fair presentation of (1) the resources invested in a business and (2) the profitability of operations. Financial accounting is complemented by **managerial accounting,** which deals primarily with re-

[1]Peat, Marwick, Mitchell & Co., *Your Career in Professional Accounting*, p. 12.

porting the results of operations to managers and interested parties within an organization. By its very nature and the audience to which it is directed, managerial accounting deals heavily in the areas of planning, control, and decision making.

The Accountant: A Glorified Bookkeeper?

Many people tend to confuse bookkeeping with accounting. They often express the opinion that these two occupations are identical, or that the accountant is nothing more than a glorified bookkeeper. Both of these notions are incorrect.

The **bookkeeper** is basically concerned with recording, summarizing, and processing data into information. Accountants may become involved with this type of work at times, but usually their duties are more complex and sophisticated. The accountant deals primarily with the use and interpretation of information as opposed to transaction record keeping. The bookkeeper, then, assists the accountant in generating the information needed for financial reporting and analysis.

Normally, bookkeepers lack the training and background to function effectively in financial management. A successful accountant is one who is skilled not only in accounting but in other business and management techniques as well. Indeed, the accountant must assume a key role in supervising an organization's survival in a constantly changing financial climate.

THE ACCOUNTING PROFESSION

The profession of accounting can be traced back almost five hundred years. Thus there has been considerable time for growth and development. Still, the accounting profession has not reached full maturity. Accounting rules frequently change. National programs (e.g., energy conservation, pollution control, pension, and health care) are enacted that influence income tax law and impose new record-keeping requirements. Regulatory agencies constantly dictate new reporting provisions for firms under their domain. Events such as these make it necessary for the accounting profession to adapt to a dynamic environment. For the most part accounting has met the challenge.

Unfortunately, there have been some problems. Lawsuits filed by stockholders against accounting firms are increasing in number. There is discontent in the financial community with the rule-making bodies within the accounting profession. In addition, the reports produced by accountants are criticized by many as being deficient. Several of these complex issues will be discussed later in this text. At this point, however, a brief overview of the various facets of the profession is helpful.

Public Accounting

Firms engaged in **public accounting** render accounting services to all types of enterprises (e.g., hotels, publishers, equipment manufacturers, and professional sports clubs). In view of the size and multiple locations of many of their clients, several public accounting firms have offices from coast to coast and in foreign countries. The largest firms are known collectively as the Big Eight. They are as follows:

Arthur Andersen & Co.
Arthur Young & Co.
Coopers & Lybrand
Deloitte Haskins & Sells
Ernst & Whinney
Peat, Marwick, Mitchell & Co.
Price Waterhouse & Co.
Touche Ross & Co.

Rather than operate on such a large scale, many public accounting firms are established on a regional or local basis. All these firms, regardless of scope, employ certified public accountants (CPAs). **CPAs** are individuals who, like doctors, dentists, and lawyers, are licensed to practice their profession. The CPA certificate is granted to those who pass a rigorous two-and-a-half-day examination and meet certain accounting experience and educational requirements.[2]

Public accounting firms perform numerous services for their clients. Most often their work is in the fields of auditing, income tax, and management advisory services (MAS).

Auditing

Audit work represents the major source of business for most public accounting firms, particularly those organized on the national or international level. **Auditing** involves the investigation and examination of the transactions that underlie an organization's financial reports. The investigation is accomplished by an auditor, who studies the accounting and administrative controls that have been built into a client's information-processing system for purposes of error detection and fraud prevention. In addition, the auditor often performs statistical tests on accounting data to verify the data's accuracy.

A major purpose of the audit process is to increase the credibility of the financial statements (reports) prepared by a business. The statements are sent to the owners of the business, to financial analysts, and frequently to government agencies. These parties are vitally concerned that the reports result in a fair presentation of the financial activities of the enterprise. The employment of an *external independent auditor,* who performs certain audit tasks, enhances this process.

Income tax

Public accounting firms also perform **income tax services.** These services are very specialized and include much more than the preparation and filing of tax returns. In fact, many of the mechanical procedures associated with tax returns have been computerized, thus eliminating considerable drudgery for the accountant. Tax accountants must be experts in the many and often confusing tax laws. Not only do they figure the amount of taxes

[2]Education and experience requirements vary from state to state.

owed to the Internal Revenue Service (IRS), but tax accountants also ensure compliance with tax laws and plan for the future. They advise clients on various alternatives that might minimize taxes. The suggested courses of action are within the legal boundaries of the tax statutes and therefore center on techniques of tax avoidance, not tax evasion.

The tax accountant's duties may include working with individuals other than clients, namely, employees from the IRS or the various state and local departments of taxation. When tax returns of individuals and businesses are reviewed (audited), the tax accountant may meet with revenue agents in order to answer questions. Or the accountant may contact the IRS or state agencies to obtain rulings in advance of proposed business transactions.

Tax accounting is extremely exacting and challenging. As the various legislatures pass new laws and enact new programs, the field of taxation will grow and require more skilled tax practitioners and accounting technicians.

Management advisory services

Management advisory services (MAS) are the broadest of the services performed by public accounting firms. MAS essentially involves the operation of a management consulting practice for clients. Often the work is only indirectly related to traditional accounting matters. As a result, the larger accounting firms have hired specialists for various consulting areas, some of whom have had little or no accounting training. Examples include physicians (if a firm has extensive involvement with hospitals), educators (if the firm does considerable work in university administration), computer experts, and engineers. The smaller CPA firms generally cannot afford the luxury of hiring a specialist in a nonaccounting area. Consequently, their MAS activities are typically not as broad nor as sophisticated as those performed by the larger firms.

It is an impossible task to list all the advisory services performed by accountants. However, the following projects seem fairly representative: inventory control, analysis and design of information-processing systems, implementation of production scheduling systems, cost analysis of buy-versus-lease alternatives, and assistance in product pricing.

Private Accounting

Private accounting, sometimes referred to as industrial accounting, is another major branch of the profession. Rather than perform accounting services for many different clients, a private accountant is employed by an individual business to render services exclusively for that organization. As you can imagine, there is considerable variety within this field. Typical opportunities for employment include jobs with retailers, manufacturers (in such diverse industries as petroleum and filmmaking), and service enterprises (such as airlines, banks, and amusement parks).

There are several other significant distinctions between public and private accounting. Although many CPAs are employed in the private sector, there is no specific licensing procedure for private accountants. The only accounting "license" is the CPA. There are, however, examinations and programs designed to measure competence in the private field. The *Certificate in Management Accounting* (*CMA*) requires candidates to pass a broad two-and-a-half-day examination. This test covers such disciplines as managerial finance and economics, principles of organizational behavior, business ethics, financial and managerial accounting practices, and quantitative methods. Another program has been designed to measure proficiency in internal auditing. Individuals passing an examination and meeting work experience requirements may receive the *certified internal auditor* (*CIA*) designation.

Much of the work performed in the private field can be subdivided into specialized areas. These areas include the following tasks.

Cost accounting

Every successful business uses some form of cost accounting. **Cost accounting** deals with the collection, assignment, control, and evaluation of costs. A manufacturer such as Ford Motor Company incurs many different costs in its vast network of plants and offices. To compute the cost of producing an automobile, Ford must collect cost data and assign the data to the company's diverse manufacturing activities. This procedure is one of the necessary steps for correctly determining the selling price of the vehicle. Service enterprises follow essentially the same procedures. As an example, hospitals collect and assign cost data for purposes of calculating patient billing rates for hospital rooms and services.

The costs incurred by an enterprise will impact its overall profitability. Therefore most businesses are cost-conscious and have extensive programs of cost control. These programs often utilize *budgets*, which are plans of expected performance. Actual costs are compared against planned costs, and a variance is calculated. The *variance* is generally labeled unfavorable or favorable, depending on whether actual costs are more or less than originally anticipated. On the basis of an analysis of the variances, appropriate corrective action is then taken by management.

Cost accounting not only helps to evaluate past activity, but it also aids management in making decisions regarding the future. Consider United Airlines, the largest air carrier in the United States. Like other airlines, United has been affected by deregulation of the airline industry and the subsequent start-up of new routes and cities to service. In addition, increasing inflation has produced a consumer outcry for discounted airfares. Energy problems have caused United's jet fuel cost per gallon to rise over 200% since 1976. Furthermore, spiraling costs have prompted United to help launch a new generation of wide-body, fuel-efficient aircraft. The firm has entered into an agreement

> *. . . for 30 Boeing 767s to be delivered beginning in 1982. The 767 will seat 197 passengers and have transcontinental range. Cost of the aircraft, engines and support equipment is expected to be $1.2 billion (including the effect of projected inflation).*

Cost accounting will be of great assistance to United in terms of evaluating such problems as the following:

Route structures. Should new routes be sought, or service on existing routes expanded?

Airfares. Should fares be increased to cover rising costs? Are discounted fares and the accompanying increase in passenger volume profitable?

Equipment. Can existing planes be flown more hours per day, thus raising total seat capacity without the acquisition of expensive new aircraft? What should be done with the older aircraft that the 767s are expected to replace?

Financing. What is the most profitable means of financing new aircraft acquisitions?

Internal auditing

Large organizations often have their own personnel to review and monitor established accounting procedures and controls. The review process, which determines whether the procedures and controls are functioning as originally intended, helps to (1) safeguard the company's resources and (2) check the reliability and accuracy of the accounting information being produced. The individuals performing this work are known as **internal auditors.** While their duties and responsibilities are similar to those of auditors employed in public accounting (i.e., external auditors), the internal-auditing orientation is somewhat different. The internal auditor focuses mainly on controls and procedures. The independent external auditor, while also investigating accounting controls, is concerned primarily with the fairness of the financial statements prepared by a business.

Other activities

Depending on size, many companies engage in accounting activities other than cost accounting and internal auditing. Larger businesses maintain separate *systems departments* to design the methods, procedures, and forms needed to process accounting data. Frequently, computers are involved.

The systems field is a very fertile area for accountants. Many accountants, especially those who earned degrees prior to the mid-1960s, had minimal exposure to computers and data processing work in their degree programs. To complicate matters, systems and computer personnel often have little or no accounting background. Thus the accountant with considerable computer training is a very employable individual.

Many businesses have established *planning departments* that deal heavily with budgeting and forecasting. Planning work is very interesting, because the activities involved are both internal and external in orientation. Planning personnel must work with managers within the firm to establish proper budgets. At the same time planners must monitor the general business environment, including such factors as actions of competitors, the gross national product (GNP), trends in interest rates, and inflation.

Finally, large businesses frequently operate their own *tax departments.* These departments offer in-house advice on various issues and engage in tax-planning activities.

Governmental Accounting

The last major segment of the accounting profession is composed of those accountants employed by governmental agencies. Employment may be at the local, state, or federal level. The accountant's duties range from helping the Federal Bureau of Investigation (FBI) in a fraud case to assisting in local property tax collections to auditing defense contracts for the U.S. Department of Defense (DOD).

Among the many governmental agencies that employ accountants, three are very well known for either their work in or their influence on the accounting profession. They are as follows:

Internal Revenue Service (IRS). This body is responsible for processing the millions of tax returns that are filed each year. In addition, the IRS administers the tax laws that are passed by Congress and the rulings handed down by the courts. These actions frequently result in the audit of taxpayers' returns to determine whether proper procedures have been followed.

Securities and Exchange Commission (SEC). The SEC was established to administer the Securities Act of 1933 and the Securities Exchange Act of 1934. This agency reviews the financial statements of firms that offer securities for sale to the public and has the authority to impose certain reporting standards. The work and influence of the SEC will be cited later in this text.

General Accounting Office (GAO). The GAO is often called the "watchdog" of Congress because it evaluates other governmental agencies and programs. Its work is varied and sometimes far removed from "traditional" accounting. The GAO has investigated the status of missile programs, medical standards of pilots for the Federal Aviation Administration (FAA), and tax collection procedures of the IRS.

KEY UNDERLYING CONCEPTS

As we noted earlier, accounting is supported by a set of underlying principles and concepts. An in-depth presentation of these concepts will be given in Chapter 18. The discussion is postponed so that you may gain an understanding of the mechanics and procedures of accounting, thus making a conceptual presentation more meaningful. To comprehend how accounting measures financial activity, you should have knowledge of three of these concepts—the entity assumption, the cost principle, and the accounting equation—at this time.

Entity Assumption

The **entity assumption** holds that a business must be viewed as a unit that is separate and apart from its owners and from other firms. If this assumption was not made, personal economic activities of the owners (e.g., the purchase of a home, the payment of a child's college tuition) would be merged with the transactions of their businesses, thus combining the affairs of two separate and distinct units—owner and business. The resulting financial statements that are constructed to report the business's financial condition and profitability, therefore, would not be meaningful.

The entity assumption also notes that a business should be viewed aside

CONSIDERING ACCOUNTING AS A CAREER?

Well below rock stars and sex symbols in earning power but well above the typical corporation president stand the nation's top professionals—doctors and lawyers—thousands of whom earn upwards of $100,000 a year. These wealthy professionals are in many ways the economic aristocrats of our affluent society. They have far more security and independence than a high-paid corporate executive and a far longer career span than most entertainers or sports figures.

Now add to this elite professional group the certified public accountants. Their business is growing by leaps and bounds, and their earning power now equals that of lawyers and is approaching that of physicians.

What is happening is clear enough in Adam Smith terms. The demand for accounting services is expanding faster than the supply. It is not, of course, "natural" demand in the sense that people want more bookkeeping. It is manufactured demand created by laws and regulations in a society that seems to feel it can cure all human ills simply by passing laws and regulations—happiness through red tape. Every year fewer and fewer Americans are even trying to do their own income taxes. Every year additional requirements are laid on business for record keeping and disclosure.

As a result more people are practicing public accounting. Some have phenomenal records. Consider the case of Russell Palmer. Fresh out of Michigan State University, Palmer took a job in the Big Eight accounting firm Touche Ross. "I thought I'd make a little money and go to law school," the trim, fair-haired CPA recalls. Just 16 years later, at 37, he became the firm's managing partner at a salary of around $300,000 a year.

Russell Palmer's success is one reason why bright students are jamming accounting classrooms today. Obviously, the accounting profession can be a very, very fast track to high pay and heady responsibility. However, Palmer's case is the exception. Most accountants don't make partner at a Big Eight firm. Many go to smaller firms and become partners there. Or they create their own practices. Many join private industry's burgeoning financial staffs.

The occasional CPA may rise above his or her specialty and become a corporate treasurer, chief financial officer, and even chief executive officer. Of the United States' 800 highest-paid chief executives, over 20% boast financial backgrounds. They are not necessarily CPAs, though many are.

Ours is daily becoming a more complex society requiring more and more specialists—and new kinds of specialists. In such a situation the accountant is exalted as far above the old-fashioned bookkeeper in a green eyeshade as a surgeon or psychiatrist is exalted above the old-fashioned country doctor with a battered bag. The accountant is a member of a rapidly expanding and prestigious profession.

SOURCE Adapted from "The U.S.' Newest Glamour Job," Forbes, September 1, 1977, pp. 32–36.

and apart from other businesses. It would be impossible to measure the activities of an enterprise without this assumption. Imagine the difficulty of evaluating the operations of Anheuser-Busch if they could not be distinguished from those of Pabst Brewing and the Coors Brewing Company. These are three separate units and their activities must be accounted for accordingly.

This textbook will view the accounting activities of three popular entity forms. The simplest in structure is the **sole proprietorship,** which is a business owned by one individual. A step above the proprietorship is the partnership; the **partnership** is a business owned by two or more individuals and managed according to a contractual agreement among them. The third basic form of entity is the **corporation** in which the owners are its stockholders.

Cost Principle

Accounting is based on the **principle of historical cost.** That is, the acquisitions of goods, services, and other resources by a business are entered in the accounting records at cost. For example, if a company pays $55,000 to acquire a parcel of land for use as a future plant site, the land cost is recorded at $55,000. Thus the exchange or transaction price serves as the basis for entries into the accounting records.

The rationale for the use of historical cost is twofold. First, historical cost is objective and definite. The land above may have cost the original seller $32,000, may have been assessed for property taxes at $40,000, and may have been appraised by two independent appraisal services at $58,000 and $53,000. Which of these figures are correct? They all are. The cost of $55,000 is entered in the records, however, because the buyer and seller have negotiated an "arms-length" transaction and have agreed that the land is to be exchanged at a price of $55,000. The use of definite cost figures helps to make accounting reports and information more objective. In contrast, appraisal or market values can vary and often incorporate personal opinion and bias.

The second reason for the use of historical cost is that cost can be verified. Recall from our earlier discussion that auditors examine the financial statements of an enterprise to determine whether the statements result in a fair presentation of financial activity. The use of definite, objective cost-based information lends itself to this process. Evidence of the cost of goods and services normally exists in the form of documents and canceled checks. In addition, complicated transactions and exchanges can be examined by different accountants. Because of the objectivity of the cost basis, the accountants should reach the same conclusions and report the same facts. When subjective market and appraisal values are used, the same results would probably not occur.

Although it is objective, the use of historical cost does create problems. Recording a long-term resource in the accounting records at cost at the time of acquisition is satisfactory. Maintaining that resource over its lifetime at cost can result in a severe misstatement of financial condition and profitability. Picture what has happened to the real estate market, for example, over the past ten to fifteen years. Prices have soared because of high annual inflation rates. The historical-cost basis ignores these increases, however. To illustrate, suppose the land purchased for $55,000 is now worth $94,000. The land, nevertheless, remains in the accounting records at $55,000. As a result, the cost basis is criticized by many financial statement users as not being in accord with economic reality. The use and limitations of the cost basis of accounting will be cited throughout this text.

The Accounting Equation

Activities of accounting entities range from preparation of the weekly payroll at Joe's Grocery to the acquisition of a foreign subsidiary by a large international corporation. From the simple to the complex, all business transactions have one common feature: their accounting treatment is based on the fundamental accounting equation. Before we illustrate this equation, though, we must explain some associated terminology. As you progress through the study of accounting, these terms will be encountered with increasing frequency. Proper understanding, therefore, is mandatory.

Assets

Assets are the economic resources owned by a company that are expected to benefit future time periods. Examples include the cash that a business has on hand and in the bank, its investments in stocks and bonds, inventories maintained for sale or for use in production, buildings, land, and equipment. Two assets in need of further explanation at this point are receivables and prepaid expenses.

Receivables are the amounts that a business expects to collect at some future date. The most commonly encountered receivable, *accounts receivable,* represents the amounts owed to a firm by its customers. This asset generally arises from the sale, on credit, of goods and services. Other receivables may include interest receivable and notes receivable. The former indicates that a business expects to receive some interest that is owed to it in the near future. A note receivable, on the other hand, indicates ownership of a signed document (called a note) by which one party promises to pay another party a certain sum of money on a future date.

Prepaid expenses are goods and services that have been purchased for future consumption and paid for in advance (prepaid). A common example is insurance, which is generally paid on a quarterly, semiannual, or annual basis. At the time of purchase a service has been acquired, the insuring of assets. The ownership rights to this service are an asset appropriately known as prepaid insurance. Other examples of goods and services that are frequently prepaid include rent, advertising, and supplies.

Liabilities

Amounts owed by an enterprise are known as **liabilities.** As we will show shortly, liabilities also represent the creditors' "interest" or equity in a company's assets. Most liabilities, because they will be paid in the future, have the term "payable" within their names. Examples include salaries payable, taxes payable, and interest payable. A substantial liability for many firms is *accounts payable,* which represents the amounts owed to creditors for goods purchased or services rendered.

You should be able to visualize the relationship between accounts receivable and accounts payable; that is, an account receivable of one firm is represented by an account payable on someone else's records. As an example, suppose Joe Martin purchased gasoline by using a credit card issued by Exxon Corporation. Immediately after the purchase and until payment with cash, Exxon is considered an account payable by Martin since he owes the firm money for the gasoline. In contrast, Exxon carries Martin as an account receivable since the company has a claim against him for the purchase. This same relationship exists between other assets and liabilities, for example, notes receivable and notes payable, and interest receivable and interest payable.

Owners' equity (capital)

Owners' equity, or capital, represents the owners' net worth or "interest" in the assets of a business. It is equal to the company's net assets, that is, assets minus liabilities. Importantly, owners' equity is a concept that exists *only* on a piece of paper. To explain, many accounting students are under the impression that capital is equivalent to a company's cash on hand and in the bank. This notion is incorrect; there is no direct relationship between capital and cash. Capital is not spent, nor is it placed in a vault for safe storage; it is only the result of a mathematical operation.

During a given time period changes in owners' equity result from the following factors.

Investments by the owner

Owners of an enterprise often take some of their personal assets and put **(invest)** them in a business. Frequently, this investment is in the form of cash. Investments by the owner are not loans, because the owner is relinquishing asset control and ownership to the enterprise. Since the investment causes company assets to increase, the owners' net "interest" or equity in these assets will also increase.

Withdrawals by the owner

A **withdrawal** is just the opposite of an investment. The owners are removing assets from the business for their own personal use. Thus withdrawals decrease the equity of the owners in the firm's assets. A common example of a withdrawal is the payment of a cash dividend by a corporation to its owners, the stockholders.

Net income

A third factor affecting owners' equity is net income. **Net income** is the excess of a company's revenues over expenses for a given time period. When an individual states that a business is "making money," he or she normally means that a net income is being generated. Like owner investments, net income causes the owners' equity in the assets of an enterprise to increase.

To fully comprehend the concept of net income, you must understand the terms "revenue" and "expense." **Revenues** refer to the amounts charged to customers for goods sold or services rendered. Revenues take different forms, as the following list shows:

Entity	*Revenue Form*
The Seven-Up Company	Soft drink sales
Ryder System, Inc.	Vehicle-leasing revenue
Dallas Cowboys	Ticket revenue
Lawyer	Fees earned
Salesperson	Commissions earned

Note that revenues are *not* equivalent to the cash receipts of an enterprise. For example, assume Signet Company had the following activity during October:

Credit sales to customers	*$25,000*
Cash sales to customers	*8,000*
Cash collections from credit sales	*10,000*

Signet had total cash receipts during October of $18,000: $8,000 from cash sales and $10,000 from the collection of accounts receivable. The firm's revenues totaled $33,000: $25,000 from credit sales plus $8,000 in cash sales. The $10,000 of collections on credit sales is not considered in the latter computation because the revenue was recognized in an earlier period, when the credit sales occurred.

Expenses are the costs incurred in producing revenue. Unlike assets, expenses do not benefit future time periods; instead the related benefits are received currently. Examples of expenses include salaries and wages incurred for employee services, utility costs incurred for gas and electricity, and interest incurred for the use of borrowed money. Note that many assets that render future benefits eventually become expenses. To illustrate, suppose on January 1 of the current year Hernandez Corporation paid $600 for a one-year insurance policy. Hernandez has acquired a prepaid expense that will provide benefits (insurance against casualties) for one year. By January 31, or one month after purchase, $\frac{1}{12}$ of the policy has expired; that is, the policy has rendered benefits for the current accounting period (January). As a result, $50 ($600 × $\frac{1}{12}$) becomes insurance expense. The remaining $550 is still an asset—a prepaid expense that will benefit the next eleven months.

Two final points about expenses are in order. First, do not equate expenses with cash payments. It was shown earlier that a company's revenues are not necessarily equal to its cash receipts. Likewise, expenses are not equivalent to cash payments. For example, many businesses incur expenses at the end of one accounting period that are paid in the following period. Thus when one is calculating total expenses and cash payments for the initial period, it is easily recognized that the two amounts will not be equal.

Also not all cash payments are for expenses. A business may purchase a piece of equipment for cash. Since an asset has been acquired, total cash payments again will not equal total expenses.

Second, withdrawals are not expenses. Expenses and withdrawals may both involve an outflow of cash from the firm. Recall, however, that an expense is incurred in producing revenue. A withdrawal, on the other hand, is a removal of assets for personal use and is not associated with the revenue-producing process.

Net loss

A **net loss** is computed in the same fashion as net income; that is,

net loss = revenues − expenses

In this case, however, a company's expenses have exceeded its revenues. A net loss causes the owners' equity of an enterprise to decrease.

Now that we have defined these terms, let us view their interrelationships by studying the fundamental accounting equation. Imagine that Deborah Gardner has just graduated from college. Her parents have given her a graduation gift of $7,000 to purchase a car. After choosing a model and making the best deal with the car agency, Deborah finds that the cost of the car is exactly $7,000. She gives the dealer a check for $7,000. The car is now fully paid for, and Deborah takes possession the next day.

Consider the impact of this transaction in accounting terms. Deborah has the car, an asset, which cost $7,000. Her interest or equity in the car is also $7,000. The following equation expresses this relationship:

assets = owners' equity

$7,000 = $7,000

Now we will alter the example slightly. Suppose Deborah's parents gave her only $2,000. To purchase the $7,000 car, Deborah has secured a loan for the remaining $5,000. She now has the $7,000 car, and she also owes $5,000. Looking at the transaction from a different perspective, we see that Deborah's net interest or net worth in the car is $2,000, which is represented by her payment to the dealer. The loan company, her creditor, has a $5,000 interest in the car. Stated differently, the owners' equity in the $7,000 asset is $2,000, and the creditor's equity is $5,000. The foregoing statement can be expressed as follows:

assets = liabilities + owners' equity

$7,000 = $5,000 + $2,000

The mathematical relationship above is known as the fundamental **accounting equation.** In one form or another all transactions have some impact on the equation. As you will see, the equation will always balance, unless an error has been made.[3] The reason for this balancing is the *double-entry system of bookkeeping* that is employed by accountants. Under the double-entry system a transaction will always affect two or more accounts, such as two or more assets, an asset and a liability, an asset and owners' equity, and so on. Consequently, the equation's balance is always maintained.

The accounting equation: an illustration

The following example will help you understand the impact of transactions on the accounting equation and an enterprise. Assume Ray Davis has organized the Davis Furniture Repair Company as a sole proprietorship. The business opened on January 3, 1983, and had several transactions during the first month of operation. These transactions are described and explained on pages 17–19, and their effect on the accounting equation is shown.

A warning

The foregoing illustration shows that transactions can affect the accounting equation in many different ways. Assets, liabilities, and owners' equity can each remain the same or change in combination with one another. There are numerous possibilities. Therefore if your approach to learning this material is memorization, you will be fighting a losing battle. An analysis of the accounts affected by each transaction must be made. *Successful accounting students are those who develop the abilities to reason and analyze, not memorize.*

FINANCIAL STATEMENTS

One of the objectives of accounting is to convey financial information to owners, managers, lenders, and other interested parties. A significant portion of this information is contained within formal financial reports that are compiled and distributed by companies. Four reports are normally prepared: income statement, statement of owners' equity, balance sheet, and statement of changes in financial position. Discussion of the latter statement, which shows a firm's sources and uses of financial resources, will be postponed until Chapter 17. Let us now address the other three reports.

Income Statement

The **income statement** summarizes the results of a business's operations by disclosing the revenues earned and the expenses incurred. The expenses are subtracted from the revenues, yielding either a net income or a net loss. The income statement conveys information concerning an entity's profitability and the relation of expenses to revenues. From our presentation thus far it would appear that the net income or loss figure is very precise. Once we progress deeper into the study of accounting, we will show that net income is really a very arbitrary number based heavily on alternative practices and techniques that are selected for use by the accountant.

[3]To the frustration of many students, numerous errors can occur that have no effect on the equation's balancing. These errors will be explored in Chapter 2.

Jan. 3 Davis withdrew $9,000 from his personal savings account and invested it in the firm. As a result of this transaction, Davis Furniture Repair now has an asset, Cash, of $9,000. In addition, Ray Davis has obtained an interest (owners' equity) in the business's assets of $9,000. For the sake of clarity the elements affecting owners' equity are listed individually. Revenues and expenses will be combined later to generate the company's net income or net loss.

	Assets	= Liabilities +	Owners' Equity			
	Cash		**(+) Investments**	**(−) Withdrawals**	**(+) Revenues**	**(−) Expenses**
Jan. 3	+$9,000		+$9,000			

Jan. 4 Davis leased a shop and paid the first month's rent of $700. The cash payment reduces the firm's assets by $700. Because the business has incurred an expense, total expenses are increased.

	Assets	= Liabilities +	Owners' Equity			
	Cash		**(+) Investments**	**(−) Withdrawals**	**(+) Revenues**	**(−) Expenses**
Balances	$9,000		$9,000			$ —
Jan. 4	−700					+700 (Rent)
	$8,300		$9,000			$700

Note: *The equation remains in balance at $8,300.*

Jan. 4 Davis contacted Furniture Refinishers, a wholesaler, and purchased $1,100 of supplies and $450 of tools. Davis paid $300 in cash and agreed to remit the balance of $1,250 ($1,100 + $450 − $300) shortly. A liability, Accounts Payable, has been created, because the business now owes money to the wholesaler. This type of purchase, where money is owed, is commonly called a purchase on account.

	Assets			= Liabilities +	Owners' Equity			
	Cash	**Supplies**	**Tools**	**Accounts Payable**	**(+) Investments**	**(−) Withdrawals**	**(+) Revenues**	**(−) Expenses**
Balances	$8,300	$ —	$ —	$ —	$9,000			$700
Jan. 4	−300	+1,100	+450	+1,250				
	$8,000	$1,100	$450	$1,250	$9,000			$700

Note: *Assets are normally listed in order of liquidity or nearness to cash. As we will now show, receivables are listed before supplies and tools since collections from customers are forthcoming in a relatively short period of time.*

Jan. 15 During the past two weeks Davis provided repair services for six different customers and billed them a total of $870. This transaction is representative of Davis's earnings process, necessitating an increase in revenues. The customers have been billed and will pay at a later date. An asset, Accounts Receivable, has been created, since Davis has a claim against these individuals. This type of transaction is known as a sale of services on account.

	Assets				= Liabilities +	Owners' Equity			
	Cash	**Accounts Receivable**	**Supplies**	**Tools**	**Accounts Payable**	**(+) Investments**	**(−) Withdrawals**	**(+) Revenues**	**(−) Expenses**
Balances	$8,000	$ —	$1,100	$450	$1,250	$9,000		$ —	$700
Jan. 15		+870						+870	
	$8,000	$870	$1,100	$450	$1,250	$9,000		$870	$700

Jan. 19 Because he was in need of cash for personal activities, Davis withdrew $950 from the business. In addition, he paid the $35 utilities bill of his residence by using business funds. Both cash outlays are considered withdrawals. The latter is not an expense of Davis Furniture Repair, for it is not a cost incurred in a revenue-producing activity (repair work).

	Assets				= Liabilities +	Owners' Equity			
	Cash	**Accounts Receivable**	**Supplies**	**Tools**	**Accounts Payable**	**(+) Investments**	**(−) Withdrawals**	**(+) Revenues**	**(−) Expenses**
Balances	$8,000	$870	$1,100	$450	$1,250	$9,000	$ —	$870	$700
Jan. 19	−985						+985		
	$7,015	$870	$1,100	$450	$1,250	$9,000	$985	$870	$700

Jan. 20 The morning mail brought checks of $310 from two customers who were previously billed. Checks are accounted for as Cash. Is this revenue to Davis? The answer is no. Davis performed the services during the first two weeks of January. On January 15 revenue of $870, which includes the $310, was recorded. To record the $310 as revenue again would be double counting. The customers are paying their bills, thereby necessitating a reduction in Accounts Receivable. This type of transaction is referred to as a payment on account.

	Assets				= Liabilities +	Owners' Equity			
	Cash	**Accounts Receivable**	**Supplies**	**Tools**	**Accounts Payable**	**(+) Investments**	**(−) Withdrawals**	**(+) Revenues**	**(−) Expenses**
Balances	$7,015	$870	$1,100	$450	$1,250	$9,000	$985	$870	$700
Jan. 20	+310	−310							
	$7,325	$560	$1,100	$450	$1,250	$9,000	$985	$870	$700

Jan. 31 Davis paid two bills: one-half the amount due to Furniture Refinishers for the purchase on January 4 and a telephone bill of $25. The purchase was initially established as a liability to be paid at some future date. Because payment is now occurring, the account payable must be eliminated. The $25 expenditure is for a cost related to Davis's revenue-producing activity and is, thus, an expense of doing business.

	Assets				= Liabilities +	Owners' Equity			
	Cash	**Accounts Receivable**	**Supplies**	**Tools**	**Accounts Payable**	**(+) Investments**	**(−) Withdrawals**	**(+) Revenues**	**(−) Expenses**
Balances	$7,325	$560	$1,100	$450	$1,250	$9,000	$985	$870	$700
Jan. 31	−625				−625				
	−25								+25 (Telephone)
	$6,675	$560	$1,100	$450	$ 625	$9,000	$985	$870	$725

Jan. 31 Davis noted that $680 of supplies were used during the month. To reflect properly the firm's financial condition, he must reduce Supplies. Since $680 reflects the cost of supplies used in repair work, it is charged to an expense. This is an example of a prepaid expense (an asset), which eventually, upon consumption, becomes an expense.

	Assets				= Liabilities +	Owners' Equity			
	Cash	**Accounts Receivable**	**Supplies**	**Tools**	**Accounts Payable**	**(+) Investments**	**(−) Withdrawals**	**(+) Revenues**	**(−) Expenses**
Balances	$6,675	$560	$1,100	$450	$625	$9,000	$985	$870	$ 725
Jan. 31			−680						+680 (Supplies)
	$6,675	$560	$ 420	$450	$625	$9,000	$985	$870	$1,405

Jan. 31 Davis billed customers $2,100 for repair services performed during the second half of the month. This transaction is recorded in the same manner as that on January 15.

	Assets				= Liabilities +	Owners' Equity			
	Cash	**Accounts Receivable**	**Supplies**	**Tools**	**Accounts Payable**	**(+) Investments**	**(−) Withdrawals**	**(+) Revenues**	**(−) Expenses**
Balances	$6,675	$ 560	$420	$450	$625	$9,000	$985	$ 870	$1,405
Jan. 31		+2,100						+2,100	
	$6,675	$2,660	$420	$450	$625	$9,000	$985	$2,970	$1,405
		$10,205			= $625 +		$9,580		

The income statement, like the other three statements, is divided into two sections: heading and body. The heading reveals the company's name, the name of the statement, and the period of time covered by the statement. The income statement is known as a period statement because it discloses the net income or loss generated by a business over a period of time. The period is usually a month, a quarter, or a year. If the latter is employed, the year selected may be any of the following:

Type	*Explanation*
Calendar year	Runs from January 1–December 31
Fiscal year	Any one-year period other than the above (e.g., July 1–June 30)
Natural business year	Ends at the conclusion of the natural business year (e.g., October 31 for a professional baseball club, which is after the play-offs and World Series)

The statement's body contains detailed accounting information. For the income statement this information consists of an itemized listing of revenues and expenses.

The income statement for Davis Furniture Repair appears on the top of Exhibit 1-1. Observe how the statement is developed from the revenue and expense columns of the accounting equation. Since revenues exceed expenses, Davis has generated a net income.

Statement of Owners' Equity

The purpose of the **statement of owners' equity** is to disclose the causes of change in owners' equity during the accounting period. Like the income statement, then, the owners' equity statement also reveals financial information for a period of time. Given the statement's purpose, you should be able to picture its content. Recall that the following items impact owners' equity:

Increase	*Decrease*
Owner investments	Owner withdrawals
Net income	Net loss

Consequently, these four items compose the heart of this statement.

The owners' equity statement varies with the form of business organization. The statement for a corporation is considerably different, both in content and name, from the statement of a proprietorship. To be consistent with the Davis Furniture Repair example, we will illustrate the statement of owners' equity for a sole proprietorship.

During January the repair service had owner investments of $9,000 and withdrawals of $985. In addition, as shown by the income statement, net income amounted to $1,565. Davis's statement of owners' equity appears in the middle of Exhibit 1-1. Because owners' equity is affected by the net income generated from operations, the income statement should be con-

Exhibit 1-1

Financial statements of Davis Furniture Repair

DAVIS FURNITURE REPAIR
Income Statement
For the Month Ended January 31, 1983

Repair sales		$2,970
Less expenses		
Rent	$700	
Telephone	25	
Supplies	680	
Total expenses		1,405
Net income		$1,565

DAVIS FURNITURE REPAIR
Statement of Owners' Equity
For the Month Ended January 31, 1983

Beginning balance, Jan. 1		$ —
Increases		
Owner investments	$9,000	
Net income	1,565	10,565
		$10,565
Decreases		
Owner withdrawals		985
Ending balance, Jan. 31		$ 9,580

DAVIS FURNITURE REPAIR
Balance Sheet
January 31, 1983

Assets		
Cash	$6,675	
Accounts receivable	2,660	
Supplies	420	
Tools	450	
Total assets		$10,205
Liabilities		
Accounts payable		$ 625
Owners' equity		
Ray Davis, capital		9,580
Total liabilities & owners' equity		$10,205

structed first. The January 31 balance of $9,580 will carry over to become the beginning owners' equity balance on February 1, 1983.

Balance Sheet

The **balance sheet,** sometimes called the statement of financial position, is a formalized listing of the accounting equation's components: assets, liabilities, and owners' equity. The balance sheet shows that the sum of the individual equity interests, the owners' and creditors', is equal to and in balance with the firm's assets; that is, assets = liabilities + owners' equity. This equality is shown for some particular *point* in time, not for a *period.* The statement's heading, therefore, reflects a single date rather than a time period. Since the other financial statements summarize activity for a period, it is only logical that the date given the balance sheet be the last day of the accounting period.

The balance sheet of Davis Furniture Repair, which appears at the bottom of Exhibit 1-1, is based on the January 31 final balances of the accounting equation illustration with one minor exception. So that the information already contained in the income statement and statement of owners' equity is not duplicated, the January 31 (ending) owners' equity balance is reported as a single amount labeled Ray Davis, Capital.

Statement Interrelationships

The three statements are distinct, with each presenting different types of financial information. While they do differ, the statements are also interrelated. The income statement furnishes the necessary net income figure for the statement of owners' equity, which, in turn, provides the ending capital balance for the balance sheet.

The statements are also interrelated in another sense. The balance sheet depicts a company's financial condition as of a specific date, for example, January 31 in the Davis illustration. Going one step further, the same balance sheet represents Davis's position at the start of business on February 1. The income statement and statement of owners' equity would then be prepared for the month of February to summarize activities that affect owners' equity (net income or net loss, withdrawals, and investments). A balance sheet would be prepared again on February 28 to summarize the financial condition as of that date. Thus the income statement and statement of owners' equity bridge the gap between successive balance sheets.

Financial Statements: Added Complexities

Unlike the financial statements of many companies, the statements of Davis Furniture Repair are very simplistic. Income statements and balance sheets are usually presented in more detail to facilitate understanding and analysis and to improve reader comprehension. Ordinarily, this detail takes the form of added captions within the statement's body and accompanying footnotes.

Within the income statement revenues are frequently classified as to their origin. Profit on the sale of merchandise is disclosed, and expenses are generally categorized by type or nature. Taxes are highlighted and unusual items are noted. Balance sheets are also complex. The asset and liability sections are normally subdivided for purposes of disclosure and analysis. In addition, the owners' equity section often contains capital stock accounts, thus informing the statement reader that the business is organized as a corporation.

Chapter 6 presents an in-depth view of financial statements. Many of the techniques necessary for the development and, more importantly, the understanding of financial statements will be presented throughout this text. Others can be gained only after a thorough study of topics in intermediate and advanced accounting courses. We hope this text will serve to "whet your appetite" for further exploration of the complex environment in which the accountant operates.

SUMMARY PROBLEM

On October 2, 1983, John Tunis opened the Tunis Realty Company. The following transactions occurred during the month.

Oct. 2 Invested $25,000 cash in the business.
3 Rented an office for the year and paid the first month's rent of $1,000.
4 Purchased $700 of office supplies for cash.
10 Received the cash for a home sold for a client. Tunis's commission on the home was $3,600.
15 Paid $400 in automobile expenses during the month. (Tunis uses his personal auto for business and bills the firm for all business expenses.)
16 Withdrew $500 for personal use.
21 Sold another home. The commission on this home was $3,200, but Tunis will not receive the cash until November.
23 Purchased furniture for the office at a cost of $6,500. Paid a down payment of $2,000 and agreed to remit the balance owed next month.
24 Paid utility bills of $350 for the month.
31 Tunis calculated that $450 of office supplies had been used during the month.

INSTRUCTIONS

a **Analyze the effects of these transactions on the individual elements of the accounting equation.**

b **Prepare an income statement for the month ended October 31.**

c **Prepare a statement of owners' equity for the month ended October 31.**

d **Prepare a balance sheet as of October 31.**

SOLUTION

a

	Assets				= Liabilities +	Owners' Equity			
	Cash	Accounts Receivable	Office Supplies	Office Furniture	Accounts Payable	(+) Investments	(−) Withdrawals	(+) Revenues	(−) Expenses
Oct. 2	+$25,000					+$25,000			
3	−1,000								+$1,000 (Rent)
4	−700		+$700						
10	+3,600							+$3,600	
15	−400								+400 (Auto)
16	−500						+$500		
21		+$3,200						+3,200	
23	−2,000			+$6,500	+$4,500				
24	−350								+350 (Utilities)
31			−450						+450 (Supplies)
	$23,650	$3,200	$250	$6,500	$4,500	$25,000	$500	$6,800	$2,200

b

TUNIS REALTY
Income Statement
For the Month Ended October 31, 1983

Commissions		$6,800
Less expenses		
Rent	$1,000	
Automobile	400	
Utilities	350	
Supplies	450	
Total expenses		2,200
Net income		$4,600

c

TUNIS REALTY
Statement of Owners' Equity
For the Month Ended October 31, 1983

Beginning balance, Oct. 1		$ —
Increases		
Owner investments	$25,000	
Net income	4,600	29,600
		$29,600
Decreases		
Owner withdrawals		500
Ending balance, Oct. 31		$29,100

d

TUNIS REALTY
Balance Sheet
October 31, 1983

Assets		
Cash	$23,650	
Accounts receivable	3,200	
Office supplies	250	
Office furniture	6,500	
Total assets		$33,600
Liabilities		
Accounts payable		$ 4,500
Owners' equity		
John Tunis, capital		29,100
Total liabilities & owners' equity		$33,600

KEY TERMS AND CONCEPTS

accounting 3
accounting equation 15
assets 12
auditing 5
balance sheet 22
bookkeeper 4
certified public accountant (CPA) 5
corporation 11
cost accounting 7
cost principle 11
entity assumption 9
expense 14
financial accounting 3
fiscal year 20
General Accounting Office (GAO) 9
income statement 16
income tax services 5
internal auditors 8
Internal Revenue Service (IRS) 9
liabilities 12
management advisory services (MAS) 6
managerial accounting 3
natural business year 20
net income 13
net loss 15
owner investments 13
owner withdrawals 13
owners' equity (capital) 13
partnership 11
prepaid expense 12
private accounting 6
public accounting 4
receivables 12
revenue 14
Securities and Exchange Commission (SEC) 9
sole proprietorship 11
statement of owners' equity 20

QUESTIONS

Q1-1 How does financial accounting differ from managerial accounting?

Q1-2 How does bookkeeping differ from accounting?

Q1-3 Paul Martin is contemplating an investment in the Indiana Company. He has secured the firm's audited financial statements, which have been reviewed by a certified public accountant. How can Martin be sure that the statements do not present false and incorrect information to purposely mislead investors?

Q1-4 Would cost accounting be of any value to a public accounting firm in managing its own internal operations? How?

Q1-5 Differentiate between internal and external auditing.

Q1-6 Explain the entity assumption.

Q1-7 Mr. P, the president of Fairwood Company, recently purchased a new car solely for personal use. He asked Mr. A, Fairwood's accountant, to record the car as a miscellaneous expense of the company's current accounting period. Mr. A refused. Explain the reason behind A's action.

Q1-8 Discuss the use of historical cost in the accounting process. Why is historical cost used, and what is one of its chief limitations?

Q1-9 Differentiate between an asset and an expense. When does a prepaid expense, which is an asset, become an expense?

Q1-10 To calculate owners' equity on December 31, a beginning accounting student made the following computation:

Beginning cash, Jan. 1	*$19,000*
+Cash receipts	*41,000*
	$60,000
−Cash payments	*24,000*
Owners' equity, Dec. 31	*$36,000*

Is he correct? Why?

Q1-11 Gifford's December income statement is in the process of being prepared. Through December 30 the firm has generated a $2,600 net income. The only transaction on December 31 is a withdrawal by the owner of $3,000. Would it be correct to say that Gifford incurred a $400 net loss during December? Why?

Q1-12 The Harter family owns a service station in Vermont. After his first lecture in principles of accounting, the youngest of the Harter sons, Teddy, decided to review the accounting records for the year just ended. He noted that net income of $15,800 was generated. At the same time the balance in the Cash account declined $5,300. Teddy felt that this situation was not possible and that a mistake had been made. Is Teddy correct? Explain and cite several examples to support your answer.

Q1-13 The text suggested that the income statement should be prepared first, the statement of owners' equity second, and the balance sheet last. Explain how this order of preparation facilitates the accounting process.

Q1-14 Juarez and Rodriguez are having a heated debate regarding the order in which certain items should be listed on the balance sheet. Their views are as follows:

Juarez. Cash, Accounts Receivable, Equipment, Rent Expense
Rodriguez. Equipment, Accounts Receivable, Rent Expense, Cash

Who is correct? Why?

EXERCISES

E1-1 Pants Palace is a firm that specializes in the sale of jeans and related accessories. Stores are operated in shopping malls throughout the country. State whether each of the following is an asset, a liability, a revenue, or an expense from Pants Palace's viewpoint.

a Monthly rental charges paid to a mall.
b The inventory of jeans and tops owned by the firm.
c A loan that is due to Second Federal Savings.
d Daily sales that are made to customers.
e Supplies that have been consumed in operations.
f Amounts owed by customers from sales made on credit.
g Land that is held by the company for future development of a new national headquarters.
h Cash on hand in each store for paying small miscellaneous expenses.

E1-2 The Murphy Company's books showed the following totals on January 1 and December 31.

	Jan. 1	Dec. 31
Total assets	$81,000	$74,000
Total liabilities	38,000	46,000

Jack Murphy invested $4,000 and had withdrawn $10,000 on various dates throughout the year. Calculate Murphy's net income or net loss by analyzing the change in owners' equity during the year.

E1-3 The following accounts and balances were obtained from the records of the Jenkins Company.

	Jan. 1	Dec. 31
Cash	$5,100	$4,200
Equipment	2,600	3,900
Accounts payable	3,800	5,400
Accounts receivable	1,800	2,000

Additional information is as follows:

Withdrawals during the year	*$ 800*
Net loss for the year	*900*
Fees earned during the year	*2,100*

Calculate

a Owners' equity on January 1 and December 31.
b Total expenses for the year.
c Investments by the owner during the year.

E1-4 The following balances pertain to the Bonati Company as of December 31, 1983.

Accounts payable	*$ 3,000*	*Prepaid insurance*	*$1,500*
Accounts receivable	*5,100*	*Supplies*	*600*
Advertising expense	*500*	*Supplies expense*	*300*
Cash	*9,000*	*Utilities expense*	*800*
Commission revenue	*15,000*	*Wages expense*	*2,100*
Insurance expense	*1,000*	*Wages payable*	*700*

At the beginning of 1983 Pat Bonati, Capital, had a balance of $2,900. Owner investments and withdrawals totaled $1,200 and $1,900, respectively, through December 31.

a Determine Bonati's total assets as of December 31.
b Determine Bonati's total liabilities as of December 31.
c Compute Bonati's ending capital balance as of December 31.
d Determine Bonati's net income or net loss for the year.

E1-5 Write the accounting equation on a piece of paper. By using "+" and "−", indicate the effect of each of the following transactions on total assets, liabilities, and owners' equity.

a Rendered services on account.
b Purchased a new machine for cash.
c Customers paid on account.
d Recorded the receipt of a utilities bill to be paid next month.
e Paid the weekly salaries of the employees.

f Purchased land of $18,000 by paying $6,000 down and signing a note payable for the remainder.
g Paid the utilities bill that was previously recorded in (d).
h Returned a new desk purchased earlier in the month on account. The bill had not as yet been paid.

E1-6 You are in the process of reviewing the income statement, statement of owners' equity, and balance sheet of the Weissman Company. On which financial statement(s), if any, would the following information be found?

a The amount of equipment owned.
b Withdrawals by the owner.
c Supplies used in operations.
d Cash payments during the period.
e Ending owners' equity.
f Amounts owed to creditors.
g Fees earned for services rendered.
h Amounts owed by customers.

E1-7 The Hirsch Company recorded the following two items in the accounting records during July.

1 Purchased $4,900 of equipment for cash at a "going-out-of-business" sale. The equipment normally sold for $7,500. The transaction was recorded as follows:

Equipment	*+$7,500*
Cash	*−4,900*
Revenue from purchase	*+2,600*

2 Increased the value of the company's main manufacturing plant by $80,000 to reflect the real estate boom in the Sun Belt. The $80,000 figure was obtained from the Dade County Appraisal Company and was recorded as follows:

Building	*+$80,000*
Hirsch, capital	*+80,000*

Hirsch's July 31 balance sheet contained the following information:

Total assets	*$254,000*
Total liabilities	*102,000*
Owners' equity	*152,000*

Assume that net income for July was $18,700.

a Criticize the treatment of the items above.
b Determine corrected figures for the following:
  1 Net income
  2 Total assets
  3 Total liabilities
  4 Total owners' equity

E1-8 The Baxter Company is a successful office machine repair service. In the first few years of operation John Baxter invested considerable funds in the business. Lately, owner investments have not been necessary. Baxter's accountant prepared the following balance sheet for the year just ended:

Assets		
Cash		$ 7,000
Accounts receivable		14,000
Supplies		2,000
Other assets, including equipment		29,000
Total assets		$52,000
Liabilities		
Accounts payable	$4,000	
Loan payable	9,000	
Total liabilities		$13,000
Owners' equity		
John Baxter, capital		39,000
Total liabilities & owners' equity		$52,000

Baxter now desires to withdraw the $28,000 that he has invested in the firm over the years.

a How would Baxter's accountant respond to his client concerning the request for $28,000?

b Suppose the Baxter Company desired to honor the request of its owner. How could this be done, and what effect could this action possibly have on company operations?

PROBLEMS

P1-1 ***Identification of transactions***

The tabulation below summarizes several transactions of the Loftus Company.

	Assets			= Liabilities +	Owners' Equity			
	Cash	Accounts Receivable	Equip-ment	Accounts Payable	(+) Invest-ments	(−) With-drawals	(+) Revenues	(−) Expenses
Balances	$5,000	$8,000	$15,000	$12,000	$16,000	$11,000	$20,000	$9,000
(a)	+900						+900	
(b)	−800		+4,000	+3,200				
(c)				+700				+700
(d)	−400			−400				
(e)			−500	−500				
(f)		+1,800					+1,800	
(g)	+600	−600						
	$5,300	$9,200	$18,500	$15,000	$16,000	$11,000	$22,700	$9,700

INSTRUCTIONS

Write a brief explanation of the nature of each transaction (*a*)–(*g*).

P1-2 ***Statement preparation***

The following balances are taken from the books of Gibson Enterprises at the close of their fiscal year on June 30, 1983.

Accounts payable	$19,200	Mortgage note payable	$48,000
Accounts receivable	13,500	Prepaid expenses	6,500
Building	50,000	Rent expense	15,000
Cash	10,000	Repair expense	3,000
Charla Gibson, capital	14,000*	Service revenue	70,000
Insurance expense	4,000	Supplies expense	2,000
Interest expense	1,000	Tax expense	5,000
Interest payable	1,000	Utilities expense	7,000
Investment in IBM stock	5,700	Wage expense	20,000
Land	11,000		

* *This amount represents Gibson's capital balance on July 1, 1982. Owner withdrawals and investments during the year totaled $4,500 and $6,000, respectively.*

The building and land were acquired on June 18, 1983, by paying $13,000 cash and obtaining a mortgage note for $48,000.

INSTRUCTIONS

a Prepare the income statement for Gibson Enterprises in good form.
b Prepare the statement of owners' equity for Gibson in good form.
c Prepare Gibson's balance sheet in good form.

P1-3 ***Transaction analysis and statement preparation***

On August 2 of the current year Steve Stockton organized Stockton Cleaning Services, a sole proprietorship. The following transactions occurred during the first month of operation.

Aug. 2 Stockton withdrew $7,000 from his savings account and invested it in Stockton Cleaning Services.
3 Rented the necessary equipment from Page Equipment. Page required Stockton to prepay the first 4 months' rental costs of $1,600.
4 Purchased $180 of supplies on account from Thomas Wholesale.
9 Billed customers $720 for cleaning services performed.
15 Paid $210 to the *Daily Citizen* for advertising during the first half of the month.
17 Two customers, previously billed, paid a total of $240.
18 Steve wrote himself a check for $350 so he could pay his personal expenses.
19 Paid Thomas Wholesale $160 for the supplies purchased on August 4. Returned $20 of supplies issued by Thomas's warehouse personnel in error and received the appropriate credit.
20 Recorded the receipt of a customer's check for $130 for services performed on August 20.
22 Paid Thomas Wholesale for the purchase of $100 of additional supplies.
25 Received a $90 bill from B&W Repair for the repair of cleaning equipment. Payment is due on September 8.
28 Billed customers $1,400 for services performed.
30 Issued a $300 check to a customer to settle a claim for damage caused by defective cleaning solution. The manufacturer of the solution agreed to reimburse Stockton within ten days for the entire amount.

31 Stockton issued a check to himself for the use of his van by the business: 450 miles at $0.30 per mile.

31 Stockton determined that $110 of supplies remained on hand. He also noted the accounting for his equipment rental should be updated to reflect that one of the 4 months had passed.

INSTRUCTIONS

a Determine the impact of each of the preceding transactions on Stockton's assets, liabilities, and owners' equity. Use the following format:

Assets				= Liabilities +	Owners' Equity			
Cash	Accounts Receivable	Supplies	Prepaid Rent	Accounts Payable	(+) Invest- ments	(−) With- drawals	(+) Revenues	(−) Expenses

Record each transaction on a separate line. Calculate balances only after the last transaction has been recorded.

b Prepare an income statement, statement of owners' equity, and balance sheet in good form.

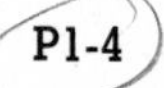

P1-4 *Net income determination from transactions*

The Barron Company, a service business, was formed on January 1 of the current year by John Barron. Karl Barron, the owner's son, was placed in charge of keeping the books for the company. Unfortunately, he had minimal training in accounting and kept very sketchy records. Karl has furnished you with the following information:

Cash receipts	
From fees	$23,000
From client payments on account	4,000
Borrowed from First National Bank	12,000
Owner's investment	9,000
Receipts from rental of land to city	3,000
	$51,000
Cash disbursements	
Salary payments	$18,000
Purchase of land	16,000
Utilities expense	1,600
Supplies expense	2,000
Withdrawals by John Barron	3,000
	$40,600

Additional data follows:

Fees still owed by clients	$8,300
Interest owed to the bank on the First National loan	900
Salaries not yet paid but owed to employees	500

INSTRUCTIONS

John Barron desires to learn whether the firm was profitable during the first year of operation. Furnish him with the information he desires by preparing an income statement in good form.

P1-5 ***Identification of income statement errors***

The following income statement was prepared by the bookkeeper of the Okun Pest Control Service.

OKUN PEST CONTROL
Profit and Loss Statement
June 30, 1983

Income			
Services rendered		$19,000	
Accounts receivable		4,500	$23,500
Owner investments			13,000
Total income			$36,500
Expenses			
Salaries		$11,200	
Taxes		2,100	
Prepaid rent		600	
Utilities		1,000	
Insurance		800	
Office equipment		200	
Loan payment (includes $400 interest)		1,700	
Miscellaneous		10,000	
Supplies			
On hand	$700		
Used	250	450	
Owner withdrawals		2,400	
Total expenses			30,450
Net loss			$ 6,050

INSTRUCTIONS

a Identify and explain the errors in the above statement. Tell what should be done to correct the errors.

b Computers are often used by small businesses to assist in information processing and statement generation. Given the nature of Okun's problems, do you feel computers will help to improve the accuracy of the firm's statements? Why?

P1-6 ***Error analysis***

The financial statements of Western Company revealed the following information for the year ended December 31.

Net income	$64,000
Total assets	97,000
Total liabilities	26,000
Ending owners' equity	71,000

Unfortunately, the following errors were made:

a Accidentally overlooked check no. 186 to Eastern Associates for $1,500 in payment of Western's account balance.
b Failed to record a $600 receipt on account from a customer.
c Accidentally ignored December's utility bill of $1,000. The bill will be paid in January.
d Accidentally recorded $500 of supplies on hand as supplies expense.
e Failed to record a withdrawal of $4,000 by Western's owner.
f Incorrectly charged $900 of rent expense to miscellaneous expense.
g Omitted $1,700 of cash received for services rendered.

INSTRUCTIONS

Prepare corrected figures for net income, total assets, total liabilities, and ending owners' equity. *Hint:* Recall that net income affects owners' equity.

P1-7 ***Balance sheet preparation and evaluation***

On May 15, 1983, Al Lightburn formed a sole proprietorship to operate a small restaurant. The proprietorship was financed by a $4,000 cash investment from Lightburn and a $20,000 loan from the bank. On May 16 Lightburn purchased Bruno's Pizzeria for $22,500. This price included Bruno's building valued at $15,000, land of $2,000, restaurant equipment of $4,200, and cooking supplies of $2,600. In addition, Lightburn assumed Bruno's accounts payable of $1,300.

At the end of the month Lightburn determined that his cooking supplies inventory had decreased by $1,200. Bruno's had not made any payments on the loan. The amounts owed to creditors dropped from $1,300 to $700, not including a utility bill of $150 due in June. Lightburn made no additional investments and was able to withdraw $400 during the month. The ending cash balance was $900.

INSTRUCTIONS

a Prepare Bruno's balance sheet as of May 16, 1983.
b Prepare Bruno's balance sheet as of May 31, 1983. Account balances not specifically mentioned as changing are assumed to remain constant between May 16 and May 31.
c Compare the two balance sheets that you have prepared. Evaluate the success or failure (profitability) of Lightburn's investment during May.

P1-8 ***Identification of transactions (alternate to P1-1)***

The tabulation below summarizes several transactions of the Kramer Company.

	Assets				= Liabilities +	Owners' Equity			
	Cash	Accounts Receivable	Supplies	Equipment	Accounts Payable	(+) Investments	(−) Withdrawals	(+) Revenues	(−) Expenses
Balances	$ 8,000	$10,000	$2,000	$ 4,000	$ 9,000	$15,000	$4,000	$ 6,000	$2,000
(a)	−1,000		+1,000						
(b)	−1,000			+10,000	+9,000				
(c)	+4,500	−4,500							
(d)			−1,500						+1,500
(e)		+2,800						+2,800	
(f)			−500				+500		
(g)	+2,100							+2,100	
	$12,600	$ 8,300	$1,000	$14,000	$18,000	$15,000	$4,500	$10,900	$3,500

INSTRUCTIONS
Write a brief explanation of each transaction (*a*)–(*g*).

P1-9 ***Statement preparation (alternate to P1-2)***
The following balances are taken from the books of Day and Associates at the close of their year on December 31, 1983.

Accounts payable	$ 8,700	Prepaid expenses	$ 500
Accounts receivable	16,400	Rent expense: building	6,000
Cash	15,000	Rent expense: car	2,400
Paul Day, capital	26,800*	Repair expense	5,600
Insurance expense	3,800	Service revenue	65,000
Interest expense	50	Supplies expense	1,400
Interest payable	50	Tax expense	3,900
Investment in land	9,000	Utilities expense	2,500
Loan payable	5,500	Van	8,000
		Wage expense	34,000

* This amount represents Day's capital balance on January 1, 1983. Owner investments and withdrawals during the year totaled $10,000 and $7,500, respectively.

The van was acquired on December 19, 1983, by paying $2,500 cash and securing a loan payable for the remainder.

INSTRUCTIONS
a Prepare Day's income statement in good form.
b Prepare Day's statement of owners' equity in good form.
c Prepare Day's balance sheet in good form.

P1-10 ***Transaction analysis and statement preparation (alternate to P1-3)***
On May 3 of the current year Tony Gomez organized Viscount Carpet Cleaning, a sole proprietorship. The following transactions occurred during the first month of operation.

May 3 Gomez withdrew $6,200 from his savings account and invested it in Viscount Carpet Cleaning.
4 Rented the necessary equipment from Bell Distributors at $400 per month. Bell required Viscount to prepay the first 3 months' rental costs.
4 Purchased $280 of supplies on account from Montgomery Sales.
10 Billed customers $550 for cleaning services performed.
14 Paid $225 to the *Arlington Daily* for advertising during the first half of the month.
16 Two customers, previously billed, paid a total of $150.
19 Paid Montgomery Sales $200 for the supplies purchased on May 4. Returned $80 of supplies issued by Montgomery's warehouse personnel in error and received the appropriate credit.
22 Recorded the receipt of a customer's check for $180 for services performed on May 22.
23 Paid Montgomery Sales for the purchase of $350 of additional supplies.
24 Gomez issued a check to himself for $600 so he could pay his personal expenses.
28 Received a $75 bill from Eastside Repair for the repair of cleaning equipment. Payment is due on June 8.
30 Billed customers $1,100 for services performed.

31 Issued a $400 check to a customer to settle a claim for damage caused by defective cleaning solution. The manufacturer of the solution agreed to reimburse Viscount within ten days for the entire amount.

31 Gomez issued a check to himself for the use of his van by the business: 500 miles at $0.30 per mile.

31 Gomez determined that $100 of supplies remained on hand. He also noted the accounting for his equipment rental should be updated to reflect that one of the 3 months had passed.

INSTRUCTIONS

a Determine the impact of each of the preceding transactions on Viscount's assets, liabilities, and owners' equity. Use the following format:

Assets				= Liabilities +	Owners' Equity			
Cash	Accounts Receivable	Supplies	Prepaid Rent	Accounts Payable	(+) Investments	(−) Withdrawals	(+) Revenues	(−) Expenses

Record each transaction on a separate line. Calculate balances only after the last transaction has been recorded.

b Prepare an income statement, statement of owners' equity, and balance sheet in good form.

P1-11 ***Net income determination from transactions (alternate to P1-4)***

/ The Shannon Company, a service business, was formed on January 1 of the current year by Mary Shannon. Larry Shannon, the owner's son, was placed in charge of keeping the books for the company. Unfortunately, he had minimal training in accounting and kept very sketchy records. Larry has furnished you with the following information:

Cash receipts	
From services rendered	$37,200
From client payments on account	11,600
Borrowed from City Bank and Trust	20,000
Owner's investment	6,000
Miscellaneous receipts from consulting activities	4,800
	$79,600
Cash disbursements	
Salary payments	$25,400
Advertising	3,200
Purchase of land	15,000
Supplies expense	5,500
Withdrawals by Mary Shannon	18,000
	$67,100

Additional data follows:

Fees still owed by clients	$9,900
Interest owed to City Bank and Trust for the loan	800
Salaries incurred but not yet paid	1,400

INSTRUCTIONS

Mary Shannon desires to learn whether the firm was profitable during the first year of operation. Furnish her with the information she desires by preparing an income statement in good form.

P1-12 ***Error analysis (alternate to P1-6)***

The following balances were taken from the books of Masters Company for the year ended December 31.

Net income	*$ 14,500*
Total assets	*104,000*
Total liabilities	*75,000*
Ending owners' equity	*29,000*

Certain errors were made in determining the figures above:

a Services provided of $2,500 on account were not recorded on the last day of the year.

b Equipment purchased on account for $6,000 was not entered in the accounting records.

c A prepaid expense of $800 was erroneously expensed.

d Wages of $4,000, owed to employees as of December 31, were not recorded.

e Cash of $650 received from a client on account was erroneously recorded as revenue.

f An asset was acquired for cash of $600. The bookkeeper recorded the asset at $1,000 and recognized revenue of $400 because he felt the purchase price was a bargain.

g A $500 cash withdrawal by the owner was not recorded.

INSTRUCTIONS

Prepare corrected figures for net income, total assets, total liabilities, and ending owners' equity. *Hint:* Recall that net income affects owners' equity.

CASE 1
OCEANSIDE TRANSPORTATION COMPANY

The Oceanside Transportation Company was founded three years ago to serve the small but growing city of Oceanside. Ed Weber, the firm's owner, was recently involved in a fatal automobile accident. His widow, Marian, assumed ownership, and to everyone's surprise she promptly announced that Oceanside Transportation was for sale. After negotiating with her attorney, accountant, and several prospective buyers, Marian stated that the business had been purchased by George Lazar, a longtime family friend. The selling price was $80,000 plus 25% of the net income generated during Lazar's first year of ownership.

Lazar became sole owner on January 1, 1983. Thirteen months later Marian Weber received a check in the mail along with the following note:

> *Marian:*
> *I have enclosed a check for $50. We had a very poor year with net income amounting to only $200. Ridership was down and expenses increased faster than expected. We're going to do a complete analysis of operations and hopefully get things turned around shortly. See you at Joan's party.*
>
> *George*

Marian was very disappointed. While Ed was running the firm, net income had steadily increased. Even until the day of his death Ed claimed that "business was great and everything looked fine."

Marian and George discussed the problem and agreed to arrange a meeting with her accountant. At the meeting George presented the income statement he had constructed. (See Exhibit 1-2.) The accountant questioned certain items and noted the statement contained several errors. Under questioning, George admitted he had computed net income himself and that his knowledge of accounting was minimal. George and Marian both agreed to have the accountant examine Oceanside's records to render a complete and correct evaluation of 1983 operations.

Lazar submitted Oceanside's books and supporting records to the accountant. In the course of his examination the accountant discovered the following items:

a Oceanside opened a savings account at the American Savings Bank for $1,900 on January 3, 1983. Interest earned totaled $100.

Exhibit 1-2

OCEANSIDE TRANSPORTATION COMPANY
Income Statement
For the Year Ended December 31, 1983

Revenues		
Fare revenue	$46,500	
Charter revenue	17,200	
Amounts owed by customers	3,800	
Interest revenue	100	
Cash receipts from customers on account	13,400	
Increase in value of firm	5,000	
		$86,000
Expenses		
Vehicle leasing	$12,000	
Owner withdrawals	14,800	
Insurance	16,000	
Gas and oil	10,100	
Rent	1,800	
Supplies	400	
Wages	17,900	
Payroll taxes	3,500	
Advertising	500	
Payments on account to suppliers	4,200	
Maintenance and repairs	1,500	
License expense	2,000	
Miscellaneous	1,100	
		85,800
Net income		$ 200

b All charter trips were billed to customers on account.

c During his first year of ownership Lazar felt he made considerable progress toward improving customer service and satisfaction with Oceanside Transportation. Many residents agreed with him. He, therefore, increased the value of the firm by $5,000.

d Cape Cod Auto Leasing provided vans for Oceanside. A one-year contract was signed for $12,000, payable in three equal installments.

e Insurance Expense represents a two-year automobile policy that became effective on January 1, 1983.

f Maintenance and Repairs are itemized as follows:

Van repairs	$1,200
Repairs to Lazar's personal car	300
	$1,500

A review of Oceanside's cash receipts revealed that the firm was reimbursed $150 from Cape Cod Auto Leasing. This amount was for work Cape Cod should have performed prior to leasing the vans to Oceanside. The reimbursement is not reflected in the above figures.

g License Expense includes $800 for a two-year city operating license granted on July 1, 1983. In addition, the accountant determined that a license fee of $700 pertaining to 1983 and payable in 1984 was incorrectly recorded as an addition to Accounts Payable and a deduction from Fare Revenue.

INSTRUCTIONS

Assume the role of Marian's accountant and determine whether your client's concern over the size of Oceanside's net income is justified. Recalculate net income.

2 PROCESSING ACCOUNTING INFORMATION

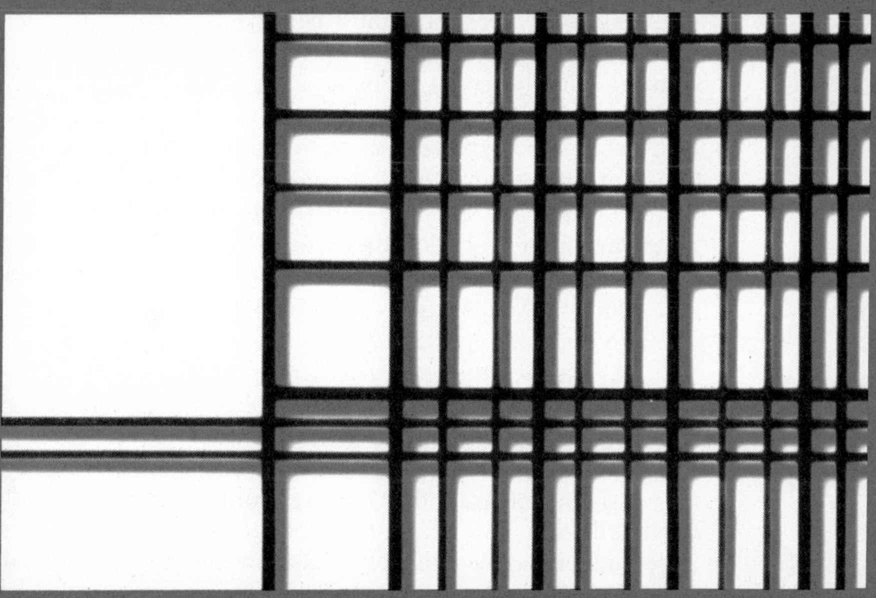

LEARNING OBJECTIVES

After reading this chapter you should:

1 Understand accounts, debits and credits, journals, the chart of accounts, and their interrelationships.

2 Be able to journalize and post transactions.

3 Understand what a trial balance is and how it is constructed.

4 Be aware of the impact of errors on the trial balance and the various steps necessary to locate an error.

CHAPTER 2

The businesses that operate in our economy are involved with a multitude of financial events and transactions, such as the sale of goods and services to customers, the payment of cash to creditors and employees, the purchase of merchandise and equipment, and investments and withdrawals by the owners. These examples, while not all-inclusive, illustrate the variety of transactions a company must be capable of handling and recording. Add to this variety the frequency with which these transactions occur and a genuine record-keeping problem is created.

The Davis Furniture Repair example in Chapter 1 showed that a business could process transactions by increasing and decreasing the components of the fundamental accounting equation. While this processing method was satisfactory for illustrative purposes, some modification is necessary in a more realistic environment. It is not uncommon for an enterprise to process thousands of transactions each day. In addition, complex organizations may have dozens of asset, liability, and owners' equity elements that must be updated on a timely basis.

To illustrate the record-keeping problems of real firms, consider the Atlanta Braves and PepsiCo, Inc. The Braves, a professional baseball team owned by Turner Broadcasting System, Inc., is a relatively small organization by today's standards. Operating in one primary location, the club generates revenues of around $9 million and fields a team for approximately two-thirds of a year. At first glance, accounting for the Braves would not appear much more complex than the accounting for Davis Furniture Repair. However, a deeper probe into the operations of a professional sports club such as the Braves discloses the following:

Multiple sources of revenue from gate receipts, concession operations, and the sale of broadcast rights.
Guaranteed salaries under long-term player contracts.
Participation in the Major League Baseball Players Benefit Plan.

In addition, the Braves lease sports facilities. Rentals are dependent on paid attendance or revenues at sports events, subject to specified minimum amounts.

PepsiCo, considerably larger than the Atlanta Braves, has annual revenues approaching $7 billion and conducts operations in five different business segments. PepsiCo's holdings and operations include the following:

Business Segment	***Company***
Beverage	Pepsi-Cola Co.
Food products	Frito-Lay, Inc.
Food service	Pizza Hut, Inc., Taco Bell
Transportation	North American Van Lines, Inc., Lee Way Motor Freight, Inc.
Sporting goods	Wilson Sporting Goods Co.

Producing tennis balls, moving household goods across the country, feeding thousands of people in restaurants, and producing snack foods are only a small part of PepsiCo's daily activities that need summarization for inclusion in its financial statements. In addition, management must have ready and efficient access to operating information for use in planning, control, and decision-making activities.

Naturally, not all businesses possess the magnitude and complexity of PepsiCo. Many, however, approach the size of the Atlanta Braves. The small, locally owned restaurant, manufacturer, or grocery can easily have revenues into the millions. Accompanying these revenues are a number of expenses, asset acquisitions, and governmental reporting requirements (such as tax) that companies must properly account for or satisfy. Over the years accountants have found it is beneficial to formalize the processing of transactions by employing several basic tools. Whether or not these tools are used, the end result is the same: the production of financial statements. The tools, however, improve efficiency and help to reduce the cost of the statement generation process.

For learning purposes this text will focus on the presentation of a simple manual accounting system. Although many large businesses use computers, their complex systems are designed around the basic fundamentals illustrated in these chapters.

TOOLS OF ACCOUNTING

The four tools of accounting needed to process transactions and summarize financial activity are *accounts, debits and credits, journals,* and the *chart of accounts.* The tools are closely interrelated.

Accounts

As we explained in Chapter 1, financial transactions affect the fundamental accounting equation and the equation's component parts. To provide useful information to managers and other interested parties, a business must keep detailed records of its assets, liabilities, and owners' equity. Assets, for example, should be subdivided into more specific elements such as cash, accounts receivable, and equipment, with individual accountings made for each element.

The records that are kept for the individual asset, liability, and owners' equity components are known as **accounts.** If a company employs manual accounting methods, the record keeping for each account is performed on a separate sheet of paper. If electronic data processing is utilized, the account is located somewhere in a computer's memory. No matter which medium is employed, however, the account is used to record the increases and decreases that result from transactions. All the accounts taken together comprise a firm's **general ledger.** Essentially, the general ledger is a book that contains separate listings for each account appearing on an organization's financial statements.

The account may assume several different forms. One form of the account is the **T-account,** so named because of its shape. A Cash T-account

THE IMPORTANCE OF GOOD PROCESSING SYSTEMS

Good accounting systems are a key ingredient to effective management. In recognition of this fact many organizations have taken steps to ensure the adequacy of their systems. Consider the federal government, for example. In the early 1950s Congress required the comptroller general to prescribe standards that executive agencies were to follow in their accounting systems. The comptroller general did so and proceeded to grant formal approval to systems that conformed to the standards.

Unfortunately, good intentions can go awry. In the late 1970s close to 40% of the eligible accounting systems were still not approved. This situation led to several problems. For example, the Department of the Army experienced a serious breakdown in the financial management of and control over approximately $225 million of procurement appropriations. The breakdown was accompanied by a loss in integrity of accounting information and an inability to pay hundreds of contracts. The Army spent over 28,000 staff days in an effort to correct the involved accounts. Another case involved the Social Security Administration (SSA) in the mid-1970s. Estimates showed that by the end of 1975 the SSA had made nearly a billion dollars in erroneous Supplemental Security income payments. A primary cause was that the SSA had to assemble the computer system for this program under a tight deadline and did well to make any payments at all.

Other cases can be cited but the point has been made. A good accounting system is mandatory to manage operations more efficiently and economically. Accountants must show management in both the public and private sectors that good systems mean good information, which, in turn, leads to better operational control.

SOURCE Adapted from "A Good Accounting System—A Key to Good Management," Journal of Accountancy, February 1978, pp. 66–69.

appears as follows:

Cash			
1983			
2/1	1,000	2/4	450
2/12	200	2/18	290
2/24	600		740
(1,060)	1,800		

Observe that the T-account has both a left and a right side. The left side of any account is known as the *debit* side, and the right side is known as the *credit* side. In this particular case Cash has entries totaling $1,800 on the debit side (debits) and $740 on the credit side (credits).[1] The Cash account presently has a debit balance of $1,060 ($1,800 – $740). If credits are larger than debits, the account is said to possess a credit balance.

The T format presents a concise picture of the various transactions affecting a given account and is useful for understanding how transactions increase or decrease assets, liabilities, and owners' equity. For these reasons the T-account is used throughout the text. In actual practice, however, the **running balance form of account** is encountered more frequently. Using the same information that appeared in the Cash T-account, the running-balance form is illustrated as follows:

Cash — Account No. 11

Date		Explanation	Post Ref	Debit	Credit	Balance
1983						
Feb.	1			1,000		1,000
	4				450	550
	12			200		750
	18				290	460
	24			600		1,060

Entries on the left side of the T-account are recorded in the debit column; entries on the right side appear in the credit column.

The running balance account form offers the advantage of maintaining an up-to-date account balance after each transaction. In addition, an expla-

[1]The small handwritten figures are commonly known as *footings*.

nation column is provided for descriptive purposes should an unusual entry arise. Normally, however, this column is left blank. The use of the posting reference (Post Ref) column will be explained shortly.

At this point you should understand the concepts of establishing an account and determining an account's balance. However, two important questions have probably occurred to you:

1 Should the dollar amounts be entered as debits or credits?
2 Which amounts in the Cash account represent increases in cash and which are decreases?

The answers to these questions will become clear in the explanation of a second key accounting tool, debits and credits.

Debits and Credits

Debits and credits are tools used by the accountant to increase and decrease account balances. Certain accounts are debited to record an increase; that is, entries are made on the debit (left) side or in the debit column of the account. These accounts, in turn, are credited to reduce their balance; that is, entries are made on the right side (credit) or in the credit column. To keep the accounting equation balanced, other accounts employ the opposite rule; namely, increases are recorded by credits and decreases are recorded by debits. Exhibit 2-1 summarizes the debit/credit rules used in accounting.

Exhibit 2-1

Debit/credit rules

Account Type	*Normal Balance*	*To Increase*	*To Decrease*
Assets	Debit	Debit	Credit
Liabilities	Credit	Credit	Debit
Owners' equity	Credit	Credit	Debit
Revenues	Credit	Credit	Debit
Expenses	Debit	Debit	Credit

To understand the rules, remember that the three elements of the accounting equation are assets, liabilities, and owners' equity. In addition, recall that owners' equity changes, in part, due to net income and net loss. These two items are calculated by comparing a business's revenues and expenses. Therefore it is safe to say there are five basic account types: assets, liabilities, owners' equity, revenues, and expenses.

The balance of each account is obtained by offsetting or netting the total debits against the total credits. Certain account types tend to contain more debits than credits and will almost always possess a debit balance. Their **normal balance,** then, is a debit balance. According to Exhibit 2-1, assets and expenses normally have debit balances. In contrast, liabilities, owners' equity, and revenue accounts generally have more credits than debits and usually possess a credit balance. This discussion should *not* be taken to mean that accounts always possess a normal balance. Certain accounts may, at times, carry opposite balances; for example, Accounts Receivable, an asset, could have a credit balance by a customer overpaying his or her account. Opposite balances in some accounts, however, can only be created by an error. To illustrate, a credit balance in Machinery is not possible, since a company cannot have "negative" equipment.

The normal balances of accounts correspond to the fundamental accounting equation: assets = liabilities + owners' equity. An enterprise's assets (debit balances) are matched against their ownership interests—the creditors' (credit balances) and the owners' (credit balances). Since revenues increase owners' equity, they normally have credit balances. Expenses, on the other hand, reduce owners' equity and therefore possess debit balances.

As we noted earlier, debits and credits are used to increase and decrease account balances. To increase the balance of any asset account, the account must be debited. This same rule applies to expense accounts. For example, consider Six Flags, Inc., which operates a chain of amusement parks. The salaries earned by the firm's employees would be debited to the Salaries Expense account since the company's total salary expense is increasing. In contrast, credits are used to record increases in liabilities, owners' equity, and revenues. Thus Six Flags would credit an Amusement Revenue account to record the admission fees received from visitors entering the company's various parks. The observant accounting student should note that the increase column of the debit/credit chart matches perfectly with the normal-balance column. Consequently, once the normal balance column is mastered, all you need to remember is to give the account "more of the same" to record an increase.

Note that the decrease column of the debit/credit chart is the opposite of the increase column. Therefore when Six Flags pays its suppliers on account, the Accounts Payable account (a liability) is debited to record the reduction in the amounts owed to creditors.

Let us return now to the two questions raised on page 46 that relate to the Cash account illustration. The answers are as follows:

1 The dollar amounts will be entered as debits or credits, depending on whether the amounts increase or decrease the account. Since Cash is an asset, receipts or increases are recorded as debits. Conversely, decreases to Cash are recorded on the right side as credits, or in the credit column.
2 This question has really been answered above. Debits of $1,800 ($1,000 + $200 + $600) represent increases to the Cash account, while the credits ($450 and $290) are reductions.

Misconceptions about debits and credits

There are two common misconceptions about debits and credits. From their experiences with retail stores many people believe that credits *always* reduce account balances. When they pay on account or return merchandise, customers are often told that their account will be credited. Because the amounts owed by customers are an asset to the retail establishment, these two transactions generate credits to reduce Accounts Receivable. Keep in mind, however, that credits also increase certain account balances, specifically, liability, owners' equity, and revenue accounts.

A second misconception is that credits are good and debits are bad. This notion is incorrect. While credits reduce your account on someone else's books ("good"), credits also increase the amounts you owe as shown in your Accounts Payable account ("bad"). Overall, then, it is a matter of perspective.

Beginning students would do well to forget these thoughts and simply concentrate on the rules presented in Exhibit 2-1. These rules form the basis for the proper recording and processing of all business transactions.

Journals

The transactions that affect a business arise from many different sources. Evidence of these transactions is often provided by the receipt or issuance of accounting forms known as **source documents.** Examples of source documents include inventory receiving reports, bills from suppliers, customer sales slips, and customer checks. These documents show that a transaction has occurred and thus trigger the recording process. For a proper recording of the account changes caused by a transaction, the source document must be translated into a debit/credit format. This translation takes place in the journal.

The **journal,** sometimes called the book of original entry, serves as the entry or starting point for transactions into a company's formalized accounting system. Many students feel that the journal is a needless repetition of the information contained on the source documents. This is not so. Frequently, transactions are complicated; they affect numerous accounts and are supported by many different documents. Depending on the type, source documents are often filed in a variety of locations once they are no longer needed. Imagine the difficulty faced by an employee who is asked a basic question about a particular transaction. Without the journal the employee would be forced to go scurrying through different documents, which may be filed in various locations. The journal avoids this unfortunate situation and brings order to the recording process by summarizing in one place all relevant information regarding a transaction.

The recording process

To record its many transactions, a business may utilize different types of journals. For example, sales transactions may be entered in a specialized sales journal, purchases in a purchases journal, cash receipts in a cash receipts journal, and so forth. The journal illustrated in this chapter is commonly referred to as a *two-column general journal.* It has two amount columns (debit and credit) and is used to record a variety of transactions.

Recording transactions in the journal is a three-step process known as **journalizing.** The transactions are first analyzed in terms of the accounts that are affected. Next, the appropriate debits and credits are determined. Finally, in their new debit/credit format, the transactions are formally recorded in the journal.

To illustrate these procedures, let us examine the following transaction of the Wise Advertising Agency. The agency was founded on May 1, 1983, when Gary Wise invested $9,000 of his personal savings into the business. Analyzing the effect of this transaction, we see that the investment by the owner increased the agency's cash balance along with owners' equity. In the format utilized in Chapter 1 the investment would appear as follows:

Assets	=	**Liabilities**	+	**Owners' Equity**
Cash				(+) **Investments**
+$9,000				+$9,000

Once the proper accounts are determined, the transaction is next translated into debits and credits. Since Cash is an asset, a $9,000 debit is needed to record the appropriate increase. As we noted above, the investment has also increased owners' equity, namely, Gary Wise, Capital. According to the debit/credit rules, increases to owners' equity are recorded by credits. This analysis is summarized in the following general journal entry:

Date		**Accounts**	**Post Ref**	**Debit**	**Credit**
1983					
May	1	Cash		9,000	
		Gary Wise, Capital			9,000
		Owner investment			

Observe the debits are recorded first and appear next to the date column. Credits are entered next by using a slight indentation. Finally, a short description of the transaction is recorded since the general journal will eventually contain a variety of transactions. The explanation documents the purpose of the entry; that is, to record an investment by the owner. The posting reference (Post Ref) column is left blank at the time the entry is recorded.

Upon completion of the recording process, debits of $9,000 equal credits of $9,000, and the entry is said to be in balance. *In any transaction total debits must equal total credits.* Naturally, this equality would not be possible if a transaction affected only one account. Recall, however, that accountants employ the double-entry system of bookkeeping in which a transaction always affects a minimum of two accounts.

To conclude, note that we are really performing the same operation that was illustrated in Chapter 1; that is, increasing and decreasing the various components of the accounting equation. Now, however, we are recording the increases and decreases in a journal by using a system of debits and credits. The overall objective of recording changes in the account balances has remained the same; only the methodology has changed.

Chart of Accounts

Accounts in the general ledger are usually arranged in the following order: assets, liabilities, owners' equity, revenues, and expenses. Within each grouping each individual account is assigned an account number according to the chart of accounts. The **chart of accounts** is a detailed listing of a company's accounts along with associated account numbers. For example, the asset portion of a chart of accounts may appear as follows:

Assets (100s)	
Cash	*101*
Accounts receivable	*110*
Inventory	*120*
Prepaid insurance	*130*
Supplies	*140*
Land	*150*
Building	*160*

Liabilities might be numbered in the 200s, owners' equity accounts in the 300s, and so on. The determination of a suitable numbering scheme is an important issue in systems design work. Sufficient gaps should be left when assigning account numbers for the possible insertion of additional accounts at a later date.

The chart of accounts is very useful in helping to determine proper transaction recording. To illustrate, suppose Binkert Company paid an electric bill of $1,800 on March 31. The correct analysis should reveal that Binkert's total electrical costs have increased, necessitating a debit to an expense account. Also Cash has decreased. Therefore the following entry appears to be needed:[2]

Mar. 31	*Utilities Expense*	*1,800*	
	Cash		*1,800*
	Paid utilities bill		

However, a review of the chart of accounts might reveal that Binkert does not use a Utilities Expense account. Rather, in light of rising energy costs, the company has established separate accounts for:

Electricity expense
Natural gas expense
Fuel oil expense

[2]This entry is recorded in general-journal format. Observe the manner in which the account titles and amounts are staggered, thus duplicating the appearance of the entry in the general journal. It is not necessary to write the words "debit" and "credit" next to the accounts or amounts since the format is well recognized and understood by accountants.

Telephone expense
Water and sewer expense

Separate accounts furnish management with more detailed information. The proper entry, then, which could only be made after inspecting the chart of accounts, requires a debit to Electricity Expense.

In addition to assisting with transaction recording, the chart of accounts also reveals how organizations can differ. While virtually every company has accounts such as Cash, Accounts Receivable, Loans Payable, Sales, and Salaries Expense, businesses often establish accounts that are attuned to their specific area of operation. A review of annual corporate reports revealed the specialized accounts listed in Exhibit 2-2.

Exhibit 2-2

Specialized corporate accounts

Firm	*Account*	*Account Type*
Philip Morris, Inc.	Leaf tobacco inventory	Asset
Northwest Airlines, Inc.	Advance payments on new flight equipment	Asset
Vail Associates, Inc.	Ski lifts	Asset
Cleveland Professional Basketball Company	Advance season ticket sales	Liability
American Broadcasting Companies, Inc.	Recorded music revenue	Revenue
Walt Disney Productions	Design projects abandoned	Expense

POSTING: INTERACTION OF THE BASIC TOOLS

The journal alone is not sufficient to handle the recording process. Many transactions in the journal have affected the same component of the accounting equation. To facilitate financial statement preparation, we must summarize these transactions in the business's accounts. The transactions in the journal and the accounts in the ledger are linked together by a process called **posting.**

Posting transfers the debits and credits of the transactions that were entered in the journal to the appropriate ledger accounts. The necessary posting for the entry on May 1 of Wise Advertising appears in Exhibit 2-3. The circled numbers represent the order in which the posting steps are performed.

To explain: ① The transaction recorded in the journal requires a debit to Cash of $9,000. This amount is transferred to the debit column of the Cash account. ② Next, the date of the transaction (May 1) is posted. ③ J1 is then entered in the posting reference column of the Cash account. Why? The debit to Cash was transferred from page 1 of the general journal. The "J" indicates that the entry was initially recorded in the general journal, as opposed to one of the other journals noted earlier. The source of the entry is

Exhibit 2-3
Posting transactions from journal to ledger

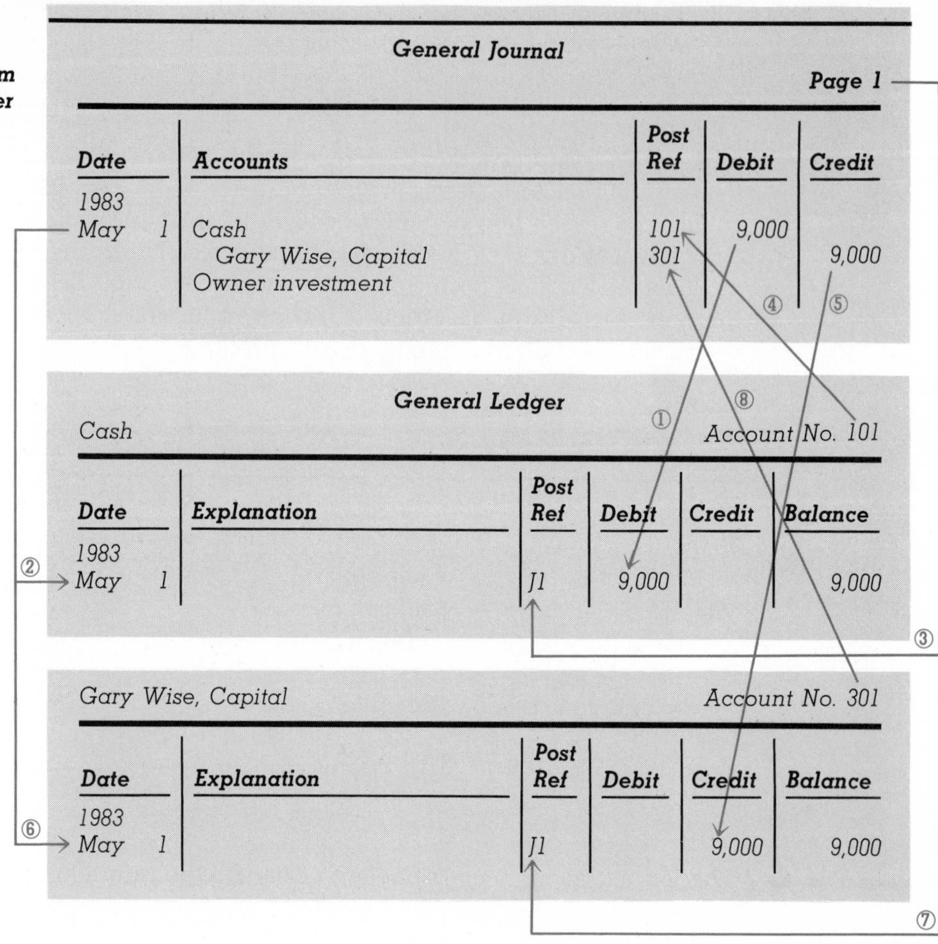

recorded in the account should the need arise to trace a ledger entry back to its origin. This concept, known as an *audit trail,* is discussed more fully in Chapter 5. ④ 101 is placed in the posting reference column of the journal. This step serves two purposes:

1 The posting reference facilitates the tracing process by showing the accountant the account to which the debit was actually transferred.
2 The posting reference signifies completion of the posting process. Accountants interpret a blank in the posting reference column to mean that an entry has not yet been posted. This procedure is important if a number of entries are being transferred and an interruption occurs. The person performing the process can easily find the proper place to resume his or her work.

The Cash account has now been increased by $9,000. If there were additional debits in the journal entry, they, too, would be posted in this fashion.

Once the debit is posted, the credit is transferred in a similar manner. ⑤ The investment generated a credit to Gary Wise, Capital. Therefore $9,000 is posted from the journal to Wise's account. ⑥ Next, May 1 is transferred to the date column. ⑦ The source of the entry, J1, is then entered in the ledger account. ⑧ Finally, the account to which the credit was transferred (301) is entered in the journal. The credit has now been posted and the process is complete.

AN EXTENDED ILLUSTRATION

The interrelationships between debits and credits, journal entries, and ledger accounts are best viewed by means of an extended illustration. Transactions of the Wise Advertising Agency are presented below, along with the proper journal entries. You should concentrate on each transaction and its analysis *prior* to viewing the correct entry. Again, follow the process by reasoning, not memorizing. Account numbers appear in the journal, thus indicating that the entries have already been posted to the general ledger accounts.

May 1 Wise invested $9,000 in the business.

Analysis See page 49.

Entry

Page 1

1983					
May	*1*	*Cash*	*101*	*9,000*	
		Gary Wise, Capital	*301*		*9,000*
		Owner investment			

May 3 Paid monthly office rent of $800.

Analysis Expenses have increased; thus Rent Expense: Office is debited. Since Cash has decreased, this asset account must be credited to record the payment.

Entry

3	*Rent Expense: Office*	*520*	*800*	
	Cash	*101*		*800*
	Paid May rent			

May 6 Agreed to rent office equipment from Knox Rental at $1,500 per month. Paid $1,000 down with the remainder due in ten days.

Analysis Rent Expense: Equipment is debited to record the appropriate increase. Cash is credited due to the payment. In addition, Accounts Payable is credited for $500 ($1,500 − $1,000), because the amount owed to Knox, a liability, has increased.

Entry

6	*Rent Expense: Equipment*	*530*	*1,500*	
	Cash	*101*		*1,000*
	Accounts Payable	*210*		*500*
	Paid partial equipment rental; balance due in 10 days			

Note: *All necessary debits are recorded first, followed by the required credits. Observe that total debits of $1,500 equal total credits of $1,500.*

May 14 Billed clients for services rendered, $1,700.

Analysis The amounts owed by clients have increased; Accounts Receivable, an asset, is therefore debited. The revenues earned by the agency have also increased, necessitating a credit to Agency Revenue.

Entry

14	*Accounts Receivable*	*120*	*1,700*	
	Agency Revenue	*410*		*1,700*
	Billed customers			

May 15 Paid the $500 balance due to Knox Rental from the transaction on May 6.

Analysis The $500 payment has reduced Wise's cash balance and the amounts owed to creditors. Accounts Payable, a liability, is debited and Cash is credited.

Entry

15	*Accounts Payable*	*210*	*500*	
	Cash	*101*		*500*
	Paid Knox Rental on account			

May 23 Received $950 from clients on account.

Analysis Two assets are involved in this transaction, Cash and Accounts Receivable. Cash has increased and must be debited. Because the amounts owed to Wise have decreased, Accounts Receivable is credited.

Entry

23	*Cash*	*101*	*950*	
	Accounts Receivable	*120*		*950*
	Receipts on account from customers			

May 24 Gary Wise withdrew $700 from the business for personal use.

Analysis Withdrawals decrease owners' equity. Rather than debit Gary Wise, Capital, accountants use a separate **drawing account** to accumulate withdrawals. The drawing account is a contra- (opposite) owners' equity account that reduces capital and, as such, normally possesses a debit balance. Gary Wise, Drawing is debited and Cash is credited.

Entry

24	*Gary Wise, Drawing*	*320*	*700*	
	Cash	*101*		*700*
	Owner withdrawal			

May 25 Received a $125 electric bill, due in June.

Analysis Total expenses have increased, requiring a debit to Electricity Expense. Accounts Payable is credited to record the increase in the amounts owed to creditors.

Entry

Page 2

1983				
May 25	*Electricity Expense*	*540*	*125*	
	Accounts Payable	*210*		*125*
	Received May's electric bill; due in June			

May 27 Received a call from Kathy Howard, a client, stating that she had not paid her bill of May 14 because of a $100 overcharge. Wise checked his records and found the client was correct.

Analysis Refer to the entry of May 14. Accounts Receivable and Agency Revenue were each overstated by $100 and must therefore be reduced. The original entry is left intact to improve accountability.

Entry

27	*Agency Revenue*	*410*	*100*	
	Accounts Receivable	*120*		*100*
	Corrected error of 5/14 to Kathy Howard			

May 28 Paid office salaries of $825.

Analysis Similar to the transaction of May 3.

Entry

28	*Salaries Expense*	*510*	*825*	
	Cash	*101*		*825*
	Paid May salaries			

May 31 Billed customers for services rendered, $1,350.

Analysis Similar to the transaction of May 14.

Entry

31	*Accounts Receivable*	*120*	*1,350*	
	Agency Revenue	*410*		*1,350*
	Billed customers			

The general ledger accounts relevant to the foregoing journal entries are illustrated in Exhibit 2-4. Trace each transaction from the journal to the ledger to understand how information is processed through an accounting system.

TRIAL BALANCE

Earlier in the chapter we noted that in any given journal entry total debits must equal total credits. Because journal entries are transferred (posted) to the ledger, it stands to reason that total debits entered in the ledger accounts must equal total credits. If debits do not equal credits, the accounting records are out of balance.

Many errors can occur in the transaction-recording and posting processes. To determine whether the general ledger accounts are in balance, accountants construct a trial balance. The **trial balance** checks the equality of debits and credits in the ledger by listing each account along with its ending balance. Unlike the balance sheet, income statement, and statement of owners' equity, the trial balance is not a formal financial statement; it is not issued to such parties as owners and creditors. The trial balance of the Wise Advertising Agency appears in Exhibit 2-5.

The trial balance is a two-column report. Debit balances appear in the left column and credit balances are in the right column. Wise's trial balance proves that the books are in balance at $12,075.

Equality Does Not Ensure Accuracy

Unfortunately, a trial balance with equal debit/credit totals does not always mean the accounting process was free from error. Several errors can occur that have no effect on the required equality. To illustrate, examine the

Exhibit 2-4

General ledger accounts for Wise Advertising Agency

Cash — *Account No. 101*

Date		Explanation	Post Ref	Debit	Credit	Balance
1983						
May	1		J1	9,000		9,000
	3		J1		800	8,200
	6		J1		1,000	7,200
	15		J1		500	6,700
	23		J1	950		7,650
	24		J1		700	6,950
	28		J2		825	6,125

Accounts Receivable — *Account No. 120*

Date		Explanation	Post Ref	Debit	Credit	Balance
1983						
May	14		J1	1,700		1,700
	23		J1		950	750
	27		J2		100	650
	31		J2	1,350		2,000

Accounts Payable — *Account No. 210*

Date		Explanation	Post Ref	Debit	Credit	Balance
1983						
May	6		J1		500	500
	15		J1	500		—
	25		J2		125	125

Gary Wise, Capital — *Account No. 301*

Date		Explanation	Post Ref	Debit	Credit	Balance
1983						
May	1		J1		9,000	9,000

Gary Wise, Drawing — Account No. 320

Date	Explanation	Post Ref	Debit	Credit	Balance
1983					
May 24		J1	700		700

Agency Revenue — Account No. 410

Date	Explanation	Post Ref	Debit	Credit	Balance
1983					
May 14		J1		1,700	1,700
27		J2	100		1,600
31		J2		1,350	2,950

Salaries Expense — Account No. 510

Date	Explanation	Post Ref	Debit	Credit	Balance
1983					
May 28		J2	825		825

Rent Expense: Office — Account No. 520

Date	Explanation	Post Ref	Debit	Credit	Balance
1983					
May 3		J1	800		800

Rent Expense: Equipment — Account No. 530

Date	Explanation	Post Ref	Debit	Credit	Balance
1983					
May 6		J1	1,500		1,500

Electricity Expense					Account No. 540
Date	**Explanation**	**Post Ref**	**Debit**	**Credit**	**Balance**
1983					
May 25		J2	125		125

Exhibit 2-5

Trial balance for Wise Advertising Agency

WISE ADVERTISING AGENCY
Trial Balance
May 31, 1983

Cash	$ 6,125	
Accounts receivable	2,000	
Accounts payable		$ 125
Gary Wise, capital		9,000
Gary Wise, drawing	700	
Agency revenue		2,950
Salaries expense	825	
Rent expense: office	800	
Rent expense: equipment	1,500	
Electricity expense	125	
	$12,075	$12,075

transaction recorded in the journal by Wise on May 28:

May 28	Salaries Expense	825	
	Cash		825
	Paid May salaries		

This entry increased the balance in the Salaries Expense account from zero to $825. In addition, as shown by the ledger account, Cash decreased from $6,950 to $6,125. Consider the following error possibilities:

1 *Transaction omission.* If a transaction is accidentally omitted in the recording process, the trial balance will still balance. Omitting the May 28 transaction as an example, we see that Salaries Expense and Cash would have balances of zero and $6,950, respectively. Salaries Expense is understated and Cash is overstated. Because both accounts have debit balances, the overstatement is offset by the understatement, and equal debit/credit totals of $12,075 are still generated.

2 *Transaction duplication.* If Wise's transaction was accidentally entered and posted twice, Salaries Expense would increase from zero

to $1,650. In addition, Cash would decrease from $6,950 to $5,300. The overstatement in Salaries Expense is counterbalanced by an understated Cash account, and, again, the debit/credit equality remains intact at $12,075.

3 *Posting errors.* Posting an entry to an incorrect account will not affect the equality of the totals. Assume, for example, that the $825 credit to Cash was erroneously posted as a credit to Accounts Payable. Cash would be listed in the trial balance at $6,950; at the same time Accounts Payable would have a balance of $950 ($125 + $825). Each account is therefore overstated by $825. Since Cash has a debit balance and Accounts Payable a credit balance, the trial balance totals are each raised to $12,900 ($12,075 + $825). The totals are incorrect; yet the ledger remains in balance.

4 *Transaction errors.* Account and amount errors within a journal entry will also not destroy the trial balance's debit/credit equality. To illustrate, assume that Wise incorrectly debited the $825 salaries payment to Accounts Receivable. Accounts Receivable is thereby overstated, but it is offset by an understated Salaries Expense account. The trial balance totals remain intact at $12,075.

As another example, suppose Salaries Expense and Cash were respectively debited and credited for $1,825 rather than the correct amount of $825. This error increases Salaries Expense by an additional $1,000, while Cash is reduced by the same amount. Because both accounts appear in the debit column of the trial balance, the overstatement is counterbalanced by the understatement.

The foregoing errors prove frustrating to accountants. After producing a trial balance with equal debit/credit totals, how do accountants know whether the trial balance contains an error or is error-free? Indeed, they do not want to borrow trouble by completely double-checking their work to look for a problem that might not exist. Unfortunately, there is no answer book in the "real world" that can be used to check for the proper solution. If equality is achieved, we assume that no errors have been made. Later in the text we will discuss other tests and procedures that accountants and auditors perform to verify the validity of this assumption.

Unequal Totals

Many errors are made that cause the trial balance to have unequal totals. These errors must be located and corrected to reinstate the necessary equality. Locating the errors, however, can be a problem, since the trial balance is really a summarization of the journalizing and posting processes. For example, mistakes can be made when (1) transactions are placed in the journal, (2) journal entries are posted to the ledger, and (3) the trial balance is constructed. It is generally suggested that one work backward through the process in attempting to pinpoint problems. The following sequence of steps may prove helpful.

1 Re-add the trial balance columns.
2 Calculate the difference between the debit and credit totals. If the difference is evenly divisible by 9, there is a good chance that a transposition or slide has occurred.
   a *Transposition.* A **transposition** means that two digits of a given number have been accidentally reversed (e.g., the number 560 appears as 650, 125 as 152, and so on). Observe that the difference between the correct and incorrect number is divisible by 9 with no remainder. Refer to Wise's trial balance in Exhibit 2-5. Suppose debits amounted to $11,625 while credits were $12,075. The difference of $450, which is evenly divisible by 9, may mean that the hundreds' digit and the tens' digit of an account balance were interchanged. Reviewing the trial balance, we see there is only one number capable of producing the $450 difference: the $1,500 balance of Rent Expense: Equipment. The account balance was probably copied from the ledger to the trial balance as $1,050.
   b *Slide.* A **slide** occurs when the decimal point of a number is improperly moved to the left or right (e.g., the number 895 might appear as 8,950 or 89.5). As in the case of the transposition, the difference between the correct number and incorrect number is divisible by 9 with no remainder.
3 Calculate one-half the difference between the debit and credit totals, and then look for that amount in the trial balance. If the amount can be located, a debit balance may have been entered in the credit column or vice versa. This type of error always causes the trial balance totals to differ by twice the amount of the improperly placed account balance. To illustrate, suppose Wise's trial balance totals were $11,375 (debits) and $12,775 (credits). The $1,400 difference when halved yields $700. Thus Wise's Drawing account was probably placed in the incorrect column to generate this error condition.
4 After thoroughly checking the trial balance, return to the ledger. Examine individual accounts and recompute balances.
5 Return to the journal and examine individual entries. Trace the entries to the ledger accounts to verify the accuracy of posting.

It should now be evident that a variety of errors can occur in the preparation of a trial balance. Error detection for a business of modest complexity and size can be extremely frustrating. A large number of accounts combined with a high volume of transactions complicate the process. In addition, the possibility exists that several errors may have occurred which have counterbalancing effects on one another. Indeed, error determination and location is often more challenging than the recording and processing of transactions and the preparation of financial statements.

A BRIEF OVERVIEW

The concepts presented in this chapter have laid the groundwork for comprehending the manner in which accounting information is produced. A transaction starts the entire process in motion. The transaction generates a source document, which is translated into debits and credits and recorded in the journal. The entries in the journal are then transferred to accounts in the ledger by posting. Next, the trial balance is prepared to determine whether the ledger accounts are in balance. This sequence of events can be summarized as shown in Exhibit 2-6.

Exhibit 2-6

Basic sequence in the accounting process

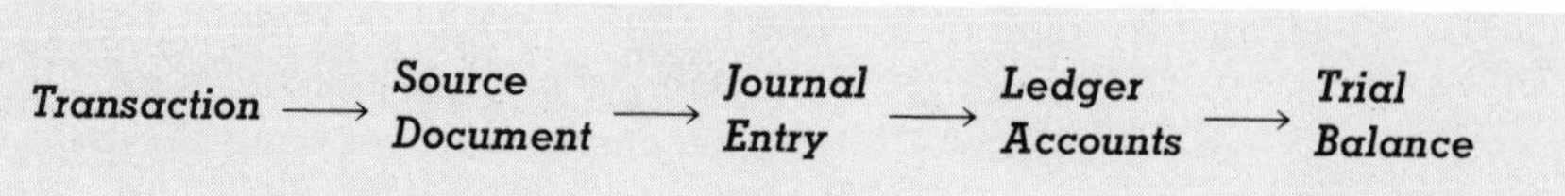

The trial balance is not the end of the process; it is only an intermediate step in the processing cycle. The next chapter will illustrate the remaining procedures that must be performed before a transaction finds its way into a company's financial statements.

SUMMARY PROBLEM

Below are a chart of accounts and a list of transactions for operations of the Drake Company during March 1983.

Cash	*101*	*John Drake, drawing*	*302*
Accounts receivable	*110*	*Service revenue*	*401*
Office equipment	*120*	*Salaries expense*	*501*
Accounts payable	*201*	*Rent expense*	*510*
John Drake, capital	*301*		

Mar. 1 John Drake, owner, invested $40,000 in the business.
7 Paid rent for March of $175.
18 Services rendered to date: cash, $15,500; credit, $12,200.
20 Paid employees' salaries of $10,500.
24 Purchased $4,000 of office equipment from Peach Equipment Company. Paid $3,200 down and agreed to remit the balance owed in ten days.

INSTRUCTIONS

a ***Record the transactions in a general journal.***
b ***Post the transactions from the journal to the ledger.***
c ***Prepare a trial balance as of March 31, 1983.***

SOLUTION

a

Page 1

Date		Accounts	Post Ref	Debit	Credit
1983					
Mar.	1	Cash	101	40,000	
		John Drake, Capital	301		40,000
		Owner investment			
	7	Rent Expense	510	175	
		Cash	101		175
		Paid monthly rent			
	18	Cash	101	15,500	
		Accounts Receivable	110	12,200	
		Service Revenue	401		27,700
		Recorded service revenue from operations			
	20	Salaries Expense	501	10,500	
		Cash	101		10,500
		Paid employees' salaries			
	24	Office Equipment	120	4,000	
		Cash	101		3,200
		Accounts Payable	201		800
		Purchased office equipment; balance due in 10 days			

b

Cash — Account No. 101

Date		Explanation	Post Ref	Debit	Credit	Balance
1983						
Mar.	1		J1	40,000		40,000
	7		J1		175	39,825
	18		J1	15,500		55,325
	20		J1		10,500	44,825
	24		J1		3,200	41,625

Accounts Receivable — Account No. 110

Date	Explanation	Post Ref	Debit	Credit	Balance
1983					
Mar. 18		J1	12,200		12,200

Office Equipment — Account No. 120

Date	Explanation	Post Ref	Debit	Credit	Balance
1983					
Mar. 24		J1	4,000		4,000

Accounts Payable — Account No. 201

Date	Explanation	Post Ref	Debit	Credit	Balance
1983					
Mar. 24		J1		800	800

John Drake, Capital — Account No. 301

Date	Explanation	Post Ref	Debit	Credit	Balance
1983					
Mar. 1		J1		40,000	40,000

John Drake, Drawing — Account No. 302

Date	Explanation	Post Ref	Debit	Credit	Balance

Service Revenue — *Account No. 401*

Date	Explanation	Post Ref	Debit	Credit	Balance
1983					
Mar. 18		J1		27,700	27,700

Salaries Expense — *Account No. 501*

Date	Explanation	Post Ref	Debit	Credit	Balance
1983					
Mar. 20		J1	10,500		10,500

Rent Expense — *Account No. 510*

Date	Explanation	Post Ref	Debit	Credit	Balance
1983					
Mar. 7		J1	175		175

c

DRAKE COMPANY
Trial Balance
March 31, 1983

Cash	$41,625	
Accounts receivable	12,200	
Office equipment	4,000	
Accounts payable		$ 800
John Drake, capital		40,000
Service revenue		27,700
Salaries expense	10,500	
Rent expense	175	
	$68,500	$68,500

KEY TERMS AND CONCEPTS

account 43
chart of accounts 50
credit 46
debit 46
drawing account 55
general ledger 43
journal 48
journalizing 48
normal balance 46
posting 51
running balance account 45
slide 61
source document 48
T-account 43
transposition 61
trial balance 56

QUESTIONS

Q2-1 Explain why a business needs a formal accounting system to process transactions.

Q2-2 Explain the concept of debits and credits to someone with no background in business or accounting.

Q2-3 Explain the relationship between the fundamental accounting equation and normal account balances.

Q2-4 Explain how Accounts Payable could have a debit balance.

Q2-5 In terms of debits and credits, liabilities are decreased by ________, expenses are increased by ________, and revenues are increased by ________.

Q2-6 Les Howard accidentally debited an expense account rather than an asset account. As a result of this error, the following occur:

a Total assets will be ________.
b Total expenses will be ________.
c Net income will be ________.
d Ending owners' equity will be ________.

Q2-7 What is a source document? How are source documents used in the accounting process?

Q2-8 Explain the functions of the chart of accounts.

Q2-9 A student once commented: "I don't understand the purpose of the ledger account. It seems as though the account is an unnecessary duplication of the journal." Is the student correct? Why?

Q2-10 "All information about a transaction is recorded in the ledger and then posted to the journal." Is this statement correct? Why?

Q2-11 Why is the posting reference column in the journal left blank at the time an entry is recorded?

Q2-12 Would the drawing account appear on the income statement or the statement of owners' equity? Why?

Q2-13 What is the purpose of a trial balance?

Q2-14 What types of errors will not affect the equality of the trial balance totals?

Q2-15 The general journal of the Sprint Company contained the following entry:

Date	Accounts	Post Ref	Debit	Credit
May 19	Accounts Payable	210	800	
	Cash			800

Will the totals of the trial balance be in agreement? Why?

EXERCISES

E2-1 Classify each of the following as an asset, liability, revenue, or expense. Also indicate the normal account balance of each item.

a Administrative costs incurred by a flower shop.
b Machinery and equipment.
c Amounts owed to creditors.
d Property taxes incurred by a flower shop.
e Long-term loan owed to a bank from the borrower's point of view.
f Admission charges to games from a football team's viewpoint.
g Cash in the bank.
h Land held as an investment.
i Fuel costs of an airline.
j Sales of a department store.
k Short-term loan owed to a bank from the bank's point of view.

E2-2 Brian Mullins has just enrolled at Southwest State University in Small Town, Arizona. Since this was his first experience living away from home, he opened a checking account at a local bank to help manage his cash transactions. After one month Brian's checkbook contained the following entries:

Date	Check No.	Description	Amount	Balance
9/5	—	Deposit	$100	
9/8	101	Southwestern Bell	28	
9/14	102	Tony's Pizza	15	
9/17	103	Southwestern Bookstore	55	
9/19	—	Paycheck from Ace Delivery	30	
9/26	—	Bank service charge	3	
9/29	104	Westside Car Repair	45	

The balance column was left blank because Brian's calculator was not working properly.

a Show how the checkbook entries would appear in a Cash T-account. Foot the account and determine its balance.
b If Brian prepared personal financial statements, on which statement and under what classification (assets, liabilities, owners' equity, revenues, or expenses) would his Cash account appear? Why?

E2-3 Record the following transactions in general-journal form. Include explanations.

a Purchased equipment on account, $900.
b Buzz Sawyer, the owner, withdrew $600 from the business.
c Received $300 from customers on account.
d Paid advertising expense, $400.
e Paid for the equipment purchased in (a) above.
f Rendered services to customers on account, $750.
g Received a $75 telephone bill that will be paid next month.

E2-4 The following accounts appear on the books of the Lyon Company. Each account has a normal balance.

Land	*$7,000*	*Utilities expense*	*$ 2,800*
Salary expense	*8,000*	*Accounts receivable*	*2,700*
Accounts payable	*3,000*	*George Lyon, drawing*	*1,200*
Prepaid expenses	*500*	*Rent expense*	*?*
Loan payable	*5,600*	*Fees earned*	*14,000*
George Lyon, capital	*5,900*	*Cash*	*1,800*
Interest expense	*900*		

Calculate the balance in the Rent Expense account.

E2-5 Consider each of the following items individually. Which items would cause the trial balance totals to be unequal?

a Recorded a $500 payment on account as a debit to Salaries Expense and a credit to Cash.
b Failed to record the receipt of $200 from a customer for services rendered.
c Recorded the $700 purchase of a machine on account as a debit to Machinery and a debit to Accounts Payable.
d Incorrectly computed the drawing account's balance by $100.
e Recorded the $1,500 balance of the Equipment account in the credit column of the trial balance.
f Recorded a $72 utility bill due next month as a $27 debit to Utilities Expense and a $27 credit to Accounts Payable.

E2-6 The bookkeeper of the Tulsa Towing Company is attempting to locate an error in the trial balance. Which of the figures below was probably listed incorrectly? Why?

Debit	***Credit***
$ 650	
200	
460	
	$ 780
	250
270	
370	
$1,950	$1,030

E2-7 The Arbor Company correctly determined the balance in the Accounts Receivable account to be $15,225.07. Yet when adding the amounts owed by individual customers, the bookkeeper generated the following figures:

J. Brown	$ 4,856.22
S. Black	1,465.71
L. White	2,369.46
R. Green	2,735.00
G. Gray	3,528.68
	$14,955.07

Which account was probably listed incorrectly? Why?

PROBLEMS

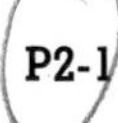

P2-1 ***Transaction analysis and trial balance preparation***

The T-accounts that follow were taken from the records of Hinsdale Enterprises on December 31, 1983. Letters in the accounts reference specific transactions of the firm.

Cash	
(a) 5,000	(d) 900
(c) 1,800	(i) 2,500
(g) 6,000	
(h) 1,900	

Accounts Receivable	
(e) 2,400	(h) 1,900

Land	
(a) 15,000	(g) 6,000

Equipment	
(b) 3,500	(f) 1,000

Accounts Payable	
(f) 1,000	(b) 3,500
(i) 2,500	

Hinsdale, Capital	
	(a) 20,000

Service Revenue	
	(c) 1,800
	(e) 2,400

Advertising Expense	
(d) 600	

Salary Expense	
(d) 300	

INSTRUCTIONS

a Write a sentence or two describing the nature of transactions (*a*)–(*i*).

b Determine the balance in each account and prepare a trial balance.

P2-2 ***Journal entry and trial balance preparation***

Consider the following transactions of the Vance Service Organization.

Feb. 2 The owner, Victor Vance, opened a bank account in the name of the business by depositing $8,000.

9 Rendered services on account, $1,900.

15 Paid $1,500 of expenses: rent, $700; salaries, $800.
17 Purchased $2,400 of office equipment on account.
22 Customers, previously billed, paid $900 on account.
26 Paid one-half the amount due for the equipment purchased on February 17.
28 Purchased a building for $40,000. Paid $5,000 down and secured a loan from the bank for the remainder.
28 Recorded the receipt of the February utility bill of $250. The bill will be paid in March.

INSTRUCTIONS

a Show how the transactions would appear in the following T-accounts: Cash; Accounts Receivable; Office Equipment; Building; Accounts Payable; Loan Payable; Vance, Capital; Service Revenue; Rent Expense; Salaries Expense; and Utilities Expense. Then determine the balance of each account.

b Prepare a trial balance.

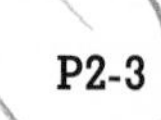

P2-3 ***Entry, trial balance preparation, and analysis of operations***

In an effort to rejuvenate the center-city area of Los Frisco, Bill Conti has agreed to reopen and operate the Palace Theater. The following transactions occurred during September.

Sept. 1 Deposited $9,000 of personal savings in a bank account in the name of the business.
1 Paid the first month's rent of $1,200.
4 Entered into an agreement for the operation of a refreshment stand. The operator agreed to pay the Palace Theater 10% of his net income with a monthly minimum of $350. Accountings and related cash payments will be made at the end of each month.
7 Received a film rental invoice of $2,300, which is due in ten days.
10 Recorded cash admissions of $3,150 and a $350 billing to the Valley Women's Club.
14 Paid $380 for September advertising in the *Times Herald*.
15 Paid salaries of $1,800.
17 Discovered a billing error to the Valley Women's Club on September 10. The correct amount should have been $530.
17 Paid the film rental invoice received on September 7.
19 Recorded cash admissions of $1,900 and billings of $420.
23 Received $550 from customers on account.
24 Paid a repair bill of $680 on Conti's personal car by using business funds.
26 Purchased new office equipment for $4,000. Paid $1,000 down and agreed to pay the balance by November 30.
30 Paid salaries of $1,800.
30 Recorded cash admissions of $1,750. There were no billings.
30 Received the proper amount due from the concession operator. Concession sales were $8,500. The operator noted that the cost of food and refreshments sold amounted to $4,100 and other expenses incurred totaled $1,580.

The Palace's accounts and account numbers are as follows:

Cash	110	Admissions revenue	401
Accounts receivable	120	Concession revenue	410
Office equipment	130	Salaries expense	501
Accounts payable	201	Building rent expense	510
Bill Conti, capital	310	Film rental expense	520
Bill Conti, drawing	330	Advertising expense	530

INSTRUCTIONS

a Record the transactions in the general journal.

b Post the transactions to running balance ledger accounts.

c Prepare a trial balance as of September 30. Omit accounts with zero balances.

d Evaluate the success or failure of the Palace Theater in September.

P2-4 ***Entry, trial balance preparation, and statement analysis***

The trial balance of Sahaido Enterprises follows.

SAHAIDO ENTERPRISES
Trial Balance
March 31, 1983

Cash	$10,000	
Accounts receivable	8,900	
Land	26,000	
Accounts payable		$ 9,400
Loan payable		17,000
Miki Sahaido, capital		23,500
Miki Sahaido, drawing	18,800	
Service fees		38,700
Salaries expense	17,400	
Interest expense	1,500	
Miscellaneous expense	6,000	
	$88,600	$88,600

The following transactions occurred during April.

Apr. 2 Sahaido withdrew $1,800 from the business.
6 Sold one-quarter of the land to a neighboring business for $6,500.
10 Billed customers $6,400 for services rendered.
15 Paid salaries of $3,000 and miscellaneous expenses of $900.
19 Collected $4,000 from customers on account.
23 Paid $600 to the bank in partial payment of the loan. The payment includes interest of $150.
27 Paid $1,500 to creditors on account.

INSTRUCTIONS

a Record the necessary journal entries for April.

b Prepare a trial balance as of April 30, 1983.

c Creditors often review financial statements in deciding whether to do business with a company. Determine which of Sahaido's assets (Cash, Accounts Receivable, or Land) would be of interest in a credit-granting decision. Explain your answer.

P2-5 ***Error analysis and correcting entries***

The Bates Company has just hired a new bookkeeper. In reviewing some of his work, the firm's accountant found the following:

a A $900 withdrawal by the owner was debited to Jane Bates, Capital. The credit was recorded properly.

b The receipt of $700 from a customer on account was recorded as follows:

Accounts Receivable	*700*	
Cash		*700*

c A payment of $400 to a creditor was recorded as follows:

Accounts Payable	*40*	
Cash		*40*

d A $1,500 purchase of equipment for cash was not recorded.

e A $500 payment for rent was properly recorded in the journal but was accidentally posted to the Advertising Expense account in the ledger.

f A $1,000 investment by the owner was recorded and posted twice.

g A $570 purchase of equipment on account was entered in the proper accounts. However, an investigation revealed the amount of the purchase was recorded as $750.

INSTRUCTIONS

Assuming all transactions have been posted to ledger accounts, prepare a brief narrative analysis of each of the bookkeeper's errors. Then record the necessary entry or entries to correct the errors. Transaction (*a*) is done as an example.

Analysis The withdrawal should have been recorded in the drawing account. The capital account was reduced by $900 from the debit and must be increased to eliminate the impact of the error.

Entry

Jane Bates, Drawing	*900*	
Jane Bates, Capital		*900*

P2-6 ***Preparation of corrected trial balance***

The bookkeeper of the Nettles Company was having difficulty with the following December 31 trial balance:

Cash	$ 31,300	
Accounts receivable	26,100	
Building	50,000	
Accounts payable		$ 13,200
Loan payable		65,000
Ralph Nettles, capital		25,600
Ralph Nettles, drawing	6,900	
Service revenue		61,000
Salaries expense		38,900
Utilities expense	4,100	
Advertising expense	7,600	
	$126,000	$203,700

The following facts have been called to his attention.

a All accounts have normal balances.

b Receipts of $2,900 from customers on account were debited to Cash and credited to Ralph Nettles, Drawing.

c Debits in the Accounts Receivable account were incorrectly stated as $5,500 rather than $4,500.

d The Building account includes the land on which the building is sitting. Correspondence indicates that 80% of the complex's cost is attributed to the building.

e The December utility bill of $500, due in January, was not recorded.

f A withdrawal of $1,200 in December was accidentally debited to Ralph Nettles, Capital. The credit was recorded correctly.

g A $2,900 salary payment was debited to Cash and credited to Salaries Expense.

h A $3,200 advertising bill was inadvertently recorded and paid as $2,300. The advertising agency agreed to accept the balance due in January.

i The Miscellaneous Expense account of $1,900 was accidentally omitted from the trial balance.

j Credits of $1,000 to the Service Revenue account were overlooked when calculating the account's balance.

INSTRUCTIONS

Prepare a corrected trial balance for the Nettles Company.

P2-7 ***Transaction analysis and trial balance preparation (alternate to P2-1)***

The T-accounts below were taken from the books of the MacWithey Company on December 31, 1983. Letters in the accounts reference specific transactions of the firm.

Cash	
(a) 20,000	(c) 350
(e) 2,000	(d) 500
(f) 550	(g) 375
(i) 50	

Accounts Receivable	
(e) 1,000	(f) 550

Supplies	
(c) 350	(i) 50

Equipment	
(b) 4,800	
(h) 2,100	

Accounts Payable	
	(b) 4,800

MacWithey, Capital	
	(a) 20,000
	(h) 2,100

Fees Earned	
	(e) 3,000

Advertising Expense	
(d) 500	

Utilities Expense	
(g) 375	

INSTRUCTIONS

a Write a brief explanation of each of the transactions (*a*)–(*i*).

b Determine the balance in each account and prepare a trial balance.

P2-8 ***Journal entry and trial balance preparation (alternate to P2-2)***
Consider the following transactions of the Johnson Service Organization.

May *4* Marcus Johnson, the owner, withdrew $10,000 from his savings and opened a bank account in the name of the business.
5 Marcus rented office space in a nearby shopping center. Rental payments total $850 a month and the landlord required that 3 months' rent be paid immediately.
10 Office supplies of $275 were purchased on account.
15 Revenues collected from clients during the first week of operation totaled $1,500.
18 Office equipment costing $4,800 was purchased by paying $800 down; the balance was borrowed on a note payable.
29 Revenues for the 2 weeks just ended totaled $1,600; $750 was collected.
31 Office salaries of $1,800 were paid to Marcus's two employees.
31 Rent expense for the month was recorded.

INSTRUCTIONS

a Establish T-accounts for Cash; Accounts Receivable; Prepaid Rent; Supplies; Equipment; Accounts Payable; Notes Payable; Marcus Johnson, Capital; Service Revenue; Salaries Expense; and Rent Expense. Enter the transactions in the T-accounts and determine the balance of each account.
b Prepare a trial balance.

P2-9 ***Entry, trial balance preparation, and analysis of operations (alternate to P2-3)***
In an effort to help rejuvenate the downtown area of Metroville, Frank Rhoden agreed to reopen and operate the Majestic Cinema. The following transactions occurred during August.

Aug. *1* Deposited $10,000 of personal savings in a bank account in the name of the business.
2 Paid the first month's rent of $1,000.
3 Completed the hiring of personnel whose monthly salaries will total $4,000.
3 Entered into an agreement for the operation of a concession stand. The operator agreed to pay the Majestic Cinema 15% of his net income with a monthly minimum of $400. Accountings and related cash payments will be made at the end of each month.
6 Received a film rental invoice of $2,900, which is due by August 25.
9 Recorded cash admissions of $3,800 and a $400 billing to the Fine Arts League.
12 Paid $300 for August advertising in the *Metroville Herald.*
15 Paid salaries of $2,000.
19 Purchased new projection equipment for $3,800. Paid 25% down and agreed to pay the balance in September.
22 Recorded cash admissions of $1,800. There were no billings.
24 Paid the film rental invoice received on August 6.
26 Received partial payment of $275 from the billing to the Fine Arts League.

29 Paid salaries of $2,000.
31 Recorded cash admissions of $1,200 and billings of $650.
31 Received the proper amount due from the concession operator. Concession sales were $7,200. The operator noted that the cost of food and refreshments sold amounted to $3,800 and miscellaneous expenses incurred totaled $400.

Majestic's accounts and account numbers are as follows:

Cash	101	Admissions revenue	410
Accounts receivable	110	Concession revenue	420
Equipment	120	Salaries expense	510
Accounts payable	210	Building rent expense	520
Frank Rhoden, capital	310	Film rental expense	530
Frank Rhoden, drawing	320	Advertising expense	540

INSTRUCTIONS

a Record the necessary journal entries for August.
b Post the entries to running balance ledger accounts.
c Prepare a trial balance as of August 31. Omit accounts with zero balances.
d Evaluate the success or failure of Rhoden's operation in August.

P2-10 ***Entry, trial balance preparation, and statement analysis (alternate to P2-4)*** The trial balance of Moore Services follows. Only accounts with balances are listed.

MOORE SERVICES
Trial Balance
April 30, 1983

Cash	$ 2,700	
Accounts receivable	2,500	
Accounts payable		$ 1,800
Sally Moore, capital		6,000
Sally Moore, drawing	5,000	
Professional fees		29,500
Salaries expense	15,000	
Rent expense	8,200	
Utilities expense	3,900	
	$37,300	$37,300

The following transactions occurred during May.

May 2 Paid $800 to creditors on account.
5 Billed customers $4,000 for services rendered.
9 Received $3,300 from Sally Moore as an investment.
14 Paid $1,500 for rent and $2,200 for salaries.
18 Received May's utility bill of $600 to be paid in June.

25 Received $750 from customers on account.
31 Acquired $8,000 of equipment. Paid $1,000 down and secured a short-term bank loan for the remainder.

INSTRUCTIONS

a Record the necessary journal entries for May.
b Prepare a trial balance as of May 31, 1983.
c A new creditor, Wade Distributors, is considering doing business with Moore. Wade has requested certain account balance information to judge Moore's debt-paying ability. By analyzing the data as of April 30 and May 31, comment on Moore's ability to pay new creditors such as Wade.

P2-11 ***Error analysis and correcting entries (alternate to P2-5)***

The Ortiz Company has just hired a new bookkeeper. In reviewing some of her work, the firm's accountant found the following:

a A $1,200 purchase of equipment on account was credited to Accounts Receivable. The debit was recorded properly.
b An investment of $6,000 by the owner was recorded as follows:

Jose Ortiz, Capital	*6,000*	
Cash		*6,000*

c A $350 purchase of supplies for cash was recorded as follows:

Supplies	*35*	
Cash		*35*

d A $2,000 withdrawal by the owner was not recorded.
e A $700 payment for utilities was properly recorded in the journal but was accidentally posted to the Rent Expense account in the ledger.
f A $750 customer receipt on account was recorded and posted twice.
g A $10,500 purchase of land for cash was recorded in the proper accounts. However, an investigation revealed that the cost of the land was incorrectly recorded as $15,000.

INSTRUCTIONS

Assuming all transactions have been posted to ledger accounts, prepare a brief narrative analysis of each of the bookkeeper's errors. Then record the necessary entry or entries to correct the errors. Transaction (*a*) is done as an example.

Analysis The credit should have been recorded in the Accounts Payable account. The Accounts Receivable account was reduced by $1,200 from the credit and must be increased to eliminate the impact of the error.

Entry

Accounts Receivable	*1,200*	
Accounts Payable		*1,200*

CASE 2
BARKMAN AND ASSOCIATES

Don Pruitt is a staff accountant with Meredith and Meredith, CPAs. On December 3 Pruitt and a co-worker were on assignment at a client's, Barkman and Associates. Barkman and Associates is a small service business whose accounting records are maintained by Bev Wright, a bookkeeper. Pruitt and his colleague were in the process of completing a discussion with Phil Barkman, the firm's owner, regarding several tax problems. All of a sudden Wright burst into the office in distress. She apologized and explained that she had been frustrated in trying to get the November 30 trial balance to balance. Pruitt volunteered his services to help her locate the problem(s).

The following transactions were recorded in the journal and posted to the ledger during November.

Nov. *1* Barkman invested $7,500 and opened a bank account in the name of the business.
3 Paid office rent for November, $900.
7 Purchased office equipment on account, $2,200. Paid $700 down, with the remaining balance due in December.
11 Billed clients for services rendered, $980.
15 Paid office salaries, $750.
19 Returned $300 of the office equipment purchased on November 7 and received credit from the seller.
24 Received $460 from customers on account.
27 Barkman withdrew $1,000 from the business.
28 Recorded the November utilities bill of $80. The bill is due on December 10.
30 Paid office salaries, $750.

In the process of assisting Wright, Pruitt found the following two documents:

Richard Kale
8703 Landover Ct.
Arlington, Tx. 76017

1301

Nov 29 19 83

RECEIVED
11-30-83
B&A

Pay to the Order of Barkman and Associates $ 80.00

Eighty and 00/100 Dollars

NATIONAL CITY
BANK OF ARLINGTON
Arlington, Texas 76010

Richard Kale

memo Payment of bill of 11/11

⑆111922789⑆ 25 788 4⑈

RECEIVED
12-03-83
B&A

INVOICE

WEAVER OFFICE EQUIPMENT
11 East Division
Arlington, Texas 76019

Invoice Date: 12/2/83

To: Barkman and Associates
751 West Maple
Arlington, Texas 76019

Date	Qty	Description	Cost
12/1/83	1	12-710 Calculator	$60.00
		Sales Tax	3.00
		Amount Due	$63.00

Barkman's general journal and ledger accounts follow.

Page 1

Date		Accounts	Post Ref	Debit	Credit
1983					
Nov.	1	Cash	110	7,500	
		Phil Barkman, Capital	310		7,500
	3	Rent Expense	510	900	
		Cash	110		900
	7	Office Equipment	130	2,200	
		Accounts Payable	210		1,500
		Cash	110		700
	11	Accounts Receivable	120	980	
		Service Revenue	410		980
	15	Salaries Expense	520	750	
		Accounts Payable	210		750
	19	Accounts Payable	120	300	
		Office Equipment	130		300
	24	Cash	110	640	
		Accounts Receivable	120		640
	27	Phil Barkman, Drawing	320	1,000	
		Cash	110		1,000
	28	Utilities Expense	530	80	
		Accounts Payable	210		80
	30	Salaries Expense	520	750	
		Cash	110		750

Cash 110

11/1	J1	7,500	11/3	J1	900
11/24	J1	640	11/30	J1	750
11/27	J1	1,000			1,650
	(7,490)	9,140			

Accounts Receivable 120

11/11	J1	980	11/24	J1	640
11/19	J1	300			
	(640)	1,280			

Office Equipment 130

11/7	J1	2,200	11/19	J1	300
	(1,800)				

Accounts Payable 210

			11/7	J1	1,500
			11/15	J1	750
			11/28	J1	80
					2,330

Phil Barkman, Capital 310

			11/1	J1	7,500

Phil Barkman, Drawing 320

11/27	J1	1,000			

Service Revenue 410

			11/11	J1	980

Rent Expense 510

11/3	J1	900			

Salaries Expense 520

11/15	J1	750			
11/30	J1	750			
		1,500			

Utilities Expense 530

11/28	J1	80			

Wright's trial balance and the related calculator tape are shown below.

BARKMAN AND ASSOCIATES
Trial Balance
November 30, 1983

Cash	$ 7,490	
Accounts receivable	640	
Office equipment	1,800	
Accounts payable		$ 2,330
Phil Barkman, capital		7,500
Phil Barkman, drawing		1,000
Service revenue		980
Rent expense	900	
Salaries expense	15,000	
Utilities expense	80	
	$25,910	$20,630

```
0· *

7490· +
640· +
1800· +
900· +
15000· +
80· +
25910· *

0· *

2330· +
7500· +
1000· +
9800· +
20630· *
```

INSTRUCTIONS
Assume the role of Don Pruitt in assisting Bev Wright.

a Identify the errors that Wright has made.
b Prepare entries to correct the errors that are contained in the accounts.
c Prepare a corrected trial balance.
d Suggest a course of action to Barkman's office manager as to how these errors can be avoided in the future.

3 COMPLETION OF THE ACCOUNTING CYCLE

LEARNING OBJECTIVES

After reading this chapter you should:

1 Be able to explain the impact of accounting periods on financial accounting.

2 Understand the underlying differences between the cash basis and the accrual basis of accounting.

3 Know why the adjusting process is needed and which items typically need adjusting entries.

4 Be able to prepare adjusting entries and understand their impact on the financial statements.

5 Be able to prepare a work sheet and the accompanying financial statements.

6 Know how to close a set of books and how to prepare a post-closing trial balance.

7 Be able to describe the various steps in the accounting cycle.

CHAPTER 3

As we move into Chapter 3, you should have some familiarity with the tools accountants use to process transactions. We saw that debits and credits record increases and decreases in the accounts kept by a business. In addition, we observed that entries are posted from the journal to the ledger to summarize the effect of various transactions on a given account. Finally, we noted a trial balance proves the equality of the account balances in the ledger.

You may think that we can now generate financial statements by using the information contained in the trial balance. Unfortunately, we cannot. The preparation of statements at this particular point would result in misleading reports of financial condition and profitability. While daily transactions have been recorded in the journal and posted to the proper accounts, a company's books may still not reflect the correct status of its financial affairs at the end of the period.

To illustrate, consider the problem of **prepaid expenses,** that is, goods or services purchased for future consumption and paid for in advance. As the goods or services are used or expire, the prepaid expense becomes an expense. Because many prepaid expenses are consumed on a daily basis (e.g., rent and insurance), theoretically a business should record a small amount of usage each day. This procedure is not followed in practice, however. Daily recording of consumption is needless and necessitates an unwieldy amount of bookkeeping. Instead, at the end of an accounting period, the prepaid expense is reduced by the *total* portion used during that period. You received a short exposure to this technique in the Davis Furniture Repair illustration in Chapter 1.

Other items also require updating at the end of the period. The accountant must carefully analyze a business and the business's accounts to determine exactly what updating is necessary. Two factors affect the manner in which this process is performed: the accounting period and the cash and accrual bases of event recognition.

THE ACCOUNTING PERIOD

Events and transactions that affect the financial well-being of a firm occur continually over its life. For purposes of reporting the results of operations to owners, creditors, and other interested parties, the life of a firm is divided into discrete **accounting periods.** The periods can vary in length and may be, among others, a month, a quarter, or a year. No matter which period is selected, a basic accounting problem arises when breaking the life of a company into divisible "chunks," since many financial events relate to more than a single reporting period. To illustrate, we cite the cases of R. H. Macy & Co., Inc., and Ramada Inns, Inc.

R. H. Macy & Co., Inc., operates 92 retail department stores in 13 states. Approximately 68% of the company's total sales are generated by men's, women's, and children's ready-to-wear apparel. It is essential, then, that Macy stock the right merchandise at the right time. A recent balance sheet revealed that the firm had $436.5 million of inventory or goods purchased for resale to customers. The acquisition, holding, sale, and customer payment for these goods could easily involve several accounting periods. For example, assume that toward the end of a given period, Macy placed orders with manufacturers to acquire needed inventory. The goods arrived during the next period and were distributed to various stores. Near the end of this period Macy paid its suppliers and began to sell the merchandise to customers on account. The customers were billed and, let us imagine, paid their bills during a third accounting period.

In view of these events two basic questions arise for purposes of measuring financial performance. First, in which period does the merchandise become an asset of Macy? In period 1 when Macy placed the orders, or in period 2 when the inventory arrived and the suppliers were paid? Second, when should revenue from the sales of merchandise be recognized? In period 2 when the sales were made, or in period 3 when the customers paid their bills? The answers to these questions are dependent on the accounting policies selected by the firm. Different policies will have differing effects on the income statement and the balance sheet.

The practice of using discrete accounting periods also creates problems for companies possessing assets that provide long-term benefits. Ramada Inns, Inc., is a classic example. Ramada, the third largest hotel chain in the world, generates the bulk of its revenues from furnishing room, gaming, food, and beverage services. These services are made possible, in part, by the firm's buildings, furniture, and equipment. The following lives have been established for these assets:

Buildings	40 years
Furniture	7–10 years
Equipment	3–15 years

The assets above render benefits for a number of years. Over time they are subject to wear and tear, and by the end of their lives the assets are "fully consumed." In each accounting period, then, a portion of the assets is "used up" in helping to generate Ramada's revenues. The portion consumed must be charged to the period benefited as an expense, that is, a cost incurred in the revenue-producing process. Why is this procedure necessary? Once again the explanation lies in the accounting period. We desire to measure financial activity for a specific segment of a business's life. It is therefore mandatory to consider *all* events and transactions occurring during that period, including the expiration of long-term assets.

REVENUE AND EXPENSE RECOGNITION

Many examples can be cited of activities that bridge two or more periods, especially those involving revenues and expenses. Should revenues be recognized when generated or when ultimately collected by a company? Should expenses be recognized when incurred or when finally paid? The answers to these questions vary and are dependent on whether a business employs the cash or accrual basis of accounting.

Cash Basis Accounting

As its name implies, the **cash basis** of accounting focuses on the cash flows connected with revenues and expenses. Revenues are recognized in the accounting period of *receipt;* similarly, expenses are recognized in the period of *payment.* Observe that it makes no difference when the revenues are generated or when the expenses are incurred. Recognition is determined by the timing of the related cash flows.

To illustrate the cash basis system, we will consider the following data of Denton Enterprises during June 1983.

Sales. Cash sales totaled $8,000 and credit sales amounted to $22,000. Customers paid $12,000 of the latter after being billed.
Operating expenses. Denton incurred $10,000 of operating expenses, of which $7,000 were paid.
Prepaid expenses. Denton prepaid 3 months' rent at $2,000 per month at the beginning of June.
Loan. In the middle of the month Denton secured a $20,000 loan. As of June 30, $100 of interest had been incurred; the interest will be paid to the bank in July.
Withdrawal. The owner withdrew $5,000 during the month.

Denton's cash basis income statement appears in Exhibit 3-1.

Exhibit 3-1

Cash basis income statement for Denton Enterprises

DENTON ENTERPRISES
Income Statement
For the Month Ended June 30, 1983

Service revenue		*$20,000*
Less expenses		
Operating	*$7,000*	
Rent	*6,000*	
Total expenses		*13,000*
Net income		*$ 7,000*

Note that the statement concentrates on cash flows. Denton's sales in June, for example, total $30,000 ($8,000 + $22,000). Cash receipts from sales, however, amount to $20,000 ($8,000 + $12,000), and this is the amount recognized as revenue. Only $7,000 of the operating expenses are recognized in June; the remaining $3,000 will be recognized in future months when paid. Turning to the prepaid rent, the entire payment of $6,000 is recognized as rent expense in June. Although $4,000 applies to July and August, this fact is ignored under the cash basis. The loan, which is a cash receipt, is not considered revenue because it has not been generated by Denton's earnings process. The $100 of interest, applicable to June, can also be ignored, because payment will not take place until July. Finally, as we noted in Chapter 1, withdrawals are not expenses but are considered reductions in owners' equity.

The cash basis of accounting is criticized as not being in accord with economic reality. Why? The receipt and disbursement of cash do not adequately measure financial activity within a given time period. This fact is apparent when examining Denton's June transactions. Although the company rendered services amounting to $30,000, only those services for which cash is received in June are recognized as June revenue. As far as expenses are concerned, Denton incurred and became legally liable for $10,100 of operating and interest expense in June. Under cash basis accounting, however, only $7,000 is recognized. Finally, expensing the entire $6,000 rental payment in June overstates Denton's "true" rent expense, because $4,000 really relates to July and August.

Overall, the cash basis does not properly **match** revenues and expenses. In a measurement of net income the expenses incurred in producing revenue should be matched against (deducted from) the revenues they helped to produce. In Denton's case several expenses that helped to generate June revenues will not be deducted until paid in future months. Furthermore, certain expenses were deducted (e.g., two months' rent) that failed to assist in the revenue-generating process. The foregoing treatment is contrary to the basic definition of an expense as discussed in Chapter 1.

Accrual Basis Accounting

The **accrual basis** of accounting overcomes the chief limitation of the cash basis—a possible mismatch of revenues and expenses. Under the accrual basis revenues are recognized when earned, which for most businesses occurs when goods are sold or when services are rendered. The recognition of expenses, in turn, parallels the recognition of revenue. If revenues are recognized in the *current* period, the costs incurred in the revenue-generating process are expensed. On the other hand, if a business incurs costs that help to produce revenues in a *future* period, the costs are not expensed until that same future period. When we account for revenues and expenses in this manner, expenses are matched against the revenues they helped to create, resulting in improved measurement of financial activity.

Denton's accrual basis income statement appears in Exhibit 3-2. Ser-

Exhibit 3-2

Accrual basis income statement for Denton Enterprises

DENTON ENTERPRISES
Income Statement
For the Month Ended June 30, 1983

Service revenue		$30,000
Less expenses		
Operating	$10,000	
Rent	2,000	
Interest	100	
Total expenses		12,100
Net income		$17,900

vice revenue is $30,000 ($8,000 + $22,000) because the firm rendered services and earned $30,000 in June. The expenses incurred in producing this revenue are deducted to determine June's net income. Note that only $2,000 ($\frac{1}{3}$ of the rental payment) is deducted as an expense, because the remaining $\frac{2}{3}$ is applicable to future months. Finally, interest of $100 is recognized since Denton had the use of the loan proceeds to help finance June operations.

Cash and Accrual Methods in Practice

Because of the possible mismatch of revenues and expenses and the subsequent misstatement of financial position, few businesses utilize a strict cash basis of accounting. The cash basis is probably employed most frequently in the preparation of income tax returns for individual taxpayers. The problem faced by businesses is that many firms have substantial investments in long-term assets such as buildings, machinery, and equipment. Under a strict cash basis these resources would be expensed when paid despite the fact that benefits are rendered for a number of years. In light of the large number of dollars involved, the cash basis would severely distort reported earnings.

Consequently, most businesses that desire to use the cash basis adopt a **modified cash basis** system. The modified system is really a combination of both the cash and accrual systems; that is, expenditures benefiting more than one accounting period are established as assets when acquired. As an asset's benefits are consumed or used up, the long-term asset is written off as an expense. The modified cash basis is often employed by dental, law, accounting, and other professional practices.

Outside of professional practices almost all large companies use the accrual basis of accounting. Usually, the majority of a large firm's purchase, sale, and expense transactions are made on account. Thus it is highly probable that event occurrence and subsequent payment will take place in different periods. In view of the possible mismatch that can occur with the cash basis, the accrual method is preferred and is therefore featured throughout this text.

ADJUSTING ENTRIES

Keeping the accrual basis in mind, let us return to the trial balance for a moment. The account balances in the trial balance are calculated by summarizing numerous transactions. Many of these transactions affect only the accounting period under examination. Others, of course, affect several periods. Still others affect the current period but may *not* as yet have been recorded on the books.

To illustrate, assume employees of a company are paid each Friday and that wages average $20,000 per week. The following entry is made at the end of the week:

Wage Expense	*20,000*	
Cash		*20,000*
Paid weekly wages		

In January, suppose the last Friday of the month falls on January 27. If the company is closed on the 28th and 29th, what happens to the wages earned by employees on the 30th and 31st? These wages are properly charged to January because they were incurred in January. Unless some special accounting procedure is employed, however, the wages will be incorrectly charged to February's expense when the next payroll is paid on Friday, February 3.

Financial statements that fairly present and measure financial activity cannot be produced by relying solely on information contained in the trial balance. Many accounts need updating to reflect their proper status. At the end of a period, therefore, a process known as adjusting takes place. In the **adjusting process** the accountant analyzes the various accounts maintained by a business to determine whether or not the accounts are up to date. If updating is necessary, adjusting entries (adjustments) are recorded in the journal and posted to the ledger.

Frequently, the adjusting process centers on two specific situations:

1 Multiperiod costs and revenues that must be split among two or more accounting periods.
2 Revenues and expenses that have been earned or incurred in a given period but not as yet recorded in the accounts.

The adjusting process is an outgrowth of the accrual basis of accounting. In attempting to measure net income for a given period, we are concerned with the revenues *earned* as opposed to those received. Furthermore, we recognize the expenses *incurred* in producing revenue, not just those that have been paid. Once these ideas are mastered, the adjusting process is straightforward.

Many students have a difficult time with adjustments because they attempt to memorize this material without attempting to understand why they are doing what they are doing. Keep the accrual basis in mind. Also, realize that all we are doing is updating the accounts so the accounts reflect their proper status at the end of the accounting period.

To illustrate the adjusting process, we will continue the Wise Advertising Agency example we introduced in Chapter 2. At this time, however, it is necessary to present several additional transactions that occurred during May.

Multiperiod Costs and Revenues

As we noted earlier, many of the costs and revenues encountered by a business benefit more than a single accounting period. For a correct measure of financial activity these costs and revenues must be split or apportioned among the periods affected. Examples of such items include prepaid expenses, depreciation, and unearned revenues.

Prepaid expenses

Earlier in the chapter we explained that *prepaid expenses* are assets that provide future benefits. By the end of an accounting period a portion of these assets has typically been consumed in the revenue-producing process. For a proper match of the costs incurred in producing revenue against the revenues generated, a portion of the prepaid expense must be written off as expense. This write-off is done in the adjusting process.

The Wise Advertising Agency had transactions during May that involved prepaid insurance and supplies. The proper accounting treatment for both follows.

Prepaid insurance

On May 1 Wise paid $480 for a 2-year insurance policy. The purchase, which creates an asset known as Prepaid Insurance, is recorded by the following journal entry:

May 1	Prepaid Insurance	480	
	Cash		480
	Purchased 2-year policy		

As each day passes, a portion of the insurance policy expires. Thus at the end of the period, the Prepaid Insurance account must be updated by an adjusting entry.

The policy acquired provides insurance protection for 2 years or 24 months at a cost of $20 per month ($480 ÷ 24). By the end of May $20 of the policy has expired. To record the proper decrease in Wise's asset, we must credit Prepaid Insurance. The $20 represents an expense and, accordingly, Wise's total expenses are increased by a debit to Insurance Expense. The necessary adjusting entry to update the accounts is as follows:

May 31	Insurance Expense	20	
	Prepaid Insurance		20
	Adjusting entry		

The insurance accounts now appear as follows:

Prepaid Insurance			
5/1	480	5/31	20
	460		

Insurance Expense			
5/31	20		

The Prepaid Insurance balance of $460 represents the 23 months of insurance that are still prepaid and appears on the May 31 balance sheet in the asset section. The Insurance Expense account, which contains the 1 month of expired insurance at $20, appears on the May income statement.

Supplies

On May 4 Wise purchased $340 of supplies for cash. Because the supplies will be used in future periods, the purchase is recorded in an asset account as follows:

May 4	Supplies	340	
	Cash		340
	Purchased supplies for cash		

During the month various supplies were consumed in business operations. On May 31 Wise determined that $260 of supplies remained on hand. Thus $80 ($340 – $260) was used and the accounts must be updated.

An adjusting entry must reduce the asset Supplies from $340 to $260 to reflect the amount owned as of the end of the period. Since Supplies presently has a debit balance of $340, a credit of $80 yields the desired result. The $80, which represents the portion of the asset consumed, is an expense. Because Wise's expenses have increased, Supplies Expense is debited. The necessary adjusting entry follows:

May 31	*Supplies Expense*	*80*	
	Supplies		*80*
	Adjusting entry		

Similar to the insurance transaction, the Supplies Expense balance of $80 would appear on the May income statement. The Supplies account contains a balance of $260 ($340 – $80) after adjustment and would appear on the May 31 balance sheet.

Depreciation

For most businesses the amount of money spent for prepaid expenses is relatively small. Considerable sums are expended, however, for the acquisition of other assets, such as buildings, machinery, and equipment, that benefit multiple accounting periods. These assets normally assist in the revenue-producing process for a longer period of time than the typical prepaid expense. Nevertheless, the same basic accounting practice is used for these assets as is used for the prepaid expense: the asset's balance is reduced and written off to an expense upon consumption. This expense is called **depreciation.**

Unfortunately, accountants are unable to determine the exact portion of a long-term asset that is consumed in a given period. Thus it is common practice to systematically expense a fraction of the asset's cost each year the asset is used. There are several different methods for doing this. The simplest approach, called the *straight-line method,* takes an equal amount of depreciation during each year of the asset's life.

To illustrate, assume Wise acquired a used car for cash on May 1 for use in the business. The car cost $4,500 and was estimated to have a service life of 3 years. The following entry was made:

May 1	*Car*	*4,500*	
	Cash		*4,500*
	Purchased used car		

Each year Wise will record $1,500 ($4,500 ÷ 3 years) of depreciation. On a monthly basis this amounts to $125 ($1,500 ÷ 12). Therefore the following adjusting entry is made on May 31 to update the accounting records.

May 31	*Depreciation Expense*	*125*	
	Accumulated Depreciation: Car		*125*
	Adjusting entry		

The Depreciation Expense account is debited and increases the agency's total expenses. Notice that the Car account is not credited for the appropriate reduction. Generally, accountants prefer to leave the cost of a long-term asset intact in the account where initially recorded. Thus a separate account is established—Accumulated Depreciation: Car. This account appears as a *reduction* in the asset section of the balance sheet and is appropriately termed a **contra asset.** As its name implies, the Accumulated Depreciation account keeps a running total of the depreciation taken during the various accounting periods. The car would appear on the May 31 and June 30 balance sheets as follows:

	May 31	June 30
Assets		
⋮		
Car	$4,500	$4,500
Less: Accumulated depreciation	125	250
	$4,375	$4,250

The net figures ($4,375 and $4,250) represent the car's **book value;** that is, the amount that the car is carried at on the books of the business. Book value is the numerical difference between an asset's cost and the depreciation taken to date and in no way should be equated with the true value of the asset in the marketplace.

Unearned revenues

The last of the multiperiod items to be discussed is unearned revenue. **Unearned revenue** represents future revenues that have been collected but not as yet earned. Sometimes called prepaid or deferred revenues, realization (earning) of revenue will occur when some type of service is performed.

At the time of collection, unearned revenue represents a liability to the recipient, because goods or services are owed in return. Magazine publishers, for example, often establish an Unearned Subscription Revenue account. On receipt of a subscription the publisher owes the subscriber a number of issues of the magazine. As another example, airlines often report unearned revenue accounts on their balance sheets. Consider USAir, which serves cities predominantly in the northeastern and midwestern United States. Recently, USAir reported $80.1 million in a liability account entitled Traffic Balances Payable and Unused Tickets. An explanation of this account was found in the following footnote that accompanied the financial statements:

> *Passenger ticket sales are not recognized as revenue until the transportation service is rendered. At the time of sale a liability is established (Traffic Balances Payable and Unused Tickets) and subsequently eliminated either through carriage of the passenger by the Company, through billing from another carrier who renders the service, or by refund to the passenger.*

Returning to the Wise Advertising Agency example, Wise received $10,400 on May 16 to design and run a 52-week advertising program for

McConnell and Associates. The necessary work on the program began immediately. The following entry records the receipt of cash.

May 16	***Cash***	*10,400*	
	Unearned Agency Revenue		*10,400*
	Receipt for 52-week program		

Unearned Agency Revenue is a liability account, because Wise owes McConnell a service (advertising work). Observe that the credit increases Wise's liability to clients.

By the end of May, 2 weeks of work had been performed on the contract. Because revenue is earned at the rate of $200 per week ($10,400 ÷ 52), $400 must be recorded as Agency Revenue for May for inclusion on the income statement. In addition, the amount of advertising work owed to McConnell has been reduced to $10,000 ($10,400 − $400) and will appear in the liability section of Wise's balance sheet. The appropriate updating is achieved by the following adjusting entry:

May 31	***Unearned Agency Revenue***	*400*	
	Agency Revenue		*400*
	Adjusting entry		

The impact of the entry is shown by the following T-accounts:[1]

Unearned Agency Revenue			
5/31	400	5/16	10,400
			(10,000)

Agency Revenue			
		5/31	400

Accruals

Accruals are revenues and expenses that gradually accumulate throughout an accounting period. Unlike the multiperiod costs and revenues just presented, accruals have not as yet been recorded in the accounts. Thus an adjusting entry is needed so that these items are properly considered when the financial statements are prepared.

Accruals are consistent with the accrual basis of accounting. **Accrued expenses** are expenses that have been incurred but not as yet paid. Examples include the wages incurred by businesses during the last few days of an accounting period and the interest owed to creditors on loans. Both these expenses gradually accumulate and are likely to be paid in the subsequent period. **Accrued revenues,** on the other hand, have been earned although not as yet received. Common examples of accrued revenues include the interest mentioned above from the creditors' viewpoint, commissions earned, and unbilled revenues. As you can see, we are focusing on revenues *earned* and expenses *incurred* and *not* on the related cash receipt or dis-

[1] In Chapter 2 the Agency Revenue account was affected by transactions on May 14, 27, and 31. These transactions are omitted here so we can focus solely on the unearned revenue concept.

bursement. These concepts can be clarified by returning to the Wise Advertising illustration.

Accrued expenses

On May 1 Wise obtained a $6,000 loan. Payments are due on the first of each month; interest is computed at the rate of 1% per month on the unpaid balance. The proceeds from the loan are recorded in the following entry:

May 1	*Cash*	*6,000*	
	Loan Payable		*6,000*
	Recorded loan proceeds		

As of May 31 interest charges have been incurred because Wise has had the use of the borrowed funds for 1 month. Although the interest will not be remitted until the first payment date on June 1, interest was incurred during May and should appear on May's financial statements. Thus an adjusting entry is needed to update the accounts. Interest is computed at the rate of 1% per month on the unpaid balance of the loan. For May the interest is $6,000 × 0.01, or $60. Since the $60 increases Wise's total interest costs for the accounting period, Interest Expense is debited. Because no payment is made until June 1, the $60 must also be placed in a liability account to show the firm's obligation as of May 31. Interest Payable is therefore credited. The adjusting entry is as follows:

May 31	*Interest Expense*	*60*	
	Interest Payable		*60*
	Adjusting entry		

Wise has another accrued expense: salaries. Employees are paid on the last Friday of each month, and payday was May 28 (see page 56). Because May 29 and 30 are not working days, Wise has incurred 1 day of expense in May (May 31), which will not be paid until the end of June. This expense properly belongs to May and should be recorded by an adjustment. If salaries for May 31 amount to $50, the proper adjusting entry is as follows:

May 31	*Salaries Expense*	*50*	
	Salaries Payable		*50*
	Adjusting entry		

The expense is debited because the agency's total salary cost has increased. Salaries Payable, a liability, is credited and indicates the total amounts owed by Wise have also increased.

Accrued revenues

To illustrate accrued revenue, assume that on May 14 Wise agreed to provide services for Holmes Corporation during the next 5 months. As of May 31 Wise rendered services totaling $710. The $710 is properly considered as May revenue since the service was provided during May; yet, to date, no entry has been made in the accounting records. The correct adjusting entry is as follows:

May 31	*Accounts Receivable*	*710*	
	Agency Revenue		*710*
	Adjusting entry		

Accounts Receivable is debited because the amounts owed by clients have increased. In addition, Agency Revenue is credited to record the increase in the revenue earned from business activity.

Adjustment Errors

The adjusting process is very important as far as the accountant is concerned. Failure to properly adjust the books at the end of the period will produce errors in the financial statements. To illustrate, assume that Wise's accountant failed to adjust for the expiration of a prepaid expense. As a result, an expense account was not debited and an asset account was not credited. By failing to debit the expense account, expenses were not increased and are therefore understated. When expenses are subtracted from revenues to determine net income, net income will be overstated and the income statement will be in error. Recall that net income is transferred to the statement of owners' equity. Because net income increases owners' equity and net income is overstated, ending owners' equity will be overstated as well. Ending owners' equity also appears on the balance sheet. The equality between assets and the total of liabilities and owners' equity is still maintained, however. In failing to make the adjustment, Wise did not credit (reduce) the appropriate asset account. Total assets, therefore, are overstated and the balance sheet, although incorrect, remains in balance. The entire process is depicted in Exhibit 3-3.

Turning to accruals, the analysis of errors can proceed in the same fashion. Assume that Wise failed to make the $710 adjustment for accrued revenues. The failure to credit Agency Revenue will understate revenues on the income statement. If revenues are understated, net income will be too small. This, in turn, depresses ending owners' equity on both the statement of owners' equity and the balance sheet. The balance sheet will balance, however, since Wise failed to debit (increase) Accounts Receivable.

THE WORK SHEET

Having gone through the adjusting process to determine the accounts in need of updating, the accountant can now begin to concentrate on the preparation of financial statements. A tool that is extremely useful in performing the necessary underlying work for this job is the work sheet. The **work sheet** is a columnar form that (1) aids in the construction of the financial statements and (2) assists in the performance of other tasks that will be explained shortly. In effect, one could consider the work sheet to be the "accountant's scratch pad."

The work sheet for the Wise Advertising Agency for the month ended May 31, 1983, appears in Exhibit 3-4. Observe that it is divided into four parts: trial balance, adjustments, income statement, and balance sheet. We will explain the preparation of the work sheet based on these sections. First, however, a word of encouragement is needed. Students often take a quick glance at the work sheet and conclude that it is extremely complex and beyond their comprehension. Despite its appearance, a work sheet is *not* difficult to construct. You have already been exposed to its most rigorous

ADJUSTING ENTRIES IN COURT?

Approximately twenty years ago the failure to properly adjust the accounts at the end of the period landed a company and its auditors in court. Yale Express, an overnight trucker, kept its books on the modified cash basis system. Yale acquired Republic Carloading, a freight forwarder that used the accrual system. Republic felt the accrual system was best because in their line of work transportation bills frequently arrived months after freight had been moved. Thus for a better match of revenues and expenses, accrual adjustments were made at the end of the period. The adjustments charged expense accounts and created liabilities for expenses incurred but not yet paid.

Despite the nature of Republic's operation, Yale proposed converting Republic to the modified cash basis. Unfortunately, the chief accounting personnel of the two companies rarely spoke to each other. In addition, the data processing systems of Yale and Republic were incompatible. However, the conversion was made and profits were reported of $1,140,000.

It was later discovered that information concerning millions of dollars of accrued expenses was either temporarily lost, not found by the auditors, or deliberately withheld from the auditors by management. These expenses, if properly recognized, would have converted the $1.14 million net income into a loss of $1.88 million. As a result of the misleading financial statements that were issued, stockholders and creditors sued, giving the adjusting entry its day in court.

SOURCE Adapted from "The Big Skid at Yale Express," Fortune Magazine.

Exhibit 3-3

Prepaid expense adjustment errors

Entry omitted:

Expense	*XXX*	
Asset		*XXX*
To record the expiration of a prepaid expense		

Income Statement

Revenues		$ OK
Less expenses		Understated
Net income		$ Overstated

Statement of Owners' Equity

Beginning owners' equity		$ OK
Add net income	$Overstated	
Less withdrawals	OK	Overstated
Ending owners' equity		$Overstated

Balance Sheet

Assets	$Overstated
Liabilities	$ OK
Owners' equity	Overstated
Total liabilities & owners' equity	$Overstated

elements—the preparation of a trial balance that balances and the determination of the proper adjusting entries. The rest is a matter of extending what you have already learned.

Trial Balance

The starting point for the work sheet and subsequent financial statement preparation is the trial balance. Rather than being a separate report, the trial balance now appears as the first two columns of the work sheet. Close examination of the trial balance columns reveals several differences from the trial balance for the Wise Advertising Agency that appeared in Exhibit 2-5. (A review of Exhibit 2-5 is helpful at this time.) The differences are caused by the five additional transactions of May presented in this chapter and are reconciled as follows:

Cash: $6,125 + $10,400 (unearned revenue) + $6,000 (loan) − $480 (insurance) − $340 (supplies) − $4,500 (car)	**$17,205**
Prepaid insurance: $0 + $480 (purchase on 5/1)	**$480**
Supplies: $0 + $340 (purchase on 5/4)	**$340**

Exhibit 3-4

WISE ADVERTISING AGENCY
Work Sheet
For the Month Ended May 31, 1983

Account Title	Trial Balance		Adjustments		Income Statement		Balance Sheet	
	Debit	Credit	Debit	Credit	Debit	Credit	Debit	Credit
Cash	17,205						17,205	
Accounts receivable	2,000		(g) 710				2,710	
Prepaid insurance	480			(a) 20			460	
Supplies	340			(b) 80			260	
Car	4,500						4,500	
Accounts payable		125						125
Unearned agency revenue		10,400	(d) 400					10,000
Loan payable		6,000						6,000
Gary Wise, capital		9,000						9,000
Gary Wise, drawing	700						700	
Agency revenue		2,950		(d) 400 (g) 710		4,060		
Salaries expense	825		(f) 50		875			
Rent expense: office	800				800			
Rent expense: equipment	1,500				1,500			
Electricity expense	125				125			
	28,475	28,475						
Insurance expense			(a) 20		20			
Supplies expense			(b) 80		80			
Depreciation expense			(c) 125		125			
Accumulated depreciation: car				(c) 125				125
Interest expense			(e) 60		60			
Interest payable				(e) 60				60
Salaries payable				(f) 50				50
			1,445	1,445	3,585	4,060	25,835	25,360
Net income					475			475
					4,060	4,060	25,835	25,835

Car: $0 + $4,500 (purchase on 5/1)	*$4,500*
Unearned agency revenue: $0 + $10,400 (receipt on 5/16)	*$10,400*
Loan payable: $0 + $6,000 (obtained on 5/1)	*$6,000*

Note that the trial balance summarizes daily transaction information only; adjustments are not considered.

Adjustments

Once the trial balance is completed, the adjustments illustrated earlier in the chapter are entered in the adjustment section next to the proper accounts. The first adjusting entry is as follows:

May 31	*Insurance Expense*	*20*	
	Prepaid Insurance		*20*

On the work sheet both halves of an adjustment (i.e., debit and credit) are keyed or referenced by a letter, the letter (*a*) in the case of insurance. The purpose of this procedure is to facilitate the examination of the adjustments by anyone who reviews the work sheet. There are no rules regarding the assignment of specific letters to particular adjustments.

In several cases an account that is needed in an adjusting entry does not appear in the trial balance. When this situation occurs, the account is simply written on the lines below the trial balance. After all the adjustment information is entered, the adjustment columns are totaled to check the equality of debits and credits.

Income Statement and Balance Sheet

The income statement and balance sheet sections of the work sheet serve as the foundation for preparation of the formal financial statements. After updating by any applicable adjustments, each account listed is extended to either the income statement or balance sheet columns. This process is performed on a line-by-line basis, starting at the top of the work sheet. *Revenues and expenses go to the income statement. Assets, liabilities, and owners' equity accounts, the latter of which includes the drawing account, are transferred to the balance sheet.* Although the drawing account does not appear on a formal balance sheet,[2] extension to the balance sheet columns is necessary because withdrawals reduce owners' equity.

To illustrate the extension process, let us review the accounts. The first account encountered is Cash, which is an asset. Its $17,205 debit balance is transferred from the trial balance to the balance sheet debit column. Accounts Receivable, also an asset, has a $2,000 debit balance from daily transactions, along with a $710 debit (increase) from an adjusting entry. The resulting $2,710 balance is also placed in the balance sheet debit column. Next, the Prepaid Insurance balance of $480 is credited or reduced by a $20 adjusting entry. The account's $460 ending balance is also extended to the balance sheet. Each account, then, is handled in the same manner: the

[2] Withdrawals appear on the statement of owners' equity.

balance listed in the trial balance is combined with the adjustment, and the result is placed in the proper financial statement column.

When all accounts have been extended, the income statement and balance sheet columns are totaled. Focusing on the income statement, the credit column contains the accounts with credit balances, that is, the revenues. In contrast, the debit column contains the expense accounts. Therefore:

Total revenues (credits)	*$4,060*
Total expenses (debits)	*3,585*
Net income	*$ 475*

The net income figure is entered beneath the smaller of the debit or credit totals and is added to bring both columns into agreement with one another.

Turning to the balance sheet, the net income figure is entered in the credit column. Why? Recall that owners' equity is increased by net income. A study of the work sheet, however, reveals that the revenues and expenses needed for calculating net income are located in the income statement columns. Therefore the $9,000 owners' equity figure, which appears in the balance sheet credit column, has not as yet been increased by Wise's $475 net income. Thus the $475 is placed in the credit column and added to bring the balance sheet into a balanced condition.

Wise generated a net income; if the agency had operated at a loss, the procedure for balancing the statements would be slightly different. In the case of a net loss, expenses exceed revenues. Therefore in the income statement columns, the loss would be entered in the credit column to achieve balancing. On the balance sheet the net loss must reduce owners' equity. Since appropriate reductions are recorded by debits, the net loss would be listed in the debit column.

Uses of the Work Sheet

The work sheet performs several useful functions for the accountant. As is evident from its form, the work sheet lays the groundwork for formal financial statement preparation. In addition, it serves as the basis for completing the adjusting process and assists in the closing process at the end of the accounting period.

Financial statements

Once the work sheet is completed, the preparation of financial statements is a relatively easy task. Virtually all the information necessary for this process is found in the work sheet's income statement and balance sheet sections. The income statement, for example, is simply a formalized listing of the income statement debit and credit columns.

The statement of owners' equity cannot be constructed by relying solely on the work sheet. Any investments made by the owner are already included in the capital account, which appears in the trial balance. Thus one must go back to the general ledger and examine the underlying detail of the owners' equity account (see Exhibit 2-4).

Finally, the balance sheet is prepared from the information contained in the debit and credit columns of the balance sheet section with two minor exceptions. First, the drawing account appears on the statement of owners' equity and not on the balance sheet. Second, the owners' equity account of $9,000 has not been updated by the withdrawal of $700 and Wise's $475 net income. Thus the ending balance from the statement of owners' equity, which includes these items, should appear on the formal balance sheet. This procedure was discussed in Chapter 1 and is illustrated in Wise's financial statements, which are shown in Exhibit 3-5.

Adjusting entries

Although we have already discussed adjusting entries in depth, one additional point must be stressed. To achieve consistency with the updated balances that appear in the financial statement columns of the work sheet, the accounts that are housed in the general ledger must *also* be updated. This procedure is accomplished by recording the adjustments in the journal and then posting to the appropriate ledger accounts. The work sheet, which already contains the adjustments, serves as the basis for this process. For illustrative purposes we will assume the adjusting entries presented on the work sheet and earlier in the chapter have already been journalized and posted.

The closing process

Discussion of the **closing process** should help to tie several loose ends together. As we emphasized in Chapter 1, four items cause owners' equity to change during an accounting period: investments, withdrawals, net income, and net loss. The statement of owners' equity of Wise Advertising in Exhibit 3-5 reports Wise's ending balance at $8,775. Presently, however, the Gary Wise, Capital *account* on the work sheet and in the ledger contains a balance of $9,000. This latter amount reflects only the investment on May 1, which was recorded directly in the account. Withdrawals are located in Gary Wise, Drawing, and net income is composed of the various revenue and expense accounts. It is naturally desirable that the ending balance reported on the statement of owners' equity be in agreement with the ending balance found in the owners' equity account. This agreement is achieved by placing a set of *closing entries* on the books at the end of the accounting period.

Purpose

The purpose of the closing process is twofold. First, closing corrects the aforementioned lack of agreement between the owners' equity account and the owners' equity statement. Second, closing reduces the balances in certain accounts to zero. The income statement and the statement of owners' equity each report financial activity for a period of time. On conclusion of a given period a business must start anew in its accumulation of information for these two statements. *Thus revenue, expense, and drawing accounts must be closed, or reduced to zero, at the end of the period so there is no carry-over from one period to the next.* These accounts are accordingly known as **temporary accounts.**

Because the balance sheet reports information at a particular point in time as opposed to a period, *balance sheet accounts (assets, liabilities, and ending owners' equity) are never closed.* Wise, for example, reported a cash balance of $17,205 on May 31. It does not make any sense to reduce this account to zero so that the firm could begin accounting all over again on June 1. Wise has $17,205 of cash on June 1, not zero.

Technique

Most companies close their books only once a year. For illustrative purposes, however, we will demonstrate the necessary closing process for Wise

Exhibit 3-5

Financial statements of Wise Advertising Agency

WISE ADVERTISING AGENCY
Income Statement
For the Month Ended May 31, 1983

Agency revenue		$4,060
Less expenses		
Salaries expense	$ 875	
Rent expense: office	800	
Rent expense: equipment	1,500	
Electricity expense	125	
Insurance expense	20	
Supplies expense	80	
Depreciation expense	125	
Interest expense	60	
Total expenses		3,585
Net income		$ 475

WISE ADVERTISING AGENCY
Statement of Owners' Equity
For the Month Ended May 31, 1983

Beginning balance, May 1		$ –
Increases		
Owner investments	$9,000	
Net income	475	9,475
		$9,475
Decreases		
Owner withdrawals		700
Ending balance, May 31		$8,775

Advertising on May 31, the conclusion of the agency's first month of activity.

Closing is a four-step process that requires the establishment of a new account entitled **Income Summary.** The Income Summary account is used only in the closing process and summarizes the net income or net loss of a business. The four steps to closing are as follows:

1 Close all revenue accounts.
2 Close all expense accounts.
3 Close the Income Summary account.
4 Close the drawing account.

The information necessary to perform these steps is obtained from the work sheet.

Closing revenue accounts

Revenue accounts normally possess credit balances. To reduce them to zero, the closing entry debits revenue accounts for the amount of their balance and credits Income Summary. This process transfers all revenues earned to the credit side of the Income Summary account and is shown in Exhibit 3-6.

WISE ADVERTISING AGENCY
Balance Sheet
May 31, 1983

Assets			
Cash		$17,205	
Accounts receivable		2,710	
Prepaid insurance		460	
Supplies		260	
Car	$4,500		
Less: Accumulated depreciation	125	4,375	
Total assets			$25,010
Liabilities			
Accounts payable		$ 125	
Unearned agency revenue		10,000	
Loan payable		6,000	
Interest payable		60	
Salaries payable		50	
Total liabilities			$16,235
Owners' equity			
Gary Wise, capital			8,775
Total liabilities & owners' equity			$25,010

Exhibit 3-6

Closing revenue accounts

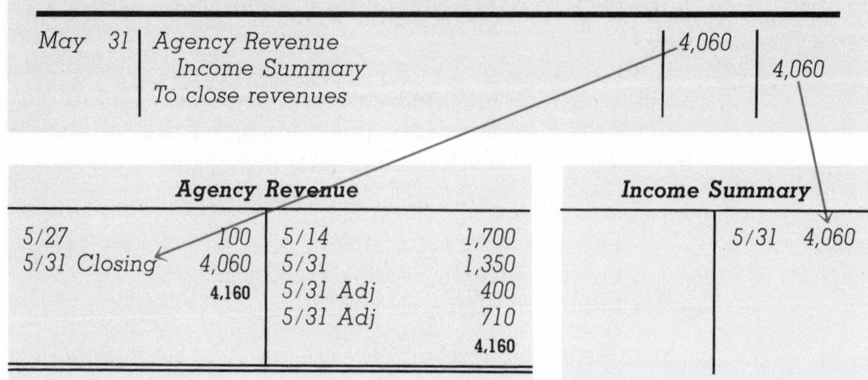

May 31	Agency Revenue	4,060	
	Income Summary		4,060
	To close revenues		

Agency Revenue

5/27	100	5/14	1,700
5/31 Closing	4,060	5/31	1,350
	4,160	5/31 Adj	400
		5/31 Adj	710
			4,160

Income Summary

	5/31 4,060

To explain, the Agency Revenue account contains charges from May 14, 27, and 31 (see Exhibit 2-4) and two adjusting entries (see Exhibit 3-4). The balance *prior* to closing is \$4,060 (\$4,160 – \$100). The closing entry debits Agency Revenue for \$4,060, thereby equalizing total debits and credits and reducing the account's balance to zero.

Closing expense accounts

The closing of expense accounts is performed in essentially the same manner. Expense accounts are credited to eliminate their debit balances. The closing entry's corresponding debit, then, is to Income Summary, which transfers the expenses incurred to the debit side of this account. Rather than closing the expense accounts individually, a combined or *compound journal entry* is employed to reduce posting. Exhibit 3-7 illustrates the proper entry and the related postings.

Closing the income summary account

The Income Summary account presently contains revenues (credits) of \$4,060 and expenses (debits) of \$3,585. The resulting credit balance of \$475 (\$4,060 – \$3,585) represents Wise's net income for May. The next step in the closing process is to reduce or close the Income Summary account to zero. The foregoing is achieved by debiting the Income Summary for \$475. In a completion of the entry, Gary Wise, Capital, is credited, because net income increases owners' equity. The resulting entry transfers the agency's net income into Wise's capital account, as shown in Exhibit 3-8.

Businesses, of course, do not always generate a net income. In the case of a net loss, expenses exceed revenues. Since the total debits in the Income Summary account would be greater than the total credits, a debit balance results. The Income Summary is thus closed by a credit entry. The corresponding debit goes to the capital account for the reduction that is caused by the net loss.

Exhibit 3-7

Closing expense accounts

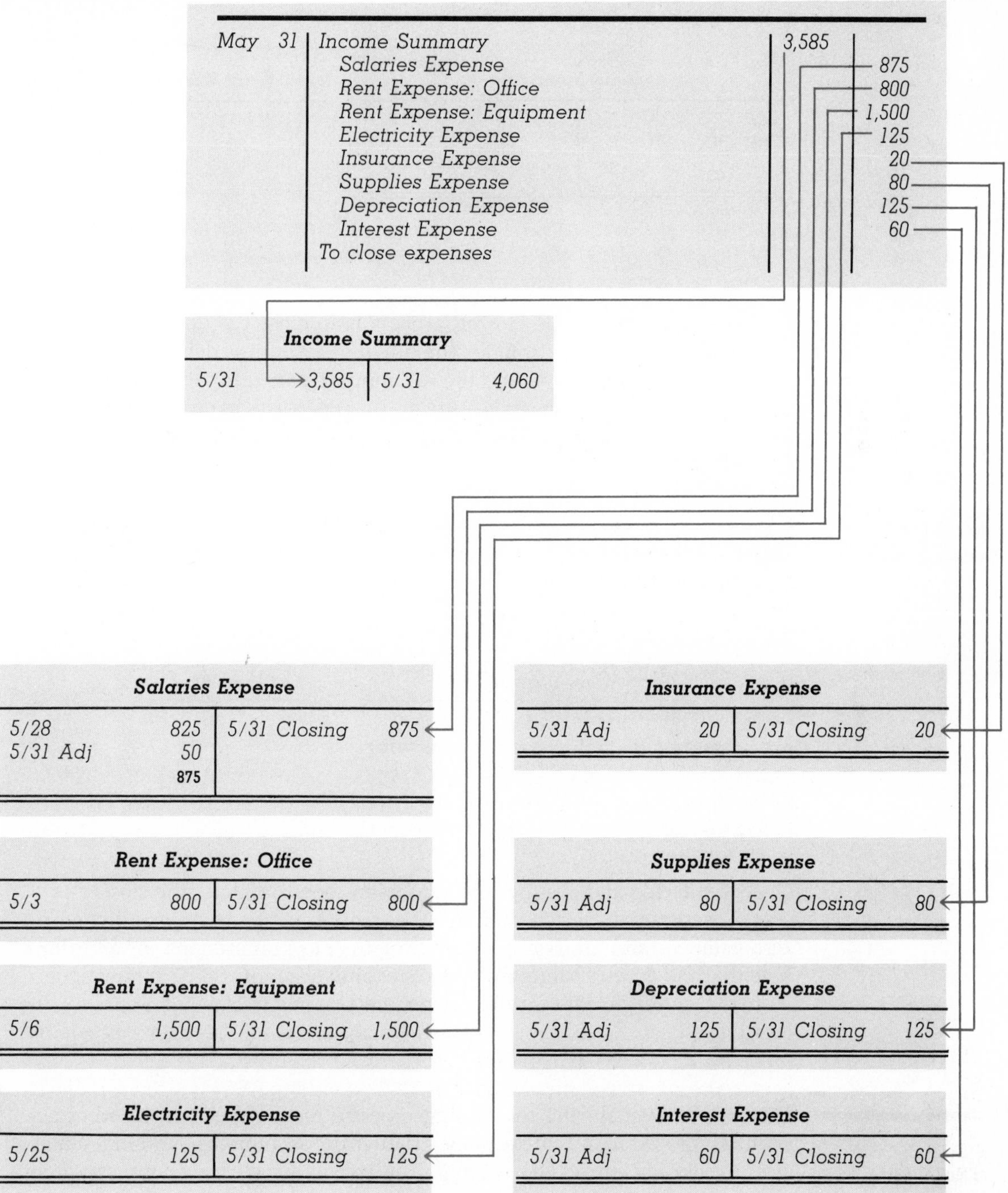

May 31	Income Summary	3,585	
	Salaries Expense		875
	Rent Expense: Office		800
	Rent Expense: Equipment		1,500
	Electricity Expense		125
	Insurance Expense		20
	Supplies Expense		80
	Depreciation Expense		125
	Interest Expense		60
	To close expenses		

Income Summary

5/31	3,585	5/31	4,060

Salaries Expense

5/28	825	5/31 Closing	875
5/31 Adj	50		
	875		

Rent Expense: Office

5/3	800	5/31 Closing	800

Rent Expense: Equipment

5/6	1,500	5/31 Closing	1,500

Electricity Expense

5/25	125	5/31 Closing	125

Insurance Expense

5/31 Adj	20	5/31 Closing	20

Supplies Expense

5/31 Adj	80	5/31 Closing	80

Depreciation Expense

5/31 Adj	125	5/31 Closing	125

Interest Expense

5/31 Adj	60	5/31 Closing	60

Exhibit 3-8

Closing the income summary account

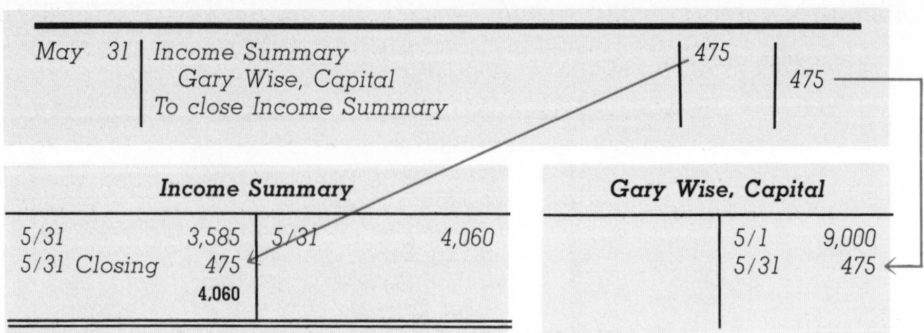

May 31	Income Summary	475	
	Gary Wise, Capital		475
	To close Income Summary		

Income Summary

5/31	3,585	5/31	4,060
5/31 Closing	475		
	4,060		

Gary Wise, Capital

		5/1	9,000
		5/31	475

Closing the drawing account

The final step in the closing process is to close the drawing account. Each time a withdrawal is made, the drawing account is debited. Therefore a credit is required to reduce the account's balance to zero. Because (1) withdrawals decrease owners' equity and (2) decreases to owners' equity are recorded by debits, the necessary entry appears as shown in Exhibit 3-9.

Exhibit 3-9

Closing the drawing account

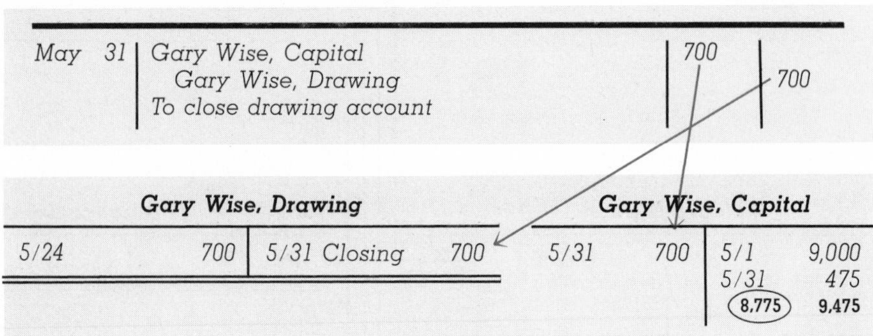

May 31	Gary Wise, Capital	700	
	Gary Wise, Drawing		700
	To close drawing account		

Gary Wise, Drawing

5/24	700	5/31 Closing	700

Gary Wise, Capital

5/31	700	5/1	9,000
		5/31	475
		8,775	9,475

By entering and posting this final entry, one completes the closing process. Observe that the revenue, expense, and drawing accounts all contain zero balances and are ready to accumulate June transactions. In addition, note that the ending balance of Wise's capital account ($8,775) now agrees with the ending balance reported on the statement of owners' equity in Exhibit 3-5.

POST-CLOSING TRIAL BALANCE

Errors can occur during the closing process, just as they can in other accounting procedures. To determine whether the accounts are still in balance after the closing entries have been journalized and posted, accountants often prepare a **post-closing trial balance.** The post-closing trial balance examines ledger account balances to determine if total debits equal total credits. Because this trial balance is constructed after completion of the closing process, no balances remain in the drawing, revenue, and expense accounts. In addition, the owners' equity account has been increased (decreased) by any net income (net loss) that has been generated and decreased by owner withdrawals. The post-closing trial balance for Wise Advertising appears in Exhibit 3-10.

Exhibit 3-10

Post-closing trial balance

WISE ADVERTISING AGENCY
Post-Closing Trial Balance
May 31, 1983

Cash	$17,205	
Accounts receivable	2,710	
Prepaid insurance	460	
Supplies	260	
Car	4,500	
Accumulated depreciation: car		$ 125
Accounts payable		125
Unearned agency revenue		10,000
Loan payable		6,000
Interest payable		60
Salaries payable		50
Gary Wise, capital		8,775
	$25,135	$25,135

A LOOK BACK: THE ACCOUNTING CYCLE

A review of the material presented in this chapter and the previous one reveals that we have been studying the **accounting cycle.** The cycle represents the various tasks performed during an accounting period to process transactions. Specifically, (1) transactions are recorded in the journal and then (2) posted to appropriate ledger accounts. In a determination of whether the ledger accounts are in balance, (3) a trial balance is prepared. The trial balance is updated by certain adjustments in the process of (4) preparing a work sheet. From the work sheet (5) formal financial statements are produced, and (6) adjusting entries are entered in the journal and posted to the ledger. Finally, (7) temporary accounts are closed and (8) a post-closing trial balance is prepared.

Do not memorize these steps. Instead it is more beneficial if you reason through transaction processing to gain a basic understanding of *what* tasks are necessary and *why* they are needed to summarize, report, and account for financial activity.

SUMMARY PROBLEM

The trial balance of the Gottom Company as of December 31, 1983, appears below.

GOTTOM COMPANY
Trial Balance
December 31, 1983

Cash	$ 65,000	
Accounts receivable	4,200	
Office supplies	800	
Prepaid insurance	2,000	
Office furniture	16,000	
Accumulated depreciation: office furniture		$ 4,000
Accounts payable		6,000
Notes payable		20,000
Paul Gottom, capital		16,600
Paul Gottom, drawing	14,000	
Service revenue		80,000
Rent revenue		5,000
Salaries expense	24,000	
Rent expense	3,000	
Utilities expense	2,000	
Other expense	600	
	$131,600	$131,600

The following adjustment information has come to your attention.

1. ***Ending office supplies inventory: $300.***
2. ***Prepaid insurance expired during the period: $1,600.***
3. ***Depreciation expense on the furniture: $2,000.***
4. ***Accrued interest on the note payable: $150.***

INSTRUCTIONS

a. ***Prepare Gottom's required adjusting entries.***
b. ***Compute the firm's net income for the year ended December 31.***
c. ***Compute the firm's total assets as of December 31.***
d. ***Prepare the company's required closing entries.***

SOLUTION

a	Dec. 31	Office Supplies Expense	500	
		Office Supplies		500
		Adjusting entry		

31	Insurance Expense	1,600	
	Prepaid Insurance		1,600
	Adjusting entry		
31	Depreciation Expense	2,000	
	Accumulated Depreciation: Office Furniture		2,000
	Adjusting entry		
31	Interest Expense	150	
	Interest Payable		150
	Adjusting entry		

b

Revenues		
Service revenue	$80,000	
Rent revenue	5,000	
Total revenue		$85,000
Expenses		
Salaries expense	$24,000	
Rent expense	3,000	
Utilities expense	2,000	
Office supplies expense	500	
Insurance expense	1,600	
Depreciation expense	2,000	
Interest expense	150	
Other expense	600	
Total expenses		33,850
Net income		$51,150

c

Assets		
Cash		$65,000
Accounts receivable		4,200
Office supplies ($800 – $500)		300
Prepaid insurance ($2,000 – $1,600)		400
Office furniture	$16,000	
Less: Accumulated depreciation ($4,000 + $2,000)	6,000	10,000
Total assets		$79,900

d

Service Revenue	80,000	
Rent Revenue	5,000	
Income Summary		85,000
To close revenues		
Income Summary	33,850	
Salaries Expense		24,000
Rent Expense		3,000
Utilities Expense		2,000
Office Supplies Expense		500
Insurance Expense		1,600
Depreciation Expense		2,000
Interest Expense		150
Other Expense		600
To close expenses		

Income Summary	*51,150*	
Paul Gottom, Capital		*51,150*
To close Income Summary		
Paul Gottom, Capital	*14,000*	
Paul Gottom, Drawing		*14,000*
To close drawing account		

KEY TERMS AND CONCEPTS

accounting cycle 105
accounting period 82
accrual basis 85
accrued expense 91
accrued revenue 91
adjusting process 87
book value 90
cash basis 84
closing process 99
contra asset 90
depreciation 89
income summary 101
matching expenses and revenues 85
modified cash basis 86
post-closing trial balance 104
prepaid expense 82, 87
temporary accounts 99
unearned revenue 90
work sheet 93

QUESTIONS

Q3-1 Why aren't financial statements prepared directly from the account balances reported in the trial balance?

Q3-2 What basic accounting problem arises from dividing the life of a business into discrete periods for reporting purposes?

Q3-3 Explain when expenses and revenues are recognized under both the cash basis and the accrual basis of accounting.

Q3-4 Explain, by citing several examples, how the cash basis can result in a mismatch of revenues and expenses in a given accounting period.

Q3-5 Explain how the accrual basis helps to enforce the matching of revenues and expenses.

Q3-6 The Wilson Company agreed to perform a service for Dan Melton. Details were finalized in April and the service was performed in May. Melton was billed and paid Wilson in June. If Wilson employs the accrual basis of accounting, in which month is revenue recognized? Why?

Q3-7 Fuller Corporation uses a calendar year and issues quarterly reports to its owners. On August 1 the firm prepaid a 6-month, $600 insurance premium. What is the proper amount of insurance expense to recognize for the third quarter under the (a) cash basis, (b) accrual basis, and (c) modified cash basis?

Q3-8 What types of items frequently require adjusting entries?

Q3-9 In reviewing the records of Yager Company, you find that 3 months' rent of $750 was prepaid to Savage Property Management on November 1. Both companies use the accrual basis of accounting. In view of this transaction,

a What account and amount would you show on Yager's income statement for the month ended November 30? On Savage's income statement for the month ended November 30?

b What account and amount would you show on Yager's November 30 balance sheet? On Savage's November 30 balance sheet?

Q3-10 What is meant by the term "depreciation"? What is the purpose of recording depreciation in the accounting records?

Q3-11 A large retailer offers service contracts with the purchase of major appliances by customers. When a contract is sold, the following entry is made:

Cash	*XXX*	
Unearned Service Contract Revenue		*XXX*
To record sale of service contract		

On which financial statement and in what section would the Unearned Service Contract Revenue account appear? What is the rationale behind your answer?

Q3-12 The Hoffman Company earned $100 of interest in May that will not be received until June. Present the proper adjusting entry to record this interest on May 31.

Q3-13 In the process of preparing a company's formal financial statements, why isn't the owner's capital balance that appears in the trial balance transferred directly to the balance sheet?

Q3-14 Why are the adjusting entries that appear on the work sheet also recorded in the general journal?

Q3-15 What are the objectives of the closing process?

Q3-16 Which accounts are closed at the end of the accounting period and which are not closed?

Q3-17 What are the differences between the trial balance and the post-closing trial balance?

EXERCISES

E3-1 The Prepaid Insurance account of the Robbins Company had a balance on December 31, 1983, after adjustment, of $4,580. During the year Robbins purchased insurance that cost $6,420. The adjusting entry revealed that 1983 insurance expense amounted to $5,180. Given this information, calculate the balance in the Prepaid Insurance account on January 1, 1983.

E3-2 The Maris Company purchased some machinery on January 1, 1981, for $24,000. The machinery had an 8-year life. Assuming Maris uses straight-line depreciation, calculate 1983 depreciation expense, record the proper adjusting entry, and show how the machine would appear on Maris's December 31, 1983, balance sheet.

E3-3 At the start of a new season most professional football clubs have significant amounts of unearned revenue on their books.

a What is the likely source of this unearned revenue?

b On what financial statement and in which section does unearned revenue appear?

c As the football season progresses, what happens to the unearned revenue? Be specific.

E3-4 The accountant for Olson Services failed to adjust the Unearned Advertising Revenue account to recognize the portion that was earned during March. As a result of this error, will the following items be overstated, understated, or unaffected?

a March revenues will be ________.
b March expenses will be ________.
c March net income will be ________.
d Ending owners' equity as of March 31 will be ________.
e Assets as of March 31 will be ________.
f Liabilities as of March 31 will be ________.

E3-5 Campbell Enterprises began operations on January 1, 1983. The following tax accounts, after adjusting and closing, were extracted from the company's general ledger on December 31, 1983.

Prepaid Property Tax			
5/1	900	12/31 Adj	500

State Taxes Payable			
		12/31 Adj	100

Tax Expense			
4/1	150	12/31 Closing	1,050
8/1	150		
12/1	150		
12/31 Adj	500		
12/31 Adj	100		

a Which of the accounts above will appear on Campbell's balance sheet? On the income statement?
b During 1983 how much cash was *paid* for taxes?
c How much of the tax that was paid during 1983 really relates to 1984?
d How much of the tax that will be paid in 1984 really relates to 1983 operations?

E3-6 On August 1 the Heath Company paid the *Victorville Gazette*, a weekly newspaper, $650 for a series of 10 advertisements. By the end of the month ads had appeared in 3 issues. On August 15 Heath received a bill and paid the *Georgetown Daily* $85 for 2 ads that had run the previous week. Finally, on August 29 Heath received a bill of $340 for August advertising in the *Bryan Buzzword*. The bill will be paid in September. Heath uses the accrual basis of accounting.

a Record the proper entries for August 1, 15, and 29.
b Record the necessary adjusting entries on August 31.
c Calculate total advertising expense for August.

E3-7 Record the adjusting entries necessary for Witt and Associates as of September 30, the end of the firm's fiscal year.

a Accrued interest owed to the bank, $1,400.
b Supplies used during September, $150.

c Insurance purchased during the year totaled $2,400. Of this amount $800 is applicable to the next period.

d Sales of $178,000 were made during September. Witt pays the sales force a 5% commission; no commissions had been paid by the end of the month.

e Witt earned $3,200 of an $8,000 payment made by a client for consulting services. The payment was initially recorded in the Unearned Consulting Revenue account.

E3-8 The Phoenix Company uses the accrual basis of accounting and pays its employees each Friday. For a 5-day week (Monday–Friday), the payroll amounts to $2,800. In April the last payday of the month fell on April 26.

a Record the April 30 adjusting entry for accrued salaries.

b When employees are paid on the first Friday in May, how much of the payroll is considered an expense of May? Why?

E3-9 The trial balance of the Ohio Company as of December 31 appears below.

Cash	$ 1,500	
Accounts receivable	2,900	
Investment in land	6,000	
Accounts payable		$ 4,000
Jones, capital		8,400
Jones, drawing	3,100	
Service revenue		14,800
Rent expense	6,800	
Advertising expense	5,300	
Utilities expense	1,600	
	$27,200	$27,200

Assuming there were no adjusting entries, present the closing entries Ohio would record on December 31.

PROBLEMS

P3-1 ***Cash and accrual basis***

The following information pertains to the Springfield Company for June.

Services rendered during June to customers on account	$5,090
Cash receipts from	
Owner investment	4,200
Customers on account	3,600
Cash customers for services rendered in June	2,800
Cash payments to	
Creditors for expenses incurred during June	3,200
Creditors for expenses incurred prior to June	700
Stockbroker for the purchase of a short-term investment	2,300
Expenses incurred during June to be paid in future months	1,700

INSTRUCTIONS

Calculate Springfield's net income for June using the:

a Cash basis of accounting

b Accrual basis of accounting

P3-2 ***Cash and accrual basis, adjustments***

In an examination of the books of the Sanchez Property Management Company, you encountered the following transactions for January:

Jan. 1 Received $2,400 as a rental prepayment for the 6-month period beginning January 1. The following entry was made:

Cash	2,400	
Unearned Rental Revenue		2,400

5 Paid $140 for the December utility bill, which was received on December 29.

8 Miguel Sanchez, the owner, invested $4,000 in the business.

14 Paid $800 for salaries, which includes $50 of salaries incurred in the previous month.

19 Received $1,100 from clients who were billed last month for December rentals.

25 Paid $2,850 for operating expenses incurred during January.

29 Billed clients $3,300 for rental services provided during January.

31 Bills arrived totaling $630 for expenses incurred during January. The bills will be paid during February.

INSTRUCTIONS

a Fill in the blank:

Under the ______________ basis of accounting, revenues are recognized when collected regardless of when they are earned, and expenses are recognized when paid regardless of when incurred.

b Is an adjusting entry needed at the end of January for the January 1 transaction under the basis of accounting cited above? If so, present it.

c Using the basis of accounting cited in (a) above, calculate January's net income or net loss.

d What is the other chief basis of accounting?

e Is an adjusting entry needed at the end of January for the January 1 transaction under the basis of accounting cited in (d)? If so, present it.

f Using the basis cited in (d), calculate January's net income or net loss.

g Generally, which basis of accounting (cash or accrual) better measures financial activity? Why?

P3-3 ***Working backward to derive adjustments***

Account balances of the Brown Company before and after adjustment appear below. All accounts have normal balances.

	Before Adjustment	After Adjustment
Cash	$ 9,000	$ 9,000
Accounts receivable	15,800	18,800
Prepaid advertising	9,100	5,600
Prepaid taxes	800	450
Equipment	30,000	30,000
Accumulated depreciation: equipment	14,000	16,400
Accounts payable	7,900	7,900
Wages payable	—	1,800
Interest payable	—	300

Taxes payable	—	280
Unearned consulting revenue	4,800	3,600
Loan payable	15,000	15,000
Frank Brown, capital	35,700	35,700
Frank Brown, drawing	16,000	16,000
Consulting revenue	71,600	75,800
Wage expense	37,400	39,200
Tax expense	5,100	5,730
Advertising expense	16,300	19,800
Rent expense	24,000	24,000
Depreciation expense	—	2,400
Interest expense	1,500	1,800

INSTRUCTIONS

Journalize the adjusting entries that Brown recorded as of December 31. After each entry present a brief narrative description of the adjustment. The adjusting entry for depreciation is done as an example.

Entry	*Depreciation Expense*	2,400	
	Accumulated Depreciation: Equipment		2,400

Description Recorded annual depreciation expense of $2,400.

P3-4 ***Adjusting entries***

You have been called in to examine the records of the Gem Corporation as of December 31, 1983, the close of the current reporting period. In the course of your examination you discover the following:

a Accrued interest on loans owed by Gem totals $15,800 as of December 31.

b On January 1, 1983, the Supplies account had a balance of $1,470. Additional purchases made during the year amounted to $4,420. As of December 31 supplies of $1,950 remain on hand.

c Prepaid Advertising contains a debit balance of $1,080 on December 31. The balance represents the amount Gem paid on August 1 for a series of ads in a monthly magazine. The ads will run over 6 months, beginning with the magazine's November issue.

d During the accounting period Gem paid insurance premiums as follows, each time debiting Prepaid Insurance:

Date Paid	*Policy No.*	*Length of Policy*	*Amount Paid*
Jan. 1	168AQ4	1 year	$450
July 1	77462J	2 years	400
Dec. 1	AB14492	2 years	360

e The Unearned Agency Revenue account contains a balance of $4,800, which represents payments from two clients. The first client paid $3,600 on March 1 for services to be performed from April through November. The second payment of $1,200 was received on August 1 for 6 months of services to be performed starting in September.

f Gem rendered services to clients in December amounting to $6,400. The services have not as yet been entered in the accounting records.

g Depreciation on equipment amounted to $8,500 for the year.

INSTRUCTIONS

The accounts were last adjusted on December 31, 1982. Present the adjusting entries required on December 31, 1983, under the accrual basis of accounting.

P3-5 ***Journal entries and adjustments***

Each summer in Pennsylvania the McGill Music Center sponsors a series of rock, classical, and country and western concerts. The center is located in a small town between two large cities. To avoid parking problems, McGill has arranged for Keystone Transit to provide bus service for each performance. The following information has come to your attention concerning McGill's operations in June:

1 At the beginning of the concert season, McGill offered patrons the opportunity to buy season tickets for the 20 concerts to be presented. From June 1 through 14, season tickets cost $200 (box seats) and $100 (lawn seating). On June 15 the prices jumped to $220 and $110, respectively. During June, 9,100 season tickets were sold as follows:

	Reduced Price	Increased Price
Box	2,500	600
Lawn	4,000	2,000

2 On June 2 McGill paid Fargo Printing $52,000 for programs for the first 10 concerts of the season.

3 On June 8 McGill purchased an insurance policy from Cox and Associates to insure against damage to the center. The amount paid was computed as follows:

Rock concerts (5)	$280 per concert	$1,400
Other concerts (15)	$150 per concert	2,250
		$3,650

4 In February, McGill signed the Ventures to do rock concerts on June 29 and 30 and July 1. The Ventures' contract stipulated that McGill would pay 10% of the performances' total gate receipts (including season tickets) upon conclusion of the third concert.

5 To meet expenses, McGill obtained a short-term bank loan for $9,000 on June 18. Accrued interest by the end of the month totaled $60.

6 During June, 4 concerts were performed:

June 19	Classical
22	Country and western
29	Rock
30	Rock

In addition to the season ticket holders, walk-in (single-ticket) sales averaged $21,000 per concert.

7 Although no bill had been received, McGill noted that 217 bus trips had been made for the concerts presented in June. The agreement between Keystone and McGill specified that McGill would pay $50 per trip.

8 A review of McGill's general ledger revealed the following selected accounts:

Unearned Ticket Revenue
Ticket Revenue
Prepaid Concert Programs
Concert Program Expense
Musicians Expense
Musicians Payable
Transportation Expense

INSTRUCTIONS

a Record the necessary journal entries for the following:
(1) Sale of season tickets during June.
(2) Payment to Fargo Printing on June 2.
(3) Payment to Cox and Associates on June 8.
(4) Receipt of the bank loan on June 18.
(5) Walk-in (single-ticket) sales; combine all 4 concerts and prepare one entry dated June 30.

b Record all necessary adjusting entries as of June 30. For simplicity, assume all season ticket holders attended each concert.

P3-6 ***Adjustment alternatives and financial statements***

Garland's is a discount store in the Pacific Northwest. Like many other discount operations, the firm leases several departments within the store to outsiders. The outsiders are given full responsibility to run their departments and pay Garland's a rental fee. Garland's requires that new lessees prepay 3 months of rental fees in advance. On October 15 Roy Chan contacted Garland's about running the jewelry department. The papers were signed on November 1 and the operation began on December 1. Chan paid $4,500 on December 1, and Garland's bookkeeper made the following entry:

Dec. 1	*Cash*	*4,500*	
	Rental Revenue		*4,500*
	Receipt from R. Chan		

INSTRUCTIONS

a How much of the $4,500 should appear on Garland's income statement for the year ended December 31? Why?

b Taking your answer above into consideration, where should the remainder of the $4,500 appear as of December 31? Be specific.

c To achieve your answers in (a) and (b) above, what adjusting entry is needed on December 31?

d Suppose the bookkeeper recorded the cash receipt from Chan as follows:

Dec. 1	*Cash*	*4,500*	
	Unearned Rental Revenue		*4,500*

How would your answers to parts (a), (b), and (c) differ?

e Suppose Garland's adjusts the books only at the end of its year on December 31. If Chan paid the 3-month rental fee on June 1 and began operations on the same date, would there be any advantage to recording the entire payment initially as revenue? Explain.

P3-7 ***Adjustment errors***

Accounting personnel for the Charles Williams Company discovered the following errors after the financial statements had been prepared. Williams's fiscal year ends on June 30, 1983.

a Failed to record $5,000 of depreciation.

b Overlooked $1,500 of accrued interest that is owed to the firm.

c Accidentally recorded the adjustment for the expiration of $500 of insurance as follows:

Insurance Expense	*5,000*	
Prepaid Insurance		*5,000*

d A $2,200 customer payment for services to be performed from June 1, 1983, through October 31, 1983, was recorded in the Unearned Agency Revenue account on May 10. No adjusting entry was recorded on June 30.

e Failed to record $7,200 of revenue for services performed in June. The revenue will be collected in July.

INSTRUCTIONS

Using a tabular format similar to the following, determine the effect of each error, individually, on Williams's financial statements. *Hint:* Remember that net income affects owners' equity. Error (a) is done as an example.

	1983 Income Statement			*Balance Sheet as of June 30, 1983*		
Error	***Revenue***	***Expense***	***Net Income***	***Assets***	***Liabilities***	***Owners' Equity***
(a)		−$5,000	+$5,000	+$5,000		+$5,000

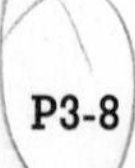

P3-8 ***Closing entries***

The Love Company operates several indoor tennis courts. For the year just ended Love incurred a net loss of $17,000. The income statement revealed that revenues from court fees amounted to $108,000. Expenses were as follows:

Advertising	*$ 15,000*
Salaries	*52,000*
Utilities	*8,000*
Rent	*50,000*
	$125,000

Love's statement of owners' equity follows.

Beginning capital, Jan. 1		*$46,000*
Increases		
Owner investments		*10,000*
		$56,000
Decreases		
Owner withdrawals	*$21,000*	
Net loss	*17,000*	*38,000*
Ending capital, Dec. 31		*$18,000*

INSTRUCTIONS

Prepare the closing entries for the year ended December 31.

P3-9 ***Cycle starting with work sheet***

The Androvich Company has the following trial balance as of December 31.

Cash	*$ 5,800*	
Accounts receivable	*8,200*	
Prepaid insurance	*2,000*	
Supplies	*2,700*	
Equipment	*40,000*	
Accumulated depreciation: equipment		*$ 10,000*
Accounts payable		*7,250*
Loan payable		*18,500*
S. Androvich, capital		*7,050*
S. Androvich, drawing	*4,000*	
Service revenue		*72,000*
Salaries expense	*30,500*	
Rent expense	*12,000*	
Advertising expense	*6,600*	
Interest expense	*3,000*	
	$114,800	*$114,800*

Additional accounts maintained by the business include Salaries Payable, Interest Payable, Income Summary, Insurance Expense, Supplies Expense, and Depreciation Expense. Androvich's accountant has derived the following adjustment data:

1. Insurance applicable to future periods: $700.
2. Supplies used: $1,800.
3. Depreciation on the equipment: $1,000.
4. Accrued interest on the loan: $400.
5. Accrued salaries incurred but not paid: $1,200.
6. Unrecorded service revenue to be collected in future months: $2,200.

During the year the owner invested $3,000.

INSTRUCTIONS

a. Complete a work sheet in good form for the Androvich Company for the year ended December 31.
b. Prepare an income statement, statement of owners' equity, and balance sheet in good form.
c. Record Androvich's adjusting entries in the journal.
d. Record Androvich's closing entries in the journal.

P3-10 ***Accounting cycle***

The Frost Company, which began operations on August 1, had the following transactions:

Aug.	*1*	Sylvia Frost, the owner, invested $5,000 cash and $6,000 of office equipment in the business. The office equipment has a life of 5 years.
	1	Paid $360 for a 3-month insurance policy.
	7	Received $440 from a client to render services over the next 8 weeks.
	11	Paid rent expense, $900.
	14	Billed clients for services rendered, $1,500.

17 Applied for a loan for the purchase of additional office equipment. The loan was in the amount of $5,500.
19 Received $780 from clients on account.
23 Received the proceeds from the loan that was applied for on August 17.
24 Purchased $9,000 of new office equipment; paid $5,500 down and agreed to pay the balance in September. This office equipment will not be depreciated until September.
27 Paid the salaries of the office staff, $2,100.
29 Recorded $650 of miscellaneous expenses that were incurred in August but will be paid during September.

Frost's chart of accounts appears below.

Cash	110	Sylvia Frost, capital	310
Accounts receivable	120	Sylvia Frost, drawing	320
Prepaid insurance	130	Income summary	330
Office equipment	140	Service revenue	410
Accumulated depreciation:		Rent expense	510
office equipment	150	Office salaries expense	520
Accounts payable	210	Insurance expense	530
Office salaries payable	220	Depreciation expense	540
Interest payable	230	Interest expense	550
Unearned service revenue	240	Miscellaneous expense	560
Loan payable	250		

As of August 31 Frost had accrued interest on the loan of $50 and accrued salaries of $180. In addition, since the last billing to clients on August 14, the firm had rendered $1,900 of services. Finally, Frost has earned 3 weeks of revenue from the prepayment received on August 7.

INSTRUCTIONS

a Record the transactions of August in the general journal.
b Post the journal entries to the proper ledger accounts.
c Complete a work sheet for the month ended August 31. Be certain to analyze *all* data presented to correctly determine Frost's adjustments.
d Prepare an income statement, statement of owners' equity, and balance sheet in good form.
e Record Frost's adjusting entries in the journal and post them to the proper ledger accounts.
f Record Frost's closing entries in the journal and post them to the proper ledger accounts.
g Prepare a post-closing trial balance.

P3-11 ***Cash and accrual basis (alternate to P3-1)***

The following information pertains to the Bailey Company for September.

Services provided during September to customers on account	$8,110
Cash receipts from	
Bank loan	6,000
Customers on account	7,450
Cash customers for services rendered during September	3,720
Cash payments to	
Creditors for expenses incurred during September	5,440

Creditors for expenses incurred prior to September	*2,790*
Real estate broker for down payment on a parcel of land	*6,500*
Owner for withdrawal	*1,500*
Expenses incurred during September to be paid in future months	*2,090*

INSTRUCTIONS

Calculate Bailey's net income for September using the:

a Cash basis of accounting

b Accrual basis of accounting

P3-12 ***Adjusting entries (alternate to P3-4)***

You have been requested to examine the records of the Daqqar Corporation as of September 30, 1983, the close of the current reporting period. In the course of your examination you discover the following:

a Accrued interest on loans receivable by Daqqar totals $17,500 as of September 30.

b On October 1, 1982, the Office Supplies account had a balance of $1,350. Additional purchases made during the year amounted to $2,480. As of September 30, 1983, office supplies of $1,200 remain on hand.

c Prepaid Rent contains a debit balance of $12,000 on September 30. The balance represents the amount Daqqar paid on August 1, 1983, for 6 months' rent.

d During the accounting period Daqqar paid insurance premiums as follows, each time debiting Prepaid Insurance:

Date Paid	Policy No.	Length of Policy	Amount Paid
Oct. 1, 1982	467292	1 year	$ 600
Feb. 1, 1983	638PQ2	2 years	1,920
Aug. 1, 1983	5794RS	3 years	1,620

e Daqqar provided services to clients in September amounting to $8,200. The services have not yet been entered in the accounting records.

f The Unearned Service Revenue account contains a balance of $6,600, which represents payments from two clients. The first client paid $4,800 on March 1 for services to be performed from April 1 through November 30. The second payment of $1,800 was received on August 1 for 6 months of services to be performed starting in September.

g Depreciation on equipment amounted to $9,600 for the year.

INSTRUCTIONS

The accounts were last adjusted on September 30, 1982. Present the adjusting entries required on September 30, 1983, under the accrual basis of accounting.

P3-13 ***Adjustment errors (alternate to P3-7)***

Accounting personnel for the Victor Giammarco Company discovered the following errors after the financial statements had been prepared. Giammarco's fiscal year ends on August 31, 1983.

a Overstated the adjustment for depreciation by $1,000.

b Overlooked $2,000 of accrued salaries that are owed by the firm.

c Accidentally recorded the adjustment to recognize $8,000 of rental revenue earned as follows:

Unearned Rental Revenue	*800*	
Rental Revenue		*800*

d An $1,800 payment by Giammarco for advertising services to be performed from July 1, 1983, through December 31, 1983, was recorded in the Prepaid Advertising account on June 15. The account has yet to be adjusted.

e Failed to record $1,500 of accrued interest that is owed to the firm.

INSTRUCTIONS

Using a tabular format similar to the following, determine the effect of each error, individually, on Giammarco's financial statements. *Hint:* Remember that net income affects owners' equity. Error (*a*) is done as an example.

	1983 Income Statement			Balance Sheet as of August 31, 1983		
Error	**Revenue**	**Expense**	**Net Income**	**Assets**	**Liabilities**	**Owners' Equity**
(a)		+$1,000	−$1,000	−$1,000		−$1,000

P3-14 ***Cycle starting with work sheet (alternate to P3-9)***

The Strickland Company has the following trial balance as of December 31.

Cash	$ 4,750	
Accounts receivable	9,840	
Prepaid advertising	2,600	
Supplies	1,420	
Building	50,000	
Accumulated depreciation: building		$ 12,650
Accounts payable		4,900
Loan payable		15,000
S. Strickland, capital		38,845
S. Strickland, drawing	10,000	
Fee revenue		68,400
Salaries expense	39,600	
Utilities expense	10,460	
Advertising expense	6,850	
Insurance expense	1,800	
Interest expense	2,475	
	$139,795	$139,795

Additional accounts maintained by the business include Salaries Payable, Interest Payable, Income Summary, Supplies Expense, and Depreciation Expense. Strickland's accountant has derived the following adjustment data:

1 Prepaid advertising applicable to future periods: $625.
2 Supplies used: $875.
3 Accrued interest on the loan: $520.
4 Accrued salaries incurred but not paid: $1,850.
5 Unrecorded fee revenue to be collected in future months: $1,550.
6 Depreciation on the building: $2,500.

During the year the owner invested $6,000.

INSTRUCTIONS

a Complete a work sheet in good form for the Strickland Company for the year ended December 31.

b Prepare an income statement, statement of owners' equity, and balance sheet in good form.

c Record Strickland's adjusting entries in the journal.
d Record Strickland's closing entries in the journal.

P3-15 ***Accounting cycle (alternate to P3-10)***
The Goldberg Company, which began operations on December 1, had the following transactions:

Dec.	*1*	Jan Goldberg, the owner, invested $10,000 cash, $6,000 of office equipment, and a building valued at $75,000 in the business. The office equipment has a life of 4 years and the building has a life of 25 years.
	1	Paid $720 for a 6-month insurance policy.
	7	Received $950 from a client to render services over the next 5 weeks.
	13	Paid $250 for computer services for the month.
	14	Billed clients for services rendered, $2,500.
	17	Applied for a loan for the purchase of additional office equipment. The loan was in the amount of $4,500.
	20	Received $1,550 from clients on account.
	23	Received the proceeds from the loan that was applied for on December 17.
	26	Purchased $10,000 of new office equipment; paid $4,500 down and agreed to pay the balance in January. This office equipment will not be depreciated until January.
	29	Paid the salaries of the office staff, $4,200.
	29	Recorded $800 of miscellaneous expenses that were incurred in December but will be paid during January.

Goldberg's chart of accounts appears below.

Cash	*110*
Accounts receivable	*120*
Prepaid insurance	*130*
Office equipment	*140*
Accumulated depreciation: office equipment	*150*
Building	*160*
Accumulated depreciation: building	*170*
Accounts payable	*210*
Office salaries payable	*220*
Interest payable	*230*
Unearned service revenue	*240*
Loan payable	*250*
Jan Goldberg, capital	*310*
Jan Goldberg, drawing	*320*
Income summary	*330*
Service revenue	*410*
Computer service expense	*510*
Office salaries expense	*520*
Insurance expense	*530*
Depreciation expense	*540*
Interest expense	*550*
Miscellaneous expense	*560*

As of December 31 Goldberg had accrued interest on the loan of $30 and accrued salaries of $250. In addition, since the last billing to clients on December 14, the firm had rendered $2,700 of services. Finally, Goldberg has earned 3 weeks of revenue from the prepayment received on December 7.

INSTRUCTIONS

a Record the transactions of December in the general journal.
b Post the journal entries to the proper ledger accounts.
c Complete a work sheet for the month ended December 31. Be certain to analyze *all* data presented to correctly determine Goldberg's adjustments.
d Prepare an income statement, statement of owners' equity, and balance sheet in good form.
e Record Goldberg's adjusting entries in the journal and post them to the proper ledger accounts.
f Record Goldberg's closing entries in the journal and post them to the proper ledger accounts.
g Prepare a post-closing trial balance.

CASE 3

MARK NEWHART

Mark Newhart lives in a middle-class suburb of Chicago. He is happy with his life-style and recently has been busier than ever. Mark performs the required maintenance on service contracts that Dolphin Pool Sales has sold to owners of new swimming pools. Customers prepay the entire service contract to Dolphin at the time of purchase. Dolphin keeps 10% and remits the remainder to Newhart, who purchases the necessary supplies and performs required servicing during the spring, summer, and fall months. For the rest of the year Newhart operates a small snowplow service. Owing to recent severe winters, he has gained several new clients. Snowplow clients are billed and pay by the month.

Because a significant portion of Newhart's revenues are received in advance (pool service contracts), his accountant has been using the accrual basis of accounting. Newhart's year ends on June 30. He has just received the income statement, which appears in Exhibit 3-11.

The net income of $20,370 is a record high, and Newhart wants to withdraw $2,000 from the business. Unfortunately, the present cash balance is insufficient to cover current bills. Comparative balance sheets in Exhibit 3-12 reveal a cash balance of $3,400 as of June 30, 1983.

All purchases of pool supplies are on account. Other expenses, except depreciation, are paid as incurred. During the year just ended Newhart withdrew $15,000 from the business.

INSTRUCTIONS

Assume the role of Newhart's accountant. Prepare a schedule of cash receipts and cash disbursements for the period July 1, 1982–June 30, 1983, and explain to Mark why cash declined $4,420 ($7,820 – $3,400) despite profitable operations. To determine cash receipts and disbursements and to view the interrelationships between the balance sheet and income statement, establish T-accounts for Snowplow Receivables, Pool Supplies, Accounts Payable, and Unearned Service Contract Revenue.

Exhibit 3-11

MARK NEWHART
Income Statement
For the Year Ended June 30, 1983

Revenues		
Pool service	$18,400	
Snowplow service	9,000	$27,400
Expenses		
Pool supplies	$ 3,550	
Truck repairs	860	
Depreciation expense	1,250	
Accounting fees	300	
Gasoline	1,070	7,030
Net income		$20,370

Exhibit 3-12

MARK NEWHART
Comparative Balance Sheets

	June 30, 1983	July 1, 1982
Assets		
Cash	$ 3,400	$ 7,820
Short-term investment	4,000	—
Snowplow receivables	3,325	600
Pool supplies	4,250	2,600
Truck	8,750	8,750
Less: Accumulated depreciation	(3,750)	(2,500)
Total assets	$19,975	$17,270
Liabilities		
Accounts payable	$ 3,800	$ 2,000
Unearned service contract revenue	3,705	8,170
Total liabilities	$ 7,505	$10,170
Owners' equity		
Mark Newhart, capital	12,470	7,100
Total liabilities & owners' equity	$19,975	$17,270

4 ACCOUNTING FOR MERCHANDISING OPERATIONS

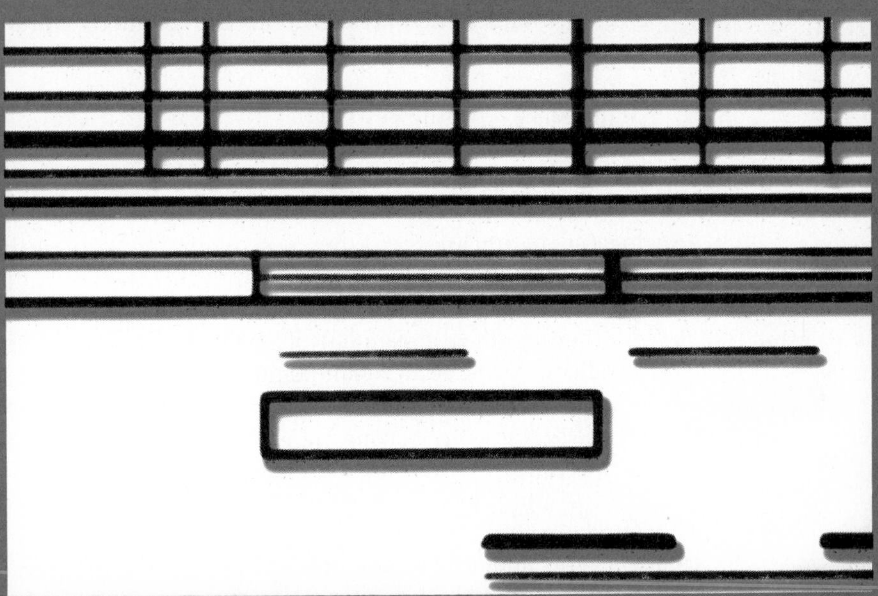

LEARNING OBJECTIVES

After reading this chapter you should:

1 Understand the importance of inventories to business enterprises.

2 Understand the flow of information and paperwork in a merchandising system.

3 Be able to record sales, returns and allowances, discounts, and freight for a seller of merchandise.

4 Be able to record purchases, returns and allowances, discounts, and freight for a buyer of merchandise.

5 Understand the difference between the gross and net methods of accounting for purchases.

6 Be able to compute cost of goods sold and prepare the financial statements and work sheet for a merchandising concern.

7 Be able to prepare the closing entries for a merchandising enterprise.

CHAPTER 4

Question: What do the following organizations have in common?

Pittsburgh Steelers Football Club
Blue Cross/Blue Shield
Chase Manhattan Bank
Federal Express Corporation
University of Connecticut

Answer: While these organizations are distinctly different, all are engaged in providing services.

Giant service businesses similar to those listed above collectively employ millions of individuals, as do smaller enterprises such as the local hairstylist, car wash, or medical clinic. Producing annual revenues in excess of $1 trillion,[1] firms and associations in service industries are a rapidly growing and significant factor in our economy. In the first three chapters of this text we emphasized the service business via the Davis Furniture Repair and Wise Advertising Agency illustrations.

Another significant segment of our economy must also be addressed: merchandising firms. A merchandising business acquires goods for resale to others (commonly known as **merchandise inventory**) and is typified by the retailer and wholesaler. Accounting for retailers and wholesalers is not completely different from accounting for service businesses. Thus the material presented in the previous chapters is also applicable to the merchandiser. The purchase and sale of inventory, however, are accompanied by and create several added complexities for the accountant. These complexities form the basis for this chapter's presentation. Before proceeding, a few words are necessary about the nature and importance of inventory.

INVENTORY: A CAUSE FOR CONCERN

Inventories have a far-reaching impact on several different areas within an organization. The marketing department, for example, is vitally concerned that a business carry sufficient quantities of the "right" goods in order to attain a high level of customer service. Marketing desires to avoid out-of-stock situations, which could result in lost sales and, even worse, an occasional lost customer.

The finance department also has a keen interest in inventory. Financial personnel generally have the responsibilities of securing operating funds and overseeing investments. Inventories represent the investment of a significant portion of these funds for a business. J. C. Penney, for example, recently reported $1.58 billion of inventories, which represented 25% of the firm's total assets. The Gap, a much smaller retailer of sportswear, had inventories of $78.2 million, which amounted to 54% of total assets.

In addition to the money tied up in inventory, the basic commitment to

[1]U.S. Department of Commerce, *Statistical Abstract of the United States, 1980* (Washington, D.C.: Government Printing Office, 1980), p. 557.

an inventory operation gives rise to storage costs, insurance, and local inventory taxes. And, frequently, companies must raise the necessary funds to finance inventory purchases by obtaining short-term loans. These loans, in turn, obligate a firm to substantial interest payments. Overall, then, an investment in inventory is very costly. Thus unlike the marketing department, the finance department wants as little inventory on hand as possible.

Lost sales, lost customers, and the funds committed to an inventory investment eventually affect a company's net income. For this reason inventory is also a primary concern for the accountant.

MERCHANDISING SYSTEMS

A **merchandising system** processes the transactions and events related to a merchandising business, specifically, the sales and purchases of inventory. Let us concentrate on the sales function for a moment since this is the area of merchandising with which you are probably most familiar. The recording of a sale may take many different forms. At a garage sale, for example, a sale is often recorded by tossing the money received into a shoe box and noting the amount of the sale on a piece of scratch paper. In a more formalized environment a clerk may record the details of a sale on a preprinted sales slip and enter the receipt of cash, if any, in a cash register. In other businesses, employees may record the sale directly into a terminal that is connected to a computer. At the close of the business day the computer can prepare an analysis of the day's sales and can also deduct the units sold from the store's inventory on hand.

The processing of purchasing activities may also vary in form. Frequently, for example, the purchaser prepares a formal document known as a **purchase order.** The purchase order itemizes the details (e.g., catalog numbers, descriptions, quantities, and prices) of the merchandise that the purchaser desires to acquire. The purchase order is then mailed to a supplier, who subsequently ships the goods. In other instances a wholesaler may visit a retail establishment, quickly review the stock levels, and write a purchase order on the spot for items that need replenishment.

While the form may differ, virtually all merchandising concerns have formalized sales and purchasing systems. As shown in Exhibit 4-1, these two systems are closely integrated and have a common focal point, the general ledger.[2] A description of Exhibit 4-1 is necessary if you are to properly understand its interrelationships.

The Sales System

The **sales system** is concerned with the customer and the proper recording and processing of sales transactions. Generally, two departments perform the bulk of the necessary work: order processing and accounts receivable.

[2]Part of the discussion in this section is adapted from *Accounting and Information Systems* by John Page and Paul Hooper (Reston, Va.: Reston Publishing, 1979).

Exhibit 4-1

Merchandising system

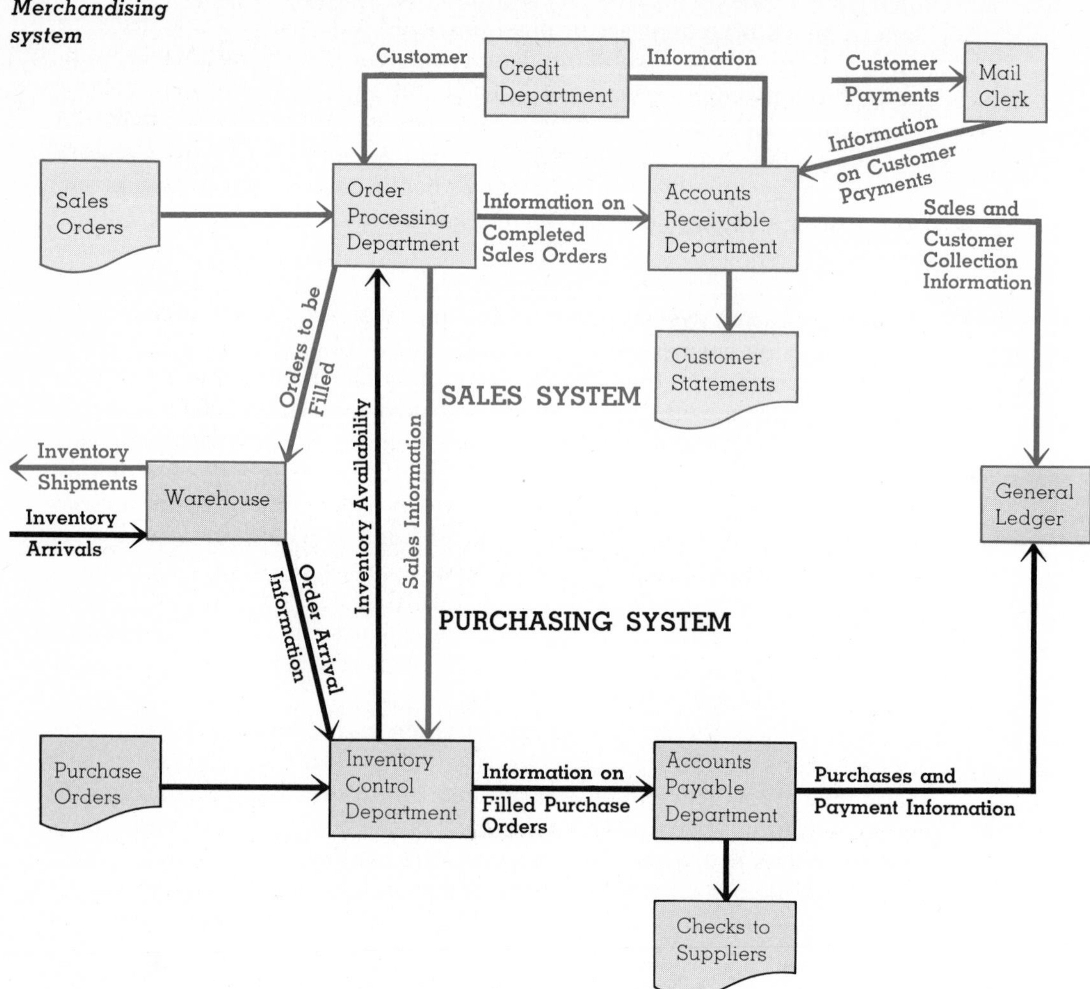

Order processing department

The **order processing department,**[3] as its name implies, is involved with the processing of sales orders. Order processing records sales of merchandise on a source document known as a sales slip or **invoice** (see Exhibit 4-2). In addition, customer credit is checked from information provided by the credit department. Finally, item availability is determined by using information furnished from inventory control. If the required inventory is on hand, the order is filled and sales information is forwarded to the accounts receivable department. If an out-of-stock situation exists, order processing keeps track of all unfilled customer orders.

[3]This illustration focuses on credit sales because of their dominance in our economy.

Exhibit 4-2

Sales invoice and customer statement

Sales Invoice

LINDSEY DISTRIBUTORS
741 W. Harrison
Wichita, Kansas 67209

No. 497

Sold to:
Burger Hut
1309 Lancaster
Wichita, Kansas 67210

Date: 6/4/83

Customer Order No.: 3940
F.O.B.: Warehouse
Terms: 2/10, n/30

Quantity	Description	Unit Price	Total
2 cases	108 napkins	15.40	30.80
3 cases	16 oz cups	25.00	75.00
2 cases	no. 8 mustard	7.60	15.20
1 only	mop	11.90	11.90
			132.90

Thank you!

Customer Statement

LINDSEY DISTRIBUTORS
741 W. Harrison
Wichita, Kansas 67209

Burger Hut
1309 Lancaster
Wichita, Kansas 67210

Balance due: $941.10
Amount paid ________

Please return this portion with payment.

Date	Reference No.	Purchases	Payments
6/1	485	110.50	
6/4	497	132.90	
6/15	674		110.50
6/21	586	550.20	
6/30	610	258.00	

Closing Date: June 30, 1983

Previous Balance	+	Finance Charge	+	Purchases	−	Payments	=	Balance Due
—		—		1,051.60		110.50		941.10

Again you are reminded that merchandising systems differ from company to company. In many large department stores, for example, the sales invoice is originated by a salesperson. In addition, customer credit is often checked by this same individual by entering the customer's account number into a computer terminal. The computer then informs the clerk whether the credit sale is allowed or disallowed. Although the form and the exact sequence of events may vary slightly, the general principles and procedures presented here apply to most businesses.

Accounts receivable department

The **accounts receivable department** closely monitors the amounts owed by customers and therefore serves as a useful source of information for credit decisions. To properly perform its function, the accounts receivable department must obtain information regarding credit sales and customer payments. Credit sales information is forwarded from order processing via the sales invoice. Customer payment information is obtained from the mail clerk, who typically receives payments on account. The mail clerk forwards a list of customer remittances, not the actual checks and/or cash received. As you will learn in Chapter 5, it is desirable to separate the physical handling of an asset from the asset's record keeping. This procedure improves control and reduces the possibility of errors, fraud, and embezzlement.

Given the sales and payment information, the accounts receivable department updates customer accounts. This process produces two important items: customer statements and information for general ledger updating.

Customer statements

The **customer statement** is a detailed listing of all purchases and payments made by a customer during the billing period. The statement is usually prepared on a monthly basis and mailed to the customer. An example appears in Exhibit 4-2.

As Exhibit 4-2 illustrates, invoices and customer statements are closely related. The invoice documents a given sale of either goods or services, while the statement summarizes all the sales and collections on account from a given customer. Observe the manner in which the invoice appears on the statement. Both documents are necessary for a successful sales and billing system.

General ledger updating

Up to this point a business has authorized a sale, documented the transaction on a sales invoice, and billed the customer. Because sales affect financial condition and profitability, they must be entered in the formal accounting records. Filling out a sales slip, billing the customer, and performing other similar activities do not accomplish this task.

Information concerning sales on account and customer collections is the second important output of the accounts receivable department. This information forms the basis for the journal entries that are necessary to update the accounts.

The Purchasing System

Prior to the sale of goods a company must acquire the merchandise it intends to resell. The **purchasing system** handles the record keeping for this acquisition process and ensures that adequate stock levels are on hand to meet demand. Two departments are essential for an effective purchasing system: inventory control and accounts payable.

Inventory control department

The **inventory control department** maintains close watch over the inventory items on order as well as those on hand. Purchase orders initiated by the purchasing department are forwarded here. Inventory control monitors which purchase orders have been filled by suppliers and which are unfilled. In addition, based on information received from the warehouse and order processing concerning order arrivals and sales, respectively, inventory control keeps a running count of the goods on hand. The running count is useful to the order processing department, which desires information about item availability. By analyzing its records, inventory control can provide insight regarding the following:

Goods that need to be reordered.
Goods that are selling rapidly and thus assisting in income generation.
Goods that are not selling and should be dropped from future marketing programs.

Finally, the inventory control department forwards information regarding filled purchase orders to the accounts payable department.

Accounts payable department

The **accounts payable department** monitors the balances owed to suppliers. Based on information received from inventory control, accounts payable establishes records that permit the proper payment of all purchase invoices (bills) as the invoices come due. In addition to maintaining creditor account records, the accounts payable department performs two useful, related functions: check issuance and the generation of information for general ledger updating.

Check issuance

Since accounts payable is aware of the amounts that are owed to individual creditors, this department is responsible for the issuance of checks to suppliers. Checks are issued only after extensive verification of purchase invoices. Mathematical accuracy of the invoice is checked. In addition, because the purchaser does not want to pay for goods that were never ordered or delivered, the invoice is compared against the initial purchase order and a warehouse report of the actual goods received. The purpose of this process is to integrate checks and balances into the accounting system. In larger firms the purchasing, payment, and receiving functions are often performed in different locations and thus "the right hand does not always know what the left hand is doing." This verification procedure brings these functions together and improves accountability.

General ledger updating

Similar to accounts receivable, the accounts payable department supplies important information for journal entries and subsequent general ledger updating. In this case accounts payable provides the basis to record purchase transactions and payments to creditors on account.

MERCHANDISING TRANSACTIONS

In light of the activities of the sales and purchasing functions, let us now view the impact of selected merchandising transactions on the financial statements. To do so, we will study the operations of Peachtree Jeans, a wholesale distributor of pants, shirts, and related accessories located in Atlanta. We will continue our approach of viewing a merchandising operation from its two chief components, sales and purchasing.

Accounting for the Seller

Accounting for the seller focuses on the proper recording of sales. The necessary record keeping includes accounting for the basic sale plus related sales returns, discounts granted by the seller, and applicable freight charges.

Recording sales

The revenues of a merchandising concern are generated from its sales of merchandise. Consequently, a revenue account entitled Sales is established. If desired, a business could keep separate accounts for different types of sales. For example, Peachtree could establish the following accounts: Pants Sales, Shirt Sales, and Accessories Sales. The Sales account is used *strictly* to record sales of merchandise; sales of other assets are treated differently. To illustrate, if Peachtree sold some extra office supplies for cash, Cash would be debited and Office Supplies would be credited. The Sales account is not affected.

A business must properly record both cash and credit sales. Although the exact procedure varies, the following is fairly representative of the practices of many companies. When a cash sale is made, a sales invoice is completed by a sales clerk. The amount of the sale is entered into a cash register, and as this is done, the register prints a tape of the transaction. The clerk, at the same time, places the cash received in the register. At the end of the day the total cash collected is compared with the total cash sales as noted on the tape. If Peachtree had cash sales of $325 on April 3 and no discrepancies were noted, the following journal entry would be made:

Apr. 3	Cash	325	
	Sales		325
	Daily cash sales		

Credit sales are handled in much the same fashion. Depending on the system employed, either the sales invoice or the register tape can provide the basis for the necessary journal entry. The use of the register tape may seem unwarranted; yet more and more businesses are using their registers to record both cash and credit sales. The registers are designed to generate separate totals at the end of the day in addition to analyzing total sales by product line, department, salesperson, or by any other breakdown management deems desirable.

To illustrate the credit sale, suppose Peachtree sold $700 of merchandise on account to Midtown Pants on April 7. Peachtree would record the sale as follows:

Apr. 7	***Accounts Receivable***	***700***	
	Sales		***700***
	Sale on account to Midtown Pants		

Sales returns and allowances

Sales of merchandise often give rise to returns. Customers frequently change their minds, find that merchandise does not fit well once they get it home, or notice defects. If an exchange of goods is not possible or desired, most merchandisers either grant a refund or reduce the customer's account balance. Sometimes, particularly in the case of defects or damaged goods, the seller will grant the buyer an *allowance*, that is, a price reduction as incentive to keep the merchandise.

Once a return or allowance is authorized, the seller documents the transaction on a form known as a **credit memorandum.** For a sale on account, a copy is given to the customer and a copy is forwarded to the accounts receivable department. The credit memo informs accounts receivable to credit or reduce a particular customer's account.

The proper accounting treatment for sales returns and allowances is shown by the following example. Suppose that on April 16 Midtown Pants returned $180 of shirts for credit that it had purchased on April 7. Peachtree Jeans, the seller, would record the transaction as follows:

Apr. 16	***Sales Returns & Allowances***	***180***	
	Accounts Receivable		***180***
	Merchandise returned by Midtown Pants		

The net amount of the sale is $520 ($700 – $180). Rather than reduce the Sales account by a debit, one can establish a separate account, Sales Returns & Allowances. Notice the word "can." While either Sales or Sales Returns & Allowances can be debited, the latter account is preferable. In this manner management and other readers of financial statements can easily see the amount of returns and allowances in comparison with sales. This relationship, particularly if returns and allowances are significant, provides considerable insight into such factors as customer satisfaction with the merchandise and problems with shipments of damaged or defective goods.

Peachtree's sales on April 3 and 7 and the return on April 16 would appear on the company's income statement as follows:

Revenues	
Sales	***$1,025***
Less: Returns & allowances	***180***
Net sales	***$ 845***

Notice how separate disclosure of both gross sales *and* returns—rather than just the single net sales figure of $845—provides more information to the readers of the statement.

Trade discounts

Sellers frequently offer discounts to purchasers, more so to businesses than to individual consumers. One type of discount is a **trade discount.** To explain, manufacturers and wholesalers spend considerable time and money to publish catalogs of the merchandise they offer for sale. These catalogs often show the merchandise at a basic catalog or **list price.** Purchasers, however, do not pay list price. Rather they pay **invoice price,** that is, list price less applicable trade discounts.

Trade discounts are a convenient means of reducing list prices to invoice prices. This procedure may seem rather strange, since it would appear to be easier to just print the invoice price in the first place. The use of trade discounts offers several distinct benefits, however. If a change in market conditions necessitates price changes, it is much easier (and cheaper) to quote a different trade discount than to update and reprint an entire catalog. In addition, trade discounts can be altered as needed to give customers more incentive to purchase larger quantities (e.g., the larger the quantity purchased, the greater would be the discount).

Trade discounts are *not* entered in the accounting records. Why? As we noted earlier, the trade discount is used only to arrive at the invoice price, that is, the actual amount of the sale by the seller. To illustrate the proper record keeping, assume that Peachtree Jeans stocks a particular style of jeans with a list price of $25. If Peachtree received an order for 600 pairs and granted a 30% trade discount, the invoice price would be computed as follows:

List price 600 pairs × $25	*$15,000*
Less: 30% trade discount	*4,500*
Invoice price	*$10,500*

An invoice would be prepared for $10,500, and this amount would be recorded in the Accounts Receivable and Sales accounts. A separate trade discounts account is not established.

Cash discounts

When merchandise is sold on account, the seller usually gives the buyer a certain period of time to settle his or her account balance. Often sales on account must be paid within thirty days of the invoice date. Sellers, however, normally desire to collect the amounts due more rapidly to cover expenses and for purposes of investment. Therefore to encourage prompt payment, they offer incentives called **cash discounts.** From the seller's point of view the cash discount is termed a **sales discount.** The use of sales discounts not only stimulates rapid collections but also tends to reduce the likelihood of losses resulting from uncollectible accounts. The sales discount offers the purchaser a financial incentive to pay the balance owed promptly, thus reducing the probability that a given customer will not pay at all.

Cash discounts are normally expressed in the following format:

2/10, n/30

Or perhaps as

3/10, n/eom

In both examples the first set of numbers indicates the discount rate and the discount period. The second set discloses the invoice due date. The terms of sale are read as follows:

2/10, n/30. A 2% discount from the invoice price is allowed if payment is made within 10 days of the invoice date; otherwise the total invoice price is due within 30 days.

3/10, n/eom. A 3% discount from the invoice price is allowed if payment is made within 10 days of the invoice date; otherwise the total invoice price is due by the end of the month (eom).

Among a number of alternatives of accounting for sales discounts, the most popular method records both Accounts Receivable and Sales at the total invoice price as if a cash discount was not involved. The rationale is that at the time of sale the seller does not know whether the discount will be taken. Subsequently, if a cash discount is taken, the difference between the cash received and the original amount owed is recorded as a discount. If the cash discount is not utilized, the amount paid by the customer is recorded in the same manner as any other receipt on account.

To illustrate, assume Peachtree Jeans sold $1,500 of merchandise on account to a customer on April 10, terms 2/10, n/30. The sale and payment by the customer are shown below.

Apr. 10	Accounts Receivable	1,500	
	Sales		1,500
	Sale on account; terms 2/10, n/30		

Case A: Customer pays on Apr. 19 and takes the discount

Apr. 19	Cash	1,470	
	Sales Discounts	30	
	Accounts Receivable		1,500
	Collection on account; discount taken		

Case B: Customer pays on Apr. 26 and forgoes the discount

Apr. 26	Cash	1,500	
	Accounts Receivable		1,500
	Collection on account; discount missed		

Observe that the sale is recorded at the total invoice price of $1,500. If the customer settles the account by April 20, a $30 discount ($1,500 × 0.02) can be taken and the customer will pay $1,470 ($1,500 – $30). Although only $1,470 is received, Accounts Receivable is credited for the full $1,500. This reduces Accounts Receivable to zero, thus indicating the customer has no further obligation to Peachtree. The $30 is debited to Sales Discounts and reduces the total revenues earned by the firm. Like Sales Returns & Allowances, Sales Discounts appears on the income statement as a reduction from the Sales account.

Freight charges

The sale of goods to manufacturers, wholesalers, retailers, service businesses, and individuals often gives rise to freight charges. These charges can be significant, especially when a company deals in bulky or heavy items. Freight costs are borne by either the seller of the goods or the buyer; the exact party is determined by an order's freight terms.

Freight terms are usually expressed as F.O.B. shipping point or F.O.B. destination. **F.O.B.,** or free on board, means the seller will place the merchandise sold on board a freight carrier at no charge. Whether the seller or buyer incurs the freight charges thereafter is dependent on "shipping point" or "destination." These terms refer to the point where the seller's responsibility for incurring the transportation charges ceases. For example, if the terms are **F.O.B. shipping point,** the seller's responsibility for freight stops when the goods are loaded for shipment. Thus the buyer incurs all freight charges. Under **F.O.B. destination** the seller's responsibility ceases when the goods arrive at their ultimate destination (e.g., the buyer's warehouse). In contrast, then, the seller incurs the freight costs. We will concentrate on F.O.B. destination at this time because of our present focus on accounting for the seller.

Assume that Peachtree Jeans, which is located in Atlanta, sold $2,800 of merchandise on account to Smokey Pants in Nashville, Tennessee. Freight charges amounted to $160 and terms were F.O.B. Nashville (i.e., F.O.B. destination). Peachtree would record the following entries:

Accounts Receivable	*2,800*	
Sales		*2,800*
Sale on account to Smokey Pants		
Freight-out	*160*	
Cash		*160*
Payment to freight company		

Since Peachtree bears the cost of the freight, an expense is recorded by debiting the Freight-out account. The "out" in the account title refers to freight on outgoing shipments. The Freight-out account contains the costs incurred in completing the sale and is listed with Peachtree's expenses on the income statement.

Occasionally, the seller might not want to pay the necessary cash to the freight company even under terms of F.O.B. destination. The seller will therefore ship the goods *freight collect,* meaning the buyer must pay the freight company for the transportation charges. Because the freight is still the seller's responsibility, the buyer simply deducts the freight payment when subsequently paying the seller for the merchandise acquired.

Accounting for the Purchaser

Every sale of goods is represented by a purchase of those goods by another business, organization, or individual consumer. Accounting for the purchaser, therefore, is just the other side of accounting for the seller. The purchaser must account for the basic purchase plus, as before, related returns, discounts, and freight charges.

Recording purchases

During the course of a year a business will make many purchases. The proper recording of purchases in the accounting records is determined by the purpose for which the goods or services are acquired. To illustrate, assume Peachtree Jeans purchased $9,000 of merchandise on account on April 16. The entry would be as follows:

Apr. 16	Purchases	9,000	
	Accounts Payable		9,000
	Purchased merchandise on account		

The Purchases account is used *strictly* to record purchases of merchandise for resale to customers. Purchases of other items that will be used in the business, such as office equipment, supplies, or a company car, are recorded in their own respective accounts. For example, the acquisition of supplies results in a debit to the Supplies account and not the Purchases account.

The Purchases account has a debit balance and appears on the income statement in a section entitled "cost of goods sold." Cost of goods sold and the income statement of a merchandising concern will be illustrated shortly.

Purchases returns and allowances

As was true for sales, purchase transactions involve returns and allowances. Returns and allowances are caused by many factors, such as the arrival of merchandise (1) in a damaged condition, (2) much later than a requested delivery date, or (3) in error. Before a return or allowance is formally recorded in the accounts, the purchaser prepares appropriate documentation of the transaction in the form of either a letter or a **debit memorandum.** The debit memo informs the seller that its account, an account payable, has been debited (reduced) by the purchaser.

Proper accounting for purchases returns and allowances is shown by continuing the previous example. Suppose that $650 of the goods purchased on April 16 arrived past a requested delivery date. On April 30 Peachtree received authorization from the supplier and returned this merchandise. The following entry would be recorded:

Apr. 30	Accounts Payable	650	
	Purchases Returns & Allowances		650
	Returned merchandise to supplier		

The net amount of the purchase is $8,350 ($9,000 – $650). Rather than crediting the Purchases account for the appropriate reduction, it is again preferable to establish a separate account for returns and allowances. This procedure allows management and others to better examine the percentage relationship between returns and allowances and gross purchases, thus providing some insight into the effectiveness of the purchasing department. A large percentage of returns could be caused by sloppy ordering or dealings with unreliable suppliers.

The purchase and return would appear on Peachtree's income statement as follows:

Cost of goods sold

⋮

Purchases	*$9,000*
Less: Returns & allowances	*650*
Net purchases	*$8,350*

⋮

Trade and cash discounts

Recall that sellers frequently offer purchasers two types of discounts, trade and cash. The trade discount was used to arrive at the invoice price of the merchandise sold. The invoice price then became the basis for the sale and the related journal entry. Just as the invoice price was the true amount of the sale, it also represents the true cost of the purchase by the buyer. Consequently, the Purchases account is debited for the invoice price of merchandise acquired, that is, list price minus applicable trade discounts.

Turning to the cash discount, the sales discount offered by the seller for prompt payment becomes a **purchases discount** to the buyer. If at all possible, buyers should take advantage of this potential reduction in the cost of merchandise acquired. Why? The reason becomes apparent in the example that follows.

Suppose Peachtree Jeans purchased $10,000 of merchandise subject to terms of 2/10, n/30. Peachtree can do one of two things:

1 Pay $9,800 [$10,000 – 0.02 ($10,000)] within 10 days of the invoice date.
2 Pay $10,000 within 30 days of the invoice date.

If Peachtree forgoes the discount and settles the invoice when due, the firm must pay an additional $200. The $200 allows Peachtree to have the use of $9,800 for a period of 20 days (30 – 10) and is appropriately deemed interest. For the 20-day period, then, the effective interest rate is 2.04% ($200 ÷ $9,800). Most interest rates are expressed on an annual basis of 360 days. Thus the 2.04% rate translates into an exceedingly high annual rate of 36.72% ($\frac{360}{20}$ × 2.04%). Purchasers should therefore utilize available cash discounts even if it means borrowing money from the bank. Generally, short-term bank loans are available at interest rates well below 36.72%.

Gross method

One of the most popular methods of accounting for purchases discounts corresponds to the previously illustrated method for sales discounts. The **gross method** records both purchases and accounts payable at the total invoice cost of the merchandise acquired. This technique is logically sound, because at the time of purchase the buyer does not always know whether the discount will be taken. If the discount is taken, it is recorded in a separate Purchases Discounts account.

Using the gross method, let us assume Peachtree purchased $4,000 of sportswear on account from Wrangler Corporation on April 14, subject to terms of 2/10, n/30. The purchase and subsequent payment would be recorded by Peachtree as follows:

Apr. 14	*Purchases*	*4,000*	
	Accounts Payable		*4,000*
	Purchase on account; terms 2/10, n/30		

Case A: Peachtree pays on Apr. 23 and takes the discount

Apr. 23	*Accounts Payable*	*4,000*	
	Purchases Discounts		*80*
	Cash		*3,920*
	Paid on account; discount taken		

Case B: Peachtree pays on Apr. 27 and forgoes the discount

Apr. 27	*Accounts Payable*	*4,000*	
	Cash		*4,000*
	Paid on account; discount missed		

While Case B is straightforward, Case A needs some explanation. By paying the invoice before the 10-day discount period expires, Peachtree is entitled to an $80 discount ($4,000 × 0.02). Although only $3,920 is remitted to Wrangler, Accounts Payable is debited for the entire $4,000 because the account is paid in full. The Purchases Discounts account, like Purchases Returns & Allowances, possesses a credit balance and is deducted from the Purchases account on the income statement to arrive at a net purchases figure.

In this particular example the discount was calculated on the basis of the $4,000 invoice cost. If any of the merchandise acquired had been returned to Wrangler prior to payment, the discount would have been figured on the net purchase only. Furthermore, discounts are computed on merchandise cost only. Cash discounts are not permitted on freight charges incurred by the buyer to acquire the goods.

Net method

Because of the high interest costs associated with missing discounts, many companies follow a policy of taking all discounts offered, even if it means obtaining a loan. In anticipation of securing these reductions in cost, businesses may follow an alternative recording procedure for purchases called the **net purchases method.** The net method records purchases and accounts payable at the net cost of the purchase, that is, total invoice cost less the anticipated cash discount. If the discount is taken, the liability is removed from the books in similar fashion to other payments on account. Any discounts missed, on the other hand, are entered in an account entitled Purchases Discounts Lost.

To illustrate the net method, we will use the same transaction that appeared in the discussion of the gross method—a $4,000 purchase subject to terms of 2/10, n/30. Under the net method the April 14 purchase and subsequent payment on account would be recorded as follows:

Apr. 14	Purchases	3,920	
	Accounts Payable		3,920
	Purchase on account; terms 2/10, n/30		

Case A: Peachtree pays on Apr. 23 and takes the discount

Apr. 23	Accounts Payable	3,920	
	Cash		3,920
	Paid on account; discount taken		

Case B: Peachtree pays on Apr. 27 and forgoes the discount

Apr. 27	Accounts Payable	3,920	
	Purchases Discounts Lost	80	
	Cash		4,000
	Paid on account; discount missed		

Under Case A, since the liability is already established at the net figure of $3,920, no additional discount is recorded. Under Case B, $4,000 must be paid: $3,920 for the merchandise acquired and $80, which is viewed as a penalty for late payment.

The Purchases Discounts Lost account appears on the income statement as an expense. The presence of a large balance in this account means that a business has missed a considerable number of discounts and may raise questions concerning managerial effectiveness. The discounts may have been missed because of carelessness in the accounts payable department or perhaps because of a very tight cash position. Whatever the cause, the firm is incurring extremely high interest rates as a result.

The major advantage associated with the net method is its enforcement of a concept known as **management by exception.** Generally, for purposes of operational control, management is interested in learning more about the exception rather than the rule. In the area of purchases discounts, for example, management desires information regarding the discounts missed (i.e., what is going wrong) rather than the discounts taken (i.e., what is going right). While some insight into this issue can be gained by studying percentage relationships of discounts and purchases under the gross method, the accumulation of discounts lost is the focal point of the net method.

Freight charges

As we noted earlier, freight charges may be borne by either the buyer or seller of merchandise. Under terms of F.O.B. shipping point the buyer incurs any related transportation costs.

Transportation charges incurred increase the cost of merchandise acquired. Rather than bury these costs in the Purchases account, one establishes a separate account, Freight-in. Used only for freight on incoming merchandise, this account is added to the Purchases account on the income statement to arrive at a net delivered cost of merchandise acquired. Establishment of a separate account for freight improves accountability and provides information for control and analysis. Alternative modes of transportation as well as full-load versus less-than-full-load purchases are often available to a firm. Rates differ dramatically among these options, and the Freight-in account generates information that assists in choosing the proper course of action.

To illustrate accounting for the purchaser under terms of F.O.B. shipping point, assume that Peachtree purchased $3,000 of footwear on account from Sport Shoe Company on April 22, F.O.B. shipping point. Freight charges amounted to $80. Peachtree will record the following entry:

Apr. 22	*Purchases*	*3,000*	
	Freight-in	*80*	
	Accounts Payable		*3,080*
	Purchased merchandise; terms F.O.B. shipping point		

The credit of $3,080 to Accounts Payable shows that Peachtree owes Sport Shoe for the freight. Apparently, as a matter of convenience to the purchaser, Sport Shoe prepaid the freight and expects to be reimbursed. If the freight was not prepaid, Peachtree would owe the seller $3,000, necessitating a credit of $3,000 to Accounts Payable. Peachtree would also owe and pay $80 to the freight company, which is recorded by a credit to the Cash account.

INVENTORY ACCOUNTING

Merchandising businesses stock a variety of goods for resale to customers. The cost of these goods is carried in an account called Inventory or Merchandise Inventory. Interestingly, however, when we look back at the methods of recording purchases and sales that were presented earlier in the chapter, we never debited or credited the Inventory account. All merchandise acquisitions were debited to Purchases, and all sales were recorded in the Sales account. Apparently, then, the balance found in the Inventory account at the beginning of the period remains there throughout the year.[4] This type of inventory system is known as the **periodic system.** At the end of the accounting period the Inventory account must be updated to reflect the proper amount of goods owned by the firm.

The periodic system is in direct contrast to a **perpetual inventory system** in which the Inventory account is increased for each purchase and decreased for each sale made during the period. The inventory control department, discussed earlier in the chapter, uses a perpetual (running) count of the units on hand to closely monitor inventory levels. While the perpetual method of accounting for *units* is simple, the maintenance of a running count of *dollar* values in the Inventory account creates several unique record-keeping problems. We will therefore use the periodic system for the remainder of this chapter.

[4]We will illustrate shortly how a balance gets into the Inventory account.

Although the Inventory account under a periodic system is not always up to date, a company can readily determine the amount of goods it has available for sale. **Goods available for sale** is computed by taking the beginning balance in the Inventory account and adding net purchases. For example, if Peachtree Jeans has a $67,000 beginning inventory and acquires $146,000 of merchandise throughout the year, $213,000 ($67,000 + $146,000) of goods is available for sale to customers. By the end of the year part of the goods available for sale has been sold and part is still owned.

On conclusion of the accounting period a business employing the periodic system must take a physical hand count of the merchandise that is unsold. Once a proper count is determined, the units are multiplied by their respective costs to obtain an ending inventory valuation. Suppose this calculation yields $48,000. As shown in Exhibit 4-3, Peachtree must therefore have sold $165,000 ($213,000 − $48,000) of inventory.

Exhibit 4-3

Breakdown of goods available for sale

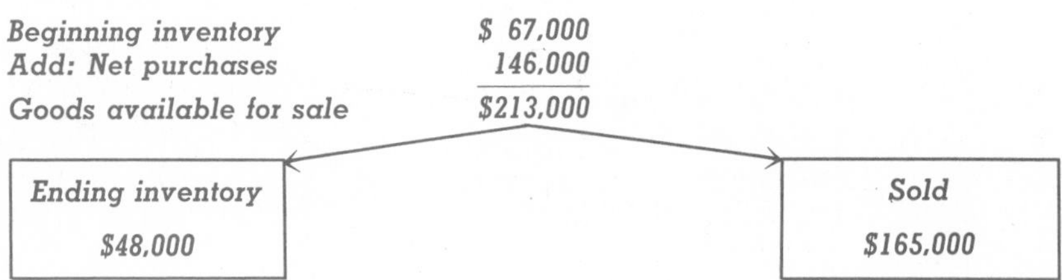

Note that $165,000 is the *cost* of inventory sold and not the inventory's sales value. A company, of course, will attempt to sell goods at a price in excess of cost to generate a profit. What happens to the cost of the ending inventory and the cost of goods that were sold? Here is where financial statements come into the picture.

FINANCIAL STATEMENTS OF A MERCHANDISING CONCERN

Thus far we have concentrated on three financial statements: the income statement, statement of owners' equity, and the balance sheet. Because the income statement is the first statement prepared and, regarding inventory, the most complex of the three statements, it is an appropriate place to begin.

Income Statement

The income statements of a service business and a merchandising firm differ considerably. While both statements measure net income, the introduction of inventory necessitates several modifications. See Exhibit 4-4, for example, which contains the income statement of Peachtree Jeans.[5]

Consistent with the matching concept, which was introduced in Chap-

[5] The account balances contained in Exhibits 4-4 through 4-7 were obtained from Peachtree's general ledger as of December 31, 1983.

Exhibit 4-4

Income statement of a merchandising firm

PEACHTREE JEANS
Income Statement
For the Year Ended December 31, 1983

Revenues				
Sales				$307,000
Less: Sales discounts			$ 5,000	
Sales returns & allowances			2,000	7,000
Net sales				$300,000
Cost of goods sold				
Beginning inventory, Jan. 1			$ 67,000	
Add: Purchases		$148,000		
Freight-in		5,000		
		$153,000		
Less: Purchases discounts	$3,000			
Purchases returns & allowances	4,000	7,000		
Net purchases			146,000	
Goods available for sale			$213,000	
Less: Ending inventory, Dec. 31			48,000	
Cost of goods sold				165,000
Gross profit				$135,000
Operating expenses				
Rent expense			$ 15,000	
Salaries expense			61,000	
Utilities expense			11,000	
Freight-out			7,000	
Advertising expense			13,000	
Depreciation expense			10,000	
Insurance expense			9,000	
Total expenses				126,000
Net income				$ 9,000

ter 3, the costs incurred in producing sales are deducted from the sales revenues generated. These costs are operating expenses and cost of goods sold. **Operating expenses** refer to expenses incurred in the selling and administrative activities of a business and include rent, advertising, wages, utilities, and repairs.

Cost of goods sold

Cost of goods sold, sometimes called cost of sales, represents exactly what its name implies, the total cost of inventory that a company has sold. For the information introduced in Exhibit 4-3, cost of goods sold is normally

GROSS PROFIT: A CLUE BEHIND THOSE SKYROCKETING PRICES

Did you ever go into a store and think the prices were out of line in comparison with those charged by other sellers for the same merchandise? Did you ever wonder how much profit a store was making on a given sale? A firm's gross profit rate provides substantial assistance in answering these questions.

The gross profit rate is computed by dividing gross profit by net sales. Because businesses operate in different markets, they have considerably different gross profit characteristics. Observe the variations, for instance, in the following representative industry averages:

Gross Profit Industry Averages, Retail Establishments	
Restaurants	*53.0%*
Flowers and plants	*47.8*
Jewelry	*47.3*
Vending machine operations	*44.9*
Furniture stores	*40.2*
Family clothing	*39.3*
Sporting goods and bicycles	*33.7*
Building materials	*26.9*
Boat dealers	*24.9*
Motorcycles	*23.7*
Groceries and meats	*21.5*
Campers and trailers	*20.7*
Liquor	*20.5*

The target rate of gross profit in an industry is dependent on many factors. Included among them are (1) the anticipated level of operating expenses, (2) the price the consumer is willing to pay, (3) the levels of spoilage and perishability of inventory, and (4) the volume of inventory sold. To illustrate, flower shops and restaurants tend to have high levels of spoilage with inventory; therefore a high gross profit is necessary for financial well-being. With vending machine operations consumers are willing to pay an extra nickel or dime just for the sake of convenience. In contrast to the foregoing, grocery stores tend to generate a fairly low gross profit. Why? Grocery stores are a high-volume operation that actively compete for a consumer's weekly purchases. Specials and a constant demand for lower prices continuously cut into the profits generated.

Obviously, the four factors cited above cannot explain all the differences between industries. However, by picturing the nature of specific industries, you can see that these factors do differ. So the next time you are complaining that a store's prices are too high, consider the operating characteristics of the business. These characteristics collectively contribute toward the target of your complaint.

SOURCE *Gross profit percentages are from* '81 Annual Statement Studies, *Robert Morris Associates (Philadelphia, 1981).*

presented in the following format:

Cost of goods sold	
Beginning inventory, Jan. 1	$ 67,000
Add: Net purchases	146,000
Goods available for sale	$213,000
Less: Ending inventory, Dec. 31	48,000
Cost of goods sold	$165,000

On an income statement the cost-of-goods-sold section appears immediately below net sales. By viewing Exhibit 4-4, you will see the placement of the cost-of-goods-sold section and the income statement's expansion to include all the accounts we have been discussing. Net sales is computed by deducting Sales Discounts and Sales Returns & Allowances from Sales. The breakdown of net purchases into its elements of Purchases, Freight-in, Purchases Discounts, and Purchases Returns & Allowances provides the financial statement user with information about Peachtree's purchasing activity. Finally, Freight-out, an expense related to the sale of merchandise, is listed among the operating expenses.

Gross profit

Cost of goods sold is subtracted from net sales to yield **gross profit** (sometimes called gross margin). Gross profit represents the profit that a company generates from the sales of inventory. In the case of Peachtree, for example, gross profit totaled $135,000. Thus for every $1 of net sales, Peachtree has earned $0.45 ($135,000 ÷ $300,000) from inventory to help cover operating expenses and produce a net income. The gross profit computation furnishes considerable insight into the nature of a firm's operations, as the accompanying article indicates.

Statement of Owners' Equity

The statement of owners' equity, which summarizes the changes in the owners' equity account during the period, is identical for both a service business and a merchandising concern. The owners' equity statement for Peachtree Jeans appears in Exhibit 4-5.

Exhibit 4-5

Statement of owners' equity of a merchandising firm

PEACHTREE JEANS
Statement of Owners' Equity
For the Year Ended December 31, 1983

Beginning balance, Jan. 1		$163,200
Increases		
Net income (from Exhibit 4-4)	$ 9,000	
Decreases		
Owner withdrawals	22,000	(13,000)
Ending balance, Dec. 31		$150,200

Balance Sheet

The balance sheets of a service business and a merchandising business are also similar, with the exception of inventory. The inventory of a merchandising firm is an asset and, accordingly, an Inventory account appears in the statement's asset section. The balance reported in the Inventory account represents the amount of merchandise owned as of the balance sheet date. In the case of Peachtree the inventory would be listed at $48,000, which agrees with the ending balance reported in Exhibits 4-3 and 4-4. Peachtree's balance sheet as of December 31, 1983, appears in Exhibit 4-6.

Exhibit 4-6

Balance sheet of a merchandising firm

PEACHTREE JEANS
Balance Sheet
December 31, 1983

Assets		
Cash		$ 25,700
Accounts receivable		19,600
Inventory		48,000
Prepaid insurance		4,800
Equipment	$124,800	
Less: Accumulated depreciation	34,800	90,000
Total assets		$188,100
Liabilities		
Accounts payable		$ 36,400
Salaries payable		1,500
Total liabilities		$ 37,900
Owners' equity		
Gene Rosen, capital (from Exhibit 4-5)		150,200
Total liabilities & owners' equity		$188,100

GOING BEHIND THE SCENES: THE WORK SHEET

Recall from Chapter 3 that the work sheet is the underlying foundation for the preparation of financial statements. The work sheet that was used for Peachtree's financial statements appears in Exhibit 4-7.

The trial balance columns contain the accounts with balances as of the trial balance date. New accounts presented in this chapter are highlighted by the use of capital letters. Each of the accounts, with the exception of Inventory, has been updated by the transactions that occurred during the period. Remember that the Inventory account under a periodic system is not affected by sales and purchases; thus the $67,000 inventory balance is properly labeled as the January 1 balance.

As before, data in the adjustment columns are gathered after analyzing each account to determine the necessary updating. These adjustments,

Exhibit 4-7 *Work sheet of a merchandising firm*

PEACHTREE JEANS
Work Sheet
For the Year Ended December 31, 1983

Account Title	Trial Balance		Adjustments		Income Statement		Balance Sheet	
	Debit	Credit	Debit	Credit	Debit	Credit	Debit	Credit
Cash	25,700						25,700	
Accounts receivable	19,600						19,600	
INVENTORY, JAN. 1	67,000				67,000			
Prepaid insurance	13,800			(b) 9,000			4,800	
Equipment	124,800						124,800	
Accumulated depreciation: equipment		24,800		(a) 10,000				34,800
Accounts payable		36,400						36,400
Gene Rosen, capital		163,200						163,200
Gene Rosen, drawing	22,000						22,000	
SALES		307,000				307,000		
SALES DISCOUNTS	5,000				5,000			
SALES RETURNS & ALLOWANCES	2,000				2,000			
PURCHASES	148,000				148,000			
FREIGHT-IN	5,000				5,000			
PURCHASES DISCOUNTS		3,000				3,000		
PURCHASES RETURNS & ALLOWANCES		4,000				4,000		
Rent expense	15,000				15,000			
Salaries expense	59,500		(c) 1,500		61,000			
Utilities Expense	11,000				11,000			
FREIGHT-OUT	7,000				7,000			
Advertising expense	13,000				13,000			
	538,400	538,400						
Depreciation expense			(a) 10,000		10,000			
Insurance expense			(b) 9,000		9,000			
Salaries payable				(c) 1,500				1,500
			20,500	20,500				
INVENTORY, DEC. 31						48,000	48,000	
					353,000	362,000	244,900	235,900
Net income					9,000			9,000
					362,000	362,000	244,900	244,900

when combined with the amounts listed in the trial balance, produce the updated balances appearing in the financial statement columns. The January 1 inventory balance of $67,000 is extended to the income statement debit column because of its use in the computation of cost of goods sold.

Because we wish to report the actual amount of goods owned, the $48,000 ending inventory balance must be recorded in the balance sheet debit column. This is accomplished by entering the ending inventory beneath the accounts that are required for the adjustments. The ending inventory is also entered in the credit column of the income statement. As shown earlier, the ending inventory is deducted from goods available for sale to determine cost of goods sold. Placement in the credit column serves as a reduction, because the beginning inventory and net purchases have debit balances. The end result is shown in Exhibit 4-8 by reproducing, in part, the income statement columns of the work sheet. The work sheet columns are compared against the cost-of-goods-sold computation on Peachtree's income statement in Exhibit 4-4.

Exhibit 4-8

Calculation of cost of goods sold

	Work Sheet		Formal Income Statement
	Debit	Credit	Cost of Goods Sold
Beginning inventory, Jan. 1	$ 67,000		$ 67,000
Purchases	148,000		
Freight-in	5,000		
Purchases discounts		$ 3,000	146,000
Purchases returns & allowances		4,000	
			$213,000
Ending inventory, Dec. 31		48,000	(48,000)
	$220,000	$55,000	$165,000
	$165,000		

ADJUSTING AND CLOSING ENTRIES

The work sheet not only assists in the preparation of financial statements but also serves as the basis for adjusting and closing entries. The techniques illustrated in Chapter 3 relating to adjusting entries for the service business also pertain to merchandising firms. Because there are no differences, we refer you to the previous chapter for a refresher of the proper procedures.

The closing process for a merchandising concern does differ somewhat from that of a service business because of the added complexities and accounts that appear on the income statement. In the closing process, income statement accounts with debit balances are credited, and, conversely, accounts with credit balances are debited. New accounts with debit balances include Sales Discounts, Sales Returns & Allowances, Purchases, Freight-in, and Freight-out. In contrast, Sales, Purchases Discounts, and Purchases Returns & Allowances have credit balances.

A new account not cited above is Inventory. Why? The Inventory account is given special treatment. Both the beginning and ending inventories are found in the cost-of-goods-sold computation on the income statement. Consequently, these amounts have a direct bearing on gross profit and net income. Recall from Chapter 3 that the balance in the Income Summary account (after all appropriate accounts have been closed) is the net income or loss of the business. The conclusion? The beginning and ending inventories must be entered in the Income Summary. At the same time we must update the Inventory account. Although it is now December 31, the January 1 balance still remains, because the account has not been updated by purchases or sales. To achieve the desired results, we need the following entries:

Dec. 31	Income Summary	67,000	
	Inventory		67,000
	To close beginning inventory		
31	Inventory	48,000	
	Income Summary		48,000
	To record ending inventory		

After posting, the Inventory and Income Summary accounts appear as follows:

Inventory

Debit		Credit	
1/1/83	67,000	12/31/83	67,000
12/31/83	48,000		

Income Summary

Debit		Credit	
12/31/83	67,000	12/31/83	48,000

The Inventory account now reflects the goods currently owned by Peachtree.

The remainder of the closing process is handled in the normal manner. In Chapter 3 we closed all the revenues and then all the expenses. When a firm has a wide variety of accounts, it is easier if we modify this procedure somewhat. Although accounts such as Sales Returns and Sales Discounts have debit balances, they are not expenses. As shown, these accounts appear on the income statement in the calculation of net revenues. It is easier, then, to close all income statement accounts with debit balances, followed by those with credit balances. This procedure is illustrated as follows.

Dec. 31	*Income Summary*	286,000	
	Sales Discounts		5,000
	Sales Returns & Allowances		2,000
	Purchases		148,000
	Freight-in		5,000
	Rent Expense		15,000
	Salaries Expense		61,000
	Utilities Expense		11,000
	Freight-out		7,000
	Advertising Expense		13,000
	Depreciation Expense		10,000
	Insurance Expense		9,000
	To close income statement accounts with debit balances		
31	*Sales*	307,000	
	Purchases Discounts	3,000	
	Purchases Returns & Allowances	4,000	
	Income Summary		314,000
	To close income statement accounts with credit balances		

After these two entries are posted, the Income Summary account appears as shown:

Income Summary

12/31/83	67,000	12/31/83	48,000
12/31/83	286,000	12/31/83	314,000
	353,000	(9,000)	362,000

The Income Summary's $9,000 credit balance corresponds to Peachtree's net income. The entries to close the Income Summary and the owner's drawing account follow.

Dec. 31	*Income Summary*	9,000	
	Gene Rosen, Capital		9,000
	To close Income Summary		
31	*Gene Rosen, Capital*	22,000	
	Gene Rosen, Drawing		22,000
	To close drawing account		

SUMMARY PROBLEM

The following trial balance pertains to Spry Company as of December 31, 1983.

SPRY COMPANY
Trial Balance
December 31, 1983

Cash	$ 37,800	
Accounts receivable	54,800	
Inventory, Jan. 1	77,200	
Prepaid advertising	24,800	
Supplies	7,400	
Equipment	179,200	
Accumulated depreciation: equipment		$ 49,600
Accounts payable		61,200
Spry, capital		291,600
Spry, drawing	52,000	
Sales		573,600
Sales returns & allowances	11,400	
Sales discounts	4,000	
Purchases	349,000	
Purchases returns & allowances		3,800
Purchases discounts		6,600
Freight-in	8,800	
Wages expense	117,000	
Insurance expense	5,200	
Rent expense	33,000	
Freight-out	7,600	
Utilities expense	17,200	
	$986,400	$986,400

Additional accounts maintained by the company include Wages Payable, Income Summary, Advertising Expense, Supplies Expense, and Depreciation Expense. Spry's accountant has generated the following adjustment data:

1. **Advertising applicable to future periods: $15,400.**
2. **Supplies on hand: $4,200.**
3. **Depreciation on the equipment: $11,000.**
4. **Accrued wages: $3,000.**

On December 31 a hand count revealed that $95,800 of inventory was still owned by the firm.

INSTRUCTIONS

a. **Complete a work sheet in good form for the Spry Company for the year ended December 31, 1983.**
b. **Prepare Spry's closing entries.**
c. **Compute the company's (1) net sales, (2) cost of goods sold, and (3) gross profit.**

SOLUTION

a

SPRY COMPANY
Work Sheet
For the Year Ended December 31, 1983

Account Title	Trial Balance		Adjustments		Income Statement		Balance Sheet	
	Debit	Credit	Debit	Credit	Debit	Credit	Debit	Credit
Cash	37,800						37,800	
Accounts receivable	54,800						54,800	
Inventory, Jan. 1	77,200				77,200			
Prepaid advertising	24,800			(a) 9,400			15,400	
Supplies	7,400			(b) 3,200			4,200	
Equipment	179,200						179,200	
Accumulated depreciation: equipment		49,600		(c) 11,000				60,600
Accounts payable		61,200						61,200
Spry, capital		291,600						291,600
Spry, drawing	52,000						52,000	
Sales		573,600				573,600		
Sales returns & allowances	11,400				11,400			
Sales discounts	4,000				4,000			
Purchases	349,000				349,000			
Purchases returns & allowances		3,800				3,800		
Purchases discounts		6,600				6,600		
Freight-in	8,800				8,800			
Wages expense	117,000		(d) 3,000		120,000			
Insurance expense	5,200				5,200			
Rent expense	33,000				33,000			
Freight-out	7,600				7,600			
Utilities expense	17,200				17,200			
	986,400	986,400						
Advertising expense			(a) 9,400		9,400			
Supplies expense			(b) 3,200		3,200			
Depreciation expense			(c) 11,000		11,000			
Wages payable				(d) 3,000				3,000
			26,600	26,600				
Inventory, Dec. 31						95,800	95,800	
					657,000	679,800	439,200	416,400
Net income					22,800			22,800
					679,800	679,800	439,200	439,200

b

		Debit	Credit
Dec. 31	Income Summary	77,200	
	Inventory		77,200
	To close beginning inventory		
31	Inventory	95,800	
	Income Summary		95,800
	To record ending inventory		
31	Income Summary	579,800	
	Sales Returns & Allowances		11,400
	Sales Discounts		4,000
	Purchases		349,000
	Freight-in		8,800
	Wages Expense		120,000
	Insurance Expense		5,200
	Rent Expense		33,000
	Freight-out		7,600
	Utilities Expense		17,200
	Advertising Expense		9,400
	Supplies Expense		3,200
	Depreciation Expense		11,000
	To close income statement accounts with debit balances		
31	Sales	573,600	
	Purchases Returns & Allowances	3,800	
	Purchases Discounts	6,600	
	Income Summary		584,000
	To close income statement accounts with credit balances		

Income Summary

12/31	77,200	12/31	95,800
12/31	579,800	12/31	584,000
	657,000	**(22,800)**	**679,800**

		Debit	Credit
Dec. 31	Income Summary	22,800	
	Spry, Capital		22,800
	To close Income Summary		
31	Spry, Capital	52,000	
	Spry, Drawing		52,000
	To close drawing account		

c (1)

Sales		$573,600
Less: Sales returns & allowances	$11,400	
Sales discounts	4,000	15,400
Net sales		$558,200

(2) Beginning inventory, Jan. 1			$ 77,200
Add: Purchases		$349,000	
Freight-in		8,800	
		$357,800	
Less: Purchases returns & allowances	$3,800		
Purchases discounts	6,600	10,400	
Net purchases			347,400
Goods available for sale			$424,600
Less: Ending inventory, Dec. 31			95,800
Cost of goods sold			$328,800

(3) Net sales	$558,200
Cost of goods sold	328,800
Gross profit	$229,400

KEY TERMS AND CONCEPTS

accounts payable department 131
accounts receivable department 130
cash discount 134
cost of goods sold 143
credit memorandum 133
customer statement 130
debit memorandum 137
F.O.B. destination 136
F.O.B. shipping point 136
goods available for sale 142
gross method of recording purchases 138
gross profit 145
inventory control department 131
invoice 128
invoice price 134
list price 134
management by exception 140
merchandise inventory 126
merchandising system 127
net method of recording purchases 139
operating expense 143
order processing department 128
periodic inventory system 141
perpetual inventory system 141
purchase order 127
purchases discounts 138
purchases returns and allowances 137
purchasing system 131
sales discount 134
sales returns and allowances 133
sales system 127
trade discount 134

QUESTIONS

Q4-1 The vice-presidents of marketing and finance of the Rucker Company are having a debate regarding the proper levels of inventory to carry. Explain the probable position of each vice-president and why she favors that position.

Q4-2 Explain the interrelationships between the order processing and inventory control departments.

Q4-3 What functions are performed in the accounts receivable department?

Q4-4 Explain the relationship between a sales invoice and a customer statement.

Q4-5 Although sales invoices and purchase orders help to document sales and purchases transactions, why is it still necessary to record these transactions in the journal?

Q4-6 Would the inventory control department be more apt to use a periodic or perpetual inventory system? Why?

Q4-7 What verification procedures are generally performed prior to the issuance of a check by a merchandising concern? Why are they performed?

Q4-8 Rather than publish catalogs that contain invoice prices, many companies follow the practice of printing list prices and then granting a trade discount to purchasers. What advantages are associated with this procedure?

Q4-9 Differentiate between F.O.B. shipping point and F.O.B. destination.

Q4-10 The Gomez Company sells an item that has a list price of $1,000. Management is contemplating whether to ship the item F.O.B. shipping point or F.O.B. destination. Compare the trade discounts that would probably be quoted under the two alternatives. Which trade discount would probably be smaller? Why?

Q4-11 Ye Old Card Shoppe has just acquired a new desk and chair on account for the bookkeeper's office. The purchase price of $490 was recorded as follows:

Purchases	*940*	
Accounts Payable		*940*
Purchased desk and chair		

Criticize the above entry.

Q4-12 Explain why a purchaser should take advantage of cash discounts even if it means obtaining a bank loan to do so.

Q4-13 Contrast the gross and net methods of recording purchases. What is the most important advantage associated with the latter approach?

Q4-14 A student once commented: "The Freight-in account is very similar to the Purchases Returns account. Both appear in the cost-of-goods-sold section of the income statement as a reduction to determine net purchases." Evaluate the student's comment.

Q4-15 What is the basic difference between a periodic and a perpetual inventory system?

Q4-16 Explain the difference between gross profit and net income.

Q4-17 The Ames Company sells its products at approximately 35% above cost. Yet at the end of the current year a net loss of $15,000 was incurred. Explain how this situation is possible.

EXERCISES

E4-1 The G. W. Brady Company is a large wholesale distributor of books and magazines. Brady carries thousands of different titles and employs a merchandising system similar to that illustrated in Exhibit 4-1.

a Explain, on a step-by-step basis, how an order from the Fireside Book Shop would be processed through Brady's sales system.
b Explain, on a step-by-step basis, how an order to Dell Publishing would be processed through Brady's purchasing system.

E4-2 Prater Auto Supply sold $680 of merchandise on account to Finn's Garage. Finn's later returned $450 of the merchandise because it was shipped in error by Prater's warehouse personnel. Show two different journal entries Prater could use to record the return. Which entry is preferred? Why?

E4-3 At the beginning of the year the balance in the Accounts Receivable account of the Morton Company was $11,400; at the end of the year the balance was $18,500. During the year cash sales to customers amounted to $63,700. Sales on account totaled $171,700, of which $10,800 were returned to Morton for various reasons. Sales discounts taken by customers for prompt payment amounted to $3,100. Calculate the total cash received from customers throughout the year.

E4-4 On August 14 the Diamond Company purchased $4,200 of merchandise from Roth Distributing, terms 3/10, n/20. The merchandise was shipped F.O.B. destination, with Roth paying the freight company $80. Because of a shipping error, Diamond returned $500 of the merchandise on August 17. Finally, on August 23 Diamond paid the proper amount due to Roth.
a Record all necessary journal entries on Diamond's books, assuming Diamond uses the gross method of accounting for purchases.
b Record all necessary journal entries on Roth's books.

E4-5 You are in charge of purchasing some merchandise for the Fox Corporation. There are two possible suppliers, Petrone Distributing and Mitchell Wholesale. Petrone has an excellent reputation; Mitchell, on the other hand, has only been in business for three weeks. Petrone has a list price of $16,400 for the merchandise you need. They offer a 25% trade discount and terms of 1/10, n/30. Freight is F.O.B. Petrone's warehouse and will amount to $400. Mitchell's list price is $16,000. They offer a 20% trade discount and, in order to land the sale, will absorb the $400 of freight charges. Mitchell's terms of sale are 3/10, n/eom.
a Based on a financial analysis, where will you acquire the needed merchandise? What appears to be the key issue?
b Aside from dollars, what other factors should you consider in your decision? Explain.

E4-6 Ricardo Company recently acquired 10 machines for resale to customers from Lemco Manufacturing. The following information pertains to this purchase.

Invoice date: 5/17
Payment date: 5/26
List price per machine: $1,200
Terms: 2/10, n/60
Trade discount: 30%
Freight: $250, F.O.B. shipping point, prepaid by Lemco

Ricardo returned one of the machines to Lemco on May 21. *Note:* Disregard freight on the return.
a Compute the amount that was paid to Lemco in full settlement of the purchase.

b Prepare journal entries for Ricardo to record the purchase on May 17, the return on May 21, and the payment on May 26. Ricardo uses the gross method of accounting for purchases.

E4-7 The Computer Store, a business specializing in the sale of small computers and prewritten computer programs, had the following transactions with one of its suppliers:

Purchases of small computers	*$164,000*
Purchases of prewritten programs	*45,000*
Returns & allowances	*4,000*
Purchases discounts taken	*1,350*

Purchases were made throughout the year on terms of 3/10, n/60. All returns and allowances took place within five days of purchase and prior to any payments on account.

a If The Computer Store used the gross method of accounting for purchases, determine the balance in the Purchases Discounts account at the end of the year.
b Would the net method of accounting for purchases provide more useful information to The Computer Store's management than the gross method? Why?
c Suppose The Computer Store could obtain a bank loan at an annual interest rate of 15% to take advantage of the discounts offered. In view of their past record, would it have been to the firm's advantage to secure the bank loan? Why?

E4-8 The Princeton Company purchased $1,400 of merchandise on account on April 3, terms 1/10, n/eom.

a Assuming Princeton uses the gross method of accounting for purchases, present entries to record the following:
(1) The purchase on April 3.
(2) Payment of the invoice if payment was made on April 12.
(3) Payment of the invoice if payment was made on April 30.

b Assuming Princeton uses the net method of accounting for purchases, present entries to record the following:
(1) The purchase on April 3.
(2) Payment of the invoice if payment was made on April 12.
(3) Payment of the invoice if payment was made on April 30.

E4-9 A review of the records of Oregon Distributing revealed the following information:

Purchases	*$141,600*	*Freight-in*	*$ 1,700*
Rent expense	*14,600*	*Sales*	*240,000*
Salaries expense	*35,000*	*Inventory, Jan. 1*	*19,400*
Freight-out	*5,800*	*Inventory, Dec. 31*	*22,200*
Advertising expense	*12,400*	*Sales returns*	*900*

a Compute cost of goods sold, gross profit, and net income for Oregon Distributing.
b Oregon makes all purchases on account. On January 1 Accounts Payable had a balance of $16,800; on December 31 the balance was $14,000. The $1,700 of freight-in was paid directly to trucking companies and did not affect Oregon's liabilities. Assuming all operating expenses were paid as in-

curred, compute total cash payments for purchases of merchandise during the year.

E4-10 The following information was obtained from the records of the Ting and Sumi companies.

	Ting	Sumi
Net purchases	$ (a)	$27,400
Sales	64,500	39,200
Net income (loss)	18,200	(3,800)
Cost of goods sold	24,300	28,800
Sales returns & allowances	(b)	3,400
Beginning inventory	17,100	(c)
Gross profit	38,100	(d)
Operating expenses	19,900	(e)
Ending inventory	21,400	21,700

Compute the amounts that are indicated by the letters (*a*)–(*e*).

E4-11 The following account balances, after adjustment, were obtained from the records of the Southside Auto Parts Company.

Cash	$ 7,400	
Accounts receivable	11,900	
Merchandise inventory, Jan. 1	15,600	
Accounts payable		$ 4,300
Joe Burke, capital		37,900
Joe Burke, drawing	18,000	
Sales		96,400
Sales returns	1,900	
Purchases	58,700	
Freight-in	1,100	
Purchases returns		800
Salaries expense	14,900	
Rent expense	8,600	
Advertising expense	1,300	
	$139,400	$139,400

The physical inventory taken on December 31 amounted to $17,500. Present all necessary closing entries for Southside Auto Parts on December 31.

PROBLEMS

P4-1 ***Merchandising journal entries***

The Haden Corporation had the following transactions during June:

June 1 Sold $3,000 of merchandise on account to Phipps Company, terms 3/10, n/30.

4 Purchased $7,500 of merchandise on account from Walker Enterprises, terms 2/10, n/30. The merchandise was shipped F.O.B. shipping point; freight charges amounted to $80 and were paid by Walker.

7 Issued a credit memorandum for $350 to the Phipps Company for defective merchandise sold on June 1.
8 Purchased a computer on account for business use from Data Resources for $11,400, terms n/eom.
10 Received the proper amount due from Phipps Company.
13 Paid the proper amount due to Walker Enterprises.
14 Received a purchase order from Uptown Distributing for merchandise having a list price of $5,500. The order was subject to a 30% trade discount and terms of 3/10, n/30. Haden shipped the merchandise F.O.B. shipping point and prepaid $75 of freight charges as a convenience to Uptown.
21 Phipps returned an additional $400 of the goods purchased on June 1. Because Phipps had already paid for the merchandise, Haden issued a cash refund.
29 Received the proper amount due from Uptown Distributing.
30 Paid the amount due to Data Resources.

INSTRUCTIONS

Prepare journal entries for the June transactions, assuming Haden uses the gross method of accounting for purchases. All terms of sale are strictly followed.

P4-2 ***Gross versus net purchases methods***

Beautiful Face operates several small cosmetics stores in shopping malls. During July store no. 108 had the following purchases transactions:

July 7 Purchased $950 of cosmetics on account from Lovely Lady, terms 2/10, n/30. Freight charges of $25 were prepaid by Lovely Lady and appear on the invoice.
12 Purchased $125 of store supplies on account from Atlas Office Supplies.
14 Returned $30 of the supplies purchased on July 12.
17 Purchased $450 of cosmetics on account from the Charles Norman Company, terms 1/10, n/30.
20 Paid the proper amount due to Lovely Lady.
21 Returned $80 of the cosmetics purchased on July 17 because of a shipping error made by the Charles Norman Company.
26 Paid the proper amount due to the Charles Norman Company.

INSTRUCTIONS

a Record the transactions above, assuming Beautiful Face uses the gross method of accounting for purchases. All terms of sale are strictly followed.

b Record the transactions above, assuming Beautiful Face uses the net method of accounting for purchases. All terms of sale are strictly followed.

P4-3 ***Periodic inventory method and theft***

The Hopkins Company uses a periodic inventory system. On December 31 a hand-count inventory revealed $29,900 of goods owned by the firm. This figure is included in the cost-of-goods-sold computation on the following income statement:

HOPKINS COMPANY
Income Statement
For the Year Ended December 31, 1983

Net sales		$79,400
Cost of goods sold		
Beginning inventory	$25,600	
Add: Net purchases	62,400	
Goods available for sale	$88,000	
Less: Ending inventory	29,900	58,100
Gross profit		$21,300
Operating expenses		16,700
Net income		$ 4,600

INSTRUCTIONS

a Suppose Hopkins thinks that some theft and shoplifting occurred during the year. Explain the impact of the theft and shoplifting on ending inventory, cost of goods sold, and resulting net income.

b Automatically, because of the effect on ending inventory, in what section of the income statement would the cost of theft and shoplifting be included (and somewhat buried)?

c Is there anything Hopkins could do to improve inventory control so that the actual cost of theft and shoplifting can be pinpointed? Explain.

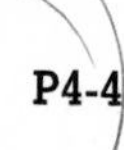

P4-4 ***Income statement construction and analysis***

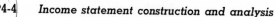

The William Sherwin Company sells paint, wallpaper, and related tools and supplies. The following balances appear in the accounts after adjustment on June 30, 1983, the close of the fiscal year.

Cash	$ 5,600	
Accounts receivable	7,750	
Inventory, July 1, 1982	25,480	
Prepaid insurance	2,400	
Supplies	790	
Store equipment	25,000	
Accumulated depreciation: store equipment		$ 7,500
Accounts payable		19,650
William Sherwin, capital		52,390
William Sherwin, drawing	15,600	
Sales: paint		55,920
Sales: wallpaper		38,620
Sales: tools & supplies		15,740
Sales returns & allowances	870	
Purchases	59,460	
Freight-in	2,130	
Purchases returns & allowances		650
Purchases discounts		280
Salaries expense	31,300	
Insurance expense	1,550	
Rent expense	9,600	
Supplies expense	1,820	
Depreciation expense	1,000	
Delivery expense	400	
	$190,750	$190,750

Sherwin's June 30, 1983, ending inventory was $29,925.

INSTRUCTIONS

a Prepare an income statement for the William Sherwin Company for the year ended June 30, 1983, in good form.

b Notice that Sherwin records sales by type: paint, wallpaper, and tools and supplies. What changes must be incorporated into Sherwin's record-keeping system to furnish additional profitability information to income statement users?

P4-5 *Income statement construction from partial information*

Kathy Brown has just been promoted to a new position in the accounting department of Continental Wholesale Corporation. To celebrate, she has taken her husband out to dinner. On arriving home later in the evening, Kathy is horrified to find that her dog had a good time eating some paperwork that was needed in a loan presentation the following morning. Rover completely destroyed Continental's income statement. In addition, he partially consumed the firm's balance sheet and some cash receipts and payments information. Kathy was able to salvage the following:

	12/31/82	12/31/83
Cash	$ 19,800	$ 25,500
Accounts receivable	68,800	63,600
Merchandise inventory	115,700	121,400
Equipment (net of accumulated depreciation)	25,100	22,900
Accounts payable	70,400	75,300

All merchandise purchases and sales were made on account. There were no purchases or sales of equipment during 1983. Operating expenses, except for depreciation, were paid as incurred. Fragmented evidence left by Rover showed the following:

Payments to suppliers for merchandise amounted to $421,100.
Receipts from customers on account amounted to $589,400.
The owners had withdrawn $46,000 during the year.

INSTRUCTIONS

Using the accrual basis of accounting, prepare the 1983 income statement of Continental Wholesale Corporation.

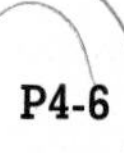

P4-6 ***Work sheet, financial statements, and closing entries***

The Clayton Company has the following trial balance as of December 31:

Cash	$ 18,900	
Accounts receivable	27,400	
Merchandise inventory, Jan. 1	38,600	
Prepaid advertising	12,400	
Supplies	3,700	
Equipment	89,600	
Accumulated depreciation: equipment		$ 24,800
Accounts payable		30,600
D. Clayton, capital		145,800
D. Clayton, drawing	26,000	
Sales		286,800
Sales returns & allowances	5,700	
Sales discounts	2,000	
Purchases	174,500	
Freight-in	4,400	
Purchases returns & allowances		1,900
Purchases discounts		3,300
Wage expense	58,500	
Insurance expense	2,600	
Rent expense	16,500	
Freight-out	3,800	
Utilities expense	8,600	
	$493,200	$493,200

Additional accounts maintained by the business include Wages Payable, Income Summary, Advertising Expense, Supplies Expense, and Depreciation Expense. Clayton's accountant has derived the following adjustment data:

1 Advertising applicable to future periods: $7,700.
2 Supplies on hand: $2,100.
3 Depreciation on the equipment: $5,500.
4 Accrued wages: $1,500.

Clayton's capital account includes $4,000 of owner investments made during the year. The December 31 physical inventory count revealed that goods costing $47,900 remained on hand.

INSTRUCTIONS

a Complete a work sheet in good form for the Clayton Company for the year ended December 31.

b Prepare an income statement, statement of owners' equity, and balance sheet in good form.

c Record Clayton's closing entries in the journal.

P4-7 ***Merchandising journal entries (alternate to P4-1)***

The Nolan Corporation had the following transactions during March:

March 2 Purchased $9,200 of merchandise on account from Thomas Company, terms 1/10, n/eom. The merchandise was shipped F.O.B. shipping point; freight charges amounted to $120 and were paid by Thomas.

4 Sold $4,100 of merchandise on account to Moritz Company, terms 2/10, n/30.

9 Purchased office furniture on account for business use from Victory Office Equipment for $5,800, terms n/eom.

10 Issued a credit memorandum for $500 to Moritz Company for merchandise shipped in error on March 4.

11 Paid the proper amount due to Thomas Company.

13 Received the proper amount due from Moritz Company.

16 Received a purchase order from USA Imports for merchandise having a list price of $7,700. The order was subject to a 20% trade discount and terms of 2/10, n/30. Nolan shipped the merchandise F.O.B. shipping point and prepaid $110 of freight charges as a convenience to USA.

21 Moritz returned an additional $300 of the goods purchased on March 4. Because Moritz had already paid for the merchandise, Nolan issued a cash refund.

30 Received the proper amount due from USA Imports.

31 Paid the amount due to Victory Office Equipment.

INSTRUCTIONS

Prepare journal entries for the March transactions, assuming Nolan uses the gross method of accounting for purchases. All terms of sale are strictly followed.

P4-8 ***Gross versus net purchases methods (alternate to P4-2)***

Magic Cutlery operates several small cutlery shops in shopping malls. During June store no. 875F had the following purchases transactions:

June 4 Purchased $1,200 of knives on account from Wilkerson, Inc., terms 2/10, n/30. Freight charges of $50 were prepaid by Wilkerson and appear on the invoice.

10 Purchased $200 of store supplies on account from Barnwell Office Supplies.

12 Returned $40 of the supplies purchased on June 10.

18 Purchased $1,450 of scissors on account from the Arthur Wise Company, terms 1/10, n/30.

20 Paid the proper amount due to Wilkerson, Inc.

23 Returned $150 of the scissors purchased on June 18 because of an overshipment of left-handed scissors.

27 Paid the proper amount due to the Arthur Wise Company.

INSTRUCTIONS

a Record the transactions above, assuming Magic Cutlery uses the gross method of accounting for purchases. All terms of sale are strictly followed.

b Record the transactions above, assuming Magic Cutlery uses the net method of accounting for purchases. All terms of sale are strictly followed.

P4-9 ***Income statement construction and analysis (alternate to P4-4)***

The Kowalski Company sells musical instruments, sheet music, and miscellaneous accessories. The following balances appear in the accounts after adjustment on August 31, 1983, the close of the fiscal year.

Cash	$ 6,400	
Accounts receivable	9,800	
Inventory, Sept. 1, 1982	24,200	
Prepaid advertising	3,500	
Office supplies	1,200	
Store equipment	19,400	
Accumulated depreciation: store equipment		$ 8,700
Accounts payable		11,300
Ralph Kowalski, capital		50,500
Ralph Kowalski, drawing	15,000	
Instrument sales		72,000
Sheet music sales		15,900
Accessories sales		22,600
Sales returns & allowances	3,100	
Purchases	64,000	
Freight-in	900	
Purchases returns & allowances		2,200
Purchases discounts		3,000
Wage expense	18,500	
Insurance expense	1,400	
Advertising expense	7,300	
Rent expense	9,600	
Supplies expense	800	
Depreciation expense	1,100	
	$186,200	$186,200

Kowalski's August 31, 1983, ending inventory was $30,100.

INSTRUCTIONS

a Prepare an income statement for the Kowalski Company for the year ended August 31, 1983, in good form.

b Notice that Kowalski records sales by type: instruments, sheet music, and accessories. What changes must be incorporated into Kowalski's record-keeping system to furnish additional profitability information to income statement users?

P4-10 ***Income statement construction from partial information (alternate to P4-5)***

Willie Johnson, recently promoted by Marvin Electric Company, was working on some financial statements at home when his eighteen-month-old son spilled a full cup of coffee on the papers. Only a few figures from the financial statements were readable. These figures are summarized as follows:

	12/31/82	12/31/83
Cash	$21,300	$28,750
Accounts receivable	54,700	52,500
Merchandise inventory	98,300	92,700
Equipment (net of accumulated depreciation)	20,400	28,900
Accounts payable	45,200	37,600

All merchandise purchases and sales were made on account. Equipment costing $12,000 was purchased for cash during 1983. Operating expenses, except for depreciation, were paid as incurred. Fragmented evidence undamaged by the coffee showed the following:

Payments to suppliers for merchandise amounted to $147,900.
Receipts from customers on account amounted to $282,400.
The owners had withdrawn $52,500 during the year.

INSTRUCTIONS
Using the accrual basis of accounting, prepare the 1983 income statement of Marvin Electric Company.

P4-11 ***Work sheet, financial statements, and closing entries (alternate to P4-6)***
The Ginn Company has the following trial balance as of December 31.

Cash	*$ 7,540*	
Accounts receivable	*11,980*	
Merchandise inventory, Jan. 1	*22,400*	
Prepaid insurance	*1,850*	
Store supplies	*2,630*	
Equipment	*38,500*	
Accumulated depreciation: equipment		*$ 12,650*
Accounts payable		*16,820*
R. Ginn, capital		*57,710*
R. Ginn, drawing	*19,000*	
Sales		*186,490*
Sales returns	*1,570*	
Sales discounts	*3,680*	
Purchases	*88,350*	
Freight-in	*1,970*	
Purchases returns		*520*
Purchases discounts		*1,750*
Salaries expense	*47,400*	
Advertising expense	*11,820*	
Rent expense	*10,800*	
Utilities expense	*2,460*	
Delivery expense	*3,990*	
	$275,940	*$275,940*

Additional accounts maintained by the business include Salaries Payable, Income Summary, Insurance Expense, Store Supplies Expense, and Depreciation Expense. Ginn's accountant has derived the following adjustment data:

1 Store supplies used: $880.
2 Insurance applicable to future periods: $1,020.
3 Depreciation on the equipment: $2,460.
4 Accrued salaries: $750.

Ginn's capital account includes $6,500 of owner investments made during the year. The December 31 physical inventory count revealed that goods costing $27,600 remained on hand.

INSTRUCTIONS

a Complete a work sheet in good form for the Ginn Company for the year ended December 31.

b Prepare an income statement, statement of owners' equity, and balance sheet in good form.

c Record Ginn's closing entries in the journal.

CASE 4
KWIK-KLEEN, INC.

Kwik-Kleen, Inc., is a medium-sized wholesaler of a broad line of industrial cleaning supplies. The company has experienced cash problems in recent months because its customers are not paying as promptly as they did in prior years. In fact, the average collection period has increased by 25%, from 20 to 25 days.

Kwik-Kleen sells on terms of 1/10, n/30. In an attempt to improve collections a new provision was added to the current credit terms to encourage more prompt payment by customers. An interest penalty of 1% per month would be applied to all account balances that are outstanding for more than 30 days. Kwik-Kleen selected the 1% per month rate because of its experience with a local bank. Management had recently negotiated a favorable 11% annual rate on a loan when most businesses were paying as much as 15% annually. The 1% rate charged to customers is 12% on an annual basis or one percentage point higher than the rate the company is paying.

After three months' experience with the revised credit terms, the average collection period did not improve. To achieve the original objective of reducing the length of time in which payments are received, Kwik-Kleen's CPA has presented two alternatives to top management:

1 Increase the cash discount from 1% to 2% and maintain the 1% per month interest penalty.

2 Increase the interest penalty from 1% to $1\frac{1}{2}$% per month and maintain the 1% cash discount.

INSTRUCTIONS

a To finance current operations and purchases of inventory, many businesses must obtain short-term loans. Explain to management why the 1% per month interest penalty did not reduce Kwik-Kleen's average collection period.

b Discuss each of the two alternatives presented to Kwik-Kleen's top management in terms of (1) their attractiveness to customers and (2) their attractiveness to Kwik-Kleen, Inc.

(CMA modified.)

5 INFORMATION-PROCESSING SYSTEMS AND INTERNAL CONTROL

LEARNING OBJECTIVES

After reading this chapter you should:

1 Understand the concept of an audit trail.

2 Understand what internal controls are and how they are integrated into an accounting system.

3 Be able to distinguish between administrative controls and accounting controls.

4 Understand the Foreign Corrupt Practices Act and its implications for accountants.

5 Be familiar with the relationship between control accounts and subsidiary ledgers.

6 Understand how special journals are used in an accounting system and the procedures related to special journals.

7 Be familiar with the interaction between accounting and computers, including the advantages and problems arising from such interaction.

CHAPTER 5

The creation and flow of information concerns many individuals engaged in day-to-day business operations. Large volumes of data must be processed into information usable by management and other readers of financial statements. From the material presented in the first four chapters of this text, you may think that the generation of information is a relatively straightforward and simple operation. Unfortunately, many problems can arise. Managers frequently complain that (1) they lack the necessary information to properly perform their duties and (2) reports arrive too late to be useful. Furthermore, some employees are so overwhelmed with computer printouts that there is not enough time in a working day to study all the facts flowing across their desks.

The network that processes transactions and ultimately produces financial statements and other reports is known as an **accounting information system.** An accounting information system generates financial information from data by utilizing a set of people, procedures, and facilities. Observe the distinction between information and data. **Information** is meaningful data that is used in reporting, planning, control, and decision-making activities. **Data,** on the other hand, refers to facts and figures. An example will help to clarify the difference. Throughout an accounting period a business participates in numerous activities, many of which culminate in a transaction. The individual transactions are recorded and then grouped, totaled, and summarized for inclusion in the financial statements. The financial statements, in turn, are used by investors, creditors, and other parties to analyze financial condition and profitability. The individual transactions are facts and figures (or data); that is, the raw material for generation of the final account balances. When organized, processed, summarized, and employed in the reporting and management process, the data becomes information.

SYSTEM FEATURES

Successful information-processing systems possess several common characteristics. Although a detailed discussion of some of these characteristics is clearly suited for a more advanced text, two features deserve attention at this early stage in your accounting education. Successful accounting systems contain a good *audit trail* and adequate *internal control.*

Audit Trails

Recall from Chapter 1 that the credibility of financial statements is strengthened through the audit process. Among its many activities, auditing includes an independent examination of the accounting records. The auditor is concerned that the financial statements result in a fair presentation of business activity. Accordingly, the auditor must determine if appropriate accounting standards and principles have been implemented and whether the financial statements are free from material error.

A considerable portion of the auditor's work involves verification of the transactions and the information on which the financial statements are based. Verification is achieved by verbal inquiry, observation, examination, confirmation by letter, and, frequently, the tracing of transactions through an accounting system from start to finish. To explain the latter, an amount appearing in a general ledger account may be selected for examination. The auditor can proceed backward through the system to determine the correctness of the amount. The original journal entry is examined along with the related documentation (e.g., an invoice) that initiated the entry. This process is facilitated if the accounting system contains an adequate **audit trail,** that is, a means to trace and access the details that underlie summarized information.

The use of posting references helps to create this audit trail. To illustrate, we present Exhibit 5-1. Notice how the Advertising Expense balance of $1,170 on the income statement of Aspen Enterprises can be traced back to general ledger account no. 516. The source of each entry in the ledger account is indicated in the posting reference column. Thus if the $650 charge on January 24 were to be verified, the proper journal entry should be found on page 3 of the general journal. The entry on page 3 informs the auditor or any other person doing verification work that the $650 expenditure represents a payment to Modern Media, Inc. Working backward even further, Aspen has probably maintained a file of its paid invoices and canceled checks. If this is the case, an individual seeking to verify the transaction need only locate Modern Media's invoice and Aspen's canceled check no. 126.

Our example has shown that the audit trail helps the accountant gather evidence. Realize, however, that the example is somewhat simplistic; companies often process thousands of transactions each day. An inadequate audit trail significantly increases the time and cost of tracing the details of operating activity when specific information is needed.

Internal Control

Errors frequently occur when data is processed through an accounting system. These errors may be accidental or intentional, the latter resulting from employee sabotage, fraud, and/or embezzlement. Although the design of a perfect system that detects and prevents all errors is an impossibility, various features can and should be built into a system to minimize the probability of error occurrence. These features are known collectively as **internal controls.** The American Institute of Certified Public Accountants defines internal control as

> *. . . the plan of organization and all of the coordinate methods and measures adopted within a business to safeguard its assets, check the accuracy and reliability of its accounting data, promote operational efficiency, and encourage adherence to prescribed managerial policies.*[1]

Internal controls are often subdivided into administrative and accounting controls. **Administrative controls,** including such activities as produc-

[1] American Institute of Certified Public Accountants, *Codification on Auditing Standards—Numbers 1 to 23* (New York: AICPA, 1979), p. 53.

Exhibit 5-1

The audit trail

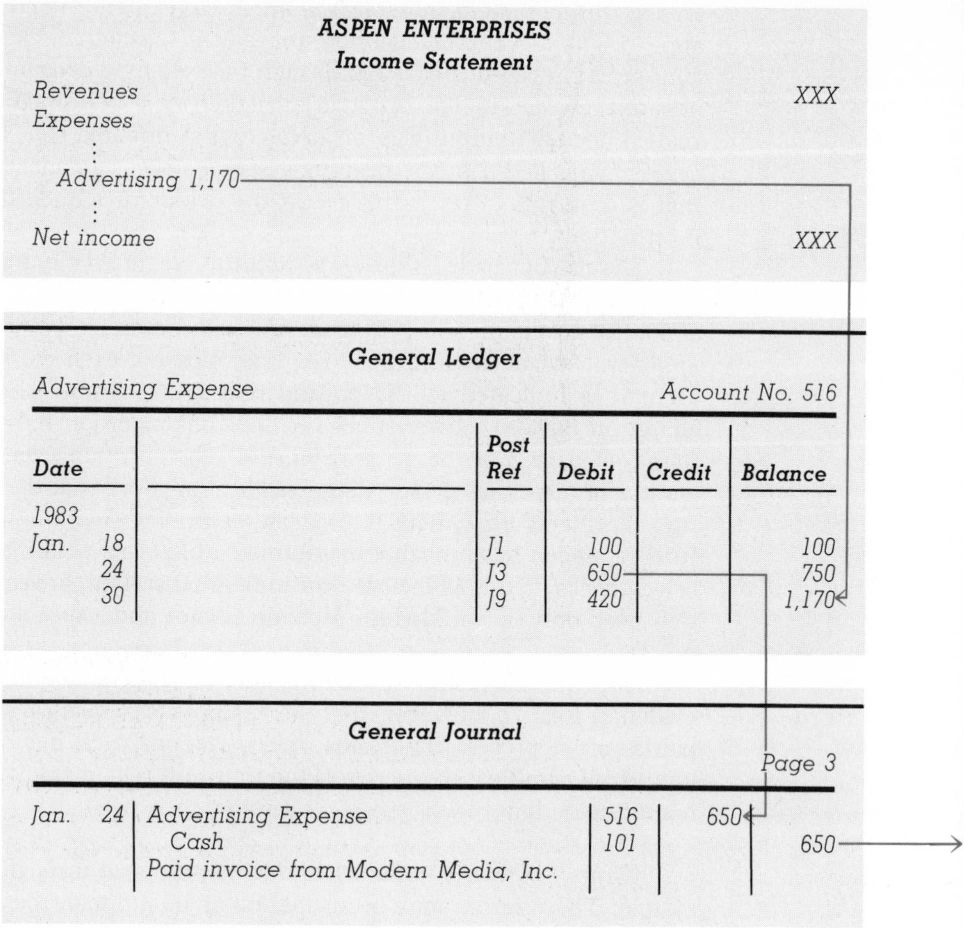

ASPEN ENTERPRISES
Income Statement

Revenues	XXX
Expenses	
⋮	
Advertising 1,170	
⋮	
Net income	XXX

General Ledger

Advertising Expense — Account No. 516

Date			Post Ref	Debit	Credit	Balance
1983						
Jan.	18		J1	100		100
	24		J3	650		750
	30		J9	420		1,170

General Journal

Page 3

Jan.	24	Advertising Expense	516	650	
		Cash	101		650
		Paid invoice from Modern Media, Inc.			

tion quality control, employee training programs, and statistical analysis, are established to promote operational efficiency and encourage adherence to management policies. In contrast, **accounting controls** assist a firm in protecting its assets and checking the reliability and accuracy of the financial information generated. You are probably very familiar with some commonly used accounting controls. For example, did you ever notice the following?

Checks and other important documents are usually prenumbered.

Cash registers and similar devices normally make a noise (buzz, bell rings) when they are opened.

Two signatures are required on some checks.

Often when obtaining a cash refund in a store, the refund must be authorized by someone in a managerial capacity.

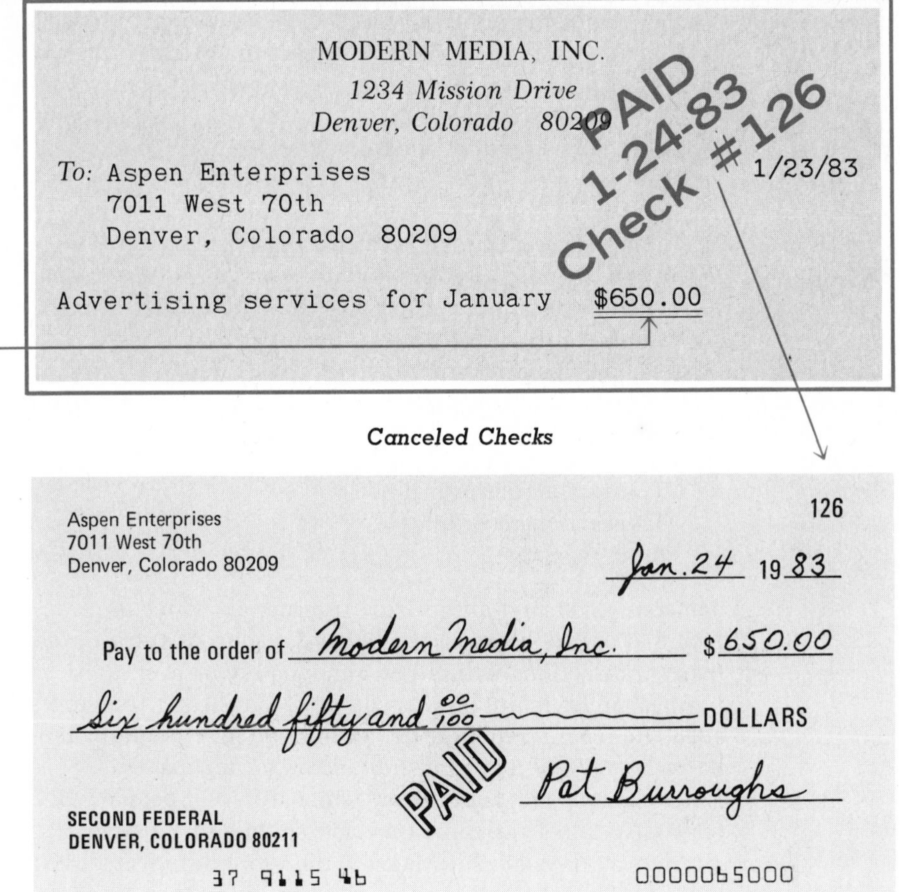
Paid Invoice File

MODERN MEDIA, INC.
1234 Mission Drive
Denver, Colorado 80209

PAID
1-24-83
Check #126

1/23/83

To: Aspen Enterprises
7011 West 70th
Denver, Colorado 80209

Advertising services for January $650.00

Canceled Checks

Aspen Enterprises
7011 West 70th
Denver, Colorado 80209

126

Jan. 24 1983

Pay to the order of Modern Media, Inc. $650.00

Six hundred fifty and 00/100 DOLLARS

PAID

Pat Burroughs

SECOND FEDERAL
DENVER, COLORADO 80211

37 9115 46 0000065000

All these procedures are types of accounting controls and, incidentally, of keen interest to accountants. Why? Accounting controls have a direct bearing on the financial statements. Weak controls can lead to a loss of assets and incorrect reports of financial condition and profitability.

Although controls vary extensively from business to business, the following general control features should be incorporated into most accounting systems.

Limited access to assets

The safeguarding of assets is a stated objective of internal control. One way to achieve this objective is by **limiting the access to assets** to only a few authorized personnel. Limited access may take different forms. For example, customers normally are not permitted in the back of a store to roam freely through the merchandise awaiting sale. This area is reserved for employees only. Furthermore, access to a company's computer and valuable computer time and data files is usually gained only after a secret password is entered into a computer terminal. The password is known by a select few. And, finally, when many retail establishments close for business at the end of the day, the cash that has been collected is often counted in a locked room. All these procedures are designed to ensure that assets are adequately protected from theft and unauthorized use.

Separation of duties

Many different functions (duties) performed within a company pertain to the firm's financial activities. To improve the accuracy and reliability of financial information and protect the assets, a firm must provide for an adequate **separation of duties.** Incompatible duties or functions must be divided; that is, they must be performed by different employees.

To explain, three basic types of financial activities are performed within a business:

Transaction authorization
Transaction recording
Asset custody

Someone must first authorize a transaction. Later the transaction must be recorded on the books in the form of a journal entry. In addition, because many transactions will either immediately or eventually affect an asset, a business must maintain custody of or physically protect its assets. For an adequate separation of duties, authorization, recording, and custody should be performed by different individuals or departments. Separation of these functions helps to detect errors, since different people will be handling different aspects of the same transaction. The likelihood that an error will go all the way through the system is therefore diminished, because employees will, in effect, be checking each other's work.

In addition to assisting in error detection, separation of authorization, recording, and custody makes fraud and embezzlement more difficult. To illustrate, let us create a situation where an employee can steal a company's assets by altering the books of account. This situation arises if an individual who maintains physical control over an asset (custody) is also permitted to handle the asset's record keeping. Assume that Howard Shelton, a clerk for Weber's Clothing Store, has the authority to operate the firm's cash register to record sales. Shelton also assists Weber's bookkeeper on a part-time basis in recording transactions. Suppose that Steve Rocco, a charge customer, arrived at Weber's to pay his $150 bill. To keep matters simple, Rocco paid in cash rather than writing a check. If the transaction is handled properly, Shelton should enter the $150 receipt of cash on the register and place the money in the register's cash drawer. In addition, the following journal entry should be made:

Cash	*150*	
Accounts Receivable		*150*
Receipt on account from S. Rocco		

In this manner the $150 receipt in the cash drawer is represented by a $150 debit or increase to the Cash account in the general ledger.

Because duties are not separated, the following could easily occur. Rather than enter the $150 in the register, Shelton could steal the cash to help satisfy his own financial problems. He must still update the accounts to reflect Rocco's payment; however, Cash cannot be debited because an increase in the Cash account would not be matched by an increase in the cash drawer. Shelton, therefore, constructs the following entry:

Sales Returns & Allowances	*150*	
Accounts Receivable		*150*
Return on account from S. Rocco		

Rocco's receivable has been reduced to zero, and he will not be billed again. An invalid sales return has been recorded to cover the theft. Shelton has gained; Weber's has lost.

You should note two important points. First, this scheme would have been more difficult to undertake if Shelton had access to the register only rather than to both the books and the register. Of course, even if duties were separated, Shelton could conspire with the bookkeeper and the fraud would still be possible. Second, the intent of this example was not to be a primer entitled "How to Embezzle in One Easy Lesson." Its purpose was to show the importance of separating incompatible duties in order to improve accounting control.

Accountability procedures

A business can adopt different measures to achieve financial accountability. These measures, known as **accountability procedures,** may help to pinpoint responsibility within an organization, protect the assets, or detect errors. The measures vary depending on the size and nature of a business. Common accountability procedures include duty authorization, prenumbered documents, and verification of records.

Duty authorization

Pinpointing responsibility is essential in medium and large organizations. In small businesses many of the accounting and financial activities are handled by the owner/manager. In larger organizations, however, there are too many tasks for one individual to perform. Consequently, the accounting duties are divided among the various employees. Each employee is authorized to perform certain functions and, as a result, is held responsible or accountable for those functions.

Frequently, the actions taken by employees result in some form of documentation to provide the necessary basis for accountability. Did you ever notice, for example, that store clerks often initial customer checks, sales invoices, and other similar documents? These procedures assist management in pinpointing responsibility and are especially helpful should a question or problem arise. Management can quickly determine the employee responsible and then take any necessary corrective action.

Prenumbered documents

Important forms such as checks, sales invoices, and purchase orders are usually serially prenumbered and subsequently accounted for. During a review of these forms a missing document is easily spotted because of a break in the numbering scheme. An investigation can then commence to locate the source of the problem.

Verification of records

Another widely practiced accountability procedure is verification of company records by comparison with company assets. For example:

At the end of the day a cash register is emptied, and the cash collected is compared against the register's tape.

At the end of a month a business compares the amount of cash in its checkbook against a statement issued by the bank.

Periodically, a firm counts inventory and compares the actual hand count against a perpetual book count.

If the comparisons do not agree, suspicions may be raised regarding errors in the recording process or possible theft.

Qualified personnel

A business may limit access to assets, separate incompatible duties, and install many sophisticated accountability procedures. Yet all these elements of internal control will be wasted unless one other essential element is present, **qualified personnel.** A certain way to destroy any system is to introduce incompetency. It's like putting a ten-year-old child behind the wheel of a $150,000 city transit bus and telling him to "have a good time and go for a ride." The outcome is highly predictable.

In addition to being competent, employees must be honest. As we noted earlier, every accounting system can be beaten. This statement is especially true after employees have been working with a system and have gained knowledge of its design. Familiarity with design can result in circumvention of the system's built-in controls.

Several personnel practices have been implemented by businesses to reduce the likelihood of errors and losses due to fraud. Some firms administer polygraph (lie detector) examinations in the hiring process. Other companies bond certain employees who handle cash and other "desirable" assets by obtaining a fidelity bond. A **fidelity bond** is essentially an insurance policy that reimburses a company for losses suffered from the dishonest practices of bonded employees. Annual employee vacations are another popular personnel practice. A number of frauds have been committed by individuals who faithfully serve their employers year after year with no break for vacations. An employee could undertake an embezzlement scheme by slightly changing a specific accounting procedure each day that he or she is on the job. Because this alteration occurs with regularity, the theft can be concealed. By forcing all employees to take a vacation, it is possible that the regular routine will be broken and that the scheme will surface.

Independent review

Businesses continuously review and evaluate their accounting controls. In smaller companies the review is usually performed by the owner/manager or perhaps by another key employee. In larger firms an internal auditor frequently becomes involved.

This review process sometimes has several inherent problems. In smaller organizations the owner/manager or key employee may be too close to the action to take an objective look at the process being examined. Furthermore, the owner/manager may possess minimal knowledge about accounting controls. Turning to larger companies, the internal audit department may be viewed as just one of many departments in the organizational hierarchy. If the internal audit department is given little recognition and treated as a low-level operating unit, its audit findings will be lightly regarded.

The integrity of information systems and internal controls is strengthened by a review performed by an external party, namely, the independent auditor. Such a review is usually performed as a matter of course. The transactions processed through a system and its controls affect a business's financial statements. Because the auditor must express an opinion about the fairness of the statements, an evaluation must be made of the internal controls in operation.

The independent auditor's internal control evaluation is delivered to management for internal use. Occasionally, though, management makes comments to external parties concerning internal control practices. As an example, the following paragraphs were excerpted from a recent annual report of Scott Paper Company:

> *. . . Management has a system of internal accounting controls designed to provide reasonable assurance that assets are safeguarded, transactions are executed in accordance with management's authorization and financial records are reliable as a basis for preparation of financial statements. Management is continually modifying and improving its system of internal accounting controls in response to changes in business conditions and operations. Continuous support for this system is provided by the Company's internal audit staff through their periodic audits of Scott's worldwide operations . . . .*
>
> *The Company's Board of Directors has had an Audit Committee composed solely of outside directors since 1969. This Committee reviews the Company's accounting controls and policies as well as its practices in financial reporting to shareholders and the public. It*

meets on a timely basis with the internal auditors, the independent accountants and management to review their work and to ensure that each is properly fulfilling its responsibilities. In addition, the independent accountants meet periodically with the Committee, without management present, to discuss the results of their audit work and related matters.

Costs and benefits

Any business can design a system with elaborate controls. But exactly how far should companies go? Should a very small business hire several additional employees just to maintain an adequate separation of duties? Should a company bond an employee who, on a part-time basis, issues cash refunds to customers? For many businesses these and related questions are difficult to answer.

When designing and installing specific internal controls, the accountant must treat each business individually, because no two businesses are alike. The accountant must study the errors that can occur and the probability of occurrence. Once the probability is determined, controls must be selected for which the *benefits of use exceed the costs of implementation and operation.* If this practice is followed, an organization will have a positive and financially beneficial approach to internal control.

Foreign Corrupt Practices Act

During the 1970s the American public began to question the ethical conduct of U.S. businesses engaged in international trade. The public was shocked to learn that corporations had paid hundreds of millions of dollars in bribes or questionable payments to foreign firms, governments, and political officials. After considerable deliberation Congress enacted the **Foreign Corrupt Practices Act (FCPA),** which outlaws these payments and makes them a criminal offense. Companies in violation of the FCPA can be fined up to $1 million. In addition, directors, officers, and stockholders of offending companies can be fined up to $10,000 and/or imprisoned for up to five years.

The FCPA has had a significant impact on accountants. Many of the questionable payments involved falsifying accounting records or maintaining secret funds that were not carried on a business's books. On occasion these practices were conducted without the knowledge of top management. To help curtail the preceding problems, the FCPA requires large corporations to follow certain record-keeping and internal control provisions. Reasonably detailed records must be kept, which accurately depict financial activities. Furthermore, internal control systems must provide reasonable assurance that transactions are properly authorized by management and recorded and that access to assets is limited. These requirements have been practiced for many years; the FCPA, however, now makes their absence a violation of the law.

Ernst & Whinney, a Big Eight CPA firm, makes two realistic observations about the FCPA. First, they note the following:

> *While a company making illegal foreign bribes can be fined up to $1,000,000, there are no stated financial penalties for violations of the accounting provisions. However, such violations may subject a company to other sanctions under the federal securities laws and the embarrassment of adverse publicity. This is in addition to the possible effect of misleading financial statements or unauthorized loss of assets that may arise from the deficiency in the system of internal accounting control.*[2]

And in reinforcement of a point made earlier in this chapter, they observe:

> *The legislative history indicates that the accounting provisions were enacted to strengthen the anti-bribery rules. The intent was to require companies to install and maintain accounting systems which would prevent or detect foreign bribes. However, it should not be concluded that compliance with the accounting provisions achieves the purpose of preventing or detecting all foreign bribes. Even the best system of internal control may not prevent or detect employee collusion or circumvention.*[3]

TYPES OF SYSTEMS

Having introduced you to audit trails and internal control, we can now proceed with a description of several different types of processing systems. The systems range in scope from the simple to the sophisticated; all are found in practice.

Journal/Ledger System

The general journal/general ledger processing system was introduced in Chapter 2. In this system transactions are listed chronologically in the general journal and then posted to accounts in the general ledger. The ledger serves to summarize the various transactions that affect a given account. The processing is orderly and appears to be efficient. When the volume of transactions is small, this system is acceptable, since it provides a business with some basic information-processing capability. There are, however, several problems with the general journal/general ledger system, which will be illustrated shortly.

Special Journals

A step above the general journal/general ledger system is a system that employs special journals. As their name implies, **special journals** handle specialized (specific) types of transactions. A business will normally find this type of system beneficial whenever it has a large number of a given type of transaction to process. The following special journals are commonly encountered:

---

[2]Ernst & Whinney, *The Foreign Corrupt Practices Act: Focus on Internal Control,* September 1978, p. 3.
[3]Ibid.

Journal	Transactions Contained
Sales journal	Sales of merchandise on account
Purchases journal	Purchases of merchandise on account
Cash receipts journal	All cash receipts
Cash payments journal	All cash payments

We will concentrate on these four journals. If needed, special journals may also be established to record sales returns and purchases returns.

Advantages

Special journals offer two distinct advantages to the user. First, they allow a company to spread its work load, since each journal can be maintained by a different employee. All credit sales can be accounted for by one person, all cash receipts by another, and so on. Second, special journals significantly reduce the amount of posting necessary to process transactions. A short example will illustrate the bookkeeping efficiency associated with special journals and, at the same time, explain the use and operation of the sales journal. Before this example can be presented, however, the concept of subsidiary ledgers and control accounts must be explored.

Subsidiary ledgers and control accounts

Earlier in the text the general ledger was defined to contain the various accounts that appear on a company's financial statements. Frequently, it is necessary to divide the balances appearing in several of these accounts into further detail. Common examples include the following:

General Ledger Account	Subdivided by
Accounts Receivable	Customer
Accounts Payable	Creditor
Merchandise Inventory	Individual inventory items
Salary Expense	Department

A business must keep track of the amounts owed by each customer, the balances owed to individual creditors, and other specific information. Separate accounts are therefore established for each of these subdivisions. These accounts are collectively known as a **subsidiary ledger,** that is, a group of lower-level accounts that comprise a general ledger account. The general ledger account that is composed of subsidiary ledger accounts is, in turn, known as a **control account.** A separate subsidiary ledger is established for each control account a company uses.

If all accounting procedures are properly followed, the balance in a control account should equal the sum of the individual account balances contained within its subsidiary ledger. Thus if Football, Inc., lists $15,000 of Accounts Receivable on its December 31 balance sheet, the subsidiary ledger should contain customer accounts whose balances total $15,000. The equality between the subsidiary ledger and control account is checked on a periodic basis, often monthly, when a supporting schedule is prepared. The schedule is a listing of each account in the subsidiary ledger along with the account's balance. The schedule of Accounts Receivable for Football, Inc., appears in Exhibit 5-2.

Exhibit 5-2

FOOTBALL, INC.
Schedule of Accounts Receivable
December 31, 1983

Earl Dorsett	$ 4,000
Dan Harris	3,000
Richard Simpson	2,500
Jack Younger	5,500
	$15,000

Sales journal

As we stated earlier, the **sales journal** is employed to record sales of merchandise on account. To illustrate its use and the bookkeeping efficiency associated with special journals, we will examine the processing techniques of Stereo Unlimited. The firm, a wholesale distributor of stereo equipment, records and tapes, and miscellaneous accessories, had the following credit sales during January:

Jan. 4 Sold $1,350 of stereo equipment on account (invoice no. 101) to House of Music.
12 Opened an account for the Sound Center and sold $400 of records and tapes on account (invoice no. 102).
18 Sold $150 of stereo accessories on account (invoice no. 103) to Treetops Disco.
25 Sold $1,200 of stereo equipment and $200 of records and tapes on account (invoice no. 104) to Wallace's Hi-Fi Shop.

If Stereo Unlimited employed only a general journal, the following entry would be made for the transaction on January 4:

1983					
Jan.	4	Accounts Receivable: House of Music		1,350	
		Sales			1,350
		Sale on account; invoice no. 101			

Accounts Receivable must be debited to record the appropriate increase. In view of the previously mentioned control account/subsidiary ledger relationship, a separate account for House of Music is established in the Accounts Receivable subsidiary ledger. Like Accounts Receivable control, House of Music's account is also debited for $1,350. The Sales account is credited to complete the transaction. Stereo Unlimited's general and subsidiary ledgers after posting appear in Exhibit 5-3.

Exhibit 5-3

Posting the general journal

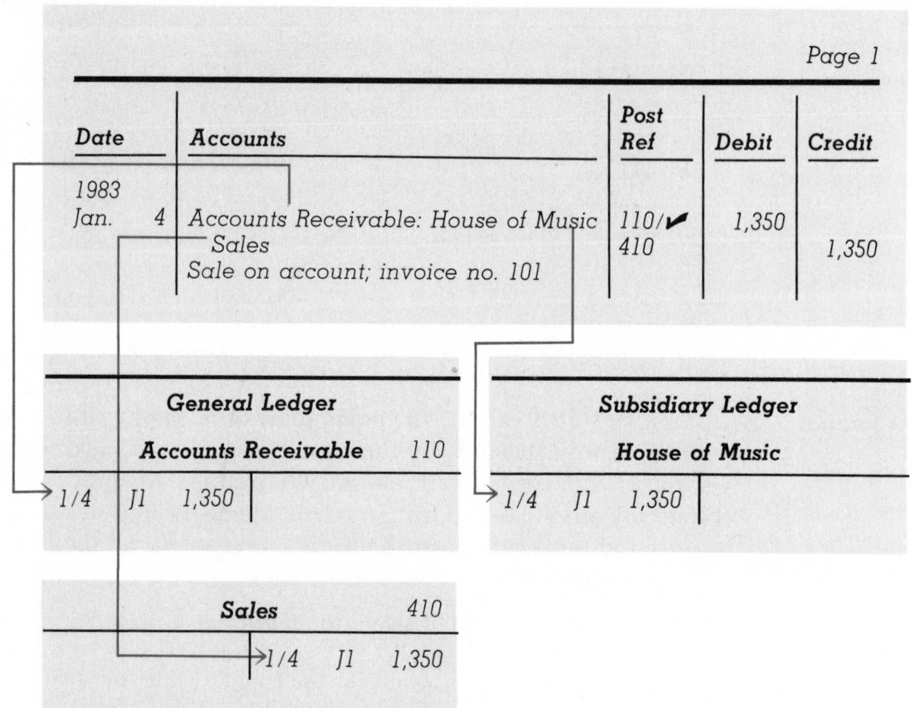

The posting reference column in the general journal contains a new feature (110/✓), because the $1,350 debit is posted to two places: account no. 110 in the general ledger and House of Music's account in the subsidiary ledger. House of Music's account does not have an account number; thus a check mark is used to indicate completion of the posting process. Many companies do not assign account numbers when dealing with individual customer and creditor accounts. Instead the subsidiary ledger is arranged alphabetically, thereby allowing for expansion and contraction without having to modify numbering schemes.

Observe that the balance in the control account (Accounts Receivable no. 110) is equal to the sum of the account balances in the subsidiary ledger (House of Music). The trial balance, when constructed, will contain *only* general ledger accounts. Therefore debits of $1,350 (Accounts Receivable control) will equal credits of $1,350 (Sales).

One basic problem should be evident from this illustration: three postings (Accounts Receivable, House of Music, and Sales) were necessary to record the debits and credits in the proper accounts. A total of twelve postings would therefore be required to process the four January transactions. As you can well imagine, the bookkeeping that accompanies a large number of monthly transactions would be overwhelming. A sales journal can be used to help overcome this problem. Keep our objectives in mind: We must update the customer's account, the Accounts Receivable control account, and Sales. Rather than post each individual sale to Accounts Receivable and Sales, we can achieve the same result by posting the total sales figure to these two accounts. Individual sales, however, must still be posted to the subsidiary ledger. Stereo Unlimited's sales journal, general ledger, and subsidiary ledger appear in Exhibit 5-4.

Posting the sales journal

After the date, customer, invoice number, and amount have been entered in the sales journal, the posting process can begin. The date and amount of each sale are posted daily to the appropriate customer's account in the subsidiary ledger. Daily posting is necessary to keep up-to-date customer balances. To signify completion of posting to the ledger and to provide an audit trail, one enters the notation S1 (sales journal, page 1) as a reference in the customer's account. Finally, a check mark is placed in the sales journal to indicate that the transaction was transferred to the subsidiary ledger. The process is repeated until all transactions are posted.

The control account must now be updated to maintain the necessary equality. Since the only type of transaction recorded in the sales journal is a sale of merchandise on account, the total of the sales journal is posted periodically (often monthly) as a debit to Accounts Receivable and a credit to Sales. The notation S1 is then entered in the Accounts Receivable and Sales accounts in the general ledger. To complete the posting process the numbers of the accounts to which the $3,300 was posted, 110 and 410, are written beneath the total. With a special journal the four transactions are transferred to the proper accounts by a total of six postings (Accounts Receivable, four customer accounts, and Sales), half the number required if only a general journal is used. As the number of credit sales increase, the savings in postings becomes more pronounced. (The end result of the posting process can be seen by viewing Stereo Unlimited's general and subsidiary ledgers, which appear in Exhibit 5-9 on pages 190–194.)

Journal variations

The journals illustrated in this chapter are general models that can be altered to meet the needs of individual businesses. For example, if a company was charging its customers for sales taxes, an additional column could be added in the sales journal to accumulate the total sales taxes collected.

The modification of journals to meet specific needs can be shown by returning to the Stereo Unlimited example. Suppose Stereo Unlimited de-

Exhibit 5-4

Sales journal and related postings

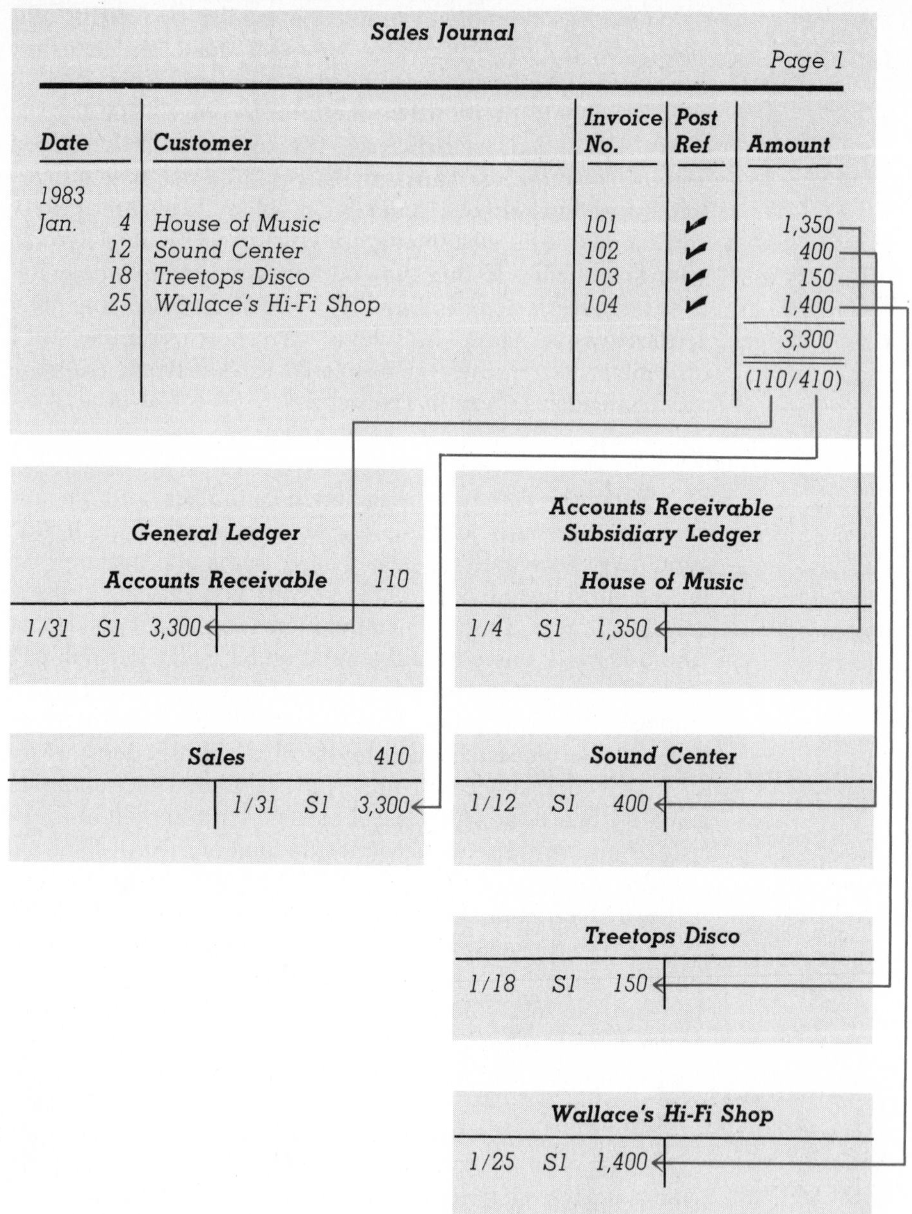

Sales Journal

Page 1

Date		Customer	Invoice No.	Post Ref	Amount
1983					
Jan.	4	House of Music	101	✓	1,350
	12	Sound Center	102	✓	400
	18	Treetops Disco	103	✓	150
	25	Wallace's Hi-Fi Shop	104	✓	1,400
					3,300
					(110/410)

sires to report its sales by product line. As shown in Exhibit 5-5, a slight modification of the sales journal will generate the required information.

General Ledger
Accounts Receivable 110
1/31 S1 3,300
Sales 410
1/31 S1 3,300
Accounts Receivable Subsidiary Ledger
House of Music
1/4 S1 1,350
Sound Center
1/12 S1 400
Treetops Disco
1/18 S1 150
Wallace's Hi-Fi Shop
1/25 S1 1,400

As before, individual entries in the Accounts Receivable column are posted daily as debits to customer accounts in the subsidiary ledger. At the end of the month the journal is totaled and the equality of debits ($3,300) and credits ($2,550 + $600 + $150 = $3,300) is determined. To maintain

Exhibit 5-5

Sales journal to accumulate product line information

Sales Journal

Page 1

Date		Customer	Invoice No.	Post Ref	Accounts Receivable Dr	Stereo Equipment Sales Cr	Record and Tape Sales Cr	Accessories Sales Cr
1983								
Jan.	4	House of Music	101	✓	1,350	1,350		
	12	Sound Center	102	✓	400		400	
	18	Treetops Disco	103	✓	150			150
	25	Wallace's Hi-Fi Shop	104	✓	1,400	1,200	200	
					3,300	2,550	600	150
					(110)	(411)	(412)	(413)

the necessary equality with the subsidiary ledger, one then posts the $3,300 debit total to the Accounts Receivable control account. When the single-column sales journal was used, the $3,300 total was also posted as a credit to the Sales account. Now, with sales being subdivided, $2,550 is posted as a credit to a newly established Stereo Equipment Sales account in the general ledger, $600 to a Record and Tape Sales account, and $150 to Accessories Sales.[4]

We have stressed the superiority of the sales journal over the general journal in terms of bookkeeping efficiency. When a company has few credit sales, however, there is no need to establish a formal sales journal. Instead the sales invoices that arise from credit sales may be bound together in numerical order. Individual invoices are then posted to customer accounts in the subsidiary ledger, and the invoices' total is posted periodically to the Accounts Receivable control and Sales accounts.

Purchases journal

The **purchases journal** is used to record only one type of transaction, purchases of merchandise on account. Other types of purchases, such as cash purchases of merchandise and purchases of equipment on account, are recorded elsewhere. The proper procedures for these latter acquisitions will be illustrated shortly.

Every purchase of merchandise on account increases a company's total purchases and liabilities. Thus the Purchases account must be debited and

[4]This journal was employed strictly to illustrate that variations in journal design are possible. We will assume that Stereo Unlimited uses the sales journal shown in Exhibit 5-4 and does not divide sales by product line.

Accounts Payable must be credited. Because a business needs detailed information regarding the balances owed to each supplier, an Accounts Payable subsidiary ledger is established. As before, the sum of the individual accounts in the subsidiary ledger must equal the balance in the control account (Accounts Payable in this case).

Exhibit 5-6

Purchases journal and related postings

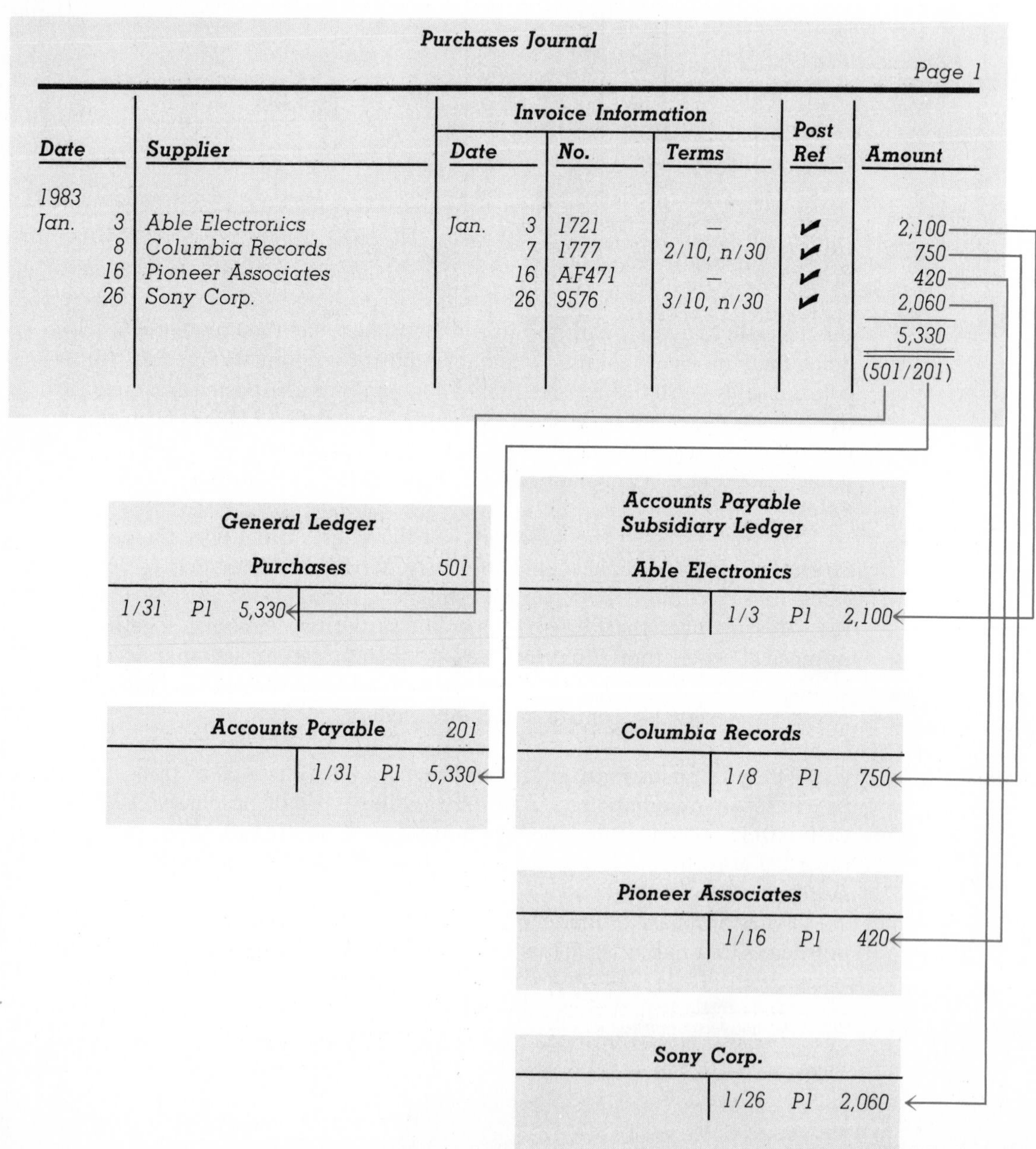

Purchases Journal

Page 1

Date		Supplier	Invoice Information Date		No.	Terms	Post Ref	Amount
1983								
Jan.	3	Able Electronics	Jan.	3	1721	—	✓	2,100
	8	Columbia Records		7	1777	2/10, n/30	✓	750
	16	Pioneer Associates		16	AF471	—	✓	420
	26	Sony Corp.		26	9576	3/10, n/30	✓	2,060
								5,330
								(501/201)

Stereo Unlimited's purchases journal and related postings appear in Exhibit 5-6. Individual amounts for purchases are credited daily to suppliers' accounts in the Accounts Payable subsidiary ledger, because the balances owed have increased. As before, completion of posting is denoted by placing a check mark in the journal. The journal's total is then posted monthly as a debit to the Purchases account and a credit to Accounts Payable control. The P1 references in the ledger accounts indicate that the entries were transferred from page 1 of the purchases journal.

Overall, you should have observed a very close parallel between the sales and purchases journals:

Individual amounts affecting subsidiary ledgers are posted daily to the subsidiary ledger accounts.

Totals affecting control accounts are posted monthly to the general ledger.

Cash receipts journal

A company receives cash from many different sources, including cash sales, customer payments on account, the sale of old equipment, bank loans, and owner investments. The possibilities are numerous. The **cash receipts journal** must therefore have multiple amount columns since all cash receipts are recorded here. Separate columns are normally established for transactions that occur frequently, such as cash sales, customer payments on account, and so on.

Stereo Unlimited had the following cash receipts during January:

Jan. 2 Patricia Monroe, owner of Stereo Unlimited, invested $2,000 in the business.

9 Sold $650 of stereo equipment and $150 of tapes for cash to Central Stereo.

13 Received a check from the House of Music in payment of its purchase on January 4, less the correct discount.

17 California Trust Company granted Stereo Unlimited a $4,800 loan to acquire several new display cases.

22 Sold $100 of records and $100 of accessories to Burrows Music Company for cash.

28 The Sound Center paid the balance due from its purchase on January 12.

Proper recording of these transactions is shown in Exhibit 5-7. Assume all credit sales were subject to terms of 2/10, n/30.

Operation of the cash receipts journal

Transactions are entered in the cash receipts journal in their usual debit/credit format. To illustrate, examine the $400 payment on account from the Sound Center on January 28. An entry for $400 is placed in both the Cash debit column and the Accounts Receivable credit column. The Sound Center appears in the Account space because the firm's subsidiary ledger account must be updated.

Exhibit 5-7

Cash receipts journal and related postings

Cash Receipts Journal

Page 1

Date		Account	Post Ref	Cash Debit	Sales Discounts Debit	Accounts Receivable Credit	Sales Credit	Sundry Accounts Credit or (Debit)
1983								
Jan.	2	Patricia Monroe, Capital	301	2,000				2,000
	9	—		800			800	
	13	House of Music	✓	1,323	27	1,350		
	17	Loans Payable	210	4,800				4,800
	22	—		200			200	
	28	Sound Center	✓	400		400		
				9,523	27	1,750	1,000	6,800
				(101)	(413)	(110)	(410)	(X)

Transactions that do not arise often are recorded in the Sundry or miscellaneous column. On January 2, for example, Patricia Monroe, Stereo Unlimited's owner, invested $2,000 in the business. The required entry in general journal form is as follows:

Cash	2,000	
Patricia Monroe, Capital		2,000
To record investment by owner		

In terms of the cash receipts journal, $2,000 is entered in the Cash debit column. No column has been established for Patricia Monroe, Capital, because owner investments are infrequent. Thus $2,000 is placed in the Sundry column and Patricia Monroe, Capital, is entered in the Account space.

Note that the Account column is left blank for cash sales. Stereo Unlimited (and many other companies) make no attempt to gather the names of cash sale customers. An explanation of the transaction may be entered if desired (e.g., Daily Cash Sales).

Posting the cash receipts journal

Individual amounts appearing in the Accounts Receivable and Sundry columns are posted during the month. Customer collections from credit sales are generally posted daily in order to maintain up-to-date account balances. Thus receipts from the House of Music and Sound Center are credited to their respective accounts in the Accounts Receivable subsidiary ledger.

Entries in the Sundry column are posted as they occur to minimize work during the hectic period at the end of the month. During January Patricia Monroe, Capital (account no. 301), and Loans Payable (account no. 210) are credited for $2,000 and $4,800, respectively. The posting process transfers these amounts to the general ledger.

Column totals are posted monthly to their respective accounts in the general ledger. Prior to posting, however, the equality of debits and credits must be determined. In the case of Stereo Unlimited the required equality is maintained:

Debits		**Credits**	
Cash	$9,523	Accounts receivable	$1,750
Sales discounts	27	Sales	1,000
	$9,550	Sundry accounts	6,800
			$9,550

All column totals are posted, with one exception: Sundry. As the X indicates, the total of the Sundry column is not posted, because its components ($2,000 and $4,800) have already been transferred to the proper accounts in the general ledger. The $6,800 total is generated only for use in determining whether total debits are equal to total credits. (The results of the posting process can be seen by studying Exhibit 5-9. References of CR1 indicate those entries that were transferred from page 1 of the cash receipts journal.)

Cash payments journal

The **cash payments journal** is used to record virtually all cash disbursements that are made by a business.[5] Because cash outlays are made for many different purposes, the journal utilized for their recording must be multicolumn in format. Separate columns are again established when the same type of transaction occurs frequently or when more detailed accounting information is desired.

Stereo Unlimited's cash payments journal appears in Exhibit 5-8. The journal possesses a Cash credit column since each payment reduces the company's cash balance. Because the firm's merchandise purchases are on account, an Accounts Payable debit column is needed to record reductions in the amounts owed to creditors when payment is made. Furthermore, a Purchases Discounts column is utilized for cash discounts generated from the prompt payment of invoices. Finally, a Sundry column is used to record cash payments for other purposes. The cash payments journal has one additional feature, a check number column. All significant cash payments are made by check for purposes of safety and accountability. The check's number is entered in the journal to facilitate the audit trail process.

[5] A minor exception occurs with small miscellaneous payments that are made under a petty cash system. The operation of a petty cash system is discussed in Chapter 7.

Exhibit 5-8

Cash payments journal and related postings

Cash Payments Journal

Page 1

Date		Check No.	Payee	Account	Post Ref	Cash Credit	Purchases Discounts Credit	Accounts Payable Debit	Sundry Accounts Debit or (Credit)
1983									
Jan.	4	101	Kraft Management Association	Rent Expense	530	750			750
	11	102	Central Stereo	Sales Returns & Allowances	414	100			100
	14	103	Columbia Records		✓	735	15	750	
	19	104	John Harrison	Sales Commissions	540	650			650
	27	105	Able Electronics		✓	2,100		2,100	
						4,335	15	2,850	1,500
						(101)	(504)	(201)	(X)

Stereo Unlimited's cash payments during January were as follows:

Jan. 4 Paid January rent of $750 to Kraft Management Association by issuing check no. 101.

11 Issued check no. 102 for $100 to Central Stereo for the return of stereo equipment purchased for cash on January 9.

14 Paid invoice no. 1777 dated January 7 of Columbia Records by issuing check no. 103. The invoice totaled $750 and was subject to terms of 2/10, n/30.

19 Paid $650 of sales commissions to John Harrison by issuing check no. 104.

27 Issued check no. 105 to Able Electronics for $2,100, in payment of the purchase made on January 3.

Translate each transaction into the correct debits and credits and then examine how the transactions are recorded in the cash payments journal appearing in Exhibit 5-8.

Posting the cash payments journal

Posting the cash payments journal is very similar to posting the cash receipts journal. Both journals are multicolumn, both have a Sundry column to record miscellaneous transactions, and both deal with a control account/subsidiary ledger arrangement. Throughout the month individual amounts in the Sundry column are posted to the proper accounts in the general ledger (e.g., Rent Expense, Sales Returns & Allowances, and Sales Commissions). Entries in the Accounts Payable debit column are transferred daily to creditors' accounts in the Accounts Payable subsidiary ledger. At the end of the month the columns are totaled, and equality of debits and credits is checked. Then all column totals are posted to their respective accounts in the general ledger, with the exception of Sundry. As before, individual elements of the Sundry column have already been transferred. The outcome of the posting process can be observed in Exhibit 5-9 by noting the entries referenced by CP1 (cash payments journal, page 1).

General journal

During an accounting period a business will have a number of transactions that cannot be accommodated in its special journals. Consider, for example, the journals that have been designed for Stereo Unlimited. Suppose on January 19 the firm bought a piece of display equipment on account from Store Outfitters for $2,600. Because the purchases journal contains only purchases of merchandise, this transaction must be recorded elsewhere, specifically, in the general journal. The general journal is used to record transactions that cannot be placed in special journals (e.g., miscellaneous transactions, adjusting entries, and closing entries). The necessary entry appears at the top of page 190.

As the posting references indicate, the transaction was transferred to the Display Equipment account and the Accounts Payable control account in the general ledger. In addition, Store Outfitters was credited in the Accounts Payable subsidiary ledger. The effect of this transaction can be seen by view-

General Journal

Page 1

1983					
Jan.	19	Display Equipment	130	2,600	
		Accounts Payable: Store Outfitters	201/✓		2,600
		Purchased equipment on account			

ing these accounts in Exhibit 5-9 and their related J1 (general journal, page 1) references.

Some final comments on special journals

Exhibit 5-9 contains the general ledger and Accounts Receivable and Accounts Payable subsidiary ledgers of Stereo Unlimited. The trial balance appearing in Exhibit 5-10 shows that the general ledger is in balance. The schedules of Accounts Receivable and Accounts Payable prove that the subsidiary ledgers are in agreement with the balances found in the control accounts.

The order of posting the special journals is not crucial since all transactions eventually wind up in the same place, the ledger accounts. Accountants prefer, however, to post the sales journal before the cash receipts journal and the purchases journal before the cash payments journal. In this manner sales and purchases are entered in the appropriate accounts prior to payment by customers and the firm, respectively.

Exhibit 5-9

General and subsidiary ledgers of Stereo Unlimited

General Ledger

Cash — Account No. 101

Date		Explanation	Post Ref	Debit	Credit	Balance
1983						
Jan.	31		CR1	9,523		9,523
	31		CP1		4,335	5,188

Accounts Receivable — Account No. 110

Date		Explanation	Post Ref	Debit	Credit	Balance
1983						
Jan.	31		S1	3,300		3,300
	31		CR1		1,750	1,550

Display Equipment — Account No. 130

Date		Explanation	Post Ref	Debit	Credit	Balance
1983						
Jan.	19		J1	2,600		2,600

Accounts Payable — Account No. 201

Date		Explanation	Post Ref	Debit	Credit	Balance
1983						
Jan.	19		J1		2,600	2,600
	31		P1		5,330	7,930
	31		CP1	2,850		5,080

Loans Payable — Account No. 210

Date		Explanation	Post Ref	Debit	Credit	Balance
1983						
Jan.	17		CR1		4,800	4,800

Patricia Monroe, Capital — Account No. 301

Date		Explanation	Post Ref	Debit	Credit	Balance
1983						
Jan.	2		CR1		2,000	2,000

Sales — Account No. 410

Date		Explanation	Post Ref	Debit	Credit	Balance
1983						
Jan.	31		S1		3,300	3,300
	31		CR1		1,000	4,300

Exhibit 5-9
Continued

Sales Discounts — *Account No. 413*

Date		Explanation	Post Ref	Debit	Credit	Balance
1983						
Jan.	31		CR1	27		27

Sales Returns & Allowances — *Account No. 414*

Date		Explanation	Post Ref	Debit	Credit	Balance
1983						
Jan.	11		CP1	100		100

Purchases — *Account No. 501*

Date		Explanation	Post Ref	Debit	Credit	Balance
1983						
Jan.	31		P1	5,330		5,330

Purchases Discounts — *Account No. 504*

Date		Explanation	Post Ref	Debit	Credit	Balance
1983						
Jan.	31		CP1		15	15

Rent Expense — *Account No. 530*

Date		Explanation	Post Ref	Debit	Credit	Balance
1983						
Jan.	4		CP1	750		750

Sales Commissions — Account No. 540

Date	Explanation	Post Ref	Debit	Credit	Balance
1983					
Jan. 19		CP1	650		650

Accounts Receivable Subsidiary Ledger

House of Music
642 Ocean Way San Francisco, Calif. 94118

Date	Explanation	Post Ref	Debit	Credit	Balance
1983					
Jan. 4		S1	1,350		1,350
13		CR1		1,350	—

Sound Center
7701 2nd Ave. Hayward, Calif. 94521

Date	Explanation	Post Ref	Debit	Credit	Balance
1983					
Jan. 12		S1	400		400
28		CR1		400	—

Treetops Disco
108 Madison Ave. San Francisco, Calif. 94113

Date	Explanation	Post Ref	Debit	Credit	Balance
1983					
Jan. 18		S1	150		150

Wallace's Hi-Fi Shop
7743 Burnt Oak San Francisco, Calif. 94115

Date	Explanation	Post Ref	Debit	Credit	Balance
1983					
Jan. 25		S1	1,400		1,400

Exhibit 5-9

Continued

Accounts Payable Subsidiary Ledger

Able Electronics
5550 West Fairview Los Angeles, Calif. 90036

Date		Explanation	Post Ref	Debit	Credit	Balance
1983						
Jan.	3		P1		2,100	2,100
	27		CP1	2,100		—

Columbia Records
943 West 7th New York, N.Y. 10006

Date		Explanation	Post Ref	Debit	Credit	Balance
1983						
Jan.	8		P1		750	750
	14		CP1	750		—

Pioneer Associates
942 Superior Ave. San Francisco, Calif. 94115

Date		Explanation	Post Ref	Debit	Credit	Balance
1983						
Jan.	16		P1		420	420

Sony Corp.
1190 Highland San Francisco, Calif. 94114

Date		Explanation	Post Ref	Debit	Credit	Balance
1983						
Jan.	26		P1		2,060	2,060

Store Outfitters
7746 Meadowbrook San Francisco, Calif. 94116

Date		Explanation	Post Ref	Debit	Credit	Balance
1983						
Jan.	19		J1		2,600	2,600

Exhibit 5-10

Trial balance and schedules of accounts receivable and accounts payable

STEREO UNLIMITED
Trial Balance
January 31, 1983

Cash	$ 5,188	
Accounts receivable	1,550	
Display equipment	2,600	
Accounts payable		$ 5,080
Loans payable		4,800
Patricia Monroe, capital		2,000
Sales		4,300
Sales discounts	27	
Sales returns & allowances	100	
Purchases	5,330	
Purchases discounts		15
Rent expense	750	
Sales commissions	650	
	$16,195	$16,195

STEREO UNLIMITED
Schedule of Accounts Receivable
January 31, 1983

Treetops Disco	$ 150
Wallace's Hi-Fi Shop	1,400
	$1,550

STEREO UNLIMITED
Schedule of Accounts Payable
January 31, 1983

Pioneer Associates	$ 420
Sony Corp.	2,060
Store Outfitters	2,600
	$5,080

To conclude, the transaction-recording and posting processes associated with special journals are usually performed by bookkeepers, not accountants. Why, then, did we spend considerable time on these topics? Many accountants are employed to audit and review financial activity; part of this job includes an examination of the information-processing system and related internal controls. The accountant must therefore possess a fundamental knowledge of how transactions are processed and summarized into the account balances found in the trial balance. In addition, accountants are frequently involved with the design of new information systems for their employers or clients. Even though the systems may be highly technical and involve a computer, a basic understanding of data flow and systems procedures is necessary to complete this assignment.

Computers

Manual accounting systems are not always suitable for use in business applications. Frequently, these systems are too slow and become very expensive to operate. Companies with a large volume of transactions have found that the computer is the most cost-effective method of processing data.

Computers accept data as input and process it according to a *program*, or set of instructions. The processed data eventually exits from the system as output, usually in the form of a printed report or as a message on a video display screen. A description of the technical details underlying the operation of a computer is clearly beyond the scope of this text. All business students, however, should have some familiarity with the interaction between accounting and computers.

The computer has had an enormous impact on accountants. This impact is growing each year as (1) more companies find the computer is the answer to many of their record-keeping and management problems and (2) computer costs continue to decline. Because of technological advances, costs have decreased to the point where computers are now an acceptable data processing alternative for even the smallest of organizations.

Mini- and microcomputers

A related factor that partially explains the growing use of computers in accounting is a dramatic increase in the availability of small (*mini- and micro-*) computers. In their earlier years computers were designed for large firms only. Recently, however, considerable engineering effort has been directed toward developing computers for the small business. Computers that provide adequate data processing capability can now be purchased for less than $12,000,[6] an amount that often approximates the annual salary and fringe benefit costs of one bookkeeper.

Small computers have several very attractive features. They can process large volumes of data quicker and more efficiently than manual systems.

[6]These computers are used by large businesses also.

In addition, their implementation and use requires no special preparation or expensive remodeling cost. Small computers are accordingly known as "turnkey" systems, because you just plug them in ("turn the key") and away they go. Finally, many small computers are easy to operate and require minimal programming effort on the part of the user. Prewritten or canned programs are available for all aspects of a company's accounting activities, including payroll, billing, inventory control, and report generation. Thus a business using a small computer need not add a computer specialist to its staff.

Advantages of computers

Organizations have realized many benefits by employing both small and large computers in their data processing activities. These benefits include the reduction of data processing costs, better information for management control, and quick response to system queries.

Reduction of data processing costs

As the volume of data to be processed increases, manual accounting systems become incapable of handling the necessary work load. When additional personnel are necessary to process a company's daily transactions, a firm may find it is advantageous to acquire some computer capability. The options include purchasing or renting a small computer or contracting an outside service bureau to do some of the firm's processing work. No matter which alternative is selected, the cost per transaction processed when volumes are high is usually lower on a computer than on manual systems.

Better information for management control

Because of their speed, computers can generate reports faster than manual accounting systems. The receipt of information on a more timely basis often results in improved control of operations by allowing prompt corrective action in troubled areas. In addition, computers can also update accounts faster to reflect recent transactions. Imagine a company that has many receipts and sales of a variety of inventory items. Computers can easily maintain a perpetual inventory system and furnish management with an up-to-date count of the units on hand. A business can therefore monitor its inventory levels very closely, resulting in more effective purchasing programs. Also, higher customer service levels can be attained by avoiding frequent out-of-stock situations.

Computers are also more cost-effective than manual systems in producing detailed information. For example, a manual system can easily generate information concerning a company's sales, such as total sales and sales by product line. Suppose, however, that management desires sales and gross profit to be broken down by department, by salesperson, and by customer. Generation of this information will be burdensome if produced by an employee using a calculator. A computer, on the other hand, can provide management with the desired information in a matter of seconds. More detailed

THE NAGGING FEELING OF UNDETECTED FRAUD

The computer has brought both good and bad news to the accountant. The good news is that it has simplified many time-consuming tasks and provided easier access to a company's financial data. Chances for errors have been diminished considerably. "Unlike humans, computers never have a bad day," says Donald L. Adams, managing director of administrative services for the American Institute of Certified Public Accountants.

But at the same time, fraud has become easier to commit and harder to detect. "An extremely small amount of money—fractions of a cent—can be siphoned off each entry by a simple change in a computer program," Adams says. The diverted funds could add up to a large sum, but since the amount taken from each transaction is very small, the scheme would be difficult to find.

As an example, a programmer at a mail-order sales company had the computer round down odd cents (e.g., $0.003 in the case of $8.523) in the company's sales commission accounts and channeled the money into a dummy account that was discovered only when the company decided, by chance, to single out the holder of that particular account for a public relations ceremony.

In another case the head teller at a New York bank used a computer to skim off more than $1.5 million in customer accounts over four years. The scheme was upset only when police raided a gambling operation and discovered that one of its principal clients was the teller, who was betting up to $30,000 a day on an annual salary of $11,000.

Manipulation by computer is also subject to less scrutiny because little paper changes hands, Adams explains. There's no trail of paper that auditors can use to trace transactions and the culprit.

With the advent of the small, relatively inexpensive minicomputer, the potential for fraud and embezzlement has increased. In the large firms that have many minis, security is a growing problem as supervision becomes difficult. These units are as easy to use as electric typewriters—and equally easy to misuse.

In small companies one or two low-level employees often operate the only mini with little, if any, supervision. In this situation the operators may program the computer for their own advantage. That's what happened in an aerospace firm where a junior accountant paid himself an extra $1,000 a month for two years. He had the computer issue checks to fictitious employees, assumed the false identities, and cashed the checks. The fraud was detected when a company officer noticed unfamiliar names as he looked through canceled checks.

Most large accounting firms have hired computer specialists and trained auditors in computer science to guard against problems the computers present. Still, says Adams, "I have the nagging feeling that there is more fraud out there than we're catching. What we're seeing now is all so poorly done. I wonder what the real computer experts are doing—the ones who really know how a computer works."

SOURCE Adapted from U.S. News & World Report, *December 19, 1977, p. 42.*

information gives better insight into operations and can lead to better control.

Quick response to system queries

A computerized information system can provide users with instantaneous answers to a host of questions. Many of the resultant benefits, like the inventory example cited, are oriented toward improving customer service and, thus, profitability. Several common applications of query-oriented information systems by large corporations include those listed below.

Corporation	System Query	Benefit Provided
Eastern Air Lines	Seat availability on a particular flight	Improved customer service
J. C. Penney	Customer credit status	Better credit decisions
Holiday Inns	Room availability at a particular location	Improved customer service

Computer problems

It may appear from the discussion thus far that the computer is infallible and the answer to the problems of every business. This is not the case. Companies not familiar with computers expect immediate improvements from their installation. Unfortunately, success does not happen overnight. Several years often pass before a firm experiences the full benefits of computer implementation. Users must therefore be trained to expect initial delays and difficulties. Occasionally, the anticipated benefits never materialize. For example:

> *. . . Both TWA and United Air Lines had horrendous results with early ticketing and reservations systems. TWA spent a total of $26.5 million on a reservation system that it later had to abandon. The firm recovered some of the money in a lawsuit against the supplier, but the payment could not make up for the lost time and effort. In all, the airline spent five years trying to set up the system before scrapping it, and another two in litigation.*
>
> *In the United case, the firm invested an estimated $39 million and several years of effort in its ticketing and reservation system before abandoning the project. Then the firm had to spend an additional $60 million to get a system that worked.*[7]

Computer fraud

The possibility of fraud is another basic problem associated with computerized systems. **Computer fraud**, which involves the use of the computer to aid and abet in a fraud or embezzlement, seems to be occurring with increasing frequency. Schemes have been perpetrated involving employees at all levels of the organizational hierarchy. Sometimes even outsiders have gotten into the act. How? Ingenious individuals have used telephones along

[7] "Getting Control of the System," *Dun's Review*, July 1977, pp. 68, 71.

with secret passwords found in trash bins to successfully gain access to centralized computer systems. The cause of a computer fraud is often lack of adequate internal controls in a firm's data processing network.

KEY TERMS AND CONCEPTS

accountability procedures 173
accounting controls 170
accounting information system 168
administrative controls 169
audit trail 169
cash payments journal 187
cash receipts journal 185
computer fraud 199
control account 178
data 168
fidelity bond 174
Foreign Corrupt Practices Act 176
independent review 175
information 168
internal control 169
limited access to assets 171
purchases journal 183
qualified personnel 174
sales journal 179
separation of duties 172
special journals 177
subsidiary ledger 178

QUESTIONS

Q5-1 Distinguish between data and information.
Q5-2 Why would an auditor trace a transaction through an accounting system?
Q5-3 In addition to signifying completion of the posting process, what other function does a posting reference serve? Why is this function so important?
Q5-4 Differentiate between administrative and accounting controls.
Q5-5 In general, which accounting functions should be separated because of a lack of compatibility?
Q5-6 What benefits are provided by an adequate separation of duties?
Q5-7 What is the purpose behind the serial prenumbering of important documents?
Q5-8 What ultimate guideline should be used to decide which controls to build into a system?
Q5-9 Why are accountants so concerned about the Foreign Corrupt Practices Act?
Q5-10 Why are special journals employed in an accounting system?
Q5-11 Explain and briefly illustrate the interrelationships between control accounts and subsidiary ledger accounts.
Q5-12 Perkins Company recorded and posted the following sales return in its general journal:

		Post Ref		
May 16	Sales Returns & Allowances	415	125	
	Accounts Receivable: Sue Hall	110/		125

Observe the posting reference column. Which items (journals, ledgers, accounts, and so on) will not be in balance with one another? Why? Briefly describe the procedure performed to detect this type of error.

Q5-13 When special journals are designed, what rule should be followed if a firm has a high frequency of the same type of transaction?

Q5-14 What benefits have resulted from the use of computerized accounting systems?

EXERCISES

E5-1 The Sylvania Corporation is a small company that has just acquired a minicomputer to perform its accounting functions. The computer has been placed near the firm's receptionist for "showcasing" to company visitors. All the computer's programs and files of data are stored in Sylvania's office supply closet, which is frequented daily by many employees. Various computer forms such as blank checks and purchase orders are stored in the same location. John Apple is the only employee authorized to operate the computer by Sylvania's management. For amusement during lulls in the working day, Apple purchased a program that permitted him to challenge the computer to games of tic-tac-toe. He had such a good time that he gave his friends the computer's password so that they, too, could participate. Comment on any control weaknesses in Sylvania's computer operation.

E5-2 Mark Kahn has been given the responsibility of handling all aspects of inventory receipts for the Hanley Corporation. He supervises the arrival of merchandise at the loading dock and subsequently completes a receiving report. He later enters the quantities that appear on the receiving report into the perpetual (running-count) inventory that Hanley maintains. Do Kahn's present job assignment and duties present any inherent problems for Hanley? Explain.

E5-3 Multiple Charities conducts a large door-to-door fund-raising campaign each year to assist local charitable organizations. Contributions in the form of cash and checks are received by volunteer workers who, in turn, issue an official Multiple Charities' receipt. The fund-raising campaign lasts one week. This year the officers of Theta Theta Beta fraternity have pledged the services of the entire membership to canvass the homes in Mountain Way, a small college town located approximately one hundred miles from the headquarters of Multiple Charities. On Thursday afternoon of the campaign the brothers of Theta Theta Beta ran out of official Multiple Charities' receipts. Because it was too late to obtain an additional supply, the fraternity's treasurer designed the following form and had it printed on the chapter's mimeograph machine. The form would be given to each contributor.

MULTIPLE CHARITIES

Date ____________

Contributor ______________________________

Amount Received ____________

Theta Theta Beta

After dinner on Thursday, each member grabbed a handful of the forms for use in Friday's collections. Discuss this system in terms of internal control. Does the system ensure that all contributions collected by Theta Theta Beta will be submitted to Multiple Charities? Why?

E5-4 The Posh Dress Shop employs the following journals:

Sales
Purchases
Cash receipts
Cash payments
General

All journals are multicolumn and similar in format to those illustrated in this chapter. The following transactions took place during March of the current year:

a Prepaid a one-year fire insurance policy.
b Received $200 from Joan Bench on account.
c Returned two defective dresses to the manufacturer for credit.
d Mary Whelan, a customer, purchased three dresses on account.
e Acquired new inventory from suppliers; terms 2/10, n/eom.
f Recorded daily cash sales.
g Purchased several new display counters on account.
h Received a bill for printing done in connection with the store's current advertising program. The bill will be paid in April.
i Wrote checks in settlement of the weekly payroll.
j Adjusted the Supplies account for usage during the month.

Indicate the journal in which each of these transactions would be recorded.

E5-5 At the end of September the Farr Company's bookkeeper could not obtain equality between the Accounts Payable control account and its subsidiary ledger. The following information is provided for your review.

Accounts Payable — *Account No. 210*

Date		Post Ref	Debit	Credit	Balance
9/1	Balance				3,230
9/18		J6	480		2,750
9/30		P8		4,650	7,370
9/30		CP9	3,570		3,800
9/30		J8	250		3,550

Subsidiary Ledger

Becker Corp.

Date	Ref	Debit	Date	Ref	Credit
9/16	CP9	1,450	9/1	Balance	1,450
			9/23	P8	920
					920

Howell, Inc.

Date	Ref	Debit	Date	Ref	Credit
9/19	P8	1,100	9/1	Balance	600
			9/7	P8	1,300
					800

Rogers & Smith

9/5	CP9	800	9/1 Balance		1,000
9/18	J6	480	9/22	P8	880
					(600)

Weaver Corp.

9/21	CP9	630	9/1 Balance		180
			9/10	P8	450

You may assume that all posting references are correct. Prepare a list of the errors made by Farr Company.

E5-6 The Swanson Corporation uses a single-column sales journal similar to that illustrated in this chapter. During August all transactions were recorded correctly, but the bookkeeper accidentally underadded the total sales by $100. Assume all postings were made to the proper accounts.

a Will the trial balance remain in balance? Why?

b Will the Accounts Receivable control account equal its subsidiary ledger? Why?

c If your answer to part (b) is no, is the control account or subsidiary ledger smaller?

E5-7 The sales journal of Brunson's Apparel appears below.

Date		Customer	Post Ref	Accounts Receivable Dr	Suit Sales Cr	Shirt Sales Cr	Other Sales Cr
1983							
May	8	Al Green	✓	180	180		
	15	Art Black	✓	20		20	
	22	Sam White	✓	240	200		40
	29	Joel Brown	✓	100		30	70
				640	380	50	110
				(110)	(401)	(402)	(403)

Observe the addition error in the Accounts Receivable column. After the postings are made,

a Will the general ledger still be in balance? Explain.

b Will the Accounts Receivable control account be in agreement with its subsidiary ledger? Why?

c If the answer to part (b) is no, is the subsidiary ledger or control account larger?

E5-8 The Dennison Company is a small firm that uses special journals. Dennison recently gained several new customers because of the bankruptcy of a competitor, and the increase in business is taxing the capacity of its system. Customer statements are going out late, and Dennison's president is complaining that monthly reports have not been arriving on a timely basis. Discuss the use of the computer to help ease the company's record-keeping and reporting problems.

PROBLEMS

P5-1 ***Internal control: Separation of duties***

The Rostomily Company has three employees and the following functions to perform:

1 Maintain the general ledger.
2 Maintain the accounts receivable subsidiary ledger.
3 Maintain the accounts payable subsidiary ledger.
4 Prepare checks for management's signature.
5 Maintain the cash payments journal.
6 Issue credits for sales returns.
7 Prove the equality of the balance of the Cash account in the general ledger with the cash balance as reported by the bank (i.e., prepare a bank reconciliation).
8 Handle and deposit cash receipts.

Issuing credits for sales returns and preparing the bank reconciliation take a minimal amount of time. The other functions are equally time-consuming and require a significant number of hours to perform.

INSTRUCTIONS

a Your objective is to achieve a high degree of internal control. Divide the functions among the three employees to achieve this goal. You may assume that an employee will perform only those functions you have assigned.
b List several incompatible functions that should not be assigned to any one employee.

(CPA adapted.)

P5-2 ***Internal control weaknesses***

The Whitehall Company, a small distributor of dental products, has been in business for four months. The firm's accounting system was designed by Buck Whitehall, the owner, and operates in the following manner. All sales are made on account. Each morning sales invoices are typed, recorded in the sales journal, and posted to the Accounts Receivable subsidiary ledger by Betty Clark. Clark has been with Whitehall since the company opened. She had several courses in high school bookkeeping and is presently working to earn money for her college education. Because the company is new and has a relatively low sales volume, Betty serves as a general secretary and receptionist for the majority of the day. Between greeting customers and answering the phone, Betty opens the mail, which often contains customer payments on account. Because of the long distance to the bank, she accumulates the payments during the week and hides them in an envelope buried at the bottom of a desk drawer. Betty carefully records these transactions in the journal and updates customers' accounts in the subsidiary ledger.

At the end of each month Betty prepares a schedule of Accounts Receivable so that Whitehall can follow up on slow-paying accounts. In addition, she bills customers and performs a bank reconciliation. The bank reconciliation compares the firm's general ledger cash balance with the cash balance as reported by the bank.

Whitehall is very pleased with Clark's performance. She is quiet and efficient, and she has not missed a day of work since the company opened. Betty, too, is quite pleased. On her $250 weekly salary she has been able to open a savings account for her education, rent a very nice apartment, and make a substantial down payment on a Datsun 280-ZX.

INSTRUCTIONS

Identify the internal control weaknesses in Whitehall's system. Explain why they are weaknesses.

P5-3 ***Internal control: Collusion***

The Kansas Owls, a minor league baseball team, play at Owl Stadium and attract approximately 2,500 people per game. All tickets are sold on the day of a game; there are no season ticket holders. Fans buy either bleacher seats for $2 (blue tickets) or reserved seats for $3 (red tickets). All tickets are serially prenumbered and are sold by two cashiers located in a ticket booth outside the stadium's entrance. On entering the stadium, a fan must give a ticket to a ticket taker, who tears it in half. Half the ticket is returned to the customer to save as a rain check; the other half is deposited in a locked box at the entrance.

INSTRUCTIONS

a What internal control features are present in the Owls' system?

b To achieve accountability in the ticket operation, what should be done at the end of each game?

c Suppose Ray Dodson, a cashier, and Marv Starr, a ticket taker, conspire to defraud the Owls. What type of scheme could they undertake to achieve their goal? For simplicity, assume the stadium has only one ticket booth and one entrance.

d Suppose the Owls install a turnstile at the entrance that registers the number of people entering the stadium. How would the turnstile affect Dodson and Starr's plans?

P5-4 ***Detection of processing errors***

The Hartman Company uses special journals to record sales, purchases, cash receipts, and cash payments. Hartman also employs a general journal to record miscellaneous transactions and adjusting and closing entries. During August the following errors were made:

a The correct total of the single-column sales journal, $7,510, was posted to the Sales account in the general ledger as $5,710. The debit to Accounts Receivable was posted correctly.

b The total of the single-column sales journal was accidentally overadded by $10.

c A cash receipt on account from Norman Dresser was entered in the general journal.

d A sale on account to Bob Smith was accidentally posted to Bill Smith's account in the Accounts Receivable subsidiary ledger.

e A purchase of merchandise on account from Modern Equipment Sales was not recorded on the books.

f A cash payment on account to Hardware Wholesalers was properly recorded in the cash payments journal. The bookkeeper neglected to post the payment to Hardware Wholesalers' account in the Accounts Payable subsidiary ledger.

INSTRUCTIONS

State how each error is likely to be discovered. If discovery is unlikely, tell why.

P5-5 *Analysis of special journal errors*

The following errors occurred in recording, adding, and posting the multicolumn cash receipts and cash payments journals of the McCurdy Company.

1 The Accounts Receivable column in the cash receipts journal was underadded by $40.

2 The Sales and Cash columns in the cash receipts journal were each overadded by $100.

3 The Accounts Payable and Sundry columns in the cash payments journal were each overadded by $1,000.

4 A $700 receipt on account from Don Stern was accidentally recorded in the general journal rather than the cash receipts journal.

INSTRUCTIONS

a Observe the chart below. Indicate by yes or no whether the trial balance will still be in balance after the errors have been posted. Consider each case independently.

b Indicate by yes or no whether the appropriate control account and subsidiary ledger will still be in agreement. If they will not be, indicate which of the two balances (control or subsidiary) will be larger.

	a	*b*	*b*
Error	***Yes or No***	***Yes or No***	***Control or Subsidiary***
1	_____	_____	__________
2	_____	_____	__________
3	_____	_____	__________
4	_____	_____	__________

P5-6 *Special journals, transaction processing, and schedules*

Bryson Stamp and Coin began operations on May 1. A partial listing of its accounts follows.

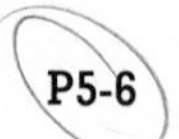

Cash	*101*	*Sales*	*410*
Accounts receivable	*110*	*Sales returns*	*420*
Merchandise inventory	*120*	*Purchases*	*510*
Prepaid insurance	*130*	*Purchases returns*	*520*
Store equipment	*140*	*Purchases discounts*	*530*
Accumulated depreciation:		*Rent expense*	*610*
store equipment	*150*	*Salaries expense*	*620*
Accounts payable	*210*	*Insurance expense*	*630*
Loan payable	*220*	*Utilities expense*	*640*
Ed Bryson, capital	*310*	*Interest expense*	*650*
Ed Bryson, drawing	*320*		

Bryson's accounting system generates total sales and profitability information; in other words, no attempt is made to produce information on a product line basis. Bryson uses a single-column sales journal, a single-column purchases journal, multicolumn cash receipts and payments journals, and a general journal. Merchandise is purchased from wholesale distributors and agencies such as the U.S. Mint and the Postal Service. Wholesale distributors grant terms of 3/10, n/30, while agencies require cash with the order. Bryson uses a periodic inventory system. The transactions for May follow.

May 1 Ed Bryson invested $6,000 in Bryson Stamp and Coin. In addition, he obtained a $4,000 bank loan to help finance his inventory.
2 Purchased $6,500 of merchandise on account from the El Diego Stamp Company (invoice no. 1786 dated May 2).
3 Paid the first month's store rent of $700; issued check no. 101 to Plaza Way Shopping Center.
5 Purchased $400 of recent issues from the U.S. Postal Service; issued check no. 102.
6 Purchased a 1-year inventory insurance policy from Balley Insurance. The yearly premium of $500 was due in 15 days.
8 Purchased several store counters on account from Deaton Office Equipment for $1,600.
12 Sold $250 of stamps on account to Del Aaron (invoice no. 1000).
13 Paid the balance owed to El Diego Stamp Company; issued check no. 103.
14 Cash sales for the week ended May 14 amounted to $1,050.
15 Purchased $1,700 of merchandise on account from Mar Vista Wholesalers (invoice no. 384 dated May 15).
17 Sold $450 of stamps and $150 of coins on account to Robert Barnhard (invoice no. 1001).
19 Issued check no. 104 to Balley Insurance in payment of the insurance policy purchased on May 6.
20 Because of a purchasing error, Bryson returned $300 of the merchandise purchased on May 15 from Mar Vista Wholesalers.
21 Received the amount due from Del Aaron.
21 Cash sales for the week ended May 21 amounted to $1,450.
22 Robert Barnhard returned $50 of stamps purchased on May 17. He also paid his remaining balance.
23 Paid the amount due to Mar Vista Wholesalers; issued check no. 105.
25 Paid $120 to California Edison for utilities as follows: store, $90; personal residence, $30. Issued check no. 106.
28 Cash sales for the week ended May 28 amounted to $1,100.
29 Purchased $1,500 of merchandise on account from El Diego Stamp Company (invoice no. 1804 dated May 29).
30 Paid the first installment due on the May 1 loan. Issued check no. 107 to American Trust for $400, of which $80 is interest.
31 Paid Deaton Office Equipment for the purchase of May 8; issued check no. 108.
31 Sold $900 of coins on account to Wilbur Burns (invoice no. 1002).

INSTRUCTIONS

a Record the transactions in the correct journals. Post the proper individual amounts and general journal entries daily. At the end of the month post the appropriate totals.

b Prepare a trial balance, schedule of Accounts Receivable, and schedule of Accounts Payable.

P5-7 *Special journals, transaction processing, and schedules*

The Lakeside Appliance Company is a small appliance store owned by James Horton. The company's fiscal year runs from July 1 through June 30. Credit sales and merchandise purchases are subject to terms of 2/10, n/30. The general ledger contained the following balances on May 31:

Cash (101)	*$ 4,000*
Accounts receivable (110)	*1,700*
Inventory (120)	*22,000*
Prepaid insurance (130)	*80*
Accounts payable (201)	*1,300*
James Horton, capital (301)	*39,000*
James Horton, drawing (302)	*12,000*
Sales (401)	*71,500*
Sales discounts (402)	*800*
Sales returns (403)	*1,000*
Miscellaneous revenue (450)	—
Purchases (501)	*46,200*
Purchases discounts (502)	*500*
Salaries expense (510)	*18,900*
Advertising expense (520)	*520*
Insurance expense (530)	*400*
Rent expense (540)	*4,700*

The Accounts Receivable subsidiary ledger showed that Hal Jamison, a builder, purchased $1,700 of appliances on May 28. The Accounts Payable ledger revealed that Lakeside owes $1,300 to Metro Distributors for a purchase on May 27.

The following transactions took place during June.

June 2 Sold a $600 television on account to Starbright TV (invoice no. 548).
3 Hal Jamison paid the proper amount due in settlement of his account balance.
4 Paid the proper amount due to Metro Distributors for the purchase on May 27; issued check no. 1252.
7 Purchased $2,800 of merchandise on account from Vista Distribution Corporation (invoice no. 4706 dated June 7).
7 Cash sales for the week amounted to $1,000.
10 Starbright TV paid the proper amount due in settlement of its account balance.
10 Issued check no. 1253 for $400 to Midtown Printers for brochures announcing Lakeside's June sale.
14 Cash sales for the week totaled $800.
14 Issued check no. 1254 to Vista Distribution Corporation in payment of the purchase on June 7.
15 Issued check no. 1255 to Butch Graybark in payment of his $1,700 salary.
18 Received $175 for consulting services rendered to the builder of a new apartment complex.
20 Sold a $400 television and a $200 dryer on account to Walt's Home Center (invoice no. 549).
21 Sold a $300 washing machine on account to Ken Perry (invoice no. 550).
21 Cash sales for the week amounted to $600.

24 Purchased $800 of appliances on account from Metro Distributors (invoice no. 1555 dated June 23).
24 Ken Perry returned the washing machine purchased on June 21 and his account was adjusted. He paid Lakeside $25 to cover the labor and delivery costs associated with the return.
24 Paid $500 to Atlas Insurance for an insurance policy covering the next fiscal year; issued check no. 1256.
25 Received a $60 check from Midtown Printers. An accompanying note stated that Lakeside's bill for the printing job on June 10 had been computed incorrectly.
26 Sold a $500 television on account to Maxwell Stereo and TV (invoice no. 551).
28 Cash sales for the week amounted to $1,000.

Lakeside employs single-column sales and purchases journals and multicolumn cash receipts and cash payments journals similar to those illustrated in this chapter. In addition, a general journal is used for miscellaneous transactions.

INSTRUCTIONS

a Open Lakeside's accounts in the general ledger and the Accounts Receivable and Accounts Payable subsidiary ledgers. *Note:* This step is not necessary if you are using the preprinted working papers that accompany this text.
b Record the transactions in the correct journals. Post the proper individual amounts and general journal entries daily. At the end of the month post the appropriate totals. All terms of sale are strictly followed.
c Prepare a trial balance, a schedule of Accounts Receivable, and a schedule of Accounts Payable as of June 30.

P5-8 ***Internal control weaknesses (alternate to P5-2)***

Betty Barnwell has been a trusted employee of Mitchell and Associates, interior designers, for twenty-five years. She has worked her way into the position of secretary-treasurer for the firm. Because Donald Mitchell and his partner, James McDonald, occupy their time consulting with clients, traveling, attending shows and markets, and planning with builders, Betty is in charge of the office. While she does not actively work on the furniture sales floor or in the gift gallery, Betty approves all credit sales. She also opens all mail and posts billings and payments to the Accounts Receivable subsidiary ledger.

Betty's taste in furniture and gift items is excellent, and she has started to assist in the purchasing activities of the firm. In this capacity she is permitted to buy antiques and decorative accessories that she often finds through extensive personal travel. Betty is also authorized to write company checks; these are cosigned by one of the two owners.

Betty's expertise in buying has made her the authority on costing for the firm's inventory. She hand-prices all merchandise on the sales floor and keeps inventory records. Because the firm has expanded over the years, two additional full-time office employees have been hired to assist Betty. These employees often relieve Betty of some of the record keeping. Because of a high level of turnover in the positions, however, Betty is reluctant to delegate too much responsibility to her subordinates.

INSTRUCTIONS

Identify the internal control weaknesses in Mitchell and Associates' system. Explain why they are weaknesses.

P5-9 ***Detection of processing errors (alternate to P5-4)***

The Perez Company uses special journals to record sales, purchases, cash receipts, and cash payments. Perez also employs a general journal to record miscellaneous transactions and adjusting and closing entries. During March the following errors were made:

a A cash receipt on account from Joe Ellis was accidentally posted to Jay Ellis's account in the Accounts Receivable subsidiary ledger.

b A clerk who also served as a part-time bookkeeper kept the cash received from a $100 cash sale and made no entry for the sale in the accounting records.

c The total of the purchases journal was accidentally underadded by $1,000.

d The $150 total of the Sales Discounts column in the cash receipts journal was posted to the Sales Discounts account as $1,500.

e A $600 sale on account to Jerry Avery was both entered in the sales journal and posted to Avery's account as $500.

f A cash receipt on account from Sue Cepeda was properly recorded in the cash receipts journal. The bookkeeper neglected to post the payment to Cepeda's account in the Accounts Receivable subsidiary ledger.

INSTRUCTIONS

State how each error is likely to be discovered. If discovery is unlikely, tell why.

P5-10 ***Analysis of special journal errors (alternate to P5-5)***

The following errors occurred in recording, adding, and posting the multicolumn cash receipts and cash payments journals of the Ullrich Company.

1 The Cash column in the cash receipts journal was overadded by $100.

2 The Sales and Accounts Receivable columns in the cash receipts journal were each underadded by $50.

3 The Cash and Sundry columns in the cash payments journal were each overadded by $800.

4 A $900 payment on account to Lee Wholesale was accidentally recorded in the general journal rather than the cash payments journal.

INSTRUCTIONS

a Observe the chart below. Indicate by yes or no whether the trial balance will still be in balance after the errors have been posted. Consider each case independently.

b Indicate by yes or no whether the appropriate control account and subsidiary ledger will still be in agreement. If they will not be, indicate which of the two balances (control or subsidiary) will be larger.

	a	*b*	*b*
Error	***Yes or No***	***Yes or No***	***Control or Subsidiary***
1	_____	_____	_______________
2	_____	_____	_______________
3	_____	_____	_______________
4	_____	_____	_______________

P5-11 ***Special journals, transaction processing, and schedules (alternate to P5-6)***

Hickory Clocks began business on December 1. Selected accounts follow.

Cash	*100*	*Sales*	*400*
Accounts receivable	*110*	*Sales returns*	*401*
Merchandise inventory	*120*	*Purchases*	*550*
Prepaid insurance	*130*	*Purchases returns*	*551*
Store equipment	*140*	*Purchases discounts*	*552*
Accumulated depreciation: store equipment	*150*	*Rent expense*	*660*
		Salaries expense	*670*
Accounts payable	*200*	*Insurance expense*	*680*
Loan payable	*210*	*Utilities expense*	*690*
James Hickory, capital	*300*	*Interest expense*	*695*
James Hickory, drawing	*310*		

In operating the clock shop, Hickory uses a single-column sales journal, a single-column purchases journal, multicolumn cash receipts and payments journals, and a general journal. Merchandise is purchased from individuals, estates, dealers, and antique shops. Dealers usually grant terms of 2/10, n/30; other purchases are individually negotiated. A periodic inventory system is used. December transactions follow.

Dec. *1* James Hickory invested $25,000 in Hickory Clocks. In addition, a $25,000 bank loan was obtained.
1 Purchased $12,500 of clocks on account from Bavarian Timepieces, Ltd. Invoice no. 5406 was dated December 1.
2 Paid rent of $1,450 for December. Check no. 001 was issued to Raintree Mall.
2 Acquired a 3-year insurance policy on the clock inventory from Marsh Insurance. The total premium of $3,600 was due December 25.
4 Purchased $750 of antique clocks from the Montrose Estate; issued check no. 002.
8 Sold a grandfather clock on account to D. Hinckle for $2,050 (invoice no. 100).
10 Paid the amount owed Bavarian Timepieces, Ltd.; issued check no. 003.
13 Cash sales of smaller clocks totaled $1,750 for the week.
15 Purchased $2,500 of merchandise on account from Thomas Antiques (invoice no. 007 dated December 15; terms 3/10, n/30).
16 Sold 3 antique clocks on account to Gloria Max for $1,250 (invoice no. 101).
18 Because of damage in shipment, Hickory returned a $300 clock to Thomas Antiques.
19 Collected half the balance owed by D. Hinckle.
20 Cash sales totaled $1,900 for the week.
21 Gloria Max returned 1 antique clock purchased on December 16. The returned clock had been sold for $250. She also paid half of her remaining account balance.
22 Purchased several display counters for smaller clocks from Riverside Counters. Payment of $1,500 is due within 30 days.
24 Paid the amount owed Thomas Antiques; issued check no. 004.
24 Paid Marsh Insurance for the insurance policy purchased on December 2; issued check no. 005.

26 Paid utilities to Southern Power of $240; issued check no. 006.
27 Cash sales for the week totaled $1,950.
28 Paid a $1,000 installment on the December 1 loan, which included interest of $250. Issued check no. 007 to U.S. Bank & Trust.
31 Paid salaries for the month of $1,200; issued check no. 008 to John Russ.

INSTRUCTIONS

a Record the December transactions in the correct journals. Post the proper individual amounts and journal entries daily. At the end of the month post the appropriate totals.

b Prepare a trial balance, schedule of Accounts Receivable, and schedule of Accounts Payable.

P5-12 ***Special journals, transaction processing, and schedules (alternate to P5-7)***

Midtown Camera Distributors is owned by Diane Pettit. Credit sales and merchandise purchases are subject to terms of 2/10, n/30. The general ledger contained the following balances on November 30:

Cash (110)	$ 14,700
Accounts receivable (120)	2,600
Inventory (130)	56,700
Prepaid advertising (140)	1,600
Accounts payable (210)	3,700
Diane Pettit, capital (310)	85,300
Diane Pettit, drawing (320)	15,000
Sales (410)	146,600
Sales discounts (420)	2,200
Sales returns (430)	3,700
Miscellaneous revenue (450)	—
Purchases (510)	98,500
Purchases discounts (520)	1,600
Wage expense (530)	24,400
Advertising expense (540)	3,200
Rent expense (550)	11,500
Utilities expense (560)	3,100

The Accounts Receivable subsidiary ledger showed that Evertson Photo purchased $2,600 of merchandise on November 28. The Accounts Payable ledger revealed that Midtown owes $3,700 to Tokyo Camera Works for a purchase on November 29.

The following transactions took place during December.

Dec. 3 Evertson Photo paid the proper amount due in settlement of its account balance.
4 Sold $500 of merchandise on account to Duke's Camera Shop (invoice no. 642).
5 Purchased $2,900 of merchandise on account from Polaroid Corporation (invoice no. 6847 dated December 5).
6 Paid the proper amount due to Tokyo Camera Works for the purchase on November 29; issued check no. 4305.
7 Cash sales for the week amounted to $2,330.
9 Issued check no. 4306 for $520 to Smith and Son Printers for brochures to be used in January's advertising program.

12 Duke's Camera Shop paid the proper amount due in settlement of its account balance.
14 Cash sales for the week totaled $3,230.
14 Issued check no. 4307 to Polaroid in payment of the purchase on December 5.
15 Issued check no. 4308 to Susan Woodard in payment of her $1,800 salary.
17 Sold $2,200 of cameras and $650 of accessories on account to Dave's Studio (invoice no. 643).
19 Received $225 for consulting services rendered to a suburban newspaper's photography staff.
21 Cash sales for the week amounted to $1,120.
22 Sold a $580 camera on account to Hawthorne Photo Supply (invoice no. 644).
23 Purchased $1,950 of merchandise on account from Tokyo Camera Works (invoice no. 8041 dated December 23).
24 Hawthorne Photo Supply returned the camera purchased on December 22 and its account was adjusted. Because the camera was a special order for Midtown, Hawthorne paid Midtown $20 to cover the labor and shipping costs associated with the return.
24 Paid $85 for utilities to South Carolina Power and Light; issued check no. 4309.
26 Received a $50 check from Smith and Son Printers. An accompanying note stated that Midtown's bill for the printing job on December 9 had been computed incorrectly.
28 Sold a $620 camera on account to Hay Photography (invoice no. 645).
29 Cash sales for the week totaled $910.

Midtown employs single-column sales and purchases journals and multicolumn cash receipts and payments journals similar to those illustrated in this chapter. In addition, a general journal is used for miscellaneous transactions.

INSTRUCTIONS

a Open Midtown's accounts in the general ledger and the Accounts Receivable and Accounts Payable subsidiary ledgers. *Note:* This step is not necessary if you are using the preprinted working papers that accompany this text.

b Record the December transactions in the correct journals. Post the proper individual amounts and general journal entries daily. At the end of the month post the appropriate totals. All terms of sale are strictly followed.

c Prepare a trial balance, a schedule of Accounts Receivable, and a schedule of Accounts Payable as of December 31.

CASE 5
THE UNIVERSITY CLUB

The University Club was formed five years ago by faculty members at Midwestern State University to promote interaction among the various departments and colleges on campus. To achieve this goal, the club sponsored several discussion sessions and held numerous social events. In addition, food service was provided at the noon hour for dues-paying members and their guests.

The University Club's food service was operated by a catering company. The catering company signed a contract with club officials, agreeing to provide meals at a reasonable cost during the academic year. Although the original contract called for lunches only, there was a substantial demand for breakfast and catered parties. The contract was later changed to include these additional services. The catering company handled most aspects of the club's operations, including the purchase of food, employment of personnel, payment of bills, and deposit of daily cash receipts. The club obtained a liquor license and maintained control over bar revenues and expenses.

The club was never intended to be a profit-making entity and had been operated more as a social organization than a small business. After sustaining several years of heavy operating losses, the club's existence was threatened. Recognizing that a change in philosophy was needed, club members appointed two professors from the business school to their board of directors. The directors were charged with turning the entity around to become a break-even operation.

The club's contract with the catering company was about to expire. After lengthy deliberations the board decided to operate the food service independently of a catering company. The board hired the manager who had supervised club activities while an employee of the catering company. In addition, they agreed to employ a member of the university's accounting department on a part-time basis to handle the required record keeping. The accountant studied past operations and noted that an accounting system was needed to process required financial information. Conversations with the club's manager revealed the following:

1 Virtually all daily food service and bar sales were for cash. The club operated in a state where food and bar sales were subject to a 5% sales tax.
2 The club was frequently booked for private parties by academic departments on campus.
3 Credit sales averaged about seven per week.
4 Bar purchases were made by the club's manager. Liquor sales were under state control, which resulted in cash payment upon purchase. The manager took the necessary cash out of the day's cash receipts.
5 Charge accounts existed with approximately ten different companies for purchases of food and supplies.
6 Each of the club's 12 employees was paid weekly.

INSTRUCTIONS

a To record club activity, the accountant decided it would be most efficient to use a "hybrid" (combination) journal, which would accommodate all transactions except for adjusting and closing entries (to be recorded in a separate general journal). Design a hybrid journal that would be appropriate for the University Club by specifying columnar headings.
b Do you see any control weaknesses with the liquor-purchasing procedure? Explain.

6 FINANCIAL STATEMENTS: AN IN-DEPTH VIEW

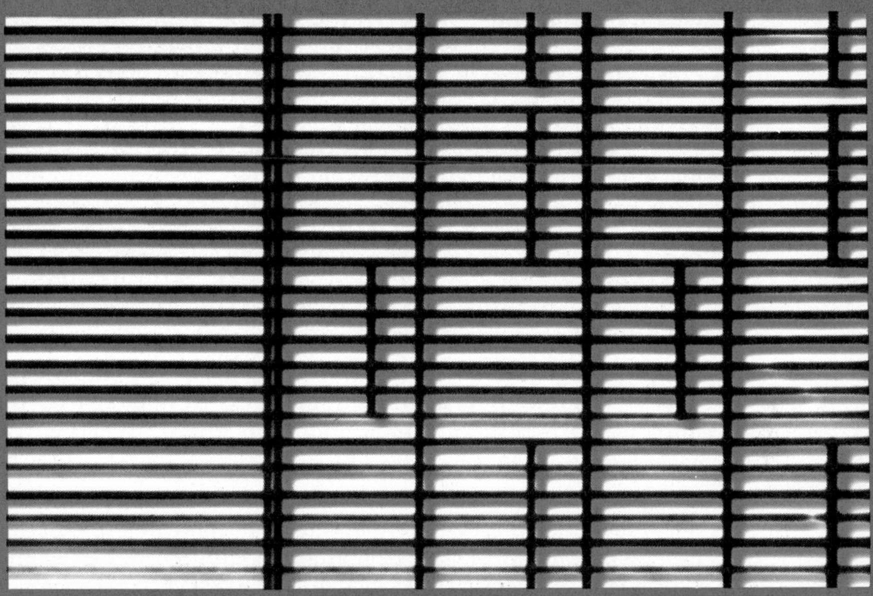

LEARNING OBJECTIVES

After reading this chapter you should:

1 *Be able to describe the form and content of a detailed balance sheet, income statement, and statement of owners' equity.*

2 *Understand the concept of an operating cycle.*

3 *Be able to compute the current ratio and working capital for a company and understand the use of these financial measures.*

4 *Be able to distinguish extraordinary items from other transactions.*

5 *Understand the meaning of earnings per share.*

6 *Be familiar with the content of footnotes and parenthetical disclosures.*

CHAPTER 6

Each financial statement prepared by a business presents information pertaining to the business's financial activities. The statements convey information useful for decision making by both individuals within a company (e.g., managers) and concerned external parties (such as suppliers and lenders). These decisions relate to such diverse areas as inventory management, long-term financing, and even the funds available for employee pay raises.

The decision-making process is facilitated if businesses follow a generally accepted set of accounting practices. To illustrate the related benefits, suppose that General Motors has just concluded an extremely profitable year; Chrysler's operating performance, on the other hand, was somewhat marginal. Imagine that, to prevent owners, analysts, and other parties from learning about Chrysler's poor performance and present financial condition, management decided not to release the current year's financial statements. Naturally, the decisions made by external parties would be stymied. Furthermore, accounting and its measurement process might be viewed with suspicion if individual businesses were allowed to play by their own rules. As another example, suppose that a firm had an embarrassingly low level of cash at the time that a balance sheet was to be prepared. The owner may think about regrouping the accounts in a more imaginative and advantageous way to hide this fact, such as having a combined Cash and Accounts Receivable account rather than separate accounts for each asset.

Businesses must follow accepted accounting practices to (1) provide users with a clear picture of financial activities and (2) lend reliability and credibility to the reporting process. Financial reporting rests on a set of underlying assumptions and principles that have been generally accepted by the accounting profession. In addition, various authoritative bodies have issued pronouncements that have had a significant impact on financial statement presentation and preparation. These bodies include the *Securities and Exchange Commission* (*SEC*), the *Accounting Principles Board* (*APB*), and the *Financial Accounting Standards Board* (*FASB*). The work and pronouncements of the SEC, APB, and FASB will be cited throughout the text as we study the reporting environment in which an organization operates.

FINANCIAL STATEMENTS

A complete set of financial statements includes the following formally prepared, interrelated statements:

1 *Balance sheet.* Provides information about a company's financial condition at a single point in time.
2 *Income statement.* Furnishes information concerning a firm's revenue-producing activities over a period of time.
3 *Statement of owners' equity.* Provides insight into the changes in owners' equity over a period of time.
4 *Statement of changes in financial position.* Presents a summary of how a firm acquires and uses its capital funds.

These statements present vital information about an organization in different ways; unless all are prepared, valuable perspectives are lost.

We now present an in-depth view of the first three statements just listed. The statement of changes in financial position is discussed later in the text because of its complex nature.

Balance Sheet

The balance sheet provides information about a company's assets, existing liabilities, and the capital provided by the owners. Balance sheet information is useful in many ways to many different groups of individuals. For example, the manager of a rapidly growing company can study the level of merchandise inventory at the end of an accounting period to judge the effectiveness of a new ordering policy. Stable inventory levels may prompt the manager to question why the ordering policy has not kept pace with significant changes in sales. Creditors review the asset and liability relationships on a balance sheet to determine the adequacy of cash balances for settling the firm's current and upcoming obligations. Creditors also analyze the balance sheet to determine if the owners are investing their own capital in the business or relying on other creditors (e.g., banks) to finance operations. Lenders, in particular, want the owners to have a sizable stake in the business should financial problems develop. The feeling is that owners will probably work harder if they have more of their own money to lose.

While the balance sheet is extremely useful, it suffers from several limitations. First, current values are not usually employed for asset valuation. As we noted in Chapter 1, accounting is based on the *historical-cost principle.* That is, assets are recorded in the accounts at acquisition cost. With only a few exceptions, cost remains in the records until the asset is sold. Thus although a company may have purchased a parcel of land ten years ago for $50,000 and that parcel is currently worth $380,000, the land remains on the books at $50,000. This lack of currentness on the balance sheet is partially overcome by the use of disclosure techniques that are discussed later in the chapter. A second problem is that many of the assets important to the profitability and future existence of a business are not measurable in dollars. These assets, which include a good management, a skilled work force, a prime location, and business contacts and relationships, are therefore omitted from the balance sheet. No one would dispute the value of these items to a firm. Yet no one can objectively value them for accounting purposes.

Form

The balance sheet can be presented in two different ways, the **account form** or the **report form.** Both forms are commonly encountered in practice and are shown in Exhibit 6-1.

The account form takes its name from the T-account. The asset accounts are presented on the left side of the statement since these accounts normally have debit balances. The liability and owners' equity accounts are presented on the right side since they normally possess credit balances. In contrast, the report form presents asset accounts above the liability and owners' equity accounts.

Exhibit 6-1

Balance sheet formats

Account Form

Assets	*$XXX*	*Liabilities*	*$XXX*
⋮		⋮	
		Owners' equity	*XXX*
		⋮	
Total assets	*$XXX*	*Total liabilities & owners' equity*	*$XXX*

Report Form

Assets	*$XXX*
⋮	
Total assets	*$XXX*
Liabilities	*$XXX*
⋮	
Owners' equity	*XXX*
⋮	
Total liabilities & owners' equity	*$XXX*

Statement classification

Generally accepted practice for balance sheets (and other financial statements, too) dictates the classification or grouping of accounts so that important relationships and subtotals can be obtained. Standard classifications improve statement utility because users can better analyze the accounts and relationships important to them. Visualize the plight of bankers, for example, if all loan applicants classified accounts differently. Bankers would have to spend countless hours rearranging the applicants' financial statements to gather needed information. Having general classification standards does not mean complete uniformity, however. With the approval of their accountant, businesses may make slight deviations from the general schemes when they believe that such departures are needed and justified.

The balance sheet's classifications are shown in Exhibit 6-2 and will be discussed on the next few pages.

Exhibit 6-2

Balance sheet classifications

Balance Sheet

Assets	**Liabilities & owners' equity**
Current assets	*Current liabilities*
Long-term investments	*Long-term liabilities*
Property, plant, & equipment	*Owners' equity*
Intangible assets	
Other assets	

Assets

Current assets. **Current assets** are those assets management intends to convert into cash or consume in the normal course of business within a relatively short period of time. The time period depends on the **operating cycle** of the entity, that is, how long it takes a firm to buy merchandise inventory, sell the inventory, and ultimately collect the cash. For companies selling goods on credit, the operating cycle appears as shown in Exhibit 6-3.

Exhibit 6-3

Operating cycle

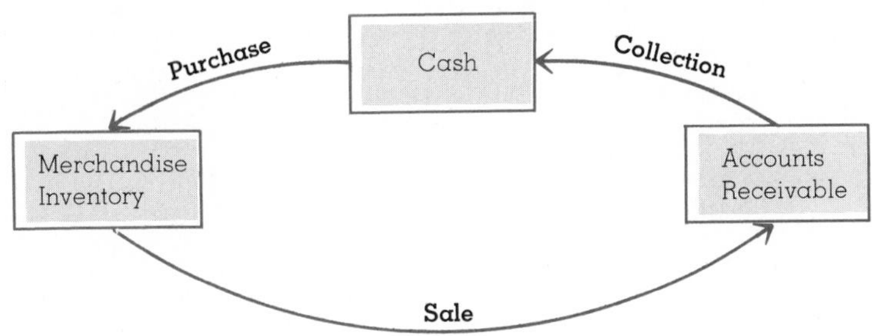

Most businesses have numerous operating cycles within a year and use one year as the minimum time parameter for classifying current assets. Be aware, however, that some firms have operating cycles well over one year in length. Examples include tobacco companies, which must cure their tobacco leaf, and liquor firms, which must age their inventory. Thus the time period for purposes of the current asset definition is *one year or the operating cycle, whichever is longer.*

Current assets include cash, short-term investments purchased with idle cash, receivables, inventories, and prepaid expenses. These accounts are sequenced on the balance sheet in order of **liquidity,** that is, how close a current asset is to becoming cash. For instance, examine the asset section of the balance sheet for The Williamsburg Company in Exhibit 6-4. Presented directly after Cash is a short-term investment, the Certificate of Deposit. While this certificate matures six months from the time of origination, it can be converted into cash immediately if necessary. Accounts Receivable is listed next and represents claims against customers for inventory already sold or services rendered. The receivables are often collected in a month or two, depending on the credit and collection practices of the firm. The merchandise inventory has yet to be sold and is presented next. Depending on the type of business involved, several months could elapse before the existing goods are purchased by customers and cash is collected. Prepaid expenses, such as rent, insurance, and supplies, are commonly listed as the final current asset. Unlike receivables and inventory, prepaid expenses will not be converted to cash; they will, however, be consumed within a relatively short period of time.

Exhibit 6-4

THE WILLIAMSBURG COMPANY
Balance Sheet
December 31, 1983

ASSETS			
Current assets			
Cash		*$ 181,000*	
Certificate of deposit (6-month maturity)		*50,000*	
Accounts receivable		*1,389,000*	
Merchandise inventory		*2,375,000*	
Prepaid expenses		*36,000*	
Total current assets			*$4,031,000*
Long-term investments			
Land (held for future use)			*1,000,000*
Property, plant, & equipment			
Land		*$2,000,000*	
Buildings	*$3,000,000*		
Less: Accumulated depreciation	*1,250,000*	*1,750,000*	
Equipment	*$1,000,000*		
Less: Accumulated depreciation	*175,000*	*825,000*	
Vehicles	*$ 45,000*		
Less: Accumulated depreciation	*40,000*	*5,000*	
Total property, plant, & equipment			*4,580,000*
Intangible assets			
Patents on inventions			*40,000*
Other assets			
Long-term receivables (due 1999)			*850,000*
Total assets			*$10,501,000*
LIABILITIES & OWNERS' EQUITY			
Current liabilities			
Accounts payable		*$2,100,000*	
Property taxes payable		*900,000*	
Salaries payable		*500,000*	
Unearned revenues		*400,000*	
Current portion of mortgage payable		*100,000*	
Total current liabilities			*$ 4,000,000*
Long-term liabilities			
Mortgage payable (due 1990)			*1,500,000*
Total liabilities			*$ 5,500,000*
Owners' equity			
Charles E. Quittmeyer, capital			*5,001,000*
Total liabilities & owners' equity			*$10,501,000*

Long-term investments. The next asset classification on the balance sheet is **long-term investments.** These investments are made with the intention of being retained for a long period of time. Examples include land purchased for either speculation or a future plant site, investments set aside for the employees' pension fund, and investments made to acquire other firms.

Property, plant, and equipment. **Property, plant, and equipment** are assets that are used in the operation of a business and not held for resale to customers. These assets are tangible and have a long-term usefulness to a firm. Examples of property, plant, and equipment include land, buildings, machinery, furniture and fixtures, and vehicles. With the exception of land, the costs of assets in this category are gradually charged to expense through the depreciation process discussed in Chapter 3. Items of property, plant, and equipment are normally listed on the balance sheet in order of the length of their service lives, from the longest to the shortest. A typical presentation is shown on the balance sheet appearing in Exhibit 6-4.

Intangible assets. **Intangibles** are assets that lack physical existence but represent valuable long-term rights to the business that has acquired or developed them. Examples include franchises, patents, copyrights, trademarks, and product formulas. The Coca-Cola Company's balance sheet, for instance, lists the firm's secret formulas for soft drinks as an intangible asset. Each year a portion of the costs of intangible assets is expensed as the rights are used up or expire. Intangibles are discussed further in Chapter 11.

Other assets. Any asset account that cannot be placed in one of the previous classifications is presented in the other assets category. For example, The Williamsburg Company lists Long-Term Receivables as an other asset (see Exhibit 6-4).

Liabilities

Current liabilities. Generally stated, liabilities that will be liquidated within one year or the operating cycle, whichever is longer, are called **current liabilities.** Observe the consistency with the current asset definition. Examples of current liabilities include payables to suppliers and utilities, wages payable to employees, taxes payable to governmental units, and interest payable to banks. Another type of current liability is the unearned or prepaid revenue discussed in Chapter 3. Unearned revenues represent cash received in advance of goods or services provided. These prepayments are liabilities until the goods or services are given in return, which generally occurs in less than a year's time.

Current liabilities are normally paid or reduced by current assets. Thus the relationship between current assets and current liabilities is important, especially from a creditor's point of view. Creditors and other financial statement users periodically study this relationship by dividing the total current assets by the total current liabilities. The result, called the **current ratio,** provides insight into a firm's ability to pay short-term obligations on time and maintain its credit rating. Bankers and other lenders often prefer to see total current assets at least twice as large as total current liabilities. This 2:1 ratio essentially means that for every $1 owed and payable in the near future, a business has $2 of current assets available or soon available for payment.[1] Usually, a high current ratio is preferable to a low one. However, an abnormally high current ratio may indicate that too much cash or inventory is held for the volume of business being generated. By having excessive cash balances or inventory levels, a company may be forced to forgo other more profitable investment opportunities.

The relationship between current assets and current liabilities can also be studied by calculating **working capital,** the mathematical difference between total current assets and total current liabilities. Working capital is the amount that would remain if all current obligations were paid immediately. Working capital, therefore, provides an assessment of a company's ability to pay debts as they come due. The amount of working capital should be sufficient to meet day-to-day expenses and provide for some expansion.

From the data shown in Exhibit 6-4 we see that The Williamsburg Company's current ratio and working capital appear somewhat tenuous. The firm's current ratio is 1.01 : 1 ($4,031,000 : $4,000,000), while working capital stands at only $31,000 ($4,031,000 − $4,000,000). Should an unexpected event arise, management may be forced to go scurrying for cash. Why? Although Williamsburg's current assets do exceed its current liabilities, observe the current asset composition. Approximately 93.4% of the current asset total is comprised of receivables and inventory, both of which will require some time until ultimate conversion into cash. Creditors may thus be reluctant to conduct business with the firm for fear of nonpayment.

Long-term liabilities. Obligations that are expected to be paid after one year or the operating cycle, whichever is longer, are classified as **long-term liabilities.** Examples of such liabilities include certain bank loans and mortgages payable. Many long-term obligations are paid in annual installments, that is, $X per year. As a result, the portion of a long-term liability that will be paid within one year or the operating cycle is properly presented as a current liability. To illustrate, we will examine the balance sheet in Exhibit 6-4. Williamsburg owes $1,600,000 from a mortgage due in 1990. The liability is split according to its payment dates: $100,000 within one year and $1,500,000 after one year.

Owners' equity

As we noted in Chapter 1, owners' equity represents the net worth or "interest" of the owners in the assets of a business. The owners' equity section of the balance sheet varies with the three forms of business organization: sole proprietorship, partnership, and corporation.

Sole proprietorship. A **sole proprietorship** is a business owned by one

[1] Remember that current assets include cash *and* assets that will be converted into cash in the near future (e.g., accounts receivable, inventories, and short-term investments). The exception is prepaid expenses.

person in which owner investments and withdrawals, as well as the net income (or net loss), are merged into a single account at the end of the period. For The Williamsburg Company, the account is labeled Charles E. Quittmeyer, Capital. The balance sheet of a sole proprietorship will contain only one owners' equity account: the name of the owner followed by the term "Capital."

Partnership. A **partnership** is a business owned by two or more persons, with a separate capital account established for each partner. For example, if Charles E. Quittmeyer entered into a partnership with Paul Ziegler, the owners' equity section of Williamsburg's balance sheet would contain two accounts: Charles E. Quittmeyer, Capital, and Paul Ziegler, Capital. Similar to what occurs in the proprietorship, each capital account after closing will contain a partner's investments, withdrawals, and an appropriate share of the partnership's net income or net loss. Net income or net loss can be divided among the partners in any fashion. Generally, a written partnership agreement stipulates the profit-sharing arrangements; if no written agreement exists, net income or net loss is usually divided equally. Accounting problems for partnerships are presented later in the text, in Chapter 13.

Corporation. A third form of business organization is the **corporation.** The owners (called *stockholders*) are the investors who have purchased shares of stock in the corporation. The most prevalent form of stock is **common stock.** Shares of common stock are easily acquired or sold, resulting in frequent and sometimes rapid changes in ownership interests.

The stockholders of a corporation, which can number from one to several million, annually elect the corporation's *board of directors.* The board of directors, in turn, hires the management. This routine always appears overly legalistic in a small family corporation where the stockholders, board of directors, and managers are all the same four or five individuals. It is a different story for a giant firm like Procter & Gamble, however, where the ownership (stockholders) and control of operations (the board of directors and managers) are in the hands of different parties.

Unlike the owners' equity sections for the sole proprietorship and the partnership, the owners' equity section for a corporate balance sheet does *not* combine (1) owner investments, (2) net income and net losses, and (3) withdrawals in one capital account. Instead different accounts are maintained for the investments made by stockholders and the net income or losses achieved by management. Owner investments are recorded in a Common Stock account. A separate account called **Retained Earnings** is used to keep track of the profits generated by the business. Just as sole proprietorships and partnerships permit owner withdrawals, corporations follow a similar practice. Corporate withdrawals are termed **dividends** and represent distributions of profits to the stockholders. At any point in time, then, the balance in the Retained Earnings account represents the firm's undistributed profits, that is, the earnings that are left (retained) in the business.

A simplified owners' (stockholders') equity section of a corporate balance sheet would appear as follows:

Stockholders' equity	
Common stock, 10,000 shares authorized and issued	*$100,000*
Retained earnings	*42,500*
Total stockholders' equity	*$142,500*

In practice, accounting for corporate equity can become quite complex. Further discussion of corporations is presented in Chapters 13 and 14.

Income Statement

Almost all businesses are started with the objective of producing a profit or "making money." These phrases, when put into accounting terms, mean the generation of net income. Some businesses do produce sizable amounts of net income for their owners. For example, witness the large profits of oil companies in the late 1970s. On the other hand, many businesses are only marginally profitable and are operated on the proverbial shoestring before the owners decide to sell their interests.

The meaning of profit

The quest for profits is an integral part of the capitalist system. Profits (or losses) are the result of managers using the economic factors of production—land, labor, and capital—in an effective (or ineffective) manner. Before the profits of a business can be tabulated, we must have a clear understanding of the meaning of "profit." Economists define "profit" in terms of being "better off." That is, profit constitutes the amount by which a business is better off at the end of a period compared to the beginning of the period. Profit would therefore represent a comparison of worth or value at two different points in time.

Unfortunately, use of the term "better off" is very subjective and is often an outgrowth of personal opinion and moods. How would an accountant measure being better off? How would you measure it for yourself? Accountants would have to rely on the opinion of an appraiser or team of appraisers at the end of each period. What happens if the appraisers disagree on changes in worth or "well-offness"? Should the accountant use an average of opinions or perhaps discard the high and low opinion and average the others? Obviously, the economic concept of profit does not allow for the precision and objectivity needed for the preparation and presentation of the income statement.

As a result, accountants have developed a different definition of income (or profit). Accounting income is measured by subtracting an organization's expenses from its revenues. Revenues and expenses, in turn, are entered in the accounts as a result of *transactions,* that is, financial events and activities that produce a change in an entity's assets, liabilities, and/or owners' equity. Examples of such events and activities include the sale of merchandise, the payment of employee salaries, and the placement of advertising in a newspaper. Essentially, then, the accountant has abandoned the economic concept of profit and employs a **transactions approach** when determining and measuring net income.

Usefulness of the income statement

The income statement provides detailed information concerning a company's profitability by disclosing sources of revenue and the dollar amount of each source; the discounts, allowances, and returns related to sales or other revenues; the cost of goods sold; a breakdown of expenses into functional categories such as selling and administrative; income tax expense; and net income. The income statement also includes the results of extraordinary events and, for corporations, the earnings per share. Extraordinary events and earnings per share are discussed later in the chapter.

By reviewing a series of income statements of a business, users can determine how fast sales are increasing and whether the rate of increase exceeds the inflation rate. They can judge if cost of goods sold and expenses are increasing too rapidly or are being controlled by management. In addition, income statement readers can examine the income tax rates imposed on the reporting company and study overall profitability.

Over the years the income statement has become the most important of the financial statements. As evidence, when newspapers report the financial activities of large corporations, they often publish only sales, net income, and earnings-per-share information. All three of these figures come from the income statement. Why is there such an emphasis on income? The existence of future income will enable a corporation to pay dividends or expand operations to meet expected customer demands. (Previously earned income probably has already been spent, committed to various projects, or distributed to owners.) Users of income statements therefore review past and current profitability as a means of forecasting what future profitability will be. Future profitability from operations will partially prove whether today's business decisions are correct.

Income statement format

There are two methods of presentation for accounts on the income statement, the single-step approach and the multiple-step approach. With a **single-step income statement,** there is one section for revenues and another section for costs and expenses.[2] The single-step format offers the advantage of simplicity, since net income (or loss) before income tax is determined with one step (i.e., one subtraction). Because many unsophisticated users of financial information are confused by a detailed income statement, an increasing number of companies prefer to report their net income (or loss) in a single-step presentation. A single-step income statement of American Greetings Corporation, a manufacturer of greeting cards and gift wrap, is shown in Exhibit 6-5.

In a **multiple-step income statement,** accounts are presented by association so that important relationships can be seen easily by readers. Merchandising firms, for example, deduct cost of goods sold from net sales to arrive at gross profit. In addition, many companies segregate interest expense and interest revenue into a category called nonoperating or other income (expense) that is placed after operating income from normal busi-

[2]Income taxes may be shown separately.

Exhibit 6-5

Single-step income statement

AMERICAN GREETINGS CORPORATION **Consolidated Statements of Income** **For the Year Ended February 28, 1982** **(000 omitted)**	
Net Sales	$605,970
Other income	17,634
Total revenue	$623,604
Costs and expenses:	
Material, labor and production costs	$276,071
Selling, distribution and marketing	179,021
Administrative and general	76,494
Depreciation and amortization	12,752
Interest	21,647
	$565,985
Income before income taxes	$ 57,619
Income taxes	24,776
Net income	$ 32,843

ness activities. The rationale for this placement is that interest is not derived from operations (such as selling a product or rendering a service) but from a financing condition of having or needing extra cash. Many accountants believe that specific placements and the generation of important subtotals such as gross profit make the multiple-step statement more informative and useful.

The multiple-step income statement of The Waikiki Trading Company, Inc., is presented in Exhibit 6-6. Note the grouping of accounts by association and the number of steps involved before net income is presented.

Given the single- and multiple-step formats, we will now take a look at the various components on the income statement.

Revenues

Revenues are the amounts charged to customers for goods sold or services rendered. As we noted in Chapter 1, revenues take different forms, depending on the entity involved (e.g., sales, fees, commissions, and so on). Revenues are usually listed on the income statement at gross amounts. Direct reductions caused by such items as sales discounts and sales returns and allowances are then made to arrive at net revenues.

Expenses

Expenses are the costs incurred in the production of revenues that are reported on the income statement. The expenses are matched against and

Exhibit 6-6

Multiple-step income statement

THE WAIKIKI TRADING COMPANY, INC.
Income Statement
For the Year Ended December 31, 1983

Revenues				
Sales				$510,000
Less: Sales discounts			$ 10,000	
Sales returns & allowances			5,000	15,000
Net sales				$495,000
Cost of goods sold				
Beginning inventory, Jan. 1			$100,000	
Add: Purchases		$120,000		
Freight-in		5,000		
		$125,000		
Less: Purchases discounts	$4,000			
Purchases returns & allowances	1,000	5,000		
Net purchases			120,000	
Goods available for sale			$220,000	
Less: Ending inventory, Dec. 31			50,000	
Cost of goods sold				170,000
Gross profit				$325,000
Operating expenses				
Selling expenses				
Advertising		$ 45,000		
Sales salaries		27,000		
Depreciation expense: building		10,000		
Depreciation expense: store equipment		13,000		
Depreciation expense: delivery vans		14,000		
Miscellaneous		8,000		
Total selling expenses			$117,000	
General & administrative expenses				
Executive salaries		$ 95,000		
Office salaries		43,000		
Insurance		18,500		
Depreciation expense: building		5,000		
Miscellaneous		12,500		
Total general & administrative expenses			174,000	
Total operating expenses				291,000
Income from operations				$ 34,000
Other expenses				
Interest expense				4,000
Net income before income taxes				$ 30,000
Income taxes				10,000
Net income				$ 20,000

deducted from these revenues. Expenses are typically categorized as follows:

Cost of goods sold
Selling expenses
General and administrative expenses
Nonoperating expenses
Income tax expense

Cost of goods sold is subtracted from net sales revenues to yield gross profit. Selling and general and administrative expenses are known collectively as **operating expenses,** that is, expenses that relate to normal business activities and operations. For presentation purposes operating expenses are usually divided into those expenses incurred in generating sales and those pertaining to administration of the business. Certain individual expenses may need to be split between selling and general and administrative because they relate to both functional areas. An example would be depreciation on a building that houses both selling activities and administrative offices.

Companies frequently incur expenses (and revenues) that are not directly related to normal business activities. As an example, assume a retail store leased some extra space to a charitable organization for use as an office. The retail store would earn rental revenue and may incur some added expense (such as maintenance) as a result of the lease. In the single-step income statement the revenue and expense would be presented as part of total revenues and total expenses. On the multiple-step income statement, however, items related to the lease affecting net income would be presented in a separate nonoperating (other) category. As noted earlier, interest revenue and interest expense also appear in this classification (see Exhibit 6-6).

Income tax expense is typically deducted separately from other firm expenses in both the single- and multiple-step formats. This practice is evident by reexamining the income statements of American Greetings Corporation and The Waikiki Trading Company. Income taxes are afforded special treatment because the amount of the tax is dependent on the calculation of a company's net income before tax. In Waikiki's case, for example, the company is subject to a $33\frac{1}{3}\%$ tax rate. Income taxes amounting to \$10,000 (\$30,000 $\times$ $33\frac{1}{3}\%$) are deducted to yield a final net income figure of \$20,000. In essence, income tax expense can be viewed as a sharing of net income with the government, as opposed to an expense incurred in the generation of revenue.

Measuring net income

Businesses enter into a variety of earnings transactions. Many transactions are routine, such as sales to customers and payments for salaries and supplies; others, however, are not. For example, a business may only occasionally sell a piece of equipment, a building, or a long-term investment. These assets may have been purchased years ago, with management having no intention of selling them. Market and economic conditions change, however, and management may ultimately decide that disposal is the proper course of action to follow. Transactions involving the sale of property, plant, and equipment or investments, as well as other events, often give rise to a gain or loss. To illustrate, suppose a firm purchased a parcel of land for $56,000 for use as a future plant site in a companywide expansion program. At some later date the company may sell the land because of a change in plans. If the land is sold for $100,000, there is a gain of $44,000 ($100,000 – $56,000) on the sale. Gains and losses affect profitability and are therefore disclosed on the income statement. Gains increase net income, while losses cause a reduction. For businesses using a multiple-step income statement, such gains and losses are usually placed in the other income (expense) category. As an example, a recent income statement of Northwest Airlines, Inc., contained the following gain (figures are in thousands):

Operating income		*$1,747*
Other income (expenses)		
Interest	*$(14,135)*	
Gain on sale of flight equipment	*16,975*	
Other	*3,322*	*6,162*
Earnings before income taxes		*$7,909*

Extraordinary gains and losses

On occasion a firm may be involved with a transaction or event that (1) is clearly different from the firm's customary business activities and (2) results in a sizable gain or loss. In other words, the transaction or event is both unusual in character and occurs infrequently, possibly only once in the lifetime of the business. This type of transaction or event results in **extraordinary gains or losses.** Extraordinary gains and losses may arise from such events as earthquakes, tornadoes, hurricanes, floods, and other acts of God. In addition, the loss suffered because of a newly enacted law or regulation that forced the closing of a plant or a halt in the production of certain products is normally classified as extraordinary.

Treatment of a gain or a loss as extraordinary is dependent on whether the event that gave rise to the gain or loss is both unusual and infrequent for the particular business. For example, consider the loss suffered, as a result of an earthquake, by a store that deals in fine china and porcelain figurines. If the store was located in Iowa, the loss would be classified as extraordinary. On the other hand, if the store was located in northern California, which is prone to earthquakes, the loss would not qualify for extraordinary treatment.

Extraordinary gains and losses are presented separately on the income statement and, importantly, after the results of normal and usual operating activities. The proper presentation method is shown in Exhibit 6-7.

In addition to separate disclosure, a firm must show the related tax effect of the extraordinary gain or loss. Extraordinary gains increase net income and thereby increase income tax expense. Conversely, extraordinary losses reduce net income and income taxes, thus providing a company with a tax savings. In Mincer's case the net income tax expense is $54,000:

Exhibit 6-7

Income statement presentation of extraordinary items

MINCER WHOLESALE COMPANY
Income Statement
For the Year Ended December 31, 1983

Net sales		$600,000
Cost of goods sold		240,000
Gross profit		$360,000
Operating expenses		
Selling	$110,000	
General & administrative	80,000	190,000
Income from operations		$170,000
Other expenses		20,000
Net income before income taxes		$150,000
Income taxes		60,000
Net income before extraordinary items		$ 90,000
Extraordinary loss	$ 20,000	
Less: Tax savings	6,000	14,000
Net income		$ 76,000

$60,000 of taxes based on usual recurring activities less a $6,000 tax savings from the extraordinary loss.

Observe that all earnings transactions and events that occurred during the accounting period, including extraordinary items, are presented on the income statement. This approach to the measurement and presentation of net income is called the **all-inclusive approach.** With the all-inclusive approach the income statement includes operating and nonoperating revenues and expenses, gains and losses from occasional sales of assets, and extraordinary gains and losses. Such a comprehensive measure of profit may inadvertently draw some attention away from the normal recurring earnings of the firm. By separate disclosures, however, readers are made aware that the all-inclusive net income figure is composed of earnings (losses) resulting from (1) ordinary business activities and (2) events that just happened to occur during the accounting period. The use of a section for extraordinary gains and losses is an example of this disclosure procedure. Knowledge of normal versus highly unusual and infrequent events is especially useful when performing any type of comparative analysis, such as studying the net income of a given company from one year to the next or comparing the net income of one company with that of another.

Earnings per share

As we discussed earlier, corporations issue shares of common stock to represent ownership interests in the business. Some corporations issue only a handful of shares; thus each share represents a substantial ownership percentage of the company. In contrast, other firms issue millions of shares. Because corporations have different levels of profitability and different numbers of shares, a computation called **earnings per share** is frequently used to compare businesses on a common basis. At this point in your accounting career, earnings per share will be defined as follows:

net income ÷ number of common shares

In Chapter 14 a more complex discussion of the calculation of earnings per share is presented.

Earnings per share is really a summarization of every item included on the income statement on a per-share basis; it is somewhat like the won-loss record of a sports team at the end of a long and grueling season. Earnings-per-share amounts are widely circulated in the financial press as soon as they are available. Investors and other users of financial statements make decisions based on past trends and future prospects of this key business figure. Because of its importance, earnings per share must be disclosed on the face of the income statement. To be consistent with the material just presented, the earnings per share attributed to extraordinary gains and losses, if any, should also be revealed. Kennington, Ltd., a manufacturer of leisurewear for men and boys, reported the earnings-per-share information shown in Exhibit 6-8 in a recent annual report.

Exhibit 6-8

Earnings-per-share disclosure of Kennington, Ltd.

KENNINGTON, LTD.
Statement of Income
For the Year Ended December 31, 1981

Net sales	$75,073,000
Cost of sales	55,236,000
Gross profit	19,837,000
Operating expenses	12,930,000
Operating income	6,907,000
Interest income (net)	4,445,000
Income before provision for income taxes	11,352,000
Provision for income taxes	3,059,000
Net income	$ 8,293,000
Earnings per share of common stock	$1.46

Statement of Owners' Equity

The statement of owners' equity discloses changes in the owners' equity during the accounting period. Remember that increases to owners' equity arise from investments by the owner(s) and net income, while decreases result from withdrawals and net losses. An example of a statement of owners' equity for a sole proprietorship is shown on page 21.

The owners' equity statement of a corporation is somewhat different from that of a proprietorship. As we noted earlier in the chapter, corporations maintain a separate account for the capital contributed by the stockholders (Common Stock) and for the firm's earnings less dividends distributed (Retained Earnings). Any changes in the owners' equity accounts for a corporation are presented in a *statement of stockholders' equity.* If the only transactions affecting owners' equity result from net income (or net loss) and the distribution of dividends, the statement of owners' equity contains changes only in the Retained Earnings account. Accordingly, the statement is known as the **statement of retained earnings.** The retained earnings statement of The Maytag Company, a manufacturer of appliances, appears in Exhibit 6-9.

Exhibit 6-9

Statement of retained earnings

THE MAYTAG COMPANY
Statement of Retained Earnings
For the Year Ended December 31, 1981

Retained earnings at beginning of year	*$140,674,052*
Net income for the year	*37,436,063*
	$178,110,115
Cash dividends, $2.15 per share	*(30,252,833)*
Retained earnings at end of year	*$147,857,282*

DISCLOSURE

The financial activities and policies of companies that operate in today's business environment are complex and often beyond the comprehension of the average financial statement user. For example, businesses often do the following:

Use a variety of different accounting policies.
Operate in a number of different industries.
Merge with other companies.
Change accounting policies from those followed in the previous year.

Although only a sampling, the practices above complicate the reporting process. It is virtually impossible for financial statements to convey a clear picture of financial condition and profitability unless some additional information is presented. For this reason we wish to acquaint you with **disclosure,** an important area sometimes overlooked by investors and other statement users. Adequate disclosure can be achieved in several different ways. Keeping our discussion at a basic level, we will focus on the techniques of footnotes, parenthetical information, and comparative data.

Footnotes

The set of financial statements issued by a firm normally includes **footnotes.**[3] Footnotes provide an expansion of the information contained in the body of the financial statements to assist in statement interpretation. Unfortunately, much of this supplemental information is quite technical and often flavored with specialized accounting jargon that confuses rather than clarifies. The excerpt from *CA Magazine* illustrates the magnitude of the problem (see p. 234).

Contingencies

Footnotes are a supplemental, yet integral, part of financial statements. Despite the possible reading problem, they contain a wealth of valuable (and interesting) information. As an example, Dr Pepper Company recently made the following footnote disclosure regarding contingencies:

> *In 1979, a private antitrust action was filed in Louisiana in which the plaintiff contends that the Company's decision to license the Coca-Cola bottler in Lake Charles, Louisiana, to produce Dr Pepper soft drinks, rather than the plaintiff (a 7-Up/Pepsi bottler) was violative of federal antitrust laws. Damages are sought in the amount of $15 million, trebled. The Company intends to defend this action vigorously, and believes that the plaintiff's claims are unfounded, without merit, and that the Company has substantial defenses to the plaintiff's claims.*

Contingencies are circumstances such as those above where the outcome is uncertain. The footnotes provide an excellent forum to disclose contingencies that may ultimately involve either future revenue or future expense. To record such contingencies in the accounts is generally premature, but to disclose their existence is prudent.

Commitments

Important contracts and **commitments** of a company with other entities should also be disclosed via footnotes. For example, a recent annual report of CBS Inc., contained the following footnote concerning broadcasting and recording commitments:

> *The Company routinely enters into commitments to purchase the rights to broadcast programs, including feature films and sports events, on television. These contracts permit the broadcast of such properties for various periods ending no later than December 31, 1998. The Company also enters into long-term contracts with recording artists and companies for the production and/or distribution of records and tapes. These contracts cover various periods through December 31, 1989. As of December 31, 1981 the Company was committed to make payments under such broadcasting and recorded music contracts of $818,874,000 and $192,484,000, respectively.*

Because this topic is somewhat advanced, a brief explanation is in order. Contracts and commitments are not entered in the accounting records until their related financial transactions actually take place. The underlying

[3] A complete set of footnotes accompanies the financial statements of Wendy's International, Inc., appearing in Appendix A at the end of the book.

THE READABILITY OF FINANCIAL STATEMENT FOOTNOTES

Footnotes to financial statements play an important role by providing additional information that cannot be disclosed in a few words or by a single number in the body of the financial statements. The information may pertain to such areas as restrictions, commitments, or pending litigation by or against a company. To communicate, however, footnotes to financial statements must possess certain characteristics, one of which is readability.

The U.S. accounting profession is aware of the increased participation and interest in investing by average citizens and recommends that financial information should be expressed in a form and with terminology adapted to the users' range of understanding. The consequences, if the footnotes are not written appropriately, are that the average investors will not be provided with the information they are entitled to and that the auditors may be subjected to lawsuits by the owners.

Writing footnotes that are easy to understand is a particularly difficult and frustrating task for accountants; difficult because they must express involved technical matters in language or style that persons without technical accounting training will understand; frustrating because the primary concern is with the accounting information, not with writing style. Have accountants followed the recommendations and written footnotes appropriate for average investors?

In the mid-1970s a sample of 927 footnotes from 96 of the 500 largest U.S. corporations was tested for readability, using a well-known readability formula. The results showed that only 64% of American stockholders, those who have some amount of college education, would be able to understand and comprehend the footnotes of 88% of the companies selected. The 36% who had no college education could only comprehend the footnotes of 7% of the firms because these companies wrote footnotes at the 11th-12th grade reading level. Five percent of the companies had footnotes understandable only by college graduates.

Little improvement, if any, has been made in the readability of footnotes since the study was done. This means, of course, that financial footnotes are still understood only by an audience considerably more sophisticated in reading ability than are the average investors.

SOURCE Adapted from James S. Worthington, "Making Financial Statement Footnotes More Readable," CA Magazine, September 1977, pp. 469–478.

reason behind this practice is that a company's obligation to pay money usually depends on the ability of another party to provide certain goods or services according to the terms of an agreement (contract). Since such performance normally cannot be guaranteed ahead of time, it would be improper to record such contracts in the accounts prior to their execution. Thus footnote disclosure is the proper treatment for these agreements.

Segment reporting

Footnotes to the financial statements also contain information concerning the different **segments** (parts) of a company if the company is involved in more than one business activity. Firms meeting certain criteria must provide selected accounting data by industry segment according to prescribed guidelines. Reporting information in this manner assists the financial statement user in assessing the profitability and the importance of each segment to the business. To illustrate, The Gillette Company has five operating segments: Blades and Razors, Toiletries and Grooming Aids, Writing Instruments (Paper Mate and Liquid Paper), Braun AG (a manufacturer of small appliances), and Other Products. A recent financial statement footnote (see Exhibit 6-10) revealed the composition of the firm's total sales and operating profit. The footnote shows that while Blades and Razors generated approximately one-third of net sales, this segment accounted for nearly 70% of segment-produced profit. Furthermore, Other Products appears to have experienced financial difficulties, as evidenced by recent losses. Both of these informative disclosures would have been "buried" in Gillette's overall income statement, which, like others, simply shows *total* sales and profit figures.

Exhibit 6-10

Segment reporting by The Gillette Company

Net sales (in millions)	**1981**		**1980**	
	$	**%***	**$**	**%***
Blades and razors	775.6	33.2	743.0	32.1
Toiletries and grooming aids	661.4	28.3	597.1	25.8
Writing instruments	303.5	13.0	289.3	12.5
Braun products	451.4	19.4	496.1	21.4
Other products	142.5	6.1	189.8	8.2
Total	2,334.4	100.0	2,315.3	100.0

Profit from operations (in millions)	**1981**		**1980**	
	$	**%***	**$**	**%***
Blades and razors	234.7	70.9	204.6	68.9
Toiletries and grooming aids	57.9	17.5	49.6	16.7
Writing instruments	26.7	8.0	31.9	10.7
Braun products	22.8	6.9	23.6	8.0
Other products	(10.9)	(3.3)	(12.9)	(4.3)
Total	331.2	100.0	296.8	100.0

*Percentages computed by the authors.

Accounting policies

Footnotes are also used to disclose the accounting policies a business employs in keeping its accounting records. Information is normally furnished regarding a company's treatment of various assets, income taxes, pension costs, and other significant matters. The purpose of disclosing accounting policies is to inform the statement reader of the procedures used in the computation of certain account balances. This practice is especially useful when a firm can choose from among different accounting alternatives. Policy disclosure allows a clearer understanding of the information presented.

Parenthetical Information

Rather than use separate footnotes, many companies make **parenthetical disclosures** in the body of the financial statements. Parenthetical information was provided on the balance sheet of The Williamsburg Company in Exhibit 6-4 to assist you in better understanding the presentation. See the certificate of deposit, land investment, long-term receivables, and mortgage payable as examples.

Sometimes parenthetical disclosure is furnished for assets that have increased in value. For instance, suppose that many years ago a company purchased 10 diamonds for $40,000 as an investment. If the diamonds are now worth $120,000, the firm would have the following balance sheet presentation:

Investments: diamonds (estimated market value, $120,000) $40,000

Notice that the original cost of the investment, $40,000, is not changed in the accounting records even though the value has increased. The original cost remains in the accounts, because it is the outgrowth of the only transaction that has taken place, the purchase of the diamonds. To use value or worth instead of cost for the investment account would permit a subjective opinion to supersede a known, objective fact.

Comparative Data

Except for the first period of operation, financial statements are often presented on a **comparative basis.** Thus, for example, when the 1983 financial statements of a business are issued, they are presented in side-by-side columns along with the statements of 1982. Likewise, in quarterly financial statements, information for the second quarter of 1983 may be presented with that of the second quarter of 1982. Disclosures in this manner assist users in making comparisons and assessing the direction of a business over time. As an example of comparative disclosure, restudy Exhibit 6-10, which contains segment (and comparative) data of The Gillette Company.

KEY TERMS AND CONCEPTS

account form balance sheet 217
all-inclusive approach 230
commitments 233
common stock 223
comparative data 236
contingencies 233
corporation 223
current assets 219
current liabilities 221
current ratio 221
disclosure 232
dividends 223
earnings per share 231
extraordinary gains and losses 229
footnotes 233
intangible assets 221
liquidity 219
long-term investments 221
long-term liabilities 222
multiple-step income statement 225
operating cycle 219
operating expenses 228
parenthetical disclosure 236
partnership 223
property, plant, and equipment 221
report form balance sheet 217
retained earnings 223
segment information 235
single-step income statement 225
sole proprietorship 222
statement of retained earnings 232
transactions approach 224
working capital 222

QUESTIONS

Q6-1 How do the balance sheet and the income statement differ in portraying the financial activities of a business? How do the balance sheet and the statement of owners' equity differ?

Q6-2 Discuss the limitations of the balance sheet.

Q6-3 Define the operating cycle and explain how the cycle is lengthened. Should businesses attempt to shorten the cycle or lengthen it? Why?

Q6-4 How should current assets be organized on the balance sheet?

Q6-5 What is an intangible asset? Present three examples of intangible assets.

Q6-6 Discuss the use of the current ratio in making credit decisions.

Q6-7 How does the form of business organization (sole proprietorship, partnership, or corporation) affect the owners' equity section of the balance sheet?

Q6-8 Explain the transactions approach to determining a company's net income or net loss.

Q6-9 What is an extraordinary gain or loss? How are extraordinary gains and losses presented on a company's income statement?

Q6-10 What is meant by the all-inclusive approach of determining net income or net loss?

Q6-11 Must earnings per share be computed for all business entities or just corporations? Why? Where should earnings per share be disclosed in the financial statements?

Q6-12 What is the purpose of providing footnotes?

Q6-13 What is a contingency?

Q6-14 How are important contracts and commitments between a business and other entities (unions, suppliers, customers) disclosed in the financial statements? Why are they disclosed in this manner?

Q6-15 Why must companies that are involved in numerous business activities disclose segment information in their financial statements?

Q6-16 Stanback Company bought some land for $50,000 in 1959; the land is currently valued at $200,000. How should Stanback disclose the value of the land in its financial statements?

EXERCISES

E6-1 The balance sheet of the Vicks Company is similar to that appearing in Exhibit 6-4. Under which classification would each of the following accounts appear?

a Salaries payable
b Accumulated depreciation: trucks
c Prepaid rent expense
d Merchandise inventory
e Receivable from Jim Blankenship, due in 3 years
f Long-term investment in IT&T common stock
g Patents
h Accounts receivable
i Salaries expense
j John Vicks, capital

E6-2 Selected accounts of the Mercer Island Company, with current balances, are presented below.

Accounts receivable	*$ 20,000*
Accounts payable	*45,800*
Merchandise inventory	*40,400*
Sales	*100,000*
Salary expense	*30,500*
Prepaid rent expense	*1,600*
Equipment	*132,000*
Land	*12,000*
Accumulated depreciation: equipment	*66,000*
Cash	*4,000*
Note payable, due in 5 months	*14,200*
Loan payable, due in 5 years	*45,000*

a Determine the current ratio. Who would be interested in this ratio?
b Calculate Mercer Island's working capital.
c How will working capital be affected if Mercer Island has a crash program to collect its receivables?
d How will the current ratio be affected if Mercer Island has a crash program to sell a large portion of its merchandise inventory?

E6-3 Presented on the next page are the balance sheet accounts of Wenotchee Trading, Inc., together with some important subtotals.

Cash	*$ 37,100*
Land	*15,000*
Accounts receivable	*50,000*
Buildings	*54,000*
Merchandise inventory	*194,500*
Accounts payable	*68,600*
Property, plant, & equipment (total)	*82,500*
Current assets	*285,000*
Salaries payable	*2,100*
Equipment	*64,000*
Accumulated depreciation: buildings	*?*
Prepaid insurance	*?*
Interest payable	*3,000*
Current liabilities	*78,700*
*Bank loan payable, due in 1998**	*?*
Common stock	*100,000*
Retained earnings	*?*
Total liabilities	*168,700*
Accumulated depreciation: equipment	*37,000*

**During the 1984 calendar year, $5,000 of the loan is payable to the bank.*

Prepare a classified report form balance sheet for the corporation as of December 31, 1983.

E6-4 Selected account balances from Blaine, Inc., for the current year include the following:

Sales	*$353,000*	*Sales discounts*	*$ 1,000*
Income tax	*32,200*	*Beginning inventory*	*95,400*
Purchases	*201,000*	*Salesmen's salaries*	*11,000*
Advertising expense	*9,000*	*Insurance expense*	*4,400*
Administrative salaries	*25,800*	*Depreciation expense*	*10,000*
Ending inventory	*99,000*	*Sales returns*	*2,000*

One thousand shares of common stock have been issued by the corporation. Forty percent of the insurance and depreciation expense relates to Blaine's sales activities. Calculate the following:

a Net revenues
b Cost of goods sold
c Gross profit
d Total selling expenses
e Total general and administrative expenses
f Net income
g Earnings per share

E6-5 The Tacoma Company, a retailer of Indian rugs and products, uses the accrual basis of accounting. Indicate whether the following items give rise to (1) operating revenue, (2) other income (nonoperating), (3) an extraordinary item, or (4) none of the above.

______ a Sold land, carried in the accounting records as an investment, for $85,000. The original cost of the land was $25,000.

______ b A Mercedes delivery truck purchased for $15,000 has a current appraised value of $25,000.

_____ c Sold merchandise on account for $11,700.

_____ d Tacoma's warehouse was destroyed by an earthquake, the first such earthquake in the city's recorded history. Cost of the warehouse was $147,500; insurance proceeds amounted to $160,000.

_____ e Received a commitment from a customer to buy some rare artifacts from inventory for $15,000. Cost of the artifacts was $7,500.

_____ f Sold merchandise to an out-of-town customer for $750. Accepted a check from a small out-of-state bank.

E6-6 Homer City News, publisher of a weekly newspaper, is organized as a partnership. Listed below are several of the company's accounts and balances as of November 30, 1983.

Sales: over the counter	$40,100	Interest earned	$ 900
Unearned subscription sales	22,000	Utilities expense	2,900
Labor expenses	12,500	Maintenance expense	4,200
Paper costs	14,000	Loss on sale of truck	450
Interest expense	800	Juan del Rio, capital	25,400
Other expenses	5,100	Property tax expense	3,400
Gain on sale of press	4,150	Dividends received	200
Paul Wiggins, capital	50,800		

As of November 30, $18,000 of subscription sales has yet to be earned.

a Prepare a single-step income statement for the month of November. Ignore income taxes.

b Calculate the partners' capital balances at the end of the month (after closing) if net income is split $\frac{2}{3}$ for Wiggins and $\frac{1}{3}$ for del Rio.

E6-7 You have the following information concerning the Commerce Company for the year ended December 31, 1983.

Net income from operations	$70,000
Extraordinary loss (before tax)	24,000
Interest revenue	4,000
Dividends: $1 per share	10,000

Commerce is subject to a 40% tax rate. From the information presented, construct as detailed an income statement as is possible.

E6-8 The following information relates to Poster City, Inc., for the year ended December 31, 1983.

Dividends paid	$ 40,000
Common stock (end of year)	80,000
Total assets (end of year)	420,000
Net income from operations (before tax)	120,000
Gain on sale of truck	4,000
Total liabilities (end of year)	150,000

Assuming Poster City is subject to a 40% income tax rate, prepare a statement of retained earnings for the year ended December 31, 1983.

E6-9 Determine whether the following transactions or events would increase (+), decrease (−), or have no effect (0) on a company's working capital and earnings per share.

		Working Capital	Earnings per Share
a	The sale of inventory on account at a price above cost.	______	______
b	The collection of an account receivable.	______	______
c	The recording of accrued interest expense at the end of the period.	______	______
d	The signing of a contract to purchase materials.	______	______
e	The purchase of a truck for cash.	______	______
f	The purchase of merchandise inventory on account.	______	______

PROBLEMS

P6-1 *Balance sheet classification*

Presented below are the account classifications on a balance sheet.

1 Current assets
2 Long-term investments
3 Property, plant, & equipment
4 Intangible assets
5 Other assets
6 Current liabilities
7 Long-term liabilities
8 Owners' (stockholders') equity

The following accounts were taken from the general ledger of Kern Corporation.

a Pension fund: employees
b Sales
c Prepaid commissions expense
d Equipment
e Copyrights
f Certificate of deposit (matures in 6 months)
g Common stock
h Accounts payable
i Merchandise inventory (ending)
j Interest receivable
k Office supplies
l Loss from hurricane damage
m Land
n Notes payable (due in 1995)
o Notes receivable (matures in 3 months)
p Dividends
q Accumulated depreciation: equipment
r Interest payable
s Interest expense
t Franchise

INSTRUCTIONS

Classify Kern's accounts as to their proper placement on the balance sheet. For those accounts not appearing on the balance sheet, determine whether they appear on the income statement or the statement of retained earnings.

P6-2 *Income statement classification*

Welder's Supply Company sells its own inventory to area factories in addition to selling products for other companies on a commission basis. Presented below are the categories used in a multiple-step income statement.

1 Revenue
2 Cost of goods sold
3 Selling expenses
4 General & administrative expenses
5 Other income (expense)
6 Income taxes
7 Extraordinary items

The following accounts were taken from the firm's general ledger.

a Depreciation expense: office
b Freight-in
c Commissions earned
d Depreciation expense: delivery equipment
e Sales returns
f Commissions to salespersons
g Office supplies expense
h Inventory (ending)
i Interest expense
j Customer entertainment expense
k Sales
l Purchases
m Payroll taxes payable
n Loss from spring flood (recurring event)
o Freight-out
p J. B. Gibbons, drawing
q Interest revenue
r J. B. Gibbons, capital
s Miscellaneous expense (relates to management of the business)

INSTRUCTIONS

Classify the accounts of Welder's Supply as to their proper placement on the income statement. If any of the accounts do not appear on the income statement, determine whether they appear on the balance sheet or the statement of owners' equity.

P6-3 ***Classified balance sheet***

Assume that Case Company, a partnership, has the following balance sheet accounts at the end of 1983.

Jack Feltner, capital	*$13,000*
Building	*82,000*
Accumulated depreciation: office furniture	*800*
Note receivable (due May 1984)	*4,200*
Cash	*5,150*
Merchandise inventory	*41,570*
Note payable (due 1995)	*48,560*
Office furniture	*8,000*
Land held for speculation	*18,320*
Receivable from former partner (due 1990)	*3,355*
Temporary investments	*22,000*
Joan Miller, capital	*20,000*
Salaries payable	*750*
Accounts receivable	*31,500*
Current portion of bank loan payable	*2,000*
Accounts payable	*52,100*
Accumulated depreciation: building	*19,000*
Land	*37,500*
Note payable (due June 1984)	*71,800*
Patents	*10,000*
Prepaid insurance	*900*
Office supplies	*750*
Property taxes payable	*5,400*
Bank loan payable (long-term)	*24,000*
Paul Starz, capital	*7,835*

INSTRUCTIONS

Prepare a classified report form balance sheet in good form as of December 31, 1983.

P6-4 ***Error identification; preparation of balance sheet***

The balance sheet for Butler Co., a sole proprietorship, follows:

BUTLER CO.
Balance Sheet
For the Year Ended December 31, 1983

ASSETS			
Current assets			
Cash		$ 5,000	
Prepaid insurance		420	
Short-term investments (cost $20,000), at market		22,000	
Receivables (40% to be collected in 1989)		45,250	$ 72,670
Property, plant, & equipment			
Land	$412,000		
Buildings	142,500		
Equipment	25,600		
	$580,100		
Less: Accumulated depreciation	120,700	$459,400	
Merchandise inventory		80,000	539,400
Other assets			
Claim against former supplier for breach of contract (lawsuit pending)			4,000,000
Total assets			$4,612,070
LIABILITIES			
Current liabilities			
Accounts payable		$ 75,200	
Salaries payable		4,700	
Interest payable		2,350	
Property taxes payable		12,400	
Unearned rental revenue		400	$ 95,050
Long-term liabilities			
Mortgage payable (payable $10,000 per year for 35 years)		$ 350,000	
Sued by former employee for sex discrimination (lawsuit pending)		2,000,000	2,350,000
James Butler, original capital		$ 212,000	
James Butler, retained earnings		1,955,020	2,167,020
Total liabilities			$4,612,070

INSTRUCTIONS

a Indicate the deficiencies in the balance sheet above.

b Prepare a corrected classified report form balance sheet for the company. Assume that 90% of the accumulated depreciation relates to the building.

P6-5 ***Income statement preparation***

Presented below is financial information for the Prince Corporation for the year ended December 31, 1983.

General & administrative expenses	
Executive salaries	$ 84,000
Depreciation expense: building	47,000
Insurance expense	3,540
Merchandise inventory (beginning)	55,000
Interest revenue	10,000
Interest expense	8,000
Sales returns & allowances	2,200
Selling expenses	
Advertising	15,400
Sales salaries	54,100
Depreciation expense: building	24,300
Depreciation expense: store equipment	12,200
Freight-out	5,000
Purchases	342,000
Loss on sale of forklift	12,000
Sales	722,200
Loss due to flooding (extraordinary)	55,000
Dividends received	24,140
Freight-in	5,000
Sales discounts	20,000
Purchases discounts	19,800
Dividends paid	40,000
Purchases returns	16,600
Merchandise inventory (ending)	62,000

The corporation has issued 50,000 shares of common stock and is subject to a tax rate of 40%.

INSTRUCTIONS

a Prepare a multiple-step income statement for 1983.

b Discuss the advantages of the multiple-step format over the single-step format.

P6-6 ***Error identification, preparation of income statement and statement of owners' equity***

The multiple-step income statement for the Tigeress Company, a sole proprietorship owned by A. Trump, is presented on page 245. Tigeress operates a wholesale produce business near the equator.

Income Statement

Sales		$712,400
Interest earned		3,000
Purchases discounts		2,000
		$717,400
Less: Purchases		302,000
		$415,400
Less: Sales salaries	$ 22,000	
Administrative salaries	27,500	
Owner withdrawals	42,500	
Rent expense	5,400	
Advertising expense	11,800	
Insurance expense	7,540	
Depreciation expense	13,360	
Sales returns	10,000	
Loss on sale of equipment	16,000	
Utilities expense	25,400	
Lost key employee (estimated value)	7,000	
Sales discounts	2,400	
Loss due to freeze damage	100,000	290,900
Net income		$124,500

Other information:

1 Beginning inventory, $200,000; ending inventory, $50,000.
2 Trump's capital balance at the beginning of the year was $75,000.
3 Rent, insurance, depreciation, and utilities should be divided as follows:

	Selling	Administrative
Rent	80%	20%
Insurance	90%	10%
Depreciation	70%	30%
Utilities	70%	30%

INSTRUCTIONS

a Indicate any deficiencies in the income statement above.
b Prepare a corrected income statement for the year ended October 31, 1983, using the multiple-step format. Ignore income taxes.
c Prepare a statement of owners' equity for the company.

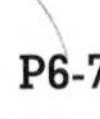

P6-7 ***Comprehensive problem: Income statement, statement of retained earnings, and balance sheet***

Presented next are the account balances of Haworth Library, Inc., a retail bookstore. The balances were taken from the work sheet after all adjustments were made by the bookkeeper. Haworth uses the periodic inventory method.

Accounts payable	***$101,500***
Accounts receivable	***9,500***
Accumulated depreciation: furniture & fixtures	***8,000***
Accumulated depreciation: store equipment	***12,000***
Accumulated depreciation: van	***3,000***
Administrative salaries	***20,000***
Advertising expense	***32,000***
Cash	***7,600***
Common stock (10,000 shares)	***10,000***
Depreciation expense: furniture & fixtures	***4,000***
Depreciation expense: store equipment	***6,000***
Depreciation expense: van	***3,000***
Dividends paid	***30,000***
Furniture & fixtures	***40,000***
Heat & light expense	***21,000***
Income tax expense	***15,600***
Interest expense	***5,000***
Merchandise inventory	
Jan. 1, 1983	***97,300***
Dec. 31, 1983	***100,000***
Payable to officers (long-term)	***50,000***
Prepaid rent expense	***2,600***
Purchases	***702,700***
Rent expense	***48,600***
Retained earnings, Jan. 1, 1983	***5,700***
Salaries expense: sales force	***43,400***
Salaries payable	***7,100***
Sales	***950,000***
Sales returns	***20,000***
Store equipment	***24,000***
Van	***15,000***

INSTRUCTIONS

a Prepare a multiple-step income statement and a statement of retained earnings for the year ended December 31, 1983. Depreciation expense should be divided as follows:

	Selling	***Administrative***
Store equipment	100%	—
Furniture & fixtures	50%	50%
Van	10%	90%

Rent and heat & light expenses should be allocated 80% to selling and 20% to administrative.

b Prepare a classified report form balance sheet as of December 31, 1983.

P6-8 ***Balance sheet classification (alternate to P6-1)***

Presented below are the account classifications on a balance sheet.

1 Current assets
2 Long-term investments
3 Property, plant, & equipment
4 Intangible assets
5 Other assets
6 Current liabilities
7 Long-term liabilities
8 Owners' equity

The following accounts were taken from the general ledger of Lansford Company.

a Delivery truck
b Cash
c Salaries payable
d Receivable from employee (matures in 1989)
e Patent
f Depreciation expense
g C. Lansford, drawing
h Merchandise inventory
i Unearned rental income
j Interest receivable
k Land held for future plant site
l Accumulated depreciation: building
m Trademark
n Office supplies expense
o Prepaid insurance
p Portion of long-term note payable (due within 6 months)
q Loss from truck accident
r Short-term investment in marketable securities
s Accounts receivable
t Parts inventory

INSTRUCTIONS

Classify Lansford's accounts as to their proper placement on the balance sheet. For those accounts not appearing on the balance sheet, determine whether they appear on the income statement or the statement of owners' equity.

P6-9 ***Income statement classification (alternate to P6-2)***

Skall's, Inc., sells menswear in a fashionable suburb of Minneapolis. The categories below were extracted from the firm's multiple-step income statement.

1 Revenue
2 Cost of goods sold
3 Selling expenses
4 General & administrative expenses
5 Other income (expense)
6 Income taxes
7 Extraordinary items

The following accounts appear in the general ledger.

a Purchases returns
b Office supplies
c Advertising expense
d Dividends earned on short-term investments
e Sales commissions
f Transportation-in
g Rental income (from tenant who occupies extra space in rear of store)
h Loan interest expense
i Computer expense (incurred from processing payroll)
j Sales returns
k Depreciation expense: store equipment
l Delivery expense
m Loan payable
n Loss on sale of delivery equipment
o Inventory (beginning)
p Officers' salaries
q Store counters
r Travel expense (to view new lines of inventory)
s Common stock

INSTRUCTIONS

Classify Skall's accounts as to their proper placement on the income statement. If any of the accounts do not appear on the income statement, determine whether they appear on the balance sheet or the statement of retained earnings.

P6-10 ***Classified balance sheet (alternate to P6-3)***

Assume that Clifford Clothiers, Inc., a corporation, has the following balance sheet accounts at the end of 1983:

Land held as a future plant site	$ 45,810
Note receivable (due in 1988)	21,200
Delivery equipment	10,000
Accumulated depreciation: building	74,000
Accounts receivable	34,560
Prepaid insurance	1,800
Prepaid rent	1,200
Office supplies	700
Note receivable (due in 1 month)	9,400
Certificate of deposit (matures in 2 months)	10,000
Accumulated depreciation: store equipment	14,700
Trademark	520
Accounts payable	47,000
Notes payable (due in 9 days)	25,000
Retained earnings	41,110
Store equipment	52,100
Cash	6,200
Payable to P. T. Wog (due in 1988)	52,000
Income taxes payable	18,500
Accumulated depreciation: delivery equipment	8,500
Merchandise inventory	52,600
Salaries payable	2,500
Building	124,000
Common stock	86,780

INSTRUCTIONS

Prepare a classified report form balance sheet in good form as of December 31, 1983.

P6-11 ***Income statement preparation (alternate to P6-5)***

Presented below is financial information of the Chiu Corporation for 1983.

Sales	$611,100
Freight-in	9,970
Interest expense	5,500
Interest revenue	7,200
Sales discounts	4,750
Purchases discounts	6,210
Gain on sale of truck	9,710
Merchandise inventory (ending)	49,200
Merchandise inventory (beginning)	43,500
Loss from tornado (extraordinary)	35,000
Dividends received	7,500
Purchases	212,100
Sales returns	10,000
Administrative expenses	
Officer salaries	55,000
Depreciation expense: buildings	27,000
Maintenance expense	15,200
Miscellaneous expense	5,700
Selling expenses	
Freight-out	14,200
Salespersons' salaries	27,200
Advertising expense	5,400
Depreciation expense: delivery equipment	12,500
Maintenance expense	2,900

The corporation has issued 50,000 shares of common stock to the public; the officers and employees own another 50,000 shares. The tax rate is 40%.

INSTRUCTIONS

a Prepare a multiple-step income statement for the year ended November 30, 1983.

b Would a tornado loss always be classified as an extraordinary item? Explain.

P6-12 ***Comprehensive problem: Income statement, statement of retained earnings, and balance sheet (alternate to P6-7)***

Presented below are the account balances of Bairdford Galleries, Inc., a retail dealer of original art and prints. The balances were taken from the work sheet after all adjustments were made by the bookkeeper. Bairdford uses the periodic inventory method.

Accounts payable	$ 20,300
Accounts receivable	1,900
Accumulated depreciation: automobile	1,600
Accumulated depreciation: office equipment	2,400
Accumulated depreciation: store equipment	600
Administrative salaries	4,000
Advertising expense	6,400
Automobile	8,000
Cash	1,520
Common stock (1,000 shares)	2,000
Depreciation expense: automobile	800
Depreciation expense: office equipment	1,200
Depreciation expense: store equipment	600
Dividends paid	6,000
Heat & light expense	4,200
Income tax expense	3,120
Interest expense	1,000
Merchandise inventory	
Jan. 1, 1983	19,460
Dec. 31, 1983	20,000
Office equipment	4,800
Payable to officers (long-term)	10,000
Prepaid rent expense	520
Purchases of merchandise	140,540
Rent expense	9,720
Retained earnings, Jan. 1, 1983	1,140
Salaries expense: sales	8,680
Salaries payable	1,420
Sales	190,000
Sales discounts	3,000
Sales returns & allowances	1,000
Store equipment	3,000

INSTRUCTIONS

a Prepare a multiple-step income statement and a statement of retained earnings for the year ended December 31, 1983. Depreciation expense should be divided as follows:

	Selling	Admin-istrative
Automobile	20%	80%
Office equipment	30%	70%
Store equipment	100%	—

Rent and heat & light expenses should be allocated 70% to selling and 30% to administrative.

b Prepare a classified report form balance sheet as of December 31, 1983.

CASE 6
ROYAL CROWN COMPANIES

Royal Crown Companies, Inc., is involved in four major business segments: soft drinks, fast-food, citrus production, and home furnishings. The soft drink division produces Royal Crown (RC) Cola, Diet Rite Cola, and Nehi soft drinks. The fast-food division has over 1,000 Arby's Restaurants. The citrus division produces Texsun and Adams fruit juices. Finally, home furnishings manufactures products that appeal to a wide range of customers of different ages, incomes, and life-styles via Frederick Cooper lamps, Couroc serving ware, Athens furniture, and Hoyne mirror tiles.

Presented below are portions of simplified balance sheets for Royal Crown Companies from 1979 and 1980 as well as segment income information (in thousands of dollars).

	December 31	
	1980	1979
Current assets		
Cash	$ 4,325	$ 6,585
Receivables	42,758	39,937
Inventories	53,380	51,458
Other	6,664	4,982
	$107,127	$102,962
Current liabilities		
Current portion of long-term debt	$ 3,991	$ 1,339
Notes payable	20,510	10,773
Dividends payable	2,132	2,132
Accounts payable	21,751	21,009
Accrued payables	19,874	26,500
	$68,258	$61,753

1980	*Soft Drink*	*Fast Food*	*Citrus*	*Home Furnishings*
Net sales	$220,731	$69,880	$78,706	$68,759
Operating profit	$ 13,942	$ 6,666	$ 9,704	$ 1,827
1979				
Net sales	$204,399	$75,497	$73,454	$68,025
Operating profit	$ 14,859	$11,058	$ 9,274	$ 5,306

INSTRUCTIONS

a Compute the amount of working capital of Royal Crown Companies at the end of 1980 and 1979. What is the trend in the firm's working capital?

b Compute the current ratio at the end of 1980 and 1979. Evaluate your findings.

c Which segment was the most profitable in 1980 and 1979 (1) in terms of absolute dollars and (2) as a percentage of sales? What additional information is generated by expressing profitability as a percentage of sales?

d What are some reasons for the disclosure of segment information? What problem might a large diversified company encounter in providing and generating segment information?

7 CASH AND SHORT-TERM INVESTMENTS

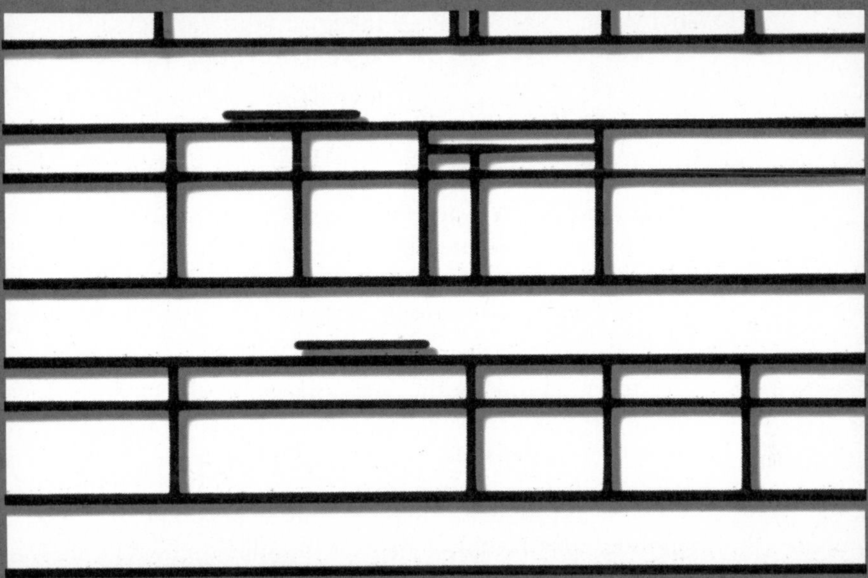

LEARNING OBJECTIVES

After reading this chapter you should:

1 Understand the composition of cash and how cash is presented on a balance sheet.

2 Understand why cash management is important and be familiar with the various controls and procedures related to cash receipts and disbursements.

3 Be able to reconcile a bank account.

4 Be familiar with the operation of a petty cash system.

5 Understand the proper accounting treatments for short-term investments, especially the lower-of-cost-or-market method.

6 Be familiar with the operation of a voucher system.

CHAPTER 7

As we noted in the previous chapter, financial statements provide a variety of information for decision making. The balance sheet, for example, discloses important relationships between the resources owned by a business and the amounts owed to creditors. Two balance sheet accounts of key interest to a number of parties are *cash* and *short-term investments.* Cash and short-term investments are the most liquid of the current assets. Thus lenders, creditors, and prospective suppliers study the amounts of these assets in comparison with current liabilities when judging a firm's debt-paying ability. Investors review the cash and short-term investments of a business to gauge the funds available for dividend distributions as well as for medium- and long-term investments that are important to future profitability. Even employees are interested in cash and short-term investments, because salary increases are often directly related to the funds available and the balances in these two accounts. It is imperative, then, that cash and short-term investments be properly accounted for and presented in the financial statements.

CASH

The items reported in the Cash account on the balance sheet must be (1) acceptable to a bank for deposit and (2) free from restriction for use in satisfying current debts. Cash therefore includes *coins, currency, funds on deposit with a bank (checking accounts and savings accounts), checks, and money orders.* The following items are not considered to be cash for accounting purposes: certificates of deposit, postdated checks, IOUs, travel advances, and postage stamps.

1 *Certificates of deposit (CDs).* Securities issued by banks to allow companies and individuals to invest cash for short periods of time. CDs pay a guaranteed interest rate and may be cashed in any time after purchase. However, a substantial interest penalty usually results unless they are held until their due date. Consequently, certificates of deposit are not classified as cash but are considered to be short-term investments.

2 *Postdated checks.* Checks that become payable on a date subsequent to the issue date. For example, suppose Buck Company issued a check to Foy Company on April 15, 1983. Buck dated the check April 22, 1983, because it lacked sufficient funds on the 15th. Since Foy cannot cash or deposit the check until the 22nd, the postdated check is not classified as cash. Postdated checks are receivables until the date they can be deposited.

3 *IOUs.* Acknowledgments of debts. Since IOUs are not negotiable, they usually cannot be used to pay off liabilities. IOUs are therefore classified as receivables until the time of collection.

4 *Travel advances.* Cash given by a company to employees to cover out-of-pocket expenses while traveling on company business. Because the employees owe the firm both any excess monies advanced plus receipts from their business trips, travel advances are normally classified as receivables on the balance sheet.

5 *Postage stamps.* Classified as supplies or prepaid expenses.

Balance Sheet Presentation

The Cash account is listed on the balance sheet in the current asset section. For concise reporting, all cash items are normally combined and listed as a single figure.

As we noted earlier, the amount reported for cash must be available for use in satisfying current debts. Frequently, many corporations establish special funds that allow for the accumulation of cash for specific purposes. For example, a special fund may be established to repay money borrowed (often termed a *sinking fund*) or to expand a manufacturing plant. Amounts deposited in these funds should not be classified as current assets on the balance sheet because they are restricted and not available to settle current obligations. Likewise, amounts held in foreign banks should not be reported as current assets if governmental regulations restrict the transfer of funds out of the foreign country.

Compensating Balances

During the past few years many banks have required that a portion of any amount loaned to customers remain on deposit in the bank for the duration of the loan period. These required deposits are termed **compensating balances.** Customers borrowing money under these circumstances are affected in two distinct ways. First, the amount of cash available to the borrower is reduced, and, second, the effective interest rate that the borrower pays for the use of the funds is increased. For example, suppose a customer agreed to pay $6,000 of interest for a $50,000 one-year loan. This amount represents a 12% interest rate ($6,000 ÷ $50,000). If a $5,000 compensating balance must be kept at the bank, the customer has the use of only $45,000. Thus the effective rate of interest is raised to 13.3% ($6,000 ÷ $45,000).

In the early 1970s a study by the SEC found that many corporations having problems meeting current obligations were, at the same time, reporting sizable cash balances in their financial statements. In many cases the amount of cash available to pay creditors was much less than the reported cash balance, because a portion was legally restricted by compensating balances with lenders. The SEC subsequently issued reporting guidelines for compensating balances. The SEC recommended that restricted deposits held against short-term borrowings be stated separately in the current assets section of the balance sheet. In this manner the statement user is made aware of a business's restricted funds.

Frequently, agreements are made whereby compensating balances are not legally restricted and are available to companies for operating purposes. In this situation footnote disclosure is appropriate. Such was the case with K mart Corporation, which made the following compensating balance disclosure:

> *At January 27, 1982, the company had bank lines of credit aggregating $853.3 million with interest rates approximating the "prime" lending rate. In support of certain lines of credit, it is expected that compensating balances will be maintained on deposit with the*

banks, which will average 10% of the line to the extent that it is not in use and an additional 10% on the portion in use whereas other lines require fees in lieu of compensating balances. The company is free to withdraw the entire balance in its accounts at any time.

Cash Management

Effective cash management is important to the success of any company. Care must be taken to ensure that sufficient cash is available to meet current obligations but that unnecessarily large cash balances do not remain in checking accounts. Why? Most checking accounts do not pay interest. Recently, a congressional bill was enacted to permit **negotiated orders of withdrawal or NOW accounts.** NOW accounts allow customers to write checks on their interest-bearing savings; the interest rate is fairly low, however, when compared with other available investment alternatives. Thus large cash balances held in regular checking or NOW accounts represent a loss of earnings potential. Cash not currently needed should be invested in short-term securities to earn higher rates of return or be used for new programs and projects.

The amount of cash necessary to meet current obligations varies among businesses. Consider the information that appeared in recent financial statements of Resorts International, Black and Decker Manufacturing, and the Carnation Company as presented in Exhibit 7-1.

Exhibit 7-1

Current asset composition of Resorts International, Black and Decker Manufacturing, and the Carnation Company (in thousands)

	Resorts International		Black and Decker Manufacturing		Carnation Company	
	$	%*	$	%*	$	%*
Cash	$ 16,449	8.5	$ 53,752	6.4	$ 33,184	2.8
Short-term investments	148,586	76.3	17,399	2.1	194,909	16.6
Receivables	20,427	10.5	297,896	35.4	375,457	32.0
Inventories	4,294	2.2	453,925	54.0	553,723	47.1
Prepaid expenses	4,864	2.5	17,912	2.1	18,114	1.5
	$194,620	100.0	$840,884	100.0	$1,175,387	100.0

* *Percentages calculated by the authors.*

Resorts International's (RI's) major line of business is the operation of gaming casinos. Thus, the company needs a relatively large cash balance to support daily operations. This circumstance is reflected by the fact that cash constitutes over 8% of the company's total current assets. More importantly, however, notice the size of the firm's short-term investment portfolio. As we will discuss later in the chapter, short-term investments are easily converted into cash should the need arise. Nearly 85% of RI's current assets, then, are cash or near cash. For Black and Decker and Carnation it is an entirely different story. These firms must stock inventories for production and sale and, given the nature of their activity, carry large amounts of customer receivables. As a result, both these companies have lower cash balances as a percentage of total current assets and a significantly lower percentage of short-term investments.

Planning and control

The management of cash is subdivided into cash planning and cash control. **Cash planning systems** consist of those procedures adopted to ensure that adequate cash is available to meet current obligations and that any excess cash is invested. A major component of cash planning systems is the cash budget. The **cash budget** is an overall plan of activity that depicts cash inflows and outflows for a stated period of time. The cash budget is a very useful tool in the management of any organization, because it pinpoints when any cash surpluses and shortages will occur. Predicting surpluses and shortages before they take place enables a business to analyze potential high-return investments and low-cost sources of funds and thereby improve investment and financing decisions. The cash budget is discussed in detail in Chapter 23.

Cash control systems are the procedures adopted to ensure the safeguarding of an organization's funds. These systems establish adequate internal control over cash. Recall that adequate internal control aids a company in safeguarding its assets, checking the reliability and accuracy of accounting data, promoting operational efficiency, and encouraging adherence to prescribed managerial policies. A strong cash control system is essential, because employees and others regard cash as a very desirable asset. In addition, cash is difficult to trace because it has no readily identifiable means to establish ownership. Although currency does have serial numbers, a business makes no attempt to record these numbers in view of the overwhelming amount of bookkeeping that would be required.

Internal control for cash

The internal control system for cash is based on the general internal control features discussed in Chapter 5. An organization should limit the access to cash to a few authorized personnel only. Furthermore, incompatible duties such as the authorization of cash transactions, the entry of cash transactions in the accounting records, and the custody of cash should be separated. Finally, the following accountability procedures should be implemented: prenumbered checks, verification of invoices prior to payment, and verification of the cash balance as reported in the general ledger. These general control features become apparent when studying typical accounting procedures for cash receipts and cash disbursements.

Cash receipts

The control of cash receipts attempts to ensure that all cash inflows are safeguarded from the time they are received by a company until the time of deposit in a bank account. There are two major types of cash receipts: *cash sales* and *collections of credit sales*. Control over cash sales is facilitated by the use of a cash register. A cash register requires a salesperson to record each sale in full view of the customer and to provide the customer with a receipt. As the clerk enters the sale on the register, the sale is simultaneously recorded on a cash register tape. At the end of the business day a store manager compares the cash collected in the register's drawer with the total cash sales reported by the tape. The tapes are then forwarded to the accounting department and recorded in the company records. The cash is kept in a vault until deposited in the bank or picked up by a courier service such as Brinks or Wells Fargo.

The internal control over cash received through the mail from credit sales should be based on the principle of separation of duties. Thus the following procedures are usually employed.

1 The daily counting of cash receipts is assigned to one person or, in large businesses, to a group of specific personnel. The personnel open the mail, prepare a list of checks received, and forward the list to the accounting department.[1]
2 The checks are forwarded to a cashier, who prepares a deposit slip and deposits all receipts intact on a *daily* basis. Daily deposits prevent bills from being paid out of current receipts; they also minimize the amount of cash left on the premises at the end of the business day, thus reducing the possibility of large losses from theft. A duplicate deposit slip is then sent to the accounting department.
3 The accounting department compares the list of cash receipts with the deposit slip and records the daily mail-in receipts in the accounting records. Naturally, any discrepancies between the deposit slip and the list of receipts require investigation.

Cash disbursements

The control over disbursements includes procedures that will allow only authorized payments for actual company expenditures. A cash disbursements system with proper internal control should include the following procedures:

1 All significant disbursements are made by check so that a record (i.e., written evidence) exists for these expenditures.
2 Periodic comparisons are made of an organization's cash account in the general ledger with the cash account as reported by the bank.
3 Certain small payments are made by using a *petty cash system*. (The operation of a petty cash system will be explained later in this chapter.)
4 Before any checks are written or disbursements are made from a petty cash system, the expenditure is verified and approved. Verification may take the form of examining invoices and receiving reports, as discussed in Chapter 4.

[1] As discussed in Chapter 4, a separate accounts receivable department may be established.

These procedures, like so many others, are aided by a proper separation of duties. For example, the person signing the checks should not be the same individual who prepares the checks. In addition, the comparison of a company's general ledger cash balance with the cash balance as reported by the bank (record-keeping function) should not be performed by an employee who handles the cash (custody function). Separation of duties helps in the detection of errors and also makes theft or fraud more difficult.

Bank reconciliations

As we previously noted, adequate internal control requires the use of checks for significant cash payments. Canceled checks and their endorsements furnish written evidence that payments have been made. In addition, checking accounts provide security and safety for the large cash balances that many businesses must carry.

As you can well imagine, a company will have many cash receipts and disbursements during a given accounting period. Because of the high frequency of transactions and the potential for error, it is necessary to periodically examine the accuracy of the balance of the Cash account in the general ledger (or your checkbook). This process, called a **bank reconciliation,** is based on the Cash account and a document called a **bank statement.**

Bank statements versus cash accounts

Businesses and individuals receive monthly bank statements for every checking account they maintain. An example of a bank statement appears in Exhibit 7-2. Bank statements summarize the activity in a checking account and report the ending monthly balance. It is important to understand that although the Cash account of a depositor (such as Johnson Manufacturing) is an asset, the depositor's account is carried on the bank's books as a *liability.* Thus checks and other debits by the bank *reduce* Johnson's account, while deposits and other credits *increase* the account.

At the end of a month the bank statement cash balance and the company's cash records will normally not agree. A major reason for this discrepancy is the timing differences associated with the use of a checking account. Timing differences result in an item being recorded on the depositor's books or the bank's books, but not both, in a given accounting period. Some of the timing differences arise from the operation of the Postal Service and the check-processing procedures of the Federal Reserve System. For example, suppose a check is written by Johnson Manufacturing and mailed to Hobart Distributors. Hobart receives the check and deposits it in its bank account. Hobart's bank then sends the check to Johnson's bank (First City Bank Trust), which deducts the funds from Johnson's account. This entire process may take several days and sometimes weeks, particularly if Johnson and Hobart are thousands of miles apart. As a result, disbursements may be recorded in Johnson's accounting records prior to their appearance on the bank statement.

Common examples of timing differences include the following:

Exhibit 7-2
Bank statement

FIRST CITY BANK TRUST
101 North James Ave.
Chicago, Ill. 60638

Johnson Manufacturing Corporation
1800 South Main
Chicago, Illinois 60634

Account No. 0008564201 — *Page No.* 1

Statement Period
From 7/31/83 — *To* 8/31/83

Beginning Balance	*No. of Debits*	*Total Debits*	*No. of Credits*	*Total Credits*	*Service Charge*	*Ending Balance*
19,507.50	18	40,239.75	11	42,178.50	20.00	21,426.25

Checks/Debits			Deposits/ Credits	Date	Balance
				7/31	19,507.50
1,250.40			3,984.40	8/3	22,241.50
940.20			3,150.43	8/5	24,451.73
1,960.85			2,897.04	8/6	22,747.92
2,640.00					
375.00			4,925.75	8/7	26,558.52
740.15					
2,470.80			5,242.70	8/9	18,689.52
10,640.90					
127.90 DM			4,600.80 NC	8/13	22,022.04
675.18			75.00 IC		
540.20					
728.40			4,167.10	8/20	25,321.24
139.50					
650.53			5,145.18	8/22	29,378.60
437.29					
2,147.90			4,752.30	8/27	30,993.95
989.05					
12,785.50			3,237.80	8/30	21,446.25
20.00 SC				8/31	21,426.25

Code Explanation: CM *Credit Memo* IC *Interest Collection* SC *Service Charge*
DM *Debit Memo* NC *Note Collection*

1 Items recorded on company records but not yet reported on the bank statement, such as:
   a ***Deposits in transit.*** Receipts recorded on company records but not yet recorded at the bank. This situation often occurs when deposits are mailed to the bank. Deposits in transit are determined by comparing deposits on the bank statement with deposits reported in the firm's Cash account.
   b ***Outstanding checks.*** Checks written but not yet processed by the bank. Johnson's check to Hobart Distributors is an example. Outstanding checks are determined by comparing checks reported on the bank statement against checks written on the company's records.

2 Items reported on the bank statement but not yet entered in company records, such as:
   a ***Nonsufficient funds (NSF) checks.*** Customer checks returned because of a lack of funds. NSF checks are frequently reported on the bank statement via a debit memo notation, because the bank has reduced the depositor's account.
   b Bank service charges for account processing.
   c Notes receivable and interest collected by the bank. The collection of a note and interest is sometimes reported with a credit memo notation because of the increase in the depositor's account balance.
   d Interest added to NOW accounts by the bank.

In addition to timing differences, errors may cause a discrepancy between the bank statement balance and company accounting records. Errors are possible by either the company or the bank and naturally must be corrected as quickly as possible.

Reconciliation process

Several different types of reconciliations can be prepared. The most commonly encountered form results in determining the amount of cash a company has control over and reports on its balance sheet at the end of the accounting period. An example appears in Exhibit 7-3.

The exhibit reveals the thrust of a reconciliation. That is, we strive to isolate specific items that cause a difference between the depositor's records and the bank statement balance. The accountant considers these items and adjusts one cash balance or the other to bring both balances into agreement.

If the balances do not agree and the reconciling items are deemed correct, there is an excellent chance that a record-keeping error has been made. Errors must be determined and then added or subtracted on the reconciliation to arrive at the corrected cash balance. For example, if a check written by the firm for $94.50 was incorrectly entered in the accounting records as $49.50, the accounting records will be overstated by $45.00 ($94.50 – $49.50). This amount ($45) should therefore be deducted from

Exhibit 7-3

Illustrative bank reconciliation

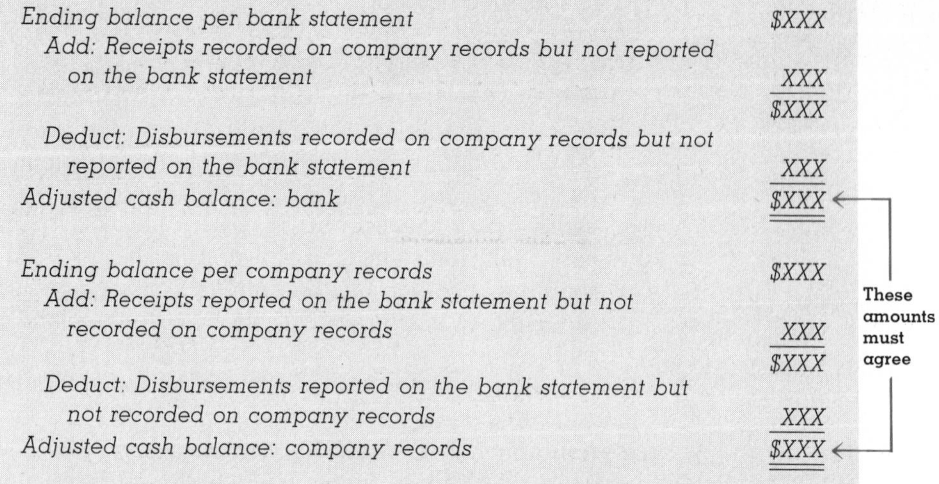

Ending balance per bank statement	*$XXX*
Add: Receipts recorded on company records but not reported on the bank statement	*XXX*
	$XXX
Deduct: Disbursements recorded on company records but not reported on the bank statement	*XXX*
Adjusted cash balance: bank	*$XXX*
Ending balance per company records	*$XXX*
Add: Receipts reported on the bank statement but not recorded on company records	*XXX*
	$XXX
Deduct: Disbursements reported on the bank statement but not recorded on company records	*XXX*
Adjusted cash balance: company records	*$XXX*

These amounts must agree

the ending cash balance per company records, since the company's books are in error. The bank, of course, will deduct the correct amount of the check ($94.50) when it is received for payment. The reconciliation, then, not only highlights timing differences but also identifies errors made by either the bank or the depositor.

Most bank reconciliations contain adjustments to both the ending cash balance per bank statement and the ending balance per company records. After the reconciliation is completed, general journal entries must be prepared for adjustments made to company records. These adjustments are necessary to update the Cash account (and others) for corrections of company errors and information already recorded at the bank. No journal entries are required for adjustments made to the ending bank statement balance. Why? These adjustments reflect items that have already been entered in company records; thus no further updating is needed.

Exhibit 7-4 contains summarized data and the bank reconciliation of Johnson Manufacturing Corporation for the month ended August 31, 1983. It is helpful if you refer back to Johnson's bank statement (see Exhibit 7-2), which serves as the source for much of the data.

The reconciliation reveals two increases to the bank statement cash balance: (1) the deposit that was mailed prior to the end of the month but not recorded by the bank and (2) the checks that were recorded by Johnson and are awaiting deposit. Johnson had control over each of these items as of August 31, and they should be included in the ending cash balance. The decrease to the bank statement cash balance was necessitated by checks Johnson had written that had not yet cleared the bank. The bank will receive these checks shortly, and the funds will then be deducted from the firm's account.

Exhibit 7-4

Data and bank reconciliation of Johnson Manufacturing Corporation

Data

a Cash balance per bank statement, $21,426.25.

b Cash balance per company records, $17,473.35.

c A customer's check for $127.90 was returned because of insufficient funds.

d A customer's note receivable for $4,600.80 plus $75.00 of interest was collected by the bank and reported on the August bank statement.

e A deposit for $1,430.00, mailed to the bank on August 30, did not appear on the bank statement.

f Monthly bank service charge, $20.00.

g Customers' checks totaling $420.00 were on hand awaiting deposit.

h The following checks written by Johnson were outstanding at the end of the month:

No. 638	$410.00
No. 640	320.00
No. 641	240.00
No. 642	323.00

i Check no. 627, written for $675.18, was erroneously recorded as $657.18 in the company's records. The check involved a payment to a supplier on account.

JOHNSON MANUFACTURING CORPORATION
Bank Reconciliation
August 31, 1983

Ending balance per bank statement		$21,426.25
Add: Deposit in transit	$1,430.00	
Checks on hand	420.00	1,850.00
		$23,276.25
Deduct: Outstanding checks		
No. 638	$ 410.00	
No. 640	320.00	
No. 641	240.00	
No. 642	323.00	1,293.00
Adjusted cash balance: bank		$21,983.25
Ending balance per company records		$17,473.35
Add: Note receivable collected by bank	$4,600.80	
Interest on note	75.00	4,675.80
		$22,149.15
Deduct: NSF check	$ 127.90	
Monthly service charge	20.00	
Error in recording check no. 627	18.00	165.90
Adjusted cash balance: company records		$21,983.25

TRUNCATION: A NEW ERA IN CHECKING ACCOUNTS?

Could you get by if your canceled checks were not returned along with your monthly bank statement? Would you accept such a situation, particularly if some financial incentive were offered by the institution that has your account? These are two questions that many bankers are asking, rhetorically and otherwise, as they study truncation—a technique now in its infancy among American financial institutions. Truncation, a $10 word that the banking industry uses to refer to the nonreturn of canceled checks to customers after payment has been made, may very well be the rule rather than the exception in the next decade.

The cause of its arrival on the scene, as might be expected, is economic. With more than 30 billion checks expected to be written in the United States this year and about 50 billion in 1985, and with the cost of operations involved in processing a check estimated at somewhere between $0.25 and $2, billions could theoretically be saved every year by reducing this flow of paper.

Reducing is never easy, however, whether it is paperwork or [weight]. The public has been sold on the value of having checks returned for more than thirty years. Most consumers are aware of good reasons to receive canceled checks with their statements, such as help in balancing their accounts or proof of payment. One banker calls the return of canceled checks "a paper security blanket."

The biggest jumps into truncation so far have been taken by savings institutions and credit unions. Some commercial banks have ventured into the area, too. Although the number of institutions now participating is relatively small, their enthusiasm and initial success make many banking observers predict that truncation is likely to increase. "We had some reservations when we first went into it," says Ernest C. Williamson, a vice-president of Reliance Federal Savings and Loan Association of New York. "But the reaction from the customers has been surprisingly good."

Initially, bankers are focusing on internal truncation, where checks are kept at the payor bank—the last point in the clearing process. The long-range goal is a national truncation system. Within such a system the receiving bank, or the bank of first deposit, stores the check; all further processing of documents through the clearing system is done electronically. The American National Standards Institute is already considering ways to implement such an arrangement.

SOURCE Adapted from Leonard Sloane, "Here Comes Truncation," Parade Magazine, July 15, 1979, p. 22.

The increase to company records arose from the note receivable and interest, both of which appear on the bank statement. These funds are now on deposit in Johnson's bank account and must therefore be entered in the company's records. The deductions for the NSF check and service charge are also caused by items on the bank statement but not as yet in the firm's ledger. The error in recording check no. 627 was discovered during the reconciliation. The correct amount of the check was deducted by the bank, thus requiring an adjustment to Johnson's records to bring them into agreement with those of First City.

On completion of the reconciliation, journal entries are needed for all items affecting company records. The following entries will be made on August 31.

Cash	4,675.80	
Notes Receivable		4,600.80
Interest Revenue		75.00
Note and interest collected by bank		
Accounts Receivable	127.90	
Miscellaneous Expense	20.00	
Accounts Payable	18.00	
Cash		165.90
NSF check, bank service charge, and error in recording check no. 627		

The first entry reflects the increase in cash caused by the collection of the note and $75.00 of interest. The second entry combines the firm's three cash reductions. The NSF check is debited to Accounts Receivable because Johnson still has a claim against the customer for $127.90. The bank service charge is recorded as a miscellaneous expense. Finally, the error in recording check no. 627 was found to involve a payment on account; thus Accounts Payable must be debited. These entries bring Johnson's records into agreement with the true amount of cash held by the firm, as shown by the accompanying T-account.

Cash			
8/31	17,473.35	8/31	165.90
8/31	4,675.80		
(21,983.25)	22,149.15		

In recent years there have been suggestions that the paperwork involved in reconciling bank accounts could be reduced if canceled checks were retained by the bank. This process is reviewed in the excerpted article from *Parade Magazine* on page 264.

Petty cash

Another important element in the control of cash is a petty cash system. A **petty cash system** establishes a fund that is used to make small payments, especially those that are impractical or uneconomical to make by check.

Examples of such payments include those for minor items like postage due or coffee for the office.

A petty cash fund is created by cashing a check drawn on the company's regular checking account. The proceeds from the check are placed in a petty cash box that is controlled by an individual known as the fund custodian. The custodian supervises the fund and is held accountable for any discrepancies. The petty cash fund is established at an amount estimated to be adequate to cover payments for a short period of time (e.g., several weeks). Assuming this amount is $200, the journal entry to record the establishment of the fund is as follows:

Petty Cash	200	
Cash		200
To establish petty cash fund		

Making disbursements from the fund

As payments are made from the fund, the custodian completes a petty cash voucher. A typical petty cash voucher is illustrated in Exhibit 7-5. Each petty cash voucher indicates the amount paid, the purpose of the expenditure, the date of the expenditure, and the individual receiving the money. Along with various invoices and receipts, petty cash vouchers are used as evidence of disbursements.

Exhibit 7-5

Petty cash voucher

Petty Cash Voucher No. ________

Date ________	*Payee* ________
Explanation ________	*Account* ________
________	*Amount* $ ________
________	*Approved* ________
	Received Payment ________

The completed voucher is placed in the petty cash box by the custodian. Although a payment has been made, no journal entry is recorded at this time. Preparing a formal journal entry for each disbursement would necessitate considerable bookkeeping work and posting, all for relatively small amounts. This procedure would eliminate the timesaving and economical benefits associated with using a petty cash system. At all times the following relationship should be true:

Cash remaining in the fund	$XX
+ Petty cash vouchers	XX
= Original amount of the fund	$200

Replenishing the petty cash fund

The petty cash fund is replenished when the amount of cash in the fund becomes low. For instance, assume that a count of the petty cash on hand totaled $32.40. Vouchers revealed that the following expenses had been incurred:

Postage expense	$27.50
Office supplies expense	50.80
Transportation expense	73.40
Coffee	15.90

The general journal entry to record replenishment is as follows:

Postage Expense	27.50	
Office Supplies Expense	50.80	
Transportation Expense	73.40	
Miscellaneous Expense	15.90	
Cash		167.60
To replenish petty cash fund		

Notice that the credit is to the Cash account and not Petty Cash. Although disbursements have been made from the petty cash box, the fund is restocked by writing a check for $167.60 on the company's regular checking account. Thus payment (and replenishment) is really from the Cash account. The balance in Petty Cash remains intact at the original amount of $200.

In addition to being replenished when the fund is low, the petty cash fund is also replenished at the end of each accounting period. This procedure is necessary because no formal journal entries have been recorded for individual fund disbursements. Replenishment requires a journal entry, which thus ensures that all expenses are charged to the period in which they arose.

Errors in the petty cash fund balance

Frequently, the sum of petty cash vouchers and cash in the fund does not equal the original fund balance. This discrepancy usually occurs because of errors made by the fund custodian, some in the company's favor and some against. In such cases a **Cash Short & Over** account is established to accumulate the effects of the errors. The Cash Short & Over account can also be used for discrepancies that arise when comparing a cash register's tape with cash collections.

To illustrate the use of the Cash Short & Over account, we will continue the previous petty cash illustration. Assume that on the date of replenishment, the fund contained the same vouchers totaling $167.60 but only $31.00 of cash. As the following computation shows, $1.40 has been disbursed incorrectly.

Original fund balance		$200.00
Less: Vouchers	$167.60	
Cash in box	31.00	198.60
Shortage		$ 1.40

The journal entry to replenish the fund is now as follows:

Postage Expense	*27.50*	
Office Supplies Expense	*50.80*	
Transportation Expense	*73.40*	
Miscellaneous Expense	*15.90*	
Cash Short & Over	*1.40*	
Cash		*169.00*
To replenish petty cash fund		

The balance in Cash Short & Over is usually very small. Since overpayments are more likely than underpayments, this account is normally shown as a miscellaneous (other) expense on the income statement. If Cash Short & Over possessed a credit balance, it would be listed as a miscellaneous (other) revenue.

Voucher system

Another way to increase internal control over cash is the use of a voucher system for cash disbursements. A discussion of the voucher system appears in the Appendix to this chapter.

Electronic Funds Transfer Systems (EFTS)

In our discussion of bank reconciliations we noted that the paperwork accompanying checking accounts is costly and somewhat overwhelming. Furthermore, there is frequently a time lag between the day when a depositor processes a cash transaction and the appearance of the transaction on the bank statement. In recent years the use of computerized **electronic funds transfer systems (EFTS)** has greatly reduced this time lag and the need for physical documents associated with cash handling systems.

EFTS has many applications. Banks, for example, can transfer huge sums of money among themselves or from a depositor's account to an account at another bank. No checks are written and the updating of account balances is instantaneous. Messages are merely sent back and forth electronically to deposit and disperse funds.

Other EFTS applications include telephone bill-paying systems and automated teller machines. Some banks allow their customers to pay monthly bills over the telephone by way of a telephone/bank computer hookup. Automated tellers, sometimes called "money machines," allow customers to make deposits and withdrawals from their checking and savings accounts by inserting a magnetic-stripe identification card into a computer terminal. Automated tellers are found not only in banks but in supermarkets and other retail establishments as well.

EFTS has profound implications for accountants because often much of the traditional written evidence supporting cash transactions (such as deposit tickets and checks) does not exist. Consequently, accountants must employ methods other than visual examination of documents to determine whether all cash receipts and disbursements have been properly handled and recorded.

SHORT-TERM INVESTMENTS

Earlier in this chapter we noted that firms should invest excessive checking account balances in more profitable projects and programs. Many companies find that excessive cash balances arise because the period of greatest cash inflows does not coincide with the period of greatest cash needs. Consider, for example, the seasonal sales and operations of the Topeka Company, a manufacturer of children's toys. The firm's cash flows, production, and sales are shown graphically in Exhibit 7-6.

Exhibit 7-6 **Seasonal fluctuations of the Topeka Company**

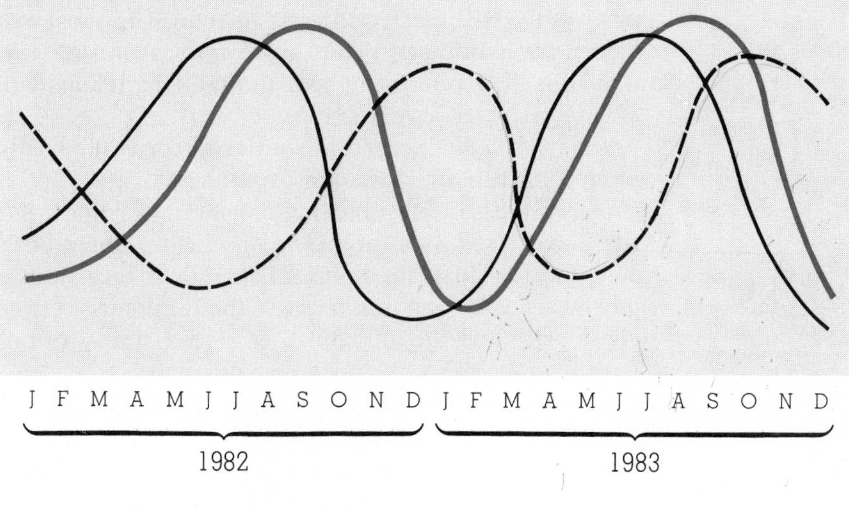

Topeka's peak sales occur during July, August, September, and October of each year. During this period retail store customers build up inventories in anticipation of the Christmas season. Notice the pattern of cash flows caused by this sales activity. The period of greatest cash needs precedes the peak sales period because Topeka must manufacture the necessary goods. Production activity naturally requires large sums of cash for materials, labor, and other factory costs. To complicate matters, the greatest cash inflows follow the period of peak sales. Why? Topeka, like most companies, extends credit to customers and balances are payable 30 days from the date of sale. Generally, then, the firm has some excess cash for several months throughout the year.

Nature of Short-Term Investments

Effective cash management dictates the investment of excess funds until a need for the funds arises by the firm. Normally, short-term investments are acquired. Typical examples of short-term investments include the following:

1 *Common stock.* The ownership rights of a corporation. As we explained in Chapter 6, corporations often distribute dividends to

stockholders, thereby providing some return on the stockholders' investment.

2 *Preferred stock.* A special class of stock in which the investor receives a dividend preference. That is, preferred stockholders are entitled to their dividend payments prior to any common stock dividends.

3 *Corporate bonds.* Securities issued by corporations that promise to repay a certain amount (usually $1,000 per security) at some future date. The investor is really loaning the corporation some money and as a result, will receive interest in return. In most cases interest is payable semiannually. Thus an investor acquiring a $1,000 bond that pays 10% interest in semiannual installments will receive $50 of interest twice a year ($\$1{,}000 \times 0.10 \times \frac{6}{12}$).

4 *Municipal bonds.* Securities similar to corporate bonds, which are offered for sale by cities and counties.

5 *Treasury bills.* Interest-bearing obligations of the U.S. government that pay a fixed amount after a specified number of days. These securities are sold at an amount below their face value so that the interest earned by the purchaser is the difference between the purchase price and the amount to be repaid. Treasury bills are offered with 91-day, 182-day, and 1-year due dates.

6 *Certificates of deposit* (*CDs*). See the discussion earlier in the chapter.

7 *Commercial paper.* Short-term notes sold by large businesses to investors and other corporations. The due dates of commercial paper usually vary between 30 and 270 days.

The short-term investments acquired by an organization are reported as current assets on the balance sheet if they are (1) readily salable and (2) intended to be converted into cash within the operating cycle or one year, whichever is longer. The key element in this reporting test is *managerial intent.* If management intends to convert a short-term investment into cash whenever the firm is in need of cash, the security is classified as a current asset.[2] Securities purchased with longer-term goals in mind, such as management control or affiliation, are classified as long-term investments.

Recording Initial Cost and Changes in Value

All short-term investments are recorded initially at their acquisition price plus any other costs related to the transaction. Examples of such costs include brokerage fees and taxes. To illustrate the proper accounting, we will assume that Phillip Corporation purchased 200 shares of Karl Corporation stock at $42 per share (for a total of $8,400). Brokerage fees of $50 were incurred on the purchase. This transaction would be recorded as follows:

[2] In practice, the "intent" guideline has created problems for auditors. Intentions, of course, can change from one period to the next. In addition, intentions may be somewhat subjective and are rarely documented in company records.

Short-Term Investment in Stock	*8,450*	
Cash		*8,450*
Purchased 200 shares of Karl Corporation stock		

Unlike the value of most other assets, the value of short-term investments fluctuates continuously and can often be determined on a daily basis. Changes in value of short-term investments (caused by the economy, investor expectations, earnings reports, and other factors) are readily obtainable from *The Wall Street Journal* or the business section of major metropolitan newspapers. In light of these characteristics, two alternative methods have been used to account for short-term investments. These methods are the historical-cost method and the lower-of-cost-or-market method.

Under the **historical-cost method** short-term investments are reported on the balance sheet at their acquisition (historical) cost until the time of sale. Accordingly, changes in the value of the securities are ignored while the securities are held. Any revenue from the investments, such as dividends and interest, is recorded as it is earned by the investor.

With the **lower-of-cost-or-market method** changes in the value of the securities are recognized and entered in the accounting records. Decreases in the market value of short-term investments are accounted for as losses, while recoveries in these market value declines are reported as revenue. Recoveries, however, are limited to the amount of previously recorded losses. As before, revenue from dividends or interest is recorded when earned.

In recent years the historical-cost and the lower-of-cost-or-market methods have each been used with regularity. The lower-of-cost-or-market method has been used with stock investments, while the historical-cost method has been employed for other short-term investments. The accounting procedures for stock investments are illustrated in the following section.

Lower of cost or market

The adoption of the lower-of-cost-or-market method for stock investments was in response to wide fluctuations in the securities market during 1973 and 1975. These fluctuations caused numerous reporting discrepancies. Consider the graph of the Dow-Jones Industrial Average for 1972–1981 appearing in Exhibit 7-7. The Dow-Jones Industrial Average is the sum of the stock prices of 30 large corporations.

Notice that the overall average of stock prices declined during 1973 and 1974 and then recovered sharply in 1975. Assume a company purchased stock as a short-term investment in 1973. If the market price of the shares purchased followed the general trend of the stock market, the cash resources expected from the sale of these securities would have fluctuated considerably during the period just cited. The company, reporting its short-term investment at historical cost in 1974, would have overstated the amount of cash anticipated upon sale, given the decline of the Dow-Jones average. Why? Remember that historical cost leaves securities valued on the books at cost and ignores changes in market value while the securities are held. For

Exhibit 7-7

Dow-Jones Industrial Average, 1972–1981

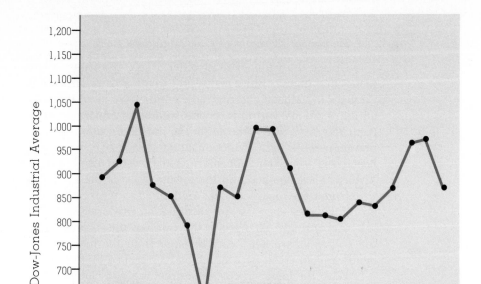

this reason the accounting profession studied the issue of proper reporting practices for short-term stock investments. In 1975 the Financial Accounting Standards Board issued a pronouncement that voiced a preference for the lower-of-cost-or-market method.[3]

The application of the lower-of-cost-or-market method is quite simple. The carrying value of the entire short-term stock investment portfolio is the lower of its *aggregate* cost or market value on each balance sheet date. That is, the total cost and total market value of all short-term stock investments are compared and the *lower* figure is used for financial statement valuation. The difference between total cost and total market value is disclosed by using a separate "valuation" account, which is offset against the original cost of the short-term investment.

To illustrate the use of the lower-of-cost-or-market method for stock

[3] As we noted in Chapter 6, the Financial Accounting Standards Board is a rule-making body of the accounting profession. For those readers desiring additional insight into the valuation of short-term investments, see "Accounting for Certain Marketable Equity Securities," *Statement of Financial Accounting Standards No. 12* (Stamford, Conn.: Financial Accounting Standards Board, 1975).

investments, we assume Carr Corporation acquired the following securities on January 1, 1983.

Security	Total Cost
200 shares of Rolph Corporation stock at $50 per share	$10,000
400 shares of Dana, Inc., stock at $100 per share	40,000
300 shares of Borg Corporation stock at $75 per share	22,500
	$72,500

The following journal entry is made to record these acquisitions.

Short-Term Investment in Stock	*72,500*	
Cash		*72,500*
Purchased Rolph, Dana, and Borg stock		

During 1983 dividends of $4,500 were received. Dividends are revenue to the recipient and are recorded as follows:

Cash	*4,500*	
Dividend Revenue		*4,500*
To record dividends received		

Declines in market value

On December 31, 1983, the market value per share of Carr's three securities was as follows: Rolph, $48; Dana, $98; Borg, $76. The accompanying table is used to summarize this information.

Security	Cost	Market*
Rolph Corporation (200 shares)	$10,000	$ 9,600
Dana, Inc. (400 shares)	40,000	39,200
Borg Corporation (300 shares)	22,500	22,800
	$72,500	$71,600

* *Number of shares times market value per share.*

The table reveals that the portfolio's total market value is $900 less than cost ($72,500 – $71,600). The entry made to record the decline in market value is as follows:

Unrealized Loss on Short-Term Investments	*900*	
Allowance for Decline in Market Value of Short-Term Investments		*900*
To record decline in market value		

As we noted earlier, decreases in the market value of short-term investments are accounted for as losses. The loss, known as an *unrealized loss*, appears on the income statement under the other expense classification.[4] Rather than credit the Short-Term Investment account directly, one establishes an Allowance account. The Allowance for Decline in Market Value is a contra

[4] In most cases gains and losses are said to be *realized* at the time of sale. Because Carr still owns the securities, the loss is labeled "unrealized."

asset that is deducted from the Short-Term Investment account on the balance sheet as follows:

Current assets	
Short-term investment in stock	*$72,500*
Less: Allowance for decline in market value of short-term investments	*900*
Short-term investments at the lower of cost or market	*$71,600*

Notice how the balance sheet discloses more information by using a separate valuation account.

Recording recoveries

During 1984 dividends of $4,800 were received. The proper entry is as follows:

Cash	*4,800*	
Dividend Revenue		*4,800*
To record dividends received		

Now suppose on December 31, 1984, market values per share were as follows: Rolph, $49; Dana, $99; and Borg, $76. This information is summarized in the accompanying table.

Security	***Cost***	***Market****
Rolph Corporation (200 shares)	$10,000	$ 9,800
Dana, Inc. (400 shares)	40,000	39,600
Borg Corporation (300 shares)	22,500	22,800
	$72,500	$72,200

** Number of shares times market value per share.*

The entry to record the recovery in market value of the portfolio from $71,600 (on December 31, 1983) to $72,200 (on December 31, 1984) is as follows:

Allowance for Decline in Market Value of Short-Term Investments	*600*	
Recovery in Value of Short-Term Investments		*600*
To record recovery in market value		

In the second and all subsequent years, losses and loss recoveries are determined by comparing the necessary balance in the Allowance account at the end of the year with the account's balance on the last previous balance sheet date. The previous amount in the Allowance for Decline account was $900. As of December 31, 1984, however, the market value of the portfolio is only $300 below cost ($72,500 – $72,200), which means that only a $300 balance is needed. Thus Carr must debit the Allowance for $600 to achieve the desired result. The $600 represents a recovery or increase in value and is revenue to the firm.

The preceding events are shown in Carr's comparative financial statements for 1983 and 1984, which appear in Exhibit 7-8.

Exhibit 7-8

Comparative financial statements of Carr Corporation

	1984	1983
Balance Sheet		
Current assets		
Short-term investment in stock	$72,500	$72,500
Less: Allowance for decline in market value of short-term investments	300	900
Short-term investments at the lower of cost or market	$72,200	$71,600
Income Statement		
Other income		
Dividend revenue	$ 4,800	$ 4,500
Recovery in value of short-term investments	600	
Other expense		
Unrealized loss on short-term investments		900

Observe that if the stocks recover the remaining $300 to their original cost, the valuation allowance would be eliminated, since the short-term investments will be carried on the books at $72,500. If the stocks continue to increase in value above $72,500, the additional increase is ignored. The lower-of-cost-or-market method would again value the securities at the lower figure, which is now the portfolio's cost. As we stated earlier, loss recoveries are only recognized to the extent of the previously recorded losses. To recognize more would increase the carrying value of the securities above cost.

It is interesting to note that we recognize losses in market value while holding securities. However, *we do not recognize increases in market value above original cost.* This practice is consistent with the accounting concept of conservatism, which is discussed in Chapter 18. The increase in market value will be recognized upon the ultimate sale of the securities by commanding a selling price in excess of cost.

APPENDIX: THE VOUCHER SYSTEM

The principles of internal control discussed in this chapter (and in Chapter 5) can be applied to the design of a detailed cash payments system, termed a **voucher system.** The voucher system improves control over all cash disbursements made by check. Every payment must be approved by a supervisor or officer of the company. In addition, documents supporting each payment are reviewed and verified before approval is granted. Improper disbursements of cash, whether intentional or unintentional, are therefore eliminated (or reduced). As you will soon see, a voucher system enforces an adequate separation of duties.

A voucher system operates in the following manner:

1 An internal company document called a **voucher** is prepared for each invoice or expenditure that requires a cash disbursement.[5] Vouchers are prenumbered, summarize the details of the cash payment, and have supporting evidence such as invoices and paid receipts attached. An example of a voucher appears in Exhibit 7-9.

***Exhibit* 7-9**

Voucher

Voucher No. 415

Date: March 1, 1983 *Payee:* Franklin Company
1420 West State St.
Chicago, Illinois 60603

ITEM	*AMOUNT*
Merchandise (2/10, n/30)	$500.00

Account Debited	Amount	Approval
Purchases	$500	*Acct Dept* J.L.
Office Supplies		*Controller* Dave S.
		Payment PAID
		Date Paid 3/10/83
		Check No. 391

2 The voucher is examined for accuracy, approved, and then recorded in a **voucher register.** The voucher register is a multicolumn journal that is somewhat similar to an all-encompassing purchases journal. All vouchers are credited to a current liability account entitled Vouchers Payable. An example of a voucher register is shown in Exhibit 7-10.

[5]Exceptions are disbursements made from a petty cash fund.

Exhibit 7-10

Voucher register

Date	Voucher No.	Payee	Check No.	Date Paid	Vouchers Payable Credit	Purchases Debit	Office Supplies Debit	Sundry Accounts Debit	Post Ref	Sundry Accounts Amount
Mar. 1	415	Franklin Co.	391	Mar. 10	500	500				
8	416	Timely Supply	392	Mar. 18	125		125			
12	417	Wheatly Corp.	393	Mar. 22	650	650				
21	418	WPED Radio			150			Adv Exp	525	150
25	419	Timely Supply			180		180			
					1,605	1,150	305			150
					(201)	(501)	(130)			(X)

3 Vouchers are then filed in an unpaid voucher file by payment date. When the payment date arrives, the voucher is sent to the individual responsible for authorizing disbursements. The voucher is approved and forwarded to the accounting department.

4 The voucher is paid by issuing a check. Each check is recorded in the **check register,** which is very similar to the cash payments journal. The check register has a debit column for Vouchers Payable and a credit column for Cash. Additionally, there is a credit column for Purchases Discounts. As each voucher is paid, the check number and the date paid are recorded in the check register and the voucher register, the latter as a means of cross-referencing. Exhibit 7-11 contains a check register.

Exhibit 7-11

Check register

Date	Payee	Check No.	Voucher No.	Vouchers Payable Debit	Purchases Discounts Credit	Cash Credit
Mar. 10	Franklin Co.	391	415	500	10	490
18	Timely Supply	392	416	125		125
22	Wheatly Corp.	393	417	650		650
				1,275	10	1,265
				(201)	(502)	(101)

5 All paid vouchers are marked "paid" and filed in a paid voucher file.

AN ILLUSTRATION

The following transactions illustrate the operation of a voucher system for Braswell Company for March 1983.

Mar. 1 Purchased $500 of merchandise (terms 2/10, n/30) from Franklin Company and completed a voucher (see Exhibits 7-9 and 7-10). The voucher is recorded in the voucher register by a debit to Purchases and a credit to Vouchers Payable.

8 Purchased $125 of office supplies from Timely Supply Company. The voucher is recorded in the voucher register as a debit to Office Supplies and a credit to Vouchers Payable.

10 Paid the Franklin Company voucher (see Exhibit 7-11) within the discount period. Paid vouchers are recorded in the check register as debits to Vouchers Payable and credits to Cash. Since Braswell paid within the discount period, the Purchases Discounts account must also be credited. The check number and date paid are recorded in both the check register and the voucher register.

12 Purchased merchandise from Wheatly Corporation for $650. The voucher is recorded as a debit to Purchases and a credit to Vouchers Payable (see Exhibit 7-10).

18 Paid the amount due to Timely Supply. The check is recorded first in the check register and then cross-referenced in the voucher register.

21 Received an invoice for $150 of advertising with radio station WPED. This transaction is recorded in the voucher register. Since there is no special column for Advertising Expense, the title of the account debited is recorded in the Sundry Accounts column and $150 is posted to the Advertising Expense account in the general ledger. The credit is recorded in the Vouchers Payable column.

22 Paid the amount due to Wheatly Corporation. The disbursement is recorded first in the check register and then cross-referenced in the voucher register.

25 Purchased $180 of office supplies from Timely Supply. This transaction is similar to the purchase of March 8 in the voucher register.

At the end of the month all column totals in the voucher register and check register are totaled to determine whether debits equal credits. The column totals, with the exception of Sundry, are then posted to the general ledger in a manner similar to the methods discussed for special journals in Chapter 5. Notice that unpaid vouchers no. 418 and no. 419 (total $330) comprise a subsidiary ledger for the Vouchers Payable control account ($1,605 − $1,275 = $330).

SUMMARY PROBLEM

The Donnell Company recently hired Steve Hampton to fill a staff accounting position. On August 1 Hampton established a $400 petty cash fund. The count of petty cash on August 31 indicated that $92.30 remained in the fund. Petty cash vouchers disclosed that the following expenses were incurred during the month.

Postage expense	*$137.40*
Office supplies expense	*102.78*
Miscellaneous selling expenses	*64.92*

Additionally, the following information concerning Donnell's checking account is available.

Balance per bank statement	*$1,671.32*
Balance per company records	*1,419.99*
Bank service charge	*22.00*
Outstanding checks	*318.46*
Undeposited receipts	*208.70*
Note and interest collected by the bank but not yet recorded on the books (note, $175.00; interest, $7.00)	*182.00*
NSF check returned by the bank with the bank statement	*18.43*

INSTRUCTIONS

a **Prepare the August 1 entry to establish the petty cash fund and the August 31 entry for replenishment.**

b **Prepare the August bank reconciliation for the firm's checking account. Assume the balance per company records has already been reduced for the petty cash replenishment.**

c **Prepare the necessary journal entries related to the bank reconciliation.**

d **Determine Donnell's total cash balance (including the petty cash fund) that would appear on the August 31 balance sheet.**

SOLUTION

a

Aug.	1	Petty Cash	400.00	
		Cash	400.00	
		To establish petty cash fund		
	31	Postage Expense	137.40	
		Office Supplies Expense	102.78	
		Miscellaneous Selling Expenses	64.92	
		Cash Short and Over*	2.60	
		Cash		307.70
		To replenish petty cash fund		

* Original fund		$400.00
Less: Vouchers ($137.40 + $102.78 + $64.92)	$305.10	
Cash in fund	92.30	397.40
Shortage		$ 2.60

b

DONNELL COMPANY
Bank Reconciliation
August 31, 1983

Ending balance per bank statement		$1,671.32
Add: Undeposited receipts	$208.70	
Deduct: Outstanding checks	318.46	(109.76)
Adjusted cash balance: bank		$1,561.56
Ending balance per company records		$1,419.99
Add: Note collection	$175.00	
Interest collection	7.00	182.00
		$1,601.99
Deduct: Bank service charge	$ 22.00	
NSF check	18.43	40.43
Adjusted cash balance: company records		$1,561.56

c **All adjustments to company records require entries.**

		Debit	Credit
Aug. 31	Cash	182.00	
	Notes Receivable		175.00
	Interest Revenue		7.00
	Note and interest collected by the bank		
31	Miscellaneous Expense	22.00	
	Accounts Receivable	18.43	
	Cash		40.43
	Bank service charge and NSF check		

d

Adjusted cash balance per company records	$1,561.56
Petty cash	400.00
Total cash	$1,961.56

KEY TERMS AND CONCEPTS

bank reconciliation 259
bank statement 259
cash 254
cash budget 257
cash control system 257
cash management 256
cash planning system 257
cash short & over 267
check register 278
compensating balance 255
deposit in transit 261
electronic funds transfer system (EFTS) 268
historical-cost method 271
lower-of-cost-or-market method 271
NOW account 256
NSF check 261
outstanding check 261
petty cash system 265
short-term investments 269
voucher 276
voucher register 276
voucher system 275

QUESTIONS

Q7-1 What items are normally included in the Cash account on the balance sheet?

Q7-2 Define each of the following items and describe how they are classified on the balance sheet.

a Certificate of deposit
b Postdated check
c IOU
d Travel advance

Q7-3 What are compensating balances? What effects do compensating balances have on borrowers? How are compensating balances disclosed in financial statements?

Q7-4 What is cash management? Briefly discuss the two subdivisions of an effective cash management system.

Q7-5 What general control features should be built into a cash control system?

Q7-6 Why should cash receipts be deposited daily?

Q7-7 What is a bank reconciliation?

Q7-8 What is the effect of a bank debit memo on a depositor's account balance?

Q7-9 What are the reasons for the discrepancy between the cash balance reported on the bank statement and the cash balance in the accounting records?

Q7-10 Which adjustments on a bank reconciliation require general journal entries in the accounting records?

Q7-11 Briefly discuss the purpose of a petty cash system.

Q7-12 Describe the journal entry that is made for individual disbursements under a petty cash system.

Q7-13 Discuss the advantages associated with electronic funds transfer systems.

Q7-14 What are short-term investments? Why do companies make short-term investments?

Q7-15 Briefly discuss the criteria that must be met to classify a short-term investment as a current asset.

Q7-16 Describe two methods that may be used to account for short-term investments. When is each method used?

Q7-17 What is the purpose of a voucher system? What two journals are used to record transactions in a voucher system?

EXERCISES

E7-1 Sam Barto is the owner of The Station, a restaurant located in a residential area of a large city. Sam is concerned about the internal control over receipts from customers. Presently, waiters record customer orders on serially prenumbered service checks and take the checks to the kitchen area, where the order is prepared. After the order is completed, the check and the order are returned to the waiter. The waiter later collects the proper amount due from the customer and goes to the cashier. At the end of the day each waiter's service checks are compared with the amount of cash received, and any discrepancies are investigated.

a What internal control procedures are present in this situation?

b What control weaknesses do you believe exist? How would you recommend strengthening Barto's internal control procedures?

E7-2 Consider each of the following independent cases:

1 The petty cash custodian took $50 out of the fund and used the money for personal use. The expenditures were charged to miscellaneous expense on a petty cash voucher.

2 An employee opening the mail for a company used the company's endorsement stamp to endorse a customer's check to himself. The employee later cashed the check.

3 The accounting clerk received a customer's check for $350 and made the following entry in the accounting records:

Sales Returns & Allowances	*350*	
Accounts Receivable		*350*

The clerk later cashed the check and kept the money.

For each of the foregoing cases indicate any apparent internal control weakness and suggest procedures that may prevent the irregularity.

E7-3 Farwell Corporation received a bank statement that indicated a cash balance on deposit of $1,520 as of February 28. The bank statement also disclosed a service charge of $15. Farwell's accountant discovered that a $400 deposit in transit had not been recorded by the bank and that outstanding checks totaled $640.

a Compute the Farwell Corporation's *unadjusted* cash balance on February 28 as per the company records.

b Determine the cash balance that should be reported on Farwell's February 28 balance sheet.

E7-4 Baez's March 31 bank statement indicated a cash balance on deposit of $5,960. In reviewing the cash transactions for the month, the company's accountant discovered that (1) a deposit in transit of $685 had not been recorded by the bank, (2) the bank service charge for the month was $20, and (3) the company's cash records, before adjustment, showed a $5,845 balance.

a Compute the total of Baez's outstanding checks on March 31.

b Determine the cash balance that should be reported on Baez's March 31 balance sheet.

E7-5 The following information was taken from the accounting records of Ardis Corporation for the month of May.

Balance per bank	$1,650.25
Balance per books	1,190.20
Note collected by the bank on May 30	200.00
Interest on the above note	25.00
Bank service charge for May	15.00
Outstanding checks	430.25
NSF check returned by the bank with the bank statement	180.20

a Prepare a bank reconciliation for Ardis Corporation for May.

b Prepare any necessary journal entries for Ardis.

E7-6 The following information is available for Pape Company on June 30.

Bank statement balance	$8,218.75
Undeposited June 30 receipts	1,951.00
Bank service charge for June	21.25
June outstanding checks	2,451.00
Note collected by the bank but not recorded on the books	2,080.00
Interest on the above note	45.00
Balance per company records	5,615.00

a Determine Pape's cash balance to be reported on the June 30 balance sheet.

b Prepare any required journal entries for Pape.

E7-7 The Tatum Corporation instituted a petty cash system on June 1 to allow for the payment of small expenditures. The following information has come to your attention.

June 1 The fund was established at $500.

30 Cash in the fund had been reduced to $102.50. The petty cash vouchers were sorted into the following expense categories and the fund was replenished.

Office supplies	$225.75
Miscellaneous expense	98.40
Postage	70.50
	$394.65

a Prepare the journal entry necessary to record the establishment of the fund on June 1.
b Prepare the journal entry necessary to record the replenishment of the fund on June 30.

E7-8 On June 30 Herblin Corporation purchased the following short-term investments:

Z-Mart	200 shares at $51 per share
4-12 Food Stores	300 shares at $20 per share

On December 31, the following market value information concerning the two short-term investments is available.

Security	*Market Value per Share*
Z-Mart	$45
4-12 Food Stores	21

a Prepare the journal entry to record the acquisition of Herblin's short-term investments.
b Prepare the journal entry to record the change in market value of the short-term investments.

E7-9 The Van Horn Company, formed during 1982, invests excess cash in common stocks of growth companies. The stocks are readily salable and management intends to sell the stocks whenever the firm is in need of cash. The accompanying table gives the cost and market values of Van Horn's short-term investments for 1982 and 1983.

	1982	*1983*
Cost	$48,000	$48,000
Market value	43,500	49,600

a Present Van Horn's journal entries in 1982 and 1983 to value the short-term securities at the lower of cost or market.
b Show how the securities would appear on Van Horn's 1982 and 1983 balance sheets.

E7-10 The Nowlin Company presented the following disclosure in the long-term investment section of its balance sheet.

Long-term investments	
Securities purchases	*$74,000*
Less: Allowance for decline in market value of short-term investments	*5,400*
Short-term investments at the lower of cost or market	*$68,600*

The securities were valued in the following fashion:

Security	Cost	Market	Lower of Cost or Market
A Corporation stock (200 shares)	$20,000	$17,200	$17,200
B Corporation stock (400 shares)	4,000	4,900	4,000
C Corporation stock (500 shares)	50,000	47,400	47,400
	$74,000	$69,500	$68,600

All securities are readily salable and will be sold in the next four months because of a cash shortage. Brokers' fees of $2,200 relating to the purchase of the securities were expensed when incurred.

Prepare a corrected balance sheet for the Nowlin Company.

E7-11 On June 1 Verkin Company established a $700 petty cash fund for incidental expenditures. On June 30 a count of cash indicated that $94.60 remained in the fund. A sorting of petty cash vouchers disclosed that the following expenses had been incurred during the month.

Postage expense	*$215.40*
Office supplies expense	*160.80*
Miscellaneous expense	*223.55*

Verkin uses a voucher system for all cash payments that are made by check. Record the following entries in general journal form.

a Preparation of voucher no. 100 to establish the petty cash fund.

b Payment of voucher no. 100 by issuing check no. 100.

c Preparation of voucher no. 101 to replenish *and* increase the petty cash fund to $750 on June 30.

d Payment of voucher no. 101 with check no. 101.

PROBLEMS

P7-1 ***Cash on the balance sheet***

The following information has been gathered from the records of Huskey Corporation as of December 31.

Certificate of deposit	*$10,000.00*
Employee's IOU	*300.00*
Cash on hand	*1,840.60*
Reconciled balance in Second National Bank checking account	*3,120.40*
Balance in Second Federal savings account	*18,950.00*
Petty cash fund	*500.00*
Reconciled balance in University Bank checking account	*3,970.50*
Postage stamps on hand	*220.00*
Customer's postdated check	*1,240.60*
Money orders on hand	*700.00*

Huskey has $50,000 on deposit in a special account at the University Bank. The money will be used to finance future construction at Huskey's main manufacturing plant. In addition, Huskey has negotiated a $15,000 short-term loan with the United National Bank that requires a 10% compensating balance. The compensating balance is restricted; that is, the funds cannot be used for current operations and activities.

INSTRUCTIONS

a Considering only those items available for current operations, compute the cash balance to be reported as a current asset on the December 31 balance sheet.

b Describe the balance sheet treatment of the items not included in the cash balance computed in part (a).

P7-2 ***Internal control***

The town of Commuter Park operates a private parking lot near the railroad station for the benefit of town residents. City Hall issues prenumbered parking stickers to commuters who submit an application form and show evidence of residency. The sticker is affixed to the auto and allows the resident to park anywhere in the lot for twelve hours if four quarters are placed in a parking meter. A guard checks to see that only residents use the lot and that no resident has parked without paying the required meter fee.

Once a week, after all personnel have gone home, the guard on duty takes the coins from the meters and places them in a locked steel box. The guard delivers the box to the town storage building, where it is opened. The coins are manually counted by a storage department clerk who records the total cash counted on a weekly cash report. This report is sent to the town accounting department. The storage department clerk puts the coins back in the locked box and places the box in the rear of a supply closet. On the following day the cash is picked up by the town's treasurer, who manually recounts the cash, prepares the bank deposit slip, and delivers the deposit to the bank. The deposit slip, authenticated by the bank teller, is sent to the accounting department, where it is filed with the weekly cash report.

INSTRUCTIONS

Describe weaknesses in the existing system and recommend one or more improvements for each weakness to strengthen internal control.

(CPA modified.)

P7-3 ***Internal control and cash shortages***

Frank Evans is employed as a sales clerk by the Bedford Variety Store. He is a close friend of Ned Fong, the store's bookkeeper. Evans is experiencing some personal financial problems and Fong has agreed to employ him a few extra hours each week to assist in the bookkeeping department. During the last two weeks of June, Fong was on vacation. The following information pertains to June 20.

Evans checked out the register at the end of the day. The register's tape read as follows:

Total cash sales	$128
Total credit sales	245
	$373

The register's drawer contained the following:

Change fund at all times	$ 50
Cash collections	125

The cash collections included two checks:

Check Date	Customer	Amount
June 20	Nancy Jordan	$40
June 24	Sam May	30

Evans helped satisfy his financial problems by stealing $20 from the register.

INSTRUCTIONS

a Present the journal entry that should have been made when checking out the register on June 20. *Hint:* Disregard the theft.

b What must Evans do to the accounting records to conceal his theft?

c Are there any apparent violations of internal control at the Bedford Variety Store? Explain.

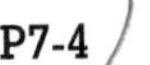

P7-4 ***Bank reconciliation and entries***

The October 31 bank statement for Ricca Supplies Company disclosed a balance of $6,956.80. On this date the Cash account in Ricca's general ledger totaled $1,961.10. The following information has come to your attention.

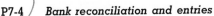

1 Deposit in transit on October 31, $700.00.

2 A note receivable of $5,000 and interest of $50 were collected by the bank but not as yet recorded in the accounts.

3 Outstanding checks amounted to $3,321.50. The outstanding checks include a duplicate check for $141.70 to G. Weiss, who notified Ricca that the original was lost. Ricca stopped payment on the original check and has already adjusted the Cash account for this amount.

4 Cash receipts of $1,280.50 for October 20 were recorded on the books and deposited at the bank. (Ricca has a duplicate of the deposit slip.) The bank recorded the deposit in the account of Rocca Toy Company.

5 Jones's NSF check returned with the bank statement, $840.80.

6 Bank service charge, $14.50.

7 A check on account from Smith for $390.80 was recorded on the books as $930.80.

INSTRUCTIONS

a Prepare a bank reconciliation for Ricca.

b Prepare the journal entries necessary for Ricca as of October 31.

P7-5 ***Bank reconciliation from bank statement***

The Union Company is in the process of reconciling its bank account with Metropolitan Bank and Trust for May. Union's bank statement follows.

METROPOLITAN BANK AND TRUST

Union Company
1502 East Woodruff
Pittsburgh, PA 15263

For the month of May

Date	Checks/Debits	Deposits/Credits	Balance
5/1			$8,440
5/2		$ 400	8,840
5/4	500, 725		7,615
5/7	690, 310	625	7,240
5/11	1,080	370	6,530
5/14	510 NSF		6,020
5/16	490, 860	1,150	5,820
5/19		2,340	8,160
5/24	665, 430, 110		6,955
5/27		850 CM	7,805
5/31	800, 1,210		5,795
5/31	10 SC		5,785

CM *Credit Memo* NSF *NSF Check* SC *Service Charge*

The credit memo represents the collection of an $830 note receivable plus $20 interest. Union's cash receipts and disbursements records for May are as follows:

Deposits

5/6	$ 625
5/10	370
5/15	1,150
5/18	3,240
5/31	780
	$6,165

Checks Written

no. 408	$ 500	no. 418	$ 120
409	690	419	555
410	310	420	440
411	Void	421	800
412	430	422	80
413	490	423	90
414	Void	424	100
415	110	425	200
416	665		$6,790
417	1,210		

An examination of the April reconciliation revealed a deposit in transit on April 30 of $400. The following checks were outstanding:

no. 384	$ 725
395	600
406	1,080
407	860

INSTRUCTIONS

a Assuming a cash balance per company records on May 1 of $5,575, prepare Union's bank reconciliation for May. Assume that any errors detected during the reconciliation process are the fault of Union's bookkeeper.

b Prepare the necessary journal entries for Union as of May 31.

P7-6 ***Petty cash fund***

Consolidated Manufacturing Corporation operates a petty cash fund for small expenditures. The following information relates to June.

June *1* Established the petty cash fund for $100.

8 Replenished the fund. The following items were found in the petty cash box.

Vouchers for postage	$27
Vouchers for supplies	43
Vouchers for miscellaneous expenses	17
Coins and currency	13

15 Replenished and raised the fund to $200. The following items were found in the petty cash box.

Vouchers for postage	$31
Vouchers for supplies	24
Vouchers for miscellaneous expenses	26
Coins and currency	15

30 Replenished the fund. The following items were found in the petty cash box.

Vouchers for postage	$48
Vouchers for supplies	45
Vouchers for miscellaneous expenses	38
Voucher stating: I owe the fund $25. Signed: Jay Huff (an employee)	
Envelope containing $35 and marked: Collections for secretary's gift	
Coins and currency	$37

INSTRUCTIONS

a Record the necessary journal entries on June 1, 8, 15, and 30.

b It is now December 14. Tom Fast, an auditor for Consolidated, believes that the petty cash custodian has been stealing from the fund for the past several months. Fast told the custodian that a detailed examination of the fund would be performed on December 15 and that "everything had better be in order." Do you see any problems in Tom's informing the custodian of the upcoming audit? Explain.

P7-7 ***Recording short-term investments***

On August 31, 1983, Bartlett Company acquired the following short-term investments:

Security	**Cost**
300 shares of Modern Co. stock	$25,000
600 shares of Dean, Inc., stock	32,000
400 shares of Awards International Corp. stock	17,000

On December 31, 1983, the following information is available.

Security	Market Value
Modern	$27,000
Dean	30,000
Awards International	14,000

On December 31, 1984, the following information is available.

Security	Market Value
Modern	$27,000
Dean	31,000
Awards International	20,000

INSTRUCTIONS

a Prepare the journal entries necessary to record the preceding information under the lower-of-cost-or-market method.

b Explain the benefits of using the lower-of-cost-or-market method rather than the historical-cost method for valuing short-term stock investments.

c How would these short-term investments appear on Bartlett's December 31, 1983, balance sheet? On the December 31, 1984, balance sheet?

d Suppose that in addition to the $25,000 outlay to acquire the Modern Company stock, Bartlett had to pay $325 of brokers' fees. Explain the proper accounting treatment for these fees.

P7-8 ***Recording short-term investments***

Schneider, Inc., reported the following information on its December 31, 1983, balance sheet.

Short-term investments	*$75,480*
Less: Allowance for decline in market value of short-term investments	*3,740*
Short-term investments at the lower of cost or market	*$71,740*

An analysis of Schneider's short-term investments on December 31, 1983, revealed the following information:

Security	Cost	Market
300 shares of Doak Manufacturing	$26,450	$25,540
400 shares of Kyle Investment Corp.	31,570	30,160
200 shares of Kerry Sales Corp.	17,460	16,040

During 1984 Schneider received the following dividends:

Doak Manufacturing	$10 per share
Kyle Investment	8 per share
Kerry Sales	6 per share

On December 31, 1984, Schneider's investments had the following market values:

Doak $86 per share
Kyle 77 per share
Kerry 76 per share

INSTRUCTIONS

a Prepare the journal entries necessary to record the preceding information on Schneider's accounting records for 1984.

b How would the short-term investments be reported on Schneider's December 31, 1984, balance sheet?

c How is Schneider's 1984 income statement affected by these transactions and events?

d Suppose the market price of the Kyle stock soared to $95 per share as of December 31, 1984. Repeat the instructions for parts (a), (b), and (c) using this new information.

P7-9 ***Voucher system***

The O'Toole Company, which uses a voucher system to control cash payments, had the following transactions during April.

Apr. *1* Issued a $500 check to establish a petty cash fund.
3 Purchased $800 of merchandise from Morisson Corporation, terms 3/10, n/30.
8 Purchased office equipment for $1,200 from the Otis Desk Company.
10 Purchased $300 of office supplies from the Larkin Supply Company.
12 Paid the proper amount due to Morisson Corporation.
18 Purchased $900 of merchandise from Upton, Incorporated, terms 2/10, n/eom.
20 Purchased $700 of merchandise from Lewis Company.
24 Paid the amount due to Larkin Supply Company.
26 Paid the amount due to Upton, Incorporated.
30 A sorting of petty cash vouchers indicated that the following expenses had been incurred during the month.

Office supplies	*$187*
Postage	*65*
Miscellaneous expense	*178*

Replenished the petty cash fund for the amount of these expenses.

O'Toole uses a voucher register and check register similar in format to those illustrated in this chapter.

INSTRUCTIONS

a Record the transactions in the appropriate journal, that is, the voucher register or the check register. Begin with voucher no. 741 and check no. 732.

b Total the voucher register and check register at the end of the month.

c Compute the balance in the Vouchers Payable account as of April 30. On what financial statement and in which section would this balance appear?

d Compute the total of unpaid vouchers as of April 30. If all procedures are properly followed, what should the total of the unpaid vouchers be? Why?

P7-10 Cash on the balance sheet (alternate to P7-1)

The following information has been gathered from the records of San Marcos Supply.

Customer's postdated check	$ 450
Reconciled balance in Northeast Bank checking account	6,905
Certificate of deposit	15,000
Investment in Treasury bills	10,000
Petty cash fund	250
Savings account balance at Hartford Federal	3,075
Cash on hand	875
Employee IOU	100
Postage stamps on hand	25

San Marcos has $40,000 on deposit in a special account at the Northeast Bank. The money will be used to finance a warehouse modernization program in three years. In addition, San Marcos has negotiated a $35,000 short-term loan with the Connecticut General Bank that requires a 10% compensating balance. The compensating balance is legally restricted and cannot be used for current operations and activities.

INSTRUCTIONS

a Considering only those items available for current operations, compute the cash balance to be reported as a current asset on the December 31 balance sheet.

b Describe the balance sheet treatment of the items not included in the cash balance computed in part (a).

P7-11 Bank reconciliation and entries (alternate to P7-4)

The February 28 bank statement of Simoni Corporation disclosed a balance of $4,825.40. On this same date the Cash account in the general ledger indicated a balance of $2,497.62. The following information has come to your attention.

1 A deposit of $823.40, mailed by Simoni on February 27, was entered in the accounting records on February 28 but was not received by the bank until March 1.

2 Outstanding checks on February 28 totaled $1,247.53, computed as follows:

Checks written in January	$ 264.10
Checks written in February	983.43
	$1,247.53

3 A customer's NSF check for $187.40 was returned with the bank statement.

4 Cash on hand on February 28 totaled $318.70.

5 Simoni's check no. 614 for a $6,700 machinery acquisition was entered in the accounts as $7,600.

6 A note receivable of $1,500 and interest of $25 were collected by the bank but not as yet recorded in the accounts.

7 Bank service charge, $15.25.

INSTRUCTIONS

a Prepare a bank reconciliation for Simoni Corporation.

b Prepare the journal entries necessary for Simoni as of February 28.

P7-12 ***Bank reconciliation from bank statement*** **(*alternate to P7-5*)**
The Whitlow Corporation received the accompanying bank statement for September from First City Bank & Trust.

FIRST CITY BANK & TRUST

Whitlow Corporation
9th & Circle Drive
Browntree, Arkansas 72330

Date	Checks/Debits	Deposits/Credits	Balance
9/1			$10,480
9/2	400, 740	150	9,490
9/5	380		9,110
9/8	500, 325, 480		7,805
9/15	640, 200	2,350	9,315
9/18	210		9,105
9/20	840, 370		7,895
9/22	610	1,820	9,105
9/25	415 NSF		8,690
9/27	720, 300	740 CM	8,410
9/28	220, 480	2,570	10,280
9/30	515, 15 SC		9,750

CM *Credit Memo* NSF *NSF Check* SC *Service Charge*

The credit memo represents the collection of a $700 note receivable plus $40 interest. Whitlow's cash receipts and disbursements records for September disclose the following:

Deposits	
9/14	$2,350
9/20	1,820
9/27	2,570
9/30	1,580
	$8,320

Checks Written			
no. 915	$380	no. 924	$ 300
916	500	925	220
917	480	926	720
918	200	928	180
919	640	929	515
920	210	930	720
921	370	931	510
922	610	932	460
923	840		$7,855

An examination of the August reconciliation revealed a deposit in transit on August 31 of $150. The following checks were listed as outstanding.

no. 890	$615
911	740
912	325
913	400

INSTRUCTIONS

a Assuming a cash balance per company records on September 1 of $8,550, prepare Whitlow's bank reconciliation. Assume that any errors detected during the reconciliation process are the fault of Whitlow's bookkeeper.

b Prepare the journal entries necessary by Whitlow on September 30.

P7-13 *Petty cash fund (alternate to P7-6)*

Pacific Enterprises operates a petty cash fund for small expenditures. The following information relates to November.

Nov. 1 Established the petty cash fund for $150.

10 Replenished the fund. The following items were found in the petty cash box.

Vouchers for postage	$36
Vouchers for supplies	72
Vouchers for miscellaneous expenses	15
Coins and currency	27

19 Replenished and raised the fund to $275. The following items were found in the petty cash box.

Vouchers for postage	$39
Vouchers for supplies	58
Vouchers for miscellaneous expenses	36
Coins and currency	19

30 Replenished the fund. The following items were found in the petty cash box.

Vouchers for postage	$ 47
Vouchers for supplies	55
Vouchers for miscellaneous expenses	29
Voucher stating: I owe the fund $30. Signed: Janet King (an employee)	
Envelope containing $50 and marked: Collections for football pool	
Coins and currency	$111

INSTRUCTIONS

a Record the necessary journal entries on November 1, 10, 19, and 30.

b Explain the probable reasoning behind the fund replenishment on November 30 despite the presence of $111 of cash in the petty cash box.

P7-14 *Recording short-term investments (alternate to P7-8)*

Fazio Corporation disclosed the following information on its December 31, 1983, balance sheet.

Short-term investments	$89,740
Less: Allowance for decline in market value of short-term investments	5,660
Short-term investments at the lower of cost or market	$84,080

An analysis of Fazio's short-term investments on December 31, 1983, revealed the following:

Security	Cost	Market
600 shares of Lyons, Inc.	$26,270	$24,050
500 shares of Madden Company	19,860	17,650
300 shares of Lipton, Inc.	32,480	29,740
400 shares of Loeb Corporation	11,130	12,640

During 1984 Fazio received the following dividends:

Lyons	$ 5 per share
Madden	6 per share
Lipton	10 per share
Loeb	3 per share

On December 31, 1984, Fazio's investments had the following market values:

Lyons	$41 per share
Madden	30 per share
Lipton	98 per share
Loeb	35 per share

INSTRUCTIONS

a Prepare the journal entries necessary to record the above information on Fazio's accounting records for 1984.

b How would the short-term investments be reported on Fazio's December 31, 1984, balance sheet?

c How is Fazio's 1984 income statement affected by these transactions and events?

d Suppose the market price of the Madden stock soared to $46 per share as of December 31, 1984. Repeat the instructions for parts (a), (b), and (c) using this new information.

CASE 7
METROPOLITAN BAR ASSOCIATION

The Metropolitan Bar Association (MBA), a professional association for practicing attorneys, is contemplating a new cash investment policy. MBA's cash receipt and disbursement situation is somewhat unique. Receipts are generated mainly from annual membership dues, and most dues are collected in the 3-month period following the mailing of invoices on May 31. (The fiscal year begins on June 1.) Therefore MBA cash balances peak during June, July, and August. On the other hand, disbursements for expenses occur almost uniformly throughout the year except for March and April, when members are reimbursed for out-of-pocket costs (such as mileage while serving on committee assignments). Thus MBA has excess cash on hand during most of the year.

Susan Hogan, the new assistant treasurer, has suggested investing the idle cash to earn additional revenue for MBA. Phil Stephens, the treasurer, agrees.

However, he notes: "We cannot afford to invest our idle cash for long enough periods to justify the additional costs such as brokerage fees and transfer taxes on stocks and bonds. Stocks and bonds must be held for relatively long periods of time to earn a reasonable return. Additionally, the association cannot speculate with members' dues. We cannot afford to take losses because the services our employees provide are funded by membership dues."

Susan Hogan believes that an idle-cash investment policy can be found that overcomes these problems. She has developed the following projected cash flow information for the upcoming fiscal year.

Month	Receipts	Disbursements
June	$150,000	$35,000
July	200,000	35,000
Aug.	100,000	35,000
Sept.	25,000	35,000
Oct.	10,000	35,000
Nov.	5,000	35,000
Dec.	2,000	35,000
Jan.	2,000	35,000
Feb.	2,000	35,000
Mar.	2,000	60,000
Apr.	1,000	75,000
May	1,000	40,000

INSTRUCTIONS

a Prepare a rough evaluation of MBA's cash flow data. Would a cash planning system benefit MBA? Why?

b Suggest several possible investment options for MBA.

c To more closely match cash disbursements, one attorney has suggested dividing the membership into groups and billing a twelfth of the membership each month. From an investment viewpoint, do you see any problems with this procedure? Explain.

8 RECEIVABLES

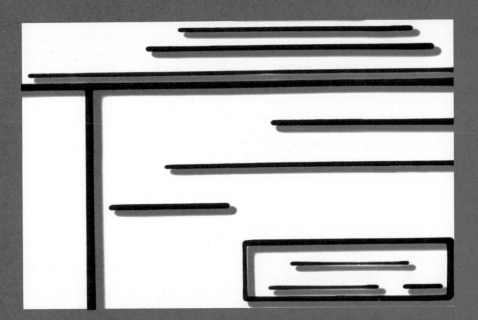

LEARNING OBJECTIVES

After reading this chapter you should:

1 Understand the costs and processes related to the credit-granting decision.

2 Understand the distinction between trade and nontrade receivables.

3 Be able to account for uncollectible accounts by using both the direct write-off and the allowance methods.

4 Understand the difference between the income statement and balance sheet approaches to estimating bad debts.

5 Be able to compute interest.

6 Be able to account for installment sales and credit card sales.

7 Understand the various options for securing immediate cash from outstanding accounts receivable: pledging, assignment, and factoring.

8 Be able to account for notes receivable, including discounted and dishonored obligations.

CHAPTER 8

THE USE OF CREDIT

The extension of credit has been a significant factor behind economic growth in the United States. The purchase of goods and services on an installment plan, by the use of in-house charge accounts, or through bank cards such as Visa and MasterCard is a way of life for today's average business or consumer.

Businesses extend credit in order to increase sales. Frequently, however, firms concentrate on this objective and lose sight of the costs related to the credit-granting decision. Credit sales often create the need for a credit department to (1) investigate customer credit ratings, (2) approve the extension of credit to customers, and (3) attempt to collect delinquent accounts.

Furthermore, a business must wait for a customer to pay the balance owed. As we saw in Chapter 4, many firms offer cash discounts to encourage prompt customer payment. These discounts, of course, result in reduced revenues. Despite the discount incentive, many customers still fail to settle their balances within requested time limits. Consequently, businesses often must sell short-term investments and secure bank loans to obtain needed operating funds. The former action may result in the loss of future interest or dividends, while the latter will give rise to interest costs.

Another cost related to credit sales is the result of nonpayment by customers. Firms rarely collect all their accounts receivable because customers go bankrupt, leave town, and so on. This cost, known as *bad debts expense,* can be especially high for a business that has tried to increase sales by being too liberal in granting credit. While some marginal customers can be profitable, the end result is often increased costs and a lack of collection by the firm.

When a company is considering whether to sell its products on credit or render services on account, it must evaluate the trade-off between the additional revenue from the credit sales and the additional expenses that the credit sales generate. The goal is to reduce receivables to the lowest possible level while maximizing profitable sales volume and minimizing related expenses. Some companies have decided that they can be more profitable by not extending credit. Although these firms will undoubtedly lose some sales, they apparently feel that the cost savings outweigh the decline in revenue.

RECEIVABLES

Credit sales and other transactions give rise to **receivables.** Receivables represent a variety of claims against customers and others arising from the operation of a business enterprise. Receivables are reported on the balance sheet as either current or noncurrent assets until they are ultimately collected. Those receivables expected to be collected within one year or the operating cycle, whichever is longer, are classified as current assets; all other receivables are classified as noncurrent.

Receivables are also subcategorized as trade receivables and nontrade receivables. The majority of receivables are **trade receivables,** which emanate from the sale of a company's products or services to customers. Trade receivables consist of accounts receivable and notes receivable. **Nontrade receivables,** on the other hand, arise from transactions not directly related to the sale of goods and services; they include accrued receivables, advances to employees, and deposits with utilities.

In this chapter we will focus on the accounting problems associated with current trade receivables. Accounting for other types of receivables is touched on in other chapters of the text.

Accounts Receivable

Accounts receivable represent the amounts that customers owe an entity for goods and services. As the figures in Exhibit 8-1 indicate, accounts receivable can be a substantial percentage of total assets for many firms.

Exhibit 8-1

Accounts receivable for various firms (000 omitted)

	American Greetings	Borden, Inc.	Federated Department Stores	NCR
Net accounts receivable	$114,051	$486,451	$1,181,040	$1,025,116
Total assets	$431,680	$2,508,816	$4,096,877	$3,386,534
Net accounts receivable as a percentage of total assets	26.4%	19.4%	28.8%	30.3%

In view of the magnitude of accounts receivable, proper valuation and presentation on the balance sheet are essential. In Chapter 4 we discussed a number of issues related to this important asset, including trade discounts, sales discounts, and sales returns and allowances. We will now focus on one additional accounting problem: *uncollectible accounts.*

Despite the use of credit standards, some uncollectible accounts (i.e., **bad debts**) almost always arise. Uncollectible accounts have both income statement and balance sheet implications for accountants. On the income statement, for example, an "adequate" amount for bad debts expense should be matched against (deducted from) the sales revenues generated. The objective is to present a fair measurement of net income. On the balance sheet the Accounts Receivable account should be reduced to reflect the amounts that a firm has a reasonable expectation of collecting.

There are two methods of accounting for uncollectible accounts: the direct write-off method and the allowance method.

Direct write-off method

Under the **direct write-off method,** bad debts are entered in the accounting records when the actual loss is incurred. That is, when a customer account is deemed uncollectible, the account is written off as an expense of the current accounting period. To illustrate, we will assume that Bill McCracken owes the Warren Company $875. After repeated collection efforts, Warren has just learned that McCracken has filed for personal bankruptcy. The Warren Company would make the following entry:

Bad Debts Expense	*875*	
Accounts Receivable: Bill McCracken		*875*
To write off uncollectible account		

The direct write-off method of accounting for bad debts is simple and has the advantage of reporting actual losses rather than estimates. There are several deficiencies with this approach, however. Frequently, a customer's account is not deemed uncollectible until a period subsequent to the period of sale. Therefore the direct write-off method could recognize the sales revenue in one period and the expense related to that revenue in the next period. Thus an improper matching of revenues and expenses has taken place. Furthermore, because the write-off may occur in a future period, Accounts Receivable is often overstated at the end of the year of sale.

Allowance method

The **allowance method** overcomes the objections to the direct write-off method by associating the revenue and expense in the same accounting period. Correct matching is achieved through the use of *estimates* of bad debts expense. Accurate estimates can normally be obtained by studying a firm's past experience with uncollectible accounts and making adjustments for current economic conditions and credit standards. The estimate, usually in the form of a percentage, is applied to current sales or the year-end accounts receivable balance to derive current estimates of uncollectible accounts.

When the estimate of bad debts is determined, a journal entry is recorded at the end of the accounting period in the form of an adjustment. The entry involves a debit to Bad Debts Expense and a credit to an account entitled Allowance for Bad Debts.[1] Bad Debts Expense is reported on the income statement as an administrative operating expense. The Allowance for Bad Debts account is a contra asset that is offset against Accounts Receivable in the current assets section of the balance sheet. It is shown as follows (account balances are assumed):

Current assets		
Accounts receivable	*$19,000*	
Less: Allowance for bad debts	*2,600*	*$16,400*

Offsetting the Allowance for Bad Debts in this manner informs financial statement users of the expected **net realizable value** ($16,400) or the amount of cash expected from the collection of present customer balances. The use of this separate valuation account is required because the actual uncollectible customer accounts are unknown when the financial statements are prepared. Thus we cannot credit individual subsidiary accounts and the Accounts Receivable control account at the time of bad debt estimation.

Bad debts expense can be estimated by observing historical relationships between the actual bad debts incurred and (1) sales or (2) accounts receivable. These relationships may be classified as follows:

1 Relationship to sales (income statement approach)

[1] The Allowance account is sometimes called the Allowance for Doubtful Accounts or the Allowance for Uncollectible Accounts.

   a Percentage of sales
   b Percentage of credit sales
2 Relationship to accounts receivable (balance sheet approach)
   a Percentage of outstanding accounts receivable
   b Aging of accounts receivable

Relationship to sales: Income statement approach

Estimating bad debts on the basis of sales results in matching current revenues with the costs incurred in producing those revenues. Because of its matching emphasis, this method is commonly referred to as the **income statement approach.**

The estimate of bad debts expense may be based on total sales or credit sales. Total sales can be used when there is a fairly stable relationship between cash and credit sales from one period to the next. If the proportion of credit sales to total sales varies substantially, the use of total sales may not be appropriate. For this reason most accountants favor estimation of bad debts on the basis of credit sales. Using credit sales is also a more rational approach since bad debts are not incurred on cash sales. To illustrate the income statement approach, assume Lukin Corporation's credit sales for the current year total $500,000 and that bad debts have historically amounted to 3% of credit sales. The following adjusting entry for $15,000 ($500,000 × 0.03) would be made.

Bad Debts Expense	*15,000*	
Allowance for Bad Debts		*15,000*
Adjusting entry		

Relationship to accounts receivable: Balance sheet approach

Bad debts may also be estimated on the basis of accounts receivable. This method, known as the **balance sheet approach,** focuses on reporting accounts receivable at net realizable value. Thus when using the balance sheet method, we must consider the previous balance in the Allowance for Bad Debts account. For example, assume Lukin has determined that bad debts normally amount to 3% of the year-end accounts receivable balance. The company's accounting records at the end of the year, prior to the adjustment for bad debts, disclose the following information:

Accounts receivable	*$600,000*
Allowance for bad debts	*2,800 (credit balance)*

Collections from customer accounts are expected to total $582,000 [$600,000 − ($600,000 × 0.03)], thereby necessitating an $18,000 balance in the Allowance for Bad Debts ($600,000 − $582,000). Because $2,800 is presently in the account, an additional $15,200 ($18,000 − $2,800) must be entered to achieve the desired result. The following adjusting entry is needed:

Bad Debts Expense	*15,200*	
Allowance for Bad Debts		*15,200*
Adjusting entry		

The effect of this entry is shown in the T-accounts below:

Bad Debts Expense			Allowance for Bad Debts	
Adj	15,200		Balance	2,800
			Adj	15,200
				18,000

The resulting balance sheet presentation of Lukin's accounts receivable is as follows:

Current assets		
Accounts receivable	*$600,000*	
Less: Allowance for bad debts	*18,000*	*$582,000*

Occasionally, the Allowance for Bad Debts account may possess a debit balance.[2] If Lukin's Allowance account had a $3,000 *debit* balance prior to the adjustment, the following entry would be necessary.

Bad Debts Expense	*21,000*	
Allowance for Bad Debts		*21,000*
Adjusting entry		

The $21,000 credit to the Allowance, when combined with the $3,000 debit balance, yields the desired $18,000 ending balance.

Aging of accounts receivable. Estimating bad debts expense as a percentage of outstanding accounts receivable ignores the due date of the many individual accounts comprising the total balance. The length of time a specific account has been outstanding is an important factor when assessing the probability of future collection. That is, a company is more likely to collect an account that is 30 days old than to collect one that is 180 days old. To overcome this problem, accountants have developed a more sophisticated approach of estimating bad debts. This method, termed **aging accounts receivable,** categorizes individual accounts based on the length of time they have been outstanding. A historically developed bad debts percentage is then applied to each age category to determine the bad debt estimate.

The aging process not only furnishes information for the bad debt estimate but also serves as a useful management tool. The analysis of individual accounts provides insight regarding the success or failure of a firm's credit and collection efforts. Furthermore, close monitoring of individual customer activity will determine if any changes in a customer's credit rating are necessary.

To illustrate estimation by the aging process, we will examine Exhibit 8-2, which contains information from the records of the Livingston Corporation. The aging of individual customer accounts indicates that the Allowance for Bad Debts must contain a balance of $9,395 on December 31, 1983.

[2] The situations that cause a debit balance are discussed later in the chapter.

Exhibit 8-2

LIVINGSTON CORPORATION
Aging Schedule of Accounts Receivable
December 31, 1983

Customer	Balance 12/31/83	Under 60 Days	61-90 Days	91-120 Days	121-180 Days	Over 180 Days
		Length of Time Outstanding				
Clark Inc.	$ 15,000			$6,000	$5,000	$4,000
Gibbs Manufacturing	36,000	$31,000	$ 5,000			
Madden Co.	19,500	15,000	4,500			
Nunley Co.	18,700	9,000	5,000	3,000	1,700	
Patrick Corporation	27,500	15,500	12,000			
Total	$116,700	$70,500	$26,500	$9,000	$6,700	$4,000

Estimated Uncollectibles

Age	Account Balances (from Above)	× Estimated % Uncollectible	= Estimated Amount of Uncollectibles
Under 60 days	$ 70,500	3%	$2,115
61-90 days	26,500	7	1,855
91-120 days	9,000	12	1,080
121-180 days	6,700	35	2,345
Over 180 days	4,000	50	2,000
	$116,700		$9,395

As before, the previous balance in the Allowance account is considered when formulating the adjusting entry. If a review of Livingston's ledger revealed a credit balance of $2,200, then $7,195 ($9,395 – $2,200) would be needed to bring the Allowance account up to the required balance. The following entry is necessary.

Bad Debts Expense	*7,195*	
Allowance for Bad Debts		*7,195*
Adjusting entry		

In general, accountants favor the income statement approach over the balance sheet method because of the emphasis on the matching of revenues and expenses and the reliance on reported net income that financial statement users now include in their decision processes.

Writing off uncollectible accounts

Under the allowance method individual accounts are written off when they are deemed uncollectible by debiting Allowance for Bad Debts and crediting Accounts Receivable. Note that Bad Debts Expense is not charged again at the time of write-off; to do so would result in double counting.

As a result of this treatment, the write-off of an uncollectible account does not affect the net realizable value of the Accounts Receivable balance. To illustrate, consider the following information that appeared on Harvey Company's December 31, 1983, balance sheet.

Current assets		
Accounts receivable	*$140,000*	
Less: Allowance for bad debts	*6,780*	*$133,220*

On January 18, 1984, assume J. Waldrup's $425 balance is judged uncollectible. Thus the following entry is made.

Allowance for Bad Debts	*425*	
Accounts Receivable: J. Waldrup		*425*
To write off uncollectible account		

The write-off will not have any effect on the net accounts receivable balance because the entry reduces both the Allowance for Bad Debts account and Accounts Receivable by the same amount. This result is shown below.

	Before	**Write-off**	**After**
Accounts receivable	$140,000	−$425	$139,575
Less: Allowance for bad debts	6,780	−425	6,355
	$133,220		$133,220

The process of writing off an uncollectible account places debits in the Allowance for Bad Debts. Therefore it is possible that at the end of the period the Allowance may possess a debit balance. This situation usually arises when a firm's estimate of expense (credits in the Allowance account) is lower than its actual write off experience. The debit balance is easily corrected by increasing the percentages used in the estimation process.

Collection of an account previously written off

Occasionally, a customer whose account has been previously written off will pay the amount owed. In such cases the customer's receivable is reestablished in the accounting records and the payment is then recorded. To illustrate, we will continue the previous example. Assume J. Waldrup now pays $225 of his $425 balance. The following journal entries are made.

Accounts Receivable: J. Waldrup	*225*	
Allowance for Bad Debts		*225*
To reinstate account		
Cash	*225*	
Accounts Receivable: J. Waldrup		*225*
To record collection on account		

Observe that the reinstatement entry simply reverses the entry that was made for the write-off. If collection of the entire $425 is likely, Waldrup's account would be reinstated for the full amount.

Notice that the net effect on the Accounts Receivable account is zero, because it is debited and credited for the same amount. Yet this two-entry procedure is preferred over one that results in a single debit to Cash and a credit to Allowance for Bad Debts. Why? By going back and reestablishing the customer's account on the books, we are showing that an attempt has been made to pay the balance owed. This action and information could be useful to management in future credit-granting decisions.

Disclosure of uncollectibles

When accounting for bad debts, you should recognize that different types of operations may experience different levels of losses. In these cases uncollectibles should be separately computed and disclosed. Exhibit 8-3 illustrates the disclosure of Caesars World, Inc., a company noted principally for the operation of hotels and casinos.

Exhibit 8-3

Accounts receivable of Caesars World, Inc., and subsidiaries (000 omitted)

	1981	*1980*
Accounts receivable		
Casino	$107,558	$75,534
Hotel	6,183	4,487
Other	15,094	14,274
	$128,835	$94,295
Less: Allowance for doubtful accounts*	49,296	30,199
	$ 79,539	$64,096

** The allowance for doubtful accounts includes allowances for doubtful casino accounts receivable of $46,877,000 at July 31, 1981, and $28,782,000 at July 31, 1980, which are provided to reduce casino receivables to amounts anticipated to be collected.*

It is interesting to note that the allowance for casino receivables amounted to 95.1% and 95.3% of the total allowance in 1981 and 1980, respectively. In a recasting of the information presented for 1981 only (see the accompanying table), it is evident that the firm's bad debt experience varied significantly among its various operations.

	Gross Receivables	−	Allowance for Doubtful Accounts	=	Net Receivables	Net ÷ Gross
Casino	$107,558		$46,877		$60,681	56.4%
Hotel and other	21,277		2,419		18,858	88.6
Total	$128,835		$49,296		$79,539	61.7%

Specifically, Caesars World expects to collect approximately 61.7% of its total receivables. Most hotel and other receivables are deemed collectible. In contrast, nearly 44¢ of every dollar owed from casino activity is not expected to materialize and will be written off the books.

INTEREST

Businesses usually give their customers a certain period of time to settle outstanding account balances. After this time period has elapsed, the seller often adds a finance charge to the amount due. Long-term agreements between a buyer and seller follow a similar procedure. Consider the purchase of a car, for example. Generally, a down payment is made. Then monthly payments are due over the next four to five years. If you total the monthly payments and add the sum to the down payment, you will find that the total amount paid is more than the car's original purchase price. Again a finance charge has been incurred.

These financing costs are really **interest,** that is, a charge made for the use of borrowed funds. In the two examples above the seller probably had to pay his creditors while waiting for the receipt of cash from customers. The buyers, then, were using funds needed by the seller; consequently, an interest charge was levied. The longer the seller had to wait, the greater the interest. Banks and finance companies, of course, charge interest on all types of loans. The interest that is charged is an expense to the individual or firm who must pay it and is revenue to the recipient.

Interest Computation

Interest rates are usually quoted on an annual basis. To compute interest for a given time period, the following formula is employed:

interest = principal × rate × time

Principal represents the amount on which the interest is computed. Principal may be the balance of an account receivable, the balance of a loan, the face value of a note (to be discussed shortly), or the amount on deposit in a savings account.

Time can be expressed in either months or days. For example, assume Joyce Company borrowed $12,000 for 2 months at a 12% interest rate. Since the term of the loan is 2 months ($\frac{2}{12}$ of a year), loan interest of $240 is computed as follows:

$$\$12{,}000 \times 0.12 \times \frac{2}{12} = \$240$$

Changing the example, suppose Joyce borrowed $6,000 for 30 days at 10%. The interest computation is now

$$\$6{,}000 \times 0.10 \times \frac{30}{360} = \$50$$

In most applications and for ease of computation, a year is considered to have 360 days. Thus if the term is quoted in months, a base of 12 is used; if quoted in days, a base of 360 is employed.

Given this fundamental calculation, we can now proceed with a discussion of several receivables that involve interest.

Installment sales

Many retail products such as automobiles and large appliances are sold on **installment payment plans.** These plans stipulate that the buyer make specified monthly payments for a predetermined number of months. When sales are made on installment plans, the receipt of cash from each installment represents three separate items: (1) a partial recovery of the cost of the product to the seller, (2) a partial receipt of the gross profit on the sale to the seller, and (3) interest revenue on the unpaid receivable. That is, the merchandise is sold at cost plus a profit margin. Interest on the amount of the debt is then added to arrive at a uniform payment per month.

The accounting profession studied the issue of installment sales and concluded that installment revenues should be recognized at the time of sale.[3] In most cases the collection of revenue is reasonably assured at this time, and, accordingly, revenue recognition should not be spread over the life of the payment plan. In cases where collection of the account is not reasonably assured, different procedures are followed (see Chapter 18). In either situation interest is recorded periodically as it is earned.

To illustrate installment accounting, assume Formar Corporation sold merchandise with a cash price of $10,000 on January 2, 1983. The customer will pay 36 monthly installments of $332.15; the interest rate charged by Formar is 12%. The total amount to be paid is thus $11,957.40 ($332.15 × 36). The difference between the total amount paid and the cash price of the sale is recorded as interest revenue over the life of the installment contract. Formar's entries for the sale and the receipt of the first two installment payments follow.

Jan. 2	*Installment Accounts Receivable*	*10,000*	
	Sales		*10,000*
	To record installment sale		
31	*Cash*	*332.15*	
	Interest Revenue		*100.00*
	Installment Accounts Receivable		*232.15*
	To record receipt no. 1		
Feb. 28	*Cash*	*332.15*	
	Interest Revenue		*97.68*
	Installment Accounts Receivable		*234.47*
	To record receipt no. 2		

To explain, installment receivables are initially recorded at the cash price of the merchandise sold. In addition, the total sales revenue of $10,000 is recognized in 1983 because collection is not in doubt. Each monthly payment, then, really represents interest and a reduction in the receivable. Accordingly, the $332.15 payment must be divided into its two components. This division is accomplished by multiplying the stated interest percentage by the amount of the unpaid receivable as of each repayment date.

On January 31, 1983, the entire receivable is outstanding. Therefore interest revenue of $100 is determined by multiplying the $10,000 receivable by the interest rate for one month ($10,000 × 0.12 × $\frac{1}{12}$ = $100). The $332.15 payment, then, consists of $100 of interest revenue and a $232.15

[3] See "Omnibus Opinion," *Opinions of the Accounting Principles Board No. 10* (New York: American Institute of Certified Public Accountants, 1966).

CREDIT CARDS: AN OPEN INVITATION TO FRAUD?

It is a well-known fact that U.S. consumers love credit cards. A recent survey noted that the 113 million cardholders in this country have a total of 579 million credit cards. The latter figure is expected to grow to 700 million by 1985.

Despite their convenience and popularity, the use of credit cards is not problem-free. Consider, for instance, the problem of credit card fraud. Annual losses from the fraudulent use of bank cards alone are expected to total in excess of $437 million in a few short years. This amount is twice that of 1982 and nearly 16% of total bank card losses from such sources as noncollectible accounts and overspending.

Currently, the biggest fraud losses are coming from alteration of the card's face by the "shave and paste" method. Criminals use razor blades to shave off embossed characters and paste them back on in a different configuration so that phony names and account numbers get through the system.

Another form of fraud results from the practice of allowing charges to be made over the telephone. In this type of transaction, the customer's signature is absent from the sales slip. Furthermore, the customer's account number is simply written on the slip by a clerk; there is no official credit card imprint. As a result, the possibility exists for widespread fraud because many people may have access to a cardholder's account number—salespeople and bookkeepers to name just a few.

Should a fraud occur, it often takes months to wipe the slate clean. Such was the case with a prominent writer, who discovered charges in excess of $500 on his American Express bill for items he never ordered. All items were purchased over the telephone. While most of the charges were removed without difficulty, trouble was encountered when dealing with the manager of a clothing store. The manager claimed that the cardholder had actually visited the store, tried on some merchandise, and later ordered the same merchandise by phone. After three months of frustration, considerable correspondence, and a signed affidavit by the cardholder that the charge was a hoax, the demand for payment was finally dropped.

Fraud has happened in the past and is here to stay, even in a technologically advanced age. Unfortunately, it is the honest consumer who is the hapless victim, as evidenced by increased finance charges and recently enacted cardholder fees. To further complicate matters, the consumer must often deal with a computer—a sometimes stubborn piece of machinery with which to interact. Credit cards, fraud, and computers are part of our society. Management must construct their systems to prevent and detect errors—and importantly, to have the capability of rapid correction if and when an error does occur.

SOURCE Adapted from Irwin Ross, "Saving the Consumer from the Computerized Snafu," Fortune, January 14, 1980, pp. 56–60, 62, 64, 66; and "The Future of Credit Cards," reprinted by permission of The Banker's Magazine, vol. 162, no. 2, Mar.–Apr. 1979,

(\$332.15 – \$100) reduction in the amount owed. As of the next repayment date, the amount owed is \$9,767.85 (\$10,000 – \$232.15). Therefore on February 28, interest revenue of \$97.68 is computed by multiplying the interest rate for one month by the principal of \$9,767.85: \$9,767.85 × 0.12 × $\frac{1}{12}$ = \$97.68. This same procedure is followed for the entire life of the installment contract and results in recording a declining amount of interest each month.

Credit card sales

Many retailers and service establishments have found that maintaining credit departments, billing customers, and collecting accounts are costly and time-consuming processes. As a result, a large number of firms have stopped handling their own accounts and have turned to the use of credit cards such as American Express, Visa, and MasterCard. A firm's acceptance of these well-known cards usually offers the benefit of increased sales. In addition, the seller assumes little or no risk. If a customer does not pay his or her bill, the credit card company suffers the loss.

When a sale is made using the foregoing or similar cards, the purchaser signs a multipart form, which includes a credit card draft. The draft authorizes the credit card company to pay the seller, which generally occurs shortly after the sale is made. The credit card company later bills the customer for the amount of the purchase. The seller, then, experiences faster cash inflows and need no longer wait thirty or more days for customers to settle their obligations.

The credit card drafts are submitted to credit card companies, such as American Express or Diners Club, or to banks in the case of Visa and MasterCard. In either situation sellers do not receive the full amount of the draft. Firms accepting credit cards are assessed a service charge. The service charge is usually a percentage of each sale and, in essence, is a fee for the use of a credit department and customer billing services. The service charge varies from 1.5% to 7% and is partially determined by the seller's annual amount of credit card sales.

When sales are made on bank cards, the seller submits the sales drafts along with daily cash receipts to the bank. The bank increases the seller's account; the service charge is generally deducted at the end of the month along with other account service charges. Thus the credit card sale made on a bank card is really a cash sale. If the sale is on a nonbank card (such as American Express), the seller mails the drafts to the credit card company. Since reimbursement is not instantaneous, Accounts Receivable is established for the amount of the sale. To illustrate, assume that Jacobs Jewelry sold \$2,000 of merchandise on a nonbank credit card. If the collection fee charged by the card company is 5%, the following entry would be made.

Accounts Receivable: Credit Card Sales	*2,000*	
Sales		*2,000*
To record credit card sale		

When the receivable from the credit card company is collected, Jacobs would record the following:

Cash	1,900	
Credit Card Expense	100	
Accounts Receivable: Credit Card Sales		2,000
To record collection on account from credit card company		

Generating cash from accounts receivable

Rather than wait until the future, firms often secure immediate cash receipts from their outstanding accounts receivable. Three methods are available to do this: (1) pledging of accounts receivable, (2) assignment of accounts receivable, and (3) sale of accounts receivable (factoring).

Pledging of accounts receivable

When a company **pledges** its accounts receivable, the company, in essence, is using the accounts as collateral for a loan. Account collection responsibilities generally remain with the borrower. As the receivables are collected, the proceeds are used to repay the loan plus any interest charges. When full payment is received by the lender, the pledge is canceled. In the event that the borrower defaults, the lender has the authority to sell any pledged accounts in order to recover the remaining balance of the loan.

Assignment of accounts receivable

When accounts receivable are **assigned,** a lending institution enters into an agreement with a company to advance cash as sales on account occur. The rights to the accounts receivable are assigned to the lender, meaning that collections on these accounts are earmarked to repay the amount of cash advanced. The borrower pays interest on the cash received from the lender plus a service charge and also suffers any losses from uncollectible accounts.

Sale of accounts receivable

In the sale or **factoring** of accounts receivable, the ownership of individual customer accounts is transferred (sold) to a finance company or bank, called a *factor.* The factor, in turn, pays cash to the selling firm. Factoring frees a company from credit and collection activities and, at the same time, accelerates the firm's cash inflows. Factoring agreements vary widely. Typically, however, the factor assumes any bad debt losses on factored accounts. As a result, the factor charges a relatively high cost for this service—often 2% to 3% above the prime lending rate, or the interest rate banks charge their best customers. Additionally, the factor usually remits only 80% to 90% of the value of the accounts receivable sold as protection against sales returns and allowances. Factoring agreements are common in the furniture and textile industries.

NOTES RECEIVABLE

The balance sheets of many firms often reveal an asset entitled notes receivable. **Notes receivable** (or promissory notes) are written promises to pay a definite amount of money on a specific future date. These instruments are used in extending credit to customers and to lengthen the repayment period of outstanding accounts receivable. Notes are popular in some industries and seldom encountered in others.

Notes receivable have two attributes not normally associated with accounts receivable. First, most notes are negotiable instruments; that is, they are legally transferable among parties by endorsement and may be used to satisfy the debts of their holders. Second, notes usually involve interest. Exhibit 8-4 illustrates a typical promissory note.

Exhibit 8-4
Promissory note

$6,000 Boise, Idaho December 11, 1983

Sixty days after date I promise to

pay to the order of Forseth Company

Six thousand and no/100------------------ dollars

for value received with interest of 12%

payable at First City Bank

Due February 9, 1984 Alfred W. Waggoner

Alfred W. Waggoner

In this particular case Alfred W. Waggoner is the **maker** of the note, that is, the person or firm that promises to pay the stipulated amount. Forseth Company is the **payee,** or the party to be paid. The stated amount (face value) of the note is $6,000 and is termed the **principal.** Finally, February 9 is the **maturity date,** or the date that the note becomes due. The maturity date is computed as follows:

Term of note		*60 days*
Days outstanding in		
December (31 − 11)	*20*	
January	*31*	*51*
Days outstanding in February until maturity		*9*

Accounting for Notes and Interest

Notes receivable are initially entered in the accounting records at face value, requiring a debit to the Notes Receivable account. Because the note is owned by the payee firm, the associated interest is revenue. Interest revenue is recorded both as it is received and as a year-end adjustment if the accounting period ends prior to the maturity date.

To illustrate, we will continue the previous example. The note appearing in Exhibit 8-4 was received on account from Alfred W. Waggoner, a customer, on December 11, 1983. Waggoner desired to extend the repayment period of a previous purchase on account. Forseth Company would record the note as follows:

Dec. 11	Notes Receivable	6,000	
	Accounts Receivable: Alfred Waggoner		6,000
	Received note on account		

Waggoner has agreed to pay Forseth $6,120 on February 9: $6,000 principal plus $120 of interest ($\$6{,}000 \times 0.12 \times \frac{60}{360}$). The amount due on the maturity date (principal plus interest) is commonly referred to as the **maturity value.**

Assume that December 31, 1983, is the end of Forseth's annual accounting period. Although no interest has been received as of this date, 20 days' interest has been earned. Therefore accrued interest revenue of $40 ($\$6{,}000 \times 0.12 \times \frac{20}{360}$) is recorded by the following adjusting entry:

Dec. 31	Interest Receivable	40	
	Interest Revenue		40
	Adjusting entry		

Also on December 31 closing entries would be recorded. The interest T-accounts, after closing, appear as follows:

Interest Receivable	
12/31 40	

Interest Revenue	
12/31 Closing 40	12/31 40

On February 9, 1984, when Waggoner pays the note, Forseth will record the following entry:

Feb. 9	Cash	6,120	
	Interest Receivable		40
	Interest Revenue		80
	Notes Receivable		6,000
	Collected note and interest from A. Waggoner		

To explain, the receipt of the maturity value results in a debit to Cash for $6,120 and a credit to Notes Receivable for the original amount of the obligation ($6,000). One-third of the interest of $120 is located in the Interest Receivable account; thus Interest Receivable must be credited for $40 since this amount is now being received. The remaining $80, which has been earned during 1984, is revenue. Observe how the adjusting entry effectively splits the $120 interest: $40 of revenue in 1983 (20 days) and $80 of revenue in 1984 (40 days).

Notes Receivable Discounted

Companies frequently find that unexpected conditions dictate the need for additional cash on a short-term basis. One of the many ways to satisfy this need involves the payee's discounting a note receivable at the bank.

Discounting allows the payee to generate cash at the time of discounting rather than wait until the note comes due and is paid by the maker. The maker is notified to pay the bank directly on the note's maturity date, but the payee guarantees payment at maturity should the maker default. Thus during the period from the discount date to the maturity date, the note represents a **contingent (possible) liability** to the payee. When a promissory note is discounted, it is common practice to record the note in a separate contra account entitled Notes Receivable Discounted. This account is deducted from Notes Receivable on any balance sheet prepared prior to the note's maturity date.[4]

Because the maker is not obligated to pay the bank until the maturity date, the bank, in effect, is lending the discounting firm a sum of money. As in all loans, interest is charged. In this case, however, the interest is termed a **discount** and is determined by the discount percentage (interest rate) assessed by the bank. At the time a note is discounted, the payee records the proceeds received, the discount charged by the bank, and any interest revenue earned on the note. The entries to record the receipt, discounting, and collection of a note receivable are illustrated in the following example.

On March 10 the Kyle Corporation received a $12,000, 90-day note on account from Walt Dailey, a customer. The note carried a 12% interest rate. On April 9, 30 days later, Kyle discounted the note at the bank at a 14% discount rate. The following entries are necessary to record these transactions.

Mar. 10	Notes Receivable	12,000	
	Accounts Receivable: Walt Dailey		12,000
	Received note on account		
Apr. 9	Cash	12,071.60	
	Interest Revenue		71.60
	Notes Receivable Discounted		12,000.00
	Proceeds from Dailey's discounted note		

The calculation of the cash proceeds from the bank is as follows:

Face amount of note	$12,000.00
Interest revenue ($\$12{,}000 \times 0.12 \times \frac{90}{360}$)	360.00
Maturity value	$12,360.00
Discount ($\$12{,}360 \times 0.14 \times \frac{60}{360}$)	288.40
Proceeds	$12,071.60

The discount is based on the maturity value of $12,360, which is the value of the note to the bank. The bank subtracts the discount from the maturity value to determine the cash proceeds. Observe that the bank's discount calculation ($288.40) is dependent on the number of days the money will be

[4] Many companies reduce the Notes Receivable account at the time of discounting rather than establish a separate Notes Receivable Discounted account. Firms following the former procedure would disclose the amount of the contingent liability in the footnotes to their financial statements.

lent to Kyle. Since Kyle held the 90-day note for 30 days, the bank expects to be repaid in 60 days. Finally, notice that Kyle received $12,071.60 for a $12,000 note, necessitating the recognition of interest revenue of $71.60. If the proceeds had been less than $12,000, the firm would have incurred interest expense. The deciding factors behind the generation of interest revenue or interest expense are the interest rate on the note, the bank's discount rate, and the holding periods involved.

The note would be presented on Kyle's April 30 balance sheet as follows:

Current assets		
Notes receivable	*$12,000*	
Less: Notes receivable discounted	*12,000*	*$-0-*

The maturity date of the note is June 8. If Dailey pays the bank when the note is due, Kyle is no longer contingently liable. Therefore the note must be removed from the books by the following entry:

June 8	*Notes Receivable Discounted*	*12,000*	
	Notes Receivable		*12,000*
	To remove contingent liability arising from Dailey's note		

Dishonoring a note

In the event Dailey does not settle the obligation, Kyle must pay the bank because of the contingent liability. Dailey is in default and the note is said to be **dishonored.** If Kyle had held the note for the full 90 days, it would have received the maturity value from Dailey. The bank, which now owns the note, expects the same amount. Thus Kyle must pay the maturity value of the note plus a service charge (termed a **protest fee**).

The Notes Receivable and Notes Receivable Discounted accounts are again canceled to remove the contingent liability from the accounting records. In addition, the total amount paid is charged back to Accounts Receivable in hopes of future collection. To illustrate, assume that on June 9 the bank notified Kyle that Dailey had defaulted and also charged Kyle a $25 protest fee. Kyle paid the amount due ($12,360 + $25 = $12,385) and recorded the following entry:

June 9	*Accounts Receivable: Walt Dailey*	*12,385*	
	Notes Receivable Discounted	*12,000*	
	Notes Receivable		*12,000*
	Cash		*12,385*
	To remove contingent liability and record payment to the bank		

If collection attempts fail, the account receivable will be written off as a bad debt, using procedures discussed earlier in the chapter.

SUMMARY PROBLEM

The Shank Corporation's balance sheet revealed the following information as of January 1.

Accounts receivable	*$75,800*	
Less: Allowance for bad debts	*6,500*	*$69,300*

The following transactions took place during the first quarter of the year.

Jan. 2 Received a $4,000, 60-day, 12% note on account from T. Abernathy.

18 Wrote off the $1,300 balance owed by Magarin Company as uncollectible.

Feb. 11 Discounted Abernathy's note at the bank at a 14% discount rate.

17 Received $180 in final settlement of Pat Young's $750 account balance. Young's account had been written off as uncollectible in the previous year.

Mar. 4 Received notification from the bank that Abernathy's note had been dishonored. Paid the bank the proper amount due plus a $15 protest fee.

Shank's credit sales for the first quarter totaled $142,000; customer collections on account amounted to $106,500.

INSTRUCTIONS

a ***Prepare journal entries for the transactions from January 2 through March 4.***

b ***Prepare the journal entry on March 31 to adjust the Allowance account, assuming bad debts are estimated at 3% of credit sales.***

c ***Compute the net realizable value of Shank's accounts receivable as of March 31.***

SOLUTION

a	*Jan. 2*	*Notes Receivable*	*4,000*	
		Accounts Receivable: T. Abernathy		*4,000*
		Received note on account		
	18	*Allowance for Bad Debts*	*1,300*	
		Accounts Receivable: Magarin Company		*1,300*
		Wrote off account as uncollectible		
	Feb. 11	*Cash*	*4,048.27*	
		Interest Revenue		*48.27*
		Notes Receivable Discounted		*4,000.00*
		Discounted note of T. Abernathy		

Calculations

Face amount of note	*$4,000.00*
Interest revenue ($\$4,000 \times 0.12 \times \frac{60}{360}$)	*80.00*
Maturity value	*$4,080.00*
Discount ($\$4,080 \times 0.14 \times \frac{20}{360}$)	*31.73*
Proceeds	*$4,048.27*

			Debit	Credit
	Feb. 17	Accounts Receivable: Pat Young	180	
		Allowance for Bad Debts		180
		To reinstate account		
		Cash	180	
		Accounts Receivable: Pat Young		180
		To record collection on account		
	Mar. 4	Accounts Receivable: T. Abernathy	4,095	
		Notes Receivable Discounted	4,000	
		Notes Receivable		4,000
		Cash		4,095
		To remove contingent liability and record payment to the bank		
b	Mar. 31	Bad Debts Expense	4,260	
		Allowance for Bad Debts		4,260
		Adjusting entry ($142,000 × 0.03)		

c

Accounts receivable	$110,095
Less: Allowance for bad debts	9,640
Net realizable value	$100,455

Calculations

Accounts receivable		
Balance, Jan. 1		$ 75,800
−Jan. 2	$ (4,000)	
−Jan. 18	(1,300)	
+Feb. 17	180	
−Feb. 17	(180)	
+Mar. 4	4,095	
+Credit sales	142,000	
−Customer collections	(106,500)	34,295
Balance, Mar. 31		$110,095
Allowance for bad debts		
Balance, Jan. 1		$6,500
−Jan. 18	$(1,300)	
+Feb. 17	180	
+Mar. 31	4,260	3,140
Balance, Mar. 31		$9,640

KEY TERMS AND CONCEPTS

accounts receivable 299
aging accounts receivable 302
allowance method of bad debts 300
assignment of accounts receivable 310
bad debts 299
balance sheet approach of accounting for bad debts 301
contingent liability 313
credit card sales 308

direct write-off method of bad debts 299
discounting notes receivable 313
dishonoring a note 314
factoring 310
income statement approach of accounting for bad debts 301
installment payment plans 306
interest 306
maker 311
maturity date 311
maturity value 312
net realizable value 300
nontrade receivables 299
notes receivable 310
payee 311
pledging of accounts receivable 310
principal 306, 311
protest fee 314
receivables 298
trade receivables 298

QUESTIONS

Q8-1 Why do businesses sell on credit? What additional costs are encountered by a business that sells on credit?

Q8-2 Distinguish between trade and nontrade receivables. Give three examples of the latter.

Q8-3 Explain why uncollectible accounts have both income statement and balance sheet implications for accountants.

Q8-4 Explain the two methods that can be used to record losses from bad debts.

Q8-5 Discuss some possible deficiencies with the direct write-off method of uncollectible accounts.

Q8-6 Explain the two general approaches that may be used when bad debts are estimated.

Q8-7 Define the term "net realizable value" as it relates to accounts receivable.

Q8-8 Discuss the advantages of aging schedules over the use of a flat percentage of accounts receivable for estimates of uncollectible accounts.

Q8-9 The Howard Corporation uses the allowance method of accounting for bad debts. Howard has just written off the $640 balance of Jewel Company as uncollectible. Determine the impact of the write-off on the following:

a Bad debts expense
b Earnings per share
c Accounts receivable
d Net realizable value of accounts receivable

Q8-10 The York Company has written off the $375 balance of Dick Peterson as uncollectible. The merchandise purchased by Peterson originally cost York $250. If Peterson subsequently pays his account, determine the additional revenue that York would generate. York uses the allowance method of accounting for bad debts.

Q8-11 What is the interest computation formula? Why is the inclusion of a time factor necessary?

Q8-12 What are installment sales? What three factors are represented by each installment payment?

Q8-13 If the collection of an installment receivable is reasonably assured, when should the revenue from an installment sale be recognized?

Q8-14 Discuss the accounting procedures required for sales of merchandise on nonbank credit cards and bank cards.

Q8-15 What is a note receivable? What attributes do notes receivable have that are not normally associated with accounts receivable?

Q8-16 Where does the Notes Receivable Discounted account appear in the financial statements?

EXERCISES

E8-1 The Tucker Company has been in business for three years and makes all sales on account. The following information concerning Tucker's sales, collections, and uncollectible accounts is available.

Year	Sales	Collections	Accounts Written Off
1	$400,000	$350,000	$ 5,000
2	550,000	500,000	18,000
3	720,000	710,000	10,000

a Determine Tucker's accounts receivable balance at the end of each year if the company uses the direct write-off method of recognizing bad debts.

b Determine Tucker's net accounts receivable balance at the end of each year if the company estimates bad debts at 2.5% of sales.

E8-2 On January 2 Maher Corporation has the following information available concerning its accounts receivable balance.

Accounts receivable	$192,500
Less: Allowance for bad debts	7,800
	$184,700

During January Maher determined that J. Smitham, a customer, was unable to pay his balance of $2,500. The account was written off the accounting records on January 31. Later, on February 18, Maher received a $2,500 check from Smitham.

a Prepare Maher's journal entries to record (1) the write-off of the Smitham account and (2) the payment by Smitham.

b What is the impact of the transactions in part (a) on the net realizable value of Maher's accounts receivable?

E8-3 The Whitten Company's comparative balance sheets revealed the following information at the end of 1982 and 1983.

	1983	1982
Accounts receivable	$163,000	$174,000
Less: Allowance for bad debts	32,000	28,000
	$131,000	$146,000

Additional data pertaining to 1983 operations are as follows:

Credit sales	$280,000
Collections on account	270,000
Accounts recovered that were previously written off	6,000
Bad debts expense	19,000
Uncollectible accounts written off	?

Present the journal entries (along with explanations) that Whitten recorded during 1983.

E8-4 The following preadjusted information for the Golden Company is available on December 31.

Cash sales	$ 85,400	
Credit sales	197,800	
Total sales		$283,200
Accounts receivable		87,600
Allowance for bad debts		4,540 (credit balance)

a Prepare the journal entries necessary to record Golden's bad debt expense under each of the following assumptions:
(1) Bad debts are estimated to be 3% of sales.
(2) Bad debts are estimated to be 5% of credit sales.
(3) Bad debts are estimated to be 8% of accounts receivable.

b How would Golden's accounts receivable appear on the December 31 balance sheet under parts (2) and (3) of part (a)?

E8-5 Fielding-Marshall has gathered the following information to estimate bad debts by the use of an aging schedule.

Age of Receivable	Amount	Estimated Percentage Uncollectible
Under 30 days	$280,000	3%
31–60 days	120,000	10
61–90 days	60,000	20
91–120 days	40,000	45
121–180 days	25,000	60
Over 180 days	15,000	75
	$540,000	

a Determine the estimated amount of uncollectible accounts.

b Prepare the journal entry to record bad debts expense assuming the previous Allowance for Bad Debts account balance was:
(1) $3,600 (debit)
(2) $2,400 (credit)

c Assuming a $2,400 credit balance in the Allowance account before adjustment [part (2) of part (b)], present the proper balance sheet disclosure for Fielding-Marshall's receivables.

E8-6 The Bradley Company sells used automobiles on the installment plan. Greg Schulte, a customer, purchased a $5,000 automobile from Bradley on November 1, agreeing to pay $166.08 per month for 36 months. The interest rate charged by Bradley was 12%. Prepare the journal entries required by Bradley to record the following:

a The sale on November 1

b The first three installment payments from Schulte

E8-7 Brindisi Sales Company sold $3,500 of merchandise during August on Charge All, a national credit card. Charge All's collection fee is 7%.

a Prepare the journal entries required by Brindisi to record (1) credit card sales and (2) subsequent reimbursement from Charge All. Assume Charge All is not a bank card.

b Discuss several of the benefits and problems of accepting credit cards.

E8-8 The Alliance Corporation has just concluded a record sales year. Because of relaxed credit standards, both the Accounts Receivable and Notes Receivable accounts are at their highest levels ever. Alliance has a desperate need for cash to pay its suppliers. The following alternatives have been proposed by the firm's accountant.

Sale of accounts receivable
Assignment of accounts receivable
Discounting of notes receivable

a Explain each of the alternatives to management.

b Alliance presently has a considerable amount of debt on its balance sheet. Determine the impact of the three alternatives on the company's total liabilities.

E8-9 The Watson Corporation received a $6,000, 90-day, 12% note from Carla London on November 11, 1983. London had previously purchased merchandise from Watson and wished to extend the repayment date of the receivable. Prepare the journal entries required by Watson to record the following:

a The receipt of the note from London.

b Accrued interest on December 31, 1983, the end of Watson's accounting year.

c The payment of the note by London on February 9, 1984.

E8-10 Barbara Beach issued a note to Sloan Sales on May 16 in payment of her account. Terms of the note were as follows:

Time 90 days
Face $8,000
Rate 10%

On June 15 Sloan discounted the note at the Second Federal Bank at 12%. Determine the following:

a The maker and payee.

b The maturity date and maturity value.

c The proceeds from discounting.

d The interest revenue or interest expense recorded by Sloan at the time of discounting. Specify which and the amount.

e The amount payable to the bank should Beach default.

f The interest revenue or expense recorded by Beach on May 31, the end of her fiscal year. Specify which and the amount.

E8-11 Record the following transactions in general journal form on the books of the May Company:

Mar. 1 Received a $9,000, 120-day, 12% note dated March 1 from the Peroy Company on account.
May 30 Discounted the note at the bank; discount rate 11%.
July 2 Received notice from the bank that Peroy dishonored the note. Paid the bank the amount due plus a $10 protest fee.

PROBLEMS

P8-1 ***Direct write-off and allowance methods, theory and practice***

The December 31 year-end trial balance of Crocker Manufacturing revealed the following account information:

	Debits	Credits
Accounts receivable	$46,000	
Allowance for doubtful accounts	590	
Sales		$186,000
Sales returns	2,000	
Sales discounts	1,000	
Salesmen's salaries	17,000	

INSTRUCTIONS

a Determine the adjusting entry for bad debts under the following conditions:
(1) An aging schedule indicates that $2,040 of accounts receivable will be uncollectible.
(2) Uncollectible accounts are estimated at 1% of net sales.

b *Conceptually,* what is the basic difference between using aging schedules and using the percentage-of-sales method?

c On January 18 of the following year, Crocker learned that Wilson Distributors, a customer, had gone bankrupt. Present the proper entry to write off Wilson's $650 balance.

d Repeat the requirement in part (c), using the direct write-off method.

e Compare the allowance and direct write-off methods by:
(1) Determining the impact on net income of the Wilson write-off.
(2) Examining the methods' ability to match revenues and expenses.

P8-2 ***Allowance method of bad debts***

Erie Corporation operates in an industry that has a high rate of bad debts. On December 31, 1983, before any year-end adjustments, the balance in Erie's Accounts Receivable account was $500,000 and the Allowance for Uncollectible Accounts had a credit balance of $25,000. The year-end balance reported on the balance sheet for the Allowance for Uncollectible Accounts will be based on the accompanying aging schedule.

Days Account Outstanding	Amount	Probability of Collection
Less than 15 days	$300,000	.98
Between 16 and 30 days	100,000	.90
Between 31 and 45 days	50,000	.80
Between 46 and 60 days	30,000	.70
Between 61 and 75 days	10,000	.60
Over 75 days	10,000	.00

INSTRUCTIONS

a What is the appropriate balance for the Allowance for Uncollectible Accounts on December 31, 1983?

b Show how accounts receivable would be presented on the balance sheet prepared on December 31, 1983.

c What is the dollar effect of the year-end bad debt adjustment on 1983 net income?

(CMA adapted.)

P8-3 ***Allowance method and errors***

The Starr Manufacturing Company reports a balance of $88,000 in its Accounts Receivable control account. An aging schedule revealed the following:

Age	Net Amount	Percentage Uncollectible
Current	$40,000	1%
31–60 days	20,000	5
61–90 days	14,000	10
91–120 days	9,000	30
Over 120 days	5,000	60
	$88,000	

In an examination of the subsidiary ledger, Starr's accountant found a $2,500 credit balance in Tampa Distributors' account resulting from an overpayment. The overpayment is included in the 31–60 day category. In addition, Starr has just learned that Hill Manufacturing, a customer, has entered bankruptcy proceedings. Hill has owed Starr $3,000 for the past five months.

A further investigation revealed that the following entry had been made on October 19 to write off a $4,000 uncollectible account balance (91–120 days).

Allowance for Bad Debts	*4,000*	
Bad Debts Expense: Joe Kline		*4,000*
To write off uncollectible account		

The December 31 balance before adjustment in the Allowance for Bad Debts account was $2,550 (credit).

INSTRUCTIONS

a Was the transaction on October 19 handled correctly? If not, how would you correct the error if the books are not as yet closed?

b Determine the proper accounting treatment for the account of Hill Manufacturing. Be specific.

c Determine the adjusting entry for bad debts that should be made on December 31. Assume proper handling of the two preceding items.

d Suppose that over the past few years Starr has experienced a growing balance in the Allowance for Bad Debts account in relation to the Accounts Receivable control account. What can be done to correct this situation?

P8-4 ***Changing the method of recording bad debts***

Phillips Manufacturing Company has employed the direct write-off method of recording bad debts expense during its first five years of operation. Increases in sales volume and the amount of uncollectible accounts have caused the firm to consider changing to the allowance method. The following information has been obtained from the accounts.

Year	Sales	Uncollectible Accounts Written Off	Year of Origin of Accounts Receivable Written Off as Uncollectible				
			1	2	3	4	5
1	$ 600,000	$ 1,000	$1,000				
2	900,000	4,200	600	$3,600			
3	1,100,000	6,800	200	1,800	$4,800		
4	1,200,000	8,600			2,200	$6,400	
5	1,500,000	10,200			400	2,400	$7,400

INSTRUCTIONS

a Assuming management desires to estimate bad debts at 0.75 of 1% of sales, determine the following for each year:

(1) The increase in expense by using the allowance method rather than the direct write-off method.

(2) The ending balance in the Allowance for Bad Debts account.

b Does the percentage being used by management closely approximate Phillips' actual bad debt experience? Why?

P8-5 ***Receivables on the balance sheet***

The balance sheet of Plaza Enterprises disclosed the following information as of January 1, 1983.

Accounts receivable	$42,900	
Less: Allowance for bad debts	3,650	$39,250
Notes receivable	$19,500	
Less: Notes receivable discounted	12,400	7,100

The notes consisted of the following:

Customer	Face Amount	Maturity Value
Thornton	$3,000	$3,200
Bellotti	8,000	8,500
Gale	4,400	4,650
Tait	4,100	4,350

During the first quarter of 1983 the following events took place.

1 Sales on account amounted to $84,500, of which $78,000 was collected. Sales returns were $1,800.
2 Customer accounts with balances of $1,620 were written off as worthless.
3 The accounts of J. Cruz and Ralph Olson had been written off during the third quarter of 1982. In February 1983 Cruz paid his total balance of $550, while Olson paid half his balance of $680. Olson's remaining balance will be forthcoming.
4 Both Bellotti and Gale's notes had been discounted at the bank late in 1982. Gale paid his note on the maturity date in January. Bellotti's note was dishonored. Plaza paid the proper amount to the bank on March 31 plus a $15 protest fee. Tait's note was dated January 1, 1983, and had a term of 6 months. Thornton paid her note in February.
5 Two additional notes were received on account:

Customer	Date	Term	Amount	Rate
Fazio	1/10/83	60 days	$4,800	12%
Smith	3/1/83	90 days	5,000	12%

Fazio's note was discounted on January 30 at 14%. The note was paid on the maturity date.

6 Uncollectible accounts were estimated at the end of the first quarter to be 1% of net credit sales.

INSTRUCTIONS

a Construct the current asset section of Plaza's balance sheet as of March 31, 1983. Disregard the Cash account.
b A student once commented: "There isn't any difference between Allowance for Bad Debts and Notes Receivable Discounted. Both accounts are contra accounts that reduce current assets." Evaluate the student's comment.

P8-6 ***Journal entries for accounts and notes receivable***

The following selected transactions pertain to the Schaeffer Corporation for the last quarter of the year.

Oct. *4* Sold merchandise on account to J. R. Konrath. Konrath issued a $5,000, 60-day, 12% note in settlement of her account.
15 Wrote off the $1,900 balance owed by Sanford Company as uncollectible.
24 Discounted Konrath's note at the bank; discount rate 14%.
Nov. *1* Sold a parcel of land to Alden and Associates; accepted Alden's $12,000, 6-month, 12% note in return.
9 Received $480 in final settlement of Bill Adams's $1,500 account balance. Adams's account had been written off as uncollectible in the previous year.
16 Received a 30-day, 12%, $800 note from Doug Campbell on account.
Dec. *1* Sold $4,000 of merchandise to Rita Paige. Paige charged $1,000 on her Visa card and signed a $3,000, 12%, 60-day note for the remainder.

4 Received notification from the bank that Konrath had paid her note.

16 Campbell dishonored his note of November 16 but agreed to pay the proper amount due within five days. Schaeffer has agreed not to charge any additional interest.

19 Campbell paid his account balance in full.

31 Recorded the necessary adjusting entries for bad debts and accrued interest. On September 30 Schaeffer reported a $6,200 credit balance in the Allowance for Bad Debts account.

On December 31 the Accounts Receivable account contained a balance of $74,900.

INSTRUCTIONS

a Record the transactions in general journal form, assuming Schaeffer uses the allowance method of accounting for bad debts. An aging schedule indicates that $5,800 of accounts receivable will be uncollectible.

b Compute the net realizable value of accounts receivable.

c Suppose Schaeffer used the income statement approach for estimating uncollectible accounts. Two percent of the total sales of $290,000 are anticipated to be uncollectible. Would you have done anything differently on December 31? Explain.

d Explain what you would have done differently on December 1 if Paige's transaction had been charged on a credit card such as American Express as opposed to a bank card.

P8-7 ***Journal entries for notes***

The following information was taken from the records of the Findley Company.

Mar. 8 Sold merchandise to J. Guevera; accepted a $4,000, 10%, 120-day note.

Apr. 27 Received a $6,000, 12%, 90-day note on account from S. Mueller, a customer.

May 27 Discounted both notes at the bank at a discount rate of 14%.

July 7 Received notification from the bank that Guevera had paid her note.

26 Received notification from the bank that Mueller had defaulted on his note; paid the amount due plus a protest fee of $15. Findley informed Mueller that 14% annual interest would be charged on the face amount of the note, the interest, and protest fee.

Aug. 10 Received the proper amount due from Mueller, including interest.

16 Received a 12%, 60-day, $6,000 note on account from Henry Manufacturing, a customer.

Oct. 15 Henry Manufacturing paid the proper amount due on the note of August 16.

INSTRUCTIONS

a Assuming Findley's year ends on December 31, prepare the journal entries to record the transactions.

b If Findley's year ends on August 31, present the necessary adjusting entry on August 31 for accrued interest. Also, present the proper entry for the receipt of cash on October 15.

P8-8 ***Direct write-off and allowance methods, theory and practice (alternate to P8-1)***
The December 31 year-end trial balance of Walsh Company revealed the following account information:

	Debits	Credits
Accounts receivable	$84,000	
Allowance for bad debts	1,520	
Sales		$285,000
Sales returns and allowances	4,300	
Sales discounts	2,700	
Selling expenses	64,750	

INSTRUCTIONS

a Determine the adjusting entry for bad debts under the following conditions:
 (1) An aging schedule indicates that $4,140 of accounts receivable will be uncollectible.
 (2) Uncollectible accounts are estimated at 2% of net sales.

b Explain the basic *conceptual* differences between the income statement and balance sheet methods of estimating bad debts.

c On January 14 of the following year, Walsh learned that Faber Company, a customer, had declared bankruptcy. Present the proper entry to write off Faber's $820 balance.

d Repeat the requirement in part (c), using the direct write-off method.

e In light of the Faber bankruptcy, examine the allowance and direct write-off methods in terms of their abilities to properly match revenues and expenses.

P8-9 ***Allowance method of bad debts (alternate to P8-2)***
Lake Corporation operates in an industry that has a high rate of bad debts. On December 31, 1983, before any year-end adjustments, the balance in Lake's Accounts Receivable account was $600,000 and the Allowance for Uncollectible Accounts had a credit balance of $32,000. The year-end balance reported on the balance sheet for the Allowance for Uncollectible Accounts will be based on the accompanying aging schedule.

Days Account Outstanding	Amount	Probability of Collection
Less than 30 days	$375,000	.97
Between 31–60 days	95,000	.80
Between 61–90 days	50,000	.70
Between 91–120 days	40,000	.60
Between 121–150 days	25,000	.50
Over 150 days	15,000	.00

INSTRUCTIONS

a What is the appropriate balance for the Allowance for Uncollectible Accounts on December 31, 1983?

b Show how accounts receivable would be presented on the balance sheet prepared on December 31, 1983.

c What is the dollar effect of the year-end bad debt adjustment on 1983 net income?

(CMA adapted.)

P8-10 ***Changing the method of recording bad debts (alternate to P8-4)***
Rather Enterprises has employed the direct write-off method of recording bad debts expense during its first five years of operation. Increases in sales volume and the amount of uncollectible accounts have caused the firm to consider changing to the allowance method. The following information has been obtained from the accounts.

Year	Sales	Uncollectible Accounts Written Off	Year of Origin of Accounts Receivable Written Off as Uncollectible				
			1	2	3	4	5
1	$ 70,000	$ 800	$800				
2	120,000	1,150	300	$850			
3	350,000	2,180	100	400	$1,680		
4	500,000	4,500		500	1,000	$3,000	
5	800,000	7,200				2,400	$4,800

INSTRUCTIONS

a Assuming management desires to estimate bad debts at 1% of sales, determine the following for each year:
 (1) The increase in expense by using the allowance method rather than the direct write-off method.
 (2) The ending balance in the Allowance for Bad Debts account.

b Does the percentage being used by management closely approximate Rather's actual bad debt experience? Why?

P8-11 ***Journal entries for accounts and notes receivable (alternate to P8-6)***
The following selected transactions pertain to the Pilot Corporation for the last quarter of the year.

Oct. 7 Sold merchandise on account to R. J. Irish. Irish issued a $10,000, 60-day, 14% note in settlement of her account.
19 Wrote off the $2,200 balance owed by Davis Company as uncollectible.
22 Discounted Irish's note at the bank; discount rate 16%.
Nov. 1 Sold a parcel of land to Courtney and Associates; accepted Courtney's $25,000, 3-month, 12% note in return.
18 Received $670 in final settlement of Doug Light's $2,400 account balance. Light's account had been written off as uncollectible in the previous year.
21 Received a 30-day, 14%, $2,000 note from Cindy Raymond on account.
Dec. 1 Sold $5,000 of merchandise to Tom Lampe. Lampe charged $1,000 on his Visa card and signed a $4,000, 12%, 60-day note for the remainder.
7 Received notification from the bank that Irish had paid her note.

21 Raymond dishonored her note of November 21 but agreed to pay the proper amount due within five days. Management has agreed not to charge any additional interest.

26 Raymond paid her account balance in full.

31 Recorded the necessary adjusting entries for bad debts and accrued interest. On September 30 Pilot reported a $4,150 credit balance in the Allowance for Bad Debts account.

On December 31 the Accounts Receivable account contained a balance of $85,600.

INSTRUCTIONS

a Record the transactions in general journal form, assuming Pilot uses the allowance method of accounting for bad debts. An aging schedule indicates that $6,300 of accounts receivable will be uncollectible.

b Compute the net realizable value of accounts receivable.

c Suppose Pilot used the income statement approach for estimating uncollectible accounts. Two percent of the total sales of $315,000 are anticipated to be uncollectible. Would you have done anything differently on December 31? Explain.

d Discuss the probable impact of Pilot's acceptance of the Visa credit card on (1) yearly bad debts expense, (2) sales, and (3) administrative billing costs.

P8-12 ***Journal entries for notes (alternate to P8-7)***

The following information was taken from the records of the Landon Corporation.

Jan. 9 Received a $10,000, 10%, 90-day note on account from Don Baker, a customer.

Feb. 8 Sold merchandise to Julie Bradford, Inc.; accepted a $5,000, 12%, 120-day note.

Mar. 10 Discounted both notes at the bank at a discount rate of 12%.

Apr. 10 Received notification from the bank that Baker had paid his note.

June 8 Received notification from the bank that Bradford had defaulted on its note; paid the amount due plus a $10 protest fee. Landon informed Bradford that 12% annual interest would be charged on the face amount of the note, the interest, and protest fee.

July 8 Received the proper amount due from Bradford, including interest.

11 Received a 12%, 60-day, $20,000 note from Kramer, Inc., for the sale of a parcel of land.

Sept. 9 Kramer, Inc., paid the proper amount due on the note of July 11.

INSTRUCTIONS

a Assuming Landon's year ends on December 31, prepare the journal entries to record the transactions.

b If Landon's year ends on July 31, present the necessary adjusting entry on July 31 for accrued interest. Also present the proper entry for the receipt of cash on September 9.

CASE 8
MARTHA'S GIFT SHOPPE

Martha's, a retail gift shop, has been in business for five years. The shop sells a variety of gift items and has shown profits for the past three years. The projected results for the current year follow.

MARTHA'S GIFT SHOPPE
Projected Statement of Income
For the Year Ended December 31, 1983

Sales	$400,000	100%
Cost of goods sold	220,000	55
Gross profit	$180,000	45%
Operating expenses	100,000	25
Net income	$ 80,000	20%

These figures are based on the current cash-only sales policy. No personal checks are accepted, nor are credit or credit card sales made. Martha de Ville, the owner, is now considering the following payment methods in addition to strict cash.

Personal checks
Bank credit cards
Both personal checks and bank credit cards

Martha believes that sales will increase if other payment methods are used. She also realizes that some cash customers will change to a different method of payment if alternative methods are available. The following schedule presents the estimated increases in sales and the percentages of sales to be made under each of the proposed alternatives.

	Percentage Increase in Sales	Percentage of Total Sales Paid by: Cash	Check	Credit Card
Payment by check	15%	50%	50%	—%
Payment by bank credit card	25	40	—	60
Payment by check and bank credit card	30	30	20	50

If checks are accepted as a method of payment, it is anticipated that 3% of all check sales will not clear because of nonsufficient funds (NSF). The merchandise paid for by NSF checks will not be recovered.

Bank credit card sales can be collected daily. However, the bank charges a 5% service fee when credit card sales are deposited.

Aside from the data pertaining to NSF checks, Martha's cost of goods sold is still expected to average 55% of sales. Present operating expenses are divided as follows:

Constant	*$ 80,000*
Vary in direct proportion to changes in sales (5% of sales)	*20,000*
	$100,000

INSTRUCTIONS

Prepare an analysis showing the attractiveness of each of the proposed payment methods. This analysis should indicate which of the three proposals, if any, you would recommend for acceptance.

(CMA modified.)

9 INVENTORY

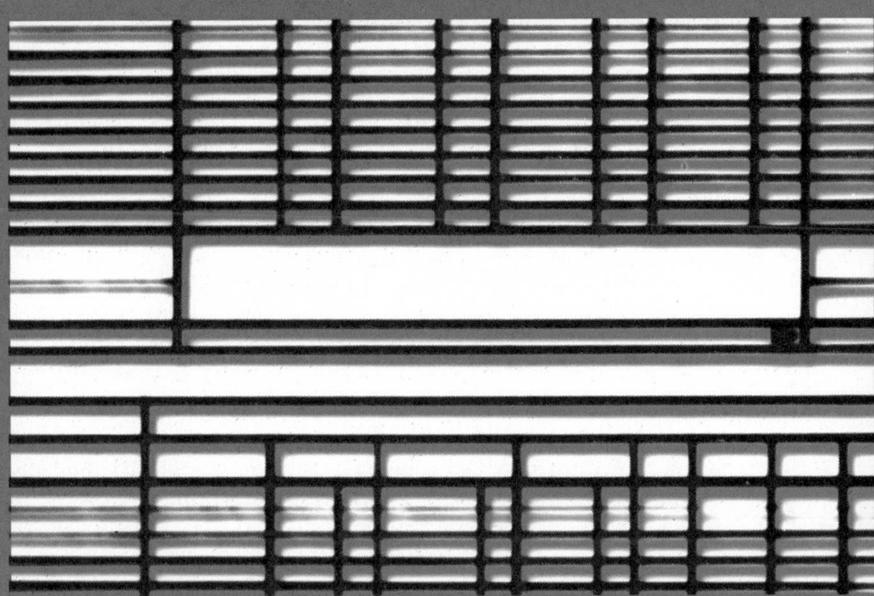

LEARNING OBJECTIVES

After reading this chapter you should:

1 *Understand the ownership issues related to goods in transit and goods on consignment.*

2 *Understand the problems of taking a physical inventory and the importance of the counting process.*

3 *Understand the effects of inventory errors on financial statements.*

4 *Be familiar with the qualitative aspects and computations related to the specific identification, FIFO, LIFO, and weighted-average inventory methods.*

5 *Understand the factors that are considered when selecting an inventory method and the effects of such a selection on financial statements.*

6 *Understand the impact of inflation on inventory, including the concept of inventory profits.*

7 *Be familiar with the lower-of-cost-or-market rule.*

8 *Understand the importance of inventory estimates and be able to formulate estimates by using the gross profit and retail methods.*

9 *Understand the differences between the periodic and perpetual inventory systems, including procedures and journal entries related to the latter.*

CHAPTER 9

In Chapter 4 we noted that inventory is a concern for both the finance and marketing functions within a business. Finance desires to reduce the amount of funds committed to the inventory investment, while marketing wants to avoid out-of-stock situations that could result in lost sales and lost customers. The accountant also has a keen interest in inventory. Excessive inventory investments, lost sales, and lost customers all affect net income. Furthermore, for many firms, especially those engaged in merchandising activities, inventories represent the largest asset on the balance sheet. These goods ultimately become a significant element on the income statement in the form of cost of goods sold.

The possession of inventory gives rise to various issues that the accountant must resolve. For example, consider Margo's Dress Shop, which overstocked a particular dress style eight months ago. Because of rapid changes in the fashion world, these dresses are now worth only a fraction of their original cost. Should Margo's continue to carry this inventory in the accounting records at original cost, or should the inventory be marked down to reflect a loss in value? Focusing on another issue, we turn to the Fast-Mix Concrete Company. Throughout the year Fast-Mix has been purchasing large quantities of sand, stone, and limestone at rapidly changing prices. Each product is piled in huge mounds near the company's production facility. If Fast-Mix used 10 tons of stone on a given day, how can the firm determine its cost? All the stone purchases have been mixed together, and it has been impossible to mark or associate each ton with its cost. Should Fast-Mix use the most recent cost, the oldest cost, or an average cost? The firm's selection will have a definite impact on profitability.

These questions and a number of other issues related to inventory must be addressed by accountants. This chapter focuses on inventory accounting, emphasizing the valuation of inventory on the balance sheet and the determination of cost of goods sold for the income statement.

WHAT IS INVENTORY?

When discussing merchandising businesses, we defined **inventory** as goods acquired for resale to customers. While this definition is satisfactory for the retailer and wholesaler, it must be expanded for the manufacturer. The manufacturer, of course, does not acquire goods for resale—it makes them. Inventories, therefore, are said to include the following:

1. *Raw materials.* Items to be processed into salable products.
2. *Work in process.* Goods started but not as yet completed.
3. *Finished goods.* Goods completed and awaiting sale.

Since most inventories will be used or sold and converted into cash within a year, they are reported as current assets on the balance sheet. Inventory is usually listed immediately following Accounts Receivable because it is one step further removed from cash via the operating cycle.

Ownership Problems

In Chapter 1 assets were defined as the economic resources owned by a firm that benefit future time periods. Let us concentrate on ownership for a moment. When the ownership of merchandise transfers to a company, the merchandise should be included as a part of that company's inventory and reported on the firm's balance sheet. Ownership is determined by the transfer of legal title to the goods from the seller to the buyer. This principle is followed even though a business may lack physical possession of the merchandise. Two areas where the issue of inventory ownership arises are goods in transit and goods on consignment.

Goods in transit

Goods in transit between the buyer and seller belong to the party that possesses legal ownership (title) to the goods. Legal ownership, in turn, is dependent on freight terms, that is, F.O.B. shipping point and F.O.B. destination. Recall from Chapter 4 that the F.O.B. point indicates the location where the seller's responsibility for shipping ceases. As a logical extension, the F.O.B. point also indicates where legal title to the goods is transferred from the seller to the buyer. Under F.O.B. shipping point, for example, title transfers to the purchaser when the goods are shipped, while under F.O.B. destination, title passes when the goods arrive at their destination (the buyer's warehouse, for instance).

When title passes, the seller should record a sale and the buyer should record a purchase. Accordingly, inventories should be respectively reduced and increased at this time, even though the goods may still be on hand or in transit. To illustrate, suppose a company buys $10,000 of merchandise, F.O.B. shipping point, on December 29. The goods are shipped on December 30 and are in transit at the end of the purchaser's accounting year. Nevertheless, the purchaser should enter a purchase in the records and include the goods in the ending inventory count because title has passed.

To simplify record keeping during the year, many companies operate on a receipt and shipment basis. That is, purchases are recorded upon receipt regardless of the F.O.B. point, and sales are recorded upon shipment. If in-transit shipments are significant, firms should examine their records and make appropriate account adjustments so that all merchandise owned is properly reflected in the ending inventory balance. Incorrect accounting for sales and purchases will influence not only inventory but also cost of goods sold, net income, owners' equity, accounts receivable, and accounts payable.

Goods on consignment

Some companies transfer merchandise to sales agents (to sell to potential buyers) without transferring ownership. This process is known as **consignment.** If the merchandise on consignment is sold, the agent receives a commission. If the merchandise is not sold, the goods are returned to the supplying company (consignor). Importantly, the consignor retains title to the transferred merchandise even though the goods are possessed by the sales agent. Consigned goods are therefore reported as part of the consignor's inventory until the time of sale. Goods on consignment should not appear in the Inventory account of the agent.

TAKING A PHYSICAL INVENTORY

We have now determined the goods that should be reported as an asset on the balance sheet. Recall that there are two types of inventory systems: periodic and perpetual. Under a periodic system the balance found in the Inventory account at the beginning of the period remains there throughout the year. In contrast, the Inventory account under a perpetual system is increased for each purchase and decreased for each sale. No matter which system is employed, a firm must hand-count the goods in its possession at the conclusion of the accounting period. The hand count provides management with the correct ending inventory and serves to verify the accounting records if a perpetual system is in use.

This process, known as **taking a physical inventory,** may involve much more than "counting." For example, many small items (such as nuts and bolts) must be weighed. Other products, such as the amount of oil in a storage tank, must be measured. In addition, an inventory counter must determine whether the goods appearing to be in the warehouse are actually there. To explain, suppose an inventory counter observes a stack of cartons 10 across by 10 deep by 15 high. A quick conclusion at the end of a long day might be that the firm has 1,500 ($10 \times 10 \times 15$) cartons on hand. A potential problem could exist, however: the middle of the stack might be hollow or less than 15 cartons high. Indeed, a more careful look at the inventory is required to avoid a serious misstatement. Proper inventory counts are so important that items may be counted a second time to check the accuracy of the original figure. This practice is especially advised for goods representing a significant portion of a firm's total inventory cost.

The counting of inventory presents additional problems. For example, it is extremely difficult to count inventory while new merchandise is arriving and existing merchandise is being sold. Picture trying to count the number of pennies in a penny jar while a friend keeps putting some in and taking some out. To avoid this troublesome situation, many companies close for business while the inventory is being taken. To assist in the counting process, part-time workers are often hired. Both these actions are costly: the former means lost sales revenues, while the latter results in additional expense.

The inventory count, although costly and time-consuming, strengthens the credibility of the inventory figure reported on the year-end balance sheet. Even so, a physical count of inventory and its observance by an outside independent auditor has not always been a required practice. It took a massive fraud case to induce change. In 1937 the financial statements of McKesson & Robbins, a drug producer, were found to contain $19 million of fictitious inventories and receivables. A fraud had been perpetrated by the president and his brothers over a period of twelve years. The fraud was finally uncovered when the controller went to a warehouse to check some reported inventory and found none in existence. As an outcome of this case, rules were enacted to require the observation of inventory and confirmation of receivables by an independent auditor.

EFFECTS OF INVENTORY ERRORS ON FINANCIAL STATEMENTS

Naturally, many errors are possible in the inventory-counting process. Inventory items may be counted incorrectly, completely omitted in the counting process, and sometimes counted twice. Furthermore, in the computation of total inventory cost, mathematical errors can be made when multiplying the number of units owned by the cost per unit. Unfortunately, these errors are carried forward to the financial statements. Incorrect inventory determination can result in incorrect current asset valuation, net income, and owners' equity.

To understand the effect of inventory errors, we will study The Backert Company. Backert failed to include $2,000 of goods on display in its showroom as part of the ending inventory balance. The firm's income statement appears in Exhibit 9-1. The figures on the left are based on the correct ending inventory of $34,000. In contrast, the figures on the right omit the display merchandise and utilize an ending inventory of $32,000.

Exhibit 9-1

THE BACKERT COMPANY
Income Statement
For the Year Ended December 31, 1983

	Correct Ending Inventory of $34,000		Incorrect Ending Inventory of $32,000	
Net sales		$80,000		$80,000
Cost of goods sold				
Beginning inventory	$26,000		$26,000	
Add: Net purchases	59,000		59,000	
Goods available for sale	$85,000		$85,000	
Less: Ending inventory	34,000		32,000	
Cost of goods sold		51,000		53,000
Gross profit		$29,000		$27,000
Operating expenses		20,000		20,000
Net income		$ 9,000		$ 7,000

Because of the understated ending inventory, Backert is subtracting a number that is too small from goods available for sale. The resulting cost-of-goods-sold figure is therefore overstated. Since an overstated cost of goods sold is subtracted from net sales, gross profit and net income will each be understated. Net income increases owners' equity. Thus ending owners' equity on both the statement of owners' equity and the balance sheet is understated by $2,000. The balance sheet will balance, however, because of a $2,000 understatement of inventory in the current assets section. Exhibit 9-2 summarizes the effects of the display merchandise error.

Exhibit 9-2

Effects of an understatement of ending inventory

Income Statement	
Cost of goods sold	*Overstated*
Gross profit	*Understated*
Net income	*Understated*
Statement of Owners' Equity	
Ending owners' equity	*Understated*
Balance Sheet	
Ending owners' equity	*Understated*
Total current assets	*Understated*

The results of an overstatement of ending inventory are just the opposite. You are again reminded not to memorize this material, since inventory errors can become quite complex. Instead trace an error through the system and analyze its impact.

Counter-balancing Errors

Inventory errors have counterbalancing effects; that is, errors causing an overstatement of net income in one year create an understatement in the following year and vice versa. Why? The ending inventory from one period becomes the beginning inventory of the next. To illustrate, assume that the goods on display in Backert's showroom were sold during 1984 and that the 1984 ending inventory count of $41,000 was correct. The firm's $2,000 ending inventory understatement in 1983 is carried forward as a $2,000 understatement of the 1984 beginning inventory. The impact on the 1984 income statement is shown in Exhibit 9-3.

Observe that the understated beginning inventory reduces goods available for sale. The ending inventory of $41,000 is not affected by the earlier error because the inventory is determined by a separate physical count. Thus cost of goods sold is understated, which produces an overstated gross profit and net income. The $2,000 understatement of net income in 1983 is therefore counterbalanced by a $2,000 overstatement in 1984. Although the 1984 income statement is in error, the ending owners' equity is correct. This result is shown as follows:

	Using Correct 1983 and 1984 Net Income	***Using Incorrect 1983 and 1984 Net Income***
Beginning owners' equity, Jan. 1, 1983 (assumed)	$50,000	$50,000
+ 1983 net income	9,000	7,000
+ 1984 net income	11,000	13,000
Ending owners' equity, Dec. 31, 1984	$70,000	$70,000

Exhibit 9-3

THE BACKERT COMPANY
Income Statement
For the Year Ended December 31, 1984

	Correct Beginning Inventory of $34,000		Incorrect Beginning Inventory of $32,000	
Net sales		$97,000		$97,000
Cost of goods sold				
Beginning inventory	$ 34,000		$ 32,000	
Add: Net purchases	71,000		71,000	
Goods available for sale	$105,000		$103,000	
Less: Ending inventory (correct)	41,000		41,000	
Cost of goods sold		64,000		62,000
Gross profit		$33,000		$35,000
Operating expenses		22,000		22,000
Net income		$11,000		$13,000

Because the initial error has been counterbalanced, you might argue that the error is of little importance. Remember, however, that net income influences financial decision making. Financial statements are used by many different groups; errors, of course, could distort trends in the data that are used for evaluation.

INVENTORY VALUATION AND INCOME MEASUREMENT

As we have just shown, inventory affects both the balance sheet and the income statement. Ending inventory valuation and the determination of cost of goods sold are probably the two most significant inventory problems faced by accountants. If a firm purchased its merchandise at the same price throughout the year, there would be little difficulty. Ending inventory could be determined by multiplying the ending quantity of merchandise owned by the unit cost. The ending inventory would then be subtracted from goods available for sale to generate cost of goods sold.

Unfortunately, purchase prices rarely remain constant during an accounting period. Further complicating matters, we are often unable to attach the price paid for an item to the item itself. Picture the concrete dealer cited at the beginning of this chapter or a business dealing in large quantities of liquids. The goods are all mixed together, and if different prices are paid, accounting becomes a problem.

Key Objective

Throughout an accounting period a business has a "pool" of inventory costs to account for. This "pool" consists of the beginning inventory cost plus the cost of merchandise acquired for resale.[1] In more familiar terms, the pool is equivalent to goods available for sale. By the end of the period many of the items available for sale have been sold while others remain on hand in inventory. Thus goods available for sale must be divided between ending inventory and cost of goods sold, as shown in Exhibit 9-4.

Exhibit 9-4

Allocation of inventory cost between the balance sheet and the income statement

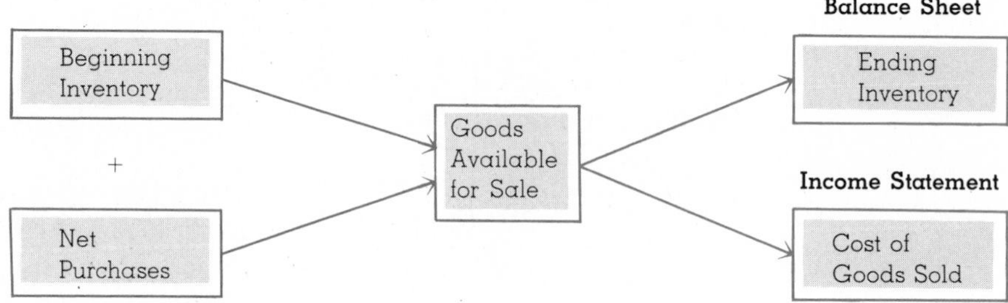

Because we have a fixed pool of dollars to apportion, the amount chosen for an ending inventory valuation will automatically affect cost of goods sold. Therefore if a relatively large amount is reported on the balance sheet as inventory, then a smaller amount will be reported as cost of goods sold.

We will soon see that several different methods can be used to allocate inventory costs between the income statement and the balance sheet. Often a given method favors one financial statement or the other, but not both. In keeping with the income statement's growth in importance, *the major objective of inventory accounting is to associate or match the costs of the items sold against the sales revenues generated.* Balance sheet valuation, then, is looked upon as a residual. That is, after assignment of costs to the income statement, those costs that remain are placed on the balance sheet.

Cost Determination

The computation of an inventory item's cost is the starting point for inventory valuation and figuring cost of goods sold. The recorded cost of inventory incorporates all expenditures related to acquisition, such as the purchase price of the merchandise (less any purchases discounts), transportation charges incurred by the purchaser, and insurance costs incurred on the merchandise while in transit.

Once the preceding expenditures are determined, the unit cost of each inventory item can be calculated. The purchase price of inventory is easily associated with specific items, but it is frequently difficult to compute unit amounts for transportation, insurance, and discounts. Why? Transportation and insurance are often incurred on shipments that consist of a variety of different inventory items. Similarly, the purchase discount on a single in-

[1]For a manufacturer the cost of merchandise acquired for resale would be replaced by the cost of goods manufactured.

voice may relate to numerous products. How, then, should these cost elements be handled?

When discounts, transportation, and insurance are traceable to a particular inventory item (i.e., the ideal situation), the cost of that item is computed accordingly. For example, suppose Baxter Corporation had the following costs for item no. 1088:

Purchase price: 500 units @ $10	*$5,000*
Add: Transportation charges	*350*
	$5,350
Less: Purchases discounts	*100*
Total cost	*$5,250*

Cost per unit: $5,250 ÷ 500 = $10.50

It is assumed that (1) these costs relate *strictly* to item no. 1088 and (2) there is no beginning inventory. If 100 units remain on hand at the end of the year, Baxter's inventory pool would be divided as shown in Exhibit 9-5.

Exhibit 9-5

Allocation of Baxter inventory pool

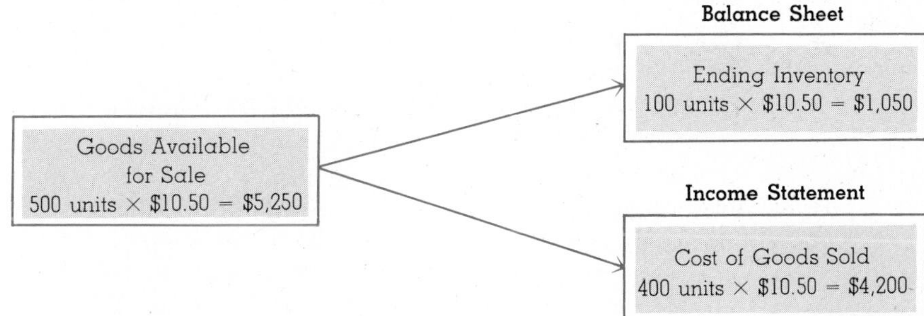

If discounts, transportation, and other acquisition costs are significant in amount and cannot be traced to specific inventory items, some form of equitable proration is necessary between the total ending inventory and cost of goods sold. The lack of such proration could result in a serious misstatement on both the balance sheet and the income statement. In many cases discounts and transportation charges are fairly small in relation to an item's purchase price. As a matter of expediency, no proration is attempted, and the Purchases Discounts and Freight-in accounts are entered in their entirety on the income statement. This latter approach was illustrated earlier in the text (see Chapter 4).

Costing Methods

Once the unit cost of each inventory item is known, a firm can begin the necessary assignment to ending inventory and cost of goods sold. The assignment process is accomplished by one of several different methods. From the viewpoint of a beginning accounting student, the specific identification method is often regarded as the most logical approach.

Specific identification

The **specific identification method** requires a business to identify each unit of merchandise with the unit's cost and retain that identification until the inventory is sold. Tags or stickers revealing a stock number are often attached to each inventory item; the stock number, in turn, is listed in a book along with the item's cost. You may have noticed, for example, that at many new car dealerships each car has a number on the windshield or side window. That number references the net invoice cost of the car in the dealer's accounting records.

To illustrate the specific identification method, we will examine the following data of the Truckee Company for 1983.

	Number of Units	×	*Cost per Unit*	=	*Total Cost*
Beginning inventory	3,000		$3.00		$ 9,000
Purchase (Feb. 28)	4,000		3.10		12,400
Purchase (May 15)	5,000		3.23		16,150
Purchase (Aug. 1)	1,000		3.50		3,500
Purchase (Oct. 31)	3,000		3.60		10,800
Goods available for sale	16,000				$51,850

During the year Truckee sold 11,800 units, leaving 4,200 units (16,000 – 11,800) in inventory.

In the process of determining cost of goods sold and the ending inventory valuation, the firm's accountant found that the units sold and on hand consisted of the following:

	Total Units	*Units Sold*	*Units on Hand*
Beginning inventory @ $3.00	3,000	3,000	—
Feb. 28 purchase @ $3.10	4,000	3,000	1,000
May 15 purchase @ $3.23	5,000	5,000	—
Aug. 1 purchase @ $3.50	1,000	800	200
Oct. 31 purchase @ $3.60	3,000	—	3,000
	16,000	11,800	4,200

The cost of the ending inventory is therefore calculated as follows:

Feb. 28 purchase	1,000 units × $3.10 =	$ 3,100
Aug. 1 purchase	200 units × $3.50 =	700
Oct. 31 purchase	3,000 units × $3.60 =	10,800
Ending inventory	4,200 units	$14,600

There are two ways to compute cost of goods sold. First, we can evaluate the cost of each batch that was sold during the year.

Beginning inventory	3,000 units × $3.00 =	$ 9,000
Feb. 28 purchase	3,000 units × $3.10 =	9,300
May 15 purchase	5,000 units × $3.23 =	16,150
Aug. 1 purchase	800 units × $3.50 =	2,800
Cost of goods sold	11,800 units	$37,250

Alternatively, because goods available for sale minus the ending inventory equals cost of goods sold, we can do the following:

Goods available for sale (see original data)	*$51,850*
Less: Ending inventory	*14,600*
Cost of goods sold	*$37,250*

The specific identification method matches the actual cost of the units sold against sales revenues. Additionally, this method allows management to manipulate net income. By selectively selling those goods with high costs or low costs, management can produce different levels of profit. Overall the specific identification method is used infrequently. Most companies find that the record-keeping costs outweigh projected benefits from the method's use. Furthermore, the physical tagging or coding of individual units of merchandise is impractical, if not impossible, in many situations. Imagine the difficulty a grocery store would experience, given the store's sales volume, the size and composition of its inventory, and the susceptibility to supplier price changes. Specific identification is most feasible when the volume of sales is low and the cost of individual units is high. This method might be used to account for jewelry, automobiles, or yachts, for example.

Cost flow assumptions

When specific identification is not employed, the accountant must make an assumption regarding the flow of costs through a firm's accounting system. That is, should cost of goods sold be computed by using the oldest costs that the firm has experienced, the most recent costs, or perhaps an average cost? If cost of goods sold is computed at the oldest costs, the most recent costs are then used for the valuation of ending inventory. This practice is consistent with splitting the goods available for sale (old costs and recent costs combined) between the income statement and the balance sheet.

It is important to recognize that a cost flow assumption pertains strictly to the *flow of cost* through the accounts and has no direct relationship to the actual *flow of goods*. In most cases a business will attempt to sell the oldest merchandise first because of a threat of obsolescence or spoilage. It is very possible that this same business will cost these goods at the most recent costs experienced. Again there is no direct connection between the physical flow of goods and the cost flow assumption used in the goods' accounting. The selection of a cost flow assumption is dependent on other factors, which will be discussed shortly.

There are three widely used cost flow assumptions: first-in, first-out (FIFO), last-in, first-out (LIFO), and weighted average. These assumptions will be illustrated by using the data from the Truckee example appearing on page 340.

First-in, first-out (FIFO)

The **first-in, first-out (FIFO) method** is based on the premise that the first goods in (purchased) are the first ones sold. This method conforms to reality for many companies, because, as we just noted, firms generally desire to sell older inventories first. The FIFO cost flow may be used, however, for any physical flow of goods. Under FIFO, since the oldest goods are assumed to be disposed of first, the ending inventory is composed of the most recent purchases. Therefore Truckee Company's 4,200-unit ending inventory would consist of the following:

Most recent purchase (Oct. 31)	3,000 units × $3.60 =	$10,800
Next most recent purchase (Aug. 1)	1,000 units × $3.50 =	3,500
Next most recent purchase (May 15)	200 units × $3.23 =	646
Ending inventory	4,200 units	$14,946

Observe that only 200 units from the May 15 purchase are needed to complete the accounting for the ending inventory; the other 4,800 units (5,000 − 200) are no longer on hand.

The cost of the 11,800 units sold can be computed as follows:

Beginning inventory	3,000 units × $3.00 =	$ 9,000
Oldest purchase (Feb. 28)	4,000 units × $3.10 =	12,400
Next oldest purchase (May 15)	4,800 units × $3.23 =	15,504
Cost of goods sold	11,800 units	$36,904

Or we can compute the cost as shown below:

Goods available for sale (see original data)	*$51,850*
Less: Ending inventory	*14,946*
Cost of goods sold	*$36,904*

Last-in, first-out (LIFO)

The **last-in, first-out (LIFO) method** charges the most recent costs (last-in) to cost of goods sold, because the newest units are assumed to be the first units sold. This assumption rarely conforms to the actual flow of goods. Because the most recent purchases are assumed to be sold, the cost of older purchases is assigned to the ending inventory. Thus the cost of Truckee's 4,200-unit ending inventory would be computed as follows:

Beginning inventory	3,000 units × $3.00 =	$ 9,000
Oldest purchase (Feb. 28)	1,200 units × $3.10 =	3,720
Ending inventory	4,200 units	$12,720

Although Truckee purchased 4,000 units on February 28, the cost of only 1,200 of these units is needed for inclusion in the ending inventory.

The cost of goods sold is $39,130:

Goods available for sale (see original data)	$51,850
Less: Ending inventory	12,720
Cost of goods sold	$39,130

Weighted average

The **weighted-average method** recognizes that there are both high and low costs during an accounting period. Rather than focus on the time when costs are incurred (i.e., currently or in the past), this method computes an average cost by weighting (multiplying) the cost per unit with the number of units purchased. Referring to page 340, observe that the outcome of this process results in $51,850, the cost of goods available for sale. The weighted average unit cost can now be computed as shown below:

cost of goods available for sale ÷ units available for sale
$51,850 ÷ 16,000 = $3.24

The unit cost of $3.24 is applied to the ending inventory as follows:

4,200 units × $3.24 = $13,608

Cost of goods sold is computed in the same manner as before; that is:

Goods available for sale	$51,850
Less: Ending inventory	13,608
Cost of goods sold	$38,242

The weighted-average method is, in effect, a compromise between FIFO and LIFO. Those who favor the weighted-average method base their argument on the belief that all goods available for sale in a period should reflect the same unit cost.

Comparison and evaluation of alternative inventory valuation methods

The effects of the four costing methods are summarized in Exhibit 9-6. The exhibit is based on the assumptions that sales and operating expenses were $125,000 and $60,000, respectively.

As you can see, each of the four methods results in reporting a different net income and ending inventory valuation. The magnitude of the differences depends on the number of units purchased and sold during the year and the extent of price changes. In light of the historical trend in purchase prices, it is evident that Truckee was experiencing an inflationary economy. Since LIFO charges recent (higher) costs to cost of goods sold, LIFO will usually report the lowest net income in a period of rising prices. FIFO, on the other hand, will report a larger net income. The results, of course, are reversed in a period of falling prices. Weighted average is a compromise between FIFO and LIFO and normally yields results somewhere between these two methods. It is difficult to generalize about specific identification

Exhibit 9-6

Alternative inventory costing methods for Truckee Company

	Specific Identification	FIFO	LIFO	Weighted Average
Sales	$125,000	$125,000	$125,000	$125,000
Cost of goods sold				
Beginning inventory	$ 9,000	$ 9,000	$ 9,000	$ 9,000
Add: Purchases*	42,850	42,850	42,850	42,850
Goods available for sale	$ 51,850	$ 51,850	$ 51,850	$ 51,850
Less: Ending inventory	14,600	14,946	12,720	13,608
Cost of goods sold	$ 37,250	$ 36,904	$ 39,130	$ 38,242
Gross profit	$ 87,750	$ 88,096	$ 85,870	$ 86,758
Operating expenses	60,000	60,000	60,000	60,000
Net income	$ 27,750	$ 28,096	$ 25,870	$ 26,758

Purchases are computed by subtracting Truckee's beginning inventory from the cost of goods available for sale: $51,850 − $9,000 = $42,850.

because the outcome is dependent on the batch of goods management selects for sale.

All four methods are acceptable accounting alternatives, and each (except specific identification) is used extensively. A survey of 1,073 large corporations disclosed the following:[2]

Method	Percentage of Corporations Using
FIFO	35.6%
LIFO	36.9
Average	22.2
Other	5.3

Which method should be selected?

It would be nice to generalize and state that a firm should always use FIFO or LIFO or one of the other inventory valuation methods. Unfortunately, we cannot. No one inventory method best meets the needs and peculiarities of all businesses. Management considers many factors when selecting an inventory method, including income taxes and their related cash outlays, financial statement presentation, and investor reaction to reported results.

Income taxes

In the past few years, LIFO has gained popularity because of the rapid price increases in our economy. By computing cost of goods sold on the basis

[2] *Accounting Trends & Techniques: 1981* (New York: American Institute of Certified Public Accountants, 1981), p. 135.

of recent (higher) costs, LIFO has produced lower net incomes and, thus, lower income tax payments for its users. The latter results in more cash available for investment purposes.

Be aware that if (1) tax rates remain constant and (2) inventory is reduced to zero, all the methods illustrated will produce the same long-run results.[3] To illustrate, assume Teal Corporation made the following purchases of a particular inventory item.

Mar.	500 units @ $ 8	$ 4,000
Sept.	1,000 units @ $10	10,000
	1,500 units	$14,000

If Teal sells all 1,500 units over the next few years, the firm's cost of goods sold will amount to $14,000 no matter which method is employed. Therefore the same taxes will be paid. The use of LIFO, however, produces a smaller net income and tax payment in earlier years, thus providing Teal with the opportunity to invest sooner and possibly generate greater dollar returns.

Financial statement presentation

The resulting financial statements must also be considered when selecting an inventory method. For example, the use of LIFO over long periods of time can generate a somewhat meaningless ending inventory valuation on the balance sheet. Why? Remember that the oldest costs are used as the basis for inventory valuation; consequently, units may be carried at costs incurred many years ago. The use of LIFO, then, could depress working capital and the current ratio. In contrast, FIFO values the ending inventory at a figure close to the cost of replacement.

While producing a reasonable balance sheet valuation, FIFO's income statement frequently results in a mismatch of revenues and expenses because cost of goods sold is determined by using older costs. Thus it is conceivable that the 1978 cost of an item could be deducted from the item's 1983 selling price when computing gross profit and net income. The meaningfulness of the net income figure is, therefore, questionable. In contrast, LIFO measures net income by charging a firm's most recent costs against sales. From an income measurement viewpoint, then, LIFO is superior to FIFO. Unfortunately, though, there is a related problem. The low tax payments associated with LIFO in an inflationary environment are based on the low net income figure LIFO generates. Given a choice, a business would rather report a larger net income to its owners than a smaller one.[4]

When choosing an inventory valuation method, management must keep in mind that the income statement and balance sheet have somewhat

[3] Inventory is rarely reduced to zero. For most businesses inventories rise because of growth and speculative buying to beat price increases.

[4] According to tax regulations in effect at the time of this writing, companies using LIFO for tax purposes must also utilize LIFO for financial reporting.

different purposes. On the income statement, cost of goods sold should reflect a fair measure of inventory cost to be matched against revenue. The balance sheet's ending inventory valuation, on the other hand, should be consistent with the definition of a current asset and indicate the amount of resources available to meet current obligations. Asset valuation and income determination are not always compatible, and it is frequently necessary to make compromises to suit an entity's reporting needs.

Investor reaction

As we have noted, the use of LIFO in periods of rising prices lowers net income. Net income, of course, is a vital element of the earnings-per-share computation—a key barometer used by investors to judge the success or failure of corporate operations. It is possible that continued use of LIFO could erode investor confidence in a firm's common stock and diminish the stock's attractiveness.

Although several widely publicized research studies have shown this statement not to be true, depressed earnings certainly must make management shudder. As a professor at the University of Michigan noted:

> *I've had two companies tell me that the only reason they stay on FIFO is because the chairman is afraid he'll be out of a job if the reported earnings are off. There are still a lot of company insiders who think the only thing the market judges is earnings per share.*[5]

Consistency in method application

The inventory method ultimately selected should be used consistently from one year to the next. Consistency helps to produce financial statements that can be compared over time and is very useful when assessing trends and performing other types of analysis. Importantly, consistency should *not* be interpreted to mean that a firm can never change inventory valuation methods. A change can and should be made when it is desirable and beneficial in measuring financial activity, for example, to achieve a better matching of revenues and expenses. If a change is made, the impact should be fully disclosed in the financial statements.

INFLATION AND INVENTORY

In recent years inflation has had a significant effect on the financial statements of most businesses. In the area of inventory, for example, companies have faced continuous cost increases in replacing the merchandise they have sold. Additionally, inflation has overstated the reported profits of many large corporations, particularly those firms using the FIFO or weighted-average methods of inventory valuation. A portion of this profit, sometimes called **inventory profit,** arises because cost of goods sold is computed by using an old (and fairly low) cost. The inventory profit is really fictitious, because a higher cost is incurred to replenish stock levels.

To illustrate the concept of inventory profit, suppose Lucerne Company

[5] "The Profit Illusion," *Business Week,* March 19, 1979, p. 111.

had the following purchases and sales of a particular inventory item:

Purchases	**Sales**
Jan. 10 units @ $6.00	10 units @ $10
Feb. 10 units @ $6.60	

Gross profit under FIFO, LIFO, and the weighted-average methods would be as follows:

	FIFO	***LIFO***	***Weighted Average***
Sales	$100	$100	$100
Cost of goods sold			
10 @ $6.00	60		
10 @ $6.60		66	
10 @ $6.30			63
Gross profit	$ 40	$ 34	$ 37

Assume that the current cost to replace this item is $6.90. Thus for every unit sold, Lucerne can keep only $3.10 ($10.00 − $6.90). The firm's "true" gross profit, then, is really $31 ($3.10 × 10 units). The use of FIFO and weighted average result in fictitious inventory profits of $9 ($40 − $31) and $6 ($37 − $31), respectively. LIFO comes closest to eliminating inventory profit (only $3 in this case) because its cost of goods sold is based on recent purchase costs.

The concept of inventory profit is important. If misunderstood by management, it is conceivable that a business could distribute the excessive profits through employee pay raises and extra dividends to the owners while, at the same time, lacking sufficient funds for inventory restocking.

The SEC and FASB

The impact of inflation on financial statements has been addressed by both the Securities and Exchange Commission (SEC) and the Financial Accounting Standards Board (FASB). In 1976 the SEC issued *Accounting Series Release No. 190.*[6] ASR 190 called for disclosure of the replacement cost of ending inventories and the amount cost of goods sold would have been if replacement cost had been used in its computation. *Replacement cost* is the cost of acquiring the same merchandise at year-end prices. Disclosure of these amounts could be done in either a special section of the financial statements or a footnote to the financial statements.

Later, in 1979, the FASB issued FASB Statement No. 33,[7] which required additional *supplemental* disclosure of inventory and cost of goods sold. With the issuance of Statement No. 33, the SEC's requirements were withdrawn. The details of the FASB's position will be presented in Chapter

[6]See "Disclosure of Certain Replacement Cost Data," *Accounting Series Release No. 190* (Washington, D.C.: Securities and Exchange Commission, 1976).

[7]See "Financial Reporting and Changing Prices," *Statement of Financial Accounting Standards No. 33* (Stamford, Conn.: Financial Accounting Standards Board, 1979).

19. The additional information provided by the disclosure rules is evident, though, when viewing recent LIFO valuations (in thousands) of the Anheuser-Busch Companies:

	Cost of Goods Sold	Inventories
As reported in the financial statements	$2,975,500	$228,400
Inflation-adjusted amounts (supplemental disclosure)	$3,038,600	$303,000
Percentage change due to inflation	+2.1%	+32.7%

Because the firm's cost of goods sold is comprised of recent prices, there is little difference between the inflation-adjusted cost of goods sold and the amount as reported in the financial statements. Turning to the balance sheet, however, it is a completely different story. The costs in LIFO ending inventory are outdated and simply not reflective of current replacement cost.

LOWER OF COST OR MARKET

Although inventories are generally valued at cost, circumstances sometimes arise where departures from cost are appropriate. As an example, assume that Art Nesbit, a loan officer at the Third Federal Bank, is examining the financial statements of Tuttle Company for purposes of granting a loan. Nesbit's primary concern is Tuttle's ability to meet loan payments as the payments come due. Nesbit is also interested in the value of certain assets that might be pledged as collateral on the loan. The following disclosure appears on Tuttle's balance sheet:

Inventories: at cost *$84,000*

Nesbit knows that accounting is based on the principle of historical cost and that several cost assignment methods are available for inventory valuation. Because Tuttle's inventory levels and purchase prices have been relatively stable, the assignment method is not an issue. Nesbit's concern is this: Can the bank get $84,000 for the inventory if Tuttle defaults on the loan? Nesbit may have some difficulty with the $84,000 figure if he knows the following information about Tuttle's merchandise.

It received considerable smoke damage from a fire next door.
It consisted heavily of electronic video games purchased a few years ago at $100 each. The games now sell at the local discount store for $29.99.
It contained numerous perishable products with a six-month shelf life that were acquired ten months ago.

Inventories are susceptible to damage, obsolescence, and spoilage. Over time the utility or usefulness of many goods declines, and a business may have to drop its selling price to ensure disposal. To achieve a better valuation of these inventory items, accountants turn to the **lower-of-cost-or-mar-**

ket method. The use of the lower-of-cost-or-market method is justified when the market potential for a particular product has been significantly reduced.

The decline in value of an inventory item is measured by the difference between its cost and its market value. Cost is determined by any one of the previously discussed methods: specific identification, FIFO, LIFO, or weighted average. **Market value** is defined as replacement cost, or the cost that would be incurred to reproduce or repurchase the item. In the case of damaged goods, market value is the amount obtainable from disposal.

To illustrate lower of cost or market, assume Tuttle stocks an electronic component that cost $170 when purchased several months ago. Owing to rapidly advancing technology, the component can now be replaced for $155. Tuttle has therefore suffered a $15 decline in value on this inventory item. To value the component at the *lower* of cost or market, we would compare $170 (original cost) with $155 (market value) and choose $155 (the lower).

There are two exceptions to the replacement cost definition of market value. First, market value cannot be greater than **net realizable value,** which is an item's selling price minus completion and disposal costs. For example, assume Tuttle carries an inventory item that originally cost $12; replacement cost is now $11.25 because of obsolescence. If Tuttle can only realize $10 by selling the item and if there are no completion and disposal costs, the true decline in value is $2 ($12 – $10). Thus the item would be valued at $10, not the higher replacement cost of $11.25.

The second exception is that market value cannot be less than net realizable value less a normal profit margin. For example, suppose a firm carries an item that originally cost $250 but can now be replaced for $200. Assume that the firm can sell this item for $300, which allows for recovery of a normal profit margin of 20%. Apparently, then, the "value" of this item is really $240 [$300 – 0.20 ($300)]. Valuing the inventory at the lower replacement cost of $200 understates asset valuation on the balance sheet.

Application of the Lower-of-Cost-or-Market Method

The lower-of-cost-or-market procedure is normally followed for each individual item in inventory. To illustrate, suppose Tuttle's inventory consisted of the following:

Item No.	(1) Quantity	(2) Per Unit Cost	(2) Per Unit Market	(1) × (2) Total Inventory Cost	(1) × (2) Total Inventory Market	Lower of Cost or Market
101	1,000	$ 12	$ 10	$12,000	$10,000	$10,000
102	500	20	23	10,000	11,500	10,000
103	3,000	15	16	45,000	48,000	45,000
104	100	170	155	17,000	15,500	15,500
				$84,000	$85,000	$80,500

The proper inventory valuation of $80,500 (right-hand column) is obtained by taking the lower of the cost and the market figures for each inventory

A CONFLICT OVER LOWER OF COST OR MARKET

"Many businesses—big and small ones—use lower of cost or market," notes James E. Power, tax partner at Deloitte Haskins & Sells, a certified public accounting firm. Under this method a lower inventory at year-end means lower earnings and thus lower income taxes. Businesses therefore have an incentive to reduce the value of their inventories for tax purposes, while the IRS has reason to strictly control inventory accounting.

In two rulings the IRS is forcing businesses using lower-of-cost-or-market accounting to stop writing down their inventories in a manner that the Supreme Court has said violates IRS regulations. Companies will have to recognize the additional income from such adjustments made in prior years, back to 1954. "Some fairly substantial amounts will be involved," Mr. Power says. For some companies more than $1 million in added taxes could result.

The Supreme Court case that resulted in these rulings involved Thor Power Tool Co. In effect, the court said Thor couldn't reduce some of its inventory to a lower "market value" unless the firm scrapped the items it was writing down or actually offered them for sale. Thor, like many businesses, reduced the book value of its inventory because experience showed that some of the items wouldn't be sold for many years, if at all.

For example, plumbing fixture companies make a lot more parts for toilets, sinks, and showers than they need for a model line. The extra parts go into inventory for sale as repair and replacement parts. It's cheaper to make all parts at once and keep some for future replacement sales than to produce the parts again in the future. But some parts won't be sold, so based on sales experience the parts inventory is written down to reflect its lower value.

Such write-downs are good accounting practice to ensure that businesses don't report larger inventory assets than they should. However, this accounting practice is in apparent conflict with IRS inventory rules. With the Thor Power decision, companies now know that such adjustments cannot be made when figuring the taxes owed to the federal government unless certain conditions are met. The adjustments are still permissible, however, when preparing a firm's financial statements.

SOURCE Adapted from "New Inventory Accounting Rules Create Unpleasant Tax Season for Many Firms."

item. Be aware, however, that other application methods are acceptable as well. Rather than evaluate each individual item, one can analyze the inventory as a whole. If Tuttle followed this latter approach, the inventory would be valued at $84,000. This figure is obtained by comparing the inventory's total cost ($84,000) with the total market value ($85,000) and selecting the lower amount. Turning to a third approach, significant inventory subclasses can be defined, with the lower-of-cost-or-market rule applied to each subclass. We will use the individual item approach, because it results in the lowest and most conservative inventory valuation.

Once the proper valuation is determined, the accounting records must be updated. If Tuttle's inventory is presently carried at cost ($84,000), a $3,500 reduction in value ($84,000 – $80,500) has occurred. This reduction is a loss and is entered in the accounts as follows:

Loss Due to Decline in Inventory Value	3,500	
Inventory		3,500
To reduce inventory to lower of cost or market		

The Inventory account now contains the lower-of-cost-or-market valuation of $80,500 and is reported as such on the balance sheet. Furthermore, Tuttle's net income is reduced by the loss. As a result of this entry, approximately normal profits are reported in the future. Why? A reduced inventory cost (because of the write-down) will be matched against reduced selling prices, the latter of which are necessary to achieve disposal.

What About Increases in Value?

While lower of cost or market appears logical on the surface, many argue that the method is inconsistent. By using the *lower* of the cost and the market figures, accountants consider write-downs in inventory valuation but not write-ups. For example, suppose a company had the following two inventory items:

Item No.	*Cost*	*Market*	*Lower of Cost or Market*
904	$40	$37	$37
905	37	40	37

Item no. 904 can be written down $3 to reflect the lower market value. Item no. 905, on the other hand, remains on the books at $37, thus ignoring an increase in valuation. A number of accountants argue that increases in value are just as important as decreases. In writing the inventory down to reflect the lower value, we are being conservative in our asset valuation practices. By writing item no. 905 up, we will have gained $3 by just holding the inventory. Is a write-up proper, however? Gain or profit from inventory is really earned upon sale. Thus the practice of increasing inventory above cost recognizes profit prematurely and results in an inflated asset valuation on the balance sheet. These actions lead to a lack of conservatism in the financial statements. Conservatism will be discussed further in Chapter 18.

INVENTORY ESTIMATES

As we noted earlier in the chapter, taking a physical inventory is a costly and time-consuming process. A physical count is mandatory, however, for determining the inventory balance that is reported in the year-end financial statements. There are numerous situations in business where an inventory valuation is needed and management desires to avoid or cannot perform a physical count. For these situations several inventory estimation procedures have been developed. These procedures allow the preparation of interim financial statements for periods between physical counts. In addition, the procedures allow businesses to estimate the goods on hand when physical counts are not possible. Such would be the case with disasters like tornadoes or fires, where inventories are destroyed or heavily damaged and estimates are needed for insurance claims. Estimation techniques, if they are reasonable, also permit a business to determine the accuracy of an actual hand count. A comparison of the hand count with the estimate could reveal gross errors in the counting process. Two widely used estimation methods are the gross profit method and the retail method.

Gross Profit Method

The **gross profit method** estimates inventory on the basis of a firm's gross profit rate, that is, gross profit expressed as a percentage of net sales. The rate, which is the key to the estimation process, is developed from past experience. Naturally, if there are known changes in a firm's recent experience, an adjustment factor should be incorporated. Once the gross profit rate is established, gross profit for the period can be estimated by applying the rate to the current period's sales. This computation then permits the user to calculate current cost of goods sold and the estimated ending inventory.

To illustrate, assume that Henderson Supply Co. desires to prepare financial statements for August without taking a physical inventory. The following information is available for the period ended August 31.

Net sales	*$80,000*
Beginning inventory, Jan. 1	*$10,000*
Net purchases	*$40,000*
Ending inventory	*?*
Cost of goods sold	*?*
Estimated gross profit percentage	*60%*

Since gross profit is estimated at 60% of net sales, current gross profit is \$48,000 (\$80,000 × 0.60). Cost of goods sold for August therefore amounts to \$32,000 (\$80,000 − \$48,000). The ending inventory is now found by the following computation:

Net sales		*$80,000*
Cost of goods sold		
Beginning inventory	*$10,000*	
Add: Net purchases	*40,000*	
Goods available for sale	*$50,000*	
Less: Ending inventory	*?*	
Cost of goods sold		*32,000*
Gross profit		*$48,000*

Ending inventory is estimated at $18,000 ($50,000 – $32,000) and would be included on any formal financial statements prepared.

Retail Method

Both department and discount stores carry a variety of different items that are tagged or marked with retail selling prices. Suppose it is the end of an accounting period and a department store takes a count of the inventory on hand. To determine the "value" of the inventory, one need only multiply the quantities found by their readily identifiable retail prices. Unfortunately, this "value" is not too helpful for financial statements. Financial statements carry inventories at cost or at the lower of cost or market, not selling prices. An inventory valued at retail could be converted to cost by inspecting numerous individual paid invoices and other records. This task is a rather formidable one, however, for businesses that carry large product lines. Alternatively, the retail method of inventory valuation can be employed.

The **retail method** is widely used by merchandising firms to value and/or estimate ending inventory. The method's thrust is to first determine the ending inventory at retail prices. This amount is subsequently converted to cost on the basis of the percentage relationship between the cost and retail valuations of goods available for sale. As you will now see, the following information must be accumulated in the accounting records to perform the necessary computations.

1 The beginning inventory valued at both cost and retail amounts
2 Net purchases priced at both cost and retail
3 Net sales for the period

To illustrate the retail method, suppose Boulder Sales Organization desires an inventory estimate as of March 31 of the current year. The required calculations follow.

	Cost	Retail
Beginning inventory, Jan. 1	$ 60,000	$ 88,000
Net purchases, Jan. through Mar.	293,600	432,000
Goods available for sale	$353,600	$520,000
Ratio of cost to retail prices		
$353,600/$520,000 = 68%		
Less: Net sales		340,000
Estimated ending inventory at retail		$180,000
Estimated ending inventory at cost ($180,000 × 0.68)		$122,400

To explain, net sales are subtracted from goods available for sale to yield an ending inventory at retail of $180,000.[8] To convert this figure to

[8] Frequently, additional factors (such as markups and markdowns to original selling prices) are considered when computing the ending inventory at retail.

cost, Boulder has computed a cost-to-retail ratio of 68%, indicating $0.68 of inventory cost for every $1.00 of retail valuation. Thus the $180,000 estimated ending inventory is multiplied by the 68% ratio to arrive at the $122,400 cost-based valuation.

In this example the retail method was used to obtain an interim estimate of inventory. This same method can also be employed to study a business's experience with theft and shoplifting. To illustrate, assume the figures in the Boulder example relate to the entire accounting year, which ends December 31. A physical count on December 31 revealed an inventory of $171,000 at retail prices. Thus Boulder has a $9,000 shortage at retail ($180,000 − $171,000), which, on a cost basis, amounts to $6,120 ($9,000 × 0.68).

The key to the retail method is the development of an accurate and realistic cost-to-retail ratio. The method assumes that the ratio observed with the goods available for sale is relevant for the ending inventory. In addition, you should realize that the ratio is an average of many different types of products; thus the likelihood is slim that *all* items in the ending inventory have identical cost-to-retail relationships. This situation is especially true in a department or discount store that carries merchandise ranging from clothes to fine jewelry to candy to lawn mowers. For improved accuracy in the retail method, ratios should be developed and applied to each major product line.

PERIODIC AND PERPETUAL INVENTORY SYSTEMS

Periodic System

Throughout this chapter and in Chapter 4 we emphasized the **periodic inventory system.** Recall that under a periodic system purchases are recorded in the Purchases account and sales are credited to the Sales account. These procedures result in a constant balance in the Inventory account throughout the year. The periodic system is frequently employed by businesses because of its minimal record-keeping requirements. The periodic system is especially attractive for firms that (1) sell slow-moving products, (2) carry a large variety of low-cost inventory items, and (3) use manual accounting systems.

Two significant problems associated with a periodic system make it undesirable for a large number of organizations. First, a business has no record of the number of units in stock at any given time. Remember, no entries are made to the Inventory account. This lack of information can lead to stockouts and poor customer service. The second problem lies in the calculation of cost of goods sold. To explain, we examine the following computations (the numbers are assumed).

Cost of goods sold	
Beginning inventory	*$19,000*
Add: Net purchases	*47,000*
Goods available for sale	*$66,000*
Less: Ending inventory	*24,000*
Cost of goods sold	*$42,000*

By subtracting the $24,000 of inventory that was obtained from the physical count, we are assuming that $42,000 of goods were sold. This assumption could be erroneous, however, because theft or errors may have occurred. Unfortunately, there is no basis of accountability, because the periodic system does not monitor the amount of inventory that *should be* on hand.

Perpetual System

The problems of the periodic system are overcome by using a **perpetual inventory system**. A perpetual system maintains a continuous record of the inflows and outflows of merchandise, resulting in a running count of the goods on hand. By maintaining records in this manner, a firm can readily answer the questions of its salespeople and customers concerning item availability. In addition, a perpetual system leads to improved inventory control. By knowing the number of units that are supposed to be on hand, a business can reorder in sufficient time to avoid stockouts. Furthermore, the extent of any theft or errors can be determined by comparing the inventory records against a physical count. We stress that although a firm has a record of the number of units in stock, a physical inventory is still necessary to verify the books at the end of the accounting period.

Perpetual systems are being used by an increasing number of businesses. This rise in popularity is partially due to the growing use of computers (especially minicomputers) and cash registers that are linked to computer systems. Computers can perform the necessary record keeping for a perpetual system in a matter of seconds, while the integration of on-line registers allows a business to update its inventory records as each sale is recorded.

Operation of a perpetual system

To illustrate the operation of a perpetual inventory system, assume that the following information regarding part no. 1058 was obtained from the records of the Bankston Company.

Beginning inventory 3,000 units @ $5.00

Purchases on Account				***Sales on Account***			
Mar. 10	2,500 units	@ $6.00 =	$15,000	Mar. 13	2,000 units	@ $9 =	$18,000
Mar. 19	1,000 units	@ $6.50 =	6,500	Mar. 22	2,800 units	@ $9 =	25,200
	3,500		$21,500		4,800		$43,200

Because the perpetual system closely monitors inventory levels, subsidiary records are normally established for each item stocked. The subsidiary record for part no. 1058 appears in Exhibit 9-7.

In this particular case Bankston is employing the FIFO method of inventory valuation. To explain, the purchase on March 10 gives rise to two different cost layers: 3,000 units at $5 and 2,500 units at $6. Because the costs differ, the layers are maintained separately and listed chronologically. The sale on March 13 reduces the inventory by 2,000 units. Although the units were sold for $9 each, they must be removed from the inventory rec-

Exhibit 9-7

PERPETUAL INVENTORY RECORD

Part No. 1058 Reorder Point 3,500 units

Date	Purchases	Sales	Balance
3/1			3,000 @ $5.00
3/10	2,500 @ $6.00		3,000 @ $5.00 2,500 @ $6.00
3/13		2,000 @ $5.00	1,000 @ $5.00 2,500 @ $6.00
3/19	1,000 @ $6.50		1,000 @ $5.00 2,500 @ $6.00 1,000 @ $6.50
3/22		1,000 @ $5.00 1,800 @ $6.00	700 @ $6.00 1,000 @ $6.50

ords at cost. With FIFO the 2,000 units are costed at the oldest purchase price of $5. This computation leaves 1,000 units from the beginning layer plus 2,500 units from the purchase of March 10 on hand. The sale of 2,800 units on March 22 is costed in similar fashion. The oldest costs (the remaining 1,000 units from the first layer plus 1,800 units from the second layer) become the cost of goods sold.

The LIFO and weighted-average methods can also be used with a perpetual system. Under LIFO, for example, the sale on March 13 would be costed at the most recent (last-in) purchase price of $6. This calculation would leave 3,000 units at $5 plus 500 units at $6 in stock. Because of special problems, a detailed study of perpetual systems coupled with LIFO and weighted average is left for more advanced accounting courses.

General ledger updating

Recall the control account/subsidiary ledger relationship that was discussed in Chapter 5. Because Bankston has been increasing and decreasing its subsidiary records for part no. 1058, the firm must also enter the purchases and sales in the general ledger control account (Inventory) to maintain the necessary equality. The transactions on March 10 and 13 are recorded as follows:

Mar. 10	*Inventory*	*15,000*	
	Accounts Payable		*15,000*
	Purchased 2,500 units at $6		

		Debit	Credit
13	*Cost of Goods Sold*	*10,000*	
	Inventory		*10,000*
	Sold 2,000 units at a cost of $5 per unit		
	Accounts Receivable	*18,000*	
	Sales		*18,000*
	Sold 2,000 units at a selling price of $9 per unit		

Observe that both the purchase and the sale are recorded in the Inventory account; the Purchases account is no longer used. Furthermore, notice that a sale now requires two entries. The first entry on March 13 reduces inventory and recognizes the cost of the units sold (via a debit to a new account entitled Cost of Goods Sold); the second entry is needed to record the appropriate sales revenue. With the use of entries such as these throughout the period, both Cost of Goods Sold and Inventory are updated continuously.

After Bankston's March transactions are journalized and posted, the Inventory, Cost of Goods Sold, and Sales accounts would appear as follows:

Inventory

3/1	*Balance*	*15,000*	*3/13*	*10,000*
3/10		*15,000*	*3/22*	*15,800*
3/19		*6,500*		**25,800**
	(10,700)	**36,500**		

Cost of Goods Sold

3/13	*10,000*		
3/22	*15,800*		
	25,800		

Sales

		3/13	*18,000*
		3/22	*25,200*
			43,200

The balance in the Inventory account agrees with the ending inventory reported in Exhibit 9-7.

700 units @ $6.00	=	$ 4,200
1,000 units @ $6.50	=	6,500
		$10,700

Additionally, the balance in the Cost of Goods Sold account agrees with the cost of sales in Exhibit 9-7:

2,000 units @ $5.00	=	$10,000
1,000 units @ $5.00	=	5,000
1,800 units @ $6.00	=	10,800
		$25,800

As you can see, the use of a perpetual inventory system entails considerable record keeping. For this reason many businesses, especially those without a computer, modify the procedures just illustrated. Numerous firms keep their subsidiary records in units only; that is, dollars are ignored. At the end of the accounting period, inventory valuation and cost of goods sold are computed by using the periodic method. By following these procedures, users are taking advantage of the benefits associated with both systems: the reduced record keeping of a periodic system along with the perpetual system's improved inventory control.

SUMMARY PROBLEM

Tiger Corporation sells a single product and uses a periodic inventory system. The following information was extracted from the accounting records.

Sales	***Purchases***	
1,500 units @ $ 8.50	Feb.	800 units @ $4.75
500 units @ $10.00	June	600 units @ $5.50
	Oct.	900 units @ $6.00

The firm's beginning inventory on January 1 totaled 300 units and cost $1,200.

INSTRUCTIONS

a ***Compute Tiger's ending inventory, cost of goods sold, and gross profit, using the following inventory valuation methods: (1) FIFO; (2) LIFO; (3) weighted average (round to the nearest cent).***

b ***Which of the methods in part (a) generates the greatest amount of inventory profits? Explain your answer.***

a ***Sales***

1,500 units @ $ 8.50 =	$12,750
500 units @ $10.00 =	5,000
2,000 units	$17,750

Goods available for sale

Beginning inventory	300 units @ $4.00 =	$ 1,200
Feb. purchase	800 units @ $4.75 =	3,800
June purchase	600 units @ $5.50 =	3,300
Oct. purchase	900 units @ $6.00 =	5,400
	2,600 units	$13,700

Ending inventory

Goods available for sale	2,600 units
Less: Sales	2,000 units
Ending inventory	600 units

FIFO ending inventory consists of the most recent costs; therefore:

600 units @ $6.00 = $3,600

LIFO ending inventory consists of the oldest costs; therefore:

300 units @ $4.00 = $1,200
300 units @ $4.75 = 1,425
$2,625

Weighted average:

$13,700 ÷ 2,600 units = $5.27 per unit

600 units × $5.27 = $3,162

	FIFO	*LIFO*	*Weighted Average*
Sales	$17,750	$17,750	$17,750
Less: Cost of goods sold			
Beginning inventory	$ 1,200	$ 1,200	$ 1,200
Add: Purchases*	12,500	12,500	12,500
Goods available for sale	$13,700	$13,700	$13,700
Less: Ending inventory	3,600	2,625	3,162
Cost of goods sold	$10,100	$11,075	$10,538
Gross profit	$ 7,650	$ 6,675	$ 7,212

* *Goods available for sale less the beginning inventory.*

b ***FIFO generates the greatest amount of inventory profit because cost of goods sold is computed by using the oldest (and in this case the lowest) purchase prices.***

KEY TERMS AND CONCEPTS

cost flow assumption 341
first-in, first-out (FIFO) 342
goods in transit 333
goods on consignment 333
gross profit method 352
inventory 332
inventory profit 346
last-in, first-out (LIFO) 342
lower of cost or market 348
market value 349
net realizable value 349
periodic inventory system 354
perpetual inventory system 355
retail method 353
specific identification 340
taking a physical inventory 334
weighted average 343

QUESTIONS

Q9-1 What items are reported as inventory for (a) merchandising and (b) manufacturing companies?

Q9-2 The Potter Corporation purchased the following merchandise on December 28.

Supplier	Terms	Amount
Pax Company	F.O.B. destination	$1,800
James Manufacturing	F.O.B. shipping point	2,500

Both purchases were shipped December 30, but neither had been received by December 31. Should the purchases be included in Potter's December 31 ending inventory? Explain.

Q9-3 What are goods on consignment? Who has title to goods on consignment?

Q9-4 Why is it necessary to take a physical count of inventory at the end of each accounting period? What problems may be encountered in taking a physical inventory?

Q9-5 The Hutton Company made the following mathematical error in determining the cost of its June 30 ending inventory.

Stock No.	Quantity	Cost per Unit	Total Cost
A674B	1,500	$3.40	$51,000

Determine the effect of the error on the following:

a Cost of goods sold for the year ended June 30
b Operating expenses for the year ended June 30
c Net income for the year ended June 30
d Owners' equity as of June 30
e Total current assets as of June 30

Q9-6 At the end of an accounting period, goods available for sale is segregated into two different costs. What are these two costs? Explain which of the costs is given primary emphasis by accountants.

Q9-7 Why is the specific identification method of inventory valuation used infrequently?

Q9-8 Discuss the difference between the physical flow of goods and a cost flow assumption.

Q9-9 Why has LIFO gained in popularity in recent years?

Q9-10 In a period of rising prices, which inventory valuation method (LIFO or FIFO) results in the following?

a Highest cost of goods sold
b Lowest inventory valuation
c Highest income taxes

Q9-11 What factors should be considered in the selection of an inventory valuation method?

Q9-12 Why do accountants object to increasing inventory valuations above cost?

Q9-13 Why do businesses frequently need to estimate their inventory balances?

Q9-14 What shortcomings are sometimes encountered when using the cost-to-retail ratio of the retail inventory method?

Q9-15 Discuss the advantages of a perpetual inventory system when compared with a periodic system. Does the perpetual system have any limitations?

Q9-16 Why are two journal entries required to record a sale under a perpetual inventory system?

EXERCISES

E9-1 The inventory count of the Barclay Corporation on December 31 indicated an ending inventory balance of $96,450. Subsequently, the following additional information was discovered by Barclay's accountant.

1 Purchases in transit of $3,200, terms F.O.B. shipping point, were not included in the ending inventory.
2 Goods consigned to Alger Corporation of $4,800 were not included in the ending inventory.
3 Purchases in transit of $5,400, terms F.O.B. destination, were not included in the ending inventory.
4 Goods on consignment from the Tower Corporation of $6,200 were included in the ending inventory.

a Determine Barclay's correct ending inventory balance.
b Determine the net effect of the inventory errors on the current year's net income.

E9-2 The income statements for the Younger Company for 1981–1983 follow.

	1981	*1982*	*1983*
Sales	$120,000	$140,000	$130,000
Cost of goods sold	72,000	82,000	78,000
Gross profit	$ 48,000	$ 58,000	$ 52,000
Expenses	18,000	22,000	20,000
Net income	$ 30,000	$ 36,000	$ 32,000

A recent review of the accounting records discovered that the 1981 ending inventory had been understated by $6,000.

a Prepare corrected 1981, 1982, and 1983 income statements.
b What is the effect of the error on Younger's ending owners' equity for 1981, 1982, and 1983?

E9-3 In December Ross Marine Supply began to carry a new type of boat. The following purchases were made:

Dec. 4	2 boats @ $7,400	$14,800
13	3 boats @ $7,700	23,100
		$37,900

All the boats are identical and all have a selling price of $9,600. During the last week in December, 3 boats were sold. Ross uses the specific identification method of inventory valuation.

a If Ross desired to maximize December net income, which boats would have been selected for sale during the last week? Why?
b If Ross desired to minimize income taxes for the year ended December 31, which boats would have been selected for sale during the last week? Why?

E9-4 The following information is available for the Chambers Corporation for the month of June.

June 1	Beginning inventory	500 units @ $4.00
8	Purchase	1,500 units @ $4.10
14	Purchase	1,000 units @ $4.15
27	Purchase	2,000 units @ $4.20

On June 30, 2,200 units were unsold and remained in inventory. The firm uses a periodic inventory system.

Compute the ending inventory balance under each of the following methods of inventory valuation.
a First-in, first-out
b Last-in, first-out
c Weighted average

E9-5 The January 1 beginning inventory of the Jahnke Corporation consisted of 200 units at a unit cost of $8. During the first quarter Jahnke purchased 500 units at $9 and then 300 units at $10. Sales during the first quarter were 550 units at $14 per unit. The firm uses a periodic inventory system.

Determine the ending inventory and cost of goods sold under each of the following inventory valuation methods.
a FIFO
b LIFO
c Weighted average

E9-6 Indicate whether LIFO or FIFO best describes each of the following:
a Gives highest profits when prices fall.
b Yields lowest income taxes when prices rise.
c Generates an ending inventory valuation that somewhat approximates replacement cost.
d Matches recent costs against current selling prices on the income statement.
e Comes closest to approximating the physical flow of goods of a sand and gravel company.
f Results in greater inventory profits in inflationary periods.
g Is acceptable for financial reporting.

E9-7 The Tenberg Company's condensed income statement for the year just ended follows.

Sales (10,000 units @ $18.40)	*$184,000*
Cost of goods sold	*129,000*
Gross profit	*$ 55,000*
Operating expenses	*38,000*
Net income	*$ 17,000*

Tenberg uses the FIFO method of inventory valuation. Cost of goods sold under LIFO and weighted average would have been $145,000 and $136,000, respectively. Replacement cost is $15.25 per unit.

a Compute the amount of inventory profit associated with FIFO, LIFO, and weighted average.

b Why are inventory profits sometimes called fictitious profits?

E9-8 The Walton Corporation sells five different products. The following information concerning their cost and market value is available on December 31.

Inventory Item	*Units*	*Cost per Unit*	*Market Value per Unit*
A	800	$5.00	$5.10
B	1,200	8.00	7.40
C	1,500	4.50	4.80
D	900	6.25	6.50
E	2,700	3.40	3.20

a Apply the lower-of-cost-or-market rule to each inventory item and determine Walton's ending inventory balance.

b Prepare the required journal entry to record the inventory at the lower of cost or market.

E9-9 On April 18 Alton's warehouse was destroyed by fire and the entire stock of inventory was lost. The accounting records disclosed the following information:

Jan. 1 inventory balance	$28,000
Purchases: Jan. 1 – Apr. 17	57,000
Sales: Jan. 1 – Apr. 17	96,000

Alton's normally experiences a 45% gross profit rate. Determine Alton's fire loss by using the gross profit method of inventory estimation.

E9-10 Sara Lynn, a women's dress store, uses the retail method of inventory valuation. The following information is available on October 31.

	Cost	*Retail*
Inventory, Jan. 1	$196,000	$310,000
Purchases, Jan.–Oct.	415,000	670,000
Sales, Jan.–Oct.		715,000
Returns & allowances		
Sales		10,000
Purchases	11,000	20,000

Determine the cost of Sara Lynn's October 31 ending inventory.

E9-11 Barto's, a well-known men's shop, had the following transactions during May.

Purchases on account	
100 shirts @ $15	*$1,500*
1 computer terminal (for use in the office)	*1,200*
Sales on account	
60 of the above shirts	*1,380*
Returns on account	
15 of the above unsold shirts	
1 typewriter	*150*

a Record the transactions above by using a periodic inventory system.

b Record the transactions above by using a perpetual inventory system.

PROBLEMS

P9-1 ***Inventory errors and the income statement***

The condensed income statement of Mayberry Products for the current year ended December 31 follows:

Sales	$120,000
Cost of goods sold	80,000
Gross profit	$ 40,000
Expenses	15,000
Net income	$ 25,000

The year-end review of the accounting records disclosed the following errors:

a A merchandise purchase of $3,000 shipped F.O.B. shipping point on December 31 was not included in the ending inventory count. The purchase was correctly entered in the accounting records.

b The ending inventory count failed to include $5,000 of goods on consignment to the Bilko Corporation. These goods were properly recorded by Mayberry when they were originally acquired.

c Credit sales of $1,500 on December 31 were not recorded. These goods were not included in the ending inventory count.

INSTRUCTIONS

Prepare a corrected income statement.

P9-2 ***Effects of inventory errors***

The Steel Corporation, which uses a periodic inventory system, made the following errors:

a An invoice of $1,800 for goods received in 1983 was not recorded until 1984. The physical count of inventory at the end of 1983 properly included these goods.

b Goods costing $2,400 were on consignment to the Gorski Company and were not included in the 1983 ending inventory count. These goods were properly recorded by Steel when purchased and were sold by Gorski in 1984.

c Goods costing $600 were sold and awaiting customer pickup on December 31, 1983. Although the sale was properly entered in the accounting records, the goods were included in the physical inventory count.

d Merchandise purchased in 1983 was properly recorded at its acquisition cost of $3,200. These goods were not received by the end of 1983 and were excluded from the ending inventory.

e Because of a clerical error, 500 units of merchandise in the 1983 ending inventory count were costed at $54 rather than the correct amount of $45. Assume that (1) these items were correctly recorded when originally purchased and (2) the error did not reoccur when costing the 1984 ending inventory.

INSTRUCTIONS

Assume that the errors above were not discovered until after Steel's 1984 financial statements had been prepared. Determine the effect of each of the errors on the items appearing in the chart that follows. Use these symbols in recording your answers: + = overstatement; − = understatement; 0 = no effect.

1983

Error	Cost of Goods Sold	Net Income	Ending Current Assets	Ending Current Liabilities	Ending Owners' Equity
(a)					
(b)					
(c)					
(d)					
(e)					

1984

Error	Cost of Goods Sold	Net Income	Ending Current Assets	Ending Current Liabilities	Ending Owners' Equity
(a)					
(b)					
(c)					
(d)					
(e)					

P9-3 ***Inventory valuation methods: Basic computations***

The Falmouth Corporation sells a single product. The following information is available for the month of March.

Mar.	1	Beginning inventory	800 units @ $6.00
	5	Purchase	600 units @ $6.05
	12	Purchase	700 units @ $6.10
	18	Purchase	550 units @ $6.20
	25	Purchase	500 units @ $6.25

During March 2,000 units were sold at $10.50 per unit. The firm uses a periodic inventory system.

INSTRUCTIONS

Determine Falmouth's ending inventory balance, cost of goods sold, and gross profit under each of the following inventory valuation methods:

a First-in, first-out

b Last-in, first-out

c Weighted average (round calculations to the nearest cent)

P9-4 ***LIFO versus FIFO: Basic computations and analysis***

The Reeder Corporation began business on January 1, 1982. Net income in 1982 amounted to $12,000; net income in 1983 was $15,000. Information pertaining to Reeder's purchases and sales of merchandise follows:

Purchases

Date of Purchase	Units	Unit Cost
Jan. 2, 1982	500	$ 6
Mar. 15, 1982	600	6
June 20, 1982	1,000	7
Aug. 7, 1982	1,200	8
Oct. 14, 1982	1,300	9
Dec. 20, 1982	1,500	10
Feb. 8, 1983	1,400	11
Apr. 14, 1983	1,200	12
July 30, 1983	1,300	13
Sept. 15, 1983	1,600	15
Nov. 10, 1983	1,800	18

Sales

1982	4,200 units
1983	5,800 units

Reeder uses the FIFO method of inventory valuation combined with a periodic inventory system.

INSTRUCTIONS

a Compute Reeder's 1982 and 1983 cost of goods sold and ending inventory balance.

b Determine Reeder's 1982 and 1983 cost of goods sold, ending inventory balance, and net income if the LIFO method of inventory valuation had been used.

c Would Reeder have been better off using LIFO rather than FIFO? Why?

P9-5 ***Analysis of inventory valuation methods***

Travis, Inc., began business on January 1, 1981. Information about the firm's inventories under different valuation methods follows:

	LIFO Cost	FIFO Cost	Market	Lower of Cost or Market
12/31/81	$10,200	$10,000	$ 9,600	$ 8,900
12/31/82	9,100	9,000	8,800	8,500
12/31/83	10,300	11,000	12,000	10,900

Purchases during 1982 totaled $20,000.

INSTRUCTIONS

a Which inventory method would produce the highest net income for 1981? Why?

b Which inventory method would produce the highest net income for 1982? Why?

c On the basis of the information presented, determine which of the following choices correctly describes the movement of prices for the items in inventory: (1) up in 1981 and down in 1983; (2) up in both 1981 and 1983; (3) down in 1981 and up in 1983; (4) down in both 1981 and 1983.

P9-6 ***LIFO versus FIFO: Elimination of product line***

In 1981 Hallmark Company began to carry a particular item in inventory. By the end of 1983 the item had been dropped from future marketing plans and all remaining inventory was sold. Purchases and sales were as follows:

	Purchases	Sales
1981	10,000 units @ $200	6,000 units @ $300
1982	16,000 units @ $220	17,000 units @ $320
1983	9,000 units @ $250	12,000 units @ $300

Hallmark uses a periodic inventory system.

INSTRUCTIONS

a If Hallmark used FIFO, compute gross profit for 1981, 1982, and 1983. What is the total gross profit for the three years together?

b If Hallmark used LIFO, compute gross profit for 1981, 1982, and 1983. What is the total gross profit for the three years together?

c Which of the two methods would be more advantageous for tax purposes? Why?

P9-7 ***Inventory profits and LIFO***

Ron Hansen, president of Carter, Inc., recently read an article that claimed that at least a hundred of the country's largest 500 companies were either adopting or considering adopting the last-in, first-out (LIFO) method for valuing inventories. The article stated that the firms were switching to LIFO to (1) neutralize the effect of inflation in their financial statements, (2) eliminate inventory profits, and (3) reduce income taxes. Hansen wonders if the switch would benefit his company.

Carter currently uses the first-in, first-out (FIFO) method of inventory valuation in conjunction with its periodic inventory system. Hansen intends to use the inventory method that is best for the company in the long run and not select a method just because it is the current fad.

INSTRUCTIONS

a Explain to Hansen what "inventory profits" are and how the LIFO method of inventory valuation could reduce them.

b Explain to Hansen the conditions that must exist for Carter to receive tax benefits from a switch to the LIFO method.

(CMA modified.)

P9-8 ***FIFO and lower of cost or market***

Kenny Company is a food wholesaler that supplies independent grocery stores in the immediate region. The first-in, first-out (FIFO) method of inventory valuation is used. Transactions and other related information regarding two of the items carried by Kenny are given on page 368 for October, the last month of Kenny's fiscal year.

	Instant Coffee	*Sugar*
Standard unit of packaging	Case containing twenty-four 1-pound jars	Bale containing twelve 5-pound bags
Inventory, Oct. 1	1,200 cases @ $53.22 per case	600 bales @ $6.50 per bale
Purchases	10/10: 1,600 cases @ $56.40 per case plus freight of $480	10/5: 640 bales @ $5.76 per bale plus freight of $320
	10/20: 1,600 cases @ $57.00 per case plus freight of $480	10/16: 640 bales @ $5.40 per bale plus freight of $320
		10/24: 640 bales @ $5.04 per bale plus freight of $320
October sales	3,400 cases @ $76.00 per case	2,200 bales @ $7.80 per bale
Returns & allowances	A customer returned 50 cases that had been shipped in error; the customer's account was credited for $3,800.	As the Oct. 16 purchase was unloaded, 20 bales were discovered to be damaged. A representative of the trucking firm confirmed the damage and the bales were discarded; credit of $108 for the merchandise and $10 for the freight was received by Kenny.

INSTRUCTIONS

a Calculate the number of cases of coffee and bales of sugar in ending inventory as of October 31.

b Kenny received a 2% discount on the coffee purchases of October 10 and 20. Compute the total cost of the firm's ending inventory under FIFO. *Hint:* Remember that discounts are not computed on freight.

c Ignoring your answers in parts (a) and (b), assume Kenny's ending inventory under FIFO was as follows:

Coffee 1,200 cases @ $55.50
Sugar 400 bales @ $ 5.25

The October 31 market values (including freight and net of purchases discounts) were as follows:

Coffee $55.20 per case
Sugar $ 5.35 per bale

Determine the lower-of-cost-or-market valuation of Kenny's ending inventory using the individual item approach. Present the necessary journal entry to value the inventory at lower of cost or market.

(CMA modified.)

P9-9 ***Gross profit method and fire loss***

On January 19, 1983, a fire heavily damaged the office and warehouse of Lexington Distributors. The following information has been obtained.

1 Lexington's condensed income statement for the year ended December 31, 1982, is as follows:

Sales		*$400,000*
Cost of goods sold		
Beginning inventory	*$180,000*	
Add: Net purchases	*310,000*	
Goods available for sale	*$490,000*	
Less: Ending inventory	*230,000*	
Cost of goods sold		*260,000*
Gross profit		*$140,000*
Operating expenses		*115,500*
Net income		*$ 24,500*

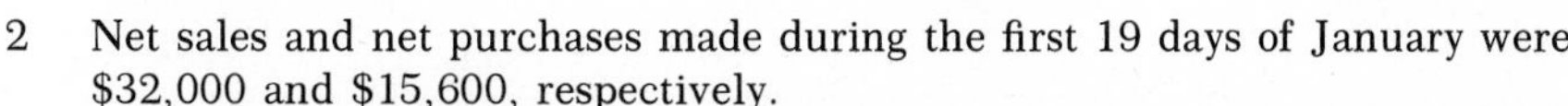

2 Net sales and net purchases made during the first 19 days of January were $32,000 and $15,600, respectively.

3 Purchases entered in the accounting records but still in transit as of January 19 amounted to $1,200.

Lexington's insurance company agreed to reimburse the firm for the fire loss on the basis of an estimate of inventory using the gross profit method. The gross profit rate will be derived by examining last year's operating results.

INSTRUCTIONS

a Determine the cost of inventory on hand on January 19.

b Taking your answer above into consideration, assume that inventory costing $20,500 was recovered and sold to a salvage firm for $4,200. Compute Lexington's total fire loss.

c In addition to computing fire losses, are there other possible uses of the gross profit method? Explain.

P9-10 ***Retail method and inventory shrinkage***

Brookline's, a department store, uses the retail method to estimate inventory. The following information was obtained from the accounting records for the year ended December 31.

Inventory, Jan. 1	
Cost	*$ 11,500*
Retail	*19,700*
Purchases	
Cost	*186,000*
Retail	*296,100*
Purchases returns	
Cost	*2,100*
Retail	*3,300*
Sales	*200,800*
Sales returns	*4,500*
Freight-in	*4,600*

INSTRUCTIONS

a Determine the cost of Brookline's estimated inventory on December 31.

b Disregarding your answer in part (a), assume Brookline's estimated ending inventory at retail totaled $68,000. If the firm's physical count on December 31 revealed an ending inventory at retail of $60,000, compute the cost of inventory shrinkage.

c List several factors that may have caused the difference between the computed inventory and the physical count in part (b).

(CPA adapted.)

P9-11 ***Perpetual inventory systems and FIFO***

The McGeorge Company carries parts that are in high demand by the automotive industry. Given the competitive nature of its business, McGeorge uses a perpetual inventory system. The following information pertains to a particular exhaust component.

June 1 Beginning inventory 800 units @ $15

Purchases		Sales	
June 10	1,100 units @ $15.50	June 7	300 units @ $22
17	600 units @ $16.00	12	400 units @ $23
20	1,000 units @ $16.25	14	600 units @ $23
		19	800 units @ $24
		28	900 units @ $24

INSTRUCTIONS

a Using a format similar to that of Exhibit 9-7, prepare a perpetual inventory record for the exhaust component. McGeorge uses the FIFO method of inventory valuation.

b Prepare summary journal entries to record total purchases and sales.

c Why do you think McGeorge implemented a perpetual inventory system rather than a periodic system?

P9-12 ***Inventory errors and the income statement (alternate to P9-1)***

The condensed income statement of Miller Distributors for the current year ended December 31 follows.

Sales	$154,300
Cost of goods sold	99,400
Gross profit	$ 54,900
Expenses	39,600
Net income	$ 15,300

The year-end review of the accounting records disclosed the following errors:

a Goods of $9,400 held on consignment from Sampson Manufacturing were accidentally included in the physical count of the ending inventory.

b A $7,200 purchase of merchandise was accidentally debited to the Equipment account on December 20. The merchandise was correctly included in the ending inventory count.

c Purchases amounting to $15,800 shipped F.O.B. destination had not arrived by December 31. The goods were debited to the Purchases account but excluded from the physical count of inventory.

INSTRUCTIONS

Prepare a corrected income statement.

P9-13 *Inventory valuation methods: Basic computations (alternate to P9-3)*

Long Sales Company began business on January 1. Purchases of merchandise during the year were as follows:

Jan. 2	500 units @ $2.00
Feb. 15	800 units @ $2.10
Apr. 8	2,200 units @ $2.40
July 30	3,500 units @ $2.50
Sept. 3	2,500 units @ $2.60
Nov. 18	3,000 units @ $2.60

During the year 10,800 units were sold: 4,000 units were sold for $3.80 per unit; the remainder were sold for $4.20 per unit. The firm uses a periodic inventory system.

INSTRUCTIONS

Determine Long's ending inventory balance, cost of goods sold, and gross profit under each of the following inventory valuation methods:

a First-in, first-out
b Last-in, first-out
c Weighted average (round all calculations to the nearest cent)

P9-14 *LIFO versus FIFO: Elimination of product line (alternate to P9-6)*

In 1981 Tyler Company began to carry a particular item in inventory. By the end of 1983 the item had been dropped from future marketing plans and all remaining inventory was sold. Purchases and sales were as follows:

	Purchases	Sales
1981	16,000 units @ $18	13,000 units @ $25
1982	21,000 units @ $20	23,000 units @ $29
1983	15,000 units @ $24	16,000 units @ $25

Tyler uses a periodic inventory system.

INSTRUCTIONS

a If Tyler used FIFO, compute gross profit for 1981, 1982, and 1983. What is the total gross profit for the three years together?
b If Tyler used LIFO, compute gross profit for 1981, 1982, and 1983. What is the total gross profit for the three years together?
c Which of the two methods would be more advantageous in terms of generating cash for Tyler's investment activities? Explain.

P9-15 *Gross profit method and tornado damage (alternate to P9-9)*

On March 11, 1983, a tornado heavily damaged the office and warehouse of Allan Wing Enterprises. The following information has been obtained.

1 Wing's condensed income statement for the year ended December 31, 1982, is as follows:

Net sales		*$280,000*
Cost of goods sold		
Beginning inventory	*$ 79,400*	
Add: Net purchases	*164,300*	
Goods available for sale	*$243,700*	
Less: Ending inventory	*92,500*	
Cost of goods sold		*151,200*
Gross profit		*$128,800*
Operating expenses		*77,300*
Net income		*$ 51,500*

2 Net sales and net purchases made through March 11 were $82,600 and $25,500, respectively.

3 Purchases entered on the accounting records but still in transit as of March 11 amounted to $2,350.

Wing's insurance company agreed to reimburse the firm for the tornado loss on the basis of an estimate of inventory using the gross profit method. The gross profit rate will be derived by examining last year's operating results.

INSTRUCTIONS

a Determine the cost of inventory on hand on March 11.

b Taking your answer above into consideration, assume inventory costing $18,500 was recovered and sold to a salvage firm for $8,400. Compute Wing's total loss from the tornado.

c Suppose Wing's inventory consisted of many different products with widely varying profit margins. What should Wing do to improve the accuracy of the inventory estimate?

P9-16 ***Retail method and inventory shrinkage (alternate to P9-10)***

Constable's, a department store, uses the retail method to estimate inventory. The following information was obtained from the accounting records for the year ended December 31.

Inventory, Jan. 1	
Cost	*$ 88,200*
Retail	*150,000*
Purchases	
Cost	*171,100*
Retail	*280,000*
Purchases returns	
Cost	*3,400*
Retail	*5,000*
Sales	*310,000*
Sales returns	*4,500*
Freight-in	*7,600*

INSTRUCTIONS

a Determine the cost of Constable's estimated inventory on December 31.

b Disregarding your answer in part (a), assume Constable's estimated ending inventory at retail totaled $110,000. If the firm's physical count on December 31 revealed an ending inventory at retail of $101,000, compute the cost of inventory shrinkage.

c Suppose Constable's accountant accidentally understated the cost-to-retail ratio at the end of the year. Determine whether this error would overstate, understate, or have no effect on the following: (1) total current assets; (2) the current year's cost of goods sold; (3) the current year's net income.

CASE 9
THE BISCAYNE COMPANY

The Biscayne Company, a newly organized Florida corporation, is composed of two divisions: Parts Manufacturing and Motor Car Sales. Both divisions presently use the LIFO method of inventory valuation. Because business is slumping, the controller has begun an in-depth review of operations.

The Parts Manufacturing division has experienced skyrocketing raw materials costs and labor difficulties. Two strikes by machinists and assemblers have been especially severe, causing Biscayne to close its plant for the past three months. Fortunately, existing finished goods inventories have been large enough to fill incoming sales orders.

The Motor Car Sales division has been hit with a sharp decline in sales, and the controller is contemplating a change from LIFO to FIFO. The year-end inventory under the LIFO method is anticipated to be $20 million. If FIFO is used, the ending inventory balance would increase to $28 million.

INSTRUCTIONS

a As the Parts Manufacturing division cuts deeper and deeper into finished goods inventory, which costs (high or low) will be charged to cost of goods sold?

b Given your answer in part (a), determine the effect of the strike on earnings per share and tax payments.

c Assuming the Motor Car Sales division is subject to a tax rate of 40%, determine the effect on net income of the shift from LIFO to FIFO.

d Present a detailed analysis to Biscayne's president regarding the advantages and disadvantages of making the shift.

10 PROPERTY, PLANT, AND EQUIPMENT: ACQUISITION AND DEPRECIATION

LEARNING OBJECTIVES

After reading this chapter you should:

1 Be able to differentiate between capital and revenue expenditures.

2 Be able to account for cash purchases of property, plant, and equipment; deferred payment plans; self-constructed assets; lump-sum purchases; and leasehold improvements.

3 Understand the meaning of "depreciation" as the term is used by accountants.

4 Understand the factors affecting the determination of service life.

5 Be able to compute depreciation by using the straight-line, units-of-output, double-declining balance, and sum-of-the-years'-digits methods.

6 Be familiar with the composite and inventory depreciation methods.

7 Understand the financial reporting issues and tax effects related to the various depreciation methods.

8 Recognize the common fallacies associated with depreciation and be able to revise a depreciation rate.

9 Understand the impact of inflation on reported property, plant, and equipment investments and on the associated depreciation computation.

CHAPTER 10

Many organizations invest large amounts of money in assets that are used to manufacture products or provide services. Greyhound Corporation, for example, recently reported an investment in such assets of over $1 billion, General Electric reported $12 billion, and IBM reported $30 billion. Assets with long lives acquired for use in business operations are termed **property, plant, and equipment** and include land, buildings, vehicles, office equipment, machinery, store equipment, and furniture and fixtures. This asset category is sometimes referred to as plant and equipment, plant assets, or fixed assets. Property, plant, and equipment is the most descriptive of these titles, however, and has gained the widest acceptance among accountants for the presentation of productive and service capacity on the balance sheet.

Long-lived assets must be currently used in a business to be classified as part of property, plant, and equipment. Idle buildings and machinery and land held for speculation or for future expansion are, thus, excluded from this asset category. These and similar assets are classified as long-term investments or other assets.

Assets appearing under the property, plant, and equipment caption are often viewed as long-term prepaid expenses. Why? Their acquisition entails an advance payment for years of future service. To explain, a firm that prepays rent for six months into the next accounting period will record a prepaid expense on its balance sheet. If that same firm purchases a building, it has, in essence, prepaid for the future services the building is expected to render.

Like prepaid expenses, items of property, plant, and equipment can only provide benefits for a certain period of time and are said to possess a limited service life. (An exception is land, which provides services indefinitely.) As a result, then, just as prepaid expenses become expenses when consumed, the amounts paid for plant and equipment are gradually charged to depreciation as the assets are used in operations.

There are several accounting issues related to property, plant, and equipment. This chapter and part of Chapter 11 will explore these issues and will serve to acquaint you with this important asset category.

DETERMINING THE COST OF PROPERTY, PLANT, AND EQUIPMENT

The cost of property, plant, and equipment includes expenditures related to acquisition (or construction) along with those required to ready the assets for business use. For the purchase of equipment such expenditures include the invoice price of the equipment, freight charges incurred by the buyer, insurance on the equipment while in transit, and installation costs such as special electrical wiring and initial testing. The cost of land includes the purchase price; attorney's fees; real estate (escrow) fees; commissions to a real estate broker; recording fees with the city or county; surveying costs; costs to clear, drain, and grade the land; and the assumption of any mortgages or delinquent property taxes from the seller. Thus if a company purchased a parcel of land by paying $45,000 and assuming $5,000 of delinquent property taxes and a $55,000 mortgage, the land is recorded at a cost of $105,000.

The rationale for the preceding accounting treatment is clear. Charging costs related to asset acquisition as expenses of the current period results in a mismatch of revenues and expenses. Property, plant, and equipment will serve a business for many years. Incidental expenditures such as freight, installation, and broker's fees are necessary for acquisition and for subsequent asset use to occur. In effect, then, these costs are providing long-run benefits and should be shown on the balance sheet as part of an asset's cost. Expenditures similar to those above that benefit future periods are commonly known as **capital expenditures.**

Expenditures related to asset acquisition and preparation that fail to provide future economic benefits are expenses. For example, if a piece of equipment was damaged while being installed, the repair costs should not be added to the cost of the equipment. Such an expenditure is an expense of the current accounting period. Likewise, if newly acquired equipment was being delivered on the buyer's truck and the truck was involved in a traffic accident, the cost of repairing the truck, any damages paid to other parties in the accident, and any fines levied on the driver are not added to the cost of the equipment. These outlays do not place the equipment in a position ready to serve the purchaser and are therefore expensed. Expenditures that fail to provide benefits to future periods are commonly known as **revenue expenditures.**

Cash Purchase

Property, plant, and equipment may be acquired in a variety of ways. One of the most frequently encountered methods is the **cash purchase.** The recorded asset cost in a cash purchase is the lowest cash price available to the buyer. For example, suppose Pizza Palace acquired a customized delivery van that has a list price of $20,000 and a negotiated purchase price of $12,000. Furthermore, assume the seller is offering a 5% cash discount if the invoice is paid within 7 days. The cost of the van is calculated as follows:

List price: irrelevant	*$20,000*
Negotiated purchase price	*$12,000*
Less: Cash discount ($12,000 × 0.05)	*600*
Accounting cost of the van	*$11,400*

The list price is totally irrelevant.[1] Recall that list price is used only as a guide in establishing the actual amount of the sale by the seller. In a discount store, for instance, you will find that virtually all items can be purchased at a cost well below their stated (and usually crossed out) list price. In a determination of the cost of the van, the negotiated purchase price is relevant; so, too, is the offer of the cash discount.

[1]The list price is sometimes referred to as the manufacturer's suggested retail price.

If Pizza Palace issued a check for $11,400, the van would be entered in the Delivery Equipment account for that amount. If the firm could not take advantage of the discount because of a lack of funds, the Delivery Equipment account would still be debited for $11,400. The $600 discount lost is treated as a financing expense of the current accounting period. The necessary journal entries for these two situations follow:

Case A: Negotiated Price of $12,000; Cash Discount of $600 Taken

Delivery Equipment	*11,400*	
Cash		*11,400*
To record purchase of van		

Case B: Negotiated Price of $12,000; Cash Discount of $600 Missed

Delivery Equipment	*11,400*	
Financing Expense	*600*	
Cash		*12,000*
To record purchase of van; discount missed		

Deferred Payment Plan

Property, plant, and equipment can also be acquired by using a **deferred payment plan.** Under such plans, a predetermined payment is sent to the seller each period (month, quarter, and so on) until the purchase price is paid off. A purchase of a new automobile through a bank loan is an example of a deferred payment plan. Each month the purchaser pays the bank a set amount. A portion of each payment represents interest for use of the bank's money; the remaining portion reduces the loan balance. At the end of the plan the bank sends the vehicle's title to the purchaser, because the loan balance has been reduced to zero. When a company purchases property, plant, and equipment on a deferred payment plan, it is important to recognize that any interest incurred is *not* included in the asset account. Interest is written off as an expense of the accounting period.

Self-Construction

Some companies construct their own assets. The cost of a **self-constructed asset** is equal to the material, labor, and indirect costs expended in the building process. Indirect costs, including such items as utilities and the salaries of supervisory personnel, often relate to more than one activity. Thus some form of allocation must be implemented to charge these costs back to specific programs and projects. The necessary allocation procedures are discussed later in this text.

Lump-Sum Purchase

Frequently, a business will purchase a number of assets together for a single amount. For example, the acquisition of developed property will often include such assets as buildings, parking lots, fences, and lawn sprinkler systems. Acquisitions of this type are termed **lump-sum purchases.** The cost of a lump-sum purchase must be apportioned among the various assets acquired for reporting and depreciation purposes. These assets generally benefit a business for different periods of time, thereby necessitating different depreciation rates.

Appraisals are frequently used to aid in the apportionment. To illustrate, we will assume that Dynamo Development Company purchased a building, land improvements (such as parking lots and lawn sprinkler systems), and land for $35,000,000 cash. The assets' appraisal values along with the necessary cost apportionment are as follows:

	Appraisal Value	Percentage of Total		Recorded Cost
Building	$20,000,000	50.0%	(20/40)	$17,500,000
Land improvements	3,000,000	7.5	(3/40)	2,625,000
Land	17,000,000	42.5	(17/40)	14,875,000
Total	$40,000,000	100.0%		$35,000,000

The acquisition cost is apportioned on the basis of an individual asset's appraised value relative to the value of the entire purchase. For example, because the building is 50% of the property's total appraised value ($20,000,000 ÷ $40,000,000), the cost of the building is established at $17,500,000 ($35,000,000 × 0.50). The recorded amounts for land improvements and land are determined in the same manner. The journal entry to record the purchase is therefore as follows:

Building	*17,500,000*	
Land Improvements	*2,625,000*	
Land	*14,875,000*	
Cash		*35,000,000*
To record acquisition of developed property		

Notice that a distinction is made between land and land improvements. It is necessary to establish separate accounts for these assets, because a parcel of land has an indefinite life while land improvements do not. As a result, land improvements are depreciated over the number of periods they render benefits or service to a business.

Companies sometimes acquire developed property and subsequently undertake a demolition program, thereby paving the way for new construction. To illustrate the necessary accounting, we will continue (and modify) the previous example. Assume that Dynamo intends to remove the building and land improvements so that the site can be used for a new sports stadium. In this instance the entire purchase price of $35,000,000 is debited to the Land account. The building and land improvements are not established as separate assets, because they will never serve the firm.

During the demolition work any costs incurred by Dynamo to prepare the land for construction are added to the Land account. Examples of such costs include the costs of razing the building or removing the improvements. Conversely, any proceeds received from selling materials that are salvaged from the demolition process are credited to Land. Thus the Land account includes all costs necessary to put the property in condition for its intended use.

Leasehold Improvements

Occasionally, buildings are constructed or land improvements are made on property leased by one party (the lessee) from another party (the lessor). The amounts expended for these assets by the lessee, called **leasehold improvements,** are recorded in an account of the same name and may be rather substantial. For example, Carter Hawley Hale Stores, Inc., an operator of department and high-fashion specialty stores, recently reported leasehold improvements of $155 million. Leasehold improvements normally become the property of the lessor at the end of the lease period. As such, the amounts expended are written off to expense over the remaining life of the lease or the life of the improvement, whichever is shorter.

Small Items of Property, Plant, and Equipment

Businesses purchase many long-lived items (such as tape dispensers, pencil sharpeners, and office clocks) that technically should be classified as property, plant, and equipment. Because of their insignificant purchase price, however, these items are not established as assets in the accounting records. Instead they are normally treated as revenue expenditures and written off as expenses in the period of acquisition. This procedure reduces paperwork costs and avoids depreciating small items over long periods of time. Imagine the record keeping associated with depreciating a $5 wastepaper basket over a ten-year life. Virtually all accountants would agree that the $0.50 annual write-off is hardly worth the effort.

To determine whether an outlay should be expensed or carried as an asset, most businesses establish a minimum cutoff in dollars. If, for example, a firm establishes a $100 cutoff, all expenditures of $100 or less would be deemed too small to be recorded as part of property, plant, and equipment and would be expensed. In contrast, expenditures exceeding $100 would be capitalized, that is, treated as assets in the accounts.

DEPRECIATION

As we previously noted, all items of property, plant, and equipment (except land) have limited lives and render services over several accounting periods. In recognition of the benefits received (and revenues generated), a portion of the cost of these assets should be expensed each year for proper matching on the income statement. A proper matching of revenues and expenses would not be attained if purchases of property, plant, and equipment were expensed entirely in the period of acquisition or, alternatively, upon retirement. In both cases many accounting periods would receive benefits from the assets' use without bearing any of the related expense.

The process used to allocate the cost of long-lived assets to the accounting periods benefited is known as **depreciation.** Be aware, however, that other definitions of depreciation are commonly encountered. For example, you may have heard new car owners mention the "depreciation" they have suffered since their purchase. To this group depreciation represents the difference between the amount paid for the car and the car's present resale value. Stated differently, depreciation is the decrease in value the owners have experienced. Observe that the preceding approach to asset measurement is used in economics but not in accounting. Property, plant, and equipment accounts make no attempt to incorporate information concerning the ever-changing market values of assets. Instead assets classified as property, plant, and equipment are recorded in the accounting records at cost. For depreciable assets this cost is subsequently allocated as expense to the years receiving service or benefits. In accounting, then, *depreciation is a process of allocation, not valuation.*

Determining Service Life

Before an asset's cost is allocated among the periods benefited, a service life must be estimated. **Service life,** sometimes called economic or useful life, is the period of time that depreciable assets provide service to a business. It is important to understand that an asset's service life is frequently different from its physical life. That is, an asset may have physical existence long after its useful life to a business has concluded. Witness, for example, the abandoned equipment around mines and the numerous railroad tracks that are no longer used by their owners.

When determining an asset's service life, we must consider three factors: physical deterioration, obsolescence, and inadequacy.

Physical deterioration

The physical deterioration of an asset, sometimes termed "wear and tear," is caused by use in the normal course of business. Repair and maintenance may prolong an asset's service life, but at some point the asset usually requires replacement because it has become worn out. Physical deterioration normally establishes the maximum limit for the estimate of service life.

Obsolescence

Obsolescence is a technological factor relating to being out of date. New technology frequently shortens the service life of assets well before their physical life is over. Businesses using obsolete machines, for example, cannot compete effectively with companies using modern, more efficient equipment. Obsolescence has been a significant factor in shortening the service life of computers. Recent advances in engineering have been dramatic. Businesses that purchased a computer three to five years ago are finding that smaller, faster, and less expensive models are now available, making their equipment out of date and less desirable.

Inadequacy

Business growth may cause certain items of depreciable property, plant, and equipment to become inadequate in their service capabilities. Plants may become unable to keep pace with demand, trucks may become too small, and equipment may become too slow. When assets are inadequate to meet the competitive needs of a business, their service lives have ended. Like obsolescence, inadequacy is an economic (as opposed to physical) determinant of service life.

All three factors above should be considered when determining the service life of a depreciable asset. It is conceivable, of course, that one factor may be more important than the others for certain assets. Consider, for example, a small commuter airline that desires to expand and begin service to large metropolitan areas. The airline may find that the service life of its flight equipment is determined primarily by the factor of inadequacy. On the other hand, a high-precision manufacturer that uses advanced electronics may view obsolescence as the most important determinant of service life for much of its equipment.

In other business situations all the factors may be equally important for a particular depreciable asset. In these cases estimating service life becomes more difficult. Companies having no experience with a particular type of asset may seek guidance from their accountants, engineers, trade associations, or the asset's seller.

Is there only one life?

Identical items of property, plant, and equipment frequently have different service lives in different businesses. And all may be correct! Managements' views of the effects of obsolescence sometimes differ. In addition, varying business objectives often make inadequacy an important factor for some companies and an irrelevant factor for others. Furthermore, assets are subjected to varying degrees of physical deterioration because of different repair schedules and different operating environments. Exhibit 10-1 contains a sample of estimated service lives obtained from recent corporate annual reports. The exhibit shows the variety inherent in the estimation decision.

Exhibit 10-1

Comparisons of estimated service life

Corporation	Asset	Service Life (Years)
Allied Department Stores	Store buildings and warehouses	40–50
Hilton Hotels	Buildings	10–55
	Furniture and equipment	8
Nabisco, Inc.	Buildings	20–40
	Machinery and equipment	3–20
Vail Associates, Inc.	Ski lifts	10–14
	Ski trails	20–30, depending on the trail
	Buildings and terminals	20–45, depending on the structure

As a depreciable asset is sold, each new owner will determine a new service life. For example, a posh limousine may have an estimated service life of 3 years to an urban limousine company before a new model must be purchased to retain wealthy clientele. Suppose that after 3 years the vehicle is sold to a shuttle service, which is concerned primarily with transporting passengers from downtown hotels to the local airport. Vehicle appearance and "snob appeal" are secondary in importance. The limousine may have a life of 7 years to the shuttle business, until a larger minibus is needed due to growth. The vehicle could then be sold again, this time to a business that offers college students discount fares for cross-country travel. Given the limousine's condition and mileage, the third owner may anticipate use for only 1 year. Importantly, notice how each company evaluated the factors affecting service life in a different way. The urban limousine company focused on obsolescence, the airport shuttle company stressed inadequacy, and the cross-country travel business emphasized physical deterioration.

Methods of Depreciation

There are several acceptable methods for computing depreciation. The four methods used most frequently are straight-line, units-of-output, double-declining balance, and sum-of-the-years'-digits. Exhibit 10-2 discloses the variation in depreciation policies of several large corporations.

Exhibit 10-2

Comparison of depreciation policies

Corporation	Depreciation Method(s)
Eastman Kodak Company	Generally sum-of-the-years'-digits for all assets in the United States and the straight-line method for assets outside the United States.
General Motors Corporation	Calculated on groups of property by using, with minor exceptions, an accelerated method which accumulates depreciation of approximately two-thirds of the depreciable cost during the first half of the estimated lives of the property.
Texas Instruments, Inc.	Double-declining balance or sum-of-the-years'-digits method, depending on the depreciable asset.
Zenith Radio Corporation	Straight-line method for additions of plant and equipment since 1972, with useful lives of 8 years or more; accelerated methods for substantially all other plant and equipment items, including shorter-lived high-technology equipment, which may be subject to rapid economic obsolescence.

Straight-line method

Largely because of its simplicity, the straight-line method is the most popular way to compute depreciation. The **straight-line method** allocates the cost of a depreciable asset, less residual value, equally over the estimated service life. The **residual value** (sometimes called salvage value) is the amount a business expects to receive upon disposal of an asset at the end of the asset's life. Given the nature of the allocation, the straight-line method is best applied to assets that provide constant, uniform service to a business.

To illustrate the straight-line method, assume WBBB-TV bought a new television camera for \$30,000. The camera has an estimated residual value of \$3,000 and an estimated service life of 5 years. The annual depreciation expense is computed as follows:

$$\frac{\text{cost} - \text{residual value}}{\text{service life in years}} = \frac{\$30{,}000 - \$3{,}000}{5 \text{ years}} = \$5{,}400 \text{ annual depreciation}$$

The deduction of the $3,000 residual value from the asset's cost of $30,000 yields a **depreciable base** of $27,000, the total amount that will be written off to depreciation expense over the asset's life.

The journal entries to record depreciation for the first two years of the camera's life are as follows:

Year 1

Depreciation Expense: TV Camera	5,400	
Accumulated Depreciation: TV Camera		5,400
To record annual depreciation expense		

Year 2

Depreciation Expense: TV Camera	5,400	
Accumulated Depreciation: TV Camera		5,400
To record annual depreciation expense		

On the income statement WBBB-TV would report annual depreciation expense of $5,400. On the balance sheet the camera would be shown as follows:

	Year 1	Year 2
Property, plant, & equipment		
Television camera	$30,000	$30,000
Less: Accumulated depreciation	5,400	10,800
	$24,600	$19,200

These figures reveal that accumulated depreciation increases by $5,400 during each year of service life. Recall that the cost of an asset less accumulated depreciation is termed **book value.** As the accompanying schedule shows, book value decreases each year and equals the residual value ($3,000) at the end of the camera's life. The asset is said to be fully depreciated at this point and no further depreciation is recorded. If the estimate of service life was correct, the camera should be of no further use to the company.

Year	Depreciation Expense	Accumulated Depreciation	Book Value
			$30,000
1	$5,400	$ 5,400	24,600
2	5,400	10,800	19,200
3	5,400	16,200	13,800
4	5,400	21,600	8,400
5	5,400	27,000	3,000

Businesses using the straight-line method often convert their service lives to percentages. For example, annual depreciation on an asset having a 50-year service life would be 2% of the depreciable base, because the fraction $\frac{1}{50}$ is equal to 2%. Likewise, an asset with a 10-year service life is depreciated at a rate of $\frac{1}{10}$ or 10% per year.

Partial periods

In the preceding example we assumed the camera was acquired on January 1. If the purchase was made later in the year, WBBB would record a prorated percentage of the annual depreciation charge. Assuming acquisition on May 1, depreciation for the first year would be \$3,600 (\$5,400 × $\frac{8}{12}$), because the asset provided services for only 8 months. The remaining depreciation expense would then be \$5,400 for Years 2, 3, 4, and 5 and \$1,800 (\$5,400 × $\frac{4}{12}$) for the first 4 months of Year 6. As before, depreciation totals \$27,000 and is recorded over 5 years of service.

Asset purchases do not always take place on the first day of the month. Most companies have established their own practices for recording depreciation in this situation. For example, when a depreciable asset is acquired during the first 15 days of a month, the purchase is often handled as if it occurred on the first day of the month. If the asset is acquired in the last half of a month, the transaction is treated as occurring on the first day of the following month, and the depreciation computation commences at this time. Other companies record one-half of the first full year's depreciation in the year of acquisition regardless of the date of purchase. Such an approach simplifies the depreciation computation because acquisition dates are ignored. These and other similar practices are acceptable as long as they are followed consistently.

Units-of-output method

The **units-of-output method**, sometimes called the units-of-production or activity method, is frequently used when an asset's service life can be expressed in terms of output (such as miles, hours, or number of times used). Under this method the asset's cost, less residual value, is divided by the total estimated output during the service life. This computation generates the depreciation rate. Annual depreciation expense is then calculated by multiplying the depreciation rate by the yearly output. To illustrate, assume a large corporation purchased a business jet for \$4,000,000 that has a residual value of \$1,500,000. The service life is estimated to be 10,000 flying hours. The depreciation rate is calculated as follows:

$$\frac{\text{cost} - \text{residual value}}{\text{service life in output}} = \frac{\$4{,}000{,}000 - \$1{,}500{,}000}{10{,}000 \text{ flying hours}} = \$250 \text{ per flying hour}$$

If the jet was used for 500 hours during the year, depreciation expense would total \$125,000 (\$250 × 500).

The units-of-output method is used when (1) the service capacity of an asset can be reasonably estimated and (2) there is a direct relationship between an asset's use and its decline in service potential. Assets that meet these two criteria include cars, trucks, and machines. In situations where the amount of an asset's output varies considerably from period to period, the units-of-output method permits a better allocation of cost than do the straight-line or other depreciation methods. For example, in years of great activity more of an asset's cost would be depreciated and matched against revenues; in years of low activity less depreciation expense is recorded. In contrast, the straight-line method produces a constant depreciation charge regardless of the services provided.

Accelerated depreciation methods

The two remaining depreciation methods are double-declining balance and sum-of-the-years'-digits. Both methods speed up or accelerate the recognition of depreciation expense. **Accelerated depreciation methods** generate relatively large amounts of depreciation in the early years of asset use and small amounts in later years.

There are a variety of reasons why businesses may prefer to use an accelerated depreciation method. First, companies recognize that the services provided by many assets are superior when the assets are new and decline over time. For example, consider the transportation services provided by a new car versus those of a less dependable older model. Or note the quality of machining obtained from a new high-precision drill press versus that from an older press with less accurate tolerances. If the services provided are actually greater in the earlier years of asset use, a proper matching of revenues and expenses dictates a gradual reduction in depreciation charges over an asset's lifetime.

Another reason for using an accelerated depreciation method is that repair and maintenance costs normally increase as an asset grows older. When combined with a decreasing amount of depreciation from an accelerated method, the total amount of yearly expense is leveled. The end result is a better matching of expenses against revenues than would be possible by the straight-line method for assets furnishing uniform service.

A final reason for using accelerated depreciation is profit- and tax-related. Because of their large write-offs, accelerated methods lower net income in the early years of asset use. With lower net income there is less demand for higher dividends from stockholders, less demand for salary increases by employees, and reduced federal income tax expense.

Depreciation and taxes

Focusing on the tax obligation for a moment, companies are permitted to use accelerated depreciation methods not only for financial reporting but for tax purposes as well. The advantage is that smaller tax payments allow a greater retention of cash for investment purposes. Sometimes, though, the best laid plans of mice and men go awry. In the late 1970s and very early 1980s, for example, the economy was sluggish and businesses were not investing. Specifically, existing plant and equipment were not being replaced with newer assets reflecting improved technology and efficiency. As a result, Congress established a new Accelerated Cost Recovery System (ACRS) as part of the Economic Recovery Tax Act of 1981.

For most property placed in service after 1980, the final depreciation calculation is no longer based on the service life of the underlying asset. Instead, *for tax purposes only*, assets are depreciated over specified predetermined "recovery periods," which are generally shorter than existing service lives. An automobile, for example, has a 3-year recovery period, while most machinery, equipment, and furniture is written off over 5 years. Furthermore, assets are depreciated by using accelerated methods that incorporate changes from one method to another, thereby resulting in a maximized tax deduction. The anticipated outcome of the ACRS is an increase in capital investment by business and overall growth in our economy.

Interestingly, businesses often use the ACRS for income tax purposes and either straight-line or units-of-output depreciation for financial reporting. This practice is neither devious nor illegal, because taxation and financial statement presentation serve different purposes. The main objectives of income taxation are to raise revenues to operate the federal government, stimulate economic growth, and redistribute wealth. In contrast, financial reporting strives to develop a comprehensive set of statements that adequately measure and disclose the results of business activity. Companies that use the straight-line depreciation method for financial reporting and the ACRS for taxes are in the enviable position of showing their owners higher profits while generating cash (via faster write-offs) for future investment.

Double-declining balance method

As we noted earlier, the **double-declining balance method** is one form of accelerated depreciation. When employing double-declining balance, a firm initially calculates a percentage depreciation rate by the straight-line method. This rate is then doubled and multiplied by the remaining book value (i.e., a declining balance) each period. Observe that residual value is ignored in the computation, thereby permitting even greater depreciation expense in the early years. Bear in mind, however, that when depreciating an asset, the asset's book value *cannot* be reduced below estimated residual value.

Applying the double-declining balance method to the television camera example cited earlier (cost, \$30,000; residual value, \$3,000; service life, 5 years), we obtain the accompanying depreciation schedule.

Year	Depreciation Expense	Accumulated Depreciation	Book Value
			\$30,000
1	\$12,000 (\$30,000 × 40%)	\$12,000	18,000
2	7,200 (\$18,000 × 40%)	19,200	10,800
3	4,320 (\$10,800 × 40%)	23,520	6,480
4	2,592 (\$6,480 × 40%)	26,112	3,888
5	888 (\$3,888 − \$3,000)	27,000	3,000

To explain, with the 5-year service life, the straight-line depreciation rate is $\frac{1}{5}$ or 20% per year. The double-declining balance rate, therefore, is 40% (2 × 20%). Depreciation expense in the first year is 40% times the \$30,000 book value, or \$12,000. The journal entry to record depreciation at the end of the year places $12,000 in the Accumulated Depreciation account, thus reducing the camera's book value to $18,000. Depreciation in the second year falls to $7,200, that is, book value of $18,000 × 40%. In the same manner, the third year's depreciation is $4,320 ($10,800 × 40%), and the fourth year's depreciation is $2,592 ($6,480 × 40%). The last year of service life is handled differently. If we continued with the same approach, depreciation expense in the fifth year would be $1,555 ($3,888 × 40%). However, the camera's book value would be reduced to $2,333 ($3,888 − $1,555), which is below the $3,000 estimated residual value. Thus depreciation expense in the fifth year amounts to only $888 ($3,888 − $3,000).

If the television camera had been purchased on October 1, depreciation expense would be computed for only 3 months in Year 1. The calculation would be [($30,000 × 40%) × $\frac{3}{12}$], or $3,000. The procedures to calculate depreciation expense in all future years are the same as in the illustration above. For example, because book value at the beginning of Year 2 would be $27,000 ($30,000 − $3,000), depreciation expense for the second year is $10,800 ($27,000 × 40%).

Sum-of-the-years'-digits method

Similar to the double-declining balance method, the **sum-of-the-years'-digits method** also produces more depreciation expense in the early years of asset use. Under this approach a successively lower depreciation rate is applied each year to a constant depreciable base (cost less residual value). The rate, which is really a fraction, is derived by setting the numerator equal to the remaining years of service life; the denominator, in turn, equals the total of the service years. In the case of the television camera, which has a 5-year life, the denominator equals 15 (5 + 4 + 3 + 2 + 1 = 15). Similarly, for assets having a 4-year life, the denominator would be 10 (4 + 3 + 2 + 1 = 10). Continuing the camera example, the numerator for the first year is 5 because 5 years of service life remain; then 4 for the second year, and so forth. WBBB's depreciation schedule using the sum-of-the-years'-digits method follows.

Year	Depreciation Expense	Accumulated Depreciation	Book Value
			$30,000
1	$9,000 ($27,000 × $\frac{5}{15}$)	$ 9,000	21,000
2	7,200 ($27,000 × $\frac{4}{15}$)	16,200	13,800
3	5,400 ($27,000 × $\frac{3}{15}$)	21,600	8,400
4	3,600 ($27,000 × $\frac{2}{15}$)	25,200	4,800
5	1,800 ($27,000 × $\frac{1}{15}$)	27,000	3,000

For assets acquired during the year, the allocation of cost over the service life is more complex. The key to understanding the necessary procedures is to recognize that each fraction ($\frac{5}{15}$, $\frac{4}{15}$, $\frac{3}{15}$, and so on) must be employed for 12 months no matter when the asset is acquired. For example, if the camera was purchased on April 1 and used for 9 months, the $\frac{5}{15}$ rate would be applied for the remainder of Year 1, producing depreciation expense of $6,750 [($27,000 × $\frac{5}{15}$) × $\frac{9}{12}$]. Depreciation expense for the second year totals $7,650 and is computed by using the $\frac{5}{15}$ rate for 3 months and the $\frac{4}{15}$ rate for 9 months; specifically,

$$\$27{,}000 \times \tfrac{5}{15} \times \tfrac{3}{12} = \$2{,}250$$
$$27{,}000 \times \tfrac{4}{15} \times \tfrac{9}{12} = 5{,}400$$
$$\underline{\underline{\$7{,}650}}$$

This process continues into Year 6 and is shown in Exhibit 10-3.

Comparison of depreciation methods

Exhibit 10-4 shows the annual depreciation expense for the three depreciation methods used for the television camera: straight-line, double-declining balance, and sum-of-the-years'-digits. The units-of-output method is disregarded here because the camera's service capacity in units could not be reasonably estimated.

As you can see, the straight-line method generates constant depreciation expense of $5,400 per year. This amount is significantly lower than the expense produced by the accelerated methods in the first year, slightly lower in the second year, equal to sum-of-the-years'-digits and greater than double-declining balance in the third year, and higher than both in the fourth and fifth years. Because of the constant charge against revenues, those companies desiring to portray financial stability on their income statements prefer the straight-line method.

Of the two accelerated methods, observe that double-declining balance produced more depreciation expense in the first year than sum-of-the-years'-digits ($12,000 versus $9,000). In the second year both methods generated identical results. Finally, in the three subsequent years, sum-of-the-years'-digits depreciation exceeded that computed under the double-declining balance approach.

By summing the annual charges, you will see that the same total amount is ultimately written off by all three methods, namely, cost less residual value ($27,000 in this example). Only the amounts of the yearly allocations differ. Which method, then, should be selected? The answer to this question depends on a number of factors, including usage patterns, the generation of revenues and operating efficiencies, obsolescence, and the timing of repair costs. Conceptually, the method selected should be the one that best follows the services delivered or benefits provided by the asset. Such a

Exhibit 10-3

Sum-of-the-years'-digits depreciation and fractional periods

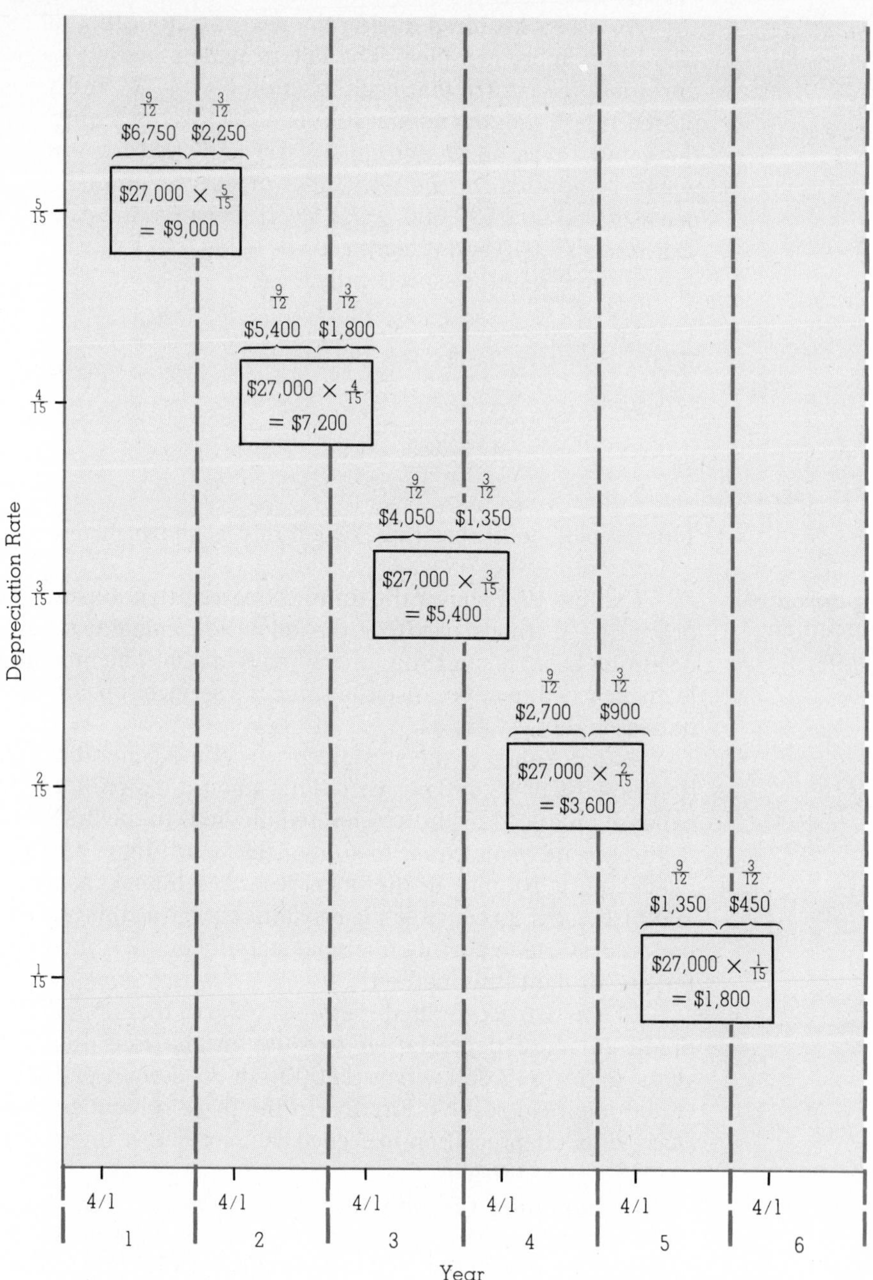

Exhibit 10-4

Comparison of annual depreciation expense

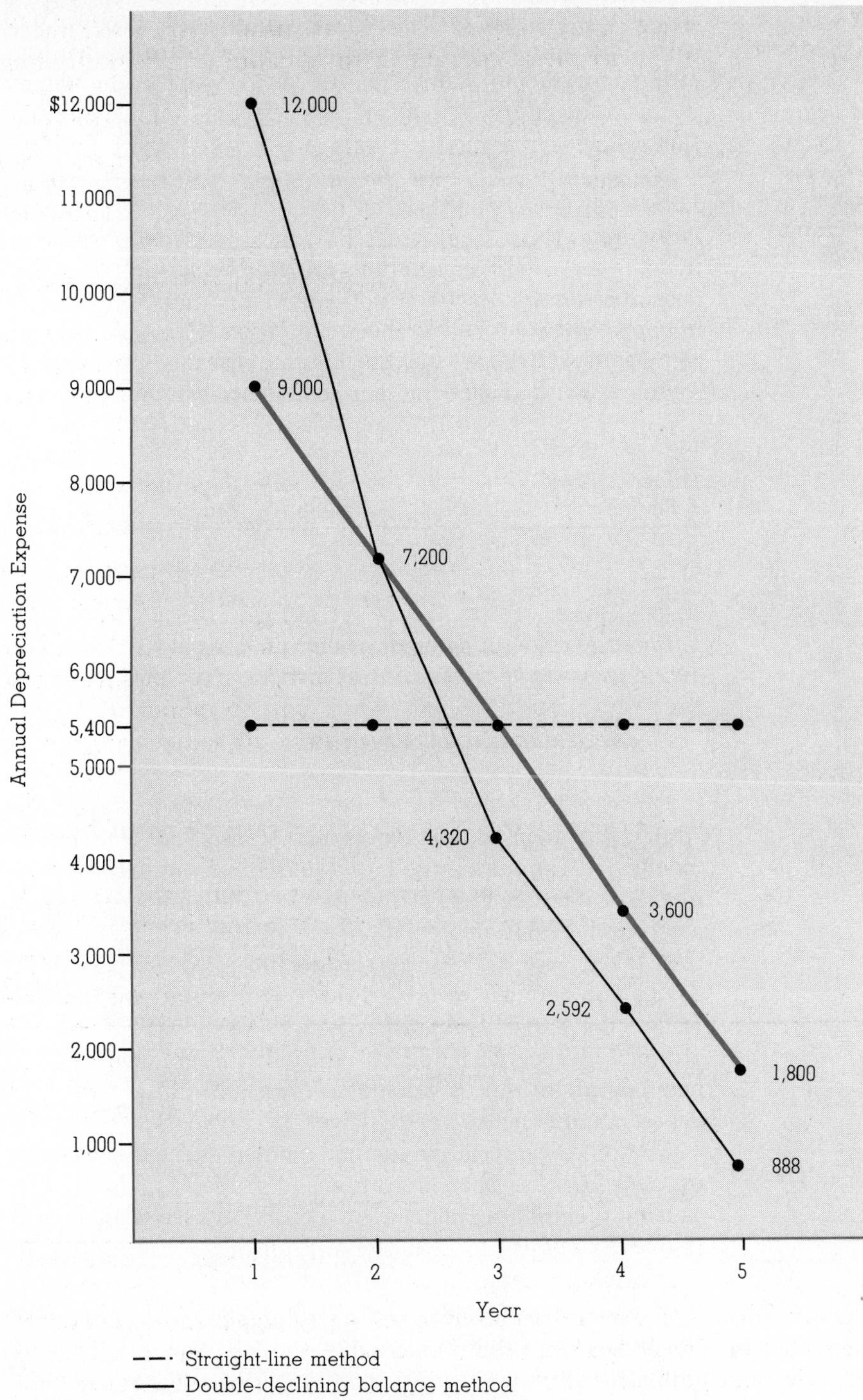

selection is consistent with proper matching of revenues and expenses. Because the pattern of service is sometimes difficult to measure, practice often differs from theory. Tax savings and attractive income statements, for example, have been known to have an "occasional" impact on the selection decision.

Other depreciation methods

In our discussion thus far, depreciation expense has been calculated on individual assets. Companies having thousands of depreciable items find that the required computations and record keeping can be extremely burdensome, even with the aid of calculators and computers. The **composite method** overcomes this problem and depreciates groups of assets by using a composite or average rate. To illustrate this method, assume that Mountain Airlines has the following depreciable assets:

Property, Plant, & Equipment	*Cost*	*Residual Value*	*Depreciable Base*	*Service Life (Years)*	*Annual Straight-Line Depreciation*
Plane	$260,000	$60,000	$200,000	20	$10,000
Ground equipment	25,000	5,000	20,000	10	2,000
Automobiles	15,000	3,000	12,000	4	3,000
	$300,000	$68,000	$232,000		$15,000

$$\textbf{composite rate} = \frac{\$15{,}000}{\$300{,}000} = 5\%$$

The composite rate is determined by (1) calculating the annual straight-line depreciation for each asset (or group of assets, as with the automobiles), (2) summing the individual annual amounts to arrive at total annual depreciation, and (3) dividing the total annual depreciation by the total asset cost. Yearly depreciation expense of $15,000 ($300,000 × 0.05) is then taken over the group's service life until the book value of the group equals $68,000 (the residual value). This situation occurs at the end of the weighted-average service life of 15.47 years ($232,000 ÷ $15,000). If the group of assets changes significantly because of acquisitions or disposals, a new composite rate is calculated for determining subsequent amounts of depreciation expense.

Another depreciation method, known as the **inventory method,** is often used for low-cost, short-lived items of property, plant, and equipment such as hand tools. These items are too costly to keep track of separately and are frequently subject to breakage and pilferage. Accounting for assets under the inventory depreciation method resembles the treatment afforded to a prepaid expense such as office supplies. Just as supplies expense represents the amount of supplies used, the amount in the Depreciation Expense account depicts the cost of the asset consumed during the period. Tool depreciation, for example, is computed by taking the value of the beginning tool inventory plus the cost of tool purchases during the year minus the value of the ending tool inventory.

Depreciation: Two Common Fallacies

There are two common fallacies about depreciation. The first is that depreciation generates funds. This belief arises because, unlike most expenses, depreciation involves no cash payment; thus many people assume a business is "saving money" and generating cash. We could make depreciation entries all day and through the night and still not have a nickel for our efforts. The Cash account is not increased nor is any current liability reduced by our debits to Depreciation Expense and credits to Accumulated Depreciation. Depreciation is simply an allocation of cost over an estimated service life. As we discussed earlier, however, depreciation does reduce income tax payments. While this reduction may allow a firm to retain cash for business purposes, the mere act of recording depreciation in the accounting records does not create funds.

The second fallacy is that the Accumulated Depreciation account contains cash that will be used to replace existing depreciable assets at the end of their service lives. There is no cash in the Accumulated Depreciation account; all cash is in the Cash account. The Accumulated Depreciation account represents the total portion of an asset's cost that has been charged to expense, nothing more, nothing less.

Revision of Depreciation Rates

The calculation of depreciation depends on two estimates: service life and residual value. Estimates, of course, are subject to change and are often incorrect. To illustrate, unanticipated suburban growth and new developments on the outskirts of town may shorten the service life of buildings located in older, central-city areas. Equipment may be useful for fewer years owing to new technology. Or residual values may need revision because of economic developments occurring after an asset was placed in service.

When new information alters the estimates used for service life and residual value, the yearly depreciation computation must be changed. This change is achieved by allocating the asset's remaining depreciable base over the remaining service life. Corrections of previous years' depreciation amounts are *not* made, because the estimates were made in good faith.

To illustrate the revision of a depreciation rate, assume Patriot Company purchased a building 10 years ago for $5,000,000. The building had a $1,000,000 residual value and an estimated 40-year service life when acquired. Assuming Patriot uses the straight-line depreciation method, depreciation of $100,000 [($5,000,000 − $1,000,000) ÷ 40] has been recorded annually for 10 years. The Accumulated Depreciation account as a result presently totals $1,000,000. Because of altered traffic patterns, management now anticipates a remaining service life of only 20 years. Beginning with the current accounting period, the revised depreciation expense will be $150,000 per year. The necessary computations follow:

THE IMPACT OF INFLATION ON PROPERTY, PLANT, AND EQUIPMENT INVESTMENTS

Comments by the Management of Holiday Inns, Inc.

Present financial reporting based on actual (historical) dollars does not reflect the economic changes caused by inflation. To help measure the impact of inflation, certain financial information has been developed using methods prescribed by the Financial Accounting Standards Board.

During inflationary times, even though the book value of property and equipment may decrease because of depreciation charges, these assets, properly maintained, tend to increase in value. . . . At the end of 1980, the current [cost] of the company's net property and equipment approximated $1.9 billion compared to a historical cost of $1.1 billion.

Current cost data for buildings and improvements, furniture, fixtures, and equipment were calculated on a property-by-property basis considering the current standards for construction and furnishings, the physical features of the property, the market served, the currently experienced cost of labor and materials, and other local conditions. Current cost of vessels was determined by applying an index of shipyard construction cost to the historical vessel cost. [Authors' note: Among its many holdings, Holiday Inns, Inc., owns Delta Steamship Lines, Inc.]

Comments by the Management of Marriott Corporation

Historical-cost accounting understates Marriott's asset values and debt capacity. . . . The company's fixed assets are principally real estate, with building and equipment depreciated according to industry accounting standards. For example, the average depreciated book value per room of Marriott's owned hotel rooms is $32,000. Yet hotels, unlike industrial plants, are appreciating assets. As reflected in the current value statement, this results in an appraisal increment of $410 million for Marriott's owned hotel assets.

In 1980, Marriott operated 16,500 rooms under management agreements with an average life of 70 years and generating $45 million in operating profits that tend to rise with inflation. These agreements have no stated value on Marriott's historical-cost balance sheet. However, they have an estimated current value of $326 million.

When the current value of Marriott's real estate assets and management agreements is reflected on its balance sheet, the magnitude of the company's debt capacity becomes more apparent. Moreover, the failure to recognize the highly liquid nature of Marriott's hotels understates the company's potential investment capacity.

SOURCE Adapted from the 1980 Annual Reports of Holiday Inns, Inc., and Marriott Corporation.

Building cost	$5,000,000
Less: Residual value	1,000,000
Depreciable base	$4,000,000
Less: Depreciation already taken	1,000,000
Remaining depreciable base	$3,000,000
Remaining life	20 years
Depreciation per year	$3,000,000 ÷ 20 = $150,000

If the remaining service life had been extended to 50 years, annual depreciation expense would have decreased to $60,000 ($3,000,000 ÷ 50).

Disclosure of Depreciation in the Financial Statements

Most companies establish separate depreciation accounts for each major group of depreciable assets, for example, buildings, equipment, furniture and fixtures, and so on. Such breakdowns are helpful for internal management analysis as well as for external reporting. For external reporting, however, practices vary widely. On the income statement, for example, most large companies combine all the depreciation expense accounts and report a single depreciation figure. Turning to the balance sheet, businesses present accumulated depreciation accounts either for each major asset group (see p. 220) or as a combined total. To illustrate the latter approach, Royal Crown Companies, Inc., recently disclosed property, plant, and equipment (in thousands) as follows:

Land	$ 13,447
Buildings	51,108
Production equipment	72,934
Delivery equipment	31,083
	$168,572
Less: Accumulated depreciation	69,097
	$ 99,475

INFLATION AND PROPERTY, PLANT, AND EQUIPMENT

Inflation has been a critical problem in the United States and throughout the world for the past fifteen to twenty years. Prices have risen significantly, and this trend is likely to continue in the future. Businesses are finding that the cost of replacing property, plant, and equipment is much higher than the original acquisition cost. This observation is especially true for firms that have substantial investments in real estate, where soaring costs have been the rule rather than the exception. To illustrate the magnitude of the problem, we present the excerpt on page 394. The excerpt contains comments by the managements of Holiday Inns, Inc., and Marriott Corporation relating to inflation's impact on historical-cost accounting systems.

Depreciation and Inflation

As you probably gathered from the excerpt, inflation can result in a serious understatement of asset valuations on the balance sheet. This understatement, in turn, leads to problems in income measurement. To explain, recording property, plant, and equipment at cost and depreciating cost over the service life seems appropriate for periods of stable prices. In inflationary times, however, the matching of old, historical costs against current revenues could mislead financial statement users. Profits may be overstated because depreciation is based on costs incurred many years ago, prior to recent inflationary spirals.

As we noted in the previous chapter, the FASB has been active in requiring companies to show the effects of inflation on their financial statements. Specifically, the FASB now requires disclosure by large corporations concerning the current cost of property, plant, and equipment and depreciation calculated on a current cost basis.[2] **Current cost** is defined as the present cost to purchase or manufacture assets having the same service potential as the assets already owned. Importantly, current cost is *not* integrated into the financial statements and used as a substitute for historical cost. Rather the necessary information is provided to statement users by supplementary comments (perhaps through a footnote).

Unfortunately, the computation of current cost is extremely troublesome. Picture the problems associated with figuring the cost to replace a large manufacturing plant. The plant may have thousands of complex machines, many of which are either custom-made or no longer obtainable from suppliers. Needless to say, the required computations would involve numerous assumptions and estimates. Even though inaccuracies are involved, many accountants believe that the FASB's rulings are a step in the right direction. The information should be interpreted with care, however. The management of Consolidated Foods, a large conglomerate known for such products as Shasta beverages, L'eggs, Sara Lee baked goods, Popsicle, and Electrolux floor care products, succinctly notes the following:

> *The corporation is in agreement with current attempts being made to provide a means of measuring inflationary effects on historical results and believes that the current cost method is more appropriate since it attempts to approximate actual costs. However, since the FASB's recommended methods require assumptions, approximations and subjective evaluations and are still in the experimental stage, the usefulness of the data can only be assessed by the future experience of preparers and users. Accordingly, this supplemental information should be viewed as an attempt to approximate, in a limited manner, the effects of changing prices rather than to measure them precisely.*[3]

SUMMARY PROBLEM

On January 1, 1982, Hardy Company acquired an automatic can labeler for $63,000, which included shipping charges of $1,000. The machine has an esti-

[2]See "Financial Reporting and Changing Prices," *Statement of Financial Accounting Standards No. 33* (Stamford, Conn.: Financial Accounting Standards Board, 1979).
[3]Consolidated Foods Corporation 1981 Annual Report, p. 57.

mated service life of 5 years (or 30,000 hours of operation) and a residual value of $6,000. Insurance on the machine while in transit was $300. Insurance on the machine against fire and water damage for one year amounted to $500. Finally, installation costs were $2,000 and test runs totaled $700.

During the five years of use (1982–1986), the machine was operated for 6,300, 6,000, 5,800, 5,700, and 6,200 hours, respectively.

INSTRUCTIONS

a Compute the machine's cost.

b Rounding final calculations to the nearest dollar, compute annual depreciation expense by using each of the following methods: (1) straight-line; (2) units-of-output; (3) double-declining balance; (4) sum-of-the-years'-digits.

c Explain why plant assets are depreciated as opposed to being expensed entirely in the year of acquisition.

SOLUTION

a

Purchase price (including shipping)	$63,000
Insurance in transit	300
Installation	2,000
Test runs	700
Total cost	$66,000

b (1) Straight-line:

$$\frac{\text{cost} - \text{residual value}}{\text{service life in years}} = \text{annual depreciation}$$

$$\frac{\$66{,}000 - \$6{,}000}{5} = \$12{,}000$$

(2) Units-of-output:

$$\frac{\text{cost} - \text{residual value}}{\text{service life in output}} = \text{depreciation per unit of output}$$

$$\frac{\$66{,}000 - \$6{,}000}{30{,}000} = \$2.00 \text{ per hour}$$

Year	Hours of Operation	×	Depreciation per Hour	=	Depreciation Expense
1982	6,300		$2.00		$12,600
1983	6,000		2.00		12,000
1984	5,800		2.00		11,600
1985	5,700		2.00		11,400
1986	6,200		2.00		12,400

(3) Double-declining balance:

$$\text{5-year life} = \frac{1}{5} = 20\% \times 2 = 40\% \text{ depreciation rate}$$

Year	Depreciation Expense	Accumulated Depreciation	Book Value
			$66,000
1982	$26,400 ($66,000 × 40%)	$26,400	39,600
1983	15,840 ($39,600 × 40%)	42,240	23,760
1984	9,504 ($23,760 × 40%)	51,744	14,256
1985	5,702 ($14,256 × 40%)	57,446	8,554
1986	2,554 ($8,554 − $6,000)*	60,000	6,000

**$8,554 × 40% would reduce the book value below residual value.*

(4) *Sum-of-the-years'-digits:*

Year	Depreciation Expense
1982	$20,000 ($60,000 × $\frac{5}{15}$)
1983	16,000 ($60,000 × $\frac{4}{15}$)
1984	12,000 ($60,000 × $\frac{3}{15}$)
1985	8,000 ($60,000 × $\frac{2}{15}$)
1986	4,000 ($60,000 × $\frac{1}{15}$)

c ***Plant assets have long lives and have years of future service potential. Expensing the entire cost when acquired would result in a mismatch of revenues and expenses on the income statement.***

KEY TERMS AND CONCEPTS

accelerated depreciation 386
book value 384
capital expenditure 377
composite depreciation 392
current cost 396
deferred payment plan 378
depreciable base 384
depreciation 380
double-declining balance depreciation 387
inadequacy 381
inventory depreciation method 392
land improvements 379
leasehold improvements 380
lump-sum purchase 378
obsolescence 381
physical deterioration 381
property, plant, and equipment 376
residual value 383
revenue expenditure 377
service life 381
straight-line depreciation 383
sum-of-the-years'-digits depreciation 388
units-of-output depreciation 385

QUESTIONS

Q10-1 List ten examples of assets that belong in the property, plant, and equipment category.

Q10-2 Do all items of property, plant, and equipment have a limited life? Explain.

Q10-3 How is the acquisition cost of a machine determined? Which of the following costs are included in the cost of an asset: purchase price, freight charges, cost of installation, medical costs of injured installer, special electrical wiring, routine maintenance?

Q10-4 What is the difference between a capital expenditure and a revenue expenditure?

Q10-5 Which price is used to record the acquisition cost of equipment: list price, negotiated price, or negotiated price less available cash discount?

Q10-6 How should the cost of property, plant, and equipment acquired in a lump-sum purchase be apportioned to the individual assets? Why is such a division necessary?

Q10-7 What does the term "depreciation" mean in accounting? Is the term used differently by others? Explain.

Q10-8 How is the service life of depreciable plant and equipment determined? Discuss the factors of physical deterioration, obsolescence, and inadequacy in the establishment of service lives.

Q10-9 Describe how identical vehicles purchased by different businesses can each be depreciated over different service lives.

Q10-10 Describe how the straight-line method of depreciation differs from the units-of-output method.

Q10-11 Is the units-of-output method of depreciation more appropriate to use for some items of plant and equipment than for others? Why?

Q10-12 Describe how the straight-line method of depreciation differs from the double-declining balance and sum-of-the-years'-digits methods.

Q10-13 Why are the accelerated methods of depreciation popular among businesses? What is the theoretical justification for these methods?

Q10-14 Describe the composite and inventory depreciation methods. Which method is applicable to groups of low-value depreciable assets?

Q10-15 What does the balance in the Accumulated Depreciation account represent? How much of the balance represents cash?

Q10-16 How does a change in the estimated remaining service life of a piece of equipment affect past and future depreciation amounts?

Q10-17 How are property, plant, and equipment assets disclosed on the balance sheet?

Q10-18 Why does the FASB require that large businesses supplementally disclose the current costs of their property, plant, and equipment and related depreciation expense?

EXERCISES

E10-1 Metro Express, a metropolitan transportation company, purchased several new buses at an invoice price of $450,000. The buses had a list price of $520,000.

By taking advantage of a cash discount, Metro paid the seller $440,000. Costs of $4,500 were incurred in transporting the buses to Metro, and insurance charges during transportation were $300. Specially trained mechanics who tested the buses were paid $550; initial test runs around the city cost another $500. On the basis of requests from the mechanics, special safety devices were installed at a cost of $750. Finally, bus registration fees amounted to $75.

a Compute the acquisition cost of the buses.
b Prepare journal entries for all preceding expenditures.

E10-2 Consider the following costs:

a Cost of initial testing of new machinery
b Painting costs of a firm's office building
c Cost of a paper stapler purchased for office use
d Finance charges on the purchase of new office equipment
e Repair costs to fix broken equipment
f Architect's fee on new building
g Surveying costs of newly acquired land
h Publicity costs related to new building
i Initial paving of parking lot for employees
j Attorney's fee related to newly acquired land

Identify each of the costs as either a capital expenditure or a revenue expenditure.

E10-3 Firestone agreed to purchase the property of the Bellanger Estate for $40,000,000 cash. Included in the purchase was land (appraised at $40,000,000), barns and tack house (appraised at $8,000,000), the main house (appraised at $1,000,000), and servant's quarters (appraised at $1,000,000).

a Allocate the purchase price of the Bellanger Estate to the individual assets acquired.
b Prepare a journal entry for the acquisition.

E10-4 Trujillo Drugs purchased a delivery van for $12,000 on January 1, 1982. The van was estimated to have a service life of 5 years and a residual value of $3,000. Trujillo is planning to drive the van 10,000 miles annually.

Compute depreciation expense for *1983* by using each of the following methods:

a Units-of-output, assuming 11,000 miles were driven during 1983
b Straight-line
c Sum-of-the-years'-digits
d Double-declining balance

E10-5 Sacramento Company paid $100,000 for a machine that has an estimated service life of 4 years. At the end of 4 years Sacramento expects to sell the machine for $10,000.

a Compute the amount of depreciation expense to be recorded each year by using the (1) sum-of-the-years'-digits method and (2) double-declining balance method.
b Compute the book value of the machine at the end of the fourth year under each method.

E10-6 A machine was purchased on October 1, 1983, at a cost of $6,000. Installation charges were $400 and freight was $200. The machine has a residual value of $600, a useful life of 6 years, and a physical life of 10 years.

a Assuming all expenditures were for cash, record the necessary journal entry to enter the machine in the accounting records.
b Record the entry for straight-line depreciation at the end of 1983.
c How would the machine and its related depreciation account appear on a balance sheet as of December 31, 1984? Use proper amounts.

E10-7 O'Henry's, a posh gourmet restaurant, purchased an ornate piano on September 1, 1983, that will be depreciated over a service life of 5 years. The cost of the piano was $15,000 and its estimated residual value is $3,000.
a Calculate depreciation expense for the year ended December 31, 1983, by using the (1) straight-line method; (2) sum-of-the-years'-digits method; (3) double-declining balance method.
b Compute O'Henry's 1984 depreciation expense using the sum-of-the-years'-digits and double-declining balance methods.

E10-8 Information taken from the records of the Hopkins Corporation follows.

Asset	*Cost*	*Residual Value*	*Service Life (Years)*
A	$100,000	$50,000	10
B	200,000	40,000	8
C	300,000	30,000	9
D	400,000	20,000	20
E	500,000	10,000	7

Assume that all of these assets are depreciable and were acquired several years ago.
a Compute the rate of depreciation and average service life by using the composite method.
b Prepare the journal entry to record annual depreciation.

E10-9 CPR, a health care company, holds clinics on how to treat heart attack victims. One year ago the firm bought a $12,000 supply of lifelike rubber bodies for seminar use. At the time of acquisition the service life and residual value were estimated to be 3 years and $300, respectively. These estimates now need revision.

Calculate yearly depreciation expense with the straight-line method under the following conditions:
a CPR now estimates that service life will be 4 more years and the residual value will be $500.
b CPR now estimates that service life will be 1 more year with no change in the residual value.
c CPR now estimates that service life will be 9 more years and the residual value will be $180.

PROBLEMS

P10-1 ***Cost treatment***
Consider the following costs of Diana Corporation:
1 Cost of grading land prior to construction

2 Cost of material spoiled during trial runs of new machinery
3 Delinquent property taxes on newly acquired land
4 Damage to equipment, which occurred during installation
5 Cost of maintaining equipment in peak condition
6 Freight charges on newly acquired equipment
7 Cost of constructing wall partitions in office building leased from Harris Properties
8 Cost of parking lot constructed on our property
9 Realtor's fees incurred on purchase of land and building
10 Cost of three wastebaskets for office
11 Cost of clearing land prior to construction
12 Cost of purchasing used equipment
13 Interest incurred to purchase machinery on credit
14 Current property taxes on land and building
15 Attorney's fees for land and building purchase
16 Cost of parking lot constructed on leased property
17 Construction costs of new building
18 Cost of sprinkling system for landscaping

INSTRUCTIONS

a Identify each of the costs as a capital expenditure or a revenue expenditure.
b For the capital expenditures only, indicate which asset account should be debited.

P10-2 ***Determining acquisition cost and annual depreciation***

On January 1, 1983, the Jenkins Packing Company agreed to purchase an electronic canning machine for $40,500, which includes shipping charges of $500. A cash discount of $1,000 was offered to Jenkins for prompt payment of the invoice, but the discount was not taken due to a lack of funds. The machine's canning capacity is 4,000 cans per hour. The cost of insurance on the machine during shipment was $100. Insurance on the machine against fire and water damage for one year cost another $800. Installation costs were $1,000, not including $200 of repairs caused by a mechanic's carelessness.

At the time of acquisition, the machine was estimated to have a service life of 5 years (20,000 operating hours) and a residual value of $2,000. During the 5 years of operation (1983–1987), the machine was used for 4,200, 3,900, 3,100, 4,000, and 4,800 hours, respectively.

INSTRUCTIONS

a Prepare journal entries to record the purchase of the machine and the other expenditures incurred by Jenkins.
b Rounding calculations to the nearest dollar, compute depreciation for 1983–1987 by using the (1) units-of-output method; (2) straight-line method; (3) sum-of-the-years'-digits method; (4) double-declining balance method.

P10-3 ***Acquisition cost, lump-sum purchase, correction of errors***

Arcadia, Inc., purchased a small farm on April 1, 1983, with the intention of converting it to a dude ranch. Arcadia agreed to pay $300,000 over the next 6 months and to assume the remaining mortgage on the property of $100,000. These costs, together with other transactions related to the ranch conversion, are presented in the Property account.

Property

4/1 Purchase price	400,000	12/31 Depreciation expense on property (estimate)	5,000
4/10 Land title	500		
4/12 Survey costs	3,500		
4/15 Land grading and draining	10,000		
4/20 Fire insurance on buildings	4,000		
5/1 Material and labor cost to refurbish buildings	20,000		
5/2 Advertising costs for grand opening	4,500		
10/1 Current year's property taxes on land	8,000		
10/10 Repaired equipment	400		

The property acquired included land (appraised value $250,000), buildings (appraised value $200,000), and equipment (appraised value $50,000). The dude ranch opened on May 2, 1983.

INSTRUCTIONS

a List the errors made by Arcadia in accounting for the purchase and related costs.

b Prepare a schedule showing how the original lump-sum purchase of property, plant, and equipment should have been handled.

c Prepare journal entries to correct the Property account on December 31, 1983. Assume the buildings and equipment have respective service lives of 20 years and 10 years from the grand opening. The straight-line method of depreciation is used; no residual value is anticipated.

d Present the property, plant, and equipment section of Arcadia's balance sheet as of December 31, 1983.

P10-4 ***Determining depreciation: Full year, fractional, and changes in rate***

Gilpin-Gorton, Inc., a food wholesaler, operates four delivery vehicles in central Kansas. Data on the four vehicles follows.

Vehicle	Date Acquired	Cost	Residual Value	Service Life (Years)	Depreciation Method
2-ton Dodge	1/1/80	$15,000	$1,000	5	Double-declining balance
2-ton Ford	1/31/80	17,000	$2,000	5	Sum-of-the-years'-digits
2-ton Chevrolet	8/31/82	21,000	—	7	Straight-line
VW bus	4/1/83	10,000	10%	6	Sum-of-the-years'-digits

INSTRUCTIONS

a Calculate depreciation expense for the 12-month period ended December 31, 1983. Round all computations to the nearest dollar.

b Compute the accumulated depreciation and book value of each vehicle owned by the firm as of December 31, 1983.

c On January 1, 1984, management determined that the 2-ton Chevrolet could be used for 10 more years, resulting in a total service life of $11\frac{1}{3}$ years. Calculate the revised annual depreciation on this vehicle for future periods.

P10-5 ***Depreciation methods, changes in rates***

George Powers Company purchased a corporate jet for $15,000,000 on May 1, 1983. The jet had an estimated residual value of 20% of cost and an 8-year (40,000-flying hour) service life. On January 1, 1984, the service life was extended to recognize 10 years (or 47,760 flying hours) of additional service from that date. At the same time residual value was decreased to 10% of cost. Flying hours during 1983 and the first quarter of 1984 totaled 5,200 and 1,616, respectively. Accumulated Depreciation accounts based on the straight-line, units-of-output, double-declining balance, and sum-of-the-years'-digits depreciation methods follow.

a

Accumulated Depreciation		
	12/31/83	*?*
	3/31/84	*532,828*

b

Accumulated Depreciation		
	12/31/83	*?*
	3/31/84	*404,000*

c

Accumulated Depreciation		
	12/31/83	*?*
	3/31/84	*312,500*

d

Accumulated Depreciation		
	12/31/83	*?*
	3/31/84	*625,000*

INSTRUCTIONS

Determine which Accumulated Depreciation account corresponds to each of the depreciation methods. Powers rounds final depreciation computations to the nearest dollar.

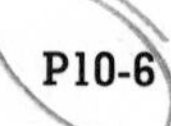

P10-6 ***Asset acquisitions and depreciation***

Moffett Company owns the following machines on January 1, 1983.

Machine	*Date Acquired*	*Purchase Price*	*Life (Years)*	*Residual Value*
489A	1/1/79	$16,000	10	$1,000
L4700	7/1/81	8,000	10	400

1,500 per year
760 per year

Both machines have been depreciated by the straight-line method. The following events took place during 1983.

Jan. 3 New technology shortened the remaining life of L4700 from $8\frac{1}{2}$ years to 5 years.

Mar. 5 A used machine, AA560, was acquired from Connor Enterprises for $13,000 cash. Connor purchased the machine 2 years ago for $20,000 and had recorded $4,000 of depreciation by using the straight-line method and a 10-year life. Moffett feels the machine will be obsolete in 5 years and anticipates a $1,000 residual value at that time. Moffett will also use straight-line depreciation.

Apr. 2 Machine 684Z was acquired for $25,500 cash. The machine required special wiring of $2,500 and installation costs of $2,000. Moffett will use double-declining balance depreciation with this machine and has estimated a life of 5 years and a residual value of $1,500.

July 2 Machine SS4900 was purchased at a cost of $13,000. This machine is estimated to have a life of 4 years and a residual value of $1,000. Sum-of-the-years'-digits depreciation will be used.

INSTRUCTIONS

a Prepare journal entries, if necessary, to record the following:
   (1) The change in the service life estimate on January 3.
   (2) The acquisition on March 5.
   (3) The acquisition on April 2.
   (4) The acquisition on July 2.
   (5) Total annual depreciation for the year ended December 31, 1983. Show a schedule of supporting computations.

b Show how the machinery would appear on Moffett's December 31, 1983, balance sheet.

c Justify the use of accelerated depreciation to an angry stockholder who is complaining that Moffett's earnings-per-share figures are depressed because of large depreciation deductions. Concentrate on financial reporting issues; disregard income taxes.

P10-7 ***Determining acquisition cost and annual depreciation (alternate to P10-2)***
On March 31, 1983, the Rando Milling Company agreed to purchase an electronic milling machine for $82,000, which includes shipping and insurance charges of $1,000. A cash discount of $1,000 was offered to Rando for prompt payment. Due to a lack of funds, however, payment did not occur within the discount period. The machine can mill 1,400 bushels of wheat per hour. Insurance on the machine for fire and explosion damage for one year cost $750. Installation costs were $1,550, test runs cost another $800, and special wiring was installed for $650. The installation costs exclude $400 of repairs, which were necessary because of a mechanic's carelessness.

At the time of acquisition, the machine was estimated to have a service life of 5 years (20,000 operating hours) and a residual value of $5,000. During the years of operation (1983–1988), the machine was used for 4,800, 5,200, 3,000, 2,500, 3,500, and 1,000 hours, respectively.

INSTRUCTIONS

a Prepare journal entries to record the purchase of the machine and the other expenditures incurred by Rando Milling.

b Rounding calculations to the nearest dollar, compute depreciation for 1983–1988 by using the (1) units-of-output method; (2) straight-line method; (3) sum-of-the-years'-digits method; (4) double-declining balance method.

P10-8 ***Acquisition cost, lump-sum purchase, correction of errors (alternate to P10-3)*** Tyrone Management recently purchased a financially troubled country club. Tyrone agreed to pay $1,200,000 over the next 9 months and to assume the remaining mortgage on the property of $300,000. These costs, together with other costs related to the acquisition, are presented in the Property account.

Property

3/1	Purchase	1,500,000	12/31	Depreciation expense on property (estimate)	10,000
3/4	Acquired fire and liability insurance	12,000			
3/18	Architect's fee for redesign of swim complex	5,000			
5/1	Promotion costs for reopening	8,000			
5/15	Installation of new plumbing and electrical systems in recreation hall	30,000			
5/25	Construction costs for swim complex	160,000			
7/8	Normal land maintenance	6,000			
11/15	Current year's property taxes on land	18,000			

The property acquired included land (appraised value $1,300,000), swim complex (appraised value $500,000), and recreation hall (appraised value $200,000). The country club reopened on June 1, 1983.

INSTRUCTIONS

a List the errors made by Tyrone in accounting for the purchase and related costs.

b Prepare a schedule showing how the original lump-sum purchase of property, plant, and equipment should have been handled.

c Prepare journal entries to correct the Property account on December 31, 1983. Assume the following service lives from the grand opening:

Swim complex	15 years
Recreation hall	10 years

The straight-line depreciation method is used; disregard residual values.

d Present the property, plant, and equipment section of Tyrone's balance sheet as of December 31, 1983.

P10-9 *Determining depreciation: Full year, fractional, and changes in rate (alternate to P10-4)*

Hozelton Products Company, a frozen food wholesaler, owns four freezers in their warehouse in southern Montana. Data on the four freezers follows.

Freezer	Date Acquired	Cost	Residual Value	Service Life (Years)	Depreciation Method
Polar Bear no. 13	2/29/80	$15,000	$1,000	7	Straight-line
Frostbite no. 3	1/1/81	21,000	$3,000	8	Sum-of-the-years'-digits
Deep Freeze no. 79	1/31/81	20,000	10%	9	Sum-of-the-years'-digits
Arctic A-82	4/1/83	24,000	None	10	Double-declining balance

INSTRUCTIONS

a Calculate depreciation expense for the 12-month period ended December 31, 1983. Round all computations to the nearest dollar.

b Compute the accumulated depreciation and book value of each freezer owned by Hozelton as of December 31, 1983.

c On January 1, 1984, management determined that Polar Bear no. 13 could be used for 5 more years, resulting in a total service life of 8 years and 10 months. Calculate the revised annual depreciation on this freezer for future years.

P10-10 *Depreciation methods, changes in rates (alternate to P10-5)*

Honeywell, Inc., purchased a bus for $160,000 on April 1, 1983. The bus has a residual value of $10,000 and a 10-year (150,000-mile) service life. On January 1, 1984, the service life was decreased to recognize 8 years (or 120,000 miles) of additional service from that date. At the same time residual value was decreased to $8,000. Miles driven during 1983 and the first quarter of 1984 totaled 16,400 and 4,700, respectively. Accumulated Depreciation accounts based on the straight-line, units-of-output, double-declining balance, and sum-of-the-years'-digits depreciation methods follow.

a

Accumulated Depreciation

	12/31/83	?
	3/31/84	8,500

b

Accumulated Depreciation

	12/31/83	?
	3/31/84	7,308

c

Accumulated Depreciation		
	12/31/83	?
	3/31/84	5,311

d

Accumulated Depreciation		
	12/31/83	?
	3/31/84	4,398

INSTRUCTIONS

Determine which Accumulated Depreciation account corresponds to each of the depreciation methods. Honeywell rounds final depreciation computations to the nearest dollar.

P10-11 ***Asset acquisitions and depreciation (alternate to P10-6)***

Martin Company owns the following machines on January 1, 1983.

Machine	Date Acquired	Purchase Price	Life (Years)	Residual Value
MGH 1	7/1/79	$26,000	10	$1,000
EK 16	1/1/80	13,000	8	3,000

Both machines have been depreciated by the straight-line method. The following events occurred in 1983.

Jan. 2 Because of new technology, the remaining service life of MGH 1 was shortened from $6\frac{1}{2}$ to 5 years.

Mar. 1 A used machine, Case no. 1921, was acquired from McNeely Company for $8,000 cash. McNeely purchased the machine 3 years ago for $20,000 and had recorded $6,000 of depreciation by using the straight-line method and a 10-year service life. Martin feels the machine will become obsolete in 5 years and anticipates a $500 residual value at that time. Martin will also use the straight-line method of depreciation.

May 2 Machine Mercer no. 1922 was acquired for $27,500 cash. The machine required special wiring of $2,000 and installation costs of $500. Martin will use the double-declining balance method with this machine and has estimated a service life of 5 years and a $1,500 residual value.

July 29 Machine Franklin no. 1919 was purchased at a cost of $26,000. This machine is estimated to have a life of 4 years and a residual value of $2,000. Sum-of-the-years'-digits depreciation will be used.

INSTRUCTIONS

a Prepare journal entries, if necessary, to record the following:
   (1) The change in the service life estimate on January 2.
   (2) The acquisition on March 1.
   (3) The acquisition on May 2.
   (4) The acquisition on July 29.
   (5) Total annual depreciation for the year ended December 31, 1983. Show a schedule of supporting computations.

b Show how the machinery would appear on Martin's December 31, 1983, balance sheet.

c Justify the use of accelerated depreciation to an angry stockholder who is complaining that Martin's earnings-per-share figures are depressed because of large depreciation deductions. Concentrate on financial reporting issues; disregard income taxes.

CASE 10
JIM'S MACHINE SHOP

Tom Ferguson and Jim Thies were fraternity brothers at Midwestern University in the 1960s. Tom graduated and took a job with a local bank, where he is now president. Jim graduated and started a machine shop with $185,000 that had been willed to him by a wealthy relative.

Jim purchased equipment on January 1, 1962, for $150,000 by paying cash; he kept the remaining cash to cover operating costs. The equipment has been depreciated by using the sum-of-the-years'-digits method over an estimated service life of 20 years.

The equipment is now worn out and must be replaced. No residual value was anticipated and none will be realized. The replacement cost of new equipment is ten times the cost of the original equipment because of an average inflation rate of slightly over 12% per year over the 20-year service life.

Jim has been fortunate enough to achieve profits in every year of operation. Each year, however, withdrawals were made from the business equal to the net income reported on the income statement. Jim is thinking of approaching Tom for a loan to finance the new equipment.

INSTRUCTIONS

a How much cash should Jim's firm have on hand? Explain your answer. Assume there were no significant changes in inventories, receivables, and payables. Disregard income taxes.

b Assuming that Jim wants to retain 20% of the present cash balance to help cover operating expenses, how much money should Tom be asked to loan?

c In light of Jim's experience with inflation and the high costs of replacing equipment, should the manner in which his business determined depreciation expense (i.e., based on historical cost) be criticized? Explain your answer and note the impact on Jim's withdrawal policy.

11 PROPERTY, PLANT, AND EQUIPMENT/INTANGIBLES/NATURAL RESOURCES

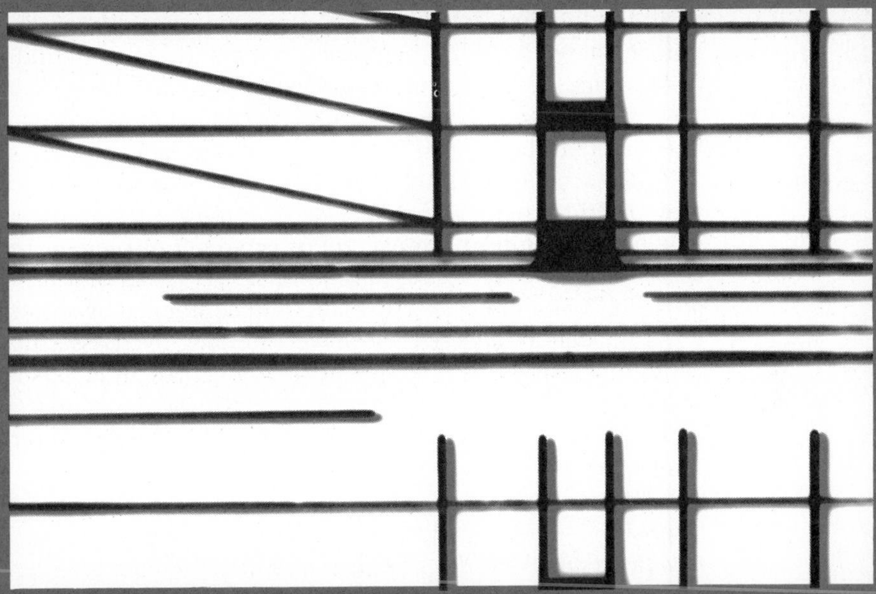

LEARNING OBJECTIVES

After reading this chapter you should:

1 *Be able to record costs that are incurred for property, plant, and equipment subsequent to acquisition.*

2 *Understand the distinction among repairs, additions, betterments, and assessments and their respective accounting treatments.*

3 *Be able to record gains and losses on the disposal of property, plant, and equipment.*

4 *Be able to account for exchanges and trade-ins for financial reporting and tax purposes.*

5 *Understand the use of subsidiary ledgers for property, plant, and equipment.*

6 *Recognize the various types of intangible assets and their legal lives and understand the amortization process.*

7 *Understand how to account for natural resources including the differences between (1) successful efforts and full-cost accounting and (2) cost and percentage depletion.*

8 *Be able to account for depreciable assets related to natural resources.*

CHAPTER 11

This chapter continues our discussion of long-lived assets. We will study several additional issues related to property, plant, and equipment and examine two other types of assets that provide long-term benefits to their owners: intangibles and natural resources.

PROPERTY, PLANT, AND EQUIPMENT

Costs Subsequent to Acquisition

Organizations invest large sums of money each year to purchase property, plant, and equipment. Frequently, expenditures related to these assets do not stop at acquisition; many costs are incurred after buildings, machines, and various pieces of equipment have started to serve a business. For example, repairs are made, new features are added to improve efficiency, major overhauls are performed, and parts are replaced.

The accountant must determine how to record these costs. Whether they are added to the depreciable base of the asset or written off as expenses may have a significant impact on reported net income for the period. If the costs are treated as *capital expenditures* (i.e., costs that benefit future periods) and debited to property, plant, and equipment accounts, net income is not immediately lowered. However, the long-lived asset now has a larger depreciable base, which results in greater depreciation expense and a reduction in future net income. Alternatively, if these costs are treated as *revenue expenditures* and expensed in the year when incurred, net income is affected immediately.

Costs related to property, plant, and equipment incurred subsequent to acquisition should be added to an asset's depreciable base if *future economic benefits result from the expenditure.* Future economic benefits occur under the following conditions:

1 The service life of an asset is prolonged.
2 The quantity of services expected from an asset has increased.
3 The quality of services expected from an asset has improved.

Expenditures that do not fulfill any one of these criteria are treated as revenue expenditures and written off as expenses of the current period. We will now examine the application of these rules to several commonly encountered items.

Repairs

Amounts spent to maintain the normal operating condition of an asset are termed **repairs.** Repairs include regular maintenance, minor parts replacement, painting, cleaning, and inspection. Repairs do not increase the future service potential of an asset; rather they assist in attaining the original service life estimate and anticipated operating efficiency. As a consequence, repair costs are debited to the Repairs Expense account when incurred.

Additions

Additions are items that will provide future benefits and be affixed to existing assets. Examples of additions include the placement of air conditioning in a building or vehicle and the construction of a new wing on a building. The cost of an addition is a capital expenditure and is therefore recorded in a property, plant, or equipment account (i.e., capitalized). Generally, the cost of an addition is entered in the same account as the original asset to simplify record keeping.

Frequently, an addition's service life is dependent on the remaining service life of the asset to which it is united. In such cases the cost of the addition should be depreciated over the remaining service life of the original asset or the addition's life, whichever is shorter. To illustrate, if a central-air-conditioning unit (life of 8 years) is placed in a building that has a remaining service life of 5 years, the air-conditioning unit should be depreciated over 5 years.

Betterments

Betterments, sometimes called improvements or extraordinary repairs, are expenditures that improve or increase the future service potential of an asset. Occasionally, a betterment occurs by replacing a major part of an existing asset with a similar but superior component. Examples include the installation of (1) a new, more efficient heating/cooling system in a building and (2) a new engine in a vehicle. In other cases the betterment may involve an extraordinary repair such as a major overhaul. Extraordinary repairs frequently extend the service life of an asset beyond the original estimate.

Often the difference between extraordinary repairs and ordinary repairs and maintenance is not readily evident. Yet the accountant must properly distinguish between these two items, because their accounting treatment differs. Ordinary repairs, as we noted earlier, are expenses. Expenditures that prolong an asset's life are capitalized in the following manner.

Assume the Simmons Company acquired a freezer on January 1, 1979, for $20,000. The freezer had an estimated service life of 5 years, with no residual value. Simmons had depreciated the asset for 4 years, using the straight-line method, resulting in the following balance sheet disclosure as of December 31, 1982:

Freezer	*$20,000*	
Less: Accumulated depreciation	*16,000*	*$4,000*

On January 1, 1983, a new motor costing $1,000 was installed, which extended the freezer's service life by 1 year. The cost of the new motor is *not* recorded in the Freezer account. Rather $1,000 is debited to Accumulated Depreciation, thereby reducing the account's balance to $15,000. The freezer's new book value of $5,000 ($20,000 − $15,000) will be depreciated over the remaining 2 years of service life at the rate of $2,500 ($5,000 ÷ 2) per year. Upon conclusion of the 6-year life, depreciation expense will total $21,000, which equals the original cost of the freezer plus the $1,000 motor.

Notice that the debit to Accumulated Depreciation increases the asset's book value, as would a debit to the Freezer account. We follow the former approach for expenditures that prolong an asset's life to, in effect, reclaim (reduce) some past depreciation. The past depreciation is then subsequently spread over the remaining service life.

Assessments

Property owners are often assessed for improvements such as new streets, curbs, sidewalks, streetlights, and sewers. These improvements are made for the benefit of the property owners and other residents of the municipality. Assessments are generally added to the Land account, because projects such as those just cited are relatively permanent and are maintained and upgraded by the municipality.

Disposals of Property, Plant, and Equipment

Items of property, plant, and equipment are acquired by a firm to render benefits for a number of years. Eventually these assets will be retired from use by being discarded, sold, or exchanged. When a company disposes of a depreciable asset, depreciation must be taken up to the date of disposal to ensure a proper matching of expenses and revenues.

To illustrate, suppose that Bennigan Corporation acquired a machine on January 1, 1981, at a cost of $15,000. The machine has a residual value of $1,000 and is being depreciated over a 7-year life by the straight-line method. As of December 31, 1982, the machine would appear in the accounting records as follows:

Machinery			
1/1/81	15,000		

Accumulated Depreciation: Machinery			
		12/31/81	2,000
		12/31/82	2,000

Assume that Bennigan discarded the machine on October 1, 1983. Because depreciation was last recorded on December 31, 1982, nine months of additional depreciation must be taken. Thus $1,500 ($2,000 × $\frac{9}{12}$) is entered in the accounts as follows:

Oct. 1	Depreciation Expense: Machinery	1,500	
	Accumulated Depreciation: Machinery		1,500
	To record 9 months' depreciation		

Removal of assets from the accounts

Once depreciation is brought up to date, any account balances associated with the depreciable asset must be removed from the books. This step is accomplished by debiting the Accumulated Depreciation account for the total depreciation taken to the date of disposal and then crediting the asset account for the asset's original cost. For Bennigan's machine the necessary journal entry is as follows:

Oct. 1	Loss on Disposal of Property, Plant, & Equipment	9,500	
	Accumulated Depreciation: Machinery	5,500	
	Machinery		15,000
	To record discarded machine		

To explain, recall that an asset's cost minus accumulated depreciation represents *book value*, that is, the "value" of the asset in the accounting records. For a proper recording of the transaction the proceeds received upon disposal, if any, must be compared with book value. If the amount received is greater than the asset's book value, a gain results; if the proceeds are less than book value, a loss arises. Since Bennigan received nothing for a machine with a $9,500 book value ($15,000 – $5,500), a $9,500 loss is incurred.

Gains and losses on the disposal of depreciable assets are common, because book value does not represent the true worth of an asset in the marketplace. Recall from Chapter 10 that depreciation is a process of allocation, not valuation. Furthermore, the service life and residual value estimates used in the depreciation computation may be incorrect. Assets are often sold before the end of their useful life at amounts that differ from residual value.

Gains and losses on disposal are normally presented on the income statement as separate, nonoperating elements of revenue (or expense); they generally do not meet the criteria noted in Chapter 6 for extraordinary items.

Sale of depreciable assets

In addition to being discarded or abandoned, depreciable assets can also be sold. To illustrate the proper accounting treatment, assume that an executive desk was acquired for $2,000. Over the years, depreciation in the amount of $1,200 has been recorded. The asset's book value of $800 ($2,000 – $1,200) appears in the accounts as follows:

Office Furniture	
2,000	

Accumulated Depreciation: Office Furniture	
	1,200

If the desk is sold for its book value, the entry to record the sale would be as follows:

Cash	800	
Accumulated Depreciation: Office Furniture	1,200	
Office Furniture		2,000
To record furniture sold at book value; no gain or loss		

No gain or loss results because furniture with a book value of $800 is replaced by $800 cash.

If the desk is sold for $500 because of a low demand for used office furniture, a loss occurs. The entry to record this transaction would be as follows:

Cash	500	
Loss on Disposal of Property, Plant, & Equipment	300	
Accumulated Depreciation: Office Furniture	1,200	
Office Furniture		2,000
To record furniture sold below book value; loss of $300		

A loss of $300 is generated because the cash received ($500) is less than the book value of the furniture ($800). The loss would have been reduced (and perhaps eliminated) if the selling price had been greater. On the other hand, the loss could have gone as high as $800 if the asset was discarded with nothing received in return.

Finally, if the furniture is sold for $1,500, a gain is generated. The proper journal entry is as follows:

Cash	1,500	
Accumulated Depreciation: Office Furniture	1,200	
Gain on Disposal of Property, Plant, & Equipment		700
Office Furniture		2,000
To record furniture sold above book value; gain of $700		

In this case a gain of $700 results from the firm's receiving $1,500 for an asset with a book value of $800.

Exchanges and trade-ins

Frequently, items of property, plant, and equipment are exchanged or traded in for newer assets. You may have had some personal experience with trade-ins when purchasing a new car. To acquire the new vehicle, you must surrender the old car, make a cash down payment, and assume an obligation (e.g., a note) for the unpaid balance. The total amount to be paid is dependent on the **trade-in allowance** granted by the dealer for the old car. Often the trade-in allowance is equal to the vehicle's **fair market value** (i.e., the current market price). Sometimes, however, the trade-in allowance varies inversely with how desperate the dealer is to make a sale. If sales are low, trade-in allowances will be high, and vice versa. Because the trade-in allowance can fluctuate for reasons unrelated to the fair value of the asset given or received, it is an unreliable measure to use for accounting purposes.

To properly account for trade-ins, we must attach a value to the old asset. Normally, the asset surrendered is valued at its fair market value (unless the fair value of the asset received is more clearly evident). The fair value of the asset surrendered rarely coincides with the asset's book value, however, thus giving rise to a gain or loss. Importantly, the accounting treatment for gains and losses differs. Briefly stated, *gains on the exchange of similar assets are ignored, while losses are recognized.*

Accounting for gains

When the fair market value exceeds the book value of the asset relinquished, an apparent gain arises. However, the gain is not recognized because an exchange of similar assets does not generate revenue. (Revenues are created by the *use and/or sale* of assets in business activity.[1]) As a result, the cost of the newly acquired asset is the sum of the old asset's book value plus any cash paid or to be paid. To illustrate, we assume the following exchange of similar assets for the Weiss Corporation.

Equipment Traded In		***Equipment Acquired***	
Cost	$10,000	Invoice price	$14,000
Accumulated depreciation	8,500	Fair market value of old equipment	2,000
Book value on date of exchange	$ 1,500	Cash paid	$12,000

The entry to record the transaction would be as follows:

Equipment (New)	*13,500*	
Accumulated Depreciation: Equipment	*8,500*	
Equipment (Old)		*10,000*
Cash		*12,000*
To record acquisition of new equipment and trade-in of old equipment		

Because the fair market value of the old equipment ($2,000) exceeds the $1,500 book value, Weiss has generated a $500 gain on the exchange. As the journal entry shows, however, no gain appears in the accounting records. Thus the new equipment is carried at $13,500: the book value of the equipment relinquished ($1,500) plus the cash paid ($12,000).

Future depreciation of the new equipment will be based on the recorded cost of $13,500, not the $14,000 invoice price. Because the gain is not recognized, the new equipment is recorded at $500 less than it otherwise would have been ($13,500 versus $14,000). Thus total depreciation expense is reduced by $500, which results in a $500 boost in profitability. Overall it is a matter of timing: a $500 gain now versus no gain now and increased net income over the asset's service life.

Accounting for losses

When the fair market value of the asset surrendered is less than the book value, a loss must be recognized. If the fair value of the old equipment in the previous illustration was only $300, a loss of $1,200 ($1,500 book value − $300 fair value) would occur. The necessary journal entry follows.

Equipment (New)	*14,000*	
Accumulated Depreciation: Equipment	*8,500*	
Loss on Exchange of Property, Plant, & Equipment	*1,200*	
Equipment (Old)		*10,000*
Cash		*13,700*
To record acquisition of new equipment and trade-in of old equipment		

[1]See "Accounting for Nonmonetary Transactions," *Opinions of the Accounting Principles Board No. 29* (New York: American Institute of Certified Public Accountants, 1973).

Observe that the cash paid increases to $13,700 ($14,000 − $300 fair market value), and the equipment is recorded at its invoice price of $14,000.

Federal income tax procedures

There are many areas in accounting where financial reporting practices differ from practices acceptable to the Internal Revenue Service. One such area is the exchange of similar assets. For federal income tax purposes, no gains *or* losses are recognized on the exchange of similar assets. The accounting shown for our first example (i.e., fair value of $2,000) is therefore consistent with tax treatment, since no gain was recognized in the accounts. For both financial accounting and income tax reporting, the new equipment is carried at a cost of $13,500.

In the second case, where book value exceeded fair value, a loss of $1,200 was recorded in the accounts and would appear on the income statement. For tax reporting, however, the loss cannot be recognized. Therefore the cost of the new equipment *for tax purposes* is $15,200. This amount is calculated in the same manner as when a gain is not recognized, that is, the sum of the old asset's book value ($1,500) and the cash given ($13,700). In effect, then, tax treatment includes the $1,200 in the cost of the new equipment. While the loss is denied, an amount $1,200 greater than invoice price ($15,200 − $14,000) will be depreciated. The higher depreciation charges, in turn, reduce taxable income and income taxes over the asset's service life. Again, it is a matter of timing.

Subsidiary Ledgers for Property, Plant, and Equipment

In Chapter 5 you were introduced to the use of control accounts and subsidiary ledgers to handle the record keeping for accounts receivable and accounts payable. Control accounts and subsidiary ledgers can also be used with long-lived assets. To explain, businesses usually maintain separate asset and accumulated depreciation accounts for each major category of property, plant, and equipment. For example, separate accounts are normally established for the following:

Land improvements
Buildings
Office equipment
Store equipment
Production equipment
Delivery equipment

Each general ledger account contains information concerning the acquisition and disposal of specific assets. For example, the Delivery Equipment account summarizes transactions involving vans, light trucks, heavy-duty trucks, and so forth.

While records of specific vehicles and equipment are necessary, it is impractical to establish separate general ledger accounts for every piece of property, plant, and equipment used in a business. If separate accounts were created for each long-lived asset, the general ledger of even a moderate-sized business would be unwieldy. Further complicating the picture, the general ledger's form and layout is normally incapable of accommodating the information needed to effectively manage the property, plant, and equipment investment.

As a result, a subsidiary ledger is often created for each major asset grouping within the property, plant, and equipment caption on the balance sheet. The subsidiary ledger can be maintained manually or on a computer. If done manually, the subsidiary ledger usually consists of many cards, with each card summarizing the details of one specific asset.

The relationship between the control account (Delivery Equipment in this case) and subsidiary ledger is illustrated in Exhibit 11-1. Each acquisition and sale of delivery equipment is entered in the control account and also on a separate card in the subsidiary ledger. In this manner all delivery equipment transactions are aggregated into a single account for reporting purposes. At the same time detailed information regarding individual assets is readily available. For example, van V-11 is included in the total cost of delivery equipment owned by the firm as of December 31, 1984 ($89,450). The depreciation for van V-11 is noted on the subsidiary ledger card and is then aggregated in the Accumulated Depreciation control account with that of other vehicles. At the end of the accounting period the balances in the control accounts should equal the sum of the balances on the subsidiary ledger cards.

Asset management

As you can see, each subsidiary ledger card contains a wealth of information regarding an asset. Some firms design their subsidiary ledger cards to gather data relating to insurance coverage and repair history. Repair histories (number of breakdowns, cost of repairs, time to repair, cooperation of suppliers, and so on) may have an important bearing on the model, specifications, and suppliers selected in the future. If designed properly, the subsidiary ledger can be of considerable assistance to a firm in managing and controlling its asset investment.

The control of an organization's asset investment is extremely important. You may have noticed that large organizations attach identification numbers to their assets through painted numbers or metal tags. Numbering the items of property, plant, and equipment assists accountants in determining whether the assets that appear in the subsidiary ledger are still on hand and serving the firm. Periodically, the subsidiary ledger should be verified by taking a physical inventory. After the inventory those assets that have been discarded or deemed missing are removed from the accounts. The importance of a physical inventory can be seen in the article on page 422.

INTANGIBLE ASSETS

Long-lived assets that lack physical existence and contribute to the earnings capability of a firm are termed **intangible assets.** Examples of intangibles include patents, copyrights, franchises, trademarks and trade names, and goodwill. Intangible assets can provide significant benefits to a firm and may

Exhibit 11-1

Control account and subsidiary ledger relationship

PROPERTY, PLANT, AND EQUIPMENT RECORD

Account No. 181

Identification No. V-11

Item Van *General Ledger Account* Delivery Equipment

Description Ford Delivery Van *Location* Lima, Ohio

Manager Responsible John Random

Purchased From Prescott Ford, Columbus, Ohio

Service Life 4 years *Estimated Residual Value* $500

Depreciation Method Straight-line

Depreciation Per Year $2,250 *Per Month* $187.50

		Asset			Accumulated Depreciation		
Date	**Explanation**	**Dr**	**Cr**	**Balance**	**Dr**	**Cr**	**Balance**
1/1/83		9,500		9,500			
12/31/83						2,250	2,250
12/31/84						2,250	4,500

Disposition of asset

Control Accounts

Delivery Equipment 181	
12/31/84 89,450 (of which $9,500 represents the cost of van V-11)	

Accumulated Depreciation: Delivery Equipment 182	
	12/31/84 23,750 (of which $4,500 represents depreciation on van V-11)

be instrumental in a business's financial success. Yet many financial statement users disagree about placing these assets on the balance sheet. Why? In comparison with the benefits of other assets such as property, plant, and equipment, the benefits of intangibles are less certain and less determinable.

Intangible assets are entered in the accounting records at cost. Cost includes all expenditures necessary to place the intangible in a service-producing capacity (e.g., the purchase price, filing fees, legal fees, and other miscellaneous costs related to acquisition). These expenditures are all capitalized, because they help to provide economic benefits for extended periods of time. Intangibles are normally presented on the balance sheet in a separate section immediately following property, plant, and equipment.

Patents

A **patent** provides its owner with the exclusive right to use, manufacture, and sell a product or process for a period of 17 years. Patents are issued by the federal government to inventors as a means of encouraging development of new products and technology. Firms may obtain patents by purchasing existing rights from inventors or by developing their own products and processes through research and development. Although the economic usefulness of a purchased patent and an internally developed patent may be the same, their costs are treated differently.

As we noted, the purchase cost of an intangible is carried as an asset. In contrast, research and development costs related to the development of a patent are expensed. Although expensing costs that result in long-term benefits may seem contrary to the accounting treatment noted in this and other chapters, research and development costs are somewhat unique. Many organizations spend considerable amounts of money for research projects that culminate in a patent. Large sums are also spent on experimental work that is unsuccessful and leads nowhere. It might seem appropriate to expense the costs of unsuccessful research projects and capitalize the costs of those that result in a favorable outcome. Unfortunately, it is often difficult to assign costs to specific patents. Frequently, for example, patents do not result from one project; instead they are the culmination of knowledge that is obtained from many different undertakings. In addition, some research costs are applicable to more than a single endeavor and thus difficult to trace to specific efforts. As a consequence of these practical problems plus the possible "go nowhere" outcome associated with many research efforts, businesses are required to expense research and development costs when incurred.[2]

Copyrights

A **copyright** provides its owners, or heirs, the exclusive right to produce and sell an artistic, musical, or published work. Like patents, these assets are issued by the federal government and can be sold or assigned to others. Formerly, a copyright was granted for 28 years and could be renewed for

[2]See "Accounting for Research and Development Costs," *Statement of Financial Accounting Standards No. 2* (Stamford, Conn.: Financial Accounting Standards Board, 1974).

INDUSTRY'S WASTED BILLIONS

When Addressograph Multigraph Corp. (AM) decided to take stock of some problems several years ago, it uncovered several unpleasant surprises. One of the most startling was that in all of its 45 years the company had never taken a physical inventory of equipment at its huge main plant. AM had been losing money for years partly because it did not know what fixed assets it actually had or how they were being used.

Unbelievable? "No . . . it is a common industry problem," said an AM executive. And he's right. For years companies have been losing huge amounts of money because of serious defects in the management of their property, plant, and equipment. The total cost to industry is difficult to measure, since no one has ever made a comprehensive study of asset management. But one estimate gives a clue to its magnitude. According to an appraisal executive, up to 15% of industry's fixed assets have disappeared from company property but are still listed on balance sheets. Over $112 billion of assets may not exist.

All kinds of property—from typewriters to expensive electronic equipment to machine tools—are sold, scrapped, destroyed, or cannibalized every year without ever being reported to the accounting department. For example, maintenance personnel routinely throw out older equipment or sell off parts as scrap in the course of their work. Engineers are considered particularly notorious for their habit of cannibalizing equipment, especially in high-technology firms, where the amount of ghost assets is said to run higher than the 15% figure above. Technical people often tear assorted electronic devices apart and use the components to build completely new machines.

Even entire buildings can disappear. For instance, when a leading southern consumer products firm launched a new building program several years ago, it had to demolish an old building on the site. Due to a mix-up in orders, the contractor also knocked down a smaller adjacent structure. But the records were so confused that when the accounting department figured the loss on the demolition, it completely missed the smaller building. Only recently was it discovered that this $1.2 million asset was still appearing faithfully on the balance sheet.

[An interesting aside from the authors: As we go to press, AM is in the process of filing for reorganization in a federal bankruptcy court. The office products maker seeks court protection while it tries to straighten its affairs and salvage its business.]

SOURCE Adapted from "Industry's Wasted Billions." Reprinted with special permission of Dun's Review, *December 1977. Copyright © 1977, Dun & Bradstreet Publications Corporation.*

another 28 years. Beginning in 1978, however, the legal life was changed to equal the life of the creator plus 50 years.

Franchises

A **franchise** gives its owner the right to manufacture or sell certain products or perform certain services. Although most people associate franchises with fast-food restaurants such as Wendy's and Pizza Inn, franchises are established for a variety of activities. Cities, for example, frequently grant franchises to firms for garbage services, towing services, and taxi services. A franchise may have an indefinite life (perpetual franchise) or a limited life; some must even be renewed yearly.

The cost of acquiring a franchise is carried in a Franchise account. A few franchises involve no acquisition costs; thus only legal costs and related fees are capitalized. Other franchises are extremely expensive and involve initial fees in excess of $100,000 plus a percentage of sales.

Trademarks

Each day, as consumers, we encounter trademarks, trade names, and symbols. These intangible assets are very important to the financial well-being of a business, since mention of a certain name or recognition of a symbol automatically denotes a specific product and/or service. Several well-known trademarks, trade names, and symbols appear in Exhibit 11-2.

Exhibit 11-2
Trademarks and symbols

The Coca-Cola Company

Metro-Goldwyn-Mayer Film Co.

Borden, Inc.

Burger King

The cost of a trademark, trade name, or special symbol includes design fees, market research costs, attorney's fees, and, importantly, registration fees. Owners can secure exclusive rights to the use of these intangible assets by registration with the federal government. Trademarks and trade names may be registered for a period of 20 years, with unlimited renewals possible for the same term.

Goodwill

The term "goodwill" means different things to different people. A business often refers to the customer goodwill that flows from an excellent reputation, superior products, and prime location. A large corporation may claim it is furthering community goodwill by sponsoring a Little League baseball team and a series of concerts open to the public. Do the foregoing types of goodwill have any value to a business? Of course they do. However, placing a dollar value on such attributes as an improved image in the community and high levels of customer satisfaction is exceedingly difficult. These attributes involve considerable personal opinion and cannot be measured objectively. If the owners and managers of a business were permitted to arbitrarily place a value on such goodwill for entry into the accounting records, the resulting financial statements could seriously misrepresent the firm's financial condition.

It is conceivable that an outside party may be of assistance in attempting to evaluate the goodwill generated by an organization. For example, suppose that Sara Trevor, millionaire owner of ten auto museums, purchased the King City Auto Museum for $500,000 cash on July 1. The current value of King City's assets and liabilities on July 1 were as follows:

Buildings	*$150,000*
Office fixtures	*15,000*
Gift shop inventory	*20,000*
Antique automobiles (15)	*300,000*
Bank loan	*(85,000)*
	$400,000

Why did Trevor pay $500,000 when the individual assets (less liabilities) were worth only $400,000? Perhaps she felt the museum had superior earnings capabilities because of such factors as a monopolistic position, good management, and/or outstanding reputation. Naturally, it is impossible to judge the value of each specific factor and whether these are all the elements Trevor evaluated. Suffice it to say that Trevor paid an extra $100,000 for all these items collectively. To an accountant, the $100,000 is an intangible asset known as goodwill. **Goodwill** represents the amount paid by the purchaser of a business in excess of the current value of the assets and liabilities acquired.

Although King City developed the goodwill, disclosure by management on the museum's financial statements is inappropriate because of the measurement difficulties cited earlier. Trevor, on the other hand, paid $100,000 for this intangible in a valid business transaction and can record it in her accounting records as follows:

Buildings	150,000	
Office Fixtures	15,000	
Gift Shop Inventory	20,000	
Antique Automobiles	300,000	
Goodwill	100,000	
Loan Payable		85,000
Cash		500,000
Acquired the assets and liabilities of the King City Auto Museum		

Observe the manner in which the current value of the assets and liabilities becomes the cost to Trevor. If King City lacked the ability to achieve superior earnings because of a marginal location or other factors, Trevor would have probably paid less than $500,000. If, for example, the agreed-upon purchase price was $400,000, Trevor would have been buying only the separate assets (less liabilities) of King City and paying nothing for the business as an operating concern. In this case no goodwill would be recorded.

Guidelines to determine goodwill

Trevor can use several methods to calculate estimated goodwill in her negotiations for the museum. The methods include the following:

A stipulated percentage of the last twelve months' sales.
A multiple of last year's earnings.
A multiple of the amount by which the business's average earnings rate on invested capital exceeds the average earnings rate for the industry.

Other Intangibles and Deferred Charges

There are many other types of intangibles, for example, customer mailing lists, secret formulas, film rights, athletic contract rights, licenses, and airline routes. Although practice varies, many companies also include deferred charges among the intangibles on their balance sheets. A **deferred charge** is really a long-term prepaid expense. Examples include plant rearrangement costs and the costs of moving company facilities and offices. Such costs are incurred with the intention of enhancing earnings for a prolonged period of time and are, thus, capitalized in the accounts. Because of the difficulty in predicting the life of a deferred charge, however, some companies follow the practice of immediately expensing these and other similar expenditures. American Airlines, for instance, expensed $29.2 million of relocation, consolidation, and training costs when it moved its general offices from New York City to Fort Worth, Texas.

Amortization of Intangibles

Both property, plant, and equipment and intangibles benefit multiple accounting periods. In Chapter 10 we stressed that the cost of property, plant, and equipment is allocated over an estimated service life through depreciation. To properly match revenues and expenses, we perform the same process with intangibles; the name is changed, however, and the process is known as **amortization.** The entry to record the periodic amortization of an intangible is a debit to Amortization Expense and a credit to the intangible asset account. This treatment differs slightly from the depreciation entry, where the credit involved the contra asset Accumulated Depreciation. An Accumulated Amortization account is seldom used.

Determining the service life

The most troublesome issue in amortization is estimating the intangible's service life. Imagine the difficulty of determining when a beer trademark, the unique flavor of a soft drink, or an ice cream franchise would have no future economic value to their owners. Lending some assistance, the Accounting Principles Board noted that the following factors (and others) should be considered when estimating the service life of intangibles:

Legal, regulatory, or contractual provisions
Provisions for renewal or extension
Effects of obsolescence, demand, competition, and other economic factors[3]

As we previously noted, many intangibles have specified legal lives, for instance, 17 years for a patent and the life of the creator plus 50 years for a copyright. Despite the legal life, the service life of an intangible may be considerably shorter. For example, although the inventor of a new electronic device can obtain exclusive rights to its manufacture and sale for 17 years through a patent, the patent may be useful for only 5 years due to intense competition and rapid technological developments in the electronics industry. Accordingly, the patent should be written off over a 5-year period. In general, an intangible should be amortized over its legal life or service life, whichever is shorter.

Some intangibles, including goodwill and certain franchise agreements, have unlimited service lives. Until 1970 these assets did not have to be amortized. It is now accepted practice, however, to amortize *all* intangibles over a period not to exceed 40 years.[4] This lengthy maximum recognizes that the majority of intangibles do not and cannot provide indefinite benefits.

Amortization in practice

Because it is difficult to measure changes in the yearly benefits provided by intangibles, most companies use the straight-line method of amortization. Similar to straight-line depreciation, an equal amount of amortization expense is recorded each period. Several examples of intangible assets and amortization practices appear in Exhibit 11-3.

Amortization procedures

To illustrate the amortization of an intangible asset, assume Kelley Corporation purchased a patent from an inventor for $720,000 on July 1, 1983.

[3] "Intangible Assets," *Opinions of the Accounting Principles Board No. 17* (New York: American Institute of Certified Public Accountants, 1970).
[4] Ibid., paragraph 29.

Exhibit 11-3

Intangible assets and amortization practices

Company	Intangible	Amortization Policy
The Coca-Cola Company	Formulas, trademarks, goodwill, and contract rights	Formulas, trademarks, goodwill, and contract rights are stated on the basis of cost and, if purchased subsequent to October 31, 1970, are being amortized, principally on a straight-line basis, over the estimated future periods to be benefited (not exceeding 40 years).
Scripps-Howard Broadcasting Co.	Film contract rights	The cost of film contract rights acquired is allocated to each showing under a method that assigns proportionately greater values to initial showings and decreasing values to each subsequent showing; films are then amortized, by charges to income, when shown.
Turner Broadcasting System, Inc.	Player contracts	The value assigned to player contracts acquired in connection with the purchase of the Atlanta Braves professional baseball team is amortized for financial reporting purposes on the basis of the estimated remaining playing careers of the individual players acquired.

The patent was originally granted to the inventor on January 1, 1978, will provide benefits to Kelley until December 31, 1990, and has no residual value. The entries to record the purchase on July 1 and amortization on December 31, 1983, follow.

July 1	*Patents*	*720,000*	
	Cash		*720,000*
	To record purchase of patent		
Dec. 31	*Amortization Expense: Patents*	*48,000*	
	Patents		*48,000*
	To record 6 months of amortization expense		

Although the patent's 17-year legal life extends until 1995, the service life to Kelley is only $7\frac{1}{2}$ years, or 90 months (July 1, 1983 through December 31, 1990). Because monthly amortization equals \$8,000 (\$720,000 ÷ 90), amortization of \$48,000 is recorded. The Patents account would appear on Kelley's December 31, 1983, balance sheet at \$672,000 (\$720,000 − \$48,000).

Revision of amortization rates

The service life of an intangible is an estimate; as such, it is subject to error and change. The revision of an amortization rate is handled in a manner similar to the revision of a depreciation rate: the remaining unamortized cost (less any residual value) is spread over the remaining service life. Continuing the Kelley example, suppose the patent's remaining service life is reduced to 2 years on January 1, 1985, because of technological advances made by competitors. The revised yearly amortization of $288,000 is computed as follows:

Cost of patent		*$720,000*
Less: Amortization		
1983	*$48,000*	
1984	*96,000*	*144,000*
Unamortized cost		*$576,000*

Remaining life: 2 years
Amortization per year: $576,000 ÷ 2 = $288,000

When an intangible asset ceases to provide future economic benefits, the remaining unamortized cost must be written off as a loss.

NATURAL RESOURCES

Natural resources represent another major group of assets that provide long-term benefits to their owners. Examples of natural resources include oil and gas wells, mineral deposits, and standing timber. These assets are often called *wasting assets* because they are actually consumed (through removal) and do not maintain their physical presence like property, plant, and equipment.

Proper accounting for natural resources is very important because of the large sums of money involved. Often billions of dollars are spent attempting to determine if commercial production of a natural resource is feasible. During a recent 12-month period, for example, Mobil Corporation reported worldwide exploration expenses of $803 million. Furthermore, the company made long-term investments in excess of $2.1 billion in acquiring and developing energy resources.

Natural resources are initially entered in the accounting records at cost. This amount includes acquisition cost of the properties, legal fees, and surveying costs. After acquisition, significant sums are usually expended for drilling and/or exploration. Consistent with the treatment of other assets that provide long-term benefits, the exploration costs of successful ventures are capitalized and written off to expense in future years.

A controversy arises, however, concerning the exploration costs related to unsuccessful projects. Some companies say that unsuccessful efforts (e.g., dry holes) are necessary to find commercially profitable ventures. In other words, valuable information is obtained, which may have a direct bearing on a later project. This philosophy has been translated into the **full-cost approach,** which charges the exploration costs of *both* successful and unsuccessful ventures to asset accounts. In contrast, other companies follow the **successful-efforts approach,** which immediately expenses exploration costs associated with nonproductive activities. Under the latter method, then, only the costs of successful projects appear on the balance sheet. At the time of this writing, both the full-cost and successful-efforts methods are acceptable for financial reporting.

Depletion

As we previously noted, property, plant, and equipment are depreciated and intangible assets are amortized. The same process is applied to natural resources; now, however, it is called depletion. **Depletion** is the allocation of natural resource cost to the resources extracted during an accounting period. The depletion computation is similar to the units-of-output depreciation method. That is, the cost of the natural resource (less any residual value) is divided by the total estimated units (e.g., tons, barrels) in the resource deposit. The result, depletion per unit of output, is then multiplied by the number of units extracted during the period to determine the depletion charge.

To illustrate the necessary computations, assume Thompson Oil Company purchased the rights to search for oil in Louisiana. The company spent $150,000 for the rights and another $1,850,000 for exploration costs. After estimated oil reserves of 2 million barrels were discovered, Thompson incurred costs of $4,000,000 to develop a well. Thompson's depletion charge of $3 per barrel is determined in the following manner:

Cost of project	
Rights	*$ 150,000*
Exploration	*1,850,000*
Well development	*4,000,000*
Total	*$6,000,000*

cost ÷ estimated units in deposit = depletion rate
$6,000,000 ÷ 2,000,000 barrels = $3 per barrel

If 300,000 barrels are extracted and sold in the first year of the well's operation, depletion expense would total $900,000 (300,000 barrels × $3). The year-end journal entry to record depletion follows.

Depletion Expense	*900,000*	
Accumulated Depletion: Oil Property		*900,000*
To record depletion expense		

The Accumulated Depletion account is a contra asset that is deducted from the cost of the natural resource on the balance sheet. Thus Thompson would disclose its oil properties as follows:

Natural resources		
Oil properties	*$6,000,000*	
Less: Accumulated depletion	*900,000*	*$5,100,000*

Companies usually establish separate asset and accumulated depletion accounts for each major category of natural resource owned.

In the example just presented, the entire $900,000 depletion charge was expensed because all extracted oil was sold. The net result was a proper matching of revenues and expenses. If some of the extracted oil was stored for future sale, a portion of the depletion charge must be allocated to an Oil Inventory account. To illustrate, if only 285,000 barrels were sold, depletion expense would total $855,000 (285,000 × $3). Because 15,000 barrels (300,000 – 285,000) remain on hand, $45,000 (15,000 × $3) is inventoried and added to other oil production costs. The Oil Inventory account is disclosed in the current asset section of the balance sheet.

Revision of depletion rates

Depletion rates are commonly revised because of errors in the estimation of recoverable resources. The procedure for the revision of depletion rates is identical to that followed for depreciation and amortization. To illustrate, we will continue the Thompson Oil example. Assume that upon conclusion of the first year of operation, an independent geologist determined that another 2,500,000 barrels of oil were recoverable. The undepleted book value of the properties is presently $5,100,000 ($6,000,000 – $900,000). Thus the remaining book value is spread over the remaining barrels, generating a new depletion rate of $2.04 ($5,100,000 ÷ 2,500,000) per barrel.

Percentage depletion

The previous example discussed **cost depletion,** that is, the allocation of natural resource cost over the estimated recoverable units of output. Another type of depletion, known as **percentage depletion,** has been allowed by the IRS to stimulate discovery of new resource deposits and the development of existing deposits. Percentage depletion is computed by multiplying the revenue generated from natural resource sales by a stipulated percentage. Some sample depletion percentages follow:

Sulfur	22%	Copper	15%
Uranium	22%	Coal	10%
Gold	15%	Clay	5%
Silver	15%	Gravel	5%

Because depletion is calculated on revenues, not costs, aggregate depletion expense over the years can easily exceed the cost of the natural resource property.

Percentage depletion is used only for tax purposes, not for financial reporting. The importance of percentage depletion has declined significantly because Congress has disallowed its use by major oil and gas producers.

Depreciable Assets Related to Natural Resources

For commercial development of a natural resource, facilities are usually built and equipment is acquired. Often the facilities and equipment cannot be moved after the resources are exhausted. Therefore it is common practice to depreciate these assets over their own lives or the life of the deposit, whichever is shorter. Frequently, the units-of-output depreciation method is used to tie depreciation to the removal of the resource.

To illustrate, assume a mining company recently constructed a building at a mine site expected to contain 300,000 tons of ore. The building cost $160,000, has a service life of 15 years, and has an estimated residual value of $10,000. The mining company expects to extract 60,000 tons each year and will terminate activity in about 5 years (300,000 tons ÷ 60,000 tons per year). Assuming the building is permanent and cannot be moved, the use of a 15-year service life for depreciation computations results in a substantial overstatement of the years of benefit. Depreciation in this instance should be based on the life of the mine and calculated in the same manner as cost depletion. Thus a depreciation rate of $0.50 per ton is appropriate:

$$\frac{\text{cost} - \text{residual value}}{\text{estimated units in deposit}} = \text{depreciation rate per unit}$$

$$\frac{\$160{,}000 - \$10{,}000}{300{,}000 \text{ tons}} = \$0.50 \text{ per ton}$$

If production in the first year totaled the anticipated 60,000 tons, depreciation would amount to $30,000 (60,000 tons × $0.50).

KEY TERMS AND CONCEPTS

addition 412
amortization 426
assessment 414
betterment 413
copyright 421
cost depletion 430
deferred charge 425
depletion 429
fair market value 416
franchise 423
full-cost approach 428
goodwill 424
intangible asset 419
patent 421
percentage depletion 430
repairs 412
successful-efforts approach 429
trade-in allowance 416
trademark 423

QUESTIONS

Q11-1 What factors should be considered to determine whether costs incurred after the acquisition of property, plant, and equipment are handled as capital expenditures or revenue expenditures?

Q11-2 Discuss the accounting treatment normally given to the following:

a Repairs
b Additions
c Betterments
d Assessments

Q11-3 Why is it necessary to update the depreciation accounts when depreciable assets are sold, discarded, or exchanged?

Q11-4 How are gains and losses from the sale of property, plant, and equipment disclosed on the income statement? How are these gains and losses calculated?

Q11-5 How are gains and losses on the exchange of similar items of property, plant, and equipment handled for financial reporting purposes? For federal income tax purposes?

Q11-6 Why are control accounts and subsidiary ledgers used to account for property, plant, and equipment? What information does the subsidiary ledger provide?

Q11-7 Why should an inventory of property, plant, and equipment be periodically taken and compared with the subsidiary ledger records?

Q11-8 Discuss the treatment of research and development costs that are incurred in the development of a patent.

Q11-9 Define "goodwill" and explain how the cost of goodwill is determined.

Q11-10 Define "deferred charge" and present an example.

Q11-11 How is the service life of an intangible asset determined?

Q11-12 What costs are commonly capitalized in a natural resource account?

Q11-13 Explain the proper accounting treatment for the exploration costs incurred with a dry hole.

Q11-14 Define the term "depletion."

Q11-15 Explain how a portion of the depletion charge can be included in the current asset section of the balance sheet.

Q11-16 What is percentage depletion? Discuss the use of percentage depletion for both income tax and financial reporting.

Q11-17 How should a company determine the service life of a company-owned railroad track adjacent to a coal mine? Explain which depreciation method may be most appropriate for the railroad track.

EXERCISES

E11-1 The following expenditures were incurred by Paulus Corporation. Determine whether each item is a capital expenditure or a revenue expenditure.

a Painted 4 offices at a cost of $650.

b Spent $1,100 for a major overhaul on machine no. 107; the machine's service life will be extended by 2 years.

c Replaced all windows on the building with new Energy Savers at a cost of $6,450.

d Rewired the building at a cost of $18,400.

e Had the delivery truck tuned up for $78.

f Subdivided a large supply area into 3 offices at a cost of $7,550.

E11-2 The Lessem Company purchased a building many years ago at a cost of $460,000. Residual value was estimated to be $100,000, and the straight-line depreciation method has been employed. The book value of the building as of June 30, 1983, was $196,000. On July 1, 1983, the beginning of the current fiscal year, *major* repairs were completed on the building at a cost of $110,000. The repairs were expected to extend the service life of the building 10 years beyond the original estimate of 30 years.

a Compute Lessem's annual depreciation expense for fiscal years ending before July 1, 1983.

b To what account should the repairs be debited? Why?

c Compute the book value of the building after the repairs have been recorded.

d Compute depreciation expense for the current and future fiscal years.

E11-3 The Harding Company had the following transactions in 1983.

a Discarded a hand-held calculator that originally cost $150. The current book value is $30.

b Sold a fully depreciated airplane for $1,000,000. The airplane cost $4,000,000 and had an estimated residual value of $750,000.

c Paid sewer assessments on property, $1,800.

d Paid $450 to repair the front end of the delivery truck.

e Paid $120 for annual maintenance on the air-conditioning unit.

f Purchased a CB unit for each of the 10 delivery trucks. Paid $120 plus $10 installation for each unit.

Prepare the necessary journal entries.

E11-4 Selmon, Inc., purchased a truck on January 1, 1980. The truck cost $45,000, had a service life of 5 years, and had an estimated residual value of $5,000. Selmon uses the straight-line method of depreciation. Consider the following *independent* cases.

a If Selmon sells the truck on April 1, 1983, for $22,500, compute the gain or loss on the sale.

b Assume Selmon's driver demolished the truck on July 1, 1983. The company carries no insurance. If depreciation was last recorded on December 31, 1982, prepare the necessary entries to (1) update depreciation and (2) remove the truck from the accounts.

c Suppose Selmon exchanged the truck on October 1, 1983, for a new truck with an invoice price of $52,800.

(1) If the truck dealer requires Selmon to pay $38,000, compute the trade-in allowance that has been granted.

(2) List several factors that the dealer probably considered when determining Selmon's trade-in allowance.

E11-5 Arvin purchased an electric typewriter on January 1, 1980, for $1,200. The typewriter had an estimated service life of 5 years and no residual value. On April 1, 1983, Arvin acquired a new electric typewriter. The invoice price of the new machine was $2,000, service life was estimated to be 10 years, and no residual value was anticipated. Arvin received a $600 trade-in allowance, which was equal to the old machine's fair value, and paid the balance due in cash. Depreciation was last recorded on December 31, 1982, by use of the straight-line method.

a Prepare Arvin's journal entry(ies) to record the trade-in. Would the cost of the new typewriter be the same for federal income tax purposes? Why?

b Repeat part (a) assuming the life of the old typewriter was 8 years (instead of 5 years).

E11-6 On September 1, 1982, the Intangible Company paid cash to acquire a patent for $100,000, a copyright for $75,000, a trademark for $42,000, and a franchise for $4,000. The patent expires in 1992 but is expected to produce benefits for only 5 more years. The copyright has a service life of 20 years, and the trademark has an unlimited service life. The franchise allows Intangible to be the exclusive sales agent for a new product for 1 year.

a Record the necessary journal entry for the acquisition of the intangibles on September 1, 1982.

b Record amortization of the intangibles at the end of the company's fiscal year on August 31, 1983.

c Present the proper balance sheet disclosure as of August 31, 1983.

E11-7 The balance sheet of the Norfolk Neptunes Football Club as of December 31, 1983, follows.

NORFOLK NEPTUNES FOOTBALL CLUB
Balance Sheet
December 31, 1983

Current assets			
Cash		$ —	
Accounts receivable		21,000	
Prepaid expenses		10,000	$31,000
Property, plant, & equipment			
Land (practice field)		$ 5,000	
Equipment	$ 8,000		
Less: Accumulated depreciation	8,000	—	
Bus	$14,000		
Less: Accumulated depreciation	12,500	1,500	6,500
Intangibles			
Franchise: California Football League			10,000
Total assets			$47,500
Current liabilities			
Accounts payable		$27,000	
Taxes payable		4,000	
Salaries payable		15,000	$46,000
Owners' equity			
Jay Sherrad, capital			1,500
Total liabilities & owners' equity			$47,500

Richard Corbett is negotiating to buy the team. An examination of Norfolk's records reveals that $4,000 of receivables will be uncollectible. In addition, $9,000 of prepaid expenses will be worthless since Corbett wants to move the team. Current values of property, plant, and equipment and intangibles are as follows:

Land	$25,000
Equipment	500
Bus	7,500
Franchise	10,000

a If Corbett assumed Norfolk's liabilities and purchased the team for $20,000, how much was paid for goodwill?

b Prepare Corbett's entry to record the purchase of the team.

E11-8 April Mining Company purchased a coal mine for $4,500,000 in 1981. An estimated 500,000 recoverable tons of coal existed in the mine at the time of purchase. Tons of coal mined and sold during 1981–1983 were as follows:

1981	100,000 tons
1982	75,000 tons
1983	125,000 tons

a Calculate depletion expense for 1981, 1982, and 1983.

b Compute the book value of the mine at the end of 1983.

c If a geologist retained by the company determined that 300,000 recoverable tons of coal remained in the mine at the beginning of 1984, calculate the new depletion rate for 1984 and future years.

E11-9 In its initial year of operation Bullock Gold Mining Company extracted 75,000 tons of gold ore. Fifty thousand tons were sold at $12 per ton. Costs for the year, exclusive of depletion and depreciation, follow.

Labor	*$100,000*
Other mining costs	*73,000*

The gold mine cost $2,000,000 and has an estimated yield of 1,000,000 tons. Mine equipment cost $100,000, has a 30% residual value and a 7-year service life, and is depreciated by the straight-line method.

a Determine total mining costs for the year.

b Compute the mining costs that would be
 (1) Expensed on the income statement
 (2) Carried as ore inventory on the balance sheet

PROBLEMS

P11-1 ***Costs incurred after purchase; disposals***

Chain-Link had the following transactions and events during the year ended December 31, 1983.

1 The company's land was assessed $4,000 because the city plans to install water and sewer lines to the property. The assessment was paid on January 1.

2 Sold store equipment on January 1 for $8,000. The equipment cost $12,000 and had a book value of $5,000 as of December 31, 1982.

3 On January 2 the company paid $23,000 for a new roof on its building. The new roof will extend the service life of the building from an original estimate of 25 years to a total life of 30 years. The subsidiary ledger shows that the building cost $400,000, has a residual value of $150,000, and had accumulated depreciation at the beginning of 1983 of $100,000. Straight-line depreciation is being used.

4 Repaired truck no. 101 on March 1 for $50. The subsidiary ledger revealed that the truck initially cost $7,000 and had accumulated depreciation at the beginning of 1983 of $1,750. Depreciation is based on a 4-year service life

and zero residual value. The straight-line depreciation method has been used.

5 Added an air-conditioning unit to truck no. 101 on July 1. The unit cost $600, has a 5-year service life, and no estimated residual value. The straight-line depreciation method will be used.

6 Discarded office furniture on September 29 at the local landfill. The subsidiary ledger showed that the furniture cost $800 and had accumulated depreciation of $700 at the beginning of the year. The furniture has been fully depreciated down to a residual value of $100 by the double-declining balance method.

7 Replaced tires on truck no. 101 on November 15. The new tires cost $210.

INSTRUCTIONS

a Prepare journal entries to record Chain-Link's transactions and events. Depreciation was last recorded on December 31, 1982.

b Determine total depreciation expense for the year ended December 31, 1983, for items of property, plant, and equipment still owned by the company.

P11-2 ***Property, plant, and equipment errors***

The Hernandez Corporation depreciates machinery by the straight-line method. The following information was found in the subsidiary equipment ledger pertaining to machine A43.

A43				
1983		1983		
1/4 Purchase	42,000	10/2 Proceeds from sale	37,400	
1/6 Installation	3,000			
7/2 Miscellaneous repairs	1,000			

Machine A43 had an estimated service life of 5 years and a $5,000 residual value. The machine was sold for $37,400 on October 2, 1983, because of a consolidation of operations. The following entry was made.

Cash	*37,400*	
Machinery		*37,400*
Disposal of machine A43		

INSTRUCTIONS

a Present all necessary journal entries to correct the accounts as of December 31, 1983. Assume the books have not been closed.

b Discuss the impact on the financial statements, both current and future, of the incorrect capitalization of a revenue expenditure.

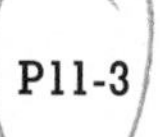

P11-3 ***Trade-ins***

On June 3, 1981, the Secrest Company purchased a specialized piece of equipment for $70,000. The equipment had an estimated service life of 10 years and an estimated residual value of $4,000. The company uses the straight-line method of depreciation on all plant assets. On June 30, 1983, Secrest traded the equipment for a new piece of equipment having an invoice price of $110,000.

The fair value of the old equipment on the date of trade was $60,000. Secrest paid $30,000 cash and signed a note payable for the remaining balance. The new equipment has a service life of 10 years and a residual value of $8,000.

In another transaction Secrest exchanged old furniture for new furniture on October 1, 1983. The old furniture was purchased on October 1, 1975, for $2,000, had a service life of 20 years, and had no estimated residual value. The new furniture cost $1,500, has a service life of 10 years, and has a residual value of $100. The fair value of the old furniture on the date of exchange was $100. Secrest promised to pay the balance owed in early 1984.

INSTRUCTIONS

a Prepare journal entries to record both trade-ins. Depreciation expense was last recorded on December 31, 1982, the end of Secrest's previous accounting year.

b Prepare journal entries to record depreciation expense on December 31, 1983, on the newly acquired assets.

c Will the newly acquired assets have the same cost for both financial reporting and federal income tax purposes? If not, which asset will be recorded differently, and what will be its acquisition cost for tax purposes?

P11-4 ***Trade-ins: Practice and theory***

On January 2, 1983, Beamer Corporation exchanged an old machine for a new machine with an invoice price of $46,000. The old machine originally cost $34,000, was carried in the accounts at a book value of $17,000, and possessed a fair market value of $16,000 on the date of exchange.

Beamer's accountant stated that the exchange could be recorded by either of the following entries:

Equipment (New)	46,000	
Accumulated Depreciation	17,000	
Loss on Exchange	1,000	
Equipment (Old)		34,000
Cash		30,000

or

Equipment (New)	47,000	
Accumulated Depreciation	17,000	
Equipment (Old)		34,000
Cash		30,000

INSTRUCTIONS

a Explain how Beamer's accountant calculated that (1) a loss of $1,000 had been incurred and (2) a cash payment of $30,000 was necessary to complete the transaction.

b Which entry would be appropriate for financial reporting purposes? Why?

c Beamer's accountant claimed that if the fair market value of the old machine had been $19,000, earnings per share for 1983 would have risen because of the immediate recognition of a gain on the exchange. Do you agree? Why?

P11-5 ***Intangibles: Acquisition cost and amortization***

On September 1, 1981, Quartz Conglomerate acquired a patent on K-82, a space-age process. Legal and filing fees amounted to $5,100; research and development costs related to the formulation of K-82 totaled $34,000. Also on September 1 Quartz purchased the patent rights on K-24 from a competitor for $120,000. The rights on K-24 have a remaining legal life of 15 years and a service life to Quartz of 10 years.

On October 1, 1981, the company acquired the copyright to a dinner theater play for $8,000 from the estate of the play's author. The author died 10 years ago. The service life of the play is estimated to be 40 years.

On November 1, 1981, Quartz acquired a perpetual franchise from Purple Punch to distribute a foamy grape-flavored drink in Alaska. The franchise was given to the company free of charge since the presidents of Quartz and Purple Punch are brothers. Similar franchises are currently selling for $18,000. Incidental costs connected with the franchise for legal and other fees totaled $6,000.

INSTRUCTIONS

a Prepare a compound (combined) entry to amortize the intangibles as of December 31, 1981.

b Prepare a compound (combined) entry to amortize the intangibles as of December 31, 1982.

c Assume that on January 1, 1983, the estimated remaining service life of the K-82 patent dropped to 4 years and the remaining life of the K-24 patent dropped to 5 years. In addition, on June 30, 1983, Quartz learned that Purple Punch went out of business; accordingly, the franchise was deemed worthless. Prepare the appropriate journal entries and record 1983 amortization.

P11-6 ***Goodwill***

After three years of negotiating between the owners, Sonju Motors agreed to purchase Blacker Motors for $32,000. The balance sheets of the companies on August 1, 1983, the date of purchase, appear on pages 439–440. A probe of Blacker's records revealed the following:

1 The books were last closed on June 30, 1983, the end of Blacker's accounting year. No adjustments have been made since that time.

2 The inventories include $2,000 of parts that are obsolete and must be discarded.

3 Prepaid expenses of $100 have expired.

4 Current market values of the building and equipment are as follows:

Building	*$25,000*
Equipment	*4,000*

5 Tools remaining on hand total $400.

6 The patent represents money spent by Blacker for research and development costs of a motor analyzer. Sonju believes the patent is worthless.

7 The deferred charge represents the cost (less amortization) of an executive training program undertaken four years ago; the account is being amortized at the rate of $500 per month. Sonju believes the training will continue to provide benefits to the firm.

INSTRUCTIONS

a Calculate the amount Sonju paid for goodwill in the acquisition of Blacker Motors.

b Prepare a balance sheet for Sonju immediately after the acquisition. Assume that Sonju paid cash for Blacker.

SONJU MOTORS CO.
Balance Sheet
August 1, 1983

ASSETS

Current assets			
Cash			$ 45,000*
Accounts receivable		$30,000	
Less: Allowance for uncollectibles		3,600	26,400
Inventories			82,000
Prepaid expenses			800
Total current assets			$154,200
Property, plant, & equipment			
Land		$80,000	
Building	$100,000		
Less: Accumulated depreciation	40,000	60,000	
Equipment	$ 20,000		
Less: Accumulated depreciation	5,000	15,000	
Total property, plant, & equipment			155,000
Intangibles			
Franchise, net of amortization			800
Total assets			$310,000

LIABILITIES & OWNERS' EQUITY

Current liabilities		
Accounts payable	$40,000	
Taxes payable	30,000	
Salaries payable	20,000	
Interest payable	1,000	
Current portion of long-term debt	5,000	
Total current liabilities		$ 96,000
Long-term liabilities		
Mortgage payable		40,000
Total liabilities		$136,000
Owners' equity		
Sonju, capital		174,000
Total liabilities & owners' equity		$310,000

*Prior to the purchase of Blacker.

BLACKER MOTORS CO.
Balance Sheet
August 1, 1983

ASSETS			
Current assets			
Cash		$ 1,500	
Accounts receivable		40,000	
Inventories		10,000	
Prepaid expenses		500	$ 52,000
Property, plant, & equipment			
Building	$50,000		
Less: Accumulated depreciation	32,000	$18,000	
Equipment	$10,000		
Less: Accumulated depreciation	8,000	2,000	
Tools		500	20,500
Intangibles			
Patent		$28,500	
Deferred charge, net of amortization		11,500	40,000
Total assets			$112,500
LIABILITIES & OWNERS' EQUITY			
Current liabilities			
Accounts payable		$15,100	
Current portion of long-term debt		10,000	$ 25,100
Long-term liabilities			
Bank loan payable			40,000
Total liabilities			$ 65,100
Owners' equity			
Blacker, capital			47,400
Total liabilities & owners' equity			$112,500

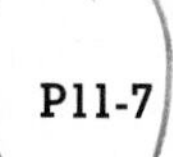
P11-7 ***Depletion***

The Shiny Metal Mining Company purchased a tract of land, together with mineral rights, for $70,000. After incurring exploration costs of $125,000 and legal fees of $5,000, Shiny Metal learned that 150,000 tons of high-grade ore could be extracted from the site. The company estimates that production will be 10,000 tons during the first year and 20,000 tons each year thereafter. The mining site is estimated to have a residual value of $20,000 since the land can be used for farming after all mining operations have ceased.

Shiny Metal plans to construct the necessary mining structures (buildings, sheds, and bunkhouses) on the site for $150,000. According to the contractor, the structures will have a service life of 20 years with no residual value. They will be abandoned when production ceases. Finally, machinery and equipment must be acquired, which costs $100,000, has a service life of 10 years, and has a residual value of $10,000. All equipment will be removed from the mine site when production ends.

INSTRUCTIONS

a Prepare a schedule for management of depletion and depreciation expense for each year the mine is anticipated to operate. The following depreciation methods will be used.

Structures	Units-of-output method
Machinery and equipment	Straight-line method

b Assume that during the first year, 12,000 tons of ore were extracted from the mine. If sales were only 8,000 tons, calculate the total depletion charge and explain how it is treated in the financial statements. Total mine-related costs, excluding depletion, amounted to $3 per ton.

c Assume that the following production has been attained.

Year	Production (Tons)
1	12,000
2	18,000
3	25,000
4	15,000
5	30,000

According to a new report received from the company geologist, 100,000 tons of ore remain in the mine at the start of Year 6. Calculate the depletion charge per ton on future production.

P11-8 ***Costs incurred after purchase; disposals (alternate to P11-1)***

Galleria, Inc., had the following transactions and events during the year ended December 31, 1983.

1 The company's land was assessed $2,800 because the city plans to install water and sewer lines to the property. The assessment was paid on January 1.

2 Sold office equipment on January 1 for $6,200. The equipment cost $15,800 and had a book value of $6,700 as of December 31, 1982.

3 On January 2 the company paid $18,000 for a new roof on its building. The new roof will extend the service life of the building from an original estimate of 30 years to a total life of 36 years. The subsidiary ledger shows that the building cost $670,000, has a residual value of $100,000, and had accumulated depreciation at the beginning of 1983 of $228,000. Straight-line depreciation is being used.

4 Repaired truck no. 118 on June 1 for $120. The subsidiary ledger revealed that the truck initially cost $10,500 and had accumulated depreciation at the beginning of 1983 of $2,100. Depreciation is based on a 5-year service life and zero residual value. The straight-line depreciation method has been used.

5 Added an air-conditioning unit to truck no. 118 on July 1. The unit cost $700, has a 5-year service life, and has no estimated residual value. The straight-line depreciation method will be used.

6 Discarded some old machinery on November 30 at the local landfill. The subsidiary ledger showed that the machinery cost $1,400 and had accumulated depreciation of $1,200 at the beginning of the year. The machinery has been fully depreciated down to a residual value of $200 by the double-declining balance method.
7 Replaced tires on truck no. 118 on December 11. The new tires cost $285.

INSTRUCTIONS

a Prepare journal entries to record Galleria's transactions and events. Depreciation was last recorded on December 31, 1982.
b Determine total depreciation expense for the year ended December 31, 1983, for items of property, plant, and equipment still owned by the company.

P11-9 ***Property, plant, and equipment errors (alternate to P11-2)***

The Hoskins Corporation depreciates machinery by the straight-line method. The following information was found in the subsidiary equipment ledger pertaining to machine L4800.

L4800					
1983			1983		
1/2	Purchase	37,000	8/1	Proceeds from sale	30,700
1/5	Installation	2,000			
7/3	Minor repairs	600			

Machine L4800 had an estimated service life of 8 years and a $3,000 residual value. The machine was sold for $30,700 on August 1, 1983, because of a consolidation of operations. The following entry was made.

Notes Receivable	30,700	
Machinery		30,700
Disposal of machine L4800		

INSTRUCTIONS

a Present all necessary journal entries to correct the accounts as of December 31, 1983. Assume the books have not been closed.
b Discuss the impact on the financial statements, both current and future, of the incorrect capitalization of a revenue expenditure.

P11-10 ***Trade-ins (alternate to P11-3)***

On October 1, 1981, the Clone Company purchased a piece of equipment for $105,000. The equipment had an estimated service life of 7 years and an estimated residual value of $7,000. The company uses straight-line depreciation on all items of property, plant, and equipment. On September 30, 1983, Clone traded the equipment for a new piece of equipment having an invoice price of $140,000. The fair value of the old equipment on the date of trade was $35,000. Clone paid $40,000 cash and signed a note for the remaining balance. The new equipment has an estimated service life of 10 years and a residual value of $15,000.

In another transaction Clone exchanged a delivery van for a new vehicle on November 1, 1983. The old van was purchased on June 1, 1980, for $8,000, had a service life of 4 years, and had an estimated $800 residual value. The new van cost $12,000, has a service life of 5 years, and has a residual value of $2,000. The fair value of the old van was $2,100 on the date of trade. Clone paid the balance due in cash.

INSTRUCTIONS

a Prepare journal entries to record both trade-ins. Depreciation expense was last recorded on December 31, 1982, the end of Clone's previous accounting year.

b Prepare journal entries to record depreciation expense on December 31, 1983, on the newly acquired assets.

c Will the newly acquired assets have the same cost for both financial reporting and federal income tax purposes? If not, which asset will be recorded differently, and what will be its acquisition cost for tax purposes?

P11-11 ***Intangibles: Acquisition cost and amortization (alternate to P11-5)***

On April 1, 1981, Bubble Machine, Inc., acquired a patent on chocolate bubble gum, which had been developed in its research and development department. Costs of research and development totaled $85,000; legal and filing fees were $1,700. Also on April 1 the company acquired a patent on tropical fruit gum from a competitor for $90,000. This patent has a remaining life of 15 years but should be useful to Bubble Machine for only 10 years, according to the firm's marketing director.

On May 1, 1981, the company paid $12,000 to acquire the copyright to a classic painting of a traffic policeman chewing gum. The artist died 20 years ago. The service life of the copyright is estimated to be 5 years.

On June 1, 1981, Bubble Machine acquired a perpetual franchise to distribute Jenny Gumball Machines. The cost of the franchise was $30,000; incidental costs connected with the franchise for legal fees totaled $3,600.

INSTRUCTIONS

a Prepare a compound (combined) entry to amortize the intangibles as of December 31, 1981.

b Prepare a compound (combined) entry to amortize the intangibles as of December 31, 1982.

c Assume that on January 1, 1983, the remaining service life of both the chocolate bubble gum and tropical fruit gum is estimated to be 5 years. Further, assume that the gumball franchise ceased operation on June 30, 1983. Prepare the appropriate journal entries and record 1983 amortization.

P11-12 ***Depletion (alternate to P11-7)***

The Red Barn Coal Company purchased a tract of land, together with mineral rights, for $275,000. After incurring exploration costs of $225,000 and legal fees of $50,000, Red Barn learned that 1,100,000 tons of coal could be extracted from the site. The company estimates that production will be 200,000 tons during the first year and 75,000 tons each year thereafter. The mining site is estimated to have a residual value of $110,000.

Red Barn plans to construct the necessary mining structures (buildings, sheds, and so on) on the site for $385,000. According to the contractor, the structures have a service life of 30 years with no residual value. The company does not intend to move the structures when production ceases. Finally, machinery and equipment, which costs $440,000, has a service life of 15 years, and has a residual value of $50,000, must be acquired for use at the mine. The equipment will be moved to other company properties after production ends.

INSTRUCTIONS

a Prepare a schedule for management of depletion and depreciation expense for each year the mine is anticipated to operate. The following depreciation methods will be used.

Structures	Units-of-output method
Machinery and equipment	Straight-line method

b Assume that during the first year 150,000 tons of coal were extracted from the mine. If sales were only 140,000 tons, calculate the total depletion charge and explain how it is treated in the financial statements. Total mine-related costs, excluding depletion, amounted to $2.50 per ton.

c Assume that the following production has been attained.

Year	Production (Tons)
1	150,000
2	100,000
3	100,000
4	75,000
5	50,000

According to a new report received from the company geologist, 1,000,000 tons of coal remain in the mine at the start of Year 6. Calculate the depletion charge per ton on future production.

CASE 11
DUDLEY FINFROCK, BANKER

Dudley Finfrock is the assistant vice-president for commercial lending of the Maplewood National Bank. He has recently been approached by two aggressive companies for business loans. Both companies are engaged in high-technology product development and sales, but each company has used a different approach to achieve its ultimate profit objective.

Linden Electronics is run by two ex-employees of Woodhaven Semiconductor, John Brown and Stan Hall. Brown has an orientation toward research; Hall's specialty is sales. With an initial capital of $150,000 the two partners have developed many valuable products. Over $80,000 has been spent on research and development, and from this effort three patents have been obtained. (Legal costs and filing fees connected with the patents were negligible because Linden's attorney is a family relative.) Advertising and sales promotion costs have consumed the remaining funds.

Rabway Electronics is also managed by two bright entrepreneurs, Harry

Scott and Jack Monroe. Scott and Monroe were finance majors at the local university and possess minimal knowledge of electronics and sales. To establish a viable company, Rabway acquired existing patents from a California firm for $100,000. To generate sales, Scott and Monroe also purchased a franchise for $40,000 to sell a product similar to their own. In this manner the two products could be marketed together. Finally, Rabway spent $10,000 for legal fees related to the patents and franchise.

In the first few years of business Linden operated at a net loss, while Rabway had impressive profits. A comparison of the financial statements and other operating information revealed that sales and production costs of the two companies were virtually identical. In addition, their products were very similar.

INSTRUCTIONS

Explain the probable cause behind Linden's net losses and Rabway's profits. If you were in Dudley's position, would you grant a loan to Linden or Rabway? Why?

12

CURRENT LIABILITIES AND PAYROLL

LEARNING OBJECTIVES

After reading this chapter you should:

1 Be familiar with the occurrence of and accounting for typical current liabilities of a business.

2 Be able to record accrued expenses, including property taxes.

3 Understand how the accounting treatment of notes payable differs when interest is included in the face value of a note and when interest is recorded separately.

4 Recognize contingent liabilities, when they are recorded in the accounts, and when footnote disclosure is appropriate.

5 Understand accounting for warranty costs.

6 Understand payroll accounting, including the role of internal control, the differentiation between employees and independent contractors, and the treatment of taxes.

CHAPTER 12

The five preceding chapters have presented various valuation and income determination issues related to current and long-term assets. We now turn our attention to another important element of the fundamental accounting equation: liabilities. Liabilities are obligations that (1) have arisen from past transactions or events and (2) are payable in cash, other assets, or services. The measurement and disclosure of liabilities in the financial statements is extremely important, because future cash outlays or services are involved. Many suppliers, for example, refuse to grant credit to businesses with high levels of liabilities for fear of nonpayment. Similarly, most investors shy away from companies heavily burdened by debt because of the risk involved. Why? Substantial debt payments are often accompanied by large outlays for interest, thus reducing an investor's chance of receiving dividends. Adding to this problem is the fact that the firm's cash position may be extremely weak in periods of a softening economy.

As we noted in Chapter 6, liabilities are classified as either current or long-term, depending on the due date (or dates). We will discuss current liabilities in this chapter and long-term liabilities in Chapter 15.

CURRENT LIABILITIES

Current liabilities are debts or obligations that will be paid within one year or the operating cycle, whichever is longer. Payment of current liabilities involves the use of current assets (usually cash) or, on occasion, the creation of another current liability. For example, an account payable could be settled by issuing a short-term interest-bearing note to the creditor.

Current liabilities are reported on the balance sheet at the amount necessary to settle the obligation. Naturally, it is desirable that all debts and obligations be disclosed. The failure to record a current liability not only understates total liabilities but also affects assets or expenses as well. Because management may deliberately try to boost net income by hiding unpaid bills, accountants must take great care in their recognition of an entity's short-term debts.

Typical current liabilities include the following:

1. Accounts payable.
2. Prepayments (advances) by customers.
3. Amounts collected for and payable to third parties.
4. The portion of long-term debt due within one year or the operating cycle, whichever is longer.
5. Accrued liabilities for expenses incurred but not yet paid.
6. Notes payable to banks and other parties.
7. Contingent liabilities.

Accounts Payable

Accounts payable, sometimes called *trade accounts payable,* represent amounts owed to suppliers for the purchase of goods or services. The creation and control of these short-term obligations was discussed in Chapters 4 and 5.

The use of accounts payable and trade credit is a convenient means of financing inventory acquisitions, particularly seasonal needs or special daily requirements. Consider a tobacco shop and a candy shop, both of which have increased sales activity just prior to holidays (e.g., Father's Day and Christmas for the former and Easter, Valentine's Day, and Mother's Day for the latter). Does it pay for these businesses to maintain high inventory levels throughout the year to accommodate these peak periods? Of course not. Idle inventory costs money in terms of interest charges and profits forgone from alternative investments. By using trade credit, businesses have the opportunity to fund the necessary buildup in inventory. The inventory can then be sold to pay suppliers within the normal 30- to 60-day credit period.

Most accounting systems are capable of recording trade payables when goods and services are acquired or rendered. More often than not, however, the payable is recorded when an invoice is received from the supplier. Unfortunately, delays, timing differences, and errors frequently permeate the process. For example, the invoice may sit in an in-basket for a few days awaiting processing. Or goods purchased under terms of F.O.B. shipping point may still be in transit at the end of the period. Although the goods legally belong to the purchaser because of the passage of title, the liability (and inventory) may be erroneously overlooked. After all, there would be no paperwork documenting the goods' arrival at the warehouse, and there is a strong possibility that the purchaser has yet to be invoiced. Because of these and other problems, the accountant must pay particular attention to transactions occurring at the beginning and end of an accounting period. In this manner, the purchases of goods and services and their associated liabilities will be correctly entered in the records.

Prepayments (Advances) by Customers

Businesses often receive **prepayments,** or advances, from customers. Insurance companies collect premiums; publishers sell magazine subscriptions; stores issue gift certificates; and transportation firms sell tickets and tokens before their service is delivered. These amounts, frequently termed *unearned revenues* or *deferred revenues*, represent liabilities to the recipient because goods or services are owed in return. You were originally introduced to unearned revenues in Chapter 3 and may find a review of this earlier material helpful.

The balance sheet should report the amount of goods and services owed as of the statement's date. As the obligations are settled, the prepayments are reduced with a corresponding increase in revenue on the income statement. For most businesses prepayments are relatively modest in amount. There are exceptions (and some sizable ones!) as shown in Exhibit 12-1.

Collections for Third Parties

In the normal course of business, organizations frequently collect money from customers and employees that is payable to others. Retailers, for example, accumulate sales tax from customers when goods are sold. Subsequently, the monies collected are remitted to the proper governmental authority. Similarly, companies often become involved in United Way or

Exhibit 12-1

Examples of customer prepayments*

Organization	*Prepayment Form*	*Amount (in Thousands)*	*Percentage of Total Current Liabilities*
Sears, Roebuck and Co.	Unearned maintenance agreement income	$ 433,500	23.3%
Cleveland Professional Basketball Company	Advance season ticket sales	660	9.3
Burroughs	Customers' deposits and prepayments	154,893	11.5
Delta Air Lines	Unused passenger tickets	245,579	41.7
U.S. Postal Service	Prepaid permit mail, box rentals, and postage	1,099,355	29.3

** Data obtained from recent annual reports.*

disaster relief activities, receiving funds that are ultimately disbursed to various social service agencies. And, as we will discuss later in this chapter, payroll deductions are customarily made from employee wages for taxes and other items, which must be forwarded to third parties.

Collections such as those above are recognized as current liabilities until cash is disbursed to the proper authority. To illustrate the necessary accounting, assume that the Yorktown Candle Shoppe sells $1,000 of merchandise on account in a state having a 5% sales tax. The entry to record the sale follows.

Accounts Receivable	*1,050*	
Sales		*1,000*
Sales Taxes Payable		*50*
To record sale and related sales tax		

A liability of $50 ($1,000 × 0.05) is established for the sales tax, which Yorktown now owes to the state treasury. When the tax is remitted, Sales Taxes Payable will be debited and Cash will be credited. The liability is thus eliminated. Other third-party collections are handled in a similar manner.

Current Portion of Long-Term Debt

As we noted, long-term liabilities will be discussed at length in a subsequent chapter. At this point, however, it is essential to understand that the portion of long-term debt due within one year or the normal operating cycle, whichever is longer, is reported as a current liability. For example, suppose a firm borrowed $200,000 through a long-term loan. If $30,000 is payable within the next 12 months, the appropriate balance sheet disclosure would be as follows:

Current liabilities	
Current portion of long-term debt	*$30,000*

Long-term liabilities		
Loan payable	*$200,000*	
Less balance due currently	*30,000*	*$170,000*

Treatment as a current liability presumes that the short-term portion will be liquidated by the use of current assets or by the creation of other current liabilities. If not, such amounts remain as long-term liabilities until paid or refinanced.

Accrued Liabilities

Accrued liabilities, often called accrued expenses, were also introduced in Chapter 3. Under the accrual basis of accounting, expenses are matched against revenues in the period when incurred. This practice generally results in the recognition of some unpaid expenses and necessitates the placement of accrued liabilities on the balance sheet. Examples of accrued liabilities include salaries and wages, income taxes (both federal and state), local property taxes, and interest.

A discussion of several of these accrued liabilities is helpful. We will now present a basic example relating to salaries and a more complex illustration dealing with property taxes.

Accrued salaries

Accrued salaries and wages result when an accounting period ends in the midst of a payroll period. For example, suppose that Rosenthal has a 5-day workweek and all employees are paid on Friday. Also assume that the end of the annual accounting period, November 30, falls on Thursday. Although employees will not be paid until December 1, Rosenthal must accrue payroll expense on November 30 for the work performed from Monday through Thursday. In so doing, revenue and expense for the period just ended will be correctly matched and current liabilities will be properly recorded. If salaries total $10,500 per day, the adjusting entry is as follows:

Salaries Expense	*42,000*	
Salaries Payable		*42,000*
*To accrue four days of salaries at $10,500 per day**		

*Payroll taxes should also be accrued at this time.

Property taxes

Most municipalities provide a variety of services for the households and businesses located within their boundaries. Examples of such services include fire and police protection, libraries, snow removal, street repair, and summer recreation programs. A major source of funding for these and other activities comes from property taxes. Property taxes are based on an assessed valuation of the property owned by local businesses and residents. Although such taxes are normally paid in one or two installments, it is logical to record accrued taxes through the year because of the continuous period of benefit.

Accounting for property taxes is complicated by the fact that the fiscal year of the taxpayer often differs from the fiscal year of the taxing authority.

Because tax rates and assessed valuations frequently change, a question arises concerning the proper period of expense recognition. The accounting profession recommends that property taxes be accrued monthly over the fiscal period of the taxing authority.[1] As a result, the property owner's expense recognition will coincide with the same period that the municipality used the tax dollars to provide services.

To illustrate, we consider the following information, which relates to the Mendoza Company.

Mendoza's fiscal year	Jan. 1, 1983, through Dec. 31, 1983
Taxing authority's fiscal year	July 1, 1983, through June 30, 1984
Tax statement received	Oct. 10, 1983
Taxes due	Nov. 15, 1983

During July Mendoza estimated property taxes for the upcoming year (July 1983–June 1984) at $24,000. The estimate was based on last year's tax bill plus knowledge of a recent rate hike. At the end of July Mendoza will record accrued taxes of $2,000 ($24,000 ÷ 12 months) as follows:

Property Tax Expense	*2,000*	
Property Taxes Payable		*2,000*
To record monthly property tax accrual		

The same entry will be repeated at the end of August and September.

On October 10 Mendoza received a tax statement from the city for $25,200, reflecting an actual monthly tax of $2,100 ($25,200 ÷ 12). Because the difference between the actual and estimated expense is small, it is permissible to correct the records when the next accrual is recorded. Mendoza would make the following entry on October 31.

Property Tax Expense	*2,400*	
Property Taxes Payable		*2,400*
To record monthly property tax accrual and correct for estimation error		

To explain, the tax expense and liability accounts have each been understated by $300 ($100 per month × 3 months). Both accounts must now be increased along with recording October's accrual of $2,100.

Next, Mendoza must pay the taxes due on November 15. The entry below is needed.

Property Taxes Payable	*8,400*	
Prepaid Property Taxes	*16,800*	
Cash		*25,200*
To record payment of property taxes		

The total amount due is $25,200. Immediately after the October 31 entry,

[1] See *Accounting Research and Terminology Bulletins—Final Edition* (New York: American Institute of Certified Public Accountants, 1961), Chapter 10, paragraph 14.

the Property Taxes Payable account has a credit balance of $8,400 [($2,000 × 3 months) + $2,400]. Because this balance represents taxes for July through October, the remaining amount remitted is a prepaid expense. That is, $16,800 ($25,200 − $8,400) covers tax payments pertaining to the period November 1983 through June 1984. Beginning on November 30 the prepayment will be written off to expense at the rate of $2,100 per month. The final adjusting entry will be made on June 30, 1984, with the entire process commencing once again in July for the next fiscal year.

Notes Payable

Short-term notes have many uses in the business world. Notes are commonly employed to purchase merchandise, equipment, real estate, and other similar assets. In addition, notes can be used to secure short-term borrowings from banks. General Mills, for example, recently reported notes payable to banks of $71.6 million on its year-end balance sheet. Such temporary use of bank credit for periods of less than one year is commonplace and serves as a vital source of funds for many businesses.

Notes payable are also issued at the request of creditors when a firm (or individual) is past due in the payment of an account payable. The note is simply substituted for the account payable on the books of the issuing business. A creditor prefers a note to a delinquent open account for two reasons. First, should the issuer fail to pay the debt on schedule, a signed note provides better security if legal remedies are necessary. Second, a note is normally an interest-generating instrument.

Accounting for notes payable

To illustrate the proper accounting for notes payable, assume that Corsica Trading Corporation borrowed $80,000 from the Mercantile National Bank on June 3 by signing the obligation shown in Exhibit 12-2. The journal entry to record the receipt of funds and issuance of the note follows.

Cash	*80,000*	
Notes Payable		*80,000*
To record note payable to bank; 180 days at 15%		

Observe that the face value of the note is equal to the amount borrowed and that no interest expense is recorded on the date of issue. Interest will be incurred on a daily basis over the term of the loan.

Next, assume that Corsica's fiscal year ends on October 31. Because the note was issued on June 3 and does not mature until November 30, interest expense must be apportioned to two fiscal periods. Thus on October 31, 150 days of interest (June 3–October 31) is accrued via the following adjusting entry:

Interest Expense	*5,000*	
Interest Payable		*5,000*
To accrue interest for 150 days: $80,000 × 0.15 × $\frac{150}{360}$		

Exhibit 12-2

Example of note payable

Date June 3, 1983 New York, New York 10059

The undersigned promises to pay the Mercantile National Bank in 180 days the sum of $80,000 with interest at the rate of 15% per year.

R. B. Thompson

Corsica Trading Corporation

Corsica's balance sheet would therefore appear as shown below:

Current liabilities		
Notes payable	*$80,000*	
Interest payable	*5,000*	*$85,000*

When the note is paid on November 30, the following entry is necessary.

Notes Payable	*80,000*	
Interest Payable	*5,000*	
Interest Expense	*1,000*	
Cash		*86,000*
To record payment to bank for note payable and interest		

The additional $1,000 represents the 30 days of interest incurred in November ($\frac{1}{6}$ of the loan term).

Notes with interest included in the face value

Many notes, especially those issued to banks and finance companies, do not state interest separately. Instead interest is included in the obligation's face value. For example, assume that Corsica Trading still needs to raise $80,000. Mercantile National Bank, however, agreed to accept the $86,000 note appearing in Exhibit 12-3.

Corsica's entry to record the loan's proceeds and issue the note follows.

Cash	*80,000*	
Discount on Notes Payable	*6,000*	
Notes Payable		*86,000*
To record note payable to bank; 180 days until maturity		

As in the previous case, the note is recorded at face value—$86,000 in this instance. Cash received remains at $80,000. The difference between these two figures, $6,000, represents 180 days of future interest, which will be incurred over the term of the note. This amount is entered in an account entitled Discount on Notes Payable, a **contra liability** that is deducted from Notes Payable on the balance sheet. If a balance sheet was prepared immedi-

Exhibit 12-3

Note payable with interest included in the face value

Date June 3, 1983 New York, New York 10059

The undersigned promises to pay the Mercantile National Bank the sum of $86,000 in 180 days.

R. B. Thompson

Corsica Trading Corporation

ately after issuance, Corsica would present the following information:

Current liabilities		
Notes payable	*$86,000*	
Less: Discount on notes payable	*6,000*	*$80,000*

The net liability on June 3 is $80,000, the amount borrowed on that day.

Discount amortization

Assume it is now October 31, the end of Corsica's year. Because 150 days have passed since the note's issuance, interest expense must be recognized. As we just stated, the discount's $6,000 balance represents 180 days of future interest charges. Thus $5,000 ($6,000 × $\frac{150}{180}$) must be removed from the Discount account and transferred to the income statement. The following adjusting entry is needed.

Interest Expense	*5,000*	
Discount on Notes Payable		*5,000*
To accrue interest for 150 days and amortize the discount		

The process of reducing the discount by recognizing interest expense is frequently referred to as **discount amortization.**

As a result of the adjustment, the Discount on Notes Payable account will have a $1,000 balance ($6,000 − $5,000) and will appear on the balance sheet as follows:

Current liabilities		
Notes payable	*$86,000*	
Less: Discount on notes payable	*1,000*	*$85,000*

The net liability is now $85,000: $80,000 borrowed plus accrued interest of $5,000. No separate account for interest payable is established because the interest is already part of the note's face value.

To complete the example, the entry on page 456 would be necessary when Corsica pays the note on November 30.

Notes Payable	*86,000*	
Interest Expense	*1,000*	
Discount on Notes Payable		*1,000*
Cash		*86,000*
To record payment of the note and amortize the discount		

This entry recognizes the remaining $1,000 of interest expense that pertains to November and cancels the balance in the Notes Payable account.

A brief comparison

Observe that with both the $80,000 and $86,000 notes, Corsica received $80,000 and ultimately paid $6,000 of interest. Furthermore, the balance sheet presentations at the end of the October 31 fiscal year both revealed a total liability of $85,000. To conclude, the notes differed in form only. In the first case interest was stated separately; in the second case interest was included in the obligation's face value.

Contingent Liabilities

All the liabilities presented thus far have been definite and absolute. Although estimates were sometimes involved (see the property tax discussion as an example), there was no uncertainty regarding a firm's legal and economic responsibility for the obligation. Frequently, an existing situation gives rise to a *potential* liability. As we saw in Chapter 8, for example, the payee of a discounted note receivable was liable to the bank if the maker defaulted and dishonored the note. Going back even further, an example was presented in Chapter 6 (see p. 233) relating to a lawsuit filed by a Seven-Up/Pepsi-Cola bottler against the Dr Pepper Company. The plaintiff contended that Dr Pepper had violated federal antitrust laws and sought damages of $15 million, trebled.

Liabilities of this nature are commonly referred to as **contingent liabilities,** because their outcome hinges on the future. Future events and happenings will convert the contingent liability into an absolute liability or eliminate it entirely. In addition to discounted notes receivable and lawsuits, other contingent liabilities include obligations related to product warranties and coupon redemptions.

Over the years the treatment of contingent liabilities has been the subject of much debate. Sometimes contingent liabilities were recorded in the accounts through a journal entry. On other occasions disclosure was made in the footnotes that accompany the financial statements. On still other occasions nothing was done for fear of misleading statement users about a liability that might never materialize. This latter approach apparently followed the "no news is good news" doctrine.

Recently, guidelines were issued to "standardize" accounting for contingent liabilities.[2] Contingent liabilities should be recorded in the accounts when (1) it is *probable* that the future event will occur and (2) the amount of

[2] See "Accounting for Contingencies," *Statement of Financial Accounting Standards No. 5* (Stamford, Conn.: Financial Accounting Standards Board, 1975).

the liability can be *reasonably estimated.* Observe the key words in italics. If only one of these criteria is met, no journal entry is made; footnote disclosure is deemed appropriate.

By their very nature, these guidelines are vague and open to interpretation. For example, how does one determine the likelihood of an event's occurrence? What differentiates an event as being *probable,* as stated in the guidelines, from being "reasonably possible"? Also, what is considered a *reasonable* estimate? Because of the subjectivity involved, the accountant cannot work in isolation. Close contact with engineers, lawyers, and other professionals is necessary to correctly implement these criteria.

Warranty costs

To illustrate accounting for a contingent liability that typically meets both guidelines, we will focus on warranty costs. A **warranty** is a promise made by a seller or manufacturer to remedy defects in product quality and performance. Most appliances, for example, are warranted for one year; the major components of automobiles often have a 50,000-mile warranty.

As we all know, a percentage of goods and services (hopefully small) will always fall into the defective category. From past experience a business can normally estimate, with reasonable accuracy, the cost of honoring warranties. Since most warranties help to promote the sale of goods and services, warranty costs should be matched against sales revenues when the revenues are generated. In attempting to follow this procedure, however, businesses are confronted with a problem. The majority of warranty costs arise in subsequent periods as products become older. As a remedy for this situation, an estimated expense is recorded in the period of sale. At the same time a contingent liability is entered in the accounts to reflect a firm's potential exposure to warranty work.

As an example, assume Drake Appliance sold 120 television sets in 1983. Each television has a one-year warranty. Drake estimates that 25% of the sets will require warranty work and that the work will average $40 per set. The journal entry to record the estimated warranty cost of $1,200 (120 sets × 0.25 × $40) and establish the liability is as follows:

Warranty Expense	*1,200*	
Estimated Liability for Warranties		*1,200*
To record warranty costs for 1983		

As the warranties are honored, Drake will reduce the liability. If 10 sets were serviced during 1983, the journal entry would be as follows:

Estimated Liability for Warranties	*400*	
Cash, Salaries Payable, Parts Inventory, and so on		*400*
To record service cost under warranties: 10 sets × $40		

The Estimated Liability for Warranties account would be reported on the December 31, 1983, balance sheet at $800 ($1,200 – $400). This amount represents the estimated warranty cost in 1984 of servicing televisions sold in 1983.

Balance Sheet Disclosure

Current liabilities are normally presented on the balance sheet according to due date (from the earliest to the latest) or maturity value (from the largest to the smallest). Reporting practices vary widely, however. To illustrate typical presentations, we show the current liability sections from recent balance sheets of NCR Corporation and RCA in Exhibit 12-4.

Exhibit 12-4

Current liability presentations (in millions)

NCR	
Current liabilities	
Notes payable	$ 132.4
Commercial paper	70.0
Current installments on long-term debt	18.8
Accounts payable	98.5
Taxes payable	172.1
Payroll payable	112.3
Customers' deposits and deferred service revenue	252.2
Other current liabilities	242.2
Total current liabilities	$1,098.5

RCA	
Current liabilities	
Notes payable	$ 277.9
Hertz debt payable within one year*	717.5
Accounts payable	609.5
Accrued wages, salaries, & other compensation	219.4
Other accrued liabilities	894.7
Accrued artist, copyright, & product royalties	126.5
Taxes on income	150.3
Dividends payable	66.9
Total current liabilities	$3,062.7

*Authors' note: RCA owns The Hertz Corporation, a subsidiary engaged in automobile- and truck-leasing activities.

ACCOUNTING FOR PAYROLL

Employees' wages, salaries, related payroll taxes, and fringe benefits are a significant expense for many businesses, particularly those engaged in providing services. For example, Arthur Andersen & Co., one of the Big Eight accounting firms, recently reported employee compensation and benefits amounting to 53.5% of fees earned. At H&R Block, salaries and related expenses of $126.3 million comprised over 57% of total operating expenses. These costs are sure to rise as employees demand higher wages and benefits to cope with inflation.

Accounting for payroll is important not only because of the large amounts of money involved but also because of the various federal and state regulations that relate to payroll records. By law, businesses must maintain detailed payroll information on individual employees and aggregate information for the business as a whole. As a consequence of these demanding requirements, many companies use computers to process payroll data. Indeed, it is hard to imagine how large corporate giants with thousands of employees worldwide could keep detailed payroll records, issue prompt and accurate paychecks, and complete reports for governmental agencies without some form of electronic data processing.

Internal Control

Payroll systems, whether manual or computerized, must contain strong internal controls to safeguard funds and ensure the accurate processing of payroll information. An absence of controls will often lead to a high frequency of errors and, on occasion, fraud. Many ingenious embezzlements have been successful in weak control environments. One of the most common frauds has been the "padded" payroll, which involves payments to fictitious employees. As one leading accountant notes:

> *Theoretically, a corrupt personnel department employee could authorize entry of a ghost on the rolls. However, the employee would also have to provide for receiving the paycheck and annual . . . tax form and make sure that no one ever wondered where "Joe" worked and why "Joe" was never seen. Complications are added if "Joe" has to submit periodic time reports (a supervisor would have to approve them) or if he has to participate in a periodic salary review program.*[3]

Although a scheme like this sounds bizarre, its probability of success is high, especially in large organizations where a lack of communication often prevails among departments.

Internal controls must be implemented to guard against not only the issuance of checks to fictitious employees but also duplicate paychecks, paychecks to persons who have been terminated or who have voluntarily quit, and overpayments to existing personnel. In addition, the payroll system must be sufficiently developed so that records are correctly maintained for new employees, employees receiving promotions, and employees receiving wage and salary increases.

Employees and Independent Contractors

For purposes of payroll accounting an organization must distinguish between employees and independent contractors. The distinction is important because payroll regulations, whether they pertain to taxes, reporting, or record keeping, apply solely to the employees of a business. **Employees** are persons who work for a specific business and are directed and closely supervised by that business. **Independent contractors,** on the other hand, frequently perform services for many different organizations at the same time or perhaps finish a project for one entity and then move on to service another. Common examples of independent contractors include certified pub-

[3] Jack C. Robertson, *Auditing*, rev. ed. (Dallas: Business Publications, Inc. Copyright © 1979), p. 560.

lic accountants, attorneys, and architects. Observe that an employer/employee relationship does not exist; rather the independent contractor is engaged to provide a service, performs that service without direct supervision from the client, and receives a fee in return.

Employee Earnings

Wages and salaries earned by employees develop either from a negotiated contract between a company and representatives of its employees or from a direct agreement between the company and individual personnel. The former is usually encountered for a firm's labor force, while the latter relates most often to management.

The wages and salaries earned are paid after the payroll period has concluded. During each period a business must maintain records of the amounts earned by individual employees. Generally, the most difficulty relates to personnel paid by the hour or on the basis of piecework. Time cards and time clocks are commonly used to ensure that each hourly worker is compensated correctly. For employees receiving wages based on productivity, a daily report must be generated indicating the output and operations performed.

Proper determination of an employee's hours or output is the first step in the calculation of total or **gross earnings.** Gross earnings are dependent on many factors, including federal regulations and company policy. According to the Federal Fair Labor Standards Act,[4] for example, businesses engaged in interstate commerce must pay overtime of at least one and one-half times the regular rate for hours worked in excess of 40 per week. In addition, many companies establish their own policies and pay premium rates for work on night shifts, split shifts, holidays, and Sundays.

To illustrate the calculation of gross earnings, assume Paula Hite worked 52 hours during a weekly payroll period at Ajax Fabricators, Inc. Paula is paid $10 per hour and the company compensates for overtime at one and one-half times the regular hourly rate. Paula's gross pay for the week would be $580: [(40 hours × $10) + (12 hours × $15)].

Deductions from Employee Earnings

As many of you know, an employee's **take-home (net) pay** is less than his or her gross pay. And normally it is much less! The difference between these two amounts arises because of required tax withholdings by the employer and voluntary deductions that have been authorized by the employee. We will now focus on several common deductions.

Social Security taxes (FICA)

The **Federal Insurance Contributions Act (FICA),** commonly called Social Security, provides retirement, financial, and medical benefits to the aged, widows, and orphans. Employers are required to withhold a portion of each employee's gross earnings to help fund these programs. Additionally, the employer must match the employee's contribution. As an example, assume that Kathy Durham earns $24,000 and that all the earnings are sub-

[4] This act is sometimes called the Wages and Hours Law.

ject to FICA taxes of 6.7%. Kathy will have $1,608 ($24,000 × 0.067) withheld from her paychecks. A total of $3,216 will ultimately be remitted to the government, comprised of Kathy's contribution and a matching amount by her employer ($1,608 × 2 = $3,216).

In recent years both the amount of earnings subject to FICA tax (termed the FICA base) and the tax rate have increased dramatically. This trend is noted by observing the figures in Exhibit 12-5. The amounts for 1983 and beyond are estimates and subject to change. Both the FICA base and tax rate can be expected to increase even more if the financial solvency of the Social Security system is further jeopardized.

Exhibit 12-5

FICA tax table

Year	*FICA Base (Earnings Subject to FICA Tax)*	×	*FICA Tax Rate (%)*	=	*Maximum FICA Tax on Employee*
1951	$ 3,600		1.50%		$ 54
1966	6,600		4.20		277
1977	16,500		5.85		965
1979	22,900		6.13		1,404
1980	25,900		6.13		1,588
1982	31,800		6.70		2,131
1983	33,900		6.70		2,271
1984	36,000		6.70		2,412
1985	38,100		7.05		2,686
1986	40,200		7.15		2,874
1987	42,600		7.15		3,046

Federal, state, and city income taxes

Employers must also withhold a portion of an employee's gross earnings to satisfy federal income tax laws and the laws of many states and local municipalities. These withholdings are later submitted to the appropriate governmental authorities in payment of the employee's tax liability. Because of the nature of the system, income taxes are actually remitted on a pay-as-you-go basis.

The amount withheld for federal income taxes depends on employee earnings, frequency of pay, marital status, and the number of **withholding allowances** claimed. One withholding allowance is permitted for the employee, one for the spouse, and one for each child and other qualifying dependent. As we will discuss in Chapter 20, additional allowances are permitted if certain age and sight requirements are met. To inform an employer of the number of allowances claimed, each employee completes a Withholding Allowance Certificate (Form W-4) at the time of hire. See Exhibit 12-6. A completed W-4 remains in effect until changed by the employee.

In an effort to secure operating revenues, many state and local governmental units have enacted laws that tax an employee's gross earnings. The amounts withheld for state and local income taxes vary widely but are often a stipulated percentage of gross pay.

Other deductions

In addition to required Social Security and income tax withholdings, many employees voluntarily authorize other deductions from their paychecks. Common examples of such deductions include payments for insurance programs (life, medical, dental) and U.S. savings bonds, contributions to a pension plan, union dues, and charitable contributions.

Calculation of take-home pay

To illustrate the computation of net or take-home pay, we will focus on Tony Disano, a married employee of Trimble Services. Assume that for the two-week period ending on December 31, Tony has earned a salary of $1,325. The following information is available.

1 According to the W-4 form shown in Exhibit 12-6, Tony is claiming 3 withholding allowances.
2 Ohio, the state of employment, has a 2% income tax (assumed).
3 FICA taxes are 6.7% on a base of $33,900.
4 Disano has authorized a $40 deduction for hospitalization insurance and a $10 contribution to the United Way.

Tony's December 31 take-home pay of $935.77 is calculated as follows:

Exhibit 12-6

Form W-4

Form **W-4** | Department of the Treasury—Internal Revenue Service
Employee's Withholding Allowance Certificate

1 Type or print your full name: TONY JOSEPH DISANO
2 Your social security number: 579-89-1111

Home address (number and street or rural route): 79 FLORA STREET
City or town, State, and ZIP code: CLEVELAND OHIO 44106

3 Marital Status: ☐ Single ☒ Married ☐ Married, but withhold at higher Single rate
Note: If married, but legally separated, or spouse is a nonresident alien, check the Single box.

4 Total number of allowances you are claiming (from line F of the worksheet on page 2) . . . 3
5 Additional amount, if any, you want deducted from each pay . . . $ —
6 I claim exemption from withholding because (see instructions and check boxes below that apply):
a ☐ Last year I did not owe any Federal income tax and had a right to a full refund of ALL income tax withheld, AND
b ☐ This year I do not expect to owe any Federal income tax and expect to have a right to a full refund of ALL income tax withheld. If both a and b apply, enter "EXEMPT" here . . . ▶
c If you entered "EXEMPT" on line 6b, are you a full-time student? . . . ☐ Yes ☐ No

Under the penalties of perjury, I certify that I am entitled to the number of withholding allowances claimed on this certificate, or if claiming exemption from withholding, that I am entitled to claim the exempt status.

Employee's signature ▶ Tony Joseph Disano Date ▶ August 10, 1979

7 Employer's name and address (including ZIP code) (FOR EMPLOYER'S USE ONLY): Trimble Services, Inc. 805 Tuck Place Cleveland, Ohio 44108
8 Office code: --
9 Employer identification number: 59-14113

Detach along this line

Gross earnings		*$1,325.00*
Less deductions		
Federal income tax	*$260.80*	
State income tax ($1,325 × 0.02)	*26.50*	
FICA taxes	*51.93*	
Hospitalization insurance	*40.00*	
United Way contribution	*10.00*	*389.23*
Net pay		*$ 935.77*

The federal income tax deduction is based on wage-bracket tables provided by the government. An excerpt from the table needed to compute Tony's withholding appears in Exhibit 12-7.

Because Tony earned $1,325 and claimed 3 allowances, $260.80 (circled figure) will be withheld from gross earnings. Note that withholdings become smaller as the number of allowances claimed increases. The result is a larger paycheck.

Turning to FICA, employees are subject to a 6.7% tax computed on a base of $33,900. Prior to the current two-week period, Tony has earned $33,125 ($1,325 × 25 periods). Thus when his salary for the last two weeks of the year is considered, the maximum taxable base of $33,900 will be exceeded. For this reason only $775 ($33,900 – $33,125) of the current earnings are subject to FICA taxation, and Trimble will deduct $51.93 ($775 × 0.067) from Tony's gross pay.

Exhibit 12-7

Federal income tax withholding table

MARRIED Persons—BIWEEKLY Payroll Period

And the wages are—		And the number of withholding allowances claimed is—										
At least	But less than	0	1	2	3	4	5	6	7	8	9	10
		The amount of income tax to be withheld shall be—										
1,200	1,220	259.20	246.10	233.10	220.50	208.60	196.60	184.70	172.80	160.90	150.80	141.20
1,220	1,240	266.00	252.90	239.90	226.80	214.80	202.80	190.90	179.00	167.10	155.80	146.20
1,240	1,260	272.80	259.70	246.70	233.60	221.00	209.00	197.10	185.20	173.30	161.30	151.20
1,260	1,280	279.60	266.50	253.50	240.40	227.30	215.20	203.30	191.40	179.50	167.50	156.20
1,280	1,300	286.40	273.30	260.30	247.20	234.10	221.40	209.50	197.60	185.70	173.70	161.80
1,300	1,320	293.20	280.10	267.10	254.00	240.90	227.80	215.70	203.80	191.90	179.90	168.00
1,320	1,340	300.40	286.90	273.90	260.80	247.70	234.60	221.90	210.00	198.10	186.10	174.20
1,340	1,360	307.80	293.70	280.70	267.60	254.50	241.40	228.30	216.20	204.30	192.30	180.40
1,360	1,380	315.20	301.00	287.50	274.40	261.30	248.20	235.10	222.40	210.50	198.50	186.60
1,380	1,400	322.60	308.40	294.30	281.20	268.10	255.00	241.90	228.90	216.70	204.70	192.80
1,400	1,420	330.00	315.80	301.60	288.00	274.90	261.80	248.70	235.70	222.90	210.90	199.00
1,420	1,440	337.40	323.20	309.00	294.80	281.70	268.60	255.50	242.50	229.40	217.10	205.20
1,440	1,460	344.80	330.60	316.40	302.20	288.50	275.40	262.30	249.30	236.20	223.30	211.40
1,460	1,480	352.20	338.00	323.80	309.60	295.30	282.20	269.10	256.10	243.00	229.90	217.60
1,480	1,500	359.60	345.40	331.20	317.00	302.70	289.00	275.90	262.90	249.80	236.70	223.80

Payroll Recording and Record Keeping

Payroll systems vary from business to business and are influenced greatly by the number of employees and the extent of computerization. Nevertheless, most systems have several common features that are necessitated either by bookkeeping convenience or governmental regulation. At the end of each payroll period, for example, the gross earnings, deductions, and net pay of all employees are recorded in a **payroll register,** a journal-like device that summarizes a firm's entire payroll. The top part of Exhibit 12-8 contains the payroll register of Trimble Services (see pages 466–467).

Observe the manner in which Tony Disano's previously illustrated net pay computation occupies one line of the register. Also note that each employee's gross pay is classified as sales salaries expense or office salaries expense, depending on the type of work performed.

After the necessary information is compiled, checks can be prepared for issuance to employees. Based on data in the register, the following entry is required to record Trimble's payroll for the two-week period ended December 31.

Sales Salaries Expense	*2,560.00*	
Office Salaries Expense	*1,942.50*	
Employees' Federal Income Taxes Payable		*778.10*
Employees' State Income Taxes Payable		*90.05*
FICA Taxes Payable		*264.82*
Employees' Insurance Program Payable		*215.00*
Savings Bonds Payable		*15.00*
United Way Contributions Payable		*50.00*
Cash		*3,089.53*
To record payroll and withholdings		

The withholdings are current liabilities to Trimble because the amounts are owed to various authorities (e.g., the federal government, the state of Ohio, and so forth) and must be paid within a relatively short period of time. At the time of remittance the proper payable is debited and Cash is credited.

Employee records

At the end of a calendar year an employer must furnish information to each employee regarding the gross wages and salaries earned and taxes withheld. Thus individual employee payroll records are a necessity. These records not only provide the above information but also assist in the proper computation of FICA and other taxes. Examine Tony Disano's earnings record, which appears in Exhibit 12-8. Observe how the cumulative earnings column signals that Tony will exceed the FICA taxable base ($33,900) when the last pay period of the year is considered.

The employer provides the necessary information to the employee on a **Wage and Tax Statement,** more commonly known as a W-2. As shown in Exhibit 12-8, the W-2 is based on the yearly totals of the employee earnings record. Upon receipt, the employee can proceed with completion of the various income tax returns that are filed with the IRS and state and local taxing authorities.

Payroll Taxes of the Employer

Thus far, our discussion of taxes has focused on the employee. Employers are also subject to payroll taxes, specifically FICA, federal unemployment, and state unemployment.

FICA tax

The most significant payroll tax levied on the employer is FICA. As we noted earlier, employers must match the contributions of their employees to the Social Security program. Consequently, FICA tax rates on the employee and the employer are identical.

Federal unemployment tax

Another tax on the employer requires payments under the **Federal Unemployment Tax Act (FUTA).** FUTA is a joint program between the federal government and the various states to financially assist the unemployed. Taxes collected are not distributed directly to those out of work; instead the funds are used to support the administrative costs of state unemployment programs.

FUTA taxes are levied only on employers. At the time this text was written, the tax was 3.4% of the first $6,000 paid to each employee. Employers, however, can receive a credit of up to 2.7% for amounts paid to state unemployment funds. Accordingly, most states have set a 2.7% rate for their own programs, resulting in a net FUTA rate of 0.7% (3.4% − 2.7%) on an employee's first $6,000 of gross earnings.

State unemployment taxes

The amounts paid to the unemployed are disbursed through the various state programs. As we just noted, most states have implemented a tax rate of 2.7%, also computed on an employee's first $6,000 of gross pay. Normally, however, a merit reduction is granted to businesses with good labor records. This practice makes sense economically because these firms have a low number of layoffs and terminations, thereby avoiding large payments for unemployment compensation. Employers receiving merit reductions can still obtain a credit for federal purposes of up to 2.7%.

Recording the employer's taxes

The entry to record the payroll taxes levied on an employer is made at the same time payroll is recorded. To illustrate, we will continue the Trimble Services example. Refer to the payroll register appearing in Exhibit 12-8; we will make the following assumptions:

1 Only Tony Disano has exceeded the FICA base of $33,900. Recall that only $775 of Tony's current gross earnings ($1,325) were taxed at the 6.7% rate.

2 Federal and state unemployment tax rates are 0.7% and 2.7%, respectively, of an employee's first $6,000 of gross earnings. All employees except Pete Roe (a new hire) have earned more than $6,000 for the year.

Exhibit 12-8 Payroll record keeping

Payroll Register for the Two-Week Period Ended December 31

Name	Sales or Office	Total Hours	Earnings: Regular	Earnings: Overtime	Earnings: Total	Federal Income Tax	State Income Tax
Al Baker	Sales	80	640.00		640.00	86.30	12.80
Tony Disano	Office	—	1,325.00		1,325.00	260.80	26.50
Sue Kennedy	Sales	80	720.00		720.00	117.30	14.40
Pete Roe	Sales	—	1,200.00		1,200.00	220.50	24.00
Alice Yurkow	Office	90	520.00	97.50	617.50	93.20	12.35
			4,405.00	97.50	4,502.50	778.10	90.05

Employee Earnings Record

Name Tony J. Disano

Address 79 Flora Street

Cleveland, Ohio 44106

Position Office Manager

Social Security Number 579-89-1111

Single ____ *Married* x

Withholding Allowances 3

Period Ending	Total Hours	Earnings: Regular	Earnings: Overtime	Earnings: Total	Earnings: Cumulative	Federal Income Tax
11/19		1,325.00		1,325.00	30,475.00	260.80
12/3		1,325.00		1,325.00	31,800.00	260.80
12/17		1,325.00		1,325.00	33,125.00	260.80
12/31		1,325.00		1,325.00	34,450.00	260.80
		34,450.00		34,450.00		6,780.80

1 Control number 22222

2 Employer's name, address, and ZIP code

Trimble Services, Inc.
805 Tuck Place
Cleveland, Ohio 44108

3 Employer's identification number 59-14113

4 Employer's State number 35-11486

5 Stat. employee ☐ Deceased ☐ Pension plan ☐ Legal rep. ☐ 942 emp. ☐ Subtotal ☐ Correction ☐ Void ☐

6

7 Advance EIC payment

8 Employee's social security number 579-89-1111

9 Federal income tax withheld 6,780.80

10 Wages, tips, other compensation 34,450.00

11 FICA tax withheld 2,271.30

12 Employee's name, address, and ZIP code

Tony Disano
79 Flora Street
Cleveland, Ohio 44106

13 FICA wages 33,900.00

14 FICA tips

16 Employer's use Ohio tax—689.00 Ins.—1,040.00

Form **W-2 Wage and Tax Statement 198X** Copy B To be filed with employee's FEDERAL tax return. This information is being furnished to the Internal Revenue Service. Department of the Treasury Internal Revenue Service

Deductions				Payment		Distribution	
FICA Tax	Insurance	Other	Total Deductions	Net Earnings	Check No.	Sales Salaries Expense	Office Salaries Expense
42.88	35.00	SB 10.00	186.98	453.02	1089	640.00	
51.93	40.00	UW 10.00	389.23	935.77	1090		1,325.00
48.24	70.00	UW 20.00	269.94	450.06	1091	720.00	
80.40	50.00	UW 20.00	394.90	805.10	1092	1,200.00	
41.37	20.00	SB 5.00	171.92	445.58	1093		617.50
264.82	215.00	65.00	1,412.97	3,089.53		2,560.00	1,942.50

SB = *Savings Bonds* UW = *United Way*

Pay $1,325 *per*

Hour ____ *Week* ____

Two Weeks x *Month* ____

Employee Number 2

Date of Birth 5/14/42

Date Hired 8/10/79

Date Terminated ____

Deductions					Payment	
State Income Tax	FICA Tax	Insurance	Other	Total Deductions	Net Earnings	Check No.
26.50	88.78	40.00		416.08	908.92	1003
26.50	88.78	40.00		416.08	908.92	1030
26.50	88.78	40.00		416.08	908.92	1056
26.50	51.93	40.00	UW 10.00	389.23	935.77	1090
689.00	2,271.30	1,040.00	10.00	10,791.10	23,658.90	

THE TRUE COST OF EMPLOYEE LABOR

Did you ever stop to think about the total cost of employee labor? Sure, there's the compensation paid and the employer's share of payroll taxes. Yet there is another element of the compensation package that cannot be overlooked—fringe benefits.

Fringe benefits provide a means to attract, motivate, and retain good employees. Besides certain tax advantages, benefits are offered on the premise that the cost per worker is much lower under group purchases than if individually acquired. However, if recent cost increases in benefit plans continue, serious doubts might be raised as to their value. General Motors, for example, has reported that auto workers' health care benefit costs exceed total expenditures for all steel purchases required for automobile production.

Just what's involved may be somewhat eye opening. Common examples of employee benefits, aside from those legally required such as FICA and FUTA tax, include the following:

- *Pensions*
- *Group insurance: life, medical, dental, travel, accident/sickness, and long-term disability*
- *Paid rest periods: lunches and breaks*
- *Payments for time not worked: vacations, holidays, sick leave, and jury duty*
- *Reimbursement for relocation, parking, work clothes, and training*
- *Executive benefits: stock purchase plans, company car, club memberships, vacation villa, and physical examinations*
- *Other: awards, educational subsidies, travel clubs, credit unions, Christmas bonuses, employee meals, and recreational programs*

No doubt the foregoing list has some omissions. Be aware, however, that fringe benefit costs can be astronomical and can amount to well over a firm's recorded wage and salary expense. Indeed, benefits must be considered when evaluating the true cost of employee compensation.

SOURCE Adapted from John B. Hanna, "Can the Challenge of Escalating Benefit Costs be Met?" Reprinted from the November 1977 issue of Personnel Administrator, *30 Park Drive, Berea, Ohio, 44017.*

Trimble's payroll tax obligation, an expense, is recorded as follows:

Payroll Tax Expense	*305.62*	
FICA Taxes Payable ($3,952.50 × 0.067)*		*264.82*
Federal Unemployment Taxes Payable ($1,200† × 0.007)		*8.40*
State Unemployment Taxes Payable ($1,200† × 0.027)		*32.40*
To record employer's payroll taxes		

*All gross earnings are subject to FICA taxes except for $550 of Disano's salary ($1,325 – $775). Thus FICA taxes are based on $3,952.50 ($4,502.50 – $550.00).

†Roe's salary; all other employees are over the limit.

Observe how Trimble's FICA tax expense is identical to the FICA taxes withheld from employee earnings. The liabilities will eventually be removed from the books upon remittance to the proper authority.

SUMMARY PROBLEM

Cater Company, which has a fiscal year-end of August 31, has been forced to use short-term borrowing to meet payroll obligations for July. Two different notes have been issued.

Note A. **Executed on July 1 to the First National Bank in the amount of $5,000. The note is due in 3 months and bears a 12% interest rate.**
Note B. **Executed on July 17 to the Second National Bank in the amount of $3,000. The note is due in 60 days and interest of $75 is included in the face value.**

At the end of July Mr. Cater met his payroll. Total salaries amounted to $30,000; 80% pertains to the sales staff and 20% to office personnel. FICA taxes are 6.7% on a base of $33,900 for each employee. All employees are under the $33,900 base except for the owner, who earned $5,000 during the month. Additional data follows.

Federal income taxes withheld	*$3,850*
State income taxes withheld	*300*
Insurance program withholdings	*680*

INSTRUCTIONS

a **Prepare entries on July 1 and July 17 to issue the notes.**
b **Prepare an entry on July 31 to record Cater's payroll.**
c **Prepare an entry on July 31 to record Cater's payroll taxes. Assume that the state and federal unemployment tax rates are 2.7% and 0.7%, respectively. Thirty percent of the gross earnings are subject to unemployment taxes.**
d **Prepare the journal entries required on August 31 to accrue interest on each of the two notes.**

SOLUTION

a	*July 1*	*Cash*	*5,000*	
		Notes Payable		*5,000*
		To record note payable to bank; 3 months at 12%		

	Date	Account	Debit	Credit
	17	Cash	2,925	
		Discount on Notes Payable	75	
		Notes Payable		3,000
		To record note payable to bank; 60 days until maturity		
b	July 31	Sales Salaries Expense	24,000*	
		Office Salaries Expense	6,000*	
		FICA Taxes Payable		1,675†
		Employees' Federal Income Taxes Payable		3,850
		Employees' State Income Taxes Payable		300
		Employees' Insurance Program Payable		680
		Cash		23,495
		To record payroll and withholdings		

* $30,000 × 0.8 = $24,000; $30,000 × 0.2 = $6,000
† ($30,000 − $5,000) × 0.067 = $1,675

	Date	Account	Debit	Credit
c	July 31	Payroll Tax Expense	1,981	
		FICA Taxes Payable		1,675*
		State Unemployment Taxes Payable		243†
		Federal Unemployment Taxes Payable		63‡
		To record employer's payroll taxes		

* ($30,000 − $5,000) × 0.067 = $1,675
† $30,000 × 0.3 = $9,000; $9,000 × 0.027 = $243
‡ $30,000 × 0.3 = $9,000; $9,000 × 0.007 = $63

	Date	Account	Debit	Credit
d	Aug. 31	Interest Expense	100	
		Interest Payable		100
		To accrue interest for 2 months: $5,000 × 0.12 × $\frac{2}{12}$		
	31	Interest Expense	56.25	
		Discount on Notes Payable		56.25
		To accrue interest for 45 days and amortize the discount: $75 × $\frac{45}{60}$		

KEY TERMS AND CONCEPTS

accounts payable 448
accrued liability 451
collections for third parties 449
contingent liability 456
contra liability 454
current liability 448
current portion of long-term debt 450
customer prepayments 449
discount amortization 455
discount on notes payable 454
employee 459
Federal Insurance Contributions Act (FICA) 460
Federal Unemployment Tax Act (FUTA) 465
gross earnings 460
income tax withholdings 461
independent contractor 459
notes payable 453
payroll register 464
state unemployment taxes 465
take-home pay 460
Wage and Tax Statement (W-2) 464
warranty 457
withholding allowance 461

QUESTIONS

Q12-1 Define the term "current liability" and present six examples.

Q12-2 Why are customer prepayments classified as liabilities?

Q12-3 Present five different situations where a business collects monies from customers and employees and reports such amounts as current liabilities.

Q12-4 Discuss several common uses of notes payable.

Q12-5 What does the Discount on Notes Payable account represent?

Q12-6 How does a contingent liability differ from an absolute liability? Present three examples of contingent liabilities.

Q12-7 What guidelines must be met in order for a contingent liability to be recorded in the accounts? What happens if only one of the guidelines is met?

Q12-8 Why is a warranty considered a contingent liability?

Q12-9 Are internal control procedures important in the area of payroll? Why?

Q12-10 Differentiate between "employees" and "independent contractors." For which group must detailed payroll records be kept?

Q12-11 What is the purpose of requiring businesses to withhold income taxes (federal, state, and local) from employee wages? How are these withholdings treated on the books of the employer?

Q12-12 How does the Employee's Withholding Allowance Certificate (Form W-4) assist in determining the amount of federal income taxes to withhold from gross earnings?

Q12-13 Discuss the interrelationships between the payroll register, employee earnings record, and Form W-2.

Q12-14 Which payroll taxes are incurred by the employer? How are these taxes treated in the accounting records?

Q12-15 Do most state unemployment programs grant merit reductions to businesses? What is the purpose behind merit reductions?

Q12-16 Explain how the real cost of maintaining a work force can exceed the costs of employee compensation and payroll taxes.

EXERCISES

E12-1 Sunshine Tours sells prepaid package tours of Europe. The accompanying information pertains to 1983.

Tour	*Number Sold*	*Selling Price per Tour*
A	500	$1,600
B	300	850
C	1,400	500

Seventy percent of the tours sold were used during the year; the remainder will be used early in 1984.

a Prepare journal entries in 1983 to record (1) the sale of the tour packages and (2) the tours used during the year.

b Present proper disclosure of the unused tour packages on Sunshine's 1983 year-end balance sheet.

E12-2 Kahn Corporation operates a single plant in the city of Mansfield. The firm maintains its records on a calendar year basis; Mansfield's fiscal year runs from June 1 through May 31. In June Kahn's accountant estimated monthly property tax accruals of $3,400. On August 7 a semiannual tax statement was received amounting to $21,180; the statement is due on September 10.

a Prepare journal entries to record Kahn's property tax accruals from June through August.

b Prepare the necessary entries for (1) payment of the tax statement on September 10 and (2) September's tax expense.

c Why is it preferable to accrue property taxes over the fiscal year of a taxing authority rather than the fiscal year of a business?

E12-3 Gruber Foods purchased three delivery trucks from Vandergriff Truck Sales on May 1, 1983, for $90,000. Gruber paid Vandergriff $15,000 cash and signed a 9-month note for $82,500. Interest is included in the note's face value. Prepare journal entries for Gruber Foods to record the following:

a The purchase of the trucks on May 1, 1983

b Accrued interest for the fiscal year ending July 31, 1983

c The payment of the note and discount amortization on February 1, 1984

E12-4 Marty Poole is a skilled machinist who earns $12 per hour. The machinists' union has a contract that calls for overtime pay at 150% of the regular rate for hours worked in excess of 40 per week. Furthermore, any work on Sundays is compensated at 200% of the regular rate.

For the week just ended, Poole worked a total of 58 hours including 7 on Sunday. His check stub revealed take-home pay of $567.85. Insurance and union dues deductions amounted to $25 and $5, respectively.

a Compute the amount of federal income taxes withheld from Poole's wages. The FICA tax rate is 6.7% on the first $33,900 earned. Poole's cumulative earnings for the year before considering the current pay period totaled $33,250.

b Poole is considering marrying a widow with two children. If he pursues his marital plans, determine and explain the probable effect on his (1) weekly take-home pay and (2) FICA tax withholdings.

E12-5 The payroll register of Starbuck Company for the month of February contained the following information.

Office salaries	*$14,000*
Sales salaries	*10,000*
Sales commissions	*5,000*

Payroll deductions were made for FICA taxes at the rate of 6.7% of total earnings, federal income taxes of $3,210, state income taxes of $2\frac{1}{2}$% of gross earnings, and dental insurance of $500.

a Prepare the necessary entry to record Starbuck's February payroll.

b Record Starbuck's payroll tax expense. Assume that unemployment taxes are 3.4% of the first $6,000 paid to each employee (2.7% for state unemployment and 0.7% for federal unemployment). All employees have earned less than $6,000 for the year.

E12-6 Payroll information of the Ling Wang Company for the month of August follows.

Gross earnings of employees	*$400,000*
Federal income taxes withheld	*49,000*
State income taxes withheld	*4,000*
Voluntary deductions (insurance, union dues, and so on)	*18,000*
Employee earnings subject to FICA tax	*300,000*
Employee earnings subject to FUTA tax	*120,000*

Tax rates are as follows:

FICA	6.7% on the first $33,900 earned per employee
State unemployment	2.7% on the first $6,000 earned per employee
Federal unemployment	0.7% on the first $6,000 earned per employee

a Why isn't the entire $400,000 payroll subject to FICA and FUTA taxes?
b Compute the employees' take-home pay during August.
c Compute Wang's payroll tax expense for August.

E12-7 Al Hall and John Garrett work part-time for the Airport Freight Company. Al earns $12 per hour; John is paid a salary of $20,000. Both men worked 1,400 hours during the year. FICA taxes are 6.7% of an employee's first $33,900 of gross earnings; unemployment taxes are computed on each employee's earnings up to $6,000. The state unemployment rate is only 2.3% because of a merit reduction, and the federal unemployment tax rate is 0.7%.
a Calculate the company's annual payroll tax expense for Al and John.
b What is the total annual cost of having Al and John on the payroll?
c Would your answer to part (b) be different if John decided to work full-time for $36,800 per year and Al was laid off? Explain.

PROBLEMS

P12-1 ***Balance sheet presentation of liabilities***

Kamar, Inc., has been producing quality children's apparel for over twenty-six years. The company's fiscal year runs from April 1 to March 31. The following information relates to the obligations of Kamar as of March 31, 1983.

Notes payable. Kamar has signed several long-term notes with financial institutions and insurance companies. The maturities of these notes are given in the schedule below. The total unpaid interest of all these notes amounts to $90,000 as of March 31, 1983.

Due Date	*Amount Due*
Apr. 1, 1983	$ 100,000
July 1, 1983	200,000
Oct. 1, 1983	100,000
Jan. 1, 1984	200,000
Apr. 1, 1984–Mar. 31, 1985	600,000
Apr. 1, 1985–Mar. 31, 1986	400,000
Apr. 1, 1986–Mar. 31, 1987	400,000
Apr. 1, 1987–Mar. 31, 1988	500,000
Apr. 1, 1988–Mar. 31, 1989	500,000
	$3,000,000

Estimated warranties. Kamar has a one-year product warranty on some selected items in its product line. The estimated warranty liability on sales made during the 1981–1982 fiscal year and still outstanding as of March 31, 1982, amounted to $55,000. The warranty costs on sales made from April 1, 1982, through March 31, 1983, are estimated at $145,000. The actual warranty costs incurred during the current 1982–1983 fiscal year are as follows:

Warranty claims honored on 1981–1982 sales	$ 55,000
Warranty claims honored on 1982–1983 sales	75,000
	$130,000

Other information is as follows:

1 *Trade payables.* Accounts payable for supplies, goods, and services purchased on open account amount to $325,000 as of March 31, 1983.

2 *Payroll-related items.* Outstanding obligations related to Kamar's payroll as of March 31, 1983, are as follows:

Accrued salaries and wages	$145,000
FICA taxes	15,000
State and federal income taxes withheld from employees	30,000
Other payroll deductions	3,000

3 *Taxes.* The following taxes were incurred or collected but not due until the next fiscal year.

State and federal income taxes	$300,000
Property taxes	125,000
Sales taxes	185,000

4 *Miscellaneous accruals.* Other accruals not separately classified amount to $50,000 as of March 31, 1983.

5 *Dividends.* On March 31, 1983, Kamar's board of directors declared a cash dividend of $0.40 per common share. The dividend is to be paid on April 12, 1983; there are 2,500,000 shares of common stock.

INSTRUCTIONS

Prepare the liability section of Kamar's balance sheet as of March 31, 1983, in good form.

(CMA modified.)

P12-2 Current liabilities and errors

Preliminary figures of Gault, Inc., revealed the following liabilities as of December 31, 1983.

Current liabilities		
Accounts payable	$146,000	
Notes payable	86,000	$232,000
Long-term liabilities		
Loan payable		$450,000

The following information has come to your attention.

1 Notes payable include a 9-month, $50,000 obligation issued on August 1 to the Second National Bank. Gault received proceeds of $46,400.

2 No accrued interest has been recorded. Excluding the Second National note, accrued interest amounted to $6,500.

3 The long-term loan was due in five equal annual installments, the first to be paid on February 15, 1984.

4 Gault operates in a state that charges a 5% sales tax. Cash sales in December (including the sales tax) were recorded as follows:

Cash	48,090	
Sales		48,090

5 Gault subleased part of its warehouse on December 1. The lessee prepaid 4 months' rent and Gault made the following entry:

Cash	3,200	
Lease Revenue		3,200

No adjusting entry has been recorded.

Assume that net income for 1983 amounted to $47,600 before considering these items. The books have not been closed.

INSTRUCTIONS

a Determine the correct net income for 1983.

b Prepare the liability section of Gault's December 31 balance sheet in good form.

P12-3 ***Unearned revenues***

It is common practice for a publisher to pay royalties to an author on the basis of the number of books sold. In addition, as a means of attracting and motivating writers, authors generally receive advances, that is, prepayments of future royalties. The writers at Rossiter Enterprises recently completed two books: *Touring Europe on $80 a Day* and *The Fast Food Diet.* The following information is available.

	Touring Europe	Fast Food Diet
Royalty rate	$0.75 per book for the first 100,000 copies sold; $0.50 per book thereafter	$0.50 per book for the first 200,000 copies sold; $0.25 per book thereafter
Minimum *annual* royalty as per contract	$25,000	None
Royalty advances (received in 1981)	$60,000	$45,000

In both cases royalties due Rossiter from the publishers are paid in the year following sale. Book sales follow.

Year	Touring Europe	Fast Food Diet
1982	25,000 copies	50,000 copies
1983	45,000 copies	37,000 copies
1984	65,000 copies	25,000 copies

INSTRUCTIONS

a Prepare all appropriate journal entries for 1981–1985 to record royalty advances, royalties earned, and royalties received. Do each book separately.

b Show how the advances would appear on Rossiter's year-end balance sheet for 1983. Again, do each book separately.

P12-4 ***Notes payable***

The Blue Smoke Company was involved in the following transactions during the fiscal year ended September 30.

June 2 Paid $10,000 cash and issued a $65,000 note to Euless Office Supply for the purchase of $75,000 of office furniture. The note was due in 180 days and carried a 12% interest rate.

July 14 Borrowed $100,000 from the Second National Bank by signing a 90-day note for $103,000.

Aug. 1 Issued a $24,000 note to Al Kinder in settlement of an overdue account payable of the same amount. The note was due in 30 days and carried an interest rate of 18%.

15 Purchased merchandise from San Diego Industries in the amount of $17,500. Issued a 30-day, 15% note in settlement of the balance owed.

31 The note to Kinder was due today, but Blue Smoke was unable to make payment. Blue Smoke issued a new 30-day, 18% note for $24,360, the maturity value of the original obligation.

Sept. 14 The note to San Diego Industries was paid in full.

30 The new note to Al Kinder was paid in full.

INSTRUCTIONS

a Prepare journal entries to record the transactions.

b Prepare adjusting entries on September 30 to record accrued interest.

c Prepare the current liability section of Blue Smoke's balance sheet as of September 30. Assume the Accounts Payable account totals $321,700 on this date.

P12-5 ***Contingent liabilities***

Consider the following independent cases.

1 From January through August of the current year, Downs Manufacturing worked on and completed a defense contract for the U.S. Air Force. Downs has been reimbursed for its costs plus a profit margin, the costs determined by following Defense Department guidelines. On December 28 Downs was informed by government auditors that the firm had computed its costs incorrectly. The Air Force requested a $74,000 reimbursement. Conversations with Downs's cost accounting department revealed that the Air Force's claim was both accurate and correct.

2 Chase Corporation offers a one-year warranty on its sole product. From past experience the probable warranty claims from a given level of sales can be determined.

3 On December 15 an explosion occurred at the Vesper Glue Company. Ten people were injured, and five houses located near Vesper's manufacturing facility were severely damaged. Although no lawsuits had been filed by the end of the year, management anticipates future court appearances and several out-of-court settlements. The company was uninsured for the casualty.

4 Washington Company has always had an excellent reputation for product quality. Thus management was shocked to learn that a governmental agency was investigating one of the firm's products for safety violations. Although the investigation has just commenced, Washington's legal counsel said there was "some chance of a product recall. On the other hand, we might get off scot-free."

5 Bonanza, Inc., was sued in February for discriminatory hiring practices. Bonanza's lawyers noted that the plaintiffs had a strong case and would likely win the suit. Although the suit was for $100,000, it would probably be settled for $40,000.

INSTRUCTIONS

a Discuss the accounting treatment for contingent liabilities.

b Indicate and discuss how each of the five cases would be treated in the financial statements. Assume each company's year ends on December 31. Present journal entries when appropriate.

P12-6 *Payroll: Journal entries and balance sheet presentation*

Judy Zoldak Cosmetics incurred salaries and wages of $138,000 during July; 75% relates to sales personnel and 25% to office personnel. FICA taxes are 6.7% on a base of $33,900 for each employee. All employees are under the $33,900 base except for the owner, who earned $6,000 during the month. Additional data follows.

Federal income taxes withheld	$14,470
State income taxes withheld	3,560
City income taxes withheld	1,380

Other deductions from payroll were authorized for pensions (3% of gross earnings), insurance (2% of gross earnings), and charitable contributions (0.2% of gross earnings).

INSTRUCTIONS

a Prepare the journal entry to record the payroll and disburse cash.

b Prepare a journal entry to record Zoldak's payroll taxes and other related payroll costs. Assume that state unemployment tax is 1% because of a merit reduction and that federal unemployment tax is 0.7%. Eighty percent of the gross earnings are subject to unemployment taxes. Also, Zoldak matches employees' deductions for pensions and insurance. Employee and employer contributions for pensions and insurance will be remitted to the Idaho Insurance Company on August 15.

c Compute the total payroll expense for July. Determine the percentage of total payroll expense to gross compensation earned. Is this percentage likely to remain constant through the remainder of the year? Why?

d Prepare the current liability section of Zoldak's balance sheet as of July 31.

P12-7 *Payroll register and entries*

The Pewter Shop has three hourly employees and two salaried employees. Payroll data for the month of November follows.

Employee	Hours Reg	Hours OT*	Pay Rate	Gross Pay for Month	Federal Income Tax Withheld	Compensation to Oct. 31
Bishop	160		$5/hr	$ 800	$ 165	$ 1,600
McConnell	160	5	$6/hr	1,005	195	6,200
Markoff	160	10	$4/hr	700	100	7,500
Ramon			$2,000/mo	2,000	220	20,000
Wykovich			$4,000/mo	4,000	830	32,000
				$8,505	$1,510	

*Overtime hours are compensated at 150% of the regular hourly rate.

Other information is as follows:

1 FICA taxes are 6.7% on a base of $33,900 for each employee.
2 Unemployment taxes are based on the first $6,000 of an employee's earnings. The state and federal rates are 2.7% and 0.7%, respectively.
3 Deductions are made for life and medical insurance (5% of gross earnings) and for contributions to the United Way (1% of gross earnings). The company matches United Way donations.
4 Ramon and Wykovich perform administrative work; other employees are involved with sales.

INSTRUCTIONS

a Prepare a payroll register for the month of November. Use the following column headings and round to the nearest cent.

		Deductions				
Employee	**Gross Pay**	**Federal Income Tax**	**FICA Tax**	**Insurance**	**United Way**	**Net Pay**

b Prepare the necessary journal entry to record the payroll. Assume employees are paid on November 30.
c Record the employer's payroll taxes and United Way contribution. The United Way contribution will be remitted on December 15.
d Prepare the current liability section of The Pewter Shop's November 30 balance sheet. Existing current liabilities prior to recording the payroll follow.

Accounts payable	$14,650
FICA taxes payable	1,210
State unemployment taxes payable	425

P12-8 **Current liabilities and errors (alternate to P12-2)**

Preliminary figures of Hoffman, Inc., revealed the following liabilities as of December 31, 1983.

Current liabilities		
Accounts payable	$41,500	
Notes payable	76,400	$117,900
Long-term liabilities		
Loan payable		$80,000

The following information has come to your attention.

1 Notes payable include a 3-month, $35,000 obligation issued on December 1 to the First City Bank. Hoffman received proceeds of $33,800.
2 No accrued interest has been recorded. Excluding the First City note, accrued interest amounted to $1,400.
3 The long-term loan was due in ten equal annual installments, the first to be paid on March 8, 1984.
4 Hoffman operates in a state that charges a 6% sales tax. Credit sales in December (including the sales tax) were recorded as follows:

Accounts Receivable	25,122	
Sales		25,122

5 Hoffman subleased part of its warehouse on November 1. The lessee prepaid 5 months' rent and Hoffman made the following entry:

Cash	4,500	
Lease Revenue		4,500

No adjusting entry has been recorded.

Assume that net income for 1983 amounted to $29,300 before considering these items. The books have not been closed.

INSTRUCTIONS

a Determine the correct net income for 1983.

b Prepare the liability section of Hoffman's December 31 balance sheet in good form.

P12-9 *Unearned revenues (alternate to P12-3)*

It is common practice for a publisher to pay royalties to an author on the basis of the number of books sold. In addition, as a means of attracting and motivating writers, authors generally receive advances, that is, prepayments of future royalties. The writers at Weinberg Enterprises recently completed two books: *Collecting U.S. Stamps* and *Exercise and Fitness.* The following information is available.

	Collecting U.S. Stamps	*Exercise and Fitness*
Royalty rate	$0.60 per book for the first 70,000 copies sold; $0.40 per book thereafter	$0.70 per book for the first 100,000 copies sold; $0.45 per book thereafter
Minimum *annual* royalty as per contract	None	$5,000
Royalty advances (received in 1981)	$40,000	$55,000

In both cases royalties due Weinberg from the publishers are paid in the year following sale. Book sales are as follows:

Year	*Collecting U.S. Stamps*	*Exercise and Fitness*
1982	40,000 copies	45,000 copies
1983	25,000 copies	30,000 copies
1984	15,000 copies	10,000 copies

INSTRUCTIONS

a Prepare all appropriate journal entries for 1981–1985 to record royalty advances, royalties earned, and royalties received. Do each book separately.

b Show how the advances would appear on Weinberg's year-end balance sheet for 1983. Again, do each book separately.

P12-10 *Notes payable (alternate to P12-4)*

The Pioneer Tube Company was involved in the following transactions during the fiscal year ended July 31.

Apr. 2 Paid $5,000 cash and issued a $30,000 note to the Dodson Company for the purchase of a $35,000 delivery truck. The note was due in 150 days and carried a 13% interest rate.

22 Borrowed $50,000 from the Rio Vista National Bank by signing a 120-day note for $53,000.

May 1 Issued a $31,500 note to Wayne Fergerson in settlement of an overdue account payable of the same amount. The note was due in 30 days and carried an interest rate of 18%.

10 Purchased merchandise from Sacramento Enterprises in the amount of $7,400. Issued a 45-day, 15% note in settlement of the balance owed.

31 The note to Fergerson was due today, but no funds were available for payment. Pioneer issued a new 30-day, 18% note for $31,972.50, the maturity value of the original obligation.

June 24 The note to Sacramento Enterprises was paid in full.

30 The new note to Wayne Fergerson was paid in full.

INSTRUCTIONS

a Prepare journal entries to record the transactions. Round to the nearest cent.

b Prepare adjusting entries on July 31 to record accrued interest.

c Prepare the current liability section of Pioneer Tube's balance sheet as of July 31. Assume the Accounts Payable account totals $210,500 on this date.

P12-11 ***Payroll: Journal entries and balance sheet presentation (alternate to P12-6)***
Womack Enterprises incurred wages and salaries of $272,000 during August; 20% relates to office personnel and the remainder to sales personnel. FICA taxes are 6.7% on a base of $33,900 for each employee. All employees are under the $33,900 base except for the owner, who earned $5,500 during the month. Federal income taxes withheld amounted to $54,300 and state income taxes withheld totaled $6,800. Other deductions from payroll were authorized for pensions (2% of gross earnings), insurance (1% of gross earnings), and United Way contributions (0.5% of gross earnings).

INSTRUCTIONS

a Prepare the journal entry to record the payroll and disburse cash.

b Prepare a journal entry to record Womack's payroll taxes and other related payroll costs. Assume that state unemployment tax is 1.4% because of a merit reduction, and that federal unemployment tax is 0.7%. Seventy percent of the gross earnings are subject to unemployment taxes. Also, Womack matches employee contributions to the United Way and insurance programs. These amounts will be remitted to the proper authorities on September 15.

c Compute total payroll expense for August. Determine the percentage of total payroll expense to gross compensation earned. Is this percentage likely to change later in the year? Why?

d Prepare the current liability section of Womack's balance sheet as of August 31.

P12-12 ***Payroll register and entries (alternate to P12-7)***
Videoland, Inc., has three hourly employees and two salaried employees. Payroll data for the month of October follows.

Employee	Hours Reg	Hours OT*	Pay Rate	Gross Pay for Month	Federal Income Tax Withheld	Compensation to Sept. 30
Duckworth	160	10	$6/hr	$ 1,050	$ 200	$ 6,100
Hyde	100		$7/hr	700	130	3,600
Manders	160	20	$8/hr	1,520	270	11,700
Powell			$3,000/mo	3,000	355	24,000
VanZandt			$4,500/mo	4,500	705	32,500
				$10,770	$1,660	

Overtime hours are compensated at 150% of the regular hourly rate.

Other information is as follows:

1 FICA taxes are 6.7% on a base of $33,900 for each employee.
2 Unemployment taxes are based on the first $6,000 of an employee's earnings. The state and federal rates are 2.7% and 0.7%, respectively.
3 Deductions are made for life and medical insurance (6% of gross earnings) and for contributions to the United Way (1% of gross earnings). The company matches United Way donations.
4 Powell and VanZandt perform administrative work; other employees are involved with sales.

INSTRUCTIONS

a Prepare a payroll register for the month of October. Use the following column headings and round to the nearest cent.

		Deductions				
Employee	Gross Pay	Federal Income Tax	FICA Tax	Insurance	United Way	Net Pay

b Prepare the necessary journal entry to record the payroll. Assume employees are paid on October 31.
c Record the employer's payroll taxes and United Way contribution. The United Way contribution will be remitted on November 12.
d Prepare the current liability section of Videoland's October 31 balance sheet. Existing current liabilities prior to recording the payroll follow.

Accounts payable	*$27,840*
Interest payable	*180*
State unemployment taxes payable	*550*

CASE 12
ARLINGTON STADIUM

The city of Arlington, Texas, owns and operates a baseball stadium used by the Texas Rangers of the American League. During the baseball season, which extends from April through the end of September, the city's personnel office must employ 300 people per game to handle food concessions, ticket sales, program/novelty sales, general cleaning, and maintenance. The Rangers play 82 home games on 63 dates, the difference being due to doubleheaders. Employees are paid $20 for a single game and $35 for a doubleheader. Few employees work more than two months; thus total earnings are subject to FICA and unemployment taxes. FICA taxes are 6.7% and federal and state unemployment taxes total 3.4%.

Close supervision is exercised over all employees. Fifteen supervisors are paid $1,000 per month for their efforts. Additionally, the city pays for insurance on all employees and supervisors at an annual cost of $12 per person. All stadium personnel are permitted to eat at the ball park for 50% of posted prices (which approximates the actual food cost). Finally, employees are furnished with uniforms, which need not be returned. The city spent $12,000 last year, but the uniform manufacturer has announced a 10% price increase for the upcoming season.

A proposal has been received by the city for staffing the stadium. The city is strongly considering this proposal because personnel turnover is high and employee processing is consuming a large amount of staff time. A temporary help company called People Power will staff the stadium (including supervisors) at a yearly cost of $575,000. People Power will pay all their employees and will incur all the payroll tax expense and insurance. The city will provide uniforms and will continue the present food policy. The city's personnel office should save $10,000 in processing costs if the outside service is used.

INSTRUCTIONS

a Prepare a schedule that indicates whether the proposal should be accepted.

b What noncost factors should be considered in the decision to use an outside independent contractor?

13 PARTNERSHIPS AND CORPORATIONS

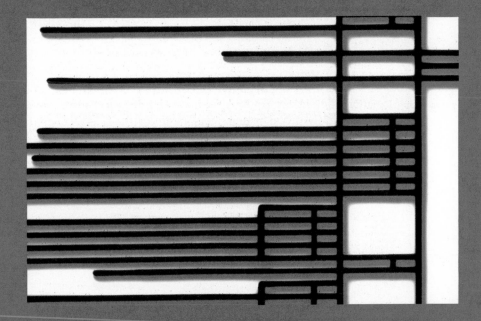

LEARNING OBJECTIVES

After reading this chapter you should:

1 Understand the distinctive features of a partnership, including the advantages and disadvantages of this entity form.

2 Be able to account for partnership formation and income distribution, including the situations that give rise to an earnings deficiency.

3 Understand partner admission (including purchase of an interest, investment, and bonuses) and partner withdrawals.

4 Be familiar with the basic steps to account for partnership liquidations.

5 Understand the distinctive features of a corporation, including the advantages and disadvantages of this entity form.

6 Understand the difference between common and preferred stock.

7 Be familiar with the concepts and accounting treatments for organization costs; par, no-par, and stated-value stock; and stock subscriptions.

8 Be able to account for dividends associated with preferred stock.

9 Be familiar with the stockholders' equity section of a corporate balance sheet.

CHAPTER 13

Economic activity in the United States is conducted through three forms of business organization: sole proprietorships, partnerships, and corporations. Although the vast majority of businesses operate as either proprietorships or partnerships, the bulk of private sector revenues and earnings are generated by corporations. The first part of this chapter presents an introduction to partnerships and related accounting issues; the second part focuses on corporations.

PARTNERSHIPS

To govern the organization and operation of partnerships, most states have adopted the Uniform Partnership Act. This act defines a **partnership** as "an association of two or more persons to carry on, as co-owners, a business for profit." Partnerships are an attractive form of organization for small firms, which often need more talent, experience, and capital than a single owner can provide. Most partnerships have fewer than five owners; others, however, are quite large. Touche Ross & Co., for example, a Big Eight public accounting firm, recently reported having 1,856 partners located in 357 offices in 82 countries. Many retail shops, light manufacturers, home builders, and service establishments are organized as partnerships. Also partnerships are commonly encountered in professional practices such as accounting, law, medicine, dentistry, and architecture.

Characteristics of a Partnership

Partnerships possess several distinctive features that have important implications for accountants. These features are discussed in the following sections.

Ease of formation

A partnership is easily created by a voluntary agreement between two or more persons. The agreement, commonly referred to as the **articles of partnership,** details the rights, responsibilities, and duties of the partners. In addition, specific policies are normally stated with regard to partner investments and withdrawals, the division of net income (and net loss), the admission of new partners, the withdrawal of partners, and procedures to be followed in the event of partner disputes or a partner's death.

No separate legal entity

A partnership is an association of people, not a separate legal entity from its owners. Although accountants treat a partnership as a separate accounting entity for reporting purposes, a partnership has no legal status under common law.

Unlimited liability

Because of the lack of legal entity, each owner of a partnership is personally liable for debts incurred by the partnership. Thus if a partnership becomes insolvent, the partners are required to furnish personal assets to settle the firm's obligations. Amounts due from partners with insufficient personal assets must be paid by wealthier partners, who are then entitled to reimbursement.

Mutual agency

Partnerships have **mutual agency;** that is, each partner acts as an agent of the partnership in business transactions. As a result, the partnership is bound to the commitments and obligations made by any partner on behalf of the firm. For this reason partners must be selected with great care, since irresponsible personnel could spell disaster.

Co-ownership of property and income

According to the Uniform Partnership Act, partners are really the co-owners of an enterprise. Thus if a partner invests a building in the firm, no personal rights to the building are retained; the asset becomes jointly owned by all partners. Similarly, the net income of a partnership belongs to all the partners and can be divided among them in any agreed-upon manner.

Limited life

Unless there is an agreement to the contrary, the death, bankruptcy, retirement, incapacity, or withdrawal of a partner ends the partnership. Other events calling for termination include accomplishment of the firm's objective and the admission of new partners. When a partnership's life has ended, the firm is *dissolved.* Dissolution does not necessarily mean that operations cease and the remaining assets must be sold. Rather, if the surviving partners agree, operations can continue uninterrupted by the formation of a new partnership.

Partnerships: Advantages and Disadvantages

There are several advantages to the partnership form of organization. Initially, there is the obvious opportunity to combine persons with capital and/or specialized skills to start and operate a business. Additionally, in comparison with corporations, partnerships have more operating flexibility because of fewer reporting requirements and less governmental regulation. Many decisions that require formal (and time-consuming) actions by stockholders and corporate management can often be settled quickly among the partnership's members.

Turning to disadvantages, the features of mutual agency, limited life, and unlimited liability frequently present problems. Unlimited liability is especially an obstacle when trying to raise substantial amounts of additional capital. Most people who invest in stocks and other alternatives (e.g., stamps, coins, art, or gold) are willing to incur a loss. However, because personal assets such as a home and car may be exposed to a partnership's creditors, many investors tend to shy away from this entity form; the risk is simply too great.

One additional factor should be considered when evaluating the partnership: income taxes. A business operating as a partnership (as opposed to a corporation) does not pay income taxes; that is, the partnership is not a taxable entity. Instead the firm's net income (or net loss) is allocated to the partners, and the partners pay income taxes personally on their share. Partners having personal tax rates lower than corporate rates are often benefited; partners with higher rates lose out. Because the tax aspect may be either pro or con, effective tax planning is mandatory when considering the partnership form of organization for a new business.

Partnership Accounting

Partnership accounting does not differ significantly from the procedures described in earlier chapters for sole proprietorships. Transactions unique to partnerships arise only in owners' equity and relate to formation, income distribution, admittance and withdrawal of partners, and liquidation.

Partnership formation

Accounting for a partnership commences when owners (i.e., partners) invest their personal assets in the firm. Investments in a partnership may take the form of cash, noncash assets such as land or buildings, and even an entire operating business. As in a sole proprietorship, the net assets (total assets minus total liabilities) invested are entered in the owner's capital account. Now, however, a separate capital account is maintained for each partner.

To illustrate the proper accounting, suppose that Steve Leake and Dotty Mueller, both CPAs, decided to form a partnership on January 1, 1983. Steve invested cash of $15,000; Dotty invested her existing accounting practice. According to the December 31 balance sheet from the preceding year, the practice had the following assets and liabilities:

Assets		
Cash		$ 3,000
Accounts receivable	$4,000	
Less: Allowance for bad debts	500	3,500
Supplies		1,000
Equipment	$5,000	
Less: Accumulated depreciation	1,200	3,800
		$11,300
Liabilities		
Accounts payable		$ 2,500

As of January 1, 1983, the equipment had a fair market value of $6,000. The necessary journal entries to record the partners' investments follow.

Cash	15,000	
Leake, Capital		15,000
To record investment by Leake in the partnership of Leake and Mueller		

Cash	3,000	
Accounts Receivable	4,000	
Supplies	1,000	
Equipment	6,000	
Allowance for Bad Debts		500
Accounts Payable		2,500
Mueller, Capital		11,000
To record investment of Mueller in the partnership of Leake and Mueller		

Observe that the Equipment account is debited for $6,000 and *not* the book value of $3,800. Noncash assets are entered in the new records at fair market value—the actual acquisition cost to the partnership. A failure to use fair market value improperly ignores increases in asset valuation. To explain, suppose the equipment was recorded at its $3,800 book value and immediately sold by the partnership for $6,000. The $2,200 gain would be shared by both partners, which is unfair to Mueller. The increase in valuation occurred while the asset was in her possession; thus she should receive full and proper credit for her investment. The use of book value in this instance would significantly understate Mueller's capital account on the books of the new entity.

Income distribution

Similar to the net income of a sole proprietorship, partnership profits include remuneration for a partner's services, interest for the use of invested capital, and a "pure" economic profit (i.e., reward) for the risks associated with operating a business. Because partners often provide differing amounts of service and/or capital contributions, most partnership agreements contain provisions for the division of net income (or loss). If no provisions are stated, profits and losses are divided equally.

Recognition of services

Partnership agreements frequently recognize differences among partners in terms of seniority, reputation, business contacts, and time devoted to the firm. Assume, for example, that Leake and Mueller's articles of partnership provide for monthly salary allowances of $1,000 and $1,200, respectively, with any remaining net income to be divided equally. If 1983 net income amounted to $38,000, the following division would be made:

	Leake	Mueller	Total
Division of net income			
Salary			
Leake ($1,000 × 12 months)	$12,000		
Mueller ($1,200 × 12 months)		$14,400	$26,400
Remainder of $11,600 ($38,000 − $26,400) divided equally	5,800	5,800	11,600
	$17,800	$20,200	$38,000

Once determined, net income is transferred to the capital accounts by the following closing entry:

Income Summary	*38,000*	
Leake, Capital		*17,800*
Mueller, Capital		*20,200*
To record the division of net income		

Observe the similarity between this entry and the entry to close the Income Summary account for a sole proprietorship (see Chapter 3).

It is important to note that partners are owners and *not* employees. Thus **salary allowances** are not business expenses; rather the allowances are only considered in the division of net income. Partners often withdraw their salary allowances throughout the year; if and when a withdrawal is made, entries are recorded in drawing accounts.[1] To illustrate the proper accounting, let's suppose Leake and Mueller have withdrawn their salary allowances along with an additional $800. End-of-period balances in the partners' drawing accounts total $12,800 ($12,000 + $800) and $15,200 ($14,400 + $800), respectively. The impact of these transactions is shown on the firm's statement of owners' equity appearing in Exhibit 13-1.

Exhibit 13-1

Statement of owners' equity

LEAKE AND MUELLER, CPAs
Statement of Owners' Equity
For the Year Ended December 31, 1983

	Leake	Mueller	Total
Investment, Jan. 1, 1983	$15,000	$11,000	$26,000
Add: Net income for the year	17,800	20,200	38,000
Subtotal	$32,800	$31,200	$64,000
Deduct			
Drawings: salary	$12,000	$14,400	$26,400
Drawings: other	800	800	1,600
Total	$12,800	$15,200	$28,000
Ending balance, Dec. 31, 1983	$20,000	$16,000	$36,000

The balances in the drawing accounts are subsequently closed by the following entry:

Leake, Capital	12,800	
Mueller, Capital	15,200	
Leake, Drawing		12,800
Mueller, Drawing		15,200
To close partners' drawing accounts		

By tracing through the entries presented, observe that the capital accounts were credited for the initial investment at the time of formation and for each partner's share of net income. The entry to close the drawing accounts will therefore reduce Leake, Capital, and Mueller, Capital, to the balances reported on the statement of owners' equity.

Interest on invested capital

Total invested capital is a major factor in the success of businesses that carry inventory or that have substantial equipment needs. Thus partnership agreements often consider differences in the amount of capital contributed by individual partners. Recognition is particularly prevalent for firms hav-

[1] As is true with capital, separate drawing accounts are maintained for each partner.

ing "silent" partners, that is, partners who provide substantial financial support but who rarely become involved in daily management activities.

The amount of a partner's invested capital is recognized by an **interest allowance.** The interest allowance can be computed on the beginning or average capital balance and is similar to the salary allowance discussed earlier. Once again the allowance is only considered in the division of net income and is not an expense of the partnership.

To illustrate the proper accounting, we will continue the Leake and Mueller example. Assume that the partnership agreement now contains the following features:

1 Monthly salaries of $1,000 and $1,200 to Leake and Mueller, respectively
2 Interest of 15% to both partners on the basis of their beginning capital balances
3 Any remaining income (or loss) to be divided equally

It is one year later and 1984 net income totals $42,000. The proper division between Leake and Mueller follows.

	Leake	Mueller	Total
Division of net income			
Salary			
Leake ($1,000 × 12 months)	$12,000		
Mueller ($1,200 × 12 months)		$14,400	$26,400
Interest*			
Leake ($20,000 × 0.15)	3,000		
Mueller ($16,000 × 0.15)		2,400	5,400
	$15,000	$16,800	$31,800
Remainder of $10,200 ($42,000 − $31,800) divided equally	5,100	5,100	10,200
	$20,100	$21,900	$42,000

** Interest is computed on the January 1, 1984 (i.e., December 31, 1983), capital balances. These balances are taken from the statement of owners' equity appearing in Exhibit 13-1.*

The necessary journal entry to close the books requires a debit to Income Summary for $42,000 and a credit to Leake, Capital, and Mueller, Capital, for $20,100 and $21,900, respectively.

Earnings deficiency

In the previous examples salary and interest allowances were less than the total earnings of the firm. Naturally, it is possible for a partnership to incur a net loss or have insufficient earnings to cover the allowances. In these cases an **earnings deficiency** arises. Unless provisions are made to the contrary, the partnership agreement is still followed; that is, authorized salary and interest allowances continue to be recognized. Because of insufficient earnings, however, a deficiency is allocated to the partners in the same ratio as that for profits and losses. Leake and Mueller, for example, would share the deficiency equally.

To illustrate the necessary procedures, suppose that Leake and Mueller's partnership agreement still stipulates respective monthly salaries of $1,000 and $1,200 and interest allowances of 15%. Now, however, assume that 1984 net income amounted to only $20,000. The proper allocation follows.

	Leake	Mueller	Total
Division of net income			
Salary	$12,000	$14,400	$26,400
Interest	3,000	2,400	5,400
	$15,000	$16,800	$31,800
Deficiency of $11,800 ($31,800 − $20,000) divided equally	(5,900)	(5,900)	(11,800)
	$ 9,100	$10,900	$20,000

The required closing entry is similar to those shown previously; specifically, Income Summary is debited for $20,000, with corresponding credits of $9,100 to Leake, Capital, and $10,900 to Mueller, Capital.

Admission of a new partner

The Leake and Mueller partnership was a new entity formed with investments from both Steve Leake and Dotty Mueller. Observe that Leake did not invest in Mueller's existing accounting practice; instead a new business was established. Frequently, individuals are admitted to existing partnerships. Admission normally occurs by (1) purchasing an interest from one or more of the present partners or (2) making an investment in the partnership. The method of entry depends on several factors. For example, interests are often purchased when existing partners wish to decrease their involvement in daily activities because of either financial well-being or retirement. Investments directly in the partnership, on the other hand, sometimes occur when firms are growing and are in need of additional capital and financing.

Purchase of an interest

When an entering partner purchases an interest from an existing partner, the assets and liabilities of the partnership remain constant. Why? Payment is made directly to the selling partner. To illustrate, we assume Leake and Mueller have present capital balances of $20,000 and $16,000, respectively. After considerable negotiation both partners have agreed to sell 50% of their respective interests in the business to Ann Thomas. Thomas will pay Leake and Mueller $15,000 each. The necessary journal entry follows.

Leake, Capital	*10,000*	
Mueller, Capital	*8,000*	
Thomas, Capital		*18,000*
To record the transfer of 50% of present capital balances to Thomas		

Notice that the price paid by Thomas is in excess of the interest acquired from each partner. This result, however, is a personal matter among the parties involved. The cash goes to Leake and Mueller personally and all that is needed on the firm's records is a transfer of ownership (i.e., capital balances).

Investment in the firm

In addition to purchasing an interest from existing partners, an incoming partner may invest directly in the firm. In this case the new partner makes payment to the partnership, and total partnership assets increase. If the partnership assets and liabilities are valued correctly, the entering partner's investment will be equal to the negotiated percentage of the new entity's total capital. To explain, we will again assume Leake and Mueller have respective capital balances of $20,000 and $16,000. Suppose both partners have agreed to grant Thomas a one-third interest in the business for an investment of $18,000. Thomas's investment will bring total firm capital to $54,000.

Leake, capital	$20,000
Mueller, capital	16,000
Investment by Thomas	18,000
Total	$54,000

Observe that the $18,000 investment represents one-third of the owners' equity of the new partnership ($54,000 $\times \frac{1}{3} =$ $18,000). Thomas paid nothing extra to gain a one-third interest; nothing extra was given to her to provide the investment. Thus the necessary journal entry is as follows:

Cash	18,000	
Thomas, Capital		18,000
To record the admission of Thomas to the partnership		

We stress that Thomas's admission does not necessarily mean she is entitled to one-third of the profits. As we noted earlier, income-sharing agreements are normally specified in the articles of partnership and often include interest and salary allowances. If unique attributes of incoming partners are to be recognized, the partnership agreement will probably be redrawn.

Bonus to existing partners. If the prospect of joining a partnership is especially appealing because of past earnings records and other favorable factors, an incoming partner may be required to pay a bonus to the existing owners. Any bonuses paid are allocated to the present partners' capital accounts according to the profit- and loss-sharing ratio in the partnership agreement.

To illustrate, assume Thomas was required to invest $24,000 for a one-third interest in the firm. Total capital would amount to $60,000.

Leake, capital	$20,000
Mueller, capital	16,000
Investment by Thomas	24,000
Total	$60,000

Thomas's one-third interest would therefore be $20,000 ($60,000 × ⅓). Apparently, then, she is paying a $4,000 bonus ($24,000 – $20,000) to Leake and Mueller for admission. If profits and losses are shared equally, the bonus is split 50–50 and the necessary journal entry is as follows:

Cash	24,000	
Leake, Capital		2,000
Mueller, Capital		2,000
Thomas, Capital		20,000
To record the investment of Thomas and bonus to existing partners		

Bonus to new partner. Frequently, a firm is anxious to attract a new partner who possesses specialized skills, significant capital, or unique managerial ability. In these instances the existing owners may grant the incoming partner a larger business interest than is justified by the partner's investment. In essence, a bonus is being given to the new partner.

To illustrate, assume Thomas was required to invest only $9,000 for her one-third interest. As the following figures show, total capital after admission would amount to $45,000.

Leake, capital	$20,000
Mueller, capital	16,000
Investment by Thomas	9,000
Total	$45,000

Because a one-third interest has been granted, Thomas's capital account must contain a balance of $15,000 ($45,000 × ⅓). She has therefore received a $6,000 bonus over and above her $9,000 investment. The bonus is provided by Leake and Mueller, resulting in a reduction of each of their capital accounts. Because Leake and Mueller share profits and losses equally, the following entry is needed.

Cash	9,000	
Leake, Capital	3,000	
Mueller, Capital	3,000	
Thomas, Capital		15,000
To record the investment of Thomas and bonus to new partner		

Withdrawal of a partner

Aside from admission, the composition of a partnership will also change when an owner withdraws or retires from the firm. The exiting owner's business interest is sometimes purchased by the remaining partners or even an outsider (if the other partners approve). In both cases the assets and liabilities of the firm remain unchanged; however, a journal entry is needed to eliminate the withdrawing partner's capital balance and to record an increase in the capital account(s) of the purchaser(s). The necessary entry is identical to the one illustrated on page 490 for the admission of a new partner who purchases an interest from an existing owner.

Purchase by the partnership

Rather than sell to new or existing partners, the partnership may agree to purchase the interest of the withdrawing owner. Negotiations between the partner and the firm may produce a selling price that coincides with the partner's capital balance. Frequently, however, the amount offered is considerably greater. Keep in mind that the accounting records are based on historical cost; thus increases in the market values of assets have been ignored. This valuation procedure, coupled with the fact that the partnership may have substantial earnings potential, could result in a somewhat unrealistic capital balance. If settlement involves a payment in excess of the withdrawing partner's equity, the capital balances of the remaining partners are reduced according to the profit- and loss-sharing ratio. In effect, a bonus is being paid to the exiting owner.

For example, assume the present capital balances of Leake, Mueller, and Thomas are $30,000, $45,000, and $25,000, respectively. Leake has decided to withdraw from the business and the firm has agreed to pay $40,000 for his interest. If net income is divided equally, Leake's withdrawal and payment of his $10,000 bonus ($40,000 – $30,000) would be recorded as follows:

Leake, Capital	*30,000*	
Mueller, Capital	*5,000*	
Thomas, Capital	*5,000*	
Cash		*40,000*
To record the purchase of Leake's interest by the partnership		

As we noted, the asset and capital balances of the partnership may be understated because of the historical-cost principle. Some firms use partner withdrawals as an occasion to review asset valuations and record appropriate increases or decreases. Once the proper accounts are adjusted, any additional valuation increase is debited to Goodwill. Each partner's capital account is then adjusted by using the profit- and loss-sharing ratio.

Liquidation of a partnership

The process of terminating a partnership and discontinuing operations is known as **liquidation.** In the usual case the noncash assets are sold, the creditors are paid, and any remaining cash is distributed to the partners. Because liquidations can be complex and are covered in advanced accounting courses, only a basic overview is presented in this text.

To illustrate the necessary accounting procedures, assume the partnership of Leake, Mueller, and Thomas has decided to suspend operations. The firm's balance sheet prior to liquidation follows.

Start Here!

Assets		*Liabilities & owners' equity*	
Cash	*$ 50,000*	*Accounts payable*	*$ 5,000*
Noncash assets	*50,000*	*Leake, capital*	*43,000*
	$100,000	*Mueller, capital*	*40,000*
		Thomas, capital	*12,000*
			$100,000

Next, suppose the noncash assets are sold for $32,000, which results in an $18,000 loss ($50,000 – $32,000) on liquidation. Gains and losses on liquidation are absorbed by the partners in the profit- and loss-sharing ratio. If the ratio calls for equal division, the journal entry to record the asset sale is as follows:

Cash	*32,000*	
Leake, Capital	*6,000*	
Mueller, Capital	*6,000*	
Thomas, Capital	*6,000*	
Noncash Assets		*50,000*
To record sale of noncash assets		

Observe that a separate loss account is not established; instead the loss is charged directly to the capital accounts, because the business is terminating.

The entry above produces the following account balances:

	Cash	+	Noncash Assets	=	Accounts Payable	+	Leake, Capital	+	Mueller, Capital	+	Thomas, Capital
Prior to asset sale	$50,000		$50,000		$5,000		$43,000		$40,000		$12,000
Asset sale	+32,000		–50,000				–6,000		–6,000		–6,000
	$82,000		—		$5,000		$37,000		$34,000		$ 6,000

Once the assets are sold, the liabilities are paid. Any cash that remains is then distributed to Leake, Mueller, and Thomas *in the amount of their capital balances.* The necessary journal entries are shown below:

Accounts Payable	*5,000*	
Cash		*5,000*
To record payment of liabilities		
Leake, Capital	*37,000*	
Mueller, Capital	*34,000*	
Thomas, Capital	*6,000*	
Cash		*77,000*
To record cash distribution to partners		

Note that the profit- and loss-sharing ratio is ignored in the disbursement of cash to the owners. This ratio is used in the division of *earnings,* not in the allocation of cash or other assets among the partners.

Capital deficiency

In the previous example each partner's capital account was of sufficient size to absorb the $6,000 share of the loss. Suppose, however, that the noncash assets are sold for only $8,000. In this case a $42,000 loss arises

($50,000 − $8,000), which reduces each of the capital balances by $14,000 ($42,000 ÷ 3). After the liabilities are paid, $53,000 cash remains in the firm, and Thomas's capital account contains a $2,000 debit balance. These figures are shown in the accompanying chart.

	Cash	+ Noncash Assets	= Accounts Payable	+ Leake, Capital	+ Mueller, Capital	+ Thomas, Capital
Prior to asset sale	$50,000	$50,000	$5,000	$43,000	$40,000	$12,000
Asset sale	+8,000	−50,000		−14,000	−14,000	−14,000
	$58,000	—	$5,000	$29,000	$26,000	$(2,000)
Payment of liabilities	−5,000		−5,000			
	$53,000	—	—	$29,000	$26,000	$(2,000)

The $2,000 debit balance is commonly referred to as a **capital deficiency.** Just as Leake and Mueller have respective claims against the partnership of $29,000 and $26,000, the partnership has a $2,000 claim against Thomas. Notice that until the deficiency is settled, insufficient cash is available for disbursement to the partners with credit balances. Thomas thus would be requested to remit $2,000 to the firm.

If Thomas pays, the partnership's cash would increase to $55,000, thereby allowing a distribution of $29,000 to Leake and $26,000 to Mueller. The required journal entries follow.

Cash	*2,000*	
Thomas, Capital		*2,000*
To record receipt of cash from Thomas to settle deficiency		

Leake, Capital	*29,000*	
Mueller, Capital	*26,000*	
Cash		*55,000*
To record cash distribution to partners		

If Thomas is unable to pay, the $2,000 deficiency is charged against the other partners according to the profit- and loss-sharing ratio. As a result, Leake and Mueller would absorb $1,000 each to allow the closing of Thomas's capital account. This procedure is illustrated by the following entry.

Leake, Capital	*1,000*	
Mueller, Capital	*1,000*	
Thomas, Capital		*2,000*
To distribute capital deficiency and close Thomas's capital account		

The cash balance of $53,000 would then be distributed, with $28,000 going to Leake and $25,000 to Mueller.

Leake, Capital	*28,000*	
Mueller, Capital	*25,000*	
Cash		*53,000*
To record cash distribution to partners		

CORPORATIONS

The corporate form of business organization dominates the U.S. economy in terms of revenues and net income generated, assets owned, and number of employees. As evidence, consider the information appearing in Exhibit 13–2, which was extracted from a recent listing of the Fortune 500, the 500 largest industrial corporations in America.

Exhibit 13-2

Excerpt from Fortune 500

Rank	Firm	Sales (000 Omitted)	Net Income (000 Omitted)	Assets (000 Omitted)	Number of Employees
1	Exxon	$ 108,107,688	$ 5,567,481	$ 62,931,055	180,000
50	Monsanto	6,947,700	445,100	6,069,200	57,391
100	Agway	3,828,262	Not available	1,335,801	17,883
150	Singer	2,833,600	38,400	1,573,200	66,000
200	Cummins Engine	1,962,461	115,211	1,415,797	22,788
250	Timken	1,427,158	101,115	1,101,431	20,920
300	Becton Dickinson	1,066,093	75,863	1,004,324	21,500
350	General Cinema	823,551	44,265	503,328	12,500
400	Varian Associates	680,057	(3,554)	495,132	12,800
450	Nucor	544,821	34,729	384,782	3,700
500	Shaklee	454,522	24,543	191,670	1,500
Totals for entire 500		$1,773,381,212	$84,223,057	$1,282,828,236	15,635,041

SOURCE Fortune, *May 3, 1982, pp. 260–279.*

Without a doubt these firms are giants. Taken collectively, the entire 500 is an impressive listing of financial strength, power, and resources. Consider, however, that these are industrial corporations only; transportation companies, banks, utilities, and many other businesses have been omitted from the totals presented. Also omitted are numerous smaller corporations, along with hundreds of thousands of family-run businesses. Indeed, the corporation is a significant factor that affects everyone's daily activities and life-style.

In the early 1800s Supreme Court Justice Marshall defined a corporation as "an artificial being, invisible, intangible, and existing only in contemplation of the law." Given this definition, the corporation is viewed as a legal entity having an existence separate and distinct from its owners. Corporations may thus buy and sell property in their own names. Additionally, corporations can enter into contracts, defend themselves in court, and conduct business in the same manner as a person would.

Corporate Form of Organization: Advantages

The corporate form of organization is often considered preferable to both a sole proprietorship and partnership for conducting business activities. This preference arises for the following reasons.

Transferability of ownership

A corporation is divided into transferable units of ownership called **shares of stock.** These shares are readily transferable from one investor to another without affecting corporate operations. Frequently, the transfer occurs in an organized market such as the New York Stock Exchange, a mechanism where the stocks of roughly 2,000 businesses can be bought or sold. With the possible exception of family-owned entities or corporations owned by a few persons (termed **closely held corporations**), the acquisition and sale of stock are routine matters and do not require the approval of other owners.

Perpetual existence

As we just noted, a transfer of ownership does not affect the operations of a corporation. The corporation is therefore said to have a continuous or perpetual existence. Contrast this feature with that of a partnership where, unless so stated in the partnership agreement, a change in ownership terminates the entity's life. Because it is not unusual for millions of shares to change hands on a single day, perpetual existence is necessary to ensure continuity of operations and the achievement of corporate objectives.

Limited liability of stockholders

The owners of a corporation are termed its **stockholders.** Because of the corporation's separate legal existence, stockholders have *limited liability;* that is, the most they can lose is the amount of their investment. Creditors of a corporation have a claim against the entity's assets only; the personal assets of the owners cannot be used to satisfy corporate debts. Recall that this feature does not apply to partnerships, as each partner may be held personally liable for the debts of the business.

Ease of raising capital

Limited liability tends to make the corporation an attractive alternative for investors. This feature, coupled with the fact that ownership is divided into many units, provides a corporation with ready access to additional capital funds. The need for and the ability to raise substantial amounts of capital have prompted virtually all large businesses to adopt the corporate form of organization.

Corporate Form of Organization: Disadvantages

Although the corporation offers many advantages, several disadvantages must be considered.

Double taxation

As we noted earlier in the chapter, a partnership pays no income taxes; instead an owner is taxed personally on his or her share of the earnings. This same feature also applies to sole proprietorships. Corporations, on the other hand, are required to pay income taxes. The taxes are heavy and often amount to approximately 50% of taxable net income. In addition, any earnings distributed as dividends are income to the recipient stockholders and are subject to personal income tax. Thus the same earnings can be taxed twice. The taxing of income to the corporation and the subsequent taxing of dividends to the stockholder is termed **double taxation.**

Heavy regulation

In comparison with sole proprietorships and partnerships, corporations are subject to heavier governmental regulation. Most corporations that sell their stock to the general public (termed **publicly held corporations**) must follow the financial reporting regulations of the Securities and Exchange

Commission (SEC). Corporations are also subject to widely varying state laws. Furthermore, depending on the activities in which it is involved, a corporation may come under the scrutiny of specialized agencies. Examples of such agencies include the Interstate Commerce Commission, the Nuclear Regulatory Commission, and the Federal Deposit Insurance Corporation.

Organization of a Corporation

A corporation is created by obtaining a **charter** from one of the states. The charter is granted after the appropriate state department reviews and approves an application for incorporation. The charter specifies, among other things, the firm's business purpose, its organizational structure, and the types and amounts of stock that can be issued.

After the corporation is created, a stockholders' meeting is usually held to adopt the bylaws that govern the conduct of business activities and to appoint the board of directors. The board of directors normally meets several times a year and has the responsibility of overseeing business affairs, determining corporate policy, and hiring the officers who manage the company.

Organization costs

Forming a corporation is more involved and costly than forming a sole proprietorship or partnership. In addition to state incorporation fees, there are legal costs connected with preparing the application for incorporation, expenses incurred by the founders, and numerous other outlays. These one-time costs are debited to an account entitled Organization Costs. Organization costs are disclosed on the balance sheet as either an intangible asset or an "other asset."

Treatment as an asset is justified because organization costs contribute to the formation of the corporation; thus the benefits derived extend over a number of years. Normally, the number of years is unknown, since most corporations have an indefinite life. A minority of accountants therefore argue that until a corporation is liquidated, organization costs should be reported on the balance sheet at the initial amount incurred.

Recall from Chapter 11 that intangible assets with indeterminant lives are amortized over a period not to exceed forty years. Most firms amortize organization costs over five years, which is the minimum period allowable under existing income tax regulations. Businesses follow this practice because organization costs are small in relation to total assets. In addition, the effect of the associated amortization charges on net income is typically insignificant.

Common Stock

The corporate charter specifies the types and number of shares of stock (sometimes called *capital stock*) that a corporation is allowed to issue. Normally, the charter allows for the issuance of more shares than are currently needed. This practice saves the time and expense of gaining repeated approvals from stockholders and state authorities for additional stock issues at a later date. The number of shares allowed by the charter is termed the **authorized stock.**

Many corporations issue different types of stock to permit flexibility in raising capital and to appeal to different types of investors. Usually, the different types of stock have different rights or privileges. All corporations issue **common stock**—an ownership interest that controls corporate management by exercising voting rights. Common stockholders are often rewarded with increased stock values when net income rises and, conversely, with decreased values when profitability falls. Overall it is the common stockholder who reaps the benefits of corporate success and pays the price of failure.

Rights of common stockholders

The owners of common stock typically have the following rights:

1 To share in any dividend distributions that may be declared by the board of directors.
2 To subscribe to any additional common stock issued by the corporation (known as the **preemptive right**). Existing stockholders are given the opportunity to maintain their respective interests in a corporation by acquiring additional shares on a pro rata basis. Thus a stockholder owning 40% of a corporation's common stock is allowed to purchase 40% of any new shares issued before those shares are offered to other investors. The preemptive right is not a hard and steadfast rule. In some cases stockholders have waived the preemptive right, thereby permitting the issuance of large blocks of stock to acquire other businesses. In other cases certain states have allowed the issuance of shares with no preemptive rights attached.
3 To share in the final disposition of assets if the corporation is liquidated. At the end of a corporation's life its assets are sold, and the cash generated is used to settle the claims of creditors. Any remaining cash (or assets) is shared proportionately by the common stockholders on the basis of the number of shares owned.
4 To elect the board of directors and to vote on other important corporate issues. Common stockholders are frequently asked to consider such matters as proposed mergers; the selection of independent auditors; changes in corporate bylaws, management compensation, and incentive programs; and the types and amounts of stock that can be issued. If common stockholders are unable to attend stockholders' meetings, they can delegate their voting rights to an agent (usually the board of directors) by signing a legal document known as a *proxy*. Most stockholders of large publicly held corporations follow the proxy alternative because of convenience and skyrocketing travel costs.

In recent years dissident stockholders have started to criticize management policies at the annual stockholders' meeting. The excerpt on page 500 relates to dissidents and their implications for the future.

HOW EFFECTIVE ARE THE DISSIDENTS?

It was forty years ago that a young stockholder named Lewis Gilbert started showing up at annual meetings to criticize management policies. As the years went by, other individuals took up the cause. But the modern era of stockholder activism really began in 1970 with the first attack by Ralph Nader's Project on Corporate Responsibility on General Motors Corporation.

After all the years of sometimes bitter give-and-take, how much has stockholder dissent actually accomplished? The dissidents have never won a showdown vote except in those rare cases where management sided with them. But that, of course, is not what they are after. Realistically, dissidents have sought only a token vote on the issues—enough to keep them alive. What they really want is to force management to grapple with issues—corporate, social, and political—that they believe business should be concerned about.

And here the dissidents have had notable success. From time to time they have even persuaded management to change its policies. In past years dissidents talked five giant U.S. oil companies into leaving Southwest Africa, convinced a computer company that it should stop supplying computers to the government of South Africa, and played a big role in calling a halt to overseas bribes and payoffs. Church groups have scored a notable first in getting a number of companies to say they will stop sponsoring violent programs on television. Over the years, too, the critics have convinced many companies to disclose to shareholders, and thus eventually to the public, information on many subjects that had previously been considered for management's eyes only.

The dissidents' most significant accomplishment, though, has been in establishing a dialogue with corporate management. In trying to keep critical proposals off the annual meeting agenda, management has had to sit down and argue about them with the proponents. Today, with more and more issues at stake, that dialogue goes on almost all year around. These private discussions, both sides agree, are often more effective than a public confrontation. Both sides admit, too, that they have gained more respect for each other in talking things over.

At a time when business is on the defensive on so many fronts, most companies try to come to some kind of agreement with dissident shareholders, especially when they are well organized and articulate. All in all, the dissidents themselves must be astonished at the impact they have had on the ways of corporate America.

SOURCE Adapted from "Dissidents Gear Up for Annual Meetings," Dun's Review, *April 1977, p. 78. Reprinted with special permission of* Dun's Review, *April 1977. Copyright © 1977, Dun & Bradstreet Publications Corporation.*

The foregoing rights apply to most common stockholders, not all. Sometimes different classes of common stock are issued with rights other than those described. The Adolph Coors Company, for example, perhaps best known for its brewing operation, has Class A and Class B common stock. Class A stock has voting rights and is retained by the Coors family; Class B stock is nonvoting and has been issued to the general public.

Preferred Stock: Nature and Characteristics

Rather than have multiple classes of common stock, some corporations have achieved differentiation by issuing **preferred stock.** As its name implies, preferred stock has several preferential rights; in comparison with common stock, however, other rights are given up in return. Normally, preferred stock appeals to investors who want a safe investment with a steady dividend. Why? The reasons become apparent in the upcoming sections where we discuss characteristics of most preferred stocks.

No voting rights

Preferred stockholders generally have no vote in corporate affairs. Exceptions are made, however, by special contracts or by state law. In some cases voting privileges are awarded after certain conditions have been met, such as the absence of dividends for a specified period of time.

Dividend preference

Voting rights are often forfeited in exchange for a preference in dividend distributions. That is, owners of preferred stock are entitled to receive dividends before any distributions are made to common stockholders. In most cases, however, preferred stockholders receive only a stipulated amount regardless of the profitability of the firm. This outcome arises because preferred stock dividends are expressed either on a per-year basis or as a percentage of par value. (Par value refers to the face value of a share of stock and is discussed later in the chapter.) A 10% preferred stock with a $25 par value, for example, has a dividend of $2.50 per year.

Although many businesses take pride in their dividend records, keep in mind that dividend distributions are not mandatory but are subject to the discretion of the board of directors. Thus when a firm's cash position is weak or when earnings are marginal, dividends may not be disbursed. For this reason most preferred stocks are **cumulative.** That is, the rights to preferred dividends that are omitted in a given year accumulate and are said to be **in arrears.** Dividends in arrears must be paid before any subsequent dividends can be declared and paid on a corporation's common stock.

To illustrate, suppose Flora, Inc., has 20,000 shares of 10%, $5 par, cumulative preferred stock and 50,000 shares of $1 par common. Dividend distributions for the past four years are listed in the second column of the table on page 502. Because the annual preferred dividend requirement is $10,000 (20,000 shares × $5 × 0.10), the dividends would be divided between preferred and common shareholders as shown.

Observe that in Year 2 only $6,000 of dividends was distributed. Since preferred stockholders are entitled to receive $10,000, dividends are $4,000 in arrears. All $6,000 goes to the preferred stockholders because of their preferential right to receive dividends before distributions to common. In

Year	Total Dividends Distributed	Annual Preferred Requirement	Dividends in Arrears	Dividends Distributed: Preferred	Dividends Distributed: Common
1	$27,000	$10,000	$ —	$10,000	$17,000
2	6,000	10,000	4,000	6,000	—
3	3,000	10,000	11,000	3,000	—
4	25,000	10,000	—	21,000	4,000

Year 3 Flora failed to cover the annual preferred requirement by $7,000 ($10,000 – $3,000), thus raising dividends in arrears to $11,000. Again preferred gets the entire distribution, in this instance $3,000. Finally, the $25,000 of dividends in Year 4 was sufficient to meet not only the annual requirement but also the arrearage. Common stockholders therefore receive the remaining $4,000 ($25,000 – $10,000 – $11,000).

Dividends in arrears are not a liability because they have never been declared by the board of directors. Arrearages are typically disclosed in the footnotes to the financial statements. Although we have emphasized the cumulative feature, realize that some preferred stock is noncumulative; that is, unpaid dividends do not accumulate and are lost. Because noncumulative preferred stock lacks investor appeal, it is rarely encountered in practice.

Participation feature

Some preferred stock **participates** with common in excess dividend distributions. To illustrate, consider Year 1 in the previous example. Preferred stockholders received a 10% dividend, with the remaining $17,000 going to common. If the preferred stock was fully participating, preferred stockholders would be entitled to extra dividends after common received an equal 10% distribution. In this case, however, the common dividend would be figured on the common equity of $50,000 (50,000 shares × $1 par value). Participating preferred stocks are seldom encountered; our discussion, therefore, has been intentionally brief.

Asset preference upon liquidation

Most preferred stock has a preference over common stock in the event of corporate liquidation. After creditor claims are settled, preferred stockholders are entitled to their share of the remaining assets, prior to any distributions to the holders of common (i.e., the residual owners).

Callable

Many preferred stock issues are **callable.** That is, the issuing corporation retains the right to reacquire (call) the stock at a preset price. So that this feature is somewhat attractive to investors, the call price is generally set slightly above the original issue price. Frequently, however, the call price limits the value of the stock in the marketplace. It would be foolish for investors to pay $119 per share, for example, when the corporation could turn around and call the stock for $105. Unless a call is unlikely, the investor stands to lose $14 per share.

The call feature allows a corporation to raise capital from a stock issuance and then cancel the stock and return the funds. This outcome may occur when the cash is no longer needed or the stock becomes financially burdensome. The latter situation is possible if the preferred stock is issued when interest (and dividend) rates are high. Should the rates drop suddenly, the stock can be called and replaced with cheaper financing.

Convertible

Some preferred stock is **convertible** into common stock at the option of the stockholder. Conversion is normally in a stipulated exchange ratio; for example, 1 share of preferred may be convertible into 5 shares of common. Convertible preferred is appealing to both investors and the issuing company. From the investors' viewpoint, they are scheduled to receive a fixed dividend return on the preferred stock. Furthermore, should the common stock of the corporation rise in value, investors have the privilege of conversion. From the company's view, investors are normally willing to accept a lower dividend rate because of the attractiveness of the conversion feature.

Par-Value Stock

The common and preferred classifications are based on the rights afforded to the respective groups of stockholders. Stocks can also be categorized as par value or no-par value. **Par-value** stock has a fixed dollar amount per share printed on the face of the stock certificate.[2] The par is specified by the corporate charter; it can be any amount and is sometimes influenced by state laws that tax the face value of shares issued.

The significance of par value is that it represents the **legal capital** per share of stock. Total legal capital, obtained by multiplying the par value per share times the number of shares issued, denotes the minimum amount of owners' equity that must be maintained for protection of the creditors. To explain, recall that stockholders have limited liability and cannot be held personally liable for corporate obligations. Consequently, in an effort to provide some protection to the creditors, state laws require a minimum permanent investment from the owners, that is, legal capital. Legal capital means that part of the stockholders' investment must be retained to help settle creditor claims on corporate assets. Dividend declarations that reduce total owners' equity below legal capital are therefore not permitted.

Issuing par-value stock

If a corporation is large or is attempting to sell a substantial amount of stock, the services of an investment banking firm will normally be utilized. Typical investment bankers include E. F. Hutton & Company and Merrill Lynch Pierce Fenner & Smith. The investment banker, often referred to as an *underwriter,* has the responsibility of selling the stock, at a set price, to the public. Underwriters charge a commission for their services and often advertise stock issuances in newspapers and business periodicals. The sale of stock is typically made on the basis of a **prospectus,** a document required by the SEC that contains information about the corporation's products, management, and financial affairs.

[2] A stock certificate is the legal document that presents evidence of corporate ownership.

Issue price

Stocks may be issued at, above, or below par value, given the arbitrary manner in which par is determined. Issuances below par are seldom encountered and are actually illegal in many states. Why? Although the sale proceeds are less than par, the stock is still considered fully paid. However, the stockholder is held contingently liable to the corporation's creditors for the difference between the sale price and the amount printed on the face of the certificate. Should corporate assets be insufficient to settle creditor claims if operations cease, the original stockholders may be called upon to furnish additional cash. To avoid this situation, virtually all corporations issue stock at or above par.

The issue price for new stock is determined by the corporation along with an underwriter or financial advisors. The following factors are considered: past, present, and future corporate earnings; financial position; expected dividend rates; market position of the firm's products and services; current state of the investment market; and recent prices of competitors' stock.

Once stock is issued, its **market price** (the price at which a share can be bought or sold) continually changes. The changes reflect investor evaluation of the corporation's progress and prospects. If growth prospects are evident, the price of the shares should rise, and vice versa. If a corporation sells its stock at $5 and the market price subsequently jumps to $35, the corporation receives no benefits from the increase in value. The appreciation goes to the stockholders. Of course, if more investment capital is needed, the corporation may issue additional shares at or near the existing market, in this case $35.

Accounting for par-value stock

The issuance of par-value stock may necessitate entries in more than one owners' equity account. Specifically, an amount equal to the par value of the shares issued is placed in a capital stock account, either Common Stock or Preferred Stock. Then if the stock is issued at a price greater than par, the difference between the issue price and par is recorded in an account entitled Paid-in Capital in Excess of Par Value. Stating this important allocation differently, the funds received from investors are recorded as legal capital (the par value) and as additional paid-in capital (amounts received in excess of par).

To illustrate the proper accounting, assume McCord Corporation is authorized to issue 50,000 shares of $5 par, 8% cumulative preferred stock and 20,000 shares of $10 par common. Further assume that the corporation has issued 30,000 shares of preferred at par and 10,000 shares of common at $18. The necessary journal entries follow.

Cash	150,000	
Preferred Stock		150,000
To record the issue of 30,000 shares of $5 par, 8% preferred at $5 per share		

Cash	180,000	
Common Stock		100,000
Paid-in Capital in Excess of Par Value		80,000
To record the issue of 10,000 shares of $10 par common at $18 per share		

Observe that in both cases the par value of the issued shares was placed in a capital stock account. In addition, note that the $80,000 paid in excess of par was recorded separately. When stock is issued at a price above par, the difference between the issue price and the par value is often called a **premium.** Alternatively, then, an account termed Premium on Common Stock could have been credited for $80,000.

We stress that these entries are made *only at the time of stock issuance.* Daily purchases and sales of shares by stockholders normally involve shares that have been previously issued; thus no additional cash is received by the corporation. In these instances the corporation does not record a formal journal entry; all that is needed is an updating of the list of stockholders.

Balance sheet presentation

The owners' (stockholders') equity section of McCord's balance sheet would appear as shown in Exhibit 13-3. Notice how the balance sheet discloses the two major sources of corporate equity: stockholder investments (**paid-in capital**) and **retained earnings.** Retained earnings represent capital generated from profitable operations that is kept in the business; an in-depth discussion will be presented in Chapter 14. At this point assume the account's $240,000 balance was obtained from McCord's general ledger.

Exhibit 13-3

Stockholders' equity of McCord Corporation

STOCKHOLDERS' EQUITY		
Capital stock		
Cumulative 8% preferred stock, $5 par, 50,000 shares authorized, 30,000 shares issued and outstanding	$150,000	
Common stock, $10 par, 20,000 shares authorized, 10,000 shares issued and outstanding	100,000	$250,000
Paid-in capital in excess of par value: common		80,000
Total paid-in capital		$330,000
Retained earnings		240,000
Total stockholders' equity		$570,000

The stockholders' equity section also reveals two other important points. First, considerable detail is required in terms of disclosure. The features of the various stock issues are described along with the number of shares authorized by the corporate charter, issued by the firm, and held by

[3]The number of shares issued and outstanding can differ. This situation will also be shown in Chapter 14.

the stockholders (termed **outstanding shares**).[3] Second, note that the $80,000 paid by stockholders in excess of par value is not revenue or a profit. It is merely additional invested capital that is shown separately from the capital stock accounts.

Our illustration has focused on the issuance of stock at par and in excess of par. Should stock be issued below par the difference between par and the issue price, called a **discount,** is debited to an account entitled Discount on Capital Stock. The discount account is subtracted from the capital stock accounts when determining total paid-in capital.

No-Par Stock

In the early days of corporations the issuance of par-value stock sometimes misled investors. By printing par value on the face of the certificate, investors occasionally equated this amount with the "true" value of the stock, that is, its market value. This factor, coupled with the contingent liability problem should issuance take place at a discount, prompted many corporations to consider **no-par stock.** Because the par-value concept is absent, no premium or discount is recorded at the time of issue. Thus the entire proceeds are credited to a capital stock account. To illustrate, assume Canton Corporation is authorized to issue 20,000 shares of no-par common stock. If 10,000 shares are issued at $18 per share, the required journal entry would be as follows:

Cash	*180,000*	
Common Stock		*180,000*
To record the issue of 10,000 shares of no-par common at $18 per share		

This example has deliberately used the same numbers as the McCord Corporation illustration on page 504. Notice that both issues of common stock generated identical proceeds: $180,000. With no-par stock, however, total invested capital is recorded in one equity account rather than two.

Stated-value stock

Although most states permit the issuance of no-par stock, some states require corporations to set a minimum issue price. This price, known as the stock's **stated value,** allows for protection of the creditors in terms of legal capital. In essence, then, stated value can be likened to par value.

Because of the similarity, accounting for stated-value stock closely parallels accounting for par-value stock. To illustrate, we will continue the Canton Corporation example. Assume that to comply with state law, Canton's board of directors has assigned a $10 stated value to each share. The issuance of 10,000 shares at $18 per share would be recorded as follows:

Cash	*180,000*	
Common Stock		*100,000*
Paid-in Capital in Excess of Stated Value		*80,000*
To record the issue of 10,000 shares of no-par common (stated value, $10) at $18 per share		

The stated value of the issued stock is recorded in the Common Stock account. Any excess above the stated value is recorded as Paid-in Capital in

Excess of Stated Value, which is similar to additional paid-in capital received on par-value shares.

Stock Subscriptions

Rather than use the services of an underwriter, small corporations occasionally sell stock directly to investors on a subscription basis. Investors agree to purchase the stock at a given price, with payment taking place on a future date or through installments. After the subscriber pays in full, the shares of stock are issued.

For example, assume investors subscribed to 1,000 shares of Glover Corporation $5 par common stock at $22 per share. The following journal entry would be made.

Subscriptions Receivable: Common Stock	*22,000*	
Common Stock Subscribed		*5,000*
Paid-in Capital in Excess of Par Value		*17,000*
To record subscriptions to 1,000 shares of $5 par common at $22 per share		

Subscriptions Receivable is established to indicate that $22,000 will be forthcoming from investors. This account is similar to other receivables and normally appears as a current asset on the balance sheet. Common Stock Subscribed is a temporary paid-in capital account that is credited for the par value of the shares subscribed (1,000 shares × $5). Observe that at this point it would be incorrect to credit Common Stock, because the shares have not yet been issued. Finally, the $17,000 premium is placed in the Paid-in Capital in Excess of Par Value account.

Next, assume investors subscribing to 750 shares paid in full. Glover would therefore issue the stock and record the following entries:

Cash	*16,500*	
Subscriptions Receivable: Common Stock		*16,500*
To record collections from subscribers of 750 shares (750 × $22 = $16,500)		
Common Stock Subscribed	*3,750*	
Common Stock		*3,750*
To record issuance of 750 shares under subscription agreements		

The first entry is similar to other receipts of cash on account. The second entry removes $3,750 (750 shares × $5 par) from Common Stock Subscribed and recognizes the issuance of common shares. Consistent with previous illustrations, the capital stock account is again carried at par value.

Should subscribers to the remaining 250 shares now pay 40% of their balances due, no additional shares would be issued. Why? Shares are issued only when full payment is made; thus the only journal entry would be as follows:

Cash	*2,200*	
Subscriptions Receivable: Common Stock		*2,200*
To record partial payment on subscriptions for 250 shares (250 shares × $22 × 0.40)		

Issuing Stock for Assets Other Than Cash

Thus far we have concentrated on stock issues that generate cash. The cash, in turn, was used for the purchase of assets, payment of expenses, and other similar purposes. Frequently, corporations issue stock in direct exchange for land, buildings, and even other businesses. In addition, stock is sometimes used to settle claims of attorneys and other professionals for services rendered, particularly at the time of corporate formation, when cash balances may be low.

The issuance of shares for noncash assets or services creates a valuation problem. Specifically, at what value should the transaction be recorded? The general rule is that the assets or services acquired are recorded at their fair market value or the fair market value of the stock, whichever is more clearly discernible. If the corporation's shares are actively traded on one of the stock exchanges, determining the stock's market value is a relatively simple matter. *The Wall Street Journal* and the financial pages of most metropolitan newspapers will furnish the necessary information. When stock is not actively traded, as in a closely held corporation, an appraisal of the asset's (or service's) market value may be more appropriate.

To illustrate the proper accounting treatment, assume Fuqua Industries is a small family-run business located in Wyoming. Fuqua's attorney has agreed to accept 40 shares of $5 par common for $850 of legal work performed in organizing the corporation. The required journal entry follows.

Organization Costs	850	
Common Stock		200
Paid-in Capital in Excess of Par Value		650
To record the issuance of common stock for attorney's services		

Because Fuqua's stock is not actively traded, the $850 billing is more clearly determinable as the market value of the transaction.

In another case, suppose Fuqua later issued 40,000 shares of $5 par common to acquire a building complex. An appraiser has indicated that the property has a $280,000 fair market value, subdivided as follows: land, $60,000; building, $220,000. The required journal entry is as follows:

Land	60,000	
Building	220,000	
Common Stock		200,000
Paid-in Capital in Excess of Par Value		80,000
To record the issuance of common stock for building complex		

Corporate Equity: A Comprehensive Illustration

The stockholders' equity section in Exhibit 13-4 brings together several of the concepts discussed in the chapter. Notice that preferred stock is presented first, followed by common stock. Next, additional paid-in capital is disclosed to complete total equity contributed by stockholders. The final element is retained earnings. Although variations in terminology and presentation exist in practice, the exhibit is representative and should convey the message that corporate equity is more complex than equity of sole proprietorships and of partnerships.

Exhibit 13-4

Corporate equity

STOCKHOLDERS' EQUITY		
Capital stock		
Cumulative 9% preferred stock, $10 par, 30,000 shares authorized, 20,000 shares issued and outstanding		$200,000
Common stock, no-par, $5 stated value, 15,000 shares authorized, 10,000 shares issued and outstanding	$ 50,000	
Common stock subscribed, no-par, $5 stated value, 2,000 shares	10,000	60,000
Total capital stock		$260,000
Additional paid-in capital		
Paid-in capital in excess of par value: preferred	$120,000	
Paid-in capital in excess of stated value: common	48,000	168,000
Total paid-in capital		$428,000
Retained earnings		150,000
Total stockholders' equity		$578,000

KEY TERMS AND CONCEPTS

PARTNERSHIPS

articles of partnership 484
bonus to new or existing partners 491, 492
capital deficiency 495
earnings deficiency 489
liquidation 493
mutual agency 485
partnership 484
salary and interest allowances 487, 489

CORPORATIONS

authorized stock 498
callable preferred stock 502
charter 498
closely held corporation 497
common stock 499
convertible preferred stock 503
corporation 496
cumulative preferred stock 501
discount on capital stock 506
dividends in arrears 501
double taxation 497
legal capital 503
market price 504
no-par-value stock 506
organization costs 498
outstanding shares 506
paid-in capital 505
participating preferred stock 502
par-value stock 503
preemptive right 499
preferred stock 501
premium on capital stock 505
prospectus 503
publicly held corporation 497
retained earnings 505
shares of stock 496
stated-value stock 506
stockholders 497
stock subscriptions 507

QUESTIONS

Q13-1 Describe "mutual agency" and "unlimited liability" as related to partnerships. How do these features influence the selection of partners?

Q13-2 A partnership is said to have a limited life. Does the death of a partner terminate business activities? Explain.

Q13-3 Akers and Howard have formed a partnership. Akers invested a minicomputer that cost $24,000 and has a $15,000 fair market value. Which amount will be recorded in Akers's capital account? Why?

Q13-4 Discuss the accounting treatment of salary allowances that are provided to partners. Are the allowances considered an expense? Why?

Q13-5 Baker has a $24,000 capital interest in the ABC partnership and is entitled to one-third of all profits and losses. Assume Baker sells her entire interest to Doane for $60,000. What amount will be recorded in Doane's capital account on the partnership's books? How much cash will be received by the partnership?

Q13-6 Suppose James is withdrawing from the JKL partnership. Why might the remaining partners be willing to pay James more than the balance in her capital account? How would this difference be recorded?

Q13-7 How are liquidation gains and losses divided among a firm's partners? Assuming no capital deficiency, how is any remaining cash divided among the partners?

Q13-8 Capital deficiencies may occur during the liquidation of a partnership. What is a "capital deficiency" and how is it treated for accounting purposes?

Q13-9 What is a corporation? Discuss the advantages of the corporate form of organization.

Q13-10 What is meant by the double taxation of corporate earnings? Are there other disadvantages of the corporate form of organization? Explain.

Q13-11 List the rights typically possessed by common stockholders.

Q13-12 What is "callable preferred stock"? Why do corporations issue such stock?

Q13-13 Discuss the meaning of "legal capital."

Q13-14 Why is stock rarely issued below par value?

Q13-15 Discuss the impact of par value in determining the market price of a new stock issue.

Q13-16 Discuss the difference between "par value" and "stated value."

Q13-17 Discuss the process of selling par-value stock on a subscription basis.

Q13-18 When stock is issued in exchange for services or noncash assets, at what amount should the transaction be recorded?

EXERCISES

E13-1 John Holck decided to form a partnership with Peter Holmes. John contributed cash of $20,000; Peter contributed the assets from a business he has operated for the past five years. A recent balance sheet from this business revealed the following information:

Cash		$ 500
Accounts receivable	$2,000	
Less: Allowance for bad debts	300	1,700
Merchandise inventory		5,400
Machinery	$7,000	
Less: Accumulated depreciation	2,400	4,600
Total assets		$12,200

Other information is as follows:

a The allowance for bad debts is understated by $200.

b The fair market value of the merchandise inventory is $6,500.

c The fair market value of the machinery is $12,000.

Present the necessary journal entries to record the partners' investments.

E13-2 Bradshaw, Crane, and McDougall recently invested $10,000 each and formed the BCM partnership. The articles of partnership contained the following stipulations:

1 Partners are allowed 15% interest on investments.

2 Bradshaw and Crane each have salary allowances of $11,000.

3 Remaining profits and losses are shared equally among the three partners.

Determine the proper division of net income (or net loss) among Bradshaw, Crane, and McDougall for the following independent cases:

a Net income of $44,500

b Net income of $23,200

c Net loss of $10,100

E13-3 Smithfield and Dean are partners in a food distribution business and have capital balances of $63,000 and $72,000, respectively. Net income (or net loss) is shared equally. Prepare journal entries to record the admission of a new partner, Monastra, assuming each of the following independent situations:

a Monastra invests $45,000 and receives a 25% interest in the new partnership.

b Monastra invests $65,000 in the partnership for a 25% interest. Is a bonus being awarded to Dean and Smithfield or to Monastra?

c Monastra invests $45,000 in the partnership for a 30% interest. Is a bonus being awarded to Dean and Smithfield or to Monastra?

E13-4 Keystone, Nesbitt, and Sunshine are partners in a machinery business. On January 1 of the current year the capital balances of the three partners were $10,000, $20,000, and $30,000, respectively. All profits and losses are shared equally. Prepare journal entries to record the withdrawal of Nesbitt from the partnership for each of the following independent situations:

a Acosta purchased Nesbitt's interest for $24,500; the purchase was approved by the other partners.

b The partnership purchased Nesbitt's interest for $28,000. Will total partnership capital increase or decrease?

c The partnership purchased Nesbitt's interest for $15,000. Will total partnership capital increase or decrease?

E13-5 Sidinger, Smith, and Swanson formed a partnership in 1975 to practice law. On June 10, 1983, the partners decided to liquidate. The firm's balance sheet follows.

SIDINGER, SMITH, AND SWANSON
Balance Sheet
June 10, 1983

Assets	
Cash	$ 75,000
Noncash assets	125,000
	$200,000
Liabilities & owners' equity	
Payables	$ 10,000
Sidinger, capital	20,000
Smith, capital	80,000
Swanson, capital	90,000
	$200,000

Assume that profits and losses are divided equally. Prepare entries to record (1) the sale of noncash assets, (2) payment of the liabilities, (3) distribution of capital deficiencies (if any), and (4) cash distributions to the partners for the following independent situations:

a The noncash assets are sold for $101,000, all creditors are paid, and all cash is distributed.

b The noncash assets are sold for $41,000, all creditors are paid, and all cash is distributed. Should a capital deficiency arise, assume none of it is paid by the deficient partner.

E13-6 The Alvis-Baker-Coe partnership recently liquidated. Noncash assets were sold for $64,000, and all creditors have been paid. Partners share profits as follows: Alvis, 20%; Baker, 30%; Coe, 50%. Balances in each partner's capital account before and after the asset sale follow.

	Alvis	Baker	Coe
Before assets were sold	$24,000	$ 6,000	$31,000
After assets were sold	$16,400	$(5,400)	$12,000

a Determine the book value of the assets that were sold.

b Calculate the amount of cash on hand at the present time. Assume Baker has not yet settled his capital deficiency.

c If Baker pays $2,600 of his capital deficiency, determine the amount of cash Alvis and Coe would receive in final settlement of their account balances.

E13-7 The following information was extracted from the balance sheet of the O'Connor Corporation.

Capital stock		
Cumulative, nonparticipating 12% preferred stock, $100 par, 1,000 shares authorized, issued, and outstanding		*$100,000*
Common stock, $10 par, 20,000 shares authorized, 15,000 shares issued and outstanding		*150,000*
Total capital stock		*$250,000*
Additional paid-in capital		
Paid-in capital in excess of par: preferred	*$15,000*	
Paid-in capital in excess of par: common	*60,000*	*75,000*
Total paid-in capital		*$325,000*

Dividends declared for the past four years were as follows:

Year	*Dividends Declared*
1	$18,000
2	5,000
3	16,000
4	24,000

a Calculate the dividends paid to preferred and common stockholders during each of the four years.

b Calculate the dividends in arrears that would be shown as a current liability on O'Connor's balance sheet at the end of Year 2 and Year 3.

c Repeat requirement (a), assuming the preferred stock is noncumulative.

E13-8 Prepare journal entries to record the issuance of 500,000 shares of common stock at $18.75 per share for each of the following independent cases:

a Ajax Corporation has common stock with a par value of $5.00 per share.

b Brown Corporation has no-par common with a stated value of $17.50 per share.

c Crown Corporation has no-par common; no stated value has been assigned.

E13-9 The Kalamazoo Corporation was incorporated in June. The firm's charter authorized the sale of 100,000 shares of $5 par-value common stock. The following transactions occurred during the year.

June 2 Sold 18,000 shares of common stock to the founders of the corporation for $6 per share. Cash was collected and the shares were issued.

3 Issued 300 shares to Domingo Chavez, attorney-at-law, for services rendered during Kalamazoo's organizational phase. Chavez charged $1,850 for his work.

July 2 Sold 20,000 shares to the citizens of Kalamazoo for $16 per share. Cash was collected and the shares were issued.

Sept. 5 Issued 4,000 shares to the Grande Company for a building valued at $50,000 and a used van valued at $8,000.

a Prepare journal entries to record each of the transactions.

b Prepare the stockholders' equity section of Kalamazoo's balance sheet as of December 31, assuming a Retained Earnings balance of $17,400.

E13-10 The stockholders' equity sections of Discount Mart at the end of 1983 and 1982 follow.

	1983	1982
Preferred stock, $100 par value, 12%	$1,000,000	$ 600,000
Common stock, $20 par value	2,000,000	1,800,000
Paid-in capital in excess of par value		
Preferred	16,000	—
Common	4,350,000	3,750,000
Retained earnings	80,000	180,000
Total stockholders' equity	$7,446,000	$6,330,000

a How many shares of preferred stock were issued during 1983? At what price were the shares issued?

b How many shares of common stock were issued during 1983? At what price were the shares issued?

c Did Discount Mart's total legal capital increase or decrease during 1983? By what amount?

d Did Discount Mart's total paid-in capital increase or decrease during 1983? By what amount?

PROBLEMS

P13-1 ***Investment by partners; financial statements***

On September 5, 1983, Lopes, Matlack, and Norris formed a partnership to distribute paper products. Lopes invested cash of $85,000 and a vehicle that originally cost $7,500. The vehicle's fair market value at the time of investment was $5,000. Matlack contributed the following items from his existing business.

	Recorded Value	Fair Market Value
Accounts receivable	$32,000	$32,000
Allowance for bad debts	(2,000)	(6,000)
Merchandise inventory	51,000	57,000
Delivery equipment (net)	0*	7,000
Accounts payable	10,500	10,500

** Fully depreciated.*

Finally, Norris contributed short-term marketable securities consisting of 1,000 shares of U.S. Paper common stock (cost per share, $40; market value per share, $70).

INSTRUCTIONS

a Prepare journal entries to record the investments of Lopes, Matlack, and Norris in the partnership.

b Prepare a classified balance sheet for the partnership immediately after the investments.

c Assume that net income of $72,600 was generated through the end of 1983. Cash withdrawals of $25,000 were made by Lopes, $30,000 by Matlack, and $45,000 by Norris. If the partners divide all profits and losses equally, prepare the owners' equity section of the balance sheet as of December 31. Show all computations.

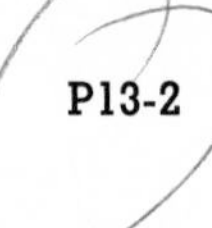

P13-2 ***Income distribution; statement of owners' equity***

McCormick, Quinn, and Saldi are partners in a restaurant. The partners' beginning and average capital balances for 1983 follow.

	Beginning	***Average***
McCormick	$80,000	$85,000
Quinn	50,000	50,000
Saldi	10,000	30,000

Investments during the year amounted to $10,000 for McCormick and $50,000 for Saldi. Net income totaled $32,000.

INSTRUCTIONS

a Prepare a schedule to show the distribution of net income among the partners for each of the following independent cases:
 (1) The partners are granted a 10% interest allowance on beginning capital and share any remaining income equally.
 (2) McCormick, Quinn, and Saldi are granted a 12% interest allowance on average capital and respectively share any remaining income on a 4:4:2 basis.
 (3) Each partner is granted a 10% interest allowance on average capital and a monthly salary allowance of $800. McCormick, Quinn, and Saldi respectively share remaining profits or losses on a 5:3:2 basis.

b Focusing on case (1) in part (a), assume that the interest allowances were withdrawn during the year along with other withdrawals as follows:

McCormick	$3,800
Quinn	4,600
Saldi	8,900

All withdrawals were recorded in the partners' drawing accounts. Prepare the statement of owners' equity for the year ended December 31, 1983.

P13-3 ***Partner admission and withdrawal; division of net income***

Holiday and Imke invested $20,000 and $30,000, respectively, on January 2, 1981, and formed a partnership. Holiday has been granted a $700 monthly salary allowance; any remaining profits and losses are divided equally. During 1981 total withdrawals for Holiday and Imke amounted to $8,000 and $6,000, respectively. Net income for the year was $1,800.

On January 3, 1982, Jackson was admitted to the partnership. Jackson purchased 30% of Holiday's interest for $12,200; payment was made directly to Holiday. The partnership agreement was redrawn so that Holiday would now receive a monthly salary of $500; remaining profits and losses are to be divided equally among the three partners. Withdrawals for the year follow.

Holiday	$6,000
Imke	4,500
Jackson	2,200

Net income for 1982 amounted to $15,600.

On January 3, 1983, Imke retired from the partnership. The firm purchased his interest for $25,400.

INSTRUCTIONS

a Determine Holiday's and Imke's shares of the 1981 net income.
b Calculate Holiday's and Imke's capital balances as of December 31, 1981.
c Present the proper entry to record the admittance of Jackson to the partnership.
d Determine each partner's share of the 1982 net income.
e Calculate each partner's capital balance as of December 31, 1982.
f Present the proper entry to record Imke's retirement from the partnership.
g Suppose that on January 3, 1982, Jackson was admitted to the partnership by investing $12,200 in the firm rather than purchasing Holiday's interest.
  (1) If Jackson received a 30% interest for his investment, determine if any bonus was involved and who received it.
  (2) Discuss the general situations which give rise to (a) a bonus to an entering partner and (b) a bonus to existing partners.

P13-4 ***Partnership liquidation***

Athens, Logan, and Marietta operate a dry-cleaning business as a partnership and share net income (and net losses) in a 5:3:2 ratio, respectively. Because the business was not as successful as planned, the partners decided to liquidate. A post-closing trial balance disclosed the following account balances as of December 31, 1983.

Post-Closing Trial Balance
December 31, 1983

Cash	$ 15,000	
Short-term investments	40,000	
Accounts receivable	45,000	
Allowance for bad debts		$ 7,000
Supplies	10,000	
Equipment	95,000	
Accumulated depreciation: equipment		20,000
Accounts payable		9,000
Notes payable		44,000
Athens, capital		62,000
Logan, capital		58,000
Marietta, capital		5,000
	$205,000	$205,000

The noncash assets were sold in 1984 as follows:

Jan. 2 The short-term investments were sold for $35,000.
8 Accounts receivable were sold to a finance company for $30,000.
10 Supplies were sold back to the vendor for $4,000.
12 The equipment was sold to another cleaner for $25,000.

The liabilities were paid on January 15 and cash was distributed to the partners on January 27.

INSTRUCTIONS

a Prepare journal entries to record the transactions of January 2–15.

b Determine the balance in each partner's capital account prior to any cash distributions on January 27.

c Assume that any partner with a capital deficiency is able to pay the balance due to the partnership. Prepare journal entries on January 27 to record (1) the receipt of cash from the deficient partner and (2) distribution of the firm's ending cash balance to the remaining partners.

d Assume that any partner with a capital deficiency is unable to pay the balance due to the partnership. Prepare journal entries on January 27 to (1) allocate the deficiency to the remaining partners and (2) distribute the firm's ending cash balance.

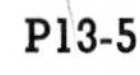

P13-5 ***Issuance of stock***

The Mark Corporation began operations on April 1 and is authorized to issue 100,000 shares of $50 par-value common stock. The following transactions took place during the first year of operation.

Apr. 1 Sold 30,000 shares to the corporation's founders at $58 per share.
3 Issued 300 shares to Mark's attorneys for $19,500 of legal work relating to corporate start-up and formation.
May 13 Issued 50,000 shares to the Atlas Company in exchange for a building (appraised at $2,000,000) and land (appraised at $1,000,000). These assets originally cost Atlas $1,800,000 and were carried at $1,150,000 on Atlas's balance sheet.
July 18 Issued 10,000 shares to Neptune Company at $64 per share.
Dec. 30 Received a subscription contract from a wealthy investor for 4,700 shares. The subscription price was $72 per share; payment will be made in the following year.

Revenues for the year amounted to $100,400. Expenses totaled $79,750 excluding the amortization of organization costs. Mark amortizes organization costs over five years.

INSTRUCTIONS

a Prepare journal entries to record the transactions through December 30.

b Prepare the stockholders' equity section of Mark's December 31 balance sheet.

c What would you have done differently on July 18 if Mark's stock was no-par value with a $50 stated value?

d Assume Mark's stock is not actively traded on a stock exchange. The investor in the transaction of December 30 agreed to pay $72 per share after lengthy negotiation with Mark's officers. What factors did both parties probably consider in arriving at the $72 price?

P13-6 ***Stock issues and subscriptions***

The Tangerine Corporation was organized on January 15. The firm's charter authorized the issuance of the following:

Preferred stock, $100 par, cumulative, 9%, 1,000 shares
Common stock, no-par, 25,000 shares

The board of directors has established a $2.50 stated value on the common stock. The following transactions occurred during the year.

Jan. 20 Sold 13,000 shares of common stock to the corporation's founders for $4.00 per share. Cash was received and the shares were issued.

30 Sold 750 shares of preferred stock to the Alliance Church for $105 per share. Cash was received and the shares were issued.

Mar. 1 Received subscription contracts from various investors to purchase 2,000 shares of common stock at $6 per share.

10 Received $8,500 from the subscribers representing full payment for 1,200 shares and partial payment on 800 shares. The appropriate number of shares were issued.

28 Received $1,000 from the subscribers in partial payment of the remaining 800 shares. No shares were issued at this time.

INSTRUCTIONS

a Prepare journal entries to record the transactions.
b Prepare Tangerine's stockholders' equity section as of March 31, assuming a Retained Earnings balance of $8,100.
c Compute the remaining amount due from subscribers.

P13-7 ***Stock subscriptions***

The Alvarez Corporation is authorized to issue 12,000 shares of no-par common stock that have a stated value of $0.50 per share. The following transactions occurred during the year.

Mar. 1 The company issued 5,200 shares to the corporation's founders for $5,200. Cash was received and the certificates were issued.

Apr. 1 The company received subscription contracts for 4,800 shares at $2.25 per share. No cash was collected at this time.

May 1 Forty percent of the amounts due under the subscription contracts were received. No shares were issued at this time.

June 1 Subscribers paid 30% of their contracts. Two thousand shares were now fully paid and the certificates were issued.

July 1 Subscribers paid the final 30% of their contracts and the appropriate certificates were issued.

INSTRUCTIONS

a Prepare journal entries to record the transactions.
b Prepare the stockholders' equity section of Alvarez's balance sheet as of June 30. Retained earnings on this date amounted to $16,800.
c Prepare the stockholders' equity section of Alvarez's balance sheet as of July 31. Retained earnings on this date amounted to $18,100.
d Determine the impact of the issuance of previously subscribed shares on (1) total common stock as reported on the balance sheet; (2) total paid-in capital; (3) total stockholders' equity.

P13-8 ***Preparation of stockholders' equity section***

Vecchio's corporate charter authorized the issuance of 40,000 shares of $10 par, 12% cumulative preferred stock and 70,000 shares of no-par common. The board of directors has assigned a $5-per-share stated value to the common stock. Through December 31 of the current year the firm has issued 25,000 of the preferred shares, generating $450,000. In addition, common shares were issued as follows:

Twenty thousand shares were sold to investors at $14 per share.

Eleven thousand shares were issued to subscribers at $16 per share. These shares were part of subscriptions for 14,000 shares; remaining subscribers have paid 70% of their balances due.

Five thousand shares were exchanged for land and buildings having a fair market value of $31,000 and $47,000, respectively.

Dividends on the preferred stock were $18,000 in arrears at the beginning of the current year. Dividend distributions in the past twelve months have amounted to $35,500.

On December 17 Vecchio's finance department learned that one of the initial investors in the corporation sold his entire holding of 3,900 shares to Harold Lundgen for $22 per share. The investor originally paid $14 per share.

INSTRUCTIONS

a Prepare Vecchio's stockholders' equity section as of December 31 of the current year along with any appropriate footnotes. The Retained Earnings balance on this date, after the appropriate dividend deductions, totals $156,200.

b What would you have done differently in part (a) if dividends distributed during the past twelve months amounted to $55,500 rather than $35,500?

P13-9 ***Analysis of stockholders' equity accounts***

The following accounts appear on the balance sheet of Hayashi, Inc.

Preferred stock, $100 par value	$230,000
Paid-in capital in excess of par value: preferred	80,500
Common stock, $5 par value	525,000
Paid-in capital in excess of par value: common	275,000
Common stock subscribed	5,000
Retained earnings	190,000
Bonds payable	400,000
Subscriptions receivable: common stock	40,000

INSTRUCTIONS

a How many shares of preferred and common stock have been issued?

b What was the average issue price of the preferred stock?

c How many shares of common stock have been subscribed but not yet issued?

d How much remains to be paid on the common stock subscriptions?

e In which account(s) would the fully paid subscribed shares be reflected? Explain.

f Compute the total amount of legal capital. *Note:* Consider common stock subscribed as part of legal capital.

g Compute the total paid-in capital.

h Compute the total stockholders' equity.

P13-10 ***Investment by partners; financial statements (alternate to P13-1)***
On July 5, 1983, Brown, Cooper, and Daugherty agreed to form a partnership to distribute office furnishings. Brown invested cash of $64,000 and a vehicle that originally cost $10,200. The vehicle's fair market value at the time of investment was $8,000. Cooper contributed the following items from her existing business.

	Recorded Value	*Fair Market Value*
Accounts receivable	$26,000	$26,000
Allowance for bad debts	(1,500)	(1,950)
Merchandise inventory	47,000	52,800
Delivery equipment (net)	13,600	15,900
Accounts payable	19,700	19,700

Finally, Daugherty contributed short-term marketable securities consisting of 600 shares of Visual Systems common stock (cost per share, $45; market value per share, $82).

INSTRUCTIONS

a Prepare journal entries to record the investments of Brown, Cooper, and Daugherty in the partnership.

b Prepare a classified balance sheet for the partnership immediately after the investments.

c Assume that net income of $49,800 was generated through the end of 1983. Cash withdrawals of $20,400 were made by Brown, $23,500 by Cooper, and $31,000 by Daugherty. If the partners divide all profits and losses equally, prepare the owners' equity section of the balance sheet as of December 31. Show all computations.

P13-11 ***Income distribution; statement of owners' equity (alternate to P13-2)***
Tanner, Umana, and Vasquez are partners in a bookkeeping service. The partners' beginning and average capital balances for 1983 follow.

	Beginning	*Average*
Tanner	$30,000	$40,000
Umana	50,000	50,000
Vasquez	70,000	80,000

Investments during the year amounted to $20,000 for Tanner and $20,000 for Vasquez. Net income totaled $27,000.

INSTRUCTIONS

a Prepare a schedule to show the distribution of net income among the partners for each of the following independent cases:
   (1) The partners are granted a 12% interest allowance on beginning capital and share any remaining income equally.
   (2) Tanner, Umana, and Vasquez are granted a 15% interest allowance on average capital and respectively share any remaining income on a 3:3:4 basis.
   (3) Each partner is granted a 10% interest allowance on average capital

and a monthly salary allowance of $700. Tanner, Umana, and Vasquez respectively share remaining profits or losses on a 4:1:5 basis.

b Focusing on case (1) of part (a), assume that the interest allowances were withdrawn during the year along with other withdrawals as follows:

Tanner	$2,900
Umana	4,100
Vasquez	5,700

All withdrawals were recorded in the partners' drawing accounts. Prepare the statement of owners' equity for the year ended December 31, 1983.

P13-12 ***Partnership liquidation (alternate to P13-4)***

Myers, Stevens, and Woods operate a repair business as a partnership and share net income (and net losses) in a 3:4:3 ratio, respectively. Because the business was not as successful as planned, the partners decided to liquidate. A post-closing trial balance disclosed the following account balances as of December 31, 1983.

Post-Closing Trial Balance
December 31, 1983

Cash	$ 16,000	
Short-term investments	9,600	
Accounts receivable	19,400	
Allowance for bad debts		$ 2,500
Supplies	5,100	
Equipment	56,300	
Accumulated depreciation: equipment		7,500
Accounts payable		10,800
Notes payable		22,600
Myers, capital		33,100
Stevens, capital		23,300
Woods, capital		6,600
	$106,400	$106,400

The noncash assets were sold in 1984 as follows:

Jan. 3 The short-term investments were sold for $12,600.
6 Accounts receivable were sold to a finance company for $12,000.
9 Supplies were sold back to the vendor for $2,600.
14 The equipment was sold to another repair shop for $25,600.

The liabilities were paid on January 17, and cash was distributed to the partners on January 24.

INSTRUCTIONS

a Prepare journal entries to record the transactions of January 3–17.

b Determine the balance in each partner's capital account prior to any cash distributions on January 24.

c Assume that any partner with a capital deficiency is able to pay the balance due to the partnership. Prepare journal entries on January 24 to record (1) the receipt of cash from the deficient partner and (2) distribution of the firm's ending cash balance to the remaining partners.

d Assume that any partner with a capital deficiency is unable to pay the balance due to the partnership. Prepare journal entries on January 24 to (1) allocate the deficiency to the remaining partners and (2) distribute the firm's ending cash balance.

P13-13 ***Issuance of stock (alternate to P13-5)***

The Craig Corporation began operations on October 1 and is authorized to issue 11,000 shares of $1 par-value common stock. The following transactions took place during the first year of operation.

Oct. *1* Sold 6,000 shares to the corporation's founders for $2.50 per share.

3 Issued 900 shares to the company's attorney for $2,700 of legal work relating to corporate start-up and formation.

Nov. 13 Issued 2,000 shares to Rosebud Company in exchange for a delivery truck presently valued at $8,000. The truck originally cost Rosebud $20,000 and was carried at $14,000 on Rosebud's balance sheet.

21 Issued 1,000 shares to the general public at $5 per share.

Dec. 30 Received a subscription contract from a prominent politician for the remaining shares. The subscription price was $8 per share; payment will be made in the following year.

Revenues for the year amounted to $40,000. Expenses totaled $35,000 excluding the amortization of organization costs. Craig amortizes organization costs over five years.

INSTRUCTIONS

a Prepare journal entries to record the transactions through December 30.

b Prepare the stockholders' equity section of Craig's December 31 balance sheet.

c Craig's president feels that organization costs should be expensed immediately. Do you agree with the president or disagree? Explain the reasoning behind your answer.

d Assume that an important vote will be taken at the upcoming annual meeting of stockholders. Who will control the outcome if they vote together?

P13-14 ***Analysis of stockholders' equity accounts (alternate to P13-9)***

The following accounts appear on the balance sheet of the Amity Corporation.

Preferred stock, $10 par value	$ 85,000
Paid-in capital in excess of par value: preferred	51,000
Common stock, $100 par value	160,000
Paid-in capital in excess of par value: common	240,000
Common stock subscribed	8,000
Retained earnings	419,000
Bonds payable	130,000
Subscriptions receivable: common stock	59,000

INSTRUCTIONS

a How many shares of preferred and common stock have been issued?

b What was the average issue price of the preferred stock?

c How many shares of common stock have been subscribed but not yet issued?

d How much remains to be paid on the common stock subscriptions?

e In which account(s) would the fully paid subscribed shares be reflected? Explain.

f Compute the total amount of legal capital. *Note:* Consider common stock subscribed as part of legal capital.

g Compute the total paid-in capital.

h Compute the total stockholders' equity.

CASE 13
SKI-MATIC

Jim Seagram is the manager of a local sporting goods store. Recently, during some spare time, he invented a device called Ski-Matic, which allows users to improve their skiing skills and balance. Jim has approached Professor Pujak at the local university's school of business to assist him in developing a budget for mass production of the device. Pujak believes that $400,000 in capital will be needed to establish manufacturing facilities, commence production, and effectively advertise the product. Pujak is excited about the project and is willing to invest $10,000 for a share of the company. Because Seagram can only invest $20,000, considerable outside funding is necessary.

There are three options open to Jim to finance his venture. First, he can establish a partnership and solicit investments. Second, he could incorporate and try to sell common stock to the public. Finally, he could incorporate and (1) sell 12% preferred stock to outside investors and (2) issue common stock to both himself and Pujak.

INSTRUCTIONS

a Discuss several advantages and disadvantages of each of the three financing alternatives. Disregard income tax considerations.

b Which alternative would appear to have the best chance of success in raising capital? Explain your answer.

c Assuming that Ski-Matic was a tremendous success, which alternative would most likely be in the best interests of Seagram? Explain your answer.

14 CORPORATIONS: ADDITIONAL EQUITY ISSUES AND INCOME REPORTING

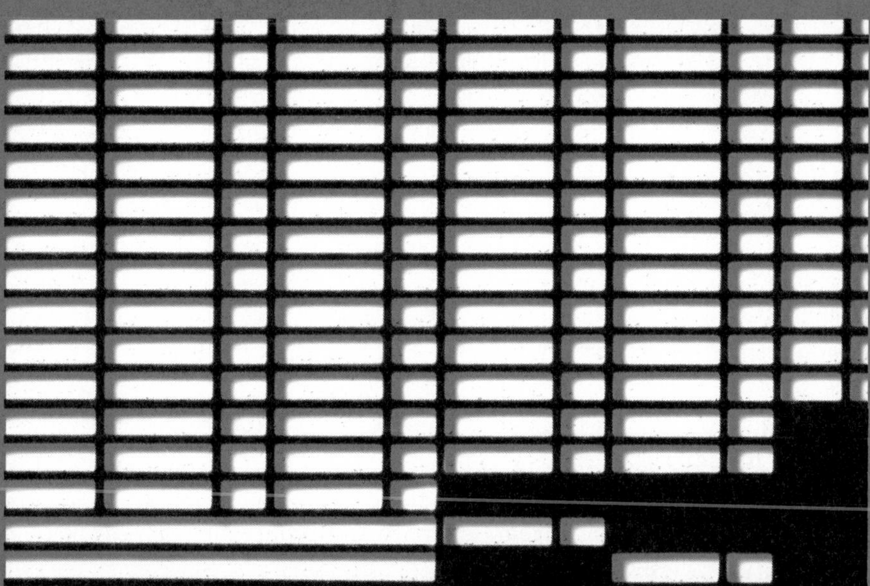

LEARNING OBJECTIVES

After reading this chapter you should:

1 Understand what treasury stock is and how to account for its acquisition and reissuance.

2 Be able to account for donated capital.

3 Be familiar with corporate income reporting, including the proper treatment of discontinued operations, extraordinary items, and intraperiod tax allocation.

4 Have a basic knowledge of earnings per share.

5 Understand the distinctions among cash dividends, property dividends, stock dividends, and stock splits, and be able to account for each of these items.

6 Be familiar with prior period adjustments, appropriations of retained earnings, and the construction of a statement of retained earnings.

7 Understand book value per share, including both computation and meaning.

CHAPTER 14

In the preceding chapter we presented an introduction to the corporate form of business organization. The discussion included the advantages and disadvantages of corporations along with the proper accounting treatment for preferred and common stock issuances. This chapter continues our presentation of corporate equity. Specifically, we will discuss (1) the reacquisition of stock by corporations, (2) retained earnings, (3) corporate reporting of income and earnings per share, (4) dividends and stock splits, and (5) the determination of book value per share.

Before progressing, we offer two pieces of advice. First, read this material slowly and with great care. Although our discussion will focus on the basics only, several of the topics presented are highly technical and detailed. To avoid difficulties in comprehension, you must study the material intensively. Second, much of this material relates to practical problems faced by investors. Newspapers consistently publish articles with headlines similar to the following:

General United's Earnings per Share Falls 15%
Largent Corporation Has 3-for-2 Stock Split
Garrett, Inc., Declares 10% Stock Dividend

The investing public must have a fundamental understanding of these events to correctly determine the impact on both corporate financial affairs and, more importantly, investment holdings. While your present financial position may not (and probably does not) permit "wheeling and dealing" in the stock market, the future often brings change. Our goal is to provide you with an introduction to the topics noted in the first paragraph so that some analysis of corporate equity and profitability is possible.

TREASURY STOCK

Corporations frequently find it advantageous to reacquire shares of their own stock. These shares, which are commonly reissued at a later date, are termed **treasury stock.** Treasury stock is purchased for a variety of reasons. Some corporations have reacquired their own shares for use in company retirement and employee stock purchase programs. Other firms have purchased treasury stock to rid themselves of a particular stockholder or group of stockholders. For example, large corporations sometimes purchase the interests of very small investors (i.e., those owning ten shares or less) to save the costs of mailing annual reports, processing minute dividend checks, and so forth. Treasury stock is also acquired for use in future acquisitions of other companies and for investment purposes. Corporations purchasing treasury shares for this latter reason do so when the market price is depressed, hoping to achieve an attractive return on their invested funds. Finally, some firms have secured treasury holdings in an attempt to boost earnings per share.

Whatever the purpose, the acquisition of treasury stock is commonplace. A review of recent annual reports disclosed the treasury stock holdings appearing in Exhibit 14-1.

Exhibit 14-1

Treasury stock holdings

Corporation	Number of Treasury Shares	Percentage of Total Shares Issued	Acquisition Cost of Treasury Shares
AMF	925,698*	3.9%	$27,686,000
Emery Air Freight	216,494	1.4	4,168,000
Jonathan Logan	809,950	14.8	10,862,000
Kimberly-Clark	1,833,160	7.7	96,800,000
Stanley Works	541,088	2.0	5,349,000
Tandy (principally known for Radio Shack)	2,723,000	2.6	17,325,000

*Common and preferred stock combined. All other citations refer to common stock only.

Corporate action to purchase treasury stock reduces the number of shares outstanding; however, the number of shares issued is unaffected. Issued shares can only be reduced if they are formally retired and canceled by the corporation. Because treasury stock is no longer outstanding, it is not entitled to voting privileges or any cash dividends declared by the board of directors.

Acquisitions of Treasury Stock

The most common treatment for treasury stock records acquisitions at cost by debiting a Treasury Stock account. Thus if Hunt Corporation purchased 5,000 shares of its $10 par-value common stock at $70 per share, the journal entry would be as follows:

Treasury Stock	350,000	
Cash		350,000
To record the purchase of 5,000 shares of treasury stock at $70 per share		

Treasury stock is *not* regarded as an asset, even if the shares are purchased for investment purposes. In plain and simple terms, a corporation cannot own part of itself. The acquisition of treasury stock really involves a reduction in stockholders' equity, because funds are being returned to the selling stockholders. To illustrate, assume Hunt had authorization to issue 15,000 shares of $10 par-value common stock. Further, assume that all the shares have been issued at $90 per share and that retained earnings amount to $440,000. After the acquisition of the 5,000 treasury shares, the firm's stockholders' equity section would appear as follows:

STOCKHOLDERS' EQUITY

Common stock, $10 par value, 15,000 shares authorized and issued, 10,000 shares outstanding	$ 150,000
Paid-in capital in excess of par value	1,200,000
Total paid-in capital	$1,350,000
Retained earnings	440,000
	$1,790,000
Deduct: Treasury stock (5,000 shares) at cost	350,000
Total stockholders' equity	$1,440,000

Observe that the Common Stock and Paid-in Capital in Excess of Par Value accounts are not reduced by the treasury stock purchase. However, the cost of the 5,000 shares is deducted later in the stockholders' equity section. Finally, note that the number of shares issued and the number outstanding now differ because of the shares held "in the treasury."

Reissuance of Treasury Stock

At the time of reissuance the Treasury Stock account is credited for the acquisition cost of the reissued shares. If the reissue price exceeds the acquisition cost, the difference is recorded as additional paid-in capital. For example, assume Hunt now sells 1,000 of the treasury shares for $79 per share. The necessary journal entry follows.

Cash	*79,000*	
Treasury Stock		*70,000*
Paid-in Capital from Treasury Stock		*9,000*
To record sale of 1,000 shares of treasury stock at $79 per share		

The $70,000 credit to the Treasury Stock account is based on the $70-per-share acquisition cost. Importantly, the $9,000 excess over cost is not a gain to be reported on the income statement. Why? Gains and losses arise from the sale of goods and services, that is, earnings activities. Transactions involving the issuance (or reissuance) of capital stock, however, affect paid-in capital. In Hunt's case investors were willing to pay $79,000 for shares having an original acquisition cost of $70,000; thus paid-in capital must increase by $9,000. The increase is recorded in a separate account entitled Paid-in Capital from Treasury Stock.

The stockholders' equity section immediately after the reissuance follows.

STOCKHOLDERS' EQUITY

Capital stock		
Common stock, $10 par value, 15,000 shares authorized and issued, 11,000 shares outstanding		*$ 150,000*
Additional paid-in capital		
Paid-in capital in excess of par value	*$1,200,000*	
Paid-in capital from treasury stock	*9,000*	*1,209,000*
Total paid-in capital		*$1,359,000*
Retained earnings		*440,000*
		$1,799,000
Deduct: Treasury stock (4,000 shares) at cost		*280,000*
Total stockholders' equity		*$1,519,000*

Total stockholders' equity has increased by $79,000 ($1,519,000 vs. $1,440,000), reflecting the amount of funds generated (invested) from the treasury stock sale.

Reissuance below cost

Treasury shares can also be reissued at or below cost. We will now illustrate the latter case because of the complexities involved. Just as reissuance above cost gave rise to additional paid-in capital, reissuance below cost necessitates a reduction of paid-in capital. For example, assume Hunt sells an additional 2,000 treasury shares. This time, however, the selling price is only $66 per share. The journal entry to record the sale follows.

Cash	*132,000*	
Paid-in Capital from Treasury Stock	*8,000*	
Treasury Stock		*140,000*
To record sale of 2,000 shares of treasury stock at $66 per share		

As before, the Treasury Stock account is credited for the cost of the reissued shares, in this case $140,000 (2,000 shares × $70). Because the sale has generated only $132,000, paid-in capital must be reduced by $8,000 ($140,000 − $132,000). In effect, the reduction is a cancellation of paid-in capital from earlier treasury stock sales, thereby requiring a debit to the Paid-in Capital from Treasury Stock account for $8,000. If the account's balance is insufficient to absorb the entire (or any of the) reduction, the remaining debit is entered in the Retained Earnings account. To illustrate, if the 2,000 shares were sold for $128,000, paid-in capital must be reduced by $12,000 ($140,000 − $128,000). As shown in the stockholders' equity section on page 528, the Paid-in Capital from Treasury Stock account has a balance of only $9,000. Thus the required journal entry would debit this account for $9,000 and charge the remaining $3,000 against Retained Earnings.

Donated Capital

Occasionally, a stockholder may donate shares to a corporation for subsequent resale to others. Donation usually occurs in a small firm that is attempting to finance a new project or program and is having difficulty attracting outside capital. The shares, often contributed by the project's developers, are more easily marketed than unissued shares. The reason is that donated stock can be sold at any price, even below par or stated value, with no worry of creating a contingent liability. Recall from Chapter 13 that some states prohibit new stock issuances at a discount to avoid this very problem.

Donated shares are considered treasury stock because of the high likelihood of reissuance. With the cost basis of accounting, no formal journal entry is needed at the time of donation since no cost is involved. The donation is noted by placing a memorandum in the journal, for example, "June 4—Received 1,000 shares of donated common stock." If the shares are subsequently sold for, say, $81 per share, the journal entry would be as follows:

Cash	*81,000*	
Donated Capital		*81,000*
To record the sale of 1,000 shares of donated common stock at $81 per share		

The Donated Capital account is listed among the additional paid-in capital accounts (e.g., Paid-in Capital in Excess of Par Value, Paid-in Capital from Treasury Stock, and so on) in the stockholders' equity section of the balance sheet.

RETAINED EARNINGS

We now turn our attention to the last major element of stockholders' equity: retained earnings. **Retained earnings** represents the portion of owners' equity that has been generated by profitable operations. Notice the use of the term "retained." Corporations often distribute part of their earnings as dividends. As a result, the balance in the Retained Earnings account is increased by periodic earnings and reduced by the declaration of dividends.

Net income is entered in the Retained Earnings account during the closing process by debiting Income Summary and crediting Retained Earnings; dividend entries will be illustrated shortly. Like most of the owners' equity accounts, Retained Earnings normally possesses a credit balance. On occasion, though, a debit (negative) balance can arise, which is commonly referred to as a **deficit.** Deficits are usually caused by firms operating at a loss for a number of years or having a sizable loss in one period that wipes out years of profitability.

In addition to net income, net losses, and dividends, other items affect Retained Earnings, for example, prior period adjustments and appropriations. We will consider all these items; our emphasis, however, will be on corporate income and dividends because of their importance in determining total stockholders' equity.

Corporate Income Reporting

Investors are vitally interested in the periodic net income earned by corporations. Net income provides the basis for dividend distributions and in many cases influences the market price of the corporation's common stock. Because of these factors, the income statement must provide adequate disclosure of earnings activities and be constructed in a format that is useful and informative to investors and other users.

To achieve these goals, the accounting profession has stipulated the segregation of ordinary business income from income caused by unusual or infrequent transactions and events. Why? Imagine the difficulty in evaluating corporate earnings if significant losses from major catastrophies and other nonrecurring events were buried in operating expenses without separate disclosure. The resultant low earnings could be interpreted as being typical, even though they were caused by onetime and unusual happenings.

In an effort to present a clear picture of corporate earnings, current accounting practice dictates separate disclosure for the results of continuing operations, discontinued operations, extraordinary items, and the financial effects of changes in accounting principles. An example of the latter is a switch from accelerated to straight-line depreciation. Because accounting changes are complex and covered in advanced accounting courses, they will not be discussed in this text.

Discontinued operations

Many corporations are involved in diverse types of business activities. Consider, for example, the Colgate-Palmolive Company, which is known for such household and personal care products as Colgate and Ultra Brite toothpastes, Ajax cleanser, Palmolive dishwashing liquid, and Curity bandages. The firm is also engaged in the manufacture and sale of rice products, candy, pet food, health care equipment, cotton and rayon, hostess and decorator accessories, clothing, shoes, and hobby products. Colgate-Palmolive, like many other corporations, conducts activities in several distinct business segments. A **segment** is defined as a "component of a company whose activities represent a major line of business or class of customer.[1] Normally, the assets and operating results of a given segment are clearly distinguishable from the other assets and operations of the firm.

Often after an in-depth review of corporate activity and profitability, a business will decide to dispose of one or more of its segments. A disposal usually results from inadequate earnings or disappointing expectations about the segment's future. Sometimes, however, a segment is sold not because of weak financial performance but because the firm desires to concentrate in other activities.

When a segment is sold, abandoned, or otherwise disposed of, the segment's operations are said to be **discontinued.** The results of discontinued operations are disclosed in a separate category on the income statement immediately after income from continuing operations. Specifically, the operating results of the disposed segment along with any gain or loss on the disposal must be shown net-of-tax.[2]

To illustrate the proper accounting treatment, we return to the Colgate-Palmolive Company. In December 1979 management approved plans to discontinue activities in certain business lines (including Helena Rubinstein, Inc.) and accrued estimated operating and investment losses. Additional losses were recorded in 1980 pertaining to these divestments and the plan to dispose of a condominium complex of a property development subsidiary. The firm's income statements for 1979–1981 are presented in Exhibit 14-2.

As you can see by analyzing the data, the disposed properties significantly depressed Colgate-Palmolive's earnings, especially in 1979. The bulk of the losses were not from operations but instead from losses on the sale or abandonment of company assets. It should now be apparent that separate disclosure of discontinued operations in this manner helps financial statement users better assess and predict the future of a business's continuing activities.

Extraordinary items

Income statements strive to disclose earnings from both continuing operations and normal business activities. Occasionally, sizable gains and losses arise from events that are clearly different from the ordinary and usual affairs of a firm. Such events, known as **extraordinary items,** are afforded special accounting treatment.

To achieve uniformity in reporting, the accounting profession has stipulated that extraordinary items must be *unusual in nature* and *occur infre-*

---

[1] "Reporting the Results of Operations," *Opinions of the Accounting Principles Board No. 30* (New York: American Institute of Certified Public Accountants, 1973), paragraph 13.

[2] Net-of-tax reporting will be discussed shortly.

Exhibit 14-2

Colgate-Palmolive Company consolidated statement of income, 1979–1981 (thousands of dollars except per-share figures)

	1981	1980	1979
Net sales	$5,261,364	$5,130,464	$4,494,464
Cost of sales	3,345,448	3,328,959	2,897,140
Gross profit	$1,915,916	$1,801,505	$1,597,324
Operating and other expenses			
Marketing	$1,077,802	$1,023,639	$ 915,502
General and administrative	419,317	371,871	332,262
Interest expense	70,867	69,165	53,832
Interest income	(46,976)	(26,998)	(19,171)
Total operating and other expenses	$1,521,010	$1,437,677	$1,282,425
Income from continuing operations before income taxes	$ 394,906	$ 363,828	$ 314,899
Provision for income taxes			
United States	$ 60,053	$ 47,101	$ 37,154
Foreign	126,454	122,110	92,780
Total	$ 186,507	$ 169,211	$ 129,934
Income from continuing operations	$ 208,399	$ 194,617	$ 184,965
Discontinued operations			
Loss from operations (net of income tax benefits of $2,682 in 1980 and $14,815 in 1979)	—	(3,149)	(25,933)
Loss on disposal (net of income tax benefits of $7,488 in 1980 and $10,480 in 1979)	—	(19,878)	(46,947)
Net income	$ 208,399	$ 171,590	$ 112,085
Net income (loss) per common share from			
Continuing operations	$2.55	$2.38	$2.26
Discontinued operations	—	(0.04)	(0.31)
Disposal of discontinued operations	—	(0.24)	(0.58)
Total	$2.55	$2.10	$1.37

quently.[3] Importantly, note that *both* criteria must be satisfied. A transaction or event is considered unusual if it has a high degree of abnormality and is unrelated to the ordinary and typical activities of the entity. To judge whether the first criterion is met, one must consider a firm's scope of operation, lines of business, operating policies, and environment. The environment includes such factors as industry characteristics, geographical location of facilities and activities, and the extent of governmental regulation. Turning to the second criterion, an event or transaction of a type not reasonably

[3] "Reporting the Results of Operations," *Opinions of the Accounting Principles Board No. 30* (New York: American Institute of Certified Public Accountants, 1973), paragraph 20.

expected to recur in the foreseeable future is considered to occur infrequently. Past experience and the environment in which a business operates are primary considerations.

Applying the guidelines

Events that meet the two criteria are rare. Examples *may* include major casualties such as earthquakes, floods, and hurricanes; a seizure of assets by a foreign government; and the financial effects caused by a prohibition under a newly enacted law or regulation. As we explained in Chapter 6, it is difficult to generalize whether a particular happening is always extraordinary. Consider a flood loss, for instance. Suppose a business is located in a low-lying area prone to flooding once every four or five years. If a heavy rainstorm and its flood waters cause considerable damage to the firm's inventory, the loss is not considered extraordinary because it fails the infrequency-of-occurrence criterion. That is, on the basis of past history, another flood will probably occur in the foreseeable future. Changing the example slightly, suppose the flood loss is caused by a dam that breaks in a nearby valley. The break is highly unusual and, once repaired, not likely to happen again. Because both tests are met, this flood loss is labeled extraordinary.

An interesting example of an extraordinary item surfaced several years ago. Most readers would probably agree that lawsuits are fairly common in our society and fail both the unusual and infrequent guidelines. Yet a review of corporate annual reports uncovered the following footnote by the Alberto-Culver Company, which is noted for Alberto VO5 hair care products, among others.

> *. . . The company received $4,250,000 in an out-of-court settlement of litigation against The Gillette Company and its former advertising agency, J. Walter Thompson Company. The proceeds, net of related expenses and $919,000 of income taxes, resulted in an extraordinary gain of $2,128,576 or 51 cents per share. The company had sued the defendants for severely damaging the Alberto Balsam trademark and brand name and impairing the reputation and goodwill of the company by the use of misleading and disparaging television commercials and antitrust violations.*

This example and its predecessor reiterate the point that we cannot generalize about extraordinary items. Each case must be evaluated on its own merits.

The following items are not considered extraordinary by the accounting profession.[4]

1 Write-down or write-off of receivables, inventories, and intangible assets.
2 Gains and losses from the sale or abandonment of property, plant, and equipment used in a business.

[4] Ibid., paragraph 23.

3 Effects of a strike, including those against competitors and major suppliers.

Such items, if material, are normally presented among nonoperating (other) revenues and expenses.

Disclosure of extraordinary items

Extraordinary items are disclosed in a separate section of the income statement immediately following discontinued operations. If a firm has no discontinued operations, extraordinary items are presented after earnings from continuing activities. Again, a net-of-tax amount must be shown. The following section lends further insight into the proper disclosure procedure.

Intraperiod tax allocation

Examine the income statement of the Antero Corporation, which is presented in Exhibit 14-3. Observe how the statement clearly distinguishes between income and losses from continuing operations, discontinued operations, and extraordinary items. In addition, notice the treatment of Antero's

Exhibit 14-3

ANTERO CORPORATION
Income Statement
For the Year Ended December 31, 1983

Sales		$2,000,000
Cost of goods sold		1,200,000
Gross profit		$ 800,000
Operating expenses		
Selling	$280,000	
Administrative	170,000	450,000
Income from operations		$ 350,000
Other income (expense)		
Loss on sale of machinery		50,000
Income from continuing operations before tax		$ 300,000
Income tax on continuing operations		120,000
Income from continuing operations		$ 180,000
Discontinued operations		
Earnings from Sunrise Division operations less applicable taxes ($110,000 − $44,000)	$ 66,000	
Loss on disposal of Sunrise facilities less tax savings ($250,000 − $100,000)	(150,000)	(84,000)
Income before extraordinary item		$ 96,000
Extraordinary item		
Flood loss less tax savings ($60,000 − $24,000)		36,000
Net income		$ 60,000

tax expense as it relates to these elements. The practice of relating income tax to the items that gave rise to the tax is referred to as **intraperiod tax allocation.** Intraperiod tax allocation recognizes that various factors contribute to a corporation's tax bill. In an effort to provide added disclosure within the financial statements, a firm's tax expense is divided among the following contributing (or tax-saving) elements: continuing operations, discontinued operations, extraordinary items, changes in accounting principle, and prior period adjustments (to be discussed later in the chapter).

To explain, suppose Antero is subject to a 40% income tax rate. Items that raise net income result in a 40% tax expense; items that reduce net income generate a 40% tax savings. From the information presented in Exhibit 14-3, Antero's net tax expense totals $40,000.

Tax on continuing operations	*$120,000*
Tax on Sunrise Division operations	*44,000*
Tax savings on disposal of Sunrise facilities	*(100,000)*
Tax savings on flood loss	*(24,000)*
Net tax expense	*$ 40,000*

Without intraperiod tax allocation the income statement would appear as follows:

Income from continuing operations before tax	*$300,000*	
Income tax	*40,000*	*$260,000*
Discontinued operations		
Earnings from Sunrise Division operations	*$110,000*	
Loss on disposal of Sunrise facilities	*250,000*	*(140,000)*
Income before extraordinary item		*$120,000*
Extraordinary item		
Flood loss		*(60,000)*
Net income		*$ 60,000*

Although the bottom line is the same as that shown in Exhibit 14-3, an uninformed statement user could erroneously interpret Antero's tax rate on continuing operations as being only 13.33% ($40,000 ÷ $300,000). From the data presented, however, we know the firm's actual tax rate is 40%. Furthermore, as the net expense computations reveal, Antero actually experienced substantial *onetime* tax savings from the loss on disposal of Sunrise facilities and the flood loss. Most accountants will agree that intraperiod tax allocation results in a more meaningful presentation of financial results, which is less apt to mislead statement users.

Earnings per share

The income statement provides considerable insight into the profitability of corporate activities. Rather than take the time to study all the statement's intricacies, investors frequently rely on a single computation called **earnings per share (EPS)** of common stock. As we noted in Chapter 6, earnings per share is similar to the won-loss percentage of a sports club at the end of the season. That is, EPS represents a summarization of all items affecting profitability. Earnings-per-share data is widely disseminated in the financial press and, because of its importance, must be disclosed on the face of the income statement. No other ratio is afforded such prominance.

Earnings per share is frequently analyzed to assess future prospects for corporate income and dividends. If current earnings are favorable and the financial outlook is bright, investors are usually willing to pay a higher price to acquire shares of the corporation's common stock. Generally stated, a higher EPS will result in a higher market price, and vice versa.[5] To study the relationship between market price and earnings per share, analysts often utilize a popular measure called the **price-earnings (P/E) ratio.** The ratio is computed by dividing the market price of a share of common stock by the annual earnings per share. P/E ratios can vary considerably. For example, at the time this text is being written, the price-earnings ratios of Bethlehem Steel and Polaroid Corporation are 10 and 27, respectively. By showing a willingness to pay more for each dollar of reported earnings, investors must feel that the financial future of Polaroid will be more prosperous than that of the mammoth steel producer.

Because of the widespread use of earnings per share, numerous computational and disclosure rules have been established to achieve reporting uniformity throughout the financial community.[6] Our discussion will concentrate on the basics only since the specific rules are technical and complex. Like several other topics presented in this chapter, earnings per share is typically covered in depth in an advanced accounting course.

Calculating earnings per share of common stock involves two steps: (1) determining the weighted-average number of shares outstanding and (2) computing the earnings available to common stockholders.

Weighted-average shares outstanding

The computation of earnings per share begins with an assessment of the number of common shares outstanding. In some firms the number of common shares remains constant during the accounting period. For many corporations, however, outstanding shares will change because of new stock issues, the purchase of treasury stock, and other similar transactions. In these situations earnings per share is based on a weighted average. The weighted average is calculated by multiplying the number of common shares outstanding by the fraction of the year the shares are in the hands of stockholders.

To illustrate, assume that Briarwood Manufacturing had 60,000 common shares outstanding at the beginning of the year. On September 1 an additional 15,000 shares were issued. The weighted-average number of shares would be computed as follows:

[5]As we noted in Chapter 13, earnings is only one of several factors affecting the market price of common stock.

[6]See "Earnings Per Share," *Opinions of the Accounting Principles Board No. 15* (New York: American Institute of Certified Public Accountants, 1969).

Outstanding Shares		Fraction of Year Outstanding		Weighted Average
60,000	×	$\frac{8}{12}$	=	40,000
75,000	×	$\frac{4}{12}$	=	25,000
				65,000

The weighted average represents the number of equivalent shares that have been outstanding for the entire year. That is, the initial 60,000 shares were outstanding for 12 months. In contrast, the 15,000-share issuance has been outstanding for only 4 months, which is equivalent to 5,000 shares for the entire year ($15{,}000 \times \frac{4}{12} = 5{,}000$). Thus Briarwood's weighted-average total is 65,000 (60,000 + 5,000). The weighting procedure is necessary because the capital provided by the new stock has helped to generate earnings for only a fraction of the accounting period.

Earnings available to common stockholders

Keep in mind that our goal is to derive the earnings per share *of common stock.* For corporations that have only common shares outstanding, all reported earnings belong to the common stockholders. If some preferred stock is outstanding, however, a different procedure is followed. Preferred stock is a *senior security,* so called because of its preferential treatment in dividend distributions and corporate liquidations. As a result, dividend claims of preferred stockholders must be deducted from net income to arrive at the earnings attributable to common shares.

For example, assume that Briarwood issued 5,000 shares of $100 par-value, 10% preferred stock in addition to the common shares described earlier. If net income for the year amounted to $180,000, the earnings available to common stockholders would total $130,000.

Net income	$180,000
Less: Dividends on preferred stock (5,000 shares × $100 × 0.10)	50,000
Earnings available to common stockholders	$130,000

Earnings per share of common stock can now be computed as follows:

$$\text{earnings per share} = \frac{\text{earnings available to common stockholders}}{\text{weighted-average common shares outstanding}}$$

$$EPS = \frac{\$130{,}000}{65{,}000}$$

$$EPS = \$2.00$$

Primary versus fully diluted earnings per share

As we noted in the previous chapter, many preferred stocks are convertible into common shares. If these or other types of convertible securities are ultimately exchanged for common stock, the number of common shares will increase and earnings per share will be reduced (i.e., *diluted*). To inform common stockholders of the potential dilution, firms must disclose additional EPS information. Specifically, corporations with potentially dilutive securities must report both **primary earnings per share** and **fully diluted earnings per share.**

Primary earnings per share is calculated by ignoring the dilutive effect of convertible securities.[7] Fully diluted EPS, on the other hand, is based on the *assumption* that all dilutive securities were converted into common shares at the beginning of the accounting period. If the securities were issued during the current period, we assume conversion as of the date of issuance. Notice that the conversion is merely an assumption. Again the intention is to show how earnings per share would be affected if common stock was issued to satisfy all existing dilutive commitments.

To illustrate the required computations and disclosure, we will continue the Briarwood Manufacturing example with one modification. Assume that each of the firm's preferred shares is convertible into seven common shares at the option of the preferred stockholder. If we assume conversion at the beginning of the period, then the following conditions hold.

No dividends would be paid on the preferred stock.
An additional 35,000 shares of common stock (5,000 preferred shares × 7) would be outstanding.

Briarwood's required earnings-per-share calculations are as follows:

	*Primary**	*Fully Diluted*
Net income	$180,000	$180,000
Less: Dividends on convertible preferred stock (5,000 shares × $100 × 0.10)	50,000	—
Earnings available to common stockholders	$130,000 ÷	$180,000 ÷
Weighted-average common shares outstanding		
For primary earnings per share	65,000	
For fully diluted earnings per share (65,000 shares + 35,000 shares from assumed conversion)		100,000
Earnings per share	$2.00	$1.80

* *This is the same computation that appeared on page 537.*

EPS disclosure

The reporting of earnings per share must be consistent with the information shown on the income statement. Thus if a corporation has discontinued operations or extraordinary items, per-share data for these elements become required disclosures. The proper earnings-per-share presentation for

[7] If convertible securities (and others) meet certain tests, the securities are considered as being equivalent to common stock and enter into primary-earnings-per-share calculations. These tests are beyond the scope of this text and will be ignored.

Exhibit 14-4

EPS disclosure for Midway Corporation

	1983	1982
Income from continuing operations (net-of-tax)	$100,000	$80,000
Income from discontinued operations (net-of-tax)	50,000	(20,000)
Income before extraordinary item	$150,000	$60,000
Extraordinary item (net-of-tax)	(10,000)	–
Net income	$140,000	$60,000
Earnings per share		
Primary		
Income from continuing operations	$1.00	$0.80
Income from discontinued operations	0.50	(0.20)
Extraordinary item	(0.10)	–
Net income	$1.40	$0.60
Fully diluted		
Income from continuing operations	$0.50	$0.40
Income from discontinued operations	0.25	(0.10)
Extraordinary item	(0.05)	–
Net income	$0.70	$0.30

Note: *Primary and fully diluted per-share computations are based on 100,000 and 200,000 common shares, respectively.*

Midway Corporation, which has potentially dilutive securities, is shown in Exhibit 14-4.

Disclosure in this fashion assists in the performance of comparative analysis. Dealing with primary earnings per share as an example, newspapers and other financial periodicals frequently publish net EPS figures only. In the case of Midway Corporation a headline might reveal that earnings more than doubled (from $0.60 to $1.40). While this statement is true, a substantial portion of the increase was caused by discontinued operations. Thus if an analyst is concerned with profitability from normal recurring activities, the headline would be misleading. A quick review of the data reveals that EPS from continuing operations rose only $0.20 ($1.00 vs. $0.80), or 25%. By requiring earnings-per-share disclosures to correspond with the major income statement sections, a clearer picture of financial performance is presented.

Dividends

Another factor affecting retained earnings is dividends. **Dividends** represent a distribution by a corporation to its stockholders. Dividends are not expenses; rather they are similar to the owner withdrawals of a proprietorship and partnership. Distributions may be in the form of cash, property, or additional shares of stock.

Many corporations attempt to attract investors by establishing a consistent dividend policy, which is either made public or is apparent to the public. American Telephone and Telegraph (AT&T), for example, increases dividends per share as earnings rise. As the following figures show, the firm's **payout ratio** (dividends per share ÷ earnings per share) has averaged approximately 62% in recent years.

Year	Dividends per Share	Earnings per Share	Payout Ratio
1974	$3.24	$5.27	61.5%
1975	3.40	5.13	66.3
1976	3.80	6.05	62.8
1977	4.20	6.97	60.3
1978	4.60	7.74	59.4
1979	5.00	8.04	62.2
1980	5.00	8.17	61.2
1981	5.40	8.55	63.2

Not all corporations are as generous as AT&T; numerous businesses distribute no dividends or severely restrict dividends. Many of these firms are referred to as *growth companies* because they are continually reinvesting profits in expansionary projects to achieve even greater income levels. Investors in growth companies expect to realize a return on investment by selling their shares at a substantial gain.

Occasionally, in addition to a corporation's regular dividend, a special (extra) dividend is distributed. The special dividend usually results from a corporation having an especially profitable year; its labeling as "special" implies no commitment to an increased payout in the future.

Dividend dates

There are three important dates connected with dividend distributions.

1 *Date of declaration.* All dividends must be declared (approved) by the board of directors. The declaration date is the date when the dividend is formally approved and the corporation becomes legally liable for payment.

2 *Date of record.* The stockholders of a corporation constantly change. To determine who will receive the dividend, the corporation establishes a record date. All stockholders as of the date of record are entitled to the declared dividend even if they dispose of their holdings prior to the date the dividend is distributed. Thus stock sold between the record date and the date of distribution is sold without the current dividend rights attached, that is, *ex-dividend.* The record date follows the date of declaration by a few weeks, thereby allowing the completion of transactions in process.

3 *Date of payment.* As specified in the dividend declaration, the date of payment is the date when the dividend will be distributed to the stockholders. Generally, the date of payment is several weeks after the record date.

Cash dividends

Most dividends are paid in cash. To distribute a cash dividend, firms must meet two conditions. First, a firm must obviously have an adequate cash balance. A lack of cash or an extremely tight cash position can easily force a corporation to skip or omit a dividend payout.

The second condition for a dividend requires an adequate balance in the Retained Earnings account. Keep in mind that dividends are distributions of earnings; thus total corporate profits must be sufficient to *support* amounts given to stockholders. Importantly, dividends are not *paid* with earnings; payments take place with cash. It is, of course, entirely possible to have a profit-rich but cash-poor corporation. The corporation has a large retained earnings balance but is limited in terms of dividend distributions by a lack of funds.

Accounting for cash dividends

To illustrate the necessary accounting for cash dividends, assume Dale Corporation has 100,000 shares of common stock outstanding. On July 15 the board of directors declared a $0.25 quarterly dividend to stockholders of record on August 14. The dividend will be distributed on September 1. The proper journal entries follow.

July 15	*Retained Earnings*	*25,000*	
	Dividends Payable		*25,000*
	To record declaration of cash dividend of $0.25 per share		
Aug. 14	*No entry required*		
Sept. 1	*Dividends Payable*	*25,000*	
	Cash		*25,000*
	To record payment of dividend declared on July 15		

Observe that the cash dividend is based on the number of shares outstanding. Thus if Dale had issued 100,000 shares and held 10,000 as treasury stock, the board of directors would declare a quarterly dividend of $22,500 (90,000 shares × $0.25). Should a balance sheet be prepared after the date of declaration but prior to the date of payment, Dividends Payable would be disclosed as a current liability.

Some corporations follow an alternative recording practice on the declaration date. Rather than reduce Retained Earnings directly, the debit is recorded in a temporary account called Dividends. The Dividends account is then closed to Retained Earnings at the end of the accounting period.

Property dividends

Sometimes a corporation will distribute assets other than cash as dividends. These distributions, known as **property dividends,** allow a corporation to conserve funds while providing stockholders with a return on their investment. Property dividends have been paid in the form of merchandise, real estate, and investments in the stock of other companies and have occasionally bordered on the imaginative and bizarre. A mining company, for example, recently paid dividends in gold bars. Because it wasn't practicable

WHEN BAD NEWS IS GOOD NEWS

Let's say you're kicking tires in a used car lot when a secondhand jalopy arrives, hanging backward from a tow truck, its engine smoking. Would you buy that car? Investors tend to look just as slit-eyed at companies that cut or omit their dividends. Instinctively, most investors feel it's the height of financial folly to buy into a company that is forced to take such extreme action.

Not all financial analysts agree, however. William Kent notes that the failure to make a scheduled dividend payment is among his top three or four positive indicators that a stock is a good buy. Kent does agree that it is important to determine why the dividend was cut or omitted. But he adds, "Even without knowing, I'm saying that if you bought every company that omitted a dividend, you'd come out, on average, ahead of the market. And if you went one step further and weeded out the ones that <u>had</u> *to skip a dividend, you'd do even better!"*

To prove Kent's theory, two studies were performed of randomly chosen corporations that cut or omitted their dividends. In the first study, stock prices of companies that reduced their dividends rose an average of 48% over a one-year period, while stocks of corporations that passed their dividends entirely rose 100%. During the same period the Dow-Jones Industrial Average climbed only 8.66%. In the second study, which took place ten years later, stocks of corporations that cut their dividends were up an average of 33.8%, while the Dow rose only 3.7%.

Kent claims there is good reason for such stock price behavior. He admits that some firms omit a dividend because they are in trouble with creditors and can't afford to pay it. But he claims that more often the reason lies in a "positive" decision by management. "Either they've decided they'd rather put the money back into the business, or they're trying to depress the company's stock before buying it themselves. In either case, that's bullish." He adds that another possibility is that management is "facing up to reality and taking matters in hand"—a good sign in anybody's book.

What do other stock market experts say? In general they agree with Kent. As one analyst notes, a dividend omission usually means "the company is admitting that things are as bad as they can be." And he adds, "If you start from the blackest point on the market, it's pretty likely that things will have to improve."

SOURCE Adapted from "When Bad News is Good News," Financial World, November 15, 1979, pp. 67–68.

to deliver a gold dividend of less than 2.5 grams, stockholders had to own 600 to 700 common shares to qualify.[8]

Stock dividends

Many corporations distribute additional shares of their own stock as dividends. The distribution, referred to as a **stock dividend,** most frequently involves the issuance of common shares to existing common stockholders. Additional shares are issued in proportion to stockholders' present ownership in the firm. For example, suppose Ellen Bagley owns 20,000 shares of a cosmetics company she founded several years ago. Assuming a total of 100,000 shares are outstanding, Ellen has a 20% ownership interest. If the board of directors declares a 10% stock dividend, an additional 10,000 shares (100,000 shares × 0.10) will be distributed to stockholders. Ellen is entitled to 20% of the additional shares, which results in the following figures:

	Before Stock Dividend	10% Stock Dividend	After Stock Dividend
Corporation	100,000 shares	10,000 shares	110,000 shares
Ellen Bagley	20,000 shares	2,000 shares	22,000 shares
Ownership interest	20%	20%	20%

As you can see, a stockholder's percentage ownership remains the same. Furthermore, the corporation's assets and liabilities are unaffected because they are not involved in the distribution. Why, then, are stock dividends issued and what is the effect, if any, on corporate equity? The answers to these questions should become apparent in the following sections.

Reasons for issuing stock dividends

Several reasons have been advanced for the issuance of stock dividends. First, stock dividends enable a corporation to engage in a distribution to shareholders while, at the same time, conserving cash. The cash can then be invested in expanding operations, new projects, and similar undertakings.

Second, stock dividends result in an increased yield to the stockholder. Cash dividends are taxable when received. Stock dividends, on the other hand, are not income and therefore no taxes are involved. Income taxes are assessed, however, when and if the shares are sold.

Finally, some accountants feel that stock dividends improve a stock's attractiveness by decreasing the market value (to be discussed shortly) and expanding the ownership base. To explain the latter, stock dividends increase the number of shares outstanding. As investors sell all or part of their holdings, the number of stockholders will ultimately increase. More stockholders may make the sale of new shares easier because of the existing owners' willingness to consider larger investments in the corporation.

---

[8] "Mining Company Plans to Pay Golden Dividend," *The Wall Street Journal,* February 11, 1981, p. 8.

Accounting for stock dividends

The accounting treatment for stock dividends depends on the size of the distribution. Most stock dividends are small, involving issuances of less than 20–25% of the existing shares outstanding. For small stock dividends the accounting profession recommends a reduction in retained earnings equal to the market value of the additional shares issued. Market value is used because stockholders view the dividend's "true worth" as being equivalent to the fair market value of the shares received.

To illustrate the proper accounting, assume Mastercraft Corporation had the following stockholders' equity section on June 1.

STOCKHOLDERS' EQUITY	
Common stock, $20 par value, 800,000 shares authorized, 300,000 shares issued and outstanding	$ 6,000,000
Paid-in capital in excess of par value	1,000,000
Retained earnings	12,000,000
Total stockholders' equity	$19,000,000

On June 15 the board of directors declared a 10% stock dividend that will be distributed on July 15. The closing market price of Mastercraft's common stock on June 15 was $33 per share. Because the stock dividend is small, the declaration would be recorded as follows:

June 15	Retained Earnings	990,000	
	Stock Dividend Distributable		600,000
	Paid-in Capital in Excess of Par Value		390,000
	To record declaration of 10% stock dividend		

To explain, the declaration involves the future issuance of 30,000 shares (300,000 shares × 0.10); thus Retained Earnings must be debited for $990,000 (30,000 shares × $33).[9] Next, an account entitled Stock Dividend Distributable is established for the par value of the dividend (30,000 shares × $20 = $600,000). Importantly, Stock Dividend Distributable is not a liability because Mastercraft has no obligation to distribute either cash or any other asset. If a balance sheet is prepared between the date of declaration and the ultimate distribution of the shares, this account would be presented in the stockholders' equity section as an addition to the Common Stock account. Finally, consistent with the material presented in Chapter 13, the difference between the "issue price" ($990,000) and par value ($600,000) is credited to Paid-in Capital in Excess of Par Value.

The following entry is made on July 15 to record issuance of the common shares.

[9] The stock dividend in this example is based on the 300,000 shares outstanding. When treasury stock is involved, practice varies. That is, some corporations base the dividend on outstanding shares only; others compute the dividend on total shares issued, including those held by the firm.

July 15	*Stock Dividend Distributable*	*600,000*	
	Common Stock		*600,000*
	To record issuance of stock dividend of 30,000 shares		

Stock dividends and corporate equity

The net effect of the stock dividend is to transfer $990,000 of retained earnings to Common Stock and other paid-in capital accounts. The accompanying schedule, constructed by utilizing the entries on June 15 and July 15, shows that total stockholders' equity remains unchanged.

Account	***Before Stock Dividend***	***Declaration and Issuance****	***After Stock Dividend***
Common stock	$ 6,000,000	$+600,000 (I)	$ 6,600,000
Paid-in capital in excess of par value	1,000,000	+390,000 (D)	1,390,000
Stock dividend distributable	—	+600,000 (D) −600,000 (I)	—
Retained earnings	12,000,000	−990,000 (D)	11,010,000
	$19,000,000	$ —	$19,000,000

**D = declaration on June 15; I = issuance on July 15.*

Overall, then, a stock dividend is merely a shifting or recapitalization of the stockholders' equity section. The end result is that (1) $990,000 of retained earnings is no longer available for future dividend distributions and (2) additional shares of common stock are outstanding.

Stock dividends and market value

Stock dividends usually affect the market price of a corporation's stock. To illustrate, we will continue the previous example. Observe that the fair market value of Mastercraft's common shares on the date of declaration amounted to $9,900,000 (300,000 shares × $33). Since an additional 30,000 shares will soon be outstanding, the market price should drop to $30 per share ($9,900,000 ÷ 330,000 shares). However, as we noted both in this chapter and in Chapter 13, a stock's market price is dependent on a variety of factors. Thus when there is a very small stock dividend, there is a strong likelihood that the decrease in price could be obscured by other market influences.

Large stock dividends, namely, those in excess of 20%–25%, are a different matter. Because of a substantial increase in the number of shares outstanding, the market price per share will drop significantly. For example, if a firm doubles the outstanding shares by a 100% stock dividend, the market price should fall by about 50%. Large stock dividends are therefore afforded different accounting treatment from that of small stock dividends. Rather than value the distribution at fair market value, the Retained Earnings account is debited for the par or stated value of the dividend, with a corresponding credit to Stock Dividend Distributable. This treatment is a logical outgrowth of accounting for stock splits, the next topic for discussion. As we will now see, large stock dividends are very similar to stock splits.

Stock splits

Most publicly held corporations are interested in maintaining the marketability of their stock. Frequently, when a share's market price rises substantially, many small investors look for other investment alternatives. Why? Investors prefer to purchase round lots of stock (i.e., 100-share multiples) to take advantage of lower commission rates from brokers. Naturally, a high-priced stock would place the round lot beyond the reach of those individuals with limited funds. As a consequence, corporations often attempt to reduce the market price per share.

One way to accomplish a reduction in market price is by the issuance of a large stock dividend; another way is a stock split. A **stock split** involves increasing the number of shares outstanding and, at the same time, reducing the stock's par or stated value per share. To illustrate, assume a corporation has 200,000 shares of $10 par-value stock outstanding, which is currently selling for $80 per share. The firm wants to reduce the market price to $20 per share and, accordingly, a 4-for-1 stock split is approved by the board of directors. The split results in a reduction of par value from $10 to $2.50 ($10 ÷ 4) and an increase in the number of outstanding shares from 200,000 to 800,000 (200,000 × 4). Total corporate equity thus remains unchanged. A stockholder owning 200 shares prior to the split will receive a certificate for 800 shares of the new issue. Observe that the stockholder is not better off, since the total market value of his or her shares remains at $16,000: 200 shares × $80 versus 800 shares × $20. The stockholder's position is only improved if the market value of the stock subsequently increases.

Because a stock split does not change the balance in any of the corporation's accounts, no formal entry is required. However, a memorandum should be recorded in the journal to note that a stock split has occurred and that the number of shares issued and outstanding has increased. The accounting treatment for stock splits therefore differs from that of large stock dividends, the latter of which requires a transfer from Retained Earnings to capital stock accounts. The reason for the differing treatments is that although both splits and dividends increase the number of shares, stock dividends do not affect a share's par or stated value. Thus an entry is needed to record the increased amount of legal capital caused by the distribution.

Other Items Affecting Retained Earnings

Although our presentation has concentrated on net income and dividends, other items affect retained earnings as well. As we noted earlier in the chapter, for example, the reissuance of treasury stock at a price below cost could necessitate a reduction in retained earnings. Retained earnings are also influenced by prior period adjustments and appropriations.

Prior period adjustments

Accountants, like other professionals, are not perfect. Even with a strong system of internal control, errors sometimes enter the accounting records. Most errors are detected soon after occurrence; some, however, may go unnoticed for several years. Naturally, once an error is found, the books must be corrected immediately.

Errors affecting the net income of previous periods are corrected by the use of **prior period adjustments.** To illustrate the proper accounting treatment, assume Mercer Corporation overlooked several pieces of equipment in 1982 and thereby understated depreciation expense by $10,000. If the error is not discovered until a subsequent accounting period, say 1983, the prior period adjustment to correct the records would be as follows:

Retained Earnings	*10,000*	
Accumulated Depreciation: Equipment		*10,000*
To correct the 1982 understatement of depreciation expense		

Correcting 1982 depreciation expense directly is impossible since all revenue and expense accounts have been closed. The understated expense overstated net income, which in turn overstated the balance in the Retained Earnings account at the end of 1982. Retained Earnings is therefore debited to record the appropriate reduction.

Prior period adjustments are reported as an adjustment to the Retained Earnings balance at the beginning of the year in which the correction is made, 1983 in Mercer's case. The adjustment is shown on a net-of-tax basis and is disclosed on the statement of retained earnings (to be discussed shortly).

Appropriations of retained earnings

Corporations occasionally transfer part of their retained earnings balances into separate accounts termed **appropriations.** The purpose of this practice is to inform financial statement readers that a portion of retained earnings is unavailable for dividend distributions. Appropriations may be made by the board of directors for such items as plant expansion, replacement of existing machinery and equipment, or a possible assessment of additional federal income taxes. In some cases an appropriation may be required because of contractual or legal restrictions. For example, many states require a retained earnings appropriation equal to the cost of any treasury stock acquired. In this manner legal capital is maintained by substituting a restriction on retained earnings in place of the treasury shares held by the corporation.

Appropriations are sometimes handled by formal journal entries in the accounting records. To illustrate, assume Husky Corporation appropriated one-third of its $150,000 retained earnings balance for future plant expansion. The necessary journal entry follows.

Retained Earnings	*50,000*	
Retained Earnings Appropriated for Plant Expansion		*50,000*
To record retained earnings appropriation		

The stockholders' equity section of the balance sheet would reveal the following:

Retained earnings	
Appropriated for future plant expansion	$ 50,000
Unappropriated	100,000
Total	$150,000

Observe that the appropriation does not reduce total retained earnings; it does, however, restrict earnings available for dividends. When the restriction is no longer needed, Husky will debit the appropriation and credit Retained Earnings.

The use of an appropriation does not mean that cash has been set aside for the stated purpose. As evidence, examine Husky's journal entry, which failed to credit the Cash account. To accumulate the necessary funds, corporations frequently establish special asset accounts and make deposits at the time of an appropriation. Again the appropriation *by itself* is not sufficient to restrict cash.

Rather than use the journal entry approach just illustrated, an increasing number of corporations disclose retained earnings restrictions (and others) in the footnotes that accompany the financial statements. As an example, Pizza Inn recently reported a retained earnings balance of $5,507,208 on its balance sheet, along with the following:

> *The Company is subject to a number of covenants under its various credit agreements, the most restrictive of which are that the Company is required to (1) maintain a minimum tangible net worth of $12,000,000; (2) maintain a ratio of current assets to current liabilities of not less than .90 to 1; and (3) restrict payment of cash dividends. Unrestricted retained earnings under these covenants is approximately $2,175,000. . . . The agreements, among other things, also provide restrictions on additional borrowings and require the maintenance of various other financial ratios.*

Statement of Retained Earnings

Changes in the Retained Earnings account are normally disclosed on a separate **statement of retained earnings**, as illustrated in Exhibit 14-5.

The form of the retained earnings statement varies widely. Some corporations divide their statements into appropriated and unappropriated sections, disclosing increases and decreases in each section during the year. Other corporations prepare a combined statement of income and retained earnings, thereby doing away with a separately prepared income statement. The combined statement has received mixed reviews from accountants. The major advantage of this approach is that all items affecting retained earnings are combined in a single statement and are less apt to be overlooked by financial statement users. However, many accountants assert that the combined statement downplays the importance of earnings by burying net income in the midst of other, less important financial data.

Exhibit 14-5

Statement of retained earnings

DONLEY CORPORATION
Statement of Retained Earnings
For the Year Ended December 31, 1983

Retained earnings, 12/31/82 (as reported)		$ 80,000
Less: Correction of prior period inventory error (net of $6,000 tax)		9,000
Retained earnings, 12/31/82 (restated)		$ 71,000
Add: Net income		100,000
		$171,000
Less: Cash dividends on preferred stock	$15,000	
Stock dividends on common stock	45,000	60,000
Retained earnings, 12/31/83 (note A)		$111,000

Note A: *The company has various debt agreements restricting the amount of retained earnings that can be used for dividend distributions. As of December 31, 1983, income retained in the business of $74,000 was free of such restrictions.*

BOOK VALUE PER SHARE

As we have noted, stockholders have a substantial interest in earnings per share and dividends per share. Another corporate financial measure is book value per share. **Book value per share** is the amount of stockholders' equity allocable to an individual share of stock. Stated differently, book value represents a corporation's net assets (total assets minus total liabilities) per share.

The calculation of book value per share depends on the number of classes of stock outstanding. If a corporation has only common stock, book value per share is computed by dividing total stockholders' equity by the number of common shares outstanding at the end of the accounting period. To illustrate, assume Ranger Corporation has the following stockholders' equity on August 31, the end of the firm's fiscal year.

STOCKHOLDERS' EQUITY

Common stock, $1 par value, 100,000 shares authorized, 50,000 shares issued and outstanding	$ 50,000
Paid-in capital in excess of par value	350,000
Retained earnings	600,000
Total stockholders' equity	$1,000,000

The book value per share is therefore $20 ($1,000,000 ÷ 50,000 shares).

An Example with Two Classes of Stock

If a corporation has two classes of stock (e.g., common and preferred), total stockholders' equity must be allocated among the respective ownership interests. The allocation is achieved by first assigning the call value (sometimes referred to as the *redemption or liquidating value*) of the preferred stock plus any dividends in arrears[10] as preferred equity. The sum of these two items is next subtracted from total stockholders' equity to generate equity attributable to the common shareholders. The book value per common and preferred shares can then be determined by dividing the equity relating to the two stock classes by their respective outstanding shares.

To illustrate the necessary accounting, we present the stockholders' equity section of Orleans, Inc.

STOCKHOLDERS' EQUITY

Preferred stock, $100 par value, 5% cumulative, callable at $110, 1,000 shares authorized, 400 shares issued and outstanding	$ 40,000	
Common stock, $1 par value, 100,000 shares authorized, 30,000 shares issued and outstanding	30,000	$ 70,000
Additional paid-in capital		
Paid-in capital in excess of par: preferred	$ 5,000	
Paid-in capital in excess of par: common	200,000	205,000
Total paid-in capital		$275,000
Retained earnings		595,000
Total stockholders' equity		$870,000

Further information reveals that dividends on the preferred stock are $4,000 in arrears.

The allocation of Orleans' stockholders' equity follows.

Total stockholders' equity		$870,000
Allocated to preferred stock		
Call value: 400 shares × $110	$44,000	
Dividends in arrears	4,000	48,000
Allocated to common stock		$822,000

Observe that the $5,000 paid-in capital in excess of par on the preferred stock is not allocated to preferred equity. This amount will not be returned to the preferred shareholders should their stock be called.

The book value per share for each class of stock can now be calculated.

Preferred stock	$48,000 ÷ 400 shares = $120.00 per share
Common stock	$822,000 ÷ 30,000 shares = $27.40 per share

Meaning of Book Value

As we stated earlier, book value is equivalent to a corporation's net assets per share of stock. Some stockholders therefore believe that should the corporation terminate operations and liquidate, they would receive an amount equal to the book value per share. Rarely, however, does this belief become reality. When a corporation liquidates, the assets are usually sold at a price far different from their valuation on a balance sheet. Remember, the balance sheet is cost-based and ignores increases in valuation due to inflation. Furthermore, because the corporation is selling out, the amounts re-

[10] Dividends in arrears apply solely to cumulative preferred stock.

ceived for certain assets may only be a small percentage of their original cost. Adding to this is the fact that liabilities are often settled at less than the amount due. These events alter corporate equity and the amounts disbursed to stockholders upon liquidation.

The importance of book value lies in its inclusion in many legal contracts. In a small corporation, for example, stockholders may agree to sell their holdings to the other owners at the book value per share existing on specified future dates. Or banks may lend funds to a corporation subject to the maintenance of a minimum book value. Under no circumstances should book value per share be equated with a stock's market value; these two measures normally differ. Consider, for example, the following figures, which were in existence at the time this text was written.

Corporation	*Book Value per Share*	*Market Value per Share*
Apple Computer	$ 3.21	$15.75
Firestone Tire & Rubber	25.00	10.63
Nike	4.74	29.75
Northwest Orient Airlines	38.43	28.00

Book value, a measure based on historical cost, is just one of the many factors investors use in assessing the appropriateness of a stock's market price.

KEY TERMS AND CONCEPTS

appropriation of retained earnings 547
book value per share 549
cash dividend 541
date of declaration 540
date of payment 540
date of record 540
deficit 530
discontinued operations 531
dividend 539
donated capital 529
earnings per share 535
extraordinary items 531
fully diluted earnings per share 538
intraperiod tax allocation 535
payout ratio 540
price-earnings ratio 536
primary earnings per share 538
prior period adjustment 547
property dividend 541
retained earnings 530
segment 531
statement of retained earnings 548
stock dividend 543
stock split 546
treasury stock 526

QUESTIONS

Q14-1 What is treasury stock? Why do corporations purchase treasury stock?

Q14-2 Should purchased treasury stock be disclosed as an asset? Why?

Q14-3 Explain how the Retained Earnings account can have a debit balance.

Q14-4 Why should a corporation segregate ordinary business income from income caused by unusual and infrequent transactions or events?

Q14-5 How are the financial results of discontinued operations disclosed on the income statement?

Q14-6 What two criteria must be satisfied for an event or transaction to be classified as an extraordinary item? Discuss each of the criteria and present three examples of possible extraordinary items.

Q14-7 Briefly discuss the practice of intraperiod tax allocation. Explain what the practice is and why it is used.

Q14-8 Why do stockholders pay so much attention to earnings per share?

Q14-9 Differentiate between primary and fully diluted earnings per share.

Q14-10 What does it mean when a corporation's common stock sells ex-dividend?

Q14-11 What two conditions must be satisfied to declare and distribute a cash dividend?

Q14-12 The XYZ Corporation has an extremely tight cash position and wishes to distribute a dividend to its stockholders. Suggest several courses of action that XYZ might follow.

Q14-13 Discuss the effect of a stock dividend on (1) a stockholder's percentage ownership position and (2) total stockholders' equity of the issuing corporation.

Q14-14 Differentiate between a small and large stock dividend. Are both of these dividends accounted for in the same manner? Explain.

Q14-15 Differentiate between a large stock dividend and a stock split.

Q14-16 What is a prior period adjustment? Explain the proper accounting and reporting treatment for prior period adjustments.

Q14-17 What is the purpose of appropriating retained earnings? How are appropriations disclosed in the financial statements?

Q14-18 Suppose a corporation appropriated $60,000 of retained earnings for future equipment purchases. Discuss the effect of the appropriation on the company's Cash account.

EXERCISES

E14-1 Nevada Corporation reacquired 10,000 shares of its common stock ($15 par value) on January 23 for $80 per share. These shares were subsequently sold as follows:

Feb. 15 2,000 shares at $80 per share
May 30 4,000 shares at $100 per share
Dec. 10 4,000 shares at $55 per share

Prepare all necessary journal entries for Nevada Corporation.

E14-2 The following information pertains to Stovall Corporation for the year ended December 31, 1983.

Sales	*$1,000,000*
Cost of goods sold	*600,000*
Selling expenses	*150,000*
Administrative expenses	*200,000*

In 1983 Stovall disposed of its retail division. The retail division generated 20% of the firm's total sales and accounted for 25% and 30% of total cost of goods sold and operating expenses, respectively. The division was sold at a before-tax gain of $25,000. Prepare Stovall's 1983 income statement, assuming a 40% tax rate.

E14-3 Which of the following events and transactions would be accounted for as an extraordinary item of Gavin Corporation? Discuss the reasoning behind your answer.

a The company experienced an unusually devastating flood in its southern warehouse. Flood damage in the area occurs approximately once every six years.

b The company experienced an unusually long strike at one of its plants, causing the plant to lose $150,000.

c The company sold its midwestern division to another corporation and realized a sizable gain on the sale.

d The company had to write off its entire inventory of toys because the toys failed to meet an obscure federal safety standard.

e The company experienced an unusual loss from hailstorm damage in the Central American division. Hailstorm damage in this location is rare.

E14-4 Neptune Corporation began the year with 100,000 common shares outstanding. On April 1, 10,000 shares were reacquired as treasury stock. All treasury shares were subsequently reissued on June 1. Finally, on September 1, 50,000 newly issued shares were sold to the public for $5 per share. Calculate the weighted-average shares outstanding during the year.

E14-5 Tabor Corporation reported aftertax net income for the current year of $235,000. The company had 100 common shares outstanding on January 1 and sold another 100 shares on July 1. Preferred dividends of $10,000 ($5 per share) were paid during the year. Compute Tabor's earnings per share of common stock.

E14-6 Dombroski, Inc., has the following stock outstanding:

Common stock, $10 par, 100,000 shares	$1,000,000
10% preferred stock, $50 par, 10,000 shares	500,000

Each share of preferred is convertible into 6 shares of common stock. Net income for the year totaled $200,000.

a Compute primary earnings per share.

b Compute fully diluted earnings per share.

E14-7 CROWNOVER HOTEL REPORTS 20% RISE IN EPS

Phoenix—Stan Crownover, president of the Crownover Hotel, today reported a 20% rise in earnings per share. The company, an Arizona-based hotel operator, reported $3.60 earnings per share for the year ended December 31, 1983. This compares favorably with $3 per share for the previous year. At the annual stockholders' meeting, Crownover expressed sorrow over an explosion that occurred in August and claimed three lives. The explosion was caused by a bomb that was detonated when Crownover refused to meet the demands of an extortionist. Because the company carried insurance based on the replacement cost of its hotel and not on the original acquisition cost, the bombing netted Crownover a $50,000 gain after tax.

Assuming Crownover has 50,000 shares of common stock outstanding, evaluate the company's success or failure during 1983.

E14-8 The Chavez Corporation has the following equity accounts:

Common stock, $1 par value	*$ 500,000*
Paid-in capital in excess of par value	*1,000,000*
Retained earnings	*4,000,000*
Total stockholders' equity	*$5,500,000*

a Record each of the following events in the accounting records. Consider each event individually.
   (1) Declared a 2% stock dividend; market value at the time of declaration was $9 per share. The dividend will be distributed in the next accounting period.
   (2) Authorized a 5-for-1 stock split.
   (3) Declared a $0.40-per-share cash dividend, to be distributed in the next accounting period.

b Compute total stockholders' equity immediately after each of the independent events in part (a).

E14-9 Korb Corporation has the following data:

Total earnings in profitable years since inception	*$2,100,000*
Current appropriations for general contingencies	*400,000*
Current appropriations for plant expansion	*200,000*
Current appropriations for possible tax assessments	*250,000*
Total of net losses since inception	*500,000*
Paid-in capital from treasury stock	*100,000*
Total dividends declared and paid since inception	*150,000*
Common stock, $1 par value	*1,000,000*
Treasury stock: 5,000 shares at cost	*75,000*

The firm's state of incorporation requires that retained earnings be appropriated for the cost of treasury stock acquisitions.

Determine the present balance of unappropriated retained earnings.

E14-10 Grant Corporation had an ending retained earnings balance on December 31, 1982, of $1,800,000. The following information pertains to 1983.

a Cash dividends of $200,000 ($1 per share) were paid to common stockholders. The last distribution took place on October 31.

b A 4% common stock dividend was declared and distributed on December 31. The stock's fair market value at the time of declaration was $12 per share.

c Income was $175,000 before tax.

d An error was discovered on April 10 that occurred in 1981 and understated before-tax net income of that year by $50,000.

e Grant is subject to a 40% income tax rate.

Prepare the corporation's 1983 statement of retained earnings.

E14-11 Irvine Corporation has the following stockholders' equity:

Common stock, $2 par value	*$250,000*
Paid-in capital in excess of par value: common	*350,000*
Retained earnings	*(250,000)*
	$350,000

a Explain the probable cause of the debit balance in Irvine's Retained Earnings account.

b Determine Irvine's book value per share.

c Assume Irvine also had a preferred stock issue of 1,000 shares ($100 par value) with a call price of $125. Compute the book value per share of both the preferred and common stock. There are no dividends in arrears.

PROBLEMS

P14-1 ***Corporate financial reporting***

The following information pertains to Sierra Corporation for the current year ended December 31.

Net sales	*$540,000*
Cost of goods sold	*320,000*
Selling expenses	*60,000*
Administrative expenses	*85,000*
Retained earnings appropriation for plant expansion	*20,000*
Loss on vehicle disposal	*15,000*
Loss on plant seizure and destruction	*150,000*
Dividends declared and paid	*28,000*
Discontinued operations	
Earnings from discontinued segment activities	*30,000*
Loss on disposal of segment facilities	*55,000*
Sale of treasury stock in excess of cost (cost, $47,000; proceeds, $72,000)	*25,000*

The plant seizure and destruction was caused by militants in a normally stable foreign country; the loss is unusual and not likely to recur in the foreseeable future. Sierra is subject to a 40% income tax rate; all figures above are before tax. Ten thousand shares of common stock have been outstanding during the year.

INSTRUCTIONS

a Identify those items that should not be considered when calculating net income. Briefly explain the reason(s) behind your selection.

b Prepare an income statement for Sierra Corporation in good form.

c At the beginning of the current year Sierra reported total retained earnings (unappropriated and appropriated) of $164,500. Determine the company's ending retained earnings balance.

d Does the retained earnings appropriation indicate that $20,000 cash has been set aside for plant expansion purposes? Explain.

P14-2 ***Extraordinary items and discontinued operations***

Liberty Lou, Inc., is aggressively acquiring small retail health food shops. In

January 1983 two representatives of Liberty Lou visited a prospective acquisition candidate, Raisins and Nuts, and obtained an income statement from the preceding year. The statement follows.

RAISINS AND NUTS
Income Statement
For the Year Ended December 31, 1982

Sales (net)		$250,000
Cost of goods sold	$125,000	
Selling expenses	30,000	
Administrative expenses	20,000	175,000
Net income before extraordinary items		$ 75,000
Extraordinary items		
Correction of error, 1981	$ 40,000	
Rain damage to roof	(10,000)	
Write-down of inventory	(20,000)	10,000
Net income before tax		$ 85,000
Income taxes, 40%		34,000
Net income		$ 51,000

The following information was obtained during a conversation with management of Raisins and Nuts.

1 In 1982 Raisins and Nuts closed a small branch operation at a local shopping center when several major occupants moved to a new location. During 1982 the branch had generated a gross profit of 30% on sales of $80,000. Payroll costs of branch sales personnel totaled $13,000; administrative costs amounted to $4,000.
2 The error correction related to a mistake in accounting for operating costs at the store's main warehouse. The mistake was discovered on February 3, 1982.
3 According to the company's president, the roof damage resulted from "an extraordinarily hard summer downpour" at the main warehouse. A local meteorologist claims that heavy summer rains are common to the area.
4 The write-down of inventory occurred because of a TV broadcaster's attack on the cholesterol content of nuts and a resultant drop in sales.
5 All extraordinary items are before the consideration of income taxes.
6 During the year 10,000 shares of common stock were outstanding.

INSTRUCTIONS

a Identify the deficiencies in the income statement.
b Prepare a corrected income statement for Raisins and Nuts in good form.
c Should Raisins and Nuts have closed the branch operation? Explain your answer.

P14-3 ***Earnings per share***

The following information was extracted from the records of Winfield, Inc.

1. Preferred stock, 6%, $100 par value, 100,000 shares outstanding during the entire year. Each share is convertible into $2\frac{1}{2}$ shares of common stock.
2. Common stock, $1 par value, 1,000,000 shares outstanding at the beginning of the year. Additional shares were sold as follows:

Apr. 1	200,000 shares
June 1	200,000 shares
Sept. 1	100,000 shares

3. Net income for the year, $7,100,000.

INSTRUCTIONS

a. Calculate primary earnings per share.
b. Calculate fully diluted earnings per share. Round to the nearest cent.
c. A stockholder believes that the fully diluted computation should be based on 1,750,000 shares outstanding, calculated as follows:

Original issuance	*1,000,000*
Additional common shares sold	*500,000*
Actual shares issued to stockholders from preferred conversion	*250,000*
	1,750,000

The stockholder has made two errors. Identify and briefly discuss each error.

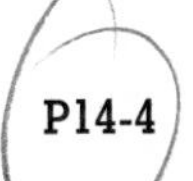

P14-4 ***Equity transactions: Journal entries and balance sheet, analysis of dividends***

An examination of the ledger of Lia Enterprises revealed the following accounts on January 1.

Common stock, $10 par, 50,000 shares authorized, 30,000 shares issued	*$300,000*
Paid-in capital in excess of par value	*90,000*
Appropriation for plant expansion	*70,000*
Appropriation for treasury stock	*25,000*
Retained earnings (unappropriated)	*145,000*
Treasury stock, 2,000 shares at cost	*25,000*

The following transactions occurred during the year.

Jan. 15	Declared a $0.65 dividend per share to stockholders of record on January 30. The dividend will be distributed on February 15.
Feb. 1	Increased the appropriation for plant expansion by $15,000.
15	Paid the dividend declared on January 15.
Apr. 10	Sold 1,500 shares of treasury stock for $21,000 and reduced the treasury stock appropriation by $18,750.
Sept. 1	Declared a 4% stock dividend on the shares outstanding to stockholders of record on September 15. The dividend will be distributed on October 1. Fair market value on the date of declaration was $15 per share.
Oct. 1	Issued the stock dividend declared on September 1.
Dec. 31	Net income for the year amounted to $105,000. Closed the Income Summary account to Retained Earnings.

INSTRUCTIONS

a Prepare journal entries to record Lia's transactions.

b Prepare the stockholders' equity section of Lia's December 31 balance sheet.

c A financial assistant noted that if the stock dividend had been declared in December for distribution during the next accounting period, the company would have reported increased liabilities on its balance sheet. Do you agree? Why?

P14-5 ***Analysis of equity transactions***

Brown, Inc., had the following transactions during the year.

Jan. 4	Declared a cash dividend.
Feb. 4	Distributed the dividend above.
18	Received 300 shares of donated treasury stock.
Mar. 30	Authorized a 3-for-1 stock split.
Apr. 10	Declared a 15% stock dividend.
May 10	Distributed the dividend above.
June 28	Purchased 500 shares of treasury stock for $30 per share.
Sept. 6	Sold 200 shares of the treasury stock purchased on June 28 for $36 per share.
Dec. 15	Appropriated retained earnings for plant expansion.

INSTRUCTIONS

Using the accompanying chart, determine the effect of each of Brown's transactions on total assets, total liabilities, total ending retained earnings, and total stockholders' equity. Use the following notation: I = increase, D = decrease, and NE = no effect. The January 4th transaction is done as an example.

Transaction Date	***Total Assets***	***Total Liabilities***	***Total Ending Retained Earnings***	***Total Stockholders' Equity***
Jan. 4	NE	I	D	D

P14-6 ***Dividends and stock split***

The Pittsburgh Corporation has the following stockholders' equity section on January 1 of the current year.

STOCKHOLDERS' EQUITY

Preferred stock, $100 par value, 9%, 10,000 shares authorized, 9,000 shares issued and outstanding	*$ 900,000*
Common stock, $1 par value, 800,000 shares authorized, 100,000 shares issued and outstanding	*100,000*
Paid-in capital in excess of par value: common	*1,400,000*
Retained earnings	*7,000,000*
Total stockholders' equity	*$9,400,000*

The following transactions occurred during the year.

Jan. 18	Declared the regular semiannual cash dividend of $4.50 per share on the preferred stock and a special cash dividend of $0.50 per share on the common stock to stockholders of record on February 5. Both dividends will be distributed on February 28.
Feb. 28	Distributed the dividends declared on January 18.

July 18 Declared the regular semiannual cash dividend of $4.50 per share on the preferred stock to stockholders of record on August 5. The dividend will be distributed on August 28.

Aug. 28 Distributed the dividend declared on July 18.

Sept. 1 Declared a 10% common stock dividend to common shareholders of record on September 15. The dividend will be distributed on September 30. The September 1 market price of the common stock was $5 per share.

30 Distributed the stock dividend declared on September 1.

Oct. 1 Sold 40,000 shares of common stock to the general public at $8 per share.

Dec. 15 The board of directors authorized a 4-for-1 split of the common stock. The market price of the stock was $12 per share.

INSTRUCTIONS

a Prepare journal entries to record the transactions.

b Prepare the stockholders' equity section of Pittsburgh's December 31 balance sheet. Net income for the year amounted to $800,000.

c On September 5 Pittsburgh received a letter from a stockholder who noted that "the corporation's financial position is already weak and the 10% stock dividend could jeopardize the financial well-being of the business." Comment on the stockholder's claim.

P14-7 ***Analysis of stock dividends and splits***

This problem consists of two unrelated questions pertaining to stock dividends and stock splits.

Part I Evaluate the following statements for the management of Dakota, Inc., and decide whether the statements apply to:

1 Stock dividends only
2 Stock splits only
3 Both stock dividends and stock splits
4 Neither stock dividends nor stock splits

_____ a The par or stated value of the stock is changed.
_____ b Total stockholders' equity remains unchanged.
_____ c The distribution is considered an expense to the issuing corporation.
_____ d There is a transfer from Retained Earnings to capital stock accounts.
_____ e The distribution results in income when received by the stockholder.
_____ f The distribution results in a larger percentage of corporate ownership for an individual stockholder.
_____ g The distribution generally results in some (perhaps very small) movement in the stock's market price.

Part II On December 31, 1982, Dakota, Inc., had the following stockholders' equity section.

Common stock, $100 par	*$2,000,000*
Paid-in capital in excess of par value	*400,000*
Retained earnings	*1,900,000*
Total stockholders' equity	*$4,300,000*

During 1983 net income of $340,000 was generated. Four independent stockholders' equity sections for Dakota as of December 31, 1983, follow. The sections differ because of different transactions that occurred during the year. Fair market value of the common stock when each transaction occurred was $120 per share. By using the following code, indicate the type of transaction that took place.

1 Small stock dividend
2 Large stock dividend
3 Stock split
4 None of the above

	A	B	C	D
Shares outstanding	21,000	40,000	26,000	20,000
Common stock	$2,100,000	$2,000,000	$2,600,000	$2,000,000
Paid-in capital in excess of par value	420,000	400,000	400,000	400,000
Retained earnings	2,120,000	2,240,000	1,640,000	2,240,000
Transaction type				

P14-8 ***Comprehensive stockholders' equity: Analysis and presentation***

On January 1 of the current year Hart Distributors reported a retained earnings balance of $4,675,000. The following information has been obtained from a review of the company's records.

1 On June 10 Hart declared a cash dividend of $0.75 per share.
2 Stockholders' equity as of September 30 follows.

Common stock, $10 par, 2,000,000 shares authorized	$ 6,000,000
Paid-in capital in excess of par value	1,800,000
Retained earnings	5,350,000
	$13,150,000

3 On November 3 Hart reacquired 20,000 shares of its own stock for $350,000. Eight thousand of these shares were reissued on December 4 at $21 per share.
4 Another cash dividend of $0.75 per share was declared on December 10.
5 Net income for the fourth quarter of the year amounted to $385,000.

INSTRUCTIONS

a Compute Hart's total net income for the current year.
b Compute the number of shares outstanding as of December 31.
c Determine the balance in the Retained Earnings account as of December 31.
d Prepare the stockholders' equity section of Hart's December 31 balance sheet in good form. Hart is required to restrict retained earnings for treasury stock purchases and discloses such restrictions in the footnotes to the financial statements.
e Compute the book value per share as of December 31. Round to the nearest cent.

P14-9 ***Book value per share***

The stockholders' equity section of Limestone, Inc., revealed the following information on January 1.

Preferred stock, $100 par value, 8% cumulative, callable at $104	*$ 100,000*
Common stock, $5 par value	*500,000*
Paid-in capital in excess of par value: preferred	*2,000*
Paid-in capital in excess of par value: common	*1,700,000*
Retained earnings	*(802,000)*
Total stockholders' equity	*$1,500,000*

Dividends in arrears on the preferred stock totaled $16,000.

INSTRUCTIONS

a Calculate the book value per share of both the preferred and the common stock.

b Calculate the book value per common share immediately after each of the following transactions and events, rounding to the nearest cent. Consider each item independently.

(1) An additional 10,000 shares of common stock were sold to the public at $17 per share.

(2) Net income for the year totaled $1,200,000; no preferred dividends were paid.

(3) Four thousand shares of common stock were purchased as treasury stock at $14 per share.

c Does book value per share indicate the amount stockholders would receive if a corporation sold its assets, paid its bills, and liquidated? Explain.

P14-10 ***Corporate financial reporting (alternate to P14-1)***

The following information pertains to Regency Corporation for the current year ended December 31.

Net sales	*$280,000*
Cost of goods sold	*125,000*
Selling expenses	*38,000*
Administrative expenses	*51,000*
Retained earnings appropriation	*24,000*
Gain on machinery sale	*7,000*
Inventory loss	*84,000*
Dividends declared and paid	*16,500*
Discontinued operations	
Loss from discontinued segment activities	*34,000*
Gain on disposal of segment facilities	*41,000*
Sale of treasury stock in excess of cost (cost, $19,000; proceeds, $28,000)	*9,000*

The inventory loss was caused by a seizure of certain inventory items by a foreign government. Regency is subject to a 40% income tax rate; all figures above are before tax. Two thousand shares of common stock have been outstanding during the year.

INSTRUCTIONS

a Identify those items that should not be considered when calculating net income. Briefly explain the reason(s) behind your selection.

b Prepare an income statement for Regency Corporation in good form.
c At the beginning of the current year Regency reported total retained earnings (unappropriated and appropriated) of $75,000. Determine the company's ending retained earnings balance.
d Explain the rationale behind the separate disclosure of discontinued operations when reporting income.

P14-11 ***Earnings per share (alternate to P14-3)***

The following information was extracted from the records of Haxton, Inc.

1 Preferred stock, 8%, $50 par value, 200,000 shares outstanding during the entire year. Each share is convertible into 4 shares of common stock.
2 Common stock, $10 par value, 500,000 shares outstanding at the beginning of the year. Additional shares were sold as follows:

Apr. 1	100,000 shares
Aug. 1	300,000 shares
Oct. 1	100,000 shares

3 Net income for the year, $3,700,000.

INSTRUCTIONS

a Calculate primary earnings per share.
b Calculate fully diluted earnings per share. Round to the nearest cent.
c Explain the purpose behind the fully-diluted-earnings-per-share presentation on the income statement.

P14-12 ***Equity transactions: Journal entries and balance sheet, analysis of dividends (alternate to P14-4)***

An examination of the ledger of Carlson Enterprises revealed the following accounts on January 1.

Common stock, $5 par, 30,000 shares authorized, 20,000 shares issued	*$100,000*
Paid-in capital in excess of par value	*60,000*
Appropriation for plant expansion	*34,000*
Appropriation for treasury stock	*18,000*
Retained earnings (unappropriated)	*109,600*
Treasury stock, 1,000 shares at cost	*18,000*

The following transactions occurred during the year.

Jan. 10	Declared a $0.30 dividend per share to stockholders of record on January 25. The dividend will be distributed on February 10.
Feb. 4	Increased the appropriation for plant expansion by $7,000.
10	Paid the dividend declared on January 10.
May 15	Sold 700 shares of treasury stock for $16,100 and reduced the treasury stock appropriation by $12,600.
Oct. 10	Declared a 5% stock dividend on the shares outstanding to stockholders of record on October 30. The dividend will be distributed on November 10. Fair market value on the date of declaration was $22 per share.
Nov. 10	Issued the stock dividend declared on October 10.
Dec. 31	Net income for the year amounted to $42,700. Closed the Income Summary account to Retained Earnings.

INSTRUCTIONS

a Prepare journal entries to record Carlson's transactions.

b Prepare the stockholders' equity section of Carlson's December 31 balance sheet.

c Management is contemplating a change in dividend policy. Suppose you owned 300 shares of Carlson and were given a choice between receiving (1) an annual cash dividend of $2.20 per share or (2) a 10% stock dividend at a time when the stock's fair market value was $22 per share. Which alternative would you prefer? Why?

P14-13 *Comprehensive stockholders' equity: Analysis and presentation (alternate to P14-8)*

On January 1 of the current year Dillard Enterprises reported a retained earnings balance of $3,315,000. The following information has been obtained from a review of the company's records.

1 On May 18 Dillard declared a cash dividend of $0.80 per share.

2 Stockholders' equity as of September 30 follows.

Common stock, $10 par, 5,000,000 shares authorized	$ 9,000,000
Paid-in capital in excess of par value	2,400,000
Retained earnings	3,545,000
	$14,945,000

3 On October 7 Dillard reacquired 45,000 shares of its own stock for $495,000. Thirty thousand of these shares were reissued on December 24 at $14 per share.

4 Another cash dividend of $0.80 per share was declared on December 30.

5 Net income for the fourth quarter of the year amounted to $520,000.

INSTRUCTIONS

a Compute Dillard's total net income for the current year.

b Compute the number of shares outstanding as of December 31.

c Determine the balance in the Retained Earnings account as of December 31.

d Prepare the stockholders' equity section of Dillard's December 31 balance sheet in good form. Dillard is required to restrict retained earnings for treasury stock purchases and discloses such restrictions in the footnotes to the financial statements.

e Compute the book value per share as of December 31. Round to the nearest cent.

P14-14 *Book value per share (alternate to P14-9)*

The stockholders' equity section of Granite, Inc., revealed the following information on January 1.

Preferred stock, $100 par value, 9% cumulative, callable at $106	$ 200,000
Common stock, $10 par value	400,000
Paid-in capital in excess of par value: preferred	12,000
Paid-in capital in excess of par value: common	1,900,000
Retained earnings	(552,000)
Total stockholders' equity	$1,960,000

Dividends in arrears on the preferred stock totaled $36,000.

INSTRUCTIONS

a Calculate the book value per share of both the preferred and the common stock.

b Calculate the book value per common share immediately after each of the following transactions and events, rounding to the nearest cent. Consider each item independently.

(1) An additional 10,000 shares of common stock were sold to the public for $24 per share.

(2) Net income for the year totaled $950,000; no preferred dividends were paid.

(3) Two thousand shares of common stock were purchased as treasury stock at $20 per share.

c Explain the meaning of book value per share to one of Granite's stockholders. Assume the stockholder has a weak accounting background.

CASE 14
THE PUB

During one winter evening at The Pub, the bartender overheard the following investment "maxims."

a Look for a corporation that buys its own stock as treasury stock. If the corporation is buying, you should be too.

b Look for a company that has the guts to report fully diluted earnings per share. Companies that do not must be hiding the facts.

c Look for a corporation that pays large cash dividends. A dollar today is worth two tomorrow.

d Look for a company that is about to split its stock. You'll receive some free shares.

e Look for a company whose book value per share exceeds the market price per share. You'll make a handsome profit when the stock market adjusts for the difference.

INSTRUCTIONS

Comment on the wisdom of each of these investment "maxims."

15 LONG-TERM LIABILITIES

LEARNING OBJECTIVES

After reading this chapter you should:

1 Be familiar with the basic differences between bondholders and stockholders and the implications of financing with bonds and stock.

2 Be aware of the characteristics of the different types of bonds, specifically, serial and debenture bonds, registered and coupon bonds, sinking-fund debentures, convertible bonds, and callable bonds.

3 Be able to account for bond issues, including those issued between interest dates.

4 Understand the factors affecting issue prices, including the distinction between contract and effective interest rates, premiums, and discounts.

5 Be familiar with the concept of present value, its role in determining issue prices, and the underlying computations.

6 Understand the need for amortization, the differences between the straight-line and effective-interest methods, and how to compute both.

7 Be able to account for bond retirements and convertible bonds.

8 Be able to account for mortgage notes.

9 Understand the growing importance of leases and the underlying differences between operating and capital leases.

CHAPTER 15

Businesses constantly need funds to finance their diverse activities. As we have shown in earlier chapters, funds may be obtained from various sources. For example, short-term projects and investments in current assets (e.g., inventory buildups) are typically financed by short-term credit such as accounts payable or notes payable and by the cash generated from profitable operations. These funding sources are not always adequate or satisfactory, however. Long-term projects such as an expansion of facilities or the addition of a new product line dictate the need for a more permanent source of capital. Imagine the difficulty of financing a new office complex with notes that had to be renewed every three months. Indeed, the prospect of scurrying around to secure the necessary credit four times a year for the next thirty or forty years is unappealing.

Generally speaking, long-term investments are financed by long-term capital. Examples of long-term capital include capital stock and various types of debt, such as bonds and notes. Bonds and notes are commonly encountered in practice and can vary in importance as a source of asset funding (see Exhibit 15-1).

Exhibit 15-1

Bonds and notes as a source of funding

Corporation	Bonds and Notes Outstanding (000 Omitted)	Net Long-Term Assets (000 Omitted)	Bonds and Notes as a Percentage of Net Long-Term Assets
Bic Pen Corporation	$ 1,709	$ 63,320	2.7%
Black and Decker Manufacturing	269,032	376,618	71.4
The Gillette Company	259,111	608,153	42.6
MGM Grand Hotels, Inc.	211,600	447,830	47.3
Mary Kay Cosmetics	2,366	59,066	4.0
Squibb Corporation	398,771	890,874	44.8

Note: *Data obtained from recent corporate annual reports.*

This chapter explores long-term liabilities with a concentration on bonds. Other long-term liabilities, specifically, mortgages and leases, will be considered as well.

BONDS

Suppose an automobile manufacturer decided to build a new plant to produce subcompacts. The plant's construction cost, estimated at $150 million, is probably more than a single lender is capable of supplying. The manufacturer therefore has two basic financing alternatives available: the issuance of additional shares of stock or the issuance of bonds. **Bonds** enable a borrower to split a large loan into many small divisible units. Each of these units (known as a bond) is essentially a note payable, that is, a written promise to pay a sum of money on a specified future date. Like capital stock, bonds are issued through an underwriter to the investing public. Once outstanding, bonds can be bought and sold on organized securities exchanges and are thus easily transferable.

Although stocks and bonds may seem somewhat similar, their holders have distinctly different rights. Stockholders are the owners of a corporation; bondholders, on the other hand, are creditors whose claims are classified as long-term debt on the balance sheet. To protect the bondholders' interests, the issuing firm usually appoints a *trustee*. The trustee, often a large bank, plays the role of a third party to monitor the issuer's adherence to stipulated terms of the bonds. For example, bond issues frequently permit dividends to stockholders only if certain working capital levels are maintained. If provisions relating to the bonds are violated, the trustee may initiate appropriate action. Such action may involve lawsuits or perhaps the seizure and foreclosure of any property pledged as collateral on the bond issue. The provisions of a bond issue are normally stipulated in an accompanying document called a **bond indenture.**

Exhibit 15-2 summarizes two further differences between bondholders and stockholders based on the creditor/owner relationship.

Exhibit 15-2

Differences between bondholders and stockholders

	Bondholders (Creditors)	**Stockholders (Owners)**
Claim on income	Bondholders receive interest and have a yearly fixed claim on income; interest must be paid regardless of the level of income and before other investors (e.g., owners) receive any return.	Stockholders are paid dividends subject to income levels and the discretion of the board of directors.
Claim in liquidation	Bondholders have a prior claim on assets in the event of bankruptcy.	Stockholders have a residual claim on business assets; in the event of bankruptcy, the owners have last claim on any proceeds generated from asset liquidation.

Financing with Bonds and Stock

Many factors must be evaluated when deciding whether to finance with bonds or stock. One of the most important considerations is that bond interest is deductible for federal income tax purposes, whereas dividends are not. To illustrate the tax effects of a financing decision, assume Greenlaw Corporation currently has 200,000 shares of common stock outstanding and must raise $2,000,000 for modernization of plant and equipment. Two alternatives are under consideration: (1) issue 100,000 additional shares of stock at $20 per share or (2) issue 12%, 20-year bonds. Management estimates that the company will have annual earnings of $800,000 before deducting bond interest and income taxes. The accompanying figures show earnings per share (EPS) for both alternatives.

	Issue 100,000 Shares of Common Stock	Issue 12% Bonds
Total financing needed	$2,000,000	$2,000,000
Earnings before interest and taxes	$800,000	$800,000
Less: Bond interest ($2,000,000 × 0.12)	—	240,000
Earnings before income taxes	$800,000	$560,000
Less: Income taxes at 40%	320,000	224,000
Net income	$480,000	$336,000
Common shares outstanding	300,000	200,000
Earnings per share of common stock	$1.60	$1.68

Observe that Greenlaw will report a relatively higher profit if common stock is issued ($480,000 vs. $336,000) since no interest is incurred. However, earnings per share will be lower (i.e., diluted) because of the additional 100,000 shares outstanding. In this particular case the use of debt will benefit the common stockholder.

If earnings fall substantially, the bonds can take their toll. Assume the same facts as before except that projected earnings before interest and taxes now amount to only $400,000. Earnings per share figures would appear as follows:

	Issue 100,000 Shares of Common Stock	Issue 12% Bonds
Total financing needed	$2,000,000	$2,000,000
Earnings before interest and taxes	$400,000	$400,000
Less: Bond interest ($2,000,000 × 0.12)	—	240,000
Earnings before income taxes	$400,000	$160,000
Less: Income taxes at 40%	160,000	64,000
Net income	$240,000	$ 96,000
Common shares outstanding	300,000	200,000
Earnings per share of common stock	$0.80	$0.48

EPS is now more attractive with common stock financing because of the bonds' large interest charge in relation to total earnings. By extending this example, we would see that businesses with high debt levels in weak or recessionary economies are prone to poor financial performance and perhaps bankruptcy. Simply stated, interest and principal payments must be made whether or not customers are coming in the front door. Both debt and equity financing are considered further in Chapter 19.

Types of Bonds

Bonds are issued by corporations as well as other entities such as the federal government, states, school districts, and local municipalities. These entities have varying financial needs and the bonds they issue appeal to different types of investors. As a result, many types of bonds are used in the fund-raising process. Consider, for example, the recent long-term liability disclosure of Anheuser-Busch Companies, Inc., in Exhibit 15-3.

Exhibit 15-3

Long-term liability disclosure of Anheuser-Busch Companies, Inc. (in millions)

Long-term debt	
9.90% notes maturing 1986	$100.0
16.50% guaranteed notes due 1988	100.0
11.25% guaranteed bonds due 1990	100.0
9.00% convertible subordinated debentures due 2005	100.0
Sinking fund debentures	390.0
Other long-term debt	27.3
	$817.3

A footnote accompanying the financial statements explained the following:

> *In November 1981, Anheuser-Busch Overseas Capital N.V., a wholly owned subsidiary of the company, sold $100.0 million of 16.5% guaranteed notes due November 1, 1988. The notes are guaranteed as to payment of principal and interest by Anheuser-Busch Companies, Inc.*
>
> *In October 1980, the company sold $100.0 million of 9.00% convertible subordinated debentures, due October 1, 2005. The debentures are convertible prior to maturity, unless previously redeemed, at a conversion price of $35.94 per share and are subordinated to all existing and future senior debt of the company. . . .*

While this illustration is somewhat technical, the following discussion should help to clarify the firm's balance sheet presentation.

Secured and debenture bonds

Many bonds are **secured;** that is, specific assets have been pledged as security for the bondholders should the issuing firm fail to meet its obligations under the indenture agreement. Virtually any type of property can be pledged. To illustrate, mortgage bonds are generally secured by property, plant, and equipment; collateral trust bonds by negotiable securities; and so forth.

In contrast to secured bonds, **debenture bonds** have no assets pledged as security. The marketability of debenture bonds is therefore based on the general credit of the issuing company. To sell debentures, the issuer must have a long period of substantial earnings as well as favorable prospects for future earnings and solvency. Many corporations, Anheuser-Busch included, have issued *subordinated* debentures, which rank behind other unsecured debt. If liquidation occurs, the holders of subordinated debentures are paid only if sufficient assets remain after settling the claims of other unsecured and secured creditors.

Registered and coupon bonds

Bonds can also be classified by their method of disbursing interest. Most of the bonds issued in recent years have been **registered bonds;** that is, the issuing company maintains a record of the purchaser's name and address. At the time interest is paid, the disbursing company simply mails a check to the bond's registered owner. Naturally, when registered bonds are sold, the issuing company must be notified so that interest can be paid to the proper party.

Interest payments on **coupon bonds** are handled in a different manner. Coupon bonds have small detachable coupons that are made payable to the bearer and correspond to each interest period. When one of the coupons falls due, it is detached by the bondholder and deposited at a bank for collection. By shifting the responsibility for collection to the bondholder and the bank, there is no need for the issuing company to maintain an up-to-date list of bond owners.

Other bond classifications

Many bond issues have a single maturity date for the entire issue. With **serial bonds,** however, bondholders are repaid in periodic installments over a number of years. For example, a company could issue $20 million of bonds in 1983 that begin to mature in 1993 at the rate of $4 million per year. This staggering of maturity dates allows investors (i.e., lenders) to select bonds that satisfy their cash flow needs.

Issuing companies often create a special fund to repay a bond issue. Cash is set aside each year and invested in income-producing securities. The periodic cash deposits plus the investment income are then used for repayment. Funds of this type are commonly termed **sinking funds** and, appropriately, the bonds are sometimes called **sinking-fund debentures.** Sinking funds will be discussed later in this chapter.

Similar to many preferred stocks, some bonds are **convertible** into common shares at the option of the bondholder. The conversion feature allows a creditor to exchange a security with fixed interest receipts for one whose increase in market value will be substantial should the issuing company enjoy high levels of profitability. Convertible bonds are also discussed later in the chapter.

Finally, many bonds are **callable** at the option of the issuing firm. Callable bonds permit the issuer to pay bondholders prior to the stipulated maturity date, a feature that is often exercised if funds become available at lower interest rates. In return for this feature, the issuer compensates the bondholder by setting a call price that normally exceeds the bonds' face value.

Accounting for Bond Issues

Accounting for bonds can be quite complex; no doubt you will see why as we proceed through the chapter. For this reason we will start with a very basic illustration, with modifications (and realism) being added along the way. Before doing so, however, two simple facts regarding bonds must be explained. First, all bonds have a *face value*, that is, a set amount to be repaid on the bond's maturity date. The face value is usually $1,000 or some multiple thereof. Second, bonds can be issued at any price; the price, in turn, is normally expressed as a percentage of face value. For example, a $1,000 bond issued at 97 will cost the buyer $970.

Given this information, assume that on January 1 Krill Corporation issued $500,000 of 10-year, 12% bonds at 100. Interest is payable semiannually on January 1 and July 1. The entry to record the issuance follows.

Jan. 1	*Cash*	*500,000*	
	Bonds Payable		*500,000*
	To record issuance of 10-year, 12% bonds		

The Bonds Payable account is classified in the long-term liability section of the balance sheet until one year prior to the maturity date. At that time the bonds become a current liability and are disclosed accordingly. An exception to this treatment occurs when bonds will be retired by using a sinking fund, which is a noncurrent asset. Bonds retired by the use of noncurrent assets continue to be classified as long-term liabilities until the date of maturity.

The first semiannual interest date is July 1. Interest of $30,000 ($\$500{,}000 \times 0.12 \times \frac{6}{12}$) will be disbursed to bondholders and is recorded as follows:

July 1	*Bond Interest Expense*	*30,000*	
	Cash		*30,000*
	To record semiannual interest on bonds		

Upon maturity Krill must repay the $500,000 it has borrowed. The entry to record the cash outlay and bond retirement is as follows:

(Year of Retirement)			
Jan. 1	*Bonds Payable*	*500,000*	
	Cash		*500,000*
	To record retirement of bonds		

Bonds issued between interest payment dates

The interest payment dates associated with a bond issue are printed on the face of the bond certificate. Bonds, however, can be issued at any time and issuance between interest dates is a frequent occurrence. To simplify record keeping, it is common practice to collect from the bond's purchaser any accumulated interest from the last interest date to the date of issue. The issuing firm can then pay a full period's interest to the bondholder on the next semiannual interest date without having to keep track of the date of sale. This practice is especially beneficial when a bond changes hands several times during a given interest period, otherwise necessitating the allocation of a single period's interest among the bond's various owners. As we will now show, the interest that has been collected is subsequently returned to the investor.

Continuing the Krill Corporation example, we assume the same facts as before except that the bonds are issued on May 1, four months after the printed interest date. The entry to record the issuance follows.

May 1	*Cash*	*520,000*	
	Bonds Payable		*500,000*
	Bond Interest Payable		*20,000*
	To record issuance of bonds plus collection of four months' accrued interest		

Krill has received \$520,000: the \$500,000 issue price plus \$20,000 of interest, which has accumulated from January 1 through April 30 (\$500,000 × 0.12 × $\frac{4}{12}$). The interest is recorded as a current liability because it is owed to the bondholders and will be returned on the first subsequent interest date.

When semiannual interest is paid two months later on July 1, Krill will record the following entry:

July 1	*Bond Interest Payable*	*20,000*	
	Bond Interest Expense	*10,000*	
	Cash		*30,000*
	To record semiannual interest payment		

Although six months' interest is being paid, remember that the company received four months' accrued interest on May 1. Thus Krill's actual expense is for May and June only and amounts to \$10,000 (\$500,000 × 0.12 × $\frac{2}{12}$).

Factors Affecting Issue Prices

Suppose a large corporation is in the process of issuing bonds that bear a 10% interest rate. In addition to receiving approval from the board of directors, the corporation must (1) obtain permission from the SEC, (2) have the bond certificates printed, and (3) have the bond issue publicized. All these procedures take time. Thus given the dynamic nature of our economy, the original 10% interest rate may or may not be attractive to investors by the time the bonds are actually issued. Investors may therefore be willing to pay more or less than the bond's face value to secure a particular holding.

To illustrate, assume the going rate of interest is presently 11%. The corporation attempting to market the 10% issue mentioned previously may encounter some difficulty, because investors can obtain higher yields elsewhere. To make the bonds attractive, the corporation could sell the issue for less than face value. In this manner a bondholder would still receive 10% interest as printed on the certificate (often called the **contract interest rate**); however, by lending the corporation a smaller amount, the investor's actual yield is increased. For example, if a \$1,000 bond was issued at 91, the above corporation would pay \$100 of interest (\$1,000 × 0.10) for the use of \$910. Thus the actual or **effective interest rate** is greater than 10%. In conclusion, bonds are frequently issued below face value when their contract interest rate is less than the interest rate prevailing at the time of sale.

Interest rates are but one factor affecting the issue price. Consider, for instance, bond issues of companies with poor earnings records. Suppose that Chrysler Corporation issued 11% bonds at a time when the going rate of interest was 11%. Many investors might possibly be reluctant to purchase these bonds because of the automaker's past financial difficulties. Bondholders, of course, are concerned about timely interest receipts and the retirement of debt on the scheduled maturity date. As in the previous example, a drop in the issue price may be needed to make the bonds an attractive investment. When bonds are sold at less than face value, the difference between the issue price and face value is commonly referred to as a **discount.**

Naturally, the opposite situation can occur; that is, bonds can be issued at a price in excess of face value. If, for example, a company attempted to sell a 13% bond issue when the prevailing interest rate was 11%, demand could be overwhelming. Investors might be willing to pay more than face value to obtain the 13% rate, thus depressing the actual or yield rate. In this particular case the difference between the issue price and face value is called a **premium.**

Present value

The amount an investor is willing to pay for a bond is determined by three items: (1) the cash inflows connected with the bond issue, (2) the timing of the cash inflows, and (3) the rate of return acceptable to the investor. To explain, there are two cash inflows related to a bond investment: periodic interest receipts and the return of principal on the maturity date. Interest, of course, is a primary consideration; if the receipts are unattractive, the investor will turn elsewhere to find more profitable opportunities. The timing of these cash flows is also of importance. After an initial outlay investors prefer a rapid inflow of funds so that reinvestment or other projects can be pursued. Thus dollars received soon after an investment is made are looked upon more favorably than inflows occurring in later periods. Finally, all investors seek a return on their invested funds. The return they desire is dependent on a number of factors, one of which is risk. Different investments have different risk levels. Consider, for example, the purchase of a certificate of deposit at a bank (a safe investment) versus the acquisition of a race horse, which could produce large profits or large losses. Investors generally require higher rates of return as their exposure to risk increases.

A tool known as **present value** integrates cash flows, their timing, and the rate of return to determine quantitatively the amount an investor is willing to pay for a bond—or for that matter any investment. A brief introduction to present value appears in the Appendix to this chapter; a more detailed discussion is presented in Chapter 28.

Bonds issued at a discount

To illustrate the necessary accounting for bonds issued at a discount, assume Homestead Corporation sold $200,000 of 4-year, 9% bonds on January 1. The company received $193,529 because the going rate of interest in the market place was in excess of 9%. The entry to record the bond issue is:

Jan. 1	Cash	193,529	
	Discount on Bonds Payable	6,471	
	Bonds Payable		200,000
	To record sale of bond issue		

The bonds would appear on Homestead's balance sheet as follows:

Long-term liabilities		
Bonds payable	*$200,000*	
Less: Discount on bonds payable	*6,471*	*$193,529*

By deducting the Discount on Bonds Payable account from the bonds' face value, Homestead's net liability becomes $193,529, the amount borrowed on January 1. Stated differently, the bonds are shown at their **carrying value,** that is, face value less the unamortized discount.[1]

Meaning of a bond discount

As we discussed in Chapter 12, a discount represents future interest expense. This idea is best understood by examining the cash flows relating to the bond issue:

Cash to be paid		
Interest payments over 4 years ($200,000 × 0.09 × 4)	*$ 72,000*	
Face value at maturity	*200,000*	*$272,000*
Cash received		*193,529*
Total cost of borrowing		*$ 78,471*

Although Homestead is required to pay $72,000 of interest per the bond indenture, issuance at a discount has raised the cost of borrowing by $6,471 ($78,471 − $72,000). Not by accident, this increase corresponds with the balance in the Discount account as of January 1.

To reflect the higher borrowing cost, the discount must be periodically transferred to interest expense. This transfer occurs over the life of the bond issue and is commonly known as *discount amortization.* Two methods of amortization are frequently encountered in practice: the straight-line method and the effective-interest method.

Discount amortization: Straight-line method

Straight-line amortization allocates an equal amount of discount to each interest period. If we assume Homestead pays interest semiannually on June 30 and December 31, the discount will be amortized over 8 installments (4 years × 2 interest periods per year) of $809 each ($6,471 ÷ 8). The following entries are therefore necessary on each interest date.

Bond Interest Expense	*9,000*	
Cash		*9,000*
To record semiannual interest payment: $200,000 × 0.09 × $\frac{6}{12}$		
Bond Interest Expense	*809*	
Discount on Bonds Payable		*809*
To record semiannual discount amortization		

[1] Carrying value is defined differently for bonds issued in excess of face value; this definition will be presented shortly.

The two entries show that Homestead's interest expense is determined by the semiannual contractual payment of $9,000 and by amortization of the discount. Interest therefore amounts to $9,809 and grows to $78,472 ($9,809 × 8 periods) over the life of the bond issue. Notice that aside from a $1 rounding error, this figure agrees with the total borrowing cost computed on page 574.

In addition to affecting Interest Expense, the amortization entry also reduces the Discount account and forces an increase in bond carrying value. For example, Homestead's balance sheet disclosure on June 30 (six months after issuance) would be as follows:

Long-term liabilities		
Bonds payable	*$200,000*	
Less: Discount on bonds payable	*5,662**	*$194,338*

* $6,471 – $809.

By the time the maturity date is reached, the balance in Discount on Bonds Payable will be zero, which results in a $200,000 net liability.

Amortization procedures vary somewhat in practice. Many companies record amortization at the end of the accounting period rather than on each interest payment date. Furthermore, rather than have separate journal entries to record discount amortization and the payment of interest, some businesses use a compound (combined) entry. Homestead's entries on June 30, for instance, could have been recorded as follows:

Bond Interest Expense	*9,809*	
Discount on Bonds Payable		*809*
Cash		*9,000*
To record semiannual interest payment and amortization		

Discount amortization: Effective-interest method

Despite its widespread use and popularity, the straight-line amortization of bond discount has a conceptual flaw. Straight-line amortization recognizes an equal amount of interest expense each period. At the same time, however, the bond carrying value (i.e., the net amount owed) is growing. Many accountants object to the straight-line method because of this apparent inconsistency. That is, if increasing amounts are owed, the amount of interest expense recorded each period should increase throughout the bond issue's life.

This problem can be overcome by using the effective-interest method of amortization. The **effective-interest method** calculates interest expense as a constant *percentage* of bond carrying value; thus increasing carrying values are matched by increasing amounts of interest expense. Consistent with the method's name, interest computations are based on a bond's effective interest rate, not the contract rate. According to a ruling issued by the Accounting Principles Board, the effective-interest method must be used when it produces results that differ significantly from the straight-line approach.[2] Often, however, the two methods produce similar results within a given accounting period.

To illustrate discount amortization with the effective-interest method, we will use the same facts we used in the previous example; our initial approach, however, will be from a slightly different perspective. The facts are as follows:

A $200,000, 4-year, 9% bond issue.
Semiannual interest payable on June 30 and December 31.
Proceeds amounting to $193,529 resulting in a 10% effective interest rate.[3]

Recall that (1) the amount an individual or firm is willing to pay for an investment is termed present value and (2) *present value is in part dependent on the rate of return acceptable to the investor* (10% in this case). Now assume you recently inherited $193,529 from a wealthy relative. After lengthy negotiation you have agreed to open a savings account at a local bank and leave the money on deposit for the next four years. The bank will pay you $9,000 at the end of each six-month period and return $200,000 upon conclusion of the fourth year. Assuming that the $9,000 is withdrawn semiannually, your savings account would appear as follows for the first year:

	First 6-Month Period		***Second 6-Month Period***	
Beginning balance	$193,529		$194,205	
Add: Interest at 5%*	9,676		9,710	
	$203,205	+$676	$203,915	+$710
Less: Semiannual cash withdrawal	9,000		9,000	
Ending balance	$194,205		$194,915	

* *10% annual rate ÷ 2 semiannual interest periods.*

Observe that the account's balance is rising each period. Furthermore, the increase is equal to the difference between the semiannual interest of 5% and the cash withdrawal. By changing our perspective, we could say that the balance in the savings account corresponds to the carrying value of the bond issue. The increase in carrying value is caused by discount amortization, which, during the first six months outstanding, amounted to $676. These facts are reflected in the discount amortization schedule appearing in Exhibit 15-4.

[2] See "Interest on Receivables and Payables," *Opinions of the Accounting Principles Board No. 21* (New York: American Institute of Certified Public Accountants, 1971).

[3] The relationship between bond prices and the effective interest rate becomes apparent after studying the Appendix to this chapter.

Exhibit 15-4

Discount amortization schedule

Semiannual Interest Period	(A) Effective Semiannual Interest Expense (5% × Carrying Value)	(B) Semiannual Interest Payment ($4\frac{1}{2}$% × Face Value)	(C) Discount Amortization (A − B)	(D) Bond Discount Balance	(E) End-of-Period Bond Carrying Value (Face Value − D)
Issue date				$6,471	$193,529
1	$9,676	$9,000	$676	5,795	194,205
2	9,710	9,000	710	5,085	194,915
3	9,746	9,000	746	4,339	195,661
4	9,783	9,000	783	3,556	196,444
5	9,822	9,000	822	2,734	197,266
6	9,863	9,000	863	1,871	198,129
7	9,906	9,000	906	965	199,035
8	9,965*	9,000	965	—	200,000

*Difference due to rounding.

A review of the exhibit reveals that interest expense and discount amortization increase each period, a direct result of applying a constant interest rate against a growing bond carrying value.

The journal entries for the effective-interest method are the same as those noted earlier for straight-line amortization; naturally, however, the amounts differ. Using information presented in the amortization table, the entries at the end of the first semiannual interest period would be as follows:

	Debit	Credit
Bond Interest Expense	*9,000*	
Cash		*9,000*
To record semiannual interest payment		
Bond Interest Expense	*676*	
Discount on Bonds Payable		*676*
To record semiannual discount amortization		

Bonds issued at a premium

Bonds are sold at a premium when their contract interest rate exceeds the prevailing market rate for bonds of a similar grade. Why? Simply stated, investors are willing to pay more than face value to obtain a higher rate of return. To illustrate the proper accounting, we will again use the Homestead Corporation example, with one modification. Assume that the $200,000, 9% bond issue is now sold for $206,734. The entry to record the bond issue is shown below:

		Debit	Credit
Jan. 1	*Cash*	*206,734*	
	Premium on Bonds Payable		*6,734*
	Bonds Payable		*200,000*
	To record sale of bond issue		

If Homestead were to prepare a balance sheet on January 1, the bonds would be disclosed as follows:

A STRANGE BREED OF BOND

Discount! Discount! Up to 70% off! Sound strange? Not really. In the very early 1980s a number of companies began to issue low-interest bearing, deep discount bonds. For example, an announcement proclaiming a new bond issue read: "$200,000,000. J.C. Penney Company, Inc. Zero Coupon Notes Due 1989."

A bond with no interest sounds like a car with no motor. But the next line of the ad started to make sense: "Price 33.247%." Buy about $330,000 worth of bonds now and collect $1 million in eight years. Check it out on the calculator, and it turns out that the effective interest rate is 14.25%.

In part the bonds are coming to market because they have distinct advantages for the borrower. The Penney "zero coupon bond"—the first of its kind—is just the logical result of the trend to deep discount bonds triggered by sky-high interest rates. By offering buyers 6% and 7% bonds selling at discounts of between 40% and 55%, companies like Martin Marietta, Northwest Industries, Cities Service, and Alcoa have been able to cut in half the cash flow burden on borrowings with a face value of over $2 billion. Zero coupon bonds eliminated that cash flow burden altogether.

"You issue a zero coupon bond for eight years and for the whole time you don't have to worry about one penny of interest on the debt," says Denis Taura, a partner with Peat, Marwick & Co. The most significant—and frequently overlooked—advantage to deep discount and zero coupon bonds comes on the issuer's tax form. Anthony V. Dub, vice president of First Boston, the firm that underwrote J.C. Penney's highly successful zero coupon bond as well as several other deep-discount bonds, explains: "Under IRS regulations, the issuer amortizes the original issue discount over the life of the issue, which provides a tax deduction even though no interest is actually paid.

What's more, a company may actually pay less interest over time than it would with conventional issues. For example, with Penney's zero coupon issue, according to Dub, "If they had done a standard eight-year offering, they would have paid 14.9%. This paid 14.25%. Add to that the tax benefits and it was a real cost to Penney of 13.6%."

So, you say, if these bonds are such nifty little numbers, what took them so long to burst upon the scene? The fact is, zero coupon bonds aren't really a brand new idea. They were first conceived about a decade ago when increased quantities of money started flowing to the Middle East in exchange for oil. That worried investment houses because it says in the Koran that interest is prohibited. How to get around the problem? Why not zero coupon bonds? But just as the idea got rolling, religious experts in the Middle East found loopholes in the Koran to deny that those dollars you get every year from bonds are interest. Zero coupon bonds went back on the shelf. Off the shelf they came when long-term bonds became hard to sell at any price. The bond salespeople needed a gimmick and here it was.

SOURCE Adapted from "A Strange Breed of Bonds," Forbes, May 25, 1981, pp. 140, 142.

Long-term liabilities		
Bonds payable	*$200,000*	
Add: Premium on bonds payable	*6,734*	*$206,734*

The bond carrying value of $206,734 is Homestead's net liability and is calculated by adding the premium to the bonds' face value. Since only $200,000 will be repaid at maturity (per the bond indenture), the carrying value must be reduced over the life of the issue. The necessary reduction is achieved through the amortization process discussed earlier.

Meaning of bond premium

The meaning of a bond premium is best explained by examining the cash inflows and outflows relating to the bond issue.

Cash to be paid		
Interest payments over 4 years ($200,000 × 0.09 × 4)	*$ 72,000*	
Face value at maturity	*200,000*	*$272,000*
Cash received		*206,734*
Total cost of borrowing		*$ 65,266*

Notice that Homestead's cash payments for interest amount to $72,000; however, the total cost of borrowing is only $65,266. Thus a premium represents a payment by bondholders that reduces the issuing firm's interest expense, in this instance by $6,734 ($72,000 − $65,266). Observe that the reduction equals the balance in the Premium account on January 1. At this point we can conclude that a premium is the opposite of a discount given the premium's effect on interest expense and its disclosure on the balance sheet (i.e., an addition to bonds payable as opposed to a reduction).

Premium amortization

A bond premium can also be amortized by either the straight-line or effective-interest methods. If straight-line amortization is used, $842 of premium ($6,734 ÷ 8) will be written off during each semiannual interest period. The following entries are therefore required on June 30 and each interest date thereafter.

Bond Interest Expense	*9,000*	
Cash		*9,000*
To record semiannual interest payment: $200,000 × 0.09 × $\frac{6}{12}$		
Premium on Bonds Payable	*842*	
Bond Interest Expense		*842*
To record semiannual premium amortization		

The amortization entry reduces both the Premium and the Bond Interest Expense accounts, the latter resulting in a six-month borrowing cost of $8,158 ($9,000 − $842). Over the life of the bond issue, total expense will amount to $65,264 ($8,158 × 8 periods), which, except for a small rounding error, agrees with the borrowing cost calculated earlier. Finally, observe that as the premium becomes smaller, the bond carrying value decreases and will eventually become $200,000, the amount Homestead owes as of the maturity date. As partial evidence compare Homestead's January 1 balance sheet disclosure with that of June 30.

	Jan. 1	June 30
Long-term liabilities		
Bonds payable	$200,000	$200,000
Add: Premium on bonds payable	6,734	5,892*
	$206,734	$205,892

* $6,734 − $842.

We turn now to the effective-interest method. Applying a constant percentage against a declining carrying value yields decreasing amounts of interest expense each period. To illustrate, suppose the bond issue's proceeds of $206,734 came about because investors were willing to accept an 8% effective interest rate. Returning to our earlier method of explanation, assume that you have agreed to open a $206,734 savings account in exchange for a $9,000 payment at the end of each six-month period. The savings account would appear as follows for the first year.

	First 6-Month Period		Second 6-Month Period	
Beginning balance	$206,734		$206,003	
Add: Interest at 4%*	8,269		8,240	
	$215,003		$214,243	
		−$731		−$760
Less: Semiannual cash withdrawal	9,000		9,000	
Ending balance	$206,003		$205,243	

* 8% annual rate ÷ 2 semiannual interest periods.

The savings account's balance, which corresponds to the bond carrying value, declines each period because the 4% interest is less than the $9,000 cash withdrawal. The difference between these two amounts is equivalent to the premium amortization of the bond issuer. Homestead's premium amortization schedule is shown in Exhibit 15-5.

Year-end interest accruals

In previous examples we assumed that one of the semiannual interest dates coincided with the end of the issuer's fiscal year. When this situation does not occur, it is necessary to accrue interest from the last payment date until the end of the reporting period. Because premiums and discounts affect interest expense, amortization must be recorded as well.

To illustrate the necessary procedures, we will use data from the preceding example in which Homestead issued its bonds at a premium. Recalling that the interest payment dates were June 30 and December 31, assume

Exhibit 15-5

Premium amortization schedule

Semiannual Interest Period	(A) Effective Semiannual Interest Expense (4% × Carrying Value)	(B) Semiannual Interest Payment ($4\frac{1}{2}$% × Face Value)	(C) Premium Amortization (B − A)	(D) Bond Premium Balance	(E) End-of-Period Bond Carrying Value (Face Value + D)
Issue date				$6,734	$206,734
1	$8,269	$9,000	$731	6,003	206,003
2	8,240	9,000	760	5,243	205,243
3	8,210	9,000	790	4,453	204,453
4	8,178	9,000	822	3,631	203,631
5	8,145	9,000	855	2,776	202,776
6	8,111	9,000	889	1,887	201,887
7	8,075	9,000	925	962	200,962
8	8,038	9,000	962	—	200,000

the company's fiscal year now ends on August 31. Prior to preparing the financial statements, the following adjusting entries are necessary.

Aug. 31	*Bond Interest Expense*	*3,000*	
	Bond Interest Payable		*3,000*
	To accrue interest expense for 2 months		

		Straight-Line Amortization		Effective-Interest Amortization	
Aug. 31	*Premium on Bonds Payable*	*281*		*253*	
	Bond Interest Expense		*281*		*253*
	To amortize bond premium for 2 months				

The first entry recognizes the company's contractual obligation to disburse $9,000 of interest for each six-month period the bonds are outstanding. Because bondholders were last paid on June 30, Homestead has incurred and owes interest of $3,000 ($9,000 × $\frac{2}{6}$). Turning to the second entry, the Bond Interest Expense account must be credited to reduce Homestead's borrowing cost for the months of July and August. Semiannual amortization using the straight-line method amounted to $842 (see page 579); thus $281 ($842 × $\frac{2}{6}$) of amortization must be recorded. If the effective-interest method is utilized, the computation is slightly more complex. According to information appearing in Exhibit 15-5, Homestead would have recorded $731 of premium amortization upon conclusion of the first semiannual interest period and $760 at the end of the second period. Because two months of the second period have now passed, year-end amortization amounts to $253 ($760 × $\frac{2}{6}$).

On December 31, the next interest payment date, two entries are again necessary.

Dec. 31	*Bond Interest Payable*	3,000	
	Bond Interest Expense	6,000	
	Cash		9,000
	To record semiannual interest payment		

		Straight-Line Amortization		*Effective-Interest Amortization*	
Dec. 31	*Premium on Bonds Payable*	561		507	
	Bond Interest Expense		561		507
	To amortize bond premium for 4 months				

The first entry records the semiannual interest payment and another four months of interest expense (September 1–December 31). The Bond Interest Payable account is debited to eliminate the two months of interest owed as of August 31. The second entry records premium amortization as follows: straight-line, $561 ($842 × $\frac{4}{6}$); effective-interest, $507 ($760 × $\frac{4}{6}$). Similar procedures are then followed in subsequent reporting periods. Had the bonds been issued at a discount, the amortization entry would have required a debit to Bond Interest Expense and a credit to Discount on Bonds Payable.

Bond Retirement

Bonds are sold under the money and credit conditions prevailing at the time of issue. Frequently, in order to raise the necessary funds, the issuing company must incur high effective interest rates and make promises to bondholders that inhibit financing flexibility. Examples of such promises include restrictions on dividend payments and the maintenance of a certain working capital position (current assets minus current liabilities).

Most companies protect themselves and take advantage of changing market conditions (and possible lower interest rates) by including a call provision on bond issues, similar to the call feature associated with preferred stock. Issuers are permitted to reacquire the bonds at a stipulated percentage of face value. Bonds may be called and be replaced by an issue carrying a lower interest rate (known as **bond refunding**) or be retired and canceled (known as **bond retirement**).

In either case any difference between the bond carrying value and the call price is treated as a gain or a loss in the year when the call occurs. The gain or loss is reported on the income statement as an extraordinary item in accordance with guidelines issued by the Financial Accounting Standards Board (FASB).[4] This treatment may seem somewhat strange because in many instances the *unusual* and *infrequency-of-occurrence* tests for extraordinary items would not be met. However, because of market conditions existing in the early 1970s, companies were realizing sizable gains (sometimes amounting to millions of dollars) on the early retirement of debt. In an effort to call these gains to the attention of financial statement users, disclosure as an extraordinary item was authorized.

[4] See "Reporting Gains and Losses from Extinguishment of Debt," *Statement of Financial Accounting Standards No. 4* (Stamford, Conn.: Financial Accounting Standards Board, 1975).

To illustrate the proper accounting, assume Troup Manufacturing retired a $400,000, 8% bond issue that had an unamortized premium balance of $16,000. If the bonds were called at 106 on one of the semiannual interest dates,[5] Troup would record the following entry:

Bonds Payable	*400,000*	
Premium on Bonds Payable	*16,000*	
Loss on Bond Retirement	*8,000*	
Cash		*424,000*
To record retirement of bond issue at 106		

The retirement necessitates the removal of the bonds from the accounting records at their current carrying value ($416,000); thus Bonds Payable and Premium on Bonds Payable are both debited. The loss occurred because the amount paid was greater than the carrying value; the opposite situation would give rise to a gain. Overall the required accounting treatment is similar to that necessary for the retirement of a depreciable asset. That is, depreciation expense is first updated. Next, the asset's book value is removed from the records via both the asset and accumulated depreciation accounts. Finally, a gain or loss on disposal is computed by comparing book value with the proceeds from the sale.

Convertible Bonds

As we noted earlier in the chapter, some bonds can be converted into shares of common stock at the option of the bondholder. Because of the conversion feature, the value of the bond will usually rise as the market price of the issuing company's common stock increases. Should the market price of the stock remain static or even drop significantly, the bondholder will still receive periodic interest payments as well as the bond's face value on the maturity date. Conversion is therefore a desirable feature for an investor as well as the issuing company. The company benefits initially because investors are willing to accept lower interest rates in exchange for the conversion privilege. Furthermore, at conversion the company issues shares at an agreed-upon exchange price—a price per share that is typically higher than the market price of the stock at the time the convertible bond was issued.

If bonds are converted into common stock, the carrying value of the bonds must be transferred to the common stock accounts. For example, assume Maynard Corporation has the following convertible bond issue outstanding:

Long-term liabilities		
Bonds payable	*$80,000*	
Less: Discount on bonds payable	*4,000*	*$76,000*

Each $1,000 bond may be converted into 40 shares of $20 par-value common stock. If all of the bonds are converted, the following entry is needed.

[5] Prior to a recording of the retirement, journal entries are needed for related interest payments and premium (or discount) amortization.

Bonds Payable	*80,000*	
Discount on Bonds Payable		*4,000*
Common Stock		*64,000*
Paid-in Capital in Excess of Par Value		*12,000*
To record bond conversion into 3,200 shares of common stock (80 bonds × 40 shares per bond)		

In accordance with proper equity accounting, the Common Stock account is credited for the par value of the shares issued (3,200 shares × $20 par = $64,000). Thus the $12,000 difference between the carrying value ($76,000) and par value ($64,000) is recorded as paid-in capital in excess of par value. Notice that no gain or loss is recognized; the reason is that no earnings activity has occurred. The transaction is a simple exchange of long-term debt for shares of stock.

Bond Sinking Funds

In an effort to further protect the bondholders, companies are sometimes required to make periodic deposits to a special fund that is used for retiring the bonds at maturity. The fund, commonly called a **bond sinking fund,** is normally under the supervision of a trustee. The trustee is permitted to invest the company's deposits in income-producing securities. If all goes according to plan, the cash deposits plus the investment income should be sufficient to pay the bondholders the proper amount due. Any cash deficiencies would be supplemented by additional deposits; in contrast, excess cash is returned by the trustee to the contributing company.

The cash and securities in a sinking fund are restricted solely for use in bond retirement and cannot be used to meet current expenses or pay current liabilities. Sinking funds, therefore, are not current assets; instead they are disclosed in the long-term investment section of the balance sheet.

OTHER LONG-TERM OBLIGATIONS

In addition to bonds, other types of long-term obligations are frequently encountered in practice. These obligations include mortgage notes and leases.

Mortgage Notes

Mortgage notes are often used to finance the purchase of real estate. In order to secure the necessary funding, borrowers agree to pledge certain assets as collateral (security) for the note. Should the borrower fail to meet required payments or other specified conditions, the lender may foreclose on the assets pledged.

Mortgage notes are normally paid in monthly installments, with each installment representing both interest and partial payment on the note's principal. Although the total monthly payment usually remains constant, the allocation between interest and principal will differ each period. Virtually all mortgage notes, as well as other long-term loans, compute interest on the basis of the unpaid principal. Thus each successive monthly payment contains a declining interest charge because of the decreasing note balance. To illustrate, assume an entity secured a 12%, $200,000 mortgage on August 1. Based on monthly payments of $3,500, the allocation between interest and principal for payments of September through December would be as follows:

Payment Date	(A) Monthly Payment	(B) Monthly Interest (1% of Unpaid Note Balance)*	(C) Reduction in Principal (A − B)	(D) Unpaid Note Balance (Previous Balance − C)
Issuance date				$200,000
Sept. 1	$3,500	$2,000	$1,500	198,500
Oct. 1	3,500	1,985	1,515	196,985
Nov. 1	3,500	1,970	1,530	195,455
Dec. 1	3,500	1,955	1,545	193,910

**12% annual rate ÷ twelve 1-month interest periods. All figures are rounded to the nearest dollar.*

Leases

In recent years soaring interest rates have prompted businesses to look for different ways of financing the acquisition of long-term assets. Many companies have begun to shy away from an outright purchase in favor of some form of lease agreement. A **lease** is an agreement that allows one party, the *lessee,* to use the assets of another party, the *lessor,* for a stated period of time. Many different types of assets can be leased, such as machines, automobiles, buildings, computers, and airplanes.

Leasing is becoming very popular despite the fact that in the long run it is usually more expensive than purchasing. Some of the advantages of leasing from the lessee's viewpoint are the following:

1 Lease payments are 100% tax deductible in the year they are paid.
2 A lease arrangement usually permits 100% financing; that is, no down payment is necessary.
3 The risk of obsolescence on the leased asset rests with the lessor.

Operating and capital leases

There are two general categories of leases: operating and capital. Under an **operating lease** the lessee obtains the right to use leased property for a limited period of time and treats amounts paid under the agreement as expense. The lessor, in turn, recognizes amounts received as revenue and retains the leased asset on its balance sheet. The agreement signed by a person who rents a car for a day, a week, or some other short period of time is an example of an operating lease.

In contrast, many lease agreements provide usage rights for nearly the entire service life of the leased asset. Such agreements frequently contain a provision for the lessee to acquire the property at a bargain purchase price upon conclusion of the lease term. Leases that meet these or other specific criteria are known as **capital leases.**[6] With a capital lease the lessee is really

[6]See "Accounting for Leases," *Statement of Financial Accounting Standards No. 13* (Stamford, Conn.: Financial Accounting Standards Board, 1976).

acquiring an asset through an installment purchase plan. Yet prior to the mid-1970s, long-term lessees were not required to disclose the asset and obligation to future lease payments (a liability) on their balance sheets. This practice gave rise to the term *off-balance-sheet financing.* Under new regulations, however, the lessee must now record both the assets leased under a capital lease agreement and the liability to the lessor. Accounting for leases is a complex topic; our discussion represents only an introduction to the subject.

APPENDIX: PRESENT VALUE

As we noted in the body of this chapter, investors use the concept of **present value** to determine the amount they are willing to pay for a bond issue. To illustrate present value, assume that today is January 1 and you have $1,000 to invest. After studying various alternatives, you have narrowed the field to investments A and B. Both investments promise a $100 cash inflow during the next twelve months; however, as the following schedule shows, the timing differs.

	A	B
Cash outlay required on Jan. 1	$1,000	$1,000
Forecasted cash inflows		
Mar. 31	$ 25	
June 30	25	
Sept. 30	25	
Dec. 31	25	$100
	$100	$100

Although A and B both yield a 10% rate of return ($100 ÷ $1,000), most people would select investment A for two reasons. First, the future is generally unpredictable and full of uncertainty. Thus all other things being equal, a more rapid recovery of investment dollars helps to reduce the risk associated with an outlay. The dollars are in hand and the investor becomes less concerned about events that may prevent or inhibit the generation of returns. The second reason investment A is preferred is that money has a *time value;* that is, a dollar today is worth more than a dollar in the future. Why? Dollars received early in the year or in the early years of a long-lived project can be reinvested to generate additional returns. The inflows associated with investment A can, therefore, be put to work; nothing, however, can be done with the $100 from investment B until the end of the year.

Present value recognizes the time value of money and weights cash flows occurring in earlier periods more heavily than those that occur further in the future. Before we proceed, we must first examine a concept with which most of you are familiar—compound interest.

COMPOUND INTEREST AND PRESENT VALUE

Earlier in the text we introduced the computation of simple interest with the following formula:

interest = principal × rate × time

Notice that the interest is calculated on the principal only. In contrast, **compound interest** is computed on principal *and* on previously computed interest as well. For example, assume you deposited $100 in a savings account that pays 5% interest. If interest is compounded annually, the deposit will have grown to $110.25 by the end of two years.

	Year 1	Year 2
Beginning of year	$100.00	$105.00
Add: 5% interest	5.00	5.25*
End of year	$105.00	$110.25

* $105.00 × 0.05.

Approaching the same example from a slightly different perspective, suppose you are willing to accept a 5% return on your money. If an investment opportunity promises a $105 cash inflow at the end of one year, how much would you be willing to invest today to obtain that inflow? We hope you answered $100. Why? If you invest $100 today at a 5% interest rate, the investment will grow to the $105 you can receive. The $100 is termed the investment's *present value,* that is, the amount an investor is willing to pay to obtain a specified cash flow ($105) on a future date (one year from today) at a given rate of return (5%).

Observe that the foregoing question could have been phrased as follows: given a 5% rate of return, how much would you be willing to invest today to receive $110.25 at the end of two years? As before, the answer is $100.

RELATIONSHIP BETWEEN COMPOUND INTEREST AND PRESENT VALUE

By using a factor of $(1 + r)^n$, where r is equal to the interest rate and n equals the number of periods, we can illustrate the relationship between present value and compound interest. For compound interest the computations are as follows:

Beginning of Year 1	→		End of Year 1	→		End of Year 2
$100	×	$(1.05)^1$	= $105	×	$(1.05)^1$	= $110.25

Alternatively, the same results could have been achieved by the following calculation:

$$\$100 \times (1.05)^2 = \$110.25$$

In either case a present amount is compounded at a 5% interest rate and extended two years into the future.

For present value the situation is reversed; that is, a future amount is discounted and brought back to today. This process is diagrammed below.

End of Year 2	→	End of Year 1	→	Beginning of Year 1
$\$110.25 \times$	$\frac{1}{(1.05)^1}$	$= \$105 \times$	$\frac{1}{(1.05)^1}$	$= \$100$

In a manner similar to compound interest, discounting could have been illustrated as follows:

$$\$110.25 \times \frac{1}{(1.05)^2} = \$100$$

Observe that the factors used in the present value calculations $[1/(1.05)^1$ and $1/(1.05)^2]$ are the reciprocals of those employed in the compound interest example. Fortunately, tables have been developed that assist in factor computation; examples of the tables are given at the end of the book. An examination of Table 1 reveals a factor of 0.907 for a $1 cash flow occurring in 2 years at a 5% interest rate. Thus the appropriate present value computation becomes

$$\$110.25 \times 0.907 = \$100$$

PRESENT VALUE AND BOND PRICES

To illustrate the use of present value in the determination of bond prices, assume Franklin Corporation plans to issue $100,000 of 3-year, 10% bonds. Annual interest is paid in a single installment at the end of each accounting period; the prevailing interest rate in the economy is 10%. The present value of the bond issue's cash flows, using a 10% interest rate, is as follows:

Year	Cash Flow		Present Value Factor (Table 1)		Present Value
1	$ 10,000*	×	0.909	=	$ 9,090
2	10,000*	×	0.826	=	8,260
3	10,000*	×	0.751	=	7,510
3	100,000†	×	0.751	=	75,100
	Total present value				$99,960‡

*Annual interest payments: $100,000 × 0.10.
†Payment to retire the bonds at the end of Year 3.
‡Total should be $100,000; off $40 because of rounding errors in the computation of present value factors.

Ignoring the rounding error, notice how the present value coincides with the face value of the bonds. Why? Franklin's bonds pay interest equal to the prevailing market rate; thus investors are willing to pay 100% of face value for bond acquisitions.

Changing the example slightly, suppose the going interest rate for other similar bond issues is now 12%. Franklin's bonds, however, continue to pay 10%. By the use of factors for the prevailing 12% rate,[7] the present value becomes $95,220.

Year	**Cash Flow**		**Present Value Factor (Table 1)**		**Present Value**
1	$ 10,000	×	0.893	=	$ 8,930
2	10,000	×	0.797	=	7,970
3	10,000	×	0.712	=	7,120
3	100,000	×	0.712	=	71,200
	Total present value				$95,220

The bonds will be issued at a discount since investors can obtain a 12% return elsewhere. By receiving less than face value and still paying the same 10% contract interest, the effective rate is increased, in this case to 12%. Franklin's bonds have now become competitive for the limited funds of the investing public.

PERIODS LESS THAN ONE YEAR

Our example has focused on three 1-year interest periods. As we noted in the body of the chapter, bonds (and other obligations as well) pay interest on a more frequent basis, for example, semiannually, monthly, and so forth. The present value tables included at the end of the book can be used when the interest period is less than one year; however, a slight modification is necessary.

In order to select the proper present value factor, *the interest rate must correspond with the interest period.* To illustrate, we will continue the Franklin Corporation example. Observe that when the prevailing interest rate was 12%, the interest payment in Year 1 was multiplied by a factor of 0.893. Suppose that the payment schedule is now changed to a semiannual basis. As a result, the 12% annual rate must be halved to become aligned to the six-month period. Thus the present value of the *first year's* interest is calculated as follows:

[7] The prevailing rate is used in present value calculations because this rate is the lowest rate of return an investor is willing to accept.

6-Month Period	Cash Flow		Present Value Factor* (Table 1)		Present Value
1	$5,000	×	0.943	=	$4,715
2	5,000	×	0.890	=	4,450
	Total present value				$9,165

*6% interest rate.

Notice that the present value is higher when interest is paid semiannually rather than annually ($9,165 vs. $8,930). Why? Remember that present value is based, in part, on the time value of money. Semiannual interest payments generate earlier cash flows for the investor.

KEY TERMS AND CONCEPTS

bond 566
bond discount 573
bond indenture 567
bond premium 573
bond refunding 582
bond retirement 582
callable bond 570
capital lease 585
carrying value 574
compound interest 587
contract interest rate 572
convertible bond 570, 583
coupon bond 570
debenture bond 569
effective-interest amortization 575
effective interest rate 572
lease 585
mortgage note 584
operating lease 585
present value 573, 586
registered bond 570
secured bond 569
serial bond 570
sinking fund 570, 584
sinking-fund debenture 570
straight-line amortization 574

QUESTIONS

Q15-1 Are bonds normally used to meet current obligations and pay operating expenses? Explain.

Q15-2 Differentiate between the rights of stockholders and of bondholders.

Q15-3 A company is considering the issuance of either additional common stock or bonds to finance a plant expansion. Explain how earnings per share could benefit under the bond alternative despite the presence of additional interest expense on the income statement.

Q15-4 Differentiate between (1) secured and debenture bonds and (2) registered and coupon bonds.

Q15-5 Jupiter Corporation is issuing bonds that have an individual face value of $500. If the bonds are sold at 104, will Jupiter receive $104 for each bond? Explain.

Q15-6 How is interest handled on bonds that are issued between interest payment dates? Explain the purpose behind this accounting treatment.

Q15-7 Ricks, Inc., recently issued $400,000 of 9% bonds at 98.

a Were the bonds sold at a discount or premium?

b In all likelihood, was the prevailing rate of interest in the marketplace for similar bonds equal to, greater than, or less than 9%?

c Is the effective interest rate equal to, greater than, or less than the contract interest rate?

Q15-8 What is meant by the term "bond carrying value"? Will carrying value increase or decrease over the life of a bond issue when bonds are issued at a discount?

Q15-9 Differentiate between a bond discount and bond premium.

Q15-10 Differentiate between straight-line and effective-interest amortization. Which method is preferred? Why?

Q15-11 Discuss the proper accounting treatment for gains and losses incurred on the early retirement of bonds.

Q15-12 What is a bond sinking fund? Where is a sinking fund disclosed on the balance sheet?

Q15-13 Explain the concept of present value to someone with a limited business background.

Q15-14 Explain the relationship between compound interest and present value.

EXERCISES

E15-1 Monroe Company issued $300,000 of 8% bonds on January 1, 1984, for $282,000. The bonds are due on December 31, 1989, and pay interest semiannually on June 30 and December 31.

a Prepare the required journal entry to record bond issuance on January 1.

b Prepare entries to record the interest payment and discount amortization on June 30 and December 31, 1984. Monroe uses the straight-line method of amortization.

c Compute 1984 bond interest expense.

d Present the proper disclosure of the bond issue on Monroe's December 31, 1984, balance sheet.

E15-2 Arizona Enterprises issued $300,000 of 11%, 10-year secured bonds on May 1 of the current year. The bonds are dated May 1 and pay interest semiannually on May 1 and November 1. The following information was obtained from a review of the firm's general ledger.

Bonds payable	
May 1	*$300,000*
Premium on bonds payable	
May 1	*9,000*
Bond interest expense	
Nov. 1	*16,500*

Arizona records straight-line amortization at the end of the year on December 31.

a Prepare the journal entries that must be recorded on December 31.

b Compute total bond interest expense for the current year ended December 31.

c Determine Arizona's total cash outlay for interest during the current year ended December 31.

d Repeat parts (a), (b), and (c), assuming the bonds were originally issued at 98.

E15-3 Minotti Corporation issued $400,000 of 10% bonds on April 1, 1984, at 100 plus accrued interest. The bonds are dated January 1, 1984, and pay interest each June 30 and December 31.

a Prepare journal entries to record (1) bond issuance on April 1, 1984; (2) the first interest payment on June 30, 1984; (3) the second interest payment on December 31, 1984.

b Compute Minotti's 1984 bond interest expense.

E15-4 The Reese Corporation issued $200,000 of 8% bonds for $191,028 on January 1, 1984. The bonds pay interest semiannually on June 30 and December 31 and were priced to yield an effective interest rate of 9%.

a Prepare the required journal entry to record bond issuance on January 1.

b Prepare entries to record the interest payment and discount amortization on June 30 and December 31, 1984. Reese uses the effective-interest method of amortization; round to the nearest dollar.

c Compute 1984 bond interest expense.

d Present the proper disclosure of the bond issue on Reese's December 31, 1984, balance sheet.

E15-5 The Mumphrey Corporation issued $500,000 of 10% bonds at 98 on January 1, 1980. Interest is paid semiannually on June 30 and December 31. The bonds have a 10-year life from the date of issuance; Mumphrey uses the straight-line method of amortization. On July 1, 1984, the bonds were called at 106 and retired.

a Compute the amount of unamortized discount as of the call date.

b Present the entry necessary on July 1, 1984.

c Discuss possible reasons why Mumphrey exercised the call provision.

E15-6 On July 1 Pinella Corporation issued $500,000 of convertible bonds. Each $1,000 bond could be converted into 30 shares of the company's $10 par-value common stock. All the bonds were converted three years later when the unamortized bond discount stood at $9,600.

a Prepare the journal entry necessary to record the bond conversion.

b Explain why convertible bonds are attractive for (1) an investor and (2) the issuing company.

E15-7 On August 1 of the current year B. T. Taylor and Company acquired a building complex for $850,000, which included $120,000 of land. Taylor paid $200,000 down and secured a long-term mortgage note for the remaining balance. The note carried a 12% interest rate, which is computed on the unpaid balance at the beginning of each month. Taylor will repay the note in monthly installments of $8,500, with the first installment due on September 1.

a Prepare the journal entry to record Taylor's purchase on August 1.

b Prepare the journal entry to record Taylor's first payment on September 1.

c Compute Taylor's interest expense for the current fiscal year ended November 30. Round to the nearest dollar.

E15-8 Henry Company, a small family-owned corporation, is studying the possibility of signing a long-term lease for two new delivery vehicles. Walter Henry, the company's president, is skeptical of leasing and has always believed in the outright purchase of needed property, plant, and equipment.

a Discuss the advantages of leasing from Henry's viewpoint.

b Discuss the basic difference between an operating lease and a capital lease.

c Would Henry's lease probably be accounted for as an operating lease or as a capital lease? Why?

d Discuss the balance sheet impact, if any, of Henry's lease.

E15-9 Martha Wopat requires a 10% rate of return on all investments. She is contemplating an investment opportunity that will provide the following cash inflows:

At the End of Year	*Cash Inflow*	
1	$ 6,000	$14,000 (years 1–2)
2	8,000	
3	9,000	$14,000 (years 3–4)
4	5,000	
	$28,000	

a Observe how the investment results in two cash inflows of $14,000, each of which is spread over two years. Which of the $14,000 inflows is more attractive to Martha? Explain your answer.

b By using present value, compute the maximum amount Martha should be willing to pay for this investment.

E15-10 Johnnie Hui has the option of receiving (1) $400 at the end of each of the next two years or (2) $200 at the end of each six-month period for the next two years.

a Which alternative should Johnnie select? Why?

b Assuming Johnnie has a 12% rate of return, evaluate both alternatives by using present value computations.

c Comment on the consistency or inconsistency of your answers in parts (a) and (b).

E15-11 Rainbow Manufacturing is contemplating the issuance of $600,000 of 3-year bonds that have a contract interest rate of 9%. The bonds pay interest semiannually on June 30 and December 31. Assume a prevailing interest rate of 10% for similar bonds.

a Determine whether the bonds will be issued at a premium or a discount. Explain your answer. *Hint:* No computations are necessary.

b Determine the present value of the bond issue.

PROBLEMS

P15-1 ***Issuing stock versus bonds***

The Turner Corporation's balance sheet revealed the following:

8% bonds payable	*$200,000*
Common stock, $20 par, 20,000 shares issued and outstanding	*400,000*

Turner must raise $300,000 to finance the purchase of a new line of machinery. Two options are under consideration.

1 Issue 10% bonds.
2 Issue 5,000 additional shares of common stock.

Earnings of $250,000 before interest and taxes are anticipated. Turner is subject to a 40% income tax rate.

INSTRUCTIONS

a Compute earnings per share under each of the alternatives above. Round calculations to the nearest cent.
b Repeat part (a), assuming earnings before interest and taxes of $150,000 rather than $250,000.
c Briefly explain the results of your calculations.

P15-2 ***Bond accounting: Computational emphasis***

The Harrell Corporation issued $600,000 of 9% bonds on March 1, 1984. The bonds pay interest on March 1 and September 1 and mature in ten years. Assume the following independent cases:

Case A. The bonds are issued at 100.
Case B. The bonds are issued at 104.
Case C. The bonds are issued at 95.

Harrell uses the straight-line method of amortization.

INSTRUCTIONS

a Complete the following table.

	Case A	Case B	Case C
(1) Cash inflow on issuance date	______	______	______
(2) Total cash outflow through maturity	______	______	______
(3) Total borrowing cost over the life of the bond issue	______	______	______
(4) Interest expense for the year ended Dec. 31, 1984	______	______	______
(5) Amortization for the year ended Dec. 31, 1984	______	______	______
(6) Unamortized premium as of Dec. 31, 1984	______	______	______
(7) Unamortized discount as of Dec. 31, 1984	______	______	______
(8) Bond carrying value as of Dec. 31, 1984	______	______	______
(9) Net liability to investors as of Dec. 31, 1984	______	______	______

b Discuss possible causes of a bond premium.
c Discuss possible causes of a bond discount.

P15-3 ***Bond account analysis***

The Addison Company's December 31, 1984, balance sheet contained the following accounts:

9% debenture bonds	*$400,000*
12% secured bonds	*600,000*
Discount on debenture bonds payable	*15,000*
Premium on secured bonds payable	*24,000*
Bond sinking fund	*740,000*
Common stock, $10 par	*300,000*
Paid-in capital in excess of par value	*260,000*

A review of the company's accounts revealed that the following entries were made on December 31.

Bond Interest Expense	*2,500*	
Discount on Debenture Bonds Payable		*2,500*
Premium on Secured Bonds Payable	*3,000*	
Bond Interest Expense		*3,000*

Addison uses the straight-line method of amortization and records amortization only on December 31. The original life of each bond issue follows.

Debenture bonds	10 years
Secured bonds	15 years

INSTRUCTIONS

a Compute Addison's total long-term liabilities as of December 31, 1984. For those accounts that are not long-term liabilities, indicate their proper balance sheet classification.

b Both bond issues were issued on January 1 in their respective year of sale. Assuming no accrued interest, calculate Addison's proceeds from the sale of the debenture and secured bonds.

c Explain the necessity of discount and premium amortization.

d Is a bond discount similar to a cash discount as discussed earlier in the text? Explain.

P15-4 ***Bonds: Journal entries, issuance through retirement***

On April 1, 1983, Los Gatos Electronics issued $400,000 of 9%, 10-year bonds for $409,440 plus accrued interest. The bonds are dated February 1, 1983, and pay semiannual interest on February 1 and August 1.

On May 1, 1984, the entire bond issue was called at 102 plus accrued interest. Los Gatos uses the straight-line method of amortization and will amortize the premium over the 118 months the bonds are outstanding.

INSTRUCTIONS

a Prepare journal entries to record (1) the bond issuance on April 1, 1983; (2) the semiannual interest payment and premium amortization on August 1, 1983; (3) accrued interest and premium amortization on December 31, 1983.

b Compute total bond interest expense for 1983.

c Present the proper disclosure of the bond issue on Los Gatos's December 31, 1983, balance sheet.

d Prepare journal entries to record the semiannual interest payment and premium amortization on February 1, 1984.

e Prepare journal entries to record the bond retirement on May 1, 1984. *Hint:* Examine when amortization was last recorded.

P15-5 ***Bond computations***

On June 1, 1983, immediately after the issuance of $200,000 of debenture bonds, the balance sheet of Flanagan Corporation revealed the following accounts:

Current liabilities		
Bond interest payable		*$ 3,000*
Long-term liabilities		
Bonds payable, 9%, 10-year	*$200,000*	
Less: Discount on bonds payable	*6,490*	*$193,510*

The bonds are dated April 1, 1983, and pay interest semiannually on April 1 and October 1. Flanagan uses straight-line amortization and will amortize the discount over the 118 months the bonds are outstanding.

INSTRUCTIONS

a Determine the amount of cash Flanagan received from the bond sale.
b Calculate total interest expense for the year ended December 31, 1983.
c Compute bond carrying value as of December 31, 1983.
d On January 1, 1984, Flanagan called and retired 40% of the bonds at 103 plus accrued interest.
 (1) Compute the total cash paid by Flanagan upon exercising the call provision.
 (2) Compute the gain or loss on the call.
e Flanagan's bond issue consisted of debenture bonds that were backed by a sinking fund. All other things being equal, would an investor prefer (1) secured bonds or debenture bonds; (2) the use of a sinking fund or the lack of a sinking fund? Select a preferred alternative for each of parts (1) and (2) and briefly state the rationale behind your answer.

P15-6 ***Bonds with effective-interest amortization***

Kelly Manufacturing issued $500,000 of 4-year, 11% bonds on January 1 of the current year. The bonds pay interest semiannually on June 30 and December 31 and were priced to generate an effective yield of 12% to investors. The bonds were sold for $484,469.

INSTRUCTIONS

a Prepare the journal entry necessary on January 1 to record issuance of the bonds.
b Assuming Kelly uses straight-line amortization, compute (1) the annual cash outlay for interest; (2) annual discount amortization; (3) annual interest expense. Round calculations to the nearest dollar.
c Assuming Kelly uses the effective-interest method of amortization, prepare the following:
 (1) A discount amortization schedule similar in format to Exhibit 15-4. Round calculations to the nearest dollar.
 (2) Compound journal entries to record semiannual interest payments and discount amortization for the first year the bonds are outstanding.
d Why is the effective-interest method of amortization preferred over the straight-line method?

P15-7 ***Bonds: Multiple-choice questions***

The following multiple-choice questions relate to bonds. Select the best answer.

1 Montgomery Company plans to issue bonds that have a contract interest rate of 9%. If the prevailing interest rate for bonds of a similar grade is 10%, one could expect that:

a The bonds are not an attractive investment.
b The bonds will be sold at face value.
c The bonds will be sold at a premium.
d The bonds will be sold at a discount.

2 McNeil Corporation neglected to amortize $900 of bond premium during the current year. This error would:

a Understate total liabilities at the end of the current year.
b Overstate total liabilities at the end of the current year.
c Understate the current year's net income.
d Overstate the current year's net income.
e Result in more than one of the above, namely, ______, ______.

3 Korta, Inc., issued $500,000 of 10%, 10-year bonds on January 1, 1984, at 96. The bonds are dated January 1 and pay interest semiannually on June 30 and December 31. Which of the following is correct?

	Cash Paid for Interest in 1984	***1984 Interest Expense***
a	$48,000	$50,000
b	50,000	48,000
c	52,000	50,000
d	50,000	52,000
e	50,000	50,000

4 Tapper and Romo issued $400,000 of 12%, 10-year bonds and received proceeds of $415,000. The bonds were dated August 1, 1984, and were sold on August 1. Assuming the company records amortization at the close of its fiscal year on October 31, the 1984 amortization entry would include a credit to:

a Discount on Bonds Payable for $375.
b Interest Expense for $375.
c Premium on Bonds Payable for $375.
d Interest Expense for $1,500.
e None of the above is correct.

5 On June 1, 1977, Rankin Manufacturing issued $600,000 of 10-year, 8% bonds at 104. Interest is payable semiannually on June 1 and December 1. On June 1, 1984, 40% of the bonds were called in at 106 and retired. Rankin would realize:

a A loss of $7,200.
b A gain of $7,200.
c A gain of $11,520.
d A loss of $11,520.
e None of the above.

P15-8 ***Issuing stock versus bonds (alternate to P15-1)***

The Lassiter Corporation's balance sheet revealed the following:

10% bonds payable	*$300,000*
Common stock, $10 par, 50,000 shares issued and outstanding	*500,000*

Lassiter must raise $200,000 to finance an equipment modernization program. Two options are under consideration.

1 Issue 12% bonds.

2 Issue 10,000 additional shares of common stock.

Earnings of $400,000 before interest and taxes are anticipated. Lassiter is subject to a 40% income tax rate.

INSTRUCTIONS

a Compute earnings per share under each of the alternatives above. Round calculations to the nearest cent.

b Repeat part (a), assuming earnings before interest and taxes of $150,000 rather than $400,000.

c Briefly explain the results of your calculations.

P15-9 ***Bond accounting: Computational emphasis (alternate to P15-2)***

The Castle Corporation issued $800,000 of 12% bonds on April 1, 1984. The bonds pay interest on April 1 and October 1 and mature in twenty years. Assume the following independent cases:

Case A. The bonds are issued at 100.
Case B. The bonds are issued at 93.
Case C. The bonds are issued at 105.

Castle uses the straight-line method of amortization.

INSTRUCTIONS

a Complete the following table.

	Case A	*Case B*	*Case C*
(1) Cash inflow on issuance date	______	______	______
(2) Total cash outflow through maturity	______	______	______
(3) Total borrowing cost over the life of the bond issue	______	______	______
(4) Interest expense for the year ended Dec. 31, 1984	______	______	______
(5) Amortization for the year ended Dec. 31, 1984	______	______	______
(6) Unamortized premium as of Dec. 31, 1984	______	______	______
(7) Unamortized discount as of Dec. 31, 1984	______	______	______
(8) Bond carrying value as of Dec. 31, 1984	______	______	______
(9) Net liability to investors as of Dec. 31, 1984	______	______	______

b In Case B, is the contract interest rate greater than the effective interest rate? Explain.

c In Case C, suppose Castle failed to record the necessary amortization entry at the end of 1984. Will 1984 net income be overstated or understated? Explain.

P15-10 *Bonds: Journal entries, issuance through retirement (alternate to P15-4)*

On July 1, 1983, McCarty, Inc., issued $600,000 of 12%, 10-year bonds for $588,400 plus accrued interest. The bonds are dated March 1, 1983, and pay semiannual interest on March 1 and September 1.

On May 1, 1984, the entire bond issue was called at 103 plus accrued interest. McCarty uses the straight-line method of amortization and will amortize the discount over the 116 months the bonds are outstanding.

INSTRUCTIONS

a Prepare journal entries to record (1) the bond issuance on July 1, 1983; (2) the semiannual interest payment and discount amortization on September 1, 1983; (3) accrued interest and discount amortization on December 31, 1983.

b Compute total bond interest expense for 1983.

c Present the proper disclosure of the bond issue on McCarty's December 31, 1983, balance sheet.

d Prepare journal entries to record the semiannual interest payment and discount amortization on March 1, 1984.

e Prepare journal entries to record the bond retirement on May 1, 1984. *Hint:* Examine when amortization was last recorded.

P15-11 *Bond computations (alternate to P15-5)*

On April 1, 1983, immediately after the issuance of $400,000 of debenture bonds, the balance sheet of Dollar Corporation revealed the following accounts:

Current liabilities		
Bond interest payable		*$ 8,000*
Long-term liabilities		
Bonds payable, 12%, 10-year	*$400,000*	
Add: Premium on bonds payable	*14,160*	*$414,160*

The bonds are dated February 1, 1983, and pay interest semiannually on February 1 and August 1. Dollar uses straight-line amortization and will amortize the premium over the 118 months the bonds are outstanding.

INSTRUCTIONS

a Determine the amount of cash Dollar received from the bond sale.

b Calculate total interest expense for the year ended December 31, 1983.

c Compute bond carrying value as of December 31, 1983.

d On January 1, 1984, Dollar called and retired 60% of the bonds at 102 plus accrued interest.

(1) Compute the total cash paid by Dollar upon exercising the call provision.

(2) Compute the gain or loss on the call.

e Dollar's bond indenture provided for the establishment of a bond sinking fund. Explain the purpose of a sinking fund and its general method of operation.

P15-12 ***Bonds with effective-interest amortization (alternate to P15-6)***

Pleasant Oak Distributors issued $800,000 of 4-year, 11% bonds on January 1 of the current year. The bonds pay interest semiannually on June 30 and December 31 and were priced to generate an effective yield of 10% to investors. The bonds were sold for $825,821.

INSTRUCTIONS

a Prepare the journal entry necessary on January 1 to record issuance of the bonds.

b Assuming Pleasant Oak uses straight-line amortization, compute (1) the annual cash outlay for interest; (2) annual premium amortization; (3) annual interest expense. Round calculations to the nearest dollar.

c Assuming Pleasant Oak uses the effective interest method of amortization, prepare the following:
   (1) A premium amortization schedule similar in format to Exhibit 15-5. Round calculations to the nearest dollar.
   (2) Compound journal entries to record semiannual interest payments and premium amortization for the first year the bonds are outstanding.

d Can Pleasant Oak use the straight-line method of amortization for financial reporting? Explain.

CASE 15
DEXTER, INC.

The directors of Dexter, Inc., will meet in the near future to select one of two plans to finance the firm's entry into the market for small kitchen appliances. The final choice will be made between a common stock issue and a bond issue.

The company normally earns $6,000,000 before interest and taxes. However, Dexter has earned as little as $1,500,000 and as much as $7,000,000 before interest and taxes on its current resources. The company is subject to a 40% income tax rate. The assets of Dexter total $25,000,000. The assets are financed by $1,000,000 of current liabilities, $5,000,000 from a long-term loan, and stockholders' equity of $19,000,000. The long-term loan carries an 8% interest rate.

There are 2,000,000 shares of common stock outstanding. The company has paid a dividend of $0.75 per share for the past four years and expects to continue this policy in the near future.

The new investment, totaling $10,000,000, can be expected to earn an additional $1,500,000 annually before interest and taxes. However, business conditions will cause these earnings to vary anywhere from $500,000 to $2,000,000. The funds can be raised by issuing 800,000 shares of common stock at $12.50 a share or by a $10,000,000 bond issue that would bear a 14% interest rate.

INSTRUCTIONS

a The directors of Dexter, Inc., would like the following amounts to be calculated for each plan.
   1 The earnings per share at the expected income level for the company after the expansion has taken place.

2 The minimum after-expansion company earnings before interest and taxes that will permit the dividend rate of $0.75 per share to be covered by current earnings.

b Suppose the company decided to issue the bonds. Given the company's wide range of earnings, would a present stockholder have any inherent fears? Explain.

(CMA modified.)

16 LONG-TERM INVESTMENTS

LEARNING OBJECTIVES

After reading this chapter you should:

1 *Understand how to account for investments in bonds, including the initial investment, bond interest revenue, amortization using the straight-line and the effective-interest methods, and the sale of bonds before maturity.*

2 *Understand accounting for stock investments, specifically, the use and procedures associated with the lower-of-cost-or-market and the equity methods.*

3 *Be familiar with parent/subsidiary relationships.*

4 *Understand the reason for consolidated financial statements, including the concepts of intercompany transactions and elimination entries.*

5 *Be able to prepare consolidated financial statements immediately after acquisition for situations with a 100% controlling interest.*

6 *Understand how to account for minority interests.*

7 *Be able to account for subsidiaries acquired at more or less than book value.*

8 *Understand the differences between purchase and pooling-of-interests accounting.*

CHAPTER **16**

Investments in assets are a fact of life for all businesses. Companies that sell merchandise or render services must invest vast sums of money for needed inventories, machinery, equipment, and facilities. Frequently, when sufficient funds are available, a business will purchase the securities of other companies. As we saw in Chapter 7, for example, excess funds are commonly used to acquire various short-term investments. Recall that short-term investments are both *readily salable* and *intended to be converted into cash* within the current operating cycle or one year, whichever is longer.

Investments in securities that do not meet these criteria are classified as noncurrent (long-term) assets on the balance sheet. Long-term securities investments are made for a variety of reasons. Many companies desire the dividend or interest income associated with the securities. Furthermore, businesses often seek to obtain a sufficient number of shares to substantially influence or control the operations of other entities. This practice is followed by firms that want to expand activities in existing markets, diversify by adding new product lines, or ensure a steady source of raw materials and supplies. The foregoing points are illustrated in Exhibit 16-1, which lists several corporations along with selected controlled subsidiaries.

Exhibit 16-1

Corporations and selected subsidiaries

Corporation	*Primary Area of Identity*	*Subsidiaries*
Beatrice Foods	Food products	Culligan International Samsonite Corp.
General Mills	Food products	Kenner Products (toy manufacturer) Monet Jewelers Red Lobster Inns
Greyhound Corporation	Intercity bus transportation	Armour Food Company Motor Coach Industries (bus manufacturer)
Philip Morris, Inc.	Tobacco products	Miller Brewing Company The Seven-Up Company
Pillsbury	Food products	Burger King Steak and Ale Restaurants
Warner Communications	Recorded music and filmed entertainment	Atari, Inc. Cosmos Soccer Franklin Mint *Mad Magazine*

This chapter focuses on long-term investments in corporate securities. We will study investments in bonds and stocks, with a concentration on the latter. Accounting for stock investments can become quite complicated since proper record keeping depends on the percentage of shares owned.

INVESTMENTS IN BONDS

In the previous chapter we discussed bonds from the viewpoint of the issuing corporation. Now we turn our attention to bond accounting by investors. The major issues involved are recording the initial investment, treatment of interest and the related amortization of bond premium or discount, and the sale of bonds before maturity. As you will see, bond accounting for the investor is very similar to that practiced by the issuer.

Recording the Initial Investment

Bond investments are initially entered in the accounts at cost, that is, the purchase price plus brokerage fees and any other costs related to acquisition. The amount paid for a bond depends on the market price existing on the date of purchase. A bond's market price is influenced by a number of different factors, including the cash flows related to the bond issue, the timing of the cash flows, and the rate of return acceptable to the investor.

In addition to the purchase price and other incidental costs, bond investors may be required to pay accrued interest. Recall that when bonds are issued between interest dates, purchasers must pay any interest that has accumulated to the date of issuance. The corporation then reimburses the investor by returning a full period's interest on the next payment date. To illustrate, assume Foxmire Corporation purchased $200,000 of Harkness Corporation 10-year bonds on March 1. Additional facts relating to Foxmire's investment follow.

Date of bonds: January 1
Contract interest rate: 12%
Interest payment dates: June 30 and December 31
Purchase price: $194,100 plus accrued interest

The journal entry to record the bond purchase would be as follows:

Mar. 1	*Investment in Bonds*	*194,100*	
	Bond Interest Receivable	*4,000*	
	Cash		*198,100*
	To record investment in Harkness bonds		

Consistent with the proper accounting treatment for all assets, the Investment in Bonds account is established at cost. Although the bonds were purchased at an amount different from their face value, a separate discount (or premium) account is not used. Instead the discount (or premium) is commingled with the investment and will be amortized over the remaining life of the bond issue. Finally, observe that Foxmire paid $4,000 of accrued interest for the two months that have passed since January 1 ($\$200,000 \times 0.12 \times \frac{2}{12} = \$4,000$). The Bond Interest Receivable account is debited, because Foxmire expects to collect the interest from Harkness on June 30.

Bond Interest Revenue

As we illustrated in the previous chapter, bond discounts and premiums respectively increase and decrease the interest expense incurred by the issuing corporation. Similarly, discounts and premiums also affect the interest earned by the investor. In Foxmire's case, for example, the bonds were acquired below their $200,000 face value, thus giving rise to a $5,900 discount ($200,000 – $194,100). As the following computations show, the discount raises Foxmire's investment income above the total interest collected over the life of the bond issue.

Cash to be received		
Interest receipts over 10 years ($200,000 × 0.12 × 10 years)	*$240,000*	
Face value at maturity	*200,000*	*$440,000*
Cash paid for investment		
Purchase price	*$194,100*	
Accrued interest	*4,000*	*198,100*
Income from investment		*$241,900*

The $241,900 of investment income is deemed interest because it will be generated on money lent to Harkness.

Discount amortization

In addition to interest received, Foxmire must recognize $5,900 of income from the discount. This is accomplished by the amortization process described in Chapter 15. The proper procedures are slightly different, however, because of the manner in which the discount was initially recorded.

To illustrate, assume it is now June 30 and Foxmire receives the first semiannual interest payment of $12,000 ($200,000 × 0.12 × $\frac{6}{12}$). Because two months of this interest ($4,000) was recorded as Bond Interest Receivable on March 1, the following entry is necessary.

June 30	*Cash*	*12,000*	
	Bond Interest Receivable		*4,000*
	Bond Interest Revenue		*8,000*
	To record the receipt of semiannual interest		

The $8,000 credit to the revenue account shows that Foxmire has earned interest for only four months (March 1–June 30)—the length of time the company has owned the bonds.

At this same time Foxmire must amortize the discount to reflect the increase in income over the investment's life.[1] Recall that amortization may be recorded by using the straight-line method or the effective-interest method. Under the *straight-line method* an equal amount of discount (or premium) is written off during each interest period. In Foxmire's case, for example, the bonds have a life of 10 years. Because the investment was made two months after the bonds' issue date (January 1), the discount will be amortized over 118 months. Thus the following entry becomes necessary on June 30.

[1] As we discussed in Chapter 15, some companies record amortization only at the end of the accounting period.

June 30	*Investment in Bonds*	*200*	
	Bond Interest Revenue		*200*
	To record discount amortization		

To explain, Foxmire's monthly amortization amounts to \$50 (\$5,900 ÷ 118 months). Four months have passed since the bonds were acquired; thus amortization of \$200 (\$50 × 4 months) must be recorded to reflect the increase in income caused by the discount. Logically, then, the journal entry must credit the Bond Interest Revenue account. The debit to Investment in Bonds is not as easily understood. Keep in mind that Foxmire's discount is included in the Investment account. *For illustrative purposes,* however, assume that the discount had been recorded separately. The amortization entry on June 30 would therefore have had the following impact:

Account	**As of Acquisition**	**Amortization**	**As of June 30**
Investment in bonds	\$200,000		\$200,000
Less: Discount on bond investment	5,900	\$200	5,700
	\$194,100	\$200	\$194,300

The net result is a \$200 rise in the investment's carrying value. To record this increase in the accounting records, the amortization entry must appropriately debit the Investment in Bonds account. Over the life of the issue, then, the investment's carrying value will increase until the \$200,000 face value is reached. On the maturity date the carrying value will reflect the amount Foxmire will receive from Harkness in settlement of the latter's debt obligation.

Effective-interest method

As we discussed in the previous chapter, straight-line amortization is conceptually incorrect. Remember, the amortization of discount (or premium) in equal installments results in equal interest charges at a time when the issuer's bond carrying value (i.e., net amount owed) is increasing (or decreasing). To overcome this problem, we employed the *effective-interest method* to calculate interest expense as a percentage of carrying value. Thus changing carrying values were matched by changing amounts of interest.

The effective-interest method can (and should) be used with bond investments as well as bonds payable. Recall, however, that straight-line amortization is permissible if the results under the two methods do not differ significantly.[2] Effective interest amortization for bond investments is computed in a manner similar to that described for bonds payable. Specifically, the *effective* interest rate is applied against the investment's carrying value;

[2] See "Interest on Receivables and Payables," *Opinions of the Accounting Principles Board No. 21* (New York: American Institute of Certified Public Accountants, 1971).

the result, in turn, is compared against the interest received from the bond issuer.

To illustrate, assume Craig Corporation purchased $90,000 of Davidson Corporation 5-year, 11% bonds on January 1. Additional facts follow.

Date of bonds: January 1
Interest payment dates: June 30 and December 31
Purchase price: $86,688
Effective interest rate: 12%

If we liken the company's bond investment to a savings account at a local bank, the following events will occur:

An account will be opened for $86,688 (i.e., the present value of Craig's investment), and the money will be left on deposit for the next 5 years.
Craig will receive $4,950 ($\$90{,}000 \times 0.11 \times \frac{6}{12}$) at the end of each 6-month period.
The bank will return $90,000 (i.e., the maturity value) upon conclusion of the fifth year.

Assuming the bank payments of $4,950 are withdrawn semiannually, the savings account would appear as follows for the first year.

	First 6-Month Period		Second 6-Month Period	
Beginning balance	$86,688		$86,939	
Interest at 6%*	5,201		5,216	
	$91,889		$92,155	
		+$251		+$266
Less: Semiannual cash withdrawal	4,950		4,950	
Ending balance	$86,939		$87,205	

*12% annual rate ÷ 2 semiannual interest periods.

Observe that the account's balance is rising each period and that the increase equals the difference between the 6% semiannual effective interest and the cash withdrawal. By changing our perspective, we could say that the balance in the savings account corresponds to the carrying value of Craig's bond investment. The increase in carrying value is caused by amortization of the discount, which, during the first six months outstanding, amounted to $251. These facts are reflected in the discount amortization schedule appearing in Exhibit 16-2.

A review of the exhibit reveals that interest revenue and discount amortization increase each period, a direct result of applying a constant interest rate against a growing investment carrying value.

Premium amortization

Although our example has focused on the acquisition of bonds at a discount, similar procedures are followed for bonds purchased at a price in

Exhibit 16-2

Discount amortization schedule

Semiannual Interest Period	(A) Effective Semiannual Interest Revenue (6% × Carrying Value)	(B) Semiannual Interest Receipt ($5\frac{1}{2}$% × Face Value)	(C) Discount Amortization (A − B)	(D) End-of-Period Investment Carrying Value*
Date of purchase				$86,688
1	$5,201	$4,950	$251	86,939
2	5,216	4,950	266	87,205
3	5,232	4,950	282	87,487
4	5,249	4,950	299	87,786
5	5,267	4,950	317	88,103
6	5,286	4,950	336	88,439
7	5,306	4,950	356	88,795
8	5,328	4,950	378	89,173
9	5,350	4,950	400	89,573
10	5,377†	4,950	427	90,000

*Previous period carrying value plus C.
† Difference due to rounding.

excess of face value, that is, at a premium. The investment is still entered in the accounting records at cost. However, a premium has the opposite effect of a discount and reduces interest revenue over the life of the issue.

To illustrate, suppose a company purchased $200,000 of 10-year, 9% bonds at 103. Cash flows relevant to the investment follow.

Cash to be received		
Interest receipts over 10 years ($200,000 × 0.09 × 10 years)	*$180,000*	
Face value at maturity	*200,000*	*$380,000*
Cash paid for investment ($200,000 × 1.03)		*206,000*
Income from investment		*$174,000*

Notice that the average annual income, $17,400 ($174,000 ÷ 10 years), is less than the $18,000 of annual interest received. The premium must therefore be amortized by means of the entry below.

Bond Interest Revenue	*XXX*	
Investment in Bonds		*XXX*
To record premium amortization		

The debit records the reduction in interest revenue, while the credit lowers the Investment in Bonds account. Eventually, the Investment in Bonds account will approach the face value of the bonds acquired.

Sale of Bonds Before Maturity

Because of other investment opportunities or perhaps favorable conditions in the bond market, long-term bond investments are often sold prior to their scheduled maturity date. When the sale occurs, it is necessary to update amortization to the date of sale and to decrease the Investment in Bonds account. The first procedure is necessary to ensure that the correct amount of interest revenue has been recorded and also to determine the investment's carrying value as of the sale date.

To illustrate the necessary procedures, assume Bishop Corporation purchased $60,000 of 4-year, 11% bonds on January 1, 1982, for $61,937. The bonds are dated January 1 and pay semiannual interest each June 30 and December 31. The amortization schedule appearing in Exhibit 16-3 has been prepared by the corporation's accounting department, assuming a 5% semiannual effective interest rate.

Exhibit 16-3

Premium amortization schedule

Semiannual Interest Period	(A) Effective Semiannual Interest Revenue (5% × Carrying Value)	(B) Semiannual Interest Receipt ($5\frac{1}{2}$% × Face Value)	(C) Premium Amortization (B − A)	(D) End-of-Period Investment Carrying Value*
Date of purchase				$61,937
6/30/82	$3,097	$3,300	$203	61,734
12/31/82	3,087	3,300	213	61,521
6/30/83	3,076	3,300	224	61,297
12/31/83	3,065	3,300	235	61,062
6/30/84	3,053	3,300	247	60,815
12/31/84	3,041	3,300	259	60,556
6/30/85	3,028	3,300	272	60,284
12/31/85	3,016†	3,300	284	60,000

** Previous period carrying value minus C.*
† Difference due to rounding.

Suppose it is now April 30, 1984, and Bishop decides to sell the investment at 104 plus accrued interest. Amortization was last recorded on December 31, 1983; thus the accounts must be updated. If the investment had been retained, Bishop would have recorded $247 of semiannual amortization on June 30, 1984. Because four of the six months have now passed, the following entry is needed.

Apr. 30	*Bond Interest Revenue*	*165*	
	Investment in Bonds		*165*
	To record four months of premium amortization: $\$247 \times \frac{4}{6} = \$165$		

The investment's carrying value is therefore reduced to $60,897 ($61,062 − $165).

The bonds were sold at 104 plus accrued interest, the latter arising because the last interest date was four months ago. Thus total proceeds from the sale amount to $64,600.

Sale price ($60,000 × 1.04)	*$62,400*
Accrued interest ($60,000 × 0.11 × $\frac{4}{12}$)	*2,200*
Total proceeds	*$64,600*

The following entry is needed to record the sale and eliminate the investment from the books.

Apr. 30	*Cash*	*64,600*	
	Investment in Bonds		*60,897*
	Bond Interest Revenue		*2,200*
	Gain on Sale of Bonds		*1,503*
	To record sale of bond investment		

The gain arises because the bonds' selling price ($62,400) exceeds the investment's carrying value ($60,897); had the situation been reversed, a loss would have been recorded.

INVESTMENTS IN STOCK

In addition to purchasing bonds, companies can also invest in shares of stock of other entities. Like bonds, stock investments are initially entered in the accounts at cost, that is, the purchase price plus any related acquisition costs such as brokers' fees and transfer taxes. Subsequent to the initial recording, the accounting treatment to be used depends on the degree of control that can be exerted over the acquired company (known as the **investee**). Generally speaking, the degree of control is influenced by the percentage of the investee's common stock owned by the investor.

Three different accounting/reporting methods have been developed: (1) lower of cost or market, (2) equity, and (3) consolidated financial statements. The use of these methods is summarized in Exhibit 16-4.[3] The exhibit presents the general rules; there are exceptions, as we will soon note. The underlying details of the three methods along with the meaning of influence and control should become apparent in the upcoming presentation.

Exhibit 16-4

Use of accounting/reporting methods

Percentage of Investee Corporation Owned	**Degree of Influence over Investee**	**Accounting/Reporting Method**
Less than 20%	No significant influence	Lower of cost or market
Between 20% and 50%	Significant influence	Equity
Greater than 50%	Controlling interest	Equity with consolidated statements*

** If consolidated statements are prepared, another approach known as the* cost method *may be used. Because both the* cost *and* equity methods *produce the same consolidated result, we will assume use of the latter to simplify our discussion.*

[3] See "The Equity Method of Accounting for Investments in Common Stock," *Opinions of the Accounting Principles Board No. 18* (New York: American Institute of Certified Public Accountants, 1971).

Lower-of-Cost-or-Market Method

The **lower-of-cost-or-market method** is used to account for long-term stock acquisitions of investors who are unable to exercise significant influence over the investee corporation. The ability to exert influence over an investee may take several different forms, including ownership of a sizable percentage of the investee's outstanding common shares, representation on the investee's board of directors, participation in policymaking processes, interchange of managerial personnel, and technological dependency. In many instances the determination of whether an investor can influence an investee is not always clear. Thus to provide some uniformity in practice, the Accounting Principles Board has recommended that "an investment of less than 20% of the voting stock of an investee should lead to a presumption that an investor does not have the ability to exercise significant influence unless such ability can be demonstrated."[4]

Under the lower-of-cost-or-market method, stock investments are initially entered in the accounting records at cost. During the period any dividends received from the investment are recorded as revenue. Furthermore, changes in the value of the securities (subject to certain limits) are recognized and recorded in the accounts by comparing an investment portfolio's aggregate market value against its cost. If this cost-versus-market comparison sounds familiar, the technique is similar to that illustrated earlier in the text for short-term investments. Should you need a refresher, refer to Chapter 7.

To illustrate the lower-of-cost-or-market method, assume the following information relates to Savko Company.

> On January 1 Savko purchased 15,000 common shares of Fresno Manufacturing Corporation at $30 per share. Fresno has 150,000 shares of common stock outstanding.
>
> During the year Fresno reported net income of $290,000 and paid $120,000 of dividends.
>
> On December 31, the close of Savko's accounting year, Fresno's common stock had a market value of $27 per share.

Given that Savko owns 10% of Fresno (15,000 shares ÷ 150,000 shares), the following entries are necessary to record the previously mentioned transactions and events.

Investment by Savko

Investment in Fresno Manufacturing	*450,000*	
Cash		*450,000*
To record the acquisition of 15,000 shares of Fresno at $30 per share		

Announcement of Fresno's earnings

No entry necessary.

[4] Ibid., paragraph 17.

Receipt of cash dividends

Cash	12,000	
Dividend Revenue		12,000
To record the receipt of 10% of Fresno's dividends		

*Valuation at lower of cost or market on December 31**

Unrealized Loss on Long-Term Investments†	45,000	
Allowance for Decline in Market Value of Long-Term Investments		45,000
To reduce the investment in Fresno to market value: ($30 − $27) × 15,000 shares		

On the basis of the foregoing entries, Savko's investment would appear as follows on the year-end balance sheet.

Long-term investments		
Investment in Fresno Manufacturing	$450,000	
Less: Allowance for decline in market value of long-term investments	45,000	$405,000

Equity Method

When a company acquires a substantial percentage (greater than 20%) of the voting shares of a corporation, the acquiring company normally gains the ability to significantly influence both the financial and the operating policies of the investee. In such instances, unless there is evidence to the contrary, a material economic relationship is formed between the investor and investee and the **equity method** of accounting must be used.

Under the equity method long-term investments in common stock are initially recorded at acquisition cost. The Investment account is then increased or decreased to reflect changes in the retained earnings of the investee. Specifically, the Investment account is increased for the investor's share of reported investee net income and decreased for the investor's share of any investee net losses or dividends. The "investor's share" is based on the percentage of voting stock owned. Importantly, *the equity method focuses principally on the investee's retained earnings, not changes in the market value of the investee's stock.*

To illustrate the equity method, we will use the same facts we used in the previous example. Assume, however, that Savko purchased 45,000 shares of Fresno, resulting in a 30% ownership interest (45,000 shares ÷ 150,000 shares). Savko must now use the equity method, necessitating the following entries:

Investment by Savko

Investment in Fresno Manufacturing	1,350,000	
Cash		1,350,000
To record the acquisition of 45,000 shares of Fresno at $30 per share		

* For simplicity we will assume this is the only long-term investment owned by Savko.

† According to a ruling of the Financial Accounting Standards Board, unrealized gains and losses on long-term investments are not included in the current year's net income. Unrealized losses on long-term investments are shown on the balance sheet as a reduction of stockholders' equity.

Announcement of Fresno's earnings of $290,000

Investment in Fresno Manufacturing	***87,000***	
Investment Revenue		***87,000***
To record 30% share of Fresno's earnings: $290,000 × 0.30 = $87,000		

Receipt of cash dividends

Cash	***36,000***	
Investment in Fresno Manufacturing		***36,000***
To record receipt of cash dividends: $120,000 × 0.30 = $36,000		

Valuation at lower of cost or market

No entry required.

On the basis of these entries, Savko's investment would be reported on the year-end balance sheet at $1,401,000, as shown by the following T-account:

Investment in Fresno Manufacturing

Initial investment	*1,350,000*	*Share of dividend*	*36,000*
Share of net income	*87,000*		
(1,401,000)	1,437,000		

Observe that the $51,000 increase in the investment's carrying value (after the initial acquisition) corresponds to 30% of the increase in Fresno's Retained Earnings account [($290,000 net income − $120,000 dividends) × 0.30 = $51,000]. Also notice that Savko did not recognize any revenue at the time the dividend was received. Although this procedure may seem illogical, bear in mind that (1) dividends represent a distribution of earnings and (2) Savko has already recognized $87,000 of Fresno's net income. If the dividends were recorded as additional revenue, they would be double-counted. Appropriately, then, the Investment account is reduced because the dividend has decreased Savko's share of Fresno's net worth (i.e., retained earnings).

Rationale of the equity method

As we have shown on numerous occasions throughout this text, financial statements are used by a number of different parties (e.g., owners, managers, and creditors, to name just a few). To meet the varied needs of these parties, the statements must be objective and neutral. Should bias be present, some users may benefit at the expense of others. For example, if management can manipulate revenue recognition to show higher earnings, creditors and investors may make incorrect decisions regarding the financial health and well-being of the enterprise. It is in this light that the equity method was developed.

To illustrate, let's suppose a company owned 40% of an investee corporation. Also assume that the investor company was experiencing abnormally low earnings, while the investee was extremely profitable. The investor, with significant influence over investee operations because of its ownership position, could convince the investee to distribute unusually large amounts of dividends. Had the equity method not been developed, the investor would report the dividends as revenue. By influencing the investee, the investing company has essentially manipulated or controlled its own earnings and has introduced bias into the measurement process. In situations where the ownership interest is 20% or more, the equity method presents a better picture of financial performance. Why? The dividends do not affect investor earnings but instead are treated as a reduction in the Investment account.

Controlling Investments

Thus far we have studied the prescribed accounting practices for companies that have minimal effect (i.e., less than 20% ownership) and that have significant influence (i.e., between 20% and 50% ownership) on their investee corporations. We now turn our attention to a control type of relationship, that is, possession of more than 50% of the common shares outstanding. By exercising the voting rights connected with these shares, the investor can elect the board of directors of the investee corporation and thereby control the latter's policies and activities.

Legal versus economic entities

Given the relationship between the majority owner (termed the **parent**) and its majority-owned companies (termed **subsidiaries**), a question arises concerning the definition of the entity. For example, if Company A owns more than 50% of Companies B, C, and D, are four separate entities involved or is there just one large interwoven operation? To explore this issue more fully, we must further define the meaning of an entity. In our example we have four separate companies that operate as individual **legal entities**—units authorized by the relevant governmental authorities to conduct business. These companies engage in their own activities and prepare separate sets of financial statements. In essence, however, Companies B, C, and D are affiliated with Company A and together form a single **economic entity.** The relationship between the legal and economic entity is shown in Exhibit 16-5.

The economic entity is assembled to pursue the objectives of operational efficiency and profit. As we noted earlier in the chapter, for example, many companies have controlling interests in other corporations to ensure themselves of a steady source of raw materials and supplies. General Motors, for instance, owns an automotive frame manufacturer (Fisher Body) along with a firm engaged in providing financial services to customers and dealers (General Motors Acceptance Corporation). American Airlines owns Sky Chefs and AA Training Corporation, which respectively provide food service and pilot training (via simulators) to the airline industry.

These companies, along with many others, have decided to operate separate subsidiaries rather than merge all activities into a single massive legal entity. The reasons behind this practice often include a savings in income taxes, conformity with governmental regulation, and a reduction of risk. To

CONTROLLING INTERESTS ARE SOMETIMES UNWELCOMED

Corporations invest in and seek to control other companies for a number of different reasons, one of the most prominent being to increase profitability. While these acquisitions may bring joy to stockholders, corporate takeovers frequently strike terror into the hearts of management—especially of the company being acquired. Not only are there worried managers, but unions, customers, and local communities can also get agitated. After all, in addition to corporate titles, jobs and factories are at stake.

To avoid an unwanted and unfriendly takeover, some companies have developed takeover strategies, both from the offensive and defensive viewpoints. Northwest Industries (NI), for example, which encountered trouble trying to acquire B. F. Goodrich in the late sixties, has a firm policy of never participating in unfriendly takeovers. "You can't expect management to be motivated after you've gunned them to death," says an NI spokesman. And even on a friendly basis, NI will acquire only those companies whose managements agree to stay on. There is an even more important consideration: A friendly merger allows NI complete access to the books and figures in order to make a more thorough evaluation. A raid does not.

Turning to the defensive, Rubbermaid, Inc., has developed the following policy. If anyone gains controlling interest of the company's outstanding shares, the remaining minority stockholders have a right to redeem their shares at the better of three options: (1) the highest price the acquiring firm paid; (2) the highest price in the past eighteen months; (3) book value. Paying off stockholders in this manner, Rubbermaid figures, could wipe out whatever assets an unfriendly purchaser may acquire in a takeover of the company—a consideration aimed at discouraging such a move.

Unfriendly takeovers are troublesome. If some corporations persist in using their economic power to impose unfriendly takeovers on well-run companies whose stocks just happen to be bargains at the moment, then public opinion is going to demand that the government "do something." In the long run business isn't going to like what government does because it will strengthen the power of the state over business decision making. Although corporate acquisitions and takeovers serve a useful economic purpose, they are, indeed, not always welcomed or beneficial.

SOURCE Adapted from "The Mounting Backlash Against Corporate Takeovers," Forbes, *August 7, 1978, pp. 31–32.*

Exhibit 16-5

Legal versus economic entity

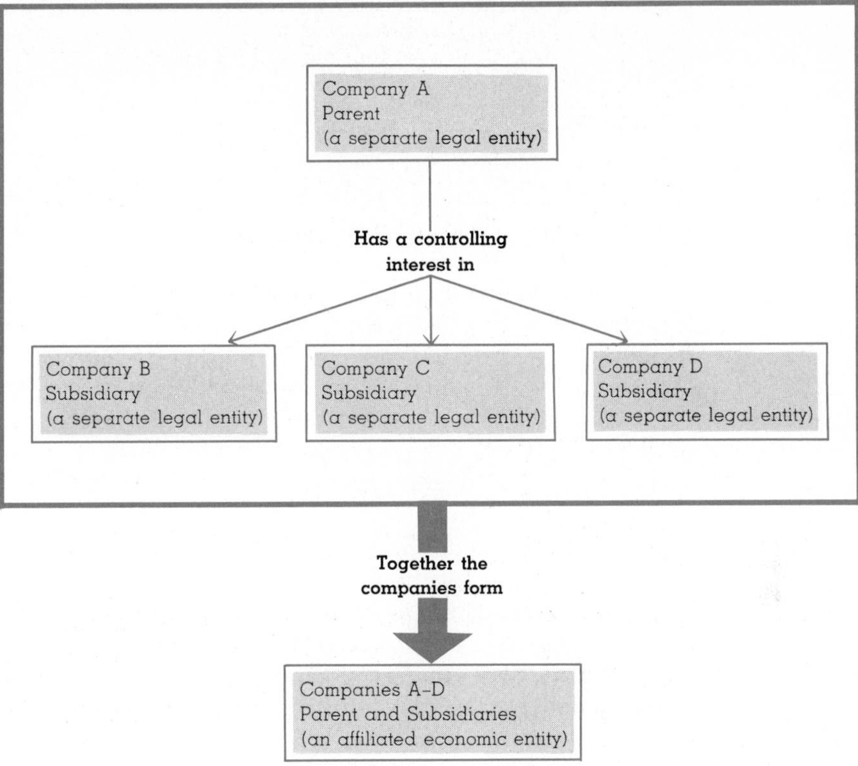

explain the latter, should a particular subsidiary encounter financial difficulties, the separate entity could be sold or liquidated without having a significant impact on the other companies in the corporate group. Depending on the nature of the subsidiary, new sources of supply may have to be found; generally, however, this is not a serious problem. Perhaps an analogy will help to further clarify this point. In essence, the subsidiary can be likened to a modular component of a complex electronic system such as a color television. Should the television need repair, it is much easier to fix or replace the module as opposed to overhauling the entire system.

Consolidated financial statements

Because of their separate legal status, a parent and its subsidiaries keep individual accounting records and prepare separate sets of financial statements. Consistent with the material presented earlier in the chapter, the parent establishes an account called Investment in Subsidiary Company and maintains the account under the equity method. To present the operating performance and financial condition of the single economic entity, the parent company also prepares a set of consolidated financial statements.

Consolidated financial statements present a combined picture of the parent and controlled subsidiaries, as if only one company existed. On a consolidated balance sheet, for instance, the Cash account shows the total cash owned by the entire affiliated group; the Accounts Payable account reveals the total amounts owed to trade creditors, and so forth. This same collective process applies to a consolidated income statement; for example, the Sales account represents the total sales revenues earned by a parent and its subsidiaries. Consolidated statements present a clear picture of the financial activities of the total enterprise, specifically, the activities that are under the control of the parent. Furthermore, the statements provide more insight than could be gained by examining the many separate statements of the various individual legal entities. For these reasons the parent company includes consolidated financial statements in the annual report to its stockholders. An example of a set of consolidated statements appears at the end of the book.

Intercompany transactions

Companies within an affiliated group frequently have transactions with one another. Parent companies often purchase materials and supplies from their subsidiaries. In addition, a parent commonly lends money to a subsidiary to help finance operations or capital improvement programs. Such transactions, referred to as **intercompany transactions,** present no special accounting problems for the individual entities involved. When consolidated financial statements are prepared, however, it is an entirely different story.

To illustrate, assume Parent Company owns a controlling interest of Sub Company. Sub is in need of funds and borrows $100,000 from Parent by signing a note payable. The transaction would appear on the balance sheets of both enterprises as follows:

PARENT COMPANY Balance Sheet	
Assets	
Notes receivable	$100,000

SUB COMPANY Balance Sheet	
Liabilities	
Notes payable	$100,000

Suppose now a consolidated balance sheet of the two companies is desired. If the two balance sheets were merely added together to reflect the financial condition of the combined entity, the results would be misleading. Why? The combined entity would report that it expects to both receive and pay $100,000 in the near future. Actually this disclosure is incorrect because the $100,000 represents a transfer of cash from Parent to Sub, both of which are in the same economic unit. The combined entity does not have a claim on any outside party nor does it owe an outsider. To properly reflect the impact of this transaction on the Parent/Sub affiliation, neither the note receivable nor the note payable should appear on the companies' consolidated balance sheet.

Work sheet and eliminations

To construct consolidated financial statements, the accountant first prepares a formal work sheet to combine the accounts of the parent and its subsidiary companies. Although the accounts are merged on the work sheet, combined accounting records are *not* established in a ledger.

As we will soon illustrate, most work sheets have two columns that are used for eliminations. **Eliminations** are required for intercompany items contained in the records of the parent and subsidiaries that do not appear in the consolidated financial statements, for example, the note receivable and note payable cited earlier. The elimination is performed by making an entry on the work sheet that debits intercompany credit balances and credits intercompany debit balances. To illustrate, the following elimination entry is needed for the $100,000 note.

Notes Payable (Sub)	***100,000***	
Notes Receivable (Parent)		***100,000***
To eliminate intercompany receivable and payable		

We stress that eliminations are made on the work sheet only; they are *never* entered in the accounts of either a parent or its subsidiaries. Entries into the accounts would formally cancel the transactions between the companies.

Consolidation upon acquisition

To illustrate the consolidation process, consider the balance sheets of Engle Corporation and Grant, Inc., appearing in Exhibit 16-6.

Exhibit 16-6

Balance sheets of Engle Corporation and Grant, Inc. (as of December 31, 1983)

	Engle	*Grant*
Cash	*$ 400,000*	*$ 25,000*
Accounts receivable (net)	*600,000*	*30,000*
Inventories	*800,000*	*40,000*
Property, plant, & equipment (net)	*1,500,000*	*230,000*
Total assets	*$3,300,000*	*$325,000*
Accounts payable	*$ 300,000*	*$ 60,000*
Bonds payable	*1,300,000*	*90,000*
Common stock	*1,000,000*	*100,000*
Retained earnings	*700,000*	*75,000*
Total liabilities & stockholders' equity	*$3,300,000*	*$325,000*

On January 1, 1984, Engle acquired 100% of Grant's outstanding stock from existing shareholders for $175,000—the stock's book value. Engle will record the acquisition as follows:

Jan. 1	***Investment in Grant***	***175,000***	
	Cash		***175,000***
	To record the acquisition of 100% of Grant, Inc.		

The only effect of this transaction on Engle's accounting records is the exchange of one asset, Cash, for another (Investment in Grant, Inc.). Grant's books are unaffected, because the exchange of outstanding shares among stockholders has no impact on the issuing firm. The balance sheets of the two companies immediately after the acquisition appear in the first two columns of the work sheet contained in Exhibit 16-7.

Exhibit 16-7

ENGLE AND GRANT
Consolidated Balance Sheet Work Sheet
January 1, 1984

Account	Engle	Grant	Intercompany Eliminations Debit	Intercompany Eliminations Credit	Consolidated Balance Sheet
Cash	225,000*	25,000			250,000
Accounts receivable (net)	600,000	30,000			630,000
Inventories	800,000	40,000			840,000
Investment in Grant	175,000			(a)175,000	
Property, plant, & equipment (net)	1,500,000	230,000			1,730,000
	3,300,000	325,000			3,450,000
Accounts payable	300,000	60,000			360,000
Bonds payable	1,300,000	90,000			1,390,000
Common stock: Engle	1,000,000				1,000,000
Common stock: Grant		100,000	(a)100,000		
Retained earnings: Engle	700,000				700,000
Retained earnings: Grant		75,000	(a) 75,000		
	3,300,000	325,000	175,000	175,000	3,450,000

*$400,000 original balance minus $175,000 acquisition cost.

The investment elimination

As Exhibit 16-7 reveals, an intercompany transaction must be eliminated in order to prepare the consolidated balance sheet. The shaded numbers in the first two columns show that the $175,000 investment by Engle (a 100% ownership interest) is represented by Grant's stockholders' equity accounts of Common Stock ($100,000) and Retained Earnings ($75,000). Stated differently, since Engle owns 100% of Grant, all common stock financing of the combined entity is provided by Engle's shareholders. Thus if the stockholders' equity accounts of the parent and subsidiary were simply combined on a consolidated balance sheet, the financing provided by Engle's stockholders and operations (i.e., retained earnings) would be counted twice. For these reasons the Investment account must be eliminated (via a credit because it has a debit balance) along with Grant's Common Stock and Retained Earnings accounts (via debits since they possess credit balances).

The result is the consolidated balance sheet, that is, the combination of Engle and Grant's individual balance sheets minus the elimination. The information appearing in the right-hand column of the work sheet is recast as shown in Exhibit 16-8.

Exhibit 16-8

ENGLE AND GRANT
Consolidated Balance Sheet
January 1, 1984

ASSETS		
Current assets		
Cash		$ 250,000
Accounts receivable (net)		630,000
Inventories		840,000
Total current assets		$1,720,000
Property, plant, & equipment (net)		1,730,000
Total assets		$3,450,000
LIABILITIES & STOCKHOLDERS' EQUITY		
Current liabilities		
Accounts payable		$ 360,000
Long-term liabilities		
Bonds payable		1,390,000
Total liabilities		$1,750,000
Stockholders' equity		
Common stock	$1,000,000	
Retained earnings	700,000	
Total stockholders' equity		1,700,000
Total liabilities & stockholders' equity		$3,450,000

The consolidated balance sheet reveals that the combined entity has $3,450,000 of assets, owes $1,750,000 to outside creditors, and has $1,700,000 of owners' equity provided solely by Engle Corporation.

Minority interest

To obtain control of a subsidiary, the parent need not acquire a 100% ownership interest as in the previous example. Acquisitions of more than 50% but less than 100% of the outstanding voting stock of other corporations are common. In such cases the parent company is said to obtain a majority interest, while the other owners of the subsidiary have a **minority interest.**

To illustrate the proper accounting for a minority interest, we will continue the Engle/Grant example. Recall that Grant had $100,000 of common stock and $75,000 of retained earnings as of December 31, 1983. Assume now that Engle purchases an 80% interest in Grant for $140,000, the purchase price corresponding to the book value of Grant's stock ($175,000 × 0.80 = $140,000). Engle will record the acquisition by the following entry:

Jan. 1	*Investment in Grant*	*140,000*	
	Cash		*140,000*
	To record the acquisition of 80% of Grant, Inc.		

The companies' ownership position is shown in Exhibit 16-9.

Exhibit 16-9

Illustration of minority interest

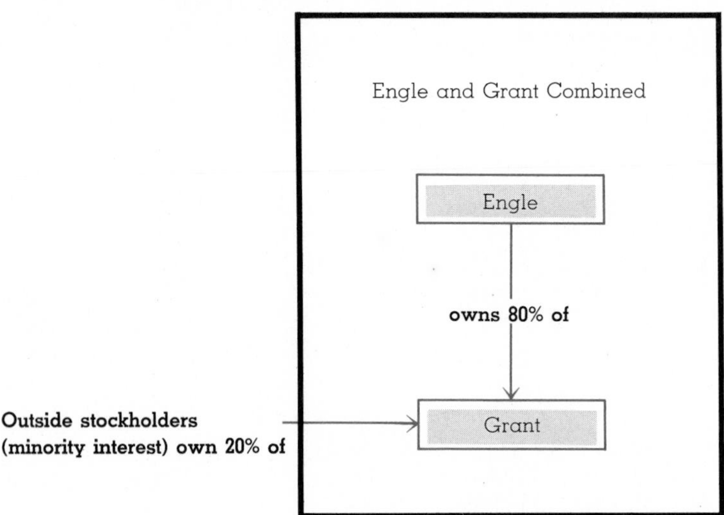

Since Engle owns 80% of Grant, 80% of the subsidiary's common stock and retained earnings balances are eliminated when consolidated financial statements are prepared. The remaining 20% of Grant's ownership represents the minority interest and is listed as such on the consolidated balance sheet (see Exhibit 16-10).

The work sheet contains two elimination entries. Entry (*a*) eliminates Engle's Investment account along with 80% of Grant's stockholders' equity, thus avoiding the possible double counting as described in the original example. Entry (*b*) transfers the remaining 20% of Grant's common stock and retained earnings into a new account entitled Minority Interest in Grant. The Minority Interest account appears on the consolidated balance sheet as follows:

Stockholders' equity	
Minority interest in Grant	*$ 35,000*
Common stock	*1,000,000*
Retained earnings	*700,000*
	$1,735,000

Exhibit 16-10

ENGLE AND GRANT
Consolidated Balance Sheet Work Sheet
January 1, 1984

Account	Engle	Grant	Intercompany Eliminations		Consolidated Balance Sheet
			Debit	Credit	
Cash	260,000*	25,000			285,000
Accounts receivable (net)	600,000	30,000			630,000
Inventories	800,000	40,000			840,000
Investment in Grant	140,000			(a) 140,000	
Property, plant, & equipment (net)	1,500,000	230,000			1,730,000
	3,300,000	325,000			3,485,000
Accounts payable	300,000	60,000			360,000
Bonds payable	1,300,000	90,000			1,390,000
Common stock: Engle	1,000,000				1,000,000
Common stock: Grant		100,000	(a) 80,000 (b) 20,000		
Retained earnings: Engle	700,000				700,000
Retained earnings: Grant		75,000	(a) 60,000 (b) 15,000		
Minority interest in Grant				(b) 35,000	35,000
	3,300,000	325,000	175,000	175,000	3,485,000

* $400,000 original balance minus $140,000 acquisition cost.

Accounting for minority interests in this manner provides added disclosure in the financial statements. The statement reader can now see that the controlling stockholders of the Engle/Grant combined entity have equity of $1,700,000 while outside stockholders of the Grant subsidiary have equity (i.e., claims against Grant) of only $35,000.

The consolidated balance sheets of some companies report the minority interest between the liability and stockholders' equity sections. Companies following this practice are stressing the limited role of the minority interest in ownership affairs.

Acquisition of subsidiary at more or less than book value

In all of our illustrations thus far, we have assumed the amount paid by the parent was equal to the book value of the ownership interest acquired. In the preceding example, for instance, Engle paid $140,000 to purchase 80% of Grant's $175,000 stockholders' equity ($\$175,000 \times 0.80 = \$140,000$). Normally, the acquisition cost of a subsidiary does not coincide with the subsidiary's book value.

Remember from Chapter 14 that book value represents a company's net assets (assets minus liabilities) and is calculated on figures extracted from the balance sheet—a cost-based financial statement. Given the impact of inflation in our economy, asset valuations and book value are frequently understated and do not reflect current market values. Adding to this problem, an ongoing business often has a number of "unrecorded assets" that a purchaser is willing to pay for. For example, a business's established reputation among clientele, its ability to earn greater-than-normal profits, and the company's top management team all enable a purchaser to begin operations in a favorable position. Finally, a business may have something of vital interest to a purchaser such as valuable patents or established product markets. Collectively, all the foregoing contribute to the fact that subsidiaries are frequently acquired at a price in excess of book value. Sometimes the difference between cost and book value is substantial. Caesars World, for example, reports a cost nearly $44 million in excess of book value on the purchase of its Caesars Palace hotel operation in Las Vegas.

An example

To illustrate the necessary accounting in this type of situation, assume Stafford Corporation acquired a 100% controlling interest in Trout, Inc., for $260,000 on December 31, 1983. The balance sheets of both companies immediately *after* the acquisition are shown in Exhibit 16-11.

Exhibit 16-11

Balance sheets of Stafford Corporation and Trout, Inc. (as of December 31, 1983)

	Stafford	Trout
Cash and other assets	$ 90,000	$ 70,000
Property, plant, & equipment (net)	140,000	180,000
Investment in Trout	260,000	—
Total assets	$490,000	$250,000
Accounts payable	$ 60,000	$ 50,000
Common stock	250,000	160,000
Retained earnings	180,000	40,000
Total liabilities & stockholders' equity	$490,000	$250,000

Stafford has paid $260,000 for a company with a book value (i.e., stockholders' equity) of $200,000. Why? Assume that during negotiations for the acquisition, Stafford's management found that Trout's property, plant, and equipment was undervalued by $35,000. In addition, Stafford was willing to pay an extra $25,000 because of favorable forecasts of Trout's future earnings and Trout's leadership position in its field of operation. To summarize, the $260,000 investment is represented by the following:

100% ownership interest	
Common stock: Trout	*$160,000*
Retained earnings: Trout	*40,000*
Increase in property, plant, & equipment (net)	*35,000*
Favorable earnings prospects, reputation, and so on	*25,000*
	$260,000

Thus in the preparation of a consolidated balance sheet, the following elimination entry is necessary.

Common Stock: Trout	*160,000*	
Retained Earnings: Trout	*40,000*	
Property, Plant, & Equipment	*35,000*	
Goodwill	*25,000*	
Investment in Trout		*260,000*
To eliminate Trout's stockholders' equity accounts against the investment account and to revalue the assets acquired		

To explain, the entry first offsets Trout's stockholders' equity accounts against Stafford's $260,000 investment. In addition, since Stafford paid an additional $35,000 to acquire the subsidiary's plant and equipment, the Property, Plant, & Equipment account is debited to reflect the increased cost. Finally, favorable earnings prospects, reputation, good management, and similar factors collectively give rise to the intangible asset *goodwill*, requiring a $25,000 debit to that account. The preceding treatment is in accordance with a ruling of the Accounting Principles Board, which states that "the excess of the cost of the acquired company over the sum of the amounts assigned to identifiable assets acquired less liabilities assumed should be recorded as goodwill."[5] Sometimes rather than debit Goodwill, a firm will use an account entitled Excess of Cost over Book Value in Subsidiary.

The net result of the elimination is the consolidated balance sheet appearing in Exhibit 16-12.

Book value in excess of cost

Our example has focused on the case of when a parent pays more than the book value of the subsidiary acquired. The opposite situation, that is, book value greater than cost, is not encountered as frequently in practice. Should it occur, however, the accounting treatment is similar to that just illustrated. The subsidiary's Common Stock and Retained Earnings accounts are offset against the parent's Investment account, and any specific subsidiary assets that may be overvalued are reduced. All remaining amounts are then credited to an account entitled Excess of Book Value of Investment in Subsidiary over Cost. The foregoing treatment is preferred

[5] "Accounting for Business Combinations," *Opinions of the Accounting Principles Board No. 16* (New York: American Institute of Certified Public Accountants, 1970), paragraph 87.

Exhibit 16-12

STAFFORD AND TROUT
Consolidated Balance Sheet
December 31, 1983

ASSETS		
Cash and other assets		$160,000
Property, plant, & equipment (net)		355,000*
Goodwill		25,000
Total assets		$540,000
LIABILITIES & STOCKHOLDERS' EQUITY		
Current liabilities		
Accounts payable		$110,000
Stockholders' equity		
Common stock	$250,000	
Retained earnings	180,000	
Total stockholders' equity		430,000
Total liabilities & stockholders' equity		$540,000

*$140,000 + $180,000 + $35,000 = $355,000.

rather than record "negative goodwill" (sometimes called badwill) in the financial statements.

Consolidated income statement

A consolidated income statement is prepared in much the same fashion as a consolidated balance sheet. Revenue and expense accounts of a parent and its subsidiaries are combined, and intercompany transactions are eliminated. The eliminations are necessary so that we can analyze the consolidated entity's profit- (or loss-) generating activities with outsiders as opposed to those activities that occur solely within the affiliated company network. As an example, consider a corporation engaged in the manufacture and sale of motion picture films. The corporation has established two separate entities: production and marketing. Production sells all its output to marketing, which, in turn, distributes the films to movie theaters and other outside establishments. It is apparent that marketing is the true generator of sales revenues for this corporation; production's revenues are strictly intercompany. Unless an elimination entry is made in the preparation of the consolidated income statement, the combination of the two Sales accounts would present an incorrect picture of corporate revenues and net income.

Two typical transactions that require an elimination entry are intercompany sales and interest on loans (or other obligations) between the parent and subsidiary. When analyzing these transactions, keep in mind that a sale by one affiliate is represented by a purchase or, if the merchandise is sold, by cost of goods sold on another affiliate's records. Similarly, interest revenue for one member of the consolidated entity becomes interest expense for another. The necessary eliminations that underlie the preparation of a consolidated income statement can become quite complex; they are more appropriately left for advanced accounting courses.

Unconsolidated subsidiaries

Consolidated financial statements strive to present a clear picture of an entity in which a parent exerts control over a subsidiary. As we noted on page 615, control is defined as the possession of more than 50% of an investee's outstanding voting shares. Despite meeting this ownership guideline, there are several situations where consolidation of parent and subsidiary financial statements is inappropriate. Sometimes subsidiaries are located in foreign countries where the ruling government has placed severe restrictions on the use or withdrawal of assets. In other cases the subsidiary may be in bankruptcy, with its assets under the supervision of trustees appointed by a court. In these instances the parent lacks control despite majority ownership. Therefore, consolidated financial statements are not prepared. Instead the subsidiary is disclosed on the parent's balance sheet as Investment in Unconsolidated Subsidiary and accounted for by using the equity method.

Consolidated statements may also be inappropriate when the operations of the parent and subsidiary differ significantly. Remember, the objective of the combined statements is to present meaningful information to users and analysts. The consolidation of two substantially different entities can result in a hodgepodge of different accounts. Practice does vary in this respect, however. For example, both Sears and J. C. Penney have separate subsidiaries to finance customer purchases and to sell insurance. Sears consolidates each of these subsidiaries; Penney consolidates neither.

Stock Investments: A Brief Overview

Although our presentation of long-term stock investments has focused on basic concepts only, you may have found this material to be somewhat detailed and complex. In an effort to briefly summarize the foregoing pages, we will study Childress Enterprises, which owns stock in the following companies:

Company	Type of Business Compared with Childress	Percentage of Investee's Voting Stock Owned by Childress
A	Similar	15%
B	Similar	30
C	Similar	60
D	Substantially different	80
E	Similar	100

From the above data, determine (1) the method used to account for each investee (i.e., lower-of-cost-or-market or equity) and (2) whether the investee's operations should be consolidated with those of Childress. The answers appear in Exhibit 16-13.

Exhibit 16-13

Methods of accounting/ reporting for Childress investees

Company	Method Used to Account for Investee	Consolidated with Childress?
A	Lower of cost or market*	No, lack of control
B	Equity	No, lack of control
C	Equity†	Yes, possess control
D	Equity	No, dissimilar businesses; however, practice may vary, like the J. C. Penney and Sears example
E	Equity†	Yes, possess control

**Less than 20% ownership.*
†See footnote in Exhibit 16-4.

The next part of the review is more difficult. Determine the proper disclosure of each investee on Childress's balance sheet. Keep in mind that in some cases the financial activities of the investee have been consolidated with those of Childress; in other cases they have not. The correct responses appear in Exhibit 16-14.

Exhibit 16-14

Disclosure of Childress investees

Company	Disclosure Form			Explanation If Appropriate
A	Investment in A	$XXX		
	Less: Allowance for decline in market value	XXX	$XXX	
B	Investment in B		$XXX	
C	Minority interest in C		$XXX	The Investment account has been eliminated along with 60% of the subsidiary's stockholders' equity; all that remains is a 40% minority interest.*
D	Investment in unconsolidated subsidiary D		$XXX	Not consolidated and thus no elimination due to dissimilar business operations.
E	—		—	The Investment account has been eliminated along with 100% of the subsidiary's stockholders' equity; no minority interest remains.*

**Subsidiary asset and liability accounts would be combined with those of Childress.*

An Addendum: Purchase Versus Pooling of Interests

In all of our illustrations the ownership interest in a subsidiary has been acquired for cash. When acquisitions are complex, the payment of cash is sometimes supplemented with notes payable and even shares of stock of the acquiring company. The form of the transaction is important when determining the proper accounting treatment. Most business combinations are treated as if a **purchase** has occurred. That is, (1) a parent has purchased an interest in a subsidiary by acquiring shares of the subsidiary's stock, and (2) the subsidiary's stockholders have terminated their investment by selling their shares to the parent.

Although the foregoing may appear clear-cut, an accounting problem arises when one company acquires virtually all the outstanding voting shares of another company in exchange for its own common stock. Specifically, has a purchase (and accompanying sale by the subsidiary's stockholders) really taken place? After all, most of the subsidiary's stockholders now own shares in the acquiring corporation. In effect, only an *exchange* of shares has occurred, and one could correctly conclude that the two companies have simply combined themselves to operate as a single economic entity. When this type of exchange transaction arises and certain other criteria are met, the combination of the two entities is deemed a **pooling of interests.**

As we noted in Chapter 13, the issuance of stock for noncash assets dictates that the transaction be entered in the accounts at fair market value. In a pooling, however, no purchase or sale occurs. Thus the Investment account is debited for the book value of the net assets (assets minus liabilities) acquired. That is, the assets and liabilities of the subsidiary are merely carried forward to the combined corporation, with no change in valuation.

Pooling and reported earnings

In comparison with the purchase method, business combinations accounted for as a pooling of interests usually result in higher consolidated earnings because of book value valuations and the policy of absorbing a subsidiary's earnings for the entire year. To explain the former, the purchase method frequently gives rise to goodwill because of an investment's cost exceeding the book value of the ownership interest acquired. In accordance with proper accounting for long-term assets, the goodwill must be amortized, thereby reducing net income. Furthermore, in compliance with a ruling of the Accounting Principles Board, specific assets acquired in a business combination that is accounted for as a purchase are assigned a cost equal to their fair market value on the date of acquisition.[6] Increased market values from inflation will result in larger depreciation deductions and depressed earnings figures. Neither of these situations would occur under a pooling because, again, assets are not revalued. Thus costs in excess of book value and market valuations would not be reflected in the accounts.

Turning to the second issue, that is, absorption of a subsidiary's earnings for the entire year, suppose Apex Company acquired a 100% interest in

[6] Ibid., paragraph 47.

Belmont Company on October 1, 1984. If the acquisition is deemed a purchase, Apex would consolidate Belmont's earnings from October 1 onward. Similar to any type of purchase, benefits accrue from the date of acquisition into the future. If the transaction is considered a pooling, however, a "purchase" does not occur. Because the two companies' figures are simply merged together, Apex is permitted to absorb Belmont's earnings for all of 1984, even though a combined relationship did not exist for the entire period. Assuming that Belmont was a profitable entity, Apex would report greater earnings under the pooling-of-interests method.

Pooling of interests in practice

Because of its favorable impact on earnings, the pooling-of-interests method has been widely used and, at times, abused. In the early 1960s a number of business combinations were accounted for as poolings when, in fact, the purchase method would have been more appropriate. For example, combinations involving the acquisition of a subsidiary in exchange for significant amounts of cash were entered in the accounts as poolings.

In 1970 the Accounting Principles Board issued strict guidelines that limited the use of the pooling-of-interests method. As we noted earlier in the discussion, for example, one of these guidelines dictates that an acquiring company must secure substantially all the voting stock of the other firm.

KEY TERMS AND CONCEPTS

bond investments 605
consolidated financial statements 617
controlling investment 615
economic entity 615
elimination entry 619
equity method 613
intercompany transaction 618
investee 611
legal entity 615
lower-of-cost-or-market method 612
minority interest 621
parent 615
pooling-of-interests method 629
purchase method 629
stock investments 611
subsidiary 615

QUESTIONS

Q16-1 Why do companies make long-term securities investments?

Q16-2 What is the proper accounting treatment for brokers' fees incurred on the purchase of corporate securities?

Q16-3 Putnam Company must pay $6,000 of accrued interest to acquire $100,000 of Zimmer Corporation bonds. If the bonds are purchased at 98, should Putnam debit the Investment in Bonds account for $104,000 ($98,000 + $6,000)? Explain.

Q16-4 Garcia Corporation recently amortized $3,000 of discount on a bond investment.

Determine the impact of the amortization entry on the following:

a Interest revenue for the year
b Interest received from the bond issuer
c The bond investment's carrying value

Q16-5 Discuss the differences in accounting for bond premiums from both the issuer's and the investor's viewpoint.

Q16-6 Louisville Machinery purchased $80,000 of Fidelity Union bonds and is contemplating use of the effective-interest method of amortization. Explain the underlying *theory* of the effective-interest method from an investor's point of view.

Q16-7 Discuss the differences between the lower-of-cost-or-market and equity methods when accounting for an investor's share of investee dividends and net income.

Q16-8 Benjamin, Inc., owns 30% of Baugh Corporation. During the current year Baugh paid total dividends of $40,000. Discuss (a) the proper treatment of the dividends on Benjamin's records and (b) the underlying reason behind that treatment.

Q16-9 Discuss the rationale underlying the equity method of accounting.

Q16-10 Distinguish between a legal and an economic entity.

Q16-11 Why are elimination entries needed in the preparation of consolidated financial statements? Are the eliminations recorded in the general ledger of the parent or of the subsidiary? Explain.

Q16-12 Explain why the acquisition cost of a subsidiary seldom agrees with the subsidiary's book value.

Q16-13 Dunn Corporation has a 70% interest in Sunny Day Distributing. Are there circumstances when consolidation of the two enterprises would not be appropriate? Explain.

EXERCISES

E16-1 Eastern Manufacturing acquired $300,000 of 12% bonds on March 1 at 100 plus accrued interest. The bonds are dated January 1 and pay interest each June 30 and December 31.

a Prepare journal entries to record (1) the bond acquisition on March 1; (2) the receipt of interest on June 30; (3) the receipt of interest on December 31.
b Compute Eastern's total interest revenue for the year ended December 31.

E16-2 Knoxville Corporation purchased $200,000 of 10% bonds on January 1, 1984, for $216,000. The bonds have an 8-year life and pay semiannual interest each June 30 and December 31.

a Prepare Knoxville's journal entry to record the bond purchase on January 1.
b Prepare entries to record the interest receipt and premium amortization on June 30 and December 31, 1984. Knoxville uses the straight-line method of amortization.
c Compute total interest revenue for 1984.
d Present the proper disclosure of the bond investment on Knoxville's December 31, 1984, balance sheet.

E16-3 On July 1, 1983, Tolbert Company purchased three different bond issues to be held as long-term investments. The following information is available.

Bond Issue	Face Value	Annual Interest Rate (%)	Remaining Years to Maturity	Purchase Price
1	$100,000	8%	5	$100,000
2	200,000	7	5	196,000
3	300,000	9	5	308,000

All bonds pay interest on June 30 and December 31. Tolbert uses the straight-line method of amortization.

a Compute the total interest received during 1983.

b Compute amortization to be recorded during 1984.

c Determine the amount of bond interest revenue to be reported on Tolbert's 1984 income statement.

d Show how the bond investments would appear on Tolbert's balance sheet as of December 31, 1984. Use proper amounts.

E16-4 Chicago Corporation acquired $300,000 of 9% bonds for $288,413 on January 1, 1984. The bonds pay semiannual interest on June 30 and December 31 and were priced to yield an effective annual interest rate of 10%.

a Prepare the required journal entry to record Chicago's investment on January 1.

b Prepare entries to record the interest receipt and discount amortization on June 30 and December 31, 1984. Chicago uses the effective-interest method of amortization and rounds to the nearest dollar.

c Compute 1984 bond interest revenue.

d Present the proper disclosure of the bond investment on Chicago's December 31, 1984, balance sheet.

E16-5 The Andrew Corporation purchased $400,000 of 10% bonds for $407,080 plus accrued interest on March 1, 1982. The bonds were dated January 1, 1982, and were scheduled to mature on December 31, 1991. Interest is paid semiannually on June 30 and December 31. On October 1, 1984, Andrew sold the bonds at 104 plus accrued interest.

a Compute the investment's carrying value as of June 30, 1984. Andrew uses the straight-line method of amortization.

b Prepare the journal entries necessary on October 1, 1984.

E16-6 On January 1 of the current year Rudder Company acquired 5,000 shares of Gibralter Corporation's common stock at $20 per share. The following information has come to your attention.

1 During the current year Gibralter generated net income of $75,000 and paid dividends totaling $24,000.

2 The year-end market price of Gibralter's common stock was $18.50 per share.

3 Rudder has no other long-term investments.

Assume Gibralter has 50,000 shares of common stock outstanding.

a Determine which method (lower-of-cost-or-market or equity) should be used to account for Rudder's investment.

b Present all appropriate journal entries for Rudder Company.

c Compute the year-end carrying value of Rudder's investment.

E16-7 On January 1 of the current year Missouri Company acquired 6,000 common shares of Hart, Inc., at $15 per share. The following information has come to your attention.

1. During the current year Hart generated net income of $42,000 and paid dividends totaling $18,000.
2. The year-end market price of Hart's common stock was $13 per share.
3. Missouri has no other long-term investments.

Assume Hart has 10,000 shares of common stock outstanding.

a. Determine which method (lower-of-cost-or-market or equity) should be used to account for Missouri's investment.
b. Present all appropriate journal entries for Missouri Company.
c. Compute the year-end carrying value of Missouri's investment.

E16-8 On June 30 Pulley Company acquired 90% of the outstanding common shares of Lopez Corporation for $270,000. The condensed balance sheets of the two companies immediately after the acquisition follow.

	Pulley	Lopez
Cash	$ 150,000	$ 90,000
Other assets	980,000	310,000
Investment in Lopez	270,000	–
	$1,400,000	$400,000
Liabilities	$ 300,000	$100,000
Common stock	600,000	240,000
Retained earnings	500,000	60,000
	$1,400,000	$400,000

a. Prepare any necessary elimination entries in general journal form.
b. Prepare a consolidated balance sheet for the two companies immediately after the acquisition. A work sheet is not required.

E16-9 On December 31 Thomas Company purchased 90% of Stark Corporation's outstanding common stock for $900,000. Stark's year-end balance sheet disclosed the following information:

Assets	$1,100,000
Liabilities	100,000
Common stock ($10 par)	750,000
Retained earnings	250,000

In negotiating the acquisition, management determined that the amounts appearing on Stark's balance sheet approximated current market values.

a. If Thomas and Stark are similar with respect to operations and financial structure, should consolidated financial statements be prepared? Why?
b. Calculate the difference between acquisition cost and the book value of the subsidiary interest purchased.
c. Calculate the minority interest. Explain (1) what minority interest represents and (2) where minority interest is reported in the financial statements.

E16-10 On October 1 of the current year Theresa Corporation acquired 6,000 shares of

Silver City, Inc., common stock for $132,000. Summarized information from the balance sheets of the two companies immediately after the acquisition follows.

	Theresa	Silver City
Net assets	$740,000	$220,000
Common stock		
100,000 shares ($5 par)	500,000	
10,000 shares ($10 par)		100,000
Retained earnings	240,000	120,000

Theresa's accountant is in the process of preparing the company's consolidated balance sheet.

a Compute the amounts to report for net assets, common stock, retained earnings, and minority interest on the consolidated balance sheet. Assume the book value of Silver City's net assets approximates fair market value.

b Compute the amount of goodwill that arose from Theresa's acquisition of Silver City. Explain how your answer was derived.

E16-11 Longman Company acquired 100% of the outstanding common shares of Pantego Electronics for $162,000. On the date of acquisition Pantego's balance sheet revealed the following information:

Cash and other current assets	$ 85,000
Property, plant, & equipment (net)	120,000
	$205,000
Accounts payable	$ 60,000
Notes payable	15,000
Common stock	100,000
Retained earnings	30,000
	$205,000

Additional information is as follows:

1 The fair market value of the property, plant, and equipment on the acquisition date totaled $135,000.

2 Pantego is expected to have higher-than-normal earnings in the next few years, a fact Longman considered when negotiating the $162,000 acquisition price.

3 Two months ago Pantego signed a note payable to Longman for $10,000. The note is still outstanding.

a The $10,000 note payable requires an elimination entry. Present the entry in general journal form and explain the implications of *not* making the elimination when preparing the consolidated financial statements.

b Prepare any other elimination entries that are necessary to consolidate the two companies' balance sheets.

c Discuss why a parent may be willing to pay an amount that differs from book value in the acquisition of a subsidiary.

E16-12 In December 1984 Petro Company acquired 95% of the outstanding common stock of Moustafa Corporation. To obtain its controlling interest, Petro issued 20,000 shares of $10 par-value common stock.

a Should this business combination be accounted for as a purchase or a pooling of interests? Why?

b Briefly explain the differences between a purchase and a pooling of interests in terms of (1) substance of the transaction and (2) probable reported earnings.

PROBLEMS

P16-1 ***Basic bond computations***

Accent Interiors purchased $400,000 of 12% bonds on June 1, 1984. The bonds pay interest on June 1 and December 1 and mature in 8 years. Assume the following independent cases:

Case A. The bonds are purchased at 106.
Case B. The bonds are purchased at 97.

Accent uses the straight-line method of amortization and has an accounting period that ends on December 31.

INSTRUCTIONS

a Complete the following table.

	Case A	Case B
(1) Cash outflow for acquisition on June 1, 1984		
(2) Total cash inflow through maturity (interest plus principal)		
(3) Total investment income over the life of the bond issue		
(4) Interest received in 1984		
(5) Amortization to be recorded in 1984		
(6) Interest revenue earned in 1984		
(7) Investment carrying value as of Dec. 31, 1984		

b Explain why premium amortization necessitates a credit to the Investment in Bonds account.

P16-2 ***Bond computations: Acquisition through sale***

On May 1, 1983, immediately after the purchase of $100,000 of 12% secured bonds, the balance sheet of International Enterprises revealed the following accounts.

Current assets	
Bond interest receivable	*$ 2,000*
Long-term investments	
Investment in bonds	*94,360*

The bonds are dated March 1, 1983, have a scheduled maturity date of March 1, 1991, and pay interest semiannually on March 1 and September 1. International uses the straight-line method of amortization.

INSTRUCTIONS

a Calculate the amount of cash International paid on May 1 to acquire the bonds.

b Calculate International's total interest revenue for the year ended December 31, 1983.

c Compute the investment's carrying value as of December 31, 1983.

d On February 1, 1984, International sold its investment at 103 plus accrued interest. Compute (1) the total cash received from the sale and (2) the gain or loss on the sale.

P16-3 ***Bond entries: Acquisition through sale***

On July 1, 1983, Kindel Corporation purchased $600,000 of 10%, 8-year bonds for $595,400 plus accrued interest. The bonds are dated March 1, 1983, and pay semiannual interest on March 1 and September 1. On May 1, 1984, Kindel sold half the bonds at 103 plus accrued interest. Kindel uses the straight-line method of amortization.

INSTRUCTIONS

a Prepare journal entries to record the following:
 (1) The bond investment on July 1, 1983.
 (2) The semiannual interest receipt and discount amortization on September 1, 1983.
 (3) Accrued interest and discount amortization on December 31, 1983.

b Compute total bond interest revenue for 1983.

c Present the proper disclosure of the bond investment on Kindel's December 31, 1983, balance sheet.

d Prepare journal entries to record the semiannual interest receipt and discount amortization on March 1, 1984.

e Prepare entries to record the bond sale on May 1, 1984. *Hint:* Examine when amortization was last recorded.

P16-4 ***Bond entries: Effective-interest method***

Lighting Unlimited purchased $400,000 of 4-year, 9% bonds on January 1, 1984, for $413,469. The bonds pay interest semiannually on June 30 and De cember 31 and were priced to generate an annual effective yield of 8% to investors. Lighting Unlimited rounds all calculations to the nearest dollar.

INSTRUCTIONS

a Prepare the journal entry necessary to record the bond acquisition, assuming the bonds are dated January 1.

b Assuming Lighting Unlimited uses straight-line amortization, compute (1) the annual amount of interest received, (2) annual premium amortization, (3) annual interest revenue.

c Assuming Lighting Unlimited uses the effective-interest method of amortization, prepare the following:
 (1) A premium amortization schedule similar in format to Exhibit 16-3.
 (2) Journal entries to record semiannual interest receipts and premium amortization for 1984.

d If Lighting Unlimited's fiscal year ended on October 31, prepare the necessary entries (assuming effective-interest amortization) to record (1) accrued interest on October 31, 1984, and (2) premium amortization on October 31, 1984.

P16-5 ***Lower-of-cost-or-market and equity methods***

The Sargent Corporation recently acquired a long-term investment in Worley, Inc. Worley has 50,000 shares of $10 par-value common stock outstanding. The following information is available.

July 18 Purchased 5,000 shares of Worley common stock at $15 per share.
Dec. 31 Received a copy of Worley's income statement disclosing net income of $40,000.
31 Worley declared and paid a cash dividend of $0.50 per share.
31 The market price of Worley's stock was $14 per share.

INSTRUCTIONS

a Which accounting method should Sargent use for its long-term investment in Worley, Inc.? Why should this method be used?

b Present Sargent's required journal entries. If no entry is needed for any of the foregoing items, explain why.

c Present the proper disclosure of the Investment account on Sargent's December 31 balance sheet.

d Repeat requirements (a), (b), and (c), assuming Sargent purchased 20,000 shares of Worley's stock at $15 per share.

P16-6 ***Long-term stock investment concepts***

Herrington Corporation, a manufacturer of heavy equipment, has long-term investments in different companies. Selected information about each company follows.

Company	*Percentage of Voting Stock Owned by Herrington*	*Other Information*
A	80%	
B	20	Operates a chain of loan companies.
C	100	
D	10	
E	70	Asset use is heavily regulated by a foreign government.

In order to prepare for the annual stockholders' meeting, Herrington's president has asked for a "crash course" in accounting for long-term stock investments.

INSTRUCTIONS

a Complete the following table.

	Company				
	A	*B*	*C*	*D*	*E*
(1) Does Herrington have a controlling interest in the company?	____	____	____	____	____
(2) What method should Herrington use to account for the investment (lower-of-cost-or-market or equity)?	____	____	____	____	____

(Continued)

	Company				
	A	B	C	D	E
(3) Should the company's financial statements be consolidated with those of Herrington?	___	___	___	___	___
(4) For those companies that are consolidated, does a minority interest appear in the consolidated financial statements?	___	___	___	___	___
(5) Are declines in the company's market value per share recognized in Herrington's financial statements?	___	___	___	___	___
(6) Would a share of the company's earnings be reflected in Herrington's financial statements?	___	___	___	___	___
(7) Would Herrington recognize a share of the company's dividends as revenue?	___	___	___	___	___

b Explain to Herrington's president the basic differences between (1) the lower-of-cost-or-market method and the equity method; (2) a consolidated and an unconsolidated subsidiary; (3) a majority interest and a minority interest.

P16-7 ***Straightforward consolidation***

For the past few years Green Distributing and Seth Distributing have been friendly business rivals. Although the companies are not affiliated, Green has borrowed money from Seth and vice versa. Part of this friendliness stems from the fact that the presidents of the two firms are brothers.

On December 31 of the current year Green acquired an 80% interest in Seth for $176,000 cash. The balance sheets of the two companies *prior to the acquisition* follow.

GREEN DISTRIBUTING

Cash	$250,000
Loan receivable from Seth	140,000
Other assets	300,000
Total assets	$690,000
Current liabilities	$160,000
Loan payable to Seth	110,000
Common stock	250,000
Retained earnings	170,000
Total liabilities & stockholders' equity	$690,000

SETH DISTRIBUTING

Cash	$120,000
Loan receivable from Green	110,000
Other assets	180,000
Total assets	$410,000
Current liabilities	$ 50,000
Loan payable to Green	140,000
Common stock	200,000
Retained earnings	20,000
Total liabilities & stockholders' equity	$410,000

INSTRUCTIONS

a Present Green's journal entry to record the acquisition of Seth.

b Prepare a consolidated work sheet similar in form to that illustrated in the text.

c Prepare a formal consolidated balance sheet for the combined entity.

P16-8 ***Consolidation and equity method***

On December 31, 1983, Brazos Oil Corporation acquired 100% of the outstanding stock of Val Verde Drilling Company for $650,000. Balance sheet information for the two companies immediately after the acquisition follows.

	Brazos	Val Verde
Cash	$ 98,300	$ 41,500
Accounts receivable (net)	112,500	57,600
Inventories	317,600	191,400
Investment in Val Verde	650,000	—
Land	60,000	12,750
Property, plant, & equipment (net)	566,100	306,950
Receivable from Val Verde	20,000	—
	$1,824,500	$610,200
Accounts payable	$ 142,000	$ 49,400
Taxes payable	39,700	13,800
Bonds payable	500,000	—
Payable to Brazos Oil	—	20,000
Common stock ($5 par)	800,000	—
Common stock ($10 par)	—	400,000
Retained earnings	342,800	127,000
	$1,824,500	$610,200

With the exception of land, the fair market value of Val Verde's assets and liabilities corresponded to the book value amounts as of the acquisition date. A recent appraisal indicated Val Verde's land was worth $65,000.

INSTRUCTIONS

a Prepare a consolidated work sheet similar in format to that illustrated in the chapter.

b Prepare a formal consolidated balance sheet.

c During 1984 Val Verde generated net income of $150,000 and paid dividends totaling $60,000.

(1) Compute the balance of Brazos's Investment account in the general ledger on December 31, 1984. Brazos uses the equity method of accounting for its investment in Val Verde.

(2) Compute the Investment account balance that would appear on the December 31, 1984, consolidated balance sheet. Disregard the amortization of goodwill.

P16-9 ***Understanding consolidated statements***

Payton, Inc., has two subsidiaries, Atlas Manufacturing and Miami Glass Corporation. A review of the companies' consolidated balance sheet revealed the following selected information.

Assets	
Investment in Atlas Manufacturing	*$ –*
Investment in Miami Glass	*180,000*
Excess of cost over book value in subsidiary investment	*45,000*
Liabilities	
Loans payable	*85,000*
Stockholders' equity	
Minority interest	*65,000*
Common stock	*150,000*
Paid-in capital in excess of par value	*50,000*
Retained earnings	*215,000*

INSTRUCTIONS

One of Payton's stockholders has been reviewing the consolidated statements and has come to you with the following questions. Prepare appropriate answers, explaining any necessary assumptions.

a Payton has two long-term investments. Why is a balance shown for Miami Glass while none appears for Atlas Manufacturing?

b What gives rise to an excess of cost over book value?

c What is meant by the Minority Interest account and to which subsidiary does it relate?

d A leading financial publication recently contained an article regarding a $750,000 loan from Payton to Atlas; yet the loan was not disclosed on the consolidated balance sheet? Why?

P16-10 ***Bond entries: Acquisition through sale (alternate to P16-3)***

On June 1, 1983, Database Corporation purchased $500,000 of 12%, 10-year bonds for $504,760 plus accrued interest. The bonds are dated May 1, 1983, and pay semiannual interest on May 1 and November 1. On July 1, 1984, Database sold half the bonds at 102 plus accrued interest. Database uses the straight-line method of amortization.

INSTRUCTIONS

a Prepare journal entries to record the following:

(1) The bond investment on June 1, 1983.

(2) The semiannual interest receipt and premium amortization on November 1, 1983.

(3) Accrued interest and premium amortization on December 31, 1983.

b Compute total bond interest revenue for 1983.

c Present the proper disclosure of the bond investment on Database's December 31, 1983, balance sheet.

d Prepare journal entries to record the semiannual interest receipt and premium amortization on May 1, 1984.

e Prepare entries to record the bond sale on July 1, 1984. *Hint:* Examine when amortization was last recorded.

P16-11 ***Bond entries: Effective-interest method*** **(*alternate to P16-4*)**

Avery Corporation purchased $300,000 of 4-year, 9% bonds on January 1, 1984, for $290,293. The bonds pay interest semiannually on June 30 and December 31 and were priced to generate an annual effective yield of 10% to investors. Avery rounds all calculations to the nearest dollar.

INSTRUCTIONS

a Prepare the journal entry necessary to record the bond acquisition, assuming the bonds are dated January 1.

b Assuming Avery Corporation uses straight-line amortization, compute (1) the annual amount of interest received, (2) annual discount amortization, (3) annual interest revenue.

c Assuming Avery Corporation uses the effective interest method of amortization, prepare the following:

(1) A discount amortization schedule similar in format to Exhibit 16-2.

(2) Journal entries to record semiannual interest receipts and discount amortization for 1984.

d If Avery Corporation's fiscal year ended on November 30, prepare the necessary entries (assuming effective-interest amortization) to record (1) accrued interest on November 30, 1984, and (2) discount amortization on November 30, 1984.

P16-12 ***Lower-of-cost-or-market and equity methods*** **(*alternate to P16-5*)**

Magnum Electronics recently acquired a long-term investment in Ion Semiconductor. Ion has 100,000 shares of $1 par-value common stock outstanding. The following information is available.

May 14 Purchased 25,000 shares of Ion common stock at $30 per share.
Dec. 31 Received a copy of Ion's income statement disclosing net income of $200,000.
31 Ion declared and paid a cash dividend of $0.20 per share.
31 The market price of Ion's stock was $27 per share.

INSTRUCTIONS

a Which accounting method should Magnum use for its long-term investment in Ion Semiconductor? Why should this method be used?

b Present Magnum's required journal entries. If no entry is needed for any of the foregoing items, explain why.

c Present the proper disclosure of the Investment account on Magnum's December 31 balance sheet.

d Repeat requirements (a), (b), and (c), assuming Magnum purchased 8,000 shares of Ion's stock at $30 per share.

P16-13 ***Straightforward consolidation*** **(*alternate to P16-7*)**

For the past few years National Toy Company and Funtime, Inc., have been friendly business rivals. Although the companies are not affiliated, National has borrowed money from Funtime and vice versa. Part of this friendliness stems from the fact that the presidents of the two firms are brothers.

On December 31 of the current year National acquired a 70% interest in Funtime for $105,000 cash. The balance sheets of the two companies *prior to the acquisition* follow.

NATIONAL TOY COMPANY

Cash	$210,000
Note receivable from Funtime	70,000
Other assets	150,000
Total assets	$430,000
Current liabilities	$ 60,000
Note payable to Funtime	30,000
Common stock	200,000
Retained earnings	140,000
Total liabilities & stockholders' equity	$430,000

FUNTIME, INC.

Cash	$ 75,000
Note receivable from National Toy	30,000
Other assets	155,000
Total assets	$260,000
Current liabilities	$ 40,000
Note payable to National Toy	70,000
Common stock	100,000
Retained earnings	50,000
Total liabilities & stockholders' equity	$260,000

INSTRUCTIONS

a Present National's journal entry to record the acquisition of Funtime.

b Prepare a consolidated work sheet similar in form to that illustrated in the text.

c Prepare a formal consolidated balance sheet for the combined entity.

P16-14 *Consolidation and equity method (alternate to P16-8)*

On December 31, 1983, Western Oil Corporation acquired 100% of the outstanding stock of Lawton Drilling Company for $470,000. Balance sheet information for the two companies immediately after the acquisition appears on page 643.

With the exception of land, the fair market value of Lawton's assets and liabilities corresponded to the book value amounts as of the acquisition date. A recent appraisal indicated Lawton's land was worth $95,000.

INSTRUCTIONS

a Prepare a consolidated work sheet similar in format to that illustrated in the chapter.

	Western	Lawton
Cash	$ 68,900	$ 36,200
Accounts receivable (net)	85,400	82,400
Inventories	215,200	77,500
Investment in Lawton	470,000	—
Land	135,000	46,500
Property, plant, & equipment (net)	275,900	246,800
Receivable from Lawton	15,000	—
	$1,265,400	$489,400
Accounts payable	$ 118,500	$ 64,100
Taxes payable	29,700	24,600
Bonds payable	400,000	—
Payable to Western Oil	—	15,000
Common stock ($10 par)	600,000	—
Common stock ($20 par)	—	200,000
Retained earnings	117,200	185,700
	$1,265,400	$489,400

b Prepare a formal consolidated balance sheet.

c During 1984 Lawton generated net income of $280,000 and paid dividends totaling $35,000.

(1) Compute the balance of Western's Investment account in the general ledger on December 31, 1984. Western uses the equity method of accounting for its investment in Lawton.

(2) Compute the Investment account balance that would appear on the December 31, 1984, consolidated balance sheet. Disregard the amortization of goodwill.

CASE 16
THE COURT APPEARANCE

"A nightmare" is the only way Charlie Reynolds can describe his recent experience in acquiring Statler Manufacturing. In what began as a normal business transaction, Charlie's acquisition has culminated in a forthcoming court battle between the two parties involved. Why? The following should serve as a short synopsis of the events leading to the present situation.

Statler Manufacturing is a small, family-owned producer of items used in the maritime industry. The company has had 10,000 shares of common stock outstanding since its inception in 1972. Over the past four years Statler's operating profits have averaged $26,000. Total income has been much higher, however, because of earnings and dividends from Statler's investment in Maple Leaf, Inc. Maple Leaf's earnings and dividends for the past four years follow.

Year	Earnings	Total Dividends Paid
1	$100,000	$ 60,000
2	150,000	80,000
3	200,000	120,000
4	250,000	120,000

From the foregoing figures Statler's accounting department computed earnings per share (EPS) as follows:

Year	(A) Operating Profit	(B) Share of Maple Leaf Profits	(C) Share of Maple Leaf Dividends	(D) Total Earnings (A + B + C)	(E) Earnings per Share (D ÷ 10,000 Shares)
1	$ 20,000	$ 20,000*	$12,000*	$ 52,000	$5.20
2	25,000	30,000*	16,000*	71,000	7.10
3	29,000	30,000†	18,000†	77,000	7.70
4	30,000	37,500†	18,000†	85,500	8.55
	$104,000	$117,500	$64,000	$285,500	

*Based on a 20% ownership interest.
†Based on a 15% ownership interest.

In January of the current year Reynolds and Statler's president were having lunch when the topic surfaced of Statler's growth in EPS. Limited information was exchanged, specifically, data appearing in columns D and E above, and Reynolds agreed to purchase a substantial interest in Statler. Included in the purchase price was $81,375 for goodwill, negotiated at $10,000 plus the average earnings over the past four years ($285,500 ÷ 4 years = $71,375 per year; $71,375 + $10,000 = $81,375). Immediately after the acquisition Reynolds performed a thorough analysis of Statler's records and felt that the latter's accounting department had furnished misleading and incorrect information. Statler disagreed and Reynolds sued to void the transaction.

INSTRUCTIONS

a Comment on Reynolds's claim that Statler's information was misleading and incorrect.

b Recompute the amount of goodwill.

c Could Reynolds be criticized in his quest to void the transaction? Explain your answer.

17 STATEMENT OF CHANGES IN FINANCIAL POSITION

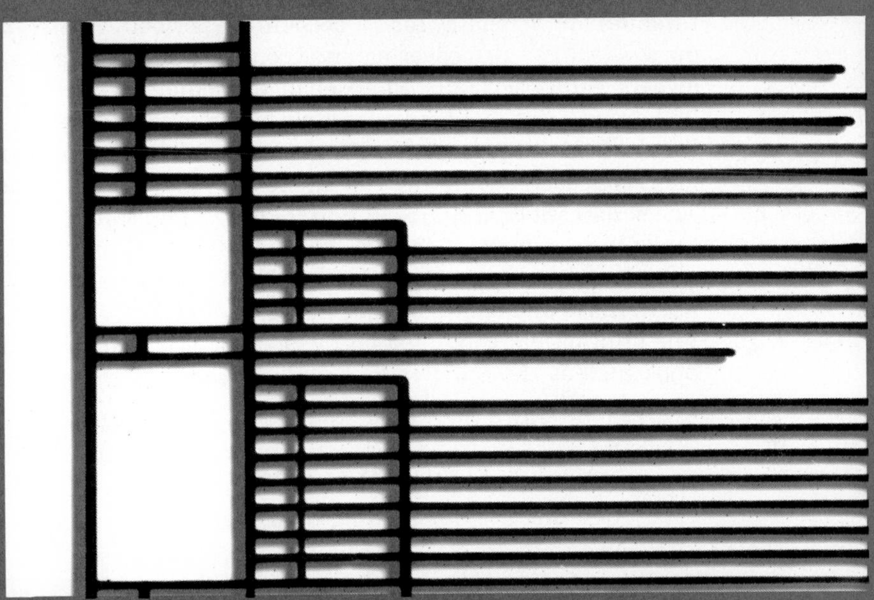

LEARNING OBJECTIVES

After reading this chapter you should:

1. *Understand the purpose of the statement of changes in financial position.*
2. *Be able to define funds and identify key sources and uses of funds.*
3. *Be able to handle significant nonfund financing and investing transactions.*
4. *Be able to prepare a statement of changes in financial position utilizing both the working capital approach and the cash approach.*

CHAPTER 17

In the preceding chapters we have examined three financial statements: the balance sheet, the income statement, and the statement of owners' equity. Recall that the balance sheet reveals information concerning the economic resources, obligations, and owners' equity of a business entity at a specific point in time. The income statement, on the other hand, discloses revenues and expenses for an accounting period. Finally, the statement of owners' equity, also covering an accounting period, reports changes in the owners' equity accounts. These changes include investments by the owners, withdrawals (or dividends), and net income (or net loss).

In 1971 the Accounting Principles Board concluded that a fourth statement is needed to improve the financial disclosure of business enterprises. The **statement of changes in financial position,** sometimes referred to as a funds flow statement, reveals the financing and investing activities of an entity. Specifically, the statement discloses the sources and uses of a business's funds and shows the net change in an enterprise's financial position. The information contained on the statement is helpful in answering questions such as the following:

Did an entity fund its activities from operations? From bank loans? From owner investments?

Were the funds obtained by an organization used to expand facilities? Reduce outstanding debt? Replace aging plant and equipment?

Were the dividends declared greater than the funds provided by business operations?

Did the firm become more solvent during the accounting period? What factors are causing the increased or decreased solvency?

Questions similar to the foregoing are routinely asked by creditors, owners, and financial analysts. By collecting information on how funds are obtained and used in an organization, the statement of changes provides operational insight that is not afforded by the other financial statements.

CONCEPTS OF FUNDS

To the general public the term "funds" means cash, both on hand and in the bank. In the business community, however, a broader definition of funds is normally employed. Funds are usually defined as **working capital,** that is, the excess of current assets over current liabilities. Current assets include cash, short-term investments, accounts receivable, short-term notes receivable, and inventories. Current liabilities, on the other hand, encompass accounts payable, notes payable, accrued payables, and other short-term obligations.

As we noted in Chapter 6, current assets such as inventories and receivables are eventually converted to cash via the *operating cycle.* To explain, inventories are sold on account and become accounts receivable; the receivables are collected and become cash. The cash, in turn, is then used to eliminate current liabilities or to purchase more inventory. Given this continual conversion, the difference between total current assets and total current liabilities represents the net short-term resources (funds) available to a business. It is now evident that when a longer time frame is considered, resources other than cash can ultimately be used to settle current debts. The working capital definition of funds, then, is a broader foundation for the statement of changes in financial position.

SOURCES AND USES OF WORKING CAPITAL

When funds are defined as working capital, the statement of changes shows the sources and uses of working capital during the accounting period. Transactions and events that increase working capital are **sources of funds;** conversely, those causing a decrease in working capital are **uses (or applications) of funds.** Fortunately, to determine sources and uses, the accountant need not individually analyze the many transactions that occurred during the year—a burdensome task to say the least. Instead aggregate end-of-period data are used. The proper procedures will be shown later in the chapter.

Over time, working capital increases or decreases because of transactions affecting both current *and* noncurrent accounts. Events and transactions that affect *only* current or *only* noncurrent accounts are neither sources nor uses of funds.[1] To illustrate, we consider the abbreviated year-end balance sheets of the Webb Corporation that appear in Exhibit 17-1.

Exhibit 17-1

Webb Corporation abbreviated balance sheets (as of December 31)

	1984	1983
Current assets	$100,000	$ 90,000
Noncurrent assets	400,000	410,000
Total assets	$500,000	$500,000
Current liabilities	$ 50,000	$ 60,000
Noncurrent liabilities	100,000	110,000
Stockholders' equity	350,000	330,000
Total liabilities & stockholders' equity	$500,000	$500,000

As the following computations show, Webb's working capital increased by $20,000 during 1984.

	1984	1983
Current assets	$100,000	$90,000
Less: Current liabilities	50,000	60,000
Working capital	$ 50,000	$30,000

+ $20,000

[1]An exception with noncurrent accounts will be noted shortly.

Notice that while the working capital increase occurred, total assets and the total of liabilities plus stockholders' equity each remained constant at $500,000. Thus the increase in working capital must have been caused by events and transactions that involved noncurrent accounts. Perhaps this is better seen by examining Exhibit 17-2, which depicts Webb's December 31, 1983, balance sheet in a diagram format.

Exhibit 17-2

Webb Corporation balance sheet

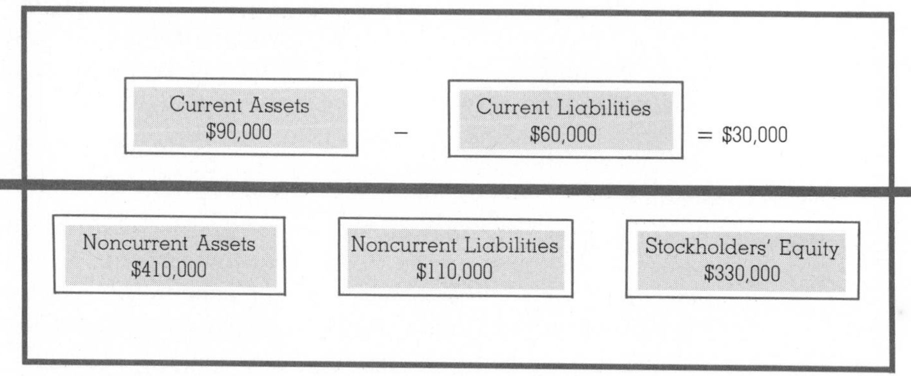

The two blocks above the bold horizontal line represent the components of Webb's $30,000 working capital balance; blocks below are the remaining items on the balance sheet. To generate a $20,000 increase in working capital through the year, transactions and events had to occur that crossed the horizontal line. To illustrate, we will study the transactions that follow; consider each item independently.

Transaction 1. Purchased $10,000 of inventory on account.

Analysis This transaction increases both the Inventory and Accounts Payable accounts by $10,000. As a result, current assets and current liabilities become $100,000 and $70,000, respectively. Working capital, however, remains at $30,000 ($100,000 – $70,000). Observe that transactions that stay entirely above the line do not affect working capital and are neither a source nor a use of funds.

Transaction 2. Acquired a building by issuing $50,000 of 20-year bonds.

Analysis This exchange transaction increases both the Building and Bonds Payable accounts. Accordingly, noncurrent assets and noncurrent liabilities are raised to $460,000 and $160,000, respectively. Again working capital remains intact at $30,000. We can therefore conclude that transactions that remain entirely below the line are neither sources nor uses of funds.

Transaction 3. Purchased $12,000 of equipment for cash.

Analysis

This transaction causes a $12,000 decrease in the Cash account, reducing current assets to $78,000. In addition, the equipment acquisition raises noncurrent assets to $422,000. Notice that working capital is now $18,000 ($78,000 − $60,000). Transaction 3 has affected balance sheet components both above and below the horizontal line, resulting in a $12,000 use of funds.

Transaction 4. Issued $50,000 of long-term bonds for cash.

Analysis

The issuance of long-term bonds raises both the Cash and Bonds Payable accounts. Thus current assets and noncurrent liabilities are increased to $140,000 and $160,000, respectively. Working capital now equals $80,000 ($140,000 − $60,000) and the transaction represents a $50,000 source of funds. As in transaction 3, components above and below the horizontal line have changed.

To conclude, a transaction or event *must* cross the horizontal line to produce a change in working capital. Transactions that remain entirely above or below the line are neither sources nor uses of funds when using the working capital definition.

Typical Sources of Working Capital

Sources (or increases) of working capital arise from many different transactions and events. Common sources include the sale of noncurrent assets, long-term borrowing, and increases in owners' (stockholders') equity.

Sale of noncurrent assets

Businesses often obtain working capital by selling buildings, equipment, land, intangibles, and other long-term assets in exchange for current assets such as cash or short-term receivables. When this type of transaction occurs, working capital is increased by the full amount of the sale. For example, suppose a company sold a parcel of land that originally cost $100,000 for $180,000 cash. The transaction produces an $80,000 gain, which would be entered in the accounting records as follows:

Cash	*180,000*	
Land		*100,000*
Gain on Land Sale		*80,000*
To record sale of land at a gain		

The only working capital component affected by the sale is the Cash account. Since Cash increased by $180,000, the transaction produced a $180,000 source of funds.

Long-term borrowing

When long-term bonds, notes, mortgages, and other noncurrent liabilities are issued, working capital is increased by the funds received from the issuance. To illustrate, if $1 million of bonds are sold at 100 for cash, the funds provided total $1 million. If the bonds are sold at 110, the sale has generated $1.1 million of working capital. The latter transaction is best seen by examining the following journal entry:

Cash	*1,100,000*	
Bonds Payable		*1,000,000*
Premium on Bonds Payable		*100,000*
To record sale of bonds at a premium		

Recall that the Premium account is shown as an addition to Bonds Payable in the noncurrent liability section of the balance sheet. Thus the only working capital item affected is cash.

Unlike long-term borrowing, short-term financing does not affect working capital. For example, if $20,000 is borrowed from a bank by signing a 180-day note, both current assets (cash) and current liabilities (notes payable) will increase. Working capital, therefore, remains unchanged.

Increases in owners' (stockholders') equity

A third source of funds results from increases in owners' or stockholders' equity. The corporate issuance of preferred or common stock for cash and the investments of current assets made by proprietors and partners raise working capital. As before, working capital is increased by the amount of funds received. For example, if a corporation issues 20,000 shares of $10 par-value common stock at a price of $20 per share, the working capital generated is $400,000 (20,000 shares × $20).

Net income

Increases in owners' equity also result from profitable operations; net income is therefore another source of working capital. To explain, revenues from the sale of products or delivery of services increase working capital. In a similar but opposite way expenses decrease working capital. Perhaps the easiest way to understand this idea is by examining two simple journal entries that record revenue recognition and expense incurrence.

Revenue Recognition		
Cash, Accounts Receivable	*XXX*	
Sales		*XXX*

Expense Incurrence		
Expense	*XXX*	
Cash, Accounts Payable		*XXX*

Remember that both sales and expenses affect owners' equity through the closing process. Consequently, these transactions cross the horizontal line depicted in Exhibit 17-2 and represent sources and uses of funds. If revenues (sources) exceed expenses (uses), we can conclude that net income is a net source of funds to the firm.

It is important to recognize that the net income figure summarizes many different transactions. Although net income is a source of funds, it is possible that certain revenues and expenses were included in the computation that have absolutely no affect on working capital. If this is the case, net income from operations will not result in a dollar-for-dollar increase in funds. To illustrate, let us consider depreciation of property, plant, and equipment and amortization of intangibles. Their proper journal entries follow.

Depreciation		
Depreciation Expense	*XXX*	
Accumulated Depreciation		*XXX*

Amortization		
Amortization Expense	*XXX*	
Patent, Copyright, and so on		*XXX*

It is evident that current assets and current liabilities are not changed by these entries; yet both expenses are deducted from revenues when computing net income. Because these expenses cause net income to decrease without an accompanying reduction in working capital, they must be added back to net income to arrive at funds from operations. Thus a corporation that has net income of $900,000, depreciation expense of $400,000, and amortization expense of $100,000 has actually provided $1.4 million of working capital from operations.

Other items affecting net income that deserve special attention are gains and losses on the sale of noncurrent assets. Returning to the example on page 649 concerning the sale of land at an $80,000 gain, we noted that the $180,000 increase in the Cash account produced a $180,000 increase in working capital. The $80,000 gain is already reflected in the amount of cash received by the firm. To recognize the gain again as a source of funds via net income would result in a double counting. Consequently, because gains increase net income, they must be subtracted to compute working capital from operations. Conversely, losses on the sale of noncurrent assets are treated as additions to net income when calculating working capital.

Typical Uses of Working Capital

Uses of working capital tend to parallel the sources. Common decreases in funds are caused by the purchase of noncurrent assets, repayment of long-term debt, and decreases in owners' (stockholders') equity.

Purchase of noncurrent assets

When noncurrent assets such as buildings and equipment are acquired by either reducing current assets or increasing current liabilities, working capital decreases by the amount of the purchase price. For example, if a business purchased $50,000 of equipment by paying $40,000 cash and issuing a 6-month note payable for the balance, working capital would decrease by $50,000. The reduction is caused by the combined effect of a $40,000 decrease in cash (current asset) and a $10,000 increase in notes payable (current liability). If the note payable had been due in 36 months (long-term), the acquisition would have only reduced working capital by the cash outlay of $40,000.

Repayment of long-term debt

When long-term debts are liquidated by using current assets, working capital decreases. For example, suppose a long-term bond issue of $400,000 is retired at 103 by using cash. Because cash (a current asset) is reduced, a $412,000 ($400,000 × 1.03) use of funds has occurred.

Decreases in owners' (stockholders') equity

Remembering the horizontal line in Exhibit 17-2, we note that a reduction in owners' equity will decrease working capital if current assets or current liabilities are also involved. Decreases in working capital are commonly caused by the purchase of treasury stock, the declaration of cash dividends, and the incurrence of a net loss.

Flow of Working Capital

Many accounting students have difficulty picturing the importance of the sources and uses of working capital within a business. Perhaps this problem will be minimized if you view sources of working capital as continuous inflows that are available for long-term investment, dividends to stockholders, debt retirement, coverage of operating losses, and a number of other items. In effect, working capital flows in and out of an organization, as shown in Exhibit 17-3.

Exhibit 17-3

Flow of working capital

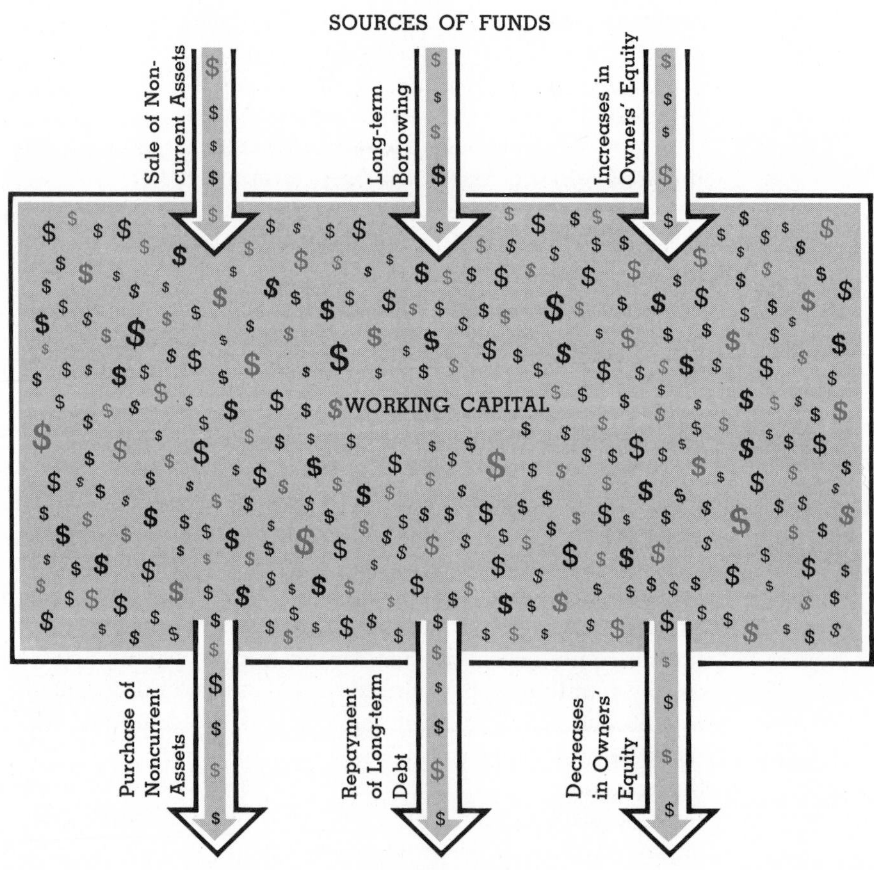

A review of recent corporate annual reports discovered a number of working capital flows in practice (see Exhibit 17-4).

Exhibit 17-4

Sources and uses of funds in practice

Source/Use	Entity	Item
Source	RCA	Insurance proceeds from loss of communications satellite
Source	Scott Paper Company	Construction funds released by trustees
Source	U.S. Postal Service	Capital contributions by U.S. government
Use	H&R Block	Acquisition of franchise operations
Use	PepsiCo, Inc.	Bottles and cases
Use	Tenneco	Natural gas pipeline cash refund

Transactions Not Affecting Funds

Several significant transactions can affect the financial position of a business but not affect funds. For example, a building may be acquired by securing a long-term loan such as a mortgage payable. Or land may be obtained in exchange for preferred or common stock. Neither transaction involves the receipt or disbursement of funds under either the working capital or cash definitions. Nonetheless, the financial position of the enterprise has changed through the increases in assets, liabilities, and stockholders' equity. A statement of changes in financial position would be incomplete if significant nonfund financing and investing transactions were omitted. Consequently, such transactions should be reported even if no funds are involved.[2]

Nonfund exchange transactions are reported on the statement of changes as both a source and a use of funds. To illustrate, assume $1 million of common stock is exchanged for a building of the same value. The issuance of common stock would be reported as a $1 million source of funds, appropriately labeled as Issuance of Common Stock for Building. The building acquisition, in turn, would be reported as a $1 million use entitled Acquisition of Building by the Issuance of Common Stock. In essence, one could visualize that the common stock is issued for cash (a source), and the cash is simultaneously disbursed to acquire the building (a use). We emphasize that this scenario is merely mentioned to assist your understanding of the exchange; keep in mind that no cash was ever involved. Although nonfund transactions have no effect on funds flow for the period, treatment as both a source and a use will at least disclose important changes in financial position to statement users.

Other examples of nonfund financing and investing transactions include (1) the exchange of one long-term asset for another, such as a long-term investment for equipment or equipment for a patent; (2) the exchange of a long-term liability for preferred or common stock; (3) the conversion of convertible preferred stock into common stock; and (4) the acquisition of assets through gifts, such as the donation of land by a municipality to entice business relocation.

[2] "Reporting Changes in Financial Position," *Opinions of the Accounting Principles Board No. 19* (New York: American Institute of Certified Public Accountants, 1971), paragraph 8.

PREPARATION OF A STATEMENT OF CHANGES IN FINANCIAL POSITION: WORKING CAPITAL APPROACH

The information needed to prepare the statement of changes in financial position comes from a variety of sources: the income statement, statement of owners' equity, comparative balance sheets, and ledger accounts. To illustrate preparation of the statement, we will utilize data of the Powell Corporation (see Exhibit 17-5). Before progressing, however, a word of encouragement is necessary. Although considerable information is presented, the statement's construction is not difficult. Keep the previous material in mind and carefully follow the three steps below. Proceed slowly and you will find a mastery of the material forthcoming.

Step 1

The first step is to determine the change in working capital during the accounting period by comparing the beginning working capital with the ending working capital. The resulting increase or decrease represents the amount that must be explained in the statement of changes in financial position. This change, of course, is caused by Powell's sources and uses of funds.

During 1984 working capital increased by $20,000. The necessary calculations appear in Exhibit 17-6.

Step 2

The second step analyzes the causes of the working capital increase or decrease. Recall that working capital is influenced by transactions and events that "cross the line," specifically, those items affecting current assets or current liabilities *and* the remaining balance sheet components. Because changes in the noncurrent accounts will reveal the funds flow that caused Powell's rise in working capital, the noncurrent accounts must now be examined. We will study these accounts in the order they appear on the balance sheet.

Land

The Land account increased by $85,000 during the year. An analysis of the ledger account revealed that land was purchased for cash on October 19.

Land			
1/1/84	Balance	115,000	
10/19/84	Purchased land for cash	85,000	
		200,000	

The increase in this noncurrent asset results from an $85,000 use of working capital, as noted below:

Uses of working capital	
Purchase of land	*$85,000*

Exhibit 17-5

Powell Corporation financial information

POWELL CORPORATION
Comparative Balance Sheets
December 31, 1984 and 1983

	1984	1983	Increase (Decrease)
ASSETS			
Current assets			
Cash	$ 100,000	$ 50,000	$ 50,000
Accounts receivable (net)	400,000	375,000	25,000
Merchandise inventory	425,000	450,000	(25,000)
Prepaid expenses	5,000	4,000	1,000
Total current assets	$ 930,000	$ 879,000	$ 51,000
Property, plant, & equipment			
Land	$ 200,000	$ 115,000	$ 85,000
Buildings	1,450,000	1,250,000	200,000
Accumulated depreciation: buildings	(50,000)	(25,000)	(25,000)
Equipment	725,000	800,000	(75,000)
Accumulated depreciation: equipment	(250,000)	(260,000)	10,000
Total property, plant, & equipment	$2,075,000	$1,880,000	$ 195,000
Other assets			
Long-term investments	$ 880,000	$1,000,000	$(120,000)
Total assets	$3,885,000	$3,759,000	$ 126,000
LIABILITIES & STOCKHOLDERS' EQUITY			
Current liabilities			
Accounts payable	$ 370,000	$ 340,000	$ 30,000
Notes payable	300,000	300,000	—
Dividends payable	15,000	20,000	(5,000)
Taxes payable	25,000	19,000	6,000
Total current liabilities	$ 710,000	$ 679,000	$ 31,000
Long-term liabilities			
Bonds payable	$1,500,000	$2,000,000	$(500,000)
Stockholders' equity			
Common stock, par value $1	$ 330,000	$ 130,000	$ 200,000
Paid-in capital in excess of par value	870,000	500,000	370,000
Retained earnings	475,000	450,000	25,000
Total liabilities & stockholders' equity	$3,885,000	$3,759,000	$ 126,000

(Continued)

Exhibit 17-5

(Continued)

POWELL CORPORATION
Income Statement
For the Year Ended December 31, 1984

Sales		$3,000,000
Cost of goods sold		1,200,000
Gross profit		$1,800,000
Expenses		
Operating and taxes	$1,675,000	
Building depreciation	25,000	
Equipment depreciation	70,000	1,770,000
		$ 30,000
Other revenue and expense		
Loss on equipment sale	$ (5,000)	
Gain on sale of long-term investments	15,000	10,000
Net income		$ 40,000

Other information
Cash dividends declared on December 30 amounted to $15,000.

Exhibit 17-6

Powell Corporation calculation of working capital

	Dec. 31, 1984	Dec. 31, 1983
Current assets		
Cash	$100,000	$ 50,000
Accounts receivable (net)	400,000	375,000
Merchandise inventory	425,000	450,000
Prepaid expenses	5,000	4,000
Total current assets	$930,000	$879,000
Current liabilities		
Accounts payable	$370,000	$340,000
Notes payable	300,000	300,000
Dividends payable	15,000	20,000
Taxes payable	25,000	19,000
Total current liabilities	$710,000	$679,000
Working capital	$220,000	$200,000

$20,000 increase

Buildings

The next noncurrent account on Powell's balance sheet, Buildings, increased $200,000, from $1,250,000 to $1,450,000. An examination of the ledger account revealed that a building was acquired on the last day of the year in exchange for shares of the company's common stock.

Buildings			
1/1/84 Balance	1,250,000		
12/31/84 Acquired building for common stock	200,000		
	1,450,000		

The acquisition does not alter working capital because no current assets or current liabilities are involved. However, the financial position of Powell Corporation has been significantly affected. Recall from our earlier discussion that such exchange transactions are reported on the statement of changes in financial position as both a source and a use of funds. Therefore the building acquisition is disclosed as follows:

Sources of working capital	
Issuance of common stock for building	*$200,000*

Uses of working capital	
Acquisition of building by the issuance of common stock	*$200,000*

Accumulated depreciation: Buildings

The Accumulated Depreciation: Buildings account increased by $25,000 during 1984 because of annual depreciation expense (see the income statement in Exhibit 17-5).

Accumulated Depreciation: Buildings			
		1/1/84 Balance	25,000
		12/31/84 Adjusting entry: annual depreciation	25,000
			50,000

Although depreciation expense reduced Powell's net income, no funds were required. As we discussed earlier, operating expenses not affecting working capital are added back to net income to determine the source of funds from operations. This addition is done in the following manner:

Sources of working capital	
Provided from operations	
Net income (to be discussed shortly)	$ XXX
Add (deduct) items not affecting working capital	
Building depreciation expense	25,000

Equipment and accumulated depreciation: Equipment

Powell's Equipment balance decreased by $75,000 during the year, perhaps caused by a discard or a sale. However, a probe of the general ledger revealed that two transactions actually occurred.

May 1 Sold $100,000 of equipment for cash.
Nov. 1 Purchased $25,000 of equipment for cash.

Equipment

1/1/84 Balance	800,000	5/1/84 Disposal for cash	100,000
11/1/84 Purchase for cash	25,000		
(725,000)	825,000		

As you can see, an over-reliance on ending account balances could result in a failure to detect all changes in working capital. In this case, for instance, Powell had a source and a use of funds that require separate disclosure; offsetting or netting is really inappropriate.

Continuing our examination of these two transactions, the Accumulated Depreciation: Equipment account reveals that (1) depreciation associated with the disposal totaled $80,000 and (2) 1984 depreciation expense amounted to $70,000.

Accumulated Depreciation: Equipment

5/1/84 Disposal	80,000	1/1/84 Balance	260,000
		12/31/84 Adjusting entry: annual depreciation	70,000
		(250,000)	330,000

From an analysis of both ledger accounts we can determine that the equipment sold on May 1 had a $20,000 book value (cost of $100,000 minus accumulated depreciation of $80,000). Furthermore, the income statement reported a $5,000 loss from equipment sales; thus Powell must have received proceeds of $15,000. The necessary calculations follow:

Equipment cost	$100,000
Accumulated depreciation	80,000
Book value	$ 20,000
Proceeds from disposal	15,000
Loss	$ 5,000

The purchase and sale of equipment, the equipment depreciation expense, and the loss are disclosed in a statement of changes in financial position, as follows:

Sources of working capital		
Provided from operations		
Net income (to be discussed shortly)	$ XXX	
Add (deduct) items not affecting working capital		
Equipment depreciation expense	70,000	
Loss on equipment sale	5,000	
Working capital provided from operations		$ XXX
Sale of equipment		15,000

Uses of working capital	
Purchase of equipment	$25,000

Long-term investments

The comparative balance sheets indicate that the Long-Term Investments account decreased from $1,000,000 to $880,000 during the year. The ledger account is shown below.

Long-Term Investments

1/1/84 Balance	1,000,000	4/15/84 Sold securities for cash	120,000
	880,000		

Powell's management reports that the securities were sold for $135,000, thus generating the $15,000 gain that appears on the income statement (see Exhibit 17-5). The gain is reflected in the selling price; inclusion via net income would result in a double counting. Consequently, Powell must deduct $15,000 from net income to arrive at working capital from operations. The securities sale is reported on the statement of changes in the following manner:

Sources of working capital		
Provided from operations		
Net income (to be discussed shortly)	*$ XXX*	
Add (deduct) items not affecting working capital		
Gain on sale of long-term investments	*(15,000)*	
Working capital provided from operations		*$ XXX*
Sale of long-term investments		*135,000*

Bonds payable

The next noncurrent account, Bonds Payable, decreased $500,000 during the period. A review of the ledger revealed that $500,000 of bonds were retired on November 14 at 100.

Bonds Payable

11/14/84 Retired bonds at face value (100) with cash	*500,000*	*1/1/84 Balance*	*2,000,000*
			(1,500,000)

The retirement is noted in the statement of changes as follows:

Uses of working capital	
Retirement of bonds payable	*$500,000*

Common stock and paid-in capital in excess of par value

During 1984 the Common Stock and Paid-in Capital accounts increased by $200,000 and $370,000, respectively. Examination of the ledger accounts revealed that two transactions occurred.

Aug. 28 Issued and received cash for 100,000 shares at $3.70 per share.
Dec. 31 Issued 100,000 shares in exchange for a $200,000 building (see p. 656).

Recall from Chapter 13 that when stock is issued at a price greater than par value, the difference between par and the issue price is placed in the Paid-in Capital in Excess account. Thus the two issuances are recorded as shown below.

Date	***Amount***	***Recorded in Common Stock Account at $1 per Share***	***Recorded in Paid-in Capital in Excess Account***
Aug. 28	$370,000	$100,000	$270,000
Dec. 31	200,000	100,000	100,000
	$570,000	$200,000	$370,000

The general ledger accounts therefore appear as follows:

Common Stock, Par Value $1			
	1/1/84	Balance	130,000
	8/28/84	Issued 100,000 shares for cash	100,000
	12/31/84	Issued 100,000 shares for building	100,000
			330,000

Paid-in Capital in Excess of Par Value			
	1/1/84	Balance	500,000
	8/28/84	Issued 100,000 shares for cash	270,000
	12/31/84	Issued 100,000 shares for building	100,000
			870,000

The stock issue on August 28 is reported in the following manner:

Sources of working capital	
Issuance of common stock for cash	$370,000

Proper disclosure of the December 31 issuance on the statement of changes was shown earlier when the Buildings account was discussed. Observe that for statement presentation purposes it is not necessary to divide a source (or use) into the individual amounts placed in the Common Stock and Paid-in Capital in Excess accounts; only the total need be shown. Such a breakdown has minimal value to financial statement users.

Retained earnings

The final noncurrent account on Powell's comparative balance sheet is Retained Earnings. During 1984 Retained Earnings increased by $25,000. According to the income statement, we know that Powell reported net income of $40,000 for the year. In addition, from the other information presented in Exhibit 17-5, we know the firm declared a $15,000 cash dividend on December 30.[3] The Retained Earnings account therefore appears as follows:

[3]The dividend has not yet been paid, as evidenced by the balance in the Dividends Payable account.

Retained Earnings			
12/30/84 Cash dividends declared	15,000	1/1/84 Balance	450,000
		12/31/84 Net income (via closing)	40,000
		(475,000)	490,000

Net income and cash dividend declarations are shown on the statement of changes in financial position as follows:

Sources of working capital	
Provided from operations	
Net income	*$40,000*

Uses of working capital	
Declaration of cash dividends	*$15,000*

Step 3

Once the noncurrent accounts are analyzed, the resulting information is pulled together and the formal statement of changes in financial position is prepared. While some flexibility is permitted in form, content, and terminology, the statement should begin with net income and add or deduct those items not affecting working capital. The resulting amount is labeled Working Capital Provided from (or, Used in, when a net loss arises) Operations. After this information is shown, other sources and then uses of working capital are disclosed.

A complete statement of changes in financial position for Powell Corporation is presented in Exhibit 17-7. The statement is merely the summation of the sources and uses illustrated in Step 2. Trace the individual sources and uses from the previous discussion (noted in shaded blocks) and observe their placement on this important financial report.

Changes in working capital components

Observe that when funds are defined as working capital, the final section of the statement is a schedule that reveals the changes in each current asset and current liability account. In this manner information is presented that explains both the increase or decrease in working capital for the business and the changes in the working capital components. Naturally, the two amounts labeled Increase (or Decrease) in Working Capital must agree.

A schedule of changes in working capital components can often reveal vital information to statement users. For example, assume Bilanin Corporation had no change in working capital for the year because sources of funds

Exhibit 17-7

POWELL CORPORATION
Statement of Changes in Financial Position
For the Year Ended December 31, 1984

Sources of working capital		
Provided from operations		
Net income	$ 40,000	
Add (deduct) items not affecting working capital		
Building depreciation expense	25,000	
Equipment depreciation expense	70,000	
Loss on equipment sale	5,000	
Gain on sale of long-term investments	(15,000)	
Working capital provided from operations		$125,000
Sale of equipment		15,000
Sale of long-term investments		135,000
Issuance of common stock for cash		370,000
Issuance of common stock for building		200,000
Total sources of working capital		$845,000
Uses of working capital		
Purchase of land	$ 85,000	
Acquisition of building by the issuance of common stock	200,000	
Purchase of equipment	25,000	
Retirement of bonds payable	500,000	
Declaration of cash dividends	15,000	
Total uses of working capital		825,000
Increase in working capital		$ 20,000

SCHEDULE OF CHANGES IN WORKING CAPITAL COMPONENTS

Increases (decreases) in current assets		
Cash	$ 50,000	
Accounts receivable (net)	25,000	
Merchandise inventory	(25,000)	
Prepaid expenses	1,000	$ 51,000
Increases (decreases) in current liabilities		
Accounts payable	$ 30,000	
Notes payable	—	
Dividends payable	(5,000)	
Taxes payable	6,000	31,000
Increase in working capital		$ 20,000

equaled uses of funds. The firm's schedule of changes in working capital components follows.

SCHEDULE OF CHANGES IN WORKING CAPITAL COMPONENTS		
Increases (decreases) in current assets		
Cash	*$(100,000)*	
Accounts receivable (net)	*(50,000)*	
Notes receivable	*(150,000)*	
Merchandise inventory	*500,000*	*$200,000*
Increases (decreases) in current liabilities		
Accounts payable		*200,000*
Change in working capital		*$ –*

The schedule shows that while total working capital remained static, there were substantive changes in working capital components. The more liquid current assets (cash, accounts receivable, and notes receivable) have all decreased, while inventory has increased. The inventory growth has been financed with funds generated from the reduction in the other current assets as well as the increase in accounts payable. These component changes provide useful information to statement users who must now assess Bilanin's ability to sell the increased inventory, pay the creditors, and regain corporate liquidity.

CASH DEFINITION

Although many organizations define funds as working capital, other definitions are permissible. Some companies use a cash concept of funds in which sources of funds are represented by cash receipts and uses of funds by cash disbursements. The most prevalent use of the cash definition occurs with banks and insurance companies, which do not classify their accounts into current and noncurrent categories.

When funds are defined as cash, the statement of changes in financial position highlights the inflows and outflows of cash and explains the change in the cash balance. Aside from a few minor differences, a statement of changes prepared by using the cash definition closely resembles the working capital statement just illustrated. The similarity is best seen by examining the diagram appearing in Exhibit 17-8.

With the working capital approach, any transaction crossing the horizontal line was either a source or a use of funds. The statement of changes in financial position was thus prepared by analyzing noncurrent assets, noncurrent liabilities, and owners' equity. Under the cash definition the same techniques are applied with some minor modification. Again any transaction that crosses the horizontal line represents an increase or decrease in

Exhibit 17-8

Statement of changes in financial position: Working capital and cash definitions

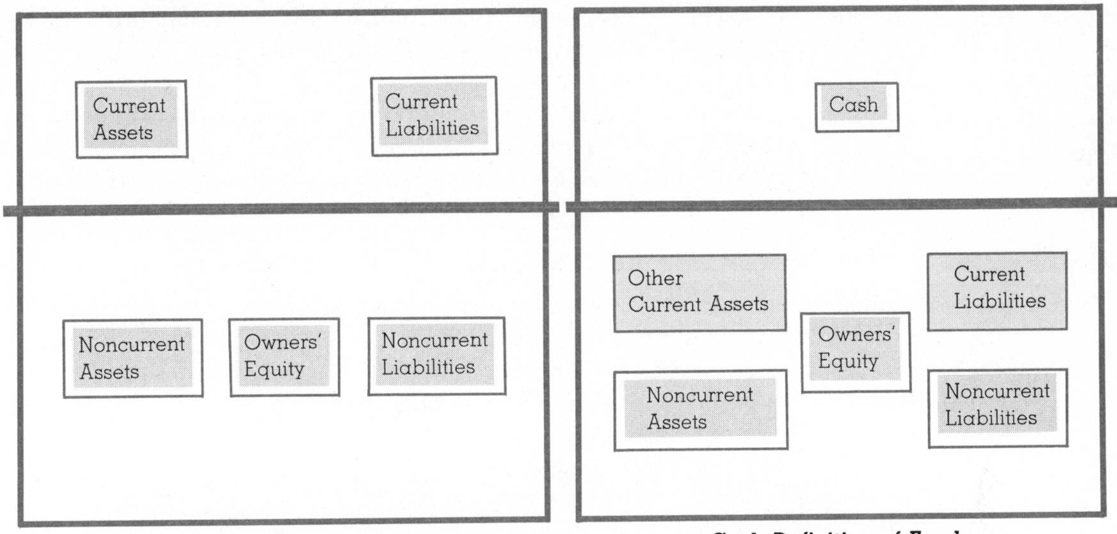

funds (cash in this case). Now, however, two *additional* balance sheet components must be reviewed: current assets other than cash and current liabilities. Stated differently, all accounts other than cash are studied to explain the change in a firm's cash position.

Sources and Uses of Cash

Sources of cash are generated from many of the same transactions and events that increase working capital, namely, sales of noncurrent assets, long-term borrowing, and increases in owners' equity. Other cash sources include decreases in current assets and increases in current liabilities. Thus a $15,000 decrease in accounts receivable and an $85,000 reduction in inventory collectively serve as a $100,000 source of cash. Similarly, a $42,000 increase in accounts payable is viewed as generating cash for the business. The reasoning for this treatment will be presented shortly.

Turning to uses of cash, many applications of working capital also decrease an organization's cash balance, for example, the purchase of noncurrent assets for cash, debt repayment, and certain decreases in owners' equity. Additional uses of cash result from increases in current assets and decreases in current liabilities. As before, the reasoning will be noted shortly.

PREPARATION OF A STATEMENT OF CHANGES: CASH APPROACH

To illustrate preparation of a statement of changes in financial position using the cash definition, we will continue the Powell Corporation example. As we proceed, observe how the preparation of this statement parallels the statement constructed when the working capital approach was employed. At this time refer to the information presented in Exhibit 17-5.

Step 1

Since the statement will concentrate on the inflows and outflows of cash, the first step is to determine the change in Powell's Cash account. According to the comparative balance sheets, the cash balance increased by $50,000 during 1984.

Step 2

Next, changes in all other balance sheet accounts are analyzed and related to their ultimate effect upon cash. Much of the analysis was shown when illustrating the working capital basis and is not repeated here. By reviewing Step 2 of the working capital discussion, you will find that the following transactions, among others, affected cash.

Sources of cash	
*Issuance of common stock for building**	*$200,000*
Sale of equipment	*15,000*
Sale of long-term investments	*135,000*
Issuance of common stock for cash	*370,000*
Uses of cash	
Purchase of land	*$ 85,000*
*Acquisition of building by the issuance of common stock**	*200,000*
Purchase of equipment	*25,000*
Retirement of bonds payable	*500,000*

**Although this exchange did not affect cash, it is an example of a significant financing and investing transaction that must be disclosed as both a source and a use of funds.*

Step 3

The statement of changes in Exhibit 17-7 disclosed that $125,000 of working capital was generated from operations. Net income served as a starting point for this computation and was adjusted for items not affecting working capital. For the Powell Corporation these items consisted of the following:

Building depreciation expense
Equipment depreciation expense
Loss on equipment sale
Gain on sale of long-term investments

Similarly, a statement developed using the cash definition works toward an amount labeled Cash Provided from Operations. Just as the four items above did not affect working capital, they also had no impact on the Cash account. Because the expenses and loss were deducted from net income, they must be added back to compute cash flow. Conversely, the gain must be subtracted.

Further complicating the picture are additional revenues and expenses included in net income that did not involve the receipt or disbursement of cash. As you have studied, net income is normally determined by using the accrual basis of accounting. Under the accrual basis, revenues are recognized when goods or services are sold or rendered, and expenses are recognized when incurred. *The accrual basis does not consider cash flows.* Yet when we are determining cash provided by operations for purposes of preparing the statement of changes, the cash flows associated with the revenues and expenses are paramount.

Frequently, timing differences arise between the recognition of revenue and expense on the income statement and the ultimate receipt and payment of cash. For example, sales on account may be made in one period and collected in another. Or prepaid insurance may be paid now and expensed in later periods. In addition, expenses such as taxes, salaries, and interest are often accrued at the end of one period, with payment occurring in the future. As a consequence of these timing differences, accrual-based net income figures must be adjusted to reflect (1) the revenues *received* in cash and (2) the expenses *paid* in cash. In other words, *a conversion to the cash basis of accounting is needed.*

Analyzing an entire year's revenue and expense transactions to determine the involvement of cash is extremely costly and time-consuming. Instead we can study changes in the current assets and current liabilities connected with operations. Decreases in current assets and increases in current liabilities are considered sources of cash and are added back to accrual-based net income. Conversely, increases in current assets and decreases in current liabilities reflect uses of cash and are deducted. *Do not memorize these rules;* they can become very confusing. Rather, reason through the material that follows.

The Powell Corporation's balance sheets (in Exhibit 17-5) show the following current asset and current liability accounts related to operations.

Account	**Dec. 31, 1984**	**Dec. 31, 1983**	**Increase (Decrease)**
Accounts receivable (net)	$400,000	$375,000	$ 25,000
Merchandise inventory	425,000	450,000	(25,000)
Prepaid expenses	5,000	4,000	1,000
Accounts payable	370,000	340,000	30,000
Notes payable	300,000	300,000	—
Taxes payable	25,000	19,000	6,000

Two current accounts are omitted from this listing: Cash and Dividends Payable. Cash is omitted because our objective is to show how changes in the other current accounts affect the cash generated from operations. Dividends Payable is not considered because dividend distributions have no effect on net income. Recall that dividends are reductions in stockholders' equity and not an expense of doing business. The correct treatment of the Dividends Payable account will be discussed shortly.

The current accounts affecting cash flow from operations will now be discussed in detail.

Accounts receivable. The ending balance of Accounts Receivable was $25,000 greater than the beginning balance, indicating that credit sales exceeded customer collections on account. Thus the accrual-based sales figure includes uncollected revenues. Accordingly, $25,000 must be deducted from Powell's net income to convert to the cash basis.

Merchandise inventory. The Inventory account declined, revealing that purchases made in a prior period were sold during 1984. As a result, cost of goods sold includes $25,000 of inventory not presently requiring a cash outlay.[4] Because the $25,000 reduced net income, it must be added back to compute current cash flow from operations.

Prepaid expenses. The balance of Prepaid Expenses increased $1,000, meaning that more prepaid expenses were acquired than consumed. Cash outlays therefore exceeded the expenses reported on the accrual-based income statement. For a conversion to the cash basis, an additional $1,000 must be deducted from Powell's net income.

Accounts payable. Accounts Payable increased by $30,000, indicating that the recognition of liabilities for goods and services exceeded cash disbursements to creditors. Because these items reduced profitability and were not paid in the current period, the accrual-based net income must be increased by $30,000 to compute cash flow from operations.

Notes payable. No change and therefore no effect on cash.

Taxes payable. The Taxes Payable account increased by $6,000. Powell thus recognized tax expense during 1984 that has not yet been paid to taxing authorities. Following the same logic we followed with Accounts Payable, $6,000 must be added to net income to arrive at cash provided from operations.

The foregoing adjustments are reflected in the statement of changes in financial position as follows:

[4]Some year-end purchases made in 1983 may actually be paid in early 1984. The soon-to-be-illustrated treatment of accounts payable compensates for this situation.

Sources of cash		
Provided from operations		
Net income		$ 40,000
Add (deduct) items to convert net income to cash basis		
Building depreciation expense	$ 25,000	
Equipment depreciation expense	70,000	
Loss on equipment sale	5,000	
Gain on sale of long-term investments	(15,000)	
Increase in accounts receivable	(25,000)	
Decrease in merchandise inventory	25,000	
Increase in prepaid expenses	(1,000)	
Increase in accounts payable	30,000	
Increase in taxes payable	6,000	120,000
Cash provided from operations		$160,000

Cash disbursed for dividends

To complete our analysis of current accounts, we must now review Dividends Payable. As we noted earlier, this account was not considered in the preceding discussion because dividends do not affect net income. The Dividends Payable balance was $20,000 at the beginning of the year and $15,000 at the end of the year. For cash flow purposes we must determine the cash paid for dividend distributions during 1984. The following ledger account indicates that $20,000 was disbursed on February 12.

Dividends Payable

2/12/84 Paid dividends	20,000	1/1/84 Balance	20,000
		12/30/84 Dividend declaration	15,000
		(15,000)	**35,000**

For purposes of the statement of changes in financial position, the cash outflow for dividends is disclosed as follows:

Uses of cash	
Payment of cash dividends	$20,000

Step 4

Once the preceding data have been determined, the formal statement is prepared. Powell Corporation's statement of changes using the cash definition of funds appears in Exhibit 17-9. Note that the change in cash agrees with the $50,000 increase as reported in Powell's comparative balance sheets.

WHAT BANKERS THINK ABOUT THE STATEMENT OF CHANGES

Don't take the statement of changes in financial position too lightly, especially if you're in need of a loan. In the late 1970s a study was made of 29 banks to determine the following:

The usefulness of the statement.

The types of information the statement provides.

The types of banking decisions that are facilitated by the statement.

Usefulness. *The study indicated convincingly that the statement of changes is providing banks of all sizes additional relevant information for banking decisions.*

Informational content. *The following table highlights the bankers' responses regarding the types of useful information provided by the statement.*

Types of Information	*Number of Bankers Responding*	*Percentage*
The resources from which funds were obtained	*28*	*96.6%*
The manner in which plant and equipment expenditures were financed	*25*	*86.2*
How debt retirement was accomplished	*20*	*70.0*
The determination of the disposition of profits	*22*	*75.8*
How and why the working capital position changed	*22*	*75.8*
The type and amount of external financing obtained	*20*	*70.0*
The amount and nature of nonfund charges	*15*	*51.7*
How and why the cash position changed	*18*	*62.1*
An indication of the change in the overall financial strength of the firm	*20*	*70.0*
An indication of the company's overall financial policies	*19*	*65.5*
The company's dividend policy	*11*	*37.9*
The relationship between a company's profitability and solvency	*11*	*37.9*

Decisions facilitated. *Bankers making lending decisions use the statement of changes to determine (1) whether external funds are obtained from the most appropriate sources, (2) if additional financing will be necessary and/or available in the near future, (3) whether the applicant will be able to meet loan obligations, and (4) if the applicant's dividend policy is appropriate. Bankers making investment trust decisions used the statement to facilitate decisions regarding the effect current sources and uses of funds will have on future earnings and whether expenditures for plant and equipment were adequate.*

Overall the bankers concluded that the statement of changes in financial position provides additional relevant and useful information. Further, they found the form and content of the statement satisfactory and were pleased that it is a required report. All but two bankers indicated that the statement of changes furnishes information that is not readily obtainable, or not obtainable at all, from the other financial statements.

SOURCE Adapted from E. Richard Brownlee, "What Bankers Think About the Funds Statement," Magazine of Bank Administration, January 1978, pp. 32–33, 37–38, 41.

Exhibit 17-9

POWELL CORPORATION
Statement of Changes in Financial Position
For the Year Ended December 31, 1984

Sources of cash		
Provided from operations		
Net income		$ 40,000
Add (deduct) items to convert net income to cash basis		
Building depreciation expense	$ 25,000	
Equipment depreciation expense	70,000	
Loss on equipment sale	5,000	
Gain on sale of long-term investments	(15,000)	
Increase in accounts receivable	(25,000)	
Decrease in merchandise inventory	25,000	
Increase in prepaid expenses	(1,000)	
Increase in accounts payable	30,000	
Increase in taxes payable	6,000	120,000
Cash provided from operations		$160,000
Sale of equipment		15,000
Sale of long-term investments		135,000
Issuance of common stock for cash		370,000
Issuance of common stock for building		200,000
Total sources of cash		$880,000
Uses of cash		
Purchase of land	$ 85,000	
Acquisition of building by the issuance of common stock	200,000	
Purchase of equipment	25,000	
Retirement of bonds payable	500,000	
Payment of cash dividends	20,000	
Total uses of cash		830,000
Increase in cash		$ 50,000

CASH VERSUS WORKING CAPITAL APPROACHES IN PRACTICE

The working capital approach of measuring changes in financial position predominates in practice. Although cash inflows and outflows are important to statement users in analyzing a firm's financial performance, condition, and investment opportunities, a consideration of all current assets and current liabilities does have merit. Because various elements of working capital will ultimately become or consume cash through the operating cycle, many accountants feel that working capital is extremely useful in generating information for prediction of *future* cash position.

Despite this attribute, a growing number of statement users appear to be shifting their allegiance to a cash-based statement of changes. A primary reason for this shift is a belief that net income computed under the accrual basis of accounting fails to present a clear picture of an entity's true earning power. These users contend that complex financial reporting practices and arbitrary allocation procedures (such as depreciation) produce results that vary greatly from cash flows. Other arguments advanced for the cash definition of funds recognize that cash (as opposed to working capital) is better understood by investors. Furthermore, if a company encounters problems in the management of its working capital, those problems frequently surface first in the area of cash flows. As a result, a cash-based statement would be more meaningful (and timely) for both internal and external financial statement users.

At the time of writing, the issue of a cash or working capital definition of funds is under study. What the final outcome will be is unknown, but it appears that the profession is leaning toward cash as the best measure for evaluating operating, financing, and investing activities.

SUMMARY PROBLEM

Colwell Corporation had the following balance sheets.

	Dec. 31, 1984	Dec. 31, 1983
ASSETS		
Cash	$ 69,000	$ 87,000
Accounts receivable (net)	189,000	223,000
Inventory	65,000	45,000
Prepaid expenses	15,000	12,000
Land	150,000	120,000
Equipment	125,000	150,000
Accumulated depreciation: equipment	(85,000)	(75,000)
Buildings	280,000	200,000
Accumulated depreciation: buildings	(85,000)	(70,000)
Patents (net of amortization)	24,000	27,000
Total assets	$747,000	$719,000
LIABILITIES & STOCKHOLDERS' EQUITY		
Accounts payable	$ 88,000	$120,000
Notes payable (current)	160,000	90,000
Dividends payable	10,000	—
Income taxes payable	50,000	70,000
Bonds payable	100,000	150,000
Common stock, $10 par	210,000	180,000
Additional paid-in capital	50,000	50,000
Retained earnings	79,000	59,000
Total liabilities & stockholders' equity	$747,000	$719,000

The following additional information was extracted from the accounting records.

1 Three thousand shares of common stock were issued for land having a fair market value of $30,000.
2 Equipment having a book value of $13,000 (cost, $25,000; accumulated depreciation, $12,000) was sold for cash at a $7,000 gain.
3 A building was constructed for $80,000 cash.
4 Cash dividends of $10,000, declared on December 30, 1984, will be paid on January 30, 1985.
5 Long-term bonds of $50,000 were retired at 100; no gain or loss was incurred.
6 The 1984 income statement revealed the following:

Net income	$30,000
Equipment depreciation expense	22,000
Building depreciation expense	15,000
Patent amortization expense	3,000

INSTRUCTIONS

a Compute the change in working capital during 1984.
b Prepare a statement of changes in financial position for the year ended December 31, 1984, using the (1) working capital definition of funds and (2) cash definition of funds.

SOLUTION

a

	Dec. 31, 1984	Dec. 31, 1983
Current assets		
Cash	$ 69,000	$ 87,000
Accounts receivable (net)	189,000	223,000
Inventory	65,000	45,000
Prepaid expenses	15,000	12,000
Total current assets	$338,000	$367,000
Current liabilities		
Accounts payable	$ 88,000	$120,000
Notes payable	160,000	90,000
Dividends payable	10,000	–
Income taxes payable	50,000	70,000
Total current liabilities	$308,000	$280,000
Working capital	$ 30,000	$ 87,000

$57,000 decrease

b(1)

COLWELL CORPORATION
Statement of Changes in Financial Position
For the Year Ended December 31, 1984

Sources of working capital		
Provided from operations		
Net income	$ 30,000	
Add (deduct) items not affecting working capital		
Equipment depreciation expense	22,000	
Building depreciation expense	15,000	
Patent amortization expense	3,000	
Gain on equipment sale	(7,000)	
Working capital provided from operations		$ 63,000
Issuance of common stock for land*		30,000
Sale of equipment†		20,000
Total sources of working capital		$113,000
Uses of working capital		
Acquisition of land by the issuance of common stock*	$ 30,000	
Construction of building	80,000	
Cash dividend declaration	10,000	
Retirement of long-term bonds	50,000	
Total uses of working capital		170,000
Decrease in working capital		$ 57,000

SCHEDULE OF CHANGES IN WORKING CAPITAL COMPONENTS

Increases (decreases) in current assets		
Cash	$(18,000)	
Accounts receivable (net)	(34,000)	
Inventory	20,000	
Prepaid expenses	3,000	$ (29,000)
Increases (decreases) in current liabilities		
Accounts payable	$ (32,000)	
Notes payable	70,000	
Dividends payable	10,000	
Income taxes payable	(20,000)	28,000
Decrease in working capital		$ 57,000

* This is a significant nonfund exchange transaction and is disclosed as both a source and a use of funds.

†Equipment cost	$25,000
Less: Accumulated depreciation	12,000
Book value	$13,000
Gain	7,000
Proceeds on disposal	$20,000

b(2)

COLWELL CORPORATION
Statement of Changes in Financial Position
For the Year Ended December 31, 1984

Sources of cash		
Provided from operations		
Net income		$ 30,000
Add (deduct) items to convert net income to cash basis		
Equipment depreciation expense	$ 22,000	
Building depreciation expense	15,000	
Patent amortization expense	3,000	
Gain on equipment sale	(7,000)	
Decrease in accounts receivable	34,000	
Increase in inventory	(20,000)	
Increase in prepaid expenses	(3,000)	
Decrease in accounts payable	(32,000)	
Increase in notes payable	70,000	
Decrease in income taxes payable	(20,000)	62,000
Cash provided from operations		$ 92,000
Issuance of common stock for land		30,000
Sale of equipment		20,000
Total sources of cash		$142,000
Uses of cash		
Acquisition of land by the issuance of common stock	$ 30,000	
Construction of building	80,000	
Retirement of long-term bonds	50,000	
Total uses of cash		160,000
Decrease in cash		$ 18,000

KEY TERMS AND CONCEPTS

nonfund (exchange) transactions 653
sources of funds 647, 649, 665
statement of changes in financial position 646
statement of changes in financial position, cash approach 666
statement of changes in financial position, working capital approach 654
uses of funds 647, 651, 665
working capital 646

QUESTIONS

Q17-1 What information does the statement of changes in financial position disclose? Give several examples. Is any of this information available from other financial statements? If so, why is a statement of changes in financial position prepared?

Q17-2 The definition of funds can vary. Explain why the working capital definition is more widely used than the cash definition.

Q17-3 Identify general sources and uses of working capital. Then present two specific examples of each source and use.

Q17-4 Why are nonfund transactions, such as the exchange of common stock for a building, included on a statement of changes in financial position? How are these nonfund transactions disclosed?

Q17-5 How much working capital is provided from each of the following transactions?

a Land, purchased for $15,000, is sold for $18,000 cash.

b Land, purchased for $15,000, is exchanged for a $15,000 short-term note receivable.

c Land, purchased for $900,000, is sold for $800,000 cash.

Q17-6 Sonny Parker purchased a television station for $500,000. He paid $75,000 cash and signed a long-term note payable for $425,000. How is Parker's working capital affected? How would the transaction be shown on a statement of changes in financial position prepared by using the working capital definition of funds?

Q17-7 Items such as depreciation expense reduce net income without a commensurate decrease in working capital. How are these and similar items treated when determining working capital provided from operations?

Q17-8 Why must a schedule of changes in working capital components be presented when a statement of changes is prepared on a working capital basis?

Q17-9 When preparing a statement of changes in financial position using the cash definition of funds, which balance sheet accounts are analyzed to explain the change in the beginning and ending cash balance?

Q17-10 What are the major differences between a statement of changes in financial position prepared by using the working capital approach and one prepared by using the cash definition of funds?

Q17-11 Summertime, Inc., uses the cash definition of funds when preparing the statement of changes in financial position. The corporation recently experienced a decrease in accounts receivable and an increase in taxes payable. Do these changes represent sources or uses of cash? Explain.

Q17-12 In a cash-based statement of changes, how is reported net income adjusted to arrive at cash provided from operations?

EXERCISES

E17-1 The Natt Company had the following transactions and events during the year.

a Sold equipment having a book value of $40,000 for $70,000 cash.

b Purchased vehicles costing $40,000 for $10,000 cash, a short-term note payable of $12,000, and a long-term note payable of $18,000.

c Purchased 2,000 shares of treasury stock at $10 per share.
d Declared a cash dividend of $1.00 per share on 100,000 common shares.
e Declared a 5% stock dividend on 100,000 shares of $1 par-value common stock. Fair market value at the time of declaration was $20 per share.
f Wrote off $5,000 of past-due accounts against the Allowance for Bad Debts.
g Net income for the year, $67,000.
h Amortization of patents for the year, $800.
i Sold long-term investments costing $40,000 for $15,000 cash.

Natt uses the working capital definition of funds.

Consider each of the items above independently. Determine whether the item (1) is a source or a use of working capital or (2) has no effect on working capital. For each source or use, indicate the amount of change in working capital.

E17-2 The Robinson Company had the following transactions and events during the year.

a Exchanged 50,000 shares of $1 par-value common stock for a building appraised at $750,000. The market value per share at the time of exchange was $15.
b Sold long-term investments costing $85,000 for $210,000 cash.
c Authorized a 5-for-1 stock split on May 1.
d Sold equipment costing $40,000 for $41,200. Accumulated depreciation at the time of sale amounted to $2,000.

Show how each transaction or event would appear on a statement of changes in financial position prepared by using the working capital definition of funds. Do each transaction separately.

E17-3 The property, plant, and equipment section of Meriweather Company's comparative balance sheet is shown below.

	Dec. 31, 1984	Dec. 31, 1983
Property, plant, & equipment		
Land	$ 18,000	$ 18,000
Machinery	980,000	720,000
Less: Accumulated depreciation	(325,000)	(360,000)

New machinery purchased during 1984 totaled $500,000. The 1984 income statement disclosed machinery depreciation expense of $100,000 and a $15,000 gain on the sale of machinery.

a Determine the cost and accumulated depreciation of the machinery sold during 1984.
b Determine the selling price of the machinery sold.
c Show how the sale of machinery would appear on a statement of changes prepared by using the working capital definition of funds.

E17-4 Jamaal Parker, Inc., included the following abbreviated income statement in its 1984 annual report to stockholders.

JAMAAL PARKER, INC.
Income Statement
For the Year Ended October 31, 1984

Sales	$2,500,000
Cost of goods sold	1,200,000
Gross profit	$1,300,000
Operating expenses, taxes, & depreciation	1,180,000
	$ 120,000
Loss on sale of long-term investment	30,000
Net income	$ 90,000

Comparative balance sheets revealed the following account balances:

	Oct. 31, 1984	Oct. 31, 1983
Trade accounts receivable	$250,000	$200,000
Merchandise inventory	200,000	280,000
Accumulated depreciation: equipment	150,000	100,000
Accounts payable	275,000	210,000
Accrued liabilities	50,000	100,000
Dividends payable (annual dividends are declared in mid-October of each year, payable in January of the next year)	200,000	100,000

There were no purchases or disposals of equipment during the year. The long-term investment had a carrying (book) value of $110,000 and was sold for cash on April 2. On the basis of the foregoing information, determine the following:

a The working capital provided from operations from November 1, 1983 through October 31, 1984.

b The cash provided from operations from November 1, 1983 through October 31, 1984.

E17-5 Federal Hills, Inc., reported net income for the year ended December 31, 1984 as follows:

FEDERAL HILLS, INC.
Income Statement
For the Year Ended December 31, 1984

Sales		$740,000
Cost of goods sold		360,000
Gross profit		$380,000
Expenses		
Depreciation	$100,000	
Amortization	30,000	
Cash operating costs	180,000	310,000
Net income		$ 70,000

Management claims that "working capital never looked better" and wants to pay an extra dividend of $50,000 in addition to the regular dividend of $60,000. The ending retained earnings and cash balances on December 31, 1984, totaled $850,000 and $240,000, respectively.

a An angry stockholder, feeling that management is trying to "pull a fast one," is demanding an explanation of how an extra dividend can be justified when net income is so small. Analyze the information presented and write a short response to the stockholder.

b What information is disclosed on the statement of changes to help clarify issues similar to the one raised by the angry stockholder?

E17-6 The comparative balance sheets of Aronstein Company follow.

ARONSTEIN COMPANY
Comparative Balance Sheets
December 31, 1984 and 1983

	Dec. 31, 1984	Dec. 31, 1983
Cash	$ 5,000	$ 7,000
Accounts receivable (net)	12,000	18,000
Merchandise inventory	35,000	28,000
Property, plant, & equipment	40,000	30,000
Accumulated depreciation	(17,000)	(10,000)
Total assets	$75,000	$73,000
Accounts payable	$25,000	$21,000
Taxes payable	20,000	17,000
Common stock	9,000	9,000
Retained earnings	21,000	26,000
Total liabilities & stockholders' equity	$75,000	$73,000

The income statement revealed sales of $120,000, cost of goods sold of $80,000, and operating expenses of $35,000 (including $7,000 of depreciation). Dividends declared and paid during 1984 totaled $10,000. Finally, Aronstein purchased $10,000 of equipment during the year for cash.

a Determine the increase or decrease in working capital during 1984.

b Prepare a statement of changes in financial position by using the working capital definition of funds. You may omit the schedule of changes in working capital components.

E17-7 Selected balance sheet accounts from Petrovide Company at the end of 1983 and 1984 follow.

	Dec. 31, 1984	Dec. 31, 1983
Accounts receivable	$ 40,000	$ 30,000
Interest receivable	5,000	3,800
Inventory	100,000	120,000
Prepaid rent	1,000	1,500
Equipment	150,000	150,000
Accumulated depreciation: equipment	40,000	30,000
Long-term investments	50,000	50,000
Accounts payable (suppliers of merchandise)	140,000	100,000

Selected income statement information for the year ended December 31, 1984, appears below.

Sales	$240,000
Cost of goods sold	180,000
Rent expense	8,000
Interest revenue	4,000
Depreciation expense	10,000

Petrovide makes all sales and purchases on account and uses the accrual basis of accounting. Determine the following:

a Cash collections from customers

b Merchandise purchases for the year

c Cash paid to suppliers of merchandise

d Interest received from long-term investments

e Cash paid for rent

E17-8 Refer to the data presented in Exercise 17-6.

a Determine the increase or decrease in cash during 1984.

b Prepare a statement of changes in financial position by using the cash definition of funds.

PROBLEMS

P17-1 ***Statement of changes in financial position: Working capital basis***

Comparative balance sheets of Bargains Company appear on page 681.

BARGAINS COMPANY
Comparative Balance Sheets
December 31, 1984 and 1983

	1984		1983	
ASSETS				
Current assets				
Cash		$ 15,000		$ 45,000
Accounts receivable (net)		100,000		115,000
Inventory		485,000		400,000
Total current assets		$600,000		$560,000
Property, plant, & equipment				
Land		$ 12,000		$ 9,000
Machinery	$ 90,000		$ 70,000	
Less: Accumulated depreciation	24,000	66,000	14,000	56,000
Total property, plant, & equipment		$ 78,000		$ 65,000
Intangible assets				
Patents (cost of $10,000 less amortization)		3,000		4,000
Total assets		$681,000		$629,000
LIABILITIES & STOCKHOLDERS' EQUITY				
Current liabilities				
Accounts payable		$390,000		$370,000
Salaries payable		10,000		8,000
Total current liabilities		$400,000		$378,000
Long-term liabilities				
Mortgage payable		6,000		7,000
Stockholders' equity				
Common stock	$200,000		$180,000	
Retained earnings	75,000	275,000	64,000	244,000
Total liabilities & stockholders' equity		$681,000		$629,000

Additional information is as follows:

a No dividends were declared or paid in 1984. The change in retained earnings is due to the net income (or net loss) for the period.

b Common stock of $20,000 was issued at par value to acquire machinery on February 4.

c Land was purchased for cash on May 10.

d The income statement revealed machinery depreciation expense of $10,000 and patent amortization expense of $1,000.

e Bargains paid $1,000 on the mortgage note during the year.

INSTRUCTIONS

Prepare a statement of changes in financial position by using the working capital definition of funds.

P17-2 ***Statement of changes in financial position: Working capital basis***

The following account balances were taken from the balance sheets of the Jackson Company, a sole proprietorship.

	Dec. 31, 1984	Dec. 31, 1983
Cash	$41,800	$28,700
Accounts receivable (net)	32,400	27,600
Notes receivable (short-term)	10,000	10,000
Merchandise inventory	92,600	88,400
Prepaid expenses	8,000	6,500
Machinery	73,400	69,700
Accumulated depreciation: machinery	11,800	9,600
Vehicles	15,750	8,800
Accumulated depreciation: vehicles	5,250	3,700
Franchise	20,000	21,000
Accounts payable	95,200	91,500
Salaries payable	6,000	7,000
Payroll taxes payable	11,000	2,000
Current portion of long-term debt	10,000	10,000
Mortgage payable (due in 15 years)	80,000	90,000
Note payable (long-term)	6,950	—
R. Jackson, capital	67,750	46,900

An examination of the ledger accounts revealed the following information:

a 1984 machinery depreciation expense totaled $9,000.
b 1984 vehicle depreciation expense totaled $1,550.
c A vehicle costing $6,950 was acquired by issuing a long-term note payable.
d Two machines were sold during 1984. Machinery costing $6,000 with a book value of $2,000 was sold for $1,000. In addition, machinery costing $4,000 with accumulated depreciation of $2,800 was sold for $5,000. New machines costing $13,700 were purchased for cash.
e Jackson amortizes its fast-food franchise (original cost, $40,000) over a 40-year life.
f During 1984 cash investments and withdrawals by the owner amounted to $5,000 and $20,000, respectively.
g Net income for 1984 totaled $35,850.

INSTRUCTIONS

Prepare a statement of changes in financial position by using the working capital definition of funds.

P17-3 ***Statement of changes in financial position: Working capital and cash definitions***

The 1984 income statement of Green Company, Inc., follows.

GREEN COMPANY, INC.
Income Statement
For the Year Ended December 31, 1984

Sales	$500,000
Less: Sales returns	10,000
Net sales	$490,000
Less: Cost of goods sold	210,000
Gross profit	$280,000
Less: Operating expenses & taxes (including depreciation expense on machinery of $15,000)	233,000
	$ 47,000
Less: Loss on sale of machinery	3,000
Net income	$ 44,000

Balance sheets for 1983 and 1984 contained the following accounts:

	Dec. 31, 1984	Dec. 31, 1983
ASSETS		
Cash	$ 5,000	$ 45,000
Accounts receivable (net)	52,000	37,000
Inventory	41,000	25,000
Machinery (net)	60,000	60,000
Total assets	$158,000	$167,000
LIABILITIES & STOCKHOLDERS' EQUITY		
Accounts payable	$ 21,000	$ 61,000
Dividends payable	6,000	3,000
Long-term note payable	5,000	20,000
Common stock, $5 par value	5,000	4,000
Paid-in capital in excess of par value	20,000	16,000
Retained earnings	101,000	63,000
Total liabilities & stockholders' equity	$158,000	$167,000

Other data follow.

1 Common stock (200 shares) was sold for $25 per share in the middle of 1984.
2 Dividends of $6 per share were declared in late 1984, payable in February 1985.
3 Machinery costing $20,000 with a book value of $13,000 was sold for $10,000. New machinery costing $28,000 was purchased for cash.
4 Changes in the Accounts Receivable and Accounts Payable accounts were caused by sales and purchases of merchandise, respectively.

INSTRUCTIONS

a Prepare a statement of changes in financial position by using the working capital definition of funds.

b Prepare a statement of changes in financial position by using the cash definition of funds.

c Analyze the two statements. Which areas should Green's management monitor more closely and control better?

P17-4 ***Statement of changes in financial position: Cash basis***

Becky Lane, owner of Squaredeal Service, is disturbed about the size of the firm's ending cash balance. The balance sheet accounts for Squaredeal follow.

	Jan. 1	Dec. 31
Cash	$15,500	$ 25
Accounts receivable	32,000	64,500
Supplies inventory	10,500	23,500
Prepaid rent	1,750	2,540
Cleaning equipment	12,000	15,000
Accumulated depreciation: cleaning equipment	9,000	11,000
Vans	18,500	18,500
Accumulated depreciation: vans	10,000	12,500
Office equipment	4,500	5,000
Accumulated depreciation: office equipment	3,000	3,750
Goodwill	6,000	5,500
Accounts payable	11,500	17,500
Current portion of long-term van notes	2,000	2,000
Notes payable on vans (long-term)	6,000	4,000
Becky Lane, capital	59,250	83,815

Other data are as follows:

1 Net income was $30,000. Cash withdrawals by the owner were made periodically throughout the year.

2 No disposals or sales of equipment occurred during the year.

3 Squaredeal purchased new cleaning and office equipment for cash.

4 Property, plant, and equipment was depreciated; the intangible was amortized.

INSTRUCTIONS

a Prepare a statement of changes in financial position by using the cash definition of funds.

b Prepare a brief evaluation of Squaredeal's current cash dilemma.

P17-5 ***Use of statement of changes in financial position to prepare a balance sheet***

A statement of changes in financial position for Bluhorn Corporation, prepared by using the cash definition of funds, follows.

BLUHORN CORPORATION
Statement of Changes in Financial Position
For the Year Ended October 31, 1984

Sources of cash		
Provided from operations		
Net income		$ 60,000
Add (deduct) items to convert net income to cash basis		
Building depreciation expense	$ 50,000	
Vehicle depreciation expense	20,000	
Patent amortization	1,000	
Loss on sale of vehicles	5,000	
Increase in accounts payable	8,000	
Increase in salaries payable	12,000	
Gain on sale of long-term investments	(8,000)	
Increase in inventory	(30,000)	
Increase in accounts receivable	(35,000)	
Increase in prepaid expenses	(2,000)	21,000
Cash provided from operations		$ 81,000
Sale of vehicles (original cost, $24,000)		13,000
Sale of long-term investments (book value, $18,000)		26,000
Issuance of preferred stock for land		300,000
Issuance of common stock at par for cash		50,000
Total sources of cash		$470,000
Uses of cash		
Acquisition of land for preferred stock	$300,000	
Purchase of patent	25,000	
Purchase of vehicle	21,000	
Retirement of bonds payable	10,000	
Payment of previously declared cash dividends	30,000	
Total uses of cash		386,000
Increase in cash		$ 84,000

The balance sheet at the beginning of the year lists the following accounts:

BLUHORN CORPORATION
Balance Sheet
November 1, 1983

ASSETS			
Current assets			
Cash		$ 42,000	
Accounts receivable (net)		70,000	
Inventory		65,000	
Prepaid expenses		4,000	$181,000
Property, plant, & equipment			
Land		$ 10,000	
Building	$400,000		
Less: Accumulated depreciation	100,000	300,000	
Vehicles	$180,000		
Less: Accumulated depreciation	60,000	120,000	430,000
Intangible assets			
Patents, at unamortized cost			5,000
Other			
Long-term investments			18,000
Total assets			$634,000
LIABILITIES & STOCKHOLDERS' EQUITY			
Current liabilities			
Accounts payable		$ 72,000	
Salaries payable		10,000	
Dividends payable		30,000	$112,000
Long-term liabilities			
Bonds payable			400,000
Stockholders' equity			
Preferred stock, $100 par value		$ —	
Common stock, $10 par value		100,000	
Retained earnings		22,000	122,000
Total liabilities & stockholders' equity			$634,000

On October 29, 1984, cash dividends of $45,000 were declared, payable to common stockholders on December 1, 1984.

INSTRUCTIONS

On the basis of the information presented, prepare a balance sheet for Bluhorn Corporation as of October 31, 1984.

P17-6 Statement of changes in financial position: Working capital basis (alternate to P17-1)

Comparative balance sheets of Washington Company are presented below.

WASHINGTON COMPANY
Comparative Balance Sheets
October 31, 1984 and 1983

	1984		1983	
ASSETS				
Current assets				
Cash		$ 100,000		$ 130,000
Short-term investments		200,000		200,000
Accounts receivable (net)		427,000		382,000
Merchandise inventory		1,000,000		918,000
Total current assets		$1,727,000		$1,630,000
Property, plant, & equipment				
Land		$ 18,000		$ 20,000
Equipment	$400,000		$300,000	
Less: Accumulated depreciation	95,000	305,000	80,000	220,000
Total property, plant, & equipment		$ 323,000		$ 240,000
Intangible assets				
Copyrights (cost of $10,000 less amortization)		6,000		8,000
Total assets		$2,056,000		$1,878,000
LIABILITIES & STOCKHOLDERS' EQUITY				
Current liabilities				
Accounts payable		$ 800,000		$ 732,000
Accrued liabilities		15,000		15,000
Taxes payable		85,000		120,000
Total current liabilities		$ 900,000		$ 867,000
Long-term liabilities				
Bonds payable		600,000		900,000
Stockholders' equity				
Common stock	$200,000		$100,000	
Retained earnings	356,000	556,000	11,000	111,000
Total liabilities & stockholders' equity		$2,056,000		$1,878,000

Additional information is as follows:

a No dividends were declared or paid in 1984. The change in retained earnings is due to the net income (or net loss) for the period.

b Common stock of $100,000 was issued at par value to acquire equipment.

c A small plot of land costing $2,000 was sold for $8,000 on July 1.

d The income statement revealed depreciation expense and amortization expense of $15,000 and $2,000, respectively.

e Washington retired $300,000 of bonds during the year; no gain or loss was incurred.

INSTRUCTIONS

Prepare a statement of changes in financial position by using the working capital definition of funds.

P17-7 ***Statement of changes in financial position: Working capital basis (alternate to P17-2)***

The following account balances were taken from the balance sheets of the Tanglewood Company, a sole proprietorship.

	Dec. 31, 1984	Dec. 31, 1983
Cash	$ 25,900	$ 31,300
Accounts receivable (net)	34,800	33,700
Notes receivable (short-term)	15,000	21,000
Merchandise inventory	87,500	68,600
Supplies	4,200	3,900
Machinery	115,500	110,800
Accumulated depreciation: machinery	41,600	38,900
Trucks	35,900	28,500
Accumulated depreciation: trucks	8,700	6,200
Franchise	60,000	62,000
Accounts payable	55,500	59,700
Salaries payable	7,100	7,300
Taxes payable	12,600	10,100
Current portion of long-term debt	9,000	9,000
Mortgage payable (due in 15 years)	150,000	159,000
Note payable (long-term)	7,400	—
L. Tanglewood, capital	86,900	69,600

An examination of the ledger accounts revealed the following information:

a 1984 machinery depreciation expense totaled $17,300.

b 1984 truck depreciation expense totaled $2,500.

c A truck costing $7,400 was acquired by issuing a long-term note payable.

d Two machines were sold during 1984. Machinery costing $9,000 with a book value of $4,800 was sold for $2,300. In addition, machinery costing $16,000 with accumulated depreciation of $10,400 was sold for $4,100. New machines costing $29,700 were purchased for cash.

e Tanglewood amortizes its franchise (original cost, $80,000) over a 40-year life.

f During 1984 cash investments and withdrawals by the owner amounted to $19,000 and $6,000, respectively.

g Net income for 1984 totaled $4,300.

INSTRUCTIONS

Prepare a statement of changes in financial position by using the working capital definition of funds.

P17-8 ***Statement of changes in financial position: Working capital and cash definitions (alternate to P17-3)***

The 1984 income statement of Taputu Company follows.

TAPUTU COMPANY
Income Statement
For the Year Ended September 30, 1984

Gross sales		$2,000,000
Less: Sales returns	$ 10,000	
Sales discounts	5,000	15,000
Net sales		$1,985,000
Less: Cost of goods sold		960,000
Gross profit		$1,025,000
Less: Rent expense	$120,000	
Utilities expense	50,000	
Salaries expense	180,000	
Advertising expense	100,000	
Depreciation expense: store equipment	10,000	
Tax expense	216,000	
Miscellaneous expense	145,000	821,000
		$ 204,000
Add: Gain on sale of long-term investments		7,000
Net income		$ 211,000

The reported income is the highest ever attained. As a result, management declared dividends totaling $41,000 in mid-September for payment in early October 1984. Balance sheets for 1983 and 1984 contained the following accounts:

	Sept. 30, 1984	Sept. 30, 1983
ASSETS		
Cash	$ 50,000	$207,000
Accounts receivable (net)	420,000	230,000
Merchandise inventory	350,000	180,000
Store equipment (net)	95,000	80,000
Long-term investments	—	8,000
Total assets	$915,000	$705,000
LIABILITIES & STOCKHOLDERS' EQUITY		
Accounts payable	$167,000	$190,000
Dividends payable	41,000	—
Bonds payable	200,000	214,000
Common stock, $10 par value	138,000	120,000
Paid-in capital in excess of par value	97,000	79,000
Retained earnings	272,000	102,000
Total liabilities & stockholders' equity	$915,000	$705,000

Other data follow.

1 Common stock (1,800 shares) was sold in February 1984 at $20 per share.
2 Store equipment having a cost of $20,000 and accumulated depreciation of $18,000 was sold for $2,000. Other store equipment was purchased for cash.
3 Taputu recently sold long-term investments costing $8,000 for $15,000 cash.
4 Taputu retired $14,000 of bonds during the year; no gain or loss was incurred.
5 Changes in the Accounts Receivable and Accounts Payable accounts were caused by sales and purchases of merchandise, respectively.

INSTRUCTIONS

a Prepare a statement of changes in financial position by using the working capital definition of funds.
b Prepare a statement of changes in financial position by using the cash definition of funds.
c Analyze the two statements. Is everything as rosy as Taputu's management believes? Explain.

P17-9 ***Statement of changes in financial position: Cash basis (alternate to P17-4)*** The Omaha Bullets, Inc., a minor league baseball team, is having great difficulty paying its bills. Management cannot understand how the firm can generate net income and continually be short of cash. The balance sheet accounts of the Bullets follow.

	Sept. 30, 1984	Oct. 1, 1983
Cash	$ –	$ 25,000
Receivable from major league affiliate	400,000	634,000
Concessions inventory	134,000	79,000
Prepaid expenses and grounds supplies	25,700	19,000
Ball park stands and structures	792,600	748,600
Accumulated depreciation: ball park	442,000	400,000
Other fixed assets	130,000	108,400
Accumulated depreciation: other fixed assets	85,000	80,000
Accounts payable	24,000	34,800
Salaries payable	46,000	54,000
Bonuses payable	51,200	176,500
Accrued taxes payable	16,000	15,000
Federal income taxes payable	–	129,000
Unearned admission revenue	5,000	15,000
Common stock	600,000	580,000
Retained earnings	213,100	129,700

Other data are as follows:

1 Net income was $100,000. Dividends declared and paid totaled $16,600.
2 No disposals of ball park stands, structures, or other fixed assets occurred during the year.
3 In February the Bullets acquired a new scoreboard and other fixed assets for cash.
4 Additional common stock was sold on May 15 for $20,000 cash.

INSTRUCTIONS

a Prepare a statement of changes in financial position by using the cash definition of funds for the year ended September 30, 1984.

b Prepare a brief evaluation of the Bullets' existing cash problem.

P17-10 *Use of statement of changes in financial position to prepare a balance sheet (alternate to P17-5)*

A statement of changes in financial position for Wedgewood Corporation, prepared by using the cash definition of funds, follows.

WEDGEWOOD CORPORATION
Statement of Changes in Financial Position
For the Year Ended December 31, 1984

Sources of cash		
Provided from operations		
Net income		$ 46,000
Add (deduct) items to convert net income to cash basis		
Building depreciation expense	$30,000	
Truck depreciation expense	8,000	
Patent amortization	2,000	
Loss on sale of long-term investments	6,000	
Decrease in inventory	11,000	
Increase in salaries payable	3,000	
Gain on sale of trucks	(4,000)	
Increase in accounts receivable	(21,000)	
Increase in prepaid expenses	(5,000)	
Decrease in accounts payable	(12,000)	18,000
Cash provided from operations		$ 64,000
Sale of trucks (original cost, $26,000)		19,000
Sale of long-term investments (book value, $13,000)		7,000
Issuance of preferred stock for cash		200,000
Issuance of common stock for land		80,000
Total sources of cash		$370,000
Uses of cash		
Acquisition of land for common stock	$ 80,000	
Purchase of patent	40,000	
Purchase of trucks	64,000	
Retirement of bonds payable	50,000	
Payment of previously declared cash dividends	28,000	
Total uses of cash		262,000
Increase in cash		$108,000

The balance sheet at the beginning of the year lists the following accounts:

WEDGEWOOD CORPORATION
Balance Sheet
January 1, 1984

ASSETS			
Current assets			
Cash		$ 51,000	
Accounts receivable (net)		85,000	
Inventory		115,000	
Prepaid expenses		9,000	$260,000
Property, plant, & equipment			
Land		$ 25,000	
Building	$580,000		
Less: Accumulated depreciation	75,000	505,000	
Trucks	$115,000		
Less: Accumulated depreciation	43,000	72,000	602,000
Intangible assets			
Patents, at unamortized cost			15,000
Other			
Long-term investments			37,000
Total assets			$914,000
LIABILITIES & STOCKHOLDERS' EQUITY			
Current liabilities			
Accounts payable		$135,000	
Salaries payable		18,000	
Dividends payable		28,000	$181,000
Long-term liabilities			
Bonds payable			500,000
Stockholders' equity			
Preferred stock, $10 par value		$ —	
Common stock, $1 par value		90,000	
Retained earnings		143,000	233,000
Total liabilities & stockholders' equity			$914,000

On November 29, 1984, cash dividends of $50,000 were declared, payable to common stockholders on January 2, 1985.

INSTRUCTIONS
On the basis of the information presented, prepare a balance sheet for Wedgewood Corporation as of December 31, 1984.

CASE 17
THE INVITED LECTURE

You are in the process of delivering an invited lecture to a group of executives concerning the statement of changes in financial position and the working capital definition of funds. During a break three executives approached you with the following comments:

Executive A. I'm confused. You say depreciation is not a source of funds because it doesn't affect working capital. Yet depreciation is normally shown in the sources section of the statement. Why?

Executive B. It seems to me that funds should always be defined as cash. After all, I don't pay my employees with accounts receivable nor do I distribute inventory to liquidate my long-term debt. Cash is the only thing that counts when it comes to funds. This working capital stuff is theory and theory only.

Executive C. I'm confused by the reports my accountant has just given me. According to her figures, our working capital from operations for the year just ended increased by $45,000. Yet our cash balance remained constant at $10,000 and we had a $5,000 net loss. These results seem contradictory. What's going on?

INSTRUCTIONS

Prepare a brief response to address the issues raised by the three executives.

18 THE FOUNDATION OF FINANCIAL ACCOUNTING

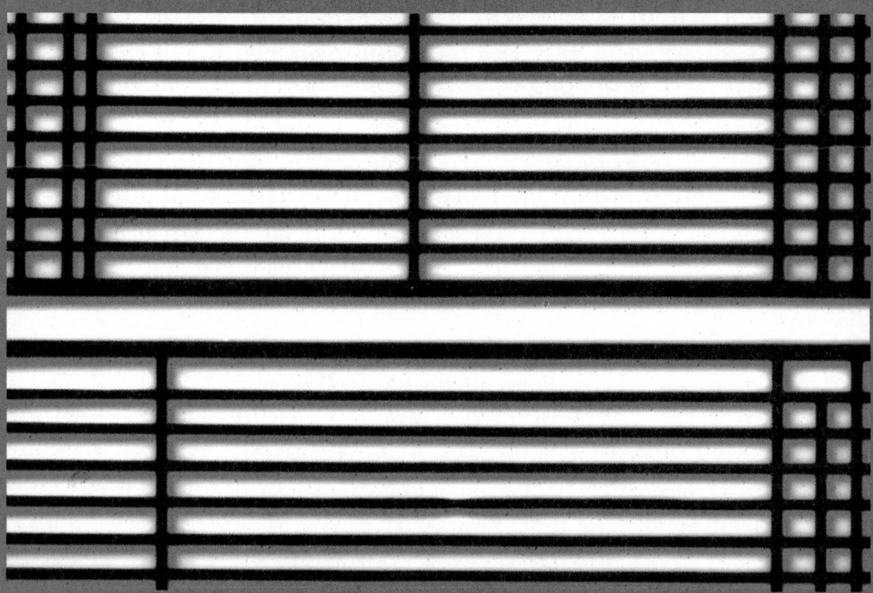

LEARNING OBJECTIVES

After reading this chapter you should:

1 Be familiar with the objectives of financial reporting.

2 Be aware of the desirable characteristics of accounting information: relevancy, reliability, comparability, and understandability.

3 Understand generally accepted accounting principles and the roles of various bodies (especially the Securities and Exchange Commission, the Accounting Principles Board, and the Financial Accounting Standards Board) in the development process.

4 Be familiar with the following assumptions and concepts: the entity assumption, the going-concern assumption, the periodicity assumption, the monetary unit assumption, the historical-cost principle, the objectivity principle, the revenue realization principle, the matching principle, the consistency principle, the disclosure principle, materiality, and conservatism.

5 Be able to apply the percentage-of-completion and installment methods of revenue realization.

6 Be aware of the potential effects of alternative reporting practices on an entity's financial statements.

CHAPTER 18

In an address before accountants and other members of the financial community, the chairman of the Securities and Exchange Commission made the following observations about accounting:

> *In many ways, accounting is unique among the professions. It does not advocate, heal, or counsel; rather it certifies. That is, it assures the public that financial statements can be accepted as credible. As such, the most important characteristic of the accounting profession is a high degree of public trust.*
>
> *During the last decade, however, much has occurred to challenge the trust which the profession has cultivated and enjoyed since the 1930s. For example, we witnessed the collapse of major corporations on the heels of financial reporting, reviewed by respected auditors, which did not communicate the threat of impending insolvency. Revelations of off-book payments to foreign officials further impeached credibility. Moreover, the relevance of traditional accounting principles came into question in an inflationary environment. . . .*
>
> *Whether these concerns were valid or not may be less important than the fact that they underscore the need for the profession to be vigilant in maintaining the public's trust. If such trust were to dissolve, calls for a greater governmental role in the profession's affairs would almost inevitably be heard.*[1]

These comments reveal that accounting and its financial reporting function have been subject to some significant criticism over the years. Perhaps this criticism has been well deserved; perhaps not.

Previous chapters of this text have focused on specific practices and procedures used to record business transactions and disclose financial affairs. In this chapter we wish to present a broad overview of financial accounting. We will study the objectives of financial reporting along with characteristics of accounting information. Our emphasis will be on the assumptions and concepts that serve as the underlying foundation for the balance sheet, income statement, statement of owners' equity, and the statement of changes in financial position, that is, generally accepted accounting principles.

OBJECTIVES OF FINANCIAL REPORTING

Stockholders, creditors, managers, taxing authorities, analysts, and a host of other parties use financial accounting information for a variety of reasons. Managers assess a segment's ability to effectively control expenses, while creditors have an interest in an enterprise's debt-paying ability. Stockholders, on the other hand, have an obvious concern about reported earnings and the probability of future dividend distributions. It goes without saying that financial statements must be *general-purpose* statements; that is, the statements must be useful in satisfying different needs of different parties. Thus

[1] "Accounting and Financial Reporting—The Challenges of the 1980s," address by Harold M. Williams, Chairman, Securities and Exchange Commission, November 3, 1980, p. 1.

unbiased determination and communication of financial information is of utmost importance.

In an effort to build a framework for attaining these attributes, the accounting profession has established several objectives of financial reporting.[2] The objectives state that financial reporting should generate information that is helpful:

1 To present and potential investors, creditors, and other users in making various types of decisions.
2 In assessing the amounts, timing, and uncertainty of an organization's cash inflows and outflows.
3 In studying an enterprise's resources, the claims to those resources by creditors and owners, and any related changes in either of the foregoing during an accounting period.
4 In examining an enterprise's financial performance, specifically, measures of earnings and its components.

Businesses *attempt* to achieve these objectives by the issuance of periodic financial statements and accompanying footnotes. Notice the emphasis on the word "attempt." Although financial statements should accomplish the desired result, many accountants, investors, and executives find fault with financial reporting as presently practiced in this country. Why? In short, these critics feel that financial statements sometimes lack certain qualities, thereby inhibiting the statements' usefulness among various user groups. These qualities will be discussed in the next section.

Characteristics of Financial Information

In the late 1970s the accounting profession studied the qualitative characteristics of financial information in an effort to improve the profession's decision-making process.[3] To explain, when given a choice among alternative policies, a decision must be made concerning the best policy to implement in a specific set of circumstances. Presumably, the selected policy would be the one that generates the most useful financial information. To judge usefulness, the profession noted that information should possess the following characteristics:

Relevancy
Reliability
Comparability
Understandability

Sometimes, as we will now see, these characteristics may conflict with one another.

---

[2] See "Objectives of Financial Reporting by Business Enterprises," *Statement of Financial Accounting Concepts No. 1* (Stamford, Conn.: Financial Accounting Standards Board, November 1978).

[3] See "Qualitative Characteristics of Accounting Information," *Statement of Financial Accounting Concepts No. 2* (Stamford, Conn.: Financial Accounting Standards Board, 1980).

Relevancy

Information is deemed relevant if it influences the actions of a decision maker. On the surface the concept of relevancy is simplistic; that is, only produce information that can be actively employed by financial statement users. A deeper probe, however, reveals several practical problems. As we noted earlier in the chapter, different users have different needs. Obviously, a given set of financial statements cannot satisfy *all* needs of *all* interested parties; thus some compromise is necessary. In addition, if the relevancy concept is implemented in the strictest sense, businesses would have to abandon the traditional cost basis of accounting. For example, consider a company that purchased $40,000 of land many years ago. If the land is now worth $500,000, the company's balance sheet would continue to reveal a valuation of $40,000. Unfortunately, the $40,000 figure is totally irrelevant for a decision maker who is attempting to evaluate the current worth of the business. This particular problem has prompted accountants to study alternative means of asset valuation and is explored further in Chapter 19.

Reliability

Financial information must be reliable; that is, the information must accurately depict the conditions it purports to represent. If net income is a reliable figure, for instance, it must truly represent a summarization of an enterprise's profit-generating activities. Similarly, the accounts payable balance reported on a balance sheet must represent the summation of trade creditor claims against the entity.

Reliability is influenced by a number of factors, one of which is bias. A measure may represent what it is supposed to, but determination of that measure may be biased. For example, suppose a company using LIFO for valuation of inventory and cost of goods sold is operating in a highly inflationary economy. Assume that management has decided to curtail purchasing activities during the last few months of the accounting period to conserve cash. As a result, inventory levels will decline and units that are sold currently will be costed at older (and cheaper) prices, given the nature of the last-in, first-out system. Cost of goods sold will therefore be lower than that computed under the firm's prior (regular) purchasing program. Overall higher earnings are reported along with a reliable but possibly biased measure of performance. Cost of goods sold is reliable in that it represents the cost of the units sold; however, the measure may be biased by showing improved profitability, caused perhaps by a purposeful manipulation of buying habits and, thus, earnings.

Bias usually benefits certain groups at the expense of others and could erode the public's confidence in financial reporting. Accounting information must be neutral; that is, it "must report economic activity as faithfully as possible without coloring the image it communicates for the purpose of influencing behavior in *some particular direction.*"[4] In so doing, accounting and its financial reporting functions are enhanced, thereby increasing their usefulness to parties with widely varying interests.

[4] Ibid., paragraph 100.

Comparability

The usefulness of accounting information is enhanced if a firm's financial statements are comparable with statements of other enterprises and of the same firm at different points in time. Comparability among enterprises is difficult because of the variety of accounting methods found in practice—a situation that is not likely to change for reasons to be noted shortly.

Comparability of a single firm's statements through time is achieved by the use of the same accounting methods from one period to the next. This practice offers the advantage of better performance evaluation. Imagine the difficulty, for example, of assessing trends in profitability if a company indiscriminantly switched depreciation methods during each financial reporting period. Indeed, an analyst would have trouble determining whether variations in earnings are due to changes in the entity's activities and efficiency or changes in its accounting methods. Our discussion here has been intentionally brief; comparability of financial statements over time is discussed further in this chapter under the heading of "Consistency Principle."

Understandability

To achieve any degree of usefulness, financial information must be understandable. Often, as is true in any technical discipline, terminology and jargon can be extremely troublesome. To illustrate, we provide the following satirical interaction between Leonard (a stockholder) and President Jones at an annual stockholders' meeting:

> *Leonard motioned for the floor and stood up. "You commented previously that total sales increased. Will you comment on our apparent decrease in earnings?"*
>
> *"Perhaps I should have pointed out," replied President Jones, "that our figures from year to year reflect changes in accounting. For example, we have used LIFO and FIFO. Our depreciation policy is flexible. There is the question of reporting per share on the total amount of shares outstanding, the average amount, or the fully converted amount. Our figures also take into account pooling of interest of our latest acquisition. This is a company making a patented banana slicer suitable for any household. Thus it fits nicely into our banana sales. Let me also point out that our final bottom line figures are reduced by some write-offs. In addition, we have written off some prepaid costs that we know we will incur in coming years. As a result, we had no taxable income this year. We were fortunate in being able to fund some of our short-term borrowings but at an increased interest cost. These and other such adjustments are included in the footnotes to our annual report."*[5]

Regrettably, to some people this parody reflects the current state of affairs in the accounting profession. Business activities have become so complex that down-to-earth explanations in everyday terms are a near impossibility.

The accounting profession services individuals with varied business and educational backgrounds. Contrary to the impression one may receive

[5]Gerald M. Loeb, "Peter and Leonard Attend an Annual Meeting," *Financial Analysts Journal*, May–June 1971, p. 30.

when reviewing corporate financial statements or a company's annual report, accountants do not strive for a presentation geared especially for bankers, financial analysts, and other long-term veterans of the business world. Our goal is to produce information that is "comprehensible to those who have a *reasonable* [emphasis added] understanding of business and economic activities and are willing to study the information with *reasonable* [emphasis added] diligence."[6]

THE FOUNDATION OF ACCOUNTING

Suppose you are pursuing your study of accounting at a university located in the heart of a major metropolitan area. You are living at home in a nice suburb and must drive 12 miles twice each week to attend class. Assume it is common knowledge that the local police department is lax in its enforcement of driving regulations. Speeding, crashing red lights, tailgating, and other offenses are common occurrences. Given the goings-on around you, your trip to campus would surely be an exciting experience. Different drivers doing their own thing results in a hectic, if not chaotic, commuting environment.

Much of the same would undoubtedly be said about financial reporting if each company could summarize business activity in its own unique way. Picture the plight of an investor who is attempting to evaluate performance of two different entities whose performance is measured by two widely divergent sets of rules. The investor's task would be formidable, to say the least.

Generally Accepted Accounting Principles (GAAP)

To bring order to the accounting and reporting process, the accounting profession has developed an underlying foundation for measuring and disclosing the results of business transactions and events. The foundation is a set of assumptions, concepts, and procedures collectively known as **generally accepted accounting principles (GAAP).** The establishment of GAAP does not mean that all organizations report and measure financial activity in the same manner. Witness, for example, the accounting alternatives illustrated in earlier chapters for depreciation computations, inventory valuation, and revenue and expense recognition. Each business is somewhat unique, and thus a rigid set of measurement and reporting techniques is not feasible. Recognizing this fact, the accounting profession has developed a generalized framework (i.e., ground rules) within which some diversity is possible.

Accounting principles differ dramatically from principles in such fields as chemistry and physics. Principles (or laws) relating to the sciences generally arise after repeated experiments and observations hold that a certain phenomenon is true. For example, by performing extensive research in their laboratories, scientists have learned that the speed of light is 186,000 miles per second and that each molecule of water consists of two atoms of hydro-

[6] "Objectives of Financial Reporting by Business Enterprises," op. cit., paragraph 34.

gen and one atom of oxygen. Unlike scientific law, accounting principles are not discovered; instead the principles are formulated to enhance the objectives of financial reporting cited earlier. To illustrate, in an effort to inform statement readers about a company's involvement with widely varying and significant lines of business, the accounting profession has stipulated the disclosure of segment information (see Chapter 6). This disclosure procedure cannot be scientifically proven as being right or wrong; it is, however, the generally accepted procedure for reporting line-of-business operations in financial statements.

The development of GAAP

For the most part, generally accepted accounting principles are an outgrowth of the profession's efforts during the past fifty years. The accounting profession made very little progress toward the establishment of principles and practices until the late 1920s and early 1930s. As happened for many developments in this country, it took a disaster to get things turned around and headed in the right direction. Both the stock market crash and the accompanying depression of those decades dictated a need for improvements in financial measurement and reporting. In many cases the financial statements of those years failed to disclose the correct financial position and profitability of an entity. Numerous businesses overstated their net income along with their financial well-being. As a result, efforts were made to protect investors and establish a generalized set of accounting principles.

The Securities and Exchange Commission

Because of a widespread belief in the 1930s that government should play an increased role in the regulation of business, Congress passed several acts pertaining to the preparation of financial statements for publicly held corporations. The **Securities and Exchange Commission (SEC),** sometimes called "the watchdog of Congress," was given the power to administer these acts and to prescribe accounting principles and reporting practices for companies issuing publicly traded securities. Although the SEC has the authority for ultimately deciding what constitutes GAAP, most of the SEC's power has been informally delegated to other rule-making bodies of the accounting profession. The SEC has principally served in an advisory role in the development of newly proposed accounting standards and has been especially active promoting the disclosure of added information to financial statement users.

The American Institute of Certified Public Accountants and the Accounting Principles Board

Several years after the SEC came into existence, the **American Institute of Certified Public Accountants (AICPA),** a national association of licensed CPAs, began publishing bulletins on suggested accounting practices and rules through its newly organized Committee on Accounting Procedure (CAP). CAP had no authority to enforce its pronouncements, and over the years it met with some criticism.

In 1959 the AICPA formed a new policymaking body called the **Accounting Principles Board (APB)** to advance the development of generally accepted accounting principles. During its existence the APB was comprised of between 18 and 21 members, most being partners with national and international accounting firms. The APB studied several different problem areas and ultimately issued 31 pronouncements (termed *Opinions of the Accounting Principles Board*) on suggested treatment of various topics. Unlike CAP, which could advise and not enforce, the AICPA and the APB collectively declared that departures from the *Opinions* (i.e., GAAP) must be detailed and explained in a company's published financial statements. Importantly, the burden of proof of using a non-GAAP procedure rests with the reporting entity. As a result, most companies follow GAAP in measuring and disclosing business activity. This practice avoids negative criticism of the firm by creditors and stockholders and, at the same time, reduces the possibility of lawsuits arising because of ill-advised reporting techniques.

In the late 1960s and early 1970s disagreement once again arose concerning the development of accounting principles. Most of the criticism dealt with the APB's response (or lack of) to contemporary issues of the profession. The APB often acted slowly and sometimes not in the best interests of the business community. Two factors are frequently cited as being the underlying causes of these problems.

1 Members of the APB were part-time, unpaid volunteers. Thus policies were formulated by professionals who could not devote their full attention to the problems at hand.
2 Board members maintained relationships with their accounting firms and clients, and may have inadvertently compromised their position and vote for fear of injuring clientele.

The AICPA reacted to this criticism by performing a thorough study of the APB's operation and policymaking procedures. In the early 1970s the APB was abolished and replaced by a body independent of the AICPA known as the Financial Accounting Standards Board. Although the APB and the Committee on Accounting Procedure are no longer in operation, their pronouncements are still in force and considered GAAP unless specifically amended or superseded by newer rulings.

The Financial Accounting Standards Board

The **Financial Accounting Standards Board (FASB)** is the private-sector organization presently in charge of formulating standards of financial reporting in the United States. The FASB consists of 7 members who are supported by a staff of 45 technical specialists and a host of administrative and other personnel. Rulings of the board are considered GAAP and are called *Statements of Financial Accounting Standards* as opposed to *Opinions.*

Aside from its independence from the AICPA, the FASB differs from the APB in three major respects. First, members of the FASB serve on a full-time basis and must sever all ties with their previous employers. Member independence is therefore increased since the chance for employer or client influence is reduced (and probably eliminated). Secondly, unlike members of the APB, FASB members are well paid for their efforts. At the time of this writing, their annual salaries were as follows: chairman, $225,000; board members, $185,000. The final difference between the FASB and APB deals with representation. Recognizing that accounting has far-reaching effects, the FASB has board members with backgrounds in public accounting as well as industry, government, academia, and the securities markets. As the FASB notes, members "have diverse backgrounds, but they must possess 'knowledge of accounting, finance, and business, and a concern for the public interest in matters of financial accounting and reporting.'"[7]

During its short existence the FASB has been more active than both the APB and CAP. Yet there is still substantial criticism that the FASB is moving too slowly and using the wrong approach to tackle troublesome reporting issues. Much of the board's work has been concerned with fighting fires, that is, issuing standards on a problem-by-problem basis as opposed to establishing a generalized framework for financial reporting. Bearing in mind that the SEC has the ultimate authority concerning financial reporting for publicly held corporations, a failure of the FASB would probably lead to increased governmental involvement in accounting policymaking.

Other influential bodies

In addition to the SEC and FASB, there are other bodies that influence the establishment of GAAP. One such body is the **Internal Revenue Service (IRS)**, which administers the tax laws passed by Congress. Tax regulations do not directly affect financial accounting; they apply solely to the filing of income tax returns. Frequently, however, businesses attempt to lessen the impact of tax law on their accounting systems by using the same accounting methods for both tax purposes and the preparation of financial statements. The result in many cases has been the adoption of methods that generate the lowest taxable income with little regard for the usefulness of the financial information produced.

Another organization, the **American Accounting Association (AAA)**, is comprised primarily of accounting instructors. The AAA strives to advance accounting knowledge, encourage accounting research, and promote the development of reporting and measurement practices. The AAA has no official stature in the development of financial accounting standards; its role is felt through education and persuasion.

The **National Association of Accountants (NAA)** is a large organization whose membership consists primarily of cost and managerial accountants. Like the AAA, the NAA plays no official role in the formulation of

---

[7] *FACTS About FASB* (Stamford, Conn.: Financial Accounting Standards Board, February 1981).

GAAP; however, it actively communicates its suggestions to various other organizations.

Add to the foregoing bodies many other professional and trade associations; public accounting and business firms; and bankers, analysts, and other financial statement users. The net result is the formula for how generally accepted accounting principles (standards) are developed in this country. The overall process is depicted in Exhibit 18-1.

Exhibit 18-1

The development of financial accounting standards

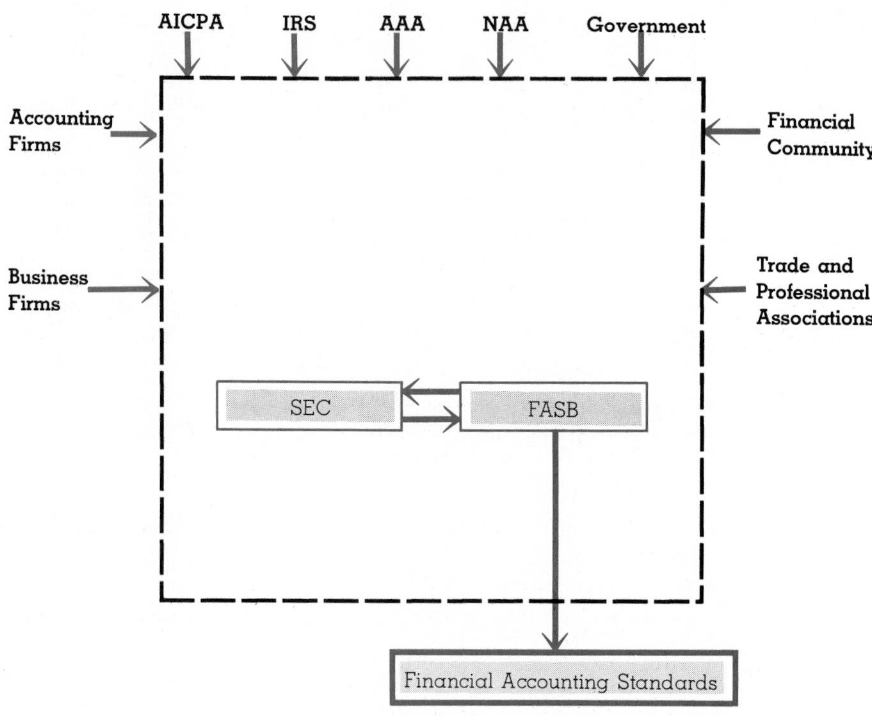

Specific Principles and Assumptions

APB *Opinions* and FASB *Statements* stipulate the proper accounting treatment that is afforded to a number of different topical areas. Throughout the first seventeen chapters of this text, you were exposed to the following pronouncements, among others:

Pronouncement	***Topic***
APB *Opinion No. 15*	Earnings per share
APB *Opinion No. 16*	Business combinations
APB *Opinion No. 17*	Intangible assets
APB *Opinion No. 21*	Interest on receivables and payables
APB *Opinion No. 30*	Discontinued operations and extraordinary items
FASB *Statement No. 12*	Short-term investments
FASB *Statement No. 14*	Segment reporting

Although the *Opinions* and *Statements* are considered GAAP by the accounting profession and the financial community, these pronouncements are not, in a true sense, "principles." Instead they are rulings that pertain to accounting practice.

Underlying accounting practice is a set of assumptions, concepts, modifying conventions, and procedures that form the basis for the FASB's work. These will be discussed in the following sections.

Entity assumption

Recall from Chapter 1 that financial reporting is based on the entity assumption. An **entity** is an economic unit organized to pursue business activity. Examples of entities include corporations, individuals, clubs, governmental units, and a host of other organizations. Importantly, each entity has its own assets, liabilities, revenues, and expenses and must be accounted for accordingly. In effect, the entity is a boundary for reporting; that is, the entity is a unit that is separate and distinct both from its owners and from other operations.

The absence of the entity assumption would make a mockery of the accounting process. To illustrate, assume Jeremy Carson, a well-to-do engineer, organized a small company to conduct research in the solar energy field. If Carson's personal transactions were merged with those of the business, the company's balance sheet would include Jeremy's personal clothing, his residence, his automobile, and other assets and liabilities that pertain solely to Jeremy's personal well-being. Similarly, the income statement would combine business transactions with personal revenues and expenses. In sum, the financial statements of the business would fail to reflect the energy company's proper financial condition and operating performance. To correctly assess the outcome of economic activity, it is mandatory that each entity maintain separate accounting records and prepare separate financial statements. That is, owner and business transactions must be separated, along with the transactions of other independent economic units.

Going-concern assumption

The **going-concern assumption** means that a business will continue to operate for a long period of time unless there is substantial evidence to the contrary. Even though all entities do not survive, the going-concern assumption is valid in the majority of cases and forms the basis for many accounting procedures encountered in practice. For example, if we assumed business termination in the near future, there would be little need for the current/noncurrent balance sheet classification of assets and liabilities. In addition, assets such as property, plant, and equipment and prepaid expenses would be more properly expensed upon acquisition because of a low probability of receiving benefits beyond the current accounting period. Finally, the going-concern assumption provides some justification for the use of an accounting system based on historical cost. Should a company plan to terminate operations in the short term, asset valuation on the balance sheet could properly take the form of liquidation (sale) prices because of the assets' impending disposal.

Periodicity assumption

Although a business is assumed to conduct operations for long periods of time, investors, creditors, governmental authorities, and other financial statement users cannot wait forever to analyze performance. The **periodicity assumption** holds that for reporting purposes, an entity's life can be divided into discrete time periods such as months, quarters, or years. As a result of this assumption, the accountant must trace business transactions back to the period being examined. In many instances this task presents no special problems. For example, a check written on March 1 in payment of March rent is easily traced to March.

Difficulty arises, however, when dealing with expenditures that span several accounting periods. To illustrate, we will consider the cost of a long-lived machine. If a company desires to produce an income statement covering a month, a quarter, or a single year, the machine's cost must be allocated to the period in question through depreciation expense. As you saw in Chapter 10, depreciation can be computed and allocated by several acceptable methods, each producing different results. Most accountants recognize that cost allocations culminate in arbitrary measures of performance and can diminish the usefulness of financial statements. In addition to depreciation, the periodicity assumption forms the basis for amortization and the adjusting process at the conclusion of an accounting period.

Monetary unit assumption

All countries have a unit of exchange. In the United States it is the dollar; in Mexico it is the peso; and in Japan it is the yen. Business organizations adopt the national currency of their home country to measure financial activity. Why? Accounting assumes that an entity's transactions can be expressed in terms of a common measuring unit, namely, money. If all organizations in a given country use the same measuring unit, extensive comparative analysis is possible by financial statement users.

Financial reporting in the United States is based on the premise that the dollar is a stable measuring unit, thereby permitting dollars of different years to be combined in the financial statements. In the computation of the balance in a company's Land account, for instance, land transactions of the 1980s are mixed with transactions occurring in prior years. This calculation is reasonable provided that the dollar is, in fact, stable. Historically, accounting policymakers have taken the position that fluctuations in the value of the dollar are small and can be ignored.

Is this a valid position, however? Consider the dollar in comparison with other units of measure, say square feet. If you were to measure the area of the room you are presently in today, next year, and five years from now, an accurate measurement would undoubtedly yield the same result each time. In contrast, consider the amount of goods and services you could purchase for $50 over the same time period. In all likelihood the goods and services acquired would decline each year due to rising prices and a reduction in the dollar's purchasing power. Because of this behavior (i.e., instability), especially in periods of rampant inflation, many accountants contend that transactions occurring today cannot be combined with those of earlier periods. The net result would be the combination of dollars of different purchasing powers and misleading financial statements. The impact of inflation on financial reporting and a recent FASB pronouncement on the subject are explored in the next chapter.

Historical-cost principle

Accountants have been faced with many problems over the years. One of the most troublesome (and debated) issues has been the financial statement valuation of goods, services, and resources acquired in business transactions. As we noted in Chapter 1, accounting is based on the **historical-cost principle.** That is, acquisitions of the foregoing items are recorded in the accounts at cost, with cost defined as the exchange or transaction price. For example, if a company purchased a building by paying $40,000 cash and signing a $200,000 note payable, the cost of the building would be $240,000.

The use of historical cost has received mixed reviews. In its favor, historical cost is objective and definite. To explain, the use of cost and exchange prices (e.g., the $240,000 figure in the preceding example) gives rise to objective valuations created by negotiation between two independent parties, a buyer and a seller. Also on the favorable end of the spectrum, cost can be verified via canceled checks, contracts, invoices, and similar documents. Thus five different accountants attempting to calculate the cost of an asset acquired in a complex transaction would probably all have similar findings.

Critics of historical cost note that the use of the cost basis *subsequent to asset acquisition* produces out-of-date asset valuations and distorted income figures. The latter arises because of cost-based depreciation and amortization computations. Critics contend that fair market values should be integrated in the financial statements. This practice, while having obvious benefits, does have an inherent problem. To illustrate, assume that the five accountants cited earlier are now trying to compute the fair market value ("current worth") of a manufacturing plant, which was constructed several years ago. The "current worth" would probably be influenced by a number of factors that are difficult to quantify, such as the plant's physical condition, its location, and the general state of the real estate market. Even competent appraisal services that specialize in this type of work would have differing ideas, culminating in dissimilar (and subjective) estimates. Subjectivity, of course, would destroy the public's confidence in a company's financial statements.

Objectivity principle

The thrust of the objectivity principle has been discussed in preceding sections of this chapter. Simply stated, the **objectivity principle** requires that accounting information be free from bias and verifiable by an independent party such as an external auditor. The resulting financial statements will therefore reflect a fair and neutral view of an organization's business affairs.

Although a high degree of objectivity is desirable, it is difficult to eliminate all personal opinion and judgment from accounting measurement. Consider the accounting procedures related to depreciable assets, for example. Although the cost of a long-lived asset can be determined objectively, estimates are needed when computing service life and residual value, and personal opinion is used when selecting a depreciation method. Naturally, variations in any of the preceding factors will produce different effects on net income and asset valuations. As long as the estimates and related decisions are reasonable, made by a competent party, and verifiable, the objectivity principle is considered to have been implemented to the greatest extent possible.

Revenue realization principle

The generation of revenue in our economy takes many different forms. Hospitals, for instance, earn revenues by rendering health care services; professional sports clubs participate in athletic competition and sell broadcasting rights; department stores sell merchandise; construction companies build roads, homes, office complexes, and a host of other items. While our list of revenue-generating activities is far from complete, a question arises as to when these enterprises should recognize revenues in their accounting records. Theoretically, revenue generation is a continuous process for most firms. Practically, however, revenue is said to be realized (earned) under the following conditions:

1 When the earnings process is complete or virtually complete.
2 When the amount of revenue can be objectively measured.

For most businesses these two tests are met when merchandise is sold or when services are rendered. In either case the transaction and earnings process is complete at this point, and the revenue is measurable on the basis of the exchange price between the buyer and the seller.

Although the time of sale (or rendering of services) is the general rule for recognizing revenue, realization is sometimes advanced or delayed, as described in the following sections.

Revenue recognized during production

Many companies earn revenues by engaging in construction projects that take several years to complete, such as ships, office complexes, and dams. Because construction firms earn revenues by building, it may be more appropriate to recognize revenue over a project's life instead of waiting until the project is completed (i.e., the point of sale). Accordingly, a method of revenue recognition termed **percentage of completion (POC)** may be used. The POC method allocates profit to each accounting period on the basis of the percentage of the total project completed. Completion is usually judged by comparing the current period's construction costs with the total expected costs over the life of the project.

To illustrate, assume Brennan Construction signed a $44,000,000 contract to build a shopping mall over the next three years. Brennan's accounting department has estimated total construction costs at $40,000,000, resulting in a $4,000,000 profit for the company. The following schedule shows the actual costs incurred along with the annual profit recognized.

Year	(A) Actual Costs Incurred	(B) Percentage of Work Completed (A ÷ $40,000,000)	(C) Profit Recognized ($4,000,000 × B)
1	$10,000,000	25%	$1,000,000
2	24,000,000	60	2,400,000
3	6,300,000	Remainder	300,000 (remainder)
	$40,300,000		$3,700,000

For the first two years the percentage of work completed is derived by dividing the actual costs incurred by the $40,000,000 total project cost. The resulting percentage is then multiplied by the $4,000,000 estimated profit to compute annual profit. Year 3, the last year of construction, is handled in a different fashion. Total construction costs amount to $40,300,000, generating an overall contract profit of $3,700,000 ($44,000,000 – $40,300,000). Since profit of $3,400,000 has already been recognized ($1,000,000 + $2,400,000), Brennan can only realize $300,000 in Year 3.

Because of the objectivity principle, the POC method is only used when a firm has the ability to make reasonably dependable estimates of contract revenues, contract costs, and the extent of progress toward completion. In those instances where substantial uncertainty surrounds the estimation process, the entire profit ($3,700,000 in this case) is best recognized at the time of project completion.

Revenue recognized at the time of receipt

As we noted in Chapter 3, many professionals (such as lawyers, dentists, and architects) use the **cash basis** of accounting for their practices. Under the cash basis, revenue is realized at the time cash is collected from customers and clients. Probably because of the method's simplicity and its acceptance by the IRS, cash basis accounting is widely used by individuals and small businesses. The cash basis is not in accord with GAAP, however, because revenue realization is delayed beyond the point where the earnings process is completed.[8] Recall that in most businesses, earnings are generated and can be objectively measured at the time of sale. The cash basis is most appropriate when revenues cannot be correctly determined at the time of sale, specifically, when collectibility of customer accounts is in serious doubt. This situation sometimes arises with installment sales.

Installment sales commonly occur in the retail field, especially home furnishings and appliances, where payments are spread over several years. Revenues can be recognized on installment sales by using a form of the cash

[8] Most professional practices do not issue "published financial statements"; that is, statements to stockholders that have been audited by a CPA. "Unpublished" statements need not be prepared in accordance with GAAP.

basis called the **installment method.** Sellers using the installment method allocate a sale's profit to different accounting periods based on the amount of cash received from customers. For example, suppose that on September 1 Beachwood Appliance sold a new freezer and microwave oven to Joyce Chambers for $1,500. Chambers paid $300 down and agreed to remit the balance owed via 24 end-of-month installments of $50 each. If the appliances cost Beachwood $900, the company has generated a $600 profit or a 40% return based on sales ($600 ÷ $1,500 = 40%). Because each dollar collected from Chambers represents a 40% profit, the company's recognition schedule would appear as follows:

Year	Cash Collected		Profit Percentage	Profit Recognized
1	$ 500*	×	40%	$200
2	600†	×	40	240
3	400‡	×	40	160
	$1,500			$600

** $300 down payment + 4 monthly installments of $50 each.*
† 12 monthly installments of $50 each.
‡ 8 monthly installments of $50 each.

Similar to the cash basis, the installment method does not conform to GAAP unless, as we noted earlier, considerable uncertainty surrounds collectibility of the receivable. The installment method is acceptable by the IRS, though, and affords users the advantage of postponing income taxes. Postponement arises because revenues are not taxed until cash is received.

Matching principle

Like revenue realization, the matching principle is another important consideration in the determination of accounting income. Under the **matching principle** all costs and expenses associated with the production of revenue are recognized when the revenue is recognized. That is, expenses are matched against and deducted from the revenues they helped to create. Perhaps this concept is best seen by examining the following simplified income statement.

Sales		$4,000
Cost of goods sold		2,400
Gross profit		$1,600
Operating expenses		
Commissions, 10%	$400	
Depreciation	900	1,300
Net income		$ 300

Observe that goods costing $2,400 and operating expenses of $1,300 were necessary to generate the company's revenue; thus $3,700 ($2,400 + $1,300) was matched against (deducted from) sales to derive net income.

The matching principle is the underlying reason behind the adjusting process. Consider, for example, the accounting treatment for depreciable assets. At the end of a reporting period, depreciation expense is recorded in the accounts via an adjusting entry. Why? Long-term assets such as plant and equipment generate revenues (or benefits) for prolonged periods of time. Thus a *portion* of the assets' cost (i.e., depreciation expense) is written off each period and matched against the revenues created by the assets' use. Notice that only part of the cost is currently expensed; the remaining cost will be expensed in future periods against the future revenues generated.

Consistency principle

Financial statements are frequently compared over periods of time to examine trends, assess growth patterns, and so forth. To enhance such studies, accountants have implemented the principle of consistency. **Consistency** holds that entities employ the same accounting practices in each reporting period. Imagine the difficulties that would result, for example, if a company indiscriminantly switched back and forth between LIFO and FIFO and other measurement techniques. Indeed, such a practice would create havoc for financial statement users who, in many cases, would be forced to compare the noncomparable.

It is important to note that consistency does not completely prohibit change. Changes in the methods of recording and reporting business transactions *are* allowable whenever the end result is a better or more fair presentation of economic activity. When such changes occur, the reason for the change and the impact on net income must be disclosed in the financial statements. The issue of consistency is so important that it is noted by auditors in a report that accompanies an organization's financial statements. See Exhibit 18-2, for example, which contains a recent auditor's report to the shareholders of CBS Inc., owner of CBS Broadcasting and a number of other companies.

Exhibit 18-2

Example of auditors' report

To the Shareholders of CBS Inc.:

We have examined the consolidated balance sheets of CBS Inc. and subsidiaries as of December 31, 1981, 1980, and 1979, and the related consolidated statements of income, retained earnings, and changes in financial position for the years then ended. Our examinations were in accordance with generally accepted auditing standards and, accordingly, included such tests of the accounting records and such other auditing procedures as we considered necessary in the circumstances.

In our opinion, the financial statements referred to above present fairly the consolidated financial position of CBS Inc. and subsidiaries at December 31, 1981, 1980, and 1979, and the results of their operations and the changes in their financial position for the years then ended, in conformity with generally accepted accounting principles applied on a consistent basis [*emphasis added*]. . . .

1251 Avenue of the Americas — *COOPERS & LYBRAND*
New York, New York 10020
February 10, 1982

Disclosure principle

So that investors, creditors, and analysts are not misled, a set of financial statements includes much more than just account balances. An entity must provide a complete reporting **(disclosure)** of all facts important enough to influence the judgment of an informed user of financial information. Just what an "informed user" really means is, itself, open to debate; however, accountants have agreed that disclosure should include the following items as a minimum:

1. A summary of the significant accounting policies used in statement preparation.
2. Principles and methods peculiar to the industry in which the entity operates, along with departures from GAAP.
3. Changes in accounting policies and the resultant impact on net income.
4. Impending lawsuits and contingencies.
5. Significant events that occurred subsequent to the accounting period being reported but prior to issuance of the financial statements, for example, stock dividends, stock splits, and major casualties such as fires and tornadoes.
6. Significant business transactions that took place during the period, such as business acquisitions and mergers.

As we discussed in Chapter 6, disclosure often takes the form of parenthetical comments within the body of the statements and separate footnotes. A complete set of footnotes can be observed by viewing the financial statements appearing on pages A-1–A-15. Normally, parenthetical and footnote disclosures provide concise information. A notable exception was found in the 1979 Annual Report of the General Public Utilities Corporation, owner of the Three Mile Island (TMI) utility plant. To explain a nuclear accident that occurred at TMI and the financial impact of the accident, the report contained a footnote spanning nearly four double-column pages. (Interestingly, the financial statements by themselves covered only four and a quarter pages!)

Materiality

There are many instances in accounting where theory gives way to expediency, especially when dealing with very small amounts or transactions. To illustrate, suppose a company recently acquired five heavy-duty wastebaskets for $75. If the principles and practices introduced in the preceding pages are followed to the letter, the wastebaskets would be entered in the accounts as long-term assets and depreciated over their lifetime. Assuming a 10-year life, annual straight-line depreciation would amount to $7.50, a pittance for almost any organization. To avoid the administrative problems and costs of keeping track of the wastebaskets over the next 10 years, most companies would expense the entire $75 outlay immediately at the time of acquisition.

This accounting treatment is justified for two reasons. First, the transaction is very small, and second, it will probably have a minimal impact on the financial statements. This example has illustrated the concept of materiality. **Materiality** dictates that the accountant must judge the impact and importance of each transaction (or event) to determine its proper handling in the accounting records. In general, an amount is said to be material if knowledge of it would influence the decisions of an informed financial statement user.

Materiality is a relative concept and is often judged by using comparative analysis. For example, a potential expense item could be compared with some type of dollar limit. If the item exceeds the limit, it is deemed material; if it is under the limit, the item is considered immaterial and would be expensed. The dollar limit and exactly what is material, of course, varies from company to company: what is immaterial for Shell Oil might be very significant to Joe's Garage. There is no guideline stating that 10% is always material or that any expenditure over $500 is always significant. Again materiality is a relative concept; it is a topic of ongoing research in the accounting profession.

Conservatism

An accountant is faced with a number of different decisions in attempting to measure and report the financial affairs of an enterprise. Frequently, the "proper" decision is difficult to determine. After exercising sound judgment and considering the objectives of financial reporting, other accounting principles, and industry practices, the accountant often turns to the doctrine of conservatism. **Conservatism** stipulates that when alternative accounting valuations and measurements are possible, the alternative selected should be that which is least likely to overstate assets and/or net income.

Over the years conservative financial statements have found favor with statement users. Conservatism allows users to downplay the impact of overly optimistic company managements who may be inclined to record revenue in the accounts before the revenue is realized, capitalize items that should be expensed, and follow other similar practices, many of which tend to improve reported financial condition and profitability. Overly optimistic financial statements could mask impending losses and mislead users.

The application of conservatism in accounting becomes evident when studying the lower-of-cost-or-market method for valuing inventories. To illustrate, suppose Casey Company and Remy Company each purchased 1,000 identical units of inventory on January 1 at $10 per unit. Assume that by December 31 the fair market value (replacement cost) had increased to $15. If Casey Company sold its units on December 31 at $15 each, a $5,000 profit is recognized. If Remy held its units in inventory, it would report no gain (profit), nor would it record any increase in inventory value in the accounts. Why? Recall that the lower-of-cost-or-market method forbids write-ups above cost. This difference in treatments by the two companies occurs even though the economic substance of both situations is essentially the same; that is, the units are worth $5,000 more than they were on January 1. Conservatism says to ignore increases in inventory values while holding the units; in line with revenue realization, gains (profits) will be recognized upon sale. Write-downs below cost and the recognition of losses, on the other hand, are acceptable. Why? The result is lower (more conservative) asset valuations and a reduced net income.

GENERALLY ACCEPTED ACCOUNTING ALTERNATIVES

The application of the previously discussed assumptions, principles, and concepts should result in accountants choosing the reporting practices that best reflect the economic activity of a business entity. Although some people argue there is too much diversity in the selection among accounting alternatives, at least there is a choice. No two businesses are alike; no two industries are alike. Thus if only one set of practices was available to all entities, financial reporting would fail to provide a logical means for statement users to analyze an organization's performance and financial well-being.

Comprehensive Example

While diversity is needed, the use of alternative accounting practices can produce widely varying results. To illustrate, assume Oklahoma Corporation was formed on January 1 of the current year by issuing 10,000 shares of no-par common stock for $500,000. The following information pertains to first year operations.

1 Equipment with a 10-year life was purchased for $200,000 cash on January 1. No salvage value was anticipated.
2 Inventory purchases were as follows:

Jan. 1	5,000 units @ $3.00	=	$ 15,000
Mar. 1	10,000 units @ $3.25	=	32,500
Aug. 1	15,000 units @ $3.40	=	51,000
Dec. 1	20,000 units @ $3.50	=	70,000
	50,000		$168,500

3 Credit sales during the year totaled $280,000 (40,000 units at $7).
4 On December 31 Oklahoma wrote off bad debts amounting to $3,000. Management estimates that uncollectible accounts will total 3% of credit sales.
5 Accounts Receivable on December 31 prior to any write-offs, $78,000. Accounts Payable on December 31, $30,000.
6 Administrative expenses paid in cash, $15,000.

Oklahoma is exploring different accounting practices for use in the preparation of its financial statements. Specifically, management desires to determine the impact of the following alternatives on the income statement and balance sheet.

Depreciation: straight-line versus double-declining balance
Inventory costing: FIFO versus LIFO
Bad debts: estimation versus direct write-off

The company has decided to prepare two sets of statements for internal review. One set, identified as "high income," will be constructed by using straight-line depreciation, FIFO inventory costing, and the direct write-off method of bad debts. The second set, identified as "conservative," will utilize double-declining balance depreciation, LIFO inventory costing, and an estimated bad debts expense. Relevant computations for depreciation, cost of goods sold, and bad debts follow.

Depreciation

Straight-line: $200,000 ÷ 10 years = $20,000.
Double-declining balance: A 10-year life means a 20% double-declining rate; $200,000 × 0.2 = $40,000.

Cost of goods sold (40,000 units)

FIFO	Jan. 1	5,000 units	@ $3.00	=	$ 15,000
	Mar. 1	10,000 units	@ $3.25	=	32,500
	Aug. 1	15,000 units	@ $3.40	=	51,000
	Dec. 1	10,000 units	@ $3.50	=	35,000
		40,000			$133,500
LIFO	Dec. 1	20,000 units	@ $3.50	=	$ 70,000
	Aug. 1	15,000 units	@ $3.40	=	51,000
	Mar. 1	5,000 units	@ $3.25	=	16,250
		40,000			$137,250

Bad debts

Direct write-off: $3,000 (given).
Estimation: 3% of credit sales = $280,000 × 0.03 = $8,400.

These alternatives are summarized in the financial statements appearing in Exhibit 18-3 (see pages 716 and 718).

Diverse results such as these give rise to the claim that accountants play games when it comes to financial reporting. One story has it that a company was in need of some audit services and interviewed several accounting firms for the job. Each firm was asked one question: "What does two plus two equal?" All the firms answered "four" except the one hired. After serious deliberation, the partner of that firm responded, "What number did you have in mind?"[9]

All kidding aside, accountants do attempt to have the financial statements present a fair picture of the enterprise. By fairness we mean that the practices selected are generally accepted and appropriate, and that "the fi-

[9] For an enlightening and candid view of the accounting profession, see Abraham Briloff, *Unaccountable Accounting* (New York: Harper & Row, 1972).

nancial statements reflect the underlying events and transactions . . . within a range of acceptable limits, that is, limits that are reasonable and practicable to attain."[10] In so doing, the statements report an unbiased and reasonable view of an entity's business transactions, financial condition, and profitability.

Exhibit 18-3

Financial statements using alternative reporting practices

Income Statement

	High Income	Conservative
Sales	$280,000	$280,000
Cost of goods sold	133,500	137,250
Gross profit	$146,500	$142,750
Operating expenses		
Depreciation	$ 20,000	$ 40,000
Bad debts	3,000	8,400
Administrative	15,000	15,000
Total expenses	$ 38,000	$ 63,400
Net income	$108,500	$ 79,350
Earnings per share (10,000 shares outstanding)	$10.85	$7.94

Balance Sheet

	High Income	Conservative
Assets		
Cash	$348,500*	$348,500*
Accounts receivable (net)	75,000†	69,600‡
Inventory	35,000§	31,250‖
Equipment (net)	180,000#	160,000**
Total assets	$638,500	$609,350
Liabilities & stockholders' equity		
Accounts payable	$ 30,000	$ 30,000
Common stock	500,000	500,000
Retained earnings	108,500	79,350
Total liabilities & stockholders' equity	$638,500	$609,350

*Cash receipts:
Stock issue ($500,000) + customer receipts of $202,000 ($280,000 credit sales − $78,000 still owed) = $702,000.
Cash payments:
Inventory purchases of $138,500 ($168,500 total purchases − $30,000 still owed) + equipment ($200,000) + administrative expenses ($15,000) = $353,500.
Cash balance = $348,500 ($702,000 − $353,500).

† $78,000 − $3,000 = $75,000.

(Continued on page 718)

[10] "The Meaning of 'Present Fairly in Conformity with Generally Accepted Accounting Principles' in the Independent Auditor's Report," *Statement on Auditing Standards No. 5* (New York: American Institute of Certified Public Accountants, 1975), p. 2.

FINANCIAL STATEMENTS: FACT OR FICTION?

During the first quarter of 1980, Union Carbide Corp. managed to increase its profit by $217.3 million, or $3.28 per share, without adding so much as $1 in cash. It did so through the use of what some analysts and auditors call "accounting magic," in this case by adopting more liberal bookkeeping methods for depreciation, taxes, and interest costs incurred during construction. Union Carbide contends that these changes—all of which are in accordance with generally accepted accounting principles—were made to present more realistic financial statements, to make its accounting more compatible with that of other chemical producers, and, in the case of interest costs, to comply with a new accounting rule. But a few financial sleuths think the company had other motives.

"It appears to me that Carbide is merely polishing its 1980 profits to make them look a lot better," says Lee Seidler, an accounting consultant. Adds a financial analyst, "Carbide's changes will have no impact on cash flow or distributable income. They're merely an accounting mirage that greatly exaggerates reported earnings."

Carbide's action is far from unique among U.S. companies. In fact, its profit-enhancing accounting techniques represent just one example of a fairly common corporate practice, broadly defined as "earnings management." Earnings management may simply involve choosing a proper liberal accounting treatment over a more conservative one. But it may also encompass more insidious techniques, such as redistributing income or expenses from good years to bad or recognizing profits in advance of sales. It may even involve outright fraud or deception—misstating inventories, for example. Whatever the method, critics say the result is financial statements that are sometimes more accounting fiction than a quantitative measure of a company's well-being.

Even the most conservative companies aren't immune. Top executives are under tremendous pressure today to keep earnings moving steadily upward; that way security analysts will recommend their company's stock, investors will buy it, and the price-earnings ratio will move up. The company will then have easier access to financing, and management will be rewarded.

Albert Murphy, a management consultant whose firm specializes in ferreting out such practices, says management often rationalizes its game playing this way: "Well, what's the harm in a little massaging anyway? Next year our operating earnings will return to normal and we can get back to solid financial reporting." Tinkering can become addictive, however. "What starts out as a little window dressing frequently turns into serious manipulative schemes," says Mr. Murphy. "That's because when that hoped-for earnings improvement doesn't materialize, management has to resort to more desperate measures to meet its specious profit projections."

Nearly everyone agrees that the task of bringing financial reporting back in line with economic reality won't be easy. For one thing, "we don't want to stamp out flexibility in financial reporting altogether," says a member of the FASB, "because no two companies are exactly alike and in some cases there are good reasons for two companies in the same industry to choose different accounting alternatives." For another, arbitrary rule changes sometimes generate an atmosphere of gamesmanship, with management and its accountants continually attempting to avoid a regulation's intent, while sticking to its strict provisions. In any event, accounting was never meant to be an exact science anyway. As one accountant explains, "It's as much art as it is anything."

SOURCE Adapted from "Slick Accounting Ploys Help Many Companies Improve Their Income," The Wall Street Journal, *June 20, 1980, pp. 1, 26. Reprinted by permission of* The Wall Street Journal,

Exhibit 18-3

(Continued)

‡	Prior to Write-off	Write-off	After Write-off
Accounts receivable	$78,000	−$3,000	$75,000
Bad debt allowance	8,400	−$3,000	5,400
	$69,600		$69,600

§FIFO inventory (50,000 units purchased − 40,000 units sold):
Dec. 1 10,000 units @ $3.50 = $35,000

‖LIFO inventory (50,000 units purchased − 40,000 units sold):

Jan. 1 5,000 units @ $3.00 = $15,000
Mar. 1 5,000 units @ $3.25 = 16,250
$31,250

Equipment ($200,000) − accumulated depreciation ($20,000) = $180,000.

** Equipment ($200,000) − accumulated depreciation ($40,000) = $160,000.

KEY TERMS AND CONCEPTS

Accounting Principles Board (APB) 702
American Accounting Association (AAA) 703
American Institute of Certified Public Accountants (AICPA) 701
cash basis 709
comparability 699
conservatism 713
consistency principle 711
disclosure principle 711
entity assumption 705
Financial Accounting Standards Board (FASB) 702
generally accepted accounting principles (GAAP) 700
going-concern assumption 705
historical-cost principle 707
installment method 710
Internal Revenue Service (IRS) 703
matching principle 710
materiality 712
monetary unit assumption 706
National Association of Accountants (NAA) 703
objectives of financial reporting 696
objectivity principle 707
percentage-of-completion method 708
periodicity assumption 706
relevancy 698
reliability 698
revenue realization principle 708
Securities and Exchange Commission (SEC) 701
understandability 699

QUESTIONS

Q18-1 Briefly explain why accountants prepare general-purpose financial statements.
Q18-2 Financial reporting attempts to generate information that is helpful in assessing

the amounts, timing, and uncertainty of an organization's cash inflows and outflows. Discuss why creditors and stockholders would be interested in this information.

Q18-3 Bearing in mind that accounting information should be relevant, discuss a possible problem of using financial statements that are based on historical cost.

Q18-4 Briefly discuss the need for an underlying foundation of financial reporting, that is, generally accepted accounting principles.

Q18-5 Why do most companies report in conformity with GAAP as opposed to "doing their own thing."

Q18-6 Which organization has ultimate authority over the reporting practices of most large corporations? Explain.

Q18-7 Discuss the basic differences between the APB and the FASB.

Q18-8 Define the entity assumption and discuss its need in financial reporting.

Q18-9 The going-concern assumption forms the basis for many of the accounting practices illustrated in this text. Define the going-concern assumption and list several of these practices.

Q18-10 Discuss the basic problem underlying the monetary unit assumption.

Q18-11 Briefly define the historical-cost principle. Why is cost preferred for asset valuations rather than other valuation methods?

Q18-12 Revenue is said to be realized when two tests are met. What are these two tests and when are they met by most businesses?

Q18-13 In 1982 Metro Delivery was founded and implemented a straight-line depreciation policy for its truck fleet.

a Should Metro use straight-line depreciation in 1983 and 1984? Why? Discuss from the viewpoint of a statement user.

b *Must* Metro use straight-line depreciation in 1983 and 1984? Explain.

Q18-14 Discuss materiality. How is the materiality of a particular item often determined?

EXERCISES

E18-1 The following accounting practices have been in use for a number of years.

a Financial statements are prepared quarterly and annually to report financial condition and profitability.

b The accounting practices adopted may not be arbitrarily changed from one year to the next.

c Revenue is normally entered in the accounts at the time of sale.

d Expenses incurred in the generation of revenue are recognized when the revenue is recognized.

e Personal transactions of the owners are not combined with the affairs of the business.

f Small expenditures for assets are expensed as incurred rather than capitalized.

g Assets and liabilities are normally classified on the balance sheet as current and long-term.

Identify the assumption, principle, or concept that serves as the basis for each of these practices.

E18-2 In 1951 the president of Wellington Candy Company began a policy of investing excess company funds in rare stamps and coins. Over the years total investments have amounted to $62,500. The company is now in need of a bank loan to finance an equipment modernization program. To impress the banker, the president proposed valuing the investment on the company's balance sheet at $174,000, the current fair market value.

a According to GAAP, at what amount should the investment be valued? Why?

b Which of the two amounts above is consistent with the principle of objectivity and the doctrine of conservatism? Explain.

c Which of the two amounts above is more relevant to the banker? Explain.

E18-3 McClary Construction recently signed a $60,000,000 contract to build a new office and shopping complex. Management has estimated total construction costs at $55,000,000 and feels the project can be completed within 3 years. Assume costs were actually incurred as follows:

Year	Cost
1	$11,000,000
2	33,000,000
3	11,800,000

Prepare a schedule that discloses annual profit recognized during the 3-year project. McClary uses the percentage-of-completion method of revenue realization.

E18-4 Lodi Appliance uses the installment method of revenue realization. On April 2, 1983, the company sold $2,000 of appliances on account to John Wallace. Wallace paid $400 down and agreed to remit the balance owed via 20 monthly installments of $80 each. The first installment was due on May 1. Assume the appliances cost Lodi $1,500.

a Prepare a schedule disclosing the yearly profit realized on the sale to Wallace. Lodi's accounting year ends on December 31.

b Briefly explain the installment method's conformity (or lack of) to GAAP.

E18-5 The president of Diaz Corporation believes that financial statements should present a conservative picture of an entity's financial condition and profitability. Accordingly, the company's accountant did the following:

1 A $10,000 major overhaul on machinery was expensed when incurred. The overhaul was expected to extend the life of the machinery by three years.

2 Obsolete inventory in the amount of $5,000 was written off as a loss.

3 Diaz recently received a $30,000 offer to sell one of its buildings, which had a book value of $33,000. The accountant therefore recorded a $3,000 loss even though the offer was ultimately rejected.

4 The company had properly recorded the receipt of $7,000 of unearned revenue related to service contracts sold throughout the year. Although $2,500 of services had been rendered, the accountant continued to show a $7,000 liability on the balance sheet.

a Discuss conservatism and why conservative statements are popular with financial statement users.

b Determine if conservatism was properly applied with items (1)–(4). If an improper application has occurred, explain why and cite other generally accepted accounting principles if appropriate.

E18-6 Kurt Elman is evaluating the following accounting and business practices for his company.

a Straight-line versus double-declining balance depreciation for the early years of an asset's life.

b FIFO, LIFO, and weighted-average inventory costing in an economy of rising prices.

c Capitalizing versus expensing minor expenditures under $100 related to asset use.

d Direct write-off versus the allowance method of accounting for bad debts. The allowance method will estimate bad debts as a percentage of total credit sales.

e Payment versus nonpayment of certain past-due invoices for equipment purchases near the end of the accounting period.

In each of the cases above, determine which accounting practice results in the lowest (most conservative) measure of net income. Assume Elman's company is in the first year of operation.

PROBLEMS

P18-1 ***Analysis of GAAP and transactions***

You are the chief accountant of Advanced Electronics. The president of the firm, Al Riverton, having graduated from college over thirty years ago, has decided to update himself in the area of financial reporting. After completing several weeks of accounting at a local university, Riverton became involved in a heated debate with Kathy Burns, one of your staff members. The following topics were discussed.

a On January 3, 1985, Advanced increased the number of shares outstanding by 30% to finance a new warehouse and distribution center. Burns proposed that this information be footnoted on the balance sheet prepared as of December 31, 1984. Riverton objected, claiming that the stock issue took place after the year-end.

b Two years ago Advanced acquired a building complex (including land) for $425,000. The current book value is $380,000. A recent appraisal indicated that the land and building are worth $90,000 and $460,000, respectively. Riverton favored the following balance sheet presentation.

Building and land	$380,000

The presentation favored by Burns was as follows:

Land	$ 90,000
Building	460,000

c Riverton used his expense account to purchase a new car solely for personal use and favored the following journal entry:

Miscellaneous Expense	9,400	
Cash		9,400

Burns was opposed for reasons she did not state.

d Advanced recently completed and occupied a new office building. Following Riverton's suggestion, all items of office equipment having a unit cost of less than $100 were expensed. The equipment had an average life of 5 years and a total cost of $84,600. Burns was opposed to this accounting treatment, again for reasons not stated.

e In reviewing several schedules of property, plant, and equipment, Burns noted that the company should depreciate its buildings by the sum-of-the-years'-digits method and its equipment by the double-declining balance approach. Riverton felt this policy was deceptive and violated the principle of consistency.

f In December 1984 Advanced spent $120,000 for 1985 advertising. Burns favored making the following entry at the end of each of the next 12 months, beginning in January.

Advertising Expense	10,000	
Cash		10,000

Riverton, on the other hand, desired to expense the entire $120,000 in 1984, because the money had been spent and was no longer available for current operations.

g A bid was received to build a loading platform for $3,900. Feeling that the amount was too high, warehouse employees built their own platform for $3,100. Burns felt that the platform should be recorded in the accounts at $3,100, while Riverton favored the following entry:

Loading Platform	3,900	
Cash, Supplies, and so on		3,100
Construction Gain		800

Assume that prior to considering any of these items, Advanced had tentatively figured 1984 net income at $325,000.

INSTRUCTIONS

Decide who, if anyone, is correct in each of the disagreements and state the logic for your answer. Cite GAAP when appropriate. In some cases more than one principle may apply.

P18-2 ***Analysis of GAAP and transactions; financial statement impact***

You are reviewing the accounting records of Dunlap Jewelers for the year just ended. The following information has come to your attention.

1 According to a local appraiser, land held as an investment increased in value by $15,000. The company made the following entry in its records.

Land Investment	15,000	
Income from Land Appreciation		15,000

2 The company, which uses the accrual basis of accounting, failed to record $5,000 of administrative salaries payable in the next accounting period.

3 On January 1 of the current year Dunlap purchased $80,000 of equipment at a going-out-of-business sale. The equipment, which normally sells for $100,000, was recorded as follows:

Equipment	100,000	
Cash		80,000
Income from Bargain Purchase		20,000

Dunlap expects to use the equipment for 10 years and employs the straight-line method of depreciation.

4 On December 30 Dunlap received a $12,000 contract for merchandise to be shipped on January 5 of the next accounting period (per the buyer's instructions). The contract was recorded on December 30 as a debit to Accounts Receivable and a credit to Sales.

5 The company, which has 10,000 shares of common stock outstanding, declared a 25¢ cash dividend on December 31, payable to stockholders on January 30. The following entry was made.

Dividend Expense	*2,500*	
Dividends Payable		*2,500*

6 Dunlap's financial statements revealed the following information:

Net income	*$ 87,000*
Assets	*248,000*
Liabilities	*110,000*
Stockholders' equity	*138,000*

INSTRUCTIONS

a Set up a four-column schedule with the following headings: net income, assets, liabilities, and stockholders' equity. By adjusting Dunlap's reported balances, compute corrected financial statement totals using the information presented in items (1)–(5).

b For items (1)–(4) only, determine if any generally accepted accounting principles have been violated. Briefly explain your answer.

P18-3 ***GAAP: Multiple-choice questions***

The following multiple-choice questions relate to GAAP. Select the best answer.

1 Which of the following is an example of the concept of conservatism?
- a Stating inventories at the lower of cost or market.
- b Stating inventories by using the FIFO method in periods of rising prices.
- c Using the percentage-of-completion method in the first year of a long-term construction contract.
- d Overestimating revenues when constructing a budget.

2 Why are certain costs of doing business capitalized when incurred and then depreciated or amortized over subsequent accounting cycles?
- a To reduce the federal income tax liability.
- b To aid management in the decision-making process.
- c To match the costs of production with revenues as earned.
- d To adhere to the accounting concept of conservatism.

3 During the lifetime of an entity accountants produce financial statements at arbitrary points in time in accordance with the basic accounting concept of:
- a Objectivity.
- b Periodicity.
- c Conservatism.
- d Matching.

4 When bad debt expense is estimated on the basis of the percentage of past actual losses from bad debts to past net credit sales, and this percentage is adjusted for anticipated conditions, the accounting concept of:

a Matching is being followed.
b Matching is not being followed.
c Substance over form is being followed.
d Going concern is not being followed.

5 Generally, revenues should be recognized at a point when:
a Management decides it is appropriate to do so.
b The product is available for sale to the ultimate consumer.
c An exchange has taken place and the earnings process is virtually complete.
d An order for a definite amount of merchandise has been received for shipment F.O.B. destination.

6 The concept of objectivity is complied with when an accounting transaction occurs that:
a Involves a transaction between two independent interests.
b Furthers the objectives of the company.
c Is promptly recorded in a fixed amount of dollars.
d Allocates revenues or expense items in a rational and systematic manner.

7 The concept referred to by the term "matching principle" is that:
a Net income should be reported on an annual basis.
b All transactions must refer to a statement of the APB or FASB.
c All cash receipts for a period be related to the cash disbursements for the period.
d Where possible, the expenses to be included in the income statement were incurred to produce the revenues.
e Current liabilities have the same period of existence as current assets.

8 The concept of conservatism often is considered important in accounting. The application of this concept means that in the event there is some doubt as to how a transaction should be recorded, it should be recorded so as to:
a Understate income and overstate assets.
b Overstate income and overstate assets.
c Understate income and understate assets.
d Overstate income and understate assets.
e Relate to the content of the president's letter that accompanies the statements, not to the statements themselves.

9 The most common test of revenue realization for most transactions is the:
a Receipt of cash.
b Receipt of a purchase order.
c Transfer of title for a product or provision of service to a customer.
d Quotation of value on a market exchange.
e Point when a product or service is ready for sale.

(CPA and CMA modified.)

P18-4 ***Revenue realization, percentage-of-completion and installment methods***
Tower Building, Inc., recently signed a long-term contract for the construction of town houses throughout the state of Florida. The contract price was $30,000,000; Tower's accounting department has estimated total construction costs of $24,000,000. The contract stipulated a $2,000,000 payment to Tower upon contract signing and periodic payments throughout the project's 3-year life.

The following information relates to the contract and the project.

	Year 1	Year 2	Year 3
Cash collected	$7,000,000*	$15,000,000	$8,000,000
Actual costs incurred	8,000,000	12,000,000	4,300,000

** Includes the $2,000,000 payment upon signing.*

The project was completed on December 24 in Year 3.

INSTRUCTIONS

a Calculate the total profit Tower Building has earned on this project.

b Assuming Tower uses the percentage-of-completion method of revenue realization, prepare a schedule that reveals the profit earned in Years 1–3.

c Assume Tower uses the installment method of revenue realization and that actual costs in Year 3 totaled $4,000,000. Prepare a schedule that reveals the profit earned in Years 1–3.

d Is the installment method or percentage-of-completion method more appropriate for Tower Building? Explain.

P18-5 ***Matching principle, income statement construction***

On January 1 of the current year Bruce Snell opened an appliance repair shop. The first year's income statement, prepared by using the cash basis of accounting, follows.

SNELL'S REPAIR SHOP
Income Statement
For the Year Ended December 31, 19XX

Cash receipts		
Owner investments	$ 3,000	
Cash sales	21,000	
Receipts from customers on account	8,500	
Interest on savings account	100	
Total receipts		$32,600
Cash disbursements		
Owner withdrawals	$ 3,200	
Wages paid to helper	11,000	
Supplies	4,400	
Delivery van	6,400	
Advertising	1,200	
Utilities	900	
Rent	2,400	
Total disbursements		29,500
Net income		$ 3,100

The following information was obtained from a review of the company's records.

1 Customers still owe $3,800 for repair services performed. Snell believes that

bad debts will total 4% of credit sales; to date, however, no accounts have been written off as uncollectible.

2 Snell owes his helper $370 for services rendered during the last two weeks of the year.

3 As of December 31 Snell owed various vendors $1,900 for purchases of supplies. An inventory count on this date revealed $2,800 of supplies remained on hand.

4 The delivery van was acquired on April 1 and was expected to have a service life of 5 years. The $6,400 figure on the income statement includes $400 of minor repairs performed on various dates subsequent to acquisition.

5 Advertising outlays include prepayments of $150.

6 On December 31 Snell owed New Hampshire Power & Light $100.

Snell recently learned from one of his customers, a CPA, that the cash basis improperly matches expenses against related revenues.

INSTRUCTIONS

a Prepare a brief explanation of the matching principle.

b Using the matching principle along with other generally accepted accounting principles, prepare a single-step income statement that better reflects financial performance. Assume straight-line depreciation for the van.

P18-6 ***Alternative accounting practices***

Filmore Corporation began operations on January 1 of the current year. The following information has come to your attention.

1 Ten thousand shares of no-par common stock were sold for $200,000.

2 The following long-lived assets were purchased for cash.

Land	$30,000
Building	80,000 (estimated life, 20 years)
Equipment	20,000 (estimated life, 5 years)

Filmore records a full year's depreciation in the year of acquisition.

3 Purchases of inventory on account follow.

Jan. 2	6,000 units @ $4.50
June 10	12,000 units @ $4.80
Nov. 15	15,000 units @ $5.30

Payments on account to suppliers totaled $124,600.

4 Filmore had credit sales as follows:

15,000 units @ $8.00
11,000 units @ $8.50

Customer payments on account have totaled $162,400. Filmore has determined that $1,100 of customer accounts are definitely uncollectible; however, management anticipates that bad debts will ultimately total 4% of credit sales.

5 Cash operating expenses throughout the year amounted to $49,700.

Management is studying the following accounting practices.

Depreciation: straight-line versus double-declining balance
Inventories: FIFO versus LIFO
Bad debts: direct write-off versus the allowance (estimation) method

INSTRUCTIONS

a Prepare an income statement and balance sheet assuming the use of straight-line depreciation, FIFO inventory costing, and the direct write-off method of bad debts. Show all supporting computations.

b Repeat the instruction in part (a), using double-declining balance depreciation, LIFO inventory costing, and the allowance method of bad debts.

c Comment on the need for diversity in financial reporting practices.

P18-7 ***Analysis of GAAP and transactions; financial statement impact*** **(*alternate to P18-2*)**

You are reviewing the accounting records of Cassidy Merchandising, a sole proprietorship, for the current year ended December 31. The following information has come to your attention.

1 The company, which uses the accrual basis of accounting, failed to record $3,500 of interest revenue. Collection will take place in the next accounting period.

2 John Cassidy, the owner, purchased a new car solely for personal use and had the bookkeeper record the following entry:

Delivery Equipment	10,800	
Cash		10,800

Depreciation pertaining to the car of $1,200 was recorded on December 31.

3 Freight charges of $1,800 relating to the purchase of equipment on December 28 were expensed when incurred.

4 Inventories costing $8,900 had a year-end fair market value of $11,500. Accordingly, the company's accountant made the following entry:

Inventories	2,600	
Income from Appreciation		2,600

5 On December 30 the company determined that a $9,000 embezzlement of cash had recently occurred. The accounts have yet to be adjusted for the amount of the theft.

6 Cassidy's financial statements for the current year revealed the following information:

Net income	$ 41,300
Assets	121,500
Liabilities	78,900
Owners' equity	42,600

INSTRUCTIONS

a Set up a four-column schedule with the following headings: net income, assets, liabilities, and owners' equity. By adjusting Cassidy's reported balances, compute corrected financial statement totals using the information presented in items (1)–(5).

b For items (1)–(4) only, determine if any generally accepted accounting principles have been violated. Briefly explain your answer.

P18-8 ***GAAP: Multiple-choice questions*** **(*alternate to P18-3*)**

The following multiple-choice questions relate to GAAP. Select the best answer.

1 Which of the following concepts states that an accounting transaction should be supported by sufficient evidence to allow two or more qualified individuals to arrive at essentially similar measures and conclusions?

a Matching
b Objectivity
c Periodicity
d Monetary unit
e None of the above

2 Howard Corporation recently recorded the following entry to reflect increased values of its real estate holdings.

Land	*70,000*	
Buildings	*340,000*	
Income from Appreciation		*410,000*

Howard Corporation:
a Has followed GAAP.
b Has violated the historical-cost principle.
c Has violated the revenue realization principle.
d Has followed nonconservative accounting practices.
e More than one of the above is correct; namely, _____, _____, _____.

3 The principle of consistency requires that:
a Entities within the same industry use the same accounting practices.
b Entities implement accounting practices that result in a consistent rate of return.
c Entities employ the same accounting practices from one period to the next.
d Entities never change accounting practices once the practices are implemented.
e More than one of the above is correct; namely, _____, _____, _____.

4 The use of accelerated depreciation recognizes that assets often provide decreasing benefits over their service lives. The accounting assumption or principle most relevant to this situation is:
a The entity assumption.
b The objectivity principle.
c The matching principle.
d The monetary unit assumption.
e None of the above.

5 The entity assumption:
a Applies only to corporations.
b Requires the allocation of cost among various periods of benefit.
c Suggests that companies follow conservative accounting practices and disclose such practices in the financial statements.
d Requires the separation of personal transactions of the owners from the affairs of the business.
e Is described by none of the above.

6 Which of the following statements regarding revenue realization is false?
a Most businesses recognize revenue at the time of sale or when services are rendered.
b The installment method of revenue recognition is in accordance with GAAP.
c Revenue should be recognized when the earnings process is complete or virtually complete.

d The percentage-of-completion method postpones revenue recognition on a construction project until such time that title to the property passes to the buyer.
e More than one of the above is false; namely, ______, ______, ______.

7 A company is considering the implementation of equally acceptable accounting practices. Which accounting principle or assumption should govern the selection decision?
a Consistency
b Full disclosure
c Periodicity
d Conservatism
e None of the above

8 Farmer Corporation, with total assets of $175,000, has a policy of expensing all items costing less than $75. In a recent office modernization program numerous items with a *total* cost of $8,450 met this guideline and were written off as expenses upon acquisition. Farmer is:
a Correctly following the doctrine of materiality.
b Incorrectly following the doctrine of materiality.
c Violating the matching principle.
d Not violating the matching principle.
e More than one of the above is correct; namely, ______, ______, ______.

9 Although challenged frequently, the historical-cost principle is still widely supported for financial reporting because historical cost:
a Is an objectively determinable amount.
b Is a good measure of current value for a going concern.
c Facilitates the calculation of economic income.
d Results in the lowest income tax accruals.
e Facilitates comparisons between years.

P18-9 ***Revenue realization, percentage-of-completion and installment methods (alternate to P18-4)***

Garwin Developers recently signed a long-term contract for the construction of apartments throughout the state of Montana. The contract price was $40,000,000; Garwin's accounting department has estimated total construction costs of $36,000,000. The contract stipulated a $700,000 payment to Garwin upon contract signing and periodic payments throughout the project's 3-year life.

The following information relates to the contract and the project.

	Year 1	Year 2	Year 3
Cash collected	$10,500,000*	$23,800,000	$5,700,000
Annual costs incurred	9,000,000	21,600,000	5,800,000

**Includes the $700,000 payment upon signing.*

The project was completed on December 28 in Year 3.

INSTRUCTIONS

a Calculate the total profit Garwin has earned on this project.
b Assuming Garwin uses the percentage-of-completion method of revenue realization, prepare a schedule that reveals the profit earned in Years 1–3.

c Assume Garwin uses the installment method of revenue realization and that actual costs in Year 3 totaled $5,400,000. Prepare a schedule that reveals the profit earned in Years 1–3.

d Given Garwin's operation, is the company allowed to use the installment method? Explain.

P18-10 ***Matching principle, income statement construction (alternate to P18-5)***
On January 1 of the current year, Ed Morrow opened a furniture repair shop. The first year's income statement, prepared by using the cash basis of accounting, follows.

MORROW'S REPAIR SHOP
Income Statement
For the Year Ended December 31, 19XX

Cash receipts		
Owner investments	$ 7,000	
Cash sales	24,600	
Receipts from customers on account	7,500	
Interest on savings account	200	
Total receipts		$39,300
Cash disbursements		
Owner withdrawals	$ 5,800	
Wages paid to helper	14,000	
Supplies	3,900	
Delivery van	6,800	
Advertising	1,500	
Utilities	1,100	
Rent	3,000	
Total disbursements		36,100
Net income		$ 3,200

The following information was obtained from a review of the company's records.

1 Customers still owe $3,500 for repair services performed. Morrow believes that bad debts will total 3% of credit sales; to date, however, no accounts have been written off as uncollectible.

2 Morrow owes his helper $420 for services rendered during the last two weeks of the year.

3 As of December 31 Morrow owed various vendors $1,700 for purchases of supplies. An inventory count on this date revealed $1,200 of supplies remained on hand.

4 The delivery van was acquired on March 1 and was expected to have a service life of 6 years. The $6,800 figure on the income statement includes $500 of minor repairs performed on various dates subsequent to acquisition.

5 Advertising outlays include prepayments of $250.

6 On December 31 Morrow owed Pacific Power & Light $85.

Morrow recently learned from one of his customers, a CPA, that the cash basis improperly matches expenses against related revenues.

INSTRUCTIONS

a Using the matching principle along with other generally accepted accounting principles, prepare a single-step income statement that better reflects financial performance. Assume straight-line depreciation for the van.

b As shown in the income statement, Morrow deducted the entire cost of the delivery van in the year of acquisition. Explain how this accounting treatment violates the matching principle.

P18-11 ***Alternative accounting practices (alternate to P18-6)***

St. Clair Distributors began operations on January 1 of the current year. The following information has come to your attention.

1 Twenty thousand shares of no-par common stock were sold for $375,000.

2 The following long-lived assets were purchased for cash.

Land	$ 48,000
Building	120,000 (estimated life, 25 years)
Equipment	35,000 (estimated life, 10 years)

St. Clair records a full year's depreciation in the year of acquisition.

3 Purchases of inventory on account follow.

Jan. 6	9,000 units @ $7.20
May 28	14,000 units @ $7.50
Oct. 17	18,000 units @ $8.00

Payments on account to suppliers totaled $214,600.

4 St. Clair had credit sales as follows:

19,000 units @ $12.50
12,000 units @ $13.00

Customer payments on account have totaled $314,500. St. Clair has determined that $3,750 of customer accounts are definitely uncollectible; however, management anticipates that bad debts will ultimately total 2% of credit sales.

5 Cash operating expenses throughout the year amounted to $119,300.

Management is studying the following accounting practices.

Depreciation: straight-line versus double-declining balance
Inventories: FIFO versus LIFO
Bad debts: direct write-off versus the allowance (estimation) method

INSTRUCTIONS

a Prepare an income statement and balance sheet assuming the use of straight-line depreciation, FIFO inventory costing, and the direct write-off method of bad debts. Show all supporting computations.

b Repeat the instruction in part (a), using double-declining balance depreciation, LIFO inventory costing, and the allowance method of bad debts.

c Suppose St. Clair adopted the accounting practices listed in part (a). Would the firm ever be allowed to switch to the practices listed in part (b)? Explain.

CASE 18
HENDERSON AND ASSOCIATES

Henderson and Associates is a corporation engaged in the development and production of television programs for commercial sponsorship. Each program is accounted for separately and is carried on Henderson's books as follows:

Program	Development Cost*
"I Live Alone"	$90,000
"Jack Gannon, M.D."	64,000
"512 Oak Lane"	31,000
"Hollywood"	18,000

*Prior to recording amortization for the current year.

An examination of contracts and records revealed the following information:

1 The first two accounts listed above represent the total cost of completed programs that were televised during the accounting period just ended. Under the terms of an existing contract, "I Live Alone" will be rerun during the next accounting period at a fee equal to 50% of the fee for the first televising of the program. The contract for the first run produced $800,000 of revenue. The contract with the sponsor of "Gannon" provides that at the sponsor's option the program can be rerun during the next season at a fee equal to 75% of the fee on the first televising of the program. There are no present indications that the program will be rerun.

2 The balance in the "512 Oak Lane" account is the cost of a new program that has just been completed and is being considered by several companies for commercial sponsorship.

3 The balance in the "Hollywood" account represents the cost of a partially completed program for a projected series that has been abandoned.

INSTRUCTIONS

a State and briefly explain the general principle (or principles) of accounting on which amortization is based.

b How would you report the balances of these accounts in Henderson's financial statements? Explain your answer by making specific references to the balance sheet and income statement.

(CPA modified.)

19 FINANCIAL STATEMENTS: ANALYSIS AND THE IMPACT OF INFLATION

LEARNING OBJECTIVES

After reading this chapter you should:

1 Be familiar with the advantages and problems of financial statement analysis.

2 Be able to perform a horizontal analysis of comparative financial statements.

3 Be able to perform a vertical analysis and understand the associated benefits of common-size statements.

4 Be familiar with ratio analysis, including its use in studying liquidity, activity, profitability, and coverage relationships.

5 Be familiar with the computation and interpretation of ratios commonly employed in statement evaluation.

6 Understand trading on the equity.

7 Understand the impact of inflation on financial statements.

8 Be familiar with the basic differences between constant dollar and current value accounting, including the FASB's disclosure requirements.

9 Understand the concept of purchasing power gains and losses.

CHAPTER 19

Financial statements, together with accompanying footnotes, provide a wealth of information to owners, managers, creditors, government agencies, employees, union officials, and prospective investors. It is important to note that the preceding groups have different interests and, therefore, different information needs. Stockholders, for example, focus on earnings because of a concern over both the market price of their investments and future dividend distributions. Creditors analyze cash and near cash assets in an effort to judge an entity's debt-paying ability. Regulatory agencies frequently study profit rates to determine if a firm's rate is in line with those of other companies in the same industry. Managers, of course, are concerned with all these factors along with operating efficiency.

Although financial statements are general purpose, the *individual* dollar amounts reported therein often fail to adequately satisfy user needs. As an example, Safeway Stores (a large supermarket operator) recently reported an ending cash balance of $44 million and net income in excess of $114 million. These two figures are of obvious interest to creditors and stockholders, respectively. When interpreted in isolation, the amounts are surely impressive. Most of you will agree, however, that perspectives might change upon learning that current liabilities totaled $1.353 billion and net income represented a mere 1¢ of every sales dollar. Hopefully, you can see a clearer picture of performance results by establishing and analyzing certain financial statement relationships.

In the following pages we will introduce various approaches to financial statement analysis. Just as your cumulative grade point average is an indicator of how well you are performing in college, the techniques illustrated provide insight into a company's financial health and well-being.

Words of Caution

Before proceeding with our discussion, we give several words of caution. First, financial statement analysis employs many different tools (e.g., ratios, trend studies) to furnish information about operating activity. These tools must be used judiciously. The tools are not ends in themselves; rather they are measures to be examined in conjunction with other, more subjective factors such as the state of the economy, industry outlooks, and management quality. Statement analysis is most effective when evaluation techniques are coupled with good judgment or decision-making experience.

Comparative standards

A second caution concerns comparative standards. When performing analysis work, accountants, creditors, stockholders, and other parties continually seek comparative standards against which to judge a company's present financial relationships. Standards commonly employed include past performance of the company and performance of other companies in the same industry.

Relating the current data of a company with data of preceding years provides insight for determining whether financial relationships are improving or deteriorating. Unfortunately, single-company comparisons do not provide a sufficiently broad basis for evaluation. For example, if a candy manufacturer incurred a net loss of $200,000 in 1983 and a net loss of only $50,000 in 1984, the firm has shown considerable improvement. However, if the manufacturer remains the only unprofitable candy producer in the country, the earnings records of both years can be viewed as being unfavorable.

The use of an external standard (or yardstick) frequently overcomes the limitations of single-company studies. That is, a business's financial performance can be compared with the performance of a similar company or the average of several companies in the same industry (called *industry norms*). Extreme care is necessary when using these comparisons, however, to make certain they are both valid and reasonable. Many firms today are diversified and cannot be neatly classified by industry lines.

To illustrate, let's suppose we desire to analyze the Coca-Cola Company. PepsiCo, Inc., the makers of Pepsi-Cola, would appear to be a natural comparison for our evaluation. Upon examination, however, we would soon find that the two companies have many significant operational differences. In addition to making soft drinks, Coca-Cola produces Minute Maid frozen concentrate, Maryland Club and Butter Nut Coffee, Hi-C fruit drinks, Taylor Wine, and water treatment equipment. Furthermore, the firm recently acquired Columbia Pictures Industries, Inc., an entity involved in the production and distribution of motion pictures, television shows and commercials, and pinball machines. PepsiCo, on the other hand, not only manufactures Pepsi-Cola but also owns Frito-Lay snack foods, Pizza Hut, Taco Bell, North American Van Lines, Lee Way Motor Freight, and Wilson Sporting Goods. Thus these two firms may not be comparable when analyzing financial statement information. Recall, however, that diversified organizations disclose business segment information in the footnotes to the financial statements (see Chapter 6). Thus some analysis may be possible by examining available figures from the soft drink segments of both companies.

Another problem in using external standards is that differences in accounting practices may reduce data comparability. For example, consider the following leisure wear firms. California, Inc., primarily uses the first-in, first-out method for costing merchandise inventories; in contrast, Ocean Fashions, Inc., uses the last-in, first-out method. Such a difference, as well as variations in depreciation methods or other accounting practices, may significantly hamper comparisons. In spite of the foregoing limitations, external standards are helpful in financial statement analysis if the standards are selected with care and the limitations are known *and* understood.

TOOLS OF ANALYSIS

Three tools are frequently used to evaluate financial statements: horizontal analysis, vertical analysis, and ratio analysis. To illustrate these tools, we will focus on a set of two-year comparative financial statements of the Handy Corporation. In addition, we will integrate other analyses that are of special interest to particular statement users.

Horizontal Analysis

The calculation of dollar and percentage changes for corresponding items in comparative financial statements is termed **horizontal analysis.** In such an analysis the earlier period is established as a base against which the later period is compared. As an example, the percentage change in the Cash account is computed by dividing the account's change between the two periods (say 1984 and 1983) by the Cash balance of the base period (1983). A complete horizontal analysis of the financial statements of Handy Corporation is presented in Exhibit 19-1.

The horizontal analysis reveals that the sizable increase in net income was mainly due to a $4,000,000 rise in sales (11.1%) coupled with reductions in cost of goods sold ($2,000,000; 8.3%), administrative expenses ($650,000; 16.3%), and interest expense ($150,000; 18.8%). These reductions, however, were offset by increases in selling expenses and income taxes, the former causing an overall hike in operating expenses of $550,000, or 6.3%.

Turning to the balance sheet, the increase in total assets ($1,360,000; 6.7%) and decrease in total liabilities ($1,400,000; 12.3%) produced a

Exhibit 19-1

Horizontal analysis of comparative financial statements

HANDY CORPORATION
Comparative Income Statements
For the Years Ended December 31, 1984 and 1983

	1984	1983	Increase (Decrease)	Percentage Change from 1983
Net sales	$40,000,000	$36,000,000	$4,000,000	11.1%
Cost of goods sold	22,000,000	24,000,000	(2,000,000)	(8.3)
Gross profit	$18,000,000	$12,000,000	$6,000,000	50.0
Operating expenses				
Selling	$ 6,000,000	$ 4,800,000	$1,200,000	25.0
Administrative	3,350,000	4,000,000	(650,000)	(16.3)
Total operating expenses	$ 9,350,000	$ 8,800,000	$ 550,000	6.3
Operating income	$ 8,650,000	$ 3,200,000	$5,450,000	170.3
Interest expense	650,000	800,000	(150,000)	(18.8)
Income before income taxes	$ 8,000,000	$ 2,400,000	$5,600,000	233.3
Income taxes, 40%	3,200,000	960,000	2,240,000	233.3
Net income	$ 4,800,000	$ 1,440,000	$3,360,000	233.3
Earnings per share*	$2.38	$0.70	$1.68	240.0

*Calculated as $\frac{\text{net income} - \text{preferred dividends}}{\text{common shares outstanding}}$

HANDY CORPORATION
Comparative Statements of Retained Earnings
For the Years Ended December 31, 1984 and 1983

	1984	1983	Increase (Decrease)	Percentage Change from 1983
Balance, Jan. 1	$ 5,900,000	$5,500,000	$ 400,000	7.3%
Net income	4,800,000	1,440,000	3,360,000	233.3
Total	$10,700,000	$6,940,000	$3,760,000	54.2
Less dividends				
Common	$ 2,000,000	$1,000,000	$1,000,000	100.0
Preferred	40,000	40,000	—	—
Total dividends	$ 2,040,000	$1,040,000	$1,000,000	96.2
Balance, Dec. 31	$ 8,660,000	$5,900,000	$2,760,000	46.8

HANDY CORPORATION
Comparative Balance Sheets
December 31, 1984 and 1983

	1984	1983	Increase (Decrease)	Percentage Change from 1983
ASSETS				
Current assets	$ 8,000,000	$ 7,000,000	$ 1,000,000	14.3%
Property, plant, & equipment (net)	12,200,000	11,500,000	700,000	6.1
Intangible assets (net)	1,000,000	1,200,000	(200,000)	(16.7)
Other assets	410,000	550,000	(140,000)	(25.5)
Total assets	$21,610,000	$20,250,000	$ 1,360,000	6.7
LIABILITIES & STOCKHOLDERS' EQUITY				
Liabilities				
Current liabilities	$ 3,500,000	$ 3,400,000	$ 100,000	2.9
Long-term liabilities	6,500,000	8,000,000	(1,500,000)	(18.8)
Total liabilities	$10,000,000	$11,400,000	$(1,400,000)	(12.3)
Stockholders' equity				
10% preferred stock, $10 par value	$ 400,000	$ 400,000	$ —	—
Common stock, $1 par value	2,000,000	2,000,000	—	—
Paid-in capital, common stock	550,000	550,000	—	—
Retained earnings	8,660,000	5,900,000	2,760,000	46.8
Total stockholders' equity	$11,610,000	$ 8,850,000	$ 2,760,000	31.2
Total liabilities & stockholders' equity	$21,610,000	$20,250,000	$ 1,360,000	6.7

$2,760,000 (31.2%) jump in stockholders' equity. Stockholders' equity would have increased even further had Handy maintained the same dividend rate in 1984 as it had in 1983. Careful examination of the balance sheet and statement of retained earnings shows that common dividends doubled to $1 per share, while the number of common shares outstanding remained constant at 2,000,000 ($2,000,000 ÷ $1 par value).

Overall, horizontal analysis provides information about the magnitude, direction, and relative importance of changes in individual and aggregate financial statement items. Such information is useful in assessing whether an enterprise has become stronger or weaker over a period of time and whether improvements are needed in particular areas.

Vertical Analysis; Common-Size Statements

Important changes and trends can also be studied by using vertical analysis. With **vertical analysis** each figure on a financial statement is related to a relevant total and stated as a percentage of that total. Examine Exhibit 19-2, which contains a vertical analysis of Handy's income statements. Observe how each item is stated as a percentage of net sales. The analysis reveals that 12¢ of every sales dollar remained as profit in 1984, up from 4¢ in 1983.

Turning to the balance sheet, each asset is stated as a percentage of total assets. In a similar fashion, each of the liability and stockholders' equity

Exhibit 19-2

Vertical analysis of income statements

HANDY CORPORATION
Comparative Income Statements
For the Years Ended December 31, 1984 and 1983

	1984		1983	
	$	Percent	$	Percent
Net sales	$40,000,000	100.0%	$36,000,000	100.0%
Cost of goods sold	22,000,000	55.0	24,000,000	66.7
Gross profit	$18,000,000	45.0	$12,000,000	33.3
Operating expenses				
Selling	$ 6,000,000	15.0	$ 4,800,000	13.3
Administrative	3,350,000	8.4	4,000,000	11.1
Total operating expenses	$ 9,350,000	23.4	$ 8,800,000	24.4
Operating income	$ 8,650,000	21.6	$ 3,200,000	8.9
Interest expense	650,000	1.6	800,000	2.2
Income before income taxes	$ 8,000,000	20.0	$ 2,400,000	6.7
Income taxes, 40%	3,200,000	8.0	960,000	2.7
Net income	$ 4,800,000	12.0%	$ 1,440,000	4.0%

accounts is stated as a percentage of the total of liabilities plus stockholders' equity. A vertical analysis of Handy's assets follows.

	1984		1983	
	$	Percent	$	Percent
ASSETS				
Current assets	$ 8,000,000	37.0%	$ 7,000,000	34.6%
Property, plant, & equipment (net)	12,200,000	56.5	11,500,000	56.8
Intangible assets (net)	1,000,000	4.6	1,200,000	5.9
Other assets	410,000	1.9	550,000	2.7
Total assets	$21,610,000	100.0%	$20,250,000	100.0%

The analysis shows that despite a $1,360,000 increase in total assets, individual components remained relatively stable. The largest change is noted for current assets, which, in terms of total assets, increased by 2.4% (37.0% − 34.6%).

Benefits of vertical analysis

Vertical analysis has two associated benefits. First, further insight is provided when interpreting performance. In the area of operating expenses, for example, Handy's comparative income statements disclose a $550,000 increase from 1983 to 1984 ($9,350,000 − $8,800,000). At first glance a manager may be upset, especially if various cost control programs had been implemented in the previous year. The use of vertical analysis shows, however, that operating expenses actually declined as a percentage of sales (from 24.4% to 23.4%). Apparently, then, the cost control programs are taking hold and functioning in an effective manner.

Second, vertical analysis results in **common-size financial statements.** That is, with all items stated on some common ground (e.g., percentages), users can evaluate financial statements in relative terms and not be concerned with differences in absolute size. This benefit becomes especially useful when comparing one company with another company or industry norms. Consider, for example, recent abbreviated income statements (in thousands) of Levi Strauss and Kennington, Ltd., both producers of apparel.

	Levi Strauss		Kennington, Ltd.	
	$	Percent	$	Percent
Net sales	$2,851,245	100.0%	$75,073	100.0%
Cost of goods sold	1,834,913	64.4	55,236	73.6
Gross profit	$1,016,332	35.6	$19,837	26.4
Operating expenses and income taxes	844,034	29.6	11,544	15.4
Net income	$ 172,298	6.0%	$ 8,293	11.0%

Levi Strauss's sales were 38.0 times ($2,851,245 ÷ $75,073) greater than those of Kennington. Yet by using vertical analysis, which eliminates differences in size, we can see that Kennington was 5.0% more profitable (11.0% − 6.0%) per sales dollar. In percentage terms the total of Kennington's cost of goods sold, operating expenses, and income taxes was lower than that of the much larger firm.

Ratio Analysis

A third method of financial statement evaluation is **ratio analysis.** Ratios can be used to study liquidity, activity, profitability, coverage of obligations, and other financial relationships. While any number of ratios can be constructed and presented, our discussion will focus only on those that are commonly encountered and widely used by statement analysts.

It is important to note that a ratio is merely a mathematical expression of relationships. In essence, one could view a ratio as being similar to a thermometer, that is, a gauge of performance. For example, suppose you're ill, you take your temperature, and the thermometer reads 102.6 degrees. The obvious conclusion? Something is wrong with your body. In no way, however, can the thermometer indicate whether you have the flu, an infected ear, or mononucleosis. The thermometer simply tells you that something is amiss and serves as a starting point for further investigation. Similarly, a ratio presents information regarding a single financial relationship; it cannot tell the complete story.

Liquidity ratios

Liquidity ratios measure the ability of a business to meet current debts as the obligations come due. Appropriately, short-term creditors have great interest in the liquidity ratios of their clients and customers, both present and potential. Weak ratios frequently indicate a high probability of nonpayment. In addition to short-term creditors, management and stockholders are also interested in liquidity ratios, especially those of their own firm. The inability to meet current obligations taints a firm's reputation, reduces its credit rating, and generally means an increase in future borrowing costs.

Current ratio

The most widely used measure of liquidity is the current ratio. As we noted in Chapter 6, the **current ratio** relates total current assets to total current liabilities. The computation of the current ratio for Handy Corporation follows.

$$\text{current ratio} = \frac{\text{current assets}}{\text{current liabilities}}$$

1984

$$\frac{\$8{,}000{,}000}{\$3{,}500{,}000} = 2.29$$

1983

$$\frac{\$7{,}000{,}000}{\$3{,}400{,}000} = 2.06$$

Handy's ratios show that by the end of 1984 the company possessed $2.29 of current assets for every $1 of current liabilities. Thus an improvement is noted from the firm's position at the end of 1983.

Although the ratio has increased, is Handy really "better off"? This is a difficult question to answer unless one has some knowledge of the current asset composition. Keep in mind that current assets include cash, short-term investments, accounts receivable, inventories, and prepaid expenses. Short-term investments can be converted into cash immediately; receivables, on the other hand, are converted upon collection, typically some 20 to 40 days in the future. Inventories eventually become cash but have yet to be sold. Finally, prepaid expenses are consumed in operations and never become cash. In judging debt-paying ability, most analysts prefer a current asset composition weighted heavily with cash and near cash items. Notice, however, that the current ratio uses a numerator of *total* current assets. Given the nature of the computation, all current assets are treated equally, with a total disregard for composition and individual component liquidities.

The current ratio also overlooks alternative uses for a business's precious capital funds. Funds committed to current assets must not exceed the level necessary to support present and prospective sales of the enterprise. Why? Normally, excess funds can be invested more profitably elsewhere, for example, in acquisitions of laborsaving equipment, new product development, and so forth. Thus abnormally high current asset levels could indicate that a company is forgoing considerable profits from other investment opportunities.

To further complicate the picture, the current ratio can be manipulated by management. A business can deliberately improve its current ratio by paying short-term obligations. Although current assets and current liabilities will both decline by the same amount, the ratio actually increases. For example, if a firm with current assets of $100,000 and current liabilities of $50,000 voluntarily paid a $10,000 account payable prior to year-end, the current ratio would improve from 2 to 2.25 ($90,000 ÷ $40,000). The practice of intentionally increasing a ratio to improve financial appearance is commonly known as *window dressing*.

Given these problems, the current ratio (and others) must be used with great care. The general rule employed by bankers and other creditors is that the current ratio should be at least 2. Be aware, however, that ratios tend to vary by type of business. For example, the median current ratio is 0.7 for restaurants, 1.3 for wholesalers of dairy products, and 2.4 for footwear manufacturers.[1] Recent current ratios of several well-known corporations follow.

---

[1] The industry figures used in this chapter are taken from '81 *Annual Statement Studies,* Robert Morris Associates, Philadelphia, Pa.

McDonald's Corporation	0.5
Fotomat Corporation	1.3
Denny's, Inc.	1.5
Hershey Foods	2.4
Whirlpool Corporation	2.9
Churchill Downs	6.1

Such variations are caused by differences in operating practices. In some industries companies carry high levels of inventories and receivables to serve their customers. Also certain industries tend to rely more heavily on trade accounts payable than others. Consequently, the general rule of 2 is just as its name implies—general. There are, as always, many exceptions.

Quick ratio

The **quick ratio** is another measure of short-term, debt-paying ability. Rather than rely on total current assets for comparison with current liabilities, the quick ratio excludes merchandise inventory and prepaid expenses from the asset base. As we noted, inventory is not an immediate source of cash since months may pass until the time of sale. In addition, prepaid expenses are consumed in operations. Thus the current assets that remain—cash, short-term investments, and accounts receivable—represent a ready or "nearly ready" source of cash to satisfy the claims of creditors. In comparison with the current ratio, the quick ratio represents a more severe test of debt-paying ability.

Handy's individual current assets appear below.

	1984	1983
Current assets		
Cash	$1,000,000	$ 400,000
Short-term investments	1,000,000	1,000,000
Accounts receivable (net)	2,000,000	1,500,000
Merchandise inventory	3,900,000	4,000,000
Prepaid expenses	100,000	100,000
	$8,000,000	$7,000,000

The firm's quick ratio is therefore computed as follows:

$$\text{quick ratio} = \frac{\text{cash + short-term investments + accounts receivable}}{\text{current liabilities}}$$

1984

$$\frac{\$1{,}000{,}000 + \$1{,}000{,}000 + \$2{,}000{,}000}{\$3{,}500{,}000} = 1.14$$

1983

$$\frac{\$400{,}000 + \$1{,}000{,}000 + \$1{,}500{,}000}{\$3{,}400{,}000} = 0.85$$

Many analysts feel that a quick ratio of 1 is satisfactory. In this manner each dollar of short-term debt is backed by $1 of cash or near cash assets. Handy's ratio improved to meet this standard by the end of 1984. Keep in mind that many of the current ratio's problems also apply to this performance measure. Especially note that the quick ratio will vary among industries; thus the standard guideline of 1 should be used with caution.

Activity ratios

Activity ratios, often termed *turnover ratios,* are employed to analyze a firm's effectiveness in using specific resources. Managers, and to a lesser extent stockholders and short-term creditors, have a keen interest in these performance measures.

Any number of activity ratios can be calculated. For example, sales can be related to the number of employees to measure employee productivity. Or sales and average plant and equipment can be compared to judge facility utilization. The two most popular activity ratios are accounts receivable turnover and inventory turnover.

Accounts receivable turnover

Accounts receivable turnover shows the number of times each year a company's receivables turn into cash. As a result, this ratio provides some indication of the quality of both the receivables and a firm's collection efforts.

Accounts receivable turnover is computed by dividing net sales by the average accounts receivable during the year. Average receivables are calculated by summing the beginning and ending receivables and dividing by 2. The 1984 accounts receivable turnover ratio for Handy Corporation follows.

$$\text{accounts receivable turnover} = \frac{\text{net sales}}{\text{average accounts receivable}} = \frac{\$40{,}000{,}000}{\frac{\$1{,}500{,}000 + \$2{,}000{,}000}{2}} = 22.86 \text{ times}$$

The fact that receivables turned over 22.86 times indicates an average collection period of about 16 days (365 days ÷ 22.86 times). Is this result good? The answer is really dependent on Handy's credit terms. If the terms are n/20 or n/30, then the company is doing an excellent job in granting credit and collecting the resulting accounts. If the terms are n/10, however, questions may surface regarding receivables management. Perhaps sales are being made to poor credit risks, or perhaps the company's collection efforts have been lax. Whatever the cause, exceeding credit terms by a few days is tolerable and somewhat expected since many customers take advantage of the full credit period. Add several days for the postal service and receipts processing and the collection period can easily increase by as much as one week.

Like other ratios, receivables turnover and collection periods vary among businesses. This fact becomes apparent when studying the following figures:

Business Segment	*Median Collection Period (Days)*
Radio and TV retailers	11
Grocery wholesalers	20
Retail furniture stores	27
Footwear wholesalers	48
Engineering, laboratory, and scientific equipment manufacturers	65

As the collection period grows longer, more funds are tied up in receivables, thus restricting the funds available for other investment opportunities. Recall from Chapter 8, however, that cash inflows can be accelerated by the sale of receivables or by the process of assignment.

Inventory turnover

The **inventory turnover ratio** shows the number of times the funds invested in inventory are turned into sales, thereby providing some insight regarding the effectiveness of a firm's inventory policies. Normally, high turnovers are indicative of sound inventory management, at least in terms of generating cash. To explain, inventory turnover is calculated by dividing cost of goods sold by the average inventory. Average inventory, in turn, is computed by adding the beginning and ending inventories and dividing by 2. As the average inventory grows, turnover will decrease unless there is a corresponding increase in sales and the accompanying cost of goods sold. Thus a company that stocks a larger-than-normal inventory will have a lower turnover than another business that can generate the same sales with a lower inventory investment.

As a result, it appears that organizations should stock low inventories to achieve high turnovers. By doing so, firms minimize funds invested in excessive (and sometimes slow-moving) goods and reduce associated inventory carrying costs (e.g., storage, insurance, taxes, obsolescence, and deterioration). Frequently, to achieve reductions in these costs, businesses stock only certain sizes and certain lines of merchandise. This practice is especially true in clothing stores, which often cater to clientele of an "average" build and are very prone to rapid style changes.

Unfortunately, too much attention on minimal inventories and high turnovers can lead to stockouts, lost sales, and lost customers. Furthermore, quantity discounts and low freight rates may be unavailable because of insufficient purchasing activity. Inventory management is, indeed, a troublesome issue.

The 1984 inventory turnover ratio for Handy Corporation is calculated as follows:

$$\textit{inventory turnover ratio} = \frac{\text{cost of goods sold}}{\text{average inventory}}$$

$$= \frac{\$22{,}000{,}000}{\frac{\$4{,}000{,}000 + \$3{,}900{,}000}{2}}$$

$$= 5.57 \text{ times}$$

The ratio shows that the inventory turned 5.57 times, or approximately once every 66 days (365 days ÷ 5.57 times). To improve turnover, management could purchase more conservatively or stimulate sales from existing stock. Before a decision is reached, however, the appropriate industry average should be studied.

Profitability ratios

Ratios are also used to examine an organization's operating success (or lack of) during an accounting period. These measures, known as **profitability ratios,** are computed on the basis of sales or investment and are of special interest to management, stockholders, union officials and employees, and creditors.

Profit margin on sales

The ratio of net income to net sales (called the **profit margin on sales**) is a popular measure of profitability. Significant decreases in this ratio from year to year necessitate investigation; consistent deterioration may indicate a need for stringent cost control programs. As noted below, Handy's profit margin for 1984 showed a great improvement over 1983.

$$\textit{profit margin on sales} = \frac{\text{net income}}{\text{net sales}}$$

1984

$$\frac{\$4{,}800{,}000}{\$40{,}000{,}000} = 12.0\%$$

1983

$$\frac{\$1{,}440{,}000}{\$36{,}000{,}000} = 4.0\%$$

Profit margins can be computed separately, as shown, or be considered an outgrowth of vertical analysis (see Exhibit 19-2).

Rate of return on assets

The **rate of return on assets,** often termed *return on investment* or *ROI,* measures profitability from a given level of asset investment. This ratio focuses on operations, specifically, the effectiveness of resources used in generating profits. Return on investment is typically calculated by dividing net income plus interest expense by the average total assets employed in business activity. The addition of interest expense produces a figure that represents earnings prior to any financing costs. Such a procedure is necessary because of ROI's operating concentration. Stated differently, we wish to focus on how well the asset investment was used, not on the related methods and costs of financing. For Handy Corporation the 1984 return on assets is computed as follows:

$$\textit{rate of return on assets} = \frac{\textit{net income} + \textit{interest expense}}{\textit{average assets}}$$

$$= \frac{\$4,800,000 + \$650,000}{\frac{\$20,250,000 + \$21,610,000}{2}}$$

$$= \frac{\$5,450,000}{\$20,930,000}$$

$$= 26.0\%$$

Handy's rate of return is quite high. For every $1 of assets employed, the company has generated $0.26 in profit.

Numerous variations of this ratio are found in corporate annual reports and other published data. Philip Morris, Inc., for example, calculates return on investment by using a numerator of net income plus *net* interest expense. Interest is a deductible expense in computing taxable income and thus results in a tax savings. Consequently, a net interest cost can be employed, that is, interest expense less the related tax benefits. Variations are also encountered in the denominator. Some companies, like K mart, compute rate of return on beginning-of-year assets; other companies employ end-of-year assets. Users of financial information must understand the manner in which a company calculates return on investment, particularly if comparisons will be made with other businesses.

Return on common stockholders' equity

Many corporations are heavily financed from investments made by common stockholders. A popular ratio, called the **return on common stockholders' equity,** measures the profits generated on the funds provided by these investors. The ratio is often calculated by dividing net income, less preferred dividends, by the average common stockholders' equity. By subtracting preferred dividends we derive the income belonging to the common shareholders, the true residual owners of a corporation. Handy's 1984 ratio is computed as follows:

$$\textit{return on common stockholders' equity} = \frac{\textit{net income} - \textit{preferred dividends}}{\textit{average common stockholders' equity}}$$

$$= \frac{\$4,800,000 - \$40,000}{\frac{\$8,450,000 + \$11,210,000}{2}}$$

$$= \frac{\$4,760,000}{\$9,830,000}$$

$$= 48.4\%$$

The common stockholders' equity figures are obtained from Exhibit 19-1 by taking total stockholders' equity and subtracting the $400,000 of preferred stock outstanding.

Handy has earned over 48¢ for each dollar invested by common shareholders, which, like the return on assets discussed earlier, is quite impressive. Notice, however, that the return on common equity is much higher than the return on assets. The difference is caused by trading on the equity.

Trading on the equity

Trading on the equity, sometimes called *leverage*, describes the process of securing funds at fixed interest and preferred dividend rates, and investing the funds to earn a return greater than their cost. To explain, Handy Corporation has rates of return on common stockholders' equity and on assets of 48.4% and 26.0%, respectively. Refer to Exhibit 19-1 and study the 1984 data. Notice that Handy is paying 10% before taxes for funds obtained via long-term debt ($650,000 interest expense ÷ $6,500,000 of long-term liabilities).[2] When considering the 40% income tax rate, the aftertax cost of debt capital is reduced to 6% [10% − 0.4(10%)]. Furthermore, the company has a $400,000 preferred stock issue outstanding. For the funds invested by preferred stockholders, Handy is paying a 10% annual dividend ($40,000 ÷ $400,000). Remember that dividends are distributions of earnings and not expenses; consequently, there are no income tax implications for the corporation.

The net result? Handy is earning 26.0% on assets but is paying 10% or less for $6,900,000 ($6,500,000 + $400,000) of asset financing. The difference benefits the common stockholders and is reflected by the 48.4% return on their equity. The firm is said to be trading on the equity at a gain; that is, it has positive financial leverage. Naturally, the opposite case is possible. Should the return on assets fall below the cost of long-term debt and preferred stock, Handy would have negative leverage and would be trading on the equity at a loss. Because the cost of financing is greater than the asset earnings, net income suffers along with the return on common stockholders' equity.

Although most people do not like to be in debt, *some* debt (and preferred stock) on the balance sheet may prove beneficial. As you have seen, the common stockholder can prosper. Of course, there can always be too much of a good thing. Substantial amounts of debt will drastically increase a company's fixed obligations, frequently putting a strain on its cash position. Furthermore, lenders and preferred stockholders view this situation as one of increased risk and a greater likelihood that interest and dividend payments will not be met. Consequently, if additional funds are needed, the interest and dividend rates may rise.

---

[2] For purposes of simplicity we are assuming the interest pertains strictly to long-term obligations.

Other profitability ratios

Several other ratios directly and indirectly concerned with profitability were introduced earlier in the text. The calculation of **earnings per share** was discussed in Chapter 14 along with the **price-earnings ratio** (the current market price of a share of common stock divided by earnings per share).

To measure the percentage of earnings distributed to stockholders, investors frequently study the **dividend payout ratio** (the annual cash dividend per share divided by earnings per share). A related ratio, the **dividend yield,** is the annual cash dividend per share divided by the current market price of the stock. This ratio furnishes investors insight regarding the short-term rate of return (from dividends) on their invested funds. Many individuals buy stocks with high yields because the dividends received may be reinvested in other profitable opportunities. In contrast, some individuals prefer firms that pay few dividends but have high growth potential accompanied by rapidly rising stock prices. As we will show in Chapter 20, gains on certain stock sales produce favorable tax benefits for the investor.

Coverage ratios

Coverage ratios are computed to judge the solvency of an entity. These ratios are of primary importance to long-term creditors, who have an obvious concern regarding the receipt of interest and the repayment of amounts borrowed.

Debt to total assets

The **debt to total assets ratio** shows the percentage of total capital provided by the creditors of a business. Debt includes all obligations, both current and long-term. The debt to total assets ratios for Handy at the end of 1984 and 1983 follow.

$$\textbf{debt to total assets} = \frac{\textbf{total debt}}{\textbf{total assets}}$$

1984

$$\frac{\$10{,}000{,}000}{\$21{,}610{,}000} = 46.3\%$$

1983

$$\frac{\$11{,}400{,}000}{\$20{,}250{,}000} = 56.3\%$$

As you can see, total liabilities outstanding declined by $1,400,000 during 1984. Furthermore, observe that debt declined in percentage terms as a means of financing Handy's asset investment. Apparently, the creditors are playing a reduced role (when compared with the owners) in terms of providing investment funds. This fact becomes evident when focusing on a *ratio of total debt to total stockholders' equity.* For Handy the debt to equity ratio at the end of 1984 was 0.86 ($10,000,000 ÷ $11,610,000), down from 1.29 ($11,400,000 ÷ $8,850,000) upon conclusion of 1983. A debt to equity ratio of 1 signifies that the creditors and owners are furnishing equal amounts of funds for business activity.

The debt to total assets ratio is of interest to both creditors and stockholders. Creditors generally prefer a low ratio, indicating that a large percentage of asset financing is provided by the owners. Low debt means low monthly outlays for principal and interest and, thus, a reduced risk of nonpayment should sales and earnings fall.

Stockholders, on the other hand, often desire a high debt to total assets ratio. As shown earlier, the presence of debt in the capital structure can give rise to positive leverage and benefit the common stockholders. Increased debt generally increases leverage. However, too much debt may actually cause the reduction or elimination of common stock dividends in periods of slow business activity. Remember, interest payments must be met; in contrast, dividends to common stockholders are subject to the discretion of the board of directors. Further complicating the picture are priorities of asset claims should a business experience financial difficulty. Creditors have first claim against an organization's assets in the event of insolvency; owners have secondary claims. Thus the lower the debt to total assets ratio, the greater is the chance that owners will share in any remaining proceeds from asset liquidation. What we have here are conflicting views. Generally, debt is fine as long as it's present in moderation. Unfortunately, the "right" amount of debt varies among industries and is extremely difficult to determine.

Times interest earned

Although a company may be heavily financed by debt, it is possible that earnings are more than adequate to cover the required interest charges. If, however, interest coverage is marginal, the creditors' position may be threatened. Insight into the amount of protection that is afforded the long-term creditors is provided by a ratio called **times interest earned.**

The times interest earned ratio is computed by dividing net income before taxes and interest by the interest charges themselves. Observe that net income *before* taxes is used, because interest, in part, determines tax expense. For Handy the number of times interest was earned improved significantly from 1983 to 1984. As the following calculations show, the more than threefold increase was due to both lower interest charges and higher earnings.

$$\textit{times interest earned} = \frac{\textit{income before income taxes and interest}}{\textit{interest charges}}$$

1984

$$\frac{\$8{,}650{,}000}{\$650{,}000} = 13.3$$

1983

$$\frac{\$3{,}200{,}000}{\$800{,}000} = 4$$

Ratio analysis: A concluding comment

Ratio analysis is an extremely useful tool for assessing financial performance. Several studies have shown, for example, that specific ratio changes are often times a forerunner (and predictor) of bankruptcy. The ratios presented in these pages will, we hope, whet your appetite for a deeper probe of financial statements. When used in conjunction with industry norms and data of other companies, a very powerful tool is at your disposal. Keep in mind, however, that ratios are not ends in themselves and cannot tell the *complete* story behind financial success or failure. They are merely a starting point for further analysis and questioning.

The ratios presented in this chapter are summarized in Exhibit 19-3.

ACCOUNTING FOR INFLATION

Horizontal and vertical analysis and ratios are basic techniques for evaluating financial statements. While the techniques are sound, many members of the financial community question the numbers these methods of analysis employ. For example, suppose Fouts, Inc., reported 1983 sales of $15 million and 1984 sales of $16.5 million. A horizontal analysis would reveal a sales increase of $1.5 million, or 10%, and management might be very satisfied with the performance of the marketing department. Undoubtedly, however, the reaction would differ if the increase was due solely to a 10% hike in selling prices necessitated by increasing product costs. In essence, there was no real growth; inflation generated the additional "revenues." If Fouts's financial statements took inflation into account, a different picture of financial condition and profitability would surely result.

As you know, the United States has experienced considerable inflation in recent years, sometimes at double-digit rates. **Inflation** is a rise in the general price level that causes a decline in the purchasing power of the dollar. Simply stated, a dollar will not buy as much today as it did, say, ten years ago. Just as you are affected by inflation in steadily rising costs for tuition, books, food, clothing, and transportation, businesses, too, have similar problems. Many profitable companies are experiencing difficulty obtaining sufficient funds to replace their inventories and productive capacity.

As we stressed in Chapter 18, financial statements are an outgrowth of historical costs and the stable dollar assumption. Criticism of measuring business income and reporting assets on this basis has been especially severe in highly inflationary times. As a result, accountants are studying methods by which the effects of inflation can be presented in the financial statements. Two approaches have been proposed: constant dollar accounting and current value accounting.

Constant Dollar Accounting

Under **constant dollar accounting,** historical cost data are adjusted for changes in the value (purchasing power) of the dollar by using a general price level index. To explain, the federal government monitors price changes in our economy by sampling various goods and services. The goods and services (often called a *market basket*) are priced at different points in time to determine how much prices have risen or fallen. The outcome is a price index, one of the most popular being the consumer price index (CPI).

Exhibit 19-3

Ratio summary

Ratio	Method of Computation	Significance
(1) Liquidity ratios		
(a) Current ratio	$\frac{\text{Current assets}}{\text{Current liabilities}}$	Measures ability to meet short-term debts
(b) Quick ratio	$\frac{\text{Cash + short-term investments + accounts receivable}}{\text{Current liabilities}}$	Measures very short-term debt paying ability
(2) Activity ratios		
(a) Accounts receivable turnover	$\frac{\text{Net sales}}{\text{Average accounts receivable}}$	Provides insight into credit and collection policies
(b) Inventory turnover	$\frac{\text{Cost of goods sold}}{\text{Average inventory}}$	Provides insight into inventory management policies
(3) Profitability ratios		
(a) Profit margin on sales	$\frac{\text{Net income}}{\text{Net sales}}$	Shows the net income generated from each sales dollar
(b) Rate of return on assets	$\frac{\text{Net income + interest expense}}{\text{Average assets}}$	Indicates effectiveness of resources used in generating profit
(c) Return on common stockholders' equity	$\frac{\text{Net income − preferred dividends}}{\text{Average common stockholders' equity}}$	Reveals the earning rate of capital provided by common shareholders
(d) Earnings per share	See Chapter 14	Measures the earnings applicable to a share of common stock
(e) Price-earnings ratio	$\frac{\text{Market price per share}}{\text{Earnings per share}}$	Shows the amount investors are willing to pay for each dollar of corporate earnings
(f) Dividend payout ratio	$\frac{\text{Cash dividend per share}}{\text{Earnings per share}}$	Reveals corporate policy regarding retention or distribution of earnings
(g) Dividend yield	$\frac{\text{Cash dividend per share}}{\text{Market price per share}}$	Indicates the investor's short-term rate of return from dividends
(4) Coverage ratios		
(a) Debt to total assets	$\frac{\text{Total debt}}{\text{Total assets}}$	Shows the percentage of assets financed by long- and short-term borrowings
(b) Times interest earned	$\frac{\text{Income before income taxes and interest}}{\text{Interest charges}}$	Measures a firm's ability to cover and meet fixed interest charges

Specifically, the CPI measures the change in retail prices of about 400 goods and services in numerous cities throughout the country. For comparative purposes the 1967 prices of these items were arbitrarily assigned an index number of 100. In subsequent years the index number is changed to correspond with the percentage increase or decrease in the price of the market basket.[3] By May, 1981, for example, the index had risen to 269.0, which means it cost $269.00 in 1981 to purchase goods that sold for $100.00 in 1967. Movements in the CPI and the effects of inflation since 1960 are noted in Exhibit 19-4.

Exhibit 19-4

The effects of inflation, 1960–1981

Year	Consumer Price Index (1967 = 100)	Purchasing Power of Dollar (1967 = $1.00)	Rate of Inflation
1960	88.7	$1.13	1.6%
1965	94.5	1.06	1.7
1970	116.3	0.86	5.9
1971	121.3	0.82	4.3
1972	125.3	0.80	3.3
1973	133.1	0.75	6.2
1974	147.7	0.68	11.0
1975	161.2	0.62	9.1
1976	170.5	0.59	5.8
1977	181.5	0.55	6.5
1978	195.4	0.51	7.7
1979	217.4	0.46	11.3
1980	246.8	0.41	13.5
1981, May	269.0	0.37	9.8

SOURCE U.S. *Department of Commerce,* Statistical Abstract of the United States, 1981 *(Washington, D.C.: Government Printing Office, 1981), pp. 458–459, 467.*

With the constant dollar approach, a general price level index is applied to account balances to adjust for transactions occurring at different times and at different price levels. In this manner financial information becomes more meaningful, because it is presented in terms of dollars of identical purchasing power. Consider, for instance, a company that purchased equipment in 1960, 1970, and 1980. The addition of purchase prices generates total equipment cost; yet the true meaning of the total is questionable. Dollars spent in 1980 are not equivalent to dollars spent in 1970 or 1960 because of different purchasing powers. In effect, calculations such as the foregoing are dealing with apples and oranges, that is, dollars of a differing size. The result is a "mixed dollar" total, not a "constant dollar" total.

The constant dollar approach recognizes this problem and converts historical cost into constant dollars by means of the following conversion formula:

[3] Several changes in market basket composition have occurred over the years because of variations in consumer tastes and buying habits.

$$\text{historical cost} \times \frac{\text{index converting to}}{\text{index converting from}}$$

To illustrate, suppose Oliva Corporation acquired a machine on December 31, 19X2, for $50,000. Assume the following price indices (simplified for purposes of this example):

December 31, 19X2	100
December 31, 19X3	120
December 31, 19X4	130
19X4 average index	125

From 19X2 to 19X3 prices increased by 20% (120 − 100). The cost of Oliva's asset is therefore reported on the December 31, 19X3, constant dollar balance sheet as $60,000 ($50,000 × 120/100). Stated differently, Oliva would need 60,000 19X3 dollars to purchase the identical machine.

Notice that our illustration used an end-of-year price index. Frequently, a business will have many transactions that occur evenly throughout the year. Typical examples of such transactions include sales, merchandise purchases, and the incurrence of operating expenses. These items are more appropriately adjusted by using an average price index. For example, if Oliva's 19X4 sales totaled $200,000, the firm's constant dollar income statement for the year ended December 31, 19X4, would report sales of $208,000 ($200,000 × 130/125). Again the same technique of adjusting is employed: index converting to divided by index converting from.

Monetary and nonmonetary items

When constant dollar financial statements are prepared, it is necessary to distinguish between monetary and nonmonetary items. **Monetary items** are contractual claims to receive or pay a fixed amount of cash in the future. Monetary items include **monetary assets** (such as cash, accounts receivable, and notes receivable) and **monetary liabilities** (such as accounts payable, notes payable, salaries payable, and bonds payable). By their very nature, monetary assets and liabilities are (1) already stated in terms of current dollars and (2) fixed by contractual obligation. That is, regardless of price level changes, a business has the legal right to collect and disburse the recorded amounts for receivables and payables. Consequently, monetary items require no adjustment for presentation in constant dollar financial statements.

The remaining items on the balance sheet, including owners' equity, are **nonmonetary items.** The prices of nonmonetary items can change over time and are not "fixed." Thus adjustments similar to those in the Oliva example are required for conversion to a common dollar. Examples of nonmonetary items include land, equipment, inventory, and warranty obligations.

Purchasing power gains and losses

The distinction between monetary and nonmonetary items is important. The analysis of *monetary* items during an accounting period will indicate whether a company has experienced a **purchasing power gain or loss.**

SAVING, BORROWING, OR SPENDING—WHAT'S BEST?

For most of her 75 years, Hilda Cloud could—and did—count on a great and dependable tradition: money in a savings account would grow in value year by year. She retired several years ago expecting that her savings would substantially supplement her Social Security income. But startling price rises have upended the world of anyone who tries to save. In 1973 the rate of inflation swept up past the rate of savings account interest and has stayed there for many years. The result? The real value of savings, even after interest is added into passbooks, drops every year.

That's why the white-haired Mrs. Cloud recently sat before a congressional subcommittee, testifying as San Francisco president of an organization called the Gray Panthers. She attacked the federal government's limit on the interest that can be paid on savings, and wore a yellow button summing up the bitter lesson she had learned: "Savings may be hazardous to your wealth."

Saving is not the only tradition that inflation has changed. Borrowing and spending have both become smart, because tax laws as well as inflation favor the borrower. Consider a young couple who want to buy a \$300 stereo. If they save \$25 a month, they will have the \$300 at the end of a year. At a $5\frac{1}{4}$% passbook savings rate, compounded quarterly, they will have earned about \$8.50 in interest. If this working couple is in a 36% federal tax bracket, they will owe about \$3 in federal taxes—leaving \$5.50 net interest after the tax bill is subtracted. In the meantime the price of the stereo will have risen to \$327, assuming a 9% rate of inflation. So the couple will have lost \$21.50 by waiting to save for the stereo.

But what if the couple instead get a \$300 cash advance on a Visa card and buy a stereo right away? In many states they'll be paying 12% interest on the advance. Minimum monthly repayment will be about \$26.50, and total interest cost at year's end when the debt is paid off will be about \$18. Since interest payments can be deducted in determining taxable income, the real aftertax interest payments will be less than \$12—the \$18 reduced by their 36% tax saving. The couple will have avoided the \$27 price increase on the stereo by buying it now. So subtracting the \$12 aftertax real interest, they'll have saved \$15—and they can disco all year in front of those big speakers.*

The moral? In periods of rampant inflation, saving money can be a bummer; the more you save, the further behind you get. Having some debt merits congratulations. Remember, though, that monthly payments must be met. Like all businesses, you need an inflation strategy, one that will help you survive our sometimes topsy-turvy economy.

** The 12% rate was in effect at the time this article was written.*

SOURCE Adapted from "Smashing Old Ideas About Money" by Jerry Edgerton, from the June 1979 issue of Money magazine by special permission.

In periods of inflation the holders of monetary assets suffer a purchasing power loss. To illustrate, let's suppose that at the beginning of a period with an annual inflation rate of 15%, you put $100 in a cookie jar to save for emergencies. Because of rising prices, goods costing $100 when the funds were put aside will cost $115 at the end of the year. Thus a $15 purchasing power loss is incurred.

In contrast, the holders of monetary liabilities experience purchasing power gains during inflationary periods, because obligations are repaid with dollars of a lower value. For example, assume a friend borrowed $500 from you and paid it back one year later without interest. If the annual inflation rate was 10%, your friend has generated a purchasing power gain of $50. Specifically, he or she received $500 of purchasing power at the time of the loan. At the end of the year the number of dollars representing the same purchasing power had risen to $550 ($500 × 1.10); yet only $500 must be repaid. Your friend's purchasing power gain is your purchasing power loss.

Given this reality, businesses attempt to incur as much debt as prudent in times of inflation to maximize purchasing power gains. The gains result from having an excess of monetary liabilities over monetary assets during the year. Note that nonmonetary items do not create purchasing power gains or losses, because they are not claims to or against specific sums of money.

To review, when constant dollar statements are prepared, monetary items are already stated at their current amount and no adjustment is necessary. An analysis of these items will indicate whether a purchasing power gain or loss has occurred. Finally, nonmonetary items must be adjusted to make all amounts equivalent on a constant (i.e., common) dollar basis.

Illustration of the constant dollar approach

To illustrate the constant dollar approach, assume Lance, Inc., was organized on January 1, 19X4, when the general price level index was 100. Lance issued $100,000 of common stock and received $40,000 of land, $50,000 of inventory, and $10,000 of cash in return. The resulting balance sheet follows.

LANCE, INC.
Balance Sheet
January 1, 19X4

ASSETS	
Cash	$ 10,000
Inventory	50,000
Land	40,000
Total assets	$100,000
LIABILITIES & STOCKHOLDERS' EQUITY	
Common stock	$100,000
Total liabilities & stockholders' equity	$100,000

Assume that no other transactions occurred during the year. By the end of 19X4, the general price level index had risen to 120, indicating a 20% inflation rate. Lance's constant dollar balance sheet as of December 31, 19X4, appears in Exhibit 19-5. For illustrative purposes the necessary adjustments are shown in parentheses.

Exhibit 19-5

LANCE, INC.
Constant Dollar Balance Sheet
December 31, 19X4

ASSETS		
Cash	$ 10,000	(monetary asset, already stated in current dollars, no adjustment necessary)
Inventory	60,000	(nonmonetary asset, adjusted $50,000 × 120/100)
Land	48,000	(nonmonetary asset, adjusted $40,000 × 120/100)
Total assets	$118,000	
LIABILITIES & STOCKHOLDERS' EQUITY		
Common stock	$120,000	(nonmonetary item, adjusted $100,000 × 120/100)
Retained earnings	(2,000)	(purchasing power loss on net monetary items, $10,000 × 0.20)
Total liabilities & stockholders' equity	$118,000	

Notice that Lance had a $2,000 purchasing power loss. By holding $10,000 of monetary assets (cash) when the inflation rate was 20%, the company suffered a $2,000 ($10,000 × 0.20) decline in purchasing power. The loss is ultimately transferred to the Retained Earnings account, to be combined with profits and losses from operations.

Income statement

A constant dollar income statement is prepared in a similar fashion. To illustrate, assume the following information pertains to Witt Company.

WITT COMPANY
Income Statement
For the Year Ended December 31, 19X5

Sales		$150,000
Cost of goods sold		90,000
Gross profit		$ 60,000
Operating expenses		
Selling	$10,000	
Depreciation: building	28,000	
Administrative	8,000	46,000
Net income		$ 14,000

The building was purchased many years ago when the price index was 70. During 19X5 the average price index was 125; at the end of the year the index stood at 130. The constant dollar income statement for Witt Company for the year ended December 31, 19X5, appears in Exhibit 19-6.

Exhibit 19-6

WITT COMPANY
Constant Dollar Income Statement
For the Year Ended December 31, 19X5

Sales		$156,000	(sales made throughout the year, adjusted $150,000 × 130/125)
Cost of goods sold		93,600	(goods purchased throughout the year, adjusted $90,000 × 130/125)
Gross profit		$ 62,400	
Operating expenses			
Selling	$10,400		(incurred evenly throughout the year, adjusted $10,000 × 130/125)
Depreciation: building	52,000		(building purchased when index was 70, adjusted $28,000 × 130/70)
Administrative	8,320		(incurred evenly throughout the year, adjusted $8,000 × 130/125)
Total expenses		70,720	
Constant dollar net income (loss)		$ (8,320)	

As you can see, inflation can hide what some consider to be the "true" results of operations. In this case a $14,000 net income was transformed into a loss of $8,320. Although there were several contributing factors, the major culprit is depreciation expense. The building was acquired when the price level index stood at 70. Now with prices nearly doubling, many accountants would argue that depreciation on a conventional (historical-cost) income statement is significantly understated. Keep in mind that if Witt had experienced a purchasing power gain or loss during the year, this amount would also be reported on the constant dollar income statement.

Current Value Accounting

The general price level index used in the constant dollar approach is, as its name implies, general. That is, a variety of goods and services are considered in the index's computation. If the prices of all nonmonetary items behaved in the same manner as the index, there would be few problems. Unfortunately, there is considerable variation. In a given year the prices of certain items may soar while others either remain the same or decline. In recent periods, for example, the costs of housing and energy have increased considerably. During the same years the costs of many electronic products (e.g., small computers, calculators, and home appliances) have decreased because of technological advances.

An alternative approach to account for the effects of inflation is termed **current value accounting.** This method recognizes price changes in the individual assets owned by an enterprise and restates the assets in terms of their current value. Although current value may be determined in various ways, the most popular method uses **replacement cost,** that is, the current cost of replacing an asset with a similar asset in similar condition. For example, the replacement cost of a company's 1979 delivery truck would be computed as the current retail selling price for a similar truck with approximately the same mileage.

Unfortunately, the computation of replacement cost is not always straightforward. While manufacturers' price lists and appraisal values (in the case of real estate) are helpful, complications are frequently encountered. Sometimes, used asset markets do not exist. Furthermore, present assets are often replaced by assets having an advanced design, improved efficiency, or larger capacity. Factors such as these must be addressed when applying the current value approach; yet the related problems are not easily overcome.

Holding gains and losses

When current value is used for asset valuation, a company will normally experience a **holding gain** or a **holding loss.** To illustrate, assume Loftus Corporation purchased 5,000 units of inventory on November 15 at $2 per unit. By December 31, the end of Loftus's accounting period, the replacement cost of the goods had increased to $2.50, for a total of $12,500 (5,000 units × $2.50). Current value financial statements would disclose the inventory at $12,500 along with a $2,500 gain [5,000 units × ($2.50 − $2.00)]. This gain is termed a *holding gain* because it relates to an increase in asset value during the period the inventory was held by the firm. If the goods had declined in value, a *holding loss* would have occurred.

There are two types of holding gains and losses: unrealized and realized. **Unrealized gains and losses** relate to assets that are still owned at the end of the accounting period. The $2,500 gain in the Loftus illustration is an example of an unrealized holding gain. If Loftus had sold some of the inventory, the computation would have been slightly different.

For instance, assume replacement cost peaked at $2.50 immediately after the purchase of 5,000 units on November 15. If the firm then sold 2,000 of the units at $8 each, Loftus would *realize* a $1,000 holding gain. To explain, **realized holding gains and losses** are calculated on the basis of assets sold or consumed. As before, Loftus must compute the difference between acquisition cost ($2.00) and replacement cost ($2.50). The firm will therefore report a $1,000 gain (2,000 units × $0.50) on the income statement. Loftus will also report a $1,500 unrealized gain relating to the 3,000 units that remain in ending inventory (3,000 units × $0.50 = $1,500).

Better disclosure

The current value method and the income statement's disclosure of holding gains and losses may provide better information to financial statement users than the traditional, historical-cost approach. To illustrate, Loftus Corporation would report profit of $12,000 by employing conventional accounting practices.

Sales: 2,000 units @ $8	*$16,000*
Cost of goods sold: 2,000 units @ $2	*4,000*
Gross profit	*$12,000*

With the current value approach, business income totals $13,500 and is subdivided into three key elements, as follows:

Sales: 2,000 units @ $8	*$16,000*
Cost of goods sold at replacement cost: 2,000 units @ $2.50	*5,000*
Gross profit	*$11,000*
Realized holding gain on units sold	*1,000*
Unrealized holding gain on units in inventory	*1,500*
Current value business income	*$13,500*

The first element is gross profit of $11,000, the difference between sales and the current replacement cost of goods sold. The second and third elements are the holding gains just discussed.

Observe that the difference between conventional and current value income is the $1,500 unrealized gain ($13,500 – $12,000 = $1,500). Disregarding this figure, the two approaches yield the same bottom line. The current value method, however, provides the advantage of additional disclosure. Income is divided into that generated from operations and that arising from price changes. The latter information is useful in appraising the effectiveness of management's business decisions.

Loftus's conventional and current value balance sheets will report an ending inventory as follows:

	Historical Cost	*Current Value*
Ending inventory		
3,000 units × $2.00	$6,000	
3,000 units × $2.50		$7,500

The $1,500 difference is balanced by an increased stockholders' equity, as shown below.

	Stockholders' Equity	
	Historical Cost	*Current Value*
Conventional income	+$12,000	
Current value income		+$13,500

Although our example dealt strictly with inventory, unrealized gains and losses relating to other assets would be treated in a similar fashion. For example, assume Loftus had previously purchased land for $100,000 which has a current value of $135,000. A current value balance sheet would report the land at $135,000; the $35,000 unrealized gain would be combined with other holding gains and losses on the current value income statement.

The FASB and Inflation

As we noted earlier in the text, both the Securities and Exchange Commission and the Financial Accounting Standards Board have issued authoritative pronouncements on accounting for inflation. Because the SEC withdrew its requirements upon issuance of the FASB statement, we will only discuss the latter's position.

The FASB noted that major changes should *not* be made in the financial statements to account for inflation. In other words, the historical-cost approach, as opposed to constant dollar or current value, must still be used in maintaining accounting records and reporting financial condition and profitability. However, approximately 1,500 of the largest publicly held companies in the United States are now required to provide selected *supplementary information* in their annual reports, allowing financial statement users to assess the impact of inflation on operations. This supplementary information includes both constant dollar and current value data. Large corporations are required to report the following for the latest year.

1 Constant dollar basis:
   a Income from continuing operations.
   b The purchasing power gain or loss on net monetary items.
2 Current value basis:
   a Income from continuing operations.

b Holding gains from inventory and property, plant, and equipment (net of inflation).

c Current values of inventory and property, plant, and equipment at the end of the reporting period.[4]

Importantly, neither the constant dollar method nor the current value method is required to be comprehensively applied in determining income from continuing operations. Restatements are necessary only for inventories; cost of goods sold; property, plant, and equipment; and depreciation, depletion, and amortization.

Investors are often shocked after reading the supplementary information required by the FASB. Consider the income data appearing in Exhibit 19-7 as an example. When historical-cost figures are adjusted for the effects of inflation, the result is normally a reduced earnings level because of increased charges for depreciation, amortization, and cost of goods sold. To the extent that financial statement users learn more about the impact of inflation through the FASB's disclosure requirements, statement analysis will become more sophisticated. Ratio analysis and other techniques illustrated in the first part of this chapter can integrate inflation data and thus make the evaluation process more meaningful.

Exhibit 19-7

Income from continuing operations (000 omitted)

	Income from Continuing Operations		
Corporation	**As Reported in the Financial Statements (Historical Cost)**	**Constant Dollar**	**Current Value**
Allied Stores Corporation	$ 88,332	$27,376	$ 65,208
American Greetings Corporation	33,843	19,656	18,049
Campbell Soup Company	129,717	73,069	80,635
Levitz Furniture Corporation	8,873	2,214	2,711
Ramada Inns, Inc.	(22,814)	(36,586)	(36,750)

KEY TERMS AND CONCEPTS

FINANCIAL STATEMENT ANALYSIS

accounts receivable turnover 743
activity ratios 743
common-size financial statements 739
coverage ratios 748
current ratio 740
debt to total assets ratio 748
dividend payout ratio 748
dividend yield 748
earnings per share 748
horizontal analysis 736
inventory turnover 744
liquidity ratios 740
price-earnings ratio 748

[4] "Financial Reporting and Changing Prices," *Statement of Financial Accounting Standards No. 33* (Stamford, Conn.: Financial Accounting Standards Board, 1979).

profit margin on sales 745
profitability ratios 745
quick ratio 742
rate of return on assets 745
ratio analysis 740
return on common stockholders' equity 746
times interest earned 749
trading on the equity 747
vertical analysis 738

ACCOUNTING FOR INFLATION

constant dollar accounting 750
current value accounting 758
holding gains and losses 758
inflation 750
monetary assets 753
monetary liabilities 753
nonmonetary items 753
purchasing power gains and losses 753
realized holding gains and losses 759
replacement cost 758
unrealized holding gains and losses 759

QUESTIONS

Q19-1 Why is financial information of a business often compared with the past performance of the same company and the performance of other companies? What difficulties exist in comparisons with other firms?

Q19-2 Distinguish between horizontal analysis and vertical analysis. Which type of analysis results in common-size financial statements?

Q19-3 A student once noted: "This ratio stuff is great. It's unbelievable how ratios can tell the complete story behind the problems of a business." Comment on the student's observation.

Q19-4 Briefly describe the following types of ratios and the users most interested in each type.

a Liquidity ratios
b Activity ratios
c Profitability ratios
d Coverage ratios

Q19-5 What is the current ratio? Present a short critique of this widely used financial measure.

Q19-6 Why do many analysts prefer the quick ratio over the current ratio for judging debt-paying ability?

Q19-7 What insight can be provided by the accounts receivable turnover ratio? The inventory turnover ratio?

Q19-8 Discuss the differences between the rate of return on assets and the return on common stockholders' equity.

Q19-9 What does it mean to "trade on the equity?" How can such trading be successful? Unsuccessful?

Q19-10 Briefly distinguish between constant dollar accounting and current value accounting.

Q19-11 Lionel Johnson, staff accountant for Martin Machinery, is attempting to compute the company's purchasing power gain or loss. Discuss the meaning of a purchasing power gain or loss, and determine whether Johnson would be more interested in monetary or nonmonetary items in completing his assignment. Explain your answer.

Q19-12 From a purchasing power viewpoint, is it better to hold monetary assets or monetary liabilities during a period of inflation? Why?

Q19-13 Discuss the meaning of unrealized and realized holding gains. Where do holding gains appear on a current value income statement?

Q19-14 Hull, Inc., desires to report the effect of inflation on corporate profits. The company's controller has suggested the use of a general price index when constructing the financial statements. Should the company prepare one set of statements using historical-cost accounting and another based on constant dollars? Explain.

EXERCISES

E19-1 The Bidwell Corporation has been operating for several years. Selected data from the 1983 and 1984 financial statements are presented below.

	1984	1983
Current assets	$ 76,000	$ 80,000
Property, plant, & equipment (net)	99,000	90,000
Intangibles	20,000	40,000
Current liabilities	40,800	48,000
Long-term liabilities	138,000	150,000
Stockholders' equity	16,200	12,000
Net sales	550,000	550,000
Cost of goods sold	440,000	450,000
Operating expenses	57,200	52,000

Prepare a horizontal analysis for 1983 and 1984. Briefly comment on the results of your work.

E19-2 Study the data appearing in Exercise 19-1 pertaining to Bidwell Corporation. Prepare a vertical analysis for 1983 and 1984, and briefly evaluate the results of your work.

E19-3 The Rio Grande Company has the following balance sheets as shown on page 764.

RIO GRANDE COMPANY
Comparative Balance Sheets
December 31, 1984 and 1983

	1984	1983
Cash	$ 21,847	$ 28,518
Accounts receivable	53,155	51,343
Inventories (costed on LIFO)	94,836	83,617
Prepaid expenses	5,527	4,695
Land & buildings (net)	34,763	34,613
Machinery (net)	69,922	71,061
Long-term receivables	2,679	1,443
	$282,729	$275,290
Accounts payable	$ 22,748	$ 17,220
Notes payable due in one year	29,000	15,000
Accrued payables	13,264	11,721
Income taxes payable	2,690	3,910
Current portion of long-term debt	8,506	5,883
Long-term debt	36,460	44,948
Stockholders' equity	170,061	176,608
	$282,729	$275,290

Compute both the current and quick ratios for 1983 and 1984. (Round calculations to two decimal places.) Comment on the trend of these liquidity ratios.

E19-4 Case, Mercer, and Franklin have the following financial information at the close of business on October 15:

	Case	Mercer	Franklin
Cash	$ 1,000	$ 2,000	$ 4,000
Short-term investments	2,000	2,000	3,000
Accounts receivable	3,000	3,000	2,000
Inventory	4,000	3,000	1,000
Prepaid expenses	100	100	100
Accounts payable	1,000	1,000	1,000
Notes payable: short-term	4,000	4,000	4,000
Accrued payables	50	50	50
Long-term liabilities	10,000	10,000	10,000

a Compute the current and quick ratios for each of the three companies. (Round calculations to two decimal places.) Which firm is the most liquid? Why?

b Suppose Case is using FIFO for inventory valuation and Franklin is using LIFO. Comment on the comparability of information between these two companies.

c If all the notes are due on October 16 at 8 A.M., comment on each company's ability to settle its obligation in a timely manner.

E19-5 The president of Vonnie Summer, Inc., has furnished you with the following selected information.

	1984	1983
Net sales	$48,008,000	$54,863,000
Cost of goods sold	35,489,000	35,243,000
Gross profit	$12,519,000	$19,620,000
Expenses	12,867,000	13,658,000
Income before taxes	$ (348,000)	$ 5,962,000
Current assets		
Cash	$ 782,000	$ 1,286,000
Short-term investments	100,000	5,716,000
Accounts receivable (net)	9,390,000	11,727,000
Inventories	14,000,000	10,642,000
Prepaid expenses	486,000	373,000

The company is planning to borrow several million dollars for the purchase of inventory by securing a 180-day bank loan.

a Compute the accounts receivable and inventory turnover ratios for 1984. Assume all sales are on account, and round calculations to two decimal places.

b Comment on the ability of the company to repay a bank loan in 180 days.

E19-6 The Athens Company has the following financial statements.

ATHENS COMPANY
Income Statement
For the Year Ended December 31, 1984

Sales		$2,000,000
Cost of goods sold		1,200,000
Gross profit		$ 800,000
Operating expenses		
Salaries	$300,000	
Rent	50,000	
Depreciation	50,000	400,000
Income before interest and taxes		$ 400,000
Bond interest expense		10,000
Income before taxes		$ 390,000
Income tax expense		160,000
Net income		$ 230,000

ATHENS COMPANY
Statement of Retained Earnings
For the Year Ended December 31, 1984

Beginning balance		$400,000
Net income		230,000
		$630,000
Less dividends		
Common	$50,000	
Preferred	20,000	70,000
Ending balance		$560,000

ATHENS COMPANY
Comparative Balance Sheets
December 31, 1984 and 1983

	1984	1983
Current assets	$1,400,000	$1,300,000
Property, plant, & equipment (net)	200,000	210,000
Other assets	246,000	306,000
	$1,846,000	$1,816,000
Current liabilities	$ 870,000	$1,000,000
Bonds payable	100,000	100,000
Preferred stock	200,000	200,000
Common stock	100,000	100,000
Paid-in capital in excess of par: common	16,000	16,000
Retained earnings	560,000	400,000
	$1,846,000	$1,816,000

a Compute the 1984 profit margin on sales and the rates of return on assets and common stockholders' equity by using the approach illustrated in the text. Round calculations to two decimal places.

b Evaluate Athens's performance given the following industry norms:

Profit margin on sales	5%
Rate of return on assets	10%
Rate of return on common stockholders' equity	25%

E19-7 Erol Company has provided you with the following data.

Operating income	$ 90,000
Bond interest expense	10,000
	$ 80,000
Income taxes	28,000
Net income	$ 52,000

Bonds payable	$100,000
Average common stock	100,000
Average paid-in capital in excess of par: common	75,000
Average retained earnings	150,000
Average total assets	500,000

Is Erol trading on the equity successfully? Explain your answer.

E19-8 Eric, Inc., has the following financial information.

	1984	1983
Current liabilities	$ 400,000	$ 500,000
Long-term liabilities	1,000,000	900,000
Common stock	500,000	500,000
Retained earnings	2,100,000	1,600,000
Total liabilities & stockholders' equity	$4,000,000	$3,500,000

During 1984 Eric incurred interest expense and income taxes of $100,000 and $250,000, respectively. No dividends were paid during the year.

Compute the following ratios for 1984, rounding calculations to two decimal places.

a Debt to total assets
b Debt to total ending stockholders' equity
c Times interest earned

E19-9 Sass, Inc., has the following accounts, among others, in its general ledger: Cash, Notes Receivable, Inventory, Accounts Payable, Common Stock, and Rent Expense.

a Which of the accounts would be needed in computing the net purchasing power gain or loss?
b Which of the accounts would probably be restated on a balance sheet prepared by using the constant dollar basis of accounting?

E19-10 The following balances were extracted from the ledger of McGregor, Inc.

Inventory	$ 150,000	(acquired evenly throughout 19X3)
Patent	120,000	(acquired on December 31, 19X0)
Equipment	240,000	(acquired on December 31, 19X0)
Building	1,040,000	(acquired on December 31, 19X1)
Notes payable	390,000	(signed on December 31, 19X1)

The general price level has steadily increased, as shown by the following index numbers.

19X0	240 (Ending)
19X1	260 (Ending)
19X2	280 (Ending)
19X3	300 (Average)
	320 (Ending)

How would the above accounts appear on McGregor's December 31, 19X3, constant dollar balance sheet? Assume the patent, equipment, and building each have a life of ten years.

E19-11 On February 3 Jeelani, Inc., purchased 6,000 electronic components at $3.50 per unit. Shortly thereafter, due to technological advances, the same component could be purchased for $3.10. On December 31, the end of Jeelani's accounting period, 1,500 components remained in inventory. The controller is now exploring the use of current value accounting.

a Compute Jeelani's realized holding loss.
b Compute Jeelani's unrealized holding loss.
c Compute Jeelani's cost of goods sold, using current value accounting.
d Compute Jeelani's cost of goods sold, using conventional accounting.
e Comment on the difference in business income when using conventional accounting and current value accounting.

PROBLEMS

P19-1 ***Horizontal and vertical analysis***
The following financial statements pertain to Rainbow Corporation.

RAINBOW CORPORATION
Comparative Income Statements
For the Years Ended December 31, 1984 and 1983

	1984	1983
Net sales	$8,000,000	$4,000,000
Cost of goods sold	4,500,000	2,500,000
Gross profit	$3,500,000	$1,500,000
Operating expenses	2,500,000	750,000
Net income before interest & taxes	$1,000,000	$ 750,000
Interest expense	40,000	40,000
Income before taxes	$ 960,000	$ 710,000
Income taxes	384,000	284,000
Net income	$ 576,000	$ 426,000

RAINBOW CORPORATION
Comparative Balance Sheets
December 31, 1984 and 1983

	1984	1983
ASSETS		
Current assets		
Cash	$ 5,000	$ 20,000
Short-term investments	—	35,000
Accounts receivable (net)	250,000	50,000
Inventories	370,000	115,000
Prepaid expenses	15,000	10,000
Total current assets	$ 640,000	$ 230,000
Property, plant, & equipment		
Land	$ 45,000	$ 15,000
Buildings (net)	440,000	450,000
Equipment (net)	250,000	200,000
Vehicles (net)	121,000	100,000
Total property, plant, & equipment	$ 856,000	$ 765,000
Trademark (net)	$ 4,000	$ 5,000
Total assets	$1,500,000	$1,000,000
LIABILITIES & STOCKHOLDERS' EQUITY		
Current liabilities		
Accounts payable	$ 300,000	$ 140,000
Notes payable	10,000	10,000
Federal taxes payable	190,000	150,000
Total current liabilities	$ 500,000	$ 300,000
Long-term debt	$ 400,000	$ 400,000
Total liabilities	$ 900,000	$ 700,000
Stockholders' equity		
Common stock, $10 par	$ 200,000	$ 50,000
Retained earnings	400,000	250,000
Total stockholders' equity	$ 600,000	$ 300,000
Total liabilities & stockholders' equity	$1,500,000	$1,000,000

INSTRUCTIONS

a Prepare a horizontal analysis of the balance sheet and income statement showing dollar and percentage changes. Round all calculations in instructions (a) and (b) to two decimal places.

b Prepare a vertical analysis of the balance sheet and income statement. On the balance sheet relate each asset to total assets and each liability and stockholders' equity account to the total of liabilities plus stockholders' equity. On the income statement relate each item to net sales.

c Briefly comment on the results of your analysis.

P19-2 ***Ratio computation***

The financial statements for Johanson Company follow.

JOHANSON COMPANY
Comparative Balance Sheets
December 31, 1984 and 1983
($000 Omitted)

	1984	1983
ASSETS		
Current assets		
Cash & short-term investments	$ 400	$ 380
Accounts receivable (net)	1,700	1,500
Inventories	2,200	2,120
Total current assets	$4,300	$4,000
Long-term assets		
Land	$ 500	$ 500
Building & equipment (net)	4,700	4,000
Total long-term assets	$5,200	$4,500
Total assets	$9,500	$8,500
LIABILITIES & EQUITIES		
Current liabilities		
Accounts payable	$1,400	$ 700
Current portion of long-term debt	1,000	500
Total current liabilities	$2,400	$1,200
Long-term debt	3,000	4,000
Total liabilities	$5,400	$5,200
Stockholders' equity		
Common stock	$3,000	$3,000
Retained earnings	1,100	300
Total stockholders' equity	$4,100	$3,300
Total liabilities & equities	$9,500	$8,500

JOHANSON COMPANY
Statement of Income and Retained Earnings
For the Year Ended December 31, 1984
($000 Omitted)

Net sales		$28,800
Less: Cost of goods sold	$15,120	
Selling expenses	7,180	
Administrative expenses	4,100	
Interest	400	
Income taxes	800	27,600
Net income		$ 1,200
Retained earnings, Jan. 1		300
		$ 1,500
Cash dividends declared and paid		400
Retained earnings, Dec. 31		$ 1,100

INSTRUCTIONS
Compute the following items for the Johanson Company for 1984, rounding all calculations to two decimal places.

a Quick ratio
b Average collection period of accounts receivable
c Number of times interest is earned
d Inventory turnover
e Dividend payout percentage
f Profit margin on sales
g Total debt to total assets
h Current ratio
i Return on common stockholders' equity

(CMA modified.)

P19-3 ***Ratio computation and interpretation***
Refer to the financial statements of Rainbow Corporation in Problem 19-1. Assume that various persons have approached you to prepare ratios to study the firm's financial condition and profitability.

INSTRUCTIONS

a For a banker, calculate the current and quick ratios at the end of each year. Prepare an analysis of your findings. *Note:* In this and subsequent parts of the problem, round all computations to two decimal places.
b For a long-term creditor, calculate the total debt to total assets ratio (use end-of-year assets) and the number of times interest was earned for both 1983 and 1984. Prepare an analysis of your findings.
c For a stockholder, calculate net income to total revenues, the rate of return on assets (use end-of-year assets), and the return on common stockholders' equity (use end-of-year equity) for both 1983 and 1984. Prepare an analysis of your findings.

d For the company treasurer, calculate accounts receivable turnover and inventory turnover for 1984. Prepare an analysis of your findings.

P19-4 ***Effect of transactions and events on ratios***

Bullet, Inc., had the following ratios based on its 1983 financial statements.

1 Current ratio: 1.5.
2 Quick ratio: 1.
3 Accounts receivable turnover: 10.3 times.
4 Inventory turnover: 12.5 times.
5 Total debt to total assets: 60%.
6 Times interest earned: 6.
7 Net income to sales: 5%.
8 Rate of return on assets: 10%.
9 Return on common stockholders' equity: 28.2%.

During 1984 the following selected transactions and events took place.

a Declared a cash dividend on common stock.
b Paid the above dividend.
c Purchased treasury stock (common) for cash.
d Sold common stock to the public for cash.
e Purchased merchandise inventory on account.
f Collected an account receivable.
g Recorded depreciation for the year.

INSTRUCTIONS

Consider items (a)–(g) individually. List the ratios affected by each transaction and event.

P19-5 ***Use and interpretation of financial ratios***

Thorpe Company is a wholesale distributor of professional equipment and supplies. The company's sales have averaged about $900,000 annually for the three-year period 1982–1984. The firm's total assets at the end of 1984 amounted to $850,000.

The president of Thorpe has asked the controller to prepare a report that summarizes the financial aspects of the company's operations for the past three years. This report will be presented to the board of directors at their next meeting.

In addition to comparative financial statements, the controller has decided to present a number of relevant financial ratios that can assist in the identification and interpretation of trends. At the request of the controller, the accounting staff has calculated the following ratios for the three-year period 1982–1984.

	1982	*1983*	*1984*
Current ratio	2.00	2.13	2.18
Quick ratio	1.20	1.10	0.97
Accounts receivable turnover	9.72	8.57	7.13
Inventory turnover	5.25	4.80	3.80
Percent of total debt to total assets	44	41	38
Percent of long-term debt to total assets	25	22	19
Sales as a percent of 1982 sales	1.00	1.03	1.06
Gross profit percentage	40.0	38.6	38.5
Net income to sales	7.8%	7.8%	8.0%
Return on total assets	8.5%	8.5%	8.7%
Return on common stockholders' equity	15.1%	14.6%	14.1%

In the preparation of his report, the controller has decided first to examine the financial ratios independently of any other data to determine if the ratios themselves reveal any significant trends over the three-year period.

INSTRUCTIONS

Answer the following questions. Indicate in each case which ratio(s) you used in arriving at your conclusion.

a The current ratio is increasing while the quick ratio is decreasing. Using the ratios provided, identify and explain the contributing factor(s) for this apparently divergent trend.

b In terms of the ratios provided, what conclusion(s) can be drawn regarding the company's use of financial leverage (trading on the equity) during the 1982–1984 period?

(CMA adapted.)

P19-6 ***Constant dollar income statement***

The Phelps Corporation reported the following income statement for 1984.

Sales		$390,000
Cost of goods sold		260,000
Gross profit		$130,000
Operating expenses		
Cash expenses	$65,000	
Depreciation (straight-line)	35,000	100,000
Net income		$ 30,000

The general price index at the beginning of the year was 120. During the year the index averaged 130 and stood at 140 by year-end. All sales and cash expenses occurred evenly throughout the year. Depreciation relates to the following equipment:

Equipment	Cost	Life (Years)	Index at Acquisition
Store	$200,000	10	80
Delivery	90,000	6	100

Assume there was no purchasing power gain or loss on net monetary items.

INSTRUCTIONS

a Prepare an income statement for the year ended December 31, 1984, using the constant dollar approach. Disregard earnings per share.

b Determine the impact of adjusting for inflation on the company's profit margin on sales ratio. Evaluate your findings.

P19-7 ***Current value financial statements***

Frontier, Inc., began operations on January 1 of the current year by acquiring the following assets in exchange for $180,000 of common stock.

Cash	$ 30,000
Inventory (15,000 units @ $6 per unit)	90,000
Land	60,000
	$180,000

During the year Frontier sold 11,000 units of inventory at $13 per unit. Additionally, the company incurred cash operating expenses of $23,000. By checking manufacturers' catalogs and recent real estate appraisals, Frontier determined the following current values for the inventory and land.

Inventory	$7.50 per unit
Land	$75,000

Assume outstanding accounts receivable total $22,000.

INSTRUCTIONS

a Prepare the firm's income statement for the current year ended December 31 by using the historical-cost basis of accounting. Disregard earnings-per-share calculations.

b Prepare the December 31 balance sheet by using the historical-cost basis of accounting.

c Determine Frontier's realized holding gain on the units sold and unrealized gain on the units remaining in inventory.

d Prepare the firm's income statement by using the current value approach. Disregard earnings-per-share calculations.

e Prepare the December 31 balance sheet by using the current value approach.

f Can Frontier issue current value statements in place of historical-cost statements? Explain your answer.

P19-8 ***Evaluation of inflation-adjusted statements***

Your friend is examining a recent annual report of the Turoff Corporation. In a section entitled "Inflation Accounting," she observed the following:

a The president has commented: "A penny saved is no longer a penny earned."

b Net income computed by using the constant dollar approach was significantly lower than historical-cost net income. The primary cause appears to have been depreciation expense.

c The company had substantial increases in cash and accounts receivable balances and, at the same time, apparently suffered a loss in purchasing power. This result seems contradictory, because more funds are or will be available to purchase needed inventory.

d On constant dollar statements land was disclosed at $135,000. In contrast, current value statements listed land at $160,000. While both approaches supposedly adjust for inflation, how can the same asset have two different values? This result seems confusing.

e The president commented: "Although the constant dollar and current value income statements disclosed substantially lower profits than the historical-cost statement, these alternative figures should be disregarded. The accounting profession has yet to perfect a suitable substitute for conventional financial statements; that's why inflation information is supplemental. In addition, the IRS taxes us on our traditionally determined net income."

INSTRUCTIONS

Discuss items (a)–(e) in depth.

P19-9 ***Horizontal and vertical analysis (alternate to P19-1)***

The following financial statements pertain to Lewisville Corporation.

LEWISVILLE CORPORATION
Comparative Balance Sheets
December 31, 1984 and 1983

	1984	1983
ASSETS		
Current assets		
Cash	$ 45,000	$ 50,000
Short-term investments	10,000	20,000
Accounts receivable (net)	64,000	80,000
Inventories	154,000	140,000
Prepaid expenses	15,000	15,000
Total current assets	$ 288,000	$ 305,000
Property, plant, & equipment		
Land	$ 50,000	$ 25,000
Buildings (net)	361,000	380,000
Equipment (net)	114,000	120,000
Vehicles (net)	128,000	160,000
Total property, plant, & equipment	$ 653,000	$ 685,000
Trademarks (net)	$ 59,000	$ 10,000
Total assets	$1,000,000	$1,000,000
LIABILITIES & STOCKHOLDERS' EQUITY		
Current liabilities		
Accounts payable	$ 196,000	$ 280,000
Notes payable	54,000	160,000
Federal taxes payable	10,000	100,000
Total current liabilities	$ 260,000	$ 540,000
Long-term debt	$ 200,000	$ 100,000
Total liabilities	$ 460,000	$ 640,000
Stockholders' equity		
Common stock, $10 par	$ 100,000	$ 100,000
Retained earnings	440,000	260,000
Total stockholders' equity	$ 540,000	$ 360,000
Total liabilities & stockholders' equity	$1,000,000	$1,000,000

LEWISVILLE CORPORATION
Comparative Income Statements
For the Years Ended December 31, 1984 and 1983

	1984	1983
Net sales	$2,200,000	$2,000,000
Cost of goods sold	1,320,000	1,000,000
Gross profit	$ 880,000	$1,000,000
Operating expenses	530,000	400,000
Net income before interest & taxes	$ 350,000	$ 600,000
Interest expense	50,000	12,000
Income before taxes	$ 300,000	$ 588,000
Income taxes	120,000	235,200
Net income	$ 180,000	$ 352,800

INSTRUCTIONS

a Prepare a horizontal analysis of the balance sheet and income statement showing dollar and percentage changes. Round all calculations in instructions (a) and (b) to two decimal places.

b Prepare a vertical analysis of the balance sheet and income statement. On the balance sheet relate each asset to total assets and each liability and stockholders' equity account to the total of liabilities plus stockholders' equity. On the income statement relate each item to net sales.

c Briefly comment on the results of your analysis.

P19-10 ***Ratio computation and interpretation (alternate to P19-3)***
Refer to the financial statements of Lewisville Corporation in Problem 19-9. Assume that various persons have approached you to prepare ratios to study the firm's financial condition and profitability.

INSTRUCTIONS

a For a banker, calculate the current and quick ratios at the end of each year. Prepare an analysis of your findings. *Note:* In this and subsequent parts of the problem, round all computations to two decimal places.

b For a long-term creditor, calculate the total debt to total assets ratio (use end-of-year assets) and the number of times interest was earned for both 1983 and 1984. Prepare an analysis of your findings.

c For a stockholder, calculate net income to total revenues, the rate of return on assets (use end-of-year assets), and the return on common stockholders' equity (use end-of-year equity) for both 1983 and 1984. Prepare an analysis of your findings.

d For the company treasurer, calculate accounts receivable turnover and inventory turnover for 1984. Prepare an analysis of your findings.

P19-11 ***Effect of transactions and events on ratios (alternate to P19-4)***
Puget, Inc., had the following ratios based on its 1983 financial statements.

1 Current ratio: 3.0.
2 Quick ratio: 1.0.
3 Accounts receivable turnover: 15.0 times.
4 Inventory turnover: 10.0 times.
5 Total debt to total assets: 80%.
6 Times interest earned: 10.
7 Net income to sales: 12%.
8 Rate of return on assets: 20%.
9 Return on common stockholders' equity: 30%.

During 1984 the following selected transactions and events took place.
a Sold 14% preferred stock to the public for cash.
b Paid an account payable.
c Purchased short-term investments for cash.
d Sold merchandise inventory on account at a higher-than-normal markup.
e Gave extended credit terms to a slow-paying, but friendly, customer.
f Paid monthly interest expense to the bank.
g Purchased merchandise inventory for cash from a competitor who was going out of business.

INSTRUCTIONS

Consider items (a)–(g) individually. List the ratios affected, if any, by each transaction and event.

P19-12 *Constant dollar income statement (alternate to P19-6)*

Minnesota Machinery, a family-owned corporation, has 2,000 shares of common stock outstanding. The company reported the following net income for 1984.

Sales		$720,000
Cost of goods sold		480,000
Gross profit		$240,000
Operating expenses		
Cash expenses	$ 90,000	
Depreciation (straight-line)	120,000	210,000
Net income		$ 30,000

The general price index at the beginning of the year was 110. During the year the index averaged 120 and stood at 130 by year-end. All sales and cash expenses occurred evenly throughout the year. Depreciation relates to the following equipment:

Equipment	Cost	Life (Years)	Index at Acquisition
Office	$250,000	5	100
Delivery	560,000	8	65

Assume there was no purchasing power gain or loss on net monetary items.

INSTRUCTIONS

a Prepare an income statement for the year ended December 31, 1984, using the constant dollar approach.
b Determine the impact of adjusting for inflation on the company's earnings per share. Evaluate your findings.

P19-13 ***Current value financial statements (alternate to P19-7)***

Woodland, Inc., began operations on January 1 of the current year by acquiring the following assets in exchange for $350,000 of common stock.

Cash	$100,000
Inventory (22,000 units @ $9 per unit)	198,000
Land	52,000
	$350,000

During the year Woodland sold 17,000 units of inventory at $15 per unit. Additionally, the company incurred cash operating expenses of $49,000. By checking manufacturers' catalogs and recent real estate appraisals, Woodland determined the following current values for the inventory and land.

Inventory	$10.20 per unit
Land	$63,000

Assume outstanding accounts receivable total $38,500.

INSTRUCTIONS

a Prepare the firm's income statement for the current year ended December 31 by using the historical-cost basis of accounting. Disregard earnings-per-share calculations.

b Prepare the December 31 balance sheet by using the historical-cost basis of accounting.

c Determine Woodland's realized holding gain on the units sold and unrealized gain on the units remaining in inventory.

d Prepare the firm's income statement by using the current value approach. Disregard earnings-per-share calculations.

e Prepare the December 31 balance sheet by using the current value approach.

f Do you see any possible conflict with current value accounting and the objectivity principle? Explain your answer.

CASE 19
JUSTIN CORPORATION

Justin Corporation operates a wholesale food business in central Virginia. The company has grown quickly in its six years of existence, necessitating substantial bank borrowing to support the higher level of sales and accompanying investments in receivables and merchandise inventory. The president of Justin, Chip Hilton, desires to increase present bank loans from $60,000 to $75,000 to provide more capital. The president of the bank, Mel Harrelson, thinks Justin should generate as much cash as possible from internal sources before it attempts to borrow more heavily. As Mel notes, "There's no interest expense on the money you can generate internally by more efficient operations."

Based on a 360-day year, Justin's average daily sales amount to $4,400 at a gross profit rate of 15%. Average receivables for the year are $88,000; average inventories are $134,640. Hilton is now evaluating alternatives to accelerate cash collections. The following policy changes are under consideration.

1 Increasing accounts receivable turnover by two by sending out invoices sooner and calling on delinquent accounts.
2 Increasing inventory turnover by one by more selective ordering of slow-moving merchandise.

INSTRUCTIONS

a If both policy changes are implemented, how much cash could be obtained to support Justin's future growth?
b What other alternatives are available to Justin to accelerate cash inflows from receivables and inventory?

20 INCOME TAXES AND BUSINESS DECISIONS

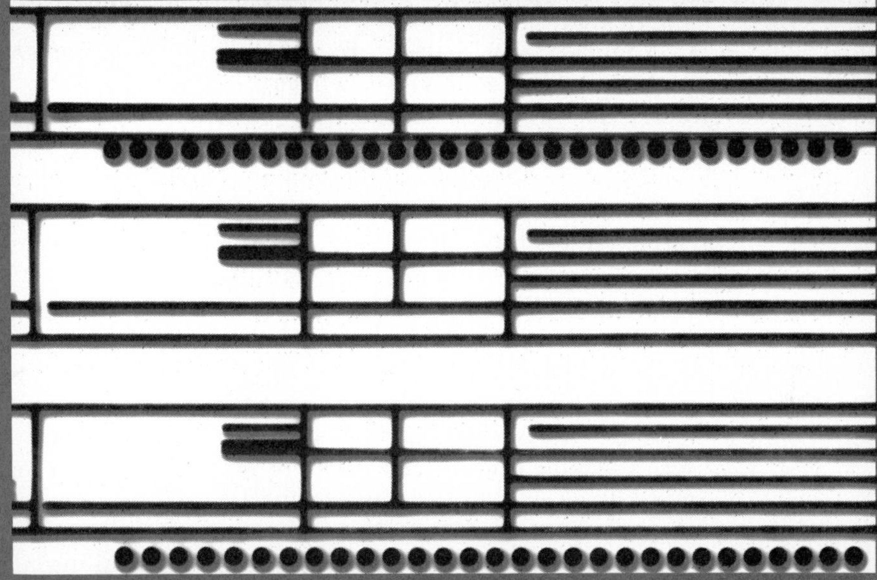

LEARNING OBJECTIVES

After reading this chapter you should:

1 Be familiar with the objectives of the federal income tax system and the functions of the IRS.

2 Be familiar with the four classes of taxpayers and understand the basic difference between the taxation of corporations and that of proprietorships and partnerships.

3 Understand the underlying differences between the cash and accrual bases of accounting.

4 Be familiar with the computation of income taxes for individuals, including the proper treatment of gross income, deductions from gross income, deductions from adjusted gross income, taxable income, withholdings, and tax credits.

5 Understand the distinction between marginal and average tax rates and the impact of inflation on taxes.

6 Have a basic knowledge of accounting for capital gains and losses of individuals.

7 Be familiar with the underlying structure of corporate taxation.

8 Be familiar with common areas for tax planning, the concept of tax shelters, and the distinction between tax evasion and tax avoidance.

9 Understand interperiod tax allocation and the treatment of deferred taxes.

CHAPTER 20

1982	May 5
1981	May 10
1980	May 4
1970	April 28
1960	April 18
1930	February 14

Confused? The dates above represent Tax Freedom Day, the day on which the average American will have earned enough to pay his or her federal, state, and local tax bills for the year. The dates are calculated by The Tax Foundation Inc., a nonprofit group, by assuming that every dollar the average worker earns starting on January 1 goes to the government. Looking at the figures a different way, the foundation noted that Americans currently spend a little more than 34% of each eight-hour workday to earn enough money to settle their tax obligations.[1]

Taxes, indeed, can be depressing. No doubt you have experienced this feeling when examining the difference between gross and net earnings on a paycheck. Don't get the impression, however, that Joe Q. Citizen is the only one helping to finance the government. Corporations are also subject to taxes, sometimes paying up to 46% of their taxable income. And this figure doesn't include certain state, local, or foreign taxes that may be assessed! Suffice it to say that with the existing level of tax rates, only the unwise disregard income taxes in planning and decision making.

This chapter presents an introduction to federal income taxes as they pertain to individuals and corporations. Although some of this material is quite detailed, our intention is to merely skim the surface. Income taxation is extremely complex; we, therefore, have no desire to make you tax experts. Everyone, though, needs some knowledge of this intricate subject in order to improve his or her future well-being.

FEDERAL INCOME TAX: BACKGROUND AND ADMINISTRATION

The first federal income tax was enacted to help finance the Civil War. Our present income tax, however, is derived from the Sixteenth Amendment to the Constitution, which was ratified in 1913. The amendment states:

> *The Congress shall have power to lay and collect taxes on incomes, from whatever source derived, without apportionment among the several States, and without regard to any census or enumeration.*

From 1913 through 1939 numerous tax-related laws were passed by Congress. In 1939, to bring the various provisions together, the laws were integrated into what is known as the Internal Revenue Code. Later, an effort to both update the tax laws and make them more understandable resulted in the Internal Revenue Code of 1954. The 1954 code, along with subsequent

[1] "Beginning Monday, Paycheck's All Yours," *Dallas Times Herald,* May 9, 1981, p. 5. Also, a telephone conversation with The Tax Foundation, Inc., conducted on June 10, 1982.

tax acts passed by Congress, provides the basic structure for today's taxation of income.

Tax Objectives

To most people, the sole objective of taxation is to raise money to support activities of the government. After all, we often hear politicians talk about increasing taxes to improve education, national defense, and a host of other services. While taxes do provide financial support for the government, other, more subtle objectives are also evident. For example, income taxation is frequently used to induce change in our economy. During a recession taxes are often reduced, thereby allowing the private sector to retain more dollars. When the dollars are spent, demand for goods and services increases and jobs may be created. Conversely, during a highly inflationary period taxes may be increased (despite the political unattractiveness of doing so) to soften demand. As demand weakens, businesses are less prone to raise prices.

Another objective of income taxation is to promote policies that are in the public interest. This objective is perhaps best illustrated by the recent legislation to encourage energy conservation. Tax reductions are currently provided to individuals for insulating their homes, installing storm or thermal windows or doors, and using solar or wind energy equipment. Businesses are given tax reductions for certain energy-related equipment, including the purchase of vans that are used primarily for transporting employees to and from work (i.e., for car pools). Turning to another area, businesses are also provided incentives for the installation of air and water pollution control equipment.

An additional objective of income taxation is to achieve certain social objectives.[2] Taxation strives to redistribute wealth through its rate structure, which taxes higher incomes at higher rates. In this manner the poor can retain more of their earnings to meet living costs. Furthermore, there are tax breaks for the elderly, the ill, the blind, and the low-wage earner. Finally, there have been incentives for companies to hire and train the handicapped, disadvantaged youths, and certain Vietnam veterans.

Administration of the Tax Law

The tax laws passed by Congress are administered by the **Internal Revenue Service (IRS)**, an agency of the Treasury Department. Probably best noted for the processing of tax returns, the IRS also interprets tax law, answers taxpayer questions, processes tax payments and refunds, and sometimes initiates legal action. Let us dwell on return processing for a moment, since this is the area of tax with which you may have had some interaction.

All returns filed with the IRS are checked for mathematical and mechanical accuracy. If a return is found to contain an error that overstates tax, any excess is either refunded or held as a credit against the subsequent period's tax liability. For errors resulting in an underpayment of tax, a bill is

[2] Programs in the public interest, such as energy conservation, could logically be discussed under this caption.

DOES THE IRS PLAY FAVORITES?

Although filling out a tax return can be sheer drudgery, most taxpayers are overjoyed when the return's bottom line indicates that a refund is in order. Normally, taxpayers can expect to wait anywhere from three to eight weeks for their precious checks. There are exceptions, however, and some notable ones. Ford Motor Company, for example, recently waited only two days for its refund—all $695 million of it. How come so much, so fast?

In 1980 Ford suffered a huge loss, $1.54 billion to be exact. A good portion of that was from U.S. operations. Under U.S. tax law companies can carryback those losses for three years, or forward for fifteen years, to lower average tax payments. By following this practice, businesses can get refunds of taxes paid in other years. Usually, Ford is fairly relaxed around tax time. But in early 1981 the rush was on to get the money.

Just after the books were closed on December 31, fourteen professionals—accountants and tax lawyers—wisked into action. They worked six-day weeks, with plenty of overtime, to prepare the IRS material. Even with computer help, they couldn't make the March 15 corporate deadline. "It's an enormous undertaking," says one Ford official. By the time their work was completed in mid-April, the filings added up to seven volumes, with more than 500,000 entries. "I don't think one guy could lift it," a Ford spokesman said.

When Ford's man arrived in Chicago to receive the refund, he found a dozen checks waiting for him. The IRS won't write a single check for more than $100 million, Ford says it was told. Besides, some of the money was against 1979 taxes, and some against 1978, and that required separate checks. One thing Ford says it's sure about: "They [the checks] added up to the right amount."

Did the IRS play favorites? While we don't like to point fingers, it certainly looks that way. No matter how desperate the "average" company or citizen is for a refund, the thought of receiving a check within two days is a sheer fantasy. In this particular case, however, the IRS can be excused. Why? The agency was merely doing its part to help our economy and keep the giant automaker going.

SOURCE Adapted from "How Ford Got Its Tax Refund Without Delay," The Wall Street Journal, *May 15, 1981, p. 25. Reprinted by permission of* The Wall Street Journal, *Copyright © Dow Jones & Company, Inc., 1981.*

sent to the taxpayer. In 1981 approximately 7.8% of the returns filed contained errors, and on a net basis the IRS collected an additional $454 million.[3]

The IRS often goes one step further in the examination of returns by performing an audit. Returns are selected for audit on the basis of several factors, including errors contained within the return, requests for abnormally large refunds, disclosure of income and expenses in excess of certain specified limits, and simply on a random basis to encourage correct reporting by taxpayers. The number of returns selected for review varies and often depends on the availability of audit personnel. Audits are conducted at an IRS office or, when supporting records and documents are voluminous, at the taxpayer's place of business. In a recent fiscal year such examinations resulted in the collection of $10.5 billion of additional taxes and penalties.[4]

CLASSES OF TAXPAYERS

According to tax law, there are four classes of taxpayers: individuals, corporations, estates, and trusts. Proprietorships and partnerships are not taxed per se; instead their income is taxed to the owner or partners whether or not such amounts have been withdrawn from the business. That is, the owner of a proprietorship reports business income from the enterprise on his or her individual tax return, together with salaries and income from other sources, and is taxed accordingly. Members of a partnership report their respective share of business income in a similar fashion.

As a separate and distinct legal entity, a corporation pays taxes on its income. Additionally, individual stockholders must report dividends received as part of their annual income. The taxing of corporate earnings and subsequent taxing of dividends to recipients is called "double taxation."

Taxation of estates and trusts is more appropriately left for advanced accounting courses and, therefore, will not be discussed in this text.

Taxpayer Accounting Methods: Cash Versus Accrual

Most small businesses and virtually all individual taxpayers use the **cash basis** of accounting when reporting to the IRS.[5] Although not in accord with generally accepted accounting principles, the cash basis is acceptable for figuring income subject to taxation. With the cash basis, revenues are recognized when cash is collected or *constructively received* (i.e., available to the taxpayer). To explain constructive receipt, income is considered taxable when it is within the taxpayer's control. Thus interest credited to a savings account on December 31, 1984, is 1984 income even if the amount is not entered in the savings passbook or withdrawn until 1985.

Turning to expenses, the general rule under the cash basis is that expenses are recognized in the period when paid. There are exceptions, how-

[3] *Annual Report of the Commissioner of the Internal Revenue Service: 1981* (Washington, D.C.: Government Printing Office, 1981), p. 5.

[4] Ibid., p. 12.

[5] As we just noted, proprietorships and partnerships do not pay taxes; however, net income is still calculated for inclusion on owners' returns.

ever. For example, disbursements for long-lived assets such as plant and equipment must be capitalized upon acquisition. Subsequently, if the assets are used for business purposes, a depreciation (i.e., cost recovery) deduction is allowed. Similarly, prepayments for business services (such as rent and insurance) are expensed not when paid but rather in the period(s) when benefits are received.

If they desire, taxpayers may elect to use the accrual basis of accounting. Under the **accrual basis,** revenues are recognized when earned, and expenses are entered in the records when incurred. Accrual accounting must be used by businesses in which inventories play a major role in operating activities. Individual taxpayers, however, voice a strong preference for cash basis accounting. Why? The cash basis is simple and eliminates the need for many year-end adjusting entries. In addition, as shown by the following decision case, cash basis taxpayers are able to defer taxes into future accounting periods.

Decision Case

A young doctor is beginning a medical practice in your town. Would the cash basis of accounting be advantageous to her? Yes. Aside from bookkeeping efficiencies, the cash basis permits the shifting of revenue and expense from one tax year to another. For example, the doctor could delay billing patients seen in December until January and thereby shift revenue into the next taxable year. By this technique, taxable income for the current year is reduced, resulting in a decreased tax bill. Obviously, this action will catch up with the doctor in the next period; however, if the same practice is repeated, the postponement of taxes will continue. The end result is the generation of additional cash for investment or to cover operating costs. Use of the accrual basis of accounting would prevent this postponement from occurring.

Tax Accounting for Individuals

Forms and instructions for the computation and filing of income taxes are available from the IRS. While the standard forms (1040 and 1040A) will not be illustrated, the calculation of an individual's tax liability can be visualized in terms of the general formula shown in Exhibit 20-1. The manner in which the formula's components actually appear on a tax return varies somewhat from our illustration. Nevertheless, the formula is a useful tool in understanding the structure of our income tax system. Each of the components appearing in the exhibit will now be explained.

Gross income

A taxpayer can receive income from hundreds of different sources. In all likelihood even the most comprehensive listing of income sources would be incomplete. Thus the Internal Revenue Code presumes that all income is reportable and taxable *unless specifically excluded by law.* A taxpayer's **gross income,** then, is his or her total income less allowable exclusions. Typical items of gross income include, but are not limited to, compensation for services (e.g., wages, salaries, tips, and bonuses), interest, dividends, rents, alimony, pensions, prizes and awards, income from a proprietorship

Exhibit 20-1

General tax formula for individuals

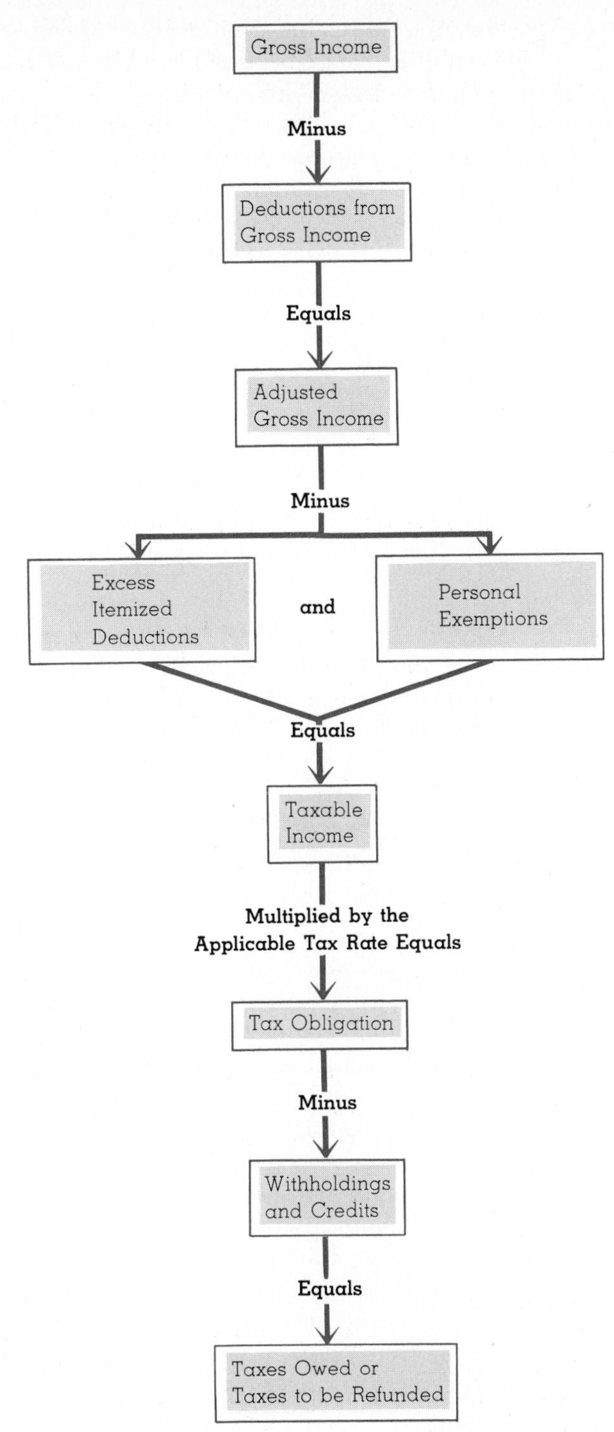

or partnership, and gains from dealings in property and securities. Even proceeds from embezzlement and gambling gains (i.e., gambling winnings minus gambling losses) are taxable!

Items excludable from gross income include life insurance proceeds, gifts and inheritances, certain scholarships, Social Security benefits, benefits from workers' compensation, interest on state and local obligations such as bonds, and the first $100 ($200 on a return filed jointly by husband and wife) of certain dividend income.[6] Thus if a single taxpayer received a $24,000 salary, a $6,000 inheritance, $900 of dividends, and a $400 prize from a quiz show, gross income would be figured as follows:

	Income Received	*Exclusions*	*Gross Income*
Salary	$24,000	$ —	$24,000
Inheritance	6,000	6,000	—
Dividends	900	100	800
Prize	400	—	400
	$31,300	$6,100	$25,200

Deductions from gross income

As shown in Exhibit 20-1, a taxpayer is entitled to several types of deductions. The first type, called **deductions from gross income,** are subtracted from gross income to yield **adjusted gross income.** These deductions generally relate to an individual's trade or business and include certain expenses incurred in the generation of gross income. No matter where a deduction appears on a tax return, the rules for deductibility are the opposite of those for income. That is, nothing is deductible *unless specifically stated in the tax laws.*

Deductions from gross income include, but are not limited to, the following:

1 *Trade and business expenses.* All ordinary and necessary expenses attributable to a taxpayer's trade or business are deductible. Such expenses include employee salaries, advertising, rent, and travel costs. In the actual tax computation business expenses are deducted from business revenues, and the net business income is included in the taxpayer's adjusted gross income.

2 *Trade and business expenses of employees.* Specific expenses incurred by taxpayers in connection with their employment are deductible. Examples include job-related travel costs away from home (such as transportation, meals, and lodging) and certain moving expenses. If any of these costs are reimbursed or partially reimbursed, only the net, nonreimbursed portion is deductible. Commuting costs from home to work are not deductible.

3 *Losses from the sale or exchange of property.* Losses from the sale or

[6] A **joint return** reports the combined income and allowable deductions of a husband and wife.

exchange of property are deductible from gross income if the property was acquired, held, or used for the production of income. Examples of such property include investments in stocks and bonds and rental property. Importantly, losses on the sale or exchange of personal property (e.g., a personal automobile or home) are not deductible.

4 *Contributions to retirement plans.* Taxpayers may establish their own retirement plan (such as an Individual Retirement Account, better known as an IRA) with a financial institution. Within certain limits amounts contributed to these plans are deductible from gross income.

5 *Deduction for two-earner married couples.* Married couples are entitled to a deduction in computing adjusted gross income if both the husband and wife are wage earners. The deduction, which is based on the earned income of the lower-earning spouse, eliminates the so-called marriage penalty of the late 1970s and very early 1980s. Previous to the deduction's introduction, there was a tax benefit associated with a couple's living together rather than taking the vows of matrimony. The deduction on a joint return is limited to 10% of the lower-earning spouse's earned income up to $30,000 (i.e., a maximum deduction of $3,000).

6 *Other deductions.* Other items that may be deducted from gross income include expenses related to rental property such as repairs, interest, taxes, and depreciation; certain alimony payments; and penalties from premature withdrawals from savings accounts and certificates of deposit.

Deductions from adjusted gross income

Exhibit 20-1 reveals that there are two types of deductions from adjusted gross income: excess itemized deductions and personal exemptions. To explain the former, all taxpayers are permitted a deduction for certain personal expenses. This practice helps promote the general welfare and provides every taxpayer with at least some tax-free income. Personal expense deductions may be taken by using the **zero bracket amount (ZBA)** or by itemizing.

The ZBA is a standard deduction that can be utilized by virtually all taxpayers. Single taxpayers are allowed a $2,300 reduction in adjusted gross income; the amount is raised to $3,400 for married individuals who file a joint return. The ZBA is already incorporated into the tax rates and tax tables published by the IRS (to be discussed shortly); thus separate deduction by taxpayers is unnecessary. The benefit of using the zero bracket amount is that the deduction is automatic. Consequently, the taxpayer need not furnish proof that allowable expenses equal to the ZBA were actually incurred.

Itemizing deductions

If taxpayers have allowable personal deductions that exceed the ZBA, a lower taxable income is produced by using an alternate procedure known as **itemizing.** With itemizing, the taxpayer lists actual allowable expenses that have been incurred during the year. The appropriate ZBA is then subtracted from the total allowable expenses, and the difference (called **excess itemized deductions**) is treated as a reduction in adjusted gross income.[7] For example, if a married couple filing a joint return has allowable personal deductions of $8,000, it would be to their advantage to deduct the $4,600 excess ($8,000 – $3,400) rather than accept the $3,400 zero bracket amount.

Unlike the ZBA, itemizing is not automatic. Thus the burden of proof shifts to the taxpayer that the expenses deducted were actually incurred. Accurate record keeping along with retention of invoices, canceled checks, and other documentation is necessary when using this method.

Deductions for personal expenses are permitted for the following:

1 *Medical and dental expenses.* Medical and dental expenses paid by the taxpayer are deductible to the extent they exceed 5% of adjusted gross income. Deductible expenses include fees paid to hospitals and doctors, outlays for medical appliances such as wheelchairs and glasses, the costs of any medical insurance premiums paid, and the costs of drugs and medicines in excess of 1% of adjusted gross income. For tax years beginning after December 31, 1983, however, the 1% test is eliminated; drugs and medicines are lumped with other medical expenses and are subject to the 5% limitation.

   To illustrate the more complicated case (i.e., for tax years ending prior to January 1, 1984), assume that a taxpayer with a $30,000 adjusted gross income paid medical costs as follows: medical insurance premiums, $1,200; hospital and doctor bills, $1,900; drugs and medicines, $400. The taxpayer is entitled to a $1,700 medical deduction, as follows.

Medical expenses		
Insurance premiums		*$1,200*
Hospital and doctor bills		*1,900*
Drugs and medicines	*$400*	
Less: 1% of adjusted gross income	*300*	*100*
		$3,200
Less: 5% of adjusted gross income		*1,500*
Total medical deduction		*$1,700*

2 *Taxes.* Real estate taxes, personal property taxes, state and local income taxes, and general sales taxes are deductible. Nondeductible taxes include federal taxes, taxes on gasoline and other motor fuels, and most licensing fees (such as driver's licenses and dog tags).

[7] As noted, the tax rates and tables already incorporate the zero bracket amount. Therefore only the excess over the ZBA is claimed as an itemized deduction.

3 *Interest.* Interest on virtually all personal debt (loans, mortgages, credit card balances, and so on) is deductible.

4 *Charitable contributions.* Subject to certain limits, contributions of money and property made to charitable, religious, educational, and other qualified organizations (usually nonprofit in nature) are deductible. Contributions to individuals, however needy, are not deductible.[8]

5 *Casualty losses.* A taxpayer can deduct the nonreimbursed portion of certain property losses resulting from casualties such as fire and theft. A deduction is permitted to the extent that a given casualty loss exceeds $100 *and* the total of all such losses exceeds 10% of adjusted gross income. A taxpayer having adjusted gross income of $25,000 and losses of $1,900 and $1,200 is thus entitled to a $400 deduction: [($1,900 – $100 + $1,200 – $100) – .10($25,000)].

6 *Expenses related to income-producing activities.* Taxpayers often incur various personal expenses related to income-producing activities. These expenses, which are not deducted from gross income because of their personal nature, are subtracted from *adjusted* gross income. Examples include uniform costs, union dues, dues to professional societies, subscriptions to professional journals, certain employment agency fees, certain legal and accounting fees, and safe deposit box rentals related to investments and income-producing properties.

Decision Case

Ted, a bachelor, rents an apartment and has an adjusted gross income of $12,000. Already this year he has paid $850 for medical and dental services, state and local income taxes of $350, sales taxes of $200, and interest on a car loan of $300. In addition, he incurred a $1,700 theft loss. Ted is paying his bills for December and among them is a $450 dental bill. Ted would like to defer payment until January and spend Christmas in Bermuda. The dentist, though, noted that dental bills are tax deductible and recommended immediate payment. Is the dentist correct? Yes, the bill is deductible; however, Ted receives no tax benefits. Examine the computations that follow.

	Itemize		ZBA
Medical and dental	$ 850		
Less: 5% of adjusted gross income	600	$ 250	
State and local income taxes		350	
Sales taxes		200	
Interest		300	
Casualty loss ($1,700 – $100)	$1,600		
Less: 10% of adjusted gross income	1,200	400	
Total expenses		$1,500	$2,300

[8] In accordance with provisions of the Economic Recovery Tax Act of 1981, nonitemizing taxpayers are also permitted a charitable contribution deduction.

Even with payment, itemized expenses will not exceed the automatic zero bracket amount. Thus, assuming his credit rating will not be affected, Ted should pay his bill in January and get a good start toward meeting (and exceeding) the ZBA in the next tax year.

Personal exemptions

In addition to excess itemized deductions or the ZBA, taxpayers are also entitled to a deduction from adjusted gross income for **personal exemptions.** A $1,000 deduction is allowed for each exemption claimed. Tax laws permit one exemption for the taxpayer, another for the spouse, and one for each person who qualifies as a dependent (to be explained shortly). Additional exemptions are granted if the taxpayer or spouse is 65 years of age or older and/or blind. For example, if John (age 68 and of good sight) and Mary (age 66 and blind) file a joint tax return, the couple would claim five exemptions, as follows:

John: regular and age	2
Mary: regular, age, and sight	3
Total exemptions	5

As noted, a taxpayer is allowed an exemption for each dependent. A **dependent** is a person who (1) has received in excess of one-half of his or her support (food, clothing, lodging, and other similar expenses) from the taxpayer, (2) is closely related to the taxpayer or has lived in the taxpayer's home for the entire year, and (3) has earned less than $1,000 of income. This last test is waived for children of the taxpayer who are under nineteen years of age or full-time students. The age and blindness exemptions noted earlier are not available for dependents.

Taxable income and the tax obligation

Adjusted gross income minus excess itemized deductions and personal exemptions equals **taxable income.** Taxable income is used in conjunction with rate schedules similar to those shown in Exhibit 20-2 to determine an individual's tax obligation.[9] The rates presented are those in effect at the time of this writing and are subject to change.

A review of the exhibit reveals the highly *progressive* nature of our tax structure; that is, the tax rates become higher as taxable income increases. Also observe that unmarried taxpayers attain higher tax rates faster (i.e., at lower taxable incomes) than their married counterparts. For example, assuming $41,000 of taxable income, a single taxpayer would pay $10,713 of federal income taxes, while a married couple would pay $8,654. The computations follow.

Single taxpayer

Tax on $34,100 as per schedule	***$ 7,953***
Tax on $6,900 excess ($41,000 − $34,100) at 40%	***2,760***
Total tax	***$10,713***

[9]In certain instances taxpayers use simplified tax tables to figure their tax obligation.

Exhibit 20-2

Tax rate schedules

SINGLE TAXPAYERS*

Taxable Income		Tax Obligation	
From	To	Amount	Of Taxable Income in Excess of
$ 2,300	$ 3,400	$ 0 + 11%	$ 2,300
3,400	4,400	121 + 13%	3,400
4,400	6,500	251 + 15%	4,400
6,500	8,500	566 + 15%	6,500
8,500	10,800	866 + 17%	8,500
10,800	12,900	1,257 + 19%	10,800
12,900	15,000	1,656 + 21%	12,900
15,000	18,200	2,097 + 24%	15,000
18,200	23,500	2,865 + 28%	18,200
23,500	28,800	4,349 + 32%	23,500
28,800	34,100	6,045 + 36%	28,800
34,100	41,500	7,953 + 40%	34,100
41,500	55,300	10,913 + 45%	41,500
55,300+		17,123 + 50%	55,300

MARRIED TAXPAYERS FILING A JOINT RETURN†

Taxable Income		Tax Obligation	
From	To	Amount	Of Taxable Income in Excess of
$ 3,400	$ 5,500	$ 0 + 11%	$ 3,400
5,500	7,600	231 + 13%	5,500
7,600	11,900	504 + 15%	7,600
11,900	16,000	1,149 + 17%	11,900
16,000	20,200	1,846 + 19%	16,000
20,200	24,600	2,644 + 23%	20,200
24,600	29,900	3,656 + 26%	24,600
29,900	35,200	5,034 + 30%	29,900
35,200	45,800	6,624 + 35%	35,200
45,800	60,000	10,334 + 40%	45,800
60,000	85,600	16,014 + 44%	60,000
85,600	109,400	27,278 + 48%	85,600
109,400+		38,702 + 50%	109,400

Note: *The ZBA has been built into these schedules.*
* *There is no tax obligation on taxable incomes under $2,300.*
† *There is no tax obligation on taxable incomes under $3,400.*

Married couple	
Tax on $35,200 as per schedule	*$6,624*
Tax on $5,800 excess ($41,000 − $35,200) at 35%	*2,030*
Total tax	*$8,654*

The disparity between the taxes paid by single and married taxpayers has generally decreased over the years because of congressional revisions of both tax rates and tax laws.

Withholdings and tax credits

Once the income tax is determined, two further items must be considered: federal income tax withholdings and tax credits. Recall that our tax system operates on a pay-as-you-go basis; that is, income taxes are withheld from employees' wages throughout the accounting period. Taxes are also withheld from certain interest and dividend distributions. These withholdings are made for two reasons. First, governmental expenditures occur during the year, so it is convenient to collect taxes on the same basis. Second, few taxpayers could (or would) pay their entire tax bill on a single date (usually April 15) because considerable savings would be necessary. Amounts withheld for federal income taxes are really prepayments of the upcoming tax obligation. These withholdings are therefore deducted from the tax obligation when figuring the total taxes owed to the IRS.

Taxpayers who anticipate owing large amounts of tax and meeting other requirements must file a *declaration of estimated tax* and pay estimated taxes in quarterly installments throughout the year. Estimated payments are also viewed as prepayments and are deducted from the taxpayer's tax obligation.

In addition to withholdings and estimated payments, taxpayers are permitted certain **tax credits.** Credits are direct dollar-for-dollar reductions from a taxpayer's total yearly tax bill. Credits exist, with specific limits, for contributions to candidates for public office, dependent child care expenses, the installation of certain energy-saving devices, and a number of other items.

Once withholdings, estimated payments, and tax credits are subtracted, the balance owed to the IRS or a taxpayer's expected refund becomes known. Sound money management dictates that requests for refunds be filed as soon as possible while taxes due be paid as late as possible. In this manner the taxpayer has more funds available for longer periods of time.

Overall the filing of a tax return represents a reporting and adjustment of the total taxes due. It is similar to "squaring up" expenses after a trip or an evening out so that everyone pays his or her fair share.

Individual tax return illustration

At this point it is helpful to review the preceding discussion in terms of a comprehensive illustration. Assume that George and Susan McGee and their three small children recently moved from another state for job-related reasons. Susan's father lives with the family and is totally dependent on the McGees for his support. George earned $44,000 working as an accountant. Susan operates a small gift shop that had sales of $57,000 and expenses (including cost of goods sold) of $39,500. The McGees earned $2,600 of interest on various savings accounts, $700 of dividends from a jointly held common stock investment, and $100 of interest on a municipal bond. Moving costs totaled $2,900; George received a $500 reimbursement from his employer. Allowable itemized deductions (medical, interest, taxes, and so on) totaled $10,200 before considering the zero bracket amount.

Total withholdings for federal income taxes from salary, interest, and dividends amounted to $9,100. The McGees paid estimated taxes of $3,200 and are entitled to a $75 tax credit for extra insulation added to their home. On the basis of the preceding information, the McGees are due a tax refund of $1,301, as shown in Exhibit 20-3.

Special Topics

From the discussion of the general tax formula, you are probably beginning to get an idea of just how complicated tax really is. And remember, we promised to just skim the surface! There are a number of topics that we have omitted from our presentation for purposes of simplification. Two of these topics, however, have a strong likelihood of affecting you in future years: tax rate analysis and capital gains and losses.

Tax rate analysis

The mechanics of using tax rates when determining an individual's tax obligation are fairly straightforward. A deeper understanding of rate struc-

Exhibit 20-3

Individual tax return filed jointly by George and Susan McGee

Gross income			
George's salary		$44,000	
Gift shop sales	$57,000		
Less: Gift shop expenses	39,500	17,500	
Interest on savings		2,600	
Dividends	$ 700		
Less: $200 dividend exclusion	200	500	
Municipal bond interest (excluded)		—	
Total gross income			$64,600
Deductions from gross income			
Two-earner married couple deduction ($17,500 × 10%)		$ 1,750	
Moving expenses	$ 2,900		
Less: Employer reimbursement	500	2,400	
Total deductions			4,150
Adjusted gross income			$60,450
Deductions from adjusted gross income			
Itemized deductions	$10,200		
Less: Zero bracket amount	3,400	$ 6,800	
Personal exemptions (6 × $1,000)		6,000	12,800
Taxable income			$47,650
Tax computation based on rates in Exhibit 20-2:			
Tax on $45,800, per schedule		$10,334	
Tax on $1,850 excess ($47,650 − $45,800) at 40%		740	
Total tax obligation			$11,074
Less: Energy tax credit		$ 75	
Taxes withheld		9,100	
Estimated payments		3,200	12,375
Taxes owed (refund)			$ (1,301)

tures and their impact is necessary, however, for achieving financial success. In discussing tax rates, we must distinguish between the average rate of tax and the marginal rate of tax. Assume, for a moment, that Linda Newton is a single taxpayer with taxable income of $34,100. Using the tax rates appearing in Exhibit 20-2, Linda's tax obligation would amount to $7,953. Stated differently, the tax **averages** 23.3% of taxable income ($7,953 ÷ $34,100).

Suppose that Linda has been offered a new job with a $4,000 salary increase. Assuming her deductions remain fairly constant, the salary increase would be taxed at the rate of 40% (from Exhibit 20-2). Forty percent is termed the **marginal rate of tax,** that is, the tax rate applied to each dollar of additional taxable income. From this simple example you can see the importance of the marginal tax rate in planning and decision making. If the government has a 40% "tax bite," Linda would keep only 60¢ of each additional dollar earned. She could easily decide that the additional take-home pay is simply too small, given the numerous problems associated with a change in employment. Should Linda be in a location where state and local income taxes have been enacted, these, too, must be considered, because they further diminish the attractiveness of the increased salary.

Inflation and income taxes

In periods of inflation most taxpayers experience a rise in both living costs and taxable income. Taxable income often increases because of higher salaries and wages offered by employers. Given the progressive structure of our tax system, higher salaries sometimes result in higher taxes as employees move from one bracket (rate) to another. To illustrate, assume that Rich Peterson, a single taxpayer, currently earns $38,000 and has a taxable income of $27,000. To keep up with a 10% annual inflation rate, Rich was recently granted a $3,800 salary increase. Assuming the use of the zero bracket amount and relatively constant deductions, taxable income will rise to $30,800 ($27,000 + $3,800). As the following computations show, total taxes jump from $5,469 to $6,765, representing a 23.7% increase.

	Taxable Income	
	$27,000	$30,800
Tax on $23,500, per schedule	$ 4,349	
Tax on $3,500 excess at 32%	1,120	
Tax on $28,800, per schedule		$ 6,045
Tax on $2,000 excess at 36%		720
Total tax	$ 5,469	$ 6,765

Is Rich really better off? No. His $3,800 raise is eaten up by higher prices for food, rent, transportation, and, importantly, a disproportionate increase in taxes. In effect, inflation increases the proportion of taxable income flowing to the federal government without raising tax rates. Beginning in 1985, the ZBA, the personal income tax brackets, and the personal exemption deduction will be indexed (adjusted) for inflation to eliminate this inequity.

Capital gains and losses

Although our taxation system appears to treat all income equally, Congress has consistently provided favorable treatment for gains and losses related to the sale or exchange of capital assets. **Capital assets** include all items of property owned by the taxpayer *except* receivables; inventories; real and depreciable business property; rights to literary, musical, and artistic compositions if in the hands of the creator; and certain governmental obligations. As the IRS notes:

> *For the most part, everything you own and use for personal purposes, pleasure, or investment is a capital asset. Some examples are: stocks and bonds held in your personal account; a dwelling owned and occupied by you and your family; household furnishings; a car used for pleasure or commuting; coin or stamp collections; gems and jewelry; gold, silver or any other metal.*[10]

Because of the advantageous tax rules, taxpayers and tax planners devote significant efforts toward achieving capital gains treatment for events and transactions. Why? Such events and transactions might otherwise be characterized as giving rise to ordinary (regular) income, which is taxed at much higher rates. The federal government has frequently clarified or changed many sections of the tax law to control imaginative interpretations.

Determination and classification of gains and losses

A capital gain or loss results from the disposal of a capital asset at an amount different from its basis. For a purchased capital asset the **basis** is the asset's cost less any depreciation (cost recovery) claimed (or that could have been claimed) for tax purposes. In many cases the determination of basis is difficult since property can be acquired in ways other than an outright purchase, for example, as an inheritance or a gift.

Once determined, a capital gain or loss is classified as either long-term or short-term. A **long-term gain or loss** results from the sale or exchange of a capital asset held more than one year. A holding period of one year or less, on the other hand, gives rise to a **short-term gain or loss.** This distinction is very important, because the tax treatments differ. As we will now see, taxpayers benefit from long-term capital gains.

Net capital gains

At the end of the tax year, all short-term gains and losses are combined to yield the net short-term gain or loss. A similar procedure is then followed for long-term gains and losses. After these two steps are performed, the *net* short-term gain or loss is combined with the *net* long-term gain or loss to form the **net capital gain or loss.**

If there is a net capital gain, it is included in gross income. Importantly, if the net long-term gains exceed the net short-term losses (if any), 60% of the excess is deducted from gross income when determining adjusted gross income. Study the examples that follow. Observe that although the net capital gain is the same in all cases, the taxable portion includable in adjusted gross income varies considerably.

---

[10] Internal Revenue Service, *Your Federal Income Tax,* November 1980, p. 113.

	Taxpayer		
	Bayer	Carver	Dunfey
Net long-term capital gain (loss)	$25,000	$12,000	$ (7,000)
Net short-term capital gain (loss)	(5,000)	8,000	27,000
Net capital gain	$20,000	$20,000	$20,000
Allowable deduction	12,000	7,200	—
Includable in adjusted gross income	$ 8,000	$12,800	$20,000

In Bayer's case the $25,000 net long-term gain exceeded the $5,000 net short-term loss by $20,000; thus $12,000 ($20,000 × 60%) can be deducted from gross income. Turning to Carver, the $12,000 net long-term gain exceeded the net short-term loss ($0 in this instance) by $12,000; consequently, $7,200 ($12,000 × 60%) is deductible. Finally, since Dunfey had no net long-term gain, the entire $20,000 is taxable.[11]

Net capital losses

Net capital losses reduce gross income subject to certain limitations. In a given year a maximum of $3,000 of net capital losses can be offset against ordinary (regular) income when figuring an individual's tax liability. As was true for net capital gains, the composition of the net capital loss must be considered when determining the proper accounting treatment.

Net short-term losses, for example, provide a dollar-for-dollar reduction in gross income. Thus a taxpayer having a $2,300 net capital loss composed entirely of short-term transactions can deduct $2,300 from gross income. In contrast, if there are net long-term capital losses, only 50% of the long-term loss can be used in taking the deduction. For example, suppose a taxpayer with gross income of $40,000 had a net capital loss of $14,000 composed entirely of long-term transactions. Part of the loss, $6,000, will be used in the current year to generate the $3,000 maximum deduction ($6,000 × 50% = $3,000). The remaining $8,000 ($14,000 − $6,000) can be carried forward into future tax years and written off against gross income subject to the normal limitation. In contrast to net capital gains, then, where long-term transactions are desirable, net capital losses show a definite bias in favor of short-term transactions.

Decision Case

David Morse has $30,000 of gross income from his salary. He has the following stock transactions.

Investment 1. Sold last month, generating a $14,000 short-term gain.

[11]There are several exceptions to the accounting treatment described in the preceding paragraphs. For example, although a personal residence qualifies as a capital asset, gains are usually not includable in gross income in the period of sale. If certain conditions are met, taxpayers can postpone gain recognition for many years. Furthermore, while both personal and investment property are capital assets, losses on the sale or exchange of *personal* property are not deductible unless they result from casualties or theft.

Investment 2. Purchased 11 months ago for $1,000; the current market value is $13,000.
Investment 3. Purchased 14 months ago for $13,000; the current market value is $1,000.

Suppose David is a calendar year taxpayer, and it is now the middle of December. Assuming that no drastic change in market value is anticipated, should he consider selling either of his two remaining investments? Yes. By selling investment 3, the $12,000 long-term loss can be offset against the $14,000 short-term gain already realized. Morse will therefore be taxed only on the $2,000 ($14,000 – $12,000) net capital gain. Investment 2 should be retained. By waiting one month, Morse will receive the benefit of having a long-term capital gain.

Tax Accounting for Corporations

Corporate taxation differs significantly from taxation of individuals. In contrast to individuals, corporations do not become involved with adjusted gross income, zero bracket amounts, and exemptions. The computation of the tax obligation assumes the form shown in Exhibit 20-4.

Determination of taxable income

The determination of taxable income is based on the same income and expense philosophy established for individuals. That is, all income is reportable and taxable unless specifically excluded by tax law, while no expense is deductible unless explicitly authorized. Although the philosophies are identical, numerous differences are encountered when dealing with taxable income's individual components. Consider, for example, dividends received and capital gains and losses.

Dividends received

Recall that individual taxpayers filing a joint return are permitted to exclude $200 of dividends received during a tax year. In contrast, corporations are entitled to deduct 85% of such dividends, a practice that takes a large step toward preventing "triple taxation." Triple taxation occurs when income is taxed to the earning corporation, taxed again as dividend income to a receiving corporation, and taxed a third time to stockholders should the receiving corporation have any dividend distributions of its own.

Capital gains and losses

Individuals are entitled to deduct 60% of the excess of net long-term capital gains over net short-term capital losses. Corporations do not receive this deduction. Rather, if there is an excess of long-term gains over short-term losses, the excess is taxed at a *maximum* rate of 28%. For corporations having less than $50,000 of taxable income, the excess is taxed at the corporation's regular tax rate (to be discussed shortly) as opposed to 28%.

If there is a net capital loss, ordinary income is not reduced. Instead the net capital loss is offset against net capital gains of the three preceding years

Exhibit 20-4

General tax formula for corporations

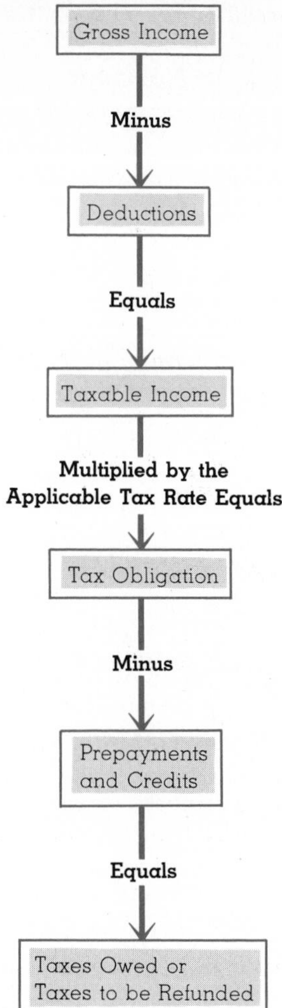

(known as a *carryback*). Then remaining amounts are used to reduce any net capital gains in the forthcoming five years (known as a *carryforward*).

Corporate tax rates

At the time of this writing, the taxable income of corporations is subject to the progressive rates shown in Exhibit 20-5. To illustrate the use of these rates, assume that a corporation has taxable income of $90,000. Income taxes would amount to $21,750: $15,750 on the first $75,000 plus $6,000 on the remaining $15,000 ($15,000 × 40% = $6,000).

Corporate tax illustration

To tie the features of corporate taxation together, we assume Century Corporation reported sales and cost of goods sold of $760,000 and $300,000, respectively, for the year just ended. Other information pertaining to the company follows.

Exhibit 20-5

Corporate tax rate schedule

Taxable Income		Tax Obligation	
From	To	Amount	Of Taxable Income in Excess of
$ 0	$ 25,000	$ 0 + 15%	$ 0
25,000	50,000	3,750 + 18%	25,000
50,000	75,000	8,250 + 30%	50,000
75,000	100,000	15,750 + 40%	75,000
100,000+		25,750 + 46%	100,000

Operating expenses, $200,000
Dividends received, $100,000
Net long-term capital gain, $80,000
Estimated tax payments, $120,000
Tax credits, $5,000

Century's tax computation is shown in Exhibit 20-6.

Exhibit 20-6

Century Corporation tax computation

Gross income			
Sales	$760,000		
Less: Cost of goods sold*	300,000	$460,000	
Dividends received		100,000	
Net long-term capital gain		80,000	
Total gross income			$640,000
Deductions			
Operating expenses		$200,000	
Dividends-received deduction ($100,000 × 85%)		85,000	
Total deductions			285,000
Taxable income			$355,000
Tax on ordinary income of $275,000 ($355,000 − $80,000)			
Tax on first $100,000		$ 25,750	
Tax on excess ($175,000 × 46%)		80,500	$106,250
Tax on net long-term capital gain ($80,000 × 28%)			22,400
Tax obligation			$128,650
Less: Estimated payments		$120,000	
Tax credits		5,000	125,000
Taxes due IRS			$ 3,650

*According to income tax regulations, cost of goods sold is considered in the computation of gross income.

TAX PLANNING

The payment of income taxes, particularly with such high and progressive tax rates, often drains businesses (and individuals) of capital needed for operations, growth, and perhaps even survival. Thus taxpayers constantly strive to minimize their tax liability to the government by careful planning. Because tax laws are complex and involve specialized knowledge, use of outside consultants on a year-round basis is common.

Tax liability may be reduced by following two courses of action: tax avoidance and tax evasion. **Tax avoidance** is achieved by the proper planning of financial events, affairs, and transactions within the legal confines of the tax statutes passed by Congress. In contrast, **tax evasion** represents a deliberate attempt to understate taxable income by the manipulation of revenues and expenses. Revenues may be intentionally understated, while fictitious and fraudulent deductions are claimed for expenses or exemptions. Tax evasion is, of course, illegal and is accompanied by severe penalties. For obvious reasons our discussion of tax planning will center on methods of tax avoidance.

Tax Avoidance: Areas to Consider

There are many areas where income taxes can be avoided by proper tax planning. Consider, for example, the following topics, which were introduced earlier in this chapter.

Cash versus accrual basis of accounting. As shown in the decision case on page 786, use of the cash basis may permit a delay in recording revenues. This action reduces taxable income, thereby postponing income taxes.

Transaction timing. As illustrated in the decision case on page 798, the timing of a sale or exchange of capital assets can be controlled to obtain favorable long-term capital gains treatment.

Taxes can also be reduced (i.e., postponed) by utilizing accelerated cost recovery write-offs and, in periods of rising prices, the LIFO method of inventory costing. Furthermore, if certain conditions are met, sellers of merchandise can employ the installment basis of revenue recognition. Installment users can defer income until such time that cash is collected over the life of an installment contract.

Finally, as we discussed in Chapter 15, there are tax planning implications of financing a business. Corporations, for example, can raise funds by issuing long-term debt, preferred stock, or common stock. Remember that interest payments on debt are tax deductible; in contrast, dividend distributions are not. Given this situation, companies often attempt to finance operations through borrowing rather than through the issuance of additional shares of capital stock. Normally, however, there is an upper limit on the amount of debt capital that is obtainable at reasonable interest rates. Each additional issuance of debt increases the chance that fixed annual interest obligations cannot be met. Creditors, therefore, often raise their rates to help offset an increased exposure to risk.

Form of organization

Tax planning should commence even before the start of business operations. Why? A very important tax consideration is the proper selection of an entity form. As we saw earlier, an entity may be organized as a proprietorship, a partnership, or a corporation. With a proprietorship or partnership, business income is reported on the owner's individual tax return and is taxed at marginal rates ranging from 11% to 50%. Corporations, on the other hand, pay their own taxes at rates that vary from 15% to 46%.

The importance of the entity selection decision is shown in the following illustration. Suppose a new company is being formed and the organizers are all affluent, paying taxes on their earnings at a marginal rate above 46%. If the venture is expected to be profitable, the corporate form of organization looks advantageous. Income would begin to be taxed at 15% and would progress toward the 46% rate; individual rates, in contrast, would be higher. Changing the example slightly, let's assume the venture is expected to be unprofitable for the first few years. With the corporate form the initial losses would provide no immediate tax benefits. With a partnership, however, an appropriate share of the losses would be transferred to the individual returns of the owners. Thus total gross income would drop, resulting in a tax reduction. In this instance the partnership form of organization appears beneficial.

As this example shows, there is no one best form of organization; each situation must be analyzed on its own merits. In addition to tax considerations, other factors such as legal liability of the owners, transferability of ownership, and governmental regulation further complicate the decision process.

An illustration

To illustrate the tax considerations surrounding the selection of the "correct" organizational form, assume that Robert Sobol is beginning a new business. Relevant information follows.

The business is expected to produce $60,000 of income per year before taxes and owner compensation. One-half of this income will be withdrawn as salaries.

Sobol and his wife, Lauren, have $6,000 of itemized deductions in excess of the zero bracket amount, claim two exemptions, and file a joint tax return.

The couple desires to learn the tax consequences of establishing either a proprietorship or a corporation. They know that corporations are permitted a tax deduction for salaries paid to owner employees; in contrast, proprietorships recognize these amounts as withdrawals, with no tax deduction allowed. Exhibit 20-7 reveals that in the Sobols' case a corporation is the preferred organizational form. Both alternatives have the same *total* taxable income of $52,000; however, the establishment of a corporation yields a net tax advantage of $5,106 ($12,814 – $7,708).

Exhibit 20-7

Taxation of corporation versus sole proprietorship

CORPORATION

Business			
Business income		$60,000	
Robert's salary		30,000	
Taxable income		$30,000	
Tax			
Tax on $25,000, per schedule*			$ 3,750
Tax on $5,000 excess at 18%			900
Individuals			
Salary		$30,000	
Less: Personal deductions	$6,000		
Personal exemptions (2 × $1,000)	2,000	8,000	
Taxable income		$22,000	
Tax			
Tax on $20,200, per schedule*			2,644
Tax on $1,800 excess at 23%			414
Total income tax			$7,708

*Corporate tax rates appear in Exhibit 20-5. Personal tax rates appear in Exhibit 20-2.

SOLE PROPRIETORSHIP†

Business income		$60,000	
Robert's salary		—	
Adjusted gross income		$60,000	
Less: Personal deductions	$6,000		
Personal exemptions	2,000	8,000	
Taxable income		$52,000	
Tax			
Tax on $45,800, per schedule*			$10,334
Tax on $6,200 excess at 40%			2,480
Total income tax			$12,814

*Corporate tax rates appear in Exhibit 20-5. Personal tax rates appear in Exhibit 20-2.
† Total income is picked up by Sobol and reported on the couple's joint return.

This outcome is quickly changed by altering one fact. Suppose that Sobol desires to withdraw the business's total earnings. Assuming salaries remain at $30,000, the corporation will therefore distribute its net income of $25,350 ($30,000 taxable income − $4,650 income taxes) as dividends. Robert and Lauren's gross income will increase by $25,150 (dividend income reduced by the $200 joint dividend exclusion), resulting in income taxes of $10,874, as shown on page 805.

Robert's salary		$30,000	
Dividend income (less $200 exclusion)		25,150	
Gross income		$55,150	
Less			
Personal deductions	$6,000		
Personal exemptions	2,000	8,000	
Taxable income		$47,150	
Tax			
Tax on $45,800, per schedule		$10,334	
Tax on $1,350 excess at 40%		540	
Total income tax			$10,874

Thus the sole proprietorship form of organization is now advantageous.

Corporation		
Tax on business (from Exhibit 20-7)	$ 4,650	
Tax on Sobols (from above)	10,874	
Total tax		$15,524
Sole proprietorship		
Total tax (from Exhibit 20-7)		12,814
Difference in favor of sole proprietorship		$ 2,710

In sum, the correct choice of an organizational form is a difficult decision. Many factors must be considered and, as we noted earlier, it is impossible to generalize about which entity form is always best.

Tax shelters

Individuals in very high tax brackets are continually searching for ways to reduce their tax burden. Many such individuals have turned to tax shelters. **Tax shelters** are investments that generate either tax-exempt income or business losses. As noted earlier in the chapter, for example, tax-exempt income is available to purchasers of state and municipal bonds. Over the years tax-sheltered investments have been available in a number of diversified areas, including oil and gas properties, motion pictures, real estate, agriculture, and cattle feeding. Unfortunately, many of the promoters of these ventures had little experience in managing such interests or properties. Thus a number of the investments turned sour, and substantial amounts of capital were lost. In recent years various changes in the tax law have eliminated most of the benefits available from tax shelters, except possibly for real estate.

Many tax-sheltered investments have been organized as partnerships. In this manner any business losses incurred could be claimed by each of the partners for tax purposes. To illustrate, suppose a partnership was formed to acquire an apartment complex. Assume that losses were incurred from the excess of mortgage interest, property taxes, maintenance, and accelerated cost recovery deductions over rental income. Each partner could then report a share of the loss on his or her individual tax return. Why be willing to incur a loss? The profit in real estate comes from (1) increasing property values because of demand and inflation and (2) long-term capital gains treatment of profits realized upon sale. From the investors' viewpoint, then, business losses in early years reduce income that is taxed at regular tax rates. Any gain on the sale of the property is taxed at a more advantageous rate in the future, after the investor has had time to reinvest tax savings from the losses.

FINANCIAL REPORTING AND INCOME TAXES

Thus far, the majority of our presentation has focused on the determination of taxable income and the related tax obligation to the IRS. Taxes, of course, must also be reported on the income statement, since they affect profitability. In so doing, a problem typically arises. Financial statements are not governed by tax law; instead they are based on generally accepted accounting principles (GAAP). The income statement, for example, strives to present a fair picture of operating results by a proper matching of revenues and expenses. Because of differences between GAAP and income tax regulations, there is often a difference between pretax income reported in the financial statements (called *pretax accounting income*) and taxable income. Consequently, the *taxes paid* (*or due*) to the government may not be an appropriate measure of a company's *tax expense* for a given accounting period. Variations between taxable income and pretax accounting income are caused by a number of factors. Collectively, these factors can be classified as permanent differences and timing differences.

Permanent Differences

Permanent differences are items that are considered in the calculation of taxable income but not pretax accounting income or vice versa. Consider, for example, the 85% dividends-received deduction for corporations. If a corporation received $200,000 of dividends during the year, the tax return would report net dividends of $30,000 [$200,000 – ($200,000 × 85%)], while the income statement would disclose the entire $200,000 as revenue. The $170,000 difference is permanent; that is, it will not be eliminated in future accounting periods. Other items that affect either taxable income or pretax accounting income but not both include tax-exempt interest on state and municipal obligations, life insurance proceeds that are also tax-exempt, and goodwill. To explain the latter, goodwill is capitalized and amortized for accounting purposes. Yet in the computation of a company's tax liability, the amortization cannot be deducted as a business expense.

Timing Differences

In several instances income tax regulations allow businesses to use methods for tax purposes that are different from those used in the accounting records. When alternative methods are employed, a **timing difference** of revenues and expenses occurs. To illustrate, assume a company uses the accelerated cost recovery system (i.e., depreciation) for tax purposes and straight-line depreciation in the preparation of financial statements. The accelerated cost recovery system results in a rapid write-off of cost, thereby lowering taxable income and a company's outlay for taxes. The straight-line method, on the other hand, allows users to stabilize the impact of depreciation on earnings by expensing the same amount year after year. Although both methods will report identical total write-offs over the life of an asset, the timing differs.

Timing differences similar to the foregoing result in either a postponement or prepayment of income taxes. This result is readily seen in the following example, which also illustrates an interesting financial reporting problem faced by the taxpayer. Assume that Dinah, Inc., has timing differences that result in the following figures:

Year	Taxable Income Reported to the IRS	Pretax Accounting Income Reported in the Financial Statements
1	$ 40,000	$ 60,000
2	60,000	60,000
3	80,000	60,000
	$180,000	$180,000

The company is subject to a 40% income tax rate.

The calculation of Dinah's liability to the IRS, as shown on the income tax return, follows.

	Year 1	Year 2	Year 3	Total
Taxable income	$40,000	$60,000	$80,000	$180,000
Income taxes, 40%	$16,000	$24,000	$32,000	$ 72,000

If the actual tax liability was integrated into the formal income statement, the results would be as shown below.

	Year 1	Year 2	Year 3	Total
Pretax accounting income	$60,000	$60,000	$60,000	$180,000
Income taxes (from tax return)	16,000	24,000	32,000	72,000
Net income	$44,000	$36,000	$28,000	$108,000

Observe that pretax accounting income is constant; net income, however, changes dramatically. Statement users may wonder why profitability is decreasing when the business appears so stable and why tax rates have skyrocketed from 26.7% of pretax accounting income ($16,000 ÷ $60,000) to 53.3% ($32,000 ÷ $60,000). Some users may even think that Dinah's financial well-being is in jeopardy and that future earnings will continue to drop.

Interperiod tax allocation

To present a clearer picture of operating performance, accountants do not deduct a company's tax obligation to the government as an expense. Instead income tax expense is computed on the basis of the information contained within the accounting records whenever timing differences are a factor. This procedure, known as **interperiod tax allocation,** results in a better matching of expenses and revenues. With interperiod tax allocation, Dinah's income statements would appear as follows:

	Year 1	Year 2	Year 3	Total
Pretax accounting income	$60,000	$60,000	$60,000	$180,000
Income taxes, 40%	24,000	24,000	24,000	72,000
Net income	$36,000	$36,000	$36,000	$108,000

These statements correctly portray the stable nature of the firm by eliminating the distortion caused by variations in income taxes. As the following computations show, the timing differences cause tax payments to be postponed. Both the tax return and the financial statements, however, disclose identical overall results.

	Year 1	Year 2	Year 3	Total
Taxes, per tax return	$16,000	$24,000	$32,000	$72,000
Taxes, per income statement with interperiod tax allocation	24,000	24,000	24,000	72,000
Difference	−$ 8,000	$ –	+$ 8,000	$ –

Deferred taxes

In Year 1 Dinah incurred tax expense of $24,000 and owed $16,000 to the IRS. The $8,000 difference between these two amounts represents a postponement or **deferral of income tax** and is recorded as follows:

Year 1	*Income Tax Expense*	*24,000*	
	Income Taxes Payable		*16,000*
	Deferred Income Taxes		*8,000*
	To record income taxes for Year 1		
Shortly Thereafter	*Income Taxes Payable*	*16,000*	
	Cash		*16,000*
	To record the payment of income taxes		

The Deferred Income Taxes account is shown on the balance sheet as a liability, thus indicating that Dinah will be subject to an $8,000 future tax payment.

The appropriate entries for Years 2 and 3 follow.

Year 2	Income Tax Expense	24,000	
	Income Taxes Payable		24,000
	To record income taxes for Year 2		
Shortly Thereafter	Income Taxes Payable	24,000	
	Cash		24,000
	To record the payment of income taxes		
Year 3	Income Tax Expense	24,000	
	Deferred Income Taxes	8,000	
	Income Taxes Payable		32,000
	To record income taxes for Year 3		
Shortly Thereafter	Income Taxes Payable	32,000	
	Cash		32,000
	To record the payment of income taxes		

In Year 2 deferred taxes are not affected because taxable income coincides with pretax accounting income. Finally, in Year 3 the postponement comes due and results in a reduction of the Deferred Income Taxes account.

The timing difference in this example worked itself out in three years. In practice, companies continuously strive to postpone taxes by the use of different accounting methods for financial reporting and tax purposes. By employing timing differences associated with depreciation, inventory, and revenue realization methods (e.g., accrual vs. installment), a company can defer payment of significant amounts of taxes until later years. As evidence, consider recent long-term tax deferral balances of the following corporations:

Corporation	Deferred Taxes (000 Omitted)	Total Liabilities (000 Omitted)	Deferred Taxes as a Percent of Total Liabilities
Brunswick Corporation	$ 32,700	$ 491,116	6.7%
Eastman Kodak Company	349,000	2,676,000	13.0
H. J. Heinz Company	79,189	1,087,139	7.3
Mary Kay Cosmetics, Inc.	2,587	39,024	6.6
R. H. Macy & Co., Inc.	45,247	777,148	5.8
Ryder System, Inc.	191,543	1,269,319	15.1

Occasionally, again due to timing differences, taxable income may exceed pretax accounting income. In this situation income taxes would be prepaid rather than postponed and would be reported as an asset on the balance sheet.

KEY TERMS AND CONCEPTS

accrual basis 786
adjusted gross income 788
average rate of tax 795
basis 797
capital assets 796
cash basis 785
deductions from adjusted gross income 789
deductions from gross income 788
deferred taxes 808
dependent 792
excess itemized deductions 790
gross income 786
Internal Revenue Service (IRS) 783
interperiod tax allocation 808
itemizing 790
joint return 787
long-term capital gains and losses 797
marginal rate of tax 795
net capital gains and losses 797
permanent differences 806
personal exemption 792
short-term capital gains and losses 797
tax avoidance 802
tax credit 794
tax evasion 802
tax shelter 805
taxable income 792
timing differences 806
zero bracket amount (ZBA) 789

QUESTIONS

Q20-1 What are the objectives of the federal taxation of income?

Q20-2 Discuss the activities performed by the IRS.

Q20-3 Compare the federal income taxation of a corporation with that of a proprietorship.

Q20-4 What is the *general* rule for determining (1) whether income is taxable and (2) whether expenditures are deductible?

Q20-5 Discuss the basic difference between deductions from gross income and deductions from adjusted gross income.

Q20-6 What is the basic benefit associated with using the zero bracket amount?

Q20-7 Karen, a single taxpayer, has deductions for interest, taxes, and medical costs amounting to $2,400. Should she itemize? Why?

Q20-8 A student once commented: "Given the nature of the tax rates for individuals, it seems that Congress has shown favoritism toward taxpayers who have low income levels." Evaluate the student's comment.

Q20-9 A single taxpayer has a marginal tax rate of 32%. Which of the following items would be most valuable to the taxpayer? Explain your answer.

a Loan interest of $500
b Doctor and hospital bills totaling $500
c Energy tax credit of $500

Q20-10 Distinguish between a net long-term capital gain and a net short-term capital gain. Which is more beneficial from a taxpayer's viewpoint? Explain.

Q20-11 Distinguish between tax avoidance and tax evasion.

Q20-12 Discuss the tax planning aspects of deciding whether to incorporate a business.

Q20-13 What are tax shelters? Why would a taxpayer be willing to incur a loss on a tax-sheltered investment that is organized as a partnership?

Q20-14 Does pretax accounting income normally differ from taxable income? Why?

EXERCISES

E20-1 Angelo Lombardi began a consulting practice in August of the current year. The practice is organized as a sole proprietorship. For the 5-month period ending December 31, Angelo billed clients $114,000 for services performed and paid $58,500 for operating expenses. Cash collections on account amounted to $71,000; there were $10,000 of unpaid bills at year-end. Lombardi rents all needed office equipment and had no prepayments during the year.

a Calculate business income for the practice using the cash basis of accounting.

b Calculate business income for the practice using the accrual basis of accounting.

c Assuming that Angelo has sufficient cash and uses the cash basis of accounting, should he pay the unpaid bills at year-end? Why?

d Discuss the benefits of using the cash basis of accounting for reporting to the Internal Revenue Service.

E20-2 Classify the items in (a)–(h) as one of the following:

1 A deduction from gross income to arrive at adjusted gross income.
2 A deduction from adjusted gross income to arrive at taxable income.
3 A tax credit deductible from the tax obligation.
4 Not deductible anywhere on the tax return.

Ignore possible limitations on the amount of the deduction or credit.

a ______ Travel expenses away from home incurred as an employee.
b ______ Dental expenses.
c ______ Subscription to a professional, work-related journal.
d ______ Fire insurance premiums on a taxpayer's personal residence.
e ______ Amounts paid for adding insulation to a personal residence.
f ______ Contribution to a retirement plan by a self-employed person.
g ______ Nonreimbursed moving expenses from New York to Denver related to a change in employment.
h ______ Costs of driving back and forth to work.

E20-3 Clarence and Sandy Hall, a married couple, file a joint return and have the following expenditures for the year just ended.

Hospital bills	*$ 210*
Medical insurance costs	*700*
Physician bills	*160*
Dentist bills	*425*
Drugs and medicines	*450*
Cash donations to church	*225*
Value of time donated to Boy Scouts	*1,500*
Safe deposit box rental for investments	*10*
Real estate taxes on personal residence	*530*
Sales taxes	*125*
Cost recovery (i.e., depreciation) on rental property	*1,800*
Mortgage interest on personal residence	*965*
Casualty loss on car accident (uninsured amount)	*250*

Assuming an adjusted gross income of $25,000, should the couple itemize their deductions? Show calculations to support your answer.

E20-4 Determine the number of allowable exemptions in each of the following independent cases:

a ______ Donald Alber, age 62, supports his wife (age 60 and blind) and his son. The son is 23, earned $1,400 during the summer, and is a full-time student. Alber and his wife file a joint return.

b ______ Robert Benton, age 43, supports his mother (age 66 and of good sight). Robert resides in Missouri; his mother, who earned $950 during the year, lives in Florida.

c ______ Mr. and Mrs. Fisher are both 66 and blind. Their son, age 25 and a part-time student, lived with the couple for eight months during the year and earned $24,500. Answer this case with respect to Mr. and Mrs. Fisher's joint return.

E20-5 Howard and Joyce Rogers, each under 65 and of good sight, have two small children. The following information was extracted from the couple's joint tax return.

Gross income	*$74,600*
Deductions from gross income	*5,900*
Itemized deductions before considering the zero bracket amount	*18,200*
Taxes withheld from salaries	*7,800*
Estimated tax payments	*2,700*
Energy tax credit	*550*

Determine the following:

a Adjusted gross income.

b Taxable income.

c The couple's tax obligation, using the rates presented in Exhibit 20-2.

d The balance owed to the IRS or the refund due. Indicate which and the amount.

E20-6 The following information was extracted from the accounting records of Glenn and Nita Dodson.

Glenn's salary	*$71,000*
Inheritance from deceased relative	*5,000*
Interest on savings account	*1,100*
Deductions from gross income	*14,500*
Itemized deductions before considering the zero bracket amount	*10,700*
Income taxes withheld	*10,400*

The Dodsons file a joint return and have three small children. Using the tax rates appearing in Exhibit 20-2, compute the amount of tax the couple owes to the IRS (or the refund due).

E20-7 Tom Burdick is married and the father of three small children. He has adjusted gross income of $52,000 and itemized expenses of $10,800 in excess of the zero bracket amount.

a Using the tax rate schedule appearing in Exhibit 20-2, compute Tom's total tax obligation to the government. Tom files a joint return with his wife.

b Compute Tom's average tax rate.

c Compute Tom's marginal tax rate.

d Assume that Tom is considering a new job that will pay an additional $500 per month. If itemized expenses remain fairly constant, how much additional cash will Tom have to meet living expenses during the upcoming year? Express your answer on an aftertax basis.

E20-8 The following information was extracted from the returns of four different taxpayers.

	Taxpayer			
	A	B	C	D
Salaries	$30,000	$30,000	$30,000	$30,000
Net long-term capital gain (loss)	24,000	10,000	(5,000)	(9,000)
Net short-term capital gain (loss)	(6,000)	8,000	23,000	(5,000)

Determine each taxpayer's adjusted gross income.

E20-9 The following information was extracted from the records of Estronics, Inc.

Sales	$1,000,000
Cost of goods sold	650,000
Operating expenses	180,000
Dividends received during the year	70,000
Prepayments of income tax	60,200
Tax credits	8,400

Using the tax rates presented in Exhibit 20-5, compute the amount of tax the corporation owes to the IRS (or the refund due).

E20-10 Mikesell Motors, Inc., postpones taxes by using alternative accounting methods for tax and financial reporting purposes. A financial forecast generated the following results for the next four years, caused entirely by timing differences.

Year	Taxable Income	Pretax Accounting Income
1	$ 38,000	$ 42,500
2	41,000	42,500
3	44,000	42,500
4	47,000	42,500
	$170,000	$170,000

Assume that Mikesell is subject to a 40% tax rate.

a Prepare a schedule listing taxes due to the IRS over the next four years.

b Prepare a schedule listing Mikesell's income tax expense over the next four years. Mikesell uses interperiod tax allocation.

c Determine the maximum amount of tax deferral and the year in which it occurs.

PROBLEMS

P20-1 ***Tax computation for individuals***

Jim and Susan Tansey have two small children and file a joint tax return. Jim is employed as a construction supervisor and earns $35,000 per year. Susan is self-employed and conducts gymnastics and exercise classes in a rented facility across town. Revenues and expenses from her business, which is organized as a sole proprietorship, amounted to $48,400 and $29,600, respectively. The couple earned $800 of interest and $1,100 of dividends from joint investments made throughout the year. The interest includes $300 from bonds issued by the state of Georgia. Additional information relating to the Tanseys follows.

Nonreimbursed moving expenses related to change in employment	*$3,000*
Hospital and doctor bills	*2,900*
Health insurance premiums	*380*
Drugs and medicines	*220*
Interest on personal residence	*2,400*
License fees for auto and pets	*40*
State income and sales taxes	*850*
Contributions to Salvation Army	*400*
Casualty losses	
Automobile accident: total loss, $1,900; reimbursement from insurance, $1,650	
Garage fire: total loss, $750; reimbursement from insurance, $350	
Federal taxes withheld	*8,200*
Estimated tax payments during the year	*900*

INSTRUCTIONS

a Compute the amount of tax the couple owes to the IRS (or the refund due) in good form. Use the tax rate schedule appearing in Exhibit 20-2, and round all calculations to the nearest dollar.

b Suppose that in addition to the foregoing data, you learned that Susan sold a stock investment in December for $10,200. The investment was acquired two years ago for $6,000. Compute the change in the Tanseys' taxable income as a result of the sale.

P20-2 ***Tax computations for individuals***

Tom and Erma Zucker are married and support three young children. The couple also provides all the support for Tom's father, who lives in a neighboring city. The following information has been extracted from the Zuckers' accounting records.

Tom's wages	*$48,410*
Rental income	*6,400*
Contributions to individual retirement plan	*1,200*
Interest on savings accounts	*850*
Prize won at raffle	*2,200*
Long-term capital gain on sale of stock	*27,000*
Short-term capital loss on sale of stock	*5,000*
Interest on municipal bonds	*400*
Dividends from jointly owned stock	*640*
Expenses on rental property	*5,100*
Medical insurance premiums	*1,240*
Medical expenses	*880*
Medicines and drugs	*460*
Property taxes on personal residence	*1,100*
Sales taxes	*180*
State income taxes	*435*
Mortgage interest on personal residence	*3,020*
Interest on car loan	*530*
Charitable contributions	*320*
Unreimbursed portion of casualty loss on residence	*410*
Food and clothing costs	*5,250*
Energy costs for personal residence	*1,450*
Income tax withholdings	*7,650*
Estimated tax payments	*1,600*
Energy tax credits	*630*

The couple plans to file a joint tax return.

INSTRUCTIONS

From the preceding information, determine the amount of tax the couple owes to the IRS (or the refund due). Use the tax rate schedule appearing in Exhibit 20-2, and round all calculations to the nearest dollar. *Hint:* The capital asset and rental property transactions should be listed with other items of gross income.

P20-3 ***Individual tax computation and tax planning***

At the beginning of the current year Dr. Jonathon Wheelwright began to lease a small animal clinic. Jonathon's brother, William, maintains the accounting records for the clinic, which is organized as a sole proprietorship. The following information is available as of December 31.

Client revenues received	*$154,000*
Operating expenses paid	*74,000*
Cash	*7,000*
Client receivables	*38,000*
Accounts payable (for services received)	*5,000*

Dr. Wheelwright is single and claims one personal exemption. He has outside income of $16,000 and itemized deductions of $8,500 in excess of the zero bracket amount. Estimated tax payments during the year amounted to $8,000.

INSTRUCTIONS

a Calculate the practice's net income by using (1) the cash basis of accounting and (2) the accrual basis of accounting. Which method should be used for tax purposes? Why?

b Considering your answer in part (a), determine the amount of tax

Dr. Wheelwright owes to the IRS (or the refund due). Use the tax rate schedules appearing in Exhibit 20-2.

P20-4 ***Capital gains and losses; tax planning***

Chris Martin is a single taxpayer entitled to one personal exemption. During 1983 he earned a $29,000 salary and sold five stock investments, as follows:

Investment	*Cost*	*Date of Purchase*	*Date of Sale*	*Selling Price*
Gadison, Inc.	$4,500	8/1/82	10/15/83	$5,100
Murphy Machinery	8,200	4/15/81	9/8/83	6,000
Rolfe Corporation	7,100	10/12/82	10/10/83	9,800
Tire City	3,400	6/4/82	7/5/83	7,500
Werner and Werner	2,000	4/6/83	8/9/83	1,800

INSTRUCTIONS

a Compute the net long-term capital gain or loss.

b Compute the net short-term capital gain or loss.

c Determine Martin's 1983 adjusted gross income.

d Determine Martin's tax obligation for the year by using the rate schedule appearing in Exhibit 20-2. Martin does not itemize expenses.

e Assuming a fairly stable stock market in October 1983, did Martin make an error in his handling of the investment in Rolfe Corporation? Explain your answer, using numbers when appropriate.

P20-5 ***Tax computations for corporations***

The following information pertains to Bobcat Corporation.

Net sales	*$2,400,000*
Cost of goods sold	*1,280,000*
Selling expenses	*420,000*
Administrative expenses	*500,000*
*Other income**	*50,000*
Other expense	*20,000*
Long-term capital gain on investment sale	*60,000*
Dividends paid to stockholders	*87,000*
Estimated tax payments	*46,000*
Tax credits	*16,500*

** Other income includes $10,000 of interest revenue and $40,000 of dividends.*

INSTRUCTIONS

From the preceding information, calculate the amount of tax Bobcat owes to the IRS (or the refund due). Use the tax rates presented in Exhibit 20-5 for taxable income and, if appropriate, the 28% rate for capital gains.

P20-6 ***Interperiod tax allocation***

Culpepper, Inc., recently completed a financial forecast covering the next four years. Pretax accounting income and taxable income are expected to be as follows:

Year	Pretax Accounting Income	Taxable Income
1	$ 35,000	$ 5,000
2	45,000	35,000
3	70,000	80,000
4	100,000	130,000
	$250,000	$250,000

The variations between pretax accounting income and taxable income are caused solely by timing differences. Culpepper is subject to a 40% tax rate.

INSTRUCTIONS

a Prepare a schedule reporting taxable income and the company's tax obligation for Years 1–4.

b Prepare a schedule reporting pretax accounting income and income tax expense for Years 1–4, assuming the use of interperiod tax allocation.

c Prepare Culpepper's journal entries for Years 1–4 to record (1) income tax expense and (2) income tax payments. Assume that payments occur on March 10 of the following year.

P20-7 ***Tax computation for individuals (alternate to P20-1)***

Bill and Amy Lamkin have three small children and file a joint tax return. Bill is employed as an architect and earns $60,000 per year. Amy is self-employed and conducts ceramics classes in a rented facility across town. Revenues and expenses from her business, which is organized as a sole proprietorship, amounted to $19,600 and $15,400, respectively. The couple earned $1,300 of interest and $500 of dividends from joint investments made throughout the year. The interest includes $400 from bonds issued by the state of West Virginia. Additional information relating to the Lamkins follows.

Nonreimbursed moving expenses related to change in employment	$ 4,800
Hospital and doctor bills	2,300
Health insurance premiums	1,250
Drugs and medicines	350
Interest on personal residence	5,700
License fees for auto and pets	70
Taxes on personal residence	1,200
Contributions to Volunteers of America	850
Casualty losses	
Automobile accident: total loss, $2,500; reimbursement from insurance, $2,200	
Garage fire: total loss, $1,000; reimbursement from insurance, $600	
Federal taxes withheld	10,700
Estimated tax payments during the year	1,600

INSTRUCTIONS

a Compute the amount of tax the couple owes to the IRS (or the refund due) in good form. Use the tax rate schedule appearing in Exhibit 20-2, and round all calculations to the nearest dollar.

b Suppose that in addition to the foregoing data, you learned that Amy sold a stock investment in December for $7,100. The investment was acquired three years ago for $10,900. Compute the change in the Lamkins' taxable income as a result of the sale.

P20-8 ***Tax computations for individuals (alternate to P20-2)***

Ken and Martha Tripott are married and support two young children. The couple also provides all the support for Ken's father (age 66) who lives in a neighboring city. The following information has been extracted from the Tripotts' accounting records.

Ken's salary	*$54,200*
Rental income	*6,000*
Employee travel expenses away from home	*500*
Interest on savings accounts	*1,200*
Dividends from jointly owned stock	*900*
Long-term capital gain on sale of stock	*8,100*
Short-term capital loss on sale of stock	*2,500*
Inheritance received from Martha's aunt	*7,000*
Expenses on rental property	*2,800*
Automobile licenses	*200*
Medical insurance premiums	*1,500*
Medical expenses	*1,800*
Medicines and drugs	*680*
Property taxes on personal residence	*2,400*
Sales taxes	*250*
Uniform costs for Ken	*600*
State income taxes	*1,400*
Mortgage interest on personal residence	*4,500*
Interest on car loan	*900*
Contribution to Goodwill Industries	*1,100*
Unreimbursed portion of casualty loss on personal residence	*400*
Union dues	*300*
Commuting costs to work	*4,600*
Subscriptions to professional journals	*100*
Income tax withholdings	*9,650*
Estimated tax payments	*700*
Energy tax credits	*1,550*

The couple plans to file a joint return.

INSTRUCTIONS

From the preceding information, determine the amount of tax the couple owes to the IRS (or the refund due). Use the tax rate schedule appearing in Exhibit 20-2, and round all calculations to the nearest dollar. *Hint:* The capital asset and rental property transactions should be listed with other items of gross income.

P20-9 ***Capital gains and losses; tax planning (alternate to P20-4)***

Ernie Cronin is a single taxpayer entitled to one personal exemption. During 1983 he earned a $36,000 salary and sold five stock investments, as follows:

Investment	Cost	Date of Purchase	Date of Sale	Selling Price
Ashford Manufacturing	$7,100	6/15/83	12/30/83	$10,800
Continental Automotive	8,900	8/19/82	8/23/83	7,500
Industrial Cleaning	3,300	2/15/81	5/17/83	7,900
Nationwide Carpet Mills	5,800	4/18/83	6/15/83	5,500
Sharp Distributors	2,600	7/15/82	11/11/83	6,200

INSTRUCTIONS

a Compute the net long-term capital gain or loss.

b Compute the net short-term capital gain or loss.

c Determine Cronin's 1983 adjusted gross income.

d Determine Cronin's tax obligation for the year, using the rate schedule appearing in Exhibit 20-2. Round all computations to the nearest dollar. Cronin does not itemize expenses.

e Assuming a fairly stable stock market in August 1983, did Cronin make an error in his handling of the investment in Continental Automotive? Explain your answer, using numbers when appropriate.

P20-10 ***Tax computations for corporations (alternate to P20-5)***

The following information pertains to Cody Corporation.

Net sales	$1,000,000
Cost of goods sold	400,000
Selling expenses	240,000
Administrative expenses	160,000
Other income*	35,000
Other expense	50,000
Long-term capital gain on investment sale	80,000
Dividends paid to stockholders	25,000
Estimated tax payments	38,000
Tax credits	2,900

*Other income includes $5,000 of interest revenue and $30,000 of dividends.

INSTRUCTIONS

From the preceding information, calculate the amount of tax Cody owes to the IRS (or the refund due). Use the tax rates presented in Exhibit 20-5 for taxable income and, if appropriate, the 28% rate for capital gains.

P20-11 ***Interperiod tax allocation (alternate to P20-6)***

Baldwin, Inc., recently completed a financial forecast covering the next four years. Pretax accounting income and taxable income are expected to be as follows:

Year	Pretax Accounting Income	Taxable Income
1	$105,000	$ 60,000
2	125,000	110,000
3	155,000	170,000
4	195,000	240,000
	$580,000	$580,000

The variations between pretax accounting income and taxable income are caused solely by timing differences. Baldwin is subject to a 40% tax rate.

INSTRUCTIONS

a Prepare a schedule reporting taxable income and the company's tax obligation for Years 1–4.

b Prepare a schedule reporting pretax accounting income and income tax expense for Years 1–4, assuming the use of interperiod tax allocation.

c Prepare Baldwin's journal entries for Years 1–4 to record (1) income tax expense and (2) income tax payments. Assume that payments occur on March 10 of the following year.

CASE 20
FEINBERG AND WYSOCKI

Feinberg and Wysocki are planning the first full year of operation of their hardware and small-appliance business. The following budgeted income statement has been assembled.

Sales	$1,000,000
Cost of goods sold	600,000
Gross profit	$ 400,000
Operating expenses	300,000
Net income	$ 100,000

Inventories and cost of goods sold were computed on a first-in, first-out basis. Operating expenses include $30,000 of equipment depreciation, calculated by using the straight-line method with a ten-year service life and no residual value.

The owners are concerned that if they adopt the corporate form of organization, net income would be heavily taxed. The result would be a drain on cash and a need for bank loans to finance inventory buildups. You suggest the following courses of action for tax purposes.

1 Adoption of the weighted-average method of inventory costing. The weighted-average method will produce a $20,000 reduction in the firm's ending inventory valuation.

2 Adoption of the Accelerated Cost Recovery System to permit a faster write-off of equipment cost. The equipment can be written off over five years by using the following percentages:

Year	Percentage Write-off
1	15%
2	22
3	21
4	21
5	21
	100%

INSTRUCTIONS

a Using the corporate tax rates presented in Exhibit 20-5, determine the tax savings that would result in Year 1 by using the suggested courses of action.

b Assuming Feinberg and Wysocki have substantial income from other businesses and investments, should the hardware and appliance operation be organized as a partnership or a corporation? Discuss fully, considering both tax and other aspects of the decision.

21 INTRODUCTION TO MANAGERIAL AND COST ACCOUNTING

LEARNING OBJECTIVES

After reading this chapter you should:

1 *Understand the distinction between financial and managerial accounting.*

2 *Be able to describe planning, control, and decision-making applications of managerial accounting.*

3 *Be familiar with the field of cost accounting, including its recent changes.*

4 *Understand the meaning of direct materials, direct labor, and factory overhead.*

5 *Understand the difference between product and period costs.*

6 *Be familiar with the unique features of the manufacturing balance sheet and income statement, especially the cost-of-goods-manufactured computation.*

7 *Understand variable and fixed cost behavior.*

8 *Be familiar with cost accounting applications in service industries.*

CHAPTER 21

As we move into Chapter 21, a look back reveals that we have presented a wide variety of topics. These topics have ranged in scope from earnings per share to the valuation of inventory on the balance sheet to the impact of inflation on net income. Although diversity appears to have characterized the previous chapters, a substantial amount of this material does have some common ground. This common ground is known as financial accounting. A brief overview of what we have been covering is helpful at this point because of the differences between financial accounting and that emphasized in the remaining chapters of the text, namely, managerial accounting.

FINANCIAL ACCOUNTING

Financial accounting is concerned primarily with external reporting, that is, reporting the results of financial activities to parties outside the firm. Interested recipients of financial accounting information include present and potential owners, suppliers, bankers, and bondholders. Owners and investors use this information in determining whether to buy, hold, or sell ownership interests (e.g., shares of stock). Suppliers, bankers, and bondholders will conduct business with a firm if they expect to be repaid. As a result, these groups find financial accounting information useful in deciding whether or not to extend credit. In general, by communicating such information as net income (income statement) and financial condition (balance sheet), financial accounting strives to present a fair picture of the business in which the foregoing parties have an interest.

Compliance Reporting

In addition to satisfying the needs of owners and creditors, financial accounting is a company's information source for meeting the demands of the many regulatory agencies in our society. Ranging in scope from the powerful Securities and Exchange Commission (SEC) to the local property tax department, these agencies must determine whether a business has complied with the laws and regulations to which it is subject. **Compliance reporting,** as it is known, is frequently troublesome.

To illustrate, we consider the case of General Electric (GE), a manufacturer of household appliances and other electronic products. GE is a large, publicly held corporation and is therefore subject to the Securities Acts of 1933 and 1934. These acts require GE to (1) have its statements certified by a public accounting firm and (2) file a detailed annual report called a 10-K with the SEC. In addition, management must issue an annual report that summarizes financial performance to each of the company's investors. Besides complying with the Securities Acts, GE is also subject to the laws of corporate taxation. Each year the firm must file a tax return with the IRS. Beyond the federal level, GE must satisfy the reporting requirements of the states and cities in which it does business. These entities desire such information as wages paid to local residents for income tax purposes and inventory and plant asset valuations for property tax determination. Information requests by unions, trade associations, and other regulatory agencies further complicate the picture.

Compliance: A costly fact of life

The generation of financial information, along with the preparation and filing of the necessary reports and forms, is a costly and time-consuming process. As an example, Nationwide Homes (a *small* manufacturer of modular homes) reported an estimated salary cost of $72,500 in a single year to comply with the reporting requirements of federal, state, and local governments. The job of filling out forms amounted to a complete year's work for $4\frac{1}{2}$ employees. While this company may be an extreme case, the Small Business Administration recently noted that the federal government could add $1 billion to small-business profits by reducing the paperwork burden by 10%.[1]

Because the information generated for external parties is mandatory, companies should attempt to minimize the cost of its production. Compliance with regulation is a fact of life in today's business environment. This fact, coupled with the objectives of corporate and earnings growth, dictates that external-reporting requirements be satisfied at the lowest possible dollar outlay.

MANAGERIAL ACCOUNTING

As its name implies, **managerial accounting** is oriented toward reporting the results of operations to managers and other interested parties within an organization. In contrast to financial accounting, managerial accounting is often concerned with generating information that pertains to small segments of activity. For example, a manufacturer may produce a quarterly income statement for stockholders that summarizes corporate activity through the financial accounting function. Managers, however, generally require more detail to properly perform their duties. Thus for internal use, income statements are often prepared on a monthly basis and subdivided by divisions, departments, and products.

Managerial accounting is also characterized by an "anything goes" philosophy. To explain, financial accounting reports the operating results of a large variety of businesses to many different parties. So that some uniformity in the reporting and measurement processes is achieved, financial accounting is based on a set of generally accepted accounting principles. As we noted in Chapter 18, the Accounting Principles Board and the Financial Accounting Standards Board have both played a role in establishing a foundation for external reporting. Thus we could say that financial accounting is based heavily on accounting theory and pronouncements of regulatory bodies. In contrast, there are no "rules and regulations" that pertain to managerial accounting. Although there are a number of widely accepted practices, a company can do whatever it pleases when reporting internally to management. For example, if a business desired to generate profitability reports for each of its vending machines, it could do so. Or if a firm wanted to ignore accumulated depreciation on internally distributed balance sheets, that, too, would be permissible. Naturally, certain reporting practices are more beneficial than others; suggested internal reporting guidelines will be presented

[1] "U.S. Paper Burden Cost Firm $72,500," *Dallas Times Herald*, January 5, 1980, p. 11.

shortly. First, however, it is helpful to view three areas in which managerial accounting plays an important role. Consistent with the functions of management, the areas are planning, control, and decision making.

Planning

Virtually every business is formulated to achieve certain goals or objectives. The owners, for example, expect a business to earn a profit and an adequate return on investment. Management strives to produce goods and services that are characterized by quality and dependability. Marketing and the sales force attempt to achieve a reasonable share of the market by attracting faithful and reliable customers.

An organization achieves its objectives by planning. **Planning** involves the formulation of methods and strategies that implement a company's objectives in definite terms. For example, to assist in achieving an adequate return for the owners and an acceptable market share, most businesses establish specified credit policies. The credit policy permits the generation of profitable sales volume without an abnormally high rate of uncollectible accounts. At the same time, if a business's credit policy is consistent with the terms offered by competitors, an acceptable market share can be attained.[2]

Sometimes the objectives of a business are in conflict with one another. As an example, suppose a company decided to enlarge its market share. To attract new customers, the firm might loosen its credit policy. Conceivably, an excessive concentration on obtaining market share could result in high levels of uncollectible accounts, thereby undermining the objective of profitability. A business must continually evaluate its objectives and the policies implemented for their attainment. While it is extremely difficult to eliminate all conflict, harmony and consistency (achieved via intensive planning) help an organization attain optimal results.

Planning takes place in all facets of an organization. Often plans are expressed quantitatively in formal reports known as **budgets.** Budgets are generated for any area that management deems critical and in need of close monitoring and evaluation. Such areas include (but are not limited to) sales, production, capital expenditures, and cash flow. Even entire financial statements can be forecast. While budgeting and forecasting are readily associated with managerial accounting, managerial accounting assists in other planning activities as well. This fact is noted in higher-level accounting courses and in the study of other business disciplines such as quantitative methods, marketing, and finance.

Control

The control function is an outgrowth of planning. No matter how extensively and effectively a business plans, unexpected events can occur. Furthermore, because plans merely reflect an organization's best guess about the future, errors are common.

[2]Many other factors influence market share, such as price, advertising policies, and product quality, to name just a few.

If management is to have insight regarding a company's progress toward its objectives, feedback is a necessity. Often the feedback is in the form of a performance report (see Exhibit 21-1). The performance report pinpoints **variances** or deviations from the budget. The individual in charge of Western Territory operations, for example, analyzes the variances, explains to management why August net income was $6,700 less than budget, and takes corrective action. Corrective action may be in the form of generating sales, cutting costs, or changing personnel. Whatever the form, the common feature is **control.** Control helps bring an organization back on target in terms of achieving the original plan. Control not only assists in eliminating deviations from budgets, but it also renders valuable perspectives for the next round of the planning process. By closely monitoring operations, management often gets a better "feel" of the business, which, in turn, leads to more effective budgeting and policy formulation. The relationship between planning and control is shown in Exhibit 21-2.

Exhibit 21-1

THORNDIKE ENTERPRISES
Western Territory Performance Report
For the Month Ended August 31, 1984

	Budget	Actual	Variance	Explanation
Sales	$68,000	$62,100	$5,900U	
Cost of goods sold	42,500	42,700	200U	
Gross profit	$25,500	$19,400	$6,100U	
Operating expenses				
Salaries	$ 6,400	$ 6,600	$ 200U	
Fuel	3,100	3,800	700U	
Advertising	4,500	4,200	300F	
Rent	2,000	2,000	—	
Total expenses	$16,000	$16,600	$ 600U	
Net income	$ 9,500	$ 2,800	$6,700U	

Note: U = unfavorable; F = favorable.

Decision Making

Managerial accounting also plays an important role in **decision making.** Decision making can be viewed as an integral part of planning and control rather than as a separate, independent management function. The implementation of a successful planning program, for example, requires that managers choose from among alternative objectives and policies. Similarly, the fine tuning and control of operations dictates that appropriate corrective action be selected and implemented.

Exhibit 21-2

Planning and control

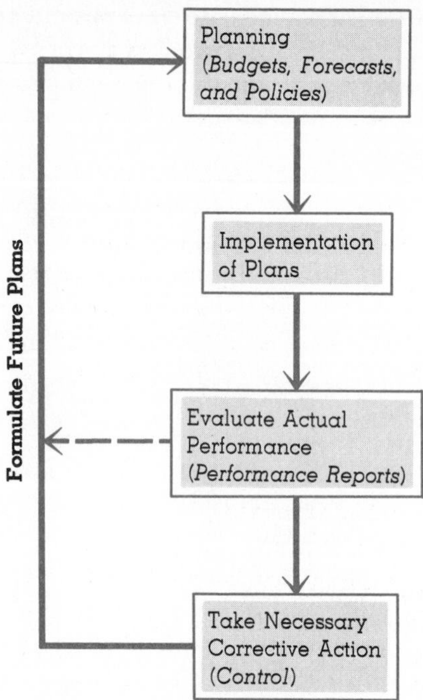

The decision process has far-reaching effects and normally involves much more than just "number crunching." Many managers, especially those involved with accounting and finance, place considerable emphasis on net income, earnings per share, and cash flow, that is, various quantitative measures of performance. Often important qualitative factors such as business ethics, corporate image, and employee morale are mistakenly disregarded.

To illustrate the importance of qualitative factors in decision making, assume that Frank Rosa is employed as a foreman by the Nicholson Manufacturing Company. Management has just decided to install some new machinery in Rosa's department. Although Rosa and his workers will be using the machines, they were not consulted in the selection process. Rosa has received minimal pay increases over the past few years, and with this latest incident, he has an extremely negative attitude about the company. His "I don't give a darn" outlook is reflected in his work and possibly in the work of his subordinates. Since negativism at the top of an organization tends to permeate lower levels of the organizational structure, Rosa's workers are probably disenchanted and have bad morale. Bad morale often affects productivity, which, in turn, impacts profitability. In Nicholson's case it is apparent that employee morale and the involvement of users in the decision process (both qualitative considerations) are indeed important. Effective decision making requires an evaluation of qualitative factors in conjunction with the quantitative outcome.

Internal Information

A business's success in planning, control, and decision making is dependent on the generation and use of **internal information,** that is, information provided for managers within a company. The information desired by management varies greatly from business to business, as the following table indicates.

Corporation	*Internal Information Desired*
Eastern Air Lines	Profitability on flights from New York to Florida
Federated Department Stores	The profit per square foot of selling space
Kellogg Company	Cash outlay necessary to manufacture and introduce a new brand of breakfast cereal
Standard Oil of Ohio	Transport cost per barrel of oil shipped via the Trans-Alaska pipeline

As a part of managerial accounting, the generation of internal information is not mandated by rules and regulations. Much internal information is highly discretionary and generated by choice. The choice is made by the firm in order to meet the needs and desires of its management. Manager Allen, for example, might desire a specific piece of information so that account collections can be monitored. Manager Bronowski, who is responsible for cost incurrence in district 18, will require other types of information. Each manager, then, has unique information needs.

Naturally, some information needs are more important than others. Because of limited resources, an organization normally cannot satisfy all the desires of its executives. As a result, an appropriate guideline must be established for the generation of discretionary information. A suggested approach employs **cost-benefit analysis.** Although it is a difficult process, a manager should compare the cost of generating a particular piece of information against the benefits (added revenues or cost savings) that will be derived by its use. The information should be produced if the benefits exceed the costs. Note that the cost minimization objective utilized for external information is not appropriate here. If management desires to minimize cost, virtually no discretionary information would be generated.

COST ACCOUNTING

All businesses need an intricate knowledge of their costs to help ensure successful performance. As we progress through the study of managerial accounting, you will find that cost analysis can be somewhat complex. Some costs vary as activity changes, while other costs remain constant. Certain costs are relevant when evaluating a decision alternative; others can be ignored. Because of management's dependence on cost information, a brief introduction to cost accounting is a logical starting point for understanding the planning, control, and decision-making functions.

Cost accounting deals with the collection, assignment, and interpreta-

COST ASSIGNMENT AT RCA AND NBC

RCA is a large diversified corporation involved in many different industries related to electronics, broadcasting, and communication. In addition, the company owns The Hertz Corporation, C.I.T. Financial Corporation, and a carpet mill. To satisfy the segment reporting requirements of the Financial Accounting Standards Board, RCA's costs and revenues are divided and assigned as follows:

- *Electronics*
  - *Consumer products and services*
  - *Commercial products and services*
  - *Government systems and services*
- *Broadcasting*
- *Transportation services*
- *Communications*
- *Financial services*
- *Other products and services*

For internal reporting, assignment relates to smaller segments of activity. Consider RCA's broadcasting subsidiary: NBC. NBC's activities include news, sports, movie, documentary, radio, and general-purpose programming. Given the wide diversity of network productions, the firm studies costs and revenues of its shows or series with interesting results. The following is a sample of revenues and costs from 1979–1980.

	Net Revenues	Cost	Profit
AFC Championship Game	$ 3,821,000	$ 3,664,000	$ 157,000
Rose Bowl	4,520,000	3,212,000	1,308,000
Orange Bowl	3,634,000	2,951,000	683,000
AFC regular season (first 8 games)	11,904,000	12,492,000	(588,000)
"Tonight Show" (per broadcast)	190,000	59,000	131,000
Late Movie (per broadcast)	12,000	79,000	(67,000)
"Another World" (per broadcast)	230,000	71,000	159,000
"Days of Our Lives" (per broadcast)	131,000	52,000	79,000
"Hollywood Squares" (per broadcast)	34,000	18,000	16,000

The cost assignment process is necessary for the effective performance of managerial functions. Advertising rates must be established, shows added and dropped, and contracts renegotiated. When Johnny Carson, star of the "Tonight Show," received a $2,000,000 pay increase to $5,000,000, many eyebrows were raised. The new salary won't cost NBC much more than a blink. The added $2,000,000 means that NBC only has to make an extra $8,000 per show.

SOURCE Adapted from the 1981 RCA Corporation Annual Report, "NBC's Day-Night Profits: The $$ from the Shows," and "NBC-TV Sport Profits: The $$ from the Shows." The latter two articles appeared in Variety, May 14 and 28, 1980, respectively.

tion of costs. Cost data are captured by an organization's information system and then assigned to various business segments and activities. Examples of such segments include territories, departments, and products. Activities, on the other hand, may encompass the design of a new advertising campaign, the operation of a summer recreation program by a city, or the implementation of a new all-day ticket plan by an amusement park. The purpose of the assignment process is to answer the age-old question, "How much does it cost?" Once cost is determined, management can proceed with an analysis of the following:

Anticipated cost for various planning needs.
Budgeted versus actual cost for control and evaluation.
Relevant costs of different alternatives for use in decision making.
Costs of producing goods and services for use in pricing and inventory valuation.

A Changing Face

The field of cost accounting has undergone three significant changes in recent years, all of which appear to be interrelated. Historically, cost accounting has had a heavy financial accounting orientation because of its use by manufacturers to determine production costs. The cost of goods produced influences inventory valuation on the balance sheet and cost of goods sold on the income statement. As we have just shown, however, cost accounting also provides information to management for planning, controlling, and decision making. Thus cost accounting is now viewed as an integral part of financial *and* managerial accounting. In many businesses the managerial emphasis is growing because of rampant inflation and dynamic operating environments.

A second change is an expanding use of cost accounting by merchandising and service organizations. Operating efficiency is a goal of all entities; thus cost information is a necessity. Retailers, wholesalers, lawyers, medical practices, governmental units, and other nonmanufacturers all use cost accounting. Although we will be stressing the manufacturer in forthcoming chapters, many of the concepts and practices presented are applicable to merchandising and service businesses as well.

The third change in cost accounting is an increased interface of the cost department with the other functional areas within an entity. The marketing department, for example, uses cost information to assist in the determination of a competitive sales price and appropriate sales strategies. The research and development department analyzes costs in design and production decisions. Finally, the personnel department utilizes cost information to assure compliance with various federal laws and union contracts. Realize that these examples represent a mere sampling of the many and varied applications of this powerful management tool.

Manufacturing Organizations

To illustrate the basics of cost accounting, we turn our attention to manufacturers. Unlike the merchandising company, which purchases goods for resale, a manufacturer acquires raw materials and uses its plant, equipment, and employees to produce a finished product. Because of their production activities, accounting for manufacturers is more complex than accounting for service businesses and merchandisers. Understand, however, that like the other two types of organizations, the manufacturer also has sales, administrative, and financial reporting responsibilities. Thus manufacturers have many of the same accounting practices and problems that service and merchandising concerns have.

Manufacturing Costs

In order to produce finished goods from raw materials, a manufacturer incurs three types of costs: direct materials, direct labor, and factory overhead.

Direct materials

Direct materials include all materials that form an integral part of the finished product and that can be easily traced to the finished product. Several examples of direct materials are major subassemblies such as the seat, back, and frame of a chair; the wheels of a bicycle; the electronic components in a calculator; and the sheet metal and glass in an automobile. Direct materials do not include minor items such as glue, varnish, and nails. Although no one would dispute the importance of these latter items to a finished product, determining and tracing their cost to the units manufactured becomes excessive. Imagine, for example, the difficulty of calculating the cost of glue consumed in producing a single piece of wooden furniture. As a result of these problems, minor materials are normally accounted for as **indirect materials** and treated as part of factory overhead.

Direct labor

Direct labor represents the gross wages of personnel who worked directly on the goods being produced. The wages of assembly-line workers and machine operators are included in this cost classification. A manufacturer employs many other personnel who indirectly contribute to the production of the finished product. Examples include maintenance workers, supervisors, plant guards, and storeroom personnel. Again the same problem arises as arose with indirect materials when attempting to trace the cost of these latter personnel to specific units produced. Thus the wages of factory employees who do not work directly on the product are accounted for as **indirect labor** and included as part of factory overhead.

Factory overhead

Factory overhead, sometimes called manufacturing expense or burden, consists of all factory-related costs other than direct materials and direct labor. Included in this label are indirect materials, indirect labor, factory and equipment depreciation, utilities, taxes, repairs, and maintenance. Observe that factory overhead includes only costs that pertain to manufacturing activity. For example, depreciation on the machinery used in production is properly considered part of overhead, while depreciation on the cars used by the sales staff is not; the latter is a selling expense. Similarly, insurance on the factory facilities is overhead. Insurance on the corporate offices, however, is treated as an administrative expense. Frequently, costs incurred by the company as a whole (e.g., utilities and maintenance) must be allocated among factory overhead, selling expense, and administrative expense to ensure proper accounting. This allocation is necessary because, as we will soon illustrate, the accounting treatment of selling and administrative expenses is considerably different from that for overhead.

Like indirect materials and indirect labor, the other elements of factory overhead are extremely difficult to trace to specific units of production. Consequently, accountants normally estimate the overhead that goes into each product as opposed to determining the actual cost incurred. Overhead is discussed in more detail in Chapter 22.

The three production cost elements are frequently combined by accountants. **Prime cost** consists of costs easily traced to the finished product, that is, direct materials plus direct labor. **Conversion cost** is the cost to convert raw material into finished product, namely, direct labor plus factory overhead.

Financial Statements of a Manufacturer

Direct materials, direct labor, and factory overhead eventually find their way to the financial statements. This process is easy to understand if we first review the accounting practices of a merchandising concern. As a merchandising business acquires goods for resale, the costs incurred are inventoried on the balance sheet as an asset. As sales are made, the inventory is taken off the balance sheet and transferred to the income statement in the form of cost of goods sold. The reason for this procedure is to match the cost of the items sold against related sales revenues.

Essentially the same practice is performed by the manufacturer. Rather than pay significant sums of money to acquire merchandise for resale, the manufacturer purchases direct materials, hires a labor force, and incurs factory overhead. These costs are all put "in process" and eventually result in the manufacture of finished product. At the end of the accounting period the finished goods still owned appear as inventory on the balance sheet, while the units sold are written off via cost of goods sold. This process is illustrated in Exhibit 21-3.

Product and period costs

The costs that go into inventory—direct materials, direct labor, and factory overhead—are termed **product costs.** These costs are attached to the units they helped to produce and are inventoried until the time of sale. The treatment of product costs can be contrasted with that of period costs. **Period costs** are costs that are not inventoried because they do not relate to the acquisition or manufacture of inventory. Instead period costs are expensed when incurred since no future benefits are said to result from their expenditure. For the manufacturer as well as the merchandising operation, period costs consist of selling and administrative expenses. Specific examples include sales commissions, advertising, bad debts, and management salaries.

To better illustrate the difference between product and period costs, assume that Conant Manufacturing Corporation began operations in 1984. Depreciation for the year amounted to $50,000; 50% relates to sales and

Exhibit 21-3

The manufacturing process

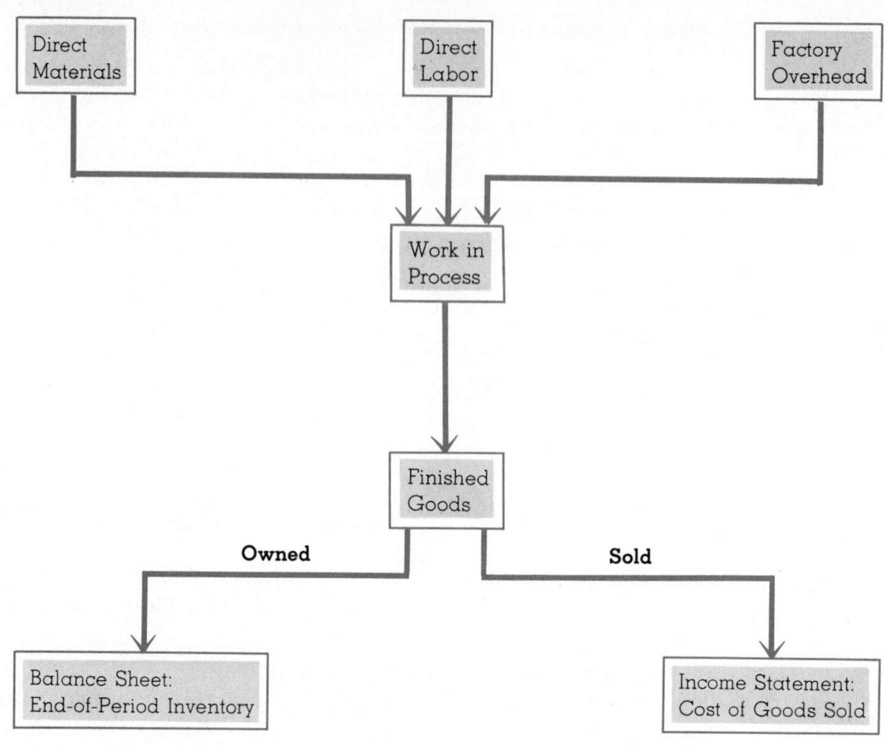

administrative facilities and 50% to the factory. Of the total units produced during the year, 80% were sold in 1984 and 20% in 1985. Assuming no ending work in process, Exhibit 21-4 depicts the timing of the 1984 depreciation on the 1984 and 1985 income statements.

To explain, the selling and administrative costs are expensed when incurred. In contrast, the factory or product cost is attached to inventory. Because only 80% of the production is sold in 1984, \$20,000 (\$25,000 × 0.80) of depreciation is initially written off through cost of goods sold; the remaining \$5,000 is included in the cost of inventory. When the inventory is sold in 1985, the remaining factory depreciation is then released to the income statement. Overall it is a matter of timing. Period costs are expensed when incurred; product costs are written off when the related inventory is sold.

The correct determination of product and period costs is important since errors will likely affect net income and reported inventory valuation. Unfortunately, however, the distinction between these two costs is not always clear. Consider, for example, the salary of the manufacturing vice-president. This individual spends considerable time administering production policies and problems. Should the salary be treated as part of factory overhead or as an administrative operating expense? Perhaps the salary should be allocated between the two cost classifications on some equitable basis. If so, what basis

Exhibit 21-4

Product and period cost timing

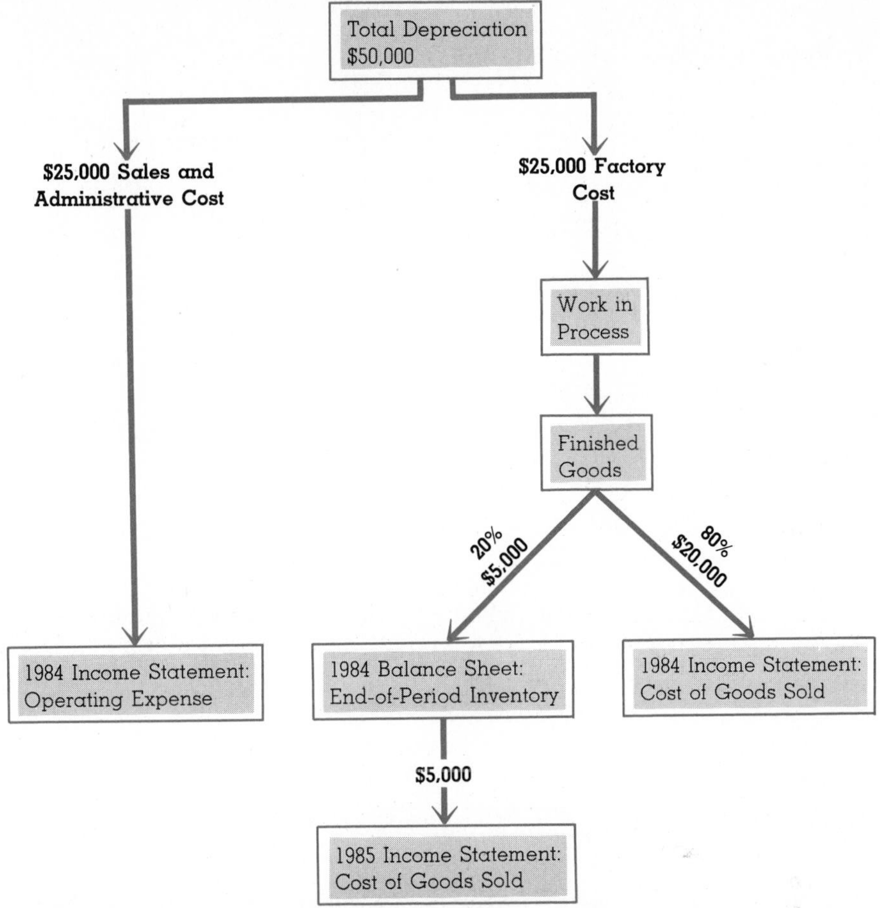

should be used? Although most companies would treat the salary of the manufacturing vice-president as an administrative expense, issues like these are difficult to resolve. Companies must therefore analyze each cost in depth, make an informed decision, and be consistent in their accounting treatment.

Balance sheet

Now that you have a better grasp of production cost flows, we can examine the manufacturer's financial statements. The balance sheet of a manufacturer is identical to that of a merchandising concern, with one exception (see Exhibit 21-5). A merchandiser normally discloses one inventory account: Inventory or Merchandise Inventory. In contrast, businesses engaged in production activities usually establish three inventory accounts: Raw Materials, Work in Process, and Finished Goods.

Raw Materials includes the items to be processed into salable goods. Specifically, the amounts of direct and indirect materials owned are housed in this account. **Work in Process** represents the cost of goods started but not

Exhibit 21-5

Merchandising and manufacturing balance sheets

MERCHANDISING FIRM

Current assets		
Cash		$ 15,000
Accounts receivable	$64,000	
Less: Allowance for bad debts	4,000	60,000
Inventory		190,000
Prepaid expenses		6,000
Total current assets		$271,000

MANUFACTURER

Current assets		
Cash		$ 10,000
Accounts receivable	$ 43,000	
Less: Allowance for bad debts	3,000	40,000
Inventories		
Finished goods	$115,000	
Work in process	51,000	
Raw materials	24,000	190,000
Prepaid expenses		11,000
Total current assets		$251,000

completed. The balance in this account is computed by totaling the direct material, direct labor, and overhead charges that pertain to the production in process. Finally, as its name implies, **Finished Goods** contains the cost of completed production that is owned by a firm.

Balance sheets in practice

Although Raw Materials, Work in Process, and Finished Goods are the traditional splits of inventory accounts, variations are frequently found in practice. For example, consider the disclosures in Exhibit 21-6, which appeared in recent corporate annual reports. These businesses have adapted the general model to meet their own needs. This practice is acceptable providing that it results in a fair measure of financial condition and adequate disclosure.

Income statement

To illustrate the determination of net income for a manufacturer, assume that Golden, Inc., produces paint and various paint supplies. Exhibit 21-7 contrasts Golden's income statement with that of Meadow Paint and Wallpaper, a retailer.

Notice that the two income statements are very similar. Meadow's cost of goods sold is computed on the basis of the firm's beginning and ending inventories and net purchases. Golden, on the other hand, does not acquire goods for resale; it makes them. Thus the cost of goods manufactured replaces net purchases. Of the three inventory accounts carried by a manufacturer, only Finished Goods is used for the cost-of-goods-sold calculation. Why? The finished goods of a manufacturer correspond to the merchandise inventory of a retailer (or wholesaler), as both inventories are offered for sale.

Exhibit 21-6

Inventory disclosures (in millions)

PHILIP MORRIS INCORPORATED

Inventories	
Leaf tobacco	$2,113.3
Other raw materials	329.0
Finished goods and work in process	510.4
Housing programs under construction*	237.3
	$3,190.0

THE PILLSBURY COMPANY

Inventories	
Grain	$ 61.0
Finished products	217.0
Raw materials, containers, and supplies	140.1
	$418.1

WARNER COMMUNICATIONS INC.

Inventories	
Consumer electronics	$233.0
Film productions for theatrical exhibition	
Released, less amortization	42.8
Completed and not released	19.8
In process	—
Film rights for television exhibition, less amortization	74.8
Direct response marketing	58.0
Records, tapes, magazines, books, and other	78.9
	$507.3

Note: *Further information relating to these corporations appears in Exhibit 16-1.*
**Philip Morris owns Mission Viejo Company, a land development corporation with operations in California and Colorado.*

Cost of goods manufactured (see the supporting schedule in Exhibit 21-7) is derived by examining the three cost elements of a manufactured product. Direct materials used, direct labor, and factory overhead are summed to arrive at the total production costs for the period. Next, the beginning and ending work in process inventories are respectively added and subtracted to generate cost of goods manufactured. The reason for involving work in process can be described as follows. At the beginning of the accounting period Golden had $7,000 of goods in production. During the period $282,000 of manufacturing costs were incurred. Therefore $289,000 ($7,000 + $282,000) of costs were "in process." If $12,000 of production remains in process at the end of the period, $277,000 ($289,000 − $12,000)

Exhibit 21-7

Income statements of a merchandising firm and a manufacturer

MEADOW PAINT AND WALLPAPER
(Merchandiser)
Income Statement

Sales		$224,000
Cost of goods sold		
Beginning inventory	$ 36,000	
Net purchases	161,000	
Goods available for sale	$197,000	
Less: Ending inventory	55,000	
Cost of goods sold		142,000
Gross profit		$ 82,000
Operating expenses		
Selling	$ 46,000	
Administrative	24,000	70,000
Net income		$ 12,000

GOLDEN, INC.
(Manufacturer)
Income Statement

Sales		$356,000
Cost of goods sold		
Beginning finished goods inventory	$ 45,000	
Cost of goods manufactured	277,000	
Goods available for sale	$322,000	
Less: Ending finished goods inventory	61,000	
Cost of goods sold		261,000
Gross profit		$ 95,000
Operating expenses		
Selling	$ 58,000	
Administrative	29,000	87,000
Net income		$ 8,000

GOLDEN, INC.
Schedule of Cost of Goods Manufactured

Direct materials used		
Beginning direct materials inventory	$ 21,000	
Net purchases	109,000	
Direct materials available	$130,000	
Less: Ending direct materials inventory	28,000	
Direct materials used		$102,000
Direct labor		79,000
Factory overhead		
Indirect materials	$ 6,000	
Indirect labor	36,000	
Utilities	15,000	
Depreciation: factory	10,000	
Depreciation: equipment	13,000	
Taxes	17,000	
Insurance	4,000	101,000
Total manufacturing costs		$282,000
Add: Beginning work in process inventory		7,000
		$289,000
Less: Ending work in process inventory		12,000
Cost of goods manufactured		$277,000

of goods must have been completed. Stated differently, $277,000 represents the cost of goods manufactured. This amount is subsequently transferred to the income statement to compute cost of goods sold.

COST BEHAVIOR

The manufacturing, selling, and administrative costs of an organization are not always presented in the traditional balance sheet and income statement formats for purposes of planning and control. Frequently, costs are subdivided and studied in terms of their behavior. As we noted earlier, some costs vary with changes in activity, while others remain constant. To illustrate the influence of cost behavior on the analysis of operations, assume the following information was excerpted from a performance report.

	Budget	*Actual*	*Variance*
Direct materials used	$60,000	$66,000	$6,000U

At first glance it appears that performance has been unsatisfactory. Suppose, however, the budget called for the manufacture of 10,000 units, each of which requires $6 of direct materials. If actual production amounted to 11,000 units because of superior labor efficiency, direct material use was right on target, that is, $6 per unit. As activity increases, the total amount of direct materials consumed will follow the same pattern. Although we will study cost behavior in depth in a later chapter, a brief introduction is necessary at this point to better understand the material that follows.

Variable Costs

Variable costs vary in direct proportion to a change in an activity base. The activity base may be sales, production, miles driven, students in a university, hours of machine operation, or any other measure of volume. To illustrate the concept of a variable cost, assume the Green Company is a manufacturer of ball-point pens. The firm's top selling model, the Smoothwriter, requires $0.30 of direct materials. Green sells the Smoothwriter for $1.20 and pays its sales force a 5% commission. Two activity bases are involved in this example. The cost of direct materials used varies with production, while total sales commissions vary with the number of pens sold. This distinction is shown below. Observe that the variable cost varies in total, but the cost per unit remains the same.

Direct Materials			*Sales Commissions*		
Number of Pens Produced	**Material Cost per Pen**	**Total Material Cost**	**Number of Pens Sold**	**Commission per Pen***	**Sales Commissions**
50,000	$0.30	$15,000	45,000	$0.06	$2,700
60,000	0.30	18,000	55,000	0.06	3,300
70,000	0.30	21,000	65,000	0.06	3,900
80,000	0.30	24,000	75,000	0.06	4,500

*$1.20 × 0.05 = $0.06.

In addition to direct materials and sales commissions, other common examples of variable costs include direct labor, supplies, and fuel.

Fixed Costs

Unlike variable costs, **fixed costs** remain constant in total when changes in the activity base occur. Examples of fixed costs include management salaries, advertising, straight-line depreciation, property taxes, and insurance. Because total fixed costs remain constant, the fixed cost per unit fluctuates. As activity increases, the fixed cost per unit decreases since a constant dollar amount is spread over a greater number of units. Opposite results occur when activity decreases.

To illustrate fixed cost behavior, we will continue the previous example. Assume the Green Company uses an $85,000 machine in its manufacturing activities. The machine has a $5,000 residual value and a 5-year service life. Thus annual straight-line depreciation amounts to $16,000 [($85,000 − $5,000) ÷ 5]. On the basis of different production levels, the depreciation per pen will be as follows:

Annual Depreciation	*Number of Pens Produced*	*Depreciation per Pen*
$16,000	50,000	$0.32
16,000	60,000	0.267
16,000	70,000	0.229
16,000	80,000	0.20

From the figures above it is apparent that the fixed cost per unit (i.e., depreciation per pen) is relevant at one activity level and *only* one activity level. That is, the calculated fixed cost per unit is true only at the level of activity used as the denominator base. The multiplication of a $0.20-per-pen depreciation rate, for example, by production levels other than 80,000 fails to yield the total depreciation charge of $16,000. When dealing with fixed costs, it is usually safer to deal in terms of total costs as opposed to unit costs.

COST ACCOUNTING: SERVICE APPLICATIONS

As we noted earlier, cost accounting is being used by an increasing number of service organizations. Banks, for example, use cost accounting to study the profitability of handling customer accounts. The costs of processing checks and deposits, issuing bank statements, and transferring funds are continually examined in relation to the revenues generated (via service charges and compensating balances). Close monitoring of checking account costs is very important because of the volume of accounts handled and the competitive nature of the banking field. Service charges that are too low will lead to unprofitable operations; in contrast, fees that are too high can result in a loss of customers.

Another application of cost accounting in a service business is flight costing by airlines. By studying passenger load rates and the costs of fuel, flight crews, meals, and landing fees, airlines can determine the profitability of individual flights. The profitability information can then be used to determine whether to:

Expand or discontinue service.
Service the route with larger or smaller aircraft.
Institute marketing programs such as discounted fares, unlimited stopovers, and vacation packages to attract a larger percentage of passenger traffic.

Nonprofit Organizations

Banks, airlines, and many other service businesses are established to make a profit. A number of service enterprises, however, are created without a profit motive to meet the needs of society. These **nonprofit organizations** include numerous colleges and universities, charitable organizations, hospitals, civic and social organizations, and churches. Nonprofit organizations are not evaluated on "the bottom line;" rather they are judged on the amount and quality of services rendered.

Despite the lack of a profit motive, managers of nonprofit organizations must still plan, control, and make decisions to allocate their resources wisely. These individuals need cost information and, hence, cost accounting. Cost accounting can be used by a college or university to study the feasibility of adding a new wing on a dormitory or offering a new course or program. Hospitals employ cost accounting to determine the costs of nursing, pharmacy, laboratory, housekeeping, and other services so that patient billing rates can be established. Even voluntary health and welfare organizations utilize cost accounting to investigate the costs of expanding counseling programs for juvenile delinquents and drug abuse.

Despite the large number of potential applications, the use of cost accounting in nonprofit organizations is handicapped because of unique measurement problems, specifically the evaluation of performance and the valuation of service. Consider net income, for example. The absence of a profit thrust makes the measurement and meaning of the earnings figure pointless. In fact, if revenues exceed costs, many individuals argue that the nonprofit organization (e.g., a hospital) is charging excessive rates for the services provided. Gross and Jablonsky note:

> *So long as the nonprofit organization has sufficient resources to carry out its objectives, there is no real need or justification for "making a profit" or having an excess of income over expense. While a prudent board may want to have a "profit" in order to provide for a rainy day in the future, the principal objective of the board is to fulfill the functions for which the organization was founded. A surplus or profit is only incidental.*[3]

[3]Malvern Gross, Jr., and Stephen Jablonsky, *Principles of Accounting and Financial Reporting for Nonprofit Organizations* (New York: Ronald Press, 1979), pp. 16–17.

To further complicate the picture, a number of nonprofit enterprises do not charge for their services. Consider your local boys' club, marriage counseling service, or suicide prevention center. These organizations provide an essential service; yet valuing their services in terms of dollars and cents is difficult, if not impossible.

In spite of these problems, managers of nonprofit organizations have found that cost accounting is still a very helpful tool. Whether or not an entity is profit making, a manager's knowledge and use of cost information assists in the attainment of effective and efficient operations.

KEY TERMS AND CONCEPTS

QUESTIONS

Q21-1 Discuss the major differences between financial and managerial accounting.

Q21-2 The generation of information is not cost-free. Discuss the difference in cost philosophies of producing external and internal information.

Q21-3 The sales manager of Snyder Company desires to maximize the firm's market share and has proposed a loosening of credit terms. Discuss the conflict that might arise between the sales manager and the vice-president of finance.

Q21-4 What is the purpose of issuing performance reports?

Q21-5 In addition to the quantitative outcome, what other factors should be considered in the decision process? Why?

Q21-6 Is cost accounting a part of financial accounting or managerial accounting? Explain.

Q21-7 What are the three cost elements of a manufactured product?

Q21-8 Why are indirect materials and indirect labor treated as part of factory overhead?

Q21-9 Differentiate between and discuss the accounting treatment of product and period costs.

Q21-10 Dave Malloy, an engineer at Lexton Manufacturing, has just spent an exhausting weekend analyzing utility costs. Management desired to know the approximate percentage of electricity consumed by the company's (1) sales and administrative offices and (2) manufacturing plant. Dave mumbled under his breath, "Who cares? Utility cost is utility cost." Explain to Malloy why his analysis is needed.

Q21-11 Discuss the balance sheet differences between a merchandiser and a manufacturer.

Q21-12 Blakely Manufacturing and Diaz Wholesalers both employ a sales manager. Discuss the differences, if any, in the accounting treatment of the salaries of the two sales managers.

Q21-13 A student once commented: "A nonprofit organization is not expected to make a profit; thus it has no need for cost accounting." Evaluate the student's comment.

EXERCISES

E21-1 The Takano Company is a manufacturer in the electronics industry. Much of Takano's work is special order and is performed on a contract basis. During Weeks 26 and 27, four contracts were in production, as shown below.

Purchaser	*Contract No.*	*Value*
Benton Electronics	A1596	$15,800
Ronald Semiconductor	A1597	62,400
B&J, Inc.	A1601	35,500
Krauss Radio	A1603	10,000

Howard Webster, Takano's production supervisor, reports to the vice-president of manufacturing. During Week 26 Webster supervised all four contracts in addition to performing other duties related to production. During Week 27, however, Webster devoted all of his efforts to contract A1601 because it was two weeks behind schedule.

a How should Webster's salary be accounted for in Week 26? Why?
b In theory, how should Webster's salary be accounted for in Week 27? Why?

E21-2 Indicate which of the following are period costs and which are product costs.

a Salary of production supervisor
b Delivery costs related to the sale of finished goods inventory
c Depreciation expense on office equipment
d Supplies used in the manufacturing process
e Salary of the vice-president in charge of production
f Property taxes paid on land held for future plant expansion

E21-3 The Showcase Manufacturing Company indicated the following inventories on recent balance sheets.

	For the Year Ended	
	Dec. 31, 1984	Dec. 31, 1983
Raw materials	$ 67,400	$ 72,200
Work in process	148,900	167,600
Finished goods	43,900	51,700

Additional information for 1984 follows.

Sales	$560,000
Total manufacturing costs incurred	287,000
Operating expenses	49,200

Compute cost of goods manufactured, cost of goods sold, and net income for 1984.

E21-4 The following information was taken from the ledger of Washington Company.

Direct labor	$ 78,000
Selling expenses	28,000
Sales	275,000
Finished goods	
Jan. 1	100,000
Dec. 31	127,000
Direct materials on hand	
Jan. 1	28,000
Dec. 31	36,000
Administrative expenses	41,000
Work in process	
Jan. 1	18,000
Dec. 31	6,000
Purchases of direct materials	71,000
Depreciation: factory	12,000
Factory supplies used	15,000
Indirect labor	23,000
Factory taxes	10,000
Factory utilities	8,000

Prepare the following:

a A schedule of cost of goods manufactured for the year ended December 31.
b An income statement for the year ended December 31.

E21-5 The Bally Manufacturing Corporation accidentally understated its work in process inventory at the end of the current accounting period. As a result of this error, determine the effect (understated, overstated, or no effect) on each of the following:

a Total current assets
b Cost of goods manufactured of the current period
c Gross profit of the current period
d Net income of the current period

E21-6 Logo Sign Manufacturing Company's income statement revealed cost of goods manufactured of $136,420. However, the following errors were noted.

a Ending work in process was understated by $4,650.
b A $6,500 utility bill was charged as an operating expense. Company engi-

neers estimate that 40% of the bill should have been allocated to the factory.

c Depreciation expense of $1,250 related to delivery equipment was included in factory overhead.

d The janitor's $8,500 salary was classified as direct labor. The janitor worked only in the manufacturing plant.

Determine the correct cost of goods manufactured.

E21-7 The planning department of Herzog Company has prepared budgets for three probable levels of operation for the upcoming year. Because of their significance, the following costs have been selected for study.

	LEVEL OF ACTIVITY (UNITS)					
	10,000		12,000		15,000	
	Total	Per Unit	Total	Per Unit	Total	Per Unit
Direct materials	$ 90,000	$ 9.00	$108,000	$ 9.00	$135,000	$ 9.00
Direct labor	120,000	12.00	144,000	12.00	180,000	12.00
Advertising	300,000	30.00	300,000	25.00	300,000	20.00
Management salaries	180,000	18.00	180,000	15.00	180,000	12.00
	$690,000	$69.00	$732,000	$61.00	$795,000	$53.00

Addressing his executive staff, Herzog's president commented: "It's imperative that we implement cost-cutting programs to reduce advertising and management salaries. As shown by the per-unit costs, these variable costs are destroying our profit margins. Our fixed costs of direct materials and direct labor (constant at $9.00 and $12.00 per unit, respectively) also need some improvement. I know our competitors are paying approximately $19.25 for these same two production factors."

Comment on the president's remarks.

E21-8 The following information was extracted from a performance report of the mixing department of Garner Manufacturing Corporation.

	Budget	Actual	Variance
Direct materials used	$ 21,000	$ 19,800	$ 1,200F
Direct labor	126,000	115,500	10,500F
			$11,700F

The head of the mixing department is about to receive a bonus based on his fine performance. You have gathered the following information:

a The budget was based on 7,000 units of activity. Actual activity amounted to 5,500 units because of problems in securing needed raw materials.

b The budgeted and actual labor rates amounted to $6 per hour.

Evaluate the performance of the mixing department. Is the true variance $11,700F? Explain.

E21-9 Consider the following nonprofit organizations and suggest several measures for performance evaluation. As an example, a police department could be evaluated on the number of citations issued, number of arrests made, the ratio of local residents to police personnel, and so on.

a A state university
b Your local library
c A hospital
d A drug abuse center

PROBLEMS

P21-1 *Quantitative and qualitative decision factors*

Templeton Manufacturing is in the process of choosing the location for a new plant that will produce rolled steel. Three locations are under consideration: Lawrence, Kansas; Youngstown, Ohio; and Plains, Georgia. Lawrence is the company's corporate headquarters and the home of other Templeton manufacturing facilities. Management feels that the firm would experience certain cost savings by locating an additional plant here.

Youngstown, Ohio, is being considered to take advantage of the city's skilled (but highly unionized) labor force. Many steelworkers were recently left without jobs when competitors closed three plants. Because of severe northern winters, it will take longer to build a plant in Youngstown. Plant management would be permanently transferred from Templeton's Los Angeles facility.

A feasibility study has indicated that a plant could be constructed in Plains, Georgia, in fourteen months, faster than in either of the other two locations. Templeton is strongly considering Plains because of economic concessions made by the city government to attract industry. Because of a lack of other similar plants in the area, extensive employee training programs would have to be developed. In addition, the company would have to transfer approximately 150 hourly employees from other Templeton facilities. Plant management would still come from Los Angeles.

INSTRUCTIONS

a List several quantitative factors that Templeton should consider in the plant location decision.
b List several qualitative factors that Templeton should consider.

P21-2 *Analysis of product cost error*

The Marshall Company began to manufacture a new product in January 1983. The following costs were incurred in the production of 12,000 units.

Direct materials	*$ 48,000*
Direct labor	*72,000*
Overhead	*36,000*
	$156,000

Demand was below expectations and by the end of 1983 production was stopped. Marshall sold 9,000 units in 1983 and 2,000 units in 1984. The firm's accountant recently discovered that Sales Salaries Expense was accidentally debited in 1983 for $18,000 of wages paid to assembly-line workers.

INSTRUCTIONS
Assuming no work in process at the end of 1983, determine the impact and amount of the error on the following:

a 1983 ending finished goods inventory and net income
b 1984 ending finished goods inventory and net income

P21-3 ***Cost classification***

The Robin Hill Company manufactures corrugated cardboard boxes for industrial use. For each of the costs listed below, determine cost behavior (variable or fixed) and whether the cost is a product or a period cost. If a product cost, identify the cost as direct materials (DM), direct labor (DL), or factory overhead (FOH). The first cost is presented as an example.

Cost	*Variable/Fixed*	*Product/Period*	*DM/DL/FOH*
a Fire insurance on the factory	Fixed	Product	FOH
b Rolls of paper used in production			
c Ink consumed in printing operations			
d Salary of the sales manager			
e Hourly wages paid to folding machine operators			
f Auditor's fees			
g Salaries of inspection personnel			
h Units-of-output depreciation on cutting machine			
i Air-conditioning costs of executive offices			
j Machine lubricant			
k Machine repair costs			
l Freight-out			

P21-4 ***Straightforward manufacturing statements***

The following information was obtained from the records of Susat Enterprises for the current year ended December 31.

Cash	$ 39,600
Accounts receivable	88,400
Accounts payable	44,700
Direct materials	
Jan. 1	140,000
Dec. 31	160,000
Work in process	
Jan. 1	30,000
Dec. 31	84,000
Finished goods	
Jan. 1	218,000
Dec. 31	310,000
Indirect labor	100,000
Direct labor	285,000
Factory supplies used	42,000
Freight on direct material purchases	18,000
Advertising expense	32,000
Salesmen's salaries	50,000
Administrative salaries	82,000
Bad debts expense	10,000
Allowance for bad debts	6,200
Direct material purchases	275,000
Direct material returns	13,000
Sales	942,000

The costs below were incurred by the factory, sales, and administrative facilities. The allocations shown are in effect.

	Costs	Factory	Sales	Administration
Utilities	$ 50,000	60%	10%	30%
Taxes	70,000	70%	15%	15%
Insurance	20,000	60%	20%	20%
Depreciation	60,000	70%	10%	20%
	$200,000			

INSTRUCTIONS

a Prepare a schedule of cost of goods manufactured in good form.

b Prepare an income statement in good form.

c If Susat's factory supplies on hand on December 31 totaled $54,000, compute the company's total current assets at the end of the period.

P21-5 ***Manufacturing statements: FIFO inventory valuation***

The following information was obtained from the records of Seaver Corporation for the current year ended December 31.

Direct materials		
Beginning inventory	*900 units @ $9.00*	
Purchase no. 1	*1,500 units @ $9.10*	
Purchase no. 2	*2,000 units @ $9.25*	
Payroll costs		
Direct labor	*$63,200*	
Indirect labor	*21,900*	
Administrative salaries	*48,600*	
Sales salaries	*34,700*	
Other costs		
Building depreciation (60% of the building is devoted to production activities, with the remainder split equally between sales and administration)		*$25,000*
Royalties paid for production patents ($0.75 per unit produced)		*?*
Other factory costs		*9,400*
Other selling expenses		*11,300*
Other administrative expenses		*16,500*

Seaver's beginning work in process inventory totaled $12,000; the ending work in process was $8,000. During the accounting period the finished goods inventory rose from 600 units to 1,100 units. Additionally, the firm sold 800 units at $150 each.

Seaver uses the FIFO method of inventory valuation for direct materials. Direct materials consumed during the period totaled 2,600 units.

INSTRUCTIONS

a Calculate the number of units produced during the accounting period.
b Compute Seaver's cost of goods manufactured.

P21-6 ***Working backward to find manufacturing costs***

The following information pertains to Companies A, B, and C.

	Company A	*Company B*	*Company C*
Cost of goods manufactured	$?	$13,800	$14,000
Operating expenses	5,000	?	?
Purchases of direct materials	10,000	?	7,700
Factory overhead	4,000	4,400	3,500
Work in process, Jan. 1	1,400	?	1,900
Work in process, Dec. 31	3,000	1,800	2,800
Sales	19,500	?	15,200
Gross profit	?	5,600	?
Direct materials, Jan. 1	3,100	3,900	?
Direct materials, Dec. 31	5,500	6,200	2,400
Finished goods, Jan. 1	4,100	4,000	?
Finished goods, Dec. 31	7,400	?	4,900
Net income	?	1,500	(400)
Direct labor	6,000	3,600	?
Direct materials used	?	5,100	6,400
Cost of goods sold	12,700	12,300	11,800

INSTRUCTIONS

Find the unknowns by preparing a schedule of cost of goods manufactured and an income statement for each company.

P21-7 ***Estimate of ending inventories***

The Breezewood Corporation's main manufacturing plant was destroyed by fire on March 31. Fortunately, all raw material inventories were stored in an adjacent warehouse. Marie Ippolito, the company's chief financial officer, has gathered the following information in an attempt to estimate the work in process and finished goods inventories destroyed.

Number of common shares outstanding: 16,000.
Beginning inventories: work in process, $24,000; finished goods, $46,000.
Sales through March 31: $450,000.
Direct labor: $70,000.
Gross profit rate: 40%.
Goods available for sale: $310,000.
Administrative expenses average 25% of total operating expenses.
Direct materials used average 30% of prime cost.
Overhead averages 60% of total manufacturing costs incurred.

Earnings per share for the first quarter amounted to $2.50. Breezewood expects full reimbursement from its insurance company for any losses suffered.

INSTRUCTIONS

Estimate the work in process and finished goods inventories destroyed. *Hint:* Prepare a detailed schedule of cost of goods manufactured and an income statement for the quarter ended March 31.

P21-8 ***Manufacturing statements and cost behavior***

The Anteau Company, a manufacturer of reading lamps, began operations on January 1 of the current year. Each lamp requires the following variable costs:

Direct materials	$12
Direct labor	8
Variable factory overhead	6
	$26

The fixed costs incurred during the current year are shown below.

Factory	$ 45,000
Selling	20,000
Administrative	65,000
	$130,000

Production totaled 20,000 lamps, of which 16,000 were sold at $55 each. Assume no work in process. Anteau carries its finished goods inventory at the average unit cost of production.

INSTRUCTIONS

a Determine the cost of Anteau's ending finished goods inventory.
b Present Anteau's income statement for the current year ended December 31.
c Suppose Anteau stepped up production to meet increased demand. If the present cost behavior patterns continue, determine the effect of the new production policy on the manufactured cost per lamp. Explain the reasoning behind your answer.

P21-9 ***Forecasted manufacturing statements and cost behavior***

The Harbour Company incurred the following costs during 1983 when 50,000 units were produced and sold.

Direct materials used	*$ 62,500*
Direct labor	*105,000*
Factory overhead	
Variable	*17,000*
Fixed	*65,000*
Selling expenses	
Variable	*7,500*
Fixed	*80,000*
Fixed administrative expenses	*40,000*
Total costs	*$377,000*

Total sales were $462,500; there were no beginning inventories. At the end of 1983, 3,000 units of direct material remained in inventory. Five units of direct material are required to produce one unit of finished product.

Management is in the process of establishing the 1984 operating plan. Harbour anticipates selling 90% of its budgeted production of 60,000 units. All cost behavior patterns observed in 1983 are expected to reoccur in 1984. The only exception is variable factory overhead; a $0.10 per unit increase is assured. The selling price will remain the same.

INSTRUCTIONS

a Prepare a schedule of cost of goods manufactured for 1984. Assume no work in process inventories.

b Prepare an income statement for 1984. Finished goods inventory will be carried at the average unit cost of production.

c The purchasing department wants to increase the direct materials inventory to 5,000 units by the end of 1984. Calculate required direct material purchases (in dollars) during 1984.

P21-10 ***Analysis of product cost error (alternate to P21-2)***

The Seaton Company began to manufacture a new product in January 1983. The following costs were incurred in the production of 40,000 units.

Direct materials	*$204,000*
Direct labor	*350,000*
Overhead	*384,000*
	$938,000

Demand was below expectations, and by the end of 1983 production was stopped. Seaton sold 24,000 units in 1983 and 13,000 units in 1984. The firm's accountant recently discovered that Store Supplies Expense was accidentally debited in 1983 for $28,000 of direct materials used in production.

INSTRUCTIONS

Assuming no work in process at the end of 1983, determine the impact and amount of the error on the following:

a 1983 ending finished goods inventory and net income

b 1984 ending finished goods inventory and net income

P21-11 ***Cost classification (alternate to P21-3)***

E. Turner & Sons manufactures barbecue grills. For each of the costs listed below, determine cost behavior (variable or fixed) and whether the cost is a product or a period cost. If a product cost, identify the cost as direct materials (DM), direct labor (DL), or factory overhead (FOH). The first cost is presented as an example.

Cost	*Variable/Fixed*	*Product/Period*	*DM/DL/FOH*
a Property taxes on the factory	Fixed	Product	FOH
b Salary of the production supervisor			
c Freight costs on shipments to out-of-state customers			
d Wages of assembly personnel			
e Grill tops and frames			
f Straight-line depreciation on factory equipment			
g Paint used to touch up production scratches			
h Miscellaneous fees paid for a new grill design			
i Heating costs for manufacturing facilities			
j Wheels attached to portable models			
k Fees paid for plant security			
l Advertising costs for new product line			

P21-12 ***Straightforward manufacturing statements (alternate to P21-4)***

The following information was obtained from the records of Milligan Enterprises for the current year ended December 31.

Cash	*$ 71,500*
Accounts receivable	*93,700*
Accounts payable	*59,500*
Direct materials	
Jan. 1	*64,100*
Dec. 31	*78,300*
Work in process	
Jan. 1	*11,400*
Dec. 31	*15,800*
Finished goods	
Jan. 1	*77,400*
Dec. 31	*85,900*
Indirect labor	*53,500*
Direct labor	*194,600*
Factory supplies used	*20,000*
Freight on direct material purchases	*2,400*
Advertising expense	*82,600*
Sales commissions	*41,500*
Administrative salaries	*50,000*
Bad debts expense	*5,500*
Allowance for bad debts	*8,900*
Direct material purchases	*187,500*
Direct material returns	*2,200*
Sales	*847,500*

The costs below were incurred by the factory, sales, and administrative facilities. The allocations shown are in effect.

	Costs	*Factory*	*Sales*	*Administration*
Taxes	$ 18,000	70%	10%	20%
Insurance	12,000	60%	20%	20%
Utilities	30,000	80%	10%	10%
Depreciation	100,000	65%	15%	20%
	$160,000			

INSTRUCTIONS

a Prepare a schedule of cost of goods manufactured in good form.
b Prepare an income statement in good form.
c If Milligan's factory supplies on hand on December 31 totaled $70,400, compute the company's total current assets at the end of the period.

P21-13 ***Manufacturing statements: LIFO inventory valuation (alternate to P21-5)***
The following information was obtained from the records of Welnack Corporation for the current year ended December 31.

Direct materials		
Beginning inventory	*2,700 units @ $6.00*	
Purchase no. 1	*3,400 units @ $6.20*	
Purchase no. 2	*2,500 units @ $6.50*	
Payroll costs		
Direct labor	*$95,700*	
Indirect labor	*37,600*	
Administrative salaries	*48,800*	
Sales salaries	*57,300*	
Other costs		
Building depreciation (70% of the building is devoted to production activities, with the remainder split equally between sales and administration)		*$42,000*
Royalties paid for production patents ($0.90 per unit produced)		*?*
Other factory costs		*14,500*
Other selling expenses		*18,900*
Other administrative expenses		*23,400*

Welnack's beginning work in process inventory totaled $15,600; the ending work in process was $12,900. During the accounting period the finished goods inventory declined from 1,750 units to 1,350 units. Additionally, the firm sold 1,100 units at $225 each.

Welnack uses the LIFO method of inventory valuation for direct materials. Direct materials consumed during the period totaled 2,800 units.

INSTRUCTIONS

a Calculate the number of units produced during the accounting period.
b Compute Welnack's cost of goods manufactured.

P21-14 ***Manufacturing statements and cost behavior (alternate to P21-8)***

The Hampton Company, a manufacturer of decorative accessories for the home, began operations on January 1 of the current year. One of its products, a metal sculpture, requires the following variable costs:

Direct materials	*$21*
Direct labor	*18*
Variable factory overhead	*9*
	$48

The fixed costs incurred during the current year are shown below.

Factory	*$13,125*
Selling	*6,600*
Administrative	*18,750*
	$38,475

Production totaled 1,500 sculptures, of which 1,200 were sold at $95 each. Assume no work in process. Hampton carries its finished goods inventory at the average unit cost of production.

INSTRUCTIONS

a Determine the cost of Hampton's ending finished goods inventory.
b Present Hampton's income statement for the current year ended December 31.

c Suppose Hampton stepped up production to meet increased demand. If present cost behavior patterns continue, determine the effect of the new production policy on (1) the $48-per-unit variable cost and (2) the fixed cost per unit. Explain the reasoning behind your answer.

CASE 21
VICEROY CORPORATION

The Viceroy Corporation is a small manufacturer of workshop tools. The company generates an adequate profit by operating a single eight-hour shift at its Lincoln plant. Presently, the plant produces 380,000 units of finished product per year. Although various products are involved, production personnel estimate that the average direct labor time to complete one unit is one quarter of an hour. Viceroy is currently utilizing 95% of its operating capacity.

Management is considering a change in operations. Part no. A402 is now purchased from outside suppliers at $4.25 per unit. Viceroy has had significant problems with supplier reliability; thus the firm is studying the feasibility of producing the part itself. The following information has been gathered.

Annual volume needed: 36,000 units.
Estimated direct material cost per unit: $1.45.
Estimated direct labor cost per unit: $\frac{1}{6}$ hour @ $6.00 = $1.00.
Estimated variable factory overhead per unit: $0.75.
Estimated fixed factory overhead: annual rental of special machine, $12,500; salary of newly hired production supervisor, $18,000.

In addition to processing on the special machine, part no. A402 will require machine time on existing equipment. The related costs are reflected in the figures above. The new machine will not significantly affect Viceroy's productive capacity.

INSTRUCTIONS

a From a productive capacity viewpoint, should Viceroy begin to manufacture part no. A402? Why?

b If your answer above was "no," what alternatives should be considered so that manufacturing activities could commence?

c From a purely financial viewpoint, should Viceroy begin to manufacture part no. A402? Why?

d What qualitative factors should be considered in reaching the proper decision?

22 COST ACCUMULATION SYSTEMS

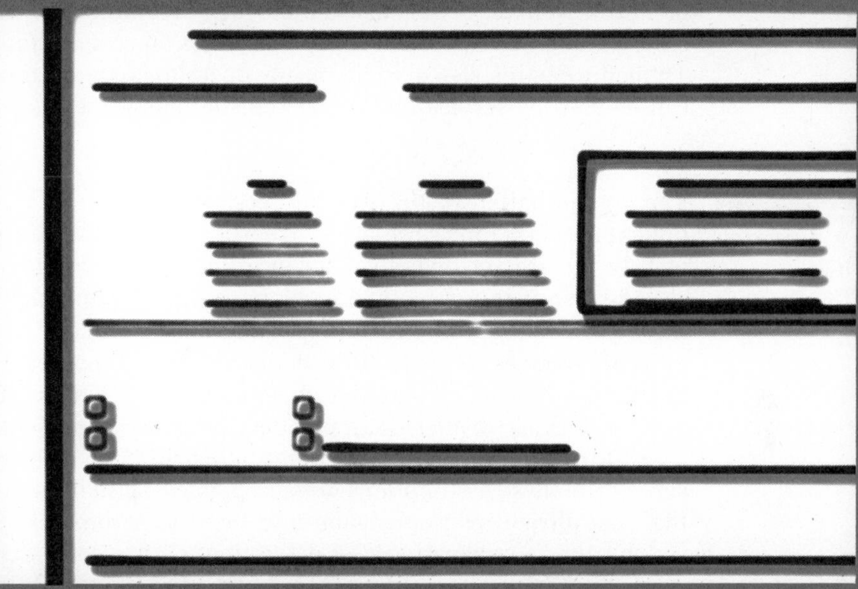

LEARNING OBJECTIVES

After reading this chapter you should:

1 Be familiar with the problem of determining the actual cost of a product or service.

2 Understand the use and operation of job order costing systems.

3 Be able to compute an overhead application rate.

4 Be familiar with the overhead application process and be able to account for over- or underapplied overhead at the end of the accounting period.

5 Understand the use and operation of process costing systems, including the computation of equivalent units.

6 Understand the applicability of cost accumulation systems in service organizations.

CHAPTER 22

As shown in the previous chapter, cost accounting generates information that both meets the needs of management and satisfies external-reporting requirements. Specifically, cost information assists in planning, control, and decision making while, at the same time, providing a basis for inventory valuation and income measurement. In order to accomplish these tasks, an organization must be able to calculate (i.e., accumulate) the cost of its goods, services, and activities. This chapter focuses on cost accumulation systems. Though we will stress manufacturing operations, the techniques illustrated can be used by service and merchandising businesses as well.

COST DETERMINATION

The determination of the "actual" cost of a good or service is extremely difficult. Several topics presented in earlier chapters of this text attest to this fact. In the area of inventory, for example, many individuals feel that the specific identification method is the most precise method of inventory costing. Recall that specific identification attaches the cost of the units to the units themselves, leaving little doubt regarding the cost of the units on hand, used, or sold. Despite this attribute, few businesses utilize this costing method because of the many practical problems it presents. Instead most firms turn to a cost flow *assumption* such as LIFO, FIFO, or weighted average. While these assumptions are acceptable, the inability to determine actual cost introduces imprecision into the costing process.

Further complicating cost determination are costs that are not easily traced to the finished product. As we noted in Chapter 21, factory overhead possesses this characteristic. Factory depreciation, utilities, plant security, and other comparable production costs are incurred by manufacturing activities as a whole; identification with specific products is extremely difficult.

A similar traceability problem exists in many divisionalized organizations where a given cost benefits several segments of activity. Picture the Trans World Corporation, for example, which owns and operates the following subsidiaries:

Subsidiary	**Area of Operation**
Canteen Corporation	Food service
Century 21	Real estate
Hilton International	Hotels
Spartan Food Systems	Food service
Trans World Airlines (TWA)	Airline

The president and others in the high-level corporate staff of Trans World make decisions and handle operating matters that benefit the corporation as a whole. Significant difficulties arise, however, when attempting to trace the cost of broad corporate activities back to smaller segments, such as a TWA flight from New York to Chicago or the sale of a home by a Century 21 broker located in Cleveland, Ohio. The flight and the home sale have probably benefited from the actions of corporate management and should, therefore, absorb a portion of corporate cost. Yet determining the proper cost that each activity should bear is a guess, at best.

Because a clear and definitive relationship between inputs (costs) and outputs (products and activities) is often lacking, cost determination frequently relies on estimates. Estimates, of course, are subjective and arbitrary. Thus although the material presented in the forthcoming pages may appear very detailed and exacting, realize that the calculation of the actual cost of a process, good, or service is a near impossibility.

COST ACCUMULATION SYSTEMS

To compute the cost of a manufactured product, a business must design an accounting system and employ an appropriate methodology for accumulating costs. Two systems, or variations thereof, are frequently found in practice: job order and process costing.

Job Order Systems

A **job order system** gathers costs by job or order. Such systems are commonly used when cost accumulation by job is a fairly easy task, a situation that often arises when goods are made (1) upon the receipt of a customer order, (2) according to customer specifications, or (3) in separate batches. Custom-home builders, for example, frequently employ job systems because of the ease in tracing costs to specific building sites. Similarly, print shops use job systems to cost individual customer orders.

The costs of each job are accumulated on a separate **job cost sheet** (see Exhibit 22-1). Direct materials used and direct labor are identified with and charged to the specific job on which they were incurred. Since factory overhead is not easily traced to a manufactured product, each job is charged with an estimated overhead cost.

The operation of a job cost system follows the flow of costs illustrated in Chapter 21. The three cost elements of direct materials, direct labor, and factory overhead are combined and put "in process" to manufacture products. Eventually, the work in process is completed. The completed goods that are sold are reported as cost of goods sold on the income statement; the unsold units are carried in the Finished Goods inventory account on the balance sheet. This process is shown in the top half of Exhibit 22-2.

To handle the necessary record keeping, a manufacturer establishes various accounts and procedures that parallel the general cost flow. These accounts appear in the bottom half of Exhibit 22-2. To illustrate their use, we will explore the August transactions of Valley Manufacturing Corporation, which uses a job order cost system.

Accounting for materials

As we noted in the previous chapter, the amounts of direct and indirect materials owned are housed in the Raw Materials inventory account. Thus when Valley purchased $80,000 of materials and factory supplies (i.e., indirect materials) on account, the following entry was made.

Raw Materials	*80,000*	
Accounts Payable		*80,000*
Purchased direct materials and factory supplies		

Exhibit 22-1

Job cost sheet

JOB COST SHEET

Manufactured for: *Job No.* ____
Stock ____
Customer ____
Date:
Needed ____
Started ____
Completed ____
Product ____ *No. of Units* ____

Direct Materials			Direct Labor				Factory Overhead	
Date	Requisition No.	Amount	Date	Ticket No.	Hours	Amount	Date	Amount

Overhead Rate: ____

COST SUMMARY

Direct materials	$____
Direct labor	____
Factory overhead	____
Total cost	$____

Materials are kept in a storeroom or warehouse and issued upon receipt of a **materials requisition.** As shown in Exhibit 22-3, $4,000 of materials have been issued for use on job no. 864. These materials are *direct materials* because they can be identified with a specific job. As a result, information appearing on the requisition is posted to the proper job cost sheet. The entry to record the issuance of the direct materials to production is shown below.

Work in Process	*4,000*	
Raw Materials		*4,000*
Issued direct materials for job no. 864		

Indirect materials (e.g., sandpaper, lubricants, and so on) are not easily traced to individual jobs; thus no attempt is made to charge specific job cost sheets. Instead indirect materials consumed are treated as part of factory overhead. During August, Valley used $2,800 of miscellaneous factory supplies in manufacturing operations. The following entry is needed.

Exhibit 22-2

Manufacturing cost flows

General Cost Flow

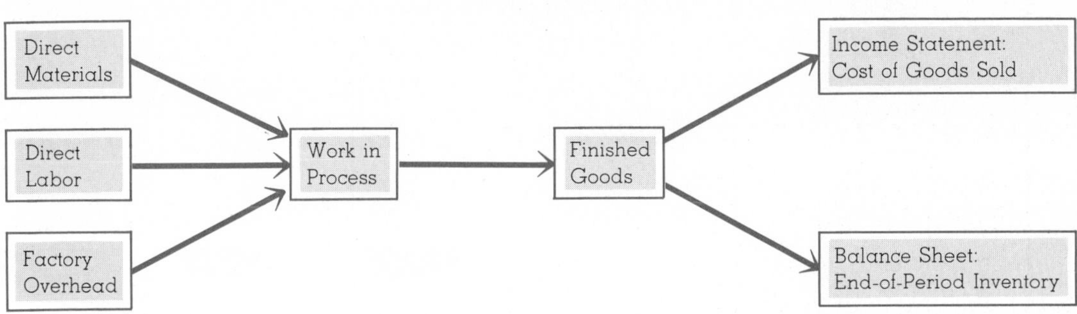

Specific Cost Flow

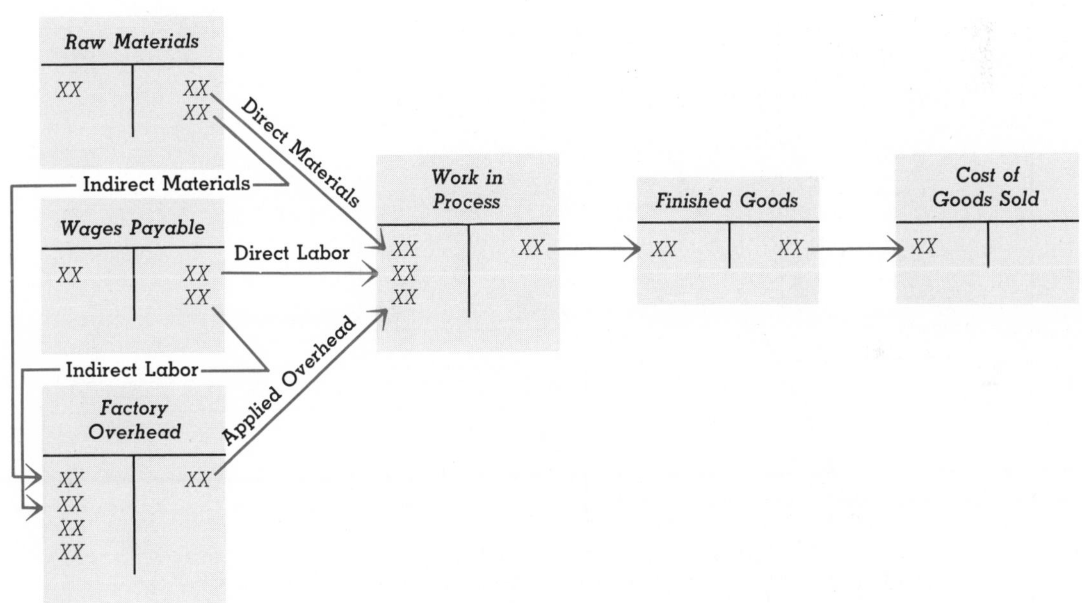

Factory Overhead	*2,800*	
Raw Materials		*2,800*
Issued indirect materials		

The Factory Overhead account is debited to record *actual* overhead charges. The manner in which each job is charged with an *estimated* share of overhead will be illustrated shortly.

Accounting for labor

The accounting treatment for labor is very similar to that of materials. Factory labor costs are classified as either direct or indirect. Recall that

Exhibit 22-3

Document interrelationships in a job order system

MATERIALS REQUISITION

Requisition No. 7602 — Date 8/3

Job No. 864

Department Assembly

Authorized by BZ

Description	Quantity	Unit Cost	Total Cost
Lamp assembly	100	$34.50	$3,450
Electric assembly	100	5.50	550
			$4,000

JOB COST SHEET

Manufactured for:
Stock X
Customer ______

Job No. 864
Date:
Needed 8/15
Started 8/3
Completed ______
Product Custom lamp no. 38
No. of Units 100

Direct Materials			Direct Labor				Factory Overhead	
Date	Requisition No.	Amount	Date	Ticket No.	Hours	Amount	Date	Amount
8/3	7602	$4,000	8/3	1146–49	28	$150		

Via labor summary

Overhead Rate: ______

COST SUMMARY

Direct materials $______
Direct labor ______
Factory overhead ______
Total cost $______

TIME TICKET

Date 8/3

Ticket No. 1146

Labor Assignment:
Job No. 864
Operation Assembly
Other Labor ______

Employee No. 1920

Start Time 1:00
Stop Time 4:30

———— Office Use Only ————

Total Hours 3.5 Total Cost $21.00
Rate per Hour $6.00

direct labor, like direct materials, is easily identified with specific jobs. Indirect labor, on the other hand, is not and is considered part of factory overhead.

Labor costs are accumulated by means of time tickets and labor summaries. Each day, each factory employee completes a **time ticket.** As shown in Exhibit 22-3, the time ticket gathers daily labor information and shows the specific job to which the employee was assigned. If the employee was not working on a job, the type of indirect labor activity performed would be noted as "Other Labor." At the end of the day the time tickets are collected, sorted, and summarized in the form of a *labor summary*. The labor summary shows the total direct and indirect labor costs. Direct labor costs are subdivided by job and then posted to job cost sheets.

The proper entry to record the direct labor on job no. 864 and the incurrence of $200 of indirect labor follows:[1]

Work in Process	*150*	
Factory Overhead	*200*	
Wages Payable		*350*
To record direct and indirect labor		

Like the cost of direct materials, the cost of direct labor is charged to Work in Process to accumulate the cost of jobs in production. When the employees are paid, Wages Payable will be debited and Cash will be credited.

Accounting for overhead

Up to this point the accumulation of job cost has not been difficult, primarily because of the ease in tracing direct materials and direct labor to individual jobs. We now turn our attention to the third and most complicated element of product cost: factory overhead.

Because of traceability and record-keeping problems, jobs are charged with an estimated (as opposed to actual) overhead cost. The use of estimated overhead charges not only is practical but also has two side benefits.

First, total job cost can be figured at the time of job completion. Timely cost information is beneficial in setting prices for customers and in other routine operating decisions that are made by management.

Second, estimated overhead charges tend to smooth product costs over a period of time. Actual costs change each month, and in addition, volume fluctuates. The cost of production is therefore dependent on when manufacturing takes place. As an example, picture the highly seasonal business of a soft drink manufacturer. Fixed manufacturing costs remain relatively stable month after month. Thus when volume peaks in the hot summer months, the actual production cost per bottle decreases. This decrease results from spreading constant fixed costs over increased activity levels. In winter months when production is lower, the production cost per bottle will rise. So that fluctuating overhead costs are avoided, estimated rates are set and implemented for a certain period of time, often one year. In this manner inventory is costed at the same rate every month.

---

[1]We are ignoring employee withholdings in this example.

Overhead application rates

The estimated overhead cost of a job or product is determined by using an overhead application rate. An **overhead application rate** relates overhead to a specific application base and is computed as follows:

$$\frac{\textit{estimated factory overhead}}{\textit{estimated application base}} = \textit{overhead application rate}$$

To explain, product costs must be determined as accurately as possible. Therefore at the beginning of a reporting period, the accountant performs an in-depth study of factory overhead. The accountant is interested in learning how overhead behaves in relation to changes in various factors of production (e.g., direct labor hours, direct labor cost, or machine hours). If a strong correlation exists between factory overhead and, say, direct labor cost, a fairly accurate estimate of overhead can be developed by applying (measuring) overhead on the basis of the labor cost identified with the job or product. In a heavily automated situation where much of the overhead is caused by the operation of machines, machine hours may be appropriate for an application base. In other cases where manual labor predominates, direct labor hours may have a strong relation to overhead.

In general, we select an application base that (1) is inexpensive to compute, (2) is easily traced to the job or product, and (3) has a strong cause and effect relationship with overhead. The latter means that the application base should have a substantial influence on the amount of overhead incurred. A strong cause and effect relationship helps to ensure accuracy in the estimation process.

Use of the overhead application rate

Once the application base is chosen, the overhead rate can be developed and used in product costing. The amount of overhead charged to an individual job is determined by multiplying the application rate by the amount of the application base associated with that job. This process is best seen by using a numerical example.

Assume that Valley Manufacturing has chosen direct labor hours as an application base because of the company's heavy emphasis on manual assembly work. On the basis of normal operations, Valley's accountant has predicted 40,000 direct labor hours of activity for the year. In addition, the following factory overhead estimates have been derived.

Indirect materials used	$ 20,000
Indirect labor	140,000
Utilities	15,000
Taxes	30,000
Insurance	10,000
Building depreciation	40,000
Equipment depreciation	25,000
Total estimated overhead	$280,000

The firm's overhead application rate of $7 per direct labor hour is computed as follows:

$$\frac{\text{estimated factory overhead}}{\text{estimated application base}} = \text{overhead application rate}$$

$$\frac{\$280{,}000}{40{,}000 \text{ direct labor hours}} = \$7 \text{ per direct labor hour}$$

The $7 rate can now be applied to individual jobs to determine the estimated overhead cost. Examine Exhibit 22-4, which contains the completed job cost sheet for job no. 864. Compare this exhibit with Exhibit 22-3,

Exhibit 22-4

Completed job cost sheet

JOB COST SHEET

Manufactured for:
Stock X
Customer ______

Job No. 864
Date:
Needed 8/15
Started 8/3
Completed 8/5
No. of Units 100

Product Custom lamp no. 38

Direct Materials			Direct Labor				Factory Overhead	
Date	Requisition No.	Amount	Date	Ticket No.	Hours	Amount	Date	Amount
8/3	7602	$4,000	8/3	1146–49	28	$150	8/5	$406
8/5	7638	1,050	8/4	1187–89	20	120		
		$5,050	8/5	2010–11	10	55		
					58	$325		

Overhead Rate: $7 per direct labor hour

COST SUMMARY

Direct materials	$5,050
Direct labor	325
Factory overhead	406
Total cost	$5,781

and notice that additional material costs (requisition no. 7638) and additional labor costs (tickets no. 1187–89 and no. 2010–11) have been incurred. On the basis of the total of 58 direct labor hours, Valley has applied or estimated an overhead cost of \$406 (58 hours × \$7).[2]

The proper entry to record the applied overhead follows.

Work in Process	406	
Factory Overhead		406
To record applied overhead		

The Work in Process account is debited to add factory overhead to the other two costs of production: direct materials used and direct labor. In this manner Work in Process now contains all the costs that pertain to job no. 864. The credit to the Factory Overhead account takes an estimated portion of Valley's total overhead and applies it to specific jobs. The credit portion of the entry should become clearer after the next two sections.

Actual overhead

The Factory Overhead account is used to accumulate both actual and applied overhead. As was shown earlier, Factory Overhead is debited to record indirect materials used and indirect labor. Other actual overhead costs are recorded in this account as well. To illustrate, assume that Valley Manufacturing experienced the following factory costs during August:

Utilities	\$ 1,300
Taxes	2,500
Insurance	900
Building depreciation	3,500
Equipment depreciation	2,200
	\$10,400

Further assume that payments for utilities and taxes are not due until September and that the insurance represents the expiration of a prepaid policy. Valley's required journal entry to record these actual overhead costs follows.

Factory Overhead	10,400	
Accounts Payable		1,300
Taxes Payable		2,500
Prepaid Insurance		900
Accumulated Depreciation: Building		3,500
Accumulated Depreciation: Equipment		2,200
To record actual overhead costs		

The entry's credits should be familiar; this procedure is the same one that was followed in the first part of the text. The expiration of a prepaid expense necessitated a reduction in an asset account; recording depreciation generated a credit to Accumulated Depreciation; and so forth. The entry's

[2] If desired, overhead could be applied daily as the number of direct labor hours becomes known. If a job is not completed by the end of the accounting period, overhead should be applied on the basis of the work performed to date to properly value the production in process.

debits, however, are different. In earlier chapters all these costs were charged to expense accounts. Now, no expenses are involved and the costs are debited to Factory Overhead. Why? The change in procedure is caused by a change in business purpose. For manufacturing firms these costs are not expenses; rather they are product costs, which must be attached to the units produced. Attachment takes place via the application of factory overhead discussed earlier.

Only factory costs are recorded in the overhead account. Selling and administrative costs such as advertising, managerial salaries, and sales commissions are still written off as expenses. Remember, these costs are period costs and, as such, never inventoried.

Applied overhead

The accumulation of actual overhead throughout the period and the application of overhead to jobs force the Factory Overhead account to assume the following status:

Factory Overhead

	Debit	Credit	
Actual overhead costs are recorded by debits as incurred	XXX	XXX	Overhead is applied to jobs via credits
	XXX	XXX	
	XXX	XXX	

It should be apparent that the application process simply takes a "chunk" of overhead and attaches it to production. By the end of the accounting period, if all goes according to plan, overhead applied will equal total overhead incurred. This rarely occurs, however. We will view the proper accounting treatment for this situation shortly.

Accounting for the completion and sale of manufactured products

By viewing Exhibit 22-5, you can see the interrelationships among the journal entries illustrated in the preceding sections, the job cost sheet, and Valley's Work in Process account. In practice, separate entries would be made on August 3, 4, and 5 to record the individual transactions.

Upon completion, jobs are transferred to the finished goods warehouse to await sale. Paralleling this physical transfer, Valley would record the following entry to recognize the completion of production.

Finished Goods	5,781	
Work in Process		5,781
Completed job no. 864		

Eventually, the finished goods inventory will be sold. Suppose, for example, that 25 of the 100 lamps produced on job no. 864 are sold on account at $80 apiece. From information found on the job cost sheet, the cost per

Exhibit 22-5

Interrelationships between manufacturing journal entries, the job cost sheet, and the Work in Process account

Job No. 864

Direct Materials			Direct Labor				Factory Overhead	
Date	Requisition No.	Amount	Date	Ticket No.	Hours	Amount	Date	Amount
8/3	7602	$4,000	8/3	1146–49	28	$150	8/5	$406
8/5	7638	1,050	8/4	1187–89	20	120		
		$5,050	8/5	2010–11	10	55		
					58	$325		

Total Cost = $5,781

Entries

Work in Process
Raw Materials

Work in Process
Wages Payable

Work in Process
Factory Overhead

Work in Process

Direct materials	5,050
Direct labor	325
Applied overhead	406
	5,781

lamp is $57.81 ($5,781 ÷ 100 lamps). Thus the following entries are needed.

Cost of Goods Sold	*1,445.25*	
Finished Goods		*1,445.25*
To record the cost of lamps sold		
Accounts Receivable	*2,000*	
Sales		*2,000*
To record sale on account		

The first entry transfers the manufactured cost of the 25 lamps sold ($57.81 × 25 = $1,445.25) from Finished Goods to the Cost of Goods Sold account. The second entry places the sales revenues generated ($80 × 25 = $2,000) in the accounting records. Valley, like most manufacturers, is using a perpetual inventory system. The perpetual system keeps a running count of the goods on hand and allows users to achieve improved inventory control. Should you need a review of inventory systems, we refer you to Chapter 9.

A recap

The sale of finished production completes the flow of manufacturing costs through the accounting system. Please reexamine the bottom half of Exhibit 22-2. Notice that material, labor, and overhead costs all begin in their own accounts. Indirect materials used and indirect labor are recognized as overhead and transferred to the Factory Overhead account to join other miscellaneous production costs. Direct materials used, direct labor, and factory overhead applied are then charged to Work in Process. As production is completed, manufacturing costs are transferred to the Finished Goods account. Finally, the sale of inventory necessitates a transfer of cost from Finished Goods to Cost of Goods Sold. Although variations are found in practice because of added complexities of manufacturing (e.g., multiple processing departments), Exhibit 22-2 accurately depicts the flow of costs for both small firms and manufacturing giants.

Work in process: A control account

In the previous example the Work in Process account housed the costs of job no. 864 until the job was completed. Normally, a business manufactures many jobs simultaneously and is unable to finish all production by the end of the accounting period. To handle the necessary record keeping, Work in Process assumes the role of a control account and is supported by individual job cost sheets.

To illustrate, assume that Wong Corporation had job no. 614 in process on January 1. Information relating to job no. 614 appears below.

Direct materials used	*$ 5,500*
Direct labor	*8,000*
Factory overhead applied, 150% of direct labor	*12,000*
	$25,500

Manufacturing activity that took place during the year is shown in Exhibit 22-6.

Exhibit 22-6

Wong Corporation manufacturing activity

	Job No. 614	Job No. 615	Job No. 616	Job No. 617	Total
Direct materials used	$ —	$ 9,000	$20,000	$ 4,000	$ 33,000
Direct labor	5,000	10,000	18,000	8,000	41,000
Factory overhead applied, 150% of direct labor	7,500	15,000	27,000	12,000	61,500
Total	$12,500	$34,000	$65,000	$24,000	$135,500
Job status	Completed	Completed and sold	In process	In process	

Wong's Work in Process account and summary journal entries appear in Exhibit 22-7. Observe that the completed jobs (no. 614 and no. 615) have been removed from Work in Process and transferred to Finished Goods. Jobs no. 616 and no. 617 are still in production; thus the $89,000 ending Work in

Exhibit 22-7

Work in Process control account of Wong Corporation

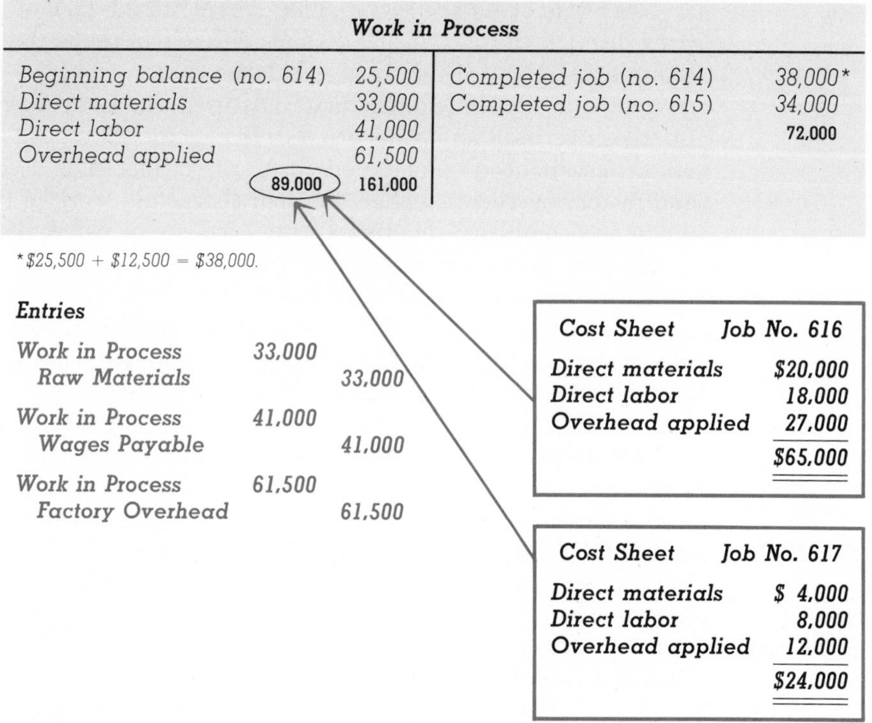

Work in Process			
Beginning balance (no. 614)	25,500	Completed job (no. 614)	38,000*
Direct materials	33,000	Completed job (no. 615)	34,000
Direct labor	41,000		72,000
Overhead applied	61,500		
89,000	161,000		

*$25,500 + $12,500 = $38,000.

Entries

Work in Process	33,000	
Raw Materials		33,000
Work in Process	41,000	
Wages Payable		41,000
Work in Process	61,500	
Factory Overhead		61,500

Cost Sheet	Job No. 616
Direct materials	$20,000
Direct labor	18,000
Overhead applied	27,000
	$65,000

Cost Sheet	Job No. 617
Direct materials	$ 4,000
Direct labor	8,000
Overhead applied	12,000
	$24,000

Process balance coincides with the total of these two jobs' cost sheets ($65,000 + $24,000 = $89,000). The Work in Process and job cost sheet relationship is an example of the control account/subsidiary ledger arrangement discussed in Chapter 5. Recall that a control account (Work in Process) appears in the general ledger and is composed of various lower-level accounts. The lower-level accounts (i.e., job cost sheets) that support a control account are collectively known as a subsidiary ledger. In a job order system the underlying detail of the Work in Process account can always be found by examining individual job cost sheets.

Overapplied and underapplied overhead

At the end of an accounting period it is unlikely that the overhead applied to production will equal the actual overhead incurred. The application rate that is used to charge overhead to jobs and products is based on two estimates: estimated overhead and an estimated application base. Unexpected price changes from suppliers, variations in production levels, and increases and decreases in plant efficiency all cause actual experience to differ from amounts originally forecast.

Overhead can be either overapplied or underapplied. If, for example, a company applied $74,000 of overhead but actually incurred $68,000, overhead is said to be **overapplied** by $6,000. If the situation was reversed, overhead would be **underapplied.** To examine the implications of over- and underapplied overhead, we will continue the Wong Corporation example.

Wong has been applying overhead to jobs at the rate of 150% of direct labor cost. The rate was computed in the following manner:

Estimated costs for the year ended December 31
Factory overhead $60,000
Direct labor cost $40,000

$$\text{application rate} = \frac{\text{estimated overhead}}{\text{estimated application base}} = \frac{\$60{,}000}{\$40{,}000} = 150\%$$

The 150% rate says that for every $1.00 of direct labor expected to be incurred, the firm anticipates $1.50 of factory overhead.

Throughout the accounting period Wong applied $61,500 of overhead to jobs no. 614–617 (see Exhibit 22-6). If we assume that actual overhead incurred amounted to $65,000, overhead would be underapplied by $3,500.

Actual overhead	*$65,000*
Applied overhead	
Direct labor cost × 150% ($41,000 × 150%)	*61,500*
Underapplied overhead	*$ 3,500*

The underapplication means that insufficient overhead has been charged to the Work in Process account; thus the account's ending balance is slightly understated. Unfortunately, the problem does not stop here, because each job produced during the period has been costed incorrectly. From the job status appearing in Exhibit 22-6, jobs no. 616 and no. 617 are still in process (Work in Process), job no. 614 has been completed but is still on hand (Finished Goods), and job no. 615 has been sold (Cost of Goods Sold). Because of the understated application rate, the ending balances in these three accounts are also understated. Consequently, an adjusting entry is needed upon conclusion of the period.

The adjusting entry first considers the status of the Factory Overhead account. In Wong's case the account appears as follows:

Factory Overhead	
Actual 65,000	Applied 61,500

The overhead account must be closed so that Wong can start anew, accumulating costs for the next period's production activities. Thus Factory Overhead is credited for $3,500. The $3,500 debit can either be (1) allocated to Work in Process, Finished Goods, and Cost of Goods Sold on some equitable basis or (2) charged entirely to Cost of Goods Sold. The first approach, which raises each account's balance to counteract the understatement, is theoretically preferred. However, because the balances in Work in Process, Finished Goods, and Cost of Goods Sold consist of the costs of individual jobs, each job cost sheet must also be adjusted. While Wong had only four jobs, the bookkeeping necessitated by this procedure in a realistic environment would be burdensome. Consequently, this approach is only used when the over- or underapplied overhead is so great that a lack of proration will result in misleading financial statements.

The second method, charging the entire $3,500 to Cost of Goods Sold, is the more popular approach. The necessary journal entry follows.

Cost of Goods Sold	*3,500*	
Factory Overhead		*3,500*
To adjust cost of goods sold for underapplied overhead		

The entry raises Cost of Goods Sold to $37,500 ($34,000 from job no. 615 + $3,500), and this amount is reported on Wong's income statement.

The procedures illustrated are reversed for overapplied overhead.

Process Costing Systems

For many manufacturing applications job order systems are not well suited to accumulate costs. Picture the automobile industry, for example. Cars continually roll off an assembly line. Although dealers frequently place special orders to fill customer requests, an assembly plant does not produce a batch of cars for one dealer, then stop, and later resume production to manufacture the cars needed by another dealer. In this type of operating environment, production is continuous; product costing by job or order becomes extremely difficult, if not impossible. Accountants, therefore, turn to a **process costing system** to accumulate costs. Process costing systems are often employed in steel, petroleum, chemical, and textile production as well as in many assembly types of industries (e.g., automobiles, appliances, and bicycles).

Measuring cost

Rather than accumulate costs by job, process cost systems accumulate costs by process or department for a specified period of time (e.g., one month). Often a process and department are synonymous. For example, the mixing process takes place in the mixing department, the assembly process in the assembly department, and so forth.

Each department typically maintains its own Work in Process account to collect production costs. Product costing and cost flow are similar to the procedures followed in a job order system. Direct materials and direct labor, costs that are easily traced to business activity, are charged to the department where consumed or incurred; factory overhead is then applied by using an overhead application rate.

Once total department cost is determined, the cost per unit can be computed. Continuous processing industries usually produce homogeneous or similar goods. Consider a manufacturer of portable typewriters, for example. Although several different models may be produced, all units of a given model are identical.[3] Thus product costing can be achieved by attaching an *average* production cost to each unit manufactured.

Measuring production

Computing the average cost per unit requires that manufacturing costs be divided by the number of units produced. As we noted earlier, process costing systems accumulate costs for a period of time. Because of the nature of continuous processing, units still in production at the end of a reporting period are a common occurrence. As the following example reveals, in-process inventories create a measurement problem.

The Paige Corporation, which uses a process cost system, began operations on January 2. The firm has established an overhead application rate of 120% of direct labor cost. The following information pertains to January.

Manufacturing Costs		***Production***	
Direct materials used	$ 90,000	Units completed	80,000
Direct labor	50,000	Units in process,	
Applied factory overhead	60,000	$\frac{1}{4}$ complete	80,000
Total manufacturing costs	$200,000		

Paige has a $200,000 cost pool that must be split between 80,000 completed units and 80,000 units in process, as shown in the following diagram:

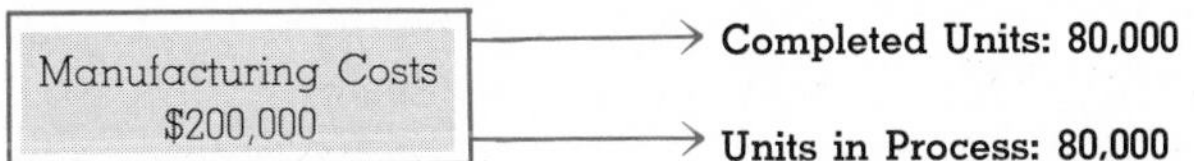

In more familiar terms, the cost pool is located in the Work in Process account at the end of January. So that the costs follow the flow of production, a portion of the $200,000 must be removed and transferred to Finished Goods.

Many individuals would say that Work in Process should be credited for $100,000 (i.e., one-half of the cost pool) since 50% of Paige's total production is completed. Stated differently, the average cost per unit is $1.25 ($200,000 ÷ 160,000 units). Thus $100,000 (80,000 completed units × $1.25) should be transferred to the Finished Goods account. While the foregoing computation is straightforward, it is, at the same time, logically unsound. We cannot add 80,000 completed units to 80,000 units in process. It's like adding apples and oranges—a meaningless total is generated.

Equivalent units

To arrive at a proper measure of performance, accountants do not use total units for unit cost computations; instead a base known as equivalent units is employed. An **equivalent unit** is a physical unit stated in terms of a

[3] An exception may be color, which generally has no impact on cost.

finished unit. For example, if a company has 16 physical units (e.g., cars, tons, gallons) that are 75% complete, 12 equivalent units (16 × 0.75) have been produced. That is, the company has done the work equivalent to manufacturing 12 finished units. Notice, however, that *none* of these units are completed. As shown by the following diagram, all 16 units are still in process.

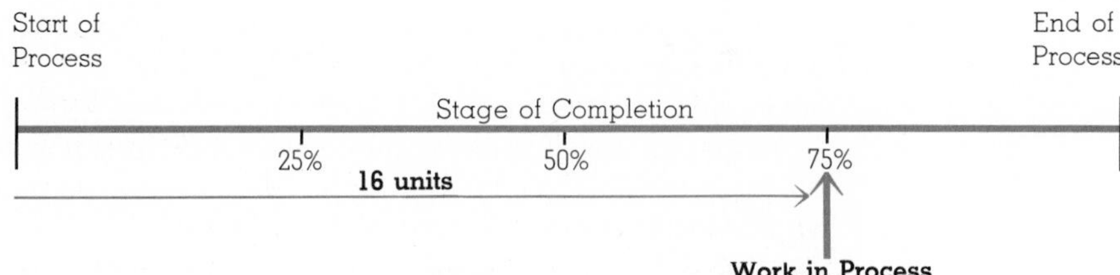

In actuality, the stage of completion is an average—some of the units have not yet reached this point, while others are beyond it.

Returning to the Paige Corporation example, 100,000 equivalent units of production took place in January.

	Physical Units	*Percentage of Work Completed During January*	*Equivalent Units*
Units completed	80,000	× 100%	= 80,000
Units in process, $\frac{1}{4}$ complete	80,000	× 25	= 20,000
			100,000

Since operations commenced at the beginning of the year, the 80,000 units completed were all started in January. Thus 100% of the work on these units occurred during the month.

Factors complicating equivalent production

Two additional factors must be considered when computing equivalent units. The first is the presence of a beginning work in process inventory. The beginning work in process must be analyzed in terms of the work performed in prior periods. If, for example, a company has a beginning inventory of 500 units that is $\frac{3}{5}$ complete, 200 equivalent units of production are necessary to complete the inventory in the current accounting period ($500 \times \frac{2}{5} = 200$). Equivalent-unit computations focus on the work performed during the *present* period because of the necessity of calculating the current average cost of production.

The second point to consider is that the three factors of production (direct materials, direct labor, and factory overhead) are generally introduced in different ways throughout the manufacturing process. Labor and overhead, collectively known as *conversion cost,* are often incurred uniformly through the process. Direct materials, however, can be introduced at different stages of production. In some products, for example, all materials enter the process at the beginning. In other products, materials enter the process at several specific points. To illustrate, certain parts may be introduced at the beginning of an assembly line. Later at the 50% stage of completion, additional parts are added, and perhaps at the 70% stage, still others are added.

The uniform introduction of certain factors of production and the introduction of others at specific points require the calculation of separate equivalent-unit figures. For example, assume that Sparks Company operates a process cost system. At the beginning of July the firm had a work in process inventory of 3,000 units, 30% complete. During July the beginning work in process was completed along with 7,500 other units that had entered production. Finally, on July 31 the production foreman determined that the ending work in process totaled 5,000 units, 20% complete. All materials are introduced at the start of the process, and labor and overhead are incurred uniformly throughout. The equivalent units for July are calculated as follows:

	Physical Units	Equivalent Units	
		Materials	Conversion
Completed			
Beginning work in process	3,000	—	2,100
Units started and completed	7,500	7,500	7,500
Ending work in process	5,000	5,000	1,000
	15,500	12,500	10,600

To explain, the beginning work in process inventory received no additional material. Remember, these units were started last period, and all material is introduced at the start of the process. To complete the beginning inventory, 70% of the work was performed in July, resulting in 2,100 (3,000 × 0.70) equivalent conversion units. Next, observe that 7,500 units were started and completed. Thus all material for these units was introduced during the month along with 100% of the processing. Consequently, 7,500 equivalent units of materials and conversion must be tallied. Finally, we assume that the ending work in process inventory was started in July. As a result, 5,000 equivalent units of material were introduced during the month. Because the ending inventory is only 20% complete, Sparks did 1,000 (5,000 × 0.20) equivalent units of conversion.

Comprehensive illustration

To tie several loose ends together, we will study the manufacturing operations of Berloff, Inc. The following information pertains to September.

Beginning work in process inventory: 4,000 units, 75% complete; cost, $23,100

Number of units started during September: 13,000
Total units completed: 11,000
Ending work in process inventory: 6,000 units, 40% complete
September manufacturing costs: direct materials used, $32,500; conversion cost, $48,880

All materials are introduced at the start of the process, and conversion costs are incurred uniformly throughout manufacturing. The following methodology is suggested to calculate the cost of goods completed during September and the cost of the ending work in process inventory.

Step 1: Analyze the physical flow

Berloff must trace the units through the manufacturing process. On the basis of the information presented, the proper physical flow is as follows:

	Physical Units	
Beginning work in process	4,000	
Units started	13,000	
Units to account for	17,000 ←	
Completed		
Beginning work in process	4,000	Must
Units started and completed	7,000	be equal
Ending work in process	6,000	
Units accounted for	17,000 ←	

The production manager must account for the beginning work in process and the units started in September. What has happened to these units? Assuming no spoilage, the units either have been completed or are still in process. The finished production must be separated into two batches: the units from the beginning inventory and those units *started* and completed during the period. The latter batch is obtained by subtracting the beginning work in process from the total units manufactured (11,000 − 4,000 = 7,000).

Step 2: Compute equivalent units

Once the physical flow is determined, current production is then translated into equivalent units. Since materials are introduced at the start of the process and labor and overhead incurred evenly throughout, the following figures are obtained (see the shaded area).

	Physical Units
Beginning work in process	4,000
Units started	13,000
Units to account for	17,000

		Equivalent Units	
		Materials	Conversion
Completed			
Beginning work in process*	4,000	—	1,000
Units started and completed†	7,000	7,000	7,000
Ending work in process‡	6,000	6,000	2,400
Units accounted for	17,000	13,000	10,400

*All materials added last period; 25% of the conversion done in this period.
†All materials and conversion introduced in this period.
‡Units were started in this period; all materials were introduced plus 40% of the conversion.

Step 3: Compute equivalent-unit costs

The cost per equivalent unit is calculated by dividing production costs by the equivalent units computed in Step 2. Just as the equivalent production figures are calculated for current activity, so, too, are the unit costs. The necessary procedures follow.

Costs	Total	Materials	Conversion
Beginning work in process	$ 23,100	$ —	$ —
Current	81,380	32,500	48,880
To account for	$104,480	$32,500	$48,880
Equivalent units (from step 2)		13,000	10,400
Cost per equivalent unit		$2.50	$4.70

Note that the cost of the beginning work in process inventory ($23,100) is ignored in unit-cost computations. Why? This cost represents work performed in the previous period. The production manager, however, is still held accountable for its incurrence.

Step 4: Cost assignment

Berloff's cost pool of $104,480 must now be assigned to the goods completed during the period and the ending work in process inventory. The assignment is accomplished by multiplying the cost per equivalent unit by the proper number of equivalent units. As shown in Exhibit 22-8, the cost of goods completed is $78,200, and the ending work in process is $26,280.

Because the prior period cost of $23,100 was not considered when computing equivalent-unit costs, it is attached entirely to the beginning work in process inventory. That is, no prior period cost is allocated to either the units started and completed or the partially completed production at the end of the period. Observe that the total cost accounted for ($104,480) agrees with the total cost to account for (as calculated in Step 3).

Exhibit 22-8

Cost assignment of Berloff, Inc.

	Equivalent Units	
	Materials	**Conversion**
Completed		
Beginning work in process	—	1,000
Started and completed	7,000	7,000
Ending work in process	6,000	2,400
Units accounted for	13,000	10,400

Completed		
Beginning work in process		
Prior period cost	$23,100	
Conversion cost:		
1,000 × $4.70	4,700	$ 27,800
Units started and completed		
Materials: 7,000 × $2.50	$17,500	
Conversion cost: 7,000 × $4.70	32,900	50,400
Total cost of completed goods		$ 78,200
Ending work in process		
Materials: 6,000 × $2.50	$15,000	
Conversion cost: 2,400 × $4.70	11,280	26,280
Total cost accounted for		$104,480

Cost of production report

All the foregoing information is summarized in Berloff's cost of production report for September, which appears in Exhibit 22-9.

Berloff's Work in Process account is reproduced below.

Work in Process		
Beginning balance	*23,100*	
Materials	*32,500*	
Conversion	*48,880*	
	104,480	

Notice the manner in which the figures in the Work in Process account tie into the production cost report. Since the cost of completed production totals $78,200, the following entry is necessary.

Finished Goods	*78,200*	
Work in Process		*78,200*
To transfer cost of completed units to finished goods		

Observe that the cost flow for a process cost system is the same as that of a job order system; only the method of cost accumulation and assignment has changed.

Problems in process costing

Although the preceding illustration may have seemed complex, several factors were ignored for the sake of simplicity. For example, continuous processing sometimes involves *joint products*. That is, two or more products may result from a single manufacturing process. Joint products are common in petroleum refining and chemical manufacturing. In addition to the normal problems associated with process costing, the accountant must now, at the same time, determine the cost of multiple products. When several prod-

Exhibit 22-9

BERLOFF, INC.
Cost of Production Report
For the Month Ended September 30, 19XX

	Physical Units			
Beginning work in process	4,000			
Units started	13,000			
Units to account for	17,000			

STEP 1

			Equivalent Units	
			Materials	Conversion
Completed				
Beginning work in process	4,000		—	1,000
Units started and completed	7,000		7,000	7,000
Ending work in process	6,000		6,000	2,400
Units accounted for	17,000		13,000	10,400

STEP 2

Costs		Total		
Beginning work in process		$ 23,100	$ —	$ —
Current		81,380	32,500	48,880
To account for		$104,480	$32,500 ÷	$48,880 ÷
Equivalent units			13,000	10,400
Cost per equivalent unit			$2.50	$4.70

STEP 3

Cost Assignment		
Completed		
Beginning work in process		
Prior period cost	$23,100	
Conversion cost: 1,000 × $4.70	4,700	$ 27,800
Units started and completed		
Materials: 7,000 × $2.50	$17,500	
Conversion cost: 7,000 × $4.70	32,900	50,400
Total cost of completed goods		$ 78,200
Ending work in process		
Materials: 6,000 × $2.50	$15,000	
Conversion cost: 2,400 × $4.70	11,280	26,280
Total cost accounted for		$104,480

STEP 4

JOB COSTING IN MASS TRANSIT?

Up until two decades ago, the urban mass transit industry had been a profitable enterprise operation. Fare box revenues not only were sufficient to cover the cost of operations but also provided capital improvement funds and a return on the owner's investment.

In the early 1960s the transit environment changed considerably, causing a reduction or elimination of profit in many systems. Because of wage increases and inflation, operating costs rose rapidly while ridership and operating revenues decreased. By the late 1960s losses totaling billions of dollars resulted, forcing numerous private systems to either cease operations entirely or be taken over by a local government body. Often to continue operating, private transit companies received subsidies from the cities and municipalities they serviced.

How can job order systems be applied to mass transit? Specifically, each transit route can be established as a "job." Then costs identifiable with a route's operation are assigned directly to that route. For example, a large portion of direct wages and fuel costs are identified with vehicles operating on specific routes; thus these costs are directly assignable. The same is true for many special and "one time" costs, such as route promotion and route development. Other costs, such as vehicle and route support services (e.g., maintenance and repair), are system overhead costs. These costs are applied to routes on the basis of a characteristic related to the service provided (e.g., miles driven). Finally, administrative costs are assigned by using a general overhead rate.

Notice that the route costing procedure is similar to product costing for a manufacturer. First, manufacturing costs easily traced to the product are assigned to the product. Then overhead is applied by using a predetermined overhead rate.

With the procedures noted above, the cost of operating an individual route can be matched with revenues, generating a reliable profit or loss figure for the route's operation. This information can then be used to formulate financing agreements. The agreements are employed by the transit system operator to obtain subsidies from communities for routes operated within the community's boundaries.

SOURCE Adapted from Paul Dierks, "Applying Cost Accounting to Transit System Financing," Management Accounting, *December 1978, pp. 20–23.*

ucts are manufactured in different departments, proper accounting can become troublesome.

Another problem encountered in a process costing environment deals with determining the stage of completion of work in process inventories. Determining the stage of completion involves estimates. In many cases, especially where goods are at virtually every stage of production, the estimates are extremely arbitrary and difficult to derive. To simplify matters, a number of companies assume a constant stage of completion (e.g., all in-process inventories are assumed to be either $\frac{1}{4}$, $\frac{1}{2}$, or $\frac{3}{4}$ complete).

Job Order and Process Costing: Service Applications

Our presentation of job order and process costing systems has focused on manufacturing applications. These two cost accumulation methods can also be used by service businesses.

Job order systems are commonly encountered in repair work, medical care, and accounting and management consulting practices. Consider the auto repair business, for example. The customer is charged for all significant materials and parts (i.e., direct materials) used in repair work. In addition, for the labor time involved, there is a stipulated charge per hour (or per job). The charge covers direct labor, overhead, and an allowance for profit. Repair charges are thus accumulated for each customer or, in other words, by job.

The use of process costing in service businesses is not as widespread as the use of job order systems. Process costing may be used to accumulate the costs incurred in continuous, multiple-step applications such as claims handling by an insurance company. Other possible applications include determining the cost of processing mail by the U.S. Postal Service and tax returns by the Internal Revenue Service.

SUMMARY PROBLEM

Riverdale Manufacturing Company uses a process costing system to accumulate product costs. The firm applies overhead to production on the basis of direct labor hours. At the beginning of the current period the following estimates were derived.

Estimated direct labor hours: 45,000.
Estimated factory overhead: $180,000.

Selected data applicable to January of the current year follow.

Beginning work in process inventory: 8,000 units, $\frac{1}{4}$ complete; cost, $17,500.
Number of units started in January: 20,000.
Total units completed: 22,000.
Ending work in process inventory: 6,000 units, $\frac{2}{3}$ complete.
Direct materials used in January: $60,000.
Direct labor incurred in January (3,500 hours): $28,000.

INSTRUCTIONS

a **Determine Riverdale's overhead application rate.**

b **Determine the overhead applied to production during January and the month's total conversion cost.**

c **Compute the equivalent production figures for January with respect to materials and conversion cost. Materials are added at the start of the process; conversion costs are incurred evenly throughout manufacturing.**

d **Compute the equivalent-unit costs for materials and conversion costs.**

e **Determine the cost of goods completed during January and the ending work in process inventory.**

f **Assume the following actual factory overhead costs for January.**

Indirect materials	$3,900
Indirect labor	7,600
Utilities	1,000
Equipment depreciation	2,000

Present entries to record (1) direct materials used; (2) direct labor incurred; (3) factory overhead incurred; (4) factory overhead applied to production; (5) cost of goods completed during the month.

g **Determine the amount of over- or underapplied overhead during January.**

SOLUTION

a $$\text{overhead application rate} = \frac{\text{estimated factory overhead}}{\text{estimated application base}} = \frac{\$180{,}000}{45{,}000\ \text{hours}} = \$4\ \text{per direct labor hour}$$

b

Overhead applied (3,500 hours × $4)	$14,000
Direct labor	28,000
Total conversion cost	$42,000

c

	Physical Units		
Beginning work in process	8,000		
Units started	20,000		
Units to account for	28,000		

		Equivalent Units	
		Materials	Conversion
Completed			
Beginning work in process*	8,000	—	6,000
Units started and completed†	14,000	14,000	14,000
Ending work in process‡	6,000	6,000	4,000
Units accounted for	28,000	20,000	24,000

*All materials added last period; $\frac{3}{4}$ of the conversion done in this period.
†All materials and conversion introduced in this period; 14,000 units derived by subtracting the beginning work in process inventory from the total units completed (22,000).
‡Units were started in this period; all materials were introduced plus $\frac{2}{3}$ of the conversion.

d

Costs	Total	Materials	Conversion
Beginning work in process	$ 17,500	$ —	$ —
Current	102,000	60,000	42,000*
To account for	$119,500	$60,000 ÷	$42,000 ÷
Equivalent units		20,000	24,000
Cost per equivalent unit		$3.00	$1.75

*From part (b).

e

Completed		
Beginning work in process		
Prior period cost	$17,500	
Conversion cost: 6,000 units × $1.75	10,500	$ 28,000
Units started and completed		
Materials: 14,000 units × $3.00	$42,000	
Conversion cost: 14,000 units × $1.75	24,500	66,500
Total cost of completed units		$ 94,500
Ending work in process		
Materials: 6,000 units × $3.00	$18,000	
Conversion cost: 4,000 units × $1.75	7,000	25,000
Total cost accounted for		$119,500

f

		Debit	Credit
(1)	*Work in Process*	60,000	
	Raw Materials		60,000
	Issued direct materials to production		
(2)	*Work in Process*	28,000	
	Wages Payable		28,000
	To record direct labor incurred		
(3)	*Factory Overhead*	14,500	
	Raw Materials		3,900
	Wages Payable		7,600
	Accounts Payable		1,000
	Accumulated Depreciation: Equipment		2,000
	To record actual factory overhead costs		
(4)	*Work in Process*	14,000	
	Factory Overhead		14,000
	To record applied overhead [see part (b)]		
(5)	*Finished Goods*	94,500	
	Work in Process		94,500
	To transfer completed units to finished goods [see part (e)]		

g **Overhead is underapplied by $500.**

Overhead incurred	$14,500
Overhead applied	14,000
Underapplied overhead	$ 500

KEY TERMS AND CONCEPTS

equivalent units 873
job cost sheet 859
job order system 859
materials requisition 860
overapplied overhead 870
overhead application rate 864
process costing system 872
time ticket 863
underapplied overhead 870

QUESTIONS

Q22-1 Discuss the general features associated with a job order costing system. In what types of applications are job order systems used?

Q22-2 What is the purpose of using job cost sheets?

Q22-3 Explain how the flow of costs through an accounting system parallels the flow of goods and materials through a manufacturing plant.

Q22-4 How does the use of a predetermined overhead rate smooth product costs over a period of time?

Q22-5 Explain how an overhead application rate is developed and used to apply overhead to specific jobs.

Q22-6 List the characteristics of a good overhead application base.

Q22-7 A manufacturing corporation computed depreciation for the current year as follows:

Factory building and equipment	*$57,000*
Office building and equipment	*33,000*
Total depreciation	*$90,000*

The following journal entry was recorded.

Factory Overhead	*57,000*	
Depreciation Expense	*33,000*	
Accumulated Depreciation		*90,000*

Explain the rationale behind the debits in the journal entry.

Q22-8 Discuss the relationship between the Work in Process account and individual job cost sheets.

Q22-9 If overhead is overapplied, will the Factory Overhead account possess a debit or credit balance? What is the probable effect of the overapplication on the Work in Process balance (before adjustment) at the end of the accounting period?

Q22-10 Which of the following businesses would be most likely to use a process costing system as opposed to a job order system?

a Bicycle manufacturer
b Shipbuilder
c Candy manufacturer
d Petroleum refinery
e Trophy shop
f Small appliance repair shop

Q22-11 Why is it permissible to cost each unit manufactured in a continuous processing environment at an average cost of production?

Q22-12 Explain the concept of equivalent units to someone who has no background in cost accounting.

Q22-13 The Gateway Company uses a process costing system. An examination of goods in production at the end of the accounting period revealed 6,000 units, $\frac{2}{3}$ complete. Would it be correct to say that 4,000 finished units were manufactured? Why?

Q22-14 Why is it usually necessary to compute separate equivalent-unit totals for direct materials and conversion cost?

EXERCISES

E22-1 The following selected transactions appeared on the books of Fastco Enterprises during February.

Feb. 4 Purchased $8,200 of direct materials and $6,400 of indirect materials on account from Jordan Wholesale.
11 Issued $2,800 of direct materials and $900 of indirect materials from the storeroom.
15 Incurred $3,900 of direct labor and $2,100 of indirect labor.
19 Recorded $800 of overhead incurred on account.

23 Applied $1,800 of overhead to production.
25 Noted that $3,100 of production had been completed.
27 Sold goods costing $6,400 on account at a profit of 20% of cost.

Prepare journal entries to record the preceding transactions.

E22-2 The Heuler Corporation applies overhead on the basis of direct labor cost. In December 1983 the company's cost accountant made the following predictions for 1984 operations.

Total direct labor cost	$350,000
Total factory overhead	$490,000

In January Heuler worked on jobs no. 119 and no. 120. The costs incurred and production status of these two jobs appear below.

	Job No. 119	*Job No. 120*
Direct materials	$34,000	$15,000
Direct labor	$22,000	$ 9,000
Production status	In process	In process

By the end of 1984, actual direct labor cost amounted to $362,000, and factory overhead incurred totaled $485,000. There was no work in process on January 1, 1984.

Compute the following:

a Heuler's overhead application rate.
b The balance of the Work in Process account on January 31, 1984.
c The amount of over- or underapplied overhead for 1984. Be sure to indicate whether overhead was overapplied or underapplied.

E22-3 Tassin Corporation's Work in Process account for the year ended December 31 appears below.

Work in Process			
Direct materials	*94,700*	*To finished goods*	*387,600*
Direct labor	*158,000*		
Applied overhead	*197,500*		

Direct materials pertaining to jobs in process on December 31 totaled $19,850. Overhead is applied on the basis of direct labor cost.

Compute the following:

a The overhead application rate used by Tassin.
b The direct labor cost related to jobs in process on December 31.
c The applied factory overhead related to jobs in process on December 31.

E22-4 Upon conclusion of the current accounting period, a Factory Overhead account contained the following amounts:

Factory Overhead	
78,900	48,700
70,100	51,200
34,200	80,600
62,700	90,500

Evaluate the following statements as true or false.

_____ a The actual overhead incurred amounted to $245,900.

_____ b Overhead was underapplied during the accounting period.

_____ c The account's $25,100 balance should be carried forward to the next accounting period.

_____ d The account's $25,100 balance could be due to errors in estimating (1) total factory overhead or (2) the base used to apply overhead to production.

_____ e The most common treatment of handling the $25,100 balance is to allocate it to Work in Process, Finished Goods, and Cost of Goods Sold.

E22-5 The Towson Manufacturing Corporation applies overhead on the basis of machine hours. The following divisional information is presented for your review.

	Division A	Division B	Division C
Actual machine hours	22,500	?	17,000
Estimated machine hours	20,000	?	?
Overhead application rate	$4.50	$5.00	?
Actual overhead	$110,000	?	$48,000
Estimated overhead	?	$90,000	$57,000
Applied overhead	?	$86,000	?
Over- (under-) applied overhead	?	$6,500	$3,000

Find the unknowns for each of the three divisions.

E22-6 The Foxboro Corporation began operations on January 1, 1984. By the end of 1984, 27 jobs had been processed, as shown below.

	No. of Jobs	Total Direct Labor Hours
In process	5	450
Completed but not sold	7	650
Sold	15	1,500
	27	2,600

The firm's overhead application rate of $12 per direct labor hour was computed by dividing estimated overhead of $30,000 by 2,500 estimated direct labor hours. The following errors were made when calculating the $12 rate.

1 Factory depreciation of $10,000 was included in the factory utility cost estimate.

2 Advertising of $5,000 was included in the estimate of total factory overhead.

a Determine the effect of Foxboro's errors on Work in Process, Finished Goods, and Cost of Goods Sold. Ignore any adjustments for over- or underapplied overhead.

b Assuming Foxboro's correct actual overhead incurred for 1984 totaled $28,500, compute the correct over- or underapplied overhead.

E22-7 Consider the following independent cases.

Case A. Beginning work in process: 800 units, $\frac{1}{4}$ complete.
Units started and completed: 2,700.
Ending work in process: 1,200 units, $\frac{1}{3}$ complete.

Case B. Beginning work in process: 1,000 units, $\frac{2}{5}$ complete.
Total units completed during the period: 4,600.
Ending work in process: 900 units, $\frac{2}{3}$ complete.

All materials are added at the start of the process, and conversion costs are incurred uniformly throughout manufacturing. Compute total equivalent units with respect to materials and conversion costs for the current accounting period for each of the above cases.

E22-8 The Nelson Manufacturing Corporation uses a process cost system. The following information pertains to operations for November.

Beginning work in process: 2,400 units, $\frac{1}{3}$ complete.
Units started and completed during November: 5,100.
Ending work in process: 1,000 units, $\frac{3}{4}$ complete.

Nelson adds material A at the start of the process; material B is added at the 50% stage of completion. Labor and overhead are incurred uniformly throughout manufacturing activities.

Assuming that none of the beginning work in process is past the 50% stage of completion on November 1, compute the equivalent units for November with respect to the following:

a Material A
b Material B
c Conversion cost

E22-9 Walther Manufacturing's cost accounting department has calculated the following equivalent production figures for August.

	Physical Units	Equivalent Units: Materials	Equivalent Units: Conversion
Completed production			
Beginning work in process	900	—	600
Units started and completed	2,600	2,600	2,600
Ending work in process	1,500	1,500	1,000
	5,000	4,100	4,200

Prior period costs pertaining to the August 1 work in process inventory amounted to $4,500. Current costs per equivalent unit follow.

Materials	$3.50
Conversion cost	5.00

Compute the following:

a The total cost of production completed in August

b The cost of the ending work in process inventory

PROBLEMS

P22-1 ***Basic job order costing with journal entries***

Friedman Manufacturing uses a job order system to accumulate production costs. On August 1 the only job in process was job no. 19. Its cost sheet appears below.

	Job No. 19
Direct materials	$ 8,500
Direct labor	7,900
Applied overhead	10,270
	$26,670

During August the following costs were incurred.

	Job No. 19	*Job No. 20*	*Job No. 21*	*Job No. 22*	*Total*
Direct materials	$2,000	$5,500	$9,400	$ 6,100	$23,000
Indirect materials					3,800
Direct labor	3,900	7,100	6,800	10,400	28,200
Indirect labor					7,400
					$62,400

Overhead is applied on the basis of direct labor cost. During August jobs no. 19 and no. 21 were completed, job no. 19 was sold on account for $45,000, and miscellaneous overhead incurred amounted to $18,400.

INSTRUCTIONS

a Determine Friedman's overhead application rate.

b Prepare journal entries for August to record the following. (*Note:* Prepare summary entries by combining individual job data.)
 (1) The issuance of direct and indirect materials
 (2) The direct and indirect labor incurred
 (3) The miscellaneous overhead charges
 (4) The application of overhead to production
 (5) The completion of jobs no. 19 and no. 21
 (6) The sale of job no. 19

P22-2 ***Computations using a job order system***

The Kothman Corporation employs a job order cost system. On June 1 the balances below were extracted from the general ledger.

Work in process	*$ 24,900*
Finished goods	*51,600*
Cost of goods sold	*115,800*

Work in Process consisted of two jobs, no. 140 ($16,800) and no. 142 ($8,100). During June direct materials requisitioned from the storeroom amounted to $75,300, and direct labor incurred totaled $71,200. These figures are subdivided as follows:

Direct Materials		Direct Labor	
Job No.	**Amount**	**Job No.**	**Amount**
140	$ 4,300	140	$ 5,000
150	15,400	142	7,500
151	17,200	150	12,600
Other	38,400	151	14,400
	$75,300	Other	31,700
			$71,200

Job no. 150 was the only job in process at the end of the month. Job no. 140 and three other jobs (material cost, $25,200; labor cost, $21,400—the costs of job no. 140 are not included in these figures) were sold during June at a profit of 30% of cost.

Kothman applies overhead daily at the rate of 200% of direct labor cost as labor summaries are posted to job orders. The firm's fiscal year ends June 30.

INSTRUCTIONS

a Compute the cost of the ending work in process inventory.
b Compute the cost of jobs completed during June.
c Compute the cost of goods sold for the year ended June 30.
d Compute the cost of the ending finished goods inventory.

P22-3 ***Comprehensive job order costing with journal entries***

The Ziegler Manufacturing Corporation uses a job order system to accumulate product costs. The books show the following account balances as of December 1.

Raw materials	$ 74,300
Work in process	233,500
Finished goods	184,500
Cost of goods sold	241,000
Factory overhead	5,400 debit

Three jobs are presently in process.

	Job No. 841	Job No. 842	Job No. 844	Total
Direct materials	$14,350	$16,800	$10,100	$ 41,250
Direct labor	28,700	31,200	17,000	76,900
Factory overhead	43,050	46,800	25,500	115,350
	$86,100	$94,800	$52,600	$233,500

Factory overhead is applied to jobs at the rate of 150% of direct labor cost when jobs are completed and at the end of the month for production in process. All over- or underapplied overhead is adjusted to Cost of Goods Sold at the end of Ziegler's year on December 31. The following transactions took place in December.

1 Purchased raw materials on account, $34,600.
2 Issued materials and incurred labor costs as follows:

	Job No. 841	Job No. 842	Job No. 844	Job No. 845	Total
Direct materials	$ —	$ 4,100	$ 6,800	$11,200	$22,100
Indirect materials					7,400
Direct labor	5,800	7,200	12,400	15,800	41,200
Indirect labor					11,500
	$5,800	$11,300	$19,200	$27,000	$82,200

3 Other costs incurred in December were as follows:

Paid in December		***To Be Paid in January***	
Factory utilities	$3,100	Advertising	$2,200
Machine repairs	3,500	Factory taxes	3,900
	$6,600		$6,100

4 Depreciation on the factory building and machinery amounted to $10,000 and $5,800, respectively.

5 Excess materials of $2,100 relating to job no. 842 were returned to the storeroom.

6 Job status on December 31 is as follows:

Job No.	*Status*
841	Completed and sold on account for $102,500
842	In process
844	Completed but unsold
845	In process

7 Job no. 839, completed in November, was sold on account for $78,500. Total job cost amounted to $65,700.

INSTRUCTIONS

a Open accounts for Raw Materials, Work in Process, Finished Goods, Cost of Goods Sold, and Factory Overhead.

b Prepare journal entries to record Ziegler's December transactions. Show supporting computations when appropriate. *Hint:* Be sure to apply overhead to completed jobs and jobs in process.

c Post the relevant entries to the accounts opened in part (a). Determine ending account balances prior to any adjustments for over- or underapplied overhead.

d Prepare the journal entry to adjust for over- or underapplied overhead. Is overhead over- or underapplied?

P22-4 ***Job order costing: Overhead and account balance computation***

The Brobst Company, a manufacturer of contemporary home furniture, uses a job order cost system. The following information pertains to the current year.

Department 203, Work in Process, January 1

Job No.	*Material*	*Labor*	*Overhead*	*Total*
1376	$17,500	$22,000	$33,000	$72,500

Department 203 costs for the year are as follows:

Incurred by Jobs	*Material*	*Labor*	*Other*	*Total*
1376	$ 1,000	$ 7,000		$ 8,000
1377	26,000	53,000		79,000
1378	12,000	9,000		21,000
1379	4,000	1,000		5,000
Not Incurred by Jobs				
Indirect materials and supplies	15,000			15,000
Indirect labor		53,000		53,000
Salesmen commissions			$10,000	10,000
Factory employee benefits			23,000	23,000
Depreciation: factory			12,000	12,000
Factory supervision		20,000		20,000
Total	$58,000	$143,000	$45,000	$246,000

Brobst applies overhead on the basis of direct labor cost. At the beginning of the year the cost accounting department forecasted direct labor cost and factory overhead of $80,000 and $128,000, respectively.

INSTRUCTIONS

a Determine total actual factory overhead for Department 203.

b Calculate the amount of over- or underapplied overhead for the year.

c Discuss several possible methods for handling the over- or underapplied overhead at the conclusion of the accounting period. Which method is most widely used in practice? Why?

d Job no. 1376 was the only job that was completed and sold during the year. Given this information, compute (1) cost of goods sold for the year (consider any over- or underapplied overhead when formulating your answer); (2) ending work in process inventory.

(CMA modified.)

P22-5 ***Job costing in a service business***

Matthews and Associates renders consulting services to a number of medical practices. To determine the cost of each consulting engagement, Matthews uses a job order cost system. All costs traceable to specific clients are charged to individual client jobs. Other costs incurred by Matthews, but not identifiable with specific clients, are charged to jobs via a predetermined overhead application rate. The overhead rate also includes a markup to provide a profit for the firm. On the basis of past experience, Matthews has prepared the following budget for the upcoming year.

Cost	*Total*	*Assignable to Specific Jobs*	*Not Assignable to Specific Jobs*
Consulting staff	$200,000	$180,000	$20,000
Office staff	30,000	12,000	18,000
Travel	20,000	15,000	5,000
Other office costs	10,000	1,000	9,000
	$260,000	$208,000	$52,000

The firm's profit objective is 25% of total cost.

INSTRUCTIONS

a Determine Matthews's overhead application rate. The rate is based on the compensation of the consulting staff assignable to client jobs (i.e., "direct labor").

b In January Matthews completed an engagement for the Cincinnati Medical Association (CMA). The following costs were directly chargeable to CMA.

Consulting staff	$4,500
Office staff	300
Travel	1,100
Other office costs	100

Clients reimburse Matthews for directly chargeable costs plus overhead (which includes the profit margin). How much will Matthews bill CMA for services performed?

c Observe that part of the consulting staff's cost is not assigned to specific jobs. List several possible underlying reasons.

P22-6 ***Flow of costs: Finding unknowns***

Selected ledger accounts for the current year for Ormsby Manufacturing appear below.

Raw Materials

Balance	17,000	84,000
	92,000	

Wages Payable

		104,000

Factory Overhead

Indirect labor	16,000	132,000
Other	120,000	

Work in Process

Balance	26,000	?
Direct materials	72,000	
Direct labor	?	
Applied overhead	?	

Finished Goods

Balance	37,000	?
	286,000	

Cost of Goods Sold	
?	

The year-end count of completed goods on hand revealed the following:

Part No.	Quantity (Units)	Unit Cost
118	4,500	$5.20
124	6,400	8.40
131	10,100	6.50

Ormsby applies overhead on the basis of direct labor cost.

INSTRUCTIONS

a Compute the amount of indirect materials used in operations.
b Compute total direct labor for the period.
c Determine Ormsby's overhead application rate.
d Compute the ending work in process balance.
e Determine total credits to the Finished Goods account.
f Ormsby adjusts over- or underapplied overhead to Cost of Goods Sold. Present the proper journal entry. Was overhead over- or underapplied?
g If sales totaled $247,000, compute Ormsby's gross profit for the year.

P22-7 ***Straightforward process costing***

Pusker Manufacturing uses a process costing system to accumulate production costs. The following information pertains to October.

Beginning work in process inventory: 1,400 units, 75% complete; cost, $23,975.
Number of units started during October: 5,100.
Total units completed: 4,700.
Ending work in process inventory: 1,800 units, 75% complete.
Costs incurred in October: direct materials used, $44,625; conversion cost, $58,200.

All materials are introduced at the start of the process, and conversion costs are incurred uniformly throughout manufacturing.

INSTRUCTIONS

a Prepare a cost of production report in good form.
b Prepare the necessary journal entry to record the completed production for October.

P22-8 ***Process costing and cost flow***

The Gunter Corporation uses a process costing system. All materials are introduced at the start of the process, and conversion costs are incurred uniformly throughout manufacturing. The following T-accounts were extracted from Gunter's records as of March 31.

Work in Process

3/1 Balance 1,800 units, $\frac{1}{3}$ complete	15,150	To finished goods: 3,300 units	?
Started 3,500 units			
Materials	19,600		
Conversion	37,380		

Finished Goods

3/1 Balance 2,500 units	35,250	To cost of goods sold: ? units	?
From work in process: 3,300 units	?		

The units completed include the beginning work in process inventory. The ending work in process inventory is $\frac{3}{4}$ complete.

INSTRUCTIONS

a Compute the following:
(1) Total equivalent units and the cost per equivalent unit for both materials and conversion cost.
(2) The cost of units started in February but completed in March.
(3) The cost of units started and completed in March.
(4) The cost of units transferred to finished goods.
(5) The cost of Gunter's ending work in process inventory.

b Gunter uses the FIFO method for costing finished goods inventory. If 3,600 units were on hand on March 31, determine (1) the ending balance in the Finished Goods account; (2) cost of goods sold during March.

P22-9 ***Comprehensive process costing and cost flows***

The Bilsky Corporation manufactures a chemical called XF-28 and accumulates costs by using a process costing system. All materials are added at the beginning of the process; conversion costs are incurred uniformly throughout manufacturing. Overhead is applied to production at the rate of $3.50 per direct labor hour.

The following information relates to production during May.

Direct materials:

May	1	Balance	3,000 pounds	$24,300
	8	Purchase	5,000 pounds	41,000
	21	Purchase	8,000 pounds	66,400
	29	Purchase	9,000 pounds	75,600

Work in process, May 1 (6,000 pounds, $\frac{1}{3}$ complete):

Direct materials	$47,400	
Direct labor @ $6.00/hour	6,600	
Factory overhead	3,850	$57,850

Direct labor for May @ $6.00/hour: $87,000.
Completed production transferred to finished goods: 20,000 pounds.
Work in process, May 31: 4,000 pounds, $\frac{1}{4}$ complete.

Bilsky uses the FIFO method of inventory valuation for direct materials. At the end of May 7,000 pounds of direct materials remained in the storeroom. The firm's year-end is May 31.

INSTRUCTIONS

a Compute the cost of direct materials issued to production during May.
b Compute total conversion cost for May.
c By preparing a cost of production report, determine the cost of XF-28 completed during May and Bilsky's ending work in process inventory.

P22-10 ***Basic job order costing with journal entries (alternate to P22-1)***
Contemporary Manufacturing uses a job order system to accumulate production costs. On May 1 the only job in process was job no. 174. Its cost sheet appears below.

	Job No. 174
Direct materials	$10,800
Direct labor	21,500
Applied overhead	38,700
	$71,000

During May the following costs were incurred.

	Job No. 174	Job No. 175	Job No. 176	Job No. 177	Total
Direct materials	$4,200	$7,300	$10,400	$12,000	$33,900
Indirect materials					5,100
Direct labor	8,600	5,500	3,000	6,400	23,500
Indirect labor					8,800
					$71,300

Overhead is applied on the basis of direct labor cost. During May jobs no. 174 and no. 176 were completed, job no. 174 was sold on account for $110,000, and miscellaneous overhead incurred amounted to $29,700.

INSTRUCTIONS

a Determine Contemporary's overhead application rate.
b Prepare journal entries for May to record the following. (*Note:* Prepare summary entries by combining individual job data.)
(1) The issuance of direct and indirect materials
(2) The direct and indirect labor incurred
(3) The miscellaneous overhead charges
(4) The application of overhead to production
(5) The completion of jobs no. 174 and no. 176
(6) The sale of job no. 174

P22-11 ***Computations using a job order system (alternate to P22-2)***
The Des Moines Corporation employs a job order cost system. On April 1 the balances below were extracted from the general ledger.

Work in process	*$ 31,600*
Finished goods	*74,200*
Cost of goods sold	*109,500*

Work in Process consisted of two jobs, no. 820 ($14,200) and no. 822 ($17,400). During April direct materials requisitioned from the storeroom amounted to $65,300, and direct labor incurred totaled $75,500. These figures are subdivided as follows:

Direct Materials		*Direct Labor*	
Job No.	***Amount***	***Job No.***	***Amount***
820	$ 4,000	820	$ 3,000
826	18,500	822	8,400
827	13,100	826	12,500
Other	29,700	827	15,200
	$65,300	Other	36,400
			$75,500

Job no. 826 was the only job in process by the end of the month. Job no. 820 and three other jobs (material cost, $19,700; labor cost, $25,300—the costs of job no. 820 are not included in these figures) were sold during April at a profit of 20% of cost.

Des Moines applies overhead daily at the rate of 150% of direct labor cost as labor summaries are posted to job orders. The firm's fiscal year ends on April 30.

INSTRUCTIONS

a Compute the cost of the ending work in process inventory.
b Compute the cost of jobs completed during April.
c Compute the cost of goods sold for the year ended April 30.
d Compute the cost of the ending finished goods inventory.

P22-12 ***Flow of costs: Finding unknowns (alternate to P22-6)***

Selected ledger accounts for the current year for Ruffin Manufacturing appear below.

Raw Materials

Balance	*19,000*	*89,000*
	?	

Wages Payable

		58,000

Factory Overhead

Indirect materials	*7,000*	*?*
All other	*97,000*	

Work in Process

Balance	?	240,000
Direct materials	?	
Direct labor	51,000	
Applied overhead	?	

Finished Goods

Balance	114,000	?

Cost of Goods Sold

296,000	

A year-end count revealed ending raw materials and work in process inventories of \$25,000 and \$14,000, respectively. Ruffin uses an overhead application rate of 200% of direct labor cost.

INSTRUCTIONS

a Compute the amount of indirect labor incurred in operations.

b Compute total direct materials used.

c Determine Ruffin's purchases of raw materials during the year.

d How much overhead was applied to production?

e Determine the cost of the ending finished goods inventory.

f Compute the cost of the beginning work in process inventory.

g If Ruffin adjusts over- or underapplied overhead to cost of goods sold, compute the cost of goods sold figure that would appear on the firm's income statement.

P22-13 ***Straightforward process costing (alternate to P22-7)***

The Norwich Company uses a process costing system to accumulate production costs. The following information pertains to April.

Beginning work in process inventory: 800 units, 25% complete; cost, \$4,430.
Number of units started during April: 1,700.
Total units completed: 2,100.
Ending work in process inventory: 400 units, 25% complete.
Costs incurred in April: direct materials used, \$6,970; conversion cost, \$12,800.

All materials are introduced at the start of the process, and conversion costs are incurred uniformly throughout manufacturing.

INSTRUCTIONS

a Prepare a cost of production report in good form.

b Prepare the necessary journal entry to record the completed production for April.

P22-14 Comprehensive process costing and cost flows (alternate to P22-9)

The Dalworth Corporation manufactures a chemical called G-108 and accumulates costs by using a process costing system. All materials are added at the beginning of the process; conversion costs are incurred uniformly throughout manufacturing. Overhead is applied to production at the rate of $3.10 per direct labor hour.

The following information relates to production during March.

Direct materials:

Mar.	1	Balance	5,000 gallons	$26,000
	4	Purchase	7,000 gallons	36,400
	18	Purchase	9,000 gallons	46,800
	24	Purchase	8,000 gallons	42,400

Work in process, March 1 (10,000 gallons, $\frac{3}{4}$ complete):

Direct materials	$49,000	
Direct labor @ $8.00/hour	9,600	
Factory overhead	4,800	$63,400

Direct labor for March @ $8.00/hour: $160,000.
Completed production transferred to finished goods: 24,000 gallons.
Work in process, March 31: 6,000 gallons, $\frac{1}{3}$ complete.

Dalworth uses the FIFO method of inventory valuation for direct materials. At the end of March 9,000 gallons of direct materials remained in the storeroom. The firm's year-end is March 31.

INSTRUCTIONS

a Compute the cost of direct materials issued to production during March.

b Compute total conversion cost for March.

c By preparing a cost of production report, determine the cost of G-108 completed during March and Dalworth's ending work in process inventory.

CASE 22

RELIABLE PRODUCTS

Susan Hume recently accepted a new job in the accounting department of Reliable Products. After only one week of employment she received the following memo from Pat Wills, her supervisor.

July 7

Susan:

Due to a death in the family, I will be gone until the 16th. As you know, I've been working on a project concerning Reliable's overhead application rates. Because the project must be completed shortly after my return, I need your assistance. Specifically, I would like you to focus on two issues. First, should overhead rates be changed every quarter to correspond with our highly seasonal business? Second, should each department set individual overhead rates in view of the significant differences that exist between departmental operations?

I know these issues might be a little difficult to understand given that (1) you've only been here one week and (2) you had minimal cost accounting while in school. Try your best and have recommendations on my desk by my return. I've attached the following material for further information. Thanks.

Pat

A: *Quarterly overhead rates*

As you know, our business is highly seasonal. Because of a lack of competition for many of our products, cost is a *major* factor in determining selling price. The following figures are for item no. 882, a representative product.

	Quarter			
	1	2	3	4
Production (units)	5,000	20,000	8,000	25,000
Direct materials	$ 25,000	$100,000	$ 40,800	$127,500
Direct labor	40,000	160,000	65,600	205,000
Variable factory overhead	10,000	40,000	16,000	52,500
Fixed factory overhead	100,000	100,000	100,000	100,000
Total cost	$175,000	$400,000	$222,400	$485,000
Cost per unit	$35	$20	$27.80	$19.40
Overhead per unit	$22	$ 7	$14.50	$ 6.10

B: *Departmental rates*

We have two primary departments: Machining and Assembly. The Machining Department uses very costly, intricate equipment in manufacturing various products. The resulting depreciation and utility costs are high. Upon completion goods are passed from Machining to Assembly. In the Assembly Department there is minimal equipment, because the emphasis is on manual labor.

A sampling of recent jobs revealed the following data:

	Hours Spent In		
Job No.	Machining	Assembly	Total
431	28	4	32
432	5	30	35
433	18	50	68
434	30	10	40

As you can see, there can be considerable variation among jobs. At present a single plantwide rate is used for product costing.

INSTRUCTIONS

a Should Reliable change its selling price each quarter to correspond with the unit-cost change? Why?

b Determine the primary cause behind the fluctuating unit costs each quarter. What can Reliable do to alleviate the problem?

c Given the nature of Reliable's operation, is a single combined overhead rate for all departments preferred, or should separate departmental rates be used? Why? Justify your answer.

23 BUDGETING

LEARNING OBJECTIVES

After reading this chapter you should:

1 Understand the benefits of budgeting.

2 Understand the distinction between top-down and bottom-up budgeting.

3 Be familiar with slack as it relates to the estimation process.

4 Understand the differences between traditional and zero-base budgeting, including the advantages and disadvantages associated with the latter approach.

5 Understand the variations in budget periods.

6 Be familiar with the limitations of budgeting, especially in the human relations area.

7 Be able to prepare a master budget.

8 Be familiar with the adaptability of budgets to computers.

CHAPTER 23

Businesses in this country continually strive to increase profitability. So that they may achieve this end, new facilities are constructed, research programs are undertaken, employees with needed skills are hired, and new product lines are introduced. These actions are usually not haphazard; rather they are part of a carefully defined plan to achieve a specific goal. Because of the increasing complexities of our society, extensive planning is necessary for effective attainment of desired results.

Planning may assume several different forms. When dealing with the long run, companies specify generalized goals along with strategies and policies to achieve those goals. For example, suppose a manufacturer of household cleaning products desired to enter the car care market. Accordingly, the company could establish a strategy to acquire an existing manufacturer of car care products or engage in an extensive research program and develop new products internally. Planning of this nature is essential, because it helps chart a company's operation over many future periods.

Another facet of planning involves budgets. A **budget** is a formal quantitative expression of management expectations. Unlike strategies and policies, budgets contain considerable detail. In effect, a budget can be likened to a blueprint, that is, an intricate plan that serves as a framework for future action.

Budgets are popular among businesses and numerous governmental units. As the following example shows, even not-for-profit entities find budgeting beneficial.

> *The American Bar Association (ABA) is a national professional organization of practicing attorneys. The purpose of the organization is to advance the professional practice of law. This purpose is accomplished (1) through various committees that study specific legal issues, (2) by furnishing advice to the United States Congress on pending legislation, and (3) by disseminating various publications to members. Most of the ABA's revenues are received during a three-month period (May–July) when annual dues are billed to members. However, the organization's activities continue throughout the year. If the ABA did not engage in a budgeting program to forecast revenues and expenditures, it could easily run out of funds before the next billing period. For this reason the budgeting process at the ABA is quite formalized, and all units must carefully adhere to the approved budgetary plan.*

BENEFITS OF BUDGETING

If done correctly, budgeting is a time-consuming and arduous process. It goes without saying that an in-depth look at the future requires numerous assumptions, much uncertainty, and often considerable employee involvement. Furthermore, managers must frequently turn their thoughts away from current, pressing problems to devote full attention to the budget effort. With all these unattractive features, the question arises, "Why budget?" Normally, the benefits of budgeting outweigh the associated problems. Budgets formalize planning, serve as a basis for performance evaluation, and assist in communication and coordination within an entity.

Formalizes Planning

Budgets are an outgrowth of the planning process. Because budgets force managers to look ahead and study the future, a formalized "plan of attack" can be constructed. To picture the related benefits, imagine building a home without the availability of the previously mentioned blueprint. Walls may be plastered or encased in plasterboard, and then one discovers that electrical outlets and heating vents were forgotten. Or the foundation may be laid and then found to be over the property line. Indeed, the building process would be chaotic at best. Similarly, the lack of a formal plan leads to considerable "fire fighting" on the part of management, thereby hampering the attainment of long-run goals and objectives.

The implementation of a budget enables companies (and individuals) to pinpoint potential problems before the problems occur. In this manner operating distractions are greatly reduced, since anticipation often leads to the introduction of preliminary corrective action. The eventual outcome of planning is a direction-oriented entity that is taking large strides toward achieving financial success and well-being.

Basis for Performance Evaluation

Although best-noted for its role in planning, a budget also assists management in the appraisal of performance and control of operations. As we explained in Chapter 21, organizations often prepare reports that compare actual results with a predetermined budget. The budget therefore serves as a yardstick in judging whether performance has been up to par. Should deficiencies arise, corrective action can be taken to bring the organization back on target.

Some businesses attempt to evaluate performance by comparing current actual results with actual results of previous accounting periods. Unfortunately, this type of comparative evaluation has an inherent deficiency. To illustrate, assume a company's total operating expenses last year amounted to $200,000. If the company was subject to a 10% inflation rate and current expenses total only $210,000, the immediate conclusion might be that management has done a creditable job in controlling costs. However, if last year's expenses were excessive because of significant inefficiencies, the entire evaluative picture could change. For instance, suppose last year's expenses would have been $180,000 under normal operating conditions. Allowing for an $18,000 increase due to inflation, current expenses would exceed the $198,000 target by $12,000 ($210,000 − $198,000).

Comparisons with past data simply do not reveal whether current performance is acceptable. Why? Past data brings all that was bad about the past into the evaluation. Furthermore, if a company's operating environment has changed significantly because of new technology, a new management team, or other factors, comparisons of past data with current data approach the meaningless level very quickly. Current performance is best judged against a budget for the same period. Although the budget relies on numerous assumptions, adequate appraisal can occur if due care has been exercised in the formulation of the budget and if all available information is considered.

Assists in Communication and Coordination

Business operations dictate the performance of many diverse activities. These activities include the production and sale of goods and services, purchasing, credit extension and the collection of accounts, data processing, and the financing of operations. In small enterprises these functions are often supervised by the same individual. In large organizations, however, operations are normally divided and are the responsibility of different managers.

So that company objectives are achieved, close coordination of activities is a necessity. Imagine the problems that could arise if coordination was lacking. For example, the marketing department could undertake a large advertising campaign for a new product and then find that production was halted due to shortages of needed raw materials. Or at a time when marketing was attempting to expand the company's market share, the credit department might be tightening credit standards because of recent problems with uncollectible accounts. In both of these cases embarrassment is sure to result.

Where do budgets fit in? When a budget for the overall organization is being constructed, individual managers must communicate their plans. The plans are then examined to determine whether they are feasible and consistent with the plans of other operating units. The budget process, therefore, serves as a gigantic blender to integrate and coordinate diverse activities to help attain company goals. Obviously, in any process where different views are represented, there must be some compromise to achieve a successful result. If each unit attempted to satisfy its own objectives rather than those of the firm, suboptimal firm performance and continuous infighting would undoubtedly occur.

Although the preceding discussion has focused on budgeting as it relates to businesses and organizations, the same principles apply to individuals, especially married couples. If you are married or contemplating marriage, you will find that considerable give-and-take is necessary when constructing an operative budget for your family. The excerpt on pages 906–907 relates this fact very clearly via the results of a simplified test.

BUDGET CONSTRUCTION CONSIDERATIONS

The construction of a budget varies dramatically from one business to another. Many companies establish formal procedures that are followed to the letter. In contrast, other companies employ "seat of the pants" management and merely scribble some hastily derived projections on the back of an envelope. Because of the wide variety of approaches found in practice, any attempt at presenting a detailed discussion on how to budget or "The Ten Easy Steps to Budgeting" is somewhat fruitless. Hence we will make no attempt to do so. There are, however, several general construction considerations with which you should be familiar. A short discussion of these considerations follows.

Construction Flows

Most medium- and large-size organizations are composed of several management levels. See Exhibit 23-1, for example, which depicts a typical organizational hierarchy.

The budget-building process generally follows the organizational structure. That is, construction proceeds from higher- to lower-management levels, or vice versa.

Exhibit 23-1

Organizational hierarchy

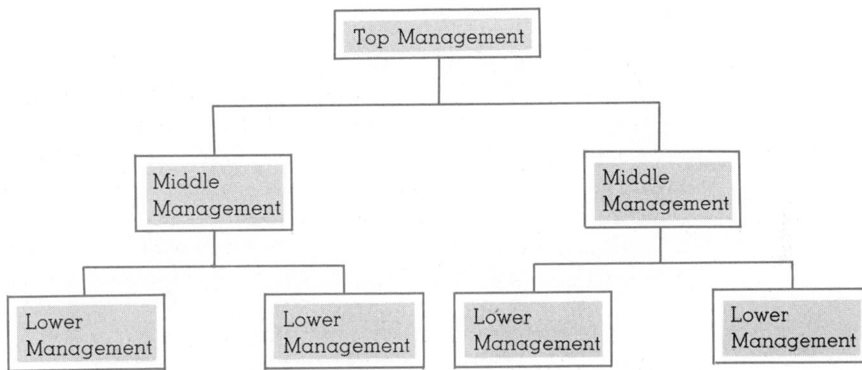

Top-down approach

With the **top-down approach** virtually all budget development takes place at the upper echelons of management. The budget is imposed on lower-level personnel, who rarely become involved in the construction process. On paper, the top-down approach offers the advantage of sound budget preparation. A budget should reflect the overall goals of an organization. Preparation in this instance is carried forth by those who have the best view of overall firm operations, that is, top management. Top management can study the interactions of the lower units and determine the consistency of the units' plans and expectations.

In most cases this apparent advantage gives rise to a significant problem. When the budget is imposed from above, lower-level managers often feel that their opinions and operating perspectives lack importance. Although lower-level employees will be evaluated against the budget, they have done little to assist in its development. This "dictatorial" approach is generally met with resentment and a "who cares" attitude, both of which result in a negative stand toward budget achievement.

Bottom-up approach

Unlike the top-down approach, **bottom-up budgeting** centers on lower-level employee participation in the development process. The bottom-up approach usually begins with the issuance of general budget guidelines by top management or perhaps by a budget committee. The budget committee normally consists of high-level executives along with representatives from

BUDGETING AND MARRIAGE

Next to sex, there are probably few areas in a marriage as emotionally charged as money. When one partner runs the family treasury and doles out funds to the other, or if one is a spender and the other a saver, the potential for endless arguments exists. If the long-range goals of one are vastly different from those of the other, at least one partner is bound to feel deeply disappointed and resentful in later years unless an early compromise is reached.

For a marriage to be successful, each partner needs insight into the way his or her spouse views money. This insight can be gained by the quiz on page 907. The rules are simple. Because families are made up of individuals, the husband and the wife should take the quiz separately. Individual answers don't count; it's the final sum that matters. Score one point for each check in column A, three points for each check in B, and five points for C. Then add up your total scores.

If your mate's score and yours are within 20 points of one another, you are very fortunate. You can choose identical strategies, and since you both view money similarly, there are likely to be few arguments over spending and saving. If your scores are between 20 and 40 points of each other, you will have to make some adjustments to each other's preferences. Trade-offs work well here. You might agree to buy less expensive clothes, for example, to satisfy your partner's craving for savings. Your spouse in turn agrees that his or her next raise will bring more fun money for each, that is, money that can be spent on anything or in any way with no questions asked.

Now let's look at what the individual scores mean. If your score is below 70, chances are that you are a very careful spender and that you value saving more than you value spending. Because you are inclined to be overcautious, you may lose money by avoiding even sensible investments that will protect you against inflation.

If your score is between 70 and 110, you have probably achieved a reasonable balance between saving, spending, and credit. Your biggest effort should go toward increasing your income by carefully monitoring interest rates, credit, dividends, and buying strategies. Finally, if your score is between 110 and 150, you probably tend to hold money very lightly and regard saving as an unnecessary evil.

Overall a family budget must be a joint venture. Like marriage, it is something that both partners must live with, and frequently, some adjustment is needed to reach a meeting of the minds. However, when you finally create a budget that works, you will rapidly learn that it's been well worth the effort.

SOURCE Adapted from Alice Priest, The Family Budget Book *(Lorenz Press, 1978), by permission of Aaron Priest Literary Agency.*

	A	B	C
1 I have managed the bulk of my own expenses since I was	16 to 18	18 to 21	over 21
2 I have my own checking account	now	at one time	never
3 I have my own savings account	now	at one time	never
4 I have trouble balancing my checkbook	never	sometimes	usually
5 I run out of money before I run out of month	never	sometimes	usually
6 I have been bothered by a creditor demanding payment on an overdue bill	never	sometimes	usually
7 I worry about money	never	sometimes	usually
8 I have been refused credit	never	once	more than once
9 I am in debt	never	sometimes	usually
10 I spend more than I planned	never	sometimes	usually
11 I can afford what I want	usually	sometimes	never
12 I regret what I buy	never	sometimes	usually
13 I save regularly	usually	sometimes	never
14 I enjoy spending money	never	sometimes	usually
15 I feel as if I've thrown my money away	never	sometimes	usually
16 My wife/husband thinks I'm a	penny pincher	prudent spender	spendthrift
17 I think I'm a	penny pincher	prudent spender	spendthrift
18 I like extravagances	never	sometimes	usually
19 Lack of money is my biggest problem	never	sometimes	usually
20 I buy on impulse	never	sometimes	usually
21 I buy ahead	usually	sometimes	never
22 I have to juggle my creditors	never	sometimes	usually
23 There are important things I want that I will _____ get	probably	possibly	never
24 I would go into debt to take a vacation	never	sometimes	usually
25 I review my net worth	each year	sometimes	never
26 I count on future raises or bonuses to pay some of my bills	never	sometimes	always
27 I write checks and then have to cover them	never	sometimes	usually
28 I have had checks bounce	never	sometimes	often
29 I estimate my expenses well	usually	sometimes	never
30 My monthly rent or mortgage payments are _____ of my monthly aftertax income	less than 25%	25%	more than 25%

functional areas such as sales, production, and finance. The guidelines normally include yearly goals, anticipated inflation rates, available resources, and similar data.

Once this information is disseminated, those employees held responsible for achieving the desired results formulate appropriate budgets. The process begins at the lower levels of the organizational structure and works its way upward. Individual budgets become grouped by major operating units, such as divisions and territories, and eventually reach top management or the budget committee. The budgets are reviewed, and suggestions for improvement are offered. Lower-level managers then make the necessary revisions, and ultimately, a compromise is reached.

Observe that the bottom-up approach is not 100% bottom-up; there is some direction and coordination from above. Nevertheless, the bottom-up approach offers several distinct advantages over a budget that is handed down from top management with a "meet it or else" attitude.

1 Bottom-up (i.e., *participative*) budgets are really self-imposed. By consulting with and incorporating the goals of lower-level employees, greater strides are made toward budget achievement. That is, individuals throughout the organization know their views are valued by top management. Thus employee morale and job satisfaction generally increase, and extensive efforts are made to meet budgeted targets.
2 The budget is constructed by employees who are close to the action and who know the "ins and outs" and intricate details of daily activity. The same cannot be said for a budget that is prepared solely by top management with no lower-level input. The bottom-up approach usually results in a more realistic and accurate target of performance.

In comparison with the top-down approach, the bottom-up approach is more time-consuming and expensive to administer because of increased employee involvement. Despite these problems, participative budgeting is a popular tool among progressive companies. Because the broad perspectives of top management are used in conjunction with the detailed operating knowledge of lower-level personnel, a powerful budget document is created, one that encompasses the views of all ranges of the organizational hierarchy.

Budget Estimation

By its nature, a budget is a series of future estimates. These estimates should not be arrived at haphazardly; instead significant care should be exercised in their determination.

Normally, budget estimates are based on both the past and the future. That is, historical information is often a good starting point for prediction. However, because of changing conditions, modification of past trends may be necessary. As an example, suppose a company is attempting to budget sales for a particular product. The company presently has a 26% market share and has increased its market share by 1% each year for the past five years. Should conditions remain relatively stable, the firm would be correct in anticipating a 27% share of total sales for the upcoming period. If, however, conditions change because of, say, new competition or technological innovations, these factors must be considered if the sales estimate is to have any meaning.

Estimation and slack

As we noted earlier, budgets are frequently used in performance evaluation. Well aware of this fact, many managers tend to build slack into their budgets. **Slack** refers to the use of padding to avoid unfavorable appraisals. Slack may be introduced in many different forms. For example, sales and operating capabilities may be underestimated and expenses may be overestimated. Thus when the actual results are tabulated and sales are "down" and expenses are "up," the manager is still deemed to have met his or her budget and, therefore, company objectives. In essence, slack has given the manager some leeway in the performance of daily activities.

Slack permeates the entire budgetary process and sometimes tends to perpetuate itself. For example, in many not-for-profit entities, operating units are given a maximum spending limit for specific types of expenditures. A governmental entity, for instance, may be authorized to spend $5,000 for new equipment acquisitions during the fiscal year. If the year-end is rapidly approaching and considerable funds have yet to be used, the unit may undertake a buying spree. Why? If funds remain, administrators might take the position that the current equipment budget was apparently in excess of what was really needed. Thus there could be a strong tendency for cutbacks in the subsequent budget period. This "use it or lose it" philosophy often presents evidence for larger (and slack-oriented) budgets in future years. Unfortunately, actions such as the foregoing frequently give rise to sloppy operating practices that are in conflict with an entity's goals and objectives.

Slack is a significant problem for most budget makers and is extremely difficult to eliminate. Although it is easier said than done, budget estimates should be realistic and should shy away from excessive optimism and pessimism. Unrealistic estimates defeat the entire purpose of the budgeting effort. The net result is aptly described by the acronym GIGO: garbage in, garbage out.

The Budget Approach

Once the estimation process is understood, the question becomes, "Where do we start?" Most companies and organizations follow a traditional budgeting approach. **Traditional budgeting** takes the most recent accounting period's operating data and makes an adjustment for anticipated cost or activity changes. For example, suppose a company spent $250,000 for factory labor during the period just ended. The company expects that production volume and the number of factory workers will remain relatively stable; however, a new union contract must be negotiated and a 10%

wage hike is likely. Thus the new budget will contain estimated labor costs of $275,000.

Although the traditional approach is frequently encountered in practice, it has an inherent problem. The budgeted amount is almost automatic—that is, take the past and adjust for the future. Little attempt is made to analyze prior productivity and costs to judge operating efficiencies. It is therefore conceivable that a company could be continuing its ineffective and inefficient ways from one year to the next and, curiously, be willing to pay more and more money to do so. If strong managerial accounting procedures are instituted, problems such as these can be identified elsewhere in the scheme of managerial control. It is possible, however, that with weak controls and a traditional budgeting approach, ineffective business practices will be perpetuated.

Zero-base budgeting

To partially overcome the limitations of traditional budgeting, firms may employ a **zero-base budgeting (ZBB)** approach. ZBB does not use last period's operating data as a starting point. Instead a manager is given an initial budget allocation of $0 and is told to start from scratch, as if the operating unit (e.g., department) was beginning anew. To obtain operating monies, the manager must then prepare a request for desired funding for the upcoming year. Importantly, this procedure forces management to take an in-depth look at the programs and activities that have been implemented so that funding requests can be justified. Presumably, ineffective operations will be identified and either improved or eliminated in the process. ZBB offers the further benefit of participative management by involving lower-level personnel in the budget construction process.

The zero-base approach is not without its problems, however. In-depth operational reviews are extremely time-consuming and costly. Furthermore, when a manager is trying to justify a request for funds, the paperwork generated can be overwhelming. After all, if you were presenting a case for budget funds and perhaps the ultimate survival of your unit, you might have a few words to say about the importance of your activity to the entire organization, the implications of not providing adequate funding, and similar matters. In an effort to remedy the paperwork problem, one zero-base user (Texas Instruments) limits funding requests to one typed page.[1]

ZBB also gives rise to a troublesome exercise in ranking. To illustrate, suppose a small city is currently evaluating funding requests from its police department and computer center operation. The city has limited funds and is unable to honor all requests; thus some paring is necessary. Somehow the requests must be evaluated and ranked in terms of importance. Obviously, it is very difficult to compare a vital service such as public safety with one that is "nice to have" such as electronic data processing. Yet the comparison (and ranking) must be made so that these units can receive funds to continue

[1] "What It Means to Build a Budget from Zero," *Business Week,* April 18, 1977, p. 160.

operations. Our example, of course, is overly simplified. Picture the difficulties that would arise when, say, twenty diverse departments are involved. Without a doubt, subjectivity plays an important role.

Critics note that because of the foregoing problems, ZBB should not be attempted every year. Many say once every five years is sufficient. Naturally, the proper frequency depends on the particular organization and the philosophy of its management. In any case, ZBB should only be used if the anticipated benefits exceed the cost of implementation. The turbine division of Westinghouse Electric saved $4.2 million in overhead costs from a one-shot ZBB experiment. Says one official, however: "It'd be many years before I'd try it again, . . . it's a very demanding exercise."[2]

The Budget Period

Budgets normally cover differing periods of time. For example, picture a company that is planning a major capital improvements program through acquisitions of needed property, plant, and equipment. These assets benefit many periods and usually involve substantial dollar outlays. Given the nature of the expenditure, the company should establish a budget for such acquisitions that extends several years into the future. In fact, capital expenditure budgets covering five to ten years are common. Such a long planning horizon is necessary so that problems can be solved long before they occur. In the capital equipment area, for example, a company may find itself in need of new assets but suddenly determine that insufficient funds are available to make the required purchases. Funding of this nature normally cannot be obtained overnight; thus long-term planning is of utmost importance.

Budgets pertaining to *operations* are generally prepared on a one-year time frame. For purposes of control and evaluation these budgets are subsequently subdivided into quarters and months. The benefit of following this latter procedure is evident after studying Exhibit 23–2.

Exhibit 23-2 depicts the budgeted monthly cash balances of a seasonal business. Notice that if we view the budget over a one-year period, we see a favorable cash position, because the cash balance increases by $20,000 (from $80,000 in January to $100,000 in December). A breakdown by months, however, shows the necessity of short-term financing from May through July because of seasonal cash needs and a dip below the minimum desired balance. Shorter budget periods usually enable a closer monitoring of operations.

In actuality, many businesses use a combination of monthly, yearly, and long-term budgets. In recent years a number of organizations have turned to continuous budgets. A **continuous budget** covers a one-year period; however, a new month is added as the current month is completed. For example, assume a budget for 1984 operations is prepared. As soon as January 1984 is completed, a budget is added on for January 1985. Continuous

[2]Ibid.

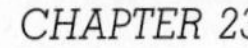

Exhibit 23-2

Cash balances of a seasonal business

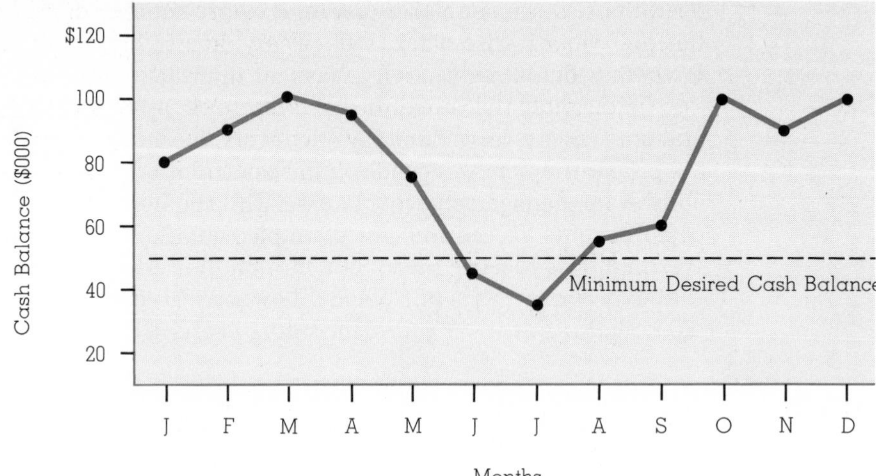

budgets offer the advantage of forcing management to continually think about the future. The planning process is not allocated to only a few months of each year but becomes an ongoing, stabilized activity.

Budget Limitations and Human Relations

Critics contend that several limitations are associated with budgeting. First, a budget is only as good as the effort that goes into its preparation. Top management must thoroughly support the budget process, or else the entire exercise will be a lesson in futility. Second, budgeting cannot replace effective day-to-day management. That is, the budget is a tool to be used by managers; it is not an end in itself and will not automatically improve a faltering operation. Although the critics' observations are correct, the preceding comments really apply to all aspects of management, not just budgeting.

Perhaps the most significant limitation of budgeting lies in the human relations and administration area. Many organizations overemphasize the use of budgets in control—and they often do it in an incorrect manner. To explain, employees are frequently disenchanted with tools used to evaluate performance. Budgets disclose weaknesses and are often studied by upper management when finding who's to blame in unfavorable times. To avoid possible negative feelings on the part of employees, management should educate personnel that budgeting is a positive tool that assists in achieving company goals, monitoring progress toward those goals, and setting standards of performance.

The administration of a budget program is a difficult task. Too often accountants become overly involved with the mechanical aspects of budget construction and lose sight of the fact that employees are people. Employees have feelings and are sensitive to management looking over their shoulders to appraise performance. Unless the budget effort considers human relations, even the best efforts will go for naught and be met with resistance.

COMPREHENSIVE BUDGETING

As we noted earlier in the chapter, the preparation of a budget normally follows a company's organizational structure. Budgets for the company's individual operating units (e.g., departments, divisions, territories, and so forth) are combined. The process culminates in the **master budget,** a comprehensive set of integrated budgets that serves as the financial plan for the entire organization. Although variations are found in practice, the master budget generally consists of the following:

1 Sales budget
2 Production budget
3 Direct material purchases budget
4 Direct labor budget
5 Factory overhead budget
6 Selling and administrative expense budget
7 Capital expenditures budget
8 Cash budget
9 Budgeted income statement
10 Budgeted balance sheet
11 Budgeted statement of changes in financial position

These budgets cannot be prepared independently. Sales levels, for example, influence production plans. The number of units produced affects direct materials, direct labor, and overhead costs, and all the foregoing have a bearing on an entity's cash budget and financial statements. The relationships within a master budget are shown in Exhibit 23-3.

These relationships become more apparent in the example that follows. At this point, however, observe how the sales budget is the starting point in the budgeting process. In addition, note how the cash budget and the budgeted financial statements serve as the focal point and the summarization of the entire planning effort.

Master Budget Illustration

To illustrate the construction of a master budget, we will focus on the Hillcroft Corporation. Hillcroft manufactures and sells a single product and desires to budget first-quarter activity for 1984. Assume that Hillcroft's master budget consists of the budgets listed above. For simplicity we will exclude the capital expenditures budget and the statement of changes in financial position from our discussion. Hillcroft's December 31, 1983, balance sheet appears in Exhibit 23-4.

Sales budget

The sales budget is probably the most important element of the master budget. Production, cash flow, the financial statements, and a number of other items are all dependent on sales, in terms of both units sold and revenues generated. A grossly incorrect sales budget will therefore be reflected throughout the entire budgeting process.

The sales budget is based on a forecast of sales volume. Forecasted volume is influenced by such factors as previous sales patterns, current and expected economic conditions, and advertising and marketing strategies.

Exhibit 23-3

Relationships within the master budget

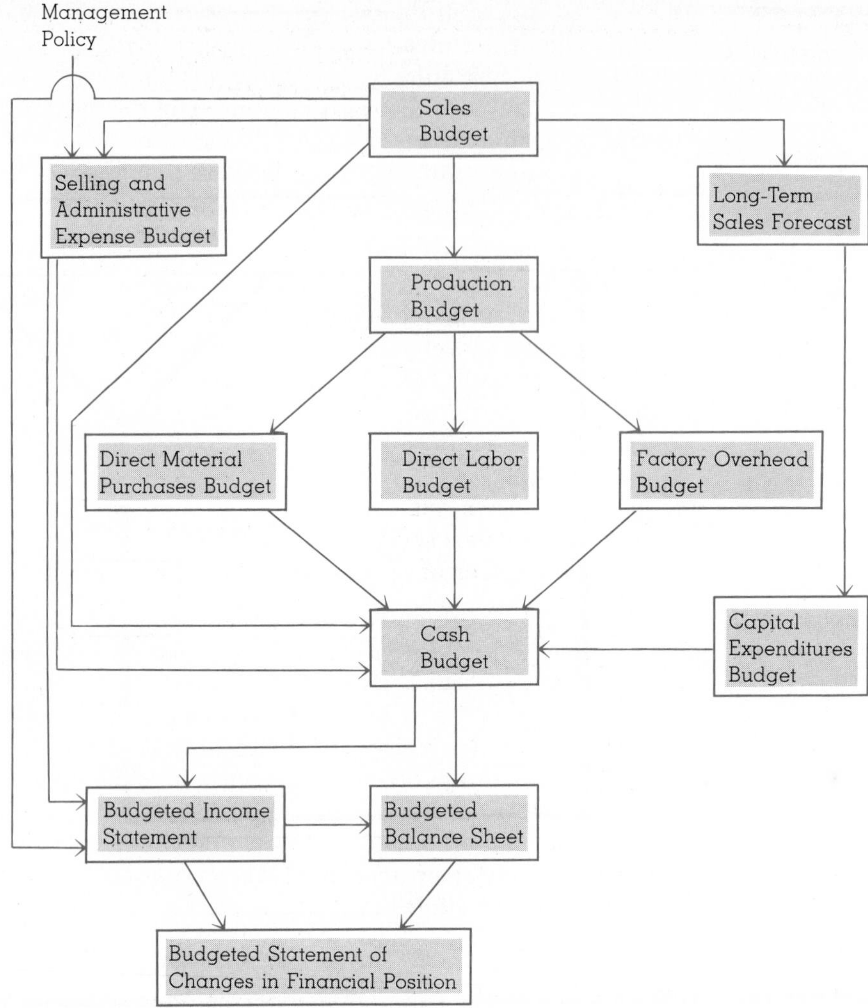

Estimated volume can be determined by using several different techniques. For example, a company can (1) study the relationship of sales to various economic indicators (such as interest rates and disposable income), (2) use various statistical forecasting methods, or (3) probe its sales staff regarding customer purchase plans for the upcoming period. Sales forecasting is extremely difficult and is more appropriately studied in advanced business courses.

Once the forecast is derived, the sales budget is constructed by multiplying the expected volume by the expected selling price per unit. Hillcroft's sales budget appears in Exhibit 23-5.

Exhibit 23-4

HILLCROFT CORPORATION
Balance Sheet
December 31, 1983

ASSETS		
Current assets		
Cash	$ 7,000	
Accounts receivable	10,000	
Finished goods (1,500 units × $7.00)	10,500	
Direct materials (6,900 units × $1.50)	10,350	$ 37,850
Property, plant, & equipment		
Plant & equipment	$70,000	
Less: Accumulated depreciation	5,000	65,000
Total assets		$102,850
LIABILITIES & STOCKHOLDERS' EQUITY		
Current liabilities		
Accounts payable		$ 8,000
Stockholders' equity		
Common stock	$40,000	
Retained earnings	54,850	94,850
Total liabilities & stockholders' equity		$102,850

Exhibit 23-5

HILLCROFT CORPORATION
Sales Budget
For the Quarter Ended March 31, 1984

	January	February	March	Total
Expected sales (units)	4,500	5,500	7,000	17,000
Selling price per unit	× $10	× $10	× $10	× $10
Budgeted sales revenues	$45,000	$55,000	$70,000	$170,000

Schedule of cash collections

Although not part of the formal sales budget, a schedule of expected cash collections is easily generated at this time. The schedule provides information that will be needed when preparing the cash budget. To illustrate the necessary procedures, assume Hillcroft's sales are all on account. Seventy percent of the sales are collected in the month of sale; the remaining 30%

Exhibit 23-6

HILLCROFT CORPORATION
Schedule of Cash Collections
For the Quarter Ended March 31, 1984

	January	February	March	Total
Accounts receivable, 12/31/83	$10,000*			$10,000
January sales ($45,000)	31,500	$13,500		45,000
February sales ($55,000)		38,500	$16,500	55,000
March sales ($70,000)			49,000	49,000
Total budgeted cash collections	$41,500	$52,000	$65,500	$159,000

*From Exhibit 23-4.
Note: Because only $49,000 of March sales are collected in March, the remaining $21,000 ($70,000 − $49,000) will appear on Hillcroft's first-quarter balance sheet as accounts receivable.

are collected in the following month. The corporation's cash collection schedule appears in Exhibit 23-6.

Production budget

Once the sales budget is completed, production requirements can be determined. Aside from sales, the number of units scheduled for production depends on raw material availability and desired finished goods inventory levels. Finished goods are often budgeted in advance so that adequate stock levels can be maintained. Excessive inventories increase storage, insurance, taxes, interest, and the possibility of deterioration and obsolescence. Precariously low inventories, on the other hand, could lead to lost sales and even lost customers.

The budgeted units of production in any given period can be calculated as follows:

Number of units to be produced	
Number of units sold	XXX
Add: Desired ending finished goods inventory (units)	XXX
Total finished units needed	XXX
Less: Beginning finished goods inventory (units)	XXX
Number of units to be produced	XXX

By adding budgeted sales to the units desired for the ending finished goods inventory, we obtain the total units needed during the period. Since some of these units already exist via the beginning finished goods inventory, the remainder will have to be produced.

Hillcroft wishes to maintain an ending finished goods inventory to cover 50% of the following month's sales. This inventory policy gives rise to the production budget shown in Exhibit 23-7.

Direct material purchases budget

Now that the production requirements are known, the direct material purchases budget can be prepared. Budgeted purchases are based on anticipated manufacturing levels and desired ending raw material inventory bal-

Exhibit 23-7

HILLCROFT CORPORATION
Production Budget
For the Quarter Ended March 31, 1984

	January	February	March	Total
Number of units sold (Exhibit 23-5)	4,500	5,500	7,000	17,000
Add: Desired ending finished goods inventory (50% × following month's sales)	2,750	3,500	3,800†	3,800‡
Total finished units needed	7,250	9,000	10,800	20,800
Less: Beginning finished goods inventory*	1,500	2,750	3,500	1,500‡
Number of units to be produced	5,750	6,250	7,300	19,300

* The beginning finished goods inventory is the ending finished goods inventory from the preceding month. January's beginning inventory of 1,500 units appears on the balance sheet presented in Exhibit 23-4.

† April's sales are assumed to be 7,600 units; thus the desired ending finished goods inventory in March is 3,800 units (7,600 units × 50%).

‡ The ending and beginning inventories are used here, not the total of the inventories. Insertion of totals will result in incorrect calculations. To illustrate, summation of the ending inventory figures yields 10,050 units (2,750 + 3,500 + 3,800), which, when added to sales, produces total finished units needed of 27,050 (10,050 + 17,000). Actually, the result is misleading because Hillcroft needs only 20,800 units during the quarter: 17,000 units to cover sales and 3,800 units to generate the desired March 31 finished goods inventory.

ances. The latter is frequently influenced by supplier delivery schedules, the availability of "specials" and quantity discounts, and management's purchasing strategy in heading off price increases.

The amount of materials to purchase can be computed in a fashion similar to that for finding the budgeted units of production.

Direct materials to be purchased	
Direct materials used in production (units)	XXX
Add: Desired ending direct materials inventory (units)	XXX
Total direct materials needed	XXX
Less: Beginning direct materials inventory (units)	XXX
Direct materials to be purchased (units)	XXX

Assume that Hillcroft uses two units of direct material in each completed product and that each direct material unit costs $1.50. Management desires to maintain an ending materials inventory equal to 60% of the direct materials needed in the following month's production. The company's direct material purchases budget is shown in Exhibit 23-8.

Schedule of cash disbursements for material purchases

Given Hillcroft's purchasing program, we can now construct a schedule of the required cash disbursements. This schedule, like the schedule of cash

Exhibit 23-8

HILLCROFT CORPORATION
Direct Material Purchases Budget
For the Quarter Ended March 31, 1984

	January	February	March	Total
Planned production, in units (Exhibit 23-7)	5,750	6,250	7,300	19,300
Units of direct material per finished unit	× 2	× 2	× 2	× 2
Direct materials used in production (units)	11,500	12,500	14,600	38,600
Add: Desired ending direct materials inventory (units)*	7,500	8,760	9,960	9,960
Total direct materials needed	19,000	21,260	24,560	48,560
Less: Beginning direct materials inventory (units)†	6,900	7,500	8,760	6,900
Direct materials to be purchased (units)	12,100	13,760	15,800	41,660
Cost per unit	× $1.50	× $1.50	× $1.50	× $1.50
Cost of direct material purchases	$18,150	$20,640	$23,700	$62,490

*The desired ending inventory equals 60% of the direct materials used in the following month's production. Ending inventories are computed as follows:

January:	60% × 12,500 = 7,500
February:	60% × 14,600 = 8,760
March:	60% × 16,600 (assumed) = 9,960

†The beginning direct materials inventory is the ending direct materials inventory from the preceding month. January's beginning inventory of 6,900 units appears on the balance sheet presented in Exhibit 23-4.

collections, is useful when preparing the cash budget. To illustrate the necessary procedures, assume Hillcroft expects to pay 60% of a given month's purchases during the month of purchase; the remaining 40% will be paid in the following month. The schedule of cash disbursements for materials appears in Exhibit 23-9.

Direct labor budget

The direct labor budget is also based on the production budget. Direct labor must be budgeted so that management can determine if sufficient personnel are available to produce the company's product. A lack of proper planning could lead to labor shortages or overstaffing, both of which introduce inefficiencies into the manufacturing process. Furthermore, employee morale could suffer because of possible layoffs or extensive overtime to meet production schedules.

Direct labor requirements are determined by multiplying the number of direct labor hours per finished unit by the number of units to be manufactured. The result is then multiplied by the estimated direct labor cost per

Exhibit 23-9

HILLCROFT CORPORATION
Schedule of Cash Disbursements for Material Purchases
For the Quarter Ended March 31, 1984

	January	February	March	Total
Accounts payable, 12/31/83	$ 8,000*			$ 8,000
January purchases ($18,150)	10,890	$ 7,260		18,150
February purchases ($20,640)		12,384	$ 8,256	20,640
March purchases ($23,700)			14,220	14,220
Total disbursements for purchases	$18,890	$19,644	$22,476	$61,010

* From Exhibit 23-4.
Note: *Because only $14,220 of March purchases are paid in March, the remaining $9,480 ($23,700 − $14,220) will appear on Hillcroft's first-quarter balance sheet as accounts payable.*

hour to generate total budgeted labor costs. To illustrate, assume Hillcroft Corporation pays its workers $6.00 per hour and that each finished unit requires 0.5 hours of direct labor time. The necessary computations appear in Hillcroft's direct labor budget, which is shown in Exhibit 23-10.

Exhibit 23-10

HILLCROFT CORPORATION
Direct Labor Budget
For the Quarter Ended March 31, 1984

	January	February	March	Total
Planned production, in units (Exhibit 23-7)	5,750	6,250	7,300	19,300
Labor time per unit (hours)	× 0.5	× 0.5	× 0.5	× 0.5
Total labor hours needed	2,875	3,125	3,650	9,650
Direct labor cost per hour	× $6	× $6	× $6	× $6
Total budgeted direct labor cost	$17,250	$18,750	$21,900	$57,900

Factory overhead budget

The factory overhead budget incorporates all production costs other than direct materials and direct labor. Such costs include indirect materials, indirect labor, depreciation, maintenance, and utilities. To construct an accurate overhead budget, individual overhead costs are first studied in terms of their behavior. Observe, for example, that several of the preceding costs vary with changes in production volume, while others remain static. Once cost behavior is determined, we then compute overhead application rates similar to those described in Chapter 22.

Assume that Hillcroft's variable overhead application rate is $1.40 per direct labor hour. Fixed overhead charges are anticipated to be $1,930 per month, which includes $700 of straight-line depreciation. Exhibit 23-11 contains the company's overhead budget.

Exhibit 23-11

HILLCROFT CORPORATION
Factory Overhead Budget
For the Quarter Ended March 31, 1984

	January	February	March	Total
Budgeted direct labor hours (Exhibit 23-10)	2,875	3,125	3,650	9,650
Variable overhead rate	× $1.40	× $1.40	× $1.40	× $1.40
Budgeted variable overhead	$4,025	$4,375	$5,110	$13,510
Budgeted fixed overhead*	1,930	1,930	1,930	5,790
Budgeted total overhead	$5,955	$6,305	$7,040	$19,300
Less: Depreciation	700	700	700	2,100
Cash disbursements for factory overhead	$5,255	$5,605	$6,340	$17,200

* The overhead budget contains total fixed overhead costs; a fixed application rate is not multiplied by the number of monthly labor hours. The reason for using total costs is that fixed costs are, indeed, fixed and do not vary with labor activity.

The overhead budget reveals two important pieces of information. First, total estimated overhead for the quarter amounts to $19,300. This figure is needed for costing Hillcroft's single product. Assuming the use of direct labor hours as an application base, the overhead application rate will amount to $2.00 per hour ($19,300 ÷ 9,650 budgeted labor hours, from Exhibit 23-10). Second, notice that there is a difference between total budgeted overhead and required cash disbursements for overhead. Depreciation, although a factory cost, does not entail a cash outlay. Thus depreciation must be subtracted from total overhead to generate monthly cash payments. We are assuming that all other overhead is paid when incurred.

Selling and administrative expense budget

All manufacturing organizations incur costs unrelated to production activities, namely, selling and administrative (S&A) expenses. Like factory overhead, S&A expenses consist of variable and fixed components. Thus an in-depth review of these costs to determine behavior is necessary prior to budget preparation.

Hillcroft's variable S&A costs consist of freight-out and sales commissions, which total $0.80 per unit. Fixed costs include salaries, advertising, insurance, and other miscellaneous costs. The firm's S&A expense budget appears in Exhibit 23-12. Importantly, observe that a new activity base is employed. That is, S&A expenses vary with sales, not production.

Exhibit 23-12

HILLCROFT CORPORATION
Selling and Administrative Expense Budget
For the Quarter Ended March 31, 1984

	January	February	March	Total
Expected sales, in units (Exhibit 23-5)	4,500	5,500	7,000	17,000
Variable S&A expense per unit	× $0.80	× $0.80	× $0.80	× $0.80
Budgeted variable expenses	$3,600	$4,400	$5,600	$13,600
Fixed S&A expenses				
Salaries	$2,000	$2,000	$2,000	$ 6,000
Advertising	600	600	600	1,800
Insurance	1,900	—	—	1,900
Miscellaneous	500	1,500	500	2,500
Total fixed expenses	$5,000	$4,100	$3,100	$12,200
Total budgeted S&A expenses	$8,600	$8,500	$8,700	$25,800

Cash budget

As we noted earlier in the chapter, the cash budget serves to summarize a considerable portion of the budgeting process. Based on many of the budgets previously discussed, the cash budget provides substantial assistance to management when assessing a firm's future cash needs. The cash budget is typically composed of four major sections:

Cash receipts
Cash disbursements
Analysis
Financing

The *receipts section* discloses the total cash available during the period before considering any disbursements. Total cash available is computed by adding the beginning cash balance to total cash receipts. For most businesses the major sources of receipts are cash sales and collections from customers on account.

The cash *disbursements section* details expected cash payments during the budget period. Such payments include disbursements for materials, labor, overhead, S&A expenses, dividends, taxes, and capital improvements.

The *analysis section* combines the information presented in the receipts and disbursements sections and discloses whether a firm has an excess of cash or a cash deficiency. Excessive cash balances should be used to retire outstanding loans or should be invested in safe short-term securities such as certificates of deposit and government notes. If the latter course of action is followed, the firm can generate a return on its investment and can reacquire the cash (if needed) in a short period of time. Should a deficiency arise, the need for additional cash is dictated. Importantly, the deficiency is disclosed prior to the time it actually occurs, thus preventing possible loan defaults, past-due bills, and other undesirable outcomes.

Finally, the *financing section* provides a schedule of borrowings and repayments that are expected to occur during the budget period. In addition, it discloses all related interest payments on borrowed funds. Overall this section enables firms to predict financing requirements and thereby give banks and other institutions advance notice of funding needs.

Cash budget illustration

To illustrate the cash budget, we will continue the Hillcroft Corporation example. Assume that Hillcroft requires a minimum cash balance of $6,000. Loans are available from a local bank in multiples of $1,000 at a 15% interest rate. For simplicity we assume that loans are obtained at the beginning of a month and are repaid at the end of the month of repayment. Interest is paid at the time of repaying principal. Finally, the company

Exhibit 23-13

HILLCROFT CORPORATION
Cash Budget
For the Quarter Ended March 31, 1984

	January	February	March
Beginning cash balance*	$ 7,000	$ 6,505	$ 6,006
Add receipts: customer collections (Exhibit 23-6)	41,500	52,000	65,500
Cash available before disbursements	$48,500	$58,505	$71,506
Less disbursements			
Material purchases (Exhibit 23-9)	$18,890	$19,644	$22,476
Direct labor (Exhibit 23-10)	17,250	18,750	21,900
Factory overhead (Exhibit 23-11)	5,255	5,605	6,340
S&A expenses (Exhibit 23-12)	8,600	8,500	8,700
Income taxes	—	—	3,000
Dividends	—	—	500
Total disbursements	$49,995	$52,499	$62,916
Cash excess (deficiency) before financing	$ (1,495)	$ 6,006	$ 8,590
Financing			
Borrowing to maintain $6,000 minimum balance (at beginning)	$ 8,000	$ —	$ —
Repayment (at end)	—	—	(2,000)
Interest at 15% per annum	—	—	(75)
Ending cash balance	$ 6,505	$ 6,006	$ 6,515

*January's beginning cash balance of $7,000 is obtained from Exhibit 23-4. Subsequent beginning balances are the ending cash balances of the preceding period.

will have a $3,000 quarterly tax payment in March and expects to distribute a $500 cash dividend on March 31. Hillcroft's cash budget appears in Exhibit 23-13.

To explain the financing section, Hillcroft requires a $6,000 minimum cash balance. Since borrowings are in $1,000 multiples, $8,000 of financing is needed in January ($8,000 − $1,495 = $6,505). All borrowings are assumed to be repaid as soon as possible, also in $1,000 multiples. Thus $2,000 of the loan obligation can be retired in March without reducing the cash balance below the desired minimum. Interest is figured for three months, because the obligation is outstanding from January 1 through March 31 ($\$2{,}000 \times 0.15 \times \frac{3}{12} = \$75$).

Budgeted income statement

The preparation of budgeted financial statements, often called **pro forma statements,** is the final step in budget construction. The first of these statements, the income statement, projects the forecasted results of operations and serves as a useful tool against which actual performance can be measured. Information necessary for its construction is taken from the various budgets discussed in preceding sections of the chapter. Hillcroft's budgeted income statement is shown in Exhibit 23-14.

The most difficult part of the statement is the computation of cost of goods manufactured and the ending finished goods inventory. As noted in

Exhibit 23-14

HILLCROFT CORPORATION
Budgeted Income Statement
For the Quarter Ended March 31, 1984

Sales (Exhibit 23-5)		$170,000
Cost of goods sold		
Beginning finished goods inventory (Exhibit 23-4)	$ 10,500	
Cost of goods manufactured (19,300 units × $7)	135,100	
Goods available for sale	$145,600	
Less ending finished goods inventory (3,800 units × $7)	26,600	
Cost of goods sold		119,000
Gross profit		$ 51,000
Less S&A expenses (Exhibit 23-12)		25,800
Income before interest and taxes		$ 25,200
Less interest expense (Exhibit 23-13)		75*
Income before taxes		$ 25,125
Income taxes (Exhibit 23-13)		3,000
Net income		$ 22,125

*For simplicity we are ignoring accrued interest on the remaining balance of the loan.

Hillcroft's production budget (see Exhibit 23-7), the firm produced 19,300 units during the quarter. The cost per unit of $7 is computed as follows:

Direct material (2 units of direct material @ $1.50 per unit; see Exhibit 23-8)	*$3.00*
Direct labor (0.5 hours per unit @ $6 per hour; see Exhibit 23-10)	*3.00*
Variable factory overhead (0.5 hours per unit @ $1.40 per hour; see Exhibit 23-11)	*0.70*
Fixed factory overhead (see Exhibit 23-11 and the following discussion)	*0.30*
Manufactured cost per unit	*$7.00*

The fixed factory overhead rate is calculated on the basis of estimated direct labor hours. Since Hillcroft anticipates $5,790 of fixed overhead and 9,650 labor hours (both figures taken from Exhibit 23-11), the rate per hour is $0.60 ($5,790 ÷ 9,650 hours). Thus each finished unit is charged with $0.30 (0.5 labor hours × $0.60) of fixed production cost.

Once the $7-per-unit manufacturing cost is computed, the ending finished goods inventory can be determined. From information appearing in Exhibit 23-7, Hillcroft has budgeted finished goods at 3,800 units as of March 31. The inventory is therefore costed at $26,600 (3,800 units × $7).

Budgeted balance sheet

The budgeted balance sheet as of March 31 is derived by combining the beginning balance sheet (see Exhibit 23-4) with the information presented in the other budgets. Hillcroft's end-of-quarter balance sheet appears in Exhibit 23-15.

BUDGETING AND COMPUTERS

No doubt you have gotten the impression that budget construction is extremely procedural. This characteristic makes budgeting very adaptable to computers. Computers help speed up the process and eliminate much of the tedious detail and drudgery for the accountant, thereby permitting more time for analysis and evaluation. In many instances computerized budgeting applications allow managers to perform "what if" testing. That is, a manager can sit at a computer terminal and key in a change in a budget variable to determine the variable's impact on the organization. For example, suppose a new credit and collections policy is under consideration. After certain data have been entered in the terminal, the computer is able to show the effects of the policy via newly generated schedules and pro forma statements in a matter of seconds. If manual computations were required, the number of "what if" tests that could be performed would surely be restricted.

Exhibit 23-15

HILLCROFT CORPORATION
Budgeted Balance Sheet
March 31, 1984

ASSETS		
Current assets		
Cash (Exhibit 23-13)	$ 6,515	
Accounts receivable (Exhibit 23-6)	21,000	
Finished goods (Exhibit 23-14)	26,600	
Direct materials (Exhibit 23-8)	14,940*	$ 69,055
Property, plant, & equipment		
Plant & equipment (Exhibit 23-4)	$70,000	
Less: Accumulated depreciation	7,100†	62,900
Total assets		$131,955
LIABILITIES & STOCKHOLDERS' EQUITY		
Current liabilities		
Accounts payable (Exhibit 23-9)	$ 9,480	
Loan payable (Exhibit 23-13)	6,000‡	$ 15,480
Stockholders' equity		
Common stock (Exhibit 23-4)	$40,000	
Retained earnings	76,475§	116,475
Total liabilities & stockholders' equity		$131,955

*9,960 units × $1.50 per unit = $14,940.

† Accumulated depreciation, Jan. 1 (Exhibit 23-4)	$5,000
Straight-line depreciation, Jan.–Mar. (Exhibit 23-11)	2,100
Accumulated depreciation, Mar. 31	$7,100

‡ Original loan − repayment ($8,000 − $2,000 = $6,000).

§ Retained earnings, Jan. 1 (Exhibit 23-4)		$54,850
Add net income (Exhibit 23-14)	$22,125	
Deduct dividends (Exhibit 23-13)	500	21,625
Retained earnings, Mar. 31		$76,475

KEY TERMS AND CONCEPTS

bottom-up approach 905
budget 902
cash budget 921
continuous budget 911
direct labor budget 918
direct material purchases budget 916
factory overhead budget 919
master budget 913
production budget 916
pro forma financial statements 923
sales budget 913
selling and administrative (S&A) expense budget 920
slack 909
top-down approach 905
traditional budgeting 909
zero-base budgeting (ZBB) 910

QUESTIONS

Q23-1 Briefly discuss the advantages of budgeting.

Q23-2 Is a budget a planning tool, a control tool, or both? Explain.

Q23-3 When evaluating performance, many organizations compare current results with the results of previous accounting periods. Are any problems encountered when following this approach? Explain.

Q23-4 Explain how a budget assists in coordinating the plans of the various operating units of an organization.

Q23-5 Define and fully explain the top-down approach to budgeting.

Q23-6 Briefly explain the bottom-up approach to budgeting.

Q23-7 Should budget data be based on the past, the future, or both? Explain.

Q23-8 Calabro Corporation, a manufacturer with annual sales approaching $75 million, is beginning the budget process for the upcoming year. Should Calabro use long-term budgets, yearly budgets, or monthly budgets? Explain your answer.

Q23-9 Why is an accurate sales forecast so important when preparing a master budget?

Q23-10 Why is it necessary to carefully budget direct labor requirements for an upcoming period?

Q23-11 Explain how a cash budget leads to effective management of an organization's cash balances.

Q23-12 Briefly discuss the use of computers in budgeting. Include in your response a description of "what if" testing.

EXERCISES

E23-1 Joe Fielder is the chief financial officer of Cronkite, Inc. Known for his autocratic approach to management, Joe has always followed the top-down approach to budgeting. He recently attended a conference on zero-base budgeting (ZBB) and came away impressed.

a Contrast traditional budgeting and ZBB.

b Briefly discuss the advantages and problems associated with ZBB.

c Is ZBB likely to be successful at Cronkite, Inc.? Explain.

E23-2 The Sunrise Community College District is preparing its budget for the coming academic year. The following information concerns the Eastern campus.

Total current enrollment: 5,000 students.
Average credit hours per student per year: 30.
Average number of students per class: 25.
Average faculty teaching load: 24 credit hours
(8 classes of 3 credit hours each).

Next year's enrollment is expected to increase by 10%. Sunrise expects to award 60 tuition-free scholarships.

a To satisfy requests from the college's board of regents,

(1) Prepare a tuition revenue budget for the upcoming year. The tuition rate is $15 per credit hour.

(2) Determine the number of faculty members needed to cover classes.

b You have been requested by the regents to construct budgets for other areas of operation (e.g., the library, grounds, and maintenance). One of the board members noted: "The most important resource of the college is its faculty. Now that you know the number of faculty needed, you can prepare the other budgets. Faculty is the key—without them, we don't operate." Does the board member really understand the budgeting process? Explain.

E23-3 Mason Corporation had December sales of $30,000. Sales for the next three months are forecasted as follows:

January	$32,000
February	35,000
March	40,000

Thirty percent of all sales are for cash; the remaining 70% are on account. Credit sales have the following collection pattern:

Sixty percent collected in the month of sale.
Thirty-five percent collected in the month following sale.
Five percent uncollectible.

Prepare a schedule of cash collections for January through March.

E23-4 Yale, Inc., anticipates the following unit sales during the first four months of the upcoming year.

January	10,000
February	10,500
March	12,000
April	13,000

The company desires to maintain its finished goods inventory at 60% of the following month's sales. The January 1 finished goods inventory will be 5,000 units.

Prepare a production budget for January through March.

E23-5 Bass Corporation manufactures a home video recorder that requires four no. S1326 circuit boards. Anticipated production of recorders for the upcoming year follows.

Quarter	***Production (Units)***
First	8,000
Second	10,000
Third	12,000
Fourth	16,000

Bass desires to stock enough circuit boards to meet 30% of the following quarter's production needs. Circuit boards cost $2.50 each; the cost has been fairly stable over the past six months.

Assuming a beginning circuit board inventory of $23,750, prepare a direct material purchases budget for the first three quarters of the year.

E23-6 The following information pertains to Knight Corporation for January.

1 Budgeted sales: 45,000 units.
2 Inventories:

On hand, Jan. 1	
Finished goods	9,400 units
Direct materials	18,600 units
Desired, Jan. 31	
Finished goods	10,200 units
Direct materials	20,500 units

3 Each finished unit requires the following materials and labor:

Direct materials	3 units @ $4 per unit
Direct labor	2 hours @ $7 per hour

4 Factory overhead is applied to production at the rate of $5.50 per direct labor hour.

Assuming no work in process, determine the following:

a The number of finished units to produce in January.
b The budgeted cost of direct materials purchased in January.
c The total budgeted direct labor costs in January.
d The total cost of goods manufactured during the month.

E23-7 Lexington Wood Products manufactures and distributes wooden baseball bats. Business is seasonal, with a large portion of the sales occurring in late winter and early spring. Production is heavy during the last quarter of the year to meet demand, and Lexington experiences a temporary cash strain during this period. Payroll costs rise because considerable overtime is scheduled. Furthermore, customer collections are low because the fall season produces only modest sales. This year there are added problems because of high inflation rates and declining sales, the latter caused by the increased popularity of aluminum bats. Also, only 25% of the customers are paying their balances in the month of sale. The average collection period is approximately 62 days.

Fortunately, the cash strain arises only during the last quarter. The Cash account builds up during the first two quarters as sales exceed production. Excessive cash is subsequently invested in U.S. Treasury bills and certificates of deposit.

Assume Lexington regularly experiences the cash strain noted above. What actions could the firm undertake to "ease the squeeze" on cash? Consider possible changes in operations when formulating your answer.

E23-8 Tennessee Merchandising has had continual problems with cash flow. The following information has come to your attention.

a The company has an opening cash balance on January 1 of $10,000. Management desires to maintain a minimum cash balance of $8,000 at all times.
b Budgeted sales for January total $200,000. Sales are expected to increase at the rate of 5% per month over the next six months. Sales from the preceding November and December amounted to $170,000 and $180,000, respectively.
c All sales are on credit and subject to the following collection pattern:

Sixty percent collected in the month of sale.
Thirty percent collected in the month following sale.
Ten percent collected in the second month following sale.

d All merchandise purchases are paid for in the month of purchase. Gross profit averages 30% of sales; inventories are expected to remain unchanged.

e Operating expenses are budgeted as follows:

	January	February	March
Selling (excluding depreciation)	$16,000	$20,000	$25,000
Administrative (excluding depreciation)	12,000	12,000	12,000
Depreciation	6,000	6,000	7,000

f The company will acquire $28,000 of new equipment in March for cash.

g Additional financing is available in $1,000 multiples at a 16% interest rate. Assume all borrowings take place at the beginning of the month and that repayments occur at the end of the month of repayment. Interest is paid at the time of repaying principal.

Analyze Tennessee's cash position by preparing a cash budget for January through March. Has the company solved its cash flow problems or will additional financing be necessary?

PROBLEMS

P23-1 ***Sales budget and slack***

Pants, Inc., specializes in the sale of jeans. Sales information follows.

Style	Selling Price	Percentage of Total Sales
Straight leg	$12	50%
Shrink to fit	14	30
Boot cut	18	20

Management is now budgeting revenues for June–August. June's total sales are forecast at 10,000 pairs, with subsequent 10%-per-month increases expected from the back-to-school rush. Customers are permitted to charge their purchases. Forty percent of total sales are for cash; the remaining 60% are on account. The company anticipates the following collection pattern for credit sales.

Fifty percent collected in the month following sale.
Forty percent collected in the second month following sale.
Ten percent never collected.

Sales in April and May totaled 8,000 pairs each month.

INSTRUCTIONS

a Prepare a sales budget in dollars for June through August.

b Prepare a schedule of cash collections for June through August.

c Define slack as it relates to budgeting.

d Management feels that June's sales could range between 8,000 and 15,000 pairs. The budget was finally established at 10,000 pairs because of conservatism. If management desired to incorporate considerable slack into the budget, which of the three sales estimates (8,000, 10,000, or 15,000) would probably be used for June? Explain.

P23-2 ***Production and purchases budgets; purchasing policy***

Hayden, Inc., manufactures and distributes various parts for bicycles. The company's main product is bicycle pedals. Each pedal requires three units of direct material at a cost of $0.25 per unit. To keep production moving smoothly, the company must maintain a direct materials inventory equal to 40% of the following month's production needs.

A sales budget for the first six months of 1984 follows.

Month	***Projected Pedal Sales***
January	14,000
February	16,000
March	18,000
April	16,000
May	15,000
June	14,000

Management desires to carry a finished goods inventory equal to 30% of the following month's sales. On December 31, 1983, the finished goods inventory totaled 7,000 pedals. On the same date 15,200 units of direct material were in the warehouse.

INSTRUCTIONS

a Prepare a production budget for January through March.

b Prepare a direct material purchases budget for January through March.

c List several factors that could cause a change in the company's present direct material inventory policy.

P23-3 ***Production budget and abbreviated cash budget***

The Halcomb Company has gathered the following information in preparation of its first-quarter budget for the coming year.

Sales and collections:

December sales (actual)	6,800 units @ $20	$136,000
January sales (estimated)	7,000 units @ $20	140,000
February sales (estimated)	7,400 units @ $21	155,400
March sales (estimated)	8,000 units @ $21	168,000
April sales (estimated)	8,200 units @ $22	180,400

Seventy percent of all sales are collected in the month of sale; the remaining 30% are collected in the following month.

Production:

Manufacturing costs are paid in the month incurred. The following costs relate to the 75,000 units produced during the current year.

Direct materials	*$225,000*
Direct labor	*525,000*
Variable factory overhead	*75,000*
Fixed factory overhead	*360,000*

No significant changes in cost behavior are anticipated. The fixed factory overhead, which includes $48,000 of depreciation, is incurred evenly throughout the year.

Inventory policies:

1 All direct materials are acquired when needed (i.e., no direct material inventory is maintained).

2 Management desires finished goods inventories equal to 40% of the following month's sales. December's ending finished goods inventory is 2,800 units.

Other data:

1 Selling and administrative expenses amount to $4 per unit and are paid in the month following their incurrence.

2 The January 1 cash balance is $18,000.

INSTRUCTIONS

a Prepare a production budget (in units only) for January through March.

b Prepare a cash budget for January through March. *Note:* The budget should end with the cash excess or deficiency before financing.

P23-4 ***Cash budget covering three months***

Riverside Corporation is a distributor of medical supplies. Management is studying cash needs for October through December and has assembled the following information.

	October	November	December
Sales	$60,000	$54,000	$50,000
Purchases of merchandise	26,000	21,000	19,000
Cash operating costs	33,000	31,000	25,000
Depreciation expense	2,000	2,200	2,500
Equipment acquisitions	8,000	5,000	—

The pro forma balance sheet on September 30 revealed the following account balances.

Cash	$ 6,500
Accounts receivable	21,000
Accounts payable	18,000

Seventy percent of all customer accounts are collected in the month of sale; 25% are collected in the following month. Because of a liberal credit policy, bad debts amounting to 5% of sales are anticipated. Management feels that only $20,000 of the accounts outstanding on September 30 will be collectible.

Forty percent of the merchandise purchases are paid for in the month of purchase to take advantage of a 2% discount. The remaining 60% are paid in the month following purchase.

Riverside maintains a $6,000 minimum cash balance at all times. Should borrowing be necessary, financing is available in $1,000 multiples at a 20% interest rate. Assume all borrowings take place at the beginning of the month and all repayments (including interest) at the end of the month of repaying principal. Principal repayments are also made in multiples of $1,000.

INSTRUCTIONS

a Prepare a schedule of cash collections for October through December.

b Prepare a schedule of cash disbursements for merchandise purchases for October through December.

c Prepare a cash budget similar to that shown in Exhibit 23-13.

P23-5 ***Cash budget and analysis***

The Triple-F Health Club is a family-oriented health club. The club's board of directors is developing plans to acquire more equipment and expand facilities. The board plans to purchase about $25,000 of new equipment each year and wants to begin a fund to purchase the adjoining property in four or five years. The adjoining property has a market value of about $300,000.

The club manager, Jane Crowe, is concerned that the board has unrealistic goals in light of its recent financial performance. She has sought the help of a club member with an accounting background to assist her in preparing a report to the board supporting her concerns. The club member reviewed the club's records, including the cash basis income statements presented below. The review and discussions with Jane Crowe disclosed the additional information that follows the statement.

TRIPLE-F HEALTH CLUB
Statement of Income (Cash Basis)
For the Years Ended October 31, 1983 and 1982

	1983	1982
Cash revenues		
Annual membership fees	$355,000	$300,000
Lesson and class fees	234,000	180,000
Miscellaneous	2,000	1,500
Total cash received	$591,000	$481,500
Cash expenses		
Manager's salary and benefits	$ 36,000	$ 36,000
Regular employees' wages and benefits	190,000	190,000
Lesson and class employee wages and benefits	195,000	150,000
Towels and supplies	16,000	15,500
Utilities (heat & light)	22,000	15,000
Mortgage interest	35,100	37,800
Miscellaneous	2,000	1,500
Total cash expenses	$496,100	$445,800
Cash income	$ 94,900	$ 35,700

Additional information:

1 Other financial information as of October 31, 1983:

Cash in checking account, $7,000.
Petty cash, $300.
Outstanding mortgage balance, $390,000.

Past-due accounts payable arising from invoices for supplies and utilities, $2,500.

2 No unpaid bills existed on October 31, 1982.
3 The club purchased $25,000 of exercise equipment during the current fiscal year. Cash of $10,000 was paid on delivery and the balance was due on October 1 but had not been paid as of October 31, 1983.
4 The club began operations in 1977 in rental quarters. In October 1979 it purchased its current property (land and building) for $600,000, paying $120,000 down and agreeing to pay $30,000 plus 9% interest annually on November 1 until the balance was paid off.
5 Membership rose 3% during 1983. This is approximately the same annual rate the club has experienced since it opened.
6 Membership fees were increased by 15% in 1983. The board has tentative plans to increase the fees by 10% in 1984.
7 Lesson and class fees have not been increased for three years. The board policy is to encourage classes and lessons by keeping the fees low. The members have taken advantage of this policy and the number of classes and lessons has grown significantly each year. The club expects the percentage growth experienced in 1983 to be repeated in 1984, thereby necessitating the hiring of additional instructors.
8 Miscellaneous revenues are expected to grow by $500 in 1984.
9 Operating expenses are expected to increase. Hourly wage rates and the manager's salary will need to be increased 15% because no increases were granted in 1983. Towels and supplies, utilities, and miscellaneous expenses are expected to increase 25%.

INSTRUCTIONS

a Construct a cash budget for 1984 for the Triple-F Health Club. *Note:* The budget should end with the cash excess or deficiency before financing.
b Identify any operating problem(s) that this budget discloses for the Triple-F Health Club. Explain your answer.
c Is Jane Crowe's concern that the board's goals are unrealistic justified? Explain your answer.

(CMA modified.)

P23-6 ***Cash budget and pro forma statements***

The Clarke Company's balance sheet as of December 31, 1983, appears on page 934. Clarke has gathered the following information relating to January 1984.

1 Budgeted sales total $250,000. Historically, cash sales have averaged 20% of total sales. Sixty percent of the firm's credit sales are collected in the month of sale; the remainder are collected in the following month.
2 Merchandise purchases are expected to total $180,000. Obligations to suppliers are settled as follows:

Forty percent are paid in the month of purchase subject to a 2% discount.
Twenty percent are paid in the month of purchase after the discount period has lapsed.
Forty percent are paid in the month following purchase.

Management has budgeted the January 31 inventory at $57,500.

CLARKE COMPANY
Balance Sheet
December 31, 1983

ASSETS		
Cash		$ 13,200
Accounts receivable		61,500
Merchandise inventory		48,600
Plant & equipment	$ 84,000	
Less: Accumulated depreciation	21,000	63,000
Total assets		$186,300
LIABILITIES & STOCKHOLDERS' EQUITY		
Accounts payable		$ 31,800
Common stock, $10 par	$ 50,000	
Retained earnings	104,500	154,500
Total liabilities & stockholders' equity		$186,300

3 Monthly operating expenses are paid as incurred and subdivided as follows:

Variable	15% of sales
Fixed (includes depreciation)	$30,500

4 The plant and equipment have a ten-year service life. Clarke uses the straight-line method of depreciation.
5 The company plans to acquire $15,000 of equipment on January 31 by paying $5,500 down and signing a short-term note for the remaining balance.
6 Clarke will declare a $0.50-per-share cash dividend on January 18. The dividend will be distributed on February 18.

INSTRUCTIONS

a Determine Clarke's January 31 cash balance by preparing a cash budget.
b Prepare a pro forma income statement for January. Disregard income taxes and earnings-per-share computations.
c Prepare a pro forma balance sheet as of January 31.

P23-7 ***Comprehensive budgeting***

The balance sheet of Watson Company as of December 31, 1983, is presented on page 935. The following information has been extracted from the company's records.

1 All sales are made on account at $20 per unit. Sixty percent of the sales are collected in the month of sale; the remaining 40% are collected in the following month. Forecasted sales for the first five months of 1984 are as follows: January, 1,500 units; February, 1,600 units; March, 1,800 units; April, 2,000 units; May, 2,100 units.

WATSON COMPANY
Balance Sheet
December 31, 1983

ASSETS		
Cash		$ 4,595
Accounts receivable		10,000
Finished goods (575 units × $7.00)		4,025
Direct materials (2,760 units × $0.50)		1,380
Plant & equipment	$50,000	
Less: Accumulated depreciation	10,000	40,000
Total assets		$60,000
LIABILITIES & STOCKHOLDERS' EQUITY		
Accounts payable to suppliers		$14,000
Capital stock	$25,000	
Retained earnings	21,000	46,000
Total liabilities & stockholders' equity		$60,000

2 Management desires to maintain the finished goods inventory at 30% of the following month's sales.

3 Watson uses four units of direct material in each finished unit. The direct material price has been stable and is expected to remain so over the next six months. Management desires to maintain the ending direct materials inventory at 60% of the following month's production needs.

4 Seventy percent of all purchases are paid in the month of purchase; the remaining 30% are paid in the subsequent month.

5 Watson's product requires 30 minutes of direct labor time. Each hour of direct labor costs $7. The company applies factory overhead at the rate of $3 per direct labor hour.

INSTRUCTIONS

a Rounding computations to the nearest dollar, prepare the following for January through March.
  (1) Sales budget
  (2) Schedule of cash collections
  (3) Production budget
  (4) Direct material purchases budget
  (5) Schedule of cash disbursements for material purchases
  (6) Direct labor budget

b Determine the balances in the following accounts as of March 31.
  (1) Accounts Receivable
  (2) Direct Materials
  (3) Finished Goods
  (4) Accounts Payable

P23-8 ***Production and purchases budgets; inventory policy (alternate to P23-2)***
McFarland, Inc., manufactures and distributes various parts for bicycles. The company's main product is bicycle pedals. Each pedal requires two units of direct material at a cost of $0.40 per unit. To keep production moving smoothly, the company must maintain a direct materials inventory equal to 30% of the following month's production needs.

A sales budget for the first six months of 1984 follows.

Month	*Projected Pedal Sales*
January	20,000
February	22,000
March	24,000
April	26,000
May	25,000
June	21,000

Management desires to carry a finished goods inventory equal to 60% of the following month's sales. On December 31, 1983, the finished goods inventory totaled 11,500 pedals. On the same date 24,800 units of direct material were in the warehouse.

INSTRUCTIONS

a Prepare a production budget for January through March.
b Prepare a direct material purchases budget for January through March.
c List several factors that could cause a change in the company's present finished goods inventory policy.

P23-9 ***Production budget and abbreviated cash budget (alternate to P23-3)***
The Deluca Company has gathered the following information in preparation of its first-quarter budget for the coming year.

Sales and collections:

December sales (actual)	10,000 units @ $10	$100,000
January sales (estimated)	10,200 units @ $10	102,000
February sales (estimated)	10,500 units @ $11	115,500
March sales (estimated)	10,800 units @ $11	118,800
April sales (estimated)	11,000 units @ $12	132,000

Sixty percent of all sales are collected in the month of sale; the remaining 40% are collected in the following month.

Production:
Manufacturing costs are paid in the month incurred. The following costs relate to the 90,000 units produced during the current year.

Direct materials	*$180,000*
Direct labor	*225,000*
Variable factory overhead	*90,000*
Fixed factory overhead	*204,000*

No significant changes in cost behavior are anticipated. The fixed factory overhead, which includes $36,000 of depreciation, is incurred evenly throughout the year.

Inventory policies:

1 All direct materials are acquired when needed (i.e., no direct material inventory is maintained).

2 Management desires finished goods inventories equal to 30% of the following month's sales. December's ending finished goods inventory is 3,060 units.

Other data:

1 Selling and administrative expenses amount to $2.20 per unit and are paid in the month following their incurrence.

2 The January 1 cash balance is $6,500.

INSTRUCTIONS

a Prepare a production budget (in units only) for January through March.

b Prepare a cash budget for January through March. *Note:* The budget should end with the cash excess or deficiency before financing.

P23-10 ***Cash budget covering three months (alternate to P23-4)***

Presswood Corporation is a distributor of sporting equipment. Management is studying cash needs for October through December and has assembled the following information.

	October	November	December
Sales	$40,000	$42,000	$52,000
Purchases of merchandise	19,000	25,000	26,000
Cash operating costs	16,400	17,000	19,000
Depreciation expense	1,400	1,800	1,800
Equipment acquisitions	9,000	—	—

The pro forma balance sheet on September 30 revealed the following account balances.

Cash	$ 5,000
Accounts receivable	15,500
Accounts payable	7,400

Sixty percent of all customer accounts are collected in the month of sale; 35% are collected in the following month. Because of a liberal credit policy, bad debts amounting to 5% of sales are anticipated. Management feels that only $14,000 of the accounts outstanding on September 30 will be collectible.

Sixty percent of the merchandise purchases are paid for in the month of purchase to take advantage of a 2% discount. The remaining 40% are paid in the month following purchase.

Presswood maintains a $4,500 minimum cash balance at all times. Should borrowing be necessary, financing is available in $1,000 multiples at an 18% interest rate. Assume all borrowings take place at the beginning of the month and all repayments (including interest) at the end of the month of repaying principal. Principal repayments are also made in multiples of $1,000.

INSTRUCTIONS

a Prepare a schedule of cash collections for October through December.

b Prepare a schedule of cash disbursements for merchandise purchases for October through December.

c Prepare a cash budget similar to that shown in Exhibit 23-13.

P23-11 ***Cash budget and pro forma statements (alternate to P23-6)***

The Shipman Company's balance sheet as of December 31, 1983, follows.

SHIPMAN COMPANY
Balance Sheet
December 31, 1983

ASSETS		
Cash		$ 8,400
Accounts receivable		42,000
Merchandise inventory		29,700
Plant & equipment	$48,000	
Less: Accumulated depreciation	17,000	31,000
Total assets		$111,100
LIABILITIES & STOCKHOLDERS' EQUITY		
Accounts payable		$ 40,000
Common stock, $1 par	$20,000	
Retained earnings	51,100	71,100
Total liabilities & stockholders' equity		$111,100

Shipman has gathered the following information relating to January 1984.

1 Budgeted sales total $150,000. Historically, cash sales have averaged 30% of total sales. Sixty percent of the firm's credit sales are collected in the month of sale; the remainder are collected in the following month.

2 Merchandise purchases are expected to total $90,000. Obligations to suppliers are settled as follows:

Fifty percent are paid in the month of purchase subject to a 2% discount.
Ten percent are paid in the month of purchase after the discount period has lapsed.
Forty percent are paid in the month following purchase.

Management has budgeted the January 31 inventory at $35,500.

3 Monthly operating expenses are paid as incurred and subdivided as follows:

Variable	20% of sales
Fixed (includes depreciation)	$20,800

4 The plant and equipment have a ten-year service life. Shipman uses the straight-line method of depreciation.

5 The company plans to acquire $24,000 of equipment on January 31 by paying $4,000 down and signing a short-term note for the remaining balance.

6 Shipman will declare a $0.10-per-share cash dividend on January 24. The dividend will be distributed on February 24.

INSTRUCTIONS

a Determine Shipman's January 31 cash balance by preparing a cash budget.

b Prepare a pro forma income statement for January. Disregard income taxes and earnings-per-share computations.

c Prepare a pro forma balance sheet as of January 31.

P23-12 ***Comprehensive budgeting (alternate to P23-7)***
The balance sheet of Mid-America Company as of December 31, 1983, is presented below.

MID-AMERICA COMPANY
Balance Sheet
December 31, 1983

ASSETS		
Cash		$ 14,800
Accounts receivable		26,000
Finished goods (1,200 units × $8.00)		9,600
Direct materials (6,000 units × $1.50)		9,000
Plant & equipment	$115,000	
Less: Accumulated depreciation	12,000	103,000
Total assets		$162,400
LIABILITIES & STOCKHOLDERS' EQUITY		
Accounts payable to suppliers		$ 12,000
Capital stock	$ 50,000	
Retained earnings	100,400	150,400
Total liabilities & stockholders' equity		$162,400

The following information has been extracted from the company's records.

1 All sales are made on account at $15 per unit. Forty percent of the sales are collected in the month of sale; the remaining 60% are collected in the following month. Forecasted sales for the first five months of 1984 are as follows: January, 2,600 units; February, 2,900 units; March, 3,100 units; April, 3,500 units; May, 3,200 units.

2 Management desires to maintain the finished goods inventory at 20% of the following month's sales.

3 Mid-America uses three units of direct material in each finished unit. The direct material price has been stable and is expected to remain so over the next six months. Management desires to maintain the ending direct materials inventory at 70% of the following month's production needs.

4 Eighty percent of all purchases are paid in the month of purchase; the remaining 20% are paid in the subsequent month.

5 Mid-America's product requires 20 minutes of direct labor time. Each hour of direct labor costs $9. The company applies factory overhead at the rate of $1.50 per direct labor hour.

INSTRUCTIONS

a Rounding computations to the nearest dollar, prepare the following for January through March.
   (1) Sales budget
   (2) Schedule of cash collections
   (3) Production budget
   (4) Direct material purchases budget
   (5) Schedule of cash disbursements for material purchases
   (6) Direct labor budget

b Determine the balances in the following accounts as of March 31.
   (1) Accounts Receivable
   (2) Direct Materials
   (3) Finished Goods
   (4) Accounts Payable

CASE 23
SPRINGFIELD CORPORATION

Springfield Corporation operates on a calendar-year basis. It begins the annual budgeting process in late August when the president establishes targets for the total dollar sales and net income before taxes for the next year.

The sales target is given to the Marketing Department; the marketing manager formulates a sales budget by product line in both units and dollars. From this budget sales quotas by product line, in units and dollars, are established for each of the corporation's sales districts. The marketing manager also estimates the cost of the marketing activities required to support the target sales volume and prepares a tentative marketing expense budget.

The executive vice-president uses the sales and profit targets, the sales budget by product line, and the tentative marketing expense budget to determine the dollar amounts that can be devoted to manufacturing and corporate office expense. The executive vice-president prepares the budget for corporate expenses and then forwards to the Production Department the product line sales budget in units and the total dollar amount that can be devoted to manufacturing.

The production manager meets with the factory managers to develop a manufacturing plan that will produce the required units when needed within the cost constraints set by the executive vice-president. The budgeting process usually comes to a halt at this point, because the Production Department does not consider the financial resources allocated to be adequate.

When this standstill occurs, the vice-president of finance, the executive vice-president, the marketing manager, and the production manager meet to determine the final budgets for each of the areas. This meeting normally results in a modest increase in the total amount available for manufacturing costs, while the marketing expense and corporate office expense budgets are cut. The total sales and net income figures proposed by the president are seldom changed. Although the participants are seldom pleased with the compromise, these budgets are final. Each executive then develops a new detailed budget for the operations in his or her area.

None of the areas has achieved its budget in recent years. Sales often run below the target. When budgeted sales are not achieved, each area is expected to cut costs so that the president's profit target can still be met. However, the profit target is seldom met because costs are not cut enough. In fact, costs often run above the original budget in all functional areas. The president, disturbed that Springfield has not been able to meet the sales and profit targets, recently hired a consultant with considerable experience in Springfield's industry. The consultant reviewed the budgets for the past four years. He concluded that the product line sales budgets were reasonable, and that the cost and expense budgets were adequate for the budgeted sales and production levels.

INSTRUCTIONS

a Discuss how the budgeting process as employed by Springfield Corporation contributes to the failure to achieve the president's sales and profit targets.

b Suggest how Springfield Corporation's budgeting process could be revised to correct the problems.

(CMA modified.)

24 COST-VOLUME-PROFIT ANALYSIS

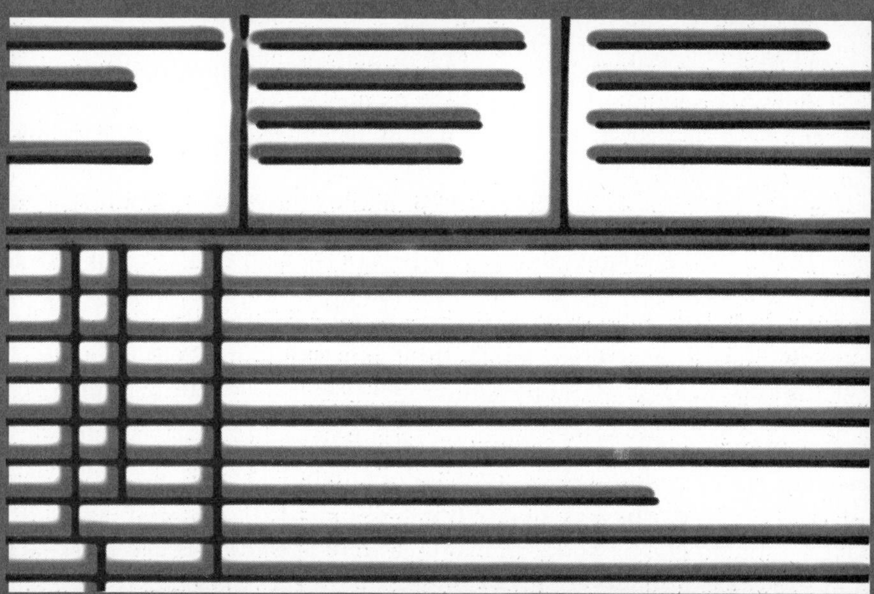

LEARNING OBJECTIVES

After reading this chapter you should:

1 Be familiar with the characteristics of variable, step, committed fixed, discretionary fixed, and mixed (semivariable) cost functions.

2 Understand the concept of the relevant range.

3 Be able to utilize the scattergraph and high-low method for studying cost behavior, and be familiar with the availability of the method of least squares.

4 Be able to perform a cost-volume-profit analysis to determine the break-even point, the sales level necessary to achieve a certain target net income, and the impact of operating changes on various profitability measures.

5 Be familiar with the computation and meaning of the contribution margin.

6 Be able to apply cost-volume-profit analysis to multiproduct firms.

7 Understand the limiting assumptions on which cost-volume-profit analysis is based.

CHAPTER 24

In recent years many firms have felt the effects of high inflation rates and increased competition. To continue the generation of adequate profitability and return on assets, companies have been forced to alter their business practices. Consider, for instance, the introduction of twilight matinees by movie theaters. By offering first-run features at deeply discounted prices, theater operators have transformed empty, dinner-hour auditoriums into thriving money-makers. Further examples are found in the fast-food industry, where franchises known mostly for hamburgers have added salad bars, speciality sandwiches, and chicken to their product lines. In addition, numerous food establishments have participated in "buy one, get one free" campaigns on selected menu items.

Operating practices such as the foregoing can be implemented only after extensive analysis. Businesses must determine how changes in revenue and volume affect both profit and total cost. As you learned in an earlier chapter, certain costs fluctuate with changes in activity, while other costs remain constant. The study of price, cost, volume, and profit interrelationships is often termed **cost-volume-profit (CVP) analysis.** Like budgeting, CVP analysis is another tool that is useful in planning.

COST BEHAVIOR

Effective CVP analysis requires a thorough understanding of cost behavior. For this reason we wish to expand on the material presented in Chapter 21. Before we do so, however, a word of caution is necessary. Keep in mind that it is extremely difficult

> *to generalize about cost behavior. Nobody can, by simple inspection of a company's chart of accounts, describe how each cost is going to fluctuate in relation to volume. Like people, costs tend to behave as individuals. Strongly influenced by their environment, costs behave differently in different places under different circumstances. What happens when revenue is down may not be repeated when revenue is up and there is more money to spend. [Also,] costs that follow a definite pattern when rigidly controlled may show erratic behavior patterns when control is relaxed or removed.*[1]

Given this warning, we will now explore three types of costs: variable, fixed, and mixed.

Variable Costs

Recall that a **variable cost** varies in direct proportion to a change in an activity base (e.g., sales, production, miles driven). Thus if an activity base triples, a true variable cost should triple; if the base is halved, a variable cost should decrease by 50%. Common examples of variable costs include direct materials, direct labor, supplies, sales commissions, and fuel.

To determine whether a cost possesses variable characteristics, one should observe the cost's behavior over wide ranges of activity. Consider, for

[1] Gerald R. Crowningshield and Kenneth A. Gorman, *Cost Accounting: Principles and Managerial Applications,* 4th ed (Boston: Houghton Mifflin, 1979), p. 350.

example, the wear and tear on automobile tires. Short daily trips and even total monthly mileage will have little effect on tire wear and tread depth. Over time—say, several years—daily driving will take its toll. Eventually, the tires will have to be replaced after a substantial number of miles have been traveled.

Because variable costs change in direct proportion to fluctuations in an activity base, the variable cost *per unit* is constant. To illustrate, assume Yellowstone Manufacturing normally produces 10,000 to 12,000 units each month. From the following total labor figures, the accounting department has calculated labor cost at $8 per unit.

A	*B*	*B ÷ A*
Production (Units)	***Total Labor Cost***	***Cost per Unit***
10,000	$80,000	$80,000/10,000 = $8
10,500	84,000	$84,000/10,500 = $8
11,000	88,000	$88,000/11,000 = $8
11,500	92,000	$92,000/11,500 = $8
12,000	96,000	$96,000/12,000 = $8

Notice that the $8-per-unit figure holds true at all volume levels.

For those readers who have taken an economics course, you may have noticed an apparent conflict in the economist's and accountant's views of variable cost behavior. Economic models generally assume that the per-unit variable cost changes with increases in production activity. For example, picture a company that produces trucks through an assembly-line process. If the firm employed only two laborers, the number of trucks manufactured would surely be low. Furthermore, efficiency would be lacking, because the employees must each perform a multitude of tasks. As demand increases, the firm could increase its output by hiring more personnel. Instead of being a "jack of all trades," a worker could specialize, improve capital utilization, and become more efficient. The net result is a decreasing variable cost per unit. Naturally, a business can improve operations only so far. At some point production problems are encountered because of capacity constraints, lack of activity and departmental coordination, bottlenecks, and other factors. The culmination is a decrease in productivity and an accompanying rise in the variable cost per unit.

The accounting and economic views of variable cost behavior are graphed as shown in Exhibit 24-1. The accountant's variable cost is graphed as a straight-line, linear function. The economist's curve, on the other hand, first depicts a decreasing cost per unit and later an increasing unit cost. The gradual upward slope to the right still indicates, however, that total variable cost increases with additional activity.

Although both views are correct, accountants normally study costs within smaller ranges of activity than those used by economists. Examine Exhibit 24-2, which shows the behavior of a curvilinear cost function. No-

Exhibit 24-1

Differing views of variable cost

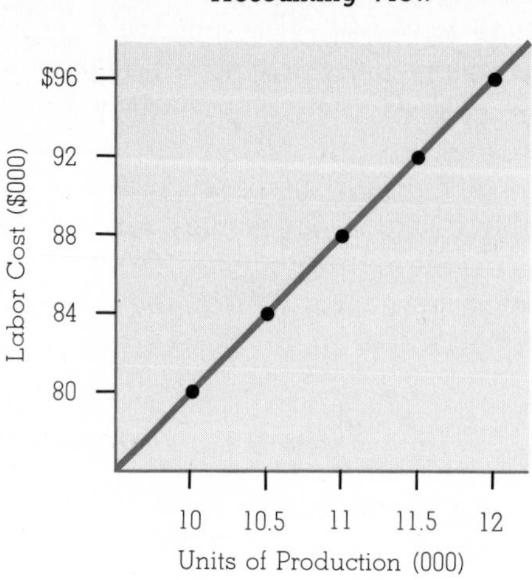

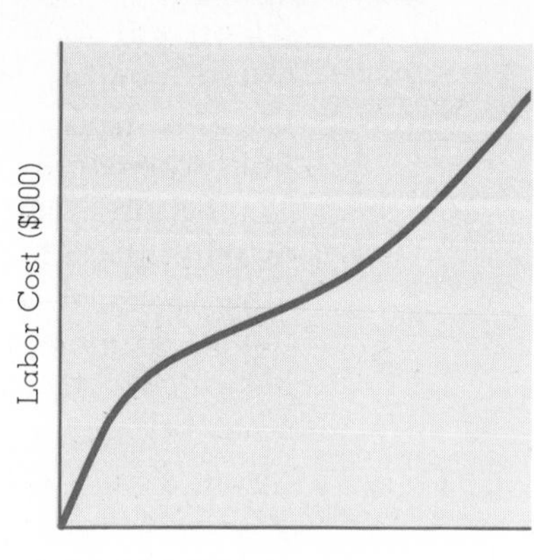

tice that within the narrow shaded band, linear behavior (and a constant cost per unit) is realistic. This band depicts the **relevant range,** or the area of activity where a cost relationship is expected to hold true. Should activity fall outside the relevant range, cost relationships may change. In the case just illustrated, for example, the accountant could be confronted with a steadily increasing or decreasing unit cost behavior and would have to make appropriate adjustments when performing analysis work. In general, the assumption of linearity within the relevant range is acceptable and not likely to result in substantial inaccuracies. Normally, the relevant range is an area in which the entity has had some recent operating activity.

Step cost

A careful inspection of variable cost functions reveals different behavior patterns. While direct materials and sales commissions change in response to small changes in production and sales, respectively, other variable costs vary only when substantial increases or decreases occur in the activity

Exhibit 24-2

Curvilinear variable cost

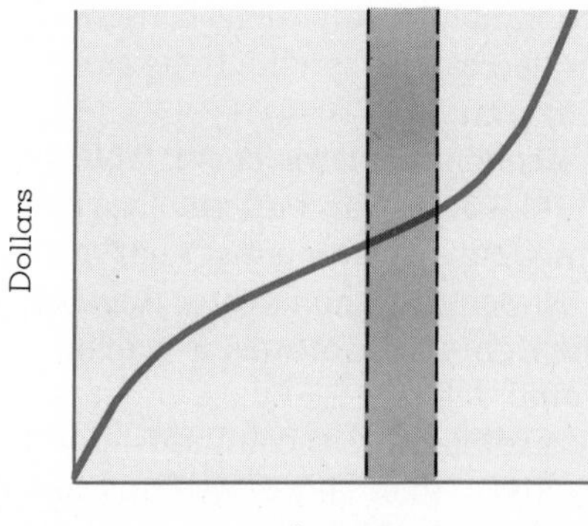

base. For example, consider the clerical staff necessary to process customer orders in a mail-order firm. By working at different paces, employees can usually handle a range of orders. The number of orders processed will be low if the office staff is working at a relaxed pace or high if efforts intensify. Thus when small fluctuations in activity occur (i.e., the number of orders to be processed), the total cost of office personnel remains constant. If orders dramatically increase, however, additional staff will be hired, and the total office costs will rise.

Because the personnel cost increases in proportion to the number of sales orders, the cost is classified as variable. In this case, though, the cost function changes only when large changes are experienced in the activity base. Specifically, the office cost will increase in "chunks" as new workers are added to the payroll. Cost functions that behave in this manner are frequently termed **step costs.** As shown in Exhibit 24-3, a step function approximates the behavior of a "true" variable cost.

Two observations are necessary with regard to step costs. First, the best place to operate on a step cost function is at the rightmost portion of a step. In this manner an organization gets the most for its money, that is, maximum activity just prior to a cost increase. Second, we have noted that the step cost resembles a variable cost and changes in response to wide fluctuations in activity. Sometimes extremely large activity changes are needed to force an increase in the cost function. In these cases the step cost tends to approximate a fixed cost.

Exhibit 24-3

Step cost function

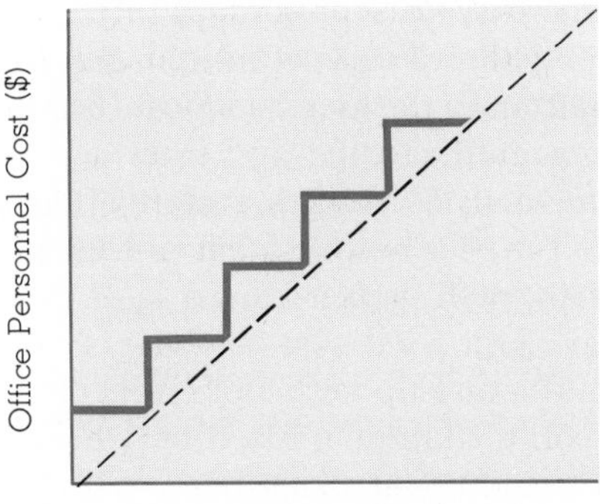

Fixed Costs

Fixed costs are costs that do not change when the activity base fluctuates. To illustrate a fixed cost, assume that Yellowstone Manufacturing leased machinery for $100,000 that is capable of producing from 40,000 to 60,000 units per year depending on utilization. Since the lease payment remains the same no matter how many units are produced, the following graph is appropriate.

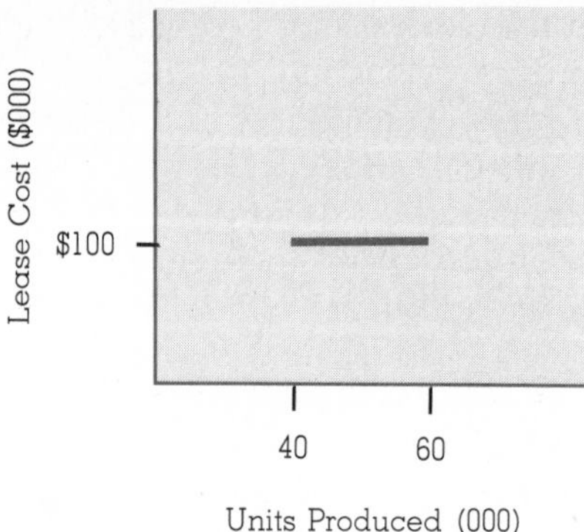

Constant dollars combined with changing activity cause variations in the fixed cost *per unit.* If Yellowstone manufactures only 40,000 units, the lease cost is $2.50 per unit ($100,000 ÷ 40,000 units). On the other hand, if production climbs to 60,000 units, the per-unit cost falls to $1.67 ($100,000 ÷ 60,000 units).

Total fixed costs can change

Although total fixed costs remain static, they can, in fact, vary. Both time and other ranges of activity readily cause increases or decreases in this significant cost element. To explain, virtually all costs change over the years because of inflation and variations in business practices. In the previous illustration, for example, Yellowstone might have leased the same equipment in future years at an increased cost or perhaps turn to another lessor to obtain newer technology. Whether a cost is, indeed, fixed depends on the time period under consideration. In the long run most costs change to match increases and decreases in manufacturing and sales activities. Normally, however, cost-volume-profit analysis studies cost relationships that have been observed in the short run. Techniques that are useful for long-term planning and decision making will be introduced later in the text.

Ranges of activity also affect fixed cost behavior. Notice that Yellowstone's equipment can manufacture up to 60,000 units per year. If production increases beyond this point, additional machinery must be leased, forcing fixed costs to rise. The additional machinery will allow the firm to handle a new range of activity, say 60,000 to 80,000 units. If production increases once again, then even more machinery must be acquired. Costs that behave in this manner can be graphed as shown in Exhibit 24-4. The graph reveals that fixed costs will change with wide fluctuations in activity. The shaded band represents Yellowstone's most recent manufacturing experience—in essence, the relevant range. If the relevant range has been properly defined, normal operations should produce fixed costs that can be graphed as a single horizontal line.

Committed and discretionary fixed costs

Fixed costs are substantial for many companies, especially those engaged in manufacturing. Heavy capital equipment and inventory requirements generate sizable depreciation write-offs, lease costs, and various re-

Exhibit 24-4

Fixed cost behavior

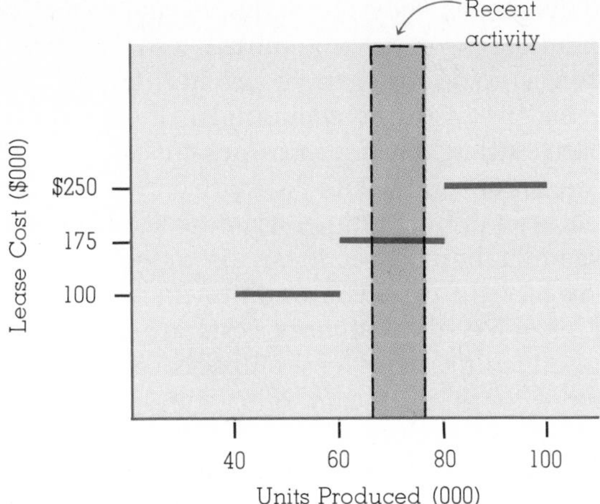

lated outlays. For purposes of planning, fixed costs are frequently subdivided into two types: committed and discretionary.

Committed fixed costs arise from an organization's commitment to engage in operations. By opening its doors and commencing activities, a firm must secure a plant, equipment, and management team. Immediately, as a result, an obligation is made to incur such costs as depreciation, rent, insurance, property taxes, and executive salaries.

By their very nature, most committed costs are not easily changed by daily business activities and decisions. Even if activity slows because of a depressed economy, many of these costs will still be incurred. Naturally, executives can vote to take salary cuts, layoffs can be instituted, and certain operations may be sold or perhaps temporarily closed. However, significant cutbacks in committed costs normally prevent a firm from achieving long-run goals.

Discretionary fixed costs are those that originate from top management's yearly appropriation decisions. That is, in preparing the annual operating budget, management will decide the amount it wishes to spend for certain forthcoming activities. Fixed costs typically determined in this fashion include advertising, research and development, employee training, and contributions.

The underlying differences

Aside from the manner in which they originate, there are two major differences between committed and discretionary fixed costs. First, when a business decides to engage in or expand operations, a careful study is performed of both the current *and* future economic position of the firm. Buildings will not be built and equipment will not be acquired unless *long-run* profitability is anticipated. Thus committed costs are geared heavily to the future. Discretionary fixed costs, on the other hand, are short term in orientation and based on management's expectations for the forthcoming accounting period.

The second distinction between committed and discretionary costs concerns cost elimination. As noted, committed costs are not easily changed. Once the decision is made for their incurrence, an organization becomes locked-in and must live with the commitment for a number of years. Because of this relative stranglehold, companies must achieve effective facility utilization as a means of coping with committed costs. Why? The associated inflexibility dictates an uphill battle in terms of cost reduction in any efforts made to improve profitability. In contrast, discretionary costs also lock in an organization; however, the period of commitment is normally much shorter. Frequently, for example, discretionary costs are set by yearly contracts. Should financial difficulties arise, cost cutbacks can be achieved more rapidly and possibly without significant damage to long-run objectives.

Mixed (Semivariable) Costs

Many cost functions contain both variable and fixed cost elements. You may have seen rental car advertisements that call for a fixed daily rental rate plus so many cents per mile. In addition, utility companies often bill a monthly fixed charge plus a certain number of cents per kilowatt-hour. Both of these cost functions are termed **mixed, or semivariable, costs.** Like a variable cost, a mixed cost changes in response to fluctuations in the activity base. Mixed cost movement, however, is not directly proportional because of the presence of a constant fixed charge. The elements of a mixed cost are shown in the graph in Exhibit 24-5.

Exhibit 24-5

Mixed cost

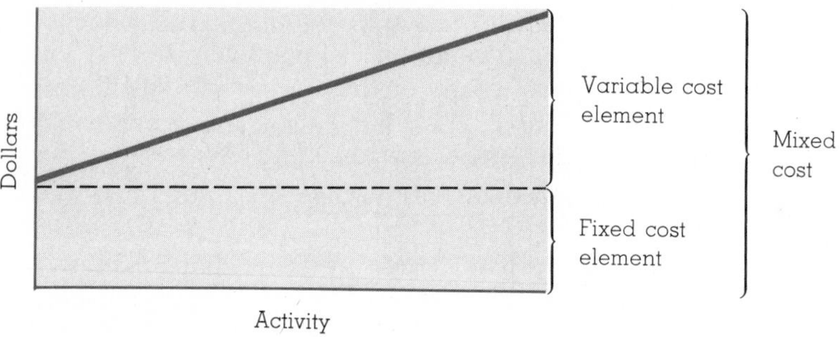

Observe that the variable and fixed cost elements are simply combined to generate the total mixed cost. To illustrate, assume you rented a car for one day and drove 300 miles. If the rental rates were \$25 per day plus \$0.30 per mile, your bill of \$115 would be computed in the following manner:

Fixed cost	\$ 25
Variable cost: 300 miles @ \$0.30	90
Total (mixed) cost	\$115

COST ANALYSIS

Most accountants and cost analysts have little difficulty understanding the differences between variable, fixed, and mixed costs. Determining how specific costs behave, however, is another matter. Recall our earlier warning—the same costs can behave differently in different environments. To further complicate matters, many costs are influenced by more than one factor at the same time. Direct materials used, for example, is normally classified as a variable cost. Use varies with production but is also influenced by material quality and worker efficiency. Turning to another area, gasoline consumption increases with the number of miles driven. However, the exact consumption is also affected by the vehicle involved, wind conditions, the type of driving (city or highway), and other factors.

You are probably beginning to realize that cost analysis is an extremely difficult task. In practice, many companies assume that cost behavior can be sufficiently explained by concentrating on only one key factor rather than the many variables that may actually affect expenditure levels. Management, as a result, must exercise judgment when examining cost functions. Cost analysis in most organizations is heavily dependent on assumptions and estimates; perfection is the exception as opposed to the rule.

Several techniques have been developed to study cost behavior. They include the scattergraph, method of least squares, and the high-low method.

Scattergraph

A **scattergraph** is a graphical representation of observed relationships between costs and activity levels. Using past operating data, one plots the costs incurred at various levels of activity. On the basis of the relationships that are observed, the costs are then identified as being fixed, variable, or mixed. To illustrate the use of a scattergraph, assume Zephyr Bus Lines desires to analyze the maintenance costs incurred to service its bus fleet. An examination of maintenance records for a recent six-month period revealed the following information:

Month	*Maintenance Labor Hours*	*Maintenance Cost*
January	1,400	$25,000
February	1,200	22,400
March	1,600	24,500
April	1,800	24,700
May	1,900	28,000
June	2,000	30,000

In a casual inspection of the data it appears that some variable cost is present, since higher levels of activity (labor hours) generate higher costs. This observation is confirmed by examining the scattergraph in Exhibit 24-6. The line through the data points, drawn by visual approximation, intersects the cost axis at $10,000, the fixed cost of Zephyr's maintenance operation. The variable cost per hour can now be found by studying the total cost of any data point that falls on the line.[2] The following computations

[2]The hourly variable cost is equal to the slope of the line.

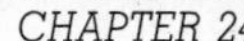

Exhibit 24-6
Scattergraph

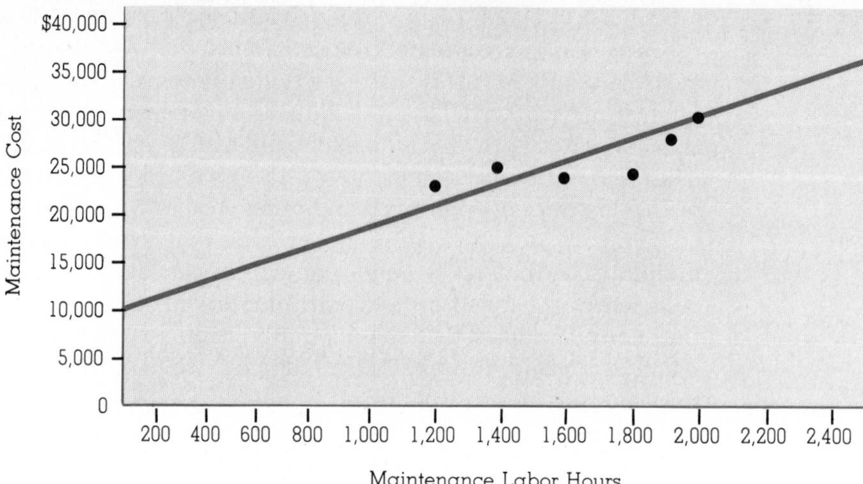

illustrate the proper methodology:

Total cost @ 2,000 hours	*$30,000*
Less fixed cost	*10,000*
Variable cost	*$20,000*

Variable cost per hour: $20,000 ÷ 2,000 hours = $10 per hour

The scattergraph is somewhat imprecise because of the manner in which the cost line is determined; yet it is a starting point for analyzing cost behavior. Further study is necessary to ensure that the observed data points are representative of the cost function's normal behavior and not caused by unusual events such as worker slowdowns, an abnormally high number of breakdowns, and so forth.

Method of Least Squares

The **method of least squares** is a statistical technique that overcomes the imprecision of the scattergraph. Rather than determine the cost line by approximation, the least-squares method uses mathematical formulas to minimize the sum of the squares of the distances from the data points to the line. With this approach the best possible fit is obtained for the line, and therefore higher accuracy is achieved. The details of the least-squares method are normally presented in most statistics courses and many advanced managerial accounting courses.

High-Low Method

Unlike the scattergraph and method of least squares, the **high-low method** uses only two data points when analyzing costs: those at the highest and lowest levels of activity within the relevant range. From these two points a generalization is made regarding variable and fixed cost behavior.

To illustrate the high-low method, we will continue the Zephyr Bus Lines example. Observe that the highest and lowest activity occurred during June and February, respectively. By studying these two points, we see that an 800-hour increase in activity caused maintenance cost to rise by $7,600. These figures are obtained from the following computations:

	Maintenance Labor Hours	Maintenance Cost
Highest activity (June)	2,000	$30,000
Lowest activity (February)	1,200	22,400
Difference	800	$ 7,600

The increase in total cost represents variable cost; thus the variable maintenance cost per hour amounts to $9.50 ($7,600 ÷ 800 hours).

Once variable cost is known, fixed cost can be determined by returning to either of the two data points. Because total cost equals variable cost plus fixed cost, the latter is found by subtraction.

	High Point (2,000 Hours)	Low Point (1,200 Hours)
Total cost	$30,000	$22,400
Less variable cost @ $9.50 per hour	19,000*	11,400†
Fixed cost	$11,000	$11,000

*2,000 hours × $9.50 = $19,000.
†1,200 hours × $9.50 = $11,400.

As the calculations show, fixed costs are the same at both points—an expected finding since we are working within one range of activity.

The high-low method is criticized by many accountants because only two points are analyzed; all other observed cost and activity relationships are ignored. Thus it is especially important that the data points selected for evaluation are representative of normal activity and not caused by unusual happenings. Because of the procedures employed, it is not surprising that the results obtained by the high-low method (fixed cost = $11,000; variable cost = $9.50 per hour) differ from those generated by using the scattergraph (fixed cost = $10,000; variable cost = $10 per hour). Both methods have inherent deficiencies and should be used with care.

COST-VOLUME-PROFIT ANALYSIS

Once variable and fixed costs are determined, cost-volume-profit analysis can begin. Managers use CVP analysis in many different ways. Various cost strategies can be explored, such as trade-offs between fixed and variable outlays. For example, management can study the benefits of acquiring new equipment that will produce savings in direct labor costs. The acquisition generates higher fixed costs while at the same time reducing the variable cost per unit. Is this commitment to additional fixed costs wise or should another strategy (e.g., increased production via incentive pay) be explored? CVP analysis can lend insight so that the proper decision is reached. CVP can also be used to examine pricing policies and their impact on market share; profit strategies such as purposely incurring a loss on a product to generate more customer traffic in a retail establishment; and similar issues.

An important and highly publicized facet of CVP analysis is break-even analysis. Break-even analysis concentrates on finding the **break-even point,** the level of activity where revenues and expenses are equal. Net income, as a result, is zero.

The break-even point can be found by using either an equation or a contribution approach. To illustrate both methods, we will assume that the University Bookstore is studying whether to add a collection of mugs to its product line. Each mug costs \$2.10 and will be sold for \$3.50. The following additional monthly costs will be incurred.

Rental cost of display case	\$200
Salary of part-time salesperson	500
	\$700

Equation Approach

As its name implies, the equation approach formulates a mathematical equation to compute the break-even point. The equation is based on the calculation of net income; that is:

Sales		*\$XXX*
Less: Variable costs	*\$XXX*	
Fixed costs	*XXX*	*XXX*
Net income		*\$XXX*

Because net income equals zero at the break-even point, the following expression is constructed:

sales − variable costs − fixed costs = 0

Transforming, we have

sales = variable costs + fixed costs

The equation requires that variable costs be expressed as a percentage of sales. For the data from the University Bookstore example, the only variable cost is the \$2.10 mug cost. The \$200 display case rental and \$500 salary are both fixed since neither cost changes with volume. Thus variable cost is 60% of sales (\$2.10 ÷ \$3.50 selling price).

The break-even point can now be found in the following manner:

$$\begin{aligned} \text{sales} &= \text{variable costs} + \text{fixed costs} \\ s &= vc + fc \\ s &= 0.6s + \$700 \\ 0.4s &= \$700 \\ s &= \$1{,}750 \end{aligned}$$

The calculations show that monthly sales must total \$1,750 to break even. Stated differently, sales in excess of 500 mugs (\$1,750 ÷ \$3.50 selling price) would generate a net income; sales less than 500 mugs would produce a net loss.

Contribution Approach

The contribution approach focuses on unit profitability. Since mugs are purchased for $2.10 and later sold for $3.50, the bookstore is better off by $1.40 for each mug sold. The $1.40 is termed the **contribution margin,** that is, selling price minus variable cost per unit. Note that the contribution margin represents the amount each unit contributes toward covering fixed costs and generating net income.

To illustrate, examine the data in the following chart.

Mugs Sold	Revenue	Total Variable Cost	Fixed Cost	Total Cost	Net Income	
0	$ 0	$ 0	$700	$ 700.00	$(700.00)	
						>$1.40
1	3.50	2.10	700	702.10	(698.60)	
						>$1.40
2	7.00	4.20	700	704.20	(697.20)	
⋮	⋮	⋮	⋮	⋮	⋮	
500	1,750.00	1,050.00	700	1,750.00	0	
						>$1.40
501	1,753.50	1,052.10	700	1,752.10	1.40	
						>$1.40
502	1,757.00	1,054.20	700	1,754.20	2.80	

The first line shows product line profitability immediately after the decision to carry the mugs. Specifically, the salesperson has been hired and the display case has been rented; however, no mugs have been sold. Subsequently, each sale contributes $1.40 toward covering the fixed costs and decreases the overall loss. Eventually, the decision to add the mugs will prove profitable. When? If each sale contributes $1.40, then 500 mugs must be sold to cover the fixed costs and break even. The break-even point is computed in the following manner:

$$\frac{\textit{fixed costs}}{\textit{unit contribution margin}} = \textit{break-even point in units}$$

$$\frac{\$700}{\$1.40} = 500 \textit{ mugs}$$

After the 500th mug is sold, profits will occur at the rate of $1.40 per unit.

The contribution margin is a very powerful tool in accounting and should not be dismissed lightly. In addition to its use in profit planning, the contribution margin also assists in performance evaluation and decision making. These applications are explored in Chapters 25 and 27, respectively.

A Graphical Representation

The break-even point and CVP relationships are frequently presented in a graphical format known as a **break-even chart.** The graph is useful because it allows managers to (1) review profits over a wide range of activity and (2) examine the effects on profitability of changes in sales and costs.

The break-even chart for our mug example appears in Exhibit 24-7.

Exhibit 24-7

Break-even chart

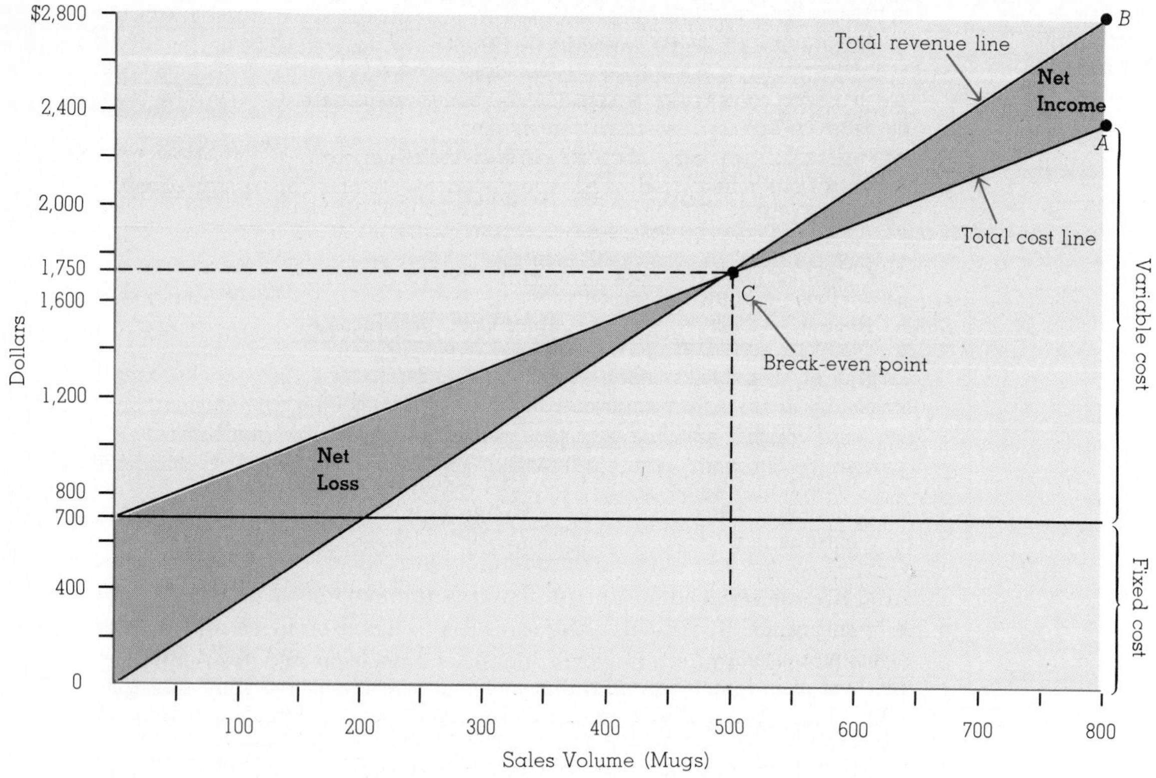

With sales volume graphed on the horizontal axis and dollars on the vertical axis, the chart is constructed in the following manner:

1 Fixed costs are represented by drawing a line parallel to the horizontal axis.

2 Total costs are represented by first computing the total cost of an arbitrarily selected volume level. If a volume of 800 mugs is selected, the total cost would be as follows:

Variable cost (800 mugs × $2.10)	*$1,680*
Fixed cost	*700*
Total cost	*$2,380*

The total cost line is then extended from the intersection of the fixed cost line and the vertical axis to $2,380 (point *A*).

3 Sales revenues are plotted in a manner similar to that for total costs. A diagonal line is extended from the graph's origin through a point representing total revenues of an arbitrarily selected activity

level. If we again choose 800 mugs, the line would be extended through point *B*, or $2,800 (800 mugs × $3.50).

Point *C* represents break-even operations: $1,750 of sales (500 mugs). The graph readily discloses that sales in excess of 500 mugs will be profitable, because total revenues exceed total costs. In contrast, should volume drop below break-even, the University Bookstore will generate a loss from its mug activity.

Target Net Income

Break-even analysis assists management in assessing the desirability of new investments and undertakings. Information is furnished regarding required minimum sales levels to maintain current firm profitability. Because of heavy start-up costs, achieving the break-even point in the early years of many projects is a significant accomplishment. Operating above break-even, of course, is highly desirable.

In addition to determining the break-even point, CVP analysis can be used to identify the level of sales necessary to generate a particular level of net income (often called the **target net income**). To illustrate, we will continue the University Bookstore example. Assume the mugs will be carried only if they generate a monthly net income of $350. Management desires to know the sales required to achieve this level of profitability. The necessary information can be found by modifying the equation and contribution approaches to break-even analysis.

Focusing on the former, we noted earlier that the following relationship was true at the break-even point:

sales − variable costs − fixed costs = 0

Because we now desire to earn a particular level of net income, the equation becomes

sales − variable costs − fixed costs = net income

or

sales = variable costs + fixed costs + net income

Recalling that variable cost is 60% of sales and fixed costs total $700, the bookstore must generate sales of $2,625. This result is shown in the following computation:

$$
\begin{aligned}
s &= vc + fc + ni \\
s &= 0.6s + \$700 + \$350 \\
0.4s &= \$1{,}050 \\
s &= \$2{,}625
\end{aligned}
$$

On the basis of the $3.50 selling price, volume must therefore total 750 mugs ($2,625 ÷ $3.50).

Turning to the contribution approach, the bookstore previously computed that each mug contributes $1.40 ($3.50 selling price − $2.10 variable cost) toward covering fixed costs and generating a profit. As shown on page

BREAK-EVEN ANALYSIS IN CONGRESS?

One of the more controversial issues during congressional hearings in the early 1970s was the economic merit of Lockheed's L-1011 TriStar program. The L-1011 TriStar is a wide-bodied commercial jet. In congressional hearings Lockheed sought a federal guarantee for $250 million of additional bank credit to complete the TriStar program. The loan guarantee was designed to help the company survive a severe cash crisis caused by cost overruns on a number of unrelated military contracts.

Spokesmen for Lockheed insisted that the TriStar program was basically sound and in jeopardy only because of the independently generated cash crisis. The opponents to the guarantee, on the other hand, argued that the program had been economically unsound from the outset and was doomed to financial failure whether or not the loan guarantee was granted.

The debate on this issue proceeded almost entirely on the basis of estimated break-even sales. In his testimony before Congress, Lockheed's chief executive asserted that the break-even point would be reached at sales of between 195 and 205 aircraft. Although at the time of the hearings Lockheed had only 103 firm and 75 optional orders, management was confident that sales would eventually reach or exceed the predicted break-even point.

When studying Lockheed's break-even computations, some analysts felt that the firm made a gross error. Because it tied up production facilities and invested funds to develop the appropriate technology, many alternative investments and projects were forgone. These forgone opportunities translated into lost profits and represented a valid cost of the TriStar program. Lockheed, however, ignored these costs in its computations. The inclusion of the costs raised the actual break-even sales to a level almost twice as high as the estimates submitted to Congress.

SOURCE Adapted from U. E. Reinhardt, "Breakeven Analysis for Lockheed's TriStar: An Application of Financial Theory," Journal of Finance, *September 1973, pp. 821–838.*

955, 500 mugs must be sold just to break even. Beyond break-even and to generate $350 of net income, *additional* sales of 250 mugs ($350 ÷ $1.40) are necessary. Therefore the break-even formula is modified as follows:

$$\frac{\text{fixed costs + net income}}{\text{unit contribution margin}} = \text{required sales in units}$$

$$\frac{\$700 + \$350}{\$1.40} = 750 \text{ mugs}$$

Operating Changes

New technology, shifts in management, and variations in efficiency are commonplace for most businesses. These events and others are usually accompanied by changes in costs and revenues, thus affecting an organization's CVP relationships. Consider, for example, the following break-even load factors[3] for several of this country's airlines.

	1981	1979	1977	1975
American Airlines	60.5%	67.3%	55.7%	57.0%
Delta Air Lines	52.5%	58.0%	50.4%	49.9%
Southwest Airlines	48.3%	53.6%	52.9%	49.2%
USAir	54.9%	60.2%	54.7%	52.1%

Observe the variation over the years and among different carriers within the same year. Although there are a number of underlying causes, several of the more significant include fleet composition in terms of size, age, and fuel efficiency; route systems and structures (e.g., long haul vs. short haul, business vs. vacation); fleet financing methods and rates; passenger fare composition (i.e., full-fare vs. discount traffic); and jet fuel contracts.

Airlines must respond to changes in these factors to stay in the black. Some have done so successfully, while others have not. Those in the latter category have incurred significant operating losses or, in some cases, been absorbed by another carrier. Airlines are not alone—all businesses are faced with variations in their cost and revenue patterns.

Because management's ability to analyze operating changes often spells the difference between prosperity or failure, we wish to focus on the impact of changes in CVP relationships. To do so, we will continue the University Bookstore example. As a refresher, recall the following data:

Selling price per mug	*$3.50*
Variable cost per mug	*2.10*
Contribution margin	*$1.40*

Fixed costs	
Display case rental	*$200*
Salary of salesperson	*500*
	$700

Previously computed break-even point: 500 mugs
Sales necessary to generate net income of $350: 750 mugs

[3]The percentage of seats that must be filled on scheduled flights to break even.

Change in fixed costs

Assume the bookstore is considering hiring a more experienced salesperson who requires a $570 monthly salary. Management wants to know the effect on the break-even point of this $70 increase in fixed cost. The necessary information can be obtained in several different ways. Employing the contribution approach, we see the new break-even volume is 550 mugs:

$$\frac{\text{fixed costs}}{\text{unit contribution margin}} = \frac{\$770}{\$1.40} = 550 \text{ mugs}$$

Or since each mug contributes $1.40 toward fixed obligations, an additional 50 mugs must be sold to cover the $70 cost increase ($70 ÷ $1.40 = 50 mugs). Thus the break-even point will jump from 500 to 550 units.

Changes in fixed costs and variable costs

Returning to the original data, assume the bookstore is exploring different compensation methods. Rather than a $500 monthly salary, a plan is under consideration that calls for a base salary of $325 plus a $0.15-per-mug sales commission. Specifically, management desires to learn the necessary sales volume to yield the target net income of $350. In this case total fixed costs fall to $525 ($325 + $200 case rental). Furthermore, since variable costs rise by $0.15, the mug's contribution margin decreases to $1.25 ($3.50 − $2.25). These two changes are combined to generate the following results:

$$\frac{\text{fixed costs + net income}}{\text{unit contribution margin}} = \text{required sales in units}$$

$$\frac{\$525 + \$350}{\$1.25} = 700 \text{ mugs}$$

The change in salary structure shows that the bookstore can suffer a drop in monthly sales of 50 mugs (750 − 700) and still produce the same target net income. Therefore the plan is advantageous and should be implemented. Not only do the numbers support the change, but an important qualitative consideration is present as well. Compensating personnel with a commission often increases employee motivation. Higher motivational levels, in turn, frequently culminate in improved sales performance.

Changes in fixed costs and sales volume

Assume that operations have been quite profitable, with monthly sales averaging 800 mugs. Management is now considering a larger display case at an increased rental cost of $75 per month. The added space will allow the bookstore to carry a larger selection, and sales are expected to total 900 units. Should the larger display case be acquired?

Because both revenues and costs change, management should compare additional revenues that arise from the decision against the additional costs. If the additional revenues exceed the additional costs, the proposal should be accepted. The following analysis reveals a net benefit in favor of the larger display case.

Additional revenues: 100 mugs × $3.50		*$350*
Less additional costs		
Variable: 100 mugs × $2.10	*$210*	
Increased rental	*75*	*285*
Net benefit		*$ 65*

Observe that we have ignored the present volume of 800 mugs in our analysis. No matter which alternative is selected (i.e., maintain the present situation or acquire the larger case), the 800 mugs will continue to be sold. The analysis should evaluate only those items that change as a result of the decision, specifically, the 100-unit increase in sales and the higher rental charge. Decisions of this nature are explored further in Chapter 27.

Changes in sales price and sales volume

Independent of the previous example (i.e., a change in fixed costs and sales volume), assume that monthly sales have averaged 800 mugs. The bookstore is contemplating an increase in selling price from $3.50 to $3.85 despite a possible lowering of volume. Before the decision is made, management needs information regarding the amount sales can decline before there is a detrimental effect on profitability.

Because current sales total 800 mugs, the present net income is $420 per month.

Sales (800 mugs × $3.50)	*$2,800*
Less variable cost (800 mugs × $2.10)	*1,680*
Contribution margin	*$1,120*
Less fixed cost	*700*
Net income	*$ 420*

With a new selling price of $3.85, the unit contribution margin becomes $1.75 ($3.85 − $2.10). Using the following technique, which was illustrated earlier in the chapter, we find that 640 mugs must be sold to maintain current profit levels.

$$\frac{\text{fixed costs + net income}}{\text{unit contribution margin}} = \text{required sales in units}$$

$$\frac{\$700 + \$420}{\$1.75} = 640 \text{ mugs}$$

Thus the bookstore can suffer a monthly sales loss of 160 mugs (800 − 640) without any impact on net income.

A word of encouragement

The preceding illustrations have shown several different methods for examining operating changes. As you become more experienced in CVP analysis, you will find this topical area is full of variety. That is, the correct solution can be found by many different approaches. As long as your logic is sound and the method of solution is not specified by the text or your instructor, feel free to use any of the techniques presented.

CVP Analysis for Multiproduct Firms

Most businesses engaged in retailing, wholesaling, and manufacturing activities sell more than one product. These products are normally sold in differing volumes and at different markups. For purposes of simplicity the University Bookstore example focused on the use of CVP analysis for a single item. With some minor modification the same procedures can be employed for a multiproduct firm.

To illustrate the use of CVP analysis when more than one product is involved, assume that Stewart Distributors sells three products: toasters, blenders, and mixers. The following data are anticipated for the upcoming year.

Product	Forecasted Sales (Units)	Selling Price	Variable Cost
Toaster	40,000	$20	$16
Blender	100,000	44	37
Mixer	60,000	34	26
	200,000		

Fixed costs: $335,000

As before, the break-even point can be found by dividing fixed costs by the unit contribution margin. Rather than dealing with the contribution margin of one product, however, Stewart has three margins to consider. To further complicate matters, the margins are not expected to occur with the same frequency. For every toaster sold, for example, the firm anticipates selling $2\frac{1}{2}$ blenders and $1\frac{1}{2}$ mixers. As a consequence, Stewart must weight the unit contribution margins by the **sales mix,** that is, the relative combination of individual product sales to total sales. The computations that follow reveal a "unit" contribution margin of $6.70.

Product	Forecasted Sales (Units)	Sales Mix*		Unit Contribution Margin†		Weighted Contribution Margin
Toaster	40,000	20%	×	$4	=	$0.80
Blender	100,000	50%	×	7	=	3.50
Mixer	60,000	30%	×	8	=	2.40
	200,000					$6.70

*Individual product sales ÷ 200,000.
†Selling price minus variable cost for each product.

Thus the break-even point is 50,000 "units" ($335,000 ÷ $6.70). Because each "unit" is really a combination of the three products in the same proportions as the predicted sales mix, the following product line sales are necessary.

Product	Sales Mix	Break-Even "Units"	Break-Even Sales by Product (Units)
Toaster	20%	× 50,000	= 10,000
Blender	50%	× 50,000	= 25,000
Mixer	30%	× 50,000	= 15,000

On the basis of the calculations presented, it is evident that if the sales mix varies, the "unit" contribution margin will differ. Consequently, the break-even volume will change.

Limiting Assumptions of CVP Analysis

The CVP model that we have presented is used to analyze the financial relationships within an organization. Businesses are constantly changing, and many of the changes affect the relationships expressed in the model. CVP studies are therefore based on several limiting assumptions, a few of which have been touched upon in the preceding pages. The assumptions are as follows:

1 All costs can be classified as fixed or variable.
2 Fixed costs remain constant through the range of analysis (i.e., the relevant range).
3 The behavior of costs and revenues is linear through the range of analysis.
4 Technology, efficiency, costs, and selling prices remain as predicted.
5 The sales mix remains as predicted (i.e., constant).
6 Inventory levels remain fairly stable. (The impact of inventory changes is considered in Chapter 25.)

Management must be fully aware of the foregoing assumptions if CVP analysis is to be used properly. Failure to recognize the limitations of the analysis and the dynamic nature of business could lead to serious deficiencies in the planning and decision processes.

SUMMARY PROBLEM

Kennett Company manufactures and sells a single product. Sales peak in March and generally bottom out in October. The following cost and volume information was extracted from the accounting records.

	March	July*	October
Production and sales (units)	25,000	19,000	14,000
Total cost incurred	$195,300	$176,200	$156,800

** An average month.*

The company's product sells for $9.00 per unit.

INSTRUCTIONS

a ***By using the high-low method, compute Kennett's variable cost per unit and monthly fixed cost.***

b Compute the firm's contribution margin per unit.
c Determine the break-even point in terms of both units and dollar sales.
d Determine the sales volume (in units) required to generate a target net income of $29,150 per month.
e Assume Kennett desires to add a second product (known as product no. 2). Data relating to the product follow.

Selling price per unit	$7.00
Variable cost per unit	$4.20
Additional fixed costs	$65,800

Management anticipates that product no. 2 will initially account for 20% of the firm's sales volume; the remaining 80% will be generated by the existing product (known as product no. 1). If Kennett adds the new product, compute the new monthly break-even point (in units).

SOLUTION

a

	Units	Total Cost
Highest activity (March)	25,000	$195,300
Lowest activity (October)	14,000	156,800
Difference	11,000	$ 38,500

Variable cost per unit = $38,500 ÷ 11,000 units = $3.50

	High Point (25,000 Units)	Low Point (14,000 Units)
Total cost	$195,300	$156,800
Less variable cost @ $3.50 per unit	87,500*	49,000†
Fixed cost	$107,800	$107,800

* 25,000 units × $3.50 = $87,500.
† 14,000 units × $3.50 = $49,000.

b

Selling price per unit	$9.00
Less variable cost per unit	3.50
Contribution margin per unit	$5.50

c

$$\frac{\text{fixed costs}}{\text{unit contribution margin}} = \text{break-even point in units}$$

$$\frac{\$107{,}800}{\$5.50} = 19{,}600 \text{ units}$$

A break-even point of 19,600 units requires a sales level of $176,400 (19,600 units × $9).

d

$$\frac{\text{fixed costs + net income}}{\text{unit contribution margin}} = \text{required sales in units}$$

$$\frac{\$107{,}800 + \$29{,}150}{\$5.50} = 24{,}900 \text{ units}$$

e

Product	Selling Price		Variable Cost		Contribution Margin	Sales Mix		Weighted Contribution Margin
1	$9.00	−	$3.50	=	$5.50	× 80%	=	$4.40
2	7.00	−	4.20	=	2.80	× 20%	=	0.56
								$4.96

Fixed costs now total $173,600 ($107,800 from product no. 1 + $65,800 from product no. 2). Therefore

$$\frac{\text{fixed costs}}{\text{"unit" contribution margin}} = \text{break-even point in "units"}$$

$$\frac{\$173{,}600}{\$4.96} = 35{,}000 \text{ "units"}$$

Each "unit" is a mixture of product no. 1 and product no. 2 in the 80–20 sales mix. The break-even point is therefore computed as follows:

Product	Sales Mix		Break-Even "Units"		Break-Even Sales by Product (Units)
1	80%	×	35,000	=	28,000
2	20%	×	35,000	=	7,000

KEY TERMS AND CONCEPTS

break-even chart 955
break-even point 954
committed fixed cost 949
contribution margin 955
cost-volume-profit (CVP) analysis 944
discretionary fixed cost 949
fixed cost 947
high-low method 952
method of least squares 952
mixed (semivariable) cost 950
relevant range 946
sales mix 962
scattergraph 951
step cost 947
target net income 957
variable cost 944

QUESTIONS

Q24-1 In evaluating the cost of operating his automobile, a professor once commented: "Fuel is a fixed cost and insurance is a variable cost. I always pay the same amount per gallon and my mileage is fairly constant. On the other hand, the cost per mile for insurance varies with the number of miles I drive." Comment on the professor's observations.

Q24-2 Differentiate between the accounting and economic views of variable cost behavior. When is the accountant's view valid?

Q24-3 What is meant by the relevant range of activity?

Q24-4 Discuss the characteristics of a step cost function. In general, where is the best place to operate on a step?

Q24-5 An accounting professor once commented: "In the long run even fixed costs are variable." Evaluate the professor's comment.

Q24-6 Distinguish between committed and discretionary fixed costs. Which is easier to eliminate should an organization encounter financial difficulties? Explain.

Q24-7 Identify the inherent problems of the scattergraph and the high-low method.

Q24-8 Define the break-even point.

Q24-9 Define the contribution margin. What does the contribution margin represent, and how is it used in finding the break-even point?

Q24-10 Product A has a negative contribution margin. Explain how a negative contribution margin can arise, and determine whether product A should continue to be sold.

Q24-11 Discuss the benefits associated with using a break-even chart.

Q24-12 Determine the effect on the break-even point of each of the following situations.

a An increase in variable cost
b A decrease in fixed cost
c An increase in sales price

Q24-13 What are the limiting assumptions of CVP analysis?

EXERCISES

E24-1 Melinda and Arthur Cooley own a fast-food restaurant in Salt Lake City. The following costs are under evaluation.

a Property taxes paid.
b Franchise fees paid ($10,000 per year plus 15% of gross sales).
c Food costs.
d Straight-line depreciation on restaurant equipment.
e Donations of food and supplies to charitable organizations.
f Local advertising.
g Paper supplies (napkins, cups, and so on).

Classify each of these costs as variable, committed fixed, discretionary fixed, or mixed.

E24-2 The following data pertains to Jenkins, Inc., during a recent six-month period.

	January	*February*	*March*	*April*	*May*	*June*
Maintenance cost	$99,300	$91,500	$87,100	$105,600	$105,800	$94,200
Direct labor hours	7,420	6,370	5,950	7,980	8,150	6,740

a Determine the variable maintenance cost per direct labor hour by using the high-low method.
b Determine monthly fixed maintenance cost by using the high-low method.

E24-3 Berry and Associates experienced the following costs when manufacturing 100 and 200 units, respectively.

	100 Units	200 Units
Direct labor	$2,400	$4,800
Supervision	1,100	1,100
Maintenance	2,600	3,200
	$6,100	$9,100

Determine the anticipated outlays for direct labor, supervision, and maintenance cost if 230 units are produced. Berry uses the high-low method for analyzing cost behavior.

E24-4 Harris Hospital has average revenue of $120 per patient day. Variable costs are $30 per patient day; fixed costs are $3,600,000 per year.

a How many patient days does the hospital need to break even?

b What level of revenue is needed to earn a net income of $450,000?

c If variable costs drop to $24 per patient day, what increase in fixed costs can be tolerated without changing the break-even point as determined in part (a)?

E24-5 The Overlook Hotel has annual fixed costs of $2,336,000 for its 500-room hotel. The average room rents for $40 per day; the daily variable cost is $8 for each room rented. The hotel is open 365 days per year.

a Compute Overlook's net income if the hotel has a 50% occupancy rate throughout the year.

b How many rooms must be rented each year to break even?

c Given your answer in part (b), what percentage of rooms must be rented during the year?

E24-6 Determine the missing amounts in each of the four independent cases below.

Case	Units Sold	Sales	Variable Costs	Contribution Margin per Unit	Fixed Costs	Net Income
A	?	$70,000	?	$6	$14,000	$10,000
B	7,000	?	$42,000	5	?	8,000
C	4,000	53,000	?	?	21,000	(2,000)
D	8,000	92,000	40,000	?	24,000	?

E24-7 M&B sells a single product. Units are purchased for $6 and sold for $14. A 10% sales commission is paid to the sales staff, and annual fixed costs amount to $72,600. The company has 2,000 shares of common stock outstanding. Current policy is to distribute 70% of the net income generated as dividends. Assume that management desires to pay an annual dividend of $3.50 per share.

a Calculate M&B's break-even point in dollar sales.

b Calculate the target net income necessary to meet the desired dividend.

E24-8 Lionel Cody manufactures two products, A and B. The following information pertains to forthcoming operations.

	A		B		
	Units	Dollars	Units	Dollars	Total
Sales	4,000	$12,000	6,000	$30,000	$42,000
Costs					
Variable		$ 6,000		$12,000	$18,000
Fixed		3,000		9,000	12,000
Total		$ 9,000		$21,000	$30,000
Income before taxes		$ 3,000		$ 9,000	$12,000

a Given the projected sales mix, calculate the contribution margin per "unit."
b To break even, how many units of A and B must be sold?
c Which of the two products would you ask the sales manager to push? Why?

E24-9 The Harrigan Company sells two products, X and Y. The following information is available.

	X	Y
Selling price	$6.00	$3.80
Variable cost per unit	$3.50	$2.60
Anticipated sales (units)	30,000	70,000

Fixed costs amount to $55,650.

a Considering the anticipated sales mix, calculate the number of units of X and Y that must be sold to break even.
b If the sales mix shifts and results in a higher percentage of product X being sold, will the break-even point rise or fall? Explain your answer.

PROBLEMS

P24-1 ***Scattergraph and high-low method***

Velez Manufacturing has a highly automated machine shop. The firm is studying utility cost behavior and has gathered the following data for a recent six-month period.

Month	Machine Hours	Utility Cost
January	22,000	$26,100
February	24,000	28,500
March	25,000	29,000
April	27,000	31,200
May	26,000	29,900
June	28,000	32,100

INSTRUCTIONS

a Prepare a scattergraph by plotting machine hours on the horizontal axis and utility cost on the vertical axis.
b By fitting a line through the plotted points, determine Velez's fixed utility cost per month and the variable utility cost per machine hour.

c Determine the variable and fixed utility costs by using the high-low method.
d In general, will the scattergraph and the high-low method yield identical results? Why?
e When using the high-low method, what must be true of the two points selected for study?

P24-2 ***Cost behavior and graphs***

The accompanying figures are graphs of different factory cost and expense data of Farris Enterprises. The vertical axes of the graphs represent *total* dollars of expense, and the horizontal axes represent production. In each case the zero point is at the intersection of the two axes.

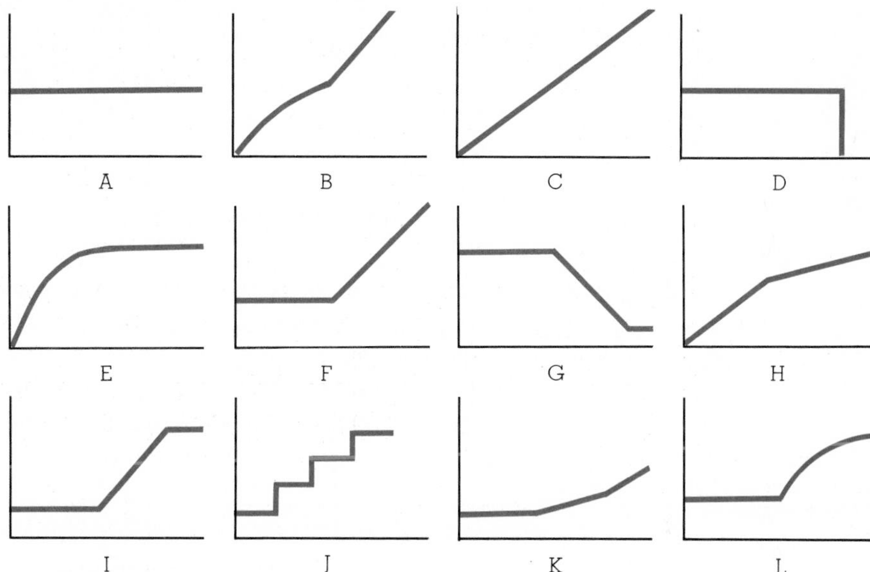

INSTRUCTIONS

Select the graph that best describes each of the following costs. The graphs may be used more than once.

1 Depreciation of equipment, where the amount of depreciation charged is computed by the units-of-output method.
2 Electricity bill: a flat fixed charge plus a variable cost after a certain number of kilowatt-hours are used.
3 City water bill, which is computed as follows:

First 1,000,000 gallons or less	$1,000 flat fee
Next 10,000 gallons	$0.003 per gallon used
Next 10,000 gallons	$0.006 per gallon used
Next 10,000 gallons	$0.009 per gallon used
And so forth	

4 Cost of lubricant for machines, where cost per unit decreases with each pound of lubricant used (e.g., if 1 pound is used, the cost is $10.00; if 2 pounds are used, the cost is $19.98; if 3 pounds are used, the cost is $29.94), with a minimum cost per pound of $9.25.

5 Depreciation of equipment, where the amount is computed by the straight-line method. When the depreciation rate was established, it was anticipated that the obsolescence factor would be greater than the wear and tear factor.
6 Rent on a factory building donated by the city, where the agreement calls for a fixed fee payment unless 200,000 man-hours are worked, in which case no rent need be paid.
7 Salaries of repairmen, where one repairman is needed for every 1,000 machine hours or less (i.e., 0 to 1,000 hours requires one repairman; 1,001 to 2,000 hours requires two repairmen, and so on).
8 Cost of raw material used.
9 Rent on a factory building donated by the county, where the agreement calls for rent of $100,000 less $1.00 for each direct labor hour worked in excess of 200,000 hours, but a minimum rental payment of $20,000 must be paid.

(CPA adapted.)

P24-3 ***Cost behavior and analysis***

The chief accountant of Patrick Corporation is studying certain costs in an effort to better control operations. The costs under study are direct labor, plant security, utilities, and maintenance. Normal production activity ranges from 2,500 to 3,000 units per month. In the past three months the following cost behavior has been observed.

	Month 1	*Month 2*	*Month 3*
Production (units)	2,550	2,970	2,720
Direct labor	$4,590	$5,346	$4,896
Plant security	3,700	3,700	3,700
Utilities	6,615	7,581	7,006

In addition, maintenance costs have displayed the following step behavior.

Activity Range (Units)	*Cost*
Up to 2,600	$4,100
2,601–2,800	5,300
2,801–3,000	6,500

Patrick uses the high-low method for analyzing mixed cost behavior.

INSTRUCTIONS

a Production for next month is expected to total 2,850 units. Calculate the cost of direct labor, plant security, utilities, and maintenance for this level of activity.
b Comment on the cost-effectiveness of producing at a 2,850-unit level of activity with respect to maintenance costs. If you feel this is an ineffective production level, describe how effectiveness could be improved.
c There is a high probability that Patrick's production volume will nearly double in forthcoming months because of a new customer. Can the data and methods used in part (a) for predicting the cost of 2,850 units be employed to estimate total costs for, say, 5,500 units? Why?

P24-4 ***High-low method; addition of new product line***

The Lombardi Corporation manufactures and sells a single product. The following information was extracted from the financial statements of the first two quarters of the current year.

	Quarter 1	Quarter 2
Sales	$2,160,000	$2,496,000
Expenses	1,850,000	2,060,000
Net income	$ 310,000	$ 436,000

Units sold in the first and second quarters totaled 45,000 and 52,000, respectively. Inventories have been fairly stable. Lombardi employs the high-low method for analyzing cost behavior.

INSTRUCTIONS

a Compute the variable cost per unit.

b Compute annual fixed costs.

c Compute the contribution margin per unit. Discuss the alternatives available to Lombardi if management feels the present contribution margin is too low.

d Assume that Lombardi desires to enter a new market by producing and selling valves. Each valve will generate a contribution margin of $9. Lombardi's accountants note that $20,000 of current fixed administrative cost will be charged to the valve line. In addition, new machinery must be leased for $8,000 per month. If 12,000 valves will be sold annually, should Lombardi enter the new market? Why? Assume current sales will not be affected by the decision.

e Suppose Lombardi enters the valve market. If the firm is now performing extensive CVP analysis, what assumption must be made regarding the sales mix of the two product lines? Why is this assumption necessary?

P24-5 ***Break-even analysis and changing fixed costs***

B. R. Ewing and Company, a manufacturer of western hats, has experienced steady sales growth over the past three years. Increased competition has led the firm to consider plans for an aggressive advertising campaign. The following information pertains to the current year.

Variable costs	
Direct labor	$12.00/hat
Direct materials	7.00/hat
Variable overhead	3.50/hat
Total variable costs	$22.50/hat
Fixed costs	
Manufacturing	$ 40,000
Advertising	66,000
Administrative & other selling	70,000
Total fixed costs	$176,000
Selling price per hat	$ 50.00
Current year's sales (12,000 hats)	$600,000

After consultation with his marketing department, Mr. Ewing has set next year's sales target at $675,000 (13,500 hats).

INSTRUCTIONS

a Determine the break-even point in units and dollars for the current year.

b Mr. Ewing believes that next year's target sales can only be achieved if the advertising budget is increased by 40%. If the additional advertising outlay is not made, sales are expected to total 12,200 hats. Should the advertising budget be increased? Why?

c If Ewing wants to achieve next year's target sales and generate net income of $160,000, what is the maximum amount of advertising expense the company can incur? Assume that the cost behavior patterns observed in the current year will continue.

P24-6 ***Break-even and other CVP analysis***

C. Gatta is a manufacturer of sportswear. The following data relate to operations of the current year.

Sales	$5,000,000
Variable costs	40% of sales
Fixed costs	$1,800,000

INSTRUCTIONS

a Compute Gatta's break-even point in dollar sales.

b Determine the current year's net income or loss.

c Next year fixed costs will increase by $500,000 because of an expansion of manufacturing facilities. Determine the *additional* sales that Gatta's marketing staff must generate if management's goal is a target net income of $1,000,000.

d Gatta was recently asked to submit a price quotation on a special order of 5,000 shirts. The variable cost per shirt is $8.50. What is the lowest price per shirt that Gatta can quote without reducing present profits? Explain your answer.

P24-7 ***Break-even and other CVP analysis***

Rosen and Tidwell manufacture a single product. The following information relates to current operations.

Sales: 200,000 units @ $9		$1,800,000
Less: Variable cost	$720,000	
Fixed cost	864,000	1,584,000
Net income		$ 216,000

INSTRUCTIONS

a The sales outlook for next year is bleak. Calculate the number of units that must be sold to break even if current revenue and cost behavior patterns continue.

b If Rosen and Tidwell wish to earn a target net income of $27,000 during the next accounting period, what level of dollar sales must be generated?

c Consider your answer in part (b). Management is contemplating a change in compensation methods during the next accounting period to boost sales. The firm presently employs five salaried salespeople who earn an average of $25,000 per year. Should a new plan be implemented that calls for a base salary of $7,000 per salesperson and a 7% commission based on gross sales? Why?

d Rosen and Tidwell's projected break-even point and target net income are the result of interactions of numerous financial events and transactions. Determine the impact of the following operating changes by filling in the blanks below with "increase," "decrease," or "not affect."

(1) A rise in property taxes will ______________ the contribution margin and ______________ the break-even point.

(2) A decrease in raw material cost will ______________ total fixed costs and ______________ the dollar sales level calculated in part (b).

P24-8 ***Straightforward break-even analysis***

All-Day Candy Company is a wholesale distributor of candy. The company services grocery, convenience, and drug stores in a large metropolitan area. Small but steady growth in sales has been achieved over the past few years while candy prices have been increasing. The company is formulating its plans for the coming fiscal year. Presented below are the data used to project the current year's net income of $184,000.

Average selling price per box	*$4.00*	
Average variable costs per box		
Cost of candy	*$2.00*	
Selling expenses	*0.40*	
Total	*$2.40*	
Annual fixed costs		
Selling		*$ 160,000*
Administrative		*280,000*
Total		*$ 440,000*
Expected annual sales volume (390,000 boxes)		*$1,560,000*

Manufacturers of candy have announced that they will increase prices of their products an average of 15% in the coming year because of increases in raw material (sugar, cocoa, peanuts, and so on) and labor costs. All-Day Candy expects that all other costs will remain at the same rates or levels as the current year.

INSTRUCTIONS

a What is All-Day Candy Company's break-even point in boxes of candy for the current year?

b What volume of sales in dollars must All-Day achieve in the coming year to maintain the same net income as projected for the current year if the selling price remains at $4 and the cost of candy increases 15%?

c To maintain the current break-even point after the 15% cost increase, what options are available to All-Day's management?

(CMA modified.)

P24-9 *Break-even and other CVP analysis*

Laraby Company produces a single product. The firm sold 25,000 units last year, with the following results:

Sales		*$625,000*
Variable costs	*$375,000*	
Fixed costs	*150,000*	*525,000*
Net income before taxes		*$100,000*

In an attempt to improve its product, Laraby is considering replacing a component part that has a cost of $2.50 with a new and better part costing $4.50 per unit in the coming year. A new machine would also be needed to increase plant capacity. The machine has a useful life of six years, no salvage value, and costs $18,000. The company uses straight-line depreciation on all plant assets.

INSTRUCTIONS

a Laraby's accountant is contemplating the use of CVP analysis. Which of the following is *not* a major assumption underlying CVP analysis?
   (1) All costs incurred by a firm can be separated into their fixed and variable components.
   (2) The product selling price per unit is constant at all volume levels.
   (3) Operating efficiency and employee productivity are constant at all volume levels.
   (4) For multiproduct situations the sales mix can vary at all volume levels.
   (5) Costs vary only with changes in volume.

b What was Laraby Company's break-even point in units last year?

c How many units would Laraby have had to sell last year to earn a net income of $140,000?

d If Laraby holds the sales price constant and makes the suggested changes, how many units must be sold in the coming year to break even?

(CMA modified.)

P24-10 *CVP: Multiple-choice questions*

Siberian Ski Company recently expanded its manufacturing capacity, which will allow it to produce up to 15,000 pairs of cross-country skis of the mountaineering model or the touring model. The sales department has assured management that it can sell between 9,000 and 13,000 pairs of either product this year. Because the models are very similar, Siberian will produce only one of the two models.

The following information was compiled by the accounting department.

	Model	
	Mountaineering	***Touring***
Selling price per pair	$88.00	$80.00
Variable costs per pair	52.80	52.80

Fixed costs will total $369,600 if the mountaineering model is produced but will be only $316,800 if the touring model is manufactured.

1 If Siberian Ski desires a target net income of $40,000, how many pairs of touring model skis will the company have to sell?

a 13,118
b 12,529
c 13,853
d 4,460
e Some amount other than those given above

2 If the sales department could guarantee the annual sale of 12,000 pairs of either model, Siberian would:
a Produce touring skis, because they have a lower fixed cost.
b Be indifferent as to which model is sold, because each model has the same variable cost per unit.
c Produce only mountaineering skis, because they have a lower break-even point.
d Be indifferent as to which model is sold, because both are profitable.
e Produce mountaineering skis, because they are more profitable.

3 How much would the variable cost per unit of the touring model have to change before it had the same break-even point in units as the mountaineering model?
a $2.68-per-pair increase
b $4.53-per-pair increase
c $5.03-per-pair decrease
d $2.97-per-pair decrease
e Some amount other than those given above

4 If the variable cost per unit of the touring skis decreases by 10% and the total fixed cost of touring skis increases by 10%, the new break-even point will be:
a Unchanged from 11,648 pairs, because the cost changes are equal and offsetting.
b 10,730 pairs
c 13,007 pairs
d 12,812 pairs
e Some amount other than those given above

5 Which one of the following statements is not an assumption made when employing a CVP study for decision analysis?
a Volume is the only relevant factor affecting costs.
b Changes in beginning and ending inventory levels are insignificant in amount.
c Sales mix is variable as total volume changes.
d Fixed costs are constant over the relevant volume range.
e Efficiency and productivity are unchanged.

(CMA modified.)

P24-11 ***Scattergraph and high-low method (alternate to P24-1)***

P. Thurmond has a highly automated machine shop. The firm is studying maintenance cost behavior and has gathered the following data for a recent six-month period.

Month	Machine Hours	Maintenance Cost
July	18,000	$36,000
August	20,000	39,500
September	18,500	37,000
October	19,000	38,200
November	22,000	36,400
December	17,000	35,400

INSTRUCTIONS

a Prepare a scattergraph by plotting machine hours on the horizontal axis and maintenance cost on the vertical axis.

b By fitting a line through the plotted points, determine Thurmond's fixed maintenance cost per month and the variable maintenance cost per machine hour.

c Determine the variable and fixed maintenance costs by using the high-low method.

d In view of Thurmond's cost behavior, which of the two methods (scattergraph or high-low) appears more accurate? Explain your answer.

e Is it possible to improve the accuracy of the results obtained by the scattergraph? Briefly explain your answer.

P24-12 ***Cost behavior and analysis (alternate to P24-3)***

The chief accountant of Lubinski Machining is studying certain costs in an effort to better control operations. The costs under study are direct materials, plant insurance, utilities, and plant supervision. Normal production activity ranges from 10,000 to 13,500 units per month. In the past three months the following cost behavior has been observed.

	Month 1	Month 2	Month 3
Production (units)	13,400	11,800	10,500
Direct materials	$10,050	$8,850	$7,875
Plant insurance	3,900	3,900	3,900
Utilities	10,840	9,880	9,100

In addition, plant supervision costs have displayed the following step behavior.

Activity Range (Units)	Cost
Up to 10,700	$28,000
10,701–12,000	42,000
12,001–13,500	56,000

Lubinski uses the high-low method for analyzing mixed cost behavior.

INSTRUCTIONS

a Production for next month is expected to total 12,400 units. Calculate the cost of direct materials, plant insurance, utilities, and plant supervision for this level of activity.

b Comment on the cost-effectiveness of producing at a 12,400-unit level of activity with respect to plant supervision costs. If you feel this is an ineffective production level, describe how effectiveness could be improved.

c Fred Braverman, Lubinski's chief accountant, has been analyzing cost incurrence over the past six months by studying the highest and lowest levels of activity. The highest activity occurred when 13,400 units were produced (Month 1 data). The lowest activity took place five months ago when only 6,400 units were manufactured. Activity was depressed because of a strike at Lubinski's main plant. Comment on the use of these activity levels when employing the high-low method.

P24-13 ***High-low method; addition of new product line (alternate to P24-4)***

The Steinmeier Corporation manufactures and sells a single product. The following information was extracted from the financial statements of the first two quarters of the current year.

	Quarter 1	Quarter 2
Sales	$534,000	$615,000
Expenses	440,200	464,500
Net income	$ 93,800	$150,500

Units sold in the first and second quarters totaled 17,800 and 20,500, respectively. Inventories have been fairly stable. Steinmeier employs the high-low method for analyzing cost behavior.

INSTRUCTIONS

a Compute the variable cost per unit.

b Compute annual fixed costs.

c Compute the contribution margin per unit. Explain the meaning of the contribution margin to someone who has a limited business background.

d Assume that Steinmeier desires to enter a new market by producing and selling faucets. The anticipated selling price and variable cost for each faucet is $14 and $6, respectively. Steinmeier will transfer a salesman who is currently earning $20,000 annually to handle faucet sales. In addition, new machinery must be leased for $6,200 per month. Assuming that 10,500 faucets will be sold annually, should Steinmeier enter the new market? Assume sales of the current product line will not be affected by the decision.

e Suppose Steinmeier entered the faucet market with great success. If faucets begin to assume an increasing *percentage* of total sales, what will happen to the firm's overall break-even point? Why?

P24-14 ***Break-even and other CVP analysis (alternate to P24-6)***

Bonfield Enterprises is a manufacturer of sporting goods. The following data relate to operations of the current year.

Sales	$6,800,000
Variable costs	55% of sales
Fixed costs	$2,790,000

INSTRUCTIONS

a Compute Bonfield's break-even point in dollar sales.

b Determine the current year's net income or loss.

c Next year fixed costs will increase by $250,000 because of an expansion of manufacturing facilities. Determine the *additional* sales that Bonfield's marketing staff must generate if variable costs decrease to 52% of sales and management's goal is a target net income of $620,000.

d Bonfield was recently asked to submit a price quotation on a special order of 7,000 basketballs. Variable manufacturing costs per basketball total $3.60; Bonfield must absorb freight charges of $2,450. What is the lowest price per basketball that Bonfield can quote without reducing present profits? Explain your answer.

P24-15 ***Break-even and other CVP analysis (alternate to P24-7)***

Miller and Choi manufacture a single product. The following information relates to current operations.

Sales: 50,000 units @ $12		*$600,000*
Less: Variable cost	*$450,000*	
Fixed cost	*120,000*	*570,000*
Net income		*$ 30,000*

INSTRUCTIONS

a The sales outlook for next year is bleak. Calculate the number of units that must be sold to break even if current revenue and cost behavior patterns continue.

b If Miller and Choi wish to earn a target net income of $18,000 during the next accounting period, what level of dollar sales must be generated?

c Management is contemplating an increase in the selling price to $14 per unit. If consumers balk and volume drops, calculate the number of units that must be sold to earn the target net income of $18,000. Should the change be implemented? Why?

d Miller and Choi's projected break-even point and target net income are the result of interactions of numerous financial events and transactions. Determine the impact of the following operating changes by filling in the blanks below with "increase," "decrease," or "not affect."

(1) An increase in direct labor cost will ______________ the contribution margin, ______________ total fixed costs, and ______________ the break-even point.

(2) A decrease in plant insurance will ______________ the break-even point and ______________ the dollar sales level calculated in part (b).

CASE 24
THE ROXY THEATER

Michelle Williams operates the concession stand at the Roxy Theater. On the basis of a study of last year's operating results, she has established the following budget for 1984.

	Food	Beverage		Total
Expected number of sales	80,000	120,000		200,000
Sales revenue	$100,000	$96,000		$196,000
Less: Variable costs	72,000	12,000		84,000
Contribution margin	$ 28,000	$84,000		$112,000
Less: 20% of gross sales paid to theater			$39,200	
Fixed costs			60,000	99,200
Net income				$ 12,800

During 1984, patrons changed their buying habits and Williams had 120,000 food sales and 80,000 beverage sales. The average sale amount and contribution margin per sale remained as budgeted.

INSTRUCTIONS

a Since Williams achieved her budget of 200,000 sales, she believes that 1984 net income will approximate $12,800. Prepare an income statement to determine the concession stand's operating performance. Explain any significant variations from the budget.

b Refer to the original budget. Assume the fixed costs can be subdivided as follows:

Food	$16,000
Beverage	8,000
General	36,000
Total	$60,000

Williams is considering the elimination of food sales because, as she notes, "The food operation is more trouble than it's worth." Determine the budgeted net income for 1984 if the food service had been dropped and the associated fixed costs could have been eliminated.

c What other factors should be considered when evaluating the possible elimination of the food operation?

25 EXTENSIONS OF CVP ANALYSIS FOR PERFORMANCE EVALUATION

LEARNING OBJECTIVES

After reading this chapter you should:

1 Understand the purpose and structure of a responsibility accounting system.

2 Be able to distinguish among cost, profit, and investment centers.

3 Understand the meaning of controllability as related to a responsibility accounting framework.

4 Be able to distinguish between direct and indirect costs.

5 Be aware of the deficiencies associated with cost allocations when measuring performance.

6 Know how to prepare a contribution income statement and be able to distinguish between the controllable contribution margin and the segment margin.

7 Understand the differences between direct (variable) costing and absorption costing, including related internal- and external-reporting issues.

8 Understand the consequences of using single, multiple, and weighted measures of performance.

CHAPTER 25

Throughout this text we have presented various measures of financial performance. Earnings per share, the current ratio, and funds provided from operations are among the many evaluative measures of interest to investors, analysts, and managers. Although our presentation has been accounting-oriented, realize that performance analysis is widespread and affects virtually everyone. For example, economists continually study unemployment rates and changes in the Consumer Price Index. Sales personnel are constantly judged against budgeted sales quotas. Baseball players are assessed on batting averages, runs batted in, and fielding percentages. And finally, you are probably being evaluated in this course on the basis of examination scores. Naturally, our list of performance measures is far from complete. Suffice it to say, however, that in one form or another, performance measurement is a way of life.

This chapter further develops the concepts discussed in Chapter 24. Cost-volume-profit (CVP) analysis and the contribution margin are extended to the area of performance evaluation. Then the direct costing method of inventory valuation is described and contrasted with inventory methods presented earlier in the text. As you will see, direct costing is a logical extension of CVP analysis because it utilizes the contribution margin in determining net income. Before we proceed, it is necessary to introduce the underlying foundation of performance measurement—responsibility accounting.

RESPONSIBILITY ACCOUNTING

Responsibility accounting is a reporting system that is based on the organizational structure of a firm. In essence, the firm is subdivided into various centers (i.e., segments) such as departments, plants, territories, or divisions. Managers are appointed to oversee individual center activities, are held accountable for operating results, and evaluated accordingly. The thrust of responsibility accounting is that centers are charged only for costs and credited only for revenues that are subject to their control. By operating in this manner, top management can better assess performance and monitor progress toward attaining specific company objectives.

Responsibility Units

As noted, responsibility centers may be organized in different ways: by territories, by departments, and so forth. Each center, in turn, may be established as a cost, profit, or investment center.

Cost center

A **cost center** is a responsibility unit in which a manager is held accountable for cost incurrence. Generally, cost centers are operations or departments that are not directly involved in revenue-generating activities. Thus managers are evaluated on the level of cost incurred, not net income. Common examples of cost centers include billing, purchasing, payroll, and janitorial departments.

Because managers are evaluated on the costs within their control, many people believe that cost centers should set a goal of cost minimization. Unfortunately, in trying to achieve this goal, a cost center would provide virtually no service to the rest of the organization. Why? Remember that many costs are variable and rise with increased activity. A cost center's manager should therefore attempt to maintain costs at a reasonably low level while at the same time furnishing adequate assistance to other segments of the firm.

Profit center

A **profit center** is a responsibility unit in which a manager is held accountable for profit, that is, revenues minus expenses. Because revenues now enter the evaluation process, profit centers must be involved in the sale of goods or services. Although it seems strange, the sales may be *intracompany,* that is, within the firm. For example, the filmmaking division of a large entertainment concern could produce and sell a "made-for-television" movie to the organization's broadcasting division. Although both divisions are part of the same company, one division is selling its output to the other. Further examples of profit centers include computer and maintenance centers, which charge other operating segments for computer services and maintenance work, respectively.

Investment center

An **investment center** is the most complex of the responsibility centers. A manager is evaluated not only on revenues and expenses but also on asset investment. That is, the head of an investment center is concerned with both profitable operations and the effective use of capital funds. Capital funds are normally disbursed for long-term projects such as the acquisition of new buildings, machinery, or equipment; investment in other companies for purposes of control and affiliation; and entry into new product lines and markets.

In effect, the investment center structure allows a manager to run his or her own small business; the business, however, is part of a larger organization. Sometimes managers lose sight of this fact and make decisions that are in the best interests of the center and not the firm. This action tends to reduce the effectiveness of the decentralized responsibility unit framework and should be avoided if at all possible.

The operations of Mattel, Inc., exemplify typical investment centers. Mattel conducts activities in the following business segments:

Segment	*Division*
Toy and hobby products	Mattel Toys U.S.A.
	Mattel Toys International
	Monogram Models, Inc.
Electronics	Mattel Electronics
Publishing and printing	Western Publishing Company, Inc.
Entertainment	Circus World, Inc., Florida

Revenue and expense data are captured at the division level and related to each division's asset investment. Next, divisional results are summarized by business segment. A breakdown of Mattel's recent operating profit and identifiable assets by segment follows.

Business Segment	Operating Profit (in Thousands)		Identifiable Assets (in Thousands)		Return on Assets*
Toy and hobby products	$ 65,522	44%	$217,520	35%	30.1%
Electronics	73,067	50	148,142	23	49.3
Publishing and printing	10,470	7	205,304	33	5.1
Entertainment**	(1,076)	(1)	56,038	9	(1.9)
	$147,983	100%	$627,004	100%	23.6%
Interest expense†	(51,394)		—		
Corporate and other†	(20,687)		20,430		
	$ 75,902		$647,434		

*Return on assets is computed by dividing operating profit by identifiable assets.
**These figures include financial data for Ringling Bros. and Barnum & Bailey Combined Shows, Inc., Ice Follies, and Holiday on Ice, Inc., all of which have been subsequently sold.
†These items relate to Mattel's overall operation.

The data show that although toy and hobby products and the publishing and printing segments employed similar asset investments in terms of size, toy and hobby products used the assets to generate a much higher return (30.1% to 5.1%). Also, the electronics segment was able to produce a much higher return than toy and hobby products (49.3% vs. 30.1%) by conducting more profitable operations with a smaller asset base.

Return on assets, commonly referred to as *return on investment* (*ROI*), is a very popular tool for examining investment center performance. This ratio shows how effectively a center utilized its assets in generating profit. Since the measurement process is placed on a percentage basis rather than absolute dollars, segments of different sizes can be compared more readily. Comparisons, however, should be done with caution since different segments often have different operating characteristics.

Reporting System

Responsibility accounting systems are tailored to a company's organization chart; that is, performance reporting begins at lower levels of the firm and continues upward. This design approach is used to reflect the pyramiding of responsibility that exists in an organizational hierarchy. The system's reports therefore show a manager's own performance plus the performance of lower-level employees in the chain of command.

To illustrate, we will examine Exhibit 25-1, which depicts the organization chart of the Sakowski Manufacturing Corporation. Sakowski has divided its operations into divisions that are organized along territorial lines. Each division, in turn, is composed of several plants. For purposes of simplicity only the details of the Eastern Division are presented. In addition, smaller responsibility units, which may be established at the plant level (e.g., departments and work stations) are omitted. Overall our example will focus on three reporting levels. From the lowest to the highest they are plant, division (vice-president), and president.

Exhibit 25-1

Sakowski Manufacturing Corporation organization chart

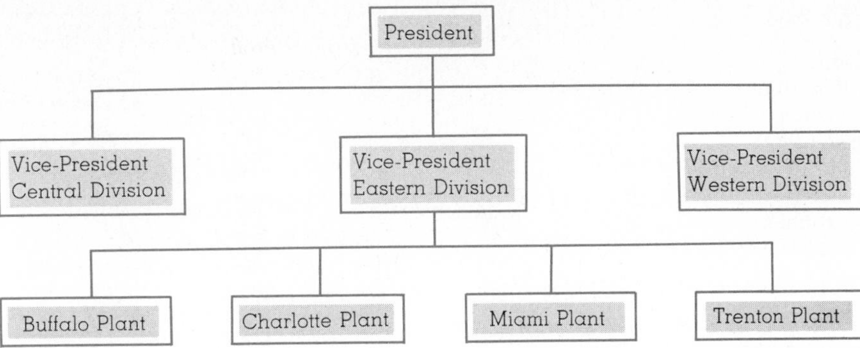

Performance reports

A formal evaluation of operations usually includes **performance reports.** Performance reports are designed to provide the manager of a responsibility center with timely feedback of operating results. Note the word "timely." The purpose of a responsibility reporting system is to assist management in the appraisal and control of operations. Reports that arrive well after a period (or manufacturing job) has concluded are frequently ineffective in trying to correct deficiencies. Why? Many managers assume their performance is satisfactory unless given some information to the contrary. Thus managers may unknowingly continue inefficient actions simply because of a lack of feedback. Timeliness is necessary to improve existing operations; yet it is a growing problem for businesses because of increasingly complex reporting requirements and the so-called paperwork blizzard. Many firms have turned to computers for assistance. As we noted earlier in the text, computers generate reports faster than manual accounting systems and provide better (more timely) information for control and performance appraisals.

The exact format and the detail level of a performance report are determined by the needs and preferences of the user as well as the type of responsibility center being evaluated. For example, the management of a manufacturing firm may desire feedback regarding units produced during a given period. A sports enterprise, on the other hand, may be concerned with attendance and sales of particular seat classifications, such as box, reserved, and general admission. Regardless of the report's specific content, most performance reports compare budgeted figures to actual figures. The differences, or variances, may be expressed in dollars or as percentages of budgeted amounts.

The reporting system utilized by Sakowski Manufacturing appears in Exhibit 25-2. Observe the bottom-up progression of operating information. The operating results at the plant level are compiled first and then included in the vice-president's report. The report of the vice-president summarizes all plants under his or her supervision and also reveals the cost of running the vice-president's office. The summarization process continues upward to the president. The president's report discloses the operating performance of

Exhibit 25-2

Sakowski Manufacturing Corporation; responsibility accounting at various organizational levels ($000 omitted)

PRESIDENT'S OCTOBER RESPONSIBILITY REPORT

	Budget	Actual	Variance: Dollars	Variance: Percentage of Budget
President's office	$ (100)	$ (95)	$ 5	5%
Central division	490	485	(5)	(1)
Eastern division	400	416	16	4
Western division	350	360	10	3
Operating income	$1,140	$1,166	$26	2%

( ) = unfavorable

EASTERN VICE-PRESIDENT'S OCTOBER RESPONSIBILITY REPORT

	Budget	Actual	Variance: Dollars	Variance: Percentage of Budget
Vice-president's office	$ (28)	$ (30)	$ (2)	(7)%
Buffalo plant	66	70	4	6
Charlotte plant	75	85	10	13
Miami plant	55	61	6	11
Trenton plant	232	230	(2)	(1)
Operating income	$400	$416	$16	4%

( ) = unfavorable

CHARLOTTE PLANT'S OCTOBER RESPONSIBILITY REPORT

	Budget	Actual	Variance: Dollars	Variance: Percentage of Budget
Sales	$360	$365	$ 5	1%
Cost of goods sold	$240	$233	$ 7	3%
Administrative expense	25	25	0	0
Selling expense	20	22	(2)	(10)
Total	$285	$280	$ 5	2%
Operating income	$ 75	$ 85	$10	13%

( ) = unfavorable

the three vice-presidents (i.e., divisions) along with the costs of maintaining the top administrative offices.

It is now apparent that the reporting system is both consistent with Sakowski's organizational structure and reflects the progression of authority and responsibility existing in most businesses. Also, it is evident that as one goes higher and higher in the structure, the reports become more summarized. This summarization reflects upper-level management's unwillingness to sift through reams of detailed data reflecting operations and activities for which subordinates are responsible. Given the nature of upper-level management positions and the type of work performed, summarized information is suitable. If for some reason more detail is needed, the reporting system is structured so that the desired information is readily accessible.

Controllability: The Key to Responsibility Accounting

When evaluating performance under a responsibility accounting system, management should consider only those revenues, expenses, and investments that a segment can control. To hold a segment and its employees accountable for uncontrollable items and events clearly diminishes the usefulness of the responsibility system. To illustrate why, imagine how you would react to the following situation. It is the first day of spring classes and your professor is explaining course policies. In discussing his grading philosophy, the professor notes: "I believe in running a rigorous course, so rigorous that I give only one A each year. Unfortunately from your point of view, I gave that A last semester." Your reaction would probably be, "What's the use in trying?" or, "I'd better find another instructor." Managers react in much the same manner. Holding personnel accountable for situations beyond their control often results in low morale and high employee turnover. If a responsibility system is to be effective, reports should clearly distinguish between those performance factors that are controllable and those that are not.

The ability to control normally means being able to influence or change. Thus if a responsibility center can significantly influence revenues, expenses, or investment funds through its own direct actions, the center's management should be held accountable for these items. Although this concept seems straightforward, it is extremely difficult to apply in practice. Often revenue generation and cost incurrence are influenced by two or more managers.

For example, the total cost of raw materials used in production is influenced by both the purchasing manager and the production manager. The production manager bears primary responsibility for raw material use since worker efficiency directly influences the materials consumed and the amount of waste incurred. The purchasing manager, on the other hand, is chiefly concerned about the prices paid to secure needed materials. In an effort to curb soaring costs in an inflationary economy, the head of purchasing may intentionally acquire lower-quality goods. Thus no matter how efficient the production workers are, material use will be partially influenced by factors beyond their control.

Even though multiple influences are brought to bear, somebody is usually in the best position to explain the level of revenue generated and cost incurred and the reasons for variances from budgeted amounts. The goal of responsibility accounting is to trace revenues and costs to their source and thereby fix responsibility for their creation. Hence an attempt is made to associate control and accountability with that person or center that has the greatest potential influence over the item in question.

CONTRIBUTION REPORTING

Advocates of responsibility accounting favor a **contribution approach** to performance evaluation. The contribution approach builds on the contribution margin presented in the previous chapter and is appropriate for evaluating both profit and investment centers. Before proceeding with an in-depth discussion, however, we must first explore a significant part of the approach's foundation—direct and indirect costs.

Direct and Indirect Costs

Direct and indirect is a classification scheme that deals with cost traceability. A **direct cost** is any cost that is easily traced to and associated with a business segment. Conversely, an **indirect cost** is one that is not easily traced to a business segment. A business segment normally refers to a responsibility center.

Given that centers are defined in different ways (e.g., a department, a division, and so on), the same cost may be considered direct with respect to certain responsibility units and indirect with respect to others. To illustrate, consider General Motors Corporation. As you probably know, General Motors is divided into various divisions, including Chevrolet, Buick, Oldsmobile, Pontiac, and Cadillac. The divisions, in turn, have numerous assembly plants throughout the country. Whether a specific cost is direct or indirect depends on the business segment being examined. For example, consider the costs of running the accounting departments of (1) General Motors Corporation, (2) the Chevrolet division, and (3) a Chevrolet assembly plant. These three costs are classified in Exhibit 25-3.

To explain, the cost of running the accounting department at GM's corporate headquarters is easily associated with the corporation as a whole.

Exhibit 25-3

Cost classification at General Motors Corporation

Cost	Direct Cost with Respect to	Indirect Cost with Respect to
Cost of running GM's corporate accounting department	Corporation	Divisions, plants, cars
Cost of running Chevrolet's divisional accounting department	Corporation, division*	Plants, cars
Cost of running a Chevrolet assembly plant's accounting department	Corporation, division,* plant	Cars

** The Chevrolet division only.*

Although part of this cost is attributed to operating the Chevrolet division and its plants, it is extremely difficult to determine and trace the exact portion back to these smaller segments of activity. Thus the cost of maintaining GM's corporate accounting department is an indirect cost with respect to the firm's divisions, plants, and cars. Similarly, the cost of operating Chevrolet's divisional accounting department is easily associated with General Motors and the Chevrolet division. Because of a lack of traceability, however, this cost is indirect with respect to smaller segments, specifically, Chevrolet's plants and cars. The reader is left to analyze the cost of the plant's accounting department; the underlying logic is identical to that just illustrated.

Cost Allocations

Despite a lack of traceability, many managers insist that indirect costs be charged to segments by using some type of allocation scheme. The cost of operating a corporate personnel department, for example, could be allocated to user departments on the basis of the number of employees in each department. Building and grounds costs could be allocated by using square feet, and so forth. The reason normally advanced for such an allocation procedure is that indirect costs are incurred to benefit multiple responsibility centers. As such, each center should absorb its "fair share."

Although this argument is sound, most accountants recognize that cost allocations have two serious deficiencies. First, as you saw with depreciation, the same cost can be allocated in several different ways. At best, then, allocations are extremely arbitrary. A given allocation method is generally viewed as adequate or inadequate by a responsibility center, depending on the amount of cost charged. Large cost allocations are branded as unfair; small cost allocations, on the other hand, receive few complaints. Turning to the second deficiency, the total cost to be allocated normally results from the decisions of other managers in the organizational hierarchy. Thus to a large degree, the amount of cost charged to a center is beyond the center's control. Overall, then, cost allocations usually result in assigning uncontrollable costs to segment managers in an arbitrary fashion.

Contribution Income Statement

The heart of the contribution approach is the contribution income statement. The **contribution income statement** provides top management with an understanding of how individual responsibility centers affect total firm profitability. Consistent with responsibility accounting and good performance evaluation, the statement incorporates the following features:

1 The contribution margin is disclosed.
2 Fixed costs directly identifiable with a segment are divided into two classifications: controllable and uncontrollable.
3 Allocations of nontraceable costs are disregarded.

To illustrate the contribution income statement, we will study EXOIL Corporation. EXOIL is divided into two divisions: Refining and Retailing. Retailing, in turn, has two major product lines: Parts and Fluids. Exhibit

25-4 contains the firm's contribution statements. The top half of the exhibit shows EXOIL's divisional operations; the bottom half displays Retailing's product lines.

The contribution statement begins by displaying a segment's contribution margin, that is, sales minus variable costs. Variable costs are considered to be controllable by responsibility centers because the costs vary with center activity. Recall from Chapter 24 that the contribution margin represents the

Exhibit 25-4

EXOIL Corporation contribution income statements (in thousands)

	Total Company	Divisions	
		Refining	Retailing
Net sales	$3,000	$2,080	$920
Less variable costs			
Cost of goods sold	$2,000	$1,390	$610
Variable selling & administrative expense	240	85	155
Total variable costs	$2,240	$1,475	$765
Contribution margin	$ 760	$ 605	$155
Less controllable fixed costs	290	225	65
Controllable contribution margin	$ 470	$ 380	$ 90
Less uncontrollable fixed costs	210	168	42
Segment margin	$ 260	$ 212	$ 48
Less nontraceable costs	115		
Net income	$ 145		

	Retailing Division	Product Lines		Non-traceable Costs
		Parts	Fluids	
Net sales	$920	$645	$275	
Less variable costs				
Cost of goods sold	$610	$440	$170	
Variable selling & administrative expense	155	100	55	
Total variable costs	$765	$540	$225	
Contribution margin	$155	$105	$ 50	
Less controllable fixed costs	65	30	10	$ 25
Controllable contribution margin	$ 90	$ 75	$ 40	$(25)
Less uncontrollable fixed costs	42	13	7	22
Segment margin	$ 48	$ 62	$ 33	$(47)

amount each unit (division and product line in this case) contributes toward covering fixed costs and generating net income. The calculation of the contribution margin is helpful not only for performance evaluation but also for further CVP analyses, such as determining the break-even point.

Controllable contribution margin

Next, the **controllable contribution margin** is computed by subtracting fixed costs that are controllable by the segment's management *and* directly traceable to the segment. Controllable fixed costs are normally discretionary fixed costs (i.e., those that arise from management's decision-making process). Examples of such costs include certain supervisory salaries, local sales promotion costs, and outlays for research and development activities.

The controllable contribution margin is really the heart of the entire statement. This important measure represents the contribution to profit that is under the direction of the responsibility center manager and is probably the best overall indicator of a manager's performance. As a result, it is a useful tool in promotion, bonus, and similar reward decisions.

Segment margin

The controllable contribution margin less uncontrollable fixed costs yields the **segment margin.** The uncontrollable costs used in this computation are incurred for the benefit of a specific responsibility center but are only minimally affected by the center's management during the reporting period. Typical examples of uncontrollable fixed costs include committed costs (such as property taxes and depreciation on factory buildings) and costs resulting from decisions made at higher levels in the organizational hierarchy (e.g., the salary of the center's manager).

The segment margin shows the contribution of each responsibility center to company profits after considering all traceable costs. Many accountants feel the segment margin is a good indicator of a center's long-run profitability because the center's total fixed costs are considered in the computation.

Controllable margin versus segment margin

Beginning accounting students often see little difference between the controllable contribution margin and the segment margin. These two performance measures actually serve different purposes. To explain, outstanding managers are frequently transferred to weak divisions to improve operations. Would you accept such an assignment if the company evaluated personnel and awarded bonuses on the basis of the "bottom line," that is, the segment margin? Probably not. No matter how hard you try, many uncontrollable factors would influence your performance appraisal. In addition, if the division was extremely weak, a heroic effort would be needed to show significant improvement in overall profitability. Thus two performance measures are utilized. The controllable contribution margin is used for personnel evaluations. The segment margin, on the other hand, is employed in exploring the long-run advisability of keeping a segment as an operating center of the business.

Nontraceable costs

As we noted, the contribution approach disregards allocations of indirect costs. By studying the top half of Exhibit 25-4, for example, you will notice that EXOIL incurred $115,000 of nontraceable costs; yet not a single penny was charged against the segment margins of Refining and Retailing. These costs could represent corporate administrative overhead incurred by the firm as a whole and not readily identified with either of the divisions.

In a similar manner, the bottom half of the exhibit reveals that Retailing's divisional manager had control of fixed costs totaling $65,000. However, when the division was further segmented by product line, only $40,000 ($30,000 + $10,000) could be traced to Parts and Fluids. The remaining $25,000 was jointly incurred by the two product lines, making traceability difficult. As an example, the Retailing division may have employed an office manager who handled clerical work relating to both areas of activity. As before, no attempt is made to charge indirect cost to segments; to do so would result in arbitrary, noncontrollable allocations.

DIRECT AND ABSORPTION COSTING

By viewing Exhibit 25-4, you will notice that (1) cost of goods sold is included under the variable cost caption and (2) fixed costs are written off entirely in the current period. This accounting treatment appears to contradict the material introduced in Chapters 21 and 22. Specifically, both variable *and* fixed overhead were included in the cost of a manufactured product and thus incorporated into the determination of cost of goods sold. Clearly, then, the earlier treatment of fixed manufacturing overhead is inconsistent with the contribution approach to income measurement.

Over the years two product costing methods have evolved: absorption costing and direct costing. The more traditional approach (and that illustrated in earlier chapters) is full or absorption costing. Under **absorption costing** all manufacturing costs are considered product costs and are included in the valuation of inventory. As you will soon see, absorption costing net income is influenced by changes in inventory and production and is therefore weak when evaluating performance.

An alternate approach is the direct costing method. **Direct costing** is more accurately called variable costing, because only variable manufacturing costs (direct materials, direct labor, and variable manufacturing overhead) are assigned to products. Fixed manufacturing costs are regarded as period costs and charged against revenues when incurred. Direct costing eliminates the effect of inventory changes on net income and presents a clearer picture of operating results than does absorption costing.

Fixed Manufacturing Overhead: The Key Difference

Observe that the basic difference between direct and absorption costing is the treatment of fixed manufacturing overhead. Absorption costing places fixed overhead in inventory on the balance sheet. At the time of sale, product cost (including fixed overhead) is transferred from the balance sheet to the income statement via cost of goods sold. Direct costing, on the other hand, writes off fixed manufacturing overhead immediately. This difference in timing is depicted in Exhibit 25-5.

Exhibit 25-5

Comparison of absorption and direct costing

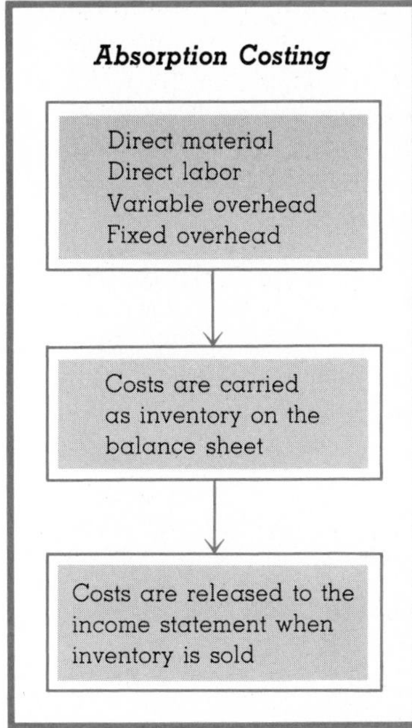

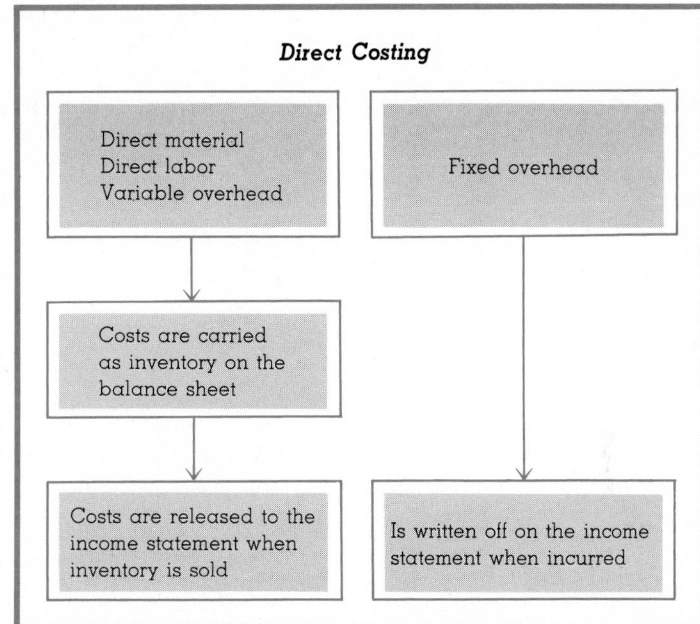

A Basic Illustration

To illustrate absorption and direct costing, examine the following information, which was obtained from the records of the Harris Corporation for the year ended December 31, 1984.

Sales: 9,500 units at $9.
Selling and administrative costs: fixed, $5,000; variable, $2 per unit.
Variable production costs per unit:

Direct materials	*$1.00*
Direct labor	*1.50*
Variable overhead (applied)	*0.50*
Total	*$3.00*

Fixed manufacturing overhead: $10,000.
Production: 10,000 units.

Under absorption costing the unit product cost is $4.00.

Variable production cost	*$3.00*
Fixed manufacturing overhead ($10,000 ÷ 10,000 units produced)	*1.00*
Total	*$4.00*

With direct costing the product cost per unit drops to $3.00, because only variable production costs are inventoried. Remember from previous chapters that selling and administrative costs are never attached to manufactured units; they are treated as expenses of the period.

Given the foregoing, Harris's income statements under both absorption and direct costing appear as shown in Exhibit 25-6.

Exhibit 25-6

Absorption and direct costing income statements

HARRIS CORPORATION
Absorption Costing Income Statement
For the Year Ended December 31, 1984

Sales (9,500 units × $9)		$85,500
Cost of goods sold (9,500 units × $4)		38,000
Gross profit		$47,500
Less selling & administrative costs		
Fixed	$ 5,000	
Variable (9,500 units × $2)	19,000	24,000
Net income		$23,500

HARRIS CORPORATION
Direct Costing Income Statement
For the Year Ended December 31, 1984

Sales (9,500 units × $9)		$85,500
Less variable costs		
Cost of goods sold (9,500 units × $3)	$28,500	
Selling & administrative (9,500 units × $2)	19,000	47,500
Contribution margin		$38,000
Less fixed costs		
Manufacturing	$10,000	
Selling & administrative	5,000	15,000
Net income		$23,000

Two important observations should be made. First, notice the similarity between the direct costing income statement and the contribution approach shown earlier in the chapter. Direct costing produces a cost of goods sold that is comprised solely of variable costs, thereby giving management the ability to calculate the contribution margin. In practice, the fixed costs appearing on the statement would be divided into those controllable by the segment manager and those that are uncontrollable.

Second, observe there is a $500 difference between absorption and direct costing net income. Although both methods utilized the same data, keep the differing treatments of fixed manufacturing overhead in mind. Under direct costing, all $10,000 of the fixed production costs were charged against revenues of the current period. With the absorption approach, however, \$1.00 of fixed overhead (\$10,000 ÷ 10,000 units manufactured) was attached to each unit produced. Recall that Harris produced 10,000 units but only sold 9,500; thus 500 units remain in inventory on the balance sheet. Because these units contain \$500 of fixed overhead (500 units × \$1), absorption costing wrote off only \$9,500 of the fixed production costs. The write off of the remaining \$500 is deferred until such time as the units are sold. The result is a larger absorption costing net income when comparing profitability under the two approaches.

The opposite situation occurs when the number of units sold exceeds the number of units produced. Under absorption costing, fixed manufacturing costs incurred in previous periods would now be matched against revenues because of the decline in inventory levels. That is, fixed costs are being pulled off the balance sheet and placed on the income statement. When combined with current fixed overhead, the result is a larger charge against revenue than would occur under the direct costing method. Thus net income under absorption costing would be lower than net income under direct costing.

An Extended Illustration

Critics of absorption costing assert that absorption costing income statements provide inadequate measures of performance. When absorption costing is used to value inventories, net income is affected by changes in production levels. This situation is a result of inventorying fixed manufacturing costs. To illustrate, we will build on the example just presented by utilizing the following information from Mintz Manufacturing.

Sales: 18,000 units at \$7.
Beginning inventory: none.
Variable manufacturing cost per unit: \$4.
Fixed manufacturing overhead: \$20,000.
Selling and administrative costs: variable, \$1.50 per unit; fixed, \$6,000.

Exhibit 25-7 shows the effect of three different production policies on absorption costing net income.

Mintz's data show that under absorption costing management can increase profit by simply stepping up production. Even though the sales level was the same in each case, profit jumped from \$1,000 to \$4,640 solely because the number of units produced increased from 18,000 to 22,000. Rising production levels accompanied by static sales result in higher ending inventories and thus a larger deferral of fixed manufacturing costs to later periods.

Most people will agree that a firm generates net income from sales of goods and services, not from stockpiling or depleting units in warehouses. *That is, sales, not production, should be the motivating force behind a given level of profit.* It is interesting to note that had the fixed overhead been written off and not inventoried, net income would have been the same for each production policy. This result is shown below Exhibit 25-7.

Exhibit 25-7

Comparative income computations, absorption costing

	Production (Units)		
	18,000	20,000	22,000
Variable manufacturing cost ($4 per unit)	$72,000	$ 80,000	$ 88,000
Fixed manufacturing cost	20,000	20,000	20,000
Total manufacturing cost	$92,000	$100,000	$108,000
Divide by units produced	÷18,000	÷20,000	÷22,000
Cost per unit	$5.11	$5.00	$4.91
Sales (18,000 units × $7)	$126,000	$126,000	$126,000
Cost of goods sold			
Beginning inventory	$ —	$ —	$ —
Cost of goods manufactured (from above)	92,000	100,000	108,000
Goods available for sale	$ 92,000	$100,000	$108,000
Less ending inventory*			
(0 × $5.11)	—		
(2,000 units × $5.00)		10,000	
(4,000 units × $4.91)			19,640
Cost of goods sold	$ 92,000	$ 90,000	$ 88,360
Gross profit	$ 34,000	$ 36,000	$ 37,640
Less selling & administrative costs			
Variable (18,000 units × $1.50)	$ 27,000	$ 27,000	$ 27,000
Fixed	6,000	6,000	6,000
Total selling & administrative costs	$ 33,000	$ 33,000	$ 33,000
Net income	$ 1,000	$ 3,000	$ 4,640

** The units in the ending inventory are computed as follows: beginning inventory + production − sales.*

	Production (Units)		
	18,000	20,000	22,000
Reported absorption costing net income	$1,000	$3,000	$4,640
Less fixed cost in inventory			
(0 × $1.11*)	—		
(2,000 units × $1.00*)		2,000	
(4,000 units × $0.91*)			3,640
	$1,000	$1,000	$1,000

** Cost per unit minus $4 variable cost. See the top of Exhibit 25-7.*

Not by accident, these computations are the essence of direct costing, which matches all fixed manufacturing overhead against revenues when incurred. Exhibit 25-8 displays the computations in a slightly different format, that is, as direct costing income statements. It is apparent that direct costing net income is not influenced by changes in production policies and

Exhibit 25-8

Comparative income computations, direct costing

	Production (Units)		
	18,000	20,000	22,000
Sales (18,000 units × $7)	$126,000	$126,000	$126,000
Less variable costs			
Cost of goods sold			
Beginning inventory	$ —	$ —	$ —
Cost of goods manufactured*	72,000	80,000	88,000
Goods available for sale	$ 72,000	$ 80,000	$ 88,000
Less ending inventory†	—	8,000	16,000
Cost of goods sold	$ 72,000	$ 72,000	$ 72,000
Selling & administrative (18,000 units × $1.50)	27,000	27,000	27,000
Total variable costs	$ 99,000	$ 99,000	$ 99,000
Contribution margin	$ 27,000	$ 27,000	$ 27,000
Less fixed costs			
Manufacturing	$ 20,000	$ 20,000	$ 20,000
Selling & administrative	6,000	6,000	6,000
Total fixed costs	$ 26,000	$ 26,000	$ 26,000
Net income	$ 1,000	$ 1,000	$ 1,000

*Number of units manufactured × $4 per unit.
†Number of units in ending inventory × $4 per unit.

inventory levels. The resulting income statements therefore become valuable evaluation and control tools.

Direct Costing: An End in Itself?

Despite widespread internal use by management, direct costing cannot be utilized for external financial reporting. The opposition to direct costing arises from its treatment of fixed manufacturing overhead. As we have noted throughout the text, expenditures that provide future benefits are established as assets in the accounting records. Fixed overhead is incurred to produce inventory, which, in turn, generates inflows of revenue. Rarely is all inventory sold in the same period that it was produced; thus some future revenues normally result. The direct costing treatment of fixed overhead is, therefore, inconsistent with accepted procedures for asset accounting.

Taking another perspective, the inventorying of fixed manufacturing costs under absorption costing results in a better matching on the income statement. At the time of sale fixed costs are released to the income statement (via cost of goods sold) and matched against the sales revenues that have just been realized. Direct costing, on the other hand, writes off fixed manufacturing costs at the time of incurrence, ignoring the fact that future revenues may result from the units produced.

Does the foregoing dampen the enthusiasm for direct costing? Not usually. Many businesses maintain internal accounting records on a direct cost basis and then report externally by using absorption costing. Although this

BIAS IN PERFORMANCE EVALUATION

Frequently, the performance evaluation process culminates in a quantified measure that expresses on-the-job achievements. When questioning management about raises, employees are often told, "It's in the numbers, and the numbers don't lie." Well perhaps the numbers are accurate and mathematically correct, but bias might be present in determining just what the numbers are.

An experiment was designed to determine whether the stated purpose of a performance evaluation affects the appraisal process. More specifically, a videotape was made of a university instructor teaching a class, and students in a junior-level management course were then asked to evaluate teaching performance. The students were divided into two experimental groups. One group was told that the purpose of the evaluation was to determine whether the instructor should be rewarded (promotion, tenure, salary increase). The other group was told that the purpose of the evaluation was to judge whether the instructor should be punished (put on probation, laid off, immediately dismissed). All students used the same evaluation questionnaire.

The results? A comparison of the groups revealed that the scores differed. In fact, the average rating of the punishment group was almost twice as large as the rating of the reward group. The students in the study generally rated the instructor contrary to the stated purpose of the evaluation. That is, if students were told that the evaluation was to determine whether the instructor should be rewarded, the instructor generally received a poor evaluation. Conversely, the punishment group generally gave the instructor higher ratings to prevent the punishment.

This experiment shows that bias can be present in the evaluation process. Management must recognize that limitations in the numbers often exist. In that way the quality and degree of objectivity of performance evaluations will improve.

SOURCE Adapted from Michael C. Gallagher, "More Bias in Performance Evaluation?" Personnel, *July–August 1978 (New York: AMACOM; a division of American Management Association, 1978), pp. 35–40.*

practice sounds complicated, conversion from a direct to an absorption cost basis is accomplished by means of a fairly simple adjustment at the end of the accounting period.

PERFORMANCE EVALUATION IN GENERAL

Our focus on responsibility accounting, contribution reporting, and direct and absorption costing has provided a foundation for performance appraisal. Realize that there are many accompanying side effects and problems of interpretation. Often, for example, when performance is judged and rewarded on a single criterion, employees tend to concentrate on that criterion and lose sight of other important issues.

To illustrate, suppose a manager's bonus is dependent solely on the controllable contribution margin. To increase this year's bonus, the manager has decided to cut repair and maintenance programs on equipment, decrease outlays for advertising, and reduce research and development activities. While all these actions will achieve the desired result, serious long-run problems could arise. Reducing repair and maintenance programs may increase the number of breakdowns and reduce the operating life of the equipment. Similarly, cutbacks in advertising and research could mean a loss of customers and new products, respectively. Because transfers and changes in employment are fairly common, this manager may be gone by the time the ultimate effects of his or her decisions are felt.

To minimize behavior of this nature, more than one evaluative criterion should be used. General Electric, for example, studies the following areas when assessing performance.[1]

1 Profitability
2 Market position
3 Productivity
4 Product leadership
5 Personnel development
6 Employee attitudes
7 Public responsibility
8 Balance between long-range and short-range goals

The use of multiple criteria allows for both qualitative and quantitative measures of performance and usually results in a more well-rounded organization. For example, suppose a manager pursues short-run profit maximization by cutting corners and reducing product quality. The end result may be customer dissatisfaction, a decrease in market share, and lower long-run profitability. If performance is judged on the basis of *both* market share and profitability, the manager will be more inclined to maintain product quality and will attempt to increase profit by some other means. For example, pro-

---

[1] E. Kirby Warren, *Long-Range Planning: The Executive Viewpoint* (Englewood Cliffs, N.J.: Prentice-Hall, 1966), p. 66.

duction efficiency may be improved or additional selling and promotional activities might be undertaken.

The use of multiple performance measures is not trouble-free. Frequently, conflicting goals are present. Overemphasis on market share, for instance, could lead to increased sales of relatively unprofitable products. Also, improvements in labor productivity are often harmful to employee morale. To overcome this problem, one can weight the performance measures in terms of their relative importance. In this manner an overall composite index is developed, one that is best suited for meeting the needs and expectations of top management.

KEY TERMS AND CONCEPTS

absorption costing 992
contribution approach 988
contribution income statement 989
controllable contribution margin 991
cost allocation 989
cost center 982
direct cost 988
direct (variable) costing 992
indirect cost 988
investment center 983
performance report 985
profit center 983
responsibility accounting 982
return on assets 984
segment margin 991

QUESTIONS

Q25-1 Briefly discuss the features associated with a responsibility accounting system.

Q25-2 Differentiate between a profit center and an investment center.

Q25-3 Why should performance reports be issued on a timely basis?

Q25-4 Describe the flow of information in a typical responsibility reporting system.

Q25-5 Why do accountants distinguish between controllable and noncontrollable costs?

Q25-6 Differentiate between direct and indirect costs. As segments become smaller and smaller, what generally happens to cost traceability?

Q25-7 Present pro and con arguments concerning the placement of cost allocations on performance reports.

Q25-8 Discuss the computations and meaning associated with the controllable contribution margin and the segment margin.

Q25-9 Differentiate between direct and absorption costing.

Q25-10 Why is absorption costing required for external reporting?

Q25-11 Discuss problems associated with using a single-criterion performance system and a multiple-goal performance system.

EXERCISES

E25-1 Crest Manufacturing produces a single product at its Albany plant. Units are processed through departments A and B and then to finished goods. The firm has a maintenance department that performs repair jobs for the producing departments.

The maintenance operation has always been evaluated as a cost center. Now with a change in management, a switch to a profit center setup is being considered. Prices charged for repair jobs would be based on the maintenance department's cost of operations.

a Discuss the difference between a cost center and a profit center.

b Mike Mizer, the head of maintenance, has always operated with a cost minimization philosophy. Will the change to a profit center alter the quality of service provided by the maintenance department? Explain your answer.

c What will be the reaction of the producing departments to the change to a profit center? Consider the probable effect on the number of service requests when structuring your answer.

E25-2 The charges below appeared on the monthly performance report of a division manager.

a General corporate overhead: $15,000.

b Wages of divisional workers: $47,000.

c Local advertising: $2,500.

d Salary of division manager: $4,000.

e Use of corporate computer facility: $2,000.

Computer costs are apportioned to divisions on the basis of use. Each user is charged $100 per hour, which represents the computer center's *actual* cost of operation.

Evaluate the five charges and determine which are controllable at the divisional level. Briefly explain your answer.

E25-3 Roxie Company is a small manufacturer of ladies' fur coats. Because of the seasonal nature of the company's business, sales and manufacturing levels are low from the beginning of April through the end of June. As a result, five skilled production employees are usually laid off during this three-month period. In an effort to boost employee morale, Roxie's president plans to change company policy and retain these workers on the payroll. The workers will perform odd jobs (cleaning, errands, and so on) in the maintenance department and will earn their usual wage of $10 per hour. Maintenance workers are normally paid $6 per hour.

The new plan was implemented, and the president thought everything was fine until the maintenance supervisor started to complain: "I just received my April performance report and it looks terrible! I have a large unfavorable variance for my labor force—actual expense was far greater than budget. It's the new policy that's wrecking my performance. I didn't want those production workers but I didn't have much choice. I'm sure that if this continues for the next two months, I'll lose my profit-sharing bonus at the end of the year. And this was supposed to improve morale?"

What would you do to improve this unexpected situation? Why? Assume Roxie has a responsibility accounting system to assist in performance appraisals.

E25-4 The following data pertain to Master Corporation's Mixer Division for the year ended December 31, 1984.

Net sales	*$4,000,000*
Variable cost of goods sold	*1,000,000*
Variable selling & administrative expenses	*600,000*
Directly traceable fixed costs	
Controllable	*1,500,000*
Uncontrollable	*500,000*
Executive office overhead allocated to the Mixer Division	*200,000*

a Prepare a contribution income statement for the Mixer Division.

b The manager of the Mixer Division is normally awarded a 1% bonus at the end of the year. Given the contribution approach, calculate the bonus the manager would expect to receive.

E25-5 The following multiple-choice questions refer to responsibility accounting and contribution reporting. Select the best answer.

1 Which of the following should not be on a monthly cost control report of a department manager?
  a Departmental labor cost.
  b Departmental supplies cost.
  c Depreciation on departmental equipment.
  d Cost of materials used in the department.

2 Periodic internal performance reports based on a responsibility accounting system should not:
  a Distinguish between controllable and uncontrollable costs.
  b Be related to the organization chart.
  c Include allocated fixed overhead in determining performance evaluations.
  d Include variances between actual and controllable costs.

3 A desirable characteristic of a factory overhead control report for a production manager is that:
  a It is more important that the report be precise than timely.
  b The report should include information on all costs chargeable to the department, regardless of their origin or control.
  c The report should be stated in dollars rather than in physical units, so that the department head knows the financial magnitude of any variances.
  d The report should specify those costs controllable by the department head.

4 The most desirable measure for evaluating the performance of the departmental manager is departmental:
  a Revenue less controllable departmental expenses.
  b Net income.
  c Contribution to indirect expenses.
  d Revenue less departmental expenses.

(CPA and CMA adapted.)

E25-6 The Arnez Company began operations on January 1 of the current year. The following information pertains to the firm's sole product.

Material cost per unit: $4.00.
Labor cost per unit: $7.00.
Variable overhead per unit: $3.50.
Variable selling cost per unit: $1.50.
Fixed manufacturing overhead (includes $50,000 of straight-line depreciation): $160,000.
Fixed selling costs: $48,000.

During the year 20,000 units were produced and 16,000 units were sold.

a Compute the cost of Arnez's ending inventory, using absorption costing.
b Compute the cost of Arnez's ending inventory, using direct costing.

E25-7 The Chen Company began operations on January 1 of the current year. The following information has been gathered from the accounting records.

Manufacturing costs:

Direct materials	$2 per unit
Direct labor	$4 per unit
Variable overhead	$6 per unit
Fixed overhead	$420,000

Selling and administrative costs:

Variable	$3 per unit
Fixed	$15,000

Production and sales amounted to 60,000 and 50,000 units, respectively. The selling price per unit is $28.

a Prepare an income statement for the year ended December 31, using direct costing.
b Prepare an income statement for the year ended December 31, using absorption costing.

E25-8 As noted in the chapter, performance can be measured in a number of different ways. Consider the following positions and performance measures.

Position	*Performance Measure*
(a) Salesperson	Total gross sales generated by the salesperson
(b) Mechanic	Number of cars serviced per day
(c) Quarterback	Percentage of passes completed
(d) Secretary	Number of words typed per minute
(e) Student	Cumulative grade point average

Evaluate each of the measures listed. If you feel a measure is inadequate, suggest other factors that should be considered when assessing performance.

PROBLEMS

P25-1 ***Responsibility accounting***

The Fillep Company uses a responsibility accounting system. Variances for each department are calculated and reported to the department manager. It is expected that the manager will use the information to improve operations. The variances are also reviewed by higher-level management when evaluating performance.

John Smith was recently appointed manager of the assembly department of the company. He has complained that the system as designed is disadvantageous to his department. Included among the variances charged to the department is one for rejected units. An inspection occurs at the end of the assembly department. The inspectors attempt to identify the cause of the rejection so that the department where the error occurred can be charged with it. Not all rejects, however, can be easily identified with a department. Unidentified rejects are therefore totaled and apportioned to the departments according to the number of identified rejects. Thus the variance for bad units in each department is a combination of the rejects caused by the department plus a portion of the unidentified rejects.

INSTRUCTIONS

a Is John Smith's claim valid? Explain the reason(s) for your answer.

b What would you recommend the company do to solve its problem with John Smith and his complaint?

(CMA adapted.)

P25-2 ***Straightforward contribution income statement***

The Miami Company has just completed a record year of sales and profits. Dave Eskew, the firm's chief accountant, is in the process of reviewing performance of the Northern Division with Hal Lyle, the divisional manager.

Lyle arrived at Eskew's office expecting to be congratulated for a job well done. Instead, it's been one complaint after another. As Eskew noted, "Look, Hal, these numbers don't lie. According to this performance report, your operation lost $23,000 for the year. Unless you get things turned around, we may have to change managers."

The performance report of the Northern Division follows.

Net sales		*$500,000*
Cost of goods sold		*300,000*
Gross profit		*$200,000*
Operating expenses		
Salaries	*$110,000*	
Travel	*8,000*	
Depreciation	*30,000*	
Administration	*40,000*	
Sales commissions (5%)	*25,000*	
Property taxes	*10,000*	*223,000*
Divisional income		*$(23,000)*

In his defense Lyle supplied the following information.

1 Inventory levels remained stable throughout the year.

2 Salaries include Lyle's $35,000 salary, which was set by Miami's vice-president. Other salaries were negotiated by Lyle.

3 Travel costs vary with sales and helped to generate $90,000 of new orders.

4 Depreciation charges can be subdivided as follows: 30% pertains to Northern Division facilities; 70% pertains to general corporate facilities.

5 Administration costs are allocated to each division on the basis of divisional sales.

6 Property taxes include $7,000 that pertain to general corporate facilities.

INSTRUCTIONS

a Examine the performance of Hal Lyle and the Northern Division by preparing a contribution income statement for the current year ended December 31. Are Eskew's complaints justified? Explain.

b What performance evaluation benefits are provided by the contribution income statement?

P25-3 ***Contribution income statement: Preparation and analysis***

Marsha Warren, president of Warren Distributors, has just finished her review of the current year's operations. She noted, "We've been lucky. Given the state of the economy, I'm really pleased with these figures. A 3% return on sales will probably beat the competition."

Marsha's comments were based on the following income statement, which was constructed by a new employee. The employee summarized information pertaining to the company's three product lines: X, Y, and Z.

WARREN DISTRIBUTORS
Income Statement
For the Year Ended December 31, 19XX

Net sales		$690,000
Less: Cost of goods sold	$444,000	
Sales commissions	63,300	
Local advertising	60,000	
Sales salaries	30,000	
Other	72,000	669,300
Net income		$ 20,700

Supplementary records revealed the following information.

1 Sales:

X 60,000 units @ $5.00
Y 70,000 units @ $3.00
Z 40,000 units @ $4.50

2 Warren purchases units from various manufacturers. The prices paid per unit were as follows:

X $3.00
Y 2.20
Z 2.75

3 Sales personnel of X and Z are paid on a commission basis. Commissions total 10% and 15% of each product's respective gross sales. Sales of Y are handled by one salesperson who receives a 3% commission plus a $30,000 salary. The salary is set by Y's management.

4 Local advertising is handled by product line managers. Advertising costs for the product lines amounted to the following:

X	$25,000
Y	20,000
Z	15,000

5 Other costs of $72,000 are subdivided as follows:
Uncontrollable costs traceable to product lines:

X	$20,000
Y	16,000
Z	12,000
	$48,000

Administrative overhead not traceable to product lines: $24,000.

INSTRUCTIONS

a Give Marsha more insight into operations by preparing a contribution income statement for the three product lines. Are things going as well as she believes or could operations be improved? Explain.

b If any of the product lines have a negative segment margin, present an analysis of the probable causes of poor performance.

P25-4 ***Contribution income statement***

Praline Products Company is a regional firm that has three major product lines: cereals, breakfast bars, and dog food. The income statement for the year ended April 30 is shown on page 1007; the statement was prepared by product line, using absorption (full) costing. Other data follow.

1 *Cost of goods sold.* The company's inventories of raw materials and finished products do not vary significantly from year to year. Factory overhead was applied to products at 120% of direct labor dollars. The factory overhead costs for the fiscal year were as follows:

Variable indirect labor and supplies	$ 15,000
Variable employee benefits on factory labor	30,000
Supervisory salaries and related benefits	35,000
Plant occupancy costs	100,000
	$180,000

There was no overapplied or underapplied overhead at year-end.

2 *Advertising.* The company has been unable to determine any direct causal relationship between the level of sales volume and the level of advertising expenditures. However, because management believes advertising is necessary, an annual advertising program is implemented for each product line. Each product line is advertised independently of the others.

3 *Commissions.* Sales commissions are paid to the sales force at the rates of 5% on the cereals and 10% on the breakfast bars and dog food.

4 *Licenses.* Various licenses are required for each product line; these are renewed annually.

5 *Salaries and related benefits.* Sales and general and administrative personnel devote time and effort to all product lines. Their salaries and wages are allocated on the basis of management's estimates of time spent on each product line.

PRALINE PRODUCTS COMPANY
Income Statement (000 Omitted)

	Total	Cereals	Breakfast Bars	Dog Food
Sales in pounds	3,000	2,000	500	500
Revenue from sales	$1,600	$1,000	$400	$200
Cost of goods sold				
Raw materials	$ 590	$ 330	$160	$100
Direct labor	150	90	40	20
Factory overhead	180	108	48	24
Total cost of sales	$ 920	$ 528	$248	$144
Gross margin	$ 680	$ 472	$152	$ 56
Operating expenses				
Selling				
Advertising	$ 100	$ 50	$ 30	$ 20
Commissions	110	50	40	20
Salaries and related benefits	60	30	20	10
Total selling expenses	$ 270	$ 130	$ 90	$ 50
General and administrative				
Licenses	$ 85	$ 50	$ 20	$ 15
Salaries and related benefits	100	60	25	15
Total general and administrative expenses	$ 185	$ 110	$ 45	$ 30
Total operating expenses	$ 455	$ 240	$135	$ 80
Operating income before taxes	$ 225	$ 232	$ 17	$ (24)

INSTRUCTIONS

a The controller of Praline Products has recommended that the company do a cost-volume-profit (CVP) analysis of its operations. As a first step, the controller has requested that you prepare a revised income statement that employs a contribution format. The statement should show the contribution margin and the segment margin for each product line and the income before taxes for the company as a whole.

b Determine the effect, if any, on income before taxes as calculated in part (a) if the April 30 inventories had increased significantly over the inventory levels of the previous year. Explain your answer.

(CMA modified.)

P25-5 *Cost classification*

The following costs were incurred by the Enberg Corporation. Reproduce the table on page 1008 and decide whether each cost is (1) a product cost under absorption costing, (2) a product cost under direct costing, and (3) a controllable cost by the managers listed. Each cost should have five yes and/or no answers.

	Product Cost Under		*Controllable Cost by*		
	Absorption Costing	*Direct Costing*	*Factory Manager*	*Manufacturing Vice-President*	*Sales Manager*
Direct labor					
Advertising					
Property taxes on factory facilities					
Salary of factory manager					
Corporate audit fee					
Interest on long-term bonds					
Factory supplies					
Salaries of plant security guards					

P25-6 ***Direct and absorption costing***

The following information pertains to Milano, Inc., for the year ended December 31, 1984.

Manufacturing costs:

Direct materials	$3 per unit
Direct labor	$4 per unit
Variable overhead	$8 per unit
Fixed overhead	$150,000

Sales: 25,000 units

Production: ?

Selling and administrative costs:

Variable	$2 per unit
Fixed	$25,000

Finished goods inventory (units):

Beginning	9,000
Ending	14,000

The unit selling price is $26. Assume that costs have been stable in recent years.

INSTRUCTIONS

a Determine the number of units produced during 1984.
b Prepare an income statement, using absorption costing.
c Prepare an income statement, using direct costing.
d Explain why absorption costing net income differed from direct costing net income.

P25-7 ***Direct and absorption costing: Performance evaluation***

Sandusky's, a small family-owned company, began operations on January 1 of the current year. The following absorption costing income statement summarizes activity for the twelve months ended December 31.

SANDUSKY'S Income Statement For the Year Ended December 31, 19XX		
Sales (30,000 units × $20)		$600,000
Cost of goods sold		
Beginning inventory	$ –	
Cost of goods manufactured*	490,000	
Goods available for sale	$490,000	
Less ending inventory†	70,000	
Cost of goods sold		420,000
Gross profit		$180,000
Less selling & administrative expenses		160,000
Net income		$ 20,000

*35,000 units × $14.
†5,000 units × $14.

Additional data revealed that Sandusky's incurred $140,000 of fixed manufacturing overhead during the year. Also selling and administrative expenses included sales commissions of $4 per unit; the remaining selling and administrative expenses were fixed.

Marty Sandusky, the firm's president, was very pleased that a profit had been generated. However, he was somewhat disturbed after talking with his daughter, a financial analyst. She observed that the company had only reached its break-even point by selling 30,000 units. "That's the trouble with traditional income statements," she noted. "They sometimes present a misleading picture of performance."

INSTRUCTIONS

a Verify the daughter's computation of the break-even point.

b Prepare Sandusky's income statement, using direct costing.

c Explain to Marty why there is a $20,000 difference between the income statement presented and his daughter's computations. *Hint:* Refer to the limiting assumptions of CVP analysis cited in Chapter 24. What does direct costing do to clarify performance?

P25-8 ***Contribution reporting, direct costing, and statement analysis***

The Busch Company began operations on January 1 of the current year. The absorption costing income statement of the Endicott Division follows.

ENDICOTT DIVISION
Income Statement
For the Year Ended December 31, 19XX

Sales (30,000 units × $20)		$600,000
Cost of goods sold		
Beginning inventory	$ —	
Cost of goods manufactured (40,000 units × $17)	680,000	
Goods available for sale	$680,000	
Less ending inventory (10,000 units × $17)	170,000	
Cost of goods sold		510,000
Gross profit		$ 90,000
Less selling & administrative expenses		
Variable	$ 45,000	
Fixed	36,000	81,000
Net income		$ 9,000

The unit manufacturing cost was computed as follows:

Direct materials	$6.00
Direct labor (0.5 hours @ $8)	4.00
Variable overhead	2.50
Fixed overhead	4.50
Total manufacturing cost	$17.00

Busch's accountant noted that the fixed overhead rate of $4.50 per unit was derived by using direct labor hours as the application base. Forecasted direct labor hours of 20,000 were divided into Endicott's fixed overhead charges. These charges amounted to $180,000 and consisted of the following:

Endicott Division's own overhead		
Controllable	$90,000	
Uncontrollable	75,000	$165,000
Allocated charges		15,000
Total fixed overhead		$180,000

$180,000 ÷ 20,000 hours = $9 per hour

$9 per hour ÷ 2 units per hour = $4.50 per unit

Busch's top management is evaluating the Endicott Division and desires that the income statement be recast to eliminate the impact of the inventory buildup and uncontrollable costs.

INSTRUCTIONS

a Prepare a contribution income statement, using direct costing. Assume that $20,000 of the fixed selling and administrative expenses are controllable by Endicott's personnel.

b On the basis of part (a), assess the performance of the divisional management and of the Endicott Division.

c Endicott's management is contemplating a $15,000 increase in local advertising, a controllable fixed cost. How much must sales increase to justify this additional expenditure?

P25-9 ***Cost allocations and performance evaluation***

The following is a conversation between Joe, the owner of a small restaurant, and an accountant/efficiency expert.[2] The topic: a new peanut rack sitting at the end of the counter.

Expert: Joe, you said you put in these peanuts because some people ask for them, but do you realize what this rack of peanuts is costing you?

Joe: It ain't gonna cost. Gonna be a profit. Sure, I had to pay $25 for a fancy rack to hold the bags, but the peanuts cost 6¢ a bag and I sell 'em for 10¢. Figure I sell 50 bags a week to start. It'll take 12½ weeks to cover the cost of the rack. After that I gotta clear profit of 4¢ a bag. The more I sell, the more I make.

Expert: That is an antiquated and completely unrealistic approach, Joe. Fortunately, modern accounting procedures permit a more accurate picture, which reveals the complexities involved.

Joe: Huh?

Expert: To be precise, those peanuts must be integrated into your entire operation and be allocated their appropriate share of business overhead. They must share a proportionate part of your expenditures for rent, heat, light, equipment depreciation, decorating, salaries for your waitresses, cook, . . .

Joe: The cook? *What's he gotta do with peanuts? He don't even know I got 'em!*

Expert: Look, Joe, the cook is in the kitchen, the kitchen prepares the food, the food is what brings people in here, and the people ask to buy peanuts. That's *why you must charge a portion of the cook's wages, as well as a part of your own salary, to peanut sales. This sheet contains a carefully calculated cost analysis, which indicates that the peanut operation should pay exactly $1,278 per year toward these general overhead* costs.

Joe: The peanuts? $1,278 a year for overhead? That's nuts!

Expert: It's really a little more than that. You also spend money each week to have the windows washed, to have the place swept out in the mornings, keep soap in the washroom, and provide free cokes to the police. That raises the total to $1,313 per year.

Joe: (Thoughtfully.) But the peanut salesman said I'd make money—put 'em on the end of the counter, he said—and get 4¢-a-bag profit.

Expert: (With a sniff.) He's not an accountant. Do you actually know what the portion of the counter occupied by the peanut rack is worth to you?

Joe: Ain't worth nothing—no stool there—just a dead spot at the end.

---

[2]The author of this conversation is unknown. Its text, which we have modified slightly, has been printed in several periodicals, including the *GAO Review.*

Expert: The modern cost picture permits no dead spots. Your counter contains 60 square feet and your counter business grosses $15,000 a year. Consequently, the square foot of space occupied by the peanut rack is worth $250 per year. Since you have taken that area away from general counter use, you must charge the value of the space to the occupant.

Joe: You mean I gotta add $250 a year more to the peanuts?

Expert: Right. That raises their share of the general operating costs to a grand total of $1,563 per year. Now then, if you sell 50 bags of peanuts per week, these allocated costs will amount to 60¢ per bag.

Joe: WHAT?

Expert: Obviously, to that must be added your purchase price of 6¢ per bag, which brings the total to 66¢. So you see, by selling peanuts at 10¢ per bag, you are losing 56¢ on every sale.

Joe: Somethin's crazy!

Expert: Not at all! Here are the figures. They prove your peanut operation cannot stand on its own feet.

Joe: (Brightening.) Suppose I sell lotsa peanuts—thousand bags a week instead of fifty?

Expert: (Tolerantly.) Joe, you don't understand the problem. If the volume of peanut sales increases, your operating costs will go up—you'll have to handle more bags, with more time, more depreciation, more everything. The basic principle of accounting is firm on that subject: "The bigger the operation, the more general overhead costs that must be allocated." No. Increasing the volume of sales won't help.

Joe: Okay. You so smart, you tell me what I gotta do.

Expert: (Condescendingly.) Well—you could first reduce operating expenses.

Joe: How?

Expert: Move to a building with cheaper rent. Cut salaries. Wash the windows biweekly. Have the floor swept only on Thursday. Remove the soap from the washrooms. Decrease the square-foot value of your counter. For example, if you can cut your expenses 50%, that will reduce the amount allocated to peanuts from $1,563 to $781.50 per year, reducing the cost to 36¢ per bag.

Joe: (Slowly.) That's better?

Expert: Much, much better. However, even then you would lose 26¢ per bag if you charge only 10¢. Therefore, you must also raise your selling price. If you want a net profit of 4¢ per bag, you would have to charge 40¢.

Joe: (Flabbergasted.) You mean even after I cut operating costs 50%, I still gotta charge 40¢ for a 10¢ bag of peanuts? Nobody's that nuts about nuts! Who'd buy 'em?

Expert: That's a secondary consideration. The point is, at 40¢ you'd be selling at a price based upon a true and proper evaluation of your then-reduced costs.

Joe: *(Eagerly.) Look! I gotta better idea. Why don't I just throw the nuts out—put 'em in the trash.*

Expert: Can you afford it?

Joe: Suré. All I got is about 50 bags of peanuts—cost about three bucks—so I lose $25 on the rack, but I'm out of this nutsy business and no more grief.

Expert: (Shaking head.) Joe, it isn't that simple. You are in the peanut business! The minute you throw those peanuts out you are adding $1,563 of annual overhead to the rest of your operation. Joe—be realistic—can you afford to do that?

Joe: (Completely crushed.) It's unbelievable! Last week I make money. Now I'm in trouble—just because I think peanuts on a counter is gonna bring me some extra profit—just because I believe 50 bags of peanuts a week is easy.

Expert: (With raised eyebrow.) That is the object of modern cost studies, Joe—to dispel those false illusions.

INSTRUCTIONS
Explain the message that this conversation conveys.

P25-10 ***Straightforward contribution income statement* (*alternate to P25-2*)**

The Cobb Company has just completed a record year of sales and profits. Lisa Day, the firm's chief accountant, is in the process of reviewing performance of the Western Division with Terry Bolton, the divisional manager.

Bolton arrived at Day's office expecting to be congratulated for a job well done. Instead, it's been one complaint after another. As Day noted, "Look, Terry, these numbers don't lie. According to this performance report, your operation lost $18,500 for the year. Unless you get things turned around, we may have to change managers."

The performance report of the Western Division follows.

Net sales		$425,000
Cost of goods sold		280,000
Gross profit		$145,000
Operating expenses		
Salaries	$90,000	
Travel	7,000	
Depreciation	22,000	
Administration	30,000	
Sales commissions	8,500	
Property taxes	6,000	163,500
Divisional income		$ (18,500)

In his defense Bolton supplied the following information.

1 Inventory levels remained stable throughout the year.
2 Salaries include Bolton's $42,000 salary, which was set by Cobb's vice-president. Other salaries were negotiated by Bolton.
3 Travel costs vary with sales and helped to generate $35,000 of new orders.
4 Depreciation charges can be subdivided as follows: 40% pertains to Western Division facilities; 60% pertains to general corporate facilities.

5 Administration costs are allocated to each division on the basis of divisional sales.

6 Property taxes include $2,900 that pertain to general corporate facilities.

INSTRUCTIONS

a Examine the performance of Terry Bolton and the Western Division by preparing a contribution income statement for the current year ended December 31. Are Day's complaints justified? Explain.

b Day and Bolton disagree about whether the Western Division should be charged with allocations of corporate office costs. Present and briefly discuss the probable positions of both employees.

P25-11 ***Contribution income statement: Preparation and analysis (alternate to P25-3)***

Harold Brandt, president of Brandt Distributing, has just finished a review of the current year's operations. He noted, "These figures look great. I was expecting overall performance to suffer given the problems we've had with the Urbana Division. However, I believe we're now on sound footing and have few financial problems."

Harold's comments were based on the following income statement, which was constructed by a new employee. The employee summarized information pertaining to the firm's three divisions: Barrington, Springfield, and Urbana.

BRANDT DISTRIBUTING
Income Statement
For the Year Ended December 31, 19XX

Net sales		$994,000
Less: Cost of goods sold	$632,000	
Sales commissions	49,700	
Salaries	130,000	
Advertising	80,000	
Other	75,000	966,700
Net income		$ 27,300

Supplementary records revealed the following information.

1 Sales:

Barrington	29,000 units @	$10
Springfield	34,000 units @	8
Urbana	48,000 units @	9

2 Each division purchases units from various manufacturers. The prices paid per unit were as follows:

Barrington	$6.00
Springfield	5.00
Urbana	6.00

3 Each division pays a 5% commission to its sales force. In addition, the Urbana Division employs a sales manager who earns $30,000 per year. The sales manager's salary is set by Urbana's divisional manager. Other salaries for high-level employees are established by Brandt and subdivided as follows:

Barrington	$ 25,000
Springfield	40,000
Urbana	35,000
Total	$100,000

4 Advertising is handled by divisional managers and is broken down as follows:

Barrington	$10,000
Springfield	20,000
Urbana	50,000
Total	$80,000

5 Other costs of $75,000 consist of the following:
Uncontrollable costs traceable to divisions:

Barrington	$ 8,000
Springfield	6,000
Urbana	27,000
	$41,000

General corporate overhead: $34,000.

INSTRUCTIONS

a Give Brandt more insight into operations by preparing a contribution income statement for the three divisions. Are things going as well as he believes or could operations be improved? Explain.

b If any of the divisions have a negative segment margin, present an analysis of the probable causes of poor performance.

P25-12 ***Cost classification (alternate to P25-5)***

The following costs were incurred by the Madden Corporation. Reproduce the table on page 1016 and decide whether each cost is (1) a product cost under absorption costing, (2) a product cost under direct costing, and (3) a controllable cost by the managers listed. Each cost should have five yes and/or no answers.

	Product Cost Under		Controllable Cost by		
	Absorption Costing	***Direct Costing***	***Factory Manager***	***Manufacturing Vice-President***	***Sales Manager***
Property taxes on corporate headquarters					
Annual maintenance contracts on factory machinery					
Travel costs of marketing staff					
Salary of factory foreman					
Costs of running annual training program for factory managers					
Direct materials used					
Cost of company's annual Christmas party					
Labor cost of reworking defective units					

P25-13 ***Direct and absorption costing (alternate to P25-6)***

The following information pertains to Gates Manufacturing for the year ended December 31, 1984.

Manufacturing costs:

Direct materials	$2 per unit
Direct labor	$4 per unit
Variable overhead	$6 per unit
Fixed overhead	$205,000

Sales: 35,000 units

Production: 41,000 units

Selling and administrative costs:

Variable	$1 per unit
Fixed	$70,000

Finished goods inventory (units):

Beginning	?
Ending	20,000

The unit selling price is $23. Assume that costs have been stable in recent years.

INSTRUCTIONS

a Determine the number of units in the beginning finished goods inventory.
b Prepare an income statement, using absorption costing.
c Prepare an income statement, using direct costing.
d Explain why absorption costing net income differed from direct costing net income.

P25-14 ***Direct and absorption costing: Performance evaluation (alternate to P25-7)*** Jernak's, a small family-owned company, began operations on January 1 of the current year. The following absorption costing income statement summarizes activity for the twelve months ended December 31.

JERNAK'S
Income Statement
For the Year Ended December 31, 19XX

Sales (15,000 units × $10)		$150,000
Cost of goods sold		
Beginning inventory	$ –	
Cost of goods manufactured*	133,000	
Goods available for sale	$133,000	
Less ending inventory†	28,000	
Cost of goods sold		105,000
Gross profit		$ 45,000
Less selling & administrative expenses		29,000
Net income		$ 16,000

* 19,000 units × $7.
† 4,000 units × $7.

Additional data revealed that Jernak's incurred $76,000 of fixed manufacturing overhead during the year. Also selling and administrative expenses included a 10% sales commission; the remaining selling and administrative expenses were fixed.

Chip Jernak, the firm's president, was very pleased that a profit had been generated. However, he was somewhat disturbed after talking with his daughter, a financial analyst. She observed that "the company was not as profitable as the income statement disclosed. In fact, the sales volume attained of 15,000 units was really the break-even point."

INSTRUCTIONS

a Verify the daughter's computation of the break-even point.
b Prepare Jernak's income statement, using direct costing.
c Explain to Chip why there is a $16,000 difference between the income statement presented and his daughter's computations. *Hint:* Refer to the limiting assumptions of CVP analysis cited in Chapter 24. What does direct costing do to clarify performance?

CASE 25
THE SHREWD PRESIDENT

Ivory Company has just concluded its worst year since commencing operations five years ago. The firm's income statement follows.

IVORY COMPANY
Income Statement
For the Year Ended December 31, 19XX

Sales (15,000 units × $10)		$150,000
Cost of goods sold		
Beginning inventory (5,000 units × $6)	$ 30,000	
Cost of goods manufactured (15,000 units × $6)	90,000	
Goods available for sale	$120,000	
Less ending inventory (5,000 units × $6)	30,000	
Cost of goods sold		90,000
Gross profit		$ 60,000
Selling and administrative costs		70,000
Net income		$ (10,000)

Cost of goods manufactured contained $30,000 of fixed overhead; the remaining production costs were variable and amounted to $4 per unit.

The company's board of directors fired the president and began the search for a successor. An applicant agreed to take the job for a bonus of 70% of any profits generated; he also agreed to reimburse the firm for any losses incurred. The board was impressed and the applicant was hired. Soon after, the new president set the factory running at full capacity.

The income statement for the next period showed a profit despite no growth in sales. The cost behavior patterns experienced were identical to those of the previous year. The president accepted his bonus and then abruptly resigned, leaving the board of directors baffled.

INSTRUCTIONS

a Does Ivory use direct costing or absorption costing? Explain your answer.

b Determine the impact on ending inventory, cost of goods sold, and net income of the new president's policy. What is the president really trying to do? *Hint:* No numerical calculations are required.

c Should the bonus have been awarded? Why?

d Suggest and evaluate an alternative reporting practice that would have hindered the new president's plans.

26 FLEXIBLE BUDGETS AND STANDARD COSTS

LEARNING OBJECTIVES

After reading this chapter you should:

1 *Know how to construct a flexible budget and understand the benefits of using flexible budgets in performance evaluation.*

2 *Know what a standard cost is and how standards are developed.*

3 *Understand the distinction between ideal and attainable standards.*

4 *Know how to calculate price and quantity variances as related to direct materials and direct labor.*

5 *Understand the calculation and meaning of the spending variance, the variable overhead efficiency variance, and the fixed overhead volume variance.*

6 *Understand the problems encountered when investigating variances and the importance of correctly placing responsibility for variance incurrence.*

7 *Know how to incorporate standard costs and variances into an accounting system (as explained in the Appendix to this chapter).*

CHAPTER 26

In Chapter 21 we noted that managerial accounting plays an important role in the control of operations. The concept of control has frequently been likened to the operation of a thermostat. That is, a room's temperature is continually monitored and compared against a preset, desired standard. Should a variation from the standard be identified, the thermostat emits a signal to a furnace (or air conditioner) to begin functioning. In business terms, control requires that managers closely observe financial performance by comparison with a plan or budget. When substantial deviations from the budget arise, some form of corrective action is initiated, such as cost cutbacks, reallocation of resources, the dismissal of certain personnel, the sale of unprofitable properties, and so forth.

In small entities the control process is generally performed by a manager who is close to the action. Sophisticated feedback reporting systems are unnecessary because the manager can personally monitor existing conditions and often knows what has happened long before any reports could be prepared and issued. In larger enterprises that have complex organizational hierarchies and highly decentralized operations, personal observation, of course, is not possible. Managers therefore require the assistance of control systems to bring operations back on target. Control systems provide feedback to managers in much the same fashion that the thermostat senses existing room conditions.

This chapter introduces two key elements of a management control system: flexible budgets and standard costs. It is important to note that unlike the thermostat, flexible budgets and standard costs cannot initiate action. These tools merely provide information; it is up to management to evaluate the information and institute needed policy changes, improvements, or remedies.

FLEXIBLE BUDGETS

As we have explained on several occasions throughout the text, budgets can be used as a yardstick against which to measure performance. Suppose it is your first day on the job as assistant to the president of Coleman Industries. On the basis of figures provided by the accounting department, the president has constructed the performance report appearing in Exhibit 26-1 for the company's Oregon plant.

The budget was based on an initial production target of 50,000 units; however, 54,000 units were actually manufactured during the quarter. The president has given you the report and desires to know whether Oregon's production manager should be praised for outstanding performance or called on the carpet for ineptness.

At first glance it appears that performance was terrible, because actual costs were $35,400 in excess of budget. When we consider only the variable costs, unfavorable variances totaled 6.6% of budgeted amounts ($37,900 ÷ $575,000), an overrun many managers would deem significant. Before proceeding with the production manager's termination from employment, though, we must consider one important underlying fact. The per-

Exhibit 26-1

COLEMAN INDUSTRIES
Oregon Plant Performance Report
For the Quarter Ended March 31, 1984

Cost	Budget	Actual	Variance*
Variable production costs			
Direct materials used	$150,000	$159,300	$ 9,300U
Direct labor	350,000	367,200	17,200U
Variable factory overhead	75,000	86,400	11,400U
Total	$575,000	$612,900	$37,900U
Fixed factory overhead	$215,000	$212,500	$ 2,500F
Total production costs	$790,000	$825,400	$35,400U

*F = favorable; U = unfavorable.

formance report compares the actual costs of producing 54,000 units against a budget calling for the manufacture of only 50,000 units. By the very nature of the comparison, a number of unfavorable variable cost variances are bound to arise because of the increase in activity.

Your conclusion about the production manager's performance? It's impossible to tell how good or bad the manager performed given the report that has been prepared. What we have illustrated is one of the classic problems associated with using a static budget for evaluative purposes. A **static budget** is a budget that is developed for one level of activity. Should output vary from the output that was anticipated (50,000 units in Oregon's case), comparisons with actual costs become meaningless. Simply stated, we cannot compare expected costs against actual costs at different activity levels. An adjustment is needed for the change in volume.

Constructing a Flexible Budget

So that the above problem is overcome, performance reports should incorporate the use of flexible budgets. A **flexible budget** covers a *range* of activity as opposed to a single level. Specifically, the relevant range of activity is determined for the forthcoming accounting period. Then individual budgets are prepared for various operating levels within the relevant range.

To illustrate the concept of a flexible budget, we will continue the Coleman Industries example. The budget that appears in Exhibit 26-1 was constructed after a thorough study of cost behavior at the Oregon plant. The following costs were judged to be realistic targets of performance for the first quarter.

Direct materials used	$3.00 per unit
Direct labor	$7.00 per unit
Variable factory overhead	$1.50 per unit
Fixed factory overhead	$215,000

A review of past accounting records revealed that quarterly production normally varies between 50,000 and 54,000 units. A flexible budget covering this range of activity is presented in Exhibit 26-2.

The flexible budget is prepared by multiplying the individual unit variable costs by the different activity levels and then adding the fixed factory overhead. We did not calculate a fixed overhead cost per unit because the unit cost will fluctuate depending on the activity level employed in the computation.

Exhibit 26-2

COLEMAN INDUSTRIES
Oregon Plant Flexible Budget
For the Quarter Ended March 31, 1984

Cost	Cost per Unit	Units of Activity 50,000	52,000	54,000
Variable production costs				
Direct materials used	$ 3.00	$150,000	$156,000	$162,000
Direct labor	7.00	350,000	364,000	378,000
Variable factory overhead	1.50	75,000	78,000	81,000
Total	$11.50	$575,000	$598,000	$621,000
Fixed factory overhead	—	$215,000	$215,000	$215,000
Total production costs		$790,000	$813,000	$836,000

Flexible Budgets and Performance Evaluation

Given the nature of flexible budgets, we can now appraise the performance of the Oregon plant's production manager. As shown in Exhibit 26-3, a properly prepared performance report enables management to compare the actual costs incurred in the manufacture of 54,000 units with budgeted costs for the same level of activity.

After the impact of the 4,000-unit variation between the original static budget and actual production has been eliminated, it appears that the manager did an acceptable job. With the exception of variable factory overhead, all costs were less than budgeted, and a total favorable variance was generated. Overall the flexible budget provides its users with a more useful tool for performance evaluations, because like volumes are compared. Activity level fluctuations no longer influence the appraisal process.

A Common Misunderstanding

Before leaving this example, we wish to clear up a common misconception about flexible budgets. Careful study of Exhibit 26-2 normally leaves the impression that many different budgets must be prepared when using the flexible approach. This is not the case. Even if this practice was followed, an organization could establish budgets for numerous volume levels and still miss the actual level of activity. For most entities the likelihood

Exhibit 26-3

COLEMAN INDUSTRIES
Oregon Plant Performance Report
For the Quarter Ended March 31, 1984

Cost	Budget, 54,000 Units	Actual, 54,000 Units	Variance*
Variable production costs			
Direct materials used	*$162,000*	*$159,300*	*$ 2,700F*
Direct labor	*378,000*	*367,200*	*10,800F*
Variable factory overhead	*81,000*	*86,400*	*5,400U*
Total	*$621,000*	*$612,900*	*$ 8,100F*
Fixed factory overhead	*$215,000*	*$212,500*	*$ 2,500F*
Total production costs	*$836,000*	*$825,400*	*$10,600F*

*F = favorable; U = unfavorable.

that a budget prepared in advance will coincide precisely with the actual volume level is extremely slim.

The preceding discussion should not be taken to mean that flexible budgets have limited application. To illustrate, suppose that the Oregon plant's output for the first quarter amounted to 53,000 units—an activity level that was not considered when establishing the budgets presented in Exhibit 26-2. Nonetheless, the manager's actual performance can still be compared against budgeted performance of $824,500, computed as follows:

Variable production costs per unit	
Direct materials used	***$ 3.00***
Direct labor	***7.00***
Variable factory overhead	***1.50***
Total	***$11.50***

Budget for 53,000 units	
Variable production costs (53,000 units × $11.50)	***$609,500***
Fixed production costs	***215,000***
Budget for 53,000 units	***$824,500***

It is apparent that flexible budgets can be prepared to coincide with any volume level. Companies determine the flexible budget characteristics (i.e., variable production costs of $11.50 per unit plus fixed production costs of $215,000) in advance. The "proper" budget and accompanying performance report must then wait until after the fact, that is, after the actual activity level is known.

DIFFERENT VIEWS ON STANDARDS

Time and time again consumers are exposed to messages such as "The quality goes in before the name goes on" (Zenith Radio Corporation) and "The dependable washer and dryer" (The Maytag Company). Quality and dependability are measures of performance, that is, standards that companies strive to achieve in the production of goods and services. The exact method of determining what "the standard" is or how standards should be measured varies greatly in practice. As evidence, consider comments that appeared in recent annual reports of Revlon, Inc., and Southwest Airlines Co.

Revlon, Inc., is engaged in the manufacture of beauty products and health products and services. Product quality, therefore, is an obvious company concern. As a result, the firm notes:

> *All our products meet or exceed uncompromised standards of quality, purity and integrity. . . . Quality assurance procedures are rigidly applied to all purchased materials and to all internal procedures. Laboratory approval is required before any product can be transferred internally, released to inventory or made available for sale. Samples of finished products regularly purchased in the marketplace are returned to local laboratories around the world for quality validation. In addition to inspections by various government authorities, each clinical laboratory is inspected three times a year by the doctoral-level team of National Health Laboratories' Scientific Advisory Board.*

Southwest Airlines has standards of a different nature. The company provides single-class, high-frequency air service to cities in the southwestern United States. By concentrating on short-haul markets, Southwest has achieved the highest operating profit margin of any domestic air carrier. Its standards? The firm focuses on productivity by having daily aircraft utilization of 11 hours; 10-minute turnaround times between most flights; and 1,900 employees, working hard and enjoying providing high-quality service. These performance goals, combined with operational simplicity (such as cash register ticketing, no baggage transfers to other airlines, and no food service) have led to a low fare structure, one that competes with bus and auto travel.

Laboratory standards and aircraft in the sky—two different types of standards for two different types of companies. Although the form varies, the intent remains the same: a preset measure against which actual activity can be compared.

SOURCE Adapted from the 1980 annual reports of Revlon, Inc., and Southwest Airlines Co.

STANDARD COSTS

Par on a golf course, a 4-minute mile, a .300 batting average, and an 8-hour workday are well-recognized standards of performance. In one form or another nearly everyone is affected by or comes in touch with standards.

Standards are popular among businesses as a means of measuring effectiveness and efficiency. **Effectiveness** refers to whether a particular goal or objective has been attained. **Efficiency,** on the other hand, relates to the amount of resources consumed in accomplishing the goal. To illustrate the difference between these two concepts, assume a manufacturer has a goal of producing 5,000 finished units per month. If each completed unit requires 3 square feet of direct material, then 15,000 square feet of material should be consumed in normal operations. Suppose that during a recent month 5,000 units were, in fact, produced. However, because of poor-quality materials and sloppy workmanship, direct materials used soared to 16,500 square feet, 10% above standard. In this particular situation the operations were effective, because the initial production goal was achieved. The process was plagued with inefficiencies, however, as evidenced by an unusually high consumption of resources (i.e., materials).

The **standards** used by businesses are norms of what should occur under reasonably efficient operating conditions. Standards are usually expressed on a per-unit basis and normally refer to the expected quantity and cost of inputs used in producing a good or service. Typical standards include the cost per pound of direct materials, the cost per direct labor hour, and the number of direct labor hours required to complete a task.

Standard Costs and Budgets

The concept of a standard cost is really nothing new. Although they were not described as such, you were introduced to standard costs in the first part of this chapter. Standard costs are used in the construction of both static and flexible budgets. Specifically, standard costs are a per-unit concept; budgets, in contrast, deal in totals.

To illustrate the difference between standards and budgets, assume that Centre Enterprises manufactures a single product that requires 5 gallons of direct material at an anticipated cost of $4 per gallon. The standard direct material cost per unit of output is computed as follows:

Standard Quantity per Finished Unit	×	Standard Price	=	Standard Cost per Unit of Output
5 gallons		$4 per gallon		$20

Once the standard cost is known, a budget (flexible in this case) can be prepared, as shown below.

	Standard Cost per Unit of Output	Flexible Budget Units of Activity		
		10,000	10,500	11,000
Direct materials	$20	$200,000	$210,000	$220,000

As our example shows, a standard cost is merely the budgeted cost for a single unit of activity.

Setting Standards

The setting of standards is a complex process, one that requires skills that often surpass the expertise possessed by the average accountant. Generally, a team effort is needed and involves participation from many different areas within the organization. In a manufacturing entity, for example, all persons who have responsibility for prices and quantities of inputs into the finished product should assist in the standard-setting process.

Recall from Chapter 21 that manufactured products contain three cost elements: direct materials, direct labor, and factory overhead. Standards must be established for each of these elements in terms of both price and quantity. Beginning with direct materials, engineering and production employees should participate in calculating standard inputs by both type and quantity of materials used. Given these calculations, the purchasing department can then price the inputs. Standard material prices should include transportation charges and be net of any contemplated cash discounts.

Direct labor standards are determined jointly by production, engineering, and personnel staffs. Standards for labor time are first established, often by using *time and motion studies.* That is, individual manufacturing operations are clocked by industrial engineers. Once labor time is calculated, the cost standard can be computed from information furnished by the personnel department. Although wage rates will vary among employees because of differences in seniority, skill levels, and other factors, many companies use a single (average) rate for costing individual manufacturing procedures. The accountant's role in the area of labor is to formalize and coordinate the standard-setting process and to establish an effective system of performance reporting once the standards have been determined.

Overhead standards are developed in the same fashion as the overhead application rate is developed, a topic that was discussed in Chapter 22. Normally, however, separate standards are established for variable overhead and fixed overhead. To illustrate the necessary procedures, we will continue the previous example relating to Centre Enterprises. Assume that Centre applies factory overhead to products on the basis of direct labor hours. Management estimates that 10,000 units will be produced in the upcoming period, requiring a total of 80,000 direct labor hours. Variable and fixed overhead at this level of activity are budgeted at $80,000 and $120,000, respectively. Centre must first compute the overhead standard per direct labor hour. The necessary calculations follow.

Variable:

$$\frac{\text{estimated variable overhead}}{\text{estimated activity}} = \frac{\$80{,}000}{80{,}000 \text{ hours}} = \$1.00 \text{ per hour}$$

Fixed:

$$\frac{\text{estimated fixed overhead}}{\text{estimated activity}} = \frac{\$120{,}000}{80{,}000 \text{ hours}} = \$1.50 \text{ per hour}$$

Since each unit requires 8 hours of production time (80,000 hours ÷ 10,000 units), the standard overhead cost per finished unit is computed in the following manner:

Variable overhead: 8 hours × $1.00 per hour	$ 8.00
Fixed overhead: 8 hours × $1.50 per hour	12.00
Standard overhead cost per finished unit	$20.00

The outcome of the standard-setting process is summarized in a *standard cost sheet,* as illustrated in Exhibit 26-4.

Exhibit 26-4

CENTRE ENTERPRISES
Standard Cost Sheet
Product No. 626

Input	Standard Quantity per Finished Unit	×	Standard Price	=	Standard Cost per Unit of Output
Direct materials	5 gallons		$4.00		$20.00
Direct labor	8 hours		6.50*		52.00
Variable overhead	8 hours		1.00		8.00
Fixed overhead	8 hours		1.50		12.00
Total standard cost					$92.00

*Assumed.

Levels of Standards

Should a standard be set high, low, or somewhere in between? How much effort should workers put forth in attempting to achieve a standard? Unfortunately, the answers to these and other related questions do not come easy. Production supervisors, engineers, laborers, and other veterans of manufacturing activities have grappled with these issues for years. Although there is a diversity of opinion, companies must address the issue and somehow determine a "correct" standard for each facet of their production operations. As we will soon see, standards that are set incorrectly are frequently rejected by employees—a definite stumbling block in attaining high levels of operational efficiency and effectiveness.

The starting point for developing standards is a look at the past. The costs incurred in prior years can provide considerable insight into a company's cost experience at different levels of activity. The past should be interpreted with care, however. Changes in the form of new suppliers, new technology, and employee training programs can rapidly make past data obsolete and not representative of a company's current manufacturing environment. Further complicating matters is the fact that past inefficiencies are often built into the data under examination. Standards strive to reflect what *should be,* not what *has been.* Management must be aware of these deficiencies when analyzing earlier experiences and make appropriate adjustments to its findings.

Ideal standards

Despite the diversity that is encountered when setting standards, most standards can be classified as either ideal or attainable. An **ideal standard** is one that can be achieved under perfect operating conditions. By essentially assuming maximum efficiency at minimum cost, ideal standards make no allowances for spoilage, machine breakdowns, worker fatigue, inefficiency, human error, and similar factors. Furthermore, since ideal standards emphasize perfection, the resulting variances tend to have little meaning when analyzing performance. Simply stated, nothing is perfect, and normal inefficiencies are a fact of life. With the employment of such high standards, variance computations combine both normal and abnormal occurrences, thereby masking the abnormalities that management desires to learn about and correct.

From our discussion many of you may wonder why any company would use such unrealistic targets of performance. Managers who favor ideal standards feel that by setting goals that are extremely difficult (if not impossible) to achieve, overall output and efficiency will increase because of the constant efforts made by employees to attain the standard. This outcome is in contrast to the outcome obtained by setting a standard that is too loose; namely, one that is easily attained with minimal work. Behavioral scientists have observed that ideal standards do cause an increase in productivity when first introduced, as employees strive for the unreachable. Subsequently, however, performance tends to fall after numerous failures and a constant barrage of unfavorable variances. Workers soon become frustrated and discouraged and adopt a "what the heck" attitude.

Attainable standards

To overcome the problems associated with ideal standards, most companies turn to attainable standards. An **attainable standard** is one that can be achieved by efficient, not perfect, operations. In the setting of standards for direct materials, for example, allowances are provided for *normal* scrap, waste, and spoilage. Similarly, in the establishment of direct labor standards, provision is made for *normal* worker inefficiencies, machine breakdowns, and so forth.

The level of attainable standards varies from firm to firm. Most organizations, however, use a high ("tight") but reachable standard. Consequently, employees must achieve high levels of operating efficiency. Yet the standard is not unreasonable and therefore avoids worker frustration and other behavioral problems.

Attainable standards offer the further benefits of improved planning and decision making. Realistic budgets can be formulated, and as we will show in the next chapter, decisions are facilitated because they are based on attainable estimates of cost. In contrast, ideal standards frequently result in faulty financial projections and errors when choosing among alternatives.

VARIANCE ANALYSIS

Standard costs provide information to management that is useful in the control of an enterprise's affairs. Much of this information comes in the form of **variances,** or deviations from standard. Actual costs are compared with standard costs to determine whether operations are running according to plan or whether significant deviations exist. Management is then alerted to departures from established targets of performance, and appropriate corrective action can be implemented. With a focus on variances managers can avoid spending countless hours reviewing what is going right. Instead their efforts can be devoted to problem areas that need attention. This process is frequently known as **management by exception.**

To illustrate the fundamentals of variance analysis, we will begin by concentrating on direct materials and direct labor. Suppose that a company reported the following results upon conclusion of a recent month's activity.

Cost	Actual	Standard	Variance
Direct materials used	$36,500	$33,000	$3,500U
Direct labor	59,400	62,700	3,300F

Notice that both direct material consumption and direct labor incurrence failed to conform to the original plan. The company spent $3,500 more than anticipated for materials, giving rise to an *unfavorable variance.* In contrast, direct labor cost was $3,300 less than planned and created a *favorable variance.*

Management now desires to know why the variances arose. Material and labor costs will stray from standard because of variations in the following factors.

1 Direct materials:
   a The per-unit acquisition cost of materials
   b The quantity of materials consumed
2 Direct labor:
   a The hourly wage rate
   b The number of hours worked

Variance Calculation

The impact of these price and quantity factors on the total variances can be determined by several relatively simple calculations. The calculations are perhaps best illustrated by the model that appears in Exhibit 26-5.

Careful study of the model reveals that the price variance is really the difference between the actual and standard prices multiplied by the actual quantities of materials or labor put into production. For direct materials the price variance is commonly known as the **materials price variance.** For labor the name changes slightly to the **labor rate variance** to be more attuned to the area of study.

The quantity variance is slightly more difficult to understand. Exhibit 26-5 shows that the quantity variance is calculated by comparing (Aq × Sp)

Exhibit 26-5

General model for variance analysis of direct materials and direct labor

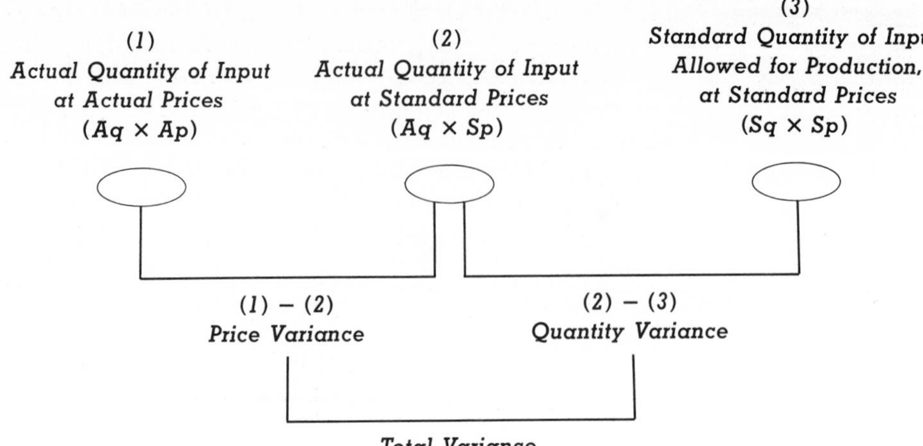

and (Sq × Sp). If we take the difference between these two expressions, the following formula is derived.

quantity variance = Sp(Aq − Sq)

The formula shows that by weighting the difference in quantities by the standard price, the quantity variance is measured in dollars.

Additionally, it is important to note that the standard quantity is subtracted from the actual quantity. The actual quantity represents the actual inputs (pounds, gallons, hours, and so on) placed in production. In contrast, *the standard quantity represents the amount of input that should have been used in production activities.* To illustrate, suppose a manufacturer produces a single product that requires 3 pounds of direct materials. For the month just ended production totaled 4,000 completed units. If 11,800 pounds of materials were consumed, Aq would be 11,800 pounds and Sq would be 12,000 pounds (4,000 completed units × 3 pounds per unit).

The quantity variance is called the **materials quantity variance** when working with direct materials. For labor the name is changed to be more descriptive of the difference between actual and standard labor hours; this variance is commonly referred to as a **labor efficiency variance.**

An Illustration of Direct Material Variances

To illustrate use of the model shown in Exhibit 26-5, assume that Sanco, Inc., has developed the following standard material cost for one of its products.

Direct materials	3 pounds at $5.00 per pound

During a recent period the following activity took place:

Direct materials purchased and used in production	6,000 pounds at $5.10 per pound
Production completed	1,900 units

Exhibit 26-6

Sanco, Inc., direct materials variances

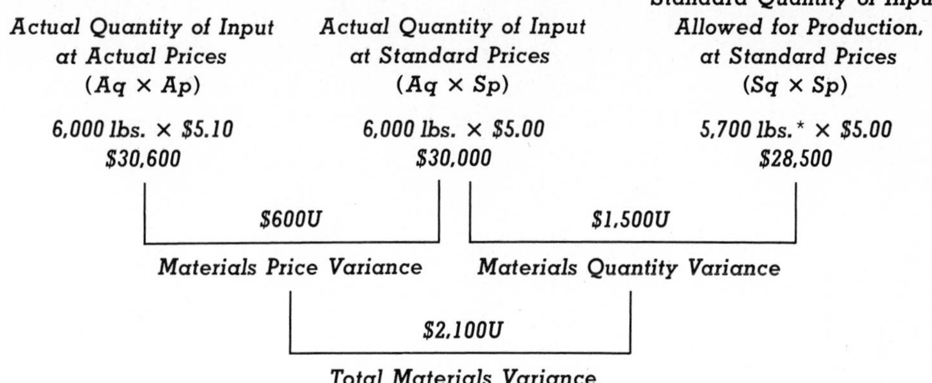

* 1,900 units × 3 lbs. per unit.

Exhibit 26-6 shows Sanco's price and quantity variances for direct materials. The variances are both unfavorable. The unfavorable price variance arose because Sanco paid $0.10 in excess of the $5.00 standard price to acquire needed materials. The unfavorable quantity variance resulted because the company used 300 pounds more than planned (6,000 vs. 5,700) in manufacturing activities.

An Illustration of Direct Labor Variances

To illustrate the computation of direct labor variances, we will continue the previous example. Assume that Sanco has established the following labor standards for each unit of its product.

Direct labor   2 hours at $6.00 per hour

In the production of the 1,900 finished units, direct labor incurred totaled 4,100 hours at $5.80 per hour, or $23,780. The company's direct labor variances are shown in Exhibit 26-7.

Exhibit 26-7

Sanco, Inc., direct labor variances

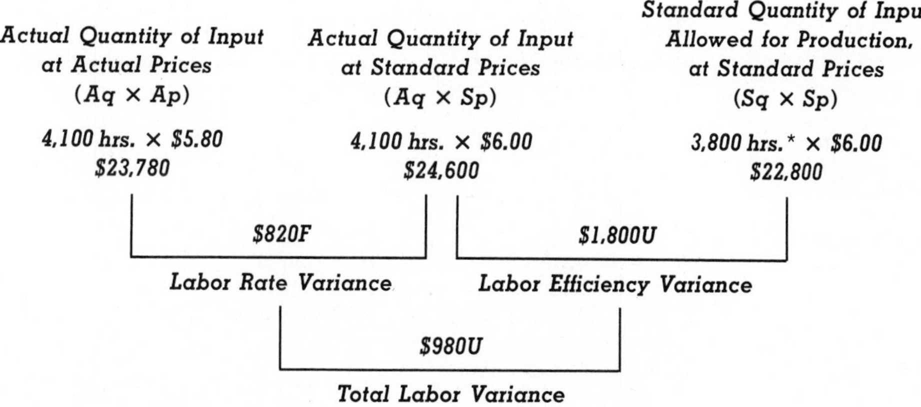

* 1,900 units × 2 hrs. per unit.

As you can see, the labor variance computations are similar to those for materials. Rather than employ pounds and the material purchase price, labor calculations require the respective use of hours worked and the wage rate. Sanco's labor rate variance was favorable because the actual rate paid ($5.80) was $0.20 less than standard. Labor efficiency was unfavorable, however, since actual hours worked exceeded the standard time allowed by 300 hours (4,100 − 3,800 = 300).

Factory Overhead Variances

Variances for the third element of product cost, factory overhead, are generally more difficult to understand than those for direct materials and direct labor. Remember that for flexible budgeting and standard costing purposes, manufacturing overhead is divided into its fixed and variable components. In addition, recall that in the setting of overhead standards an activity level is estimated to calculate the overhead rate per hour (or unit).

We can compute overhead variances by using the model illustrated in Exhibit 26-5 for direct materials and direct labor. A minor modification is necessary, however, because of the nature of overhead costs. To explain, a simplified version of the model follows.

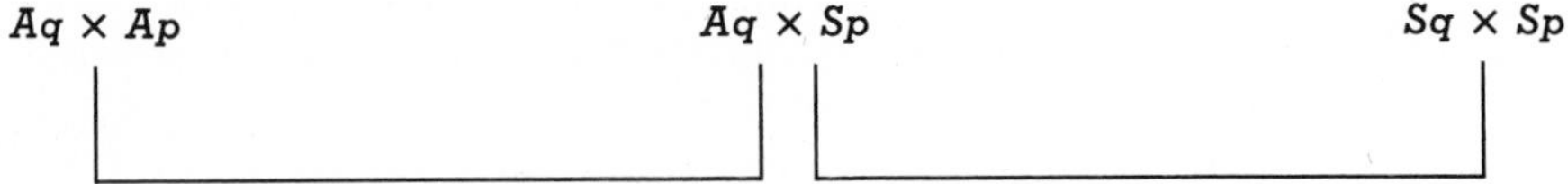

Study the middle term for a moment. The expression Aq × Sp is used to calculate the amount that the actual quantity of input should have cost. Observe that as activity increases or decreases, the amount of the Aq × Sp expression will fluctuate. This result is easily seen by picturing the computations necessary for direct materials and direct labor. As production increases, for example, the actual quantity of materials consumed and labor incurred will rise because of the variable nature of the cost functions. What happens with a fixed cost, however? No matter what the actual quantity of input is, the Aq × Sp expression must remain constant. Why? Even if the inputs go up and down, the same amount of fixed cost is incurred.[1]

Given the foregoing, we can now proceed with the calculation of overhead variances for Sanco, Inc. Assume that Sanco applies overhead to products on the basis of direct labor hours. The following information is available.

Actual factory overhead incurred (fixed plus variable)	$73,000
Standard variable overhead rate per direct labor hour	$7
Standard fixed overhead rate per direct labor hour	$10
Budgeted fixed factory overhead for the period	$40,000
Estimated activity in labor hours during the period	4,000 hours

[1]We are assuming that the firm is not moving from one activity range to another.

The company's overhead variances are shown in Exhibit 26-8.

Exhibit 26-8

Sanco, Inc., factory overhead variances

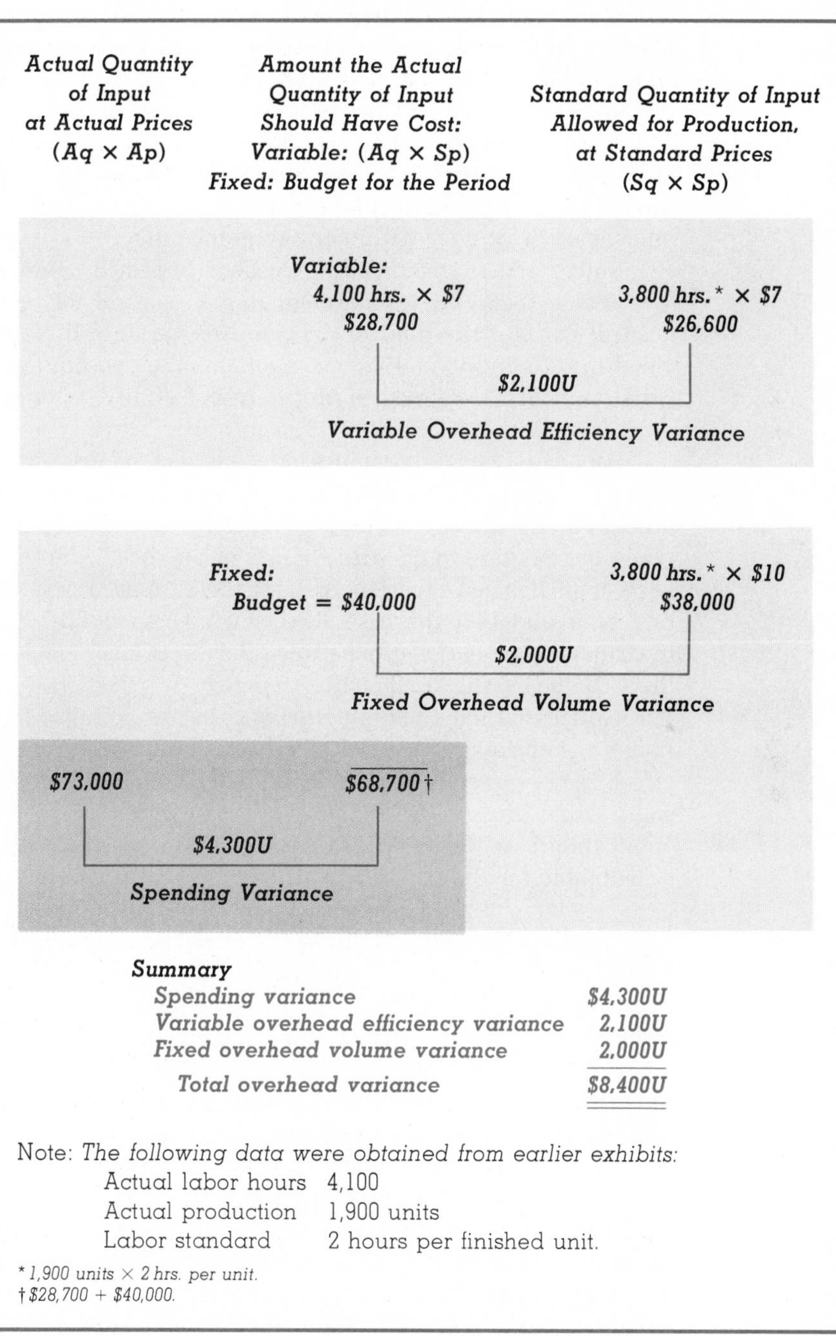

Actual Quantity of Input at Actual Prices ($Aq \times Ap$)	Amount the Actual Quantity of Input Should Have Cost: Variable: ($Aq \times Sp$) Fixed: Budget for the Period	Standard Quantity of Input Allowed for Production, at Standard Prices ($Sq \times Sp$)

Variable:
4,100 hrs. × $7 = $28,700 ; 3,800 hrs.* × $7 = $26,600
$2,100U
Variable Overhead Efficiency Variance

Fixed:
Budget = $40,000 ; 3,800 hrs.* × $10 = $38,000
$2,000U
Fixed Overhead Volume Variance

$73,000 ; $68,700†
$4,300U
Spending Variance

Summary

Spending variance	$4,300U
Variable overhead efficiency variance	2,100U
Fixed overhead volume variance	2,000U
Total overhead variance	$8,400U

Note: *The following data were obtained from earlier exhibits:*

Actual labor hours	4,100
Actual production	1,900 units
Labor standard	2 hours per finished unit.

* 1,900 units × 2 hrs. per unit.
† $28,700 + $40,000.

Spending variance

The **spending variance** measures the difference between actual overhead incurred (both variable and fixed combined) and the total overhead budgeted for 4,100 direct labor hours of production. Because Aq × Ap must equal the actual overhead incurred, we merely inserted the $73,000 figure on the left-hand side of the exhibit. The planned amount of variable overhead for the activity attained is computed in the same fashion as planned amounts for other variable cost elements (direct materials and direct labor), that is, Aq × Sp (4,100 hours × $7 = $28,700). Turning to fixed costs, Sanco has budgeted $40,000 of fixed overhead for the period. Given the nature of the expenditure, this amount should be incurred if direct labor input totals 4,100 hours, 4,200 hours, 4,000 hours, or for that matter, any other level of activity within the relevant range.

Since actual overhead exceeded budgeted amounts by $4,300 [$73,000 − ($28,700 + $40,000)], better control of overhead costs is needed. For effective control to occur, the variance must be further subdivided into its individual cost components (i.e., specific variable and fixed costs) and further related to proper responsibility centers.

Variable overhead efficiency variance

Sanco used 300 labor hours in excess of standard (4,100 hours − 3,800 hours), resulting in a $2,100 unfavorable **variable overhead efficiency variance.** The overhead efficiency variance is somewhat misleading because it really has nothing to do with the use of overhead. Rather the variance reflects inefficiencies experienced with the base used to apply the overhead, direct labor hours in this case. By reviewing Exhibit 26-7, you should be able to visualize the relationship between the direct labor efficiency variance and the variable overhead efficiency variance.

Notice that fixed manufacturing costs are excluded from the computation of the efficiency variance. Why? Small fluctuations in hours should not affect fixed overhead, because the budgeted overhead amount remains constant within the relevant range. The production supervisor in charge of the application base (labor hours, machine hours, and so on) is generally held accountable for the variable overhead efficiency variance.

Fixed overhead volume variance

The **fixed overhead volume variance** represents the fixed costs associated with an under- or overutilization of manufacturing facilities. To explain, Sanco has budgeted fixed overhead for the period of $40,000. This level of expenditure provides the company with an estimated capacity of 4,000 direct labor hours (see p. 1032). Thus each hour has an associated fixed cost of $10 ($40,000 ÷ 4,000 hours). Observe that this amount is Sp, that is, the standard fixed overhead rate per direct labor hour.

For the period just ended Sanco produced only 1,900 units. The standard hours allowed for these units total 3,800 (1,900 units × 2 hours per unit), leaving Sanco 200 hours shy of utilizing its 4,000-hour capacity. Because each hour costs $10, the volume variance amounts to $2,000. In this particular instance the volume variance is unfavorable since utilization was less than capacity. If utilization had been greater than capacity, the volume variance would have been favorable, thereby indicating a theoretical "savings" in fixed costs.

The volume variance relates strictly to fixed manufacturing costs. As production rises and falls, variable overhead will change accordingly. Fixed overhead, on the other hand, remains constant. Because the volume variance is an expression of the cost of underutilizing plant capacity, or the "savings" associated with overutilization, variable overhead is not relevant for the computation. Why? There are no variable costs of underutilization; these costs disappear when activity falls. Similarly, variable cost savings are nonexistent when production exceeds capacity, because increased activity calls for additional cost incurrence.

Volume variances are caused by a number of different factors, including an abnormally high number of machine breakdowns, strikes, sloppy production scheduling, changes in inventory policies, raw material shortages, and a lack of (or unanticipated) sales orders. In many instances volume variances are very difficult to control or eliminate. Upper-level management, though, should do some analysis to determine the cause of the variance and whether operational changes (such as improved repair programs or a larger budget for advertising) are needed.

Investigating Variances

Calculating variances from standard is only one step in achieving effective cost control. Investigating variances and taking corrective action are necessary to complete the process. Frequently, investigations are straightforward and relatively few problems are encountered. Sometimes, however, managers must assume the role of a detective to determine both the underlying cause and the correct party to hold accountable for a variance's creation.

In the simplest of cases, a variance arises because of problems directly identified with the production factor itself. For example, a direct labor rate variance may be caused by a temporary change in the labor mix required for production. Because of illness or perhaps a rush order, workers earning $7 per hour may be temporarily shifted to jobs normally performed by employees earning $6 per hour. Turning to another example, a labor efficiency variance may arise from a lack of proper employee training or morale problems among the workers.

Often a variance investigation is complicated by the strong interrelationships that exist among manufacturing activities. Difficulties with machine operation, for instance, can destroy labor efficiency and cause excessive use of raw materials. Or in a multidepartment environment, sloppy performance in a production department may lead to unfavorable efficiency and unfavorable overhead spending variances in subsequent assembly work.

Our discussion thus far has taken the position that actual operations are to blame for the creation of variances. It is possible, of course, that the standard is the problem. Variance investigators should examine standards to determine whether the standards are set correctly and up to date.

Successful standard costing systems use standards that reflect current operating performance. Standards should be reviewed periodically, usually once each year, and updated if necessary. Revisions are warranted by relatively permanent changes in prices and environmental conditions. Examples of such changes include the negotiation of a new labor contract, permanent price increases or decreases from suppliers, modification of production processes, plant renovation or rearrangement, and changes in quality control or product design.

Responsibility for Variances

Determining the cause of a variance is accompanied by a related problem: accountability. To illustrate, assume that Burdick Machinery recently installed a computerized standard costing system. The company's sales manager has just accepted a rush order for a nonstock item from a valued customer. The sales manager forwarded the order to the production supervisor. The supervisor, in turn, filed the necessary paperwork with the purchasing department to acquire needed direct materials. Unfortunately, a purchasing clerk temporarily lost the paperwork, and by the time it was located, it was too late to order from the normal supplier. A new supplier was found who quoted a very attractive price. The materials arrived and Burdick soon found why the price was so low—poor quality. The end result? In all likelihood the standard costing system will generate the following variances for materials and labor:[2]

Materials price variance: favorable because of the lower-than-normal price.
Materials quantity variance: unfavorable because of poor quality.
Labor efficiency variance: unfavorable because of difficulties encountered in working with the material.

The price variance is normally the responsibility of the purchasing department. In contrast, the production manager is usually held accountable for the materials quantity and labor efficiency variances, because use of materials and employee productivity are generally within the manager's control.

Assume it is now the Tuesday following a three-day holiday weekend. Burdick's production supervisor and the manufacturing vice-president meet to discuss the unfavorable variances in the production department and the supervisor's "inept performance." The meeting has started and the vice-president is very disturbed about the variances. The supervisor explains that the variances were undoubtedly caused by the poor quality of the materials. The vice-president knows, however, that her "computerized system doesn't lie" and concludes by presenting an ultimatum to improve operations or seek employment elsewhere.

In all likelihood the supervisor would probably leave the vice-president's office complaining about life's inequities, the unfair handling of the situation, and so forth. To compound matters, the supervisor will probably transmit his poor attitude to those employees he directs, creating low mo-

[2]We will ignore overhead variances for simplicity.

rale in the department. Low morale, in turn, will probably have an impact on future productivity.

The lesson to be learned is that the production supervisor was held accountable for a situation beyond his control, a direct violation of the tenets of responsibility accounting. For a standard costing system to function effectively, the responsibility for variances must be correctly fixed or placed. Although the production manager can usually exert some control over material use and labor efficiency, the fault here lies in the purchasing department because of the misplaced paperwork. Or one could logically argue that the sales manager was at fault for his or her initial acceptance of the rush order. In any event, the guilty party must be determined, with the appropriate manager bearing responsibility for the resulting variances.

Realize that a variance is merely the mathematical difference between two numbers and serves as a gauge of performance. Like ratios, which were discussed earlier in the text, variances present a hint that something is right or that something is wrong; only in rare circumstances can they tell the complete story. Management must therefore use variances as a springboard for further investigation.

The decision to investigate normally depends on the size of the variance involved. Large variances are of obvious concern to management; small variances are not. Most firms establish a general guideline, such as, "Review all variances that differ from standard amounts by 10% or $1,000, whichever is lower."

The reader is reminded that variance investigation costs money. The cost of determining the cause of a variance and taking the necessary corrective action may very well exceed the amount of the variance under study. Thus variance review and correction should be based on the principle of cost-benefit analysis. In this manner the evaluation and control of operations will be a profitable endeavor for all parties concerned.

APPENDIX: JOURNAL ENTRIES FOR VARIANCES

Many companies have integrated standards and variances into their formal accounting systems. This practice offers the advantage of simplifying the bookkeeping required to accumulate production costs. Firms can establish and carry a number of accounts at standard and need not keep track of daily fluctuations in input quantities and actual costs. The result is a reduction in record-keeping procedures.

To illustrate the journal entries used in a standard cost system, we will employ data from the Sanco, Inc., example appearing on pages 1030–1035.

DIRECT MATERIALS

Sanco purchased and used 6,000 pounds of direct materials in current production activities. The entry to record the purchase follows.

Raw Materials	*30,000*	
Materials Price Variance	*600*	
Accounts Payable		*30,600*
To record purchase of direct materials		

The Accounts Payable account must be established at the actual amount owed to creditors, specifically, \$30,600 (6,000 pounds × \$5.10). The price variance is recorded at this time to give management immediate feedback that a variance has occurred. As we noted in Chapter 25, rapid feedback generally results in better control. Finally, the Raw Materials account is debited for \$30,000: the actual quantity of materials purchased multiplied by the \$5.00 standard price (6,000 pounds × \$5.00 = \$30,000).

Direct materials will eventually be taken out of the storeroom and used in production. Because the materials are carried in the accounts at the \$5.00 standard price, the following entry is needed to record consumption of 6,000 pounds.

Work in Process	*28,500*	
Materials Quantity Variance	*1,500*	
Raw Materials		*30,000*
To record material use		

The quantity variance is recorded at this time because the excess use of 300 pounds (6,000 − 5,700) is now known. The net result of these two entries is that Work in Process is carried at \$28,500, the standard quantity of input times the standard price (5,700 pounds × \$5.00 = \$28,500).

Note that both the Raw Materials and Work in Process accounts are carried at the standard price and have debit balances. Thus any amounts in excess of standard (i.e., unfavorable variances) are recorded as additional costs and debited to the proper variance accounts. In contrast, favorable variances are recorded as credits.

DIRECT LABOR

Following procedures consistent with the foregoing, Sanco would record direct labor incurrence as follows:

Work in Process	*22,800*	
Labor Efficiency Variance	*1,800*	
Labor Rate Variance		*820*
Wages Payable		*23,780*
To record direct labor for the period		

Once again Work in Process is debited for the standard quantity of input multiplied by the standard price (3,800 hours × \$6.00 = \$22,800). In addition, Wages Payable is established at \$23,780, which represents Aq × Ap (the wages actually owed to employees).

FACTORY OVERHEAD

Actual factory overhead incurred is recorded as follows:

Factory Overhead	*73,000*	
Accounts Payable, Raw Materials, and so on		*73,000*
To record actual factory overhead charges		

Recall from Chapter 22 that because of difficulties in tracing overhead to finished products, each unit manufactured is charged with an estimated amount of overhead via an application rate. The application rate corresponds to the standard overhead rate, as described in the preceding pages. Sanco's variable and fixed overhead rates per direct labor hour amounted to $7 and $10, respectively. For consistency with the accounting treatments for direct materials and direct labor, the Work in Process account is again charged with the amount derived by multiplying the standard quantity of input by the standard price. From the variances computed in Exhibit 26-8, the necessary entry to apply overhead to the 1,900 units produced is as follows:

Work in Process	64,600*	
Overhead Spending Variance	4,300	
Variable Overhead Efficiency Variance	2,100	
Fixed Overhead Volume Variance	2,000	
Factory Overhead		73,000
To apply overhead to production		

* Variable + fixed ($26,600 + $38,000 = $64,600).

SUBSEQUENT ENTRIES

Upon completion of production an entry is needed to transfer the cost of the completed units to the Finished Goods account. In addition, the variance accounts are either closed to Cost of Goods Sold or, if significant, allocated on a proportional basis among Work in Process, Finished Goods, and Cost of Goods Sold. The latter treatment restates these three accounts from standard cost to actual cost to prevent the generation of misleading financial statements.

When one is working with significant variances, the cause of the variances should be determined prior to undertaking any allocation procedure. If large variances are caused by abnormal levels of inefficiency, spoilage, and similar factors, allocation to inventory accounts is inappropriate. Why? Such a procedure would result in carrying waste and ineptness as assets on the balance sheet, a treatment that is inconsistent with the principles of sound financial accounting. Charging the variances as a loss of the current period may be more appropriate.

SUMMARY PROBLEM

Mahoney Manufacturing produces a single product and uses a standard costing system. A conversation with the firm's accountant revealed that each unit of finished product has the following material and labor standards:

Direct materials	4 units @ $2.50
Direct labor	2 hours @ $6.50

Mahoney applies overhead to products on the basis of direct labor hours. Management estimates that budgeted production levels during the upcoming period will require a total of 50,000 direct labor hours. Variable and fixed overhead at this level of activity are budgeted at $150,000 and $275,000, respectively. Additional data follow.

1. ***Direct materials purchased and consumed during the period totaled 100,000 units at a cost of $2.65 per unit.***
2. ***Direct labor incurred totaled 51,000 hours at a rate of $6.70 per hour.***
3. ***Total overhead incurred amounted to $436,000.***
4. ***Actual production totaled 26,000 units, all of which were completed.***

INSTRUCTIONS

- a ***Compute the company's variable and fixed overhead rates per direct labor hour.***
- b ***Compute the total standard cost of a finished unit.***
- c ***Determine Mahoney's direct materials variances.***
- d ***Determine Mahoney's direct labor variances.***
- e ***Determine Mahoney's factory overhead variances.***

SOLUTION

a

$$\text{variable overhead rate} = \frac{\text{estimated variable overhead}}{\text{estimated activity}} = \frac{\$150{,}000}{50{,}000 \text{ direct labor hours}} = \$3 \text{ per direct labor hour}$$

$$\text{fixed overhead rate} = \frac{\text{estimated fixed overhead}}{\text{estimated activity}} = \frac{\$275{,}000}{50{,}000 \text{ direct labor hours}} = \$5.50 \text{ per direct labor hour}$$

b

Direct materials: 4 units @ $2.50	$10.00
Direct labor: 2 hours @ $6.50	13.00
Variable overhead: 2 hours @ $3.00*	6.00
Fixed overhead: 2 hours @ $5.50*	11.00
Total standard cost per finished unit	$40.00

*From part (a).

c

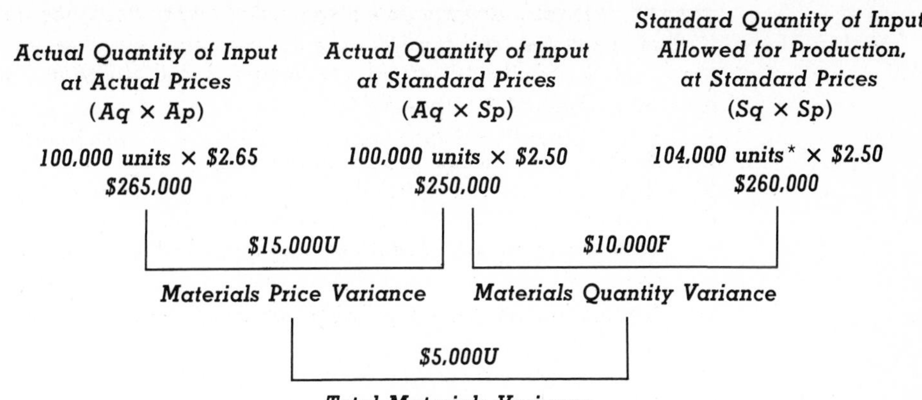

* 26,000 finished units × 4 units of direct materials.

d

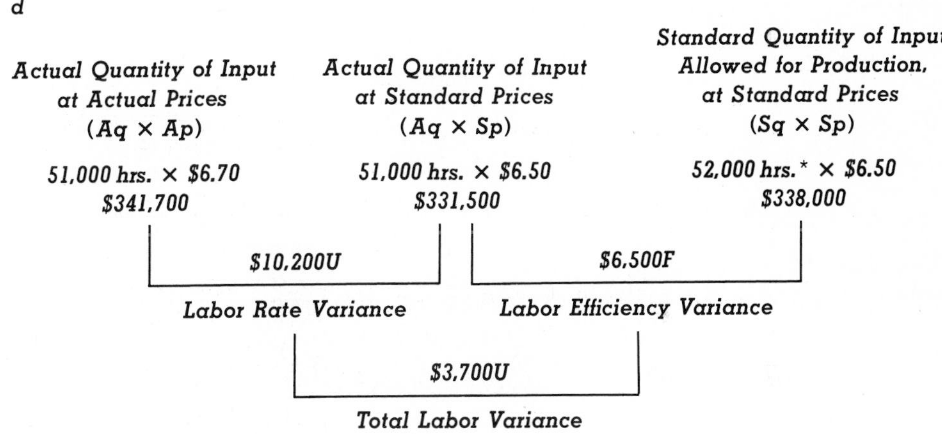

* 26,000 finished units × 2 hrs. per unit.

e

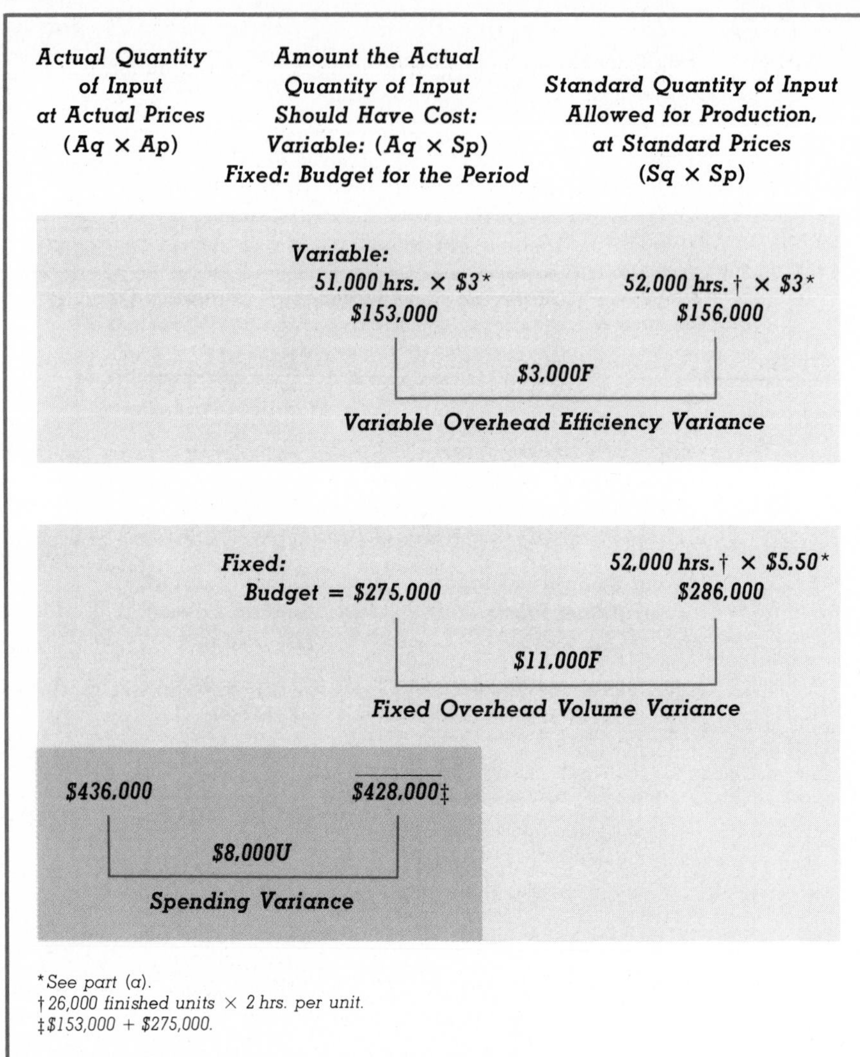

KEY TERMS AND CONCEPTS

attainable standard 1028
effectiveness 1025
efficiency 1025
fixed overhead volume variance 1034
flexible budget 1021
ideal standard 1028
labor efficiency variance 1030
labor rate variance 1029
management by exception 1029
materials price variance 1029
materials quantity variance 1030
spending variance 1034
standard 1025
static budget 1021
variable overhead efficiency variance 1034
variance 1029

QUESTIONS

Q26-1 Explain how the management control process is similar to the operation of a thermostat.

Q26-2 Why are sophisticated feedback reporting systems unnecessary in small enterprises?

Q26-3 Differentiate between a static budget and a flexible budget.

Q26-4 Differentiate between effectiveness and efficiency.

Q26-5 Explain the relationship, if any, between a standard cost and a flexible budget.

Q26-6 Identify the parties normally involved in establishing the following:

a Quantity standards for materials

b Efficiency standards for direct labor

Q26-7 An engineer once commented: "Standards must be based on a perfect operating environment. Anything less assumes inefficient working conditions." Evaluate the engineer's comment.

Q26-8 Why do some companies use ideal standards? What often occurs shortly after the introduction of ideal standards?

Q26-9 What is meant by an attainable standard?

Q26-10 Explain the concept known as "management by exception." Is variance analysis consistent or inconsistent with management by exception? Why?

Q26-11 In general, when should standards be revised? List several events that may necessitate a revision of standards.

Q26-12 Discuss a problem that could arise by holding a manager accountable for a variance beyond his or her control.

Q26-13 Should managers investigate all variances? Why?

Q26-14 List two possible methods of handling variances at the end of an accounting period. When is each method appropriate?

EXERCISES

E26-1 The following performance report of production costs was prepared by a staff assistant of the Carnahan Company.

CARNAHAN COMPANY
Performance Report
For the Month Ended January 31, 1984

Cost	Budget	Actual	Variance
Direct materials used	$ 33,000	$ 32,400	$ 600F
Direct labor	75,000	71,550	3,450F
Variable factory overhead	18,000	15,120	2,880F
Fixed factory overhead	48,000	49,300	1,300U
Total production costs	$174,000	$168,370	$5,630F

The budget was prepared by assuming a production level of 30,000 units. Because of several snowstorms in the area, Carnahan's plant was closed for seven working days and only 27,000 units were manufactured.

Management desires a performance report based on the flexible budgeting approach.

a Explain the major cause of the total favorable variance for the period.
b Prepare a performance report by using the flexible budgeting approach.
c Specifically, what does flexible budgeting do to enhance performance evaluation?

E26-2 National Corporation has established the following standards for direct materials and direct labor for one of its products.

Materials: 4.5 square feet @ $12	$54
Labor: 2.0 hours @ $8	16

During a recent month 4,200 finished units were produced. Materials purchased and consumed in operations totaled 19,500 square feet at a cost of $11.80 per square foot. In addition, National paid $8.20 per hour for 8,200 hours of factory labor. Compute National's variances for the following:

a Direct materials
b Direct labor

E26-3 Allison Corporation has two departments, both of which manufacture the same product. Information about the departments follows.

	Department	
	A	*B*
Actual direct labor hours	4,100	4,900
Actual direct labor cost	$33,620	$42,140
Units produced	4,800	6,400

Each unit has a standard manufacturing time of 45 minutes. The company's standard direct labor cost per hour amounts to $8.50.

a Compute the labor rate and efficiency variances for departments A and B.
b Examine the results obtained in part (a). Evaluate the efficiency of the two departments and determine a possible underlying cause of any differences in efficiency.
c Is the foreman of department B likely to be held accountable for the labor rate variance? Explain your answer.

E26-4 Gateway Manufacturing was in the midst of completing an order for a valued customer when a flu epidemic occurred. To finish the order on time, the production supervisor substituted skilled tool and die personnel on a job normally performed by apprentices. The job was completed in 320 hours, which was 85 hours less than the standard time allowed. The tool and die personnel earn $9.50 per hour; apprentices normally earn $6.00 per hour.

a Compute the direct labor rate and efficiency variances for this job.
b Was the production supervisor's substitution decision correct? Explain your answer.

E26-5 The Marr Manufacturing Company uses a standard cost system. The firm's accountant has provided you with certain variances along with his analysis of the variances. In each case state if you agree or disagree with the analysis. Provide a brief explanation of your answer.

Case A

Facts	Direct materials cost for 2,200 finished units of production	actual, $36,000; standard, $35,640
	Direct materials standard	3 pounds per finished unit at $5.40 per pound
	Direct materials purchased and consumed during the period	8,000 pounds

Analysis Overall we did an excellent job in controlling materials cost. The $360 variance ($36,000 – $35,640) is slightly more than 1% of standard cost, a small amount given the nature of our operation.

Case B

Facts

Materials price variance	*$ 3,400F*
Materials quantity variance	*5,100U*
Labor rate variance	*6,700F*
Labor efficiency variance	*10,800U*
Selected overhead spending variances	
Supervision	*4,500U*
Employee training	*2,300U*
Total	*$12,600U*

Analysis It appears that our poor performance this period was caused solely by the acquisition of low-grade materials from Pearl Supply. The $3,400 saved by the purchasing department came back to haunt us in other areas.

E26-6 The following information was extracted from the accounting records of Bayer and Associates.

Units manufactured during the period	20,000
Standard labor time per finished unit	$\frac{1}{2}$ hour
Standard material consumption per finished unit	$1\frac{1}{2}$ pounds
Actual direct labor cost incurred	$45,700
Direct labor efficiency variance	$4,050U
Total direct labor variance	$5,200U
Standard material cost per pound	$6
Direct materials price variance	$2,960U
Direct materials quantity variance	$2,400F

Determine the following:

a Direct labor rate variance.

b Standard direct labor rate per hour.

c Direct labor hours worked during the period.

d Pounds of direct materials purchased and consumed during the period. Assume all materials acquired were used in current operations.

e Actual price paid per pound of direct materials.

E26-7 Shattuck Manufacturing applies overhead to products on the basis of direct labor hours. At the beginning of the current year, the firm's accountant made the following estimates for the forthcoming period.

Estimated variable overhead	$150,000
Estimated fixed overhead	$87,500
Estimated direct labor hours	25,000 hours

It is now twelve months later. Actual total overhead incurred in the manufacture of 4,900 units amounted to $254,000. Actual labor hours totaled 25,600. Assuming a direct labor standard of five hours per finished unit, calculate the following:

a Variable overhead efficiency variance
b Fixed overhead volume variance
c Overhead spending variance

E26-8 Midland Industries had the following selected variances for the period just ended.

Materials price variance	$10,600F
Materials quantity variance	25,800U
Labor rate variance	8,100F
Labor efficiency variance	35,400U
Variable overhead efficiency variance	15,600U
Fixed overhead volume variance	12,700U

The company applies overhead on the basis of direct labor hours.

a Cite several causes of each of the variances listed above.
b Notice that Midland's labor efficiency variance and variable overhead efficiency variance were both unfavorable. Is it possible that in a subsequent period one of these variances could be favorable while the other is unfavorable? Explain.
c What factors should management consider in deciding whether to investigate these variances and take corrective action?

E26-9 Hutchins, Inc., has established the following standards for direct materials and direct labor for product no. 781:

Direct materials: 4 pounds @ $2.50 per pound	$10.00
Direct labor: 2 hours @ $8.00 per hour	16.00

The information below pertains to a recent month.

1 Purchases of direct materials amounted to 9,000 pounds at a total cost of $23,850.
2 Nine thousand pounds of direct materials were consumed in operations to manufacture 2,300 finished units.
3 Direct labor charges totaled 4,750 hours at $7.90 per hour.

a Compute the materials price and quantity variances.
b Determine the labor rate and efficiency variances.
c Prepare journal entries to record the transactions relating to direct materials and direct labor.

PROBLEMS

P26-1 ***Basic flexible budgeting***
Centron, Inc., has the following budgeted production costs.

Direct materials	$0.40 per unit
Direct labor	$1.80 per unit
Variable factory overhead	$2.20 per unit
Fixed factory overhead:	
Supervision	$24,000
Maintenance	18,000
Other	12,000

The company normally manufactures between 20,000 and 25,000 units each quarter. Should output exceed 25,000 units, maintenance and other fixed costs are expected to increase by $6,000 and $4,500, respectively.

During the quarter ended March 31, 1984, Centron produced 25,500 units and incurred the following costs:

Direct materials	*$ 10,710*
Direct labor	*47,175*
Variable factory overhead	*51,940*
Fixed factory overhead	
Supervision	*24,500*
Maintenance	*23,700*
Other	*16,800*
Total production costs	*$174,825*

INSTRUCTIONS

a Prepare a flexible budget for 20,000, 22,500, and 25,000 units of activity.

b Was Centron's experience in the quarter cited better or worse than anticipated? Explain your answer and show appropriate computations.

c Explain the benefit of using flexible budgets (as opposed to static budgets) when measuring performance.

P26-2 ***Flexible budgeting and performance appraisal***

Phoenix Company has just completed an in-depth study of overhead costs. The firm normally operates between 8,000 and 10,000 labor hours each month. Budgeted costs for this range of activity are presented below.

Maintenance	$22,000 plus $0.20 per direct labor hour
Supplies	$0.60 per direct labor hour
Power	$7,000 plus $0.15 per direct labor hour
Depreciation	$15,500
Overtime	$0.80 for each direct labor hour in excess of 9,500 direct labor hours per month
Indirect labor	$12,000 plus $1.20 per direct labor hour

During November Phoenix had planned to operate at 9,700 direct labor hours. Actual activity, however, amounted to only 9,200 hours at the following costs:

Maintenance	$25,570
Supplies	5,700
Power	8,440
Depreciation	15,500
Overtime	110
Indirect labor	23,500

All fixed cost elements remained as budgeted except for maintenance, which increased by $1,800.

INSTRUCTIONS

a Prepare a performance report for November that compares actual activity against a static budget. The report should list all variable costs and then all fixed costs. Split mixed costs into their variable and fixed components.

b Repeat part (a), using a flexible budgeting approach.

c The president of Phoenix prefers the static budgeting approach, "because there's no way we can predict our actual activity in advance. Furthermore, once a budget is set, it should remain in force until the month is past." Explain (1) the problems associated with using a static budget and (2) why a precise estimate of actual activity in advance is unnecessary with flexible budgets.

P26-3 ***Setting standards***

Starr Manufacturing Corporation is contemplating the implementation of a standard costing system. The following information pertains to one of the company's products, HD-24.

Direct materials used *		*$1,020,000*
Direct labor†		*348,000*
Other traceable variable costs		
Blending costs	*$148,000*	
Packaging materials	*40,700*	
Miscellaneous	*74,000*	*262,700*
Total variable costs		*$1,630,700*

* *240,000 gallons at $4.25 per gallon.*
† *58,000 hours at $6.00 per hour.*

These costs were incurred in the production of 185,000 gallons of HD-24, which are packaged 4 gallons to a case. Starr has been experiencing problems with the quality of materials used and plans to change suppliers in the forthcoming period. The price per gallon of direct materials is expected to rise to $4.40. Starr anticipates HD-24 output will total 80% of the direct materials used in production; the remainder is lost through evaporation.

Management estimates that abnormal production problems in the prior period led to the incurrence of an additional 2,500 labor hours. These problems have subsequently been corrected. Other variable costs are expected to remain stable, with the exception of packaging materials. Packaging cost is expected to increase by $0.04 per gallon.

INSTRUCTIONS

a By analyzing the data presented, compute an attainable standard variable cost for a case of HD-24.

b Compare and contrast ideal and attainable standards. What benefits normally result from the use of attainable standards?

c Discuss several problems that may be encountered by relying too heavily on past experience when setting standards.

P26-4 ***Levels of standards***

The Alton Company is going to expand its punch press department and is about to purchase three new punch presses from Equipment Manufacturers, Inc. Equipment Manufacturers' engineers report that their mechanical studies indicate that for Alton's intended use the output rate for one press should be 1,000 pieces per hour. Alton has very similar presses now in operation. At the present time production from these presses averages 600 pieces per hour.

A study of Alton's experience shows the average is derived from the following individual outputs:

Worker	Daily Output per Hour
L. Jones	750
J. Green	750
R. Smith	600
H. Brown	500
R. Alters	550
G. Hoag	450
Total	3,600
Average	600

Alton's management plans to institute a standard cost accounting system in the near future. The company's engineers are supporting a standard based on 1,000 pieces per hour, the accounting department is arguing for 750 pieces per hour, and the department foreman is arguing for 600 pieces per hour.

INSTRUCTIONS

a What arguments would each proponent be likely to use to support his or her case?

b Which alternative best reconciles the needs of cost control and the motivation of improved performance? Explain your answer.

(CMA adapted.)

P26-5 ***Straightforward variance analysis***

Streetman Enterprises uses a standard costing system. The standard cost sheet for product no. 435 is shown below.

Direct materials: 3 units @ $4.50	*$13.50*
Direct labor: 5 hours @ $6.00	*30.00*
Variable factory overhead: 5 hours @ $4.00	*20.00*
Fixed factory overhead: 5 hours @ $3.00	*15.00*
Total standard cost per unit	*$78.50*

The following information pertains to activity for March.

1 Direct materials acquired during the month amounted to 7,050 units at $4.40 per unit. All materials were consumed in operations.

2 Streetman incurred an average wage rate of $6.20 for 11,700 hours of activity.

3 Total overhead incurred amounted to $82,900. Budgeted fixed overhead totals $450,000 and is spread evenly throughout the year.

4 Actual production amounted to 2,400 completed units.

INSTRUCTIONS

a Compute Streetman's direct materials variances.

b Compute Streetman's direct labor variances.
c Compute Streetman's variances for factory overhead.

P26-6 ***Variance analysis and performance evaluation***

Baltimore Mills, a large manufacturer of textiles, uses a standard costing system to assist in the control of operations. The president has just received a performance report presenting the details of activity for a recent month. A portion of that report is reproduced below.

Total standard variable cost		*$130,200*
Less: Favorable materials variance	*$300*	
Favorable labor variance	*600*	
Favorable variable overhead variance	*100*	*1,000*
Total actual variable cost incurred		*$129,200*

The president is extremely satisfied with the figures. He notes: "It looks like we've finally gotten operations under control. Apparently the change to a new supplier did the trick. In addition, I think the new supervisor is working out well. I've noticed a much happier and more efficient work force on my daily tours through the plant."

Assume the following information has come to your attention.

1 Standard variable costs per unit of finished product:

Direct materials: 2.5 pounds @ $2.00	*$ 5.00*
Direct labor: 3.2 hours @ $7.00	*22.40*
Variable overhead: 3.2 hours @ $5.00	*16.00*
Total standard variable cost per unit	*$43.40*

2 Direct materials purchased and consumed amounted to 8,400 pounds at $1.75 per pound.
3 Direct labor incurred in the manufacture of 3,000 completed units totaled 11,100 hours at $6.00 per hour.
4 Variable factory overhead incurred amounted to $47,900.

INSTRUCTIONS

a Criticize the format and content of the performance report as presently constructed.
b Prepare a complete variance analysis for direct materials, direct labor, and variable overhead. *Note:* Compute the overhead spending variance with regard to variable overhead only.
c Explain the results of your findings to the president. Are things going as smoothly as the president believes? Discuss.

P26-7 ***Variance analysis: Working backward***

Green Power Tools has a single manufacturing department that applies factory overhead on the basis of direct labor hours. Selected departmental information follows.

Cost of materials purchased and consumed	?
Materials standard per finished unit	2 pounds
Standard material cost per pound	$6
Materials price variance	$2,000F
Materials quantity variance	$9,000U

Actual labor hours worked	?
Labor standard per finished unit	3 hours
Standard labor rate per hour	$5
Labor rate variance	$4,000F
Labor efficiency variance	$5,000U
Total actual overhead incurred	?
Variable overhead application rate	$3 per hour
Fixed overhead application rate	$4 per hour
Budgeted fixed overhead	?
Variable overhead efficiency variance	?
Fixed overhead volume variance	$7,000U
Overhead spending variance	$3,000F
Number of units manufactured	7,000

INSTRUCTIONS

Determine each of the unknowns. *Hint:* It is helpful to solve separate models simultaneously for materials, labor, and overhead by filling in the given information.

P26-8 ***Impact of events on variances***

The following independent items relate to Humphrey Industries.

a The local power company raised its rates by 5%.

b Severe winter weather caused Humphrey to close its manufacturing plant for five days.

c The firm hired ten part-time workers at premium wages to meet an unexpected increase in production levels.

d The purchasing department acquired a higher-grade material at an increased price. The material produced less waste and was more easily formed and shaped by Humphrey's workers.

e Humphrey had to absorb unexpected air freight costs on a rush order of direct materials.

f A slowdown occurred on the production line because of low morale among the workers.

INSTRUCTIONS

Determine the impact of each of these items on the following variances. Consider variance interrelationships when formulating your answer. If a revision of standards is required, assume no revision occurs until the next accounting period. Label each variance as F (favorable), U (unfavorable), or NI (no impact).

	Direct Materials		*Direct Labor*	
	Price	*Quantity*	*Rate*	*Efficiency*
a				
b				
c				
d				
e				
f				

P26-9 ***Variance analysis with journal entries***

Forrester Manufacturing has integrated standard costs and variance reporting into its formal accounting system. The following information is available.

Standard cost per finished unit:

Direct materials: 1 pound @ $2.80	*$ 2.80*
Direct labor: $\frac{1}{2}$ hour @ $11.00	*5.50*
*Variable overhead**	*3.00*
*Fixed overhead**	*1.50*
Total	*$12.80*

**Applied on the basis of direct labor hours.*

Purchases of direct materials	12,000 pounds at $3.00 per pound
Direct labor incurred	5,800 hours at a cost of $62,640

Total overhead incurred amounted to $31,400; overhead variances were as follows:

Spending variance	$3,200U
Variable overhead efficiency variance	600F
Fixed overhead volume variance	1,800U

Actual production amounted to 12,000 finished units. Direct materials consumption conformed to original predictions.

INSTRUCTIONS

a Determine Forrester's variances for direct materials.

b Determine Forrester's variances for direct labor.

c Prepare journal entries to record the following:
(1) The purchase of direct materials
(2) The issuance of direct materials to production
(3) The incurrence of direct labor
(4) The incurrence of factory overhead
(5) The application of factory overhead to production

P26-10 ***Basic flexible budgeting (alternate to P26-1)***

Westgate, Inc., has the following budgeted production costs.

Direct materials	$0.65 per unit
Direct labor	$2.20 per unit
Variable factory overhead	$3.30 per unit
Fixed factory overhead:	
Supervision	$20,000
Maintenance	14,000
Other	9,000

The company normally manufactures between 9,000 and 11,000 units each quarter. Should output exceed 11,000 units, maintenance and other fixed costs are expected to increase by $4,000 and $2,500, respectively.

During the quarter ended June 30, 1984, Westgate produced 11,400 units and incurred the following costs:

Direct materials	$ 7,752
Direct labor	25,650
Variable factory overhead	37,962
Fixed factory overhead	
Supervision	19,800
Maintenance	17,500
Other	12,000
Total production costs	$120,664

INSTRUCTIONS

a Prepare a flexible budget for 9,000, 10,000, and 11,000 units of activity.

b Was Westgate's experience in the quarter cited better or worse than anticipated? Explain your answer and show appropriate computations.

c Explain the flexibility associated with a flexible budget.

P26-11 ***Flexible budgeting and performance appraisal* (alternate to P26-2)**

Royal Company has just completed an in-depth study of overhead costs. The firm normally operates between 20,000 and 22,000 labor hours each month. Budgeted costs for this range of activity are presented below.

Maintenance	$40,000 plus $0.30 per direct labor hour
Supplies	$0.50 per direct labor hour
Power	$9,000 plus $0.18 per direct labor hour
Depreciation	$20,800
Overtime	$0.70 for each direct labor hour in excess of 21,500 direct labor hours per month
Indirect labor	$18,000 plus $1.00 per direct labor hour

During March Royal had planned to operate at 21,800 direct labor hours. Actual activity, however, amounted to only 21,300 hours at the following costs:

Maintenance	$49,050
Supplies	10,800
Power	12,900
Depreciation	20,800
Overtime	150
Indirect labor	39,600

All fixed cost elements remained as budgeted except for maintenance, which increased by $2,600.

INSTRUCTIONS

a Prepare a performance report for March that compares actual activity against a static budget. The report should list all variable costs and then all fixed costs. Split mixed costs into their variable and fixed components.

b Repeat part (a), using a flexible budgeting approach.

c Given the nature of the flexible budget, why is an in-depth study of cost behavior necessary prior to the budget's preparation?

P26-12 ***Straightforward variance analysis* (alternate to P26-5)**

Triton Enterprises uses a standard costing system. The standard cost sheet for product no. 821 is shown on page 1054.

Direct materials: 2 units @ $2.80	***$ 5.60***
Direct labor: 4 hours @ $7.00	***28.00***
Variable factory overhead: 4 hours @ $5.00	***20.00***
Fixed factory overhead: 4 hours @ $3.50	***14.00***
Total standard cost per unit	***$67.60***

The following information pertains to activity for June.

1 Direct materials acquired during the month amounted to 8,650 units at $2.76 per unit. All materials were consumed in operations.
2 Triton incurred an average wage rate of $7.10 for 16,450 hours of activity.
3 Total overhead incurred amounted to $148,700. Budgeted fixed overhead totals $732,000 and is spread evenly throughout the year.
4 Actual production amounted to 4,200 completed units.

INSTRUCTIONS

a Compute Triton's direct materials variances.
b Compute Triton's direct labor variances.
c Compute Triton's variances for factory overhead.

P26-13 ***Variance analysis: Working backward (alternate to P26-7)***

Vermont, Inc., has a single manufacturing department that applies factory overhead on the basis of direct labor hours. Selected departmental information follows.

Cost of materials purchased and consumed	$46,000
Materials standard per finished unit	4 pounds
Standard material cost per pound	?
Materials price variance	$5,000U
Materials quantity variance	$3,000F
Actual labor hours worked	6,000 hours
Labor standard per finished unit	$1\frac{1}{2}$ hours
Standard labor rate per hour	$6
Labor rate variance	$4,000U
Labor efficiency variance	?
Total actual overhead incurred	$80,500
Variable overhead application rate	?
Fixed overhead application rate	$8 per hour
Budgeted fixed overhead	$64,000
Variable overhead efficiency variance	$4,500F
Fixed overhead volume variance	?
Overhead spending variance	?
Number of units manufactured	5,000

INSTRUCTIONS

Determine each of the unknowns. *Hint:* It is helpful to solve separate models simultaneously for materials, labor, and overhead by filling in the given information.

P26-14 ***Impact of events on variances (alternate to P26-8)***

The following independent items relate to Nugent Industries.

a The company scheduled an extra day of operation (at regular wage rates) to meet increased demand.

b A machine malfunction caused higher-than-normal spoilage rates and required increased attention by the machine operator.
c The purchasing department acquired certain materials from a bankrupt supplier; the materials resulted in above-normal evaporation rates.
d The firm missed $3,000 of cash discounts caused by an unusually tight cash position.
e Several disgruntled workers caused a slowdown in production.
f Management awarded a $2,000 bonus to the foreman of the mixing department.

INSTRUCTIONS

Determine the impact of each of these items on the following variances. Consider variance interrelationships when formulating your answer. If a revision of standards is required, assume no revision occurs until the next accounting period. Label each variance as F (favorable), U (unfavorable), or NI (no impact).

	Direct Materials		Direct Labor	
	Price	Quantity	Rate	Efficiency
a				
b				
c				
d				
e				
f				

CASE 26
FLY HIGH, INC.

Fly High, Inc., produces a line of kites that are very popular with children. The manufacturing process consists of three phases: printing, cutting, and packaging. Large sheets of lightweight plastic are first printed with cartoon characters and then cut. In another department plastic rods are cut and notched to form the crosspieces for the kites. Finally, the sheets and crosspieces are packaged in a clear plastic container.

Bert Strong, the production manager, has been beset with complaints from the front office about declining gross profit. Strong countered that "costs are going up, and I can't help that." Front office investigation revealed that prices paid for direct materials and labor do not account for much of the drop in gross profit. Strong has now challenged the front office to prove that the gross profit decline is the result of production inefficiency. Because you are the assistant to the controller, you have been asked to participate in the investigation. The following information has come to your attention.

The printing operation should take five minutes per dozen kites, including setup and inspection.

The sheet-cutting operation should take ten minutes per dozen kites, including setup and inspection.
The rod-cutting operation should take ten minutes per dozen kites, including setup and inspection.
The packaging operation should take five minutes per dozen kites.
Printing, cutting, and packaging employees are normally paid $6.00 per hour.
Each plastic sheet normally costs $3.60 and can be cut into one dozen kites.
Six 12-foot plastic rods usually cost $6.00 and can be cut into 24 cross-pieces, adequate for one dozen kites.
The clear plastic packaging material costs $1.20 per dozen kites.

At the end of the month you determine that 12,000 kites have been produced. Direct labor payroll amounted to $3,900 for the 600 hours worked. Eleven hundred plastic sheets were purchased at $4.00 each; all were used. In addition, 8,000 plastic rods were purchased for $8,500; only 6,800 rods were used.

INSTRUCTIONS

a Develop the standard cost per dozen kites for materials and labor.

b Determine variances for direct materials (plastic sheets and rods only) and direct labor. Fly High computes price variances on the basis of the quantity of materials purchased.

c Explain the likely causes of the variances, including identification of those variances for which Strong is probably responsible. If he is not responsible, suggest where the responsibility does lie.

27 DECISION MAKING

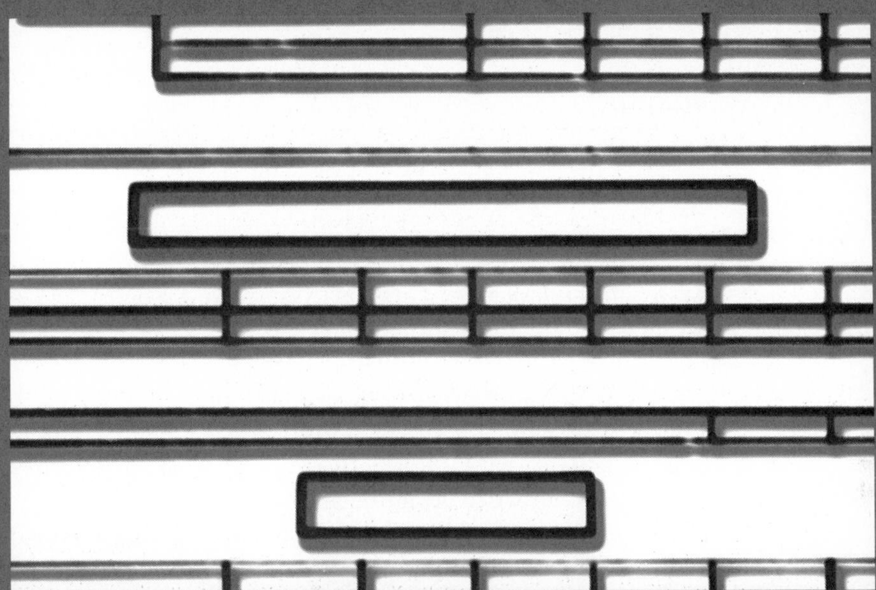

LEARNING OBJECTIVES

After reading this chapter you should:

1. *Understand the effect of relevant costs and quantitative and qualitative factors in the decision-making process.*
2. *Understand why sunk costs are ignored in the decision process.*
3. *Understand the meaning of opportunity costs.*
4. *Know how to make equipment replacement, make or buy, special order, and addition and deletion decisions.*
5. *Know why the contribution margin must be analyzed in terms of capacity constraints.*
6. *Understand the meaning of loss leaders and the related benefits of use.*
7. *Be able to differentiate between certainty and risk environments.*
8. *Know how to use probabilities in decision making, including the concepts of expected value and the expected value of perfect information.*
9. *Be familiar with decision-making constraints.*

CHAPTER 27

Business managers make decisions every day that are critical to the short- and long-term profitability and solvency of the enterprise. As evidence, examine the following recent decisions of several well-known corporations.

Corporation	Decision
Chrysler Corporation	To institute a new truck marketing program
Denny's Restaurants	To complete a new restaurant design and a new policy on site selection
Burroughs Corporation	To acquire the Memorex Corporation
American Greetings	To begin to advertise on nationwide television
Marriott Corporation	To sell an ice cream restaurant subsidiary
Southland Corporation (7-Eleven Stores)	To open 376 new stores and close 269 old stores

Future events and conditions will determine whether these decisions were wise or whether other alternatives would have been preferable.

Accountants play a significant role in decision making. Accounting information is continually generated to assist management in the problem-solving process and to monitor the impact of managerial actions. Furthermore, in many firms the accountant actually assumes the role of a decision maker and selects from among alternative courses of action. The extent of this role is dependent on the overall philosophy of top management and the accountant's position in the organizational hierarchy.

This chapter is the first of a two-chapter sequence that explores the fundamentals of decision making. Although much of our presentation will focus on the decision process from a business or firm point of view, many of the concepts illustrated have considerable relevance to individuals as well. Students, employees, and family members are continuously confronted with financial problems or issues that need attention. Knowing how to correctly evaluate alternatives is therefore of utmost importance in any attempts made to improve financial condition and well-being.

GENERAL APPROACH TO DECISION MAKING

Over time, management is faced with a number of different decisions. Certain decisions, such as the selection of a supplier for raw materials, are fairly routine; others occur with less regularity and are relatively complex (e.g., the addition or deletion of a product line). A number of decisions affect only current operations, while others have a significant impact on long-run profitability. No matter what the decision is, cost is bound to be a major factor. Simply stated, the costs involved with one course of action must be compared with those of alternative strategies and policies.

Because of the variety inherent in the decision process, a general approach to decision making is extremely useful. The general approach first involves identifying future costs that are associated with the decision at hand. To illustrate, assume management is contemplating whether to replace an existing machine with a newer, more efficient model. Expected future costs must be evaluated since they are the only ones that will be experienced as a result of making the decision. Past historical costs may serve as a basis for predicting what future costs will be, but *old costs are just memories and are not considered when selecting among alternatives.*

The next step in the general approach is to focus on **relevant costs,** that is, future costs that differ between alternatives. In the machine replacement decision, for example, any differences in maintenance costs between the old machine and the new machine are relevant and must be considered. Future costs that are expected to be identical for both machines can be ignored; they have no impact on the ultimate selection.

Full Project or Incremental Approach?

Relevant costs can be studied by using either a full project or an incremental approach. To illustrate the identification of relevant costs and these two approaches, we consider the following information. The Merchants Company must make a delivery 150 miles from its warehouse (300 miles for a round trip). Two trucks are available, A and B. Truck A gets 10 miles per gallon and consumes 1 quart of oil every 100 miles. Truck B gets 7.5 miles per gallon and uses 1 quart of oil every 150 miles. Other data are as follows:

Gasoline	$1.50 per gallon
Oil	$1.00 per quart
Driver's wage	$5.00 per hour
Trip time	8 hours
Road tolls	$10.00

The costs of operating the two trucks are shown below:

	Truck A	*Truck B*	*Difference*
Gasoline*	$45	$ 60	$15
Oil†	3	2	(1)
Driver pay (8 hours × $5)	40	40	—
Tolls	10	10	—
Total cost	$98	$112	$14

* *Truck A: [(300 miles ÷ 10 miles per gallon) × $1.50] = $45. Truck B: [(300 miles ÷ 7.5 miles per gallon) × $1.50] = $60.*
† *Truck A: [(300 miles ÷ 100 miles per quart) × $1] = $3. Truck B: [(300 miles ÷ 150 miles per quart) × $1] = $2.*

On the basis of the expected costs of delivery, the company should use truck A. By studying the difference column, observe that the driver's wage and the road tolls have no effect on the decision. Because these costs are the same for both alternatives, they can be ignored. Thus the proper decision approach would have been to focus solely on the costs of gasoline and oil. These costs are relevant since they will be incurred in the future and will differ between the trucks.

Using the **full project approach,** management would compare $48 with

SEEMINGLY GOOD DECISIONS OFTEN GO AWRY

Large corporations often possess unparalleled expertise and a wealth of information when it comes to decision making. Despite these attributes, even the big boys goof on occasion. Consider Braniff International, for example, the Dallas-based airline.

In the late 1970s the airline industry was in the midst of deregulation. To compete effectively with larger carriers, Braniff made the decision to expand—and to do so dramatically. It opened new routes across the Atlantic and the Pacific and inaugurated service to 16 new cities in the United States, an airline record. As the president of Braniff noted, "If this deregulation thing turns into a dogfight between the big and the small carriers, we want to be big enough to survive."

What looked good on paper rapidly turned into a nightmare. In the United States, for example, Braniff began flying many "dormant routes," or routes the Civil Aeronautics Board (CAB) had awarded to an airline that chose not to fly them. Says one securities analyst, "There's a reason all those routes were dormant—they were no damn good." In other cases Braniff invaded cities where other carriers were dominant and failed to pick up projected market shares. Other problems were encountered on the Atlantic and Pacific routes.

Further complicating the picture were heavy blows beyond Braniff's control. Fuel prices soared and the CAB opposed fare increases on foreign routes, making it impossible to recoup higher fuel costs there. And in the United States, traffic softened because of a recession. These factors caused huge losses for nearly all airlines. But Braniff, because of its rapid expansion, was hit harder than most. Essentially, as "an airline begins expanding with heavy costs for airplanes, crew training, new stations, and so forth, it's difficult to stop. It's like Cape [Canaveral]; once the launch begins, it's hard to abort."

The outcome of the expansion decision? Braniff was hit with losses that totaled well into the millions. In addition, the airline ran short of cash because it was unable to raise money by securities sales and was cut off from its line of credit at the bank. Braniff slashed its capacity and dropped certain routes. Additionally, management sold a number of aircraft. As one analyst observed, "In terms of financial soundness, Braniff has gone from one of the best to one of the worst airlines, and it will take them a long time to recover." As many of you may know, the analyst's observation was correct. On May 12, 1982, Braniff grounded its fleet and suspended all operations. One day later the firm filed for bankruptcy in a federal court in Fort Worth, Texas.

SOURCE Adapted from "Braniff's Cash Shortage Is Becoming Desperate, Leaving Lasting Scars," The Wall Street Journal, *July 30, 1980, pp. 1, 12. Reprinted by permission of* The Wall Street Journal, *© Dow Jones & Company, Inc., 1980. All rights reserved.*

$62 (gasoline + oil cost) to reach its decision. Specifically, the total relevant costs associated with each alternative are evaluated. With the **incremental approach** only the net differences are considered. Management would therefore focus its attention on the $14 variation among the relevant costs.[1]

While the incremental approach is often used in practice, it has two serious drawbacks. First, the incremental approach is cumbersome when more than two alternatives are being evaluated. Second, the act of netting often leads to mathematical errors. For these reasons the full project approach will be used in the remainder of this chapter.

Qualitative Factors

In addition to quantitative considerations, various qualitative factors must be addressed in the decision-making process. **Qualitative factors** are those whose evaluation in terms of dollars is impossible, or at best, difficult. Returning to our previous example, the manager of Merchants may decide to send truck B on the delivery because the truck is brand new and customer impressions are important. Or the manager may feel that the tires on truck A are unsafe for such a long delivery, and he does not want the driver subjected to any needless danger. A third qualitative factor may be air conditioning. Truck A may not be air-conditioned, and although its operating costs are less, Merchants may select truck B, which is air-conditioned. If the delivery is made on a hot summer day, the firm may feel that $14 is a small price to pay for improved employee efficiency and morale.

Most business decisions are based solely on quantitative factors. As you can see, however, qualitative considerations are important and should not be disregarded. Frequently, when the quantitative difference between alternatives is small, qualitative factors are the deciding issue.

A Summary of the Decision-Making Approach

The general approach to decision making can be summarized as follows:

1 Examine all future costs associated with each alternative. Although our example has stressed future costs, future revenues, if any, must also be considered.
2 Disregard those items that are the same among the alternatives.
3 Identify and consider the qualitative factors.
4 Make a decision on the basis of both the quantitative *and* the qualitative analysis.

EQUIPMENT REPLACEMENT AND SUNK COSTS

Observe that the thrust of the general approach is a focus on the future. As we noted earlier, past costs should be ignored in the decision process. To illustrate why, suppose that you purchased a used car for $4,000. After several months of operation you find that the car's gas consumption is so great that you have to change your eating habits and life-style. Thus you

[1]Costs that differ among alternatives are sometimes called **differential costs.**

decide to sell the car and buy a smaller model. Assume the only offer you receive is for $3,000. If you reject the offer solely because a $1,000 loss will be incurred, your analysis is incorrect. The cost of the existing automobile is an irrelevant consideration. Keeping the car for a few more years may help your pride but it does not alter the original acquisition decision. The amount paid for the car is a past cost and cannot be changed by future actions.

In the context of decision making, past costs that have already been incurred are termed **sunk costs.** Just as the cost of the car was sunk, so, too, is the book value of long-term assets. Remember that book value is an asset's cost less accumulated depreciation. To illustrate the role of book value in the decision process, we will focus on a routine business decision: equipment replacement.

Assume that Midwest Leisure, which offers river cruises in Ohio, is considering the replacement of an old cruise boat. A firm in Missouri has a used boat for sale that will enable Midwest to carry more passengers. The following information has been gathered.

Existing Boat	
Original cost	$160,000
Current book value	$50,000
Remaining service life	5 years
Current disposal value	$20,000
Residual value at the end of service life	—
Annual passenger revenue	$75,000
Annual variable operating costs	$40,000

Proposed Acquisition	
Cost to Midwest Leisure	$180,000
Estimated service life	5 years
Residual value in 5 years	—
Annual passenger revenue	$125,000
Annual variable operating costs	$55,000

Midwest's replacement analysis appears below. The analysis focuses on determining the total net income generated by each alternative over the next 5 years.

	Keep Existing Boat	***Purchase Used Boat***
Passenger revenue (annual × 5)	*$375,000*	*$625,000*
Variable operating costs (annual × 5)	*(200,000)*	*(275,000)*
Depreciation on existing boat	*(50,000)*	
Write-off of existing boat		
Book value		*(50,000)**
Current disposal value		*20,000**
Depreciation on used boat		*(180,000)*
Total net income over 5 years	*$125,000*	*$140,000*

$15,000 difference

** These two items would be reported as a loss of $30,000 if a formal income statement was prepared: $50,000 book value less $20,000 received from disposal.*

The results indicate that Midwest would be better off by $15,000 if the used boat was purchased. Notice that the increase in variable costs of $75,000 is more than offset by a $250,000 rise in passenger revenue ($625,000 – $375,000). The book value of the existing boat ($50,000) is a sunk cost and could have been ignored without altering the result. It is included for illustrative purposes to show that in addition to being a past cost, the book value is common to both alternatives.

To explain, if the present boat is retained, its book value will be written off through depreciation over the next 5 years, thus reducing profits by $10,000 per year. If the used boat is purchased, however, the book value will be written off in the year of acquisition. The treatments are identical; only the timing is different. Observe that under the purchase alternative, the $50,000 write-off is partially offset by the $20,000 received from disposal of the old boat, thereby producing a $30,000 loss. Note, however, that a vital component of the loss computation is sunk and should be disregarded. Finally, the $180,000 of depreciation is relevant for this decision because it represents a future cost that can be avoided by not acquiring the cruise equipment from the Missouri firm.

Motivational Factors

While the replacement analysis favors acquisition of the used boat, many managers may be reluctant to select this alternative. Yearly performance evaluations are often based on accrual accounting procedures and the "bottom line." Thus transfers, promotions, raises in salary, bonuses, and other fringe benefits are routinely tied to short-term profitability. Why would managers disregard the analysis when it shows total company profits will increase? The increased net income of $15,000 will occur over a five-year period; the $30,000 loss on disposal, however, penalizes the current year. Some managers will therefore attempt to avoid the loss for fear of looking bad.

As a result, we can now see how emphasis on short-term profitability may conflict with the objective of maximizing long-run income for a business. Unfortunately, only a few businesses have developed procedures whereby the outcomes of the decision process and the methods used to evaluate personnel are reconciled. Reconciliation achieves goal congruence between these two important business functions.

A further motivation problem in replacement decisions is that change involves uncertainty. Many unknowns are present with untried alternatives. Thus a number of managers would be content with the profitability generated by the existing boat. With the present situation jobs are secure. The chance that the acquisition will fail to meet expectations is one of the many qualitative factors that must be considered in the evaluation and selection process.

MAKE OR BUY AND OPPORTUNITY COSTS

Manufacturing firms often purchase needed parts for their operations from outside suppliers. For example, Ford and McDonnell Douglas contract other companies to make many of the components used in their cars and planes. Even McDonald's purchases its hamburger meat from outsiders. Interestingly, many of the firms that rely on outside sources of supply have the technical abilities to produce the needed parts and materials themselves. Apparently, an analysis has deemed the external purchase preferable.

The choice to produce internally or to rely on external suppliers is commonly known as a *make or buy* decision. To illustrate the proper approach to follow in this decision area, assume that Crane Company, a manufacturer of snowmobiles, is now producing all of its own motors. As shown in the following analysis, the motors cost $75 each, based on an output of 10,000 motors per year.

	10,000 Motors	Per Motor
Direct materials	$180,000	$18
Direct labor	390,000	39
Variable factory overhead	100,000	10
Fixed factory overhead*	80,000	8
Total cost	$750,000	$75

*Allocated on the basis of capacity used.

Crane has solicited an offer from an external supplier to provide 10,000 motors at a set price of $72 per motor. To determine whether the motors should be manufactured internally or purchased externally, management must isolate the relevant costs. Future costs that differ between the make and buy alternatives must be studied; sunk costs, on the other hand, should be ignored.

In reviewing the previous information, we see that motor production was charged with $670,000 of variable costs, specifically, direct materials, direct labor, and variable factory overhead. Being variable, these costs will be eliminated if the motors are purchased externally. Consequently, the variable costs are relevant in analyzing the make and buy alternatives. Turning to the fixed costs, Crane has allocated $80,000 of fixed factory overhead to motor production. Many of these costs are common to all operations and, being fixed, will remain unchanged even if the company decides in favor of an external supplier. Fixed overhead that does not differ among the alternatives can be ignored.

Frequently, when operations undergo a significant change, total fixed costs do not remain static. If production is discontinued, for example, it is conceivable that a production supervisor would be dismissed. Naturally, any future fixed costs that change should be included in the analysis.

Given the foregoing, the proper decision approach is to compare the relevant costs of manufacturing with the cost of purchasing. If the manufacturing costs are lower than the outside purchase price, there is a financial advantage in continuing to make the motors. In Crane's case assume fixed costs can be reduced by $20,000 if production is discontinued. The following analysis indicates that Crane should reject the supplier's offer, because there is a $30,000 advantage in favor of manufacturing internally.

	10,000 Motors		Per Motor	
	Make	Buy	Make	Buy
Purchase		$720,000		$72
Direct materials	$180,000		$18	
Direct labor	390,000		39	
Variable factory overhead	100,000		10	
Avoidable fixed factory overhead	20,000		2	
Total cost	$690,000	$720,000	$69	$72

$30,000 difference

The analysis is straightforward with the possible exception of the avoidable fixed overhead. Realize that Crane will incur $80,000 of fixed overhead if the motors are produced internally and $60,000 of fixed overhead if they are purchased from suppliers. Thus $20,000 of fixed costs must be associated with the manufacturing option.

Looking at the evaluation from a different perspective, we see that there is a $20,000 savings in fixed costs if the purchase alternative is selected. Therefore the net cost of purchasing is $700,000 ($720,000 – $20,000). The cost of production would now consist strictly of variable costs and total $670,000. Notice that the $30,000 difference in favor of production is still maintained ($700,000 – $670,000 = $30,000).

Qualitative Considerations

Given the quantitative outcome, we must also explore the qualitative factors surrounding each alternative. In make or buy decisions, the decision to purchase externally means more dependence on suppliers and the attendant worry about product quality, strikes against suppliers, transportation strikes and hazards, personnel changes at suppliers' offices, and product discontinuance. To many companies the worry about quality control alone would dictate rejection of the purchase alternative.

Sometimes a business changes back and forth between internal manufacture and external purchase. The decision to "go internal" is often made when manufacturing capacity becomes available. Should a firm later need its facilities for other production opportunities, a switch is made in favor of an outside purchase. Unfortunately, conducting operations in this manner can significantly effect dealings with suppliers. Many business relationships take years to establish and, once broken, are difficult to restore. Manufacturers may find that when they need to purchase externally, few suppliers are willing to assist them. Word travels quickly among suppliers that a specific firm's purchase commitments are short term and sporadic. In such cases purchases must often be made at premium prices. To avoid this situation, many manufacturers will use external sources of supply even when temporary productive capacity is available.

Opportunity Cost

In performing a complete analysis of make versus buy, management must also evaluate alternative uses of manufacturing facilities. If, for example, a decision is made to purchase externally, the purchaser's manufacturing facilities may remain idle. On the other hand, the decision to "go external" frequently releases facilities for use in other production applications. In the Crane Company illustration, for instance, suppose the resources committed to producing motors could be redirected toward making a new line of golf carts. Naturally, any profit from the golf cart line would be lost if the firm continues its motor manufacturing operation.

The cost of a forgone alternative is termed **opportunity cost.** If the golf carts promise to produce a contribution margin of $75,000, the make or buy decision will assume the following form:

	Make	*Buy*
Cost of buying		*$720,000*
Cost of making	*$690,000*	
Forgone contribution on golf carts	*75,000*	
Total cost	*$765,000*	*$720,000*

$45,000 difference

The analysis now shows that the company would be better off by $45,000 if it purchased the motors externally.[2] Explained differently, Crane is willing to pay an additional $30,000 per year to acquire the motors in exchange for the $75,000 of contribution margin provided by the golf carts. This analysis, like the others, assumes that the appropriate qualitative considerations have been met.

Opportunity costs are not restricted to make or buy decisions. For example, if upon graduation you turn down a $25,000 job in favor of a position that pays $23,500, the opportunity cost is $25,000. Opportunity costs permeate decision making and must be considered if the proper alternative is to be selected. Despite their importance, opportunity costs are *not* recorded in the accounting records nor do they appear on financial statements. Financial accounting concentrates on reporting transactions and events that have occurred, not those that have been rejected.

SPECIAL ORDER PRICING

The pricing of special orders is another decision faced by many firms. While businesses prefer to sell all their products at the highest prices possible,

[2]The same analysis in another format would compute the net cost of buying as $645,000 ($720,000 purchase cost − $75,000 contribution from golf carts). The decision maker would then compare $645,000 with $690,000, still noting a $45,000 advantage in favor of the buy alternative.

economic conditions often dictate otherwise. Opportunities arise where special orders are considered at prices that are less than optimum. In these situations management must again focus on the differential (or incremental) costs and revenues involved.

To illustrate, assume that Smithfield Bicycle Company received an inquiry from a large national retailer to provide 20,000 R-18 racing bicycles at a price of $57 each. The bicycles will be marketed under the retailer's brand name. Although Smithfield has sufficient (idle) manufacturing capacity, management is reluctant to accept the order because the price is well below the company's normal selling price of $99. Smithfield's accountant has prepared the following cost analysis of the R-18 bicycle.

Materials	$32.80
Labor	14.50
Factory overhead*	24.70
Variable selling costs	10.00
Total	$82.00

*Eighty percent of the factory overhead represents fixed cost.

At first glance it appears that the retailer's offer should be rejected because of a failure to cover the total cost of $82. However, further investigation reveals that variable selling costs will not be incurred on the order. Furthermore, fixed costs will remain unchanged. Thus 80% of the factory overhead ($24.70 × 0.80 = $19.76) will be present even if the offer is refused and can be disregarded. The following analysis shows that Smithfield would benefit by doing business with the retailer.

Special selling price		$57.00
Less variable costs		
Materials	$32.80	
Labor	14.50	
Variable factory overhead ($24.70 − $19.76)	4.94	52.24
Contribution margin per bicycle		$ 4.76

Acceptance of the special order will generate a contribution margin of $4.76 per bicycle and a total increase in profitability of $95,200 (20,000 bicycles × $4.76). Although each unit produces a lower-than-normal contribution margin, Smithfield does have idle manufacturing capacity. Consequently, some extra business is really "icing on the cake."

Several qualitative considerations must be addressed in this decision. They include the following issues.

Will there be a decrease in sales of Smithfield's own brand of R-18 bicycle?

Are future orders from the retailer likely?

Will plant capacity devoted to the special order soon be needed for Smithfield's regular production of R-18 bicycles?

Contribution Margin in Relation to Capacity

In addition to the special order situation, managers frequently study contribution margins when facing capacity constraints. Consider a multiple-product firm, for example, that is operating at capacity. The firm must evaluate which orders to accept and which to reject, which products to promote and which to de-emphasize, and similar issues. The goal is to maximize contribution margin of the entire business, not just of one small facet. A common error in achieving this goal is that given the resources available, items with the highest contribution margin per sales dollar are considered to be the most important.

To illustrate, assume that Metroplex Airlines has an available jet that can serve either the Boston-to-New York or Los Angeles-to-San Francisco commuter markets. The jet seats 150 people and will be filled to capacity at all times. The following information has been gathered.

	Boston-New York	***Los Angeles-San Francisco***
Round trip ticket price	$80	$75
Variable cost per round trip	40	45
Contribution margin	$40	$30
Contribution margin ratio (contribution margin ÷ selling price)	50%	40%

It appears that the company should concentrate its activity on the East Coast. However, Metroplex must evaluate the total contribution from flight operations, not just the contribution margin per ticket. Thus flight times and system capacity are critical. In view of these facts, assume that six and ten round trips per day can be scheduled on the Boston and Los Angeles routes, respectively. Total contribution margin is therefore calculated as follows:

	Boston-New York	***Los Angeles-San Francisco***
Contribution margin per seat	$ 40	$ 30
Seating capacity	× 150	× 150
Contribution margin per round trip	$ 6,000	$ 4,500
Number of round trips	× 6	× 10
Total contribution margin per day	$36,000	$45,000

The analysis shows that the Los Angeles-to-San Francisco route provides the greatest contribution given Metroplex's capacity—the number of seats flown per day. It is apparent that a firm operating at capacity may be in error by emphasizing products or services that provide the greatest contribution margin per unit or per sales dollar. Stated simply, *contribution margin must be analyzed in terms of factors that limit its generation.*

Limiting factors assume different forms, depending on the type of business. In manufacturing companies, for example, the limiting factor is often the machine hours or labor hours available for production. In retailing operations it is floor space. Finally, in entertainment situations the limiting factor may be the number of seats in a theater or an arena.

ADDITION OR DELETION OF PRODUCTS OR DEPARTMENTS

Decisions to add or delete products, departments, and other major operating units (e.g., stores, plants, or divisions) are critical. Any errors that are made can normally be corrected only after suffering years of financial strife. In-depth analysis is therefore of utmost importance.

When a business unit is eliminated, the unit's sales are lost. At the same time there is a savings in variable costs. Thus if a positive contribution margin is being generated and the unit is discontinued, overall profitability will suffer. One additional factor must be considered, however, before the proper decision can be made: fixed costs. As we noted earlier in the chapter, a significant change in operations will often influence the fixed costs incurred by an enterprise. If a department or segment is eliminated, some fixed costs can normally be avoided. Those costs that can be avoided are really differential costs and, therefore, relevant to the decision.

To illustrate addition and deletion decisions, we will study the operations of Foodway, Inc., which owns a chain of supermarkets. Each Foodway store has four major departments: groceries, meat, produce, and hardware. Earnings data for store no. 175 during the past year are shown in Exhibit 27-1. On the basis of the reported $1,100,000 loss, management feels that total profitability will increase if the hardware department is dropped.

Exhibit 27-1

Foodway, Inc., store no. 175: Departmental income statements

	Groceries	Meat	Produce	Hardware	Total
Sales	$42,000,000	$14,000,000	$7,000,000	$ 7,000,000	$70,000,000
Less variable costs	33,000,000	9,000,000	4,000,000	6,000,000	52,000,000
Contribution margin	$ 9,000,000	$ 5,000,000	$3,000,000	$ 1,000,000	$18,000,000
Less fixed costs					
Salaries	$ 2,000,000	$ 2,500,000	$1,900,000	$ 1,100,000	$ 7,500,000
Utilities	400,000	50,000	100,000	150,000	700,000
Depreciation	100,000	50,000	100,000	50,000	300,000
General and administrative	4,800,000	1,600,000	800,000	800,000	8,000,000
Total fixed costs	$ 7,300,000	$ 4,200,000	$2,900,000	$ 2,100,000	$16,500,000
Net income (loss)	$ 1,700,000	$ 800,000	$ 100,000	$(1,100,000)	$ 1,500,000

Assuming that customers remain loyal and sales in the other departments are not affected by discontinuing hardware, Foodway's profit will immediately decline by $1,000,000 because of the loss in contribution margin. Notice, though, that the hardware department has four types of fixed costs: salaries, utilities, depreciation, and general and administrative. Specific information about these costs follows.

1 The salaries represent amounts paid to employees who work in the department. If hardware is dropped, employees earning 40% of the salary amounts will be shifted to other areas; all other personnel in hardware will be discharged.
2 Utilities expense is allocated to each department on the basis of square feet. If the hardware operation is closed, total utilities cost is not expected to change significantly.
3 Depreciation relates to the building and the fixtures used in each department. If hardware is eliminated, the department's display racks and equipment will be utilized by other segments of the firm. Again, total cost is not expected to change.
4 General and administrative costs represent the costs of functions common to all departments, including purchasing, accounting, and personnel. These costs, allocated to each department on the basis of sales, will be reduced by $120,000 if hardware is dropped.

With the preceding information the following analysis can be made.

Contribution margin lost if hardware is dropped		$1,000,000
Less avoidable costs		
Salaries ($1,100,000 × 60%)	$660,000	
General and administrative	120,000	780,000
Decrease in total company profit		$ 220,000

Although hardware's bottom line indicates a loss of $1,100,000, it is still beneficial to retain the department, because the contribution produced is greater than the avoidable costs.

If desired, the same conclusion could be reached by using an analysis of earnings with and without the hardware department.

	With Hardware	Without Hardware
Sales	$70,000,000	$63,000,000
Less variable costs	52,000,000	46,000,000
Contribution margin	$18,000,000	$17,000,000
Less fixed costs		
Salaries	$ 7,500,000	$ 6,840,000
Utilities	700,000	700,000
Depreciation	300,000	300,000
General and administrative	8,000,000	7,880,000
Total fixed costs	$16,500,000	$15,720,000
Net income (loss)	$ 1,500,000	$ 1,280,000

$220,000 difference

Fixed Cost Allocations

Decisions to add or drop a product or department are often made without recognizing the impact of fixed cost allocations. In the previous example, for instance, the hardware department showed a net loss from operations. Yet when analyzing the impact of eliminating the department, we found that total company profit decreased rather than increased. This seemingly paradoxical situation is caused in part by fixed costs, specifically, those costs that are still incurred even if the hardware operation is closed.

If the hardware department is erroneously dropped, the department's unavoidable fixed costs would have to be charged to groceries, meat, and produce. This procedure would probably make the produce department a loser despite its high contribution margin in relation to sales. Conceivably, the erroneous decision making could continue with a new decision to drop produce.

It is becoming evident that when fixed costs are allocated to business segments, the final net income figure does not always present a clear measure of the segment's performance. As illustrated in Chapter 25, a divisionalized income statement can be recast in the form of a *contribution income statement* to exclude arbitrary cost allocations and focus on measuring a segment's contribution to indirect costs. That is, only the variable and fixed costs directly traceable to a segment are subtracted from sales. Although the contribution statement was shown to possess distinct benefits when evaluating performance, this same tool can also be used in decision making. The omission of arbitrary fixed cost allocations in the decision process often results in better decisions and, as a consequence, improved profitability.

Loss Leaders

In many cases a department or product will generate a loss; yet management is satisfied with the result. Although this situation may seem strange, businesses often sell products or offer services at prices below cost. Such a practice frequently attracts customers or clients who purchase other items that have a normal markup. Managerial decisions to use such **loss leaders** are made by comparing differential revenues against differential costs.

To illustrate, assume that Key Drugs has a special $0.29 price for developing all photographic film brought into the store during the week of May 15. This promotion is expected to increase Key's sales by 7% because customers, once in the store, normally browse and buy other items. Weekly sales total $20,000, with a contribution margin of 30%. Key anticipates that 300 rolls of film will be developed; company costs for processing are $1.19 per roll. Although Key loses $0.90 ($0.29 – $1.19) on processing, the following figures show that the loss leader is beneficial.

	Without Loss Leader	With Loss Leader	
Sales	$20,000		$21,400
Cost of goods sold	14,000		14,980
Contribution margin (30%)	$ 6,000		$ 6,420
Incremental contribution margin from film processing			
Sales: 300 rolls × $0.29		$ 87	
Less variable costs: 300 rolls × $1.19		357	(270)
Contribution available to cover fixed costs	$ 6,000		$ 6,150

The promotion increases store profitability by $150: the contribution margin provided by the increased sales ($1,400 × 0.30 = $420) less the negative contribution purposely incurred on film developing ($270).

Opportunities for loss leaders exist in most businesses. Sometimes the loss leader is used to stimulate general store traffic and customer purchases. On other occasions complementary goods are being promoted. For example, restaurants may offer a free souvenir glass with the purchase of a large soft drink, or a pro shop may allow customers purchasing a tennis racket to buy tennis balls at bargain prices. In either situation the objective is the same—incurring a loss to increase total profitability.

DECISION MAKING UNDER RISK

The first portion of this chapter dealt with a certainty environment. In a **certainty environment** all predicted events and outcomes are presumed to occur. Thus we can attach a probability of 1.0 to each possible event to indicate there is a 100% chance of occurrence. Decision making under certainty is fine for illustrating the basic concepts and methodologies for selecting among alternative courses of action. Organizations, however, must frequently make decisions in a rapidly changing financial climate that is full of uncertainties.

For this reason we now turn our attention to decision making in a **risk environment.** Risk refers to a situation where the possible events that can occur are known and weighted by their probability of occurrence. If, for example, a .4 probability is attached to a particular event, this means there are 4 chances in 10 that the event will take place.

Assessing Probabilities

The probability assigned to an event may be derived objectively or subjectively. An **objective probability** is based on either a statistically determined outcome or past experience. To illustrate, the probability of obtaining a head in a coin toss is .5. Assuming the coin is perfectly balanced, only two events are possible (head or tail), and each has an equal likelihood of occurrence. The probabilities in rolling dice and pulling cards from a deck are also objectively or statistically derived. Objective probabilities can also be generated from past experience. For example, suppose a business inspects its goods for defects at the end of manufacturing. In the past the business has found that 3 out of every 100 units need rework. Thus, barring any change in the production process, the firm can expect this pattern to continue and can assign .03 as the probability of a defective unit arising.

Frequently, decisions must be made that are not based on statistically generated results or where past experience is either nonexistent or radically different from a projected state of affairs. In these instances **subjective probabilities** are assigned to the possible events. Subjective probabilities are based on all relevant knowledge possessed by a decision maker and are really nothing more than "gut feelings" about the future. Because of the nature of subjective probabilities, it is likely that different decision makers will assign different probabilities to the same events and that errors will result in the estimation process.

In light of these problems, why do we bother to use subjective probabilities? Although there are imperfections, we are introducing realism into the decision process. Decisions regarding the future are based heavily on estimates and hunches. Ignoring probabilities and assuming a certainty environment when one may not exist is foolish. The use of subjective probabilities, faults and all, generally results in improved decisions. And as a manager gains more experience in the development of probabilities, the estimation process can be sharpened and refined. This outcome, of course, makes the use of probabilities more attractive and beneficial to the firm.

Expected Value

To illustrate the use of probabilities in decision making, assume that Hilltop Enterprises is in the process of selecting a new copying machine for its administrative offices. Three models are being considered.

Model	*Terms*
A	$475 monthly rental fee with an unlimited number of copies
B	$350 monthly rental fee plus $0.02 per copy
C	No monthly rental fee; $0.10 per copy

Hilltop intends to select the machine that minimizes total copying costs. A conversation with the company's office manager revealed that the following monthly volumes are possible.

Number of Copies	*Probability of Occurrence*
3,000	.1
3,500	.2
4,000	.3
4,500	.3
5,000	.1
	1.0

The most economical machine is dependent on the number of copies to be run. For purposes of making the decision, many people would evaluate the three models on the basis of the average monthly volume of 4,000 copies [(3,000 + 3,500 + 4,000 + 4,500 + 5,000) ÷ 5]. While employing an average is the proper approach, it is incorrect to use 4,000. An average calculated in this manner is a *simple average* and ignores the fact that each event (i.e., volume level) has a different chance of arising. Consequently, a *weighted average* should be computed by weighting an event with its probability of occurrence. This procedure is shown in Exhibit 27-2 for each of the models.

Exhibit 27-2

Copying machine evaluation

Model A

	Cost		Probability		Expected Value
Rental fee	$475	×	1.0*	=	$475

Model B

Number of Copies	Cost†		Probability		Expected Value
3,000	$ 60	×	.1	=	$ 6
3,500	70	×	.2	=	14
4,000	80	×	.3	=	24
4,500	90	×	.3	=	27
5,000	100	×	.1	=	10
Rental fee	350	×	1.0*	=	350
					$431

Model C

Number of Copies	Cost‡		Probability		Expected Value
3,000	$300	×	.1	=	$ 30
3,500	350	×	.2	=	70
4,000	400	×	.3	=	120
4,500	450	×	.3	=	135
5,000	500	×	.1	=	50
					$405

**A probability of 1.0 is used because the monthly rental fee is certain to occur.*

†Copying cost @ $0.02.

‡Copying cost @ $0.10.

Hilltop should select model C because it has the lowest expected value ($405) in terms of cost. The **expected value** is the mathematical outcome of multiplying the payoff of an individual event by the event's probability and then summing the results. The **payoff** is generally an event's cost or contribution margin. Since there are no revenues in this example, cost is the primary consideration in the selection decision.

Payoff Matrix

In the previous illustration the decision maker was confronted with evaluating different alternatives under different volumes of activity (i.e., events). Frequently, in this type of situation a payoff matrix is used to bring order to the decision process. The **payoff matrix** is a two-dimensional table that discloses the payoffs for all combinations of alternatives and events. A sample payoff matrix is shown in Exhibit 27-3. Because three alternatives are being evaluated and three events can occur, nine different payoffs ($) are possible.

Exhibit 27-3

Sample payoff matrix

	Events		
Alternatives	*E1*	*E2*	*E3*
A1	$	$	$
A2	$	$	$
A3	$	$	$

To illustrate the use of a payoff matrix in conjunction with expected value, assume the Arizona Bears are formulating plans for concession operations at Municipal Stadium. From last year's experience the concession staff is evaluating the number of roast beef specials to prepare for each home game. The ingredients are perishable; therefore accurate forecasting is a necessity. The following demand figures have been generated.

Demand for Roast Beef Specials (Servings)	*Probability*
8,000	.1
9,000	.4
10,000	.3
11,000	.2
	1.0

The food cost is $0.50 per serving, and the special's selling price is $2.00. Thus each serving that is sold nets $1.50 in contribution margin; unsold servings must be discarded and result in a loss of $0.50. To simplify matters, assume that the Bears will prepare either 8,000, 9,000, 10,000, or 11,000 specials.

The Bears' payoff matrix appears in Exhibit 27-4. The payoffs are computed by netting revenues and expenses. For example, if the Bears prepare

Exhibit 27-4

Payoff matrix for Arizona Bears

Alternatives (Servings Prepared)	Events (Demand) .1 8,000	.4 9,000	.3 10,000	.2 11,000	Expected Value
8,000	$12,000	$12,000	$12,000	$12,000	$12,000
9,000	11,500	13,500	13,500	13,500	13,300
10,000	11,000	13,000	15,000	15,000	13,800
11,000	10,500	12,500	14,500	16,500	13,700

8,000 specials and sell them all, total contribution margin amounts to $12,000 ($16,000 sales revenue − $4,000 food cost). Notice that no matter what the demand is, only $12,000 can be generated when 8,000 servings are made. Obviously, the team cannot sell more food than it has available.

If the Bears have 9,000 servings prepared and sell all 9,000, revenues of $18,000 (9,000 × $2.00) minus expenses of $4,500 (9,000 × $0.50) yield a contribution of $13,500. If only 8,000 of the 9,000 servings are sold, the contribution margin totals $11,500: revenues of $16,000 less expenses of $4,500. Stating the latter case differently, the 8,000 specials that are sold net the Bears $12,000 of contribution margin (8,000 × $1.50 = $12,000). Furthermore, a $500 loss is incurred on the 1,000 extra servings that must be discarded (1,000 × $0.50 = $500).

Once the payoffs are known, the expected value of the various alternatives can be computed. As before, the expected value is derived by weighting the payoff with the appropriate probability. The relevant computations follow.

Servings Prepared		*Expected Value*
8,000	($12,000 × .1) + ($12,000 × .4) + ($12,000 × .3) + ($12,000 × .2) =	$12,000
9,000	($11,500 × .1) + ($13,500 × .4) + ($13,500 × .3) + ($13,500 × .2) =	$13,300
10,000	($11,000 × .1) + ($13,000 × .4) + ($15,000 × .3) + ($15,000 × .2) =	$13,800
11,000	($10,500 × .1) + ($12,500 × .4) + ($14,500 × .3) + ($16,500 × .2) =	$13,700

Because the Bears desire to maximize contribution margin, 10,000 roast beef specials should be prepared. This action will result in an average contribution margin of $13,800 per game.

Perfect Information

The decision to prepare 10,000 specials, although best from an expected value point of view, is still not optimal. Ideally the Bears would like to meet demand head-on; that is, the team desires to avoid shortages if demand is high and discards due to excessive preparations. Both situations can be achieved if the Bears have *perfect information* about demand. For example, if the Bears knew demand would be 8,000, only 8,000 specials would be prepared; if they knew demand would be 9,000, only 9,000 specials would be prepared; and so forth. An environment of perfect information is depicted along the diagonal of a payoff matrix (see the circled figures in Exhibit 27-5).

Exhibit 27-5

Perfect information

	Events (Demand)			
Alternatives (Servings Prepared)	**.1 8,000**	**.4 9,000**	**.3 10,000**	**.2 11,000**
8,000	$12,000	$12,000	$12,000	$12,000
9,000	11,500	13,500	13,500	13,500
10,000	11,000	13,000	15,000	15,000
11,000	10,500	12,500	14,500	16,500

With perfect knowledge of demand the Bears will net either $12,000, $13,500, $15,000, or $16,500. Note, however, that none of these payoffs are certain to occur. For example, if patrons demand 8,000 specials, then 8,000 specials will be prepared. Yet this level of demand occurs only 10% of the time. Similarly, the probability of earning $13,500 is only .4. To calculate the expected contribution margin when operating in an environment of perfect information, one must make the following computations.

Payoff		Probability		Expected Value
$12,000	×	.1	=	$ 1,200
13,500	×	.4	=	5,400
15,000	×	.3	=	4,500
16,500	×	.2	=	3,300
				$14,400

How much is perfect information worth? Presently, by following the expected value strategy of preparing 10,000 servings, the team is making $13,800 (see Exhibit 27-4). With perfect information the contribution margin averages $14,400. Thus the Bears should be willing to pay up to $600 ($14,400 – $13,800) to obtain this faultless look at demand. The $600, sometimes called the **expected value of perfect information,** represents the mathematical difference between the expected value of existing conditions and the expected value of an environment where events can be predicted in advance.

Although the theory behind this concept is sound, realize that perfect information is generally unobtainable. Why, then, have we dealt with this topic? While *perfect* information is normally a fantasy, *better* information is a reality. Businesses can obtain additional information regarding customer behavior and other events through market surveys and statistical sampling. This additional knowledge often results in increased revenues or reductions in cost or both. The maximum a firm should be willing to pay for market surveys and other similar studies is the expected value of perfect information. In reality, amounts less than the maximum would be spent because businesses must usually settle for something less than perfection.

DECISION CONSTRAINTS

Managers are often restricted in their quest for effective decisions by *decision constraints.* Many of these constraints are found within the organization. For example, the opinions of superiors and subordinates affected by the decision, the risk the decision maker is willing to assume, the available capital to take full advantage of the decision analysis, and the presence of strong labor unions all have some impact on the implementation of preferred alternatives.

Other constraints are external to the entity. The economic climate may be turbulent, making forecasting of the future troublesome. New competition may be moving into the area. Congress may be talking about new legislation such as wage and price guidelines or revisions in the current tax laws. Such problems or uncertainties have forced many managers to rely heavily on short-term decisions, a strategy that often impedes long-term business growth and development.

Further constraints stem from the existing laws that regulate the conduct of business. One such law, the **Robinson-Patman Act,** forbids charging different prices to competing customers for the same goods and services unless variations in cost are experienced when serving the customers. Such cost variations may relate to manufacturing outlays or selling and distribution expenses (e.g., advertising, freight, and commissions). In essence, then, the act prohibits discriminatory pricing and is an obvious concern to businesses when conducting activity.

Robinson-Patman is not the only law affecting business decisions, however. Firms are subject to pension laws, minimum wage provisions, and a host of other regulations. Businesses do not conduct their affairs in a vacuum; thus familiarity with the surrounding legal environment is a necessity. In one way or another this environment is bound to have some impact on and constrain the decisions made by management.

KEY TERMS AND CONCEPTS

certainty environment 1072
differential cost 1061
expected value 1074
expected value of perfect information 1077
full project approach 1059
incremental approach 1061
loss leader 1071
objective probability 1072
opportunity cost 1066
payoff 1075
payoff matrix 1075
qualitative factors 1061
relevant cost 1059
risk environment 1072
Robinson-Patman Act 1078
subjective probability 1073
sunk cost 1062

QUESTIONS

Q27-1 Discuss the general approach to decision making.

Q27-2 Are all future costs relevant for decision-making purposes? Explain.

Q27-3 An educator once commented, "Not all future costs are relevant to decisions, but costs are not relevant unless they occur in the future." Evaluate the educator's comments.

Q27-4 Explain why the book value of old equipment can be disregarded in equipment replacement decisions.

Q27-5 When equipment is replaced, why are some managers hesitant to incur a loss on the disposal of an existing asset? Should managers always be reluctant to take the loss? Why?

Q27-6 List several qualitative factors related to external purchases in a make or buy decision.

Q27-7 Fred Holtz recently experienced a $16,000 opportunity cost. Discuss the concept of an opportunity cost, and present Holtz's journal entry to record the $16,000 in the accounting records.

Q27-8 The Crandall Corporation has been offered $34 per unit on a one-time special order. Variable cost and fixed cost per unit amount to $27 and $10, respectively. Assuming Crandall's facilities are available, should the offer be accepted? Why?

Q27-9 Discuss the use of the contribution margin income statement in decisions regarding the deletion of departments.

Q27-10 Why would a business purposely incur a loss on a product?

Q27-11 Differentiate between certainty and risk environments.

Q27-12 Differentiate between objective and subjective probabilities.

Q27-13 Explain the meaning of the expected value of perfect information to someone who has a limited business background.

EXERCISES

E27-1 The Landry Corporation manufactures a variety of products (e.g., mugs, shirts, pennants) that carry the insignia of teams in the Professional Football League (PFL). Recently, Landry paid $27,000 to the league for rights to market a new line of player posters. Thirty thousand posters have been printed at a total cost of $15,000. Landry has paid the printer $4,000, with the remainder scheduled to be remitted next month.

Because of a disagreement, the PFL is about to file a lawsuit to block Landry's marketing program. The league is demanding another $12,000 from Landry. Landry's attorneys agree that the PFL has a strong case and is likely to win any ensuing court battles.

To date, no posters have been sold. Landry expects to spend $8,000 for marketing and promotion costs once the disagreement is settled. Each poster sells for $2.50 and a sellout is expected.

Should Landry pay the additional $12,000 to the PFL or should the poster program be dropped? Assume the $27,000 payment for marketing rights will not be returned if the program is discontinued. Explain your answer and show all computations.

E27-2 The Lane Assembly Company purchased a truck 2 years ago for $15,000. The straight-line depreciation method has been used assuming a 6-year service life and no residual value. Ken Sero, the firm's traffic manager, has just learned of a new truck that promises to reduce operating costs by $3,800 per year. The new truck costs $18,000 and will be depreciated over a 4-year life by using the straight-line method. Lane has received a bona fide offer of $4,000 for the old truck.

Sero noted: "While I'd like to acquire the new truck, my job will be in jeopardy. Management will definitely not appreciate the $6,000 loss on disposal of the old truck. I guess we should keep our existing equipment."

Evaluate Sero's comments, showing calculations when appropriate.

E27-3 The Nedderman Manufacturing Corporation recently produced 6,000 units at a cost of $5.70 per unit. The units do not meet quality standards and can be sold as seconds to a discount chain for $3.10 each. Alternatively, Nedderman can reprocess the units at an additional cost of $3.80 per unit. The reprocessed units can then be sold for $7.70.

After evaluating the two alternatives, an assistant in the accounting department concluded: "We'd be better off to keep the units. We'll incur a loss no matter which alternative is selected."

a Show the computations that formed the basis for the assistant's remarks.
b Is the assistant's conclusion correct? Why?
c Suppose the reprocessing alternative prevents the company from producing 6,000 units of another product that has a normal selling price and a variable manufacturing cost of $10.40 and $5.50, respectively. Should Nedderman reprocess the original units or sell them as seconds? Why?

E27-4 The Robinson Corporation makes small plastic cases with built-in mirrors for sale to cosmetics manufacturers. The company's unit manufacturing costs for an annual volume of 200,000 cases (including mirrors) follow.

Direct materials	*$0.30*
Direct labor	*0.10*
Total overhead	*0.15*
Total cost	*$0.55*

All overhead is variable except for $6,000 of straight-line depreciation and $12,000 of allocated fixed production costs.

Because of manufacturing problems, Robinson desires to purchase the mirror from an outside firm. New York Glass has offered to supply a suitable mirror for $0.18. If mirror production is discontinued, material, labor, and variable overhead costs will decline by 40%, 30%, and 20%, respectively.

a Should Robinson make or buy the mirror? Why?
b Assume that if the mirror is purchased, the mirror's production space will be leased to a small manufacturer for $2,500 per month. Discuss the proper treatment of this revenue and its impact on Robinson's make or buy decision.

E27-5 The airport manager of Westerville has just received a $215,000 bid from A&L Services to perform the airport's maintenance work for the upcoming year. Maintenance is currently performed by the airport's own staff at the following yearly costs:

Supplies	*$ 30,000*
Staff salaries	*120,000*
Overhead	*100,000*
Total maintenance cost	*$250,000*

Overhead includes $15,000 of building depreciation and $40,000 of allocated administrative costs; the remaining overhead costs are variable.

The airport manager requested the bid because of soaring labor costs. The employees are bargaining for a 20% raise for next year. Despite a threatened strike, the manager feels that a 15% compromise increase is highly likely.

a Should the outside bid be accepted? Why?

b Although the amount of the raise is not as yet settled, a decision regarding the bid must now be made. How could the airport manager incorporate the uncertainty surrounding the pay increase into the decision process? Explain your answer.

E27-6 The Hashimoto Corporation produces house paint and supplies. Most of the firm's paint is sold through company-owned stores or franchises. A recent income statement of the latex division appears below.

Sales (450,000 gallons @ $6)	*$2,700,000*
Cost of goods sold	*2,025,000*
Gross profit	*$ 675,000*
Less selling & administrative expenses (fixed)	*590,000*
Net income	*$ 85,000*

Fixed costs included in cost of goods sold total $315,000.

J-Mart, a discount chain, recently approached Hashimoto with a request to purchase 40,000 gallons of latex at $4 per gallon. J-Mart will attach its own label to the can, thereby preventing disclosure of the paint's manufacturer. Hashimoto presently has idle capacity and will experience no change in fixed costs as a result of accepting the order. Per-unit variable costs are expected to remain stable.

Should Hashimoto accept the special order? Why?

E27-7 The Hallmark Corporation manufactures two products, X and Y. Pertinent data about the products follow.

	X	Y
Selling price	*$10*	*$19*
Less variable costs		
Manufacturing	*$ 5*	*$ 8*
Selling	*2*	*5*
Total	*$ 7*	*$13*
Contribution margin	*$ 3*	*$ 6*

a All other factors being equal, which product would Hallmark's sales manager instruct the sales force to push? Why?

b A study of Hallmark's manufacturing capacity revealed that 3,000 hours of machine time are available for production activities. The firm now intends to make only one product. If it takes 3 hours to manufacture a unit of X and 8 hours to manufacture a unit of Y, which product should be produced? Why? Assume Hallmark is operating at capacity.

c If your answer to part (b) is different from your answer to part (a), explain why the difference arises.

E27-8 The Travis Company manufactures three products. For the year just ended product B generated a net loss of $35,000, as shown below.

Sales	*$140,000*
Cost of goods sold	*96,000*
Gross profit	*$ 44,000*
Less selling & administrative expenses	*79,000*
Net income (loss)	*$ (35,000)*

Fixed manufacturing costs total 20% of cost of goods sold. Selling and administrative (S&A) expenses include a 10% sales commission; all other S&A costs are fixed. Management is contemplating dropping product B because of the loss. If B is dropped, Travis will lease the abandoned plant space for $18,000.

Should product B be dropped? Why?

E27-9 Jurgen's is a combination food and drug center. The following is a recent monthly income statement.

	Food	*Drugs*	*Total*
Sales	*$600,000*	*$50,000*	*$650,000*
Less variable costs	*576,000*	*45,000*	*621,000*
Contribution margin	*$ 24,000*	*$ 5,000*	*$ 29,000*
Less fixed costs			*22,000*
Net income			*$ 7,000*

Management is contemplating a change in operations by remaining open 24 hours a day. To generate store traffic, the store will deeply discount all soft drinks (cases only) from midnight to 6 A.M. for a three-month period. On the basis of the outcome, the firm will decide whether an around-the-clock operation will become a permanent feature.

Management anticipates selling 1,200 cases of soft drinks per month at a discount price of $1.25. Beverage distributors charge Jurgen's an average of $2.10 per case. Once in the store, customers normally browse and buy other items. Monthly food (excluding soft drinks) and drug sales are therefore expected to increase by 20% and 15%, respectively. Finally, because of additional staffing and utilities costs, fixed costs will rise by $3,100 per month.

a Determine whether the soft drink special will attract sufficient business to justify the expanded hours.

b Although disregarded above, what can conceivably happen to daytime sales as a result of the special?

E27-10 The ARC Radio Company is deciding whether to introduce a wrist "radiowatch" designed for shortwave reception. The radiowatch would be priced at $60, which is exactly twice its variable selling and manufacturing cost. The additional fixed costs necessitated by introducing this new product would amount to

$240,000 per year. Subjective estimates of the demand for the product are shown in the following probability distribution.

Annual Demand (Units)	Probability
6,000	.2
8,000	.2
10,000	.2
12,000	.2
14,000	.1
16,000	.1

a Determine the expected demand for the radiowatch.
b Calculate the break-even point in units.
c If the radiowatch is introduced, determine the probability that ARC's profits will not increase.

(CMA modified.)

E27-11 The Cantrell Corporation will be introducing a new product in the coming year. Anticipated demand follows.

Demand (Units)	Probability
50,000	.1
60,000	.5
70,000	.4

Because of a change in operations, a new machine will be leased to manufacture this product. Three machines are being considered.

Machine	Annual Lease Payment	Capacity (Units)
A49C	$29,500	55,000
1700	34,600	65,000
DF32	38,200	75,000

Which machine should be selected? Why?

PROBLEMS

P27-1 ***Equipment replacement***
Three years ago Rothstein, Inc., acquired a machine for $80,000. The machine has been depreciated by the straight-line method, using an 8-year life and no residual value. Operating expenses, excluding depreciation, have totaled $78,000 per year. Recently, a new machine became available that promises an annual savings in operating costs of $24,000. The new machine costs $125,000, has a 5-year service life, and no residual value. If the new machine is acquired, the

existing equipment can be sold for $18,000. No matter which machine is used, Rothstein's revenues are expected to continue at $155,000 per year.

INSTRUCTIONS

a Should Rothstein acquire the new machine? Why?

b Which of the preceding items are irrelevant for the decision? Why?

c List several qualitative factors that should be considered in the equipment replacement decision.

P27-2 ***Make or buy***

Urban, Inc., manufactures a full line of workshop tools. The manufactured cost of one of the company's products, a staple gun, appears below.

Direct materials	$ 4.80
Direct labor	8.00
Total factory overhead	9.60
Total	$22.40

Overhead is applied to products on the basis of direct labor cost. Estimated annual direct labor cost and fixed overhead chargeable to the staple gun line amount to $400,000 and $160,000, respectively.

Urban is presently producing all the staple gun's components. One of the components, part no. A461, has created a number of manufacturing problems. The company is therefore considering acquiring this part from an outside supplier.

A supplier has agreed to provide the part in lots of 1,000 for $4,800. If Urban accepts the supplier's offer, it is estimated that the gun's direct labor and variable overhead cost will decline by 25%. In addition, direct material cost should fall by approximately 15%.

INSTRUCTIONS

a Should Urban make or buy the component? Show computations to support your answer. *Note:* Each gun uses one of the no. A461 components.

b What is the maximum purchase price Urban would be willing to pay an outside supplier for the 1,000 components?

c Assume that Urban can manufacture a maximum of 50,000 staple guns per year. To eliminate the production problems, top management has proposed hiring an additional foreman for $20,000. In addition, $6,000 of existing fixed administrative costs would be allocated to the staple gun line. If both these actions take place, should Urban make or buy the component? Show computations to support your answer.

d List several qualitative factors Urban should consider in deciding whether to make or buy the component.

P27-3 ***Special order and pricing policy***

The Jessica Company makes several products that are used in the home. Revenues and costs of the Magic Kitchen Slicer appear below.

Sales		$90,000
Less		
Direct materials used	$20,000	
Direct labor	30,000	
Factory overhead	18,000	
Sales commissions, 5%	4,500	
Allocated administrative expense	10,500	83,000
Net income		$ 7,000

The figures shown are for the production and sale of 10,000 units. Factory overhead is applied on the basis of direct labor cost.

The Baskin Corporation, which advertises heavily on television, has submitted an offer to purchase 3,000 slicers at $7.75 each. Baskin will market the product under its own brand name, and Jessica's normal sales are not expected to suffer. Jessica's president feels that the offer should be rejected because the price is below the current unit cost of $8.30 ($83,000 ÷ 10,000 units).

An in-depth study revealed the following information.

1 Baskin's units will require overtime at time and one-half the regular wage rate.
2 Budgeted fixed factory overhead for the year represents two-thirds of Jessica's total overhead.
3 No sales commissions will be paid on these units.
4 Administrative expenses are allocated to product lines on the basis of sales dollars. Because of the special order, an additional $2,500 will be charged to the slicer line. Jessica's total administrative costs will remain the same, however.

INSTRUCTIONS

Should Jessica reject Baskin's offer? Why?

P27-4 ***Special order and cost concepts***

George Jackson operates a small machine shop. He manufactures one standard product available from many other similar businesses, and he also manufactures products to customer order. His accountant prepared the annual income statement shown below.

	Custom Sales	Standard Sales	Total
Sales	$50,000	$25,000	$75,000
Material	$10,000	$ 8,000	$18,000
Labor	20,000	9,000	29,000
Depreciation (straight-line)	6,300	3,600	9,900
Power	700	400	1,100
Rent	6,000	1,000	7,000
Heat & light	600	100	700
Miscellaneous variable costs	400	900	1,300
Total expenses	$44,000	$23,000	$67,000
Net income	$ 6,000	$ 2,000	$ 8,000

The depreciation charges are for machines used in the respective product lines. The power charge is apportioned on an estimate of power consumed. The rent is for the building space, which has been leased for 10 years at $7,000 per year. The rent and heat and light are apportioned to the product lines on the basis of the amount of floor space occupied. All other costs are current expenses identified with the product line causing them.

A valued customer has asked Jackson if he would manufacture 5,000 special units. Jackson is working at capacity and would have to give up some other business to take this special order. He can't renege on custom orders already agreed to, but he could reduce the output of his standard product by about one-half for one year while producing the specially requested units. The customer is willing to pay $7.00 for each unit. The material cost will be about $2.00 per unit, and the labor will be $3.60 per unit. Jackson will have to spend $2,000 for a special device, which will be discarded when the job is done.

INSTRUCTIONS

a Calculate the following costs related to the 5,000 unit custom order: (1) the differential cost of the order; (2) the opportunity cost of taking the order.

b Should Mr. Jackson take the order? Show computations and explain your answer.

(CMA modified.)

P27-5 ***New product introduction***

The Estrada Corporation is a small firm engaged in the manufacture of garden tools. The firm currently has a substantial share of the market with its product line. During the past twelve months two new products have been under development: a timer system for lawn watering and a lawn weeder. Research and development costs for the timer and weeder have totaled $72,000 and $18,000, respectively.

Company policy is to introduce only one new product a year. Customer acceptability studies performed in the past few months indicated that both products would be successful. Estrada's accounting department has gathered the following information.

	Timer System	Lawn Weeder
Customer acceptability studies	$17,000	$24,000
Projected sales (units)	9,000	18,000
Selling price	$48	$36
Sales commission (expressed as a percentage of sales)	5%	10%
Unit production costs		
Direct materials	$8.50	$5.70
Direct labor	$10.00	$8.00
Variable overhead	$18.00	$14.40
Projected advertising	$23,000	$15,000

INSTRUCTIONS

a List those costs that are irrelevant to the product introduction decision and explain why each is irrelevant.

b Compute the contribution margin per unit for each product.

c Which of the two products should be introduced? Why?

P27-6 ***Dropping an unprofitable segment***

City Mart, Inc., operates a chain of discount stores in large metropolitan areas of the United States. An abbreviated income statement for store no. 1706 for the year just ended follows.

	Total	General Merchandise	Lawn and Garden	Snack Bar
Sales	$1,260,000	$800,000	$350,000	$110,000
Less variable expenses	809,000	520,000	245,000	44,000
Contribution margin	$ 451,000	$280,000	$105,000	$ 66,000
Less fixed expenses	356,000	210,000	60,000	86,000
Net income	$ 95,000	$ 70,000	$ 45,000	$ (20,000)

Because of poor performance, management is contemplating dropping the snack bar. If the snack bar is closed, the vacated space will be divided between general merchandise and lawn and garden, with the following results.

1 General merchandise and lawn and garden sales are expected to increase by $60,000 and $40,000, respectively.
2 Fixed expenses include $55,000 of salaries earned by snack bar employees. Employees earning $26,000 would be transferred to other departments; remaining employees will be terminated.
3 All other fixed costs incurred by the snack bar will continue to be incurred.
4 The snack bar's equipment will be removed and transferred to another store. Removal and transportation costs will amount to $4,500.

INSTRUCTIONS

a Should the snack bar be dropped? Show computations to support your answer.

b Assume that Colonial Caterers has approached City Mart about taking over the snack bar operation. Colonial will pay City Mart $1,600 per month and assume all costs of operation, with the exception of $7,500 of fixed costs. Should the snack bar be retained in its present form or be turned over to Colonial Caterers? Show computations to support your answer.

P27-7 *Expected value: Computation and interpretation*

The Professional Management Institute (PMI) sponsors seminars and short courses for executives at its headquarters in Denver. The courses cover a variety of topics but normally concentrate in the accounting field. Two new courses are under consideration for development: Oil and Gas Accounting and Oil and Gas Taxation.

Each course will cost $7,000 to design and will be offered repeatedly throughout the year. Enrollees pay a $400 course fee; the variable costs of offering a course total $80 per executive. Because of limited staff, only one course can be introduced in the coming year. To determine which course to offer, PMI's management has derived the following probabilities:

Total Course Enrollments	Oil and Gas Accounting	Oil and Gas Taxation
100	.1	.2
150	.2	.4
200	.4	.2
250	.3	.2
	1.0	1.0

INSTRUCTIONS

a Discuss the relevance of the design cost in deciding which course to introduce.

b Which course should PMI select? Explain and show your computations.

c Suppose that PMI has revised its thinking regarding the taxation course. Management is now absolutely certain that taxation will attract 195 registrants. Explain which course should be offered and why.

d Ignoring the previous information, assume that PMI will introduce the Oil and Gas Accounting course. In predicting classroom and food service needs, the following enrollment figures per offering have been estimated.

Enrollment per Offering	Probability
20	.1
30	.3
35	.4
40	.2

Using the expected value approach, how many registrants should PMI expect per offering? Is it conceivable that the number of people who actually register for a session will differ from your answer above? Why?

P27-8 ***Expected value***

The Unimat Company manufactures a unique thermostat that yields dramatic cost savings from effective climatic control of large buildings. The efficiency of the thermostat is dependent on the quality of a specialized thermocoupler, which is purchased from Cosmic Company for $15.

Since early 1984 approximately 10% of the thermocouplers purchased from Cosmic have not met Unimat's quality requirements. The number of unusable thermocouplers has ranged from 5% to 25% of the total number purchased and has resulted in failure to meet production schedules.

Unimat is considering a proposal to manufacture the thermocouplers. The company has the facilities and equipment to produce the components. The engineering department has designed a manufacturing system that will produce the thermocouplers with a defective rate of 4% of the number of units produced. The schedule below presents the engineers' estimates of the probabilities that different levels of variable manufacturing cost per thermocoupler will be incurred under this system. The variable manufacturing cost per unit includes a cost adjustment for the defective units at the 4% rate. Additional annual fixed costs incurred by Unimat if it manufactures the thermocoupler will amount to $32,500.

Estimated Annual Variable Manufacturing Cost per Good Thermocoupler Unit	Probability of Occurrence
$10.00	10%
12.00	30
14.00	40
16.00	20
	100%

Unimat Company will need 18,000 thermocouplers to meet annual demand requirements.

INSTRUCTIONS

Prepare an expected value analysis to determine whether Unimat Company should manufacture the thermocouplers.

(CMA adapted.)

P27-9 ***Expected value: Payoff matrix and perfect information***

Vendo, Inc., has been operating the concession stands at the university football stadium. The university has had successful football teams for many years; as a result, the stadium is always full. From time to time Vendo has found itself very short of hot dogs, and at other times it has had many left. A review of the sales records of the past ten seasons revealed the following frequency of hot dogs sold.

Hot Dog Demand	Number of Times Sold
10,000	5
20,000	10
30,000	20
40,000	15
	50

Hot dogs sell for $1.00 and cost Vendo $0.60 each. Unsold hot dogs are given to a local orphanage without charge.

INSTRUCTIONS

a Prepare a payoff matrix to represent the four possible strategies of ordering 10,000, 20,000, 30,000, or 40,000 hot dogs.

b Determine the best strategy by using the expected value decision rule.

c Compute the expected value of perfect information.

d Can Vendo obtain perfect information? Why?

(CMA modified.)

P27-10 ***Equipment replacement (alternate to P27-1)***

Two years ago Hardesty Machinery acquired some equipment for $42,000. The equipment has been depreciated by the straight-line method, using a 6-year life and no residual value. Operating expenses, excluding depreciation, have totaled $58,000 per year. Recently, new equipment became available that promises an annual savings in operating costs of $9,500. The new equipment costs $50,000, has a 4-year service life, and no residual value. If the new equipment is acquired, the existing equipment can be sold for $17,000. No matter which equipment is used, Hardesty's revenues are expected to continue at $110,000 per year.

INSTRUCTIONS

a Should Hardesty acquire the new equipment? Why?

b Which items above are irrelevant for the decision? Why are they irrelevant?

c Terry Dubbs is the manager in charge of making the decision. Assume that her analysis revealed (1) a loss on the disposal of the old equipment and (2) an overall savings if the new equipment is acquired. Despite the overall savings, why might she still be reluctant to proceed with the acquisition?

P27-11 ***Make or buy (alternate to P27-2)***

Finch, Inc., manufactures a full line of workshop tools. The manufactured cost of one of the company's products, an electric drill, appears below.

Direct materials	$11.00
Direct labor	7.50
Total factory overhead	6.00
Total	$24.50

Overhead is applied to products on the basis of direct labor cost. Estimated annual direct labor cost and fixed overhead chargeable to the electric drill line amount to $300,000 and $160,000, respectively.

Finch is presently producing all the drill's components. One of the components, part no. B74, has created a number of manufacturing problems. The company is therefore considering acquiring this part from an outside supplier.

A supplier has agreed to provide the part in lots of 1,000 for $4,150. If Finch accepts the supplier's offer, it is estimated that the drill's direct labor and variable overhead cost will decline by 20%. In addition, direct material cost should fall by approximately 15%.

INSTRUCTIONS

a Should Finch make or buy the component? Show computations to support your answer. *Note:* Each drill uses one of the no. B74 components.

b What is the maximum purchase price Finch would be willing to pay an outside supplier for the 1,000 components?

c Assume that Finch can manufacture a maximum of 45,000 electric drills per year. To eliminate the production problems, top management has proposed hiring an additional foreman for $24,000. In addition, $5,000 of existing fixed administrative costs would be allocated to the electric drill line. If both these actions take place, should Finch make or buy the component? Show computations to support your answer.

d List several reservations Finch might have about dealing with an outside supplier.

P27-12 ***New product introduction (alternate to P27-5)***

The Seltzer Corporation is engaged in the manufacture of electronic toys. During the past eighteen months two new products have been developed: an electronic space gun and a quiz game called Super Stumper.

Seltzer recently conducted market surveys for the gun and game at a cost of $35,000 each. Although the surveys indicated that both toys could be introduced at this time, the firm has encountered difficulty in obtaining the required electronic components. Thus only one product will be manufactured.

Seltzer's accounting department has gathered the following information.

	Space Gun	***Super Stumper***
Development costs over the past 18 months	$85,000	$60,000
Production costs per unit		
Direct materials	$3.50	$7.50
Direct labor	$7.00	$9.00
Variable overhead	$2.80	$3.60
Sales commissions (expressed as a percentage of sales)	10%	5%
Selling price	$20	$28
Projected sales (units)	200,000	140,000
Projected advertising	$38,000	$30,000

INSTRUCTIONS

a List those costs that are irrelevant to the product introduction decision and explain why each is irrelevant.

b Compute the contribution margin per unit for each toy.

c Which of the two products should be introduced at this time? Why?

P27-13 *Dropping an unprofitable segment (alternate to P27-6)*

Bargain Mart operates a chain of discount stores in large metropolitan areas of the United States. An abbreviated income statement for store no. 2104 for the year just ended follows.

	Total	General Merchandise	Patio	Lunch Counter
Sales	$940,000	$500,000	$280,000	$160,000
Less variable expenses	598,000	310,000	168,000	120,000
Contribution margin	$342,000	$190,000	$112,000	$ 40,000
Less fixed expenses	256,000	130,000	77,000	49,000
Net income	$ 86,000	$ 60,000	$ 35,000	$ (9,000)

Because of poor performance, management is contemplating dropping the lunch counter. If the lunch counter is closed, the vacated space will be divided between general merchandise and patio, with the following results.

1 General merchandise and patio sales are expected to increase by $35,000 and $12,000, respectively.
2 Fixed expenses include $31,000 of salaries earned by lunch counter employees. Employees earning $19,000 would be transferred to other departments; remaining employees will be terminated.
3 All other fixed costs incurred by the lunch counter will continue to be incurred.
4 The lunch counter's equipment will be removed and transferred to another store. Removal and transportation costs will amount to $2,700.

INSTRUCTIONS

a Should the lunch counter be dropped? Show computations to support your answer.
b Assume that Quality Caterers has approached Bargain Mart about taking over the lunch counter operation. Quality will pay Bargain Mart $1,400 per month and assume all costs of operation, with the exception of $12,200 of fixed costs. Should the lunch counter be retained in its present form or be turned over to Quality Caterers? Show computations to support your answer.

P27-14 *Expected value: Payoff matrix and perfect information (alternate to P27-9)*

Hospitality Services sells pizza at the local university stadium. The university has had successful football teams for many years; as a result, the stadium is always full. From time to time Hospitality has found itself very short of pizzas, and at other times it has had many left. A review of the sales records of the past nine seasons revealed the following frequency of pizzas sold.

Pizza Demand	Number of Times Sold
5,000	4
6,000	16
7,000	12
8,000	8
	40

Pizzas sell for $2.00 and cost Hospitality $0.80 each. Unsold pizzas are discarded.

INSTRUCTIONS

a Prepare a payoff matrix to represent the four possible strategies of ordering 5,000, 6,000, 7,000, or 8,000 pizzas.

b Determine the best strategy by using the expected value decision rule.

c Compute the expected value of perfect information.

d How much should Hospitality be willing to pay for in-depth surveys of crowd demand for pizzas? Explain your answer.

CASE 27
ALONZO HARRISON

Alonzo Harrison is the highly successful manager of the Wisconsin Division of Office Interiors, Inc. The income statement of the Wisconsin Division for 1983 appears below.

OFFICE INTERIORS/WISCONSIN DIVISION
Income Statement
For the Year Ended December 31, 1983

Sales (10,000 units)	$100,000
Less variable costs	60,000
Contribution margin	$ 40,000
Less fixed costs controllable by the division manager*	30,000
Contribution controllable by the division manager	$ 10,000
Less fixed costs controllable by others	3,000
Division margin	$ 7,000

*Includes depreciation on machinery.

Harrison has just earned a 10% bonus computed on the contribution controllable by the division manager. Top management is so pleased with his performance that they have promised him a promotion to corporate headquarters if 1984's controllable contribution is close to that of 1983.

In early 1984 Harrison was confronted with an equipment replacement decision. Machinery purchased two years ago for $50,000 has been depreciated by using the straight-line method, a 5-year life, and no residual value. Because of technological advances, new machinery costing $39,000 has become available. The new machinery would be depreciated evenly over its 3-year life. No residual value is expected, and a 20% savings in variable unit costs are anticipated. The old machinery can be sold for $12,000.

To assist Harrison in the decision, the accounting and marketing departments have generated the following information.

1 Forecasted demand over the next three years:

Units	Probability
9,000	.1
10,000	.2
11,000	.3
12,000	.4
	1.0

2 Forecasted selling prices:

Year	Selling Price
1984	$10.50
1985	11.75
1986	13.00

3 Increases in cash outlays over the previous year for fixed costs controllable by the division manager:

Year	Increase
1984	$ 5,000
1985	8,000
1986	10,000

For purposes of measuring performance, all gains and losses are considered in computing a manager's controllable contribution.

INSTRUCTIONS

a Does the new machinery appear to be a good investment for Office Interiors? Explain your answer, showing appropriate computations.

b Is Harrison likely to acquire the machinery? Why? Prepare a new income statement to support your answer. Conclude the statement with the contribution controllable by the division manager.

c Is there a conflict? If so, what can be done to resolve it?

28 CAPITAL BUDGETING

LEARNING OBJECTIVES

After reading this chapter you should:

1 Understand the capital budgeting process and be able to distinguish between project screening and project ranking decisions.

2 Know the factors that management considers when evaluating capital expenditure proposals, namely, the amount of an investment, the returns from an investment, and the lowest rate of return acceptable to the firm.

3 Have a general understanding of the cost of capital.

4 Be familiar with the concept of the time value of money.

5 Understand the distinction between compound interest and present value.

6 Know how to compute and use net present value, the internal rate of return, the payback method, and the accounting rate of return when evaluating investment proposals.

7 Have a basic knowledge of how income taxes complicate the analysis of capital expenditures.

CHAPTER 28

Each year American businesses spend vast sums of money on a variety of long-term investments. As evidence, consider the following excerpts from recent annual reports of AMF International and Walt Disney Productions.

AMF International

> *Recognizing that a company, in order to achieve the near and long term goals it sets for itself, must be positioned to compete in the most efficient manner possible, AMF pays close heed to its capital spending requirements. For new plant construction, expansion and modernization of existing facilities, for tools and equipment that meet the changing production technologies, and for more energy efficient operations, AMF expended $93.2 million during [the year]. This represents 6 percent of revenue and 96 percent of pretax income.*

Walt Disney Productions

> *The Company continues to invest in the future through its capital improvements program. Over the past five years, the Company has invested approximately $655 million in property, plant and equipment and $235 million in film production for a total of almost $900 million. These investments are intended to expand services and operating capacity in the Company's entertainment and recreation businesses and to maintain and increase the productive capability (in the form of new film product) of its motion picture business. The consumer product business will also benefit from this continued expansion of product.*

Most executives will agree that a company's long-term investments often spell the difference between financial prosperity or lengthy periods of unprofitable performance. Investments such as those cited in the excerpts are costly and require the commitment of resources for many years. As a result, poor decisions are usually very difficult to reverse. Yet good decisions do not come easily, because the future is uncertain and hard to predict.

This chapter focuses on the evaluation of programs and projects that influence the financial performance of more than one accounting period. Outlays for such undertakings are commonly called *capital expenditures.* The planning and decision making related to long-term programs and projects is appropriately labeled **capital budgeting.**

CAPITAL BUDGETING DECISIONS

Most firms face the same problem when evaluating long-term investments: too many investment opportunities and not enough money. Management must therefore carefully select from among alternative courses of action. This selection process gives rise to two basic types of capital budgeting decisions. The first type of decision involves *project screening* to determine whether an investment proposal meets certain preset criteria. Examples of such criteria include a specified rate of return or perhaps the recovery of invested funds within a certain number of years. If the screening tests are met, the proposal is considered for acceptance; if not, rejection is in order.

The second type of decision concerns *ranking*. Given that a number of projects will probably be acceptable, ranking must occur because of the limited availability of investment dollars. A distinction is necessary to determine the most attractive project, the second most attractive project, and so forth. Our discussion will concentrate on screening decisions; ranking decisions are more appropriately left for advanced accounting and finance courses.

Decision Factors to Consider

Assume that you recently inherited $10,000 from a wealthy relative and are now exploring various investment possibilities. Three opportunities appear particularly attractive.

1 Purchase a six-month, $10,000 money market certificate that carries an interest rate of 14%.
2 Acquire $10,000 of stock in several so-called growth companies. The shares promise significant appreciation in market value but pay no dividends.
3 Purchase a $60,000 home by paying $9,000 down and securing a $51,000 mortgage loan. The loan will require payments over the next thirty years and carries a 13% interest rate.

Somehow you must decide which of the three investments to select. As a starting point, the following thoughts might be running through your head.

The first two investments require an immediate cash outlay of $10,000; the third requires only $9,000.
The money market certificate yields a guaranteed interest rate of 14%.
The stocks generate no dividends; however, the long-run profit may be attractive if market prices increase substantially.
The house requires monthly payments for mortgage principal and interest along with outlays for insurance, utilities, and property taxes. Furthermore, interest and property taxes are deductible for federal income tax purposes, and appreciation in housing prices has been substantial over the years.

While our list of decision factors is far from complete, these factors coincide with those studied by managers when evaluating capital expenditure proposals. Specifically, management is concerned with (1) the amount of an investment, (2) the returns from an investment, and (3) the lowest rate of return acceptable to the firm. The amount of an investment is generally measured by its associated cash outlay. Project returns and the lowest rate of return are somewhat more complex to understand; we discuss these concepts in the following sections.

Project returns

Investments are made to increase an organization's profitability. Added profitability results from projects that (1) produce income by generating revenues in excess of expenses or (2) decrease costs. Income-producing investments include the addition of new product lines, an expansion of plant capacity, and the implementation of successful marketing and advertising programs. Cost reduction investments, on the other hand, often involve the installation of more efficient equipment and the acquisition of assets to perform services presently handled by outside entities. For instance, a company could acquire its own computer to eliminate dependence on an outside service bureau.

For both income-producing and cost-saving projects, managers desire a return. That is, managers seek to recover their initial outlays *and* to provide the company with a reward for the risk associated with the investment. Returns can be measured in terms of accounting profits or net cash flows (cash inflows minus cash outflows). For long-term decisions cash flow is preferred. Why? Accounting net income is accrual-based and therefore ignores the timing of the cash flows from an investment alternative.

As we explained in the Appendix to Chapter 15 and as we will explore later in this chapter, the timing of cash flows is extremely important. Stated succinctly, a dollar received today is worth more than a dollar to be received in the future. The dollar received today can be reinvested to earn additional returns for the enterprise. Naturally, additional returns are not possible with future dollars until the dollars are actually in hand. Because of noncash charges such as depreciation and changes in the levels of receivables and payables, accrual-based net income and cash flow can differ markedly. Unlike net income, *cash* is invested and *cash* earns a return. These facts, coupled with the timing aspect, dictate a cash definition of returns when evaluating long-term investments.

The cost of capital

The analysis of investment opportunities requires the establishment of a cutoff rate of return for project acceptance or rejection. The cutoff rate (i.e., the minimum rate of return acceptable to the firm) depends on the cost of obtaining investment funds. For example, if the cost of funds is 12%, a firm would ordinarily invest only in those projects that promise a return in excess of 12%.

Calculation of the cost of investment funds is generally known as determining the **cost of capital.** The proper determination of the cost of capital is an extremely controversial issue and is related more to finance than to accounting. For these reasons our coverage will be very light.

Importantly, you should understand that the cost of capital is much more than just interest expense. Obviously, an entity can obtain substantial funding via long-term debt issuances such as bonds and mortgages and thereby obligate itself to interest payments. Remember, however, that capital stock is another popular source of financing and that stockholders desire dividends. Unlike interest payments, though, dividend outlays are not fixed by contractual commitments. Further complicating the computation is the fact that many investment projects are financed from retained earnings (i.e., operations). The cost of these latter funds is in the form of an opportunity cost, specifically, the dividends forgone by shareholders.

Suffice it to say that the calculation of an entity's cost of capital is complex and usually requires a number of assumptions. As a result, the minimum desired rate of return for investments is often set several percentage points higher than the cost of capital to compensate for computational inaccuracies. The illustrations and problems that follow this discussion will assume the cost of capital has already been determined by management and is ready for use in the decision-making process.

TIME VALUE OF MONEY[1]

Suppose a manager has an option of receiving $1,000 today or $1,000 one year from now. Virtually every manager would prefer the first alternative for two basic reasons. Receiving the $1,000 today offers the advantage of reduced risk. The future, of course, is full of uncertainty. As time passes, more and more events can occur that imperil the receipt of future sums of money. Because the $1,000 is in hand, the manager is exposed to less risk and becomes less concerned about changing conditions in the forthcoming months.

The first alternative is also preferred because of the **time value of money.** As we noted earlier, a dollar received today is worth more than a dollar received in the future. Why? Money in hand can be reinvested to earn additional returns.

We caution that the preceding example is overly simplistic. When one compares equal sums of money (e.g., $1,000) at two different times, the preferred alternative is readily apparent. Suppose we change the example, however. Assume the second alternative now calls for the receipt of $1,050 or even $1,100 in one year. The decision becomes more difficult. Maybe the extra $50 or $100 is worth the wait; maybe not. An important influence would surely be the investment opportunities available for the immediate $1,000 receipt.

Decisions such as the above are facilitated if the time value of money is quantitatively incorporated into the evaluation process. The means by which this integration is accomplished is the use of present value, a derivation of compound interest.

Compound Interest

With **compound interest,** interest is computed on principal plus previously accumulated interest. For example, assume you deposited $1,000 in a 6% savings account. If the interest is compounded annually, the deposit will grow to $1,191.02 by the end of three years, as shown below.

Year	Beginning Balance	+	Interest at 6%	=	Ending Balance
1	$1,000.00		$60.00		$1,060.00
2	1,060.00		63.60		1,123.60
3	1,123.60		67.42		1,191.02

[1] The discussion that follows is an expansion of the Appendix to Chapter 15.

Observe that the interest rate remains constant at 6%; however, the amount of interest earned each year is growing. The reason is that the interest is based on the principal and also on previously computed interest that is left on deposit.

Despite the apparent simplicity, the calculations become quite burdensome when many years are involved. Fortunately, a formula is available to determine the future value (i.e., ending value) of an investment at a given rate of interest (return). The formula follows.

$$V = P(1 + r)^n$$

where

V = *future value of the investment*
P = *present value of the investment*
r = *interest rate*
n = *number of periods*

To calculate the value of the previous deposit at the end of, say, 2 years, the formula is used as follows:

$$\begin{aligned} V &= P(1 + r)^n \\ &= \$1{,}000(1 + 0.06)^2 \\ &= \$1{,}000(1.1236) \\ &= \$1{,}123.60 \end{aligned}$$

Present Value

An investment such as the foregoing can also be evaluated from a different perspective. Restudy the preceding example. Suppose an opportunity is available that promises a cash inflow of $1,060 at the end of one year. If you are willing to accept a 6% return on your money, how much would you spend to receive this cash flow? The answer is $1,000. Why? If $1,000 is invested immediately at a 6% interest rate, the outlay will grow to the $1,060 that you can receive.

In essence we found this amount by working backward. Rather than take a present amount and extend it out to the future, as we would with compound interest, we took a future amount and brought it back to today (a process often called **discounting**). The $1,000 is termed the **present value** of the investment, that is, the amount an investor is willing to pay to secure a specified cash flow ($1,060) on a future date (one year from now) at a given rate of return (6%). Compound interest and present value can be contrasted as shown in Exhibit 28-1.

Exhibit 28-1

Compound interest versus present value

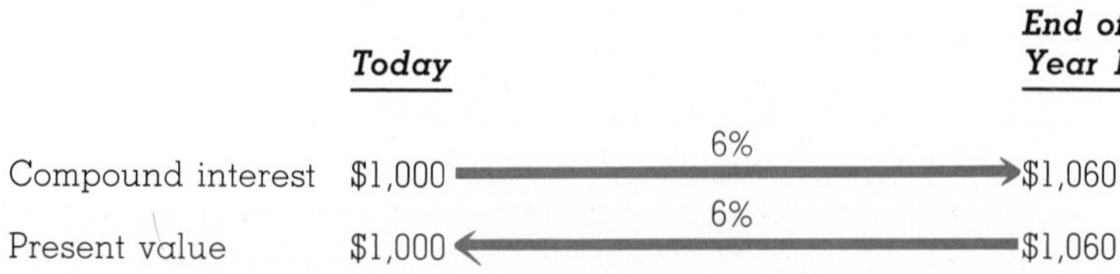

Observe that present value is merely the opposite of compound interest. Thus $1,000 invested today at 6% will grow to $1,060 in one year via compounding, whereas the present value of $1,060 to be received in one year's time given a 6% discount rate is $1,000.

The present value of a future cash flow can be found by solving the compound interest formula for P. Since

$$V = P(1 + r)^n$$

then

$$P = \frac{V}{(1 + r)^n}$$

Using the numbers from the preceding illustration, the $1,000 present value is determined as follows:

$$P = \frac{V}{(1 + r)^n}$$

$$= \frac{\$1{,}060}{(1.06)^1}$$

$$= \$1{,}000$$

Present value tables

Fortunately, tables have been developed to assist in present value computations. Examine Table 1, which appears at the end of the book, on page B-1. The table shows the present value factors of $1 at different rates of interest and for different time periods. Continuing our previous example, the present value factor for $1 to be received in one year given a 6% interest rate is 0.943. Because we are trying to find the present value of $1,060 and not $1, the following calculation is necessary.

cash flow	×	present value factor	=	present value
$1,060	×	0.943	=	$1,000

A quick review of the table reveals that as we go further into the future, the present value factors become smaller. Notice the impact of time on the aforementioned receipt of $1,060.

If Received at the End of Year	The 6% Present Value Factor Would Be	Producing a Present Value of*
1	0.943	$1,000
3	0.840	890
5	0.747	792
7	0.665	705
9	0.592	628

*$1,060 × present value factor.

The present value factors reflect the time value of money—the sooner cash inflows are received, the more valuable they are to the recipient. All other

IS PATIENCE ALWAYS A VIRTUE?

How can you tell an amateur investor from a seasoned pro? One of the most important ways concerns the amateur's way of calculating the profit on a stock. Larry is a 53-year-old salesman for one of the nation's largest chemical companies. By his own admission he "dabbles" in the market.

On February 17, 1978, Larry bought 300 shares of Itek Corp. at $26 per share. The total cost, including commissions, was $7,712. "I think I'll get a good bounce out of it," he said at the time. On February 1, 1980, he sold the 300 shares at $30, which brought him $8,950. "It's topping out," he said. "It looks to me like it's gone as far as it's going to go." The stock doesn't pay a dividend, so Larry's gain (if there were to be any) would have to come from capital appreciation. The stock's increase in price was the only source of potential profit.

How well did Larry do? In his own estimation the answer is "very." What was his reason for that judgment? "Well," he said, "I spent about $7,700. And I got back $8,950. That's a $1,250 gain on a $7,700 investment. Not bad."

Is he right? Suppose he had invested the $7,700 in a one-year money market instrument that earned him 10% per annum, the interest to be paid in a lump sum at maturity. Ignoring tax considerations for a moment, suppose he then repeated the process. Investing the $7,700 + $770 = $8,470 at 10% would have brought him $847. At the second maturity date, Larry would have had $9,317.

He held his Itek stock for approximately two years. Even taking into consideration the more favorable tax treatment accorded capital gains than interest earned, he in fact did no better than he'd have done had his $7,700 remained in a money market fund. Actually, the picture is far worse than it seems, because during the period of ownership the stock suffered a dramatic sinking spell, falling $10 per share from the original acquisition cost. At that point Larry had a $3,000 loss on a $7,700 investment.

In essence he wasn't rewarded for the added risk he took in buying stocks instead of CDs or Treasury bills. Nor, of course, did he expect a guarantee that his profit would be greater merely because he was taking more of a chance. Larry simply hoped he'd do well, and in the end he concluded that he definitely had.

Larry's view of stock market profits is entirely typical. What he omits from his calculations, the majority of investors also overlook—the time value of money. A dollar you own today differs from the one you owned yesterday, and a dollar you receive tomorrow is not the same as one you receive today. There is a date attached to every investment you make, and the longer your money is invested, the more it has to earn just for you to break even.

Generally speaking, picking a stock and staying with it for a few years has proved to be the most successful route for most investors. Yet, lately, a certain amount of agility has been required of those who expect to do well, because the underlying arithmetic has begun to change. Not only are the balance sheets and income statements of corporations being distorted by inflation, so, too, are those of the individual investor. The time value is becoming increasingly more important. When inflation rates were low, patience didn't cost you very much. Now it does.

Gaining a sense of the time value of money is essential for two reasons: it will prevent you from thinking you've made a profit, when in fact you've barely broken even, and it will bring you into closer contact with the investment climate that now prevails. That doesn't mean you'll automatically make a killing in the market. However, it will allow you to better understand the atmosphere of mild panic, which is an integral part of every period of high inflation.

SOURCE Adapted from Srully Blotnick, "The Time Value of Money," Forbes, March 3, 1980, pp. 114–115.

things being equal, companies are willing to pay greater sums of money for those investments that promise quicker dollar returns.

Multiple cash flows and annuities

Most long-term investments affect cash flows for more than a single year. To illustrate the necessary accounting, assume that a firm acquired a machine that promised annual savings in cash operating costs of $2,000 over the next five years. Management requires a return on investment of 10%. For capital budgeting purposes reductions in operating costs are viewed as cash inflows. Using the factors from Table 1, Exhibit 28-2 shows the present value of the machine's savings.

Exhibit 28-2

Discounting multiple cash flows

Year	Cash Flow	×	Present Value Factor at 10%	=	Present Value
1	$2,000		0.909		$1,818
2	2,000		0.826		1,652
3	2,000		0.751		1,502
4	2,000		0.683		1,366
5	2,000		0.621		1,242
Total present value					$7,580

Notice that in each year the present value factor is multiplied by the $2,000 cash flow. The computation would have required less work if the savings had been multiplied by the summation of the individual factors (0.909 + 0.826 + 0.751 + 0.683 + 0.621 = 3.790). As the following calculation shows, the same result is achieved.

$2,000 × 3.790 = $7,580

Our example has focused on an **annuity,** a series of equal cash flows over a number of years. To simplify calculations, an annuity table is often used (see Table 2 at the end of the book, on page B–2). The factor in Table 2 for a $1 annuity over the next five years discounted at 10% is 3.791, which varies slightly from the factor used above because of rounding. As before, the factor is multiplied by the cash flow to derive the cash flow's present value.

Sometimes annuity calculations are needed to discount cash flows that *begin* several years into the future. Suppose, for example, that the machine just illustrated promised annual operating savings of $1,000 for the first two years and $2,000 for each of the next three years. Two annuities are present here, and the present value is found as follows:

Years	Cash Flow	×	Present Value Factor at 10%	=	Present Value
1–2	$1,000		1.736		$1,736
3–5	2,000		2.055*		4,110
Total present value					$5,846

*3.791 − 1.736.

Both factors are again obtained from Table 2. The first factor (1.736) is needed to discount the savings that occur during Years 1 and 2. Turning to the second factor (2.055), the table reveals a factor of 3.791 for a 5-period annuity (Years 1–5) and 1.736 for a 2-period annuity (Years 1–2). Because we are focusing on savings that occur during Years 3–5, 1.736 must be subtracted from 3.791.

The authors have found that many students disregard the annuity concept in favor of a series of yearly multiplications as shown in Exhibit 28-2. We feel that this practice is unwise. Because the annuity factor is really the total of individual present value factors, problem solution time can be greatly reduced. Use the annuity table whenever you are confronted with a series of equal cash flows; the time that you save is well worth the effort in learning the table's operation.

CAPITAL BUDGETING EVALUATION METHODS

Four methods are frequently encountered in practice to evaluate capital budgeting proposals. These include the discounted cash flow methods of net present value and the internal rate of return; the payback method; and the accounting rate of return.

A recent survey of U.S.-based multinational corporations[2] revealed the extent of the use of these popular evaluation tools (see Exhibit 28-3). The exhibit shows that the four methods are normally used in conjunction with

Exhibit 28-3

Use of capital budgeting methods

Method	Use Method Exclusively		Use Method in Combination with Others		Total	
	Number	%	Number	%	Number	%
Net present value	3	2	59	38	62	40
Internal rate of return	11	7	96	62	107	69
Payback	2	1	116	75	118	76
Accounting rate of return	6	4	91	59	97	63
Other	0	0	15	10	15	10

Note: *A total of 155 companies responded.*
SOURCE *Vinod Bavishi, "Capital Budgeting Practices at Multinationals,"* Management Accounting, *August 1981, pp. 32–35.*

[2] A multinational corporation is a corporation that carries on business in more than one country via divisions, subsidiaries, and similar operating units.

one another. This practice prevails because each of the techniques has strengths and weaknesses and provides different information to management.

The majority of our discussion will center on the discounted cash flow methods of net present value and the internal rate of return. Both methods have conceptual advantages over the others cited and have seen increased use in recent years.

Net Present Value

The **net-present-value method** evaluates an investment by netting the present value of the investment's cash inflows against the present value of the cash outflows. The rate of return used for discounting corresponds to or is slightly in excess of the firm's cost of capital.

To illustrate the necessary procedures, assume Alpine Delivery is contemplating an expansion of service to the cities of High Point and Beeville. Two trucks must be acquired at a total cost of $95,000. The trucks have an 8-year life, will be depreciated by using the straight-line method, and are expected to generate annual net cash inflows from new business of $18,000. Alpine requires a 10% minimum return on all investments.

Some managers may be tempted to evaluate the truck acquisition as follows:

Initial investment	*$(95,000)*
Annual cash inflows ($18,000 × 8 years)	*144,000*
Difference in favor of acquisition	*$ 49,000*

This analysis is incorrect for two reasons. First, the computations imply that all the cash inflows are equivalent when, in fact, they are not. Inflows that occur in earlier years can naturally be reinvested for longer periods of time. Second, we cannot compare an immediate cash outflow with cash inflows that are spread over the next 8 years. Since the timing differs, the result is a comparison of dollars of unequal values—basically a study of apples and oranges.

The proper approach is to discount the cash flows at 10%. The correct computations follow.

	Cash Flow	×	*Present Value Factor at 10%*	=	*Present Value*
Initial investment	$(95,000)		1.000		$(95,000)
Annual cash inflows	18,000		5.335		96,030
Net present value					$ 1,030

A factor of 1.0 is utilized for the initial investment because the outlay takes place immediately; the other factor (5.335) is obtained from the annuity table (Table 2).

The net present value of $1,030 indicates that the present value of the inflows exceeds the present value of the outflows. The trucks are therefore an attractive investment and should be acquired if capital is available. Projects that produce a positive net present value are acceptable; those with a negative net present value should be rejected. As we will show shortly, a positive net present value means that the returns from an investment exceed the company's minimum desired rate of return (10% in Alpine's case).

Before leaving this example, note the impact of the discounting process on the decision. Actual cash inflows exceed actual cash outflows by $49,000; yet when discounting is introduced, the present value of the inflows and outflows differs by only $1,030. Incorporating the time value of money certainly diminished the attractiveness of the investment. It is hoped that you can now appreciate the importance of present value when making long-term decisions.

Omission of depreciation expense

Although the trucks had an 8-year life, management disregarded depreciation expense when making the acquisition decision. Depreciation is excluded from present value calculations because of the emphasis on cash flows and depreciation's noncash nature. The cost of the trucks took the form of a single cash outflow of $95,000 at the time of acquisition. Consequently, an additional deduction for depreciation would result in a double counting of the assets' cost.

Despite the noncash character of depreciation, depreciation expense affects the amount of income taxes paid to federal and state governments. Thus there is some impact on the cash flows of the firm. Income taxes, which were ignored in the Alpine example, will be discussed shortly.

An expanded example using net present value

Many decisions faced by managers are of a mutually exclusive nature. **Mutually exclusive** means that the acceptance of one alternative dictates automatic rejection of the other(s). Typical examples of such decisions include a keep-versus-replace decision and the selection of one particular asset when two or more are under consideration (e.g., the acquisition of an Apple microcomputer instead of another competing brand).

The illustration that follows shows the proper technique for evaluating mutually exclusive alternatives. In addition, we will show how the relevancy concept (as introduced in Chapter 27) continues to play an important role in decision making.

Assume the Delicious Baking Company is contemplating the replacement of some equipment acquired four years ago for $55,000. The equipment is expected to provide 6 more years of service if major repairs costing $4,000 are performed 2 years from now. Annual cash operating costs total $13,000 and are not expected to change in future periods. Delicious can sell the equipment now for $24,000; the estimated residual value in 6 years is $5,000.

Management can acquire new equipment costing $62,000. The new equipment has a service life of 6 years, is expected to reduce cash operating costs by $6,000 annually, and has an estimated residual value of $18,000. Major repairs costing $1,500 will be necessary at the end of the fourth year of operation. Company sales will total $240,000 per year, the same level experienced with the present equipment.

If Delicious has a minimum desired rate of return of 14%, should the firm keep its present equipment or acquire the new equipment?

To determine the proper course of action, we must first identify all *relevant* cash flows, namely, those that both occur in the future and differ among the alternatives. Such an analysis reveals that we can disregard the $55,000 cost of the old equipment (it is sunk) and the future sales revenues of $1,440,000 ($240,000 × 6 years), which are common to both the keep and the replace options. After the relevant cash flows are decided, they are discounted by using the present value factors that appear in Tables 1 and 2. The appropriate computations are shown in Exhibit 28-4.

Exhibit 28-4

Delicious Baking Company; analysis of keep and replace alternatives

	Year(s) of Occurrence	Cash Flow	×	Present Value Factor at 14%	=	Present Value
Keep the present equipment						
Cash operating costs	1–6	$(13,000)		3.889		$(50,557)
Major repairs	2	(4,000)		0.769		(3,076)
Disposal	6	5,000		0.456		2,280
Net present value						$(51,353)
Replace the present equipment						
Initial investment	Immediate	$(62,000)		1.000		$(62,000)
Sale of old equipment	Immediate	24,000		1.000		24,000
Cash operating costs ($13,000 − $6,000)	1–6	(7,000)		3.889		(27,223)
Major repairs	4	(1,500)		0.592		(888)
Disposal	6	18,000		0.456		8,208
Net present value						$(57,903)
Net present value in favor of keeping the present equipment						$ 6,550

The analysis reveals a negative net present value for both the keep and the replace alternatives. According to the guidelines presented earlier, a negative net present value calls for rejection. Given the nature of the decision, however, it is impossible to reject both "keep" and "replace." Because one alternative must be selected, Delicious Baking should keep the present equipment. On a discounted cash flow basis, the company stands to benefit by $6,550 [$(51,353) vs. $(57,903)].

Internal Rate of Return

Changing gears for a moment, suppose that Kim Enterprises has a minimum desired rate of return of 10%. Management is confronted with an investment opportunity that costs $12,010 and promises cash inflows of $5,000 for each of the next three years. As the following figures indicate, the investment should be considered for acceptance by virtue of its positive net present value.

Initial investment	*$(12,010) × 1.000*	*$(12,010)*
Annual cash inflows	*5,000 × 2.487**	*12,435*
Net present value		*$ 425*

**From Table 2.*

At this point it is helpful to recall the relationship between present value and compound interest. Present value takes a future amount and, through discounting, determines the amount's "current" value. Compound interest, on the other hand, takes a present amount and extends it out to the future. Now let us focus on Kim's cash inflows. With a 10% rate of return, the present value of the inflows was determined to be $12,435. Thus if $12,435 was invested at 10%, the investment would generate $15,000, specifically, three annual cash receipts of $5,000 each. The proof is shown in Exhibit 28-5 in the form of a savings account. The withdrawals in the exhibit correspond to the company's yearly cash inflows.

Exhibit 28-5

Investment in a savings account

Year	(A) Beginning Account Balance	(B) 10% Interest	(C) A + B	(D) End-of-Year Withdrawal	(E) Ending Account Balance*
1	$12,435	$1,244	$13,679	$5,000	$8,679
2	8,679	868	9,547	5,000	4,547
3	4,547	453†	5,000	5,000	—

**C − D.*
†Rounded.

A deeper probe of this example reveals that Kim does not have to invest $12,435 to generate $15,000 of receipts. Returning to the original data, the investment calls for an outlay of only $12,010. Investing a smaller amount and generating the same inflows can only happen if the investment has a rate of return in excess of 10%. This result is shown below.

Investment	Rate of Return	Cash Inflows
$12,435	10% ——→	$15,000
$12,010	>10% ——→	$15,000

Calculating the actual return

The actual return on a project or investment is termed the **internal rate of return** (sometimes called the time-adjusted rate of return). The National Association of Accountants has described this measure as "the maximum rate of interest that could be paid for the capital employed over the life of an investment without loss on the project."[3] As is evident from our presenta-

[3] *Return on Capital as a Guide to Managerial Decisions,* Research Report No. 35 (New York: National Association of Accountants, 1959), p. 57.

tion, the internal rate of return is another evaluation method that employs discounted cash flows.

The computations related to the internal rate of return are straightforward when the annual cash flows are uniform. To illustrate, consider the manner in which the cash inflows were originally discounted, that is,

cash flow × present value factor at 10% = present value
$5,000 × 2.487 = $12,435

Since the actual rate of return is unknown and Kim need only invest $12,010, we can make the following calculation:

cash flow × present value factor at ?% = present value
$5,000 × F = $12,010

$$F = \frac{\$12{,}010}{\$5{,}000}$$

$$F = 2.402$$

The rate of return on Kim's investment can now be found by determining the rate represented by a factor of 2.402. Because the investment involves a three-year annuity, we must examine Table 2, part of which is reproduced below.

Periods	6%	8%	10%	12%	14%	16%
⋮	⋮	⋮	⋮	⋮	⋮	⋮
3	2.673	2.577	2.487	2.402	2.322	2.246
⋮	⋮	⋮	⋮	⋮	⋮	⋮

Notice that by scanning the line for three periods, we find that the 2.402 factor coincides with a 12% interest rate. Thus Kim's investment yields a 12% rate of return.

Given the nature of the computation, the internal rate of return equates the present value of a project's cash inflows with the present value of the outflows, thereby producing a zero net present value. The appropriate proof follows.

Initial investment [$(12,010) × 1.000]	$(12,010)
Annual cash inflows discounted at 12% ($5,000 × 2.402)	12,010
Net present value	$ –

Should the investment be pursued? As we noted earlier, Kim has a minimum desired rate of return of 10%. Because the project promises a 12% return, it should be considered for acceptance. In contrast, rejection is in order for projects that generate a return less than a company's stipulated minimum.

Two complications

Two complications are normally encountered when computing the internal rate of return. First, the factor that equates the present value of the inflows and outflows usually does not coincide with the factors appearing in the annuity table. Returning to the Kim example, for instance, suppose the investment called for an initial outlay of $11,775 rather than $12,010. The factor for the project would now be 2.355, calculated as follows:

$$\textit{cash flow} \times \textit{present value factor at ?\%} = \textit{present value}$$
$$\$5{,}000 \times F = \$11{,}775$$
$$F = \frac{\$11{,}775}{\$5{,}000}$$
$$F = 2.355$$

Scanning Table 2 for a three-period annuity, we find that the factor falls between a return of 12% and 14%. The exact return is found by using the mathematical process of *interpolation*. The necessary procedures follow.

	Present Value Factors	
12% return	2.402	2.402
Return on Kim's investment	2.355	
14% return		2.322
Difference	0.047	0.080

$$\textit{internal rate of return} = 12\% + \frac{0.047}{0.080}(2\%)^{*}$$
$$= 13.2\%$$

*14% − 12%

The second complication relates to uneven cash flows. The Kim illustration had an immediate single outflow followed by three inflows of $5,000 each. Picture the difficulties that would arise if there were additional flows of, say, an extra payment in the second year and the receipt of a salvage value in the third year. Finding the one factor that equates all inflows and outflows would be burdensome, to say the least, and would require numerous rounds of trial and error. Fortunately, computer programs are available that perform the necessary computations. The accountant is thereby freed to concentrate on the analysis of results rather than the drudgery of calculation.

The Payback Method

Few accountants question the superiority of the discounted cash flow methods for investment analysis. Yet as shown in Exhibit 28-3, methods other than net present value and the internal rate of return are in widespread use. Discounted cash flow began to gain in popularity in the 1950s and is a relative newcomer on the project evaluation scene. For a number of reasons many managers still favor the older approaches, which ignore the time value of money. A brief overview of these approaches is therefore in order.

The **payback method** measures the amount of time it takes to recover a project's initial cash investment. To illustrate the necessary computations, assume that Hill Corporation is examining the possibility of manufacturing a new product. Plant and equipment costing $200,000 must be purchased and should result in net cash inflows of $60,000 for each of the next five years. When the cash flows are uniform, as they are in this example, the payback period is derived by use of the following formula:

$$\text{payback period} = \frac{\text{initial investment}}{\text{annual net cash inflow}}$$

$$= \frac{\$200,000}{\$60,000}$$

$$= 3.33 \text{ years}$$

When one investment replaces another, such as in the acquisition of new machinery and the scrapping of old machinery, both the numerator and denominator are changed slightly. The numerator becomes the *incremental* investment associated with the project; similarly, the denominator reflects the *incremental* net cash inflows.

Uneven cash flows

The formula just shown can only be used with uniform or even net cash inflows. In those situations where the annual inflows are unequal, the flows are summed until the amount of the original investment is reached. For example, assume that the inflows associated with Hill's $200,000 investment are now as follows: Year 1, $70,000; Year 2, $70,000; Year 3, $80,000; Year 4, $50,000; and Year 5, $30,000. The necessary computations are shown below.

Year	Annual Net Cash Inflow	Cumulative Net Cash Inflow
1	$70,000	$ 70,000
2	70,000	140,000
3	80,000	220,000
4	50,000	270,000
5	30,000	300,000

The computations reveal that $140,000 is recovered by the end of Year 2 and $220,000 by the conclusion of Year 3. Thus the 200,000th dollar arrives sometime during Year 3 as a result of the $80,000 net cash inflow. The payback method assumes that cash flows are spread evenly throughout the period. Consequently, the additional $60,000 that must be recovered in Year 3 to reach the payback ($200,000 – $140,000) is assumed to be received three quarters of the way through the year ($60,000/$80,000). The payback, then, is 2.75 years.

Use of payback: Pros and cons

The payback method provides its users with a very simple tool for project evaluation. By comparing a project's payback period against a preestablished standard, a manager can rapidly determine project acceptability. This type of comparison is especially useful for companies having limited cash balances and desiring a rapid recovery of investment dollars. Short paybacks allow cash-starved businesses to undertake additional opportunities: the sooner cash is received, the sooner reinvestment can occur.

Unfortunately, the use of payback is not problem-free. In addition to ignoring the time value of money, the payback method exhibits a serious weakness by disregarding project profitability. To illustrate, assume that a company can invest in one of the following projects.

Project	Initial Investment	Annual Net Cash Inflows	Project Life
A	$100,000	$50,000	3 years
B	100,000	40,000	6 years

If the decision is based solely on payback, project A would be selected, because the initial investment is recovered more quickly.

$$\textit{project A payback} = \frac{\$100{,}000}{\$50{,}000} = 2.0 \textit{ years}$$

$$\textit{project B payback} = \frac{\$100{,}000}{\$40{,}000} = 2.5 \textit{ years}$$

Is this the correct choice, however? Most companies make investments to generate profit, not to see how fast funds can be returned. Project B is really a better selection, because inflows will total $140,000 ($40,000 × 3.5 years) versus $50,000 ($50,000 × 1 year) for project A *after* the respective payback periods are reached. Stated differently, the payback method considers net cash inflows up until the time the initial investment is recovered; subsequent inflows are disregarded.

An astute student may observe that investment B's returns occur over a longer period of time, and thus the time value of money could be a significant factor in the selection process. This is a distinct possibility. As we noted earlier, the payback method ignores discounted cash flows. Because of this problem (and others), the payback method should not be used exclusively. Instead payback analysis should be employed in conjunction with other techniques that provide different types of information to management.

Accounting Rate of Return

In Chapters 19 and 25 we discussed a ratio called return on assets to evaluate the performance of companies and investment centers. This same measurement concept is also used to examine and screen investment proposals; however, the name changes slightly along with the method of computation. The **accounting rate of return,** sometimes known as the unadjusted rate of return, focuses on the average net income generated by a project in relation to the project's initial investment outlay. Unlike the evaluation methods discussed earlier, this capital budgeting technique emphasizes net income and *not* net cash flows. A proper measure of profit, of course, includes a deduction for depreciation expense.

The accounting rate of return is computed by the following formula·

$$\text{accounting rate of return} = \frac{\text{average annual increase in net income}}{\text{initial investment}}$$

To illustrate the necessary computations, assume that a company is considering the acquisition of some new machinery that costs \$80,000. The machinery has a service life of 10 years, no residual value, and will be depreciated by using the straight-line method. Annual net cash inflows from operations are expected to increase by \$28,000. The accounting rate of return is 25%, derived as follows:

$$\text{accounting rate of return} = \frac{\$28{,}000 - \$8{,}000}{\$80{,}000} = 25\%$$

The numerator is computed by subtracting depreciation expense of \$8,000 (\$80,000 ÷ 10 years) from the operating cash flows.

Because the machinery will be depreciated, some companies feel the accounting rate of return is more appropriately based on an average investment figure rather than on the initial outlay. The average investment can be calculated by adding the beginning and ending investment and dividing by 2, specifically, (\$80,000 + \$0) ÷ 2, or \$40,000.

Evaluation of the accounting rate of return

The accounting rate of return remains popular primarily because of its consistency with the techniques used to evaluate companywide and divisional performance. Despite this popularity, the accounting rate of return has two serious drawbacks. In theory, this method should parallel conventional accounting procedures for determining net income and asset investment. Frequently, however, there are glaring incongruities. Picture, for example, a business that desires to pursue an extensive marketing campaign. In accordance with financial accounting principles, the marketing outlays would probably be expensed. For rate of return calculations, however, the outlays should be placed in the denominator to measure required investment.

The second drawback relates to the method's disregard for the time value of money. Consider the investment proposals that appear in Exhibit 28-6. Ignoring the time value of money, both investments are equally desirable, as evidenced by identical accounting rates of return of 16.7%. Most managers, however, would voice a preference for investment B because of the earlier cash flows. The internal rate of return, which takes timing differences into consideration, is thus a better decision-making tool.

While these proposals vary greatly in terms of cash flows, the differences between the cash flows of other investments may not be so great. As a result, a simple inspection may not reveal a clear-cut favorite in terms of present value. The outcome could be that management is misled when using the accounting rate of return for selecting among alternative courses of action.

Exhibit 28-6

Analysis of investment proposals

	Investment A	Investment B
Initial investment	$120,000	$120,000
Annual net cash inflows		
Year 1	$ —	$ 60,000
Year 2	—	60,000
Year 3	180,000	60,000
Total	$180,000	$180,000
Average annual net cash inflow (total ÷ 3 years)	$ 60,000	$ 60,000
Less annual depreciation ($120,000 ÷ 3 years)	40,000	40,000
Average annual increase in net income	$ 20,000	$ 20,000
Accounting rate of return ($20,000 ÷ $120,000)	16.7%	16.7%
Internal rate of return (computed by trial and error)	14.5%	23.4%

CAPITAL BUDGETING: SOME FINAL THOUGHTS

Many students experience difficulty with capital budgeting, especially with discounted cash flow techniques. Although our presentation may have seemed extremely technical, realize that we have only skimmed the surface. Many complicating factors ordinarily considered when making decisions were omitted for the sake of simplicity. One factor that comes to mind in this respect is income tax.

Businesses pay a substantial amount of their profits to governmental authorities. Thus the revenues and expenses associated with an investment opportunity require examination in light of their impact on tax obligations and related cash flows. Even depreciation must be considered. Although it is a noncash expense, businesses are entitled to a depreciation (cost recovery) deduction when computing taxable income. Because a lower taxable income results in reduced taxes, depreciation provides a tax savings for the firm. Other items affecting taxable income, such as gains and losses, must be analyzed in a similar manner.

Capital budgeting is a powerful tool that has accounting, finance, and management implications. Since capital expenditures are a part of the activity of virtually all organizations (and individuals too), you should become well acquainted with the material presented in this chapter. At some future date you will undoubtedly be called upon to make a long-term decision of one type or another. The techniques and concepts discussed herein will be of considerable benefit when evaluating the various alternatives that require analysis.

SUMMARY PROBLEM

The Ellison Corporation is contemplating the following investment opportunity:

Initial outlay required	*$225,000*
Net cash inflows, Years 1–5	*75,000*
Disposal value at the end of Year 5	*5,000*

Ellison desires a minimum return of 12% on all investments.

INSTRUCTIONS

a **Compute the project's payback period.**

b **Compute the net present value of the project. Should the project be considered for acceptance? Explain.**

c **Compute the project's internal rate of return. For simplicity disregard the $5,000 disposal value.**

SOLUTION

a

Year	Annual Net Cash Inflow	Cumulative Net Cash Inflow
1	$75,000	$ 75,000
2	75,000	150,000
3	75,000	225,000
4	75,000	300,000
5	80,000	380,000

The payback period is 3 years.

b

	Cash Flow	×	Present Value Factor at 12%	=	Present Value
Initial investment	$(225,000)		1.000		$(225,000)
Annual net cash inflows	75,000		3.605		270,375
Disposal value	5,000		0.567		2,835
Net present value					$ 48,210

The net present value is positive, meaning the return on the project exceeds the 12% minimum. The project should therefore be considered for acceptance.

c **cash flow × present value factor at ?% = present value**

$$\$75{,}000 \times F = \$225{,}000$$
$$F = 3.000$$

Table 2 reveals that for a 5-year annuity a 3.000 factor lies between 18% and 20%. The internal rate of return is 19.9%, as shown below.

	Present Value Factors	
18% return	3.127	3.127
Return on Ellison's investment	3.000	
20% return		2.991
Difference	0.127	0.136

$$\text{internal rate of return} = 18\% + \frac{0.127}{0.136}(2\%)^* = 19.9\%$$

*20% − 18%

KEY TERMS AND CONCEPTS

accounting rate of return 1112
annuity 1103
capital budgeting 1096
compound interest 1099
cost of capital 1098
discounting 1100
internal rate of return 1108
mutually exclusive alternatives 1106
net-present-value method 1105
payback method 1110
present value 1100
time value of money 1099

QUESTIONS

Q28-1 Why should businesses exercise extreme care in the selection of long-term investments?

Q28-2 Describe the screening and ranking processes as related to capital budgeting.

Q28-3 What three factors should be considered in the evaluation of an investment opportunity?

Q28-4 Explain what is meant by the time value of money.

Q28-5 Explain the relationship, if any, between compound interest and present value.

Q28-6 What is meant by the term "present value"?

Q28-7 What is an annuity?

Q28-8 Four methods are frequently used to evaluate capital budgeting proposals. Are these methods normally used by themselves or in conjunction with each other? Why?

Q28-9 What are mutually exclusive alternatives? Present several examples.

Q28-10 Aside from ignoring the time value of money, what is another inherent problem associated with the payback method?

EXERCISES

E28-1 Calculate the present value of each of the following cash flows.

a An annual receipt of $8,000 over the next five years given a 10% rate of return.

b A single cash inflow of $14,000 in three years given a 12% rate of return.

c A single receipt of $10,000 at the end of Year 1 followed by a single receipt of $8,000 at the end of Year 2. The company has a 14% rate of return.

d An annual receipt of $6,000 for three years followed by a single receipt of $7,000 at the end of Year 4. The company has a 16% rate of return.

E28-2 The following information pertains to four independent investments.

	A	*B*	*C*	*D*
Present value	?	$19,644	$34,622	$50,850
Interest rate	10%	?	14%	12%
Investment period	4 years	5 years	?	10 years
Annual cash inflows	$8,000	$ 6,000	$ 7,000	?

Determine the unknown in each of the investments.

E28-3 The following items are independent of one another and require the use of present value computations. Round all calculations to the nearest dollar.

a You have $8,000 to invest and require a 10% minimum rate of return. Two proposals are under consideration. Investment A returns $2,000 for each of the next six years; investment B promises $2,500 for the next two years and $1,450 for each of the following five years. Which investment will you select? Why?

b You have $9,000 to invest. An opportunity is available that produces a stream of six annual inflows of $2,000 each.

(1) Compute the investment's internal rate of return.

(2) Determine the net present value of the investment if your rate of return is 8%.

E28-4 McMurray Company is investigating the possibility of installing some new equipment. Management estimates that the equipment will produce the following savings in cash operating costs over the next five years.

Year	Savings in Cash Operating Costs
1	$5,000
2	5,500
3	6,200
4	6,700
5	6,000

a Determine the maximum amount McMurray should pay for this equipment, assuming a minimum desired rate of return of 12%. Round all calculations to the nearest dollar.

b Independent of your answer in part (a), assume that McMurray paid $19,380 to acquire the equipment. Determine the payback period.

E28-5 Collins Corporation is considering the acquisition of a new delivery truck, costing $26,000, to expand its service area. Annual cash inflows are expected to increase by $6,000 over the next two years, $8,000 over the following two years, and $11,000 over the final three years of the truck's service life. The truck will be depreciated by the straight-line method and is expected to have a $2,000 disposal value.

Management evaluates investment opportunities by using the payback and net-present-value methods. Collins desires a minimum payback of four years and a minimum rate of return of 12%. Ignore income taxes.

a Should the truck be acquired? Explain your answer.

b What problems associated with the payback method are overcome by the net-present-value method?

E28-6 Specialty Parts, Inc., is contemplating the acquisition of new machinery that costs $39,000. The machinery has an estimated residual value of $6,000 at the end of its five-year service life and is expected to generate the following savings in cash operating costs:

Year	*Cash Operating Savings*
1	$12,000
2	12,000
3	10,000
4	8,000
5	5,000

Old equipment with a book value of $2,000 will be sold for $3,000 at the time the new machinery is acquired. Specialty uses straight-line depreciation and requires a 16% minimum return on all investments. Ignore income taxes.

By using the net-present-value method, determine whether the new machinery should be acquired.

E28-7 Sipe and Associates uses the payback method to evaluate investment opportunities. Three investment proposals are under consideration, each requiring an initial outlay of $150,000. Cash inflow information follows.

Investment A		*Investment B*		*Investment C*	
Year	*Net Cash Inflow*	*Year*	*Net Cash Inflow*	*Year*	*Net Cash Inflow*
1	$30,000	1	$45,000	1–3	$35,000
2	30,000	2	60,000	4	20,000
3	30,000	3	35,000	5	10,000
4	30,000	4	10,000	6	5,000
5	30,000	5	15,000		
6–10	15,000	6	27,000		

a Compute the payback period of each investment.

b Solely on the basis of payback, which of the three investments is the most attractive? Why?

c From a total cash flow viewpoint, which of the three investments is really the most attractive? Why? Disregard the time value of money.

d To provide the decision maker with additional information, what could Sipe do to the cash inflows? Why would this process be helpful?

E28-8 Kilgore Corporation is considering the purchase of a machine costing $58,280. The machine has a four-year life and will result in net cash inflows of $20,000 per year. Assume the use of straight-line depreciation, no residual value, and no income taxes.

a Determine the machine's net present value if Kilgore has a 10% rate of return.

b Compute the machine's internal rate of return.

c Determine the payback period.

d Determine the accounting rate of return on the company's initial investment.

PROBLEMS

P28-1 ***Straightforward net-present-value and payback computations***

Outdoors, Inc., is contemplating the acquisition of a sight-seeing boat for summer tours along the Ohio River. The following information is available.

Cost of boat	$360,000
Service life	8 summer seasons
Disposal value at the end of 8 seasons	$80,000
Variable operating costs per trip	$850
Fixed operating costs per season (including straight-line depreciation)	$65,000
Capacity per trip	250 passengers

Passengers will pay $5 per trip. From similar operations in other parts of the country, management anticipates that each trip will be sold out and that 75,000 passengers will be carried each season. The company's minimum desired return on all investments is 12%. Ignore income taxes.

INSTRUCTIONS

a Compute the payback period of the boat.

b By using the net-present-value method, determine whether Outdoors, Inc., should acquire the boat.

c Assume your answer in part (b) recommended against acquisition. What actions could management take to further improve the attractiveness of this investment?

P28-2 ***Cash flow schedule and net-present-value analysis***

Funtyme, Inc., operates amusement parks in the states of Florida, Texas, and California. The company is planning to expand its Florida park by acquiring a neighboring wax museum at a cost of $5,000,000. The acquisition will be financed by obtaining a 16% loan. Interest and principal will be repaid in five installments, the first payment coinciding with the conclusion of the museum's first year of operation. Interest is computed on the unpaid loan balance at the beginning of the year.

Funtyme will set a 75¢-per-person admission charge to the museum. Management estimates the following attendance:

Year of Operation	Attendance
1	1,200,000
2–4	1,500,000
5–10	1,700,000

Annual cash outlays for operating costs are estimated at $200,000 for the first two years of ownership. Costs should rise to $250,000 in Years 3 and 4 and level off at $300,000 during Years 5–10. Funtyme requires a 14% rate of return on all investments.

INSTRUCTIONS

a Prepare a schedule of cash receipts and disbursements from operations for the first five years of ownership. Will the project generate sufficient cash flows to pay the loan interest and principal?

b By using the net-present-value method, determine whether the museum meets management's 14% target rate of return.

P28-3 ***Financing decisions via net present value***

Buckner Enterprises operates a chain of franchised sporting goods stores throughout the country. Management has recently been approached by two dealers about the possibility of obtaining some inexpensive financing. The dealers will repay Buckner within three years and have agreed to pay 5% of their store's net income as interest. Payments will be made at the end of each year. The following information is available.

	Store No. 614	Store No. 724
Financing requested	$80,000	$50,000
Repayment of principal		
Year 1	$10,000	$15,000
Year 2	25,000	15,000
Year 3	45,000	20,000
Total	$80,000	$50,000
Forecasted net income		
Year 1	$200,000	$170,000
Year 2	230,000	210,000
Year 3	260,000	220,000

Management believes that the financing requests should be granted only if the return to the company exceeds the target internal rate of return on investment of 18%.

INSTRUCTIONS

a Compute the net present value of the financing requests of stores no. 614 and no. 724. Round calculations to the nearest dollar.

b Do either of the requests exceed management's 18% target rate of return? Explain your answer.

c Buckner is a strong believer of incorporating the time value of money into the decision process. Is this a wise policy? Explain.

P28-4 ***Net-present-value analysis and relevant costs***

Baxter, Inc., has just developed a new product that monitors the fuel efficiency of cars and trucks. The firm is anxious to manufacture the device and has made marketing and cost studies to assess probable demand and profit levels. The following information is available.

a The studies noted above were made last year at a cost of $35,000.

b Plant and equipment necessary to engage in production activities costs $6,000,000, has a 10-year life, and has a $400,000 residual value. Baxter uses straight-line depreciation on all assets.

c Projected annual sales in units over the next ten years are as follows:

Year 1	100,000
Year 2	150,000
Year 3	210,000
Year 4	275,000
Years 5–10	310,000

d The devices will be sold for $25 each. Unit variable costs are forecasted as follows:

Direct materials	$7
Direct labor	5
Factory overhead	4
Selling & administrative	3

e Production and sales of the new device require an immediate $450,000 investment to build direct materials and finished goods inventories. These inventories will be depleted at the end of ten years, allowing Baxter to recover its outlay.

f Fixed costs of salaries, maintenance, taxes, insurance, and depreciation related to the required plant and equipment are expected to total $680,000 per year.

g In order to gain rapid entry into the market, Baxter will advertise heavily in the early years of product sales. Forecasted annual advertising outlays follow.

Year 1	$275,000
Year 2	175,000
Years 3–10	50,000

Baxter uses the net-present-value method to analyze investments and requires a minimum rate of return of 14%.

INSTRUCTIONS

Should Baxter acquire the necessary plant and equipment and produce the monitoring device? Show all calculations and ignore income taxes.

P28-5 ***Make or buy using net present value***

Republic Products is a manufacturer of electronic components used in the automobile industry. The company is currently purchasing a particular part for $2.20. Because of problems with product quality and supplier reliability, Republic is studying whether to manufacture the part internally.

To begin production, Republic must acquire new machinery costing $320,000. The machinery, which has a four-year life and an estimated residual value of $20,000, will be depreciated by the straight-line method. Al Ortiz, a current Republic employee, will oversee manufacturing activities. Ortiz presently earns an annual salary of $22,000 but will be given a raise of $4,000 because of increased responsibilities. Ortiz's original position will remain unfilled.

The company's cost accountants and engineers have estimated unit variable production costs as follows:

Direct materials	$0.40
Direct labor	0.20
Variable factory overhead	0.30

Republic must invest $24,000 to build needed direct materials inventories. Annual production should total 80,000 units over the next four years. Manufacturing activities will then be discontinued and direct materials inventories depleted because of a planned change in Republic's product line. The machinery will be sold because of its specialized nature.

Management uses the net-present-value method to analyze investment opportunities and requires a 12% minimum rate of return. Ignore income taxes.

INSTRUCTIONS

Should Republic make or buy the part? Show computations to support your answer.

P28-6 ***Discounted cash flow and book publishing***

Agnes Princehouse, business editor of Dunbar Publishers, is contemplating the publication of a new statistics book by two well-known authors. Reviews of sample chapters have been favorable. The book, which is suitable for use in introductory statistics courses, will be sold by college bookstores. Projected sales and selling prices during the text's three-year life are presented below.

Year	***Sales Volume (Copies)***	***Selling Price per Copy***
1	40,000	$20
2	25,000	22
3	10,000	24

The bookstores keep 20% of the selling price as profit; the remainder is remitted to Dunbar. The authors each receive a 5% royalty on book sales; the royalty is based on the *net* selling price. Upon contract signing, which will occur immediately, each author will receive a $7,000 advance payment of the first year's royalties.

Book writing and production are projected to take three years. The following schedule of production and marketing outlays has been assembled.

	Production Outlays	***Marketing Outlays***
Contract signing	$ —	$ —
Year 1	2,000	—
Year 2	5,000	3,000
Year 3	825,000	50,000
Year 4 (book is published and sales commence)	—	40,000
Year 5	—	15,000
Year 6	—	—

Dunbar requires a 12% return on investment. Ignore income taxes.

INSTRUCTIONS

a By using the net-present-value method, determine whether Dunbar should publish the book. Assume royalty payments (except for the advances) are made in the year of sale. Round all calculations to the nearest dollar.

b Given the nature of book publishing, would the accounting rate of return or the internal rate of return be a better measure of performance for Dunbar? Explain your answer.

P28-7 ***Equipment replacement decision***

R. Davis Industries is contemplating the replacement of some equipment acquired for $45,000. The equipment is expected to provide five more years of service if major repairs costing $5,400 are performed in three years. Annual cash operating costs total $18,500. Davis can sell the equipment now for $25,000; the estimated residual value in five years is $1,000.

New equipment is available that will reduce annual cash operating costs to $13,000. The equipment costs $48,000, has a service life of five years, and has an estimated residual value of $6,000. Company sales will total $325,000 per year with either the existing or new equipment.

Davis has a minimum desired rate of return of 16% and depreciates all equipment by the straight-line method.

INSTRUCTIONS

a By using the net-present-value method, determine whether Davis should keep its present equipment or acquire the new equipment. Round all calculations to the nearest dollar, and ignore income taxes.

b What other factors should be considered in this decision?

P28-8 ***Real estate analysis using net present value***

W. R. Rust is a partner with one of the Big Eight public accounting firms. In recent years Rust has invested substantial sums of money in rental property. Six years ago he acquired an apartment building for $320,000 by paying $35,000 down and signing a note payable for the remaining balance. Annual note payments total $42,000; the note will be paid off in nine more years.

Rust has received an offer from Mather and Associates to sell the apartment complex. Mather will pay $210,000 now and annual payments of $75,000 over the next ten years. If he accepts the offer, Rust would pay off the mortgage note with an immediate outlay of $230,000.

Annual revenues and operating expenses related to the property follow.

Rental revenues		$124,000
Expenses		
Maintenance	$19,000	
Insurance	22,000	
Taxes	26,000	
Depreciation	15,000	
Other	5,000	87,000
Net income		$ 37,000

If he doesn't sell the apartment at this time, Rust will keep the complex for ten more years and then dispose of it at a healthy profit. Real estate agents feel that the apartment should sell for approximately four times the original acquisition cost.

Rust requires a 10% minimum rate of return on all investments. Ignore income taxes.

INSTRUCTIONS

Should Rust keep the apartment complex or sell it to Mather and Associates? Use the net-present-value method to determine your answer.

P28-9 ***Accounting and internal rates of return***

M&L, Inc., is studying the following two investments in depreciable assets.

Investment A. The initial outlay required is $50,000, with the following schedule of cash flows.

Year	Cash Inflows	Cash Outflows
1	$29,000	$ 8,000
2	36,000	15,000
3	41,000	20,000
4	45,000	24,000

Investment B. The initial outlay required is $50,000, with the following schedule of cash flows.

Year	Cash Inflows	Cash Outflows
1	$ —	$ —
2	—	—
3	—	—
4	157,500	73,500

Each investment will be depreciated by the straight-line method over a four-year life. Disregard residual values and income taxes.

INSTRUCTIONS

a Compute the accounting rate of return for each investment. M&L calculates the rate of return on the investment's initial acquisition cost.

b Compute the internal rate of return for investment A.

c Assuming the internal rate of return on investment B is 14%, compare the results obtained in parts (a) and (b). Comment on any differences that arose, and explain an underlying problem associated with the accounting rate of return.

P28-10 ***Straightforward net-present-value and payback computations (alternate to P28-1)***

Chicago, Inc., is contemplating the acquisition of a sight-seeing boat for summer tours along the Chicago River and Lake Michigan. The following information is available.

Cost of boat	$600,000
Service life	12 summer seasons
Disposal value at the end of 12 seasons	$60,000
Variable operating costs per trip	$800
Fixed operating costs per season (including straight-line depreciation)	$115,000
Capacity per trip	300 passengers

Passengers will pay $4 per trip. From similar operations in other parts of the country, management anticipates that each trip will be sold out and that 120,000 passengers will be carried each season. The company's minimum desired return on all investments is 10%. Ignore income taxes.

INSTRUCTIONS

a Compute the payback period of the boat.

b By using the net-present-value method, determine whether Chicago, Inc., should acquire the boat.

c Suppose the net present value is positive but extremely small. What other factors should be considered before the final decision is made?

P28-11 ***Make or buy using net present value (alternate to P28-5)***

Shepherd Products is a manufacturer of electronic components used in the computer industry. The company is currently purchasing a particular part for $4.10. Because of problems with product quality and supplier reliability, Shepherd is studying whether to manufacture the part internally.

To begin production, Shepherd must acquire new machinery costing $450,000. The machinery, which has a five-year life and an estimated residual value of $50,000, will be depreciated by the straight-line method. Sam Farris, a current Shepherd employee, will oversee manufacturing activities. Farris presently earns an annual salary of $24,000 but will be given a raise of $6,000 because of increased responsibilities. Farris's original position will remain unfilled.

The company's cost accountants and engineers have estimated unit variable production costs as follows:

Direct materials	$1.10
Direct labor	0.50
Variable factory overhead	0.80

Shepherd must invest $38,000 to build needed direct materials inventories. Annual production should total 90,000 units over the next five years. Manufacturing activities will then be discontinued and direct materials inventories depleted because of a planned change in Shepherd's product line. The machinery will be sold because of its specialized nature.

Management uses the net-present-value method to analyze investment opportunities and requires a 16% minimum rate of return. Ignore income taxes.

INSTRUCTIONS

Should Shepherd make or buy the part? Show computations to support your answer.

P28-12 ***Equipment replacement decision (alternate to P28-7)***

Pioneer Products is contemplating the replacement of some equipment acquired for $68,000. The equipment is expected to provide four more years of service if major repairs costing $9,500 are performed in two years. Annual cash operating costs total $23,600. Pioneer can sell the equipment now for $21,000; the estimated residual value in four years is $1,500.

New equipment is available that will reduce annual cash operating costs to $13,000. The equipment costs $71,000, has a service life of four years, and has an estimated residual value of $20,000. Company sales will total $390,000 per year with either the existing or new equipment.

Pioneer has a minimum desired rate of return of 14% and depreciates all equipment by the straight-line method.

INSTRUCTIONS

a By using the net-present-value method, determine whether Pioneer should keep its present equipment or acquire the new equipment. Round all calculations to the nearest dollar, and ignore income taxes.

b Discuss the factors Pioneer probably considered when establishing its 14% target rate of return.

P28-13 ***Real estate analysis using net present value (alternate to P28-8)***

B. J. Morrison is a partner with one of the Big Eight public accounting firms. In recent years Morrison has invested substantial sums of money in rental property. Five years ago he acquired an apartment building for $460,000 by paying $55,000 down and signing a note payable for the remaining balance. Annual note payments total $72,000; the note will be paid off in ten more years.

Morrison has received an offer from Davey and Associates to sell the apartment complex. Davey will pay $275,000 now and annual payments of $80,000 over the next eleven years. If he accepts the offer, Morrison would pay off the mortgage note with an immediate outlay of $390,000.

Annual revenues and operating expenses related to the property follow.

Rental revenues		$180,000
Expenses		
Maintenance	$31,000	
Insurance	29,000	
Taxes	35,000	
Depreciation	23,000	
Other	7,000	125,000
Net income		$ 55,000

If he doesn't sell the apartment at this time, Morrison will keep the complex for eleven more years and then dispose of it at a healthy profit. Real estate agents feel that the apartment should sell for approximately four times the original acquisition cost.

Morrison requires a 12% minimum rate of return on all investments. Ignore income taxes.

INSTRUCTIONS

Should Morrison keep the apartment complex or sell it to Davey and Associates? Use the net-present-value method to determine your answer.

P28-14 ***Accounting and internal rates of return (alternate to P28-9)***

Mitchell Company is studying the following two investments in depreciable assets.

Investment 1. The initial outlay required is $80,000, with the following schedule of cash flows.

Year	Cash Inflows	Cash Outflows
1	$56,000	$21,000
2	62,000	27,000
3	71,000	36,000
4	78,000	43,000

Investment 2. The initial outlay required is $80,000, with the following schedule of cash flows.

Year	Cash Inflows	Cash Outflows
1	$ —	$ —
2	—	—
3	—	—
4	305,400	165,400

Each investment will be depreciated by the straight-line method over a four-year life. Disregard residual values and income taxes.

INSTRUCTIONS

a Compute the accounting rate of return for each investment. Mitchell calculates the rate of return on the investment's initial acquisition cost.

b Compute the internal rate of return for investment 1.

c Assume the internal rate of return for investment 2 amounts to 15.1%. Explain why the internal rate of return differs between investments 1 and 2.

CASE 28
MARTHA AND KATY

Martha and Katy are two sisters who retired several years ago from their work as seamstresses with the Grenniston Clothing Company and are now looking for profitable investments.

An alteration business in a nearby shopping center has just become available for sale. The business is organized as a corporation and has annual sales of $128,000. Salaries total $28,000; other cash operating costs should amount to $35,000. Annual straight-line depreciation on the shop's equipment totals $5,000. Each year the ending cash balance will be withdrawn in the form of cash dividends.

The present owner will sell the business for $140,000. Martha and Katy require a minimum rate of return of 12%. The business is subject to an income tax rate of 40%.

INSTRUCTIONS

a Determine the shop's yearly net income.

b Determine the yearly dividends the women can expect. *Hint:* Remember that depreciation, although a noncash expense, affects income taxes.

c By using the internal-rate-of-return method, determine whether the alteration business is an attractive investment. Assume that Martha and Katy will operate the shop for five years.

APPENDIX A SPECIMEN FINANCIAL STATEMENTS

The next few pages contain recent financial statements of Wendy's International, Inc., a firm well-known for the operation of fast food restaurants. These statements are representative of those issued by other large corporations and reflect many of the topics discussed in this text.

Also included in these pages is a comprehensive set of footnotes. The footnotes expand upon the material presented in the statements and enlighten readers who desire further information about the firm's resources, obligations, transactions, and financial reporting practices. In addition, on page A-15, you will find an audit report to Wendy's stockholders from Coopers & Lybrand, a Big Eight accounting firm. The audit report indicates that the statements present fairly the company's financial position, changes in financial position, and results of operations.

CONSOLIDATED BALANCE SHEET

Wendy's International, Inc. and subsidiaries

December 31	(In thousands) 1981	1980
ASSETS		
Current assets:		
Cash	$ 9,210	$ 5,876
Short term investments, at cost which approximates market	12,877	7,012
Notes receivable	2,713	186
Accounts receivable	7,841	5,328
Inventories and other	5,967	6,305
	38,608	24,707
Property and equipment, at cost:		
Land	54,121	40,410
Buildings	82,212	56,920
Leasehold improvements	45,881	21,787
Restaurant equipment	75,317	48,853
Other equipment	19,016	10,808
Construction in progress	1,300	2,896
Capitalized leases	51,975	22,286
	329,822	203,960
Less accumulated depreciation and amortization	(48,814)	(29,725)
	281,008	174,235
Other assets:		
Unexpended construction funds	7,067	
Cost in excess of net assets acquired, net	19,408	8,648
Other	30,138	11,278
	56,613	19,926
	$376,229	$218,868

The accompanying notes are an integral part of the consolidated financial statements.

December 31	1981 (In thousands)	1980
LIABILITIES AND SHAREHOLDERS' EQUITY		
Current liabilities:		
Accounts payable, trade	$ 36,899	$ 24,685
Federal, state and local income taxes	4,074	6,257
Accrued expenses:		
Salaries and wages	3,486	3,440
Taxes	6,228	3,100
Other	5,853	3,220
Current portion of long term obligations	9,836	4,340
	66,376	45,042
Long term obligations, net of current portion:		
Term debt	52,242	22,458
Capitalized lease obligations	45,714	19,960
	97,956	42,418
Deferred technical assistance fees	1,433	1,644
Deferred income taxes	8,726	4,168
Shareholders' equity:		
Common stock, $.10 stated value Authorized: 40,000,000 shares Issued and outstanding: 25,550,000 and 22,436,000 shares, respectively	2,555	2,244
Capital in excess of stated value	79,827	34,126
Retained earnings	119,356	89,226
	201,738	125,596
	$376,229	$218,868

CONSOLIDATED STATEMENT OF INCOME AND RETAINED EARNINGS

Wendy's International, Inc. and subsidiaries

Years ended December 31	1981	1980	1979
	(In thousands except per share data)		
Revenue:			
Retail operations	$446,800	$310,067	$237,753
Royalties	38,619	35,555	30,565
Technical assistance fees	1,223	1,406	2,822
Other	3,787	2,999	2,903
	490,429	350,027	274,043
Costs and expenses:			
Cost of sales	257,735	187,968	146,347
Company restaurant operating costs	114,233	67,714	54,993
Direct expenses of franchise personnel	5,061	4,544	4,187
General and administrative expenses	24,521	19,831	15,742
Depreciation and amortization of property and equipment	15,308	9,782	7,356
Interest	8,919	5,467	4,358
	425,777	295,306	232,983
Income before income taxes	64,652	54,721	41,060
Income taxes:			
Federal:			
Current	20,554	20,557	15,584
Deferred	4,341	2,141	1,303
	24,895	22,698	16,887
State and local	2,905	1,927	1,077
	27,800	24,625	17,964
Net income	36,852	30,096	23,096
Retained earnings—beginning of year	89,226	65,094	47,692
Cash dividends	(6,722)	(5,964)	(5,694)
Retained earnings—end of year	$119,356	$ 89,226	$ 65,094
Per share data:			
Net income per share	$1.52	$1.34	$1.03
Weighted average shares outstanding	24,297	22,516	22,456
Dividends per share	$.28	$.27	$.27

The accompanying notes are an integral part of the consolidated financial statements.

CONSOLIDATED STATEMENT OF CHANGES IN FINANCIAL POSITION

Wendy's International, Inc. and subsidiaries

		(In thousands)	
Years ended December 31	1981	1980	1979
Sources of working capital:			
Operations:			
Net Income	$ 36,852	$ 30,096	$ 23,096
Items not involving working capital:			
Depreciation and amortization	16,291	10,274	7,663
Deferred income taxes	4,558	2,141	1,303
Other, net			(56)
	57,701	42,511	32,006
Property and equipment dispositions, net	2,649	2,280	1,602
Additional term debt	33,193	5,162	12,900
Additional capitalized lease obligations	952	1,966	2,699
Purchases of franchise owners:			
Long term obligations	41,522		2,832
Issuance of common stock:			
Public offering	33,373		
Purchases of subsidiaries	8,978		
Warrant and option exercises, and other	3,688	769	202
Assets held for resale		2,380	
Total sources of working capital	182,056	55,068	52,241
Dispositions of working capital:			
Property and equipment additions	68,749	52,073	37,340
Unexpended construction funds	7,067		
Payments on long term obligations, net of conversions to current	20,129	8,515	4,913
Cash dividends	6,722	5,964	5,694
Net increase in other assets	14,885	5,710	4,783
Purchase of franchise owners and Sisters International:			
Property and equipment, net	27,675	440	2,594
Capitalized leases	25,107		1,385
Cost in excess of net assets acquired	11,436	598	3,419
Other	4,282		80
Other changes, net	3,437	352	44
Total dispositions of working capital	189,489	73,652	60,252
Decrease in working capital	$ (7,433)	$(18,584)	$ (8,011)
Change in components of working capital:			
Increase (decrease) in current assets:			
Cash and short term investments	$ 9,199	$ (2,054)	$(13,745)
Notes and accounts receivable	5,040	611	1,654
Inventories and other	(338)	3,724	726
	13,901	2,281	(11,365)
Increase (decrease) in current liabilities:			
Accounts payable, trade	12,214	14,510	(1,491)
Federal, state and local income taxes	(2,183)	6,256	(7,840)
Accrued expenses	5,807	(350)	4,867
Current portion of long term obligations	5,496	449	1,110
	21,334	20,865	(3,354)
Decrease in working capital	$ (7,433)	$(18,584)	$ (8,011)

The accompanying notes are an integral part of the consolidated financial statements.

NOTES TO THE CONSOLIDATED FINANCIAL STATEMENTS

Wendy's International, Inc. and subsidiaries

1. Summary of Significant Accounting Policies

Consolidation:

The consolidated financial statements include the accounts of Wendy's International, Inc. and its majority owned subsidiaries. All significant intercompany accounts and transactions have been eliminated. See Note 7 regarding acquisitions accounted for as purchases during the three year period ended December 31, 1981. Certain subsidiaries of the Company are accounted for on the equity basis and are included in Other assets. These entities are not material in the aggregate.

Inventories:

Inventories are stated at lower of cost (first-in, first-out) or market, and consist of restaurant food items and paper supplies.

Property and Equipment:

Depreciation and amortization are recognized on the straight-line method in amounts adequate to amortize costs over the estimated useful lives of the assets. The costs and related accumulated depreciation for assets retired or otherwise disposed of are removed from the related accounts, and any resulting gains or losses are reflected in income.

Certain costs incurred during the period of construction of restaurants, such as ground rentals and real estate taxes, are expensed as incurred.

Cost in Excess of Net Assets Acquired:

The cost in excess of net assets acquired is being amortized on the straight-line method over periods ranging from fifteen to forty years which, for restaurants leased, include the original lease period plus renewal options, if applicable. This policy results in an average amortization period of approximately 27 years. Accumulated amortization of cost in excess of net assets acquired was $1,734,000 and $1,058,000 at December 31, 1981 and 1980, respectively.

Franchise Operations:

The Company grants franchises to private operators who in turn pay technical assistance fees and royalties for each opened restaurant. A technical assistance fee is recorded as income when each restaurant commences operations. Royalties, which are based on a percentage of monthly sales, are recognized as income on the accrual basis. Costs associated with franchise operations are expensed as incurred.

Foreign Operations:

Amounts of assets, revenues, net income or loss and exchange gains and losses related to foreign operations are not material.

2. Term Debt and Warrants

Term debt at December 31, 1981 consisted of the following:

	(In thousands)
Notes payable, at various rates from 6¼% to 15% with a weighted average rate of 13.6%, due in installments through 1997. Restaurant equipment with acquisition costs approximating $3,678,000 is pledged as collateral for certain of these notes	$25,530[1]
Various mortgages on real estate, at interest rates ranging from 7% to 16½%, with a weighted average rate of 10.0%, payable monthly through 2001. Land and buildings with acquisition costs approximating $18,753,000 are pledged as collateral for such mortgages	9,599
Obligations under industrial development revenue bonds at interest rates of 12½% and 13% being paid semi-annually, maturing in the aggregate on October 15, 1984	11,865
Notes payable, unsecured, at 9% interest, payable semi-annually in the amount of $690,000 plus interest	2,760
10½% Subordinated Sinking Fund Debentures	3,480
11% and 11½% Sinking Fund Debentures	7,000
	60,234
Less current portion	(7,992)
	$52,242

(1) Includes $17,000,000 in money market demand notes of which $15,000,000 are covered by unused long term lines of credit.

The Company has outstanding $3,480,000 principal amount of 10½% Subordinated Sinking Fund Debentures due May 15, 1985. Interest on the debentures is payable semi-annually. The debentures are subordinated as to principal, premium, if any, and interest to all superior indebtedness as defined in the Indenture. The debentures are redeemable by the Company, in whole or in part, at a premium of 4.65% beginning May 15, 1980 decreasing to no premium in 1985. The Company must redeem or deposit cash for redemption of $870,000 principal amount each May 15, beginning in 1981. The Indenture provides for certain restrictions on incurring additional debt and on maintaining the availability of retained earnings for dividends. At December 31, 1981 retained earnings of approximately $48,152,000 were not so restricted.

Attached to each $1,000 debenture was a nondetachable warrant to purchase 400 common shares of the Company at any time on or before May 15, 1985 at a price per share during the period May 15, 1981 to May 15, 1982 of $6.875, increasing at a rate of $.625 each year ending May 15, to a maximum of $8.75 per share during the last year. As of December 31, 1981, warrants to purchase 14,428 common shares were unexercised.

With the acquisition of Interpoint Corporation by a wholly owned subsidiary of the Company (see Note 7), the subsidiary assumed $7,000,000 in Sinking Fund Debentures issued August 15, 1979. The debentures consist of $1,600,000 11% debentures due August 15, 1987 and $5,400,000 11½% debentures due August 15, 1994. The Indenture associated with these debentures provides for a sinking fund for their retirement prior to their expressed maturity dates. Pursuant to the sinking fund provision, the deposit requirements each August 15 for the five years subsequent to December 31, 1981 are: 1982-$100,000; 1983-$150,000; 1984-$200,000; 1985-$300,000; and 1986-$400,000.

The Company has obligations under industrial development revenue bonds (accounted for as long term obligations) which were issued to provide funds for the acquisition, construction and improvement of real property and the acquisition and installation of personal property pertaining to 19 restaurant projects in five states. The funds have been deposited with a trustee and are restricted to the use for which they were intended. As of December 31, 1981, expenditures of $4,815,000 had been made. Any unexpended amounts at the completion of the projects will be applied to reduce the principal amount of the outstanding debt. Each issue is collateralized by a separate guaranty agreement dated October 15, 1981 under which the Company has unconditionally guaranteed the payment of principal and interest.

Future maturities of all Term debt are as follows:

Years ended December 31	*(In thousands)*
1982	$ 7,992
1983	15,700
1984	20,096
1985	2,241
1986	2,262
Thereafter	11,943
	$60,234

At December 31, 1981, the Company had unused lines of credit from various financial institutions aggregating $20,000,000 at their respective prime rates, while the amount of compensating balances was insignificant.

The cost of property and equipment includes interest incurred during construction. In 1981 and 1980, capitalized interest amounted to $1,269,000 and $825,000, respectively. In prior years, all interest was expensed.

3. Leases

The Company occupies land and buildings and uses equipment under terms of numerous lease agreements expiring on various dates through 2013. Minimum lease rentals have been segregated into those portions relating to land, buildings, and equipment. The building and equipment portions of the minimum rentals have been capitalized and the related assets and obligations have been recorded. The portion of the minimum rentals relating to land is expensed as incurred. The recorded assets are being amortized on the straight-line method over the lease terms and the amortization is included in depreciation in the accompanying Consolidated Statement of Income and Retained Earnings. Interest expense is being accrued on the basis of the outstanding lease obligations.

Capitalized leases consist of the following:

	(In thousands)	
December 31	**1981**	1980
Buildings	**$45,385**	$21,651
Equipment	**6,590**	635
	51,975	22,286
Less accumulated amortization	**(10,743)**	(4,391)
	$41,232	$17,895

Minimum lease payments under capital leases together with the present value of the net minimum lease payments are as follows:

Years ended December 31	*(In thousands)*
1982	$ 8,255
1983	8,037
1984	7,425
1985	7,189
1986	7,112
Later Years	80,286
Total minimum lease payments	118,304
Less amount representing interest	(70,746)
Present value of net minimum lease payments	47,558
Less current portion	(1,844)
Capitalized lease obligations	$45,714

Future minimum lease payments applicable to the land portion of restaurant leases and operating leases are as follows:

Years ended December 31	*(In thousands)*
1982	$ 6,612
1983	6,597
1984	6,578
1985	6,532
1986	6,491
Later Years	72,935
	$105,745

Certain leases require payment of additional contingent rent determined as a percentage of sales when annual sales exceed specified levels. Most leases also provide for renewal periods at the Company's option. Rent expense is included in Company restaurant operating costs and is as follows:

	(In thousands)		
Years ended December 31	**1981**	1980	1979
Minimum rent on operating leases	**$6,199**	$3,085	$2,822
Contingent rent on capitalized leases	**1,339**	872	723
	$7,538	$3,957	$3,545

4. Changes to Shareholders' Equity

On March 20, 1981, the Company effected a 3-for-2 split of the outstanding common shares. All data regarding common shares, common equivalent shares, options, warrants, and per share amounts has been restated to reflect the effects of the aforementioned split.

Changes in Shareholders' Equity for the three years ended December 31, 1981 are as follows:

	(In thousands)		
	Shares Outstanding	Stated Value	Capital in Excess of Stated Value
Balances, January 1, 1979	22,292	$2,229	$33,220
Exercise of stock purchase warrants	6	1	35
Exercise of stock options and tax benefits accruing to the Company from early disposition of shares	25	2	164
Additional common stock authorization costs, and other			(50)
Balances, December 31, 1979	22,323	2,232	33,369
Exercise of stock purchase warrants	3	1	15
Exercise of stock options and tax benefits accruing to the Company from early disposition of shares	110	11	742
Balances, December 31, 1980	22,436	2,244	34,126
Exercise of stock purchase warrants, and other	15	2	165
Exercise of stock options and tax benefits accruing to the Company from early disposition of shares	444	44	3,478
Shares issued for the acquisition of the remaining 80% of Sisters International, Inc. not previously owned	82	8	1,157
Cash payment in lieu of fractional shares in connection with 3-for-2 stock split			(28)
May 21, 1981 public offering of 2,100,000 previously unissued common shares of the Company, less $122,000 costs related thereto	2,100	210	33,163
Shares issued for the acquisition of Interpoint Corporation	473	47	7,766
Balances, December 31, 1981	25,550	$2,555	$79,827

5. Income Taxes

A summary of the provisions for income taxes is as follows:

		(In thousands)	
Years ended December 31	**1981**	1980	1979
Reconciliation:			
Statutory Federal rate	46%	46%	46%
Investment and jobs tax credits	(6)	(4)	(3)
State and local taxes, net of Federal tax benefit	2	2	1
Other	1	1	
Effective tax rate	43%	45%	44%
Components:			
Current	36%	41%	41%
Deferred:			
Excess of tax reporting over financial reporting depreciation and amortization	8	6	4
Excess of other financial reporting expense over other tax reporting expense	(1)	(2)	(1)
Total deferred	7	4	3
Effective tax rate	43%	45%	44%
Investment tax credits	$3,720	$2,219	$1,240

Investment tax credits are accounted for using the flow-through method.

6. Stock Options

The Company has five stock option plans which provide options for certain key employees to purchase common shares of the Company. Grants of options and the periods during which they can be exercised are at the discretion of the Board of Directors. Non-qualified options are exercisable three years from the date of grant, at which time a maximum of 50% is exercisable in the fourth year and the remainder in the fifth through tenth years. On May 21, 1981, unexercised qualified options became non-qualified and are still exercisable for five years beginning 60 days after date of grant. There were 209,000 and 77,000 non-qualified options granted in 1981 and 1980, respectively, and there were none in 1979. All options expire at the end of the exercise period. The Company makes no recognition in the financial statements until such options are exercised and no amounts applicable thereto are reflected in net income. As of December 31, 1981, approximately 1,940 employees were eligible to participate in the plans and approximately 175 employees had unexercised options to acquire the Company's common shares.

Effective May 21, 1981, there was a significant change in the Federal tax laws affecting the holders of qualified stock options. Because of this change, the Company granted interest bearing loans aggregating $2,146,000 at December 31, 1981 to certain key employees for the exercise of 309,000 options. These loans, which are due the earlier of November 20, 1985 or the employee's termination, are individually collateralized by the related shares which had a market value of approximately $4,363,000 at December 31, 1981. The amount of the loans is included in Other assets in the Consolidated Balance Sheet.

(In thousands except per share data)

	Shares			Option Price	
	Reserved	Under Option	Exercisable	Per Share	Total
Balances, January 1, 1979	938	530	42	$ .83-$22.59	$6,163
Became exercisable			83	3.12	259
Exercised	(25)	(25)	(25)	.83- 6.81	70
Cancelled		(47)	(12)		
Balances, December 31, 1979	913	458	88	3.12- 22.59	5,553
Granted		414(1)		6.00- 11.37	2,968
Became exercisable			704	5.75- 11.37	7,318
Exercised	(110)	(110)	(110)	3.12- 6.81	625
Cancelled		(218)(1)	(213)		
Balances, December 31, 1980	803	544	469	5.75- 11.37	3,984
Granted		214		10.87- 15.21	2,535
Became exercisable			7	10.87- 14.92	77
Exercised	(444)	(444)	(444)	5.75- 11.37	3,136
Cancelled		(33)	(12)		
Balances, December 31, 1981	359	281	20	$ 5.75-$15.21	$3,106

(1) Includes 195,000 options cancelled and then reissued at $6.00 per share, with an option price ranging from $13.13 to $22.59 prior to cancellation.

Expiration of Options Years ended December 31	1982	1985	1988	1990	1991
Number of shares (in thousands)	2	17	3	55	204
Average option price	$5.75	$7.84	$14.92	$8.89	$11.91

7. Acquisitions

During 1981, the Company acquired several corporations as detailed in the following table. All of the transactions were accounted for as purchases and all of the acquired companies' results of operations are included in the Consolidated Statement of Income and Retained Earnings from the dates of acquisition. Cost in excess of net assets acquired relating to these acquisitions is being amortized on the straight-line method over approximately 28 years.

Company Acquired	Principal Operation at Acquisition Date	Common Shares Issued (In thousands)	Purchase Price (In thousands)
Wendy's of Denver, Inc., The Food Group, Inc., WMR Foods, Inc., Interpoint Corporation, Wendy Restaurants (UK), Ltd.	Franchisees operating 161 Wendy's restaurants	473[1]	$11,613[1]
Sta-Fresh Buns of Ohio, Inc.	Producer of buns for approximately 630 Wendy's restaurants	0	1,750
Sisters International, Inc. (remaining 80% not already owned)	Owner and operator of 4 Sisters Chicken & Biscuits restaurants	82	1,166

(1) All common shares issued relate to the acquisition of Interpoint Corporation and were valued at $7,813,000. The net purchase price of Interpoint (after removing the effect of selling certain operations) was $5,920,000.

The following is a summary of the pro-forma results of continuing operations had the above purchase transactions occurred January 1, 1980 (after adjustment to reflect amortization of cost in excess of net assets acquired, additional interest expense, elimination of intercompany transactions and related tax effects):

(In thousands except per share data)	1981	1980
Revenue	**$541,829**	$436,121
Net income	**35,365**	27,229
Net income per share	**$1.44**	$1.18

On November 30, 1979, the Company acquired Wendy's of Virginia, Inc., a franchise owner operating 14 restaurants in the Virginia Beach, Virginia area. The acquisition was accounted for as a purchase. If the transaction had been consummated on January 1, 1979, net income per share would have increased $.02 in 1979. This acquisition was not considered material to the consolidated operations of the Company.

8. Quarterly Operating Results (Unaudited)

The following is a summary of the unaudited quarterly results of operations for the two years ended December 31, 1981.

(In thousands except per share data)

	Quarter ended			
1981	March 31	June 30	September 30	December 31
Revenue	$97,880	$121,492	$133,336	$137,721
Retail gross profit	13,992	17,985	19,944	22,911
Income before income taxes	12,675	17,191	18,052	16,734
Net income	6,971	9,815	10,606	9,460
Net income per share	$.31	$.42	$.42	$.37
1980				
Revenue	$76,308	$85,722	$91,554	$96,443
Retail gross profit	9,697	14,627	14,039	16,022
Income before income taxes	10,381	14,953	14,955	14,432
Net income	5,753	8,181	8,222	7,940
Net income per share	$.26	$.37	$.37	$.34

9. Pension Plan

The Company adopted a non-contributory pension plan effective January 1, 1978 covering all full time employees qualified as to age and service. Total pension expense and funding based on normal cost, including amortization of prior service cost over 20 years, was $650,000, $591,000 and $347,000 in 1981, 1980 and 1979, respectively. Accumulated plan benefit information and plan net assets as of the most recent actuarial valuation date are presented below:

		(In thousands)	
January 1	1981	1980	1979
Actuarial present value of accumulated plan benefits:			
Vested	$177	$106	$58
Nonvested	258	212	Not available
	$435	$318	
Net assets available for benefits	$1,194	$533	$172

The weighted average assumed rate of return used in determining the actuarial present value of accumulated plan benefits was 7½% in 1981 and 7% in 1980. In addition, certain actuarial assumptions were changed in 1981 to better reflect historical trends and to achieve desired results of the plan.

10. National Advertising Program

Wendy's National Advertising Program, Inc. ("WNAP") is a non-profit corporation which was established to collect and administer funds contributed by the Company and by all domestic franchise owners. These contributions total 1% of gross restaurant sales and are used for promotional and advertising programs designed to increase sales and enhance the reputation of the Company and its franchise owners. During 1981, 1980, and 1979, the Company contributed $4,241,000, $3,015,000 and $2,316,000, respectively, to WNAP.

11. Direct Expenses of Franchise Personnel

Direct expenses of franchise personnel consist of the salaries, travel, and related expenses of those Company personnel whose sole responsibilities are to support and assist franchise restaurant owners and operators. In addition, franchise owners receive assistance in such areas as real estate site selection, construction consulting, purchasing, and marketing from other Company personnel who also furnish these functions to Company operated restaurants. The cost and expenses of these other support functions are included in General and administrative expenses and aggregated approximately $18,719,000, $16,475,000, and $12,705,000 for 1981, 1980, and 1979, respectively.

12. Supplemental Information on the Effects of Inflation (Unaudited)

Although inflationary pressures have moderated in 1981, the average consumer price index has exhibited a double-digit growth rate for the third straight year. It appears probable that a moderating trend will continue but even moderate inflationary pressure can have a significant impact on a company's financial position and operations. Prior to 1980, generally accepted accounting principles did not require any adjustments in financial statements to indicate the impact of inflation. This creates difficulty in comparing data from year to year as historical cost dollars do not represent equal purchasing power. It is therefore difficult to assess the true economic position and operating results of a company.

In response to the need for assisting financial statement users in assessing inflationary effects on financial statements, the Financial Accounting Standards Board ("FASB") issued Financial Accounting Standard ("FAS") No. 33, *Financial Reporting and Changing Prices.* This statement requires certain supplemental disclosures using two methods of computing the effects of inflation. One method attempts to reflect the effects of general inflation ("constant dollar accounting"), and the other method attempts to measure the effects of specific price changes ("current cost accounting"). Since the results of the two methods are not significantly different for the Company, only the results obtained under constant dollar accounting are presented in the following tables.

It should be emphasized that these disclosures are experimental in nature and that the FASB has encouraged flexibility in implementing the requirements. The amounts disclosed are not meant to be precise measurements of the effects of inflation on the financial statements, but are meant to be used as a general guide to gauge the effect of inflationary pressures on the Company. These disclosures should not be used in comparison with other companies in the industry due to the judgemental and potentially diverse assumptions used in the computations.

The objective of constant dollar accounting is to provide all financial information in equivalent dollars of purchasing power so that revenues and expenses are matched in equivalent units. Financial data for several years then becomes more comparable as each year is stated in equal dollars of purchasing power. Under constant dollar accounting, property and equipment and related depreciation amounts are converted to average 1981 dollars of purchasing power using the Consumer Price Index for all Urban Consumers. Depreciation is computed using the same methods, useful lives, and salvage values used in computing historical cost depreciation.

FAS No. 33 also requires that inventory and cost of sales be converted to current year average dollars where inventories are material. Because inventories (mostly food and paper supplies) are not material, the effects of inflation were insignificant and have not been presented.

Summary of inflationary effects on the Company

Net income per share is $.14 lower in 1981 under the constant dollar method of accounting than determined under historical cost accounting. The majority of the Company's fixed assets have been added in the last three years and inflation has therefore not had a significant impact.

FAS No. 33 prohibits modifying income tax expense under inflation accounting. Therefore, the effective tax rate is higher than under historical cost accounting. This increase indicates the adverse effect that income taxes have on real earnings in times of inflation.

FAS No. 33 also requires disclosures of the net gain or loss experienced by holding monetary assets and liabilities. When a net monetary asset position is held, a loss is experienced as the purchasing power of the assets decline. A gain is experienced when a net monetary liability position is held as obligations can be paid off in dollars of lesser value. In the Company's case, a gain was experienced in 1981 from the holding of net monetary liabilities.

Consolidated Statement of Income Adjusted for Changing Prices

	(In thousands)	
Year Ended December 31, 1981	**As Reported in the Primary Statements**	**Adjusted for General Inflation (in average 1981 dollars)**
Revenue	$490,429	$490,429
Cost of sales	257,735	257,735
Depreciation	15,308	18,670
Other operating expenses	152,734	152,734
	425,777	429,139
Income before income taxes	64,652	61,290
Provision for income taxes	27,800	27,800
Net income	$ 36,852	$ 33,490
Effective tax rate	43%	45%
Purchasing power gain from holding net monetary liabilities during the year		$7,736

Five Year Comparison of Selected Supplemental Financial Data Adjusted for the Effects of Changing Prices
(in 1981 average dollars, except As reported amounts)

(In thousands except per share data)

Years ended December 31	1981	1980	1979	1978	1977
Revenue:					
As reported	$490,429	$350,027	$274,043	$228,151	$146,790
Adjusted for general inflation	490,429	386,036	343,247	317,940	220,225
Net income:					
As reported	$36,852	$30,096	$23,096	—	—
Adjusted for general inflation	33,490	30,517	27,301	—	—
Net income per share:					
As reported	$1.52	$1.34	$1.03	—	—
Adjusted for general inflation	1.38	1.36	1.22	—	—
Purchasing power gain from holding net monetary liabilities during the year	$7,736	$7,455	$5,467	—	—
Net assets at year end:					
As reported	$201,738	$125,596	$100,696	—	—
Adjusted for general inflation	260,695	185,651	155,005	—	—
Cash dividends per common share:					
As reported	$.28	$.27	$.27	$.09	$.08
Adjusted for general inflation	.28	.30	.34	.13	.12
Market price per common share at year end:					
As reported	$14.13	$10.38	$8.83	$15.09	$13.13
Adjusted for general inflation	13.67	10.94	10.46	20.25	19.21
Average Consumer Price Index	272.3	246.9	217.4	195.4	181.5

Report of Independent Certified Public Accountants

To the Shareholders
Wendy's International, Inc.

We have examined the Consolidated Balance Sheets of Wendy's International, Inc. and subsidiaries as of December 31, 1981 and 1980 and the related Consolidated Statements of Income and Retained Earnings, and Changes in Financial Position for the three years ended December 31, 1981, 1980 and 1979. Our examinations were made in accordance with generally accepted auditing standards and, accordingly, included such tests of the accounting records and such other auditing procedures as we considered necessary in the circumstances.

In our opinion, the aforementioned financial statements present fairly the consolidated financial position of Wendy's International, Inc. and subsidiaries at December 31, 1981 and 1980 and the consolidated results of their operations and changes in their financial position for the three years ended December 31, 1981, 1980 and 1979, in conformity with generally accepted accounting principles applied on a consistent basis.

Coopers & Lybrand

Columbus, Ohio
February 16, 1982

APPENDIX B PRESENT VALUE TABLES

Table 1 ***Present value of $1***

$$P = \frac{V}{(1 + r)^n}$$

Periods	4%	5%	6%	8%	10%	12%	14%	16%	18%	20%	22%	24%	26%	28%
1	0.962	0.952	0.943	0.926	0.909	0.893	0.877	0.862	0.847	0.833	0.820	0.806	0.794	0.781
2	0.925	0.907	0.890	0.857	0.826	0.797	0.769	0.743	0.718	0.694	0.672	0.650	0.630	0.610
3	0.889	0.864	0.840	0.794	0.751	0.712	0.675	0.641	0.609	0.579	0.551	0.524	0.500	0.477
4	0.855	0.823	0.792	0.735	0.683	0.636	0.592	0.552	0.516	0.482	0.451	0.423	0.397	0.373
5	0.822	0.784	0.747	0.681	0.621	0.567	0.519	0.476	0.437	0.402	0.370	0.341	0.315	0.291
6	0.790	0.746	0.705	0.630	0.564	0.507	0.456	0.410	0.370	0.335	0.303	0.275	0.250	0.227
7	0.760	0.711	0.665	0.583	0.513	0.452	0.400	0.354	0.314	0.279	0.249	0.222	0.198	0.178
8	0.731	0.677	0.627	0.540	0.467	0.404	0.351	0.305	0.266	0.233	0.204	0.179	0.157	0.139
9	0.703	0.645	0.592	0.500	0.424	0.361	0.308	0.263	0.225	0.194	0.167	0.144	0.125	0.108
10	0.676	0.614	0.558	0.463	0.386	0.322	0.270	0.227	0.191	0.162	0.136	0.116	0.099	0.085
11	0.650	0.585	0.527	0.429	0.350	0.287	0.237	0.195	0.162	0.135	0.112	0.094	0.079	0.066
12	0.625	0.557	0.497	0.397	0.319	0.257	0.208	0.168	0.137	0.112	0.092	0.076	0.062	0.052
13	0.601	0.530	0.469	0.368	0.290	0.229	0.182	0.145	0.116	0.093	0.075	0.061	0.050	0.040
14	0.577	0.505	0.442	0.340	0.263	0.205	0.160	0.125	0.099	0.078	0.062	0.049	0.039	0.032
15	0.555	0.481	0.417	0.315	0.239	0.183	0.140	0.108	0.084	0.065	0.051	0.040	0.031	0.025
16	0.534	0.458	0.394	0.292	0.218	0.163	0.123	0.093	0.071	0.054	0.042	0.032	0.025	0.019
17	0.513	0.436	0.371	0.270	0.198	0.146	0.108	0.080	0.060	0.045	0.034	0.026	0.020	0.015
18	0.494	0.416	0.350	0.250	0.180	0.130	0.095	0.069	0.051	0.038	0.028	0.021	0.016	0.012
19	0.475	0.396	0.331	0.232	0.164	0.116	0.083	0.060	0.043	0.031	0.023	0.017	0.012	0.009
20	0.456	0.377	0.312	0.215	0.149	0.104	0.073	0.051	0.037	0.026	0.019	0.014	0.010	0.007
21	0.439	0.359	0.294	0.199	0.135	0.093	0.064	0.044	0.031	0.022	0.015	0.011	0.008	0.006
22	0.422	0.342	0.278	0.184	0.123	0.083	0.056	0.038	0.026	0.018	0.013	0.009	0.006	0.004
23	0.406	0.326	0.262	0.170	0.112	0.074	0.049	0.033	0.022	0.015	0.010	0.007	0.005	0.003
24	0.390	0.310	0.247	0.158	0.102	0.066	0.043	0.028	0.019	0.013	0.008	0.006	0.004	0.003
25	0.375	0.295	0.233	0.146	0.092	0.059	0.038	0.024	0.016	0.010	0.007	0.005	0.003	0.002

Table 2 ***Present value of ordinary annuity of $1***

$$P = \frac{1}{r}\left[1 - \frac{1}{(1+r)^n}\right]$$

Periods	4%	5%	6%	8%	10%	12%	14%	16%	18%	20%	22%	24%	26%	28%
1	0.962	0.952	0.943	0.926	0.909	0.893	0.877	0.862	0.847	0.833	0.820	0.806	0.794	0.781
2	1.886	1.859	1.833	1.783	1.736	1.690	1.647	1.605	1.566	1.528	1.492	1.457	1.424	1.392
3	2.775	2.723	2.673	2.577	2.487	2.402	2.322	2.246	2.174	2.106	2.042	1.981	1.923	1.868
4	3.630	3.546	3.465	3.312	3.170	3.037	2.914	2.798	2.690	2.589	2.494	2.404	2.320	2.241
5	4.452	4.329	4.212	3.993	3.791	3.605	3.433	3.274	3.127	2.991	2.864	2.745	2.635	2.532
6	5.242	5.076	4.917	4.623	4.355	4.111	3.889	3.685	3.498	3.326	3.167	3.020	2.885	2.759
7	6.002	5.786	5.582	5.206	4.868	4.564	4.288	4.039	3.812	3.605	3.416	3.242	3.083	2.937
8	6.733	6.463	6.210	5.747	5.335	4.968	4.639	4.344	4.078	3.837	3.619	3.421	3.241	3.076
9	7.435	7.108	6.802	6.247	5.759	5.328	4.946	4.607	4.303	4.031	3.786	3.566	3.366	3.184
10	8.111	7.722	7.360	6.710	6.145	5.650	5.216	4.833	4.494	4.192	3.923	3.682	3.465	3.269
11	8.760	8.306	7.887	7.139	6.495	5.938	5.453	5.029	4.656	4.327	4.035	3.776	3.544	3.335
12	9.385	8.863	8.384	7.536	6.814	6.194	5.660	5.197	4.793	4.439	4.127	3.851	3.606	3.387
13	9.986	9.394	8.853	7.904	7.103	6.424	5.842	5.342	4.910	4.533	4.203	3.912	3.656	3.427
14	10.563	9.899	9.295	8.244	7.367	6.628	6.002	5.468	5.008	4.611	4.265	3.962	3.695	3.459
15	11.118	10.380	9.712	8.559	7.606	6.811	6.142	5.575	5.092	4.675	4.315	4.001	3.726	3.483
16	11.652	10.838	10.106	8.851	7.824	6.974	6.265	5.669	5.162	4.730	4.357	4.033	3.751	3.503
17	12.166	11.274	10.477	9.122	8.022	7.120	6.373	5.749	5.222	4.775	4.391	4.059	3.771	3.518
18	12.659	11.690	10.828	9.372	8.201	7.250	6.467	5.818	5.273	4.812	4.419	4.080	3.786	3.529
19	13.134	12.085	11.158	9.604	8.365	7.366	6.550	5.877	5.316	4.844	4.442	4.097	3.799	3.539
20	13.590	12.462	11.470	9.818	8.514	7.469	6.623	5.929	5.353	4.870	4.460	4.110	3.808	3.546
21	14.029	12.821	11.764	10.017	8.649	7.562	6.687	5.973	5.384	4.891	4.476	4.121	3.816	3.551
22	14.451	13.163	12.042	10.201	8.772	7.645	6.743	6.001	5.410	4.909	4.488	4.130	3.822	3.556
23	14.857	13.489	12.303	10.371	8.883	7.718	6.792	6.044	5.432	4.925	4.499	4.137	3.827	3.559
24	15.247	13.799	12.550	10.529	8.985	7.784	6.835	6.073	5.451	4.937	4.507	4.143	3.831	3.562
25	15.622	14.094	12.783	10.675	9.077	7.843	6.873	6.097	5.467	4.948	4.514	4.147	3.834	3.564

APPENDIX C CHECKLIST OF KEY FIGURES

This list presents key figures for your use when solving the problems in this book. Some of the key figures represent intermediate checkpoints so you can determine if you are on the right track. Other key figures represent a portion of the final solution. If your solution does not agree, you will want to review your calculations to find the error(s).

Chapter 1

P1-2 (a) Net income, $13,000
(c) Total assets, $96,700
P1-3 (b) Net income, $1,265
Total assets, $8,005
P1-4 Net income, $15,300
P1-6 Net income, $65,200
P1-7 (b) Total assets, $23,500
P1-9 (a) Net income, $5,350
(c) Total assets, $48,900
P1-10 (b) Net income, $530
(b) Total assets, $6,205
P1-11 Net income, $27,200
P1-12 Ending owners' equity, $26,750
Case 1 Net income, $6,050

Chapter 2

P2-1 (b) Total debits, trial balance, $24,200
P2-2 (b) Total credits, trial balance, $46,350
P2-3 (c) Total debits, trial balance, $20,100
P2-4 (b) Total credits, trial balance, $93,050
P2-6 Total debits, trial balance, $168,400
P2-7 (b) Total debits, trial balance, $29,900
P2-8 (b) Total debits, trial balance, $17,375
P2-9 (c) Total credits, trial balance, $21,150
P2-10 (b) Total debits, trial balance, $51,400
Case 2 (c) Total credits, trial balance, $9,760

Chapter 3

P3-1 (a) Cash basis net income, $2,500
P3-2 (f) Net income (loss), $(530)
P3-9 (a) Net income, $16,400
P3-10 (c) Net income (loss), $(535)
P3-11 (b) Accrual basis net income, $4,300
P3-14 (a) Net income, $1,045
P3-15 (c) Net income (loss), $(255)
Case 3 Cash receipts, $20,210

Chapter 4

P4-4 Net income, $7,525
P4-5 Purchases, $426,000
Net income, $45,100
P4-6 Net income, $11,400
P4-9 Net income, $14,900
P4-10 Purchases, $140,300
Net income, $68,250
P4-11 Net income, $17,000

Chapter 5

P5-6 Total debits, trial balance, $16,872
Accounts Receivable, May 31, 19XX, $900
P5-7 Total debits, trial balance, $117,482
Accounts Receivable, June 30, 19XX, $1,100
P5-11 Total credits, trial balance, $60,266
Accounts Receivable, December 31, 19XX, $1,525

P5-12 Total credits, trial balance, $247,967
Accounts Receivable, December 31, 19XX, $3,470

Chapter 6

P6-3 Total assets, $245,445
P6-4 (b) Total assets, $610,070
P6-5 (a) Net income, $66,000
P6-6 (b) Net income, $24,000
P6-7 (a) Net income, $31,400
(b) Total assets, $175,700
P6-10 Total assets, $272,890
P6-11 (a) Net income, $123,000
P6-12 (a) Net income, $6,280
(b) Total assets, $35,140

Chapter 7

P7-4 (a) Adjusted cash balance: bank, $5,615.80
P7-5 (a) Adjusted cash balance: bank, $4,380
P7-8 (b) Short-term investments at lower of cost or market, $71,800
P7-9 (c) Vouchers Payable, $1,900
P7-11 (a) Adjusted cash balance: bank, $4,719.97
P7-12 (a) Adjusted cash balance: bank, $8,845
P7-14 (b) Short-term investments at lower of cost or market, $83,000

Chapter 8

P8-2 (b) Allowance for Uncollectible Accounts, $39,000
P8-3 (c) Bad Debts Expense, $6,075
P8-5 (a) Accounts Receivable at March 31, 1983, $45,035
Notes Receivable at March 31, 1983, $9,100
P8-6 (b) Net realizable value of Accounts Receivable, $69,100
P8-9 (a) Allowance for Uncollectible Accounts, $73,750
P8-11 (b) Net realizable value of Accounts Receivable, $79,300
Case 8 Projected net income for payment by bank credit card, $105,000

Chapter 9

P9-4 (b) 1982 Net income using LIFO, $5,600
1983 Net loss using LIFO, $6,200
P9-6 (b) Total gross profit for 1981–1983 using LIFO, $3,070,000
P9-8 (b) Ending inventory, $60,630
(c) Lower of cost or market, $68,340
P9-9 (a) Estimated inventory on date of fire, $223,600
P9-10 (a) Estimated ending inventory at cost, $74,368
P9-15 (a) Estimated inventory on date of tornado, $71,046

Chapter 10

P10-2 (a) Cost of machinery, $40,600
P10-3 (d) Accumulated depreciation: buildings, $6,000
Accumulated depreciation: equipment, $2,667
P10-4 (a) 1983 depreciation expense, $8,308
P10-6 (a) 1983 depreciation expense, $16,192
P10-7 (a) Cost of machinery, $84,000
P10-9 (a) 1983 depreciation expense, $11,434
P10-11 (a) 1983 depreciation expense, $17,750

Chapter 11

P11-1 (b) 1983 depreciation expense, $10,520
P11-3 (a) Equipment cost (new), $106,250
Furniture cost (new), $1,500
P11-5 (c) Patent amortization for 1983, $21,975
P11-6 (a) Goodwill, $6,800
(b) Total assets, $375,100
P11-7 (c) Revised depletion, 60¢ per ton
P11-10 (a) Equipment cost (new), $140,000
Van cost (new), $11,750
P11-11 (c) Patent amortization for 1983, $15,155
P11-12 (c) Revised depletion, 25¢ per ton

Chapter 12

P12-2 (b) Total liabilities, $691,590
P12-4 (c) Total current liabilities, $491,900

P12-6 (d) Total current liabilities, $53,050.80
P12-7 (a) Total net pay, $6,055.56
P12-8 (b) Total liabilities, $202,622
P12-10 (c) Total current liabilities, $294,300
P12-11 (d) Total current liabilities, $114,409.40

Chapter 13

P13-5 (b) Retained earnings, $17,725
Total stockholders' equity, $5,755,625
P13-8 (a) Total stockholders' equity, $1,188,200
P13-9 (h) Total stockholders' equity, $1,305,500
P13-10 (b) Total assets, $213,950
P13-13 (b) Retained earnings, $4,865
Total stockholders' equity, $44,365
P13-14 (h) Total stockholders' equity, $963,000

Chapter 14

P14-1 (b) Net loss, $69,000
P14-2 (b) Net income, $27,000
P14-4 (b) Total stockholders' equity, $712,800
P14-6 (b) Total retained earnings, $7,619,000
P14-8 (d) Total stockholders' equity, $12,912,000
P14-9 (a) Common: book value per share, $13.80
P14-10 (b) Net loss, $2,400
P14-12 (b) Unappropriated retained earnings, $130,530
P14-13 (d) Total stockholders' equity, $14,682,000
P14-14 (a) Common: book value per share, $42.80

Chapter 15

P15-4 (c) Bond carrying value, $408,720
P15-5 (c) Bond carrying value, $193,895
(d) Loss on retirement, $4,842
P15-10 (c) Bond carrying value, $589,000
P15-11 (c) Bond carrying value, $413,080
(d) Gain on retirement, $3,048
Case 15 (a) Bond plan: earnings per share, $1.71

Chapter 16

P16-3 (e) Gain on sale of bonds, $11,050
P16-4 (c) Premium amortization on December 31, $1,520
P16-5 (d) (c) Long-term investments, $306,000
P16-7 (a) Consolidated assets, $674,000
P16-8 (a) Consolidated assets, $1,887,700
P16-10 (e) Gain on sale of bonds, $2,880
P16-11 (c) Discount amortization on December 31, $1,065
P16-13 (a) Consolidated assets, $485,000
Case 16 (b) Year 3 total earnings, $47,000

Chapter 17

P17-1 Total uses of working capital, $24,000
P17-2 Total sources of working capital, $62,550
P17-3 (a) Total uses of working capital, $49,000
P17-4 (a) Owner withdrawals, $5,435
P17-5 Total assets, $1,024,000
P17-6 Total sources of working capital, $464,000
P17-7 Increase in working capital, $10,800
P17-8 (a) Acquisition of store equipment, $27,000
P17-9 (a) Cash provided from operations, $37,200
P17-10 Total assets, $1,153,000

Chapter 18

P18-2 (a) Net income, $39,500
P18-4 (b) Year 3 profit recognized, $700,000
P18-5 (b) Net income, $12,288
P18-6 (a) Net income, $27,700
P18-7 (a) Net income, $36,200
P18-9 (b) Year 3 profit recognized, $200,000
P18-11 (b) Net income, $8,230

Chapter 19

P19-6 (a) Constant dollar net income, $14,000
P19-7 (d) Current value business income, $75,000
P19-12 (a) Constant dollar net income (loss), $(42,500)
P19-13 (d) Current value business income, $70,000

Case 19 Policy changes will increase cash by $21,040

Chapter 20

P20-1 (a) Total itemized deductions, $4,414
P20-2 Taxable income, $52,615
P20-4 (d) Tax obligation, $7,017
P20-5 Taxable income, $256,000
P20-7 (a) Total itemized deductions, $8,720
P20-8 Taxable income, $47,572
P20-9 (d) Taxable income, $41,120
P20-10 Taxable income, $239,500

Chapter 21

P21-2 (a) Understatement of net income, $4,500
P21-4 (a) Cost of goods manufactured, $766,000
P21-5 (b) Cost of goods manufactured, $138,075
P21-7 Cost of goods manufactured, $264,000
P21-8 (b) Net income, $343,000
P21-9 (b) Net income, $108,240
P21-10 (a) Understatement of net income, $11,200
P21-12 (a) Cost of goods manufactured, $546,000
P21-14 (b) Net income, $20,550
Case 21 (c) Savings of $7,300 if produced internally

Chapter 22

P22-2 (b) Cost of jobs completed during June, $260,600
P22-3 (d) Overapplied overhead, $11,200
P22-6 (d) Ending work in process, $32,000
P22-7 (a) Total cost of completed goods, $95,336
P22-8 (a) (4) Cost of units transferred to finished goods, $47,580
P22-9 (c) Total cost of completed goods, $303,850
P22-11 (b) Cost of jobs completed during April, 235,900
P22-12 (e) Cost of ending finished goods inventory, $58,000
P22-13 (a) Total cost of completed goods, $21,920

Chapter 23

P23-1 (a) Total budgeted sales revenue, June, $138,000
P23-2 (b) Cost of direct materials purchases, March, $12,540
P23-3 (a) Number of units to be produced, March, 8,080
P23-4 (c) Ending cash balance, October, $6,308
P23-5 (a) Total cash disbursements, $706,325
P23-6 (a) Ending cash balance, $33,540
P23-7 (b) (3) Finished goods, $4,200
P23-8 (b) Cost of direct materials purchases, March, $20,208
P23-9 (a) Number of units to be produced, March, 10,860
P23-10 (c) Ending cash balance, December, $5,495
P23-11 (b) Net income, $15,900
P23-12 (a) (4) Cost of direct material purchases, March, $15,129

Chapter 24

P24-5 (a) Break-even point in dollars, $320,000
P24-6 (c) Additional sales, $500,000
P24-7 (b) Required sales, $1,485,000
P24-8 (b) Break-even point in dollars, $1,920,000
P24-14 (c) Additional sales, $825,000
P24-15 (c) Units required, 27,600
Case 24 (b) Budgeted net income, $20,800

Chapter 25

P25-2 (a) Segment margin, $45,000
P25-3 (a) Segment margin, product Z, $16,000
P25-4 (a) Controllable contribution margin, dog food, $34,000
P25-8 (a) Segment margin, $(21,000)
P25-11 (a) Segment margin, Urbana, $(19,600)

Chapter 26

P26-2 (b) Total production costs, variance, $2,540U
P26-3 (a) Total standard variable cost per case, $35.04
P26-5 (a) Materials quantity variance, $675F

P26-6 (b) Variable overhead spending variance, $7,600F
P26-7 Actual labor hours worked, 22,000
P26-11 (b) Total production costs, variance, $3,326U
P26-12 (b) Total labor variance, $805F
P26-13 Fixed overhead volume variance, $4,000U
Case 26 (b) Materials quantity variance, plastic sheets, $360U

Chapter 27
P27-2 (b) Maximum price, $4,320
P27-4 (a) Total differential costs of order, $21,050
P27-6 (a) Keep snack bar; $8,500 in favor
P27-7 (b) Oil and Gas Accounting, expected value, 195
P27-9 (b) Order 30,000 hot dogs per game
P27-11 (a) Make the part; better off by 60¢ per part
P27-13 (a) Keep lunch counter; $12,600 in favor
P27-14 (b) Order 7,000 pizzas per game
Case 27 (a) Purchase new machinery; $12,600 in favor

Chapter 28
P28-1 (b) Net present value, $119,440
P28-2 (b) Net present value, $(544,940)
P28-3 (a) Net present value, store no. 724, $7,093
P28-4 Net present value, $(73,300)
P28-6 (a) Net present value, $45,968
P28-7 (a) Net present value in favor of replacing, $848
P28-9 (b) Internal rate of return, 24.55%
P28-10 (b) Net present value, $32,400
P28-12 (a) Net present value in favor of keeping, $854
P28-14 (b) Internal rate of return, 26.86%
Case 28 (c) Internal rate of return, 14.23%

GLOSSARY

absorption costing A method that assigns all manufacturing costs to products; used for external financial reporting purposes. (Chapter 25)
accelerated depreciation methods Methods that generate relatively large amounts of depreciation in the early years of asset use and smaller amounts in later years. (Chapter 10)
account A record that is kept for the individual asset, liability, and owners' equity components of an organization. (Chapter 2)
account form balance sheet A form of balance sheet taking its name from the T-account. Asset accounts are presented on the left side of the statement; liability and owners' equity accounts are presented on the right side. (Chapter 6)
accounting A set of theories, concepts, and techniques by which financial data are processed into information for reporting, planning, controlling, and decision-making purposes. (Chapter 1)
accounting controls Measures established to assist a firm in protecting its assets and checking the reliability and accuracy of the financial information generated. (Chapter 5)
accounting cycle The various tasks performed during an accounting period to process transactions, including (1) recording transactions in the journal; (2) posting; (3) preparing a trial balance, work sheet, and financial statements; (4) recording adjusting and closing entries; and (5) preparing a post-closing trial balance. (Chapter 3)
accounting equation A mathematical relationship: Assets = Liabilities + Owners' Equity. (Chapter 1)
accounting information system The network that processes transactions and ultimately produces financial statements and other reports. (Chapter 5)
accounts payable Amounts owed to suppliers for the purchase of goods or services. (Chapter 12)
Accounting Principles Board A former policy-making body of the AICPA charged with the responsibility of developing generally accepted accounting principles. (Chapter 18)
accounting rate of return A method of evaluating long-term projects or investment centers that focuses on the average net income generated in relation to the investment; sometimes called return on investment (ROI). (Chapters 25, 28)
accounts receivable Amounts that customers owe an entity for goods and services. (Chapter 8)
accounts receivable turnover An activity ratio that shows the number of times each year a company's receivables turn into cash; computed by dividing net sales by average accounts receivable. (Chapter 19)
accrual basis The accounting basis which recognizes revenues when earned and, for income determination purposes, matches expenses against the revenues they helped to create. (Chapters 3, 20)
accrued expenses Unpaid expenses which are matched against revenues under the accrual basis of accounting. (Chapter 3)
accrued liability The amount owed for an accrued expense. (Chapter 12)
accrued revenues Revenues recognized under the accrual basis of accounting as being earned although they have not as yet been received. (Chapter 3)
activity ratios Ratios used to analyze a firm's effectiveness in using specific resources; often called turnover ratios. (Chapter 19)
additions Items that provide future benefits and are affixed to existing property, plant, and equipment. (Chapter 11)
adjusted gross income Gross income of a taxpayer less allowable deductions from gross income. (Chapter 20)
adjusting process A process performed at the end of the period in which the accounts are analyzed and updated, if necessary. (Chapter 3)
administrative controls Measures established to promote operational efficiency and encourage adherence to management policies—for example, quality control and employee training programs. (Chapter 5)
aging accounts receivable Segregation of individual accounts receivable based on the length of time outstanding; used in the balance sheet approach to estimating bad debts. (Chapter 8)

all-inclusive approach A comprehensive approach which incorporates operating and nonoperating revenues and expenses, gains and losses from occasional sales of assets, and extraordinary gains and losses into the measurement of net income. (Chapter 6)

allowance method of bad debts A method of accounting for bad debts that employs a contra asset (Allowance for Bad Debts) for use in the valuation of accounts receivable. (Chapter 8)

American Institute of Certified Public Accountants (AICPA) A national organization of licensed CPAs. (Chapter 18)

amortization The allocation of the cost of intangible assets to the accounting periods benefited. (Chapter 11)

annuity A series of equal cash flows over a number of years. (Chapter 28)

appropriation of retained earnings A separation of the Retained Earnings account to inform financial statement readers that a portion of retained earnings is unavailable for dividend distributions. (Chapter 14)

articles of partnership The agreement in a partnership that details the rights, responsibilities, and duties of each of the partners. (Chapter 13)

assessments Amounts charged to property owners by government agencies for improvements such as new streets, sewers, and sidewalks. (Chapter 11)

assets The economic resources owned by a company that are expected to benefit future time periods. (Chapter 1)

assignment of accounts receivable The process of assigning selected customer accounts to a lending institution to secure cash. Collections from these accounts are earmarked to repay the amount of cash advanced plus interest and service charges. (Chapter 8)

attainable standard A standard that can be achieved by efficient, not perfect, operations; allows for normal scrap, waste, and spoilage. (Chapter 26)

auditing The investigation and examination of transactions that underlie an organization's financial statements. (Chapter 1)

audit trail A means to trace and access the underlying details of summarized information. (Chapter 5)

authorized stock The number of shares of stock a corporation is permitted to issue as specified in its charter. (Chapter 13)

average rate of tax A taxpayer's tax obligation divided by total taxable income. (Chapter 20)

bad debts Uncollectible accounts receivable. (Chapter 8)

balance sheet A financial statement that presents a firm's assets, liabilities, and owners' equity at a particular point in time. (Chapter 1)

balance sheet approach of accounting for bad debts A method that employs estimates of bad debts based on accounts receivable and focuses on reporting accounts receivable at net realizable value. (Chapter 8)

bank reconciliation A process for determining the amount of cash a company has control over and reports on its balance sheet. (Chapter 7)

bank statement A document that summarizes the activity in a checking account. (Chapter 7)

basis The cost of an asset less any depreciation claimed (or that could have been claimed) for tax purposes. (Chapter 20)

betterments Expenditures that improve or increase the future service potential of an item of property, plant, and equipment. (Chapter 11)

bond A formal written document that provides evidence of long-term indebtedness. (Chapter 15)

bond discount The difference between the face value of bonds and the issue price, when issuance occurs below face value. (Chapter 15)

bond indenture A document stipulating the provisions of a bond issue. (Chapter 15)

bond premium The difference between the face value of bonds and the issue price, when issuance occurs above face value. (Chapter 15)

bond refunding The replacement of a bond issue with other bonds that carry a lower interest rate. (Chapter 15)

bond retirement The cancellation of bonds that have been called. (Chapter 15)

bonus to new or existing partners A situation in which an amount different from the proportional owners' equity is paid by a new partner upon admission to a partnership. (Chapter 13)

bookkeeper A person who assists an accountant by recording, summarizing, and processing data into information. (Chapter 1)

book value The amount that an asset is carried at in the accounting records—namely, cost less any offsetting contra accounts. (Chapters 3, 10)

book value per share The amount of stockholders' equity allocable to an individual share of stock. (Chapter 14)

bottom-up approach A budgeting approach that centers on lower-level employee participation in the development of a budget. (Chapter 23)

break-even chart A presentation of the break-even point and other CVP relationships in a graphic format. (Chapter 24)

break-even point The level of activity where revenues and expenses are equal and net income is zero. (Chapter 24)
budget A formal quantitative expression of management expectations generated for any area that management deems critical. (Chapters 21, 23)
callable bond A bond that can be reacquired by the issuing firm prior to the maturity date. (Chapter 15)
callable preferred stock Preferred stock that can be reacquired by the issuing corporation at a preset price. (Chapter 13)
capital assets All items of property owned by a taxpayer except receivables; inventories; real and depreciable business property; rights to literary, musical, and artistic compositions if in the hands of the creator; and certain governmental obligations. (Chapter 20)
capital budgeting Planning and decision making related to long-term programs and projects. (Chapter 28)
capital expenditure An expenditure that provides long-term benefits to a company. (Chapter 10)
capital deficiency A debit balance in a partner's capital account. (Chapter 13)
capital lease A lease in which the lessee is really acquiring an asset via an installment purchase plan. (Chapter 15)
carrying value of a bond The face value of a bond less the unamortized bond discount (or plus the unamortized bond premium). (Chapter 15)
cash Items acceptable to a bank for deposit and free from restriction for use in satisfying current debts. (Chapter 7)
cash basis The basis of accounting that focuses on the cash flows connected with revenues and expenses. Revenues are recognized when received, and expenses are recognized when paid. (Chapters 3, 18, 20)
cash budget An overall plan of activity that depicts cash inflows and outflows for a stated period of time. (Chapters 7, 23)
cash control system Procedures adopted to ensure the safeguarding of an organization's funds. (Chapter 7)
cash discount A discount offered to credit customers to encourage prompt payment of invoices. (Chapter 4)
cash payments journal A special journal used to record virtually all cash disbursements made by a business. (Chapter 5)
cash planning system Those procedures adopted to ensure that adequate cash is available to meet current obligations and that any excess cash is invested. (Chapter 7)
cash receipts journal A special journal used to record all cash received by a business. (Chapter 5)
certainty environment An environment in which all predicted events and outcomes are presumed to occur. (Chapter 27)
Certified Public Accountant (CPA) An individual who is licensed by a state to practice public accounting. (Chapter 1)
charter A document that specifies a corporation's business purpose, organizational structure, and the types and amounts of stock that can be issued. (Chapter 13)
chart of accounts A detailed listing of a company's accounts and associated account numbers. (Chapter 2)
check register A journal used in a voucher system to record each check written. (Chapter 7)
closely-held corporations Corporations owned by only a few persons. (Chapter 13)
closing process A process in which the balances in all temporary accounts are transferred to the owners' capital account(s). (Chapter 3)
commitments Pledges or promises to enter into future business transactions. (Chapter 6)
committed fixed cost A cost arising from an organization's commitment to engage in operations—for example, property taxes, rent, and depreciation. (Chapter 24)
common-size financial statements Statements that reveal account balances in both dollars and percentages, thereby facilitating different types of comparative analysis. (Chapter 19)
common stock A corporate ownership interest that controls management by exercising voting rights. (Chapters 6, 13)
comparability A characteristic of financial information that allows users to make comparative evaluations among firms and within the same firm at different points in time. (Chapter 18)
comparative data A means of disclosing financial information that allows users to make comparative studies and assess the direction of an entity over several accounting periods. (Chapter 6)
compensating balance A portion of an amount loaned to a customer that remains on deposit in the bank during the loan period. (Chapter 7)
compliance reporting Financial reporting to meet the demands of regulatory agencies. (Chapter 21)
composite depreciation A depreciation method

that uses groups of assets and a composite, or average, depreciation rate. (Chapter 10)

compound interest Interest that is calculated on both principal and previously accumulated interest. (Chapters 15, 28)

computer fraud A scheme that involves a computer to aid and abet in a fraud or embezzlement. (Chapter 5)

consistency principle A principle stipulating that entities employ the same accounting practices in each reporting period. (Chapter 18)

conservatism A concept stipulating that when alternative valuations and measurements are possible, the alternative selected should be that which is least likely to overstate assets and/or net income. (Chapter 18)

consolidated financial statements A set of financial statements that combines the activities of the parent and controlled subsidiaries as if only one company existed. (Chapter 16)

constant dollar accounting An approach used to account for inflation in which historical cost data are adjusted for changes in the purchasing power of the dollar by using a general price level index. (Chapter 19)

contingencies Circumstances where the outcome is uncertain. (Chapter 6)

contingent liabilities Potential liabilities whose outcomes hinge on the future. (Chapters 8, 12)

continuous budget A budget that covers a one-year period; a new month is added when the current month is completed. (Chapter 23)

contra asset An account used to reduce asset balances in the financial statements. (Chapter 3)

contract interest rate The interest rate printed on the face of a bond certificate. (Chapter 15)

contra liability An account used to reduce liability balances in the financial statements. (Chapter 12)

contribution approach An approach to performance evaluation that uses contribution and segment margins for evaluating profit and investment centers. (Chapter 25)

contribution income statement An income statement featuring disclosure of the contribution margin and fixed costs directly identifiable with a segment, both controllable and uncontrollable. (Chapter 25)

contribution margin Selling price minus variable cost per unit. (Chapter 24)

control An activity that helps bring an organization back on target in terms of achieving its original plans. (Chapter 21)

control account A general ledger account that is composed of various subsidiary ledger accounts. (Chapter 5)

controllable contribution margin A performance measure computed by subtracting a segment's controllable fixed costs from its contribution margin. (Chapter 25)

controlling interest A greater-than-50% ownership interest in a subsidiary company. (Chapter 16)

conversion cost The cost to convert raw material into finished product—namely, direct labor plus factory overhead. (Chapter 21)

convertible bond A bond that can be converted into common stock at the option of the bondholder. (Chapter 15)

convertible preferred stock Preferred stock that can be converted into common stock at the option of the stockholder. (Chapter 13)

copyright An intangible asset that gives its owners or heirs the exclusive right to produce and sell an artistic, musical, or published work for a stipulated period of time. (Chapter 11)

corporation A form of business organization that is a separate legal entity from its owners. Ownership is in the hands of investors who have acquired shares of the corporation's stock. (Chapters 1, 6, 13)

cost accounting An area of accounting that deals with the collection, assignment, control, and evaluation of costs. (Chapters 1, 21)

cost allocation An approach for charging segments with indirect costs (such as corporate administrative expenses) that are not traceable to any single segment. (Chapter 25)

cost center A responsibility unit in which a manager is held accountable for cost incurrence. (Chapter 25)

cost depletion The allocation of natural resource cost over the estimated recoverable units of output. (Chapter 11)

cost flow assumption An assumption regarding the flow of inventory costs through a firm's accounting system. (Chapter 9)

cost of capital The cost of investment funds. (Chapter 28)

cost of goods manufactured The total of direct materials used, direct labor, and factory overhead plus the beginning work in process inventory less the ending work in process inventory. (Chapter 21)

cost of goods sold The total cost of inventory that a company has sold during an accounting period. (Chapter 4)

cost principle An accounting concept which holds that the acquisitions of goods, services, and other resources are entered in the accounting records at cost. (Chapter 1)

cost-volume-profit analysis The study of price, cost, volume, and profit interrelationships. (Chapter 24)

coupon bonds Bonds having small detachable coupons that correspond to each interest period and are payable to the bearer. (Chapter 15)

coverage ratios Ratios used to judge the solvency of an entity. (Chapter 19)

credit A tool used to increase and decrease account balances; also, the right-hand side of a T-account. (Chapter 2)

credit memorandum A document prepared by the seller for an allowance or an authorized return of merchandise. (Chapter 4)

cumulative preferred stock Preferred stock where the rights to dividends omitted in a given year accumulate. These dividends must be paid before any subsequent dividends are distributed to common stockholders. (Chapter 13)

current assets Those assets which management intends to convert into cash or consume in the normal course of business within one year or the operating cycle, whichever is longer. (Chapter 6)

current cost The present cost to purchase or manufacture assets having the same service potential as assets already owned. (Chapter 10)

current liabilities Debts or obligations that will be paid within one year or the operating cycle, whichever is longer. (Chapters 6, 12)

current ratio A measure of liquidity that relates total current assets to total current liabilities. (Chapters 6, 19)

current value accounting An approach to accounting for inflation that recognizes price changes in the individual assets owned by an enterprise and restates the assets in terms of their current value. (Chapter 19)

customer statement A detailed listing of all purchases and payments made by a customer during a billing period. (Chapter 4)

data Facts and figures. (Chapter 5)

date of declaration The date when a dividend is formally declared (approved) by the board of directors. (Chapter 14)

date of payment The date when a dividend will be distributed to stockholders. (Chapter 14)

date of record The date used to determine the stockholders entitled to a declared dividend. (Chapter 14)

debenture bond A bond that has no assets pledged as security and is issued on the general credit of the corporation. (Chapter 15)

debit A tool used to increase and decrease account balances; also, the left-hand side of a T-account. (Chapter 2)

debit memorandum A document prepared by the purchaser for an allowance or an authorized return of merchandise. (Chapter 4)

debt to total assets ratio A coverage ratio that shows the percentage of total capital provided by the creditors of a business; computed as total debt divided by total assets. (Chapter 19)

decision making An integral part of the planning and control process that requires managers to choose from among alternative courses of action. (Chapter 21)

deductions from adjusted gross income Subtractions from adjusted gross income for certain personal expenses—specifically, excess itemized deductions and personal exemptions. (Chapter 20)

deductions from gross income Subtractions from a taxpayer's income that generally relate to the generation of gross income. (Chapter 20)

deferred charge A long-term prepaid expense. (Chapter 11)

deferred payment plan A plan by which payment is made to the seller each period (month, quarter, and so on) until the purchase price is paid off. (Chapter 10)

deferred taxes A postponement or prepayment of income taxes that arises from timing differences. (Chapter 20)

deficit A debit (negative) balance in the Retained Earnings account. (Chapter 14)

dependent A person (1) who has received more than one half of his or her support from the taxpayer, (2) is closely related to the taxpayer or has lived in the taxpayer's home for the entire year, and (3) has earned less than $1,000 of income (unless 19 years of age or a full-time student). (Chapter 20)

depletion The allocation of natural resource cost to the resources extracted during an accounting period. (Chapter 11)

deposit in transit Receipts recorded on company records but not yet recorded at the bank. (Chapter 7)

depreciable base The cost of an item of property, plant, and equipment less any residual value. (Chapter 10)

depreciation The process used to allocate the cost of long-lived items of property, plant, and equipment to the accounting periods benefited. (Chapters 3, 10)

differential cost A cost that differs among alternatives. (Chapter 27)

direct cost Any cost that is easily traced to and associated with a business segment. (Chapter 25)
direct costing A method that assigns only variable manufacturing costs (direct materials, direct labor, and variable manufacturing overhead) to products; more appropriately termed variable costing. (Chapter 25)
direct labor The gross wages of personnel who work directly on the goods being produced. (Chapter 21)
direct materials All materials that form an integral part of the finished product and that can be easily traced to the finished product. (Chapter 21)
direct write-off method of bad debts A method of accounting for bad debts whereby customer accounts are written off (expensed) when determined to be uncollectible. (Chapter 8)
disclosure principle A principle holding that an entity must provide a complete reporting of all facts important enough to influence the judgment of an informed user of financial information. (Chapter 18)
discontinued operations A segment of a business which is sold, abandoned, or otherwise disposed of. (Chapter 14)
discount amortization The process of reducing a discount on notes payable (or bonds payable) by recognizing interest expense; also refers to the process of reducing a discount on bond investments by recognizing interest revenue. (Chapters 12, 15, 16)
discounting The process of taking a future amount and bringing it back to its value today. (Chapter 28)
discounting notes receivable A means of generating cash by presenting notes receivable to a bank before the maturity date and receiving the maturity value less a discount (interest) assessed by the bank. (Chapter 8)
discount on capital stock The difference between the par or stated value of stock and the issue price, when issuance occurs below par or stated value. (Chapter 13)
discount on notes payable A contra-liability account that represents future interest expense. (Chapter 12)
discretionary fixed cost A fixed cost that originates from top management's yearly appropriation decisions—for example, advertising expense and research and development expense. (Chapter 24)
dishonoring a note The process of failing to pay a note receivable as of the maturity date. (Chapter 8)
dividend payout ratio A profitability ratio (see payout ratio). (Chapter 19)
dividend yield A profitability ratio that is calculated by dividing the annual cash dividend per share by the current market price of the stock. (Chapter 19)
dividends A distribution of earnings by a corporation to its stockholders. (Chapters 6, 14)
dividends in arrears Dividends that have been omitted on cumulative preferred stock. (Chapter 13)
donated capital Shares of a corporation's own stock donated by a stockholder for subsequent resale to others. (Chapter 14)
double-declining balance depreciation A method of accelerated depreciation where the straight-line depreciation rate is doubled and applied against the remaining book value (i.e., a declining balance) each period. (Chapter 10)
double taxation The taxing of income to a corporation and the subsequent taxing of dividends to stockholders. (Chapter 13)
earnings deficiency The condition which exists when a partnership incurs a net loss or has insufficient earnings to cover salary and interest allowances. (Chapter 13)
earnings per share A widely used profitability ratio computed as earnings available to common stockholders (net income less any preferred dividend requirements) divided by the weighted-average common shares outstanding. (Chapters 6, 14, 19)
economic entity A group of companies functioning as a single entity to pursue the objectives of operational efficiency and profit. (Chapter 16)
effective interest amortization A method of bond discount and premium amortization that calculates interest expense (or revenue in the case of investments) as a constant percentage of bond carrying value. (Chapters 15, 16)
effective interest rate The actual interest rate on a bond, which may be different from the contract interest rate. (Chapter 15)
effectiveness A concept referring to whether a particular goal or objective has been attained. (Chapter 26)
efficiency A concept that relates to the amount of resources consumed in accomplishing a goal. (Chapter 26)
elimination entry An entry made on the consolidated work sheet to eliminate intercompany transactions from consolidated financial statements. (Chapter 16)
employee A person who works for a specific

business and is directly and closely supervised by that business. (Chapter 12)

entity assumption An assumption that a business is viewed as a unit that is separate and apart from its owners and from other firms. (Chapters 1, 18)

equity method A method of accounting for long-term investments in common stock, where the Investment account includes the acquisition cost and a share of the investee's net income, net losses, and dividends. (Chapter 16)

equivalent unit A physical unit stated in terms of a finished unit. (Chapter 22)

excess itemized deductions The difference between a taxpayer's total allowable personal expenses and the appropriate zero bracket amount. (Chapter 20)

expected value The mathematical outcome of multiplying the payoff of an individual event by the event's probability and then summing the results. (Chapter 27)

expected value of perfect information An amount that represents the mathematical difference between the expected value of existing conditions and the expected value of an environment where events can be predicted in advance. (Chapter 27)

expenses The costs incurred in producing revenues. (Chapter 1)

extraordinary gains and losses Gains and losses that are both unusual in character and occur infrequently. (Chapters 6, 14)

factoring The sale of accounts receivable to generate cash. (Chapter 8)

factory overhead All factory-related costs other than direct materials used and direct labor. (Chapter 21)

fair market value The current market price of an asset. (Chapter 11)

Federal Insurance Contributions Act (FICA) An act, commonly called Social Security, requiring employers to withhold a portion of each employee's gross earnings and to match the employee's contribution. (Chapter 12)

Federal Unemployment Tax Act (FUTA) Federal legislation requiring employers to pay taxes to assist the unemployed. (Chapter 12)

fidelity bond Essentially an insurance policy that reimburses a company for losses suffered from the dishonest practices of bonded employees. (Chapter 5)

financial accounting An area of accounting concerned primarily with external reporting—that is, reporting the results of financial activities to parties outside the firm. (Chapters 1, 21)

Financial Accounting Standards Board (FASB) The private sector organization presently in charge of formulating standards of financial reporting in the United States. (Chapter 18)

finished goods The inventory of completed production that is owned by a firm. (Chapter 21)

first-in, first-out (FIFO) An inventory accounting method based on the premise that the first goods in are the first ones sold or used. (Chapter 9)

fiscal year Any one-year period other than a calendar year—for example, July 1–June 30. (Chapter 1)

fixed cost A cost that remains constant in total when changes occur in an activity base. (Chapters 21, 24)

fixed overhead volume variance A variance that discloses the fixed costs associated with an under- or overutilization of manufacturing facilities. (Chapter 26)

flexible budget A budget that covers a range of activity as opposed to a single level. (Chapter 26)

F.O.B. destination Freight terms indicating that transportation charges are borne by the seller. (Chapter 4)

F.O.B. shipping point Freight terms indicating that transportation charges are borne by the purchaser. (Chapter 4)

footnotes A supplemental, yet integral, part of the financial statements that provides an expansion of the information contained in the body of the statements. (Chapter 6)

Foreign Corrupt Practices Act (FCPA) An act that outlaws bribes and questionable payments to foreign firms, governments, and political officials and makes such payments a criminal offense. (Chapter 5)

franchise An intangible asset representing rights that authorize the manufacture or sale of certain products and/or the performance of certain services. (Chapter 11)

full cost approach An approach used for natural resources in which the exploration costs of both successful and unsuccessful ventures are charged to asset accounts. (Chapter 11)

full project approach An evaluation of the total relevant costs associated with a decision alternative. (Chapter 27)

fully diluted earnings per share A calculation of earnings per share based on the assumption that potentially dilutive securities were converted into common shares at the beginning of the accounting period. (Chapter 14)

General Accounting Office (GAO) A government agency that evaluates programs and other government agencies for the U.S. Congress. (Chapter 1)

general ledger A book or computer file that houses an entity's accounts. (Chapter 2)

generally accepted accounting principles (GAAP) A set of assumptions, concepts, and procedures that provides a foundation for measuring and disclosing the results of business transactions and events. (Chapter 18)

going concern assumption An assumption that a business will continue to operate for a long period of time unless there is substantial evidence to the contrary. (Chapter 18)

goods available for sale The beginning balance of inventory plus net purchases. (Chapter 4)

goods on consignment Merchandise in the hands of sales agents. The agents possess the merchandise; ownership, however, remains with the consignor. (Chapter 9)

goodwill The amount paid by the purchaser of a business in excess of the current value of the assets and liabilities acquired. (Chapter 11)

gross earnings The total earnings of an employee before any deductions are made. (Chapter 12)

gross income A taxpayer's total income less allowable exclusions. (Chapter 20)

gross method of recording purchases A method of accounting for merchandise in which both Purchases and Accounts Payable are recorded at the total invoice cost of the merchandise acquired. (Chapter 4)

gross profit Net sales less cost of goods sold. (Chapter 4)

gross profit method An inventory estimation method based on a firm's gross profit rate—that is, gross profit expressed as a percentage of net sales. (Chapter 9)

high-low method A method of cost analysis that uses two data observations (the highest and lowest) to make generalizations about variable and fixed cost behavior. (Chapter 24)

historical cost principle The principle of recording goods, resources, and services acquired at cost, with cost defined as the exchange or transaction price. (Chapters 1, 18)

holding gains and losses Gains and losses that arise from increases and decreases in asset values during the period the assets are held; an integral part of the current value approach of accounting for inflation. (Chapter 19)

horizontal analysis The calculation of dollar and percentage changes for corresponding items in comparative financial statements. (Chapter 19)

ideal standard A standard that can be achieved only under perfect operating conditions. (Chapter 26)

inadequacy The inability of a depreciable asset to meet the competitive needs of a business. (Chapter 10)

income statement A financial statement that summarizes the results of a business's operation for a given time period by disclosing the revenues earned and the expenses incurred. (Chapter 1)

income statement approach of accounting for bad debts A method that employs estimates of bad debts based on total sales or credit sales. (Chapter 8)

income tax withholdings The portion of an employee's gross earnings withheld by the employer to satisfy federal (and sometimes state and local) income tax laws. (Chapter 12)

incremental approach An evaluation of the net difference in relevant costs associated with decision alternatives. (Chapter 27)

independent contractor A person who frequently performs services for many different organizations at the same time, or perhaps finishes a project for one entity and then moves on to service another. (Chapter 12)

independent review An internal control feature that involves the review and evaluation of accounting controls by the owner/manager, a key employee, an internal auditor, and in many instances, an independent external auditor. (Chapter 5)

indirect cost A cost that is not easily traced to a business segment. (Chapter 25)

indirect labor The wages of factory employees who do not work directly on the product; treated as part of factory overhead. (Chapter 21)

indirect materials Minor material items (such as glue, varnish, and nails) used in manufacturing a product; treated as part of factory overhead. (Chapter 21)

inflation A rise in the general price level that causes a decline in the purchasing power of the dollar. (Chapter 19)

information Meaningful data that is used in reporting, planning, control, and decision-making activities. (Chapter 5)

installment method A method of revenue recognition by which a sale's profit is allocated to different accounting periods. The allocation is based on the amount of cash received from customers. (Chapter 18)

installment payment plans Plans stipulating that a buyer make specific monthly payments for

a predetermined number of months. (Chapter 8)
intangible assets Long-term assets that lack physical existence—for example, patents, copyrights, and trademarks. (Chapters 6, 11)
intercompany transaction A transaction between two affiliated companies such as a parent and a subsidiary. (Chapter 16)
interest A charge made for the use of borrowed funds. (Chapter 8)
interest allowances A consideration used in the division of the net income of many partnerships. The allowances recognize differences in capital provided to the firm by the partners. (Chapter 13)
internal auditors Individuals in large organizations who review and monitor the organization's accounting procedures and controls. (Chapter 1)
internal control A plan of organization and policies and procedures to (1) safeguard assets, (2) provide accurate and reliable accounting data, (3) promote operational efficiency, and (4) encourage adherence to managerial policies. (Chapter 5)
internal information Information provided for managers within a company. (Chapter 21)
internal rate of return A discounted cash flow method of evaluating long-term projects that derives the actual return on an investment. (Chapter 28)
Internal Revenue Service (IRS) An agency of the U.S. Treasury Department that administers the tax laws passed by Congress and the rulings handed down by the courts. (Chapters 1, 18, 20)
interperiod tax allocation The allocation of income tax expense to different accounting periods affected by timing differences between taxable income and pretax accounting income. (Chapter 20)
intraperiod tax allocation The practice of relating income tax expense to the items that give rise to the tax. (Chapter 14)
inventory Goods acquired for resale to customers. (Chapters 4, 9)
inventory depreciation method A depreciation method often used for low-cost, short-lived items; depreciation expense represents the cost of assets consumed during the period. (Chapter 10)
inventory profit A fictitious profit that arises when cost of goods sold is computed by using an old (and fairly low) cost. (Chapter 9)
inventory turnover ratio An activity ratio that lends insight into a firm's inventory management policies; computed by dividing the cost of goods sold by average inventory. (Chapter 19)
investee A company whose shares have been acquired by an investor. (Chapter 16)
investment center A responsibility unit in which a manager is evaluated on profit and the effective use of asset investment. (Chapter 25)
invoice A source document used to record sales of merchandise. (Chapter 4)
invoice price List price less applicable trade discounts. (Chapter 4)
itemizing A process performed by a taxpayer; involves listing the actual allowable personal expenses that have been incurred during the year. (Chapter 20)
job order system A system of cost accumulation that gathers costs by job or order. (Chapter 22)
joint return A filing status for tax purposes that combines the income and deductions of a husband and wife. (Chapter 20)
journal A chronological record that serves as the entry point for transactions into a company's formalized accounting system. (Chapter 2)
journalizing The process of recording transactions in a journal in the form of debits and credits. (Chapter 2)
labor efficiency variance The difference between actual and standard labor hours multiplied by the standard wage rate. (Chapter 26)
labor rate variance The difference between actual and standard wage rates multiplied by the actual hours of labor used in production. (Chapter 26)
land improvements Improvements made to land, such as parking lots and lawn sprinkler systems. (Chapter 10)
last-in, first-out (LIFO) An inventory accounting method based on the premise that the last goods in are the first ones sold or used. (Chapter 9)
lease An agreement allowing one party, the lessee, to use the assets of another party, the lessor, for a stated period of time. (Chapter 15)
leasehold improvements Improvements made to leased property by the lessee. (Chapter 10)
legal capital The minimum amount of owners' equity that must be maintained for the protection of creditors; obtained by multiplying the par value per share times the number of shares issued. (Chapter 13)
legal entity A unit authorized by the relevant government authority to conduct business. (Chapter 16)
liabilities Debts that are owed by an enterprise. (Chapter 1)
liquidation The process of terminating a part-

nership and discontinuing operations. (Chapter 13)
liquidity How close an asset is to becoming cash. (Chapter 6)
liquidity ratios Ratios that measure the ability of a business to meet current debts as the obligations come due. (Chapter 19)
list price The basic catalog price for merchandise. (Chapter 4)
long-term capital gains and losses Gains and losses resulting from the sale or exchange of capital assets held for more than one year. (Chapter 20)
long-term liabilities Obligations expected to be paid after one year or the operating cycle, whichever is longer. (Chapter 6)
loss leader Products sold or services offered at prices below cost in order to attract customers or clients. (Chapter 27)
lower-of-cost-or-market-methods Methods that allow investments and inventories to be accounted for at acquisition cost or market value, whichever is lower. (Chapters 7, 9, 16)
lump-sum purchase The purchase of a number of assets together for a single amount. (Chapter 10)
maker The person or firm that promises to pay the stipulated amount of a note. (Chapter 8)
management advisory services (MAS) "Consulting" services performed by public accounting firms that are often unrelated to traditional accounting matters. (Chapter 1)
management by exception The practice of focusing a manager's attention on those aspects of operations that deviate from planned or expected results. (Chapters 4, 26)
managerial accounting An area of accounting oriented toward reporting the results of operations to managers and other interested parties within an organization. (Chapters 1, 21)
marginal rate of tax The tax rate applied to each additional dollar of taxable income. (Chapter 20)
master budget A comprehensive set of integrated budgets that serves as the financial plan for the entire organization. (Chapter 23)
matching principle The principle that all costs and expenses associated with the production of revenue are recognized when the revenue is recognized. (Chapters 3, 18)
materiality A concept dictating that an accountant must judge the impact and importance of each transaction (or event) to determine its proper handling in the accounting records. Minor items are treated in the most expedient manner possible. (Chapter 18)
materials price variance The difference between the actual and standard prices multiplied by the actual quantity of materials purchased and put into production. (Chapter 26)
materials quantity variance The difference between actual and standard quantities of materials used multiplied by the standard price. (Chapter 26)
materials requisition An order for materials to be issued from the storeroom. (Chapter 22)
maturity date The date that a note or obligation becomes due. (Chapter 8)
maturity value The amount due on the maturity date (principal plus interest). (Chapter 8)
merchandising system A system that processes the transactions and events related to a merchandising business—specifically, the sales and purchases of inventory. (Chapter 4)
method of least squares A statistical technique for determining cost behavior. (Chapter 24)
minority interest The portion of a subsidiary entity owned by parties other than the parent (controlling) company. (Chapter 16)
mixed (semivariable) cost A cost that contains both fixed and variable cost elements. (Chapter 24)
modified cash basis A method that utilizes features from both the cash and accrual bases of accounting. (Chapter 3)
monetary assets Contractual claims to receive a fixed amount of cash in the future; includes cash, accounts receivable, and notes receivable. (Chapter 19)
monetary liabilities Contractual claims to pay a fixed amount of cash in the future; includes accounts payable, salaries payable, and bonds payable. (Chapter 19)
monetary unit assumption An assumption that an entity's transactions can be expressed in terms of a common measuring unit, such as the U.S. dollar. (Chapter 18)
mortgage note A long-term note issued to finance the purchase of real estate. (Chapter 15)
multiple-step income statement A type of income statement in which accounts are presented by association, thereby revealing important relationships to readers. (Chapter 6)
mutual agency A feature of partnerships whereby each partner acts as an agent of the partnership in business transactions. (Chapter 13)
mutually exclusive alternatives A decision situation in which the acceptance of one alternative

dictates automatic rejection of all others. (Chapter 28)

natural business year A year that concludes at the end of "seasonal activity"—for example, October 31 for a professional baseball club, which is after the play-offs and World Series. (Chapter 1)

net capital gains or losses The combination of the net short-term gain or loss with the net long-term gain or loss. (Chapter 20)

net income The excess of a company's revenues over expenses for a given time period. (Chapter 1)

net loss The excess of a company's expenses over revenues for a given time period. (Chapter 1)

net method of recording purchases A method of accounting for merchandise in which both Purchases and Accounts Payable are recorded at the net cost of the purchase—that is, total invoice cost less the anticipated cash discount. (Chapter 4)

net present value method A method used to evaluate long-term investments in which the present value of an investment's cash inflows and cash outflows are netted against each other. (Chapter 28)

net realizable value For receivables: the amount of cash expected from the collection of present customer balances. For inventory: an item's selling price minus completion and disposal costs. (Chapters 8, 9)

non-fund (exchange) transactions Significant transactions that affect the financial position of a business but do not involve an inflow or outflow of funds. (Chapter 17)

nonmonetary items Asset, liability, and owners' equity items whose prices can change over time—for example, land, equipment, inventory, and warranty obligations. (Chapter 19)

nonprofit organization An organization that lacks a profit motive and is established to serve the needs of society. (Chapter 21)

nontrade receivables Those receivables arising from transactions not directly related to the sale of goods and services. (Chapter 8)

normal balance The type of balance (debit or credit) usually found in a ledger account; for example, assets usually have debit balances, liabilities normally have credit balances, and so forth. (Chapter 2)

notes payable Written promises to pay a definite amount of money on a specific future date. (Chapter 12)

notes receivable Written promises owned by a firm that specify the receipt of a definite sum of money on some future date. (Chapter 8)

NOW account (negotiated orders of withdrawal) An account that allows customers to write checks on their interest-bearing savings. (Chapter 7)

NSF check (nonsufficient funds) A customer's check returned by the bank because of a lack of funds. (Chapter 7)

objective probability A probability based on either a statistically determined outcome or past experience. (Chapter 27)

objectivity principle A principle requiring that accounting information be free from bias and verifiable by an independent party, such as an external auditor. (Chapter 18)

operating cycle The period of time it takes a firm to buy merchandise inventory, sell the inventory, and collect the cash. (Chapter 6)

operating expenses Expenses that relate to the normal selling and administrative activities of a business. (Chapters 4, 6)

operating lease A lease by which the lessee obtains the right to use leased property for a very limited period of time. (Chapter 15)

opportunity cost The cost of a foregone alternative. (Chapter 27)

organization costs Costs incurred to organize a corporation, such as state incorporation fees and legal costs. (Chapter 13)

outstanding checks Checks written but not yet processed by the bank. (Chapter 7)

outstanding shares Shares issued by the firm and held by the stockholders. (Chapter 13)

overapplied overhead A situation arising when the factory overhead applied to production is greater than the amount of factory overhead actually incurred. (Chapter 22)

overhead application rate The rate used to apply factory overhead to jobs or products; estimated factory overhead divided by the estimated application base. (Chapter 22)

owner investments Personal assets put into a business by the owners. The owners are relinquishing asset control and ownership to the enterprise. (Chapter 1)

owner withdrawals The removal of assets from the business by the owners for their own personal use. (Chapter 1)

owners' equity (capital) The owners' net worth or "interest" in the assets of a business; equal to the company's net assets (assets minus liabilities). (Chapter 1)

paid-in capital The amount of stockholder investments in a corporation. (Chapter 13)
parent A company that is the majority owner of another company. (Chapter 16)
parenthetical disclosure Supplemental information included in the body of the financial statements. (Chapter 6)
participating preferred stock Preferred stock that participates in excess dividend distributions after specified distributions to common stockholders. (Chapter 13)
partnership A company formed by two or more persons to carry on, as co-owners, profitable business activity. (Chapters 1, 6, 13)
par-value stock Stock that has an arbitrary fixed amount per share printed on the face of the stock certificate. (Chapter 13)
patent An exclusive right that permits its owner to use, manufacture, and sell a product or process. (Chapter 11)
payback method A method of analysis that measures the amount of time necessary to recover a project's initial cash investment. (Chapter 28)
payee The party to whom a note is made payable. (Chapter 8)
payoff The cost or contribution margin of an event. (Chapter 27)
payoff matrix A two-dimensional table that discloses the payoffs for all combinations of alternatives and events. (Chapter 27)
payout ratio Annual dividends per share divided by earnings per share. (Chapter 14)
payroll register A journal-like record that summarizes a firm's entire payroll. (Chapter 12)
percentage depletion A method of computing depletion that is used for income tax purposes. (Chapter 11)
percentage of completion method A method of revenue recognition that allocates profit to different accounting periods based on the percentage of the total project completed. (Chapter 18)
performance report A report designed to provide the manager of a responsibility center with timely feedback of operating results. (Chapter 25)
period cost A cost unrelated to the acquisition or manufacture of inventory; it is expensed when incurred. (Chapter 21)
periodic inventory system A system of accounting in which purchases and sales of inventory are not recorded in the Inventory account. (Chapters 4, 9)
periodicity assumption An assumption stipulating that for reporting purposes, an entity's life can be divided into discrete time periods such as months, quarters, or years. (Chapter 18)
permanent differences Items that are considered in the calculation of taxable income but not pretax accounting income or vice versa. (Chapter 20)
perpetual inventory system A system of accounting for inventory in which the Inventory account is respectively increased and decreased for each purchase and sale of inventory made during the period. (Chapter 4)
personal exemption A $1,000 deduction from adjusted gross income that is allowed for the taxpayer, the spouse, and each dependent claimed. (Chapter 20)
petty cash system A fund used to make small payments that are impractical or uneconomical to make by check. (Chapter 7)
planning The formulation of methods and strategies that implement a company's objectives in definite terms. (Chapter 21)
pledging of accounts receivable The process of using accounts receivable as collateral for a loan. (Chapter 8)
pooling-of-interests method A method of accounting for business combinations applicable when one company acquires virtually all the outstanding voting shares of another company in exchange for its own common stock. (Chapter 16)
post-closing trial balance An internal report that examines ledger account balances after the closing process has been completed to determine if total debits equal total credits. (Chapter 3)
posting The process by which the transactions in a journal are transferred to the appropriate ledger accounts. (Chapter 2)
preemptive right The right of existing stockholders to maintain their respective interests in a corporation by acquiring additional shares of new stock issues on a pro rata basis. (Chapter 13)
preferred stock Stock that gives its holders preference over common stockholders in dividend distributions and distributions of assets upon liquidation. (Chapter 13)
premium on capital stock The difference between the par or stated value of stock and the issue price, when issuance occurs above par or stated value. (Chapter 13)
prepaid expenses Goods or services purchased for future consumption and paid for in advance. (Chapters 1, 3)
present value The amount an investor is willing to pay to secure a specified cash flow on a

future date at a given rate of return. (Chapters 15, 28)

price-earnings ratio A profitability ratio calculated by dividing the current market price of a share of common stock by the annual earnings per share. (Chapters 14, 19)

primary earnings per share A calculation of earnings per share for firms with potential dilution which ignores the dilutive effect of convertible securities. (Chapter 14)

prime cost Those costs easily traced to the finished product—namely, direct materials used plus direct labor. (Chapter 21)

principal The amount on which interest is computed. (Chapter 8)

prior period adjustments Corrections of errors affecting the net income of previous periods. (Chapter 14)

process costing system A system of cost accumulation that gathers costs by process or department. (Chapter 22)

product cost A cost that goes into inventory—namely, direct materials, direct labor, and factory overhead. (Chapter 21)

profitability ratios Ratios that examine an organization's operating success (or lack of success) during an accounting period. (Chapter 19)

profit center A responsibility unit in which a manager is held accountable for profit. (Chapter 25)

profit margin on sales A measure of profitability that relates net income to net sales. (Chapter 19)

pro-forma financial statements Forecasted financial statements that are prepared as the final step of the budgeting process. (Chapter 23)

property dividends Dividends paid in assets other than cash. (Chapter 14)

property, plant, and equipment Assets with long lives acquired for use in business operations and not held for resale to customers. (Chapters 6, 10)

prospectus A document related to new stock issues that is required by the SEC; contains information about the corporation's products, management, and financial affairs. (Chapter 13)

protest fee A bank service charge associated with dishonored notes. (Chapter 8)

public accounting A branch of accounting in which an accountant provides services to all types of enterprises for fees. (Chapter 1)

publicly held corporation A corporation that sells its stock to the general public. (Chapter 13)

purchase method A method of accounting for business combinations. The parent acquires shares of the subsidiary's stock, and the subsidiary's stockholders terminate their interest in the company. (Chapter 16)

purchase order A document that itemizes the details (such as catalog numbers, descriptions, quantities, and prices) of merchandise that a purchaser desires to acquire. (Chapter 4)

purchases discounts A discount secured by the purchaser of merchandise for prompt payment of invoices. (Chapter 4)

purchases journal A special journal used to record purchases of merchandise on account. (Chapter 5)

purchasing power gains and losses Gains and losses resulting from changes in the purchasing power of the dollar for holders of monetary assets and monetary liabilities. (Chapter 19)

purchasing system A system that handles the record keeping for acquisitions of merchandise inventory and ensures that adequate stock levels are on hand to meet demand. (Chapter 4)

quick ratio A severe measure of short-term debt paying ability that relates the total of cash, short-term investments, and accounts receivable to total current liabilities. (Chapter 19)

rate of return on assets A ratio that measures company profitability from a given level of asset investment; net income plus interest expense divided by average total assets. Also called return on investment (ROI). (Chapter 19)

ratio analysis The use of mathematical relationships to study a firm's liquidity, activity, profitability, and coverage of obligations. (Chapter 19)

raw materials The items to be processed into salable goods—specifically, the direct and indirect materials owned. (Chapter 21)

realized holding gains and losses Holding gains and losses that are calculated on the basis of assets sold or consumed. (Chapter 19)

receivables Amounts that a business expects to collect at some future date from claims against customers and other parties. (Chapters 1, 8)

registered bond A bond whereby the issuing company maintains a record of the purchaser's name and address and mails interest to the registered bond owner. (Chapter 15)

relevancy A characteristic of financial information. Information is deemed relevant if it influences the actions of a decision maker. (Chapter 18)

relevant cost A future cost that differs between alternatives. (Chapter 27)

relevant range The area of activity where a cost relationship is expected to hold true. (Chapter 24) *reliability* A characteristic of financial information. Information is deemed reliable if it accurately depicts the conditions it purports to represent. (Chapter 18)

repairs Amounts spent to maintain the normal operating condition of an asset. (Chapter 11)

replacement cost The current cost of replacing an asset with a similar asset in similar condition. (Chapter 19)

report form balance sheet A form of balance sheet that presents asset accounts above the liability and owners' equity accounts. (Chapter 6)

residual value The amount that a business expects to receive upon disposal of an asset at the end of the asset's life. (Chapter 10)

responsibility accounting A reporting system based on the organizational structure of a firm. Managers of each segment are held accountable for operating results and evaluated accordingly. (Chapter 25)

retail method An inventory estimation method widely used by retail establishments; derives a cost to retail ratio and applies the ratio to the total retail value of inventory. (Chapter 9)

retained earnings The portion of stockholders' equity that has been generated by profitable operations and retained in the business. (Chapters 6, 13, 14)

return on common stockholders' equity A profitability ratio that measures the profits generated on funds provided by common stockholders; calculated by dividing net income less preferred dividends by the average common stockholders' equity. (Chapter 19)

revenue Amounts charged to customers for goods sold or services rendered. (Chapter 1)

revenue expenditure An expenditure that benefits only the current accounting period. (Chapter 10)

revenue realization principle The principle that revenue is earned when (1) the earnings process is complete or virtually complete and (2) the amount of revenue can be objectively measured. (Chapter 18)

risk environment A decision-making environment where the possible events that can occur are known and weighted by their probability of occurrence. (Chapter 27)

Robinson-Patman Act A law forbidding the charging of different prices to competing customers for the same goods and services unless variations in cost are experienced when serving the customers. (Chapter 27)

running balance account An account format that offers the advantage of maintaining an up-to-date balance after each transaction is posted. (Chapter 2)

salary allowances A consideration used in the division of net income in many partnerships. The allowances recognize differences in seniority, reputation, business contacts, and time devoted to the firm by the partners. (Chapter 13)

sales journal A special journal used to record sales of merchandise on account. (Chapter 5)

sales mix The relative combination of individual product sales to total sales. (Chapter 24)

sales system A system that focuses on the proper recording and processing of sales transactions. (Chapter 4)

scattergraph A graphic representation of observed relationships between costs and activity levels. (Chapter 24)

secured bond A bond by which specific assets are pledged as security for the bondholders. (Chapter 15)

Securities and Exchange Commission (SEC) An agency of the federal government that administers several securities acts and prescribes accounting principles and reporting practices for companies issuing publicly traded securities. (Chapters 1, 18)

segment A component of a company whose activities represent a major line of business or class of customer. (Chapter 14)

segment margin The controllable contribution margin less uncontrollable fixed costs. This measure shows the contribution of each responsibility center to company profits after considering all traceable costs and is a good indicator of a center's long-run profitability. (Chapter 25)

serial bond A bond issue in which bonds mature at different dates. (Chapter 15)

service life The period of time that depreciable assets provide service to a business; also known as the economic or useful life. (Chapter 10)

short-term capital gains and losses Gains and losses resulting from the sale or exchange of capital assets held for one year or less. (Chapter 20)

short-term investments Investments in readily marketable securities with the intention of conversion back to cash within the operating cycle or one year, whichever is longer. (Chapter 7)

single-step income statement A type of income statement in which there is one section for revenues and another section for costs and expenses. (Chapter 6)

sinking fund A fund established to ensure that sufficient funds are available to pay bondholders at maturity. (Chapter 15)

sinking fund debentures Bonds that are retired by using the proceeds from a sinking fund. (Chapter 15)
slack The use of padding in budgeting to avoid unfavorable appraisals. (Chapter 23)
slide An error occurring when the decimal point of a number is improperly moved to the left or right. (Chapter 2)
sole proprietorship A business owned by one individual. (Chapters 1, 6)
source document A document, such as an inventory receiving report, bill from supplier, or customer sales slip, that provides evidence that a transaction has occurred. (Chapter 2)
special journals Journals that handle specialized (specific) types of transactions (cash receipts, sales, and so forth). (Chapter 5)
specific identification method An inventory method that requires a business to identify each unit of merchandise with the unit's cost and retain that identification until the inventory is sold. (Chapter 9)
spending variance The difference between actual overhead incurred and the total overhead budgeted for production. (Chapter 26)
standard A norm used by businesses to measure what should occur under reasonably efficient operating conditions. (Chapter 26)
stated-value stock No-par stock which has had a minimum issue price established to allow for protection of the creditors in terms of legal capital. (Chapter 13)
statement of changes in financial position A financial statement that reveals the financing and investing activities of an entity. (Chapter 17)
statement of owners' equity A financial statement that discloses the changes in owners' equity during an accounting period. (Chapter 1)
statement of retained earnings A financial statement that discloses the changes in the Retained Earnings account during an accounting period. (Chapters 6, 14)
state unemployment taxes Taxes paid by employers to state governments. The taxes are disbursed to the unemployed through various programs. (Chapter 12)
static budget A budget developed for one level of activity. (Chapter 26)
step cost A cost function that increases or decreases in "chunks," namely, when substantial changes occur in the activity base. (Chapter 24)
stock dividend A dividend involving a distribution of a company's own shares of stock. (Chapter 14)
stockholders The owners of a corporation. (Chapter 13)
stock split An increase in the number of outstanding shares and an accompanying reduction of the stock's par or stated value per share. (Chapter 14)
stock subscriptions Agreements with investors to purchase stock at a given price with payment taking place on a future date or via installments. (Chapter 13)
straight-line amortization A method that allocates an equal amount of bond discount or premium to each interest period. (Chapter 15)
straight-line depreciation A depreciation method that allocates the cost of a depreciable asset, less residual value, equally over the estimated service life. (Chapter 10)
subjective probability A probability based on all relevant knowledge possessed by a decision maker; actually a "gut feeling" about the future. (Chapter 27)
subsidiary A company that has another company as its majority stockholder. (Chapter 16)
subsidiary ledger A group of lower-level accounts that comprise a general ledger account. (Chapter 5)
successful efforts approach An approach used for natural resources by which the costs associated with nonproductive exploration efforts are immediately expensed. (Chapter 11)
sum-of-the-years'-digits depreciation An accelerated method of depreciation in which a smaller fraction is applied against an asset's cost, less residual value, each period. (Chapter 10)
sunk cost A past cost that is irrelevant for decision making. (Chapter 27)
T-account A form of account named for its shape; the left side is the debit side, and the right side is the credit side. (Chapter 2)
take-home pay The amount of cash available to an employee after all appropriate payroll deductions are subtracted from gross pay. (Chapter 12)
taking a physical inventory The process of counting or measuring the goods in a company's possession upon conclusion of an accounting period. (Chapter 9)
tax avoidance The planning of financial events, affairs, and transactions within the confines of tax law to minimize the tax liability. (Chapter 20)
tax credit A direct dollar for dollar reduction from a taxpayer's total tax bill. (Chapter 20)
tax evasion The deliberate attempt to understate taxable income by the manipulation of rev-

enues and expenses; an illegal activity. (Chapter 20)

tax shelter An investment that generates either tax-exempt income or business losses to enable persons to reduce their tax burden. (Chapter 20)

taxable income Adjusted gross income minus excess itemized deductions and personal exemptions. (Chapter 20)

temporary accounts Accounts that are reduced to zero at the end of the accounting period via the closing process. (Chapter 3)

time ticket A ticket used to gather labor time that shows the specific job or jobs to which an employee was assigned. (Chapter 22)

times interest earned A coverage ratio computed by dividing net income before taxes and interest by a firm's interest charges. (Chapter 19)

time value of money A concept based on the fact that a dollar received today is worth more than a dollar received in the future. (Chapter 28)

timing differences Differences in the timing of revenues and expenses for tax and accounting purposes; that is, revenues and expenses are recognized in different accounting periods for income tax and financial reporting purposes. (Chapter 20)

top-down approach An approach in which virtually all budget development takes place at the upper echelons of management and the budget is imposed on lower-level personnel. (Chapter 23)

trade discount A discount frequently offered to customers—specifically, a reduction from the list price of merchandise. (Chapter 4)

trademark An exclusive right to use specific trade names and symbols for a period of 20 years, with unlimited renewals possible for the same term. (Chapter 11)

trade receivables Receivables that emanate from the sale of a company's products or services to customers. (Chapter 8)

trading on the equity The process of securing funds at fixed interest and preferred dividend rates and investing the funds to earn a return greater than their cost; also called leverage. (Chapter 19)

transactions approach An approach to determining and measuring net income by focusing on business transactions, which have produced changes in the entity's assets, liabilities, and/or owners' equity. (Chapter 6)

transposition An error that occurs when two digits of a given number have been accidentally reversed. (Chapter 2)

treasury stock Shares of stock reacquired by the issuing corporation. (Chapter 14)

trial balance An internal report that checks the equality of the debits and credits in the ledger. (Chapter 2)

underapplied overhead A situation arising when the factory overhead applied to production is less than the amount of factory overhead actually incurred. (Chapter 22)

understandability A characteristic of financial information. Information is deemed understandable if it is comprehensible to those who (1) have a reasonable understanding of business and economic activities and (2) are willing to study the information with reasonable diligence. (Chapter 18)

unearned revenue Future revenue that has been collected but not as yet earned. (Chapter 3)

units-of-output depreciation A depreciation method that allocates the cost of a depreciable asset, less residual value, to the accounting periods benefited based on output (miles, hours, number of times used, and so forth). (Chapter 10)

unrealized holding gains and losses Holding gains and losses on assets still owned at the end of the accounting period. (Chapter 19)

variable cost A cost that varies in direct proportion to a change in an activity base. (Chapters 21, 24)

variable overhead efficiency variance A variance that reflects inefficiencies experienced with the base used to apply variable overhead cost to production. (Chapter 26)

variances Deviations from a budget or standard. (Chapters 21, 26)

vertical analysis An analysis in which each figure on a financial statement is related to a relevant total and stated as a percentage of that total. (Chapter 19)

voucher An internal document used in a voucher system that summarizes the details of each cash payment. (Chapter 7)

voucher register A multicolumn journal used to record vouchers. (Chapter 7)

voucher system A detailed cash payments system to improve control over all cash disbursements made by check. (Chapter 7)

Wage and Tax Statement (W-2) A statement the employer must provide each employee regarding gross wages and salaries earned and taxes withheld. (Chapter 12)

warranty A promise made by a seller or manufacturer to remedy defects in product quality and performance. (Chapter 12)

weighted-average method A method of accounting for inventory that computes a weighted-average cost for goods purchased or manufactured. The average is used to value the ending inventory and to determine cost of goods sold. (Chapter 9)

withholding allowance A numerical amount used in computing the amount of federal income taxes withheld from an employee's paycheck. One withholding allowance is allowed for the employee, one for a spouse, and one for each child and other qualifying dependent. Additional allowances are permitted if certain age and sight requirements are met. (Chapter 12)

working capital The excess of total current assets over total current liabilities. (Chapters 6, 17)

work in process The inventory of goods started but not completed during the period. (Chapter 21)

work sheet A columnar form that aids in the construction of the financial statements and assists in the performance of other end-of-period tasks. (Chapter 3)

zero-base budgeting A start-from-scratch budgeting approach. Managers request funds and justify expenditures as if the budgeting unit (e.g., department) was starting anew. (Chapter 23)

zero-bracket amount (ZBA) A standard deduction that can be utilized by virtually all taxpayers. (Chapter 20)

INDEX

82 83 84 85 9 8 7 6 5 4 3 2 1